AMERICAN DEFENSE POLICY

AMERICAN DEFENSE POLICY

Eighth Edition

Edited by

PAUL J. BOLT, DAMON V. COLETTA, and COLLINS G. SHACKELFORD, Jr.

The Johns Hopkins University Press, Baltimore and London

The Johns Hopkins University Press
2715 North Charles Street
Baltimore, Maryland 21218-4363
www.press.jhu.edu

Library of Congress Cataloging-in-Publication Data

American defense policy / edited by Paul J. Bolt, Damon V. Coletta, and Collins G. Shackelford, Jr.—8th ed.
p.   cm.
Includes bibliographical references and index.
ISBN 0-8018-8093-9 (hardcover : alk. paper) — ISBN 0-8018-8094-7 (pbk. : alk. paper)
1. United States—Military policy.   I. Bolt, Paul J., 1964–   II. Coletta, Damon V.
III. Shackelford, Collins G., Jr.
UA23.A626   2005
355′.033073—dc22   2004021160

A catalog record for this book is available from the British Library.

This work was created in the performance of a Cooperative Research and Development Agreement with the Department of the Air Force. The Government of the United States has certain rights to use this work.

TO BRENT SCOWCROFT

whose long career of service to the
nation included teaching
political science in our department

and

TO J. W. "BRAD" BRADBURY

a leader in establishing political
science at USAFA fifty years ago

CONTENTS

FOREWORD

Four decades ago, the political science department of the U.S. Air Force Academy produced the first edition of this work, a book that then and later (including during my own graduate student days) was a cornerstone of teaching in the study of American defense policy. Thinking back in decade-long increments since then provides some perspective on what has changed, and what endures, about American defense policy.

The year 1965, of course, was the height of the Cold War. The United States was well on its way into the Vietnam war, but the outcome of that conflict and the costs it would exact in human, economic, and political terms were unknown and unknowable. The United States had a substantial margin of superiority over the Soviet Union, but was locked in a contest with it—a contest in which subversion, insurgency, and the black arts of covert warfare and propaganda were central.

Ten years later, the picture was grimmer. The United States had lost one of the most divisive wars in its history and seen its society torn by dissent and violence, much of it associated with that experience. The Soviet Union loomed larger from the point of view of sheer muscle—it had achieved, if such words mean anything, nuclear parity—but perhaps less so in terms of ideology. Nonetheless, the Soviets were expanding their influence in the Third World, using surrogates, as well as their own forces in Africa, Latin America, and later, Central Asia to extend their strength.

In 1985, the picture had shifted once again. Astonishingly, the United States was in an ebullient and hawkish mood, its military reinvigorating itself with a flood of money, an enthusiastic political leadership, and a professional officer corps determined to set right the numerous organizational and leadership failures of Vietnam. The Soviets were no longer an ideological threat, but still contested the Cold War. Muscle bound but sclerotic, persistent but geriatric, they remained a formidable opponent, even without momentum or much conviction.

By 1995, they no longer existed. The Cold War ended with a gentle (on the whole) collapse of the Warsaw Pact and of the Soviet Union itself. The United States was the world's only superpower, and although China loomed faintly on the horizon, and a few trouble spots flared—the Middle East, most notably, and Yugoslavia—American military power was supreme. The 1991 Gulf War confirmed for the world that America's conventional might was not only greater than that of any potential opponent, but in a class entirely of its own.

And what of today's world? The shadow that has fallen upon the United States since September 11 has replaced the optimism of the 1990s, a period one acute observer has sardonically referred to as "the Great Picnic." Two sharp wars—one in Afghanistan, one in Iraq—both reaffirmed American conventional superiority and highlighted the limits of that power. China's rise to military great power status, although less frequently discussed, is no less real. Warfare with networks of largely but not exclusively Islamic terrorists promises few quick wins and more horror.

In the face of such flux, a book such as this is invaluable, because the great questions of continuity and discontinuity are of first concern to students of American defense policy. There are some issues that are perennial: the right relationship between senior military and civilian officials, for example, where it is worth recalling that contention, tension, and even sharp disagreement have been the norm, not the exception, in our military past. There are cases in which a gradual evolution has been marked—the evolution of a more centralized and joint military system, for example, following lines laid out by General George C. Marshall's planning staff as early as 1943. And there are major disjunctions as well—take, for instance, the end of the central European scenario as the dominant force-sizing construct for the United States Army.

The student of American defense policy should begin, then, by asking him- or herself which issues, problems, or trends are persistent, and which are temporary. This is not an easy task, because often assumptions about the world are hardwired into seemingly neutral organizational decisions. The Air Force's willingness to abolish Strategic Air Command was unusual in its recognition that the end of the Cold War meant the end of Cold War–based organizations. But in many other respects, Cold War habits of mind persist. The Pentagon's proclivity for using abstract scenarios or measures of effectiveness to size the force—two nearly simultaneous major conflicts, to take a recent example—reflects Cold War methods of thinking. It is worth asking whether such thinking should survive that conflict. Not all discontinuities were products of the end of the Cold War: few changes have mattered more than the abolition of conscription in the early 1970s and the creation of a highly professional, all volunteer force, with large consequences for the budget, outlook on the use of military power, and even the design of military technology.

Perhaps no problem of change or continuity is as great as that of the American role in the world. In 1965, the United States was incomparably mighty. Today, it is mightier still, both because of developments within (its robust financial markets, its dominance of the information age technologies, and its favorable demographics, among others) but also because its chief rival has collapsed. The French have it right: the United States is a hyperpower. But as Americans have discovered in the past decade, such status brings with it uncertainty and even suffering. There are virtually no international security problems that do not come to the attention of the Pentagon or Foggy Bottom; there is no end to the demand for American forces around the world; there is no chance that American policy will simply meet with acclaim on the part of powers—some nominal allies—

animated by envy or anxiety, rivalry or dismay. The universal power—inevitably clumsy, occasionally foolish—is the universal target; it is the easy excuse and the useful villain.

America may stand astride the world, but like Gulliver, it finds itself bound, pricked, and perplexed. In a time of geopolitical confusion, rapid technological change, and pervasive violence, its armed forces are more important than ever. The problems are large, the times are urgent, the stakes are high. All the more reason, then, for a thoughtful point of departure in understanding American defense policy like this volume.

ELIOT A. COHEN
Robert E. Osgood Professor and Director of the
    Philip Merrill Center for Strategic Studies
School of Advanced International Studies
The Johns Hopkins University
Washington, D.C.

PREFACE

With the establishment in April 2002 of Northern Command, devoted to protecting the American homeland, American defense policy has come full circle. We might say without too much exaggeration that the mission of Northern Command was first performed by General George Washington and his Continental Army. Indeed, protecting the homeland was the predominant defense policy goal throughout the early years of the American republic. The burning of the White House by British forces in 1814 demonstrated how difficult this task could be.

However, by the time the Civil War was approaching, the threat of foreign attack on American soil was greatly diminished. Thus in 1838, Abraham Lincoln could proclaim that "All the armies of Europe, Asia, and Africa combined, with all the treasure of the earth (our own excepted) in their military chest; with a Bonaparte for a commander, could not by force, take a drink from the Ohio, or make a track on the Blue Ridge, in a trial of a thousand years."[1] This is not to suggest that the threat to the American homeland was ever completely eliminated. Shortly after Lincoln's speech, much of the homeland was devastated by the Civil War. During both world wars, shipping on the American coast was attacked by German submarines, and until the Battle of Midway in World War II, there were real fears of a Japanese invasion of the West Coast. During the Cold War, it was understood that Soviet missiles aimed at the United States might be deterred but could not be defeated if launched, while movies like the 1984 *Red Dawn* imagined American teenagers fighting against invading communist troops. Nevertheless, threats to Americans were predominantly seen as lying overseas.

All this changed with September 11. The hijacking of four American aircraft and the subsequent attacks on the World Trade Towers and Pentagon, along with the crash of one of the passenger jets in rural Pennsylvania, were not war in the conventional sense. Nevertheless, the deaths of approximately three thousand people, mostly Americans but also citizens from around the world, led President George W. Bush to declare war on terror. Subsequently, the American military has been used in numerous theaters. For example, American and allied forces drove the Taliban from Afghanistan in 2002. In 2003, the United States and coalition forces defeated Saddam Hussein's regime and began a violent occupation of Iraq, while the American military has also been deployed to the Philippines to help combat the Islamist terrorist group, Abu Sayyaf. Organizational changes, the most significant since the National Security Act of 1947, have also occurred in the United States, with the establishment of the Department of Homeland Security and Northern Command. In addition, new regulations and laws, such as the Patriot Act, have been implemented. Administration officials claim that these rules make Americans safer, whereas critics complain about their infringement on civil liberties and the creation of new obstacles for American business.

The heightened threat to the United States homeland due to terrorism, the growing defense budget, and the increasing frequency with which the United States has used military force since the end of the Cold War illustrate the importance of updating our understanding of American defense policy.[2] At the same time, we are also led back to a new examination of the fundamentals, such as the values and constitutional processes that undergird American defense policy, to guide us into the future.

The formulation and implementation of defense policy entail numerous choices on how to utilize scarce resources and balance competing goods. For example, political leaders must decide how much money to allocate to military vs. domestic priorities, and how to allocate money among manpower, training, and weapon systems within the defense budget. More prominent now is the need to balance civil liberties vs. increased security in the struggle against terrorism, and to prudently decide when to put the lives of American military personnel at risk in pursuing the war on terror. In the American republic, these decisions concern all citizens, not just defense planners. Thus this book is intended to reach a broad audience of undergraduate and graduate students across a wide range of colleges and universities, as well as members of the public interested in learning more about U.S. defense policy.

What exactly is defense policy? The term has several meanings. These include a plan that shapes policies toward a particular region (such as our defense policy toward Iraq), a subset of security policy that focuses on the use of the military, the political process that generates specific policies, and an academic field of study.[3] For our purposes, we will narrow our focus to two aspects of defense policy that are related but distinct. The first is the process by which defense policy is made. The second is the content of defense policy.

The process by which American defense policy is made is complex and involves numerous actors, challenging the realist simplification, which perceives states as unitary actors rationally pursuing their interests. Most importantly, the process is Janus-faced, looking in two different directions at the same time.[4] On the one hand, the process looks to the threats and opportunities posed by international politics. On the other hand, the process looks to the public mood, resource constraints, and political alignments in the domestic arena for direction in policymaking. Both are important and may sometimes be out of balance. For instance, shortly before the American entrance into World War II, the international environment seemed to demand a more robust American defense policy, but this was not supported by domestic political realities. However, the American war with Spain in 1898 was driven more by domestic demands than any necessity imposed by the international environment.

The policy process is explained through David Easton's political system model.[5] The defense policy process takes place in the context of both the international and domestic environments. These environments place demands on the government for policies that address defense issues, demands that are channeled through the media, interest groups, and the general public. Government actors, such as Congress, the president, the Department of Defense, and the various armed services, respond to these demands to make and implement policy. The subsequent policies then alter both the international and domestic environments, leading to a continuing cycle of demands and policies.

Our second element of American defense policy concerns content. Here we ask what American defense policy should look like, as well as what it actually does look like. In this regard, American defense policy is a subset of national security policy or grand strategy, a topic also covered in this volume.

Assessing national security policy entails first asking what American interests are. The core American interest is preserving territorial integrity and defending the homeland, along with maintaining a republic committed to constitutional government and liberty. Although specific emphases change over time, other long-term American interests include maintaining freedom of the seas, preventing the rise of a single dominant power in Europe or Asia, preserving American supremacy in the Western Hemisphere, promoting democracy, expanding market access for American exports, and more recently, protecting vital oil supplies.[6] National security policy utilizes diplomatic, economic, military, intelligence, and now law enforcement tools to promote these and other national interests. Defense (or military) policy is narrower, focusing on the use of military instruments to promote American national interests.

Admittedly, although the title of this book remains *American Defense Policy*, there are many elements of broader security policy in the volume as well. The line between defense policy and security policy has always been somewhat blurred, and is even more so today with what President Bush has described as the war on terrorism. For instance, special operations forces now engage in activities once reserved for CIA

operatives, regional combatant commanders engage in diplomacy in ways that can marginalize American ambassadors, and there is continuous debate on the role of the military vs. traditional public safety agencies in preventing and responding to catastrophic terrorist attacks in the United States. Nevertheless, the current volume continues to devote the most attention to specific defense policy issues, addressing broader security issues where the two types of policies intersect.

The organization of the book addresses both definitions of defense policy (process and content) in a manner that is consistent with Easton's systems model. Part I begins with the context or environment of American defense policy. This includes the values and historical factors that shape American thinking on defense policy, debates on the proper role of America in the world in light of our values, and the defining characteristics of the international setting that shape American policies. The second part of the book focuses specifically on the process of defense policymaking. This includes examining the constitutional and legal basis for American defense policies (which is also tied to American values), the domestic actors who are involved in making policy and their interactions, and the allocation of resources necessary to implement defense policies when resources are inherently scarce.

The third and fourth parts of the book move into the tools and content of American defense policy. Thus the third section explores the transformation of the United States military in light of technological and organizational changes, the integration of force with other policy instruments, and the preparation of future defense leaders. The last section examines civil-military relations, conventional forces, nuclear policy, and homeland security.

All of the articles but one (by Robert Art) in this eighth edition of *American Defense Policy* are different from those in the seventh edition. Nevertheless, there are both continuities and discontinuities in the subjects covered. Arguably, the processes used to create defense policies have changed the least, although even here, the creation of the Department of Homeland Security and the apparent concentration of decisionmaking powers regarding the use of force in the hands of the president have created a somewhat different environment. Thus this edition, like the seventh, covers the major actors and processes of defense policymaking. Both volumes also examine the context of American defense policy, American strategy, nuclear and conventional policies, civil-military relations, and military transformation.

However, what sets this volume apart is the greater strategic clarity of 2004. In 1997, there was still mystery regarding the shape of the post–Cold War world. This was inevitably accompanied by debates over the size and role of the American military, as politicians hoped for a "peace dividend" at the end of the Cold War. However, the attacks of September 11, 2001, changed this. President Bush's declaration of a war on terror gave a forceful new direction to American defense policy. This has in turn shaped the eighth edition of *American Defense Policy*. The current volume focuses more on values in an age of terrorism. It also reflects redoubled efforts to transform the American military in light of experiences in Afghanistan, Iraq, and elsewhere. It gives greater attention to the preparation of future defense leaders, focuses on very different debates over our national security strategy, addresses new thinking on American nuclear weapons and missile defense, and devotes more attention to the threat of terrorism and homeland security.

The goal of previous editions of *American Defense Policy* was to include articles of enduring value that would stand the test of time. Frankly, it has been more difficult in this edition to choose articles that we were confident would become classics due to the rapid changes in American defense policies and the unresolved debates over how best to protect the United States. Nevertheless, we are certain that the articles selected do indeed lay out the key issues clearly, present insightful analysis that help us better understand the policy choices and tradeoffs, and define the major debates that are occurring in Washington and elsewhere.

NOTES

The views expressed are the author's and in no way represent the opinions, standards, or policy of the U.S. Air Force Academy or the U.S. government.

1. Abraham Lincoln, "Address Before the Young Men's Lyceum of Springfield, Illinois: The Perpetuation of our Political Institutions," in *American Political Rhetoric: A Reader,* ed. Peter Augustine Lawler and Robert Martin Schaefer (Lanham, Md.: Rowman & Littlefield, 2001), 163.

2. For a discussion of the increased importance of the American military in foreign policy, see Andrew Bacevich, *American Empire* (Cambridge, Mass.: Harvard University Press, 2002).

3. For a detailed explanation of these four definitions, see Peter L. Hays, Brenda J. Vallance, and Alan R. Van Tassel, "What is American Defense Policy?" *American Defense Policy,* 7th edition (Baltimore: The Johns Hopkins University Press, 1997), 8–17.

4. See Samuel P. Huntington, *The Common Defense: Strategic Programs in National Politics* (New York: Columbia University Press, 1961), 1.

5. See David Easton, *A Systems Analysis of Political Life* (New York: John Wiley & Sons, 1965).

6. For one perspective on the interests of the United States, see The Commission on America's National Interests, *America's National Interests* (Commission on America's National Interests, 1996).

ACKNOWLEDGMENTS

A project of this magnitude requires the assistance and cooperation of many people. Jim Smith and the U.S. Air Force Institute for National Security Studies provided a foundation for the book by hosting a conference to discuss *American Defense Policy* and its contents. Participants included a wide variety of people across the defense education community who gave valuable inputs into the structure and contents of the book, including Hal Bidlack, Meena Bose, Ann Campbell, Tom Drohan, Gwendolyn Hall, Dick Hewitt, John Nagle, Lance Robinson, Jim Titus, Brenda Vallance, Al Willner, and James Wirtz.

Special thanks go to Brian Drohan, who helped with research in the early stages of the book. Brenda Vallance, our colleague and an editor of the seventh edition of *American Defense Policy*, patiently provided invaluable advice time after time. Anne Campbell, Rob Fredell, and Steve Fuscher gave tremendous help on legal and administrative issues. Frances Scott and staff at the U.S. Air Force Academy Cadet Library provided research advice and assistance on a wide range of media associated with military and defense policies. Henry Tom, our editor at the Johns Hopkins University Press, patiently answered questions and overcame numerous obstacles in a consummately professional manner. Doug Murray, our department head, in cooperation with the Center for the Study of Defense Policy, got the project off the ground and gave us all the encouragement and resources necessary to complete *American Defense Policy*.

Numerous people also commented on early drafts of this book. They include Richard Betts, Carl Brenner, Daniel Byman, Jim Callard, Bill Casebeer, Peter Feaver, Mick Gleason, Ole Holsti, Steve Kiser, Ed Kolodziej, Phil LaSala, James McCarthy, Jay Parker, Greg Rose, Don Snider, Jack Snyder, and Al Willner. Their comments have made this a better book. We also appreciate the efforts of those who assisted in proofreading. They are Preston Arnold, Hal Bidlack, Robin Bowman, Deron Jackson, Dan Lahman, Dan Marine, Fran Pilch, Vicki Rast, and Sharon Richardson.

Finally we thank our families, especially Jonan, Judy, and Betty Jo. Their love and support made this book possible.

PART I

THE CONTEXT OF
AMERICAN DEFENSE POLICY

INTRODUCTION

PAUL J. BOLT

The creation and implementation of American defense policy takes place in an overarching, complex environment that drives policy and tests its effectiveness. Because policymaking is Janus-faced, this environment includes both domestic considerations and the international environment. Sometimes elements of the environment go unnoticed. For instance, the values of the American Founders shape policymakers in ways that are almost subliminal. At other times, events provide such a stinging blow that a radically altered security environment captures everyone's attention, leading to a fundamental reassessment of defense policy and the reformulation of grand strategy. Such was the case with September 11.

Part I of *American Defense Policy* discusses the context in which policies are made. Admittedly, in light of multiple factors in the domestic and international environments that shape defense policy, the issues raised here are suggestive rather than comprehensive. Nevertheless, the themes of Part I regarding values, the proper role of America in the world, and the international environment thread through the rest of the volume, surfacing time and time again as they shape American policies.

This edition of *American Defense Policy* differs from previous editions in that it emphasizes values as a foundation and guide for defense policy, both in its creation and implementation. Values, or fundamental and enduring principles, have always played an important role in defense policies. The Cold War was largely a struggle between two value systems. Moreover, most questions regarding defense policies have both a moral and prudential aspect because lives are at stake, power is exercised, and resources that could be used elsewhere are being consumed.

However, two conditions lead us to refocus on values. The first is the struggle against terrorism. In an environment where al Qaeda claims it is justified in indiscriminately killing countless numbers of civilians (and postmodern critics state that moral values are functions only of power), an explicit discussion of morals is called for.[1] The second condition is the unipolar power of the United States. Debates on how to use such power inevitably have a moral component. (See, e.g., the imperative to spread freedom in the 2002 *National Security Strategy*.)[2] No longer do Americans debate whether to be isolationist or engaged. Instead, the crucial issues of the day revolve around the proper nature of our engagement.

Chapter 1, "American Defense in the Context of History and Values," sets the stage for *American Defense Policy*. Paul Carrese begins by looking to the past for guidance and calling on us to learn from the wisdom of George Washington. Washington's policies cannot be neatly labeled with any "-ism." Instead, Washington advocated prudent and moderate policies, rooted in republicanism, which carefully balanced liberty and security, interest and justice, while avoiding both militarism and weakness. Carrese argues that because the direction Washington set for the United States was a major cause of the American rise to global power, it would be foolish to ignore Washington's statesmanship now, as Americans debate how to confront both threats and opportunities.[3]

Reinhold Niebuhr's essay, published in 1960, when the United States faced an opposing superpower, is remarkably relevant to the current struggle against terrorism. Niebuhr claims that America sees itself as the most innocent nation on earth. This sense of innocence makes Americans ill suited to handle the temptations of power that confront them. Nevertheless, power must be exercised for moral ends, but in a way that both recognizes the moral ambiguity inherent in its use and builds world community.[4]

Michael Walzer approaches the issue of moral values from the just war perspective. The just war doctrine provides principles on when a war can be fought justly (just cause, last resort, competent authority, limited objectives, and reasonable hope of success) and how it must be fought justly (discrimination and proportionality). Walzer's essay is not primarily a historical piece on the development of the just war theory beginning with the Greek and Roman philosophers and Augustine, but rather, a reflection on how just war theory, which has won a place in the consciousness of both policymakers and military officers, should affect policy today. In particular, he calls on us to reflect upon "risk-free warmaking" and the obligation to establish a just peace at the conclusion of conflicts.[5]

Chapter 2, "The Role of the United States in the World," continues some of the themes of the first chapter. Minxin Pei begins by examining American nationalism, a powerful force that most Americans fail to appreciate. American nationalism is unique in that it is triumphant, forward-looking, and driven by civil society rather than by the state. This uniqueness makes it very difficult for the United States to objectively assess nationalism in other countries.

John Lewis Gaddis and David Hendrickson then address the current American approach to the rest of the world. The title of Gaddis' essay announces that, finally, with the unveiling of President Bush's national security strategy in 2002, America has produced a document worthy of the designation "grand strategy." The shock of September 11 marked the transition from an uncertain superpower, somewhat befuddled by the sudden success of its containment doctrine, to a global leader with a clear mission. The war on terror has prompted the United States to organize and deploy various means, including military force, with less restraint than was seen during the 1990s. In general, Gaddis applauds this change. Hendrickson, however, is critical of American policies. He asserts that American unilateralism and preventative war will ruin the United States. Because the quest for universal empire and absolute security are ultimately destructive to states that pursue these goals, the United States must voluntarily submit to accepted international norms and institutions to ensure the legitimacy of its power.[6]

Chapter 3, "American Defense and Security in the International Environment," looks at the international context in which American defense policy takes place.[7] Sam Tangredi begins with a broad overview. Based on an analysis of a wide range of studies on the future security environment, Tangredi identifies sixteen points of consensus among analysts on the shape of the security environment from 2001 to 2025 and nine points of disagreement.

Thomas Barnett focuses on globalization. He asserts that the countries of the world fall into two categories: the Core is embedded in globalization, whereas the Gap is outside globalization. Threats to the United States will come from the Gap, rather than from a peer competitor, so U.S. policy should focus on shrinking the Gap.[8] Denny Roy, however, asks whether China (a country now firmly in the Core) will become a peer competitor to the United States. Roy believes that although a stronger China does threaten some U.S. interests, a cooperative relationship is possible. Nevertheless, the dynamics of the security dilemma may still lead to a tragic conflict.[9]

In their contribution, Kurt Campbell and Celeste Ward focus on the overseas basing of American forces. The need to project force into the Gap and the rise of China, as well as other factors, have led Pentagon planners to rethink the location of American bases. Campbell and Ward argue that, although there may be sound military reasons to redeploy, the diplomatic and political ramifications of such changes must be considered as well. Their work reminds us that geography and alliances are important, and that the most powerful military in the world cannot unilaterally guarantee the security of its own state.

NOTES

The views expressed are the author's and in no way represent the opinions, standards, or policy of the U.S. Air Force Academy or the U.S. government.

1. See, for instance, "What We're Fighting For: A Letter from America," as well as the German and Saudi responses, at www.americanvalues.org/html/wwff.html.

2. George W. Bush, *National Security Strategy of the United States of America* (September 2002), at www.whitehouse.gov/nsc/nss.html.

3. For another article that looks to America's past for useful lessons, see Walter A. McDougall, "Back to Bedrock: The Eight Traditions of American Statecraft," *Foreign Affairs* 76 (March 1997): 134–46.

4. For an assessment of the contribution of Niebuhr and other Christian realists to political thinking and policies, see Eric Patterson, ed., *The Christian Realists: Reassessing the Contributions of Niebuhr and his Contemporaries* (Lanham, Md.: University Press of America, 2003).

5. For more on the just war tradition, see James Turner Johnson, *Just War Tradition and the Restraint of War* (Princeton, N.J.: Princeton University Press, 1981); James Turner Johnson, *Morality and Contemporary Warfare* (New Haven, Conn.: Yale University Press, 1999); Keith Pavlischek, "Just and Unjust War in the Terrorist Age," *Intercollegiate Review* 37 (Spring 2002): 24–32; James P. McCarthy, "The Ethical Implications of Kosovo Operations," in *The Sacred and The Sovereign: Religion and International Politics,* ed. J. D. Carlson and Erik C. Owens (Washington, D.C.: Georgetown University Press, 2003); and Jean Bethke Elshtain, *Just War Against Terror* (New York: Basic Books, 2003).

6. See also Edward Rhodes, "The Imperial Logic of Bush's Liberal Agenda," *Survival* 45 (Spring 2003): 131–54; Claes G. Ryn, "The Ideology of American Empire," *Orbis* (Summer 2003): 383–97; Jack Snyder, "Imperial Temptations," *National Interest* (Spring 2003): 29–40; and Andrew Bacevich, *American Empire: The Realities and Consequences of U.S. Diplomacy* (Cambridge, Mass.: Harvard University Press, 2002).

7. Another interesting analysis of the international security situation is Robert D. Kaplan, *Warrior Politics: Why Leadership Demands a Pagan Ethos* (New York: Random House, 2003), 3–16.

8. For a fuller explanation of this argument, see Thomas P. M. Barnett, *The Pentagon's New Map* (New York: G. P. Putnam's Sons, 2004). For more on globalization, see Thomas L. Friedman, *The Lexus and the Olive Tree* (New York: Farrar, Straus, & Giroux, 1997); Joseph E. Stiglitz, *Globalization and Its Discontents* (New York: W. W. Norton, 2002); and Stanley Hoffman, "Clash of Globalizations," *Foreign Affairs* 81 (July 2002): 104–15.

9. See also Robert Sutter, "China's Rise in Asia—Are US Interests in Jeopardy?" *American Asian Review* 21 (Summer 2003): 1–21; and Adam Ward, "China and America: Trouble Ahead?" *Survival* 45 (Autumn 2003): 35–56.

CHAPTER 1

AMERICAN DEFENSE IN THE CONTEXT OF HISTORY AND VALUES

AMERICAN POWER AND THE LEGACY OF WASHINGTON: ENDURING PRINCIPLES FOR FOREIGN AND DEFENSE POLICY

PAUL O. CARRESE

It is commonly said that America entered uncharted seas after the Cold War as the superpower with unrivaled military, economic, and cultural might, and that the war on terrorism further swept it into a new era as a global hegemon, yet beset by shadowy threats and unique burdens. When we ponder the course America should chart, it is less common, however, to consult our founding principles and first centuries of experience. Harvard's Stanley Hoffman opened the way to reconsider this longer view when, after the 2001 terrorist attacks and a decade of theorizing about a paradigm to explain the post–Cold War world, he suggested that new constructs—from "the end of history" to a "clash of civilizations"—in fact obscured our understanding of the enduring politics of nations and the actual demands of statecraft.[1] Moreover, although partisanship and rival schools have always marked American debates on foreign and security policy, disputes over the war on terrorism now recall the rancor of the Vietnam War era. This is partly due to the dangers, burdens, and confusion of our new situation, but our tendency to reduce international affairs to doctrines—realism, liberal-internationalism, democratic peace, postmodernism, or blends thereof—often yields not candid deliberation but contests between armed camps.

FIRST PRINCIPLES

A pause from current anxieties and entrenched quarrels to reconsider George Washington's statesmanship in founding American foreign and security policy might help us to chart a grand strategy more consonant with the better angels of our history and national character and with our justifiable interests. America was the first deliberately founded regime in history, and it would be odd to think that her subsequent rise to global dominance in both "hard" and "soft" power somehow justifies amnesia about her original aims. Another of her great statesmen, in the midst of our most terrible crisis, defined her as dedicated to propositions about liberty, equality, the pursuit of happiness, and the rule of law—not, primarily, to global empire, global commerce, global democracy, a national security state, or a global balance of power. Indeed, much of Lincoln's greatness lay in a strategy of rededication to the principles of America's founders, including great care in balancing the necessities of defense and military power with the higher ends they should serve. He knew that novel challenges required him to think and act anew, but he also understood that America was grounded in principles of natural justice and religious truths about the humility yet dignity to which mankind is called—however much we fail to abide by these ideals.

A half-century ago, Hans Morgenthau urged America to revive the realism of its founders, especially Washington and Hamilton, to guide our foreign policy in new circumstances and to transcend both isolationism and Wilsonian internationalism.[2] Morgenthau eloquently advocated his own favored theory of international affairs, but his reconception of Washington as simply a realist did not stick. Washington more typically labors under another, graver misreading: that his Farewell Address (1796) and other writings avow isolationism or passivity. Fortunately, several scholars in the post–Cold War era have explained why uncertain times call for revisiting this statesman who rarely favored "isms" or doctrines, but who offered sound principles on right, might, and diplomacy that long were cited as the guiding ideals of our republic.[3] We should expand our thinking and assess our current options by recovering the practical wisdom and distinctive American principles found in the Declaration of Independence, *The Federalist*, and the Constitution—all of which both reflect and inform Washington's statecraft.[4]

Washington closed his career as founder with advice to "Friends, and Fellow-Citizens" that he hoped would endure—offering for "solemn contemplation" and "frequent review" principles he thought "all important to the permanency of your felicity as a people."[5] Leading statesmen and thinkers did consult his Farewell Address up through Henry Cabot Lodge during the First World War and Morgenthau in the Cold War. In recent decades, a consensus has deemed it irrelevant, as isolationist or outdated. Some also consider Washington just a front for his bright aides Madison and Hamilton. Even brief engagement with the Address, however, sheds light on current dilemmas; deeper study shows that he revised every argument, hoping, as if a latter-day Thucydides, to distill advice for the ages.[6] A recent reappraisal finds him "a leader who sought explanations and explainers all his life, and who mastered both what he was told and those who told him."[7] His deeds and words are no cookbook of recipes for today, as the main lessons of the Address and the career informing it are architectonic, not specific: America must base its security policy on principle and prudence rather than power or popularity, and prize a decent republican politics over conquest or glory. The Address marked the second time Washington had relinquished near-absolute power, when such ambitious and talented men usually grasp for more. This led his countrymen to rank him with an ancient Roman renowned for leaving power after saving his country: he was the American Cincinnatus. He recalled the best of the Republic, not the Empire, for although Washington rose to fame through military command, he appraised power and security as means to higher ends. Principles of personal and civic virtue guided his policies and counsel, to a degree that Americans alternately admire and find hard to believe.

Familiarity with Washington's career makes it hard to deny that he was the real thing, his credibility demonstrated in decades of deeds and words devoted to liberty, constitutionalism, and political moderation.[8] The Address encapsulates a comprehensive approach to foreign policy, security, and war, but both his words and his specific deeds are best understood when viewed in light of one another. Indeed, as befits the words of a statesman, one can glean from the Address and the career informing it a handy set of guidelines—five broad, overlapping principles for strategic thinking: first, the priority of a decent republic, rooted in natural justice and guided by transcendent truths about humankind; second, the subordination of military to civil authority, and avoidance of either militarism or weakness; third, the balancing of liberty and security through a complex, moderate constitution that divides responsibility for foreign and defense policy; fourth, the need for statesmanship within such an order, especially an executive balancing deliberation, prudence, and flexibility in both grand strategy and tactics; and fifth, the balancing of interest, independence, and justice in foreign affairs through prudent recourse to just war principles and the classic right of nations. Washington was a practical man of policies and action, but he insisted these be chosen in light of sound principles and informed judgment. Those seeking concrete ideas on pressing issues may think these principles vague or useless. Washington knew, however, that republics typically falter on strategic thinking, instead seizing on short-term problems, adopting favored doctrines of the day, or following popular impulses. For Washington, sound judgments of the moment require candid deliberation guided by fundamental principles, especially when facing great challenges. He doubtless would admit that we face massive, new problems today—ballistic missiles and catastrophic weapons, terrorist exploitation of modern technology, the cultural and economic pressures of globalization, and the envy and mistrust accompanying our extraordinary political and military might. He might remind us, however, that for over two decades, he defeated a superpower and managed an international coalition, forged trust among members of his own federation, and navigated ruthless great-power politics—all with vastly fewer resources at his disposal than America can marshal today.

Sober judgment indeed will be needed to chart a course through the opportunities and threats facing America in this complex era. How should we conceive our role in world affairs, given our power and principles? How should we define our security and interests, our force structure and alliances, our commitments to collective security and international regimes? Is America the "Empire" that post-modern theorists and liberal internationalists deem a threat to the world, and that "America First" conservatives deem a threat to itself?[9] Washington's principles on republicanism and constitutional complexity, and on balancing interest and justice in foreign and defense policy, transcend the doctrines and quarrels of the moment to restore a larger, enduring horizon. He has been caricatured as incompetent at strategy, but in fact, his example recalls a Clausewitzian grand strategy that links security policy and larger moral and political aims—a perspective obscured today by our faith in technology and technological thinking, and by the dynamism and drive for novelty in the worlds of policy, the media, and academia alike.[10] At its peak, Washington's thought recalls the sober, humane, and complex republicanism of Thucydides, equally aware of the realities and necessity of war and of the imperial temptations to which democracies, and ambitious leaders, are prone. After surveying the principles evident in specific episodes and writings of his statesmanship, I offer some more particular lessons that his republicanism and principled prudence might suggest for current challenges and debates.

EYES ON THE PRIZE: A DECENT REPUBLIC, NATURAL RIGHTS, AND PROVIDENCE

Washington could suggest that his advice be consulted down the ages because he had proven that his deeds and words rested on principles. He first rose in stature in Virginia and beyond for his exploits and published journal as a colonial officer in the French and Indian War, and he was elected to Virginia's legislature in 1758. In the turbulent 1760s, he defended Americans' rights to liberty and self-governance, and in 1774, attended the First Continental Congress. He justified himself to a loyalist friend: "an Innate Spirit of freedom first told me" that the acts of the British government "are repugnant to every principle of natural justice." Indeed, they are "not only repugnant to natural Right, but Subversive of the Laws & Constitution of Great Britain itself," and the King's ministers are "trampling upon the Valuable Rights of Americans, confirmed to them by Charter, & the Constitution they themselves boast of" (August 24, 1774; W, 157). He supported strong measures in Congress, and after the battles at Lexington and Concord in 1775, Washington attended the Second Congress in carefully chosen attire: his Virginia uniform. Several principles forged in that crisis directly address our twenty-first-century concerns. The founders did not know of terrorism, but they knew of pirates and other outlaws. They therefore justified their rebellion with legal and philosophical principles publicly stated, and formed a professional military force reporting to a duly elected and organized civilian government.

The Declaration of Independence carefully justifies a war to protect basic natural rights and constitutional government, as a last resort; it also specifies unacceptable forms of warfare concerning civilians, property, and prisoners. This spirit of constitutional republicanism informed Washington's General Orders of July 9, 1776, ordering the Declaration read to the troops so that they might understand "the grounds & reasons" of the war (*W*, 228).

The same General Orders provide for chaplains and religious services, and call upon the "blessing and protection of Heaven"; indeed, Washington hoped every officer and enlisted man would live "as becomes a Christian Soldier defending the dearest Rights and Liberties of his country" (*W*, 228). After the war, his major writings always cite the guidance of transcendent ideals but in more careful, nonsectarian language, broadened to embrace the rights to religious liberty for which the war also had been fought. Still, Washington did not separate republicanism, justifiable and limited force, and divine guidance about decency and honorable conduct. The radical direction of the French Revolution by the mid-1790s confirmed these views, given its replacement of Christianity with a religion of reason, progress, and ferocious republicanism. The famous exhortations in the Farewell Address to instill religious faith as well as moral and intellectual virtue thus defy the categories of recent American disputes about church and state. He tempers the utility of piety and morals with genuine appreciation for them: "Of all the dispositions and habits which lead to political prosperity, Religion and morality are indispensable supports"; "A volume could not trace all their connections with private and public felicity"; just policies are "recommended by every sentiment which ennobles human Nature" (*W*, 971, 972–73). This endorses neither a secularist wall of separation between faith and government nor the sectarian view that America is a Christian nation; similarly, a republic should neither ignore the mutual influence between governmental and private morality nor adopt religious zealotry in its policies, at home or abroad. Throughout his career, he balanced respect for Christian churches and biblical religion with a modern republican's enlightened tolerance.[11] These were ideals worth dying for, but military and security measures were neither ends in themselves nor a replacement for decent republican politics at home and abroad.

CIVIL-MILITARY RELATIONS, AND NECESSARY DEFENSES, FOR A REPUBLIC

Throughout his decades in public life, from serving in colonial Virginia to establishing a sound national constitution by the 1790s, Washington noted the dangers of either militarism or weakness. He established the republican principle of civil-military relations, which many nations of the world still do not enjoy. Although he drew upon British practice, both America and the world chiefly should thank Washington for demonstrating that a professional military is both necessary to protect liberty and can be made safe for it through subordination of the former to laws and civil authority. This reflected his basic political moderation: real liberty is ordered liberty, securing self-government and political decency under law. Indeed, John Marshall, the great Chief Justice of the United States, served as a young officer under Washington and argued that without the latter's character and principles, the American cause would have failed in the war's darkest hours.[12] Washington resisted the temptations of power when the war prospects brightened, and while President under the Constitution. After the victory at Yorktown in 1781, an American colonel suggested he should be king, perhaps a tempting offer for a general admired by his army, and who—like Caesar, Cromwell, Arnold, Napoleon, or Musharraf—was ambitious and proud. The temptation might strengthen, given the great disorder in Congress: Washington long had proposed reforms concerning supplies, equipment, and pay for his men. Still, he immediately expressed "abhorrence" and "astonishment" to learn of "such ideas" in the army: "Let me conjure you then, if you have any regard for your Country, concern for yourself or posterity, or respect for me, to banish these thoughts from your Mind" (*W*, 468–69).

After more than two centuries enjoying this principle, Americans tend to forget that our civil-military relations have not been trouble-free, and that Washington's high standard is not easily met. A concern arose in post–Cold War America that the military is isolated from the civilian population it serves; in particular, that it is politically conservative. However valid this may be, regaining the perspective of Washington clarifies that America recently has become one of the first republics in history to define citizenship as requiring neither military nor any other national service. Many analyses of a civil-military gap, or demands that the military adopt the individualistic and egalitarian trends of the wider society, similarly misunderstand the need for a distinct military character, professionalism, and education, both for military missions and to inculcate an ethic of the rule of law. Washington's example also sheds light on modern debates about the strictly professional versus professional-political models of officership offered by Huntington and Janowitz. More recently, some scholars have argued that the military and its distinct services are semiautonomous interests pressing elected officials for money, personnel, capabilities, and security policies; others argue that elected civilians have a constitutional duty to challenge and manage top officers and the armed services—on everything from tactics to force structure—to ensure that larger political objectives are served.[13] Familiarity with Washington reminds us of the stakes involved for our constitutional republic, and recommends a balance between the functional and political models of officership. He was no wallflower as general, but he always respected civilian authority; conversely, as president, he selected and then closely supervised the generals fighting Indian tribes in the northwest (replacing St. Clair with Wayne) and the army that suppressed the Whiskey Rebellion.[14]

Beginning early in the revolution, Washington had urged Congress to establish executive offices and procedures for supplying the army and managing revenue. When these finally were adopted by 1781, the improvements in everything from transportation to readiness were crucial to the Yorktown campaign (*LGW*, 259–60). Simultaneously, he upheld discipline and civil authority during two troop mutinies in 1781 over pay and supplies, dealing moderately with the first but severely with the second (*LGW*, 245–48). Trouble arose again in 1783, when the peace process threatened to disband the army before its members were paid. An anonymous letter at headquarters in Newburgh, New York, summoned officers to discuss a threat of mutiny against Congress; Washington denounced that meeting but called an official one at the officers' meeting house, the Temple of Virtue (*W*, 490). His extraordinary speech warned that "sowing the seeds of discord and separation between the Civil and Military powers" would undermine "that liberty, and . . . that justice for which we contend" (*W*, 495–500). His final appeal was to both reason and emotion: "let me conjure you, in the name of our common Country, as you value your own sacred honor, as you respect the rights of humanity, and as you regard the Military and National character of America," to reject civil war (*W*, 498–500). He then stumbled in reading a letter from Congress: "Gentlemen, you will permit me to put on my spectacles, for I have not only grown gray, but almost blind, in the service of my country" (*W*, 1109; see note 496.12). The once-rebellious officers, some in tears, unanimously reaffirmed their allegiance to civil authority. The main doctrinal manual of the U.S. Army today opens with "Washington at Newburgh: Establishing the Role of the Military in a Democracy," finding there "the fundamental tenet of our professional ethos."[15]

Principled to the end, Washington disbanded the army once the peace treaty was official. After a last Circular Letter to the states, recommending national reforms, and final orders to the army with more political advice, he resigned before Congress in December 1783 (*W*, 547–48). Jefferson wrote to him: "the moderation & virtue of a single character has probably prevented this revolution from being closed as most others have been, by a subversion of that liberty it was intended to establish."[16]

A CONSTITUTIONAL AND MODERATE PATH TO FOREIGN AND DEFENSE POLICY

The Clausewitzian character of Washington's approach to foreign and security policy, placing particular forces and policies in a framework of larger political aims, is evident in his commitment to founding a constitutional order.[17] He was the most important leader in the constitutional reform movement from 1783 to 1789, both in his public acts and his quiet encouragement of Madison, Hamilton, and other framers. He had defended Congress at Newburgh as an "Hon[ora]ble Body" not to be distrusted merely because "like all other Bodies, where there is a variety of different Interests to reconcile, their deliberations are slow" (*W*, 498–99). His subsequent 1783 Circular to the States emphasized the need for a stronger federal government and executive power, and by 1787, he endorsed a complex federal government of separated powers that shared enough functions to keep one another in balance. The Circular formulates clear convictions on these issues— announcing his retirement from public life, then urging constitutional reforms to secure and perpetuate liberty. He noted that a general should abstain from politics, but it was "a duty incumbent upon me" to address these issues because, in "the present Crisis" of affairs, "silence in me would be a crime" (*W*, 516–18). The third of four "pillars" he proposed for national reorganization was "adoption of a proper Peace Establishment," which included "placing the Militia of the Union upon a regular and respectable footing." The common good required that state militias have "absolutely uniform" organization, equipment, and training—a complex system of defense that prevented militarism through citizen engagement, while providing an effective national capability (*W*, 524).[18]

From 1787 to 1789, Washington risked his reputation to establish a complex, effective constitutional order by serving as president of the Philadelphia Convention, helping to reprint *The Federalist* in Virginia, letting his name be used in state ratification debates, and serving as the first president under the new Constitution. Still, even with the Electoral College's unanimous support, he returned to office reluctantly. He knew from the war that effective statesmanship, legislative deliberation, and popular opinion did not always harmonize. He nonetheless was a strong, moderate, and faithfully constitutional executive, justifying decisions with principles and working patiently with an increasingly divided Congress. He sought to quell the partisanship gripping America by calling his countrymen to the enduring interests and higher ends that united them, in both domestic and foreign matters.

The great themes of Washington's presidency were that executive power was safe for republicanism, and that constitutional government, not populism or parties, should guide the way through domestic and foreign trials. He established the principle that presidents should recruit the best talents and characters for offices, from a range of political and regional viewpoints: his cabinet included the rival views of Hamilton and Jefferson; his ambassadors included John Jay, Gouverneur Morris, and John Quincy Adams; and he replaced General St. Clair after the disastrous campaign in the Northwest Territory. His adherence to separation of powers dictated respect for the legislative dominance of Congress: the president should recommend a few measures, mostly concerning core Article II powers of foreign and security policy. Similarly, the executive should use the veto power with care, on constitutional and not policy grounds; he qualified this only with a veto late in his second term over a core presidential power, the size of the army. The executive and Senate should collaborate on treaties while maintaining separate roles and judgments: the House had no role, given "the plain letter of the Constitution" and his knowledge of "the principles on which the Constitution was formed" (*W*, 930–32). Dear to him was the principle that the president represents all the American citizenry, its common principles and highest ideals, and not one party, region, or doctrine. This was especially so regarding war and foreign affairs, as is evident in his firm but patient conduct during both of his terms.

Washington's general principle guiding foreign and defense policy is moderation, understood as the sober balance among ideas or actions, advocated by Montesquieu—the modern philosopher most keen to instruct statesmen in practical judgment. This quality made Montesquieu the most cited philosopher in America in the 1780s and 1790s (e.g., in *The Federalist*), and later provided Clausewitz a model for capturing the complexity of war and strategy. Such moderation is familiar to us today in the more obvious elements of Montesquieuan political science, the complexity of viewpoints and balancing of interests inherent in separation of powers and federalism.[19] This same spirit, however, also animates Washington's endorsements of liberal learning and institutions "for the general diffusion of knowledge" from his First Annual Message in 1790, to the Farewell Address, to his final Annual Message in 1797, it being "essential that public opinion should be enlightened" (*W*, 972, 750). He repeatedly proposed a national university and military academy, and when Congress declined, he privately endowed schools and educational funds; Washington and Lee University is one result of this commitment (*W*, 982–83). The intellectual confidence he worked to develop allowed him to consult a wide range of intelligent advisers, and then to rely on one over another as he saw fit.[20] He tried to perpetuate this ideal of wide consultations and balanced judgment among a new generation of military and civilian leaders. Fashioning sound foreign and defense policies requires proper deliberation and judgment, within and across constitutional branches, about particular situations—a complex, messy process in a constitutional republic, but a path of political moderation and sobriety that avoids the extremes of doctrine or of momentary passion.

EXECUTIVE POWER, PRUDENCE, AND FLEXIBILITY IN STATECRAFT AND TACTICS

Washington's complex, political approach to formulating foreign and defense policy included a chief executive who balanced consultation, prudential judgment, secrecy, speed, and flexibility in both grand strategy and tactics. The arguments in *The Federalist* on the necessity of such an office to secure republican liberty employ the theories of Locke and Montesquieu, but they draw distinct shape and weight

from Washington as general and citizen-founder. Indeed, many scholars and statesmen have admired his balance of executive toughness and republican principle as embodying an ideal of the prudent statesman traceable to Thucydides, Plato, Aristotle, Cicero, and Plutarch. A recent analysis of the qualities of strategic sense he displayed as a general and field commander—marrying long-term objectives with continual short-term adjustment—could just as well describe his later record as a civilian chief executive:

He always kept the political object foremost in his considerations. He always seemed to examine his alternatives in terms of the whole strategic picture. Learning from his early mistakes, he constantly adapted his strategy to the circumstances. Recognizing the defects of his tactical instrument, he never asked too much of it.[21]

Several scholars cite Washington in rejecting any restriction of "strategy" to Napoleonic annihilation or Upton's bureaucratic war machine, arguing, as one puts it, that "Washington's military career provides a model of leadership and strategic and tactical expertise."[22] As general, he eventually discerned the blend of tactics, campaigns, and geopolitical alliances that could deny victory to his superpower opponent while ensuring an American victory that would provide geographic and political independence. He had to keep an army in the field during the dark years of conflict and forge a French alliance without succumbing to their ambitions, until he could maneuver the British into fatigue or a spectacular defeat. His understanding of the enemy, potential allies, and resources in the American character and domestic matériel dictated that he control his passion for reputation and honor, so as to retreat or fight as this strategy required. Marshall, drawing on Plutarch, compared him to two Romans who fought the great Carthaginian general Hannibal—Fabius, who harassed and retreated, and Marcellus, who attacked: "He has been called the American Fabius; but those who compare his actions with his means, will perceive as much of Marcellus as of Fabius in his character" (*LGW*, 467). A. T. Mahan, the founder of American strategy studies, credits Washington with seeing the decisive importance of naval power; he might have done better to include him when analyzing principles of grand strategy or praising such exemplars of strategic sense as Lord Nelson.[23]

Washington's development of practical judgment would be merely Machiavellian if the aims were immoral or amoral, or if the ends were thought to justify any means. The pattern throughout Washington's career, however, was to avoid either amoral expedience or an impractical moralism. The widespread rediscovery in the twentieth century of Aristotelian ethics has restored such traditional ideas about political conduct as "statesman" and "prudence," which one scholar defines as long reserved for those "who have exercised the art of ruling with sufficient excellence to earn the gratitude of their contemporaries and posterity." Recent figures like Washington, Lincoln, and Churchill exhibited "moral wisdom" in the face of extraordinary political emergencies, guided not by abstract moral principles alone but by prudence understood as "the mediating process and personal virtue through which they connected the moral ends they pursued with their everyday actions and policies."[24] Thus, as general and president, Washington employed realistic modes of intelligence and covert operations while stopping short of ruthlessness.[25] On larger matters, Tocqueville praised Washington's ability to discern a sound policy in the 1790s, when the French Revolution and Europe's great power contest unleashed a storm of ideas and passions upon the American body politic. A statesman's hand at the wheel was needed:

The sympathies of the people in favor of France were . . . declared with so much violence that nothing less than the inflexible character of Washington and the immense popularity that he enjoyed were needed to prevent war from being declared on England. And still, the efforts that the austere reason of this great man made to struggle against the generous but unreflective passions of his fellow citizens almost took from him the sole recompense that he had ever reserved for himself, the love of his country. The majority pronounced against his policy; now the entire people approves it. If the Constitution and public favor had not given the direction of the external affairs of the state to Washington, it is certain that the nation would have done then precisely what it condemns today.[26]

The same spirit informed Washington's policy on the popular protests to a federal tax on liquor that blossomed into the Whiskey Rebellion of 1794.[27] Still, his highest achievements of prudence and principled power involved the crises of foreign affairs and war in his second term. Voices of all persuasions, including both Hamilton and Jefferson, saw these clouds on the horizon in 1792 and pleaded that he postpone his wish to retire. He shelved the draft of a farewell address he had asked Madison to prepare; he again was the unanimous choice in the Electoral College. After navigating a stormy second term he asked Hamilton to redraft a parting address, but, ever moderate, he insisted that his increasingly partisan aide include ideas from the initial version by Hamilton's once partner, and now bitter rival, Madison.

BALANCING INTEREST, INDEPENDENCE, AND JUSTICE: JUST WAR AND INTERNATIONAL LAW

Washington wanted rival views joined in his Farewell Address to affirm the balanced thinking and shared principles nearly lost in the partisan 1790s. Tocqueville describes this "admirable letter addressed to his fellow citizens, which forms the political testament of that great man" as the basic charter of American foreign and defense policy.[28] As president, Washington's main policies sought an adequate federal army and navy; peace with the Indian nations and defense of existing American settlements by force if necessary, but not expansion; and protection of the republic from the European great powers but also from two rival doctrines about relations with them.

In the light of more recent disputes between doctrines of international relations, it is telling that he adopted neither the realism of Hamilton nor the liberal internationalism or idealism advocated by Madison and Jefferson in germ, and later by Woodrow Wilson more fully. Washington did not face globalization, or the temptation of Pax Americana, or postmodern relativism and pacifism; but, it is noteworthy that he neither embraced nor overreacted to the doctrines of *realpolitik* or perpetual peace of his day.[29]

The two great crises of Washington's presidency stemmed from the upheaval of the French Revolution and the radical democratic theory France sought to impress upon the world. His two measures to shield America from such storms brought partisan attacks—his 1793 Neutrality Proclamation and 1795 treaty with Britain (the Jay Treaty). He knew these policies would offend the revolutionary French republic and its zealous supporters in America. Amid charges of monarchism and of groveling to Britain, he defended his "system" as maintaining America's true independence and a just peace. His Seventh Annual Message (1795), and letter to the House rejecting its request for the Jay Treaty documents (1796), defended the Framers' principle that foreign policy should bow neither to popular passions nor abstract creeds but should be debated by those branches of government somewhat insulated from popular opinion, the Senate and the president. Indeed, despite his reservations about the Jay Treaty, he pressed to ratify it in part to quell disorder from the kinds of partisan clubs that had stoked civil and international war in France and the Whiskey Rebellion in America. The "prudence and moderation" that had obtained and ratified the treaty sought an honorable peace as the basis for America's future prosperity and strength. These "genuine principles of rational liberty" would prove essential to "national happiness"; having been "[f]aithful to ourselves, we have violated no obligation to others."[30]

The Farewell Address, published in September 1796, encapsulates and elevates the principles Washington had stood for during his entire career.[31] It was printed without a title in a newspaper to avoid the self-importance and air of demagoguery that a speech might suggest; its common title was bestowed by a newspaper editor. It opens by invoking republican virtue and civic duty, patriotic devotion to the common good, gratitude to Heaven for America's blessings and prayers for continued Providence, and the need for prudence and moderation to sustain such blessings. He pledged "unceasing vows" that his country and the world would enjoy the further blessings of Heaven's beneficence, union and brotherly affection, perpetuation of a free constitution, and wisdom and virtue in government. He further prayed that the happiness of a free people would be so prudently used as to gain for them "the glory of recommending it to the applause, the affection, and adoption of every nation which is yet a stranger to it"—an invocation of the widely held view that American was unique among the nations and in history (W, 963–64). Only after further advice on perpetuating the Union and the constitutional rule of law, on moderating partisan politics, and on ensuring both religion and education in the citizenry (*W,* 964–72) does Washington raise his final counsel—that America should seek both independence and justice in foreign affairs.

Washington's maxim "to steer clear of permanent Alliances" is among the best-known ideas of the Address (*W,* 975). That said, many accounts of his foreign policy mistakenly cite Jefferson's later maxim about "entangling alliances," which fosters the erroneous view that the Address launches a doctrine of isolationism.[32] Washington had for years criticized the French Revolution and its effects in America for imposing visions and doctrines when knowledge of human nature and practical realities supported more moderate views. His main principle was that a secure, independent nation should surrender to neither interest nor abstract justice, neither passions nor fixed doctrines, but must balance and find moderation among these human propensities. In this prudential spirit, he obliquely refers to the circumstances of the 1790s that suggest America should not be a "slave" either to hatred of Britain or adoration of France. He cites no names, presumably to avoid offense but also to state a general principle: "a predominant motive has been to endeavor to gain time to our country to settle and mature its yet recent institutions, and to progress without interruption, to that degree of strength and consistency, which is necessary to give it, humanly speaking, command of its own fortunes" (*W,* 973, 977).

His main concern was that the nation be independent enough to act wisely and justly; the fundamental principle was to be able to "choose peace or war, as our interest guided by our justice shall Counsel" (*W,* 975). He long had advocated provision for "the national security"; Theodore Roosevelt praised the maxim from Washington's First Annual Message that "[t]o be prepared for war is one of the most effectual means of preserving peace" (*W,* 749, 791–92, 848).[33] Roosevelt did not observe, however, Washington's balance, for the Address also reiterates his maxim that America must avoid "those overgrown Military establishments, which under any form of Government are inauspicious to liberty, and which are to be regarded as particularly hostile to Republican Liberty" (*W,* 966). He thus calls America to "[o]bserve good faith and justice towds. all Nations. Cultivate peace and harmony with all. Religion and morality enjoin this conduct; and can it be that good policy does not equally enjoin it?" He endorses the utilitarian maxim that "honesty is always the best policy," but also urges America to "give to mankind the magnanimous and too novel example of a People always guided by an exalted justice and benevolence" (*W,* 972, 975). This blend of principles lies within the just war tradition developed by classical philosophy, Christianity, and modern natural law and international law. Enlightenment writers on the right of nations developed more specific principles of war and diplomacy, while recognizing that prudent judg-

ment by statesmen must govern particular cases. One source for Americans was Montesquieu's effort, drawing on the international jurists Grotius, Pufendorf, and Vattel, to formulate guidance for statesmen that balanced the necessity of military power with limits to war found in natural rights of individuals and basic international right.[34] The guiding spirit of the Address thus echoes the great theme of Washington's career: intellectual, moral, and political moderation. Prudence and decency should guide private and public life; he hoped such "counsels of an old and affectionate friend" would "controul the usual current of the passions" and "moderate the fury of party spirit" in domestic and foreign affairs (*W,* 976; see also 832, 851, 924).

REPUBLICAN PRUDENCE FOR A GLOBALIZED WORLD

Our pitched battles in academia and the public journals today between schools of international relations, and the rhetoric volleyed between parties and pundits about our foreign policy since the 2001 attacks, suggest that a call for moderation and recourse to fundamental principles is not dated. We should recall that Washington steered American foreign and defense policy through such polarization and warned against it, and that the great authority on moderate republicanism, Montesquieu, warned that a free people could be as blinkered or irrational as those under despotism:

In extremely absolute monarchies, historians betray the truth, because they do not have the liberty to tell it; in extremely free states, they betray the truth because of their very liberty, for, as it always produces divisions, every one becomes as much the slave of the prejudices of his faction as he would be of a despot.[35]

Whatever the reach and technology of our power now, or the complexity of global threats or opportunities, Washington reminds us that such essential challenges remain. Still, examples of particular policy advice drawn from his legacy might spur greater engagement with our founding principles today. Just as there is overlap in these five principles, any effort to apply them to situations finds that each at once informs and presupposes the others. Moreover, such counsels of republican prudence may seem platitudes but are, in fact, difficult to practice, because they require tempering of the jealousy for power that always marks human affairs, at home or abroad.

First, we should observe the great success achieved by placing principle above power, by sticking to moderate policies amid partisan claims, and by carefully matching means to ends. America should note that her Founder, in his own moment of dominance, resisted both the fog of power and the thrill of partisanship, instead sticking to the virtues and aims that got him power and that justified the burdens of that power. A Kantian may detect Machiavelli in advice that honesty is the best policy, while some realists may sense naiveté or sheer cunning, but this maxim echoes

Washington's first principle—adherence to republicanism, natural justice, and transcendent truths about humankind. He is sure America will be "at no distant period, a great Nation" (*W*, 972), but he holds to a blend of Aristotelian teleology and biblical Providence: power and goodness ultimately coincide; power only endures if founded on virtuous aims and decent conduct; greater power brings greater temptation to pervert or lose one's true aims. Washington's other principles—and all his policies—rest on this foundation. If such discipline brought about the founding of America, and was at least partially adhered to by his successors as we rose to world power, on what grounds should we ignore it now? Our grand strategy must have this moral-political principle as its lodestar, lest like most cases in human history, ours, too, loses its grandeur. What does this mean not only for our use of military power, but for our national desire for wealth and global economic dominance, for our energy policy, or how we deliberate about any such means to these larger ends? Are our compromises with this principle—and Washington knew that human affairs always require compromises to some degree—justified by larger support for this principle itself?

Second, his insistence upon civil authority, and avoidance of either militarism or weakness, implicates a range of issues from force structure to public and private diplomacy. Washington's advice to balance the claims of republican liberty and national defense suggests restoration of a brief period of national service, military or civilian, for all young citizens—a policy long debated, but only partially engaged, by national political leaders.[36] More generally, we should recall, as the global power with vast superiority in everything from training to weaponry and technology, that the Romans lost their republic to empire and that the British gave up empire to preserve liberty under constitutional monarchy. In the post–Cold War era, such voices as George Kennan and Henry Kissinger invoked the Washingtonian warnings against power and a militarized foreign policy that had been echoed shortly after the founding by John Quincy Adams. Adams worried not about the temptation of sheer power, but that moral aims might tempt us to pursue power projection: America "goes not abroad in search of monsters to destroy," he warned, for efforts to right all wrongs in world affairs would change her focus "from *liberty* to *force*"; she "might become the dictatress of the world," but would no longer be "ruler of her own spirit."[37] Even though our armed forces need a distinct professional culture and full national support, we must not mistake this noble instrument for an end in itself or as obviating more complex means to formulate national policy—especially political debate at home, and forthright diplomacy and cultivation of good relations abroad. Thucydides' analysis of the long Athenian decline from hubris to disaster buttresses Washington's advice that patient diplomacy must always be equal to, or supersede, the claims of pride and power in making national policy. This is not to say that Wash-

ington would place a primary trust in international institutions or law, or in utopias of perpetual or democratic peace, but that we should maintain perspective and balance about our own temptations and motives, as well as those of allies and adversaries.

Third, Washington's specific constitutional ideas also touch policy at home and abroad. We should affirm a complex structure for formulating foreign and security policy as best for balancing liberty and security, and vet policies through multiple branches and actors—seeking not the lowest common denominator but the highest possible consensus on means and aims. Recent decades have emphasized the natural tendency of executive offices to dominate policy debates and decisions on the use of force, and of Congress to only reluctantly insist on full deliberation about war and deployment of force and then to snipe about subsequent problems or setbacks. Washington hoped his moderate principles would "prevent our Nation from running the course which has hitherto marked the Destiny of Nations" (*W*, 976), but this presupposed that vigilance about both necessary defenses and the perils of war would animate all elements of the complex political order he founded. Abroad, if necessity demands that we engage in regime building, we should underwrite not democracy but liberal constitutionalism—extending to new regimes the political complexity and moderation that we enjoy, or should enjoy, at home.[38]

Fourth, Washington's counsel that executives should employ consultations, prudence, and flexibility in both grand strategy and tactics is difficult to achieve today, since we embrace populism, partisanship, and permanent campaigning more than the founders ever could have. Still, those in elected office, and both the temporary and more permanent officials serving them, can strive to emulate the balanced thinking of the first administration. Such moderation also invokes the last of Washington's principles, on balancing interest and justice, but the aim of Clausewitzian grand strategy to assess the entire moral and political complexity of war has special relevance for the executive. One maxim both Thucydides and Washington might offer is to resist the temptation to let current dominance and superior technology narrow thinking about when to wage war, and instead to assess carefully what the consequences or complications might be when the battle is long over.[39]

The fifth Washington principle is to balance interest and justice through prudent recourse to just war principles and the classic right of nations—a difficult ideal for a weak and defensive power, and one that now taxes the patience of a superpower. If we think the grand strategy and international regimes America built for the Cold War are no longer relevant, what policies and tactics will satisfy both Washington's high standards and the threats and opportunities of the moment?[40] His counsels do not fit our typical menu of rival doctrines, nor the recent blend of Wilsonian zeal and realism advocated by some after the Cold War. Does Washington no longer fit our character and defining purposes, or do such doctrines fail to fully comprehend America? For example, is a policy of nonproliferation and counterterrorism not animated both by interest and benevolent justice—an enlightened self-interest of inextricably blended motives? Such a blend is as characteristic of American self-understanding as Washington hoped it would be, and perhaps we should revise our theories to recognize the propriety of balancing these motives in given situations, rather than depicting ourselves as polarized or confused.

Our challenges are indeed new in many ways, but the highest consensus of the founders is still the general aim proclaimed by all American presidents and parties—to benefit mankind and ourselves by respecting "the obligation[s] which justice and humanity impose on every Nation" (*W*, 977). Each of the doctrinal alternatives of the past century asks us to place too much faith either in ourselves or in international institutions and other states; some schools suggest we now can lead only by force, others that we should lead only by example and principle. The genius of Washington's advice is to ever seek the proper equilibrium among these tendencies in any given situation and for the long haul, so as to abide by republican principles of natural justice. He knew that international affairs always require "temporary alliances" and engagement with foreign nations while trying to "cultivate peace and harmony" with all (*W*, 975, 972). He might accept that the complexities of our age and our power now compel this engagement to a great degree, but that America could still retain independent judgment about balancing interest and justice if it was leading alliances and not dominated by them. Indeed, his advice on "permanent alliances" did not concern only alliances; the error of thinking so is evident in Jefferson's reduction of this to "entangling alliances," which tends toward an isolationist doctrine. Washington's core concern was, in fact, the blinkered thinking and "permanent, inveterate" antipathies or attachments behind such commitments (*W*, 973). He instead sought the independence and flexibility necessary to find a sound blend of the possible, the expedient, and the dutiful.

Although his basic moderation might tell us to avoid either isolationism or unilateralism, it also would counsel that America would only mark a *Novus Ordo Saeclorum* (new order of the ages) if we heeded the classic just war prudence that carefully balances power with right, necessity with decency.[41] Specific debates on a preemptive strike, or a regime change, or a humanitarian intervention must always be pulled up to that broader calculus, and there is no codebook in the sky that spells out in advance just what is right or what will succeed. Washington's counsels thus are difficult and elude snappy slogans, but are worthy of the effort—calling for both the moral principle to stand up to evil and the humility to check one's own power, to lead alone if necessary but with allies and by persuasion whenever possible.

Washington knew his standards were lofty. He knew he had barely succeeded in steering his country through international and domestic crises. He was far from sure that the American experiment would succeed at all. Still, it is precisely the gravity of the threats and the opportunities facing America today that justify recurrence to the thought of such great statesmen as Washington and Lincoln, even if our novel circumstances require new applications of their principles and prudence to our problems.

NOTES

I am grateful to Dr. Susan Carrese, Dr. Paul Bolt, and Ambassador Roger Harrison for their comments. The views expressed are mine and not those of the U.S. Air Force Academy or the U.S. government.

1. Stanley Hoffman, "Clash of Globalizations," *Foreign Affairs* 81 (Winter 2002): 104–15.

2. Hans Morgenthau, "The Mainsprings of American Foreign Policy: The National Interest vs. Moral Abstractions," *American Political Science Review* 44 (1950): 833–54. See also Joseph Cropsey, "The Moral Basis of International Action," in *America Armed,* ed. Robert Goldwin (Chicago: Rand McNally, 1963), 71–91, and more recently, Dmitri Simes, "Realism: It's High-minded . . . and It Works," *The National Interest* 74 (Winter 2003): 168–72.

3. See especially David Hendrickson, "The Renovation of American Foreign Policy," *Foreign Affairs* 71 (Summer 1992): 48–63; Patrick Garrity, "Warnings of a Parting Friend," *The National Interest* 45 (Fall 1996): 14–26; Matthew Spalding and Patrick Garrity, "Our Interest, Guided by Our Justice," in *A Sacred Union of Citizens: George Washington's Farewell Address and the American Character* (Lanham, Md.: Rowman & Littlefield, 1996), 91–139; Walter McDougall, *Promised Land, Crusader State: America's Encounter with the World since 1776* (Boston: Houghton Mifflin, 1997), and "Back to Bedrock," *Foreign Affairs* 76 (Summer 1997): 134–46.

4. Henry Kissinger argued, a decade into America's status as lone superpower, that we must recover the study of history and philosophy as essential to a clear national strategy and to genuine statesmanship, in *Does America Need a Foreign Policy? Toward a Diplomacy for the 21st Century* (New York: Simon & Schuster, 2001), 283–88.

5. "Farewell Address," in *George Washington: Writings,* ed. John Rhodehamel (New York: Literary Classics of the United States, 1997), 962, 964; hereafter cited parenthetically as *W.* Washington's writings are quoted largely as in the originals, with emphases retained and only occasional corrections of spelling. Another useful one-volume edition is *George Washington: A Collection,* ed. William B. Allen (Indianapolis: Liberty Fund, 1988).

6. For correspondence and successive drafts, see *W,* 804–6, 938–48, 950–51, 954–56, 960–61. Spalding and Garrity defend Washington's authorship in *Sacred Union of Citizens,* 46–57. See also *Washington's Farewell Address,* ed. Victor Paltsits (New York: The New York Public Library, 1935).

7. Richard Brookhiser, *Founding Father: Rediscovering George Washington* (New York: Free Press, 1996), 139; see "Morals" and "Ideas," 121–56.

8. For broader studies, see Brookhiser, *Founding Father; Patriot Sage: George Washington and the American*

Political Tradition, ed. Gary Gregg and Matthew Spalding (Wilmington, Del.: ISI Books, 1999); and my essay "Liberty, Constitutionalism, and Moderation: The Political Thought of George Washington," in Bryan-Paul Frost and Jeffry Sikkenga, eds., *History of American Political Thought* (Lanham, Md.: Lexington Press, 2003), 95–113, including the sources recommended therein.

9. For a range of recent viewpoints, see Andrew Bacevich, *American Empire: The Realities and Consequences of U.S. Diplomacy* (Cambridge, Mass.: Harvard University Press, 2002); Joseph Nye, *The Paradox of American Power: Why the World's Only Superpower Can't Go It Alone* (New York: Oxford University Press, 2002); Robert Kagan, *Paradise and Power: America and Europe in the New World Order* (New York: Knopf, 2003); Ivo Daalder and James Lindsay, *America Unbound: The Bush Revolution in Foreign Policy* (Washington, D.C.: Brookings Institution, 2003); and the *Foreign Affairs* anthology of post–Cold War writings, *America and the World: Debating the New Shape of International Politics,* eds. James Hoge and Gideon Rose (New York: Council on Foreign Relations Press, 2003).

10. On Washington and Clausewitzian grand strategy, see Donald Higginbotham, *George Washington and the American Military Tradition* (Athens, Ga.: University of Georgia Press, 1985), 5, 114, 117; and Mackubin Owens, "General Washington and the Military Strategy of the Revolution," in *Patriot Sage,* eds. Gregg and Spalding, 61–98. In general, see Paul Kennedy, *Grand Strategies in War and Peace* (New Haven, Conn.: Yale University Press, 1991); and John Lewis Gaddis, *Strategies of Containment: A Critical Appraisal of Postwar American National Security Policy* (New York: Oxford University Press, 1982).

11. See Washington's 1783 Circular to the States (*W,* 516–17), and as president, his 1789 Thanksgiving Proclamation and letters to religious minorities: Proclamation, October 3, 1789, and to Roman Catholics, March 15, 1790, in *Collection,* ed. Allen, 534–35, 546–47; to Hebrew Congregation, August 18, 1790 (*W,* 766–67).

12. John Marshall, *The Life of George Washington: Special Edition for Schools,* ed. Robert Faulkner and Paul Carrese (Indianapolis: Liberty Fund, 2000 [1838]), 75. Hereinafter cited parenthetically as *LGW.*

13. Compare Peter D. Feaver, *Armed Servants: Agency, Oversight, and Civil-Military Relations* (Cambridge, Mass.: Harvard University Press, 2003) with Eliot Cohen, *Supreme Command: Soldiers, Statesmen, and Leadership in Wartime* (New York: Free Press, 2002). For Higginbotham, the model of Washington and George C. Marshall blends professionalism and republicanism in a way that transcends Huntington's categories; *Washington and the Military Tradition,* 114–38.

14. See *LGW* (ch. 29, ch. 32); Ryan Barilleaux, "Foreign Policy and the First Commander in Chief," in *Patriot Sage,* eds. Gregg and Spalding, 141–64, at 144–50.

15. *The Army,* Field Manual 1 (Washington, D.C.: Department of the Army, 2001). See also Douglas Johnson and Steven Metz, "Civil-Military Relations in the United States," in *American Defense Policy,* eds. Peter Hays, Brenda Vallance, and Alan Van Tassel, 7th ed. (Baltimore: Johns Hopkins University Press, 1997), 495–96.

16. Jefferson to Washington, April 16, 1784, in *The Life and Selected Writings of Thomas Jefferson,* ed. Adrienne Koch (New York: Modern Library, 1944), 791. See Marshall's tribute, *LGW,* 301.

17. See Peter Paret, "Clausewitz," in *Makers of Modern Strategy: From Machiavelli to the Nuclear Age,* ed. Peter Paret (Princeton, N.J.: Princeton University Press, 1986), 187–213, arguing that Clausewitz adopted Montesquieu's theory of the complexity, or spirit, of politics. Gordon Craig and Felix Gilbert, "Reflections on Strategy in the Present and Future," ibid., 869–70, praises Washington and *The Federalist* for grand strategic thinking akin to Clausewitz's formulation that "War is the continuation of politics by other means."

18. In May 1783, he had sent Congress "Sentiments on a Peace Establishment," which mixed a small professional army with larger state militias; he also recommended forts, arsenals, a navy, coastal defenses, and a military academy but noted the political and economic limits to defense requests. See *Writings of George Washington,* ed. John Fitzpatrick, 39 vols. (Washington, D.C.: U.S. Government Printing Office, 1931–1944), 26: 374–98; Higginbotham, *Washington and the Military Tradition,* 124–25, 129–30; Barilleaux, "Foreign Policy," 156–57.

19. See Montesquieu, *The Spirit of the Laws,* eds. Anne Cohler, Basia Miller, and Harold Stone (Cambridge: Cambridge University Press, 1989 [1748]), Preface; Bk. 29 ch. 1; Bk. 9 ch. 1–3; Bk. 11 ch. 5, 6, 8, 20; Bk. 29 ch. 1; see also note 37 below on Fareed Zakaria's recent endorsement of Montesquieu on political science.

20. Higginbotham notes that Washington and George Marshall shared the unusual quality of seeking out diverse views from their aides, in *Washington and the Military Tradition,* 76–78, 121–22.

21. Mackubin Owens, "Washington and the Strategy of the Revolution," in *Patriot Sage,* eds. Gregg and Spalding, 98.

22. Albert T. McJoynt, "Washington, George (1732–99)," in *International Military and Defense Encyclopedia,* ed. Trevor Dupuy (Washington, D.C.: Brassey's U.S./Maxwell Macmillan, 1993) 6: 2932–34; see also Dave Palmer, *The Way of the Fox: American Strategy in the War for America, 1775–1783* (Westport, Conn.: Greenwood Press, 1975). Compare the treatment in Russell Weigley, "American Strategy from Its Beginnings through the First World War," in *Makers of Modern Strategy,* ed. Paret, 408–43 at 410–13.

23. Alfred Thayer Mahan, *The Influence of Sea Power Upon History, 1660–1783,* 12th ed. (Boston: Little, Brown, 1944 [1890]); on Washington, 342–43, 364–65, 387–89, 397–400; on grand strategy, 7–10, 22–23; on Nelson, 23–24.

24. Alberto Coll, "Normative Prudence as a Tradition of Statecraft," in *Ethics & International Affairs: A Reader,* ed. Joel Rosenthal (Washington, D.C.: Georgetown University Press, 1995), 58–77 at 75. On Lincoln and Churchill, see Cohen, *Supreme Command;* on Washington, see especially *LGW,* 465–69, and Brookhiser, *Founding Father,* passim.

25. Stephen Knott, "George Washington and the Founding of American Clandestine Activity," in *Secret and Sanctioned: Covert Operations and the American Presidency* (New York: Oxford University Press, 1996), 13–26; see also 27–57.

26. Alexis de Tocqueville, *Democracy in America,* eds. Harvey Mansfield and Delba Winthrop (Chicago: University of Chicago Press, 2000), Vol. 1, pt. 2, ch. 6, 220.

27. See Brookhiser, *Founding Father*, 84–91, 97–100; *W*, 789, 829, 870–73, 882–84, 887–93, 922.

28. Tocqueville, "The Manner in Which American Democracy Conducts External Affairs of State," in *Democracy in America*, Vol. 1, pt. 1, ch. 5, 217.

29. Compare Karl-Friedrich Walling, *Republican Empire: Alexander Hamilton on War and Free Government* (Lawrence, Kans.: University Press of Kansas, 1999) with Robert Tucker and David Hendrickson, *Empire of Liberty: The Statecraft of Thomas Jefferson* (New York: Oxford University Press, 1990); see also Madison's essay "Universal Peace" (1792) in *James Madison: Writings,* ed. Jack Rakove (New York: Literary Classics of the United States, 1999) 505–08.

30. *W*, 920–22, 930–32; *LGW*, ch. 30–32.

31. Classic studies are Samuel Bemis, "Washington's Farewell Address: A Foreign Policy of Independence" (1934), in *American Foreign Policy and the Blessings of Liberty* (New Haven, Conn.: Yale University Press, 1962), 240–58, and Felix Gilbert, *To the Farewell Address: Ideas of Early American Foreign Policy* (Princeton, NJ: Princeton University Press, 1961), 115–36, especially 124–36. I am indebted to the studies by Garrity, Spalding and Garrity, and McDougal cited in note 3.

32. Joshua Muravchik contrasts "Washingtonian" isolationism and "Wilsonian" internationalism in *The Imperative of American Leadership: A Challenge to Neo-Isolationism* (Washington, D.C.: AEI Press, 1996), 20–21, 210; see Patrick Buchanan's similar misreading in *A Republic, Not an Empire: Reclaiming America's Destiny,* 2nd ed. (Washington, D.C.: Regnery, 1999, 2002).

33. See Theodore Roosevelt, "Washington's Forgotten Maxim" (address at Naval War College, 1897), in *The Works of Theodore Roosevelt,* National Edition (New York: Charles Scribner's Sons, 1926), 13:182–99.

34. Montesquieu, *Spirit of Laws,* Bk. 1 ch. 3, Bk. 9, Bk. 10 (especially ch. 1–6); see also Gerhard von Glahn, *Law Among Nations: An Introduction to Public International Law,* 5th ed. (New York: Macmillan, 1986), 3,

22–25, 27–35; and David Hendrickson, "Foundations of the New Diplomacy," in *Peace Pact: The Lost World of the American Founding* (Lawrence, Kans.: University Press of Kansas, 2003), 169–76.

35. Montesquieu, *Spirit of Laws,* Bk. 19 ch. 27 (end), 333.

36. See William Galston, "Thinking About the Draft," *The Public Interest* 154 (2004): 61–73.

37. George Kennan, "On American Principles," *Foreign Affairs* 74 (Summer 1995): 116–26; and Kissinger, *Does America Need a Foreign Policy?* 237–40; see "Address of July 4, 1821" in *John Quincy Adams and American Continental Empire,* ed. Walter LaFeber (Chicago: Quadrangle Books, 1965), 45 (emphasis in original); see also Hendrickson, "Renovation of Foreign Policy."

38. Fareed Zakaria, *The Future of Freedom: Illiberal Democracy at Home and Abroad* (New York: Norton, 2003), advocates liberal constitutionalism with guidance from Montesquieu, the American framers, and Tocqueville.

39. For Clausewitzian strategy as alert to the limits of "total war" and of technology, see Andreas Herberg-Rothe, "Primacy of 'Politics' or 'Culture' over War in a Modern World: Clausewitz Needs a Sophisticated Interpretation," *Defense Analysis* 17 (Summer 2001): 175–86; and Frederick Kagan, "War and Aftermath," *Policy Review* 120 (August 2003): 3–28.

40. An analysis of the Bush administration's 2002 *National Security Strategy* from this larger perspective is John Lewis Gaddis, "A Grand Strategy," *Foreign Policy* 133 (November/December 2002): 50–57.

41. Recent examples of just war realism range from Reinhold Niebuhr, *The Irony of American History* (New York: Charles Scribner's Sons, 1952), to Michael Walzer, *Just and Unjust Wars: A Moral Argument with Historical Illustrations* (New York: Basic Books, 1977), to Jean Bethke Elshtain, *Just War Against Terror: The Burden of American Power in a Violent World* (New York: Basic Books, 2003).

AMERICA'S PRECARIOUS EMINENCE

REINHOLD NIEBUHR

In less than half a century, our nation has emerged from a condition of continental security to a position where its own security is intimately bound to the security of a whole community of free nations. Only yesterday we lived in a state of childlike innocence, in which the contentions and alarms of world politics interrupted our youthful dreams only as distant thunder may echo through the happy conversations of a garden party. Today we have become the senior partner in a vast alliance of nations, trying desperately to achieve sufficient unity and health to ward off the threat of tyrannical unification of the world. We are like some adolescent boy, suddenly called upon to assume a father's responsibility for a numerous family.

These responsibilities have come to us at the precise moment in history when technical developments have made the world potentially one, but only

This essay has been edited and is reprinted from Reinhold Niebuhr on Politics, *ed. Harry R. Davis and Robert C. Good (New York: Charles Scribner's Sons, 1960), 269–83.*

potentially so.[1] It was not exactly a kind fate that gave America so great and so precarious an eminence in the world at this precise historical moment. There is an ironic element in this destiny, for the same technical developments that have created the necessity, without achieving the actuality, of such a world community are also responsible for the power that gives our nation such an unchallenged hegemony in the Western world. Technical efficiency and the unusually generous natural resources of a continent have made us economically the most powerful nation on earth, in an era in which economic power is more quickly transmuted into political and military power than in any previous age. The same industrial production, which was so quickly transmuted into military power during World War II, is also the basis of our political hegemony in the post-war period. An impoverished world must wait upon the decisions of the American economic Colossus, not because it trusts our wisdom but because it depends upon our economic resources.[2]

To add to our perplexities, it is also the moment in history when a once-utopian creed of world unity through world revolution has become an instrument of power in the hands of a cynical group of tyrannical oligarchs, operating from the base of a powerful nation and seeking to bring the nations of the world under its dominion by their fear of its power and their confidence in its virtuous intentions.

Roman and British imperialism both had the advantage of a longer period of apprenticeship before assuming so wide a scope of responsibilities. And neither faced a foe of such formidable proportions. Our position is not an enviable one.[3]

THE PROPHETIC IDEA OF DESTINY

The prophet Amos was certain of two things. One was that Israel had been particularly chosen of God, and the other was that this special mission gave the nation not a special security but a special peril. "You only have I chosen," he declared in God's name, "therefore will I visit you with your iniquities." Only those who have no sense of the profundities of history would deny that various nations and classes, various social groups and races, are at various times placed in such a position that a special measure of the divine mission in history falls upon them. In that sense, God has chosen America in this fateful period of world history.

The world requires a wider degree of community. If this community is to be genuine, it cannot, of course, be superimposed by American or any other power. All peoples and nations must find their rightful place in the fellowship. Nevertheless neither the world community nor any other form of human society ever moves as logically or abstractly as some of the "planners" and blueprinters imagine. Some nation or group always has a higher degree of power and responsibility in the formation of community than others.

But the fact is that no nation or individual is ever good enough to deserve the position of leadership that some nations and individuals achieve. If the history that leads to a special mission is carefully analyzed, it always becomes apparent that factors, other than the virtues of the leader, are partly responsible for the position the individual or collective leader holds. Those who do not believe in God's providence in history will call these factors "accidents" or "fortunes." If they are purely accidental, then history itself has no meaning, for man is destined to live in a completely capricious world. The religious man perceives them as gifts of grace. The grace that determines the lives of men and nations is manifest in all the special circumstances, favors and fortunes of geography and climate, of history and fate, which lead to eminence despite the weakness and sinfulness of the beneficiary of such eminence.

If we know that we have been chosen beyond our deserts, we must also begin to realize that we have not been chosen for our particular task in order that our own life may be aggrandized. We ought not derive either special security or special advantages from our high historical mission. The real fact is that we are placed in a precarious moral and historical position by our special mission. It can be justified only if it results in good for the whole community of mankind. Woe unto us if we fail, for our failure will bring judgment upon both us and the world. That is the meaning of the prophetic word: "Therefore will I visit you with your iniquities." This word must be translated today into meanings relevant to our own history. If this is not done, we are bound to fail. For the natural pride of great nations is such that any special historical success quickly aggravates it until it becomes the source of moral and political confusion.[4]

In this precarious situation, our only chance of survival, with which the survival of Western civilization is inextricably joined, lies in a modest recognition of our weaknesses and inadequacies for our task. If ever a nation required the spirit of genuine contrition and humility, it is ours. The future of the world literally depends, not upon the display of our power (although the use of it is necessary and inevitable), but upon the acquisition of virtues that can develop only in humility.[5]

THE INNOCENT NATION

Yet we are (according to our traditional theory) the most innocent nation on earth. It is particularly remarkable that the two great religious-moral traditions which informed our early life—New England Calvinism, and Virginian Deism and Jeffersonianism —arrived at remarkably similar conclusions about the meaning of our national character and destiny. Calvinism may have held too pessimistic views of human nature, and too mechanical views of the providential ordering of human life. But when it assessed the significance of the American experiment, both its conceptions of American destiny and its appreciation of American virtue finally arrived at conclusions strikingly similar to those of Deism.

The New England conception of our virtue began as the belief that the church that had been established on our soil was purer than any church of Christendom. In Edward Johnson's *Wonder Working Providence of Zion's Saviour* (1650), the belief is expressed that "Jesus Christ had manifested his kingly office toward his churches more fully than ever yet the sons of men saw." Practically every Puritan tract contained the conviction that the Protestant Reformation reached its final culmination here.

Jefferson's conception of the innocence and virtue of the new nation was not informed by the Biblical symbolism of the New England tracts. His religious faith was a form of Christianity that had passed through the rationalism of the French Enlightenment. His sense of providence was expressed in his belief in the power of "nature's God" over the vicissitudes of history. In any event, nature's God had a very special purpose in founding this new community. The purpose was to make a new beginning in a corrupt world.

Whether our nation interprets its spiritual heritage through Massachusetts or Virginia, we came into existence with the sense of being a "separated" nation, which God was using to make a new beginning for mankind. We had renounced the evils of European feudalism. We had escaped from the evils of European religious bigotry. We had found broad spaces for the satisfaction of human desires in place of crowded Europe. Whether, as in the case of the New England theocrats, our forefathers thought of our "experiment" as primarily the creation of a new and purer church, or, as in the case of Jefferson and his coterie, they thought primarily of a new political community, they believed in either case that we had been called out by God to create a new humanity. We were God's "American Israel." Our pretensions of innocence therefore heightened the whole concept of a virtuous humanity that characterizes the culture of our era and involves us in the ironic incongruity between our illusions and the realities that we experience. We find it almost as difficult as the communists to believe that anyone could think ill of us, because we are as persuaded as they that our society is so essentially virtuous that only malice could prompt criticism of any of our actions.

Every nation has its own form of spiritual pride. These examples of American self-appreciation could be matched by similar sentiments in other nations. But every nation also has its peculiar version. Our version is that our nation turned its back upon the vices of Europe and made a new beginning.[6]

We lived for a century not only in the illusion but in the reality of innocence in our foreign relations. We lacked the power in the first instance to become involved in the guilt of its use. As we gradually achieved power, through the economic consequences of our richly stored continent, the continental unity of our economy, and the technical efficiency of our business and industrial enterprise, we sought for a time to preserve innocence by disavowing the responsibilities of power. The surge of our infant strength over a continent, which claimed Oregon, California,

Florida, and Texas against any sovereignty that may have stood in our way, was not innocent. It was the expression of a will-to-power of a new community, in which the land hunger of hardy pioneers and settlers furnished the force of imperial expansion. The organs of government, whether political or military, played only a secondary role. From those early days to the present moment, we have frequently been honestly deceived because our power availed itself of covert rather than overt instruments. One of the most prolific causes of delusion about power in a commercial society is that economic power is more covert than political or military power.

We believed, until the outbreak of the First World War, that there is a generic difference between us and the other nations of the world. This was proved by the difference between their power rivalries and our alleged contentment with our lot. The same President of the United States who ultimately interpreted the First World War as a crusade to "make the world safe for democracy" reacted to its first alarms with the reassuring judgment that the conflict represented trade rivalries with which we need not be concerned. We were drawn into the war by considerations of national interest, which we hardly dared to confess to ourselves. Our European critics may, however, overshoot the mark if they insist that the slogan of making "the world safe for democracy" was merely an expression of that moral cant which we seemed to have inherited from the British, only to express it with less subtlety than they. For the fact is that every nation is caught in the moral paradox of refusing to go to war unless it can be proved that the national interest is imperiled and of continuing in the war only by proving that something much more than national interest is at stake.

More significant than our actions and interpretations in the First World War was our mood after its conclusion. Our "realists" feared that our sense of responsibility toward a nascent world community had exceeded the canons of a prudent self-interest. Our idealists, of the thirties, sought to preserve our innocence by neutrality. The main force of isolationism came from the "realists," as the slogan "America First" signifies. But the abortive effort to defy the forces of history, which were both creating a potential world community and increasing the power of America beyond that of any other nation, was supported by pacifist idealists, Christian and secular, and by other visionaries who desired to preserve our innocence. They had a dim and dark understanding of the fact that power cannot be wielded without guilt, because it is never transcendent over interest, even when it tries to subject itself to universal standards and places itself under the control of a nascent worldwide community. They did not understand that the disavowal of the responsibilities of power can involve an individual or nation in even more grievous guilt.

There are two ways of denying our responsibilities to our fellow men. The one is the way of imperialism, expressed in seeking to dominate them by our power.

The other is the way of isolationism, expressed in seeking to withdraw from our responsibilities to them. Geographic circumstances and the myths of our youth rendered us more susceptible to the latter than the former temptation. This has given our national life a unique color, which is not without some moral advantages. No powerful nation in history has ever been more reluctant to acknowledge the position it has achieved in the world than we. The moral advantage lies in the fact that we do not have a strong lust of power, although we are quickly acquiring the pride of power which always accompanies its possession. Our lack of the lust of power makes the fulminations of our foes against us singularly inept. However, we have been so deluded by the concept of our innocence that we are ill prepared to deal with the temptations of power that now assail us.

The Second World War quickly dispelled the illusions of both our realists and idealists. We emerged from that war the most powerful nation on earth. To the surprise of our friends and critics, we seemed also to have sloughed off the tendencies toward irresponsibility that had characterized us in the long armistice between the world wars. We were determined to exercise the responsibilities of our power.

The exercise of this power required us to hold back the threat of Europe's inundation by communism through the development of all kinds of instruments of mass destruction, including atomic weapons. Thus an "innocent" nation finally arrives at the ironic climax of its history. It finds itself the custodian of the ultimate weapon that perfectly embodies and symbolizes the moral ambiguity of physical warfare. We could not disavow the possible use of the weapon, partly because no imperiled nation is morally able to dispense with weapons which insure its survival. All nations, unlike some individuals, lack the capacity to prefer a noble death to a morally ambiguous survival. But we also could not renounce the weapon because the freedom or survival of our allies depended upon the threat of its use. Yet if we should use it, we would cover ourselves with a terrible guilt. We might insure our survival in a world in which it might be better not to be alive. Thus the moral predicament in which all human striving is involved has been raised to a final pitch for a culture and for a nation that thought it an easy matter to distinguish between justice and injustice and believed itself to be peculiarly innocent. In this way, the perennial moral predicaments of human history have caught up with a culture that knew nothing of sin or guilt, and with a nation which seemed to be the most perfect fruit of that culture.[7]

Nations, as individuals, who are completely innocent in their own esteem, are insufferable in their human contacts. The whole world suffers from the pretensions of the communist oligarchs. Our pretensions are of a different order because they are not as consistently held. In any event, we have preserved a system of freedom in which they may be challenged. Yet our American nation, involved in its vast responsibilities, must slough off many illusions that were derived both from the experiences and the ideologies of its childhood. Otherwise either we will seek escape from responsibilities that involve unavoidable guilt, or we will be plunged into avoidable guilt by too great confidence in our virtues.[8]

THE MASTER OF DESTINY

There is a deep layer of messianic consciousness in the mind of America. We were always vague, as the whole liberal culture is fortunately vague, about how power is to be related to the allegedly universal values that we hold in trust for mankind. We were, of course, not immune to the temptation of believing that the universal validity of what we held in trust justified our use of power to establish it. Thus in the debate on the annexation of Oregon, in which the imperial impulse of a youthful nation expressed itself, a congressman could thunder: "If ours is to be the home of the oppressed, we must extend our territory in latitude and longitude to the demand of the millions which are to follow us; as well for our own posterity as for those who are invited to our peaceful shores to partake in our republican institutions."

Generally, however, the legitimization of power was not the purpose of our messianic consciousness. We felt that by example and by unexplained forces in history, our dream would become the regnant reality of history.

We have noted that in both the Calvinist and the Jeffersonian concept of our national destiny, the emphasis lay at the beginning upon providence rather than human power. Jefferson had proposed for the seal of the United States a picture of "the children of Israel, led by a cloud by day and a pillar of fire by night." Except in moments of aberration, we have not thought of ourselves as the potential masters, but as tutors of mankind in its pilgrimage to perfection.

Such messianic dreams, although fortunately not corrupted by the lust of power, have not, of course, been free of the moral pride that creates a hazard to their realization. "God has not been preparing the English-speaking and Teutonic peoples," declared Senator Beveridge of Indiana,

for a thousand years for nothing but vain and idle self-contemplation and self-admiration. He has made us the master organizers of the world to establish system where chaos reigns. He has made us adept in government that we may administer government among savage and senile peoples. Were it not for such a force this world would relapse into barbarism and night. And of all our race He has marked the American people as His chosen nation to finally lead in the regeneration of the world.

The concept of administering "government among savage and senile peoples" did of course have power implications. But once again, the legitimization of power has generally been subordinate in the American dream to the concept that the nation is committed by divine mandate "to lead in the regeneration of mankind." American government has been regarded as the final and universally valid form of political organization. It was expected to gain its ends by moral attraction and imitation. Only occasionally has a hysterical statesman suggested that we must increase our power and use it to gain the ideal ends, of which providence has made us the trustees.

The American dream is not particularly unique. Almost every nation has had a version of it. But the American experience represents a particularly unique and ironic refutation of the illusion in all such dreams. The illusions about the possibility of managing historical destiny from any particular standpoint in history always involve miscalculations both about the power and the wisdom of the managers and about the weakness and manageability of the historical "stuff" that is to be managed.

The first element of irony lies in our nation having in fact and without particularly seeking it acquired a greater degree of power than any other nation in history. The same technics, proficiency in the use of which lies at the foundation of American power, have created a "global" political situation, in which the responsible use of this power has become a condition of survival of the free world.

But the second element of irony lies in the fact that a strong America is less completely master of its own destiny than was a comparatively weak America.[9] We have grown from infancy to adolescence and from adolescence to maturity in quick and easy strides; and we were inclined to solve every problem, as young people do, by increasing our strength. Now we have suddenly come upon a mystery of life. It is that an infant in his cradle is in some respects more powerful than a man in his maturity. For the infant's every wish is fulfilled by some benevolent attendant, but the wishes of a mature man are subject to the hazards of many conflicting and competing desires. We were stronger as a nation when we rocked in the cradle of our continental security than we are today when we "bestride this narrow world like a huge colossus." For the patterns of history have grown more rapidly than our strength.[10]

The same strength that has extended our power beyond a continent has also interwoven our destiny with the destiny of many peoples and brought us into a vast web of history, in which other wills, running in oblique or contrasting directions to our own, inevitably hinder or contradict what we most fervently desire. We cannot simply have our way, not even when we believe our way to have the "happiness of mankind" as its promise. Even in the greatness of our power, we are thwarted by a ruthless foe, who is ironically the more recalcitrant and ruthless because his will is informed by an impossible dream of bringing happiness to all men if only he can eliminate our recalcitrance.

But we are thwarted by friends and allies as well as by foes. Our dream of the universal good is sufficiently valid to bring us into voluntary alliance with many peoples who have similar conceptions of the good life. But neither their conceptions of the good, nor their interests, which are always compounded with ideals, are identical with our own. In this situation, it is natural that many of our people should fail to perceive that historical destiny may be beguiled, deflected, and transfigured by human policy, but that it cannot be coerced.[11]

Moreover, a nation that believed itself to be the master of destiny must now make fateful decisions in an atmosphere of catastrophe. We share this problem with the entire world, but we face it in the most acute form because our responsibilities are very great. Our leaders inform us that our policies are "calculated risks." We have not been accustomed to calculated risks, for we have thrived for a long time on "safe" investments. Our whole culture has predisposed us to justify every action by its promise of rewards. We want to sow where and when we are certain to reap. Now we must sow with no certain guarantee of a harvest. No one can honestly promise us that a given policy will certainly avert a disastrous war or the triumph of communism. It is quite obvious that the world will not enjoy peace for a long while to come. The whole modern generation, even beyond our own nation, finds this prospect difficult to bear, more particularly because we have been informed by a culture that assumed that historical development assured man a more and more secure existence.[12]

The Christian faith offers no escape from life's vicissitudes. It preaches no craven resignation. We must act and assume responsibility within the limits of our powers. But we must also understand that our powers have limits. We are not God. Some of the hysteria in which our nation has been involved derived from the puncturing of the vain delusion that we were a kind of god, who could command the waves of history to obey us.[13]

POWER AND PRIDE

Powerful men and nations are in greater peril from their own illusions than from their neighbors' hostile designs. Their power secures them against untoward attempts upon their privileges and possessions, even though it may arouse jealous hostility in their neighbors. But their power does not protect them against their own follies, which are indeed aggravated by the privileges of power.

Our own nation has achieved a degree of power in the contemporary world community that dwarfs the dominions of the empires of the past. We are in obvious danger of being beguiled by the pride that tends to corrupt the powerful. One form of this pride is the pretension that our power is the natural fruit of our virtue.[14]

It is in fact difficult for all fortunate people to resist the conclusion that their fortune and their power must be regarded as the reward of their virtues. Usually the virtues ostensibly rewarded are those of thrift and diligence. But we add another social virtue to these traditionally respected ones. We assume that we are so fortunate because we are so "free." We do not usually mean that the basic democratic rights are best preserved among us, although we are not above that pretension. We usually mean that our economy is subject to fewer restraints than that of any nation. This is indeed true, although it may be questioned how much the freedom of our economy is the consequence rather than the cause of our productivity. The more meager the social fund to be divided, the greater is the interest in the just division of the fund. This explains why the poorer nations of Europe, although boasting of many democratic achievements that we have not attained, have more restraints upon their economic life than we do.[15]

We have forgotten to what degree the wealth of our natural resources and the fortuitous circumstance that we conquered a continent just when the advancement of technology made it possible to organize that continent into a single political and economic unit lay at the foundation of our prosperity.[16] Such religious awe before, and gratitude for, "unmerited" mercies was dissipated fairly early in American life. It remains the frame of our annual presidential Thanksgiving proclamations, which have, however, contained for many years a contradictory substance within the frame. They have congratulated God on the virtues and ideals of the American people, which have so well merited the blessings of prosperity we enjoy.[17] In this matter, we ought to heed the advice in Deuteronomy: "Understand therefore, that the Lord thy God giveth thee this good land to possess, not because of thy righteousness, for thou art a stiff-necked people." There is no greater temptation for a fortunate nation than to transmute its "uncovenanted mercies" into proofs and rewards of its alleged virtues.

Our self-esteem derives also from the fact that we are embattled with a foe who embodies all the evils of a demonic religion. We are by comparison more righteous than our foe, even as we were more righteous than the Nazi tyranny. We will probably be at sword's point with this foe for generations to come. It is difficult to discern the judgments of God upon a person or nation when that person or nation is engaged in mortal combat with an evil foe. All conflicts make for self-righteousness among the disputants. Disputants to a conflict may, in fact, be regarded as constitutionally self-righteous. But if the foe is obviously evil and when he embodies a creed in its most consistent form, which, in its less consistent form had proved to be an instrument of criticism in our own world, the temptation to discount all criticism is very great. Thus we are in danger of sinking into a mood of self-congratulation, which must be, as indeed it is, a trial to all our friends, no matter how grateful they may be that our strength is dedicated to the cause of freedom.

The distinguished English historian, Herbert Butterfield, in his book *Christianity, Diplomacy and War* (1953), has gone so far as to describe the present situation as a conflict between "two organized systems of self-righteousness." We may be offended that he makes no distinction between the quality of self-righteousness among us and that which is encouraged by an explicitly idolatrous religion. Indeed, he is too prone to equate the evils on both sides. But he has at least given us a glimpse of the effect of our national self-esteem upon our most intimate ally, Britain.[18]

Our pride is a great embarrassment in our relation to the democratic world. The more we indulge in an uncritical reverence for the supposed wisdom of our American way of life, the more odious we make it in the eyes of the world, and the more we destroy our moral authority, without which our economic and military power will become impotent. Thus we are undermining the reality of our power by our uncritical pride in it.[19]

We will incarnate the democratic cause the more truly, the more we can overcome the pretension of embodying it perfectly. We will stand the more surely if we "take heed lest we fall." Our power will be used the more justly, if we recognize that our possession of it is not a proof of our virtue. Our possession of it is either an "accident" or it is a gift of grace. It is a gift of grace if we recognize history as a realm of divine providence and not as a series of accidents. If it is recognized as a gift of grace, it must also become apparent that every gift of grace that is pretentiously appropriated as our due turns into a curse. Whether our nation can sense both the grace and the judgment of God in its history is thus the pivotal problem in our national destiny.[20]

Ideally, it is the function of a religion that possesses any prophetic dimension to mediate an ultimate divine judgment upon men and nations who would otherwise sink into a morass of self-esteem. The Christian church must therefore regard it as one of its most important missions to disturb the mood of national self-congratulation into which our nation is sinking. If the church is to perform this task, it must know, however, that the "prophetic" mission to the nation does not come easily or automatically to the church. Religion qua religion is naturally idolatrous, accentuating, rather than diminishing, the self-worship of men and nations, by assuring them of an ultimate sanction for their dearest desires. Insofar as our congregations are merely religious communities in which an uncritical piety is nourished, they also do no more than to mix patriotic self-congratulation with the worship of God. It requires both courage and astuteness to penetrate the armor of the nation's self-righteousness. But above all, it requires knowledge of and devotion to the one true God who declares to even the most righteous of nations, "You only have I chosen; therefore will I visit you with your iniquities."[21]

Thus a contrite recognition of our own sins destroys the illusion of eminence through virtue and lays the foundation for the apprehension of "grace" in our national life. We know that we have the position that we hold in the world today partly by reason of factors and forces in the complex pattern of history, which we did not create and from which we do not deserve to benefit. If we apprehend this religiously, the sense of destiny ceases to be a vehicle of pride and becomes the occasion for a new sense of responsibility.[22]

POWER AND RESPONSIBILITY

There is a fateful significance in the coincidence of America's coming of age and that period of world history when the paramount problem is the creation of some kind of world community. The world must find a way of avoiding complete anarchy in its international life, and America must find a way of using its great power responsibly. These two needs are organically related, for the world problem cannot be solved if America does not accept its full share of responsibility in solving it.[23] From an ultimate standpoint, this need not be regretted, for a nation that cannot save itself without at the same time saving a whole world has the possibility of achieving a concurrence between its own interests and "the general welfare," which must be regarded as the highest form of virtue in man's collective life.[24]

One moral resource not usually envisaged among our ideals and values is particularly necessary for a nation that wields as much power as our own. It is a resource that was known in the classical ages of Christianity but has largely disappeared in a rationalistic and sentimental age. This resource is an understanding of the moral ambiguity that power and self-interest introduce into political and economic structures. No political order, whether national or international, is ever a pure incarnation of brotherhood or the fruit of pure unselfishness. Order and justice cannot be maintained by coercion alone, but they cannot be maintained without it. The power required to preserve order is never so perfectly adjusted to the necessities of justice that one may have an easy conscience about its exercise. Self-interest is another source of moral ambiguity in the world of politics. Individuals and nations are capable of considering the interests of others. Without such a capacity for justice, human society would degenerate into an anarchy of conflicting claims. But the political order must also harness, deflect, and beguile the self-interest of individuals, classes, and nations. It can never completely suppress or transfigure particular loyalties and motives of self-interest. Politics must, as David Hume asserted, assume the selfishness of man.

Modern culture, particularly in America, has had the greatest difficulty in dealing with the moral ambiguities of the political and economic order. Our political scientists and men of affairs frequently seem to be divided into three classes: the sentimentalists imagine that the life of nations can be brought into conformity with the purest standards of generosity; the cynics deny every moral standard in political and economic life because they have discerned the morally ambiguous elements in it; and the hypocrites profess one standard and practice another. Sometimes it would seem as if the world were divided merely between sentimentalists who are afraid to exercise power and responsibility because they fear its corruption and the cynics who exercise it without a twinge of conscience. The temptations to sentimentality and cynicism have always existed, but they have increased since the decay of religion. It was one of the merits of the Christian interpretation of the human situation that it understood, as Pascal put it, both the dignity and the misery of man, both his capacity for goodness and his corruption of that goodness. It insisted that men ought to consider the rights of their fellow men, but it also knew that they never did so perfectly. It knew that human sin made coercion in government necessary, but it also knew that the lust for power of the ruler made government dangerous. It regarded all human majesties as, at the same time, derived from the divine majesty and in rebellion against it. This wholesome paradoxical attitude toward the problems of political and economic justice usually disintegrates in modern life, and the consequence is either cynicism or sentimentality.

Unlike the communists, we do not have a philosophy of life that makes us constitutionally fanatical and self-righteous. But we are constantly tempted to weaken the virtue of our cause by too unqualified claims for it and to suffer from periodic fits of disillusionment, when the moral ambiguity of our position becomes apparent. We must resist this temptation the more resolutely because we not only have great power but are called upon to exercise its responsibilities in a world situation in which there are no possibilities of pure and unequivocal justice. Yet there are tremendously important moral decisions to be made. Above all, it is important that we fulfill our responsibilities with steadiness and resolution, without the distractions of the alternate moods of cynicism and sentimentality.

We must learn to bear the responsibilities of power in America without imagining either that the exercise of our power will be perfectly just or that we would be a better nation if we disavowed our responsibilities for the sake of being pure.[25]

It is foolish to hope that America could bear its present responsibilities in the world without regard to national self-interest. It is equally foolish to deny that national self-interest may always become so narrow as to corrupt the virtue of what we are doing. The virtue of every political measure can never be assessed in terms of pure black or white.

If we succumb to the temptation of hypocrisy and claim too pure a virtue for our international politics, we shall merely invite the world's derision and contempt. This derision will be forthcoming the more readily because powerful nations are not generally popular. Moreover, we shall also relax our own moral restraints too much by such a procedure. Power ought always to be exercised with a certain uneasiness of conscience. When the conscience becomes easy, self-righteousness aggravates the moral weakness of the wielder of power. Furthermore, such hypocrisy and self-righteousness always tend to alienate a certain sensitive minority in every nation. This minority is usually quite sentimental about the realities of the political order. But it is, or ought to be, the bearer of the conscience of the nation.

All political justice and order are achieved by men and nations who have a margin of goodness or virtue beyond their self-interest. But they must not deny the interested motives that partly prompt their action. Otherwise their marginal virtue will turn to vice.[26]

A European statesman stated the issue very well recently: "We are grateful to America for saving us from communism. But our gratitude does not prevent us from fearing that we might become an American colony. That danger lies in the situation of America's power and Europe's weakness." The statesman, when reminded of the strain of genuine idealism in American life, replied:

The idealism does indeed prevent America from a gross abuse of its power. But it might well accentuate the danger Europeans confront. For American power in the service of American idealism could create a situation in which we would be too impotent to correct you when you are wrong and you would be too idealistic to correct yourself.

Such a measured judgment on the virtues and perils of America's position in the world community accurately describes the hazards we confront. Our moral perils are not those of conscious malice or the explicit lust for power. They are the perils that can be understood only if we realize the ironic tendency of virtues to turn into vices when too complacently relied on, and of power to become vexatious if the wisdom that directs it is trusted too confidently. The ironic elements in American history can be overcome, in short, only if American idealism comes to terms with the limits of all human striving, the fragmentariness of all human wisdom, the precariousness of all historic configurations of power, and the mixture of good and evil in all human virtue. America's moral and spiritual success in relating itself creatively to a world community requires, not so much a guard against the gross vices, about which the idealists warn us, as a reorientation of the whole structure of our idealism. That idealism is too oblivious of the ironic perils to which human virtue, wisdom, and power are subject. It is too certain that there is a straight path toward the goal of human happiness, too confident of the wisdom and idealism that prompt men and nations toward that goal, and too blind to the curious compounds of good and evil in which the actions of the best men and nations abound.[27]

NOTES

1. Reinhold Niebuhr, "The Conditions of Our Survival," *Virginia Quarterly Review* 26 (Autumn 1950): 481.

2. Reinhold Niebuhr, "America's Precarious Eminence," *Virginia Quarterly Review* 23 (Autumn 1947): 481–82.

3. Niebuhr, "The Conditions of Our Survival," 481–82.

4. Reinhold Niebuhr, "Anglo-Saxon Destiny and Responsibility," *Christianity and Crisis* 3 (October 4, 1943): 2–3.

5. Reinhold Niebuhr, "America's Eminence," *Christianity and Society* 13 (Summer 1948): 4.

6. Reinhold Niebuhr, *The Irony of American History* (New York: Charles Scribner's Sons, 1952), 23–28.

7. Niebuhr, *The Irony of American History*, 35–39.

8. Niebuhr, *The Irony of American History*, 42.

9. Niebuhr, *The Irony of American History*, 69–74.

10. Reinhold Niebuhr, "The Moral Implications of Loyalty to the United Nations," Hazen Pamphlet No. 29 (New Haven: Hazen, 1952), 11–12.

11. Niebuhr, *The Irony of American History*, 74–75.

12. Niebuhr, "The Conditions of Our Survival," 484.

13. Reinhold Niebuhr, "To Be Abased and To Abound," *Messenger* 16 (February 13, 1951): 7.

14. Reinhold Niebuhr, "American Pride and Power," *American Scholar* 17 (Autumn 1948): 393.

15. Reinhold Niebuhr, "The Peril of Complacency in Our Nation," *Christianity and Crisis* 14 (February 8, 1954): 1.

16. Niebuhr, *The Irony of American History*, 49.

17. Niebuhr, *The Irony of American History*, 52–53.

18. Niebuhr, "The Peril of Complacency in Our Nation," 1.

19. Niebuhr, "American Pride and Power," 394.

20. Niebuhr, "America's Eminence," 3–4.

21. Niebuhr, "The Peril of Complacency in Our Nation," 1–2.

22. Niebuhr, "Anglo-Saxon Destiny and Responsibility," 3.

23. Reinhold Niebuhr, "American Power and World Responsibility," *Christianity and Crisis* 3 (April 5, 1943): 2.

24. Niebuhr, "The Conditions of Our Survival," 482.

25. Reinhold Niebuhr, "Hazards and Resources," *Virginia Quarterly Review* 24 (Spring 1949): 201–2, 203, 204.

26. Niebuhr, "Hazards and Resources," 203.

27. Niebuhr, *The Irony of American History*, 132–33.

THE TRIUMPH OF JUST WAR THEORY
(AND THE DANGERS OF SUCCESS)

MICHAEL WALZER

I

Some political theories die and go to heaven; some, I hope, die and go to hell. But some have a long life in this world, a history most often of service to the powers-that-be, but also, sometimes, an oppositionist history. The theory of just war began in the service of the powers. At least that is how I interpret Augustine's achievement: he replaced the radical refusal of Christian pacifists with the active ministry of the Christian soldier. Now pious Christians could fight on behalf of the worldly city, for the sake of imperial peace (in this case, literally, *pax Romana*); but they had to fight justly, only for the sake of peace, and always, Augustine insisted, with a downcast demeanor, without anger or lust.[1] Seen from the perspective of primitive Christianity, this account of just war was simply an excuse, a way of making war morally and religiously possible. And that was indeed the function of the theory. But its defenders would have said, and I am inclined to agree, that it made war possible in a world where war was, sometimes, necessary.

From the beginning, the theory had a critical edge: soldiers (or, at least, their officers) were supposed to refuse to fight in wars of conquest and to oppose or abstain from the standard military practices of rape and pillage after the battle was won. But just war was a worldly theory, in every sense of that term, and it continued to serve worldly interests against Christian radicalism. It is important to note, though, that Christian radicalism had more than one version: it could be expressed in a pacifist rejection of war, but it could also be expressed in war itself, in the religiously driven crusade. Augustine opposed the first of these; the medieval scholastics, following in Aquinas's footsteps, set themselves against the second. The classic statement is Vitoria's: "Difference of religion cannot be a cause of just war." For centuries, from the time of the Crusades to the religious wars of the Reformation years, many of the priests and preachers of Christian Europe, many lords and barons (and even a few kings), had been committed to the legitimacy of using military force against unbelievers: they had their own version of jihad. Vitoria claimed, by contrast, that "the sole and only just cause for waging war is when harm has been inflicted."[2] Just war was an argument of the religious center against paci-

fists, on the one side, and holy warriors, on the other, and because of its enemies (and even though its proponents were theologians), it took shape as a secular theory—which is simply another way of describing its worldliness.

So the rulers of this world embraced the theory, and did not fight a single war without describing it, or hiring intellectuals to describe it, as a war for peace and justice. Most often, of course, this description was hypocritical: the tribute that vice pays to virtue. But the need to pay the tribute opens those who pay it to the criticism of the virtuous—that is, of the brave and virtuous, of whom there have been only a few (but one could also say: at least a few). I cite one heroic moment, from the history of the academic world: sometime around 1520, the faculty of the University of Salamanca met in solemn assembly and voted that the Spanish conquest of Central America was a violation of natural law and an unjust war.[3] I have not been able to learn anything about the subsequent fate of the good professors. Certainly, there were not many moments like that one, but what happened at Salamanca suggests that just war never lost its critical edge. The theory provided worldly reasons for going to war, but the reasons were limited—and they had to be worldly. Converting the Aztecs to Christianity was not a just cause; nor was seizing the gold of the Americas or enslaving its inhabitants.

Writers like Grotius and Pufendorf incorporated just war theory into international law, but the rise of the modern state and the legal (and philosophical) acceptance of state sovereignty pushed the theory into the background. Now the political foreground was occupied by people we can think of as Machiavellian princes, hard men (and sometimes women), driven by "reason of state," who did what (they said) they had to do. Worldly prudence triumphed over worldly justice; realism over what was increasingly disparaged as naive idealism. The princes of the world continued to defend their wars, using the language of international law, which was also, at least in part, the language of just war But the defenses were marginal to the enterprise, and I suspect that it was the least important of the state's intellectuals who put them forward. States claimed a right to fight whenever their rulers deemed it necessary, and the rulers took sovereignty to mean that no one could judge their

This essay has been edited and is reprinted from Michael Walzer, "The Triumph of Just War Theory (and the Dangers of Success)," Social Research 69 (Winter 2002): 925–44. The essay also appeared in Arguing about War *(New Haven, Conn.: Yale University Press, 2004).*

decisions. They not only fought when they wanted; they fought how they wanted, returning to the old Roman maxim that held war to be a lawless activity: *inter arma silent leges*—which, again, was taken to mean that there was no law above or beyond the decrees of the state; conventional restraints on the conduct of war could always be overridden for the sake of victory.[4] Arguments about justice were treated as a kind of moralizing, inappropriate to the anarchic conditions of international society. For this world, just war was not worldly enough.

In the 1950s and early 1960s, when I was in graduate school, realism was the reigning doctrine in the field of "international relations." The standard reference was not to justice but to interest. Moral argument was against the rules of the discipline as it was commonly practiced, although a few writers defended interest as the new morality.[5] There were many political scientists in those years who preened themselves as modern Machiavellis and dreamed of whispering in the ear of the prince; and a certain number of them, enough to stimulate the ambition of the others, actually got to whisper. They practiced being cool and tough-minded; they taught the princes, who did not always need to be taught, how to get results through the calculated application of force. Results were understood in terms of "the national interest," which was the objectively determined sum of power and wealth here and now plus the probability of future power and wealth. More of both was almost always taken to be better; only a few writers argued for the acceptance of prudential limits; moral limits were, as I remember those years, never discussed. Just war theory was relegated to religion departments, theological seminaries, and a few Catholic universities. And even in those places, isolated as they were from the political world, the theory was pressed toward realist positions; perhaps for the sake of self-preservation, its advocates surrendered something of its critical edge.

Vietnam changed all this, although it took a while for the change to register at the theoretical level. What happened first occurred in the realm of practice. The war became a subject of political debate; it was widely opposed, mostly by people on the left. These were people heavily influenced by Marxism; they also spoke a language of interest; they shared with the princes and professors of American politics a disdain for moralizing. And yet the experience of the war pressed them toward moral argument. Of course, the war in their eyes was radically imprudent; it could not be won; its costs, even if Americans thought only of themselves, were much too high; it was an imperialist adventure unwise even for the imperialists; it set the United States against the cause of national liberation, which would alienate it from the Third World (and significant parts of the First). But these claims failed utterly to express the feelings of most of the war's opponents, feelings that had to do with the systematic exposure of Vietnamese civilians to the violence of American war-making. Almost against its will, the left fell into morality. All of us in the antiwar camp suddenly began talking the language of just war—although we did not know that that was what we were doing.

It may seem odd to recall the 1960s in this way, because today, the left seems all too quick to make moral arguments, even absolutist moral arguments. But this description of the contemporary left seems to me mistaken. A certain kind of politicized, instrumental, and highly selective moralizing is indeed increasingly common among leftist writers, but this is not serious moral argument. It is not what we learned, or ought to have learned, from the Vietnam years. What happened then was that people on the left, and many others too, looked for a common moral language. And what was most available was the language of just war. We were, all of us, a bit rusty, unaccustomed to speaking in public about morality. The realist ascendancy had robbed us of the very words that we needed, which we slowly reclaimed: aggression, intervention, just cause, self-defense, noncombatant immunity, proportionality, prisoners of war, civilians, double effect, terrorism, war crimes. And we came to understand that these words had meanings. Of course, they could be used instrumentally—that is always true of political and moral terms. But if we attended to their meanings, we found ourselves involved in a discussion that had its own structure. Like characters in a novel, concepts in a theory shape the narrative or the argument in which they figure.

Once the war was over, just war became an academic subject: now political scientists and philosophers discovered the theory; it was written about in the journals and taught in the universities—and also in the (American) military academies and war colleges. A small group of Vietnam veterans played a major role in making the discipline of morality central to the military curriculum.[6] They had bad memories. They welcomed just war theory precisely because it was in their eyes a critical theory. It is, in fact, doubly critical—of war occasions and its conduct. I suspect that the veterans were most concerned with the second of these. It is not only that they wanted to avoid anything like the My Lai massacre in future wars; they wanted, like professional soldiers everywhere, to distinguish their profession from mere butchery. And because of their Vietnam experience, they believed that this had to be done systematically; it required not only a code but also a theory. Once upon a time, I suppose, aristocratic honor had grounded the military code. In a more democratic and egalitarian age, the code had to be defended with arguments.

And so we argued. The discussions and debates were wide ranging even if, once the war was over, they were mostly academic. It is easy to forget how large the academic world is in the United States: there are millions of students and tens of thousands of professors. So a lot of people were involved, future citizens and army officers, and the theory was mostly presented—although this presentation was also disputed—as a manual for wartime criticism. Our cases and examples were drawn from Vietnam and were framed to invite criticism (the debate over nuclear deterrence also used, in part, the language of just war, but this was a highly technical debate and engaged far fewer people than did Vietnam). Here was a war that we should never have fought, and that we fought badly, brutally, as if there were no moral limits. So it became, retrospectively, an occasion for drawing a line—and for committing ourselves to the moral casuistry necessary to determine the precise location of the line. Ever since Pascal's brilliant denunciation, casuistry has had a bad name among moral philosophers; it is commonly taken to be excessively permissive, not so much an application as a relaxation of the moral rules. When we looked back at the Vietnamese cases, however, we were more likely to deny permission than to grant it, insisting again and again that what had been done should not have been done.

But there was another feature of Vietnam that gave the moral critique of the war special fans: it was a war that we lost, and the brutality with which we fought the war almost certainly contributed to our defeat. In a war for "hearts and minds," rather than for land and resources, justice turns out to be a key to victory. So just war theory looked once again like the worldly doctrine that it is. And here, I think, is the deepest cause of the theory's contemporary triumph: there are now reasons of state for fighting justly. One might almost say that justice has become a military necessity.

There were probably earlier wars in which the deliberate killing of civilians, and also the common military carelessness about killing civilians, proved to be counterproductive. The Boer War is a likely example. But for us, Vietnam was the first war in which the practical value of *jus in bello* became apparent. To be sure, the "Vietnam syndrome" is generally taken to reflect a different lesson: that we should not fight wars that are unpopular at home and to which we are unwilling to commit the resources necessary for victory. But there was in fact another lesson, connected to but not the same as the "syndrome": that we should not fight wars about whose justice we are doubtful, and that once we are engaged we have to fight justly so as not to antagonize the civilian population, whose political support is necessary to a military victory. In Vietnam, the relevant civilians were the Vietnamese themselves; we lost the war when we lost their "hearts and minds." But this idea about the need for civilian support has turned out to be both variable and expansive: modern warfare requires the support of different civilian populations, extending beyond the population immediately at risk. Still, a moral regard for civilians at risk is critically important in winning wider support for the war . . . for any modern war. I will call this the "usefulness of morality." Its wide acknowledgement is something radically new in military history.

Hence the odd spectacle of George Bush (the elder), during the Persian Gulf war, talking like a just war theorist.[7] Well, not quite: for Bush's speeches and press conferences displayed an old American tendency, which his son has inherited, to confuse just wars and crusades, as if a war can be just only when the forces of good are arrayed against the forces of evil. But Bush also seemed to understand—and this was a constant theme of American military spokespersons—that war *is* properly a war of armies, a combat between combatants, from which the civilian population should be shielded. I do not believe that the bombing of Iraq in 1991 met just war standards; shielding civilians would certainly have excluded the destruction of electricity networks and water purification plants. Urban infrastructure, even if it is necessary to modern war-making, is also necessary to civilian existence in a modern city, and it is morally defined by this second feature.[8] Still, American strategy in the Gulf war was the result of a compromise between what justice would have required and the unrestrained bombing of previous wars: taken overall, targeting was far more limited and selective than it had been, for example, in Korea or Vietnam. The reasons for the limits were complicated: in part, they reflected a commitment to the Iraqi people (which turned out not to be very strong), in the hope that the Iraqis would repudiate the war and overthrow the regime that began it; in part, they reflected the political necessities of the coalition that made the war possible. Those necessities were shaped in turn by the media coverage of the war—that is, by the immediate access of the media to the battles and of people the world over to the media. Bush and his generals believed that these people would not tolerate a slaughter of civilians, and they were probably right (but what it might mean for them not to tolerate something was and is fairly unclear). Hence, although many of the countries whose support was crucial to the war's success were not democracies, bombing policy was dictated in important ways by the demos.

This will continue to be true: the media are omnipresent, and the whole world is watching. War has to be different in these circumstances. But does this mean that it has to be more just or only that it has to look more just, that it has to be described, a little more persuasively than in the past, in the language of justice? The triumph of just war theory is clear enough; it is amazing how readily military spokesmen during the Kosovo and Afghanistan wars used its categories, telling a causal story that justified the war and providing accounts of the battles that emphasized the restraint with which they were being fought. The arguments (and rationalizations) of the past were very different; they commonly came from outside the armed forces—from clerics, lawyers, and professors, not from generals—and they commonly lacked specificity and detail. But what does the use of these categories, these just and moral words, signify?

Perhaps naively, I am inclined to say that justice has become, in all Western countries, one of the tests that any proposed military strategy or tactic has to meet—only one of the tests and not the most important one, but this still gives just war theory a place and standing that it never had before. It is easier now than it ever was to imagine a general saying, "No, we can't do that; it would cause too many civilian deaths; we have to find another way." I am not sure that there are many generals who talk like that, but imagine for a moment that there are—imagine that strategies are evaluated morally as well as militarily, civilian deaths are minimized, new technologies are designed to avoid or limit collateral damage, and these technologies are actually effective in achieving their intended purpose. Moral theory has been incorporated into war-making as a real constraint on when and how wars are fought. This picture is, remember, imaginary, but it is also partly true; and it makes for a far more interesting argument than the more standard claim that the triumph of just war is pure hypocrisy. The triumph is real: what then is left for theorists and philosophers to do?

This question is sufficiently present in our consciousness that one can watch people trying to respond. There are two responses that I describe and criticize. The first comes from what might be called the postmodern left, which does not claim that affirmations of justice are hypocritical, as hypocrisy implies standards, but rather that there are no standards, no possible objective use of the categories of just war theory.[9] Politicians and generals who adopt the categories are deluding themselves—although no more so than the theorists who developed the categories in the first place. Maybe new technologies kill fewer people, but there is no point in arguing about who those people are and whether or not killing them is justified. No agreement about justice, or about guilt or innocence, is possible. This view is summed up in a line that speaks to our immediate situation: "One man's terrorist is another man's freedom fighter." On this view, there is nothing for theorists and philosophers to do but choose sides, and there is no theory or principle that can guide their choice. But this is an impossible position, for it holds that we cannot recognize, condemn, and actively oppose the murder of innocent people.

A second response is to take the moral need to recognize, condemn, and oppose very seriously and then to raise the theoretical ante—that is, to strengthen the constraints that justice imposes on warfare. For theorists who pride themselves on living, so to speak, at the critical edge, this is an obvious and understandable response. For many years, we have used the theory of just war to criticize American military actions, and now it has been taken over by the generals and is being used to explain and justify those actions. Obviously, we must resist. The easiest way to resist is to make noncombatant immunity into a stronger and stronger rule, until it is something like an absolute rule: all killing of civilians is (something close to) murder; therefore any war that leads to the killing of civilians is unjust; therefore every war is unjust. So pacifism reemerges from the very heart of the theory that was originally meant to replace it. This is the strategy adopted, most recently, by many opponents of the Afghanistan war. The protest marches on American campuses featured banners proclaiming "Stop the Bombing!" and the argument for stopping was very simple (and obviously true): bombing endangers and kills civilians. The marchers did not seem to feel that anything more had to be said.

Because I believe that war is still, sometimes, necessary, this seems to me a bad argument and, more generally, a bad response to the triumph of just war theory. It sustains the critical role of the theory vis-à-vis war generally, but it denies the theory the critical role it has always claimed, which is internal to the business of war and requires critics to attend closely to what soldiers try to do and what they try not to do. The refusal to make distinctions of this kind, to pay attention to strategic and tactical choices, suggests a doctrine of radical suspicion. This is the radicalism of people who do not expect to exercise power or use force, ever, and who are not prepared to make the judgments that this exercise and use require. By contrast, just war theory, even when it demands a strong critique of particular acts of war, is the doctrine of people who do expect to exercise power and use force. We might think of it as a doctrine of radical responsibility, because it holds political and military leaders responsible, first of all, for the well-being of their own people, but also for the well-being of innocent individuals on the other side. Its proponents set themselves against those who will not think realistically about the defense of the country they live in and also against those who refuse to recognize the humanity of their opponents. They insist that there are things morally impermissible to do even to the enemy. They also insist, however, that fighting itself cannot be morally impermissible. A just war is meant to be, and has to be, a war it is possible to fight.

But there is another danger posed by the triumph of just war theory—not the radical relativism and the near absolutism that I have just described, but rather a certain softening of the critical mind, a truce between theorists and soldiers. If intellectuals are often awed and silenced by political leaders who invite them to dinner, how much more so by generals who talk their language? And if the generals are actually fighting just wars, if *inter arma* the laws speak, what point is there in anything we can say? In fact, however, our role has not changed all that much. We still have to insist that war is a morally dubious and difficult activity. Even if we (in the West) have fought just wars in the Gulf, in Kosovo, and in Afghanistan, that is no guarantee, not even a useful indication, that our next war will be just. And even if the recognition of noncombatant immunity has become militarily necessary, it still conflicts with other, more pressing, necessities, justice still needs to be defended; decisions about when and how to fight require constant scrutiny, exactly as they always have.

At the same time, we have to extend our account of "when and how" to cover the new strategies, the new technologies, and the new politics of a global age. Old ideas may not fit the emerging reality: the "war against terrorism," to take the most current example, requires a kind of international cooperation that is as radically undeveloped in theory as it is in practice. We should welcome military officers into the theoretical argument; they will make it a better argument than it would be if no one but professors took an interest. But we cannot leave the argument to them. As the old saying goes, war is too important to be left to the generals; just war even more so. The ongoing critique of war-making is a centrally important democratic activity.

II

Let me, then, suggest two issues, raised by our most recent wars, that require the critical edge of justice.

First, risk-free war-making. I have heard it said that this is a necessary feature of humanitarian interventions like the Kosovo war: soldiers defending humanity, in contrast to soldiers defending their own country and their fellow citizens, will not risk their lives; or, their political leaders will not dare to ask them to risk their lives. Hence the rescue of people in desperate trouble, the objects of massacre or ethnic cleansing, is only possible if risk-free war is possible.[10] But obviously, it is possible: wars can be fought from a great distance with bombs and missiles aimed very precisely (compared with the radical imprecision of such weapons only a few decades ago) at the forces carrying out the killings and deportations. And the technicians/soldiers aiming these weapons are, in all the recent cases, largely invulnerable to counterattack. There is no principle of just war theory that bars this kind of warfare. So long as they can aim accurately at military targets, soldiers have every right to fight from a safe distance. And what commander, committed to his or her own soldiers, would not choose to fight in this way whenever he or she could? In his reflections on rebellion, Albert Camus argues that one cannot kill unless one is prepared to die.[11] But that argument does not seem to apply to soldiers in battle, where the whole point is to kill while avoiding getting killed. And yet there is a wider sense in which Camus is right.

Just war theorists have not, to my knowledge, discussed this question, but we obviously need to do so. Massacre and ethnic cleansing commonly take place on the ground. The awful work might be done with bombs and poison gas delivered from the air, but in Bosnia, Kosovo, Rwanda, East Timor, and Sierra Leone, the weapons were rifles, machetes, and clubs; the killing and terrorizing of the population was carried out from close up. And a risk-free intervention undertaken from far away—especially if it promises to be effective in the long run—is likely to cause an immediate speed-up on the ground. This can be stopped only if the intervention itself shifts to the ground, and this shift seems to me morally necessary. The aim of the intervention, after all, is to rescue people in trouble, and fighting on the ground, in the case as I have described it, is what rescue requires. But then it is no longer risk-free. Why would anyone undertake it?

In fact, risks of this sort are a common feature of *jus in bello*, and although there are many examples of soldiers unwilling to accept them, there are also many examples of their acceptance. The principle is this: when it is our action that puts innocent people at risk, even if the action is justified, we are bound to do what we can to reduce those risks, even if this involves risks to our own soldiers. If we are bombing military targets in a just war, and there are civilians living near these targets, we have to adjust our bombing policy—by flying at lower altitudes, say—so as to minimize the risks we impose on civilians. Of course, it is legitimate to balance the risks; we cannot require our pilots to fly suicidal missions. They have to be, as Camus suggests, prepared to die, but that is consistent with taking measures to safeguard their lives. How the balance gets worked out is something that has to be debated in each case. But what is not permissible, it seems to me, is what NATO did in the Kosovo war, where its leaders declared in advance that they would not send ground forces into battle, whatever happened inside Kosovo, once the air war began. Responsibility for the intensified Serbian campaign against Kosovar civilians, which was the immediate consequence of the air war, belongs no doubt to the Serbian government and army. They were to blame. But this was at the same time a foreseeable result of our action, and insofar as we did nothing to prepare for this result, or to deal with it, we were blameworthy too. We imposed risks on others and refused to accept them for ourselves, even when that acceptance was necessary to help the others.[12]

The second issue concerns wars' endings. On the standard view, a just war (precisely because it is not a crusade) should end with the restoration of the status quo ante. The paradigm case is a war of aggression, which ends justly when the aggressor has been defeated, his attack repulsed, and the old boundaries restored. Perhaps this is not quite enough for a just conclusion: the victim state might deserve reparations from the aggressor state, so that the damage the aggressor's forces inflicted can be repaired—a more extensive understanding of restoration, but restoration still. And perhaps the peace treaty should include new security arrangements, of a sort that did not exist before the war, so that the status quo will be more stable in the future. But that is as far as the rights of victims go; the theory as it was commonly understood did not extend to any radical reconstitution of the enemy state, and international law, with its assumptions about sovereignty, would have regarded any imposed change of regime as a new act of aggression. What happened after World War II in both Germany and Japan was something quite new in the history of war, and the legitimacy of occupation and political reconstitution is still debated, even by theorists and lawyers who regard the treatment of the Nazi regime, at least, as justified. Thus, as the Gulf War drew to a close in 1991, there was little readiness to march on Baghdad and replace the government of Saddam Hussein, despite the denunciation of that government in the lead-up to the war as Nazi-like in character. There were, of course, both military and geo-political arguments against continuing the war once the attack on Kuwait had been repulsed, but there was also an argument from justice: that even if Iraq "needed" a new government, that need could only be met by the Iraqi people themselves. A government imposed by foreign armies would never be accepted as the product of, or the future agent of, self-determination.[13]

The World War II examples, however, argue against this last claim. If the imposed government is democratic and moves quickly to open up the political arena and to organize elections, it may erase the memory of its own imposition (hence the difference between the western and eastern regimes in post-war Germany). In any case, humanitarian intervention radically shifts the argument about endings, because now the war is from the beginning an effort to change the regime that is responsible for the inhumanity. This can be done by supporting secession, as the Indians did in what is now Bangladesh; or by expelling a dictator, as the Tanzanians did to Uganda's Idi Amin; or by creating a new government, as the Vietnamese did in Cambodia. In East Timor, more recently, the United Nations organized a referendum on secession and then worked to set up a new government. Had there been, as there should have been, an intervention in Rwanda, it would certainly have aimed at replacing the Hutu power regime. Justice would have required the replacement. But what kind of justice is this? Who are its agents, and what rules govern their actions?

As the Rwandan example suggests, most states do not want to take on this kind of responsibility, and when they do take it on, for whatever political reasons, they do not want to submit themselves to a set of moral rules. In Cambodia, the Vietnamese shut down the killing fields, which was certainly a good thing to do, but they then went on to set up a satellite government, keyed to their own interests, which never won legitimacy either within or outside of Cambodia and brought no closure to the country's internal conflicts. Legitimacy and closure are the two criteria against which we can test wars' endings. Both of them are likely to require, in almost all the humanitarian intervention cases, something more than the restoration of the status quo ante—which gave rise, after all, to the crisis that prompted the intervention. Legitimacy and closure, however, are hard tests to meet. The problems have to do in part with strategic interests, as in the Vietnamese-Cambodian case. But material interests also figure in a major way: remaking a government is an expensive business; it requires a significant commitment of resources—and the benefits are largely speculative and non-material. Yet we can still point to the usefulness of morality in cases like these. A successful and extended intervention brings benefits of an important kind: not only gratitude and friendship, but an increment of peace and stability in a world where the insufficiency of both is costly—and not only to its immediate victims. Still, any particular country will always

have good reasons to refuse to bear the costs of these benefits, or it will take on the burden and then find reasons to perform badly. So we still need justice's critical edge.

The argument about endings is similar to the argument about risk: once we have acted in ways that have significant negative consequences for other people (even if there are also positive consequences), we cannot just walk away. Imagine a humanitarian intervention that ends with the massacres stopped and the murderous regime overthrown; but the country is devastated, the economy in ruins, and the people hungry and afraid; there is neither law nor order, nor any effective authority. The forces that intervened did well, but they are not finished. How can this be? Is it the price of doing well that you acquire responsibilities to do well again . . . and again? The work of the virtuous is never finished. It does not seem fair. But in the real world, not only of international politics, but also of ordinary morality, this is the way things work (although virtue, of course, is never so uncomplicated). Consider the Afghan-Russian war: the American government intervened in a major way, fighting by proxy, and eventually won a big victory: the Russians were forced to withdraw. This was the last battle of the cold war. The American intervention was undoubtedly driven by geopolitical and strategic motives; the conviction that the Afghan struggle was a war of national liberation against a repressive regime may have played a part in motivating the people who carried it out, but the allies they found in Afghanistan had a very restricted idea of liberation.[14] When the war was over, Afghanistan was left in a state of anarchy and ruin. At that point, the Americans walked away and were certainly wrong, politically and morally wrong, to do so—the Russians withdrew and were right to do so. We had acted (relatively) well; that is, in support of what was probably the vast majority of the Afghan people, and yet we were bound to continue acting well. The Russians had acted badly and were off the hook—even if they owed the Afghan people material aid (reparations), no one wanted them engaged again in Afghan affairs. This sounds anomalous, and yet I think it is an accurate account of the distribution of responsibility. But we need a better understanding of how this works and why it works the way it does, a theory of justice-in-endings that engages the actual experience of humanitarian (and other) interventions, so that countries fighting in wars like these know what their responsibilities will be if they win. It would also help if there were—what there is not yet—an international agency that could stipulate and even enforce these responsibilities.

This theory of justice-in-endings will have to include a description of legitimate occupations, regime changes, and protectorates—and also, obviously, a description of illegitimate and immoral activity in all these areas. This combination is what just war has always been about: it makes actions and operations that are morally problematic *possible* by constraining their occasions and regulating their conduct. When

the constraints are accepted, the actions and operations are justified, and the theorist of just war has to
say that, even if he or she sounds like an apologist for
the powers-that-be. When the constraints are not accepted, when the brutalities of war or its aftermath
are unconstrained, the theorist has to say so, even if
called a traitor and an enemy of the people.

It is important not to get stuck in either mode—
defense or critique. Indeed, just war theory requires
that we maintain our commitment to both modes at
the same time. In this sense, just war is like good government: there is a deep and permanent tension between the adjective and the noun, but no necessary
contradiction between them. When reformers come
to power and make government better (less corrupt,
say), we have to be able to acknowledge the improvement. And when they hold on to power for too
long, and imitate their predecessors, we have to be
ready to criticize their behavior. Just war theory is
not an apology for any particular war, and it is not a
renunciation of war itself. It is designed to sustain a
constant scrutiny and an immanent critique. We still
need that, even when generals sound like theorists,
and I am sure that we always will.

NOTES

1. Augustine's argument on just war can be found in
The Political Writings of St. Augustine (1962: 162–183);
modern readers will need a commentary: see Dean (1963:
134–171).

2. See Vitoria (1991: 302–304), and for commentary,
Johnson (1975: 150–171).

3. See Boswell (1952: 129), quoting Dr. Johnson: "'I
love the University of Salamanca, for when the Spaniards
were in doubt as to the lawfulness of conquering America,
the University of Salamanca gave it as their opinion that it
was not lawful.' He spoke this with great emotion."

4. With some hesitation, I cite my own discussion of
military necessity (and the references there to more sympathetic treatments): Walzer (1977: 144–151, 239–242,
251–255).

5. The best discussion of the realists is Smith (1986);
chapter 6, on Hans Morgenthau, is especially relevant to my
argument here.

6. Anthony Hartle is one of those veterans, who eventually wrote his own book on the ethics of war: *Moral Issues
in Military Decision Making* (1989).

7. See the documents collected in Sifry and Cerf (1991:
197–352), which include Bush's speeches and a wide range
of other opinions.

8. I made the case against attacks on infrastructural
targets immediately after the war (but others made it earlier) in DeCosse (1992: 12–13).

9. Stanley Fish's op-ed piece in the *New York Times*
(October 15, 2001): A19 provides an example of the post-
modernist argument in its most intelligent version.

10. This argument was made by several participants

at a conference on humanitarian intervention held at the
Zentrum für interdisziplinäre Forschung, Bielefeld University, Germany, in January 2002.

11. "A life is paid for by another life, and from these two
sacrifices springs the promise of a value." Camus (1956:
169). See also the argument in act I of *The Just Assassins*
(Camus 1958, especially pp. 246–247).

12. For arguments in favor of using ground forces in
Kosovo, see Buckley (2000: 293–294, 333–335, 342).

13. Bush's statement on stopping the American advance,
and his declaration of victory, can be found in Sifry and Cerf
(1991: 449–451); arguments for and against stopping can be
found in DeCosse (1992: 13–14, 29–32).

14. Artyom Borovik (1990) provides a useful, although
highly personal, account of the Russian war in Afghanistan;
for an academic history, see Goodson (2001).

REFERENCES

Augustine. *The Political Writings of St. Augustine,* ed. Henry
    Paolucci (Chicago: Henry Regnery Company, 1962).
Borovik, Artyom. *The Hidden War. A Russian Journalist's
    Account of the Soviet War in Afghanistan* (London: Faber
    and Faber, 1990).
Boswell, James. *Life of Samuel Johnson LL.D. Great Books
    of the Western World,* ed. Robert Maynard Hutchins.
    Vol. 44 (Chicago: Encyclopedia Britannica, 1952).
Buckley, William Joseph. *Kosovo: Contending Voices on
    Balkan Interventions* (Grand Rapids: William B. Eerd-
    mans Publishing Company, 2000).
Camus, Albert. *The Rebel,* trans. Anthony Bower (New York:
    Mintage, 1956).
———. *Caligula and Three Other Plays,* trans. Stuart Gil-
    bert (New York: Vintage, 1958).
Dean, Herbert A. *The Political and Social Ideas of St. Au-
    gustine* (New York: Columbia University Press, 1963).
DeCosse, David E., ed. *But Was It Just? Reflections on the
    Morality of the Persian Gulf War* (New York: Doubleday,
    1992).
Goodson, Larry P. *Afghanistan's Endless War. State Fail-
    ure, Regional Politics, and the Rise of the Taliban* (Seattle:
    University of Washington Press, 2001).
Hartle, Anthony E. *Moral Issues in Military Decision Mak-
    ing* (Lawrence: University Press of Kansas, 1989).
Johnson, James Turner. *Ideology, Reason, and the Limita-
    tion of War: Religious and Secular Concepts, 1200–1740*
    (Princeton: Princeton University Press, 1975).
Sifry, Micah L., and Cerf, Christopher, eds. *The Gulf War.
    History, Documents, Opinions* (New York: Times Books,
    1991).
Smith, Michael Joseph. *Realist Thought from Weber to
    Kissinger* (Baton Rouge: Louisiana State University Press,
    1986).
Vitoria, Francisco de. *Political Writings,* eds. Anthony
    Pagden and Jeremy Lawrance (Cambridge: Cambridge
    University Press, 1991).
Walzer, Michael. *Just and Unjust Wars* (New York: Basic
    Books, 1977).

CHAPTER 2

THE ROLE OF THE UNITED STATES IN THE WORLD

THE PARADOXES OF AMERICAN NATIONALISM

MINXIN PEI

Nearly two years after the horrific terrorist attacks on the United States, international public opinion has shifted from heartfelt sympathy for Americans and their country to undisguised antipathy. The immediate catalyst for this shift is the United States' hard-line policy toward and subsequent war with Iraq. Yet today's strident anti-Americanism represents much more than a wimpy reaction to U.S. resolve or generic fears of a hegemon running amok. Rather, the growing unease with the United States should be seen as a powerful global backlash against the spirit of American nationalism that shapes and animates U.S. foreign policy.

Any examination of the deeper sources of anti-Americanism should start with an introspective look at American nationalism. But in the United States, this exercise, which hints at serious flaws in the nation's character, generates little enthusiasm. Moreover, coming to terms with today's growing animosity toward the United States is intellectually contentious because of the two paradoxes of American nationalism: first, although the United States is a highly nationalistic country, it genuinely does not see itself as such. Second, despite the high level of nationalism in American society, U.S. policymakers have a remarkably poor appreciation of the power of nationalism in other societies and have demonstrated neither skill nor sensitivity in dealing with its manifestations abroad.

BLIND TO ONE'S VIRTUE

Nationalism is a dirty word in the United States, viewed with disdain and associated with Old World parochialism and imagined supremacy. Yet those who discount the idea of American nationalism may readily admit that Americans, as a whole, are extremely patriotic. When pushed to explain the difference between patriotism and nationalism, those same skeptics might concede, reluctantly, that there is a distinction, but no real difference. Political scientists have labored to prove such a difference, equating patriotism with allegiance to one's country and defining nationalism as sentiments of ethno-national superiority. In reality, however, the psychological and behavioral manifestations of nationalism and patriotism are indistinguishable, as is the impact of such sentiments on policy.

Polling organizations routinely find that Americans display the highest degree of national pride among Western democracies. Researchers at the University of Chicago reported that before the September 11, 2001, terrorist attacks, 90 percent of the Americans surveyed agreed with the statement "I would rather be a citizen of America than of any other country in the world"; 38 percent endorsed the view that "The world would be a better place if people from other countries were more like the Americans." (After the terrorist attacks, 97 and 49 percent, respectively, agreed with the same statements.) The World Values Survey reported similar results, with more than 70 percent of those surveyed declaring themselves "very proud" to be Americans. By comparison, the same survey revealed that less than half of the people in other Western democracies—including France, Italy, Denmark, Great Britain, and the Netherlands—felt "very proud" of their nationalities (see Table 1).

Americans not only take enormous pride in their values but also regard them as universally applicable. According to the Pew Global Attitudes Survey, 79 percent of the Americans polled agreed that "It's good that American ideas and customs are spreading around the world"; 70 percent said they "like American ideas about democracy." These views, however, are not widely shared, even in Western Europe, another bastion of liberalism and democracy. Pew found that, among the Western European countries surveyed, less than 40 percent endorse the spread of American ideas and customs, and less than 50 percent like American ideas about democracy.[1]

Such firmly held beliefs in the superiority of American political values and institutions readily find expression in American social, cultural, and political practices. It is almost impossible to miss them: the daily ritual of the Pledge of Allegiance in the nation's schools, the customary performance of the national anthem before sporting events, and the ubiquitous American flags. And in the United States, as in other countries, nationalist sentiments inevitably infuse

This essay has been edited and is reprinted from Foreign Policy 136 (May/June 2003): 31–37, *by permission of* Foreign Policy, *www.foreignpolicy.com.*

Table 1

National Pride: Percentage of People Who Say
They Are "Very Proud" of Their Nationality

Country	1990	1999–2000
Britain	53	49
Denmark	42	48
Egypt	N/A	81[a]
France	35	40
India	75	71
Iran	N/A	92[a]
Ireland	77	74
Italy	40	39
Mexico	56	80
Netherlands	23	20
Philippines	N/A	85[a]
Poland	69	71
United States	75	72
Vietnam	N/A	78[a]

Source: World Values Survey.
Note: N/A, not available.
[a]2001 survey data.

politics. Candidates rely on hot-button issues such as flag burning and national security to attack their opponents as unpatriotic and worse.

Why does a highly nationalistic society consistently view itself as anything but? The source of this paradox lies in the forces that sustain nationalism in the United States. Achievements in science and technology, military strength, economic wealth, and unrivaled global political influence can no doubt generate strong national pride. But what makes American nationalism truly exceptional is the many ways in which it is naturally expressed in daily life.

One of the most powerful wellsprings of American nationalism is civic voluntarism—the willingness of ordinary citizens to contribute to the public good, either through individual initiatives or civic associations. Outside observers, starting with the French philosopher Alexis de Tocqueville in the early nineteenth century, have never ceased to be amazed by this font of American dynamism. "Americans of all ages, all stations in life, and all types of dispositions are forever forming associations," noted Tocqueville, who credited Americans for relying on themselves, instead of government, to solve society's problems. The same grass roots activism that animates the country's social life also makes American nationalism vibrant and alluring, for most of the institutions and practices that promote and sustain American nationalism are civic, not political; the rituals are voluntary rather than imposed; and the values inculcated are willingly embraced, not artificially indoctrinated. Elsewhere in the world, the state plays an indispensable role in promoting nationalism, which is frequently a product of political manipulation by elites and consequently has a manufactured quality to it. But in the United States, although individual politicians often

try to exploit nationalism for political gains, the state is conspicuously absent. For instance, no U.S. federal laws mandate reciting the Pledge of Allegiance in public schools, require singing the national anthem at sporting events, or enforce flying the flag on private buildings.

The history of the pledge is an exquisite example of the United States' unique take on nationalism. Francis Bellamy, a socialist Baptist minister, wrote the original text in 1892; three major American civic associations (the National Education Association, the American Legion, and the Daughters of the American Revolution) instituted, refined, and expanded the ceremony of reciting it. The federal government was late getting into the game. Congress did not officially endorse the pledge until 1942, and it did not tamper with the language until 1954, when Congress inserted the phrase "under God" after being pressured by a religious organization, the Knights of Columbus.

Indeed, any blunt attempt to use the power of the state to institutionalize U.S. nationalism has been met with strong resistance because of popular suspicion that the government may be encroaching on Americans' individual liberties. In the 1930s, Jehovah's Witnesses mounted a legal challenge when some school boards tried to make the Pledge of Allegiance mandatory, arguing that the pledge compelled children to worship graven images. The flag-burning amendment has failed twice in the U.S. Congress during the past eight years.

In the United States, promoting nationalism is a private enterprise. In other societies, especially those ruled by authoritarian regimes, the state deploys its resources, from government-controlled media to the police, to propagate "patriotic values." The celebration of national days in such countries features huge government-orchestrated parades that showcase crack troops and the latest weaponry. (The huge military parade held in Beijing in 1999 to celebrate the fiftieth anniversary of China allegedly cost hundreds of millions of dollars.) Yet despite its awesome high-tech arsenal, such orgiastic displays of state-sponsored nationalism are notably absent on Independence Day in the United States. Of course, Americans hold parades and watch fireworks on the Fourth of July, but those events are largely organized by civic associations and partly paid for by local business groups.

Herein lies the secret of the vitality and durability of American nationalism: the dominance of civic voluntarism—and not state coercion—has made nationalist sentiments more genuine, attractive, and legitimate to the general public. These expressions of American nationalism have become so commonplace that they are virtually imperceptible, except to outsiders.

A POLITICAL CREED

American nationalism is hidden in plain sight. But even if Americans saw it, they would not recognize

it as nationalism. That is because American nationalism is a different breed from its foreign cousins and
exhibits three unique characteristics.

First, American nationalism is based on political
ideals, not those of cultural or ethnic superiority.
That conception is entirely fitting for a society that
still sees itself as a cultural and ethnic melting pot. As
President George W. Bush said in his Fourth of July
speech in 2002: "There is no American race; there's
only an American creed." And in American eyes, the
superiority of that creed is self-evident. American political institutions and ideals, coupled with the practical achievements attributed to them, have firmly
convinced Americans that their values ought to be
universal. Conversely, when Americans are threatened, they see attacks on them as primarily attacks
on their values. Consider how American elites and
the public interpreted the September 11 terrorist
attacks. Most readily embraced the notion that the
attacks embodied an assault on U.S. democratic freedoms and institutions.

Second, American nationalism is triumphant rather
than aggrieved. In most societies, nationalism is fueled
by past grievances caused by external powers. Countries once subjected to colonial rule, such as India
and Egypt, are among the most nationalistic societies. But American nationalism is the polar opposite
of such aggrieved nationalism. American nationalism
derives its meaning from victories in peace and war
since the country's founding. Triumphant nationalists celebrate the positive and have little empathy for
the whining of aggrieved nationalists whose formative experience consisted of a succession of national
humiliations and defeats.

Finally, American nationalism is forward looking,
whereas nationalism in most other countries is the
reverse. Those who believe in the superiority of American values and institutions do not dwell on their historical glories (although such glories constitute the
core of American national identity). Instead, they look
forward to even better times ahead, not just at home
but also abroad. This dynamism imbues American
nationalism with a missionary spirit and a short collective memory. Unavoidably, such forward-looking and
universalistic perspectives clash with the backward-
looking and particularistic perspectives of ethno-
nationalism in other countries. Haunted by memories
of Western military invasions since the time of the
Crusades, the Middle East cannot help but look with
suspicion upon U.S. plans to "liberate" the Iraqi people. In the case of China, U.S. support for Taiwan,
which the Chinese government and people alike
regard as a breakaway province, is the most contentious issue in bilateral relations. The loss of Taiwan—
whether to the Japanese in 1895 or to the nationalists in 1949—has long symbolized national weakness
and humiliation.

INNOCENTS ABROAD

The unique characteristics of American nationalism explain why one of the most nationalist countries
in the world is so inept at dealing with nationalism
abroad. The best example of this second paradox of
American nationalism is the Vietnam War. The combination of the United States' universalistic political
values (in this case, anticommunism), triumphalist
beliefs in U.S. power, and short national memory led
to a disastrous policy that clashed with the nationalism of the Vietnamese, a people whose national experience was defined by resistance against foreign
domination (the Chinese and the French) and whose
overriding goal was independence and unity, not the
spread of communism in Southeast Asia.

In its dealings with several other highly nationalistic societies, the United States has paid little attention to the role nationalism played in legitimizing
and sustaining those regimes the country regarded
as hostile. U.S. policy toward these nations has either
disregarded strong nationalist sentiments (as in the
Philippines and Mexico) or consistently allowed the
ideological, free-market bias of American nationalism to exaggerate the antagonism of communist
ideologies championed by rival governments (as in
China and Cuba). Former Egyptian President Gamal
Abdel Nasser's brand of postcolonial Arab nationalism, which rejected a strategic alliance with either the
U.S.-led West or the Soviet camp, baffled Washington officials, who could not conceive of any country
remaining neutral in the struggle against communist
expansionism. Echoes of that mind-set are heard
today in the United States' "you're either with us or
against us" ultimatum in the war against terrorism.

This ongoing inability to deal with nationalism
abroad has three immediate consequences. The first,
and relatively minor, is the high level of resentment
that U.S. insensitivity generates, both among foreign
governments and their people. The second, and
definitely more serious, is that such insensitive policies tend to backfire on the United States, especially
when it tries to undermine hostile regimes abroad.
After all, nationalism is one of the few crude ideologies that can rival the power of democratic liberalism. Look, for example, at the unfolding nuclear
drama on the Korean peninsula. The rising nationalism of South Korea's younger generation—which
sees its troublesome neighbor to the north as kin,
not monsters—has not yet figured in Washington's
calculations concerning Pyongyang's brinkmanship.
In these cases, as in previous similar instances, U.S.
policies frequently have the perverse effects of alien-
ating people in allied countries and driving them to
support the very regimes targeted by U.S. policy.

Finally, given the nationalism that animates U.S.
policies, American behavior abroad inevitably appears
hypocritical to others. This hypocrisy is especially
glaring when the United States undermines global
institutions in the name of defending American sovereignty (as in the cases of the Kyoto Protocol, the
International Criminal Court, and the Comprehensive Test Ban Treaty). The rejection of such multilateral agreements may score points at home, but
non-Americans have difficulty reconciling the universalistic rhetoric and ideals Americans espouse

with the parochial national interests the U.S. government appears determined to pursue abroad. Over time, such behavior can erode the United States' international credibility and legitimacy.

If American society had been less insulated from the rest of the world by geography and distance, these conflicting perspectives on nationalism might be less severe. To be sure, physical insularity has not diminished Americans' belief in the universalistic appeals of their political ideas. The nation was founded on the principle that all people (not just Americans) are endowed with "certain inalienable rights." That sentiment has been passed down through successive generations—from former President Franklin D. Roosevelt's vision of a world based upon "four freedoms" to President George W. Bush's "non-negotiable demands of human dignity."

But the United States' relative isolation, which unavoidably leads to inadequate knowledge about other countries, has created a huge communications barrier between Americans and other societies. According to a recent survey by the Pew Global Attitudes Project, only 22 percent of Americans have traveled to another country in the past five years, compared with 66 percent of Canadians, 73 percent of Britons, 60 percent of the French, and 77 percent of Germans. Lack of direct contact with foreign societies has not been offset by the information revolution. In the years leading up to September 11, 2001, only 30 percent of Americans claimed to be "very interested" in "news about other countries." Even after the September 11,

2001, terrorist attacks, average Americans did not sustain a strong interest in international affairs. According to polls conducted by the Pew Research Center in early 2002, only about 26 percent of the Americans surveyed said they were following foreign news "very closely," and 45 percent of Americans said that international events did not affect them.[2]

An amalgam of political idealism, national pride, and relative insularity, American nationalism evokes mixed feelings abroad. Many admire its idealism, universalism, and optimism and recognize the indispensability of American power and leadership to peace and prosperity around the world. Others reject American nationalism as merely the expression of an overbearing, self-righteous, and misguided bully. In ordinary times, such international ambivalence produces little more than idle chatter. But when American nationalism drives the country's foreign policy, it galvanizes broad-based anti-Americanism. And at such times, it becomes impossible to ignore the inconsistencies and tensions within American nationalism—or the harm they inflict on the United States' legitimacy abroad.

NOTES

1. The Pew Global Attitudes Project charts the rise of anti-American sentiments worldwide in its report "What the World Thinks in 2002" (Washington, D.C.: The Pew Research Center for the People & the Press, 2002).

2. Ibid.

A GRAND STRATEGY OF TRANSFORMATION

JOHN LEWIS GADDIS

It is an interesting reflection on our democratic age that nations are now expected to publish their grand strategies before pursuing them. This practice would have surprised Metternich, Bismarck, and Lord Salisbury, although not Pericles. Concerned about not revealing too much, most great strategists in the past have preferred to concentrate on implementation, leaving explanation to historians. The first modern departure from this tradition came in 1947, when George F. Kennan revealed the rationale for containment in *Foreign Affairs* under the inadequately opaque pseudonym "Mr. X," but Kennan regretted the consequences and did not repeat the experiment. Not until the Nixon administration did

official statements of national security strategy became routine. Despite his reputation for secrecy, Henry Kissinger's "State of the World" reports were remarkably candid and comprehensive—so much so that they were widely regarded at the time as a clever form of disinformation. They did, though, revive the Periclean precedent that in a democracy even grand strategy is a matter for public discussion.

That precedent became law with the Goldwater-Nichols Department of Defense Reorganization Act of 1986, which required the president to report regularly to Congress and the American people on national security strategy (NSS). The results since have been disappointing. The Reagan, Bush, and Clinton

This essay has been edited and is reprinted from Foreign Policy 133 (November/December 2002): 50–57, *by permission of* Foreign Policy, *www.foreignpolicy.com.*

administrations all issued NSS reports, but these tended to be restatements of existing positions, cobbled together by committees, blandly worded, and quickly forgotten. None sparked significant public debate.

George W. Bush's report on *The National Security Strategy of the United States of America,* released on September 17, 2002, has stirred controversy, though, and surely will continue to do so. For it is not only the first strategy statement of a new administration; it is also the first since the surprise attacks of September 11, 2001. Such attacks are fortunately rare in American history—the only analogies are the British burning of the White House and Capitol in 1814 and the Japanese attack on Pearl Harbor in 1941—but they have one thing in common: they prepare the way for new grand strategies by showing that old ones have failed. The Bush NSS, therefore, merits a careful reading as a guide to what is to come.

WHAT THE NSS SAYS

Beginnings, in such documents, tell you a lot. The Bush NSS, echoing the president's speech at West Point on June 1, 2002, sets three tasks: "We will defend the peace by fighting terrorists and tyrants. We will preserve the peace by building good relations among the great powers. We will extend the peace by encouraging free and open societies on every continent." It is worth comparing these goals with the three the Clinton administration put forth in its final NSS, released in December 1999: "To enhance America's security. To bolster America's economic prosperity. To promote democracy and human rights abroad."

The differences are revealing. The Bush objectives speak of defending, preserving, and extending peace; the Clinton statement seems simply to assume peace. Bush calls for cooperation among great powers; Clinton never uses that term. Bush specifies the encouragement of free and open societies on every continent; Clinton contents himself with "promoting" democracy and human rights "abroad." Even in these first few lines, then, the Bush NSS comes across as more forceful, more carefully crafted, and —unexpectedly—more multilateral than its immediate predecessor. It is a tip-off that there are interesting things going on here.

The first major innovation is Bush's equation of terrorists with tyrants as sources of danger, an obvious outgrowth of September 11. American strategy in the past, he notes, has concentrated on defense against tyrants. Those adversaries required "great armies and great industrial capabilities"—resources only states could provide—to threaten U.S. interests. But now, "shadowy networks of individuals can bring great chaos and suffering to our shores for less than it costs to purchase a single tank." The strategies that won the Cold War—containment and deterrence—will not work against such dangers, because those strategies assumed the existence of identifiable regimes led by identifiable leaders operating by identifiable means from identifiable territories. How, though, do you contain a shadow? How do you deter someone who is prepared to commit suicide?

There have always been anarchists, assassins, and saboteurs operating without obvious sponsors, and many of them have risked their lives in doing so. Their actions have rarely shaken the stability of states or societies, however, because the number of victims they have targeted and the amount of physical damage caused have been relatively small. September 11 showed that terrorists can now inflict levels of destruction that only states wielding military power used to be able to accomplish. Weapons of mass destruction were the last resort for those possessing them during the Cold War, the NSS points out. "Today, our enemies see weapons of mass destruction as weapons of choice." That elevates terrorists to the level of tyrants in Bush's thinking, and that is why he insists that preemption must be added to—although not necessarily in all situations replace—the tasks of containment and deterrence: "We cannot let our enemies strike first."

The NSS is careful to specify a legal basis for preemption: international law recognizes "that nations need not suffer an attack before they can lawfully take action to defend themselves against forces that present an imminent danger of attack." There is also a preference for preempting multilaterally: "The United States will constantly strive to enlist the support of the international community." But "we will not hesitate to act alone, if necessary, to exercise our right of self-defense by acting preemptively against such terrorists, to prevent them from doing harm against our people and our country."

Preemption in turn requires hegemony. Although Bush speaks, in his letter of transmittal, of creating "a balance of power that favors human freedom" while forsaking "unilateral advantage," the body of the NSS makes it clear that "our forces will be strong enough to dissuade potential adversaries from pursuing a military build-up in hopes of surpassing, or equaling, the power of the United States." The West Point speech put it more bluntly: "America has, and intends to keep, military strengths beyond challenge." The president has at last approved, therefore, Paul Wolfowitz's controversial recommendation to this effect, made in a 1992 "Defense Planning Guidance" draft subsequently leaked to the press and then disavowed by the first Bush administration. It is no accident that Wolfowitz, as deputy secretary of defense, has been at the center of the new Bush administration's strategic planning.

How, though, will the rest of the world respond to American hegemony? That gets us to another innovation in the Bush strategy, which is its emphasis on cooperation among the great powers. There is a striking contrast here with Clinton's focus on justice for small powers. The argument also seems at odds, at first glance, with maintaining military strength beyond challenge, for don't the weak always unite to oppose the strong? In theory, yes, but in practice and in history, not necessarily. Here the Bush team seems to have absorbed some pretty sophisticated political science, for one of the issues that discipline has been wrestling with recently is why there is still no anti-American coalition, despite the overwhelming dominance of the United States since the end of the Cold War.

Bush suggested two explanations in his West Point speech, both of which most political scientists—not all—would find plausible. The first is that other great powers *prefer* management of the international system by a single hegemon as long as it is a relatively benign one. When there is only one superpower, there is no point in anyone else's trying to compete with it in military capabilities. International conflict shifts to trade rivalries and other relatively minor quarrels, none of them worth fighting about. Compared with what great powers have done to one another in the past, this state of affairs is no bad thing.

U.S. hegemony is also acceptable because it is linked with certain values that all states and cultures —if not all terrorists and tyrants—share. As the NSS puts it: "No people on earth yearn to be oppressed, aspire to servitude, or eagerly await the midnight knock of the secret police." It is this association of power with universal principles, Bush argues, that will cause other great powers to go along with whatever the United States has to do to preempt terrorists and tyrants, even if it does so alone. For, as was the case through most of the Cold War, there is something worse out there than American hegemony.

The final innovation in the Bush strategy deals with the longer-term issue of removing the causes of terrorism and tyranny. Here, again, the president's thinking parallels an emerging consensus within the academic community. For it is becoming clear now that poverty was not what caused a group of middle-class and reasonably well-educated Middle Easterners to fly three airplanes into buildings and another into the ground. It was, rather, resentments growing out of the absence of representative institutions in their own societies, so that the only outlet for political dissidence was religious fanaticism.

Hence, Bush insists, the ultimate goal of U.S. strategy must be to spread democracy everywhere. The United States must finish the job that Woodrow Wilson started. The world, quite literally, must be made safe for democracy, even those parts of it, like the Middle East, that have so far resisted that tendency. Terrorism—and by implication, the authoritarianism that breeds it—must become as obsolete as slavery, piracy, or genocide: "behavior that no respectable government can condone or support and that all must oppose."

The Bush NSS, therefore, differs in several ways from its recent predecessors. First, it is proactive. It rejects the Clinton administration's assumption that since the movement toward democracy and market economics had become irreversible in the post–Cold War era, all the United States had to do was "engage" with the rest of the world to "enlarge" those processes. Second, its parts for the most part interconnect. There

is a coherence in the Bush strategy that the Clinton national security team—notable for its simultaneous cultivation and humiliation of Russia—never achieved. Third, Bush's analysis of how hegemony works and what causes terrorism is in tune with serious academic thinking, despite the fact that many academics have not noticed this yet. Fourth, the Bush administration, unlike several of its predecessors, sees no contradiction between power and principles. It is, in this sense, thoroughly Wilsonian. Finally, the new strategy is candid. This administration speaks plainly, at times eloquently, with no attempt to be polite or diplomatic or "nuanced." What you hear and what you read is pretty much what you can expect to get.

WHAT THE NSS DOES NOT SAY

There are, however, some things that you will not hear or read, probably by design. The Bush NSS has, if not a hidden agenda, then at least one the administration is not advertising. It has to do with why the administration regards tyrants, in the post–September 11 world, as at least as dangerous as terrorists.

Bush tried to explain the connection in his January 2002 State of the Union address when he warned of an "axis of evil" made up of Iraq, Iran, and North Korea. The phrase confused more than it clarified, though, since Saddam Hussein, the Iranian mullahs, and Kim Jong Il are hardly the only tyrants around, nor are their ties to one another evident. Nor was it clear why containment and deterrence would not work against these tyrants, as they are all more into survival than suicide. Their lifestyles tend more toward palaces than caves.

Both the West Point speech and the NSS are silent on the "axis of evil." The phrase, it now appears, reflected overzealous speechwriting rather than careful thought. It was an ill-advised effort to make the president sound, simultaneously, like Franklin D. Roosevelt and Ronald Reagan, and it has now been given a quiet burial. This administration corrects its errors, even if it does not admit them.

That, though, raises a more important question: why, having buried the "axis of evil," is Bush still so keen on burying Saddam Hussein? Especially as the effort to do so might provoke him into using the weapons of last resort that he has so far not used? It patronizes the administration to seek explanations in filial obligation. Despite his comment that this is "a guy that tried to kill my dad," George W. Bush is no Hamlet, agonizing over how to meet a tormented parental ghost's demands for revenge. Shakespeare might still help, though, if you shift the analogy to Henry V. That monarch understood the psychological value of victory—of defeating an adversary sufficiently thoroughly that you shatter the confidence of others, so that they will roll over themselves before you have to roll over them.

For Henry, the demonstration was Agincourt, the famous victory over the French in 1415. The Bush administration got a taste of Agincourt with its victory over the Taliban at the end of 2001, to which the Afghans responded by gleefully shaving their beards, shedding their burkas, and cheering the infidels—even to the point of lending them horses from which they laser-marked bomb targets. Suddenly, it seemed, American values were transportable, even to the remotest and most alien parts of the earth. The vision that opened up was not one of the clash among civilizations we had been led to expect, but rather, as the NSS puts it, a clash "inside a civilization, a battle for the future of the Muslim world."

How, though, to maintain the momentum, given that the Taliban is no more and that al Qaeda is not likely to present itself as a conspicuous target? This, I think, is where Saddam Hussein comes in: Iraq is the most feasible place where we can strike the next blow. If we can topple this tyrant, if we can repeat the Afghan Agincourt on the banks of the Euphrates, then we can accomplish a great deal. We can complete the task the Gulf War left unfinished. We can destroy whatever weapons of mass destruction Saddam Hussein may have accumulated since. We can end whatever support he is providing for terrorists elsewhere, notably those who act against Israel. We can liberate the Iraqi people. We can ensure an ample supply of inexpensive oil. We can set in motion a process that could undermine and ultimately remove reactionary regimes elsewhere in the Middle East, thereby eliminating the principal breeding ground for terrorism. And, as President Bush did say publicly in a powerful speech to the United Nations on September 12, 2002, we can save that organization from the irrelevance into which it will otherwise descend if its resolutions continue to be contemptuously disregarded.

If I am right about this, then it's a truly *grand* strategy. What appears at first glance to be a lack of clarity about who is deterrable and who is not turns out, upon closer examination, to be a plan for transforming the entire Muslim Middle East: for bringing it, once and for all, into the modern world. There has been nothing like this in boldness, sweep, and vision since Americans took it upon themselves, more than half a century ago, to democratize Germany and Japan, thus setting in motion processes that stopped short of only a few places on earth, one of which was the Muslim Middle East.

CAN IT WORK?

The honest answer is that no one knows. We have had examples in the past of carefully crafted strategies failing: most conspicuously, the Nixon-Kissinger attempt, during the early 1970s, to bring the Soviet Union within the international system of satisfied states. We have had examples of carelessly improvised strategies succeeding: The Clinton administration accomplished this feat in Kosovo in 1999. The greatest theorist of strategy, Carl von Clausewitz, repeatedly emphasized the role of chance, which can at times defeat the best of designs and at other times hand victory to the worst of them. For this reason, he

insisted, theory can never really predict what is going to happen.

Does this mean, though, that there is *nothing* we can say? That all we can do is cross our fingers, hope for the best, and wait for the historians to tell us why whatever happened was bound to happen? I do not think so, for reasons that relate, rather mundanely, to transportation. Before airplanes take off—and, these days, before trains leave their terminals—the mechanics responsible for them look for cracks, whether in the wings, the tail, the landing gear, or on the Acela, the yaw dampers. These reveal the stresses produced while moving the vehicle from where it is to where it needs to go. If undetected, they can lead to disaster. That is why inspections—checking for cracks—are routine in the transportation business. I wonder if they ought not to be in the strategy business as well. The potential stresses I see in the Bush grand strategy—the possible sources of cracks—are as follows.

MULTITASKING

Critics as unaccustomed to agreeing with one another as Brent Scowcroft and Al Gore have warned against diversion from the war on terrorism if the United States takes on Saddam Hussein. The principle involved here—deal with one enemy at a time—is a sound one. But plenty of successful strategies have violated it. An obvious example is Roosevelt's decision to fight simultaneous wars against Germany and Japan between 1941 and 1945. Another is Kennan's strategy of containment, which worked by deterring the Soviet Union while reviving democracy and capitalism in Western Europe and Japan. The explanation, in both instances, was that these were wars on different fronts against the same enemy: authoritarianism and the conditions that produced it.

The Bush administration sees its war against terrorists and tyrants in much the same way. The problem is not that Saddam Hussein is actively supporting al Qaeda, however much the Bush team would like to prove that. It is rather that authoritarian regimes throughout the Middle East support terrorism indirectly by continuing to produce generations of underemployed, unrepresented, and therefore radicalizable young people from whom Osama bin Laden and others like him draw their recruits.

Bush has, to be sure, enlisted authoritarian allies in his war against terrorism—for the moment. So did Roosevelt when he welcomed the Soviet Union's help in the war against Nazi Germany and imperial Japan. But the Bush strategy has long-term as well as immediate implications, and these do not assume *indefinite* reliance on regimes like those that currently run Saudi Arabia, Egypt, and Pakistan. Reliance on Yasir Arafat has already ended.

THE WELCOME

These plans depend critically, however, on our being welcomed in Baghdad if we invade, as we were in Kabul. If we are not, the whole strategy collapses, because it is premised on the belief that ordinary Iraqis will *prefer* an American occupation over the current conditions in which they live. There is no evidence that the Bush administration is planning the kind of military commitments the United States made in either of the two world wars, or even in Korea and Vietnam. This strategy relies on getting cheered, not shot at.

Who is to say, for certain, that this will or will not happen? A year ago, Afghanistan seemed the least likely place in which invaders could expect cheers, and yet they got them. It would be foolish to conclude from this experience, though, that it will occur everywhere. John F. Kennedy learned that lesson when, recalling successful interventions in Iran and Guatemala, he authorized the failed Bay of Pigs landings in Cuba. The trouble with Agincourts—even those that happen in Afghanistan—is the arrogance they can encourage, along with the illusion that victory itself is enough and that no follow-up is required. It is worth remembering that, despite Henry V, the French never became English.

MAINTAINING THE MORAL HIGH GROUND

It is difficult to quantify the importance of this, but why should we need to? Just war theory has been around since St. Augustine. Our own Declaration of Independence invoked a decent respect for the opinions of humankind. Richard Overy's fine history of World War II devotes an entire chapter to the Allies' triumph in what he calls "the moral contest." Kennedy rejected a surprise attack against Soviet missiles in Cuba because he feared losing the moral advantage: Pearl Harbor analogies were enough to sink plans for preemption in a much more dangerous crisis than Americans face now. The Bush NSS acknowledges the multiplier effects of multilateralism: "no nation can build a safer, better world alone." These can hardly be gained through unilateral action *unless that action itself commands multilateral support.*

The Bush team assumes we will have the moral high ground, and hence multilateral support, if we are cheered and not shot at when we go into Baghdad and other similar places. No doubt they are right about that. They are seeking U.N. authorization for such a move and may well get it. Certainly, they'll have the consent of the U.S. Congress. For there lies behind their strategy an incontestable moral claim: that in some situations, preemption is preferable to doing nothing. Who would not have preempted Hitler or Milosevic or Mohammed Atta, if given the chance?

Will Iraq seem such a situation, though, if we are not cheered in Baghdad? Can we count on multilateral support if things go badly? Here the Bush administration has not been thinking ahead. It has been dividing its own moral multipliers through its tendency to behave—on an array of multilateral issues ranging from the Kyoto Protocol to the Comprehensive Test Ban Treaty to the International Criminal Court—like a sullen, pouting, oblivious, and over-muscled teenager. As a result, it has depleted the reservoir of support from allies it ought to have in place before embarking on such a high-risk strategy.

There are, to be sure, valid objections to these and other initiatives the administration does not like. But it has made too few efforts to use *diplomacy*—by which I mean *tact*—to express these complaints. Nor has it tried to change a domestic political culture that too often relishes having the United States stand defiantly alone. The Truman administration understood that the success of containment abroad required countering isolationism at home. The Bush administration has not yet made that connection between domestic politics and grand strategy. That is its biggest failure of leadership so far.

The Bush strategy depends ultimately on *not* standing defiantly alone—just the opposite, indeed, for it claims to be pursuing values that, as the NSS puts it, are "true for every person, in every society." So this crack especially needs fixing before this vehicle departs for its intended destination. A nation that sets itself up as an example to the world in most things will not achieve that purpose by telling the rest of the world, in some things, to shove it.

WHAT IT MEANS

Despite these problems, the Bush strategy is right on target with respect to the new circumstances confronting the United States and its allies in the wake of September 11. It was sufficient, throughout the Cold War, to contain without seeking to reform authoritarian regimes: we left it to the Soviet Union to reform itself. The most important conclusion of the Bush NSS is that this Cold War assumption no longer holds. The intersection of radicalism with technology the world witnessed on that terrible morning means that the persistence of authoritarianism anywhere can breed resentments that can provoke terrorism that can do us grievous harm. There is a compellingly realistic reason now to complete the idealistic task Woodrow Wilson began more than eight decades ago: the world must be made safe for democracy, because otherwise democracy will not be safe in the world.

The Bush NSS report could be, therefore, the most important reformulation of U.S. grand strategy in over half a century. The risks are great—although probably no more than those confronting the architects of containment as the Cold War began. The pitfalls are plentiful—there are cracks to attend to before this vehicle departs for its intended destination. There is certainly no guarantee of success—but as Clausewitz would have pointed out, there never is in anything that is worth doing.

We will probably never know for sure what bin Laden and his gang hoped to achieve with the horrors they perpetrated on September 11, 2001. One thing seems clear, though: it can hardly have been to produce this document, and the new grand strategy of transformation that is contained within it.

TOWARD UNIVERSAL EMPIRE:
THE DANGEROUS QUEST FOR ABSOLUTE SECURITY

DAVID C. HENDRICKSON

When the attacks of September 11 came, the jolt was so sudden and unexpected as to convince nearly all that we had entered a fundamentally new world. Indeed, in many respects, it was obvious that we had. The sinister use of simple means to secure mass destruction was terrifying, and in the course of the weeks and months registering the disaster, the president enjoyed a virtually free hand in defining the character of the American response. That response has included not only a justified war in Afghanistan to depose the Taliban but two other changes whose significance is likely to prove far-reaching: one is a pronounced emphasis on unilateral methods in the conduct of American foreign policy, the other a new American strategic doctrine of preventive war. Both changes represent a new orientation in American foreign policy that holds peril for the future; if realized, they will give an imperial dimension to American policy unmatched in prior experience. It may be an exaggeration to say that the American government is taking "hasty and colossal strides to universal empire," as Alexander Hamilton said of the French Republic in 1798, but the line of march is very clear. It is toward a nation and an executive unburdened by traditional legal precepts and normative commitments to multilateral action, a vision that finds the constraints of international society an unwanted and unacceptable burden. It is toward universal empire.

The embrace of a doctrine of preventive war is a highly significant step. It represents a radical departure from the twin pillars of national security policy during the Cold War—containment and deterrence. It is also contrary to a long-established rule in international society that forbids the first use of force altogether or save in narrowly drawn circumstances. The norm against preventive war became embedded because experience with the contrary practice, which permitted states perfect discretion in the use of force, had led to results nearly fatal to civilization. That perception prompted the search for restraints on the first use of force and aggression that were registered, successively, in the League of Nations, the United Nations, and NATO. In the epoch of the world wars, doctrines of preventive war were closely identified with the German and Japanese strategic traditions, not with that of the United States.

The second factor that has distinguished the Bush administration is its penchant for unilateral action. This was a marked propensity before September 11, and that event served only to deepen it. Reflecting the general tendency has been the sour and unconstructive withdrawal from the Kyoto accord on climate change, the maniacal opposition to the International Criminal Court (ICC), the withdrawal from the Antiballistic Missile (ABM) Treaty, and—most astonishingly in light of the president's declared commitment to free trade—the imposition of high tariffs on steel. But the propensity toward unilateral measures has above all been marked in the conduct of the war on terrorism and in the strategic doctrine that has emerged in its course. That doctrine sees the United States as possessing a kind of carte blanche to act on behalf of the perceived exigencies of its national interest and of international security. Even when the administration makes an approach to international institutions, as it did in its September 2002 demands on the U.N. Security Council, it does so with the explicit reservation that it intends to pursue in any event its chosen course, thus impugning the authority of the council even in the appeal to it. Nor does NATO, the security arm of Western civilization, count in this reckoning. The U.S.-European disparity in military contribution and expenditure—destined to grow even larger over the next several years—is seen to legitimate a power over peace and war that belongs to us alone by virtue of our preeminent power.

The acceptance of preventive war and the rejection of multilateralism are momentous steps. They promise to change our role in the world as profoundly as the attacks of September 11 increased the perceived vulnerability of the ordinary American citizen. How far this new orientation in American foreign policy will run can only be speculative, but it is the proposition of this essay that if the tendency runs far it will lead to ruin. It stands in direct antagonism to fundamental values in our political tradition. It will almost certainly give rise to countervailing trends in the international system that are contrary to our interests. Finally, it threatens to wreck an international order that has been patiently built up for fifty years, inviting a fundamental delegitimation of American power.

THE POWER PROBLEM

The doctrine that power needs restraint, and that overbearing and unbounded power constitutes a danger to both order and liberty, is an old one. When John Adams said that "jealousies and rivalries have been my theme, and checks and balances as their

This essay has been edited and is reprinted from World Policy Journal *19 (Fall 2002): 1–10.*

antidotes, till I am ashamed to repeat the words," he expressed an idea that entered deeply into both early American diplomacy and the formation of the federal constitution. The one great work of political theory produced in the United States—*The Federalist* essays written at the time of the ratification of the Constitution—is a brilliant and relentless demonstration of the perversity of failing to provide such checks among human beings "remote from the happy empire of perfect wisdom and perfect virtue." The genealogy of the doctrine, however, reaches much further back than the eighteenth century. Long before it was instantiated in the American constitutional regime, hostility to any situation of unbounded power was a staple of constitutional thought, being registered in various ways by Aristotle, Polybius, and Cicero among the ancients, and by Locke, Montesquieu, and Bolingbroke among the moderns.

The same insight came to be applied to the international system and the sphere of diplomacy. The theme is heralded, at the very outset of Western civilization, by the resistance of the Greek city-states to the bid for universal dominion made by the Persian emperor Xerxes, who had wished to "so extend the empire of Persia that its boundaries will be God's own sky," and who believed that "there is not a city or nation in the world which will be able to withstand us, once these are out of the way." It found expression in opposition to the corruptions that befell the universal empire of Rome, which lost its republican freedom and became a menace to the world when it became too powerful. Resistance to universal empire has also been a consistent thread of modern thought since the Protestant Reformation. It gained moral authority in the struggle of the Dutch provinces against the religious intolerance and despotic ambition of the Spanish kings. It was a mainstay of British foreign policy in the eighteenth century, and the basis of the claim that Britain protected the public liberties of Europe. It then passed on to the American founders and their epigones. In thought and experience, resistance to universal empire is coeval with the history of civil liberty.

It seems to be a feature of universal empire that states that rose on the basis of opposition to it have often found in the fullness of their power a basis for departing from the doctrine of their youth. Thus did Athens move from a position of first among equals to hegemony and then to despotic empire as it went from the Persian Wars to the wars of the Peloponnesus. Thus, too, did Great Britain, after having lambasted for a century the French bid for universal monarchy, find itself the recipient of the same charge during the War of American Independence—with the Americans denouncing "those schemes of universal empire which the virtue and fortitude of America first checked, and which it is the object of the present war to frustrate."

Eighteenth-century Americans were not alone in treating universal empire as inconsistent with the preservation of the international system and the liberties of states. Montesquieu, Vattel, Hume, Robert-son, Burke, and Gibbon had all considered the theme, and were as one in regarding universal empire as, in Alexander Hamilton's words, a "hideous project." Up until the globalized age of the twentieth century, the term usually did not connote the literal domination of the earth, but rather dominance and mastery over a wide swath of peoples (who should otherwise, by virtue of proximity or interaction, form a system of states). Above all, it meant any situation in which one monarchy or state was in a position to give the law to the others; such a power, these eighteenth-century luminaries believed, was not to be borne.

Alongside the theme that universal empire was a menace was the proposition that it would recoil upon its authors. It was, in other words, not only a danger to others; it was a threat to its possessors. "Enormous monarchies," Hume wrote, "are, probably, destructive to human nature; in their progress, in their continuance, and even in their downfall, which never can be very distant from their establishment." Hume traced out, as had Montesquieu, a natural process by which unbounded power turned on itself: "Thus human nature checks itself in its airy elevation; thus ambition blindly labours for the destruction of the conqueror." The following two centuries gave ample evidence that Hume had seen a fundamental pattern in the world of states: what better summation is there of the fate of the successive bids for universal empire by Napoleonic France, Imperial and Nazi Germany, and Stalinist Russia? In the dreadful careers of these obscenely militarized powers, did not ambition blindly labor for the destruction of the conqueror?

THE AMERICAN DIFFERENCE

When America rose to superpowerdom in the course of the Second World War, it did not take these grim examples as any kind of precedent, and its leaders would have found contemptible the proposition that because the European powers did iniquitous acts when they were at the top of the international system, the United States enjoyed the right to do them too. This country stood for a different principle. Believing deeply in the normative legitimacy of a world ordered by law, American leaders not only contained the unbounded power of the Soviet Union but also created an array of international institutions that embedded American power in a system of reciprocal restraints. In their totality, these approximated a constitutional system within the Western world. At the moment of truth, America rejected both isolationism and imperialism, opting instead to construct a constitutional partnership of free nations in the struggle with the totalitarian enemy. "From the beginning," as presidential adviser Walt Rostow put it in 1967, "our objective was not to build an empire of satellites but to strengthen nations and regions so that they could become partners."

The complex web of international institutions that arose after the war owed much, nearly everything, to American leadership. Now an object of profound suspicion among apostles of the new empire, those institutions then expressed a grand design that entailed a novel bargain: we bid fair to surrender the policy of the lone hand in exchange for allied support of a liberal international order. Today's cheerleaders for unilateral methods have convinced themselves that the more our power grows, the less we have need of others, and hence the more we can consult a purely national standard. As the architects of the postwar order understood, however, the reverse is true. The more powerful the state, the more important that it submit to widely held norms and consensual methods. The more it overawes the remainder of the system, the more vital it is that restraints are laid upon that power, either by itself or by others. It is to the enduring fame of that older generation of American statesmen that they imbibed that lesson, as it was the genius of the postwar system to have instantiated it.

The importance of multilateralism is often misunderstood, even by its advocates. Usually, the subordination to international norms, of either a substantive or procedural kind, is justified simply on the grounds of interest. In fact, the central question these norms and procedures raise is one of legitimacy. It is generally true, as the multilateralists insist, that if you want to get your way in the world, you had best do so through working with others. But surrounding these calculations of interest—existing, as it were, in the atmosphere within which these passions and interests get registered and adjusted—is the more basic question of authority as distinguished from power. Like confidence in the financial markets, the aura of legitimacy is a difficult achievement, requiring years of patient labor and the steady observance of exacting standards. Also like confidence, legitimacy can vanish in a hurry and, once lost, is very difficult to regain. Once lost, even proper consultations of the national interest are called into question by others, and the whole can easily then seem a hive of imperial pretension and naked self-interest.

Unfortunately, American students of international politics are not well placed to understand the importance of legitimacy; nearly all the internal debates within the discipline have conceived of states as utility-maximizers on a primitive Benthamite model. Adopting a utilitarian conception of what motivates human beings, the discipline has little to say about what gives rise to, and what might prevent, a loss of legitimacy. Among the professors, instead, we have seen the adoption of the same view of human motivation that Madame de Staël, an astute observer, once attributed to Napoleon. The first consul, she noted, "considers every kind of morality a formula which has no more significance than the complimentary close of a letter. . . . Bonaparte believes that anyone who says he loves liberty, or believes in God, or prefers a clear conscience to self-interest, is just a man following the forms of etiquette to explain his ambitious pretensions or selfish calculations." This dreary mistake, now so common, was not made by the early adepts of the science of politics, who put questions of legitimacy or authority at the center of their investi-gations. "Men are not corrupted," wrote Tocqueville, "by the exercise of power or debased by the habit of obedience, but by the exercise of a power which they believe to be illegitimate, and by obedience to a rule they consider to be usurped and oppressive." Authoritative rule was seen as important not only in itself, and as vital to liberty, but also because the loss of authority was so crucial a factor in explaining events, especially the great turning points in history. In the estimation of the most penetrating thinkers, neither the experience of modern revolution nor the rise and fall of empire could be understood without reference to questions of legitimacy.

There is no simple way of articulating the complex bargains that have underlain the legitimacy of American power. Some multilateral restraints are substantive and consist in adherence to treaties and other rules of international law; others are procedural and require the pursuit of an international concert. So far as decisions concerning war and peace are concerned, probably the most important substantive rule is the presumptive judgment against the first use of force. So far as procedural requirements in this domain are concerned, the two most important institutions have been the U.N. Security Council and NATO. At no time in the past fifty years has the United States stood in such antagonism to both the primary norms and the central institutions of international society. The reason is not difficult to find. These rules and institutions convey a simple message to the Bush administration: by right you should not do what you want to do (invade Iraq, wage preventive wars, etc.). Hence these normative and institutional restraints have been belittled and demeaned by the administration, as relics of a former age. On present trends, they may indeed lose their relevance to international relations. If they fall, however, they will fall like a strong man, and will shake the legitimacy of American power.

DON'T GET CARRIED AWAY

The application of these considerations to particular circumstances will inevitably spawn disagreement, even among those who accept their general tenor. The doctrine that power needs constraint, and that such constraints have been and ought to be supplied by the American commitment to international law and multilateral decisionmaking, does not mean that every internationalist venture is of equal merit, or indeed of any merit at all. Nor in our awe of the formidable character of American military power should we forget that our power to resolve certain burning conflicts in the world is in fact severely limited. The controversy over the ICC illustrates the first point; the Israeli-Palestinian conflict, whose solution under American auspices is a recurring demand of European opinion, is an illustration of the second.

The ICC has a tangled history. Fostered in the early to mid-nineties climate of humanitarian intervention, it arose initially as a joint American–European–Latin American enterprise to complement the menu of U.N. peacekeeping operations. Even with the waning of a political commitment to multi-lateral intervention, and despite subsequent American reservations and nonparticipation, the Rome Statute continued to gain adherents, and in 2002, the new court opened for business.

That the ICC will have a beneficial impact on international security is often alleged, but it is in fact quite doubtful. Among the oldest rules in the diplomat's canon is the proposition that if you want to make a negotiated peace, you may need to waive punishment for previous offenses. Amnesties for previous offenses are features of nearly all conflicts that are settled by compromise and not by the all-out victory of one side. Even in cases of lopsided victory, subsequent judicial intervention may interfere with the requirements of political reconstruction. It is, however, in the cases that must be negotiated and that fall well short of decisive victory that the influence of the ICC could prove most pernicious. Experience shows that men can be persuaded to give up power or lay down their arms if they can be assured of a place where they can die in bed and in oblivion. In effect, the existence of the ICC is a standing impediment to this time-honored device. The more powerful the court seems to be—the more, that is, it seems capable of exercising the deterrent effect promised by its advocates—the more palpable this danger becomes. The ability of the court to call into question the political settlements that follow horrific conflicts is a loose cannon, and the threat of subsequent prosecution may operate to prevent such settlements from being made at all, at serious cost in human life. That is a huge penalty, and it suggests that the ICC will detract from rather than contribute to the cause of international security.

The United States, of course, has not opposed the court for this reason. Washington would have been delighted with an arrangement that allowed the international community to prosecute whom it wished while exempting U.S. soldiers and officials from exposure (which placing the ICC under the jurisdiction of the Security Council, as the Clinton administration proposed, would have done). The other signatories, however, would not agree, and hence the possibility of prosecutions against American personnel remains. The court may bring a suit only if national courts do not act or if their judgments are questionable, and to move forward, it needs the consent of the state on the territory of which the conduct occurred or the state of which the person accused is a national.

Faced with the modest danger of such prosecutions—one that could easily have been met at the time of the hypothetical evil—the administration instead threatened to veto the entire structure of U.N. peace-keeping operations, and did in fact veto the continuation of the U.N. mission in Bosnia (a step subsequently withdrawn). It then demanded from NATO members separate bilateral pacts with the United States, and said that failure to comply would threaten the American relationship with the recalcitrants in all

other areas. These were grossly excessive reactions. Opposition that might have been made on the basis of a principled adherence to the demands of international security was turned, in the administration's skillful hands, into a symbol of the very reasoning to which the world objects: we get to make the rules, but do not think they should apply to us. Unless we get our way, even in minor episodes, we'll shut down the system of international cooperation. Such dictatorial language is both insufferable and unnecessary, and our allies have every right to protest it.

If a sincere commitment to internationalism does not require us to embrace the ICC, it also cannot make us responsible for the settlement of intractable conflicts that are in fact beyond our power to resolve. A seldom-remarked liability of the imperial role is that it encourages what a British observer, D. W. Brogan, once called "the illusion of American omnipotence." As with the problem of theodicy—Why does God allow evil in the world?—an imperial America that celebrates its unbounded power is going to get the same question repeatedly. The Israeli-Palestinian conflict is a case in point. It needs no proof to show the desirability of settling this conflict, and it seems just as obvious that any settlement will constitute some variation on the terms Israeli and Palestinian negotiators came close to in the final days of the Clinton administration. At the same time, the ability of the United States to impose such a settlement is virtually nil in current circumstances. Taking the limiting case, in which we laid out the terms of a "just" settlement and threatened unacceptable consequences to the parties if they did not take it, the basis for success seems altogether lacking.

First, such an American initiative would reward the Palestinian recourse to suicide bombers, with their wanton and indiscriminate attacks against Israeli civil society. Those are methods that we, along with our friends, have an interest and a duty to oppose stoutly. Second, the Palestinians are, on present evidence, incapable of constituting a unified authority that can bring the terrorist attacks to an end. Even if we delivered the Palestinian leadership, the Palestinians cannot deliver themselves. Finally, the threat to abandon Israel would risk serious consequences in both the short and the long term. To pressure Israel to give up the settlements for peace, when peace is in prospect, is one thing, but to threaten abandonment when the Palestinians have chosen war is quite another. In addition to various lateral hazards—the absence of support in American public opinion, the likely strengthening of the extreme right in Israeli politics—such a threat would also compromise what is likely to be an essential ingredient of any future settlement: an Israeli conviction that Israel will not be isolated when its existence is imperiled and can thus safely make the sacrifices necessary for peace.

Given those constraints on policy, an American diktat would inevitably recoil on the dictator (at home as well as abroad). As the mediator of the Israeli-Palestinian conflict, the United States is indeed "the indispensable nation," but it cannot bring a settlement of that dispute unless the parties to the conflict want it. On present evidence, they don't.

THE IRAQI TEST

The immediate test of the American commitment to the norms and institutions of international society comes not in these areas but in the administration's approach to the use of force in the ongoing war on terrorism. From the first moments after the September massacres, the administration has wanted to extend its net as widely as possible. It has foreseen a series of wars, a battle of long duration and various campaigns, and it has laid bare the strategic doctrine that would justify these wars. Although styled a doctrine of "preemption," it is actually a doctrine of preventive war. Preemptive war is when force is used only when it is apparent that the enemy is on the verge of striking, "leaving no moment for deliberation." Preventive war is the first use of force to avert a more remote, although still ostensibly formidable, danger. It has a simple liturgy, historically sanctioned in the endless wars of the European state system. War, the advocates of prevention say, is inevitable anyway, so let us fight it under circumstances of our own choosing. In the present case, we are told that once Iraq or other evil states develop the capability to hit us, they will hit us. Ergo, we must strike to avert the threatened calamity, and sooner rather than later.

Such a war is entirely distinguishable in justification from that which toppled al Qaeda and the Taliban in Afghanistan. In that case, the United States justifiably made war in response to direct attacks on its soil. Since Saddam's complicity in those attacks has not been alleged by the administration, and cannot plausibly be inferred from the evidence thus far available, the justification for the war must rest on the aforementioned logic of prevention. That may not seem like much of a difference, but it is the difference in law between offensive and defensive war, and between aggression and self-defense. It is directly contrary to the principle that so often was the rallying cry of American internationalism in the twentieth century.

Deterrence will not work against a madman such as Saddam, say the advocates of preventive war. They give no persuasive reasons, however, for their verdict. The cruelties and massacres that Saddam has committed while in power confirm rather than disprove the idea that he continues to place his survival and that of his regime at the top of his priorities. Indeed, there is only one circumstance in which one must anticipate his use of any and all means: in the bunker, facing the end of his regime and himself— in the course, that is, of a war to do him in. There is considerable uncertainty over where Iraq stands in its ability to make use of chemical or biological agents currently in its possession, or at what point it could achieve a nuclear capability. But because Saddam's use of such weapons is most likely in the course of a war to eliminate him, and not likely at all as a "bolt from the blue," preventive war is a gambler's substitute for the safer method of containment and deterrence. The risk is not negligible that the first use of force could bring on the very mass destruction we fear. If that occurs anywhere as a consequence of the war, even in Iraq, the remedy must be judged far worse than the disease.

Despite being in a much more favorable military position in 2002 than in 1990, when Iraqi forces invaded Kuwait and threatened Saudi Arabia, we take no consolation from our undoubted ability to destroy the regime in the event it did lash out. The loss of faith in deterrence was a marked feature of the last phase of the Cold War, one to which both left and right made important contributions, but its record during that long conflict is far better than the historical record of preventive war. Having lost faith in deterrence, the Bush administration has an almost touching faith in the ability of war to solve our security problems. Forgotten is the old lesson that war is capable of enormous surprises and unexpected consequences, and that even victory can spawn among the defeated social consequences that constitute a profound barrier to a durable peace. Forgotten, too, is that the same things now said of Saddam Hussein and Kim Jong Il were once said of Stalin, Khrushchev, and Mao, and preventive war against their regimes was urged upon the United States with arguments no different from those used today. Was it unwise for successive administrations to resist those pleas?

None of this is to deny that there is a case for finishing the job left undone at the end of the Gulf War. The way that war ended created a far-from-ideal situation. War, it turned out, was not the father of peace. Instead hot war was followed by a decade of quasiwar, continued sanctions, and much Iraqi misery. Unexpectedly, the legacy of the Gulf War was a situation that allowed neither an American advance nor an American retreat. So long as Saddam stayed in power, we would not give up the sanctions; absent another act of Iraqi aggression, however, there was also little prospect of reconstituting the powerful army that stood on Baghdad's doorstep in 1991. Strategically, this stalemate seemed to offer no serious threats to American interests, but morally and psychologically, it was considered satisfactory proof in the Arab world that the United States viewed with cold indifference the suffering of the Iraqi masses, a political fact that was not changed by American declarations that it was entirely Saddam's fault and that we had nothing to do in the matter.

It will be unpopular to say so, but the Gulf War and its aftermath played an important role in the inculcation of that implacable hatred that led to September 11. The use of American power in the region was simply unprecedented. For the first time, the offshore maritime power made a huge commitment on land, and used force on a scale that was off the charts in comparison with its past record in the Arab world. The terrible suffering to both soldiers and civilians spawned by the war was the soil in which Osama bin Laden and al Qaeda formed their hideous purpose, and it counted at least as much as—I think more than—their hatred of the Jews or their outrage over the defilement of Saudi soil by American troops.

Would it be different this time around? Would America succeed in reconstructing the Iraqi regime, providing security for its peoples and the possibility of a new democratic start? That seems a dubious hope on which to pin a campaign, and the war in Afghanistan holds a lesson in this regard. Although it was apparent from the first moments that success in establishing a stable regime in that country would be a crucial test of American policy, the administration consistently subordinated that objective to the American way of war. Until its recent volte-face, the administration rejected not only American participation in a peacekeeping force but the extension of the force beyond Kabul and the offers of participation (since rescinded) of our European allies. Well after al Qaeda and the Taliban were routed, when securing a stable government in Afghanistan was clearly the objective to which military operations should have been subordinated, the United States continued to operate under rules of engagement that were more appropriate to the intensive days of the war—to the acute embarrassment of the Karzai government and at serious cost to its political viability.

Those failures were not accidental. At bottom, they are rooted in an American approach to war that is singularly ill-fitted to the purposes of political reconstruction. This cherishes aerial attack as the instrument of our deliverance, and is profoundly hostile to exposing American ground forces. In this view, war is conceived as a short and sharp engagement, and the purpose of American arms is to rout the enemy and then get out. The idea that war is but the beginning of a long engagement, that commitment to war, if it is to be justified, must also be a commitment to peace and political reconstruction, because these alone can atone for the massive killing that war entails—such a view does not express a deep conviction even among U.S. elites, and the American people at large have no truck with it. Although such an aim would undoubtedly be incumbent on us were we to depose Saddam Hussein, it could easily get lost in the chapter of accidents normally incident to war and occupation.

For the American people, the case for a second Iraqi war must ultimately rest not on visions of peace through conquest and enlightened imperial administration but on the ground of "ultimate national security." Such is where Henry Kissinger has placed the case for deposing Saddam. Kissinger acknowledges that preventive war to stop the development of weapons of mass destruction is a revolutionary departure from the past, but he is sufficiently alarmed by the danger (and sufficiently enthralled by a very optimistic reading of the regional political consequences flowing from the use of force) to recommend that policy. He has apparently forgotten a maxim of his first book, *A World Restored*, that "the distinguishing feature of a revolutionary power is not that it feels threatened—such feeling is inherent in the nature of international relations based on sovereign states—*but that nothing can reassure it.* Only absolute security—the neutralization of the opponent—is considered a sufficient guarantee, and thus the desire of one power for absolute security means absolute insecurity for all the others."

That depiction of the malady of the revolutionary power increasingly fits the United States; the inability to be reassured is reflected not only in the emerging doctrine of preventive war but also in the breakout from the ABM Treaty and overzealous measures for homeland security. The quest for absolute security is not only unreasonable in itself and productive of mischievous consequences for our own policy; it also gravely undermines the capacity of the United States to mediate intractable conflicts in whose peaceful resolution we have a stake. The advice the United States tenders to an India made insecure by terrorism and frightened by the development of nuclear weapons by its Pakistani adversary can then only be "do as we say, not as we do." That principle, if we may call it a principle, can only serve to undermine the efficacy of American diplomacy.

SAFE HARBOR

When September 11 occurred, the event was so shocking as to convince American leaders that we had entered a new age, and indeed the broad outlines of the new American policy have been revolutionary. They involve, in detail and in gross, a rejection of previous standards and doctrines that have long defined American statecraft and diplomacy. The embrace of preventive war is one such transgression; the rejection of containment and deterrence another; the feigned regard but real contempt for multilateralism is a third. The president has enjoyed near unlimited scope for carving out the long-term response to September 11. So far as the future of American strategy is concerned, this is what he has done with it.

There is another way. Rather than repudiating past precepts, it consists of the cultivation of those standards, doctrines, and principles that have accompanied America's rise to its present unparalleled position. Much as Americans found consolation for the terror in the bosom of their families and friends, and clung to them like a raft in a shipwreck, so must policy find in the past traditions of the United States the basis for a safe harbor. Especially in revolutionary times, it is a cardinal error to repudiate the past and to make a clean break from it, and all such attempts to do so in history are simply a catalog of disasters. As a token of the clean break, moral, legal, and institutional restraints often go under in times of war and revolutionary crisis, as they threaten to go under here. Only in retrospect do people come to understand that it is precisely in those times when such restraints are most needed.

CHAPTER 3

AMERICAN DEFENSE AND SECURITY IN THE INTERNATIONAL ENVIRONMENT

THE FUTURE SECURITY ENVIRONMENT, 2001–2025: TOWARD A CONSENSUS VIEW

SAM J. TANGREDI

Whether in business or defense, the first steps to any strategic plan include a definition of objectives and an evaluation of the environment in which those objectives will be pursued. This essay addresses the latter requirement for the next Quadrennial Defense Review (QDR) by outlining a consensus view of the future security environment for the years 2001–25.[1] It derives this consensus through an attempt to reconcile the existing group of competing assessments of the anticipated outlines of future conflicts. Mindful of the potential for bias, I also seek to identify dissenting viewpoints and potential wildcard events. The objective is to develop a baseline consensus of the probable future, but at the same time to identify those unpredictable catastrophic events—or predictable, yet unlikely, developments—against which hedging strategies could be adopted as a form of national defense insurance. Additionally, the intent is to identify issues about which a consensus could not be developed but which must be debated if any defense review is to be effective.

Like its 1997 predecessor, QDR 2001 is intended to be a strategy-driven assessment that balances the preparations of the present with the anticipated challenges and opportunities of the future.[2] On the surface, it would appear relatively easy to construct an assessment of future trends to guide the review. A recent survey identified over fifty academic or professional "futures studies" conducted since 1989, the approximate end of the Cold War.[3] But there are problems in attempting to apply the results of these studies to effective policymaking, among them their lack of coordination, the significant differences in their methodologies and the time periods examined, the broad and divergent scope of topics, the presence of underlying and often unidentified biases, and the wide range of contradictory results. Many of the individual studies were constructed from a clean slate, taking scant account of previous, related work. An unedited compilation of these studies would be capable of generating much debate, but would provide only a limited basis for policymaking.

To construct a policy requires a baseline consensus from which implications and issues can be examined and analyzed. The methodology developed by the working group and reported in this essay is straightforward. Thirty-six studies (unclassified or with pertinent unclassified sections) concerning the future security environment were selected based on standardized criteria.[4] These studies were representative of views from a wide range of organizations involved with or interested in national defense issues. The studies, with two exceptions, were published between 1996 and 2000. The choice of which studies to include here was based on the assumption that earlier themes would have been reflected in QDR 1997.

The thirty-six studies were analyzed in detail and compared on a subject-by-subject basis. Sixteen points of consensus and nine points of divergence were identified and are reported here. The points of consensus are those on which 85 percent or more of the sources agreed. Points of divergence are those on which there was no clear majority position.

The consensus and divergence points were compared with the conclusions of more than three hundred other sources, most of them specialized studies of the specific topics.[5] The purpose was to identify dissenting positions on the points of consensus, as well as to validate that the consensus represents a majority view.

Both the primary and consulted sources were also surveyed for the identification of wildcards: events that could not normally be predicted, but that could present a considerable challenge if they were to occur during the 2001–25 time period. Along with the divergence points, the wildcards indicate changes in the security environment that might require the development of hedging strategies.

The result was a consensus scenario that describes the anticipated 2001–25 future security environment, presented below in narrative form, along with a list of potential unanticipated events that merit hedging.

Sam J. Tangredi, "The Future Security Environment, 2001–2025: Toward a Consensus View," in QDR 2001: Strategy-Driven Choices for America's Security, *ed. Michèle A. Flournoy (Washington, D.C.: National Defense University Press, 2001), 25–73. Public domain.*

ESTIMATES, FORECASTS, SCENARIOS, AND CAVEATS

There are limitations, both conceptual and practical, in providing a consensus view of the future. First is the difficulty in comparing a mixture of assessments that use differing techniques. Three distinct methodologies are currently in favor for use in assessing the future security environment. *Estimates* utilize an assessment of current conditions to identify possible future events. The priority is accuracy, which requires a relatively short time horizon. *Forecasts* represent longer-range assessments, primarily relying on trends-based analysis. Most forecasts are issue-specific. *Scenarios* can be thought of as a range of forecasts, which tend to be richly developed depictions of alternate worlds based on plausible changes in current trends.

The strengths and weaknesses of the three primary methodologies for futures assessment have many implications for policy recommendations.[6] But the most important implication is the understanding that any attempt at deriving a consensus view requires the mixing of methodologies that were not necessarily designed to be compatible.

Moreover, although an assessment of the future security environment is the essential starting point for all strategic planning, history cautions against both its inappropriate use and a belief in a high degree of certainty.[7] Other factors also justify caution, including the problems of normative assessments, institutional bias, emotional reaction of individuals, and feedback effects, or the effects of taking action.[8] Futures assessments, even those that are based on linear trends in political events or the development of technology, inherently carry the biases of the assessors. Institutions and organizations, like individuals, also have inherent biases. Such biases do not have to be products of deliberate distortion, but can evolve from seeing the world from a particular viewpoint. Within the Department of Defense, for example, each service has a unique culture evolved from its historical experience and the particular mediums in which it operates and through which past, present, and future are perceived.

Perhaps the most significant difficulty in developing futures assessments and translating them into policies and actions is that all actions taken have the inherent effect of changing the future. By carrying out a plan, the conditions that inspired the plan are changed. The feedback dynamics of such change increase through the unfolding of competing actions, such as the plans of an enemy or its counterthrusts.

The limitations of futures analysis and the historical cautions concerning its use mean that the acceptance of any assessment entails risk. Even though, as a starting point for defense planning, the assessment of the future security environment is essential, it cannot guarantee the success of any policy based on its premises. Compiling a comparative assessment from a balanced mix of representative sources thus ap-

peared to the National Defense University (NDU) Working Group to be the best method of mitigating this risk.

ASPECTS OF AN ANTICIPATED FUTURE: COMMON ASSESSMENTS AND CONSENSUS PREDICTIONS

The comparative analysis generated by the survey of the thirty-six selected studies identified sixteen propositions that represent a general consensus of the sources. These propositions reflect a common assessment of the future security environment and mark the boundaries of the most likely future events. All of the propositions concern the time period 2001–25. They can be divided into three broad categories: consensus concerning potential threats, consensus concerning military technology, and consensus concerning opposing strategies.

Such a "derived consensus" does not represent absolute agreement by the majority of sources, nor does it represent complete agreement with any proposition by any particular source. It is meant to be a starting point from which choices about appropriate future strategies, policies, and force structure can be developed.

Almost every consensus point has a corresponding dissenting or contrary view. In the process of translating the implications of future assessment into policy recommendations, the contrary views deserve consideration, both as cautions against precipitous policy recommendations and also as indicators of potential events against which a prudent strategy should attempt to hedge. Therefore, the following discussions identify both the details of the consensus view and the arguments of prominent dissenters.[9]

1. **THERE WILL NOT BE AN IDEOLOGICAL COMPETITOR TO DEMOCRACY ON THE SCALE OF COLD WAR COMMUNISM**

The propellant of the Cold War was the ideological struggle between democracy and communism, as embodied in the United States and Soviet Union. With the dramatic victory of the West, ideology as an element of history did not end, but the rivalry between democratic capitalism and communism did, at least for the foreseeable future.

The majority of future security environment studies—both governmental and private—do not identify any other ideologies with global appeal, and thus do not foresee a competing ideology before at least 2025.[10] The expansion of democratic values appears to be a byproduct of globalization.[11] This does not mean that there will not be authoritarian nations claiming to be democracies, when in fact their political structure falls far short. However—with one significant dissenter discussed below—the consensus remains that the future will be one of an evolutionary increase in democratic states.[12] But the consensus view does include room for potential public discouragement and disillusionment in democracy and market capitalism.[13]

Although not professing to be a direct forecast of the future security environment, the thesis advanced by Samuel Huntington is that there are cultural challenges to Western-style democracy.[14] His view is that cultural identity plays a significant role in global politics and that there are natural frictions between the ethnic civilizations of our multipolar, multicivilizational world. In particular, he identifies the Islamic culture, with its traditional linkage between religious and political authority, as posing the greatest potential challenge to Americanized democratic liberalism by threatening a clash of civilizations.[15]

2. There Will Not Be a Rival Coalition of States to Challenge the United States Militarily

The consensus view is that economic and political globalization makes it unlikely that a rival coalition could form to challenge the United States militarily. Various nations may express their displeasure at particular U.S. foreign policies or the overall specter of American cultural imperialism, but most would have much to lose and little to gain in an anti-U.S. alliance.[16] There have been no credible forecasts that the European Union's (EU) interest in developing a unified military force independent from NATO will lead to a potential military confrontation with the United States.[17]

Supporters of the view that a rival coalition is unlikely argue that the desire of lesser-developed nations, as well as Russia and China, to join the "first tier" mitigates anti-Western hostility. The closer both nations are economically tied to the West, the consensus view argues, the less likely that an anti-U.S. coalition will be formed.

However, a representative dissenting view postulates a loose rival coalition driven by "an increasingly more assertive China aligned with a much weaker, authoritarian Russia."[18] The primary driver would be U.S. action to deter a Chinese naval blockade of Taiwan in the 2010 timeframe.[19] The argument is that "while to some extent a worst-case scenario [and "the least likely to develop by 2025"], the potential for both Japan and Europe to turn inward and leave the United States alone to face a major challenge from China and other states is plausible and, as a parameter for future planning, must be considered."[20]

Although this is an unlikely scenario, there has been evidence of a desire on the part of the Russian leadership for a symbolic rapprochement with China as a way of countering "global domination by the United States," especially U.S. criticism of Russian military actions in Chechnya.[21] Russia also sought, in late 1999, to recharge its diplomatic relations with the so-called rogue states.[22] Likewise, there have been suggestions that China would seek to put together alliances that "can defuse hegemonism by the U.S."[23]

3. There Will Be No Conventional Military Peer Competitor Capable of Sustained, Long-Term Power Projection beyond Its Immediate Region

To define peer competitor, one must ask what the military forces of the United States can do that those of other nations cannot. The succinct answer is that the United States is capable of projecting its military power on a global basis in a sustained fashion by means of its unparalleled logistics capabilities, including airlift, sealift, an extensive series of alliances, and expeditionary forces. Other nations can do so only to a limited extent.[24]

Whether "military peer competitor" is defined in terms of a "Soviet Union–equivalent" or by the capacity to sustain global power projection, the consensus view is that such a peer competitor cannot develop prior to 2025. It is not simply a question of pursuing the development of power projection capabilities; rather, 25 years appear insufficient to duplicate the unique U.S. logistics and alliance networks.

However, the QDR 1997 report held out the possibility of the emergence of a "regional great power or global peer competitor," with Russia and China "seen by some as having the potential to be such competitors, though their respective futures are quite uncertain."[25]

Additionally, a Russia-China–led alliance could pose the possibility of simultaneous conflicts in multiple regions, which would severely tax the ability of U.S. forces to respond. This would be the closest equivalent to a global peer competitor, but it would still not match U.S. power projection capabilities.

4. Economic Competitors Will Challenge U.S. Domination of the International Economic System, but This Will Not Lead to War

Propelled by the perception of increasing trade competition between the United States and Japan, the 1990s saw a series of publications suggesting the potential for military conflicts based on economic rivalry. Although the particular controversy was effectively smothered—at least for the time being—by the Asian economic downturn of the late 1990s, the view of a linkage between economic conflict and war has remained. A staple of Marxist theory and post–First World War assessments, it resurfaced in the view that the Gulf War was all about oil. The potential for China to become an economic power, along with the evolving EU, have also been cited as precursors to politico-military confrontation with the United States.[26]

Despite popular concerns, the consensus remains that economic competition need not lead to military confrontation and that it is very unlikely to do so in the 2001–2025 period. The particulars of U.S.-Japanese economic conflict are largely seen as reconcilable differences that will not affect security arrangements.[27] The prevailing view of the phenomenon of globalization is that such greater economic interconnection decreases, rather than increases, the potential for military conflict.[28]

One diverging view, however, holds a contrary view of the conflictual nature of globalization and global prosperity:

Paradoxically, increased prosperity and integration tends to increase political instability. Prosperity leads to greater economic integration and dependency resulting in greater insecurity by increasing the importance of international economic relationships and therefore increasing the opportunities for friction. This, in turn, leads to greater insecurity.[29]

5. REGIONAL POWERS MAY CHALLENGE THE UNITED STATES MILITARILY

The threat that regional powers will challenge the United States militarily and seek to prevent the United States from projecting power into their regions is universally considered the primary challenge that U.S. foreign and defense policy will face in the first decades of the twenty-first century. "Regional dangers" is the term used over and over again to describe the potential for "the threat of coercion and large-scale, cross-border aggression against U.S. allies and friends in key regions by hostile states with significant military power."[30] There is, however, disagreement over which power will pose such a challenge.

Initially, the first prime regional threat was thought to be the unpredictable actions (or collapse) of North Korea, the world's last true Stalinist state. The second was the actions of Saddam Hussein in Iraq, or the simmering hostility of Iran towards its Arabian Gulf neighbors and the West.[31]

However, these two major theater wars (MTWs) do not necessarily represent the most demanding future threats. Nations that can sustain sophisticated defense industries and produce significant quantities of relatively modern weaponry and that have access to a large pool of trainable manpower would be the most formidable foes. From that perspective, there is clearly a rank order of potential (and current) regional military powers. Within this order, almost every futures assessment identifies Russia and China as having the greatest potential for regional dominance.[32]

Several additional rogue states, such as Iraq, Iran, or Libya, have the potential of becoming military powers in their region, particularly through the acquisition of weapons of mass destruction (WMDs).[33] Rogue-state scenarios are considered the basis for two-MTW planning. Rogue states might also seek to use terrorism or other deniable means, rather than confront the United States directly.

One or more of the rogue states (North Korea, Iraq, Iran, Libya, and Syria) might seek to challenge the United States militarily in the near term. Such an assessment is based on current hostilities, plans, or desire for regional dominance, propensity for aggressive military action, or a pattern of anti-U.S. military activity. In a longer-term view, the potential for conflict with a major regional power may grow, with Russia or China as the most difficult potential military opponents. However, there is no consensus as to which regional power or rogue state is likely to take action at any particular time.

In the sources surveyed, there are no significant arguments that a regional conflict is unlikely prior to 2025. There is, however, a perception that effective U.S. actions, along with a well-trained and technologically superior military, could deter such conflict. Likewise, astute management of relations with Russia, China, and India may prevent the development of actual hostilities.[34] Some sources argue that hostile states are simply too weak to mount a credible military threat to the overwhelming power of the U.S. armed forces.[35] However, a pessimistic view of the constant potential for regional conflict is widespread.

6. THERE WILL BE MORE FAILING STATES, BUT U.S. INVOLVEMENT WILL REMAIN DISCRETIONARY

The terms "failed states" or "failing states" have been increasingly used to describe nations that cannot provide law, order, or basic human necessities to their population. Such states may be wracked by civil war, ideological or ethnic hatreds, or other conflicts that prevent the central government from providing internal security or promoting general welfare.

Although the internal consequences of such disorder have long been recognized, the external effects within the international environment have not always been considered a security threat to distant, stable nations. The question of exactly where the United States has vital or important interests fuels the argument that American efforts to restore order in failed states are largely humanitarian efforts that have little positive impact on U.S. national security. However, there are still compelling arguments for American intervention to stop genocide or massive loss of life.[36] Such arguments contributed to the American decision to prompt NATO intervention in Kosovo. But given the nature of democratic politics, such intervention ultimately remains discretionary.

Few, if any, sources are willing to predict categorically a future security environment in which significant numbers of failed states do *not* occur.[37] There are, however, optimistic scenarios that are envisioned, even in the case of Africa.[38] Although some sources suggest an increase in the desire to take action to stem such conflict, others point to an increasing reluctance on the part of most nations to become involved.[39] Additionally, arguments have been made that advocates of intervention underestimate the complexity of involvement, and that such involvement is often counterproductive.[40]

7. There Will Be More Nonstate Threats to Security, but They Will Increase Gradually, Not Dramatically

The term "nonstate threats" is used to denote those threats to national security that are not directly planned or organized by a nation-state. Today, foremost among these threats are acts of terrorism other than those sponsored by a rogue state. A loosely defined spectrum of nonstate threats includes humanitarian disasters, mass migrations, piracy, computer network attack, organized international crime and drug trafficking, terrorism with conventional weaponry, and terrorism with WMDs. Nonstate actors include international organizations, nongovernmental organizations (NGOs), multinational corporations, and multinational interest groups.

Alarmist predictions that nonstate actors, issues, and threats would overwhelm and break the abilities of most nation-states to deal with them have not materialized.[41] Nations that have collapsed into anarchy have largely been victims of civil wars, a phenomenon that long preceded the current definition of nonstate threats. Many of these civil wars have been fueled or supported by foreign parties, international actors, or other nations. To that extent, nonstate or transnational threats do contribute to such internal collapse, but in ways that are not unprecedented historically.

The consensus of the sources is that nonstate threats will increase in number and intensity in the future. However, this anticipated increase parallels vulnerabilities that are byproducts of the evolutionary process of globalization. Nonstate threats may seem more potent due to the advantages modern technologies may bring to the perpetrator. However, the same or other modern technologies can be used to strengthen defenses. But this does not solve the near-term problems of terrorism, particularly if terrorist groups come into possession of WMDs. The consensus view is of concern about the near-term potential for terrorist incidents, but the level of current and future vulnerability of societies to terrorism is still hotly debated.[42]

No sources maintain that nonstate threats will not increase in the 2001–25 timeframe. However, some sources do view the rise of these threats as exponential rather than gradual, with more alarm than the consensus view might imply. Of particular concern is the possibility of terrorism with WMDs, also known as "catastrophic terrorism."[43]

8. Advanced Military Technology Will Become More Diffused

The category of advanced military technology constitutes a spectrum of technologies or innovative uses of technology developed during the past few decades: from emerging biological weaponry and other WMDs, to new forms of nonlethal weapons, including information operations using mass media.[44] It includes highly accurate ballistic and cruise missiles; fourth-generation combat aircraft; complex surveillance, detection, tracking, and targeting equipment; surface-to-air missiles; nuclear-powered submarines; and other relatively high-cost systems.

The consensus of the sources is that advanced military technology will continue to be diffused through sales, modification of dual-use systems, and indigenous weapons development programs. Although international export control regimes may exist for certain types of advanced weapons, these agreements appear to be easily circumvented. Iran, Iraq, North Korea, Pakistan, and India have all effectively foiled the efforts of the Missile Technology Control Regime.[45] Control regimes appear to have slowed potential nuclear weapons development by rogue states, but there appear to be other covert proliferation efforts.

Although there are sources that endorse greater efforts to negotiate and strengthen weapons control regimes, none argue that military technology will not continue to become more diffused in the 2001–25 period. In fact, it is the rate at which military technologies are spreading that prompts the more urgent calls for international controls. Under current circumstances, proliferation of advanced systems appears to be simply a matter of time and resources.

9. Significant Operational Intelligence Will Become Commercially Available

Given the current trends in space launch and commercialization, the consensus is that operational intelligence—primarily satellite imagery—will increasingly become commercially available. Yet the consensus is that the United States will "maintain a preponderant edge, using its technical systems to produce timely and usable information."[46] The infrastructure necessary is simply too difficult to create except through the obvious expenditure of considerable resources. The consensus viewpoint concerning militarily significant commercial information is that although it might be available to a potential aggressor until the commencement of hostilities, it would be voluntarily or covertly shut down upon the initial attack. But the fact that operational intelligence would not remain available during conflict may be of little consolation, because the information obtained before hostilities would be sufficient to target fixed sites, such as land bases, in advance. The use of WMDs might also make the need for real-time targeting information moot.

None of the sources surveyed suggested that operational intelligence will not become commercially available in the 2001–25 timeframe. Opposition to the consensus view revolved around two points: that satellite information is largely irrelevant to the most likely threats the U.S. military will face, such as Third World anarchy and small-scale guerrilla warfare, and that a cutoff of commercial imagery during hostilities cannot be presumed.[47]

10. Other Nations Will Pursue a Revolution in Military Affairs (RMA), but the United States Will Retain the Overall Technological Lead

A number of advances in military technology are frequently cited as evidence that an RMA is under way, and even skeptics concede that these advances have had a tremendous effect on warfighting.[48] Advances in information processing and command and control are cited most frequently, with predictions of increasing availability of real-time information at the command level. Some proponents claim that new intelligence, surveillance, and reconnaissance (ISR) technologies and battle management systems can dispel the fog of war that has previously prevented commanders from having a thoroughly accurate picture of the battlefield.[49]

Also frequently linked to the RMA are precision weapons. Other technological advances, from biological weapons to miniaturized nanosystems, are also frequently seen as pushing modern warfare away from the bloody killing fields of ground combat.

Critics concede that the advances in military technology have greatly increased the striking power of modern militaries. However, they argue that such advances have not changed the fundamental concept of warfare, and that victory ultimately requires closing with the enemy and occupying territories or destroying centers of gravity.[50]

Potential opponents may pursue an RMA through the development of advanced weaponry, but—barring a catastrophic economic disaster in the West—they cannot surpass the overall U.S. lead in advanced military technologies during the 2001–25 timeframe.[51] Certain niche technologies, such as advances in chemical and biological warfare or the development of nanoweapons that would be easier to transport and deploy in space or on earth, could provide a temporary technological lead in specific areas.[52] Developing such a niche could give a state with limited resources more bang for its buck, but such a development would be unlikely to make the entire U.S. arsenal obsolete or completely paralyze decision-making. At the same time, the overall technological lead by the United States would facilitate the development of defenses against these advantages, or at least methods of mitigating the threat.

Although conceding America's current overall lead in military technology, several sources point to alarming trends. The nation is not producing enough engineers and scientists to maintain the knowledge capital to retain the overall technological lead.[53] Worse, from this perspective, the American education system is loyal to potential opponents.[54] Eventually other countries could take technological leadership.

Other sources argue that the United States is not taking the RMA seriously enough and is squandering its technological lead.[55] In this view, the Department of Defense continues to spend money on so-called "legacy systems" while underfunding both basic and advanced research and development and experimentation. This combination could give opponents an opportunity to leapfrog over the capabilities of the formidable U.S. arsenal and to make its overall technological superiority moot.[56]

11. If There Is a Technological Surprise, It Is Likely to Be Developed by the United States or One of Its Allies

A consensus of the sources examined views a truly unanticipated development in military technology as unlikely in the 2001–25 period. But if one were to occur, the consensus view holds that it would most likely be the product of a Western or developed nation, not a nation hostile to the United States. If a technological surprise were to occur in a hostile state, it is likely that it could be quickly replicated somewhere in the West. Infrastructure, knowledge base, and commercial incentive appear to be the drivers of new, surprising innovations, and these are centered in the democratic capitalist states.[57]

Among those assessments of the future security environment that identify potential wildcards, a major technological surprise was listed as an occurrence of potential concern.[58]

12. The United States Will Retain Control of the Seas and Air

The consensus is that the size and level of operational experience of the Navy and Air Force make it nearly impossible for potential opponents to mount a serious challenge in the waters and in the air space over the world's oceans.[59] This is likely to continue until 2025. Even if potential opponents are not deterred from direct competition against these American strengths, it would take at least 20 years for any competitor to build to the numbers and sophistication of the naval and air fleets. That is not to say that an opponent would not seek to contest sea and air control in its own region, or even individual force-on-force engagements outside its region. However, the investment needed to challenge the United States on a global basis in areas that the nation has long maintained operational advantages is staggering.[60]

No source suggests that U.S. naval and air assets could be decisively defeated, and particularly not within the global commons in the 2001–25 period. However, concerns are frequently expressed that the United States could become complacent with its current margin of superiority and elect not to replace aging systems with more technologically advanced first-line platforms. Over a long term, the cumulative effect of a procurement holiday might make the bulk of U.S. naval and air forces obsolete.[61] The concept of block obsolescence for legacy systems also appears in the arguments of proponents of transformation. Critics of American complacency also point to the continuing development of high-technology weaponry for export by technologically advanced nations.

Some also argue that general American dominance of sea and air is largely irrelevant in dealing with the more likely future threats of terrorism, chemical, biological, and information warfare, and failing states, as well as against the prepared anti-access or area denial strategies of regional opponents.[62]

13. Regional Powers Will Use Anti-Access and Area Denial Strategies

The potential use of anti-access or area denial strategies against American power projection capabilities has been a focal point of research by the Office of Net Assessment within the Office of the Secretary of Defense since at least the mid-1990s.[63] Originally, these studies had a maritime focus. In the logic of the anti-access approach, a potential opponent would not seek to engage the Navy at sea, where the United States holds absolute dominance. Rather, it would seek to prevent U.S. maritime forces from entering its littoral waters by massive attrition attacks using asymmetric weapons, such as WMDs.[64] However, these studies were soon expanded to include examination of all U.S. overseas presence and power projection forces.

The obvious first step in such an area denial effort would be to neutralize any existing lodgment that the armed forces already have within the region by destroying U.S. forward-presence forces while simultaneously attacking the regional infrastructure for follow-on power projection forces. Another step would be to attack the ports and airfields for the embarkation of forces in the continental United States (CONUS). However, that is generally outside of the anticipated conventional capabilities of most regional powers.[65] Additionally, a strike against the U.S. homeland could strengthen rather than discourage national resolve.[66]

With regional land bases destroyed and maritime access denied, the potential regional opponent would have effectively extended its defenses out to the entry points of its region. The United States will find itself in the position of having to undertake potentially costly forcible entry operations. Even in this war of attrition, it is likely that the United States would eventually breach the anti-access defenses, particularly through the use of standoff weapons stationed outside the region or in CONUS. However, the real goal of an anti-access strategy is to convince the United States or its allies and coalition partners that the cost of penetration is simply too high.[67]

The consensus of sources surveyed is that anti-access or area denial is the most likely campaign plan for an opponent of the United States to adopt, and thus the likely opposition that strategic U.S. power projection forces would face in an MTW. This conclusion is based not only on the proliferation of ballistic missiles and other weapons, including WMDs, but also on the underlying logic of the strategy itself.[68]

None of the sources surveyed maintain that it is unlikely that a potential opponent would adopt an anti-access strategy to prevent the United States from intervening to stop regional cross-border aggression. If such an MTW were to occur, an anti-access strategy would appear the best—perhaps only—method to blunt U.S. power projection strength. However, a number of sources see the occurrence of cross-border aggression and MTW as much less likely than the chaos of failed states and internal civil strife.

Perceptions also differ concerning the actual ability of regional aggressors to carry out regional closure in the 2001–25 timeframe.[69] Several sources suggest that, before 2025, most potential opponents will be unable to use ballistic missiles effectively against moving targets, leaving U.S. air and naval forces free to attack the weak points of an anti-access campaign.[70] Other sources suggest that the ability of rogue states to coerce potential allies into denying American access to their territory has been overstated.[71]

14. Large-Scale Combat Involving U.S. Forces is Likely to Include the Use of WMDs

The desires of certain states for WMD arsenals, the rate of actual proliferation, a seemingly growing disregard of the laws of armed conflict, and the lessons of the Gulf War suggest a potential for integration of WMDs into military operations.[72] Most sources assume that proliferation will continue in the 2001–25 timeframe and that many of the international control regimes seeking to prevent the spread of WMDs will break down or be ignored. Terrorist groups also appear interested in purchasing or developing WMDs. Underlying technologies, particularly dual-use systems, such as nuclear reactors that could enrich uranium as well as generate power, are becoming available to potential aggressors and provide cover for weapons development. Humanitarian NGOs report that the laws of war appear increasingly to be disregarded, with decreasing discrimination between attacking military forces and civilian noncombatants. Tyrannical regimes facing potential removal by outside forces—such as those of the United States or a U.S.-led coalition—appear increasingly tempted to use WMDs in combat.

The majority of the sources surveyed view the likelihood of use of WMDs during large-scale conflict in the 2001–25 period as quite high. The consensus is that use of chemical or biological weapons would be more likely than nuclear war. Many sources view WMD use as the primary future threat to American security. There seems to be agreement that, if certain rogue states have WMDs, they would be used for the survival of tyrannical regimes.

The potential of WMDs in the hands of terrorist groups is considered a more frightening situation by many sources. Terrorist attacks could be directed against vulnerable civilian populations as well as military forces.

There is a perception, however, that use of WMDs against the United States in conflict can be deterred.[73] The rate of increase in nuclear arsenals during 2001–25 does not suggest that more than perhaps two or three states, if any, could threaten the United States with mutual destruction. Because chemical and biological weapons are routinely categorized along with nuclear weapons as WMDs, there is, by definition, ambiguity as to whether use of chemical or biological weapons would provoke a U.S. nuclear retaliation. Thus, the use of WMDs against forces in large-scale armed conflict with the United States might be deterred by the U.S. nuclear arsenal.

Sources that view chemical and biological weapons as the significant threats of the 2001–25 period do not necessarily dispute the deterrent effect of the U.S. nuclear arsenal, or even the deterrent effect of conventional power projection forces. Rather, they argue that it is possible to use WMDs on American soil or against U.S. forces in a manner that could render the source of the attack unidentifiable.[74] If they could make it appear to be a terrorist attack, potential state opponents might believe that they could successfully attack the United States without retribution.[75] They might use ostensibly unsponsored terrorist groups as proxies in a WMD attack designed to paralyze American response to far-off regional aggression.

Other sources argue that technology (and the American psyche) will inevitably render such attacks attributable, mitigating the attractiveness of such a reckless course of action. An additional deterrent might be U.S. theater ballistic missile defenses. If positioned in theater prior to the actual outbreak of conflict, such defenses might deter WMD use in the initial stages, or perhaps deter the entire conflict itself.

It has also been suggested that a U.S. declaratory counterproliferation policy of pursuing regime change in the event of WMD use, or threats of use, would also have considerable deterrent effect. If the likely end result of any WMD confrontation with the United States or ally would be the decapitation of the aggressor, rogue states might reconsider any potential tactical advantages of WMD use.[76]

15. The U.S. Homeland Will Become Increasingly Vulnerable to Asymmetric Attacks

The perception that the U.S. homeland will become increasingly vulnerable in the 2001–25 period can be traced to the National Defense Panel report of 1997. It has subsequently become an almost universal forecast. In 1999, the U.S. Commission on National Security/21st Century echoed the prevailing perception that "America will become increasingly vulnerable to hostile attack on our homeland, and our military superiority will not entirely protect us."[77]

With the end of the Cold War and the agreed dealerting of nuclear forces, along with reductions in overall U.S. and Russian nuclear arsenals, it would appear that the American populace is much less directly vulnerable than they have been in at least 30 years. However, other experts point to the balance of terror that made a nuclear war between the United States and Soviet Union irrational. Rogue states, they argue, are less likely to be deterred from making

asymmetric attacks on the U.S. homeland in the event of a conflict.[78] Indeed, asymmetric attacks may be the most useful—and perhaps only—military tool in the hands of potential opponents.[79]

The consensus is that the U.S. homeland will become more vulnerable to new threats, particularly chemical and biological weapons in the hands of rogue states and terrorist groups.[80] The ability to transport such weapons in small packages that can easily be smuggled is often cited as a contributing factor. In addition, rogue regimes, such as North Korea, are attempting to develop ballistic missiles capable of reaching the continental United States. States that do not possess fissile material could opt for chemical or biological warheads.

Realization that the forward-defense posture allows for only limited defense of the U.S. coastline and airspace has increased.[81] At the same time, the Internet and the ubiquitous nature of computer control seem to have made the American infrastructure more vulnerable to information warfare. Computer network defenses are possible, but at both financial and social costs.

The consensus position differs from more alarming forecasts on questions of the degree of future vulnerability. The majority view is that the increase in such threats is evolutionary, rather than exponential. As use of the Internet continues to penetrate society, the vulnerability to disruption increases, but so will redundant and protected systems. As globalization causes a rise in transnational or nonstate threats, such as massive migrations, its economic benefits may mitigate such threats. Meanwhile, the United States appears to be taking steps to deal with the potential for catastrophic terrorism and infrastructure attack.[82]

Several sources suggest that the rate of development of future threats—fueled primarily by the malicious use of new technologies—is indeed increasing dramatically. From this perspective, increasing homeland vulnerability is inevitable, particularly if active defenses, interagency cooperation efforts, redundancy, and reconstitution do not receive substantial funding increases within the U.S. defense budget.

16. Information Warfare Will Become Increasingly Important

Information warfare refers both to the use of various measures to attack the information technology (IT) systems on which a military opponent may depend and to the control and manipulation of the information available to the civilian populace of an opposing state.[83] Computer network attack might be aimed at systems providing the ISR or command and control capabilities necessary for modern, high-technology warfare, or it might be an asymmetric strike on the civilian infrastructure of the opponent's homeland. Additionally, an IT-based public relations war could have a less lethal and more indirect effect on the populace than computer infrastructure attack, but as seen in the Vietnam War experience, it could have a more direct effect on the government's willingness to prosecute a war.[84]

The U.S. government has recently addressed computer network defense and critical infrastructure protection, but in the face of an emerging and somewhat indistinct threat, defense necessarily lags offense.[85] An aspect of concern to some is the potential anonymity of attack and the possible use of information warfare by nonstate actors, particularly terrorist groups. Hackers and terrorists could use multiple paths of entry to disguise their identities and intentions.[86] Although it is possible to trace these paths to a source, such efforts take time and resources.[87] The question remains whether a hostile state could mask an information attack to such an extent that the United States would be unable to determine the source to take timely defensive or retaliatory actions.

In classical military terms, the use of information is an attempt to lift the fog of war that envelops the battlefield. Commanders have always tried to acquire accurate information; what is now different is that modern IT appears to provide a greater opportunity to clear away the fog than ever before. Thus it is natural for U.S. forces to strive for "information dominance" or "knowledge superiority" in any conflict.[88] That there are more tools to make more information available suggests that information has become more important to victory.[89] This also implies that deception, disinformation, and the use of mass media are also of increasing value as military tools.

The consensus of sources is that information is increasing in importance as IT increases in reach and capacity. But the growing dependence on precise information for combat operations also creates greater opportunities for deception. Technologically superior armies, like open societies, appear more vulnerable to denial and deception than less interconnected forces or closed societies.

Although there is no overt disagreement with the proposition that information will be a critical element in future warfare, there is disagreement over the extent to which information—and, by extension, information warfare—will be the dominant element.

An opposing viewpoint is that modern IT does ensure that the fog of war can be lifted and suggests that the U.S. military must be radically transformed to optimize its capabilities in an information warfare–dominant future.[90]

DIVERGENCE AND CONTRADICTIONS

The sixteen points of consensus form a baseline from which an effective debate on defense planning priorities, during QDR 2001 or any other defense review, could proceed. Likely issues of such a debate can be identified from the diverging views and contradictions among the thirty-six surveyed sources. These alternative assessments of the future are presented here as "either-or" statements, but there are varying degrees of agreement, and the either-or statements generally represent the extreme ends of the range.

For the purpose of defense planning, identification of contending predictions about the future security environment is the prelude for making deliberate choices on how to prepare for and perhaps to hedge against an analytically uncertain future.

> It is unlikely that two MTWs would happen simultaneously.
> *or*
> Two nearly simultaneous MTWs will remain a possibility.

A number of critical assessments—some of which are linked to a recommended strategy or force structure different from the current posture—discount the possibility of two MTWs occurring nearly simultaneously. Preparing for two such overlapping contingencies is dismissed as unsupportable worst-case thinking. Yet, despite dismissive rhetoric, few present detailed logic as to why such an occurrence could not happen. Taking a cue from the National Defense Panel, many analysts find the two-MTW construct inconvenient to their recommendations for transformation, because readiness for the simultaneous scenarios requires considerable expenditure of resources and the maintenance of considerable standing forces.

When assessments of potential regional conflicts (derived from consensus point 5 above) are combined, the possibility of crises or conflicts developing nearly simultaneously in two or more regions seems plausible. There are both historical precedents and strategic logic for a potential regional opponent to make aggressive moves when conflicts are occurring in other parts of the world. While the United States is responding to the first conflict or contingency, an aggressor might believe that the objectives of a second conflict would be easier to achieve.

It has become common to describe recent NATO actions against Serbia—presumed to be a smaller-scale contingency—as using one MTW's worth of airpower.[91] If small-scale contingencies (SSCs) occur at a near-continuous rate, it is almost inevitable that two or more will occur nearly simultaneously. The United States may not choose to involve itself in more than one SSC, but if it did choose to handle two, what would happen if one or both were to require an effort worth two MTWs? The divergence of views on the probability of overlapping MTWs, like the other contradicting statements, forms fundamental issues of the debates to be expected in the QDR 2001 process.

> Future wars will be more brutal with more civilian casualties.
> *or*
> Information operations and precision weapons will make warfare less deadly.

The question of whether future wars will be characterized by greater brutality and greater civilian casualties or instead by more discriminate attacks and fewer civilian casualties often arises in debates concerning the existence and effect of an RMA and the importance of information warfare. At one end is the view that the trend is toward a "world of warriors" in which youthful populations of less economically developed nations are involved in ethnic, religious, or tribal conflict. This gives rise to more brutal forms of warfare, in which in the international laws of war are rarely observed.[92] The ethnic cleansing of Bosnia and Kosovo (along with a myriad of civil wars), conducted largely by paramilitary terror squads whose primary activities involved the killing of unarmed civilians, are cited as representations of the future of war.[93] Combatants and noncombatants are rarely distinguished. Victory consists of complete destruction of the lives and property of an enemy.[94] Such wars will involve ethnic cleansing, genocide, mass movement of refugees, famine, torture, and rape. Weapons can range from the primitive to the merely unsophisticated. Although armored vehicles, artillery, and shoulder-held antiaircraft missiles may be used, the dominant platform is the individual warrior—as young as 12 or even younger—and the small arms carried.[95] Commercial global positioning system receivers and cellular phones are useful, but not essential for operations. The implication is that the sophisticated precision weapons, along with the information systems, that characterize U.S. armed forces have relatively little effect against such an enemy.[96]

At the other end is the vision that precision weapons and information warfare will make warfare both less likely and less bloody. Kosovo is also used as an illustrative case, this time as an example of how precision bombing, with considerable effort to spare civilian lives and property, was able to win a modern war and reverse ethnic cleansing. Because such precision strikes rely on accurate ISR, the processing of information is a dominant feature of this style of war. Proponents of information warfare argue that the manipulation of information may, in itself, preclude physical combat in future conflicts.[97] Under perfect conditions, it is argued, the manipulation of information will prevent a populace from going to war by persuading its members that the war is unjustified or is already over, or turning them against governments intent on war.

Somewhere in between these views is the argument that future wars will not necessarily be more brutal, but that precision strike and information warfare do not presage an era of immaculate warfare. The U. S. Commission on National Security/21st Century, although generally enthusiastic about the precise effects of emerging military technology, expresses this middle ground in its findings:

Despite the proliferation of highly sophisticated and remote means of attack, the essence of war will remain the same. There will be casualties, carnage, and death; it will not be like a video game. What will change is the kinds of actors and the weapons available to them. While some societies will attempt to limit violence and damage, others will seek to maximize them, particularly against those societies with a lower tolerance for casualties.[98]

Chaos in littorals or panic in the city are more likely contingencies than MTW.
    or
MTW will remain the primary threat to security.

The issue of the separation between military personnel and civilians, or between combatants and noncombatants, underlies the question of where and how future warfare will take place. Classical warfare is assumed to take place between clearly identified armies in terrain suitable for direct engagements. History—replete with siege warfare, attacks on infrastructure, and massacres of civilian populations—may demonstrate that the ideal is actually an exception. However, there remains the popular impression that war is, or at least should be, about defeating crossborder aggression, as envisioned in the current MTW scenarios.

Of course, U.S. armed forces are used for more than MTWs. Throughout its history, America has called on its armed forces to deal with many contingencies outside of formally declared wars. These contingencies have ranged from punitive expeditions to humanitarian interventions. The number of such SSCs has greatly increased since the end of the Cold War. Along with a greater propensity on the part of American decisionmakers to intervene, American military involvement in MTW against crossborder aggression has been relatively rare. From this perspective, Operation Desert Storm represents the exception rather than the rule.[99] Given the apparent increase in the number and frequency of nonstate threats and the potential for asymmetric operations, it has been suggested that the primacy of the DoD focus on preparing for classical MTW is a mistake. The threats of the future, according to this view, will be significantly different and require a different emphasis in preparations.

One perspective is that future conflicts—particularly those within failed states—will present little opportunity for firepower-intensive warfare. There will be no front lines, no rear areas, and, in some cases, no clearly identifiable enemy force. Rather, there will be an overall atmosphere of chaos, in which the primary mission of U.S. military forces will be to establish order and to quell violence in the most humane way possible. Forecasts sponsored by the Marine Corps point to the continuing urbanization of the world's population and the continued breakdown of failed states as leading to numerous tribal-like conflicts.[100] Apropos of a naval service, Marine Corps–sponsored briefs point to the fact that more than 70 percent of the world's urban population is within the operating range of a coastline, otherwise known as the littoral region. "Chaos in the littorals" is shorthand for such future contingencies that occur within the region, intervention into which could potentially be done best by forces from the sea.[101]

A slightly different perspective can be termed "panic in the city," spurred by the potential use of chemical or biological weapons in urban areas. Proponents of this view are concerned that asymmetric or terrorist attacks could create chaotic conditions within the U.S. homeland.[102] The U.S. military would be expected to stabilize chaotic conditions not only overseas, but also to do the same at home. Although many emerging strategy alternatives call for increased military involvement in homeland security, most assume that the military would play merely a support role to civil authorities, providing resources that may not be readily available in the civil sector. In contrast, those who view panic as the new weapon envision homeland security as the preliminary or even the primary mission of the armed forces. The implication is that civilians cannot face the physical or psychological aspects of the chemical and biological warfare threat alone and that both precautions and responses should be a direct military function. Once the perception of homeland sanctuary is broken by an actual attack, the American population would panic into fleeing toward areas of perceived safety and demand that their elected officials cease whatever foreign activities may have provoked such an attack. To prevent such a scenario, sources argue, the military needs to refocus its efforts away from the less likely case—classical military response to crossborder aggression—and toward the more direct and more likely threats of asymmetric attacks against the homeland and the use of panic as a weapon of the globalized future.[103]

In contrast, a significant number of sources continue to view MTW as the most likely warfare in which the United States will become involved, and job number one for its military. From this perspective, America's large-scale warfighting capability is the primary deterrent of both chaos and asymmetric attack. The divergence of opinion on whether future warfare will *primarily* take the form of chaos in the littorals and panic in the city, or will mostly resemble the expected forms of MTW, appears to be more related to preferred prioritization of threats than any conclusive forecast of wars to come. But there is evidence on both sides of the issue.

Space will be a theater of conflict.
 or
Space will remain a conduit for information, but not a combat theater.

The question of the so-called "militarization of space" is particularly contentious. Space-based ISR is critical to U.S. military operations. Such ISR gave such an informational and command and control advantage during Operation Desert Storm that some have referred to the Gulf War as "the first space war."[104] However, there are great distinctions between the military use of space, a war *from* space, and a war in space.[105] Every future assessment predicts increasing use of space assets by the military; but there are wide differences over whether a war from or in space could occur in the timeframe prior to 2025.[106]

A number of sources are very certain of the potential for a force-on-force space war. The U.S. Commission on National Security/21st Century's "Major Themes and Implications" states explicitly that "Space will become a critical and competitive military environment. Weapons will likely be put in space. Space will also become permanently manned."[107]

An opposing viewpoint is the forecast that the militarization of space is not likely to occur prior to 2025. This reasoning projects a continuing U.S. advantage in military space systems, based on its previous investment and infrastructure development. From this posture, "the United States is in a good position to win any ensuing arms race."[108] Another potential inhibitor of space-based weapons are the international treaties governing space activities.[109]

But skeptics of treaty prohibitions tend to share a view of the inevitability of the introduction of space weaponry in the 2001–25 timeframe. As former Secretary of the Air Force Sheila Widnall argued, "We have a lot of history that tells us that warfare migrates where it can—that nations engaged in conflict do what they can, wherever they must. At a very tender age, aviation went from a peaceful sport, to a supporting function, very analogous to what we do today in space—to a combat arm. Our space forces may well follow that same path."[110] A similar argument was made by the DoD Space Architect in 1997: "To hope that there will never be conflict in space is to ignore the past."[111]

A near-peer competitor is inevitable over the long term; we need to prepare now.
 or
Preparing for a near-peer competitor will create a military competition (thus creating a near-peer).

As discussed above in consensus point 3, the development of a global military near-peer competitor to the United States prior to 2025 is unlikely. However, that forecast does not quell the debate on whether such a near-peer is inevitable in the long term. Sources that view a near-peer as inevitable base their argument on historical example; every aging leader is eventually challenged by younger, growing competitors. To ignore this is also to ignore the past. In the study of international relations, there appears always to be a struggle among states to become the hegemon that dominates the international system.[112] Even scholars who question the morality of hegemonic control—and in particular, the apparent U.S. position as the current hegemonic power—appear to believe that such a struggle is natural between states.

If the struggle for hegemonic control is the natural order of the international system, it would also be natural that those responsible for the security of the United States—including its freedom, its institutions, its population, and its prosperity—would prepare for such a struggle. Although there may be a continuous debate as to which preparations are most appropriate and how the outbreak of hostilities can be deterred in the near term, there seems to be agreement among many that a dissatisfied state could eventually build itself into a military near-peer to the United States sometime after 2025. The belief in the inevitability of a near-peer is also reflective of consensus point 8 that advanced military technology will become more diffused. As military technology becomes more diffused, it appears inevitable that any American advantage in military technology will gradually shrink, creating de facto near-peer competitors.

There is, however, an alternative view on the inevitability of military near-peer competition. In this view, it is not "natural order" that causes near-peer challengers to arise, but, rather, the actions of the leading power that cause such a competition.[113] Supporters of this view range from those observers who see a competitive international system as an anomaly of the capitalist world to those who view gradual world democratization as eventually leading to a world free from major war, under the premise that democracies do not fight democracies. Others subscribe to the belief that near-peer competition is not inevitable as an unspoken corollary to their idea that a leading power can take actions that prevent such a competition from occurring. To some extent, such a view underlies the premises of the proposal by Ashton Carter and William Perry for "preventive defense."[114]

The question of the inevitability of a near-peer competitor after 2025 is not merely an academic question. It ties directly to the choice of a future defense policy. If conflict with a near-peer competitor is inevitable after 2025, it would behoove the United States to take distinct steps to develop a defense policy and force structure that would retain military superiority sufficient to dissuade, deter, or—if necessary—defeat a potential near-peer opponent.[115]

However, if it is actual or proposed military preparations of the hegemon that propel other states to seek parity, it may be in the interest of the United States to break the cycle of increasing military expenditures to prevent the development of a near peer. Specific policies could be adopted—along the lines of preventive defense—that seek to co-opt or to manage a potential near peer by allowing a degree of American vulnerability to preserve the current balance, which appears to favor the United States.[116]

Overseas bases will be essentially indefensible.

or

Future capabilities will be able to defend overseas bases.

The potential reach of opponents into space, along with the adoption of other techniques of anti-access or area denial warfare, would have a damaging impact on the overseas bases upon which America's current power projection forces appear to depend. If the 2001–25 period is indeed one in which potential opponents strengthen their anti-access capabilities (as appears to be the consensus in point 13 above), then the threat to overseas bases would appear to increase. This forecast is commonly accepted.[117] However, there is a debate among the sources as to whether the nature of the future security environment, and the laws of physics and diffusion of technology will make an overwhelming threat to fixed land bases permanent.

To the bases-will-be-indefensible school, defensive measures simply cannot keep up with the offensive threat that places fixed military forces at grave risk.[118] In this perspective, the action-reaction phenomenon of military technological development naturally favors offensive systems. Even with theater ballistic missile defenses in place, overseas bases could be attacked with WMDs by other means of delivery, such as cruise missiles, attack aircraft, or artillery shells.

At the same time, there may be political vulnerabilities that make overseas bases, particularly those within the sovereign territory of a host nation, much more difficult to defend. The host nation may seek to placate a potential aggressor by insisting that defenses be kept minimal to maintain the current strategic balance. If the base relies on the movement of mobile defenses into the theater, such as Patriot missile batteries, then they are vulnerable to pre-emptive attack or coercion. The host nation may decide not to let the United States use its base facilities lest such permission provoke an attack by a regional aggressor. This would make mounting a power projection campaign considerably more difficult.

It may be a reaction to the implications for American power projection that causes other sources to insist that overseas bases could be successfully defended in the 2001–25 timeframe. To admit growing vulnerability could cause undesired revolutionary changes in the allocation of defense resources. However, the view that bases can be defended also argues that emerging military technologies can make defenses against WMDs more effective. The continuing and natural lead of America and its allies in emerging military technology, as identified in consensus points 10 and 11, cause some to conclude that defenses can match offenses, particularly when backed by the eventual triumph of qualitatively (and possibly quantitatively) superior U.S. power projection.[119] Likewise, the regional use of WMDs may be deterred by the vast U.S. nuclear arsenal, use of which might be provoked by significant casualties of American military personnel or host-nation civilians. Other sources argue that overseas bases can be defended by sea- or space-based systems.

Additionally, there is the argument that the vulnerability of land bases actually works to the advantage of the nation. If overseas-based U.S. forces are attacked, then it is likely that U.S. determination to push for the enemy's regime change would be reinforced. This perception could potentially deter a regional aggressor from launching such a strike. Also, the vulnerability of the host-nation's territory to an aggressor might provoke the host nation to seek greater rather than lesser military cooperation with the United States. Some also argue that any host nation that could be coerced to restrict U.S. access to bases is an ally simply not worth defending.[120]

Current (legacy) U.S. forces will not be able to overcome anti-access strategies except at high cost.

or

Techniques of deception or denial of information will remain effective in allowing legacy systems to penetrate future anti-access efforts.

The debate on the defensibility of overseas bases has a parallel with that on the continuing effectiveness of power projection forces. Supported by the same data concerning the growing development of anti-access systems and strategies (consensus point 13), a number of sources suggest that the power-projection forces of the United States—as they are currently constituted—will have increasing difficulty penetrating anti-access defenses in the 2001–25 period.

The proponents of this view, however, do not necessarily see these developments as an evolutionary challenge to which the United States can modify and adapt its current forces. Rather they see this as a revolutionary development that is enabled, in part, by foreign adaptation to the RMA. This position leads to the advocacy of radical changes in the U.S. defense posture. Indeed, the perception of the growing strength of anti-access strategies is a major impetus to calls for defense transformation.

In contrast, there remains a body of literature that characterizes anti-access strategies as natural aspects of war that require incremental improvements in U.S. power projection forces, but are not a revolutionary development requiring radical change. This view argues that current developments, particularly in theater missile defense and standoff and precision weapons, allow power projection capabilities to keep pace with anti-access systems.[121] The Army vision of a strategically responsive force that is less dependent on heavy equipment and multiple air- and sea-lifts contributes to the perception that power projection forces may become even more effective in the 2001–25 period.[122]

Nuclear deterrence will remain a vital aspect of security.

or

Nuclear deterrence will have a smaller role in future security.

Sources are split in their assessment of the importance of nuclear weapons and the validity of traditional nuclear deterrence in the 2001–15 period. On the one hand are those who see nuclear weapons as decreasingly effective tools in deterring war.[123] On the other are those experts who concede that nuclear weapons may have a different role than at the height of the Cold War, but who argue that they remain the ultimate deterrent, with considerable effect on the actions of even rogue states.[124]

Many experts who state a moral opposition to nuclear weapons have translated this into forecasts of a globalized world in which nuclear deterrence no longer makes sense. With greater economic interdependence, this argument runs, even the so-called "rogue states" will be reconciled to the international order, renouncing or reducing their overt or covert nuclear arsenals.

Sources that view future conflict as consisting primarily of brutal civil wars in undeveloped states—along with Western intervention to prevent suffering and injustice—see no utility in nuclear weapons. From a considerably different perspective, some suggest that the RMA has simply passed nuclear weapons by. If information operations will be the dominant form of conflict in an "internetted" world, the use of nuclear weapons would seem merely suicidal. Nuclear effects, such as electromagnetic pulses (EMP), hold the potential of destroying much of the technical access to information on which both war and international society are dependent. Again, there would seem to be no utility in nuclear warfighting, and therefore nuclear deterrence is confined to a background role. Others who focus on the potential for RMA advances to make national missile defenses effective argue that a defense-dominant world will eventually lead to the abolition of nuclear arsenals. Some sources argue that nuclear deterrence has little effect on irrational rogue regimes and terrorist groups, the two types of adversaries most likely to attempt asymmetric attacks on the U.S. homeland.

Other sources view nuclear weapons as retaining considerable deterrent effect, even on rogue regimes. Since, it is argued, active defenses can never be 100 percent effective, the potential for nuclear destruction will remain. Nuclear deterrence, therefore, retains a considerable role in protecting the homeland from WMDs.[125] A few sources suggest that a world in which there are more nuclear powers is a world in which interstate conflict is much less likely.[126] Peace would be even more dependent on nuclear deterrence than it is today.

Divergence of views on the importance of nuclear deterrence in the 2001–25 period seems to presage a continuing debate on that portion of future American defense policy.

Conventional military force will not deter terrorism or nonstate threats.

or

U.S. military capabilities will retain considerable deterrent or coercive effects against terrorism and nonstate threats.

Sources that focus on the increasing vulnerability of the U.S. homeland and on the potential for asymmetric attack tend to doubt the ability of conventional military force to deter such attacks. Many of these sources tend to downplay the role of nuclear weapons and assume that potential opponents would concentrate on developing chemical or biological WMDs, rather than expend resources on developing an extensive nuclear arsenal. Biological weapons, in particular, are frequently assumed to be immune to deterrence by conventional military forces, and possibly by nuclear weapons as well.[127] The logic is that opponents who would be so irrational or immoral as to use biological weapons (particularly against civilian populations) would not easily be swayed by the threat of extensive damage to their own people.[128] More importantly, terrorist groups—having no state or population to protect—do not necessarily present the vulnerabilities of a traditional military opponent. If there is an inherent difficulty in determining the actual perpetrators of a biological attack, then there may be no apparent target for conventional (or nuclear) forces to attack.

An opposing viewpoint is that there are always vulnerabilities that can be attacked—even for terrorist groups.[129] Presumably, terrorists act for causes that have overt elements, such as political independence for a certain population. Contrary to the most alarmist speculations, effective terrorist groups tend not to be crazy or self-destructive.[130] Proponents of this position point to the example of the 1986 Eldorado Canyon reprisal on Libya, which appeared to cause Muammar Qaddafi to reduce his support of terrorist activities.[131] With a combination of intelligence, overt reprisal, covert reprisal, effective law enforcement, and some degree of consequence management preparations, it would seem possible that terrorist activities—particularly with weapons as sophisticated as WMDs, which are extremely difficult to obtain or to utilize effectively—could be prevented, dissuaded, or deterred.

CONCLUSION

The nine points of divergence described above are based on differing assumptions concerning the implications of the previously identified consensus points. It is possible for opposing points of view to accept the plausibility of any or all of the consensus points and yet to advocate substantially different defense policies. This allows for the development of baseline expectations that American defense policy will need to fulfill to maintain security in 2001–25. From this baseline, alternative options for policy can be explored. In developing likely strategy choices for the QDR, the working group incorporated the differing positions on the nine points into the alternative worldviews that drive the choices.

The identification of divergent viewpoints helps to frame the more contentious issues of the defense debate. But, in addition, it suggests that there may be potential developments that future defense policies may need to hedge against. If reputable, well-informed sources differ as to the future impact of chaos and urban warfare, for example, or on the future role of nuclear deterrence, it may be prudent to develop policies that are effective under multiple alternatives. Another element that suggests the need for hedging strategies is the identification of outliers and wild cards.

NOTES

1. This chapter summarizes the details contained in Sam J. Tangredi, *All Possible Wars? Toward a Consensus View of the Future Security Environment, 2001–2025,* McNair Paper 63 (Washington, D.C.: National Defense University, 2000).

2. The future security environment for QDR 1997 was primarily derived from classified intelligence estimates and the unclassified work of two primary sources: the Global Trends 2010 project of the National Intelligence Council and assessments by the Institute for National Strategic Studies, National Defense University. This chapter proposes a more inclusive input.

3. United States Commission on National Security/ 21st Century (USCNS/21), Philip L. Ritcheson, primary author, "Study Addendum" to *New World Coming* (published on website only; not released with report text) (September 15, 1999), 10–11.

4. These standardized criteria are detailed in Tangredi, *All Possible Wars?* 8–9.

5. The three hundred secondary sources are listed in Appendix B of Tangredi, *All Possible Wars?* 161–83.

6. A detailed evaluation of these strengths and weaknesses can be found in Tangredi, *All Possible Wars?* 15–20.

7. Perhaps the most telling historical example of unwarranted belief in certainty was the British Cabinet's "Ten-Year Rule" used between the First and Second World Wars. See Brian Bond and Williamson Murray, "The British Armed Forces, 1918–39," in *Military Effectiveness,* Vol. II: *The Interwar Period* ed. Allen R. Millet and Williamson Murray (Boston: Allen & Unwin, 1988), 101.

8. See Tangredi, *All Possible Wars?* 21–29.

9. The term "prominent dissenters" here refers to analytical, political, or scholarly sources that we deemed likely to have an effect on U.S. defense policy: generally authorities used by the Department of Defense for analysis, or who have a track record of influencing the thinking of government decisionmakers.

10. A succinct statement of this argument can be found in Donald M. Snow, *The Shape of the Future: World Politics in a New Century,* 3rd edition (Armonk, N.Y.: M. E. Sharpe, 1999), 128–30.

11. Jacquelyn K. Davis and Michael J. Sweeney, *Strategic Paradigm 2025: U.S. Security Planning for a New Era* (Dulles, Va.: Brassey's, 1999), 14–15.

12. A number of previously enthusiastic authorities on the post–Cold War expansionism of democratic values now suggest that exponential growth in democracies may be over. See, for example, Larry Diamond, "Is the Third Wave Over?" *Journal of Democracy* 7 (July 1996): 20–37.

13. See, for example, Ralph Peters, "Our Old New Enemies," in *Challenging the United States Symmetrically and Asymmetrically: Can America Be Defeated?* ed. Lloyd J. Matthews (Carlisle, Pa.: U.S. Army War College, Strategic Studies Institute, July 1998), 215–38; Robin Wright, "Democracy: Challenges and Innovations in the 1990s," *The Washington Quarterly* 20 (Summer 1997): 23–36. *The National Security Strategy for a New Century* (October 1998 version) suggests that "if citizens tire of waiting for democracy and free markets to deliver a better life for them, there is real risk that they will lose confidence in democracy and free markets," iv.

14. Samuel P. Huntington, *The Clash of Civilizations and the Remaking of World Order* (New York: Simon &

Schuster, 1996); Samuel P. Huntington, "The Clash of Civilizations?" *Foreign Affairs* 72 (Summer 1993): 22–49.

15. However, other sources—including Middle East regional specialists—tend to agree that, "like their secular counterparts, on most issues many [Islamic-oriented political actors] would operate on the basis of national interests and demonstrate a flexibility that reflects acceptance of the realities of a globally interdependent world." Even some who acknowledge the potentially destabilizing effect of Islamic fundamentalism argue that fundamentalism is now waning. See John L. Esposito, "The Islamic Factor," in *Egypt at the Crossroads: Domestic Stability and Regional Role,* ed. Phebe Marr (Washington, D.C.: National Defense University Press, 1999), 61–62; Max Rodenbeck, "Is Islamism Losing Its Thunder?" *The Washington Quarterly* 21 (Spring 1998): 177–94.

16. See www.stratfor.com, "Global Intelligence Update—5 June 2000; Retrieving the Irretrievable: The Clinton Foreign Policy Legacy" (June 4, 2000).

17. However, there are discussions of how an independent European military structure could balance American power. See, for example, Jean-Marie Guehenno, "The Impact of Globalisation on Strategy," *Survival* 40 (Winter 1998–99): 16–18; Frederick Bonnart, "U.S. Starts to Fret Over EU Military Independence," *International Herald Tribune* (May 24, 2000): 8.

18. Davis and Sweeney, *Strategic Paradigm 2025,* 226. "Chinese opposition to the United States is not the result of current trends in Sino-U.S. relations . . . [but] developed following a series of poor policy choices by both Beijing and Washington that have moved them into a more antagonistic posture than either state had intended."

19. Others suggest that the People's Republic of China is more likely to employ a massive military strike without warning against Taiwan, spearheaded by ballistic missile attack. See, for example, Robert Kagan, "How China Will Take Taiwan," *Washington Post* (March 12, 2000): B7; and Gary Schmitt and Thomas Donnelly, "Our Interests Lie with Theirs," *Washington Post* (April 23, 2000): B4.

20. Davis and Sweeney, *Strategic Paradigm 2025,* 238.

21. Henry Chu and Richard C. Paddock, "Russia Looks to China as an Ally Amid West's Ire," *Los Angeles Times* (December 8, 1999): 1. Rajan Menon describes Russian-Chinese rapprochement as a "strategic convergence" directed against the United States rather than based on any mutual "trust or goodwill." Menon, "The Strategic Convergence Between Russia and China," *Survival* 39 (Summer 1997): 101–25.

22. www.stratfor.com, "Herding Pariahs: Russia's Dangerous Game," Stratfor.com, *Weekly Global Intelligence Update* (February 8, 2000).

23. Agence France-Presse in Beijing, "Alliances Can Defuse Hegemonism by U.S.," *South China Morning Post* (March 8, 2000). Arguing that an effective alliance is unlikely is Jennifer Anderson, *The Limits of Sino-Russian Strategic Partnership,* International Institute for Strategic Studies, Adelphi Paper 315 (New York: Oxford University Press, December 1997). See also Norman Friedman, "The China Puzzle Continues to Baffle the West," *U.S. Naval Institute Proceedings* 126 (March 2000): 4–6.

24. The QDR 1997 report used the analogy of the Soviet Union in the Cold War, stating that "the security environment between now and 2015 will also be marked with the absence of a 'global peer competitor' able to challenge the United States militarily around the world as the Soviet Union did during the Cold War." U.S. Department of Defense, *Report of the Quadrennial Defense Review* (Washington, D.C.: U.S. Department of Defense, May 1997), 5.

25. Ibid.

26. A recent essay on the linkage between economic and military competition with China is Dana Rohrabacher, "Q: Should Congress Be Concerned about China and the Panama Canal?" *Insight on the News* (December 27, 1999): 40. A discussion on American fears of a competition with the EU can be found in William Wallace and Jan Zielonka, "Misunderstanding Europe," *Foreign Affairs* 77 (November 1998): 65–79.

27. See C. Fred Bergsten and Marcus Nolan, *Reconcilable Differences? United States–Japan Economic Conflict* (Washington, D.C.: Institute for International Economics, June 1993). A review of recent sources on U.S.–Japanese security arrangements is Chris B. Johnstone, "Redefining the U.S.–Japan Alliance," *Survival* 42 (Spring 2000): 173–81.

28. See Thomas L. Friedman, *The Lexus and the Olive Tree: Understanding Globalization* (New York: Farrar, Straus & Giroux, 1999); Davis and Sweeney, *Strategic Paradigm,* 14–15.

29. www.stratfor.com, "Decade Forecast—Decade Through 2005" (December 24, 1994), 1.

30. QDR 1997, 3.

31. Current MTW planning focuses on Iraq, rather than Iran. However, the two contingencies are often linked when addressing American foreign policy objectives in the Gulf region. "This approach is consistent with the dual containment policy of the United States, which treats Iran and Iraq as twin pariahs. Although both reject being classified as a pair, American policy groups them together." Raymond Tanter, *Rogue Regimes: Terrorism and Proliferation* (New York: St. Martin's Press, 1998), xiii.

32. National Intelligence Council (NIC), *Global Trends 2010,* argues that internal contradictions in both states would prevent such dominance in the near term. See pages 8–10. *New World Coming* states that "Major powers—Russia and China are two obvious examples—may wish to extend their regional influence by force or the threat of force." United States Commission on National Security/21st Century, *New World Coming,* 47.

33. Rogue states are generally "those states that support aggression and terrorism. A rogue state is an outlaw country capable of instigating conflict with the United States and its allies." NDU INSS, *Strategic Assessment 1999,* 3. Raymond Tanter identifies the "primary criteria" of rogue status as "large conventional forces, [support for] international terrorism, and [desire to possess] weapons of mass destruction." Tanter, *Rogue Regimes,* 261, note 1. Five states are usually included in intelligence assessments as rogues: North Korea, Iraq, Iran, Syria, and Libya. Tanter includes Cuba under the category of rogue regimes because it appears to support international terrorism. Sudan, which is also considered a rogue because of its support for terrorism, generally is not included in the list because it is thought to be a client state of another rogue—Iran—and does not possess large conventional forces. On June 19, 2000, Secretary of State Madeleine K. Albright announced that the Clinton

administration would no longer use the term "rogue states," but that "henceforth nasty, untrustworthy, missile-equipped countries would be known as states of concern." This would appear to be a reaction to a recent meeting of the South and North Korean heads of state. See Steven Mufson, "What's in a Name? U.S. Drops Term 'Rogue State'," *Washington Post* (June 20, 2000): 16. However, the term is ubiquitous within the analytical literature, and therefore has been retained in this chapter.

34. There is a wealth of published recommendations in this regard. Prominent among them is Ashton B. Carter and William J. Perry, *Preventive Defense: A New National Security Strategy for America* (Washington, D.C.: Brookings Institution, March 1999), which discusses the immediate need for engagement of both Russia and China.

35. A particularly witty treatment of this argument is Hank H. Gaffney, "Oh, to be weak" (unpublished paper circulated in 1998; available from author at Center for Naval Analyses).

36. One argument for intervention to prevent massive but not normal levels of war-related deaths can be found in Stephen J. Solarz and Michael E. O'Hanlon, "Humanitarian Intervention: When Is Force Justified?" *Washington Quarterly* 20 (Autumn 1997): 3–14.

37. Arguing that the cumulative effect of failed states is a significant international security threat is Susan L. Woodward, "Failed States: Warlordism and 'Tribal Warfare,'" *Naval War College Review* 52 (Spring 1999): 55–68.

38. USCNS/21, *New World Coming*, 96–99. Several NGOs claim that pessimistic forecasts for Africa discourage investment, therefore perpetuating instability. The implication is that they should be balanced by more optimistic assessments. See, for example, Peter Veit, ed., *Africa's Valuable Assets: A Reader in Natural Resource Management* (Washington, D.C.: World Resources Institute, 1998).

39. Snow, *The Shape of the Future*, 170–72.

40. See James F. Miskel, "Are We Learning the Right Lessons from Africa's Humanitarian Crises?" *Naval War College Review* 52 (Summer 1999): 136–47.

41. But see Martin Van Creveld, *The Rise and Decline of the State* (Cambridge: Cambridge University Press, 1999), 336–421.

42. An argument that "superterrorism" is unlikely and that measures taken to prevent it may be counterproductive is Ehud Sprinzak, "The Great Superterrorism Scare," *Foreign Policy* 112 (Fall 1998): 110–19.

43. Zachary S. Davis, *Weapons of Mass Destruction: New Terrorist Threat?* CRS Report to Congress 97-75 ENR (Washington, D.C.: Congressional Research Service, January 8, 1997); Advisory Panel to Assess Domestic Response Capabilities for Terrorism Involving Weapons of Mass Destruction, First Annual Report: *Assessing the Threat* (Washington, D.C.: RAND, December 15, 1999). A list of current sources on the topic of catastrophic terrorism can be found in USCNS/21, *New World Coming*, footnote 95, 48.

44. A number of sources identify information operations or information warfare as "WMD." The logic of this argument is that death and destruction on a large scale can occur by attacks on the computer networks controlling public utilities and transportation. However, these sources do not convincingly demonstrate that such attacks would result in casualties as extensive as from a successful nuclear or biological attack. In USCNS/21, *New World Coming*, the more realistic term "weapons of mass disruption" is used (52).

45. Ibid., 51. See also INSS, *Strategic Assessment 1999*, 293–94.

46. On this point, USCNS/21, *New World Coming*, cites Roger C. Molander, David A. Mussington, and Richard F. Mesic, *Strategic Information Warfare Rising* (Washington, D.C.: RAND, 1998) as its source.

47. See Joseph A. Engelbrecht, Jr., et al., *Alternative Futures for 2025* (Maxwell Air Force Base, Ala.: Air University Press, 1996), 49–53, 150, 169; Larry K. Grundhauser, "Sentinels Rising: Commercial High-Resolution Satellite Imagery and Its Implications for U.S. National Security," *Airpower Journal* 12 (Winter 1998): 74–76; Frederick W. Kagan, "Star Wars in Real Life: Political Limitations on Space Warfare," *Parameters* 28 (Autumn 1998): 117–18.

48. Eliot A. Cohen, "A Revolution in Warfare," *Foreign Affairs* 75 (March 1996): 37–54; James R. FitzSimonds and Jan M. van Tol, "Revolutions in Military Affairs," *Joint Force Quarterly* 4 (Spring 1994): 24–31; and Andrew F. Krepinevich, Jr., "Cavalry to Computer: The Patterns of Military Revolutions," *The National Interest* 37 (Fall 1994): 30–42. A more skeptical discussion is Michael E. O'Hanlon, "Can High Technology Bring U.S. Troops Home?" *Foreign Policy* 113 (Winter 1998): 72–86; and O'Hanlon, *Technological Change and the Future of Warfare* (Washington, D.C.: Brookings Institution, 2000).

49. One of the more enthusiastic advocates of pursuing the RMA is Admiral William A. Owens. See William A. Owens with Ed Offley, *Lifting the Fog of War* (New York: Farrar, Straus and Giroux, 2000), especially chapter 6, "Winning the Revolution."

50. See Earl H. Tilford, Jr., *The Revolution in Military Affairs: Prospects and Cautions* (Carlisle, Pa.: U.S. Army War College, Strategic Studies Institute, June 23, 1995); Kenneth F. McKenzie, Jr., "Beyond Luddites and Magicians: Examining the MTR," *Parameters* 25 (Summer 1995): 15–21.

51. "Only one country—the United States—currently has capabilities in all [RMA] areas, thereby indicating its centrality in any discussion of the RMA." Andrew Richter, "The American Revolution? The Response of the Advanced Western States to the Revolution in Military Affairs," *National Security Studies Quarterly* 5 (Autumn 1999): 3.

52. Engelbrecht et al., *Alternative Futures for 2025*, 171–72.

53. USCNS/21, *New World Coming*, 120.

54. Michael Dorgan, "Few Surprised at Firing of Los Alamos Scientist: Tip of Iceberg Seen on Chinese Spying," *Arizona Republic* (March 14, 1999): A17; Fox Butterworth and Joseph Kahn, "Chinese Intellectuals in U.S. Say Spying Case Unfairly Cast Doubts on Their Loyalties," *New York Times* (May 16, 1999): 1, 32; David Talbot and Ed Hayward, "Students Say Focus Is Studies, Not Spying," *Boston Herald* (May 26, 1999): 030.

55. For example: Andrew F. Krepinevich, Jr., "Military Experimentation—Time to Get Serious" (March 3, 2000) at www.csbahome.org.

56. Andrew F. Krepinevich, Jr., *Restructuring for a New Era: Framing the Roles and Missions Debate* (Washington, D.C.: Defense Budget Project, April 1995), 44–47; Krepinevich, "Cavalry to Computer: The Pattern of Military Revolutions," 37.

57. "At present, the vast majority of countries in the developing world appear totally unprepared to adapt to the RMA, and thus any study that focused on them would, by definition, be brief." Richter, "The American Revolution," 1.

58. Among future studies devoted specifically to potential wildcards is John L. Petersen, *Out of the Blue: Wild Cards and Other Big Future Surprises* (Washington, D.C.: Arlington Institute, 1997).

59. Jan S. Breemer refers to this circumstance as "the end of naval strategy," implying that U.S. forces can focus on directly influencing effects on land. Jim Wirtz refers to it as "the golden age of United States seapower." See Breemer, "The End of Naval Strategy: Revolutionary Change and the Future of American Naval Power," *Strategic Review* 22 (Spring 1994): 40–53; Wirtz, "QDR 2001: The Navy and the Revolution in Military Affairs," *National Security Studies Quarterly* 5 (Fall 1999): 43–60.

60. It is likely that some competitors will seek to build or to purchase fourth-generation platforms and the most modern ocean-going warships in relatively small numbers to dominate regional opponents. If used in actual combat operations directly against the U.S. naval and air fleets, it is likely that they would operate as a high-tech guerrilla force, attacking areas of perceived weakness until they were destroyed or securely hidden from U.S. response.

61. Illustrative of this argument is John A. Tipak, "Can the Fighter Force Hold Its Edge?" *Air Force Magazine* 83 (January 2000): 25–31.

62. Martin Van Creveld maintains that the warmaking abilities of the modern state will continue to weaken, ensuring that large-scale clashes of sea or air power will not occur. In a sense, his overall argument implies that all states will become failing states. Martin Van Creveld, *The Rise and Decline of the State* (Cambridge: Cambridge University Press, 1999), 337–54, 419.

63. Arguing that "increasingly, other countries' strategies will be oriented around keeping the U.S. out of their region" is Under Secretary of Defense (Policy) 1999 Summer Study Final Report, *Maintaining U.S. Military Superiority* (assembled briefing slides and text), Newport, R.I., July 25–August 4, 1999; quotation, 19.

64. WMDs can be considered asymmetric because the U.S. Navy is largely configured for open-ocean operations. An excellent study of the historical and environmental factors influencing near-shore naval operations is Milan N. Vego, *Naval Strategy and Operations in Narrow Seas* (Portland, Ore.: Frank Cass, 1999).

65. A skeptical view of the ballistic missile threat to CONUS can be found in "NMD: The Hard Sell," *Jane's Defence Weekly* 33 (March 15, 2000): 19–23.

66. See discussion in Kenneth F. McKenzie, Jr., *Revenge of the Melians: Asymmetric Threats and the QDR*, McNair Paper 62 (Washington, D.C.: National Defense University Press, 2000), 8–10.

67. See discussion in Thomas G. Mahnken, "America's Next War," *Washington Quarterly* 16 (Summer 1993): 171–84.

68. A typology of anti-access strategies that could be used against power-projection forces can be found in McKenzie, *Revenge of the Melians*, 46–52.

69. See James R. Boorujy, "Network-Centric Concepts Can Guarantee Access," *U.S. Naval Institute Proceedings* 126 (May 2000): 60–63; Gary W. Schnurrpusch, "Asian Crisis Spurs TBMD," *U.S. Naval Institute Proceedings* 125 (September 1999): 46–49.

70. See Sam J. Tangredi, "The Fall and Rise of Naval Forward Presence," *U.S. Naval Institute Proceedings* 126 (May 2000): 28–32.

71. John P. Jumper has said, "Access is an issue until you begin to involve the vital interests of the nation that you want and need as a host. Then access is rarely an issue." Jumper quoted in "The Access Issue," *Air Force Magazine* 81 (October 1998): 42–46. See also "Operating Abroad," *Air Force Magazine* 81 (December 1998): 28–29.

72. Robert W. Chandler with John R. Backschies, *The New Face of War: Weapons of Mass Destruction and the Revitalization of America's Transoceanic Military Strategy* (McLean, Va.: AMCODA Press, 1998), 199–223; Anthony H. Cordesman and Abraham R. Wagner, *The Lessons of Modern War,* Volume IV: *The Gulf War* (Boulder, Colo.: Westview Press, 1996), 879–915.

73. "Given the West's still-sizable nuclear arsenal and its relatively robust capability to deal with other-than-nuclear WMD warfare, are WMD really asymmetrical to the West? So long as the West maintains its current capabilities, it seems rather unlikely that an adversary could decisively employ WMD against it." Charles J. Dunlap, Jr., "Preliminary Observations: Asymmetrical Warfare and the Western Mindset," in Matthews, *Challenging the United States Symmetrically and Asymmetrically,* 5.

74. Robert Kupperman and David W. Siegrist, "Strategic Firepower in the Hands of Many?" in *Countering Biological Terrorism in the U.S.: An Understanding of Issues and Status,* ed. David W. Siegrist and Janice M. Graham (Dobbs Ferry, N.Y.: Oceana Publications, 1999), 49.

75. Richard Danzig, *The Big Three: Our Greatest Security Risks and How to Address Them* (Washington, D.C.: National Defense University Press, 1999), 32–34.

76. Based on historical survey, Stuart D. Landersman maintains that "Chemical warfare is employed [only] when there is no chance of reciprocal use." Landersman, "Sulfur, Serpents, and Sarin," *U.S. Naval Institute Proceedings* 124 (August 1998): 42–43.

77. USCNS/21, *New World Coming,* 141.

78. Khalilzad and Lesser, *Sources of Conflict in the 21st Century,* 18–19.

79. McKenzie, *Revenge of the Melians,* 3–4, 10–12; USCNS/21, *New World Coming,* 49–50.

80. National Defense Panel (NDP), *Transforming Defense: National Security in the 21st Century* (Washington, D.C.: National Defense Panel, December 1997), 25. Representative arguments include Chandler with Backschies, *The New Face of War,* 177–94; Raymond S. Sheldon, "No Democracy Can Feel Secure," *U.S. Naval Institute Proceedings* 124 (August 1998): 39–44.

81. NDP, *Transforming Defense,* 26–27.

82. See F.G. Hoffman, "Countering Catastrophic Terrorism," *Strategic Review* (Winter 2000): 55–57.

83. See Steve Goldstein, "Pentagon Planners Gird For Cyber Assault," *Philadelphia Inquirer* (December 1, 1999): 1; and Robert E. Podlesny, "Infrastructure Networks Are

Key Vulnerabilities," *U.S. Naval Institute Proceedings* 125 (February 1999): 51–53.

84. A North Vietnamese commander is quoted as saying: "The conscience of America was part of its war-making capability, and we were turning that power in our favor. America lost because of its democracy; through dissent and protest it lost the ability to mobilize a will to win." From "How North Vietnam Won the War," *Wall Street Journal* (August 3, 1995): A8. For a discussion of potential future effects, see Brent Baker, "War and Peace in a Virtual World," *U.S. Naval Institute Proceedings* 123 (April 1997): 36–40; and Michael Ignatieff, *Virtual War: Kosovo and Beyond* (New York: Metropolitan Books/Henry Holt, 2000), 191–96.

85. Robert Callum, "Will Our Forces Match the Threat?" *U.S. Naval Institute Proceedings* 124 (August 1998): 51–52. E. Anders Eriksson argues that "the cyber WMD problem is likely to be transitional in the sense that as information technology matures, defense will outweigh offense. E. Anders Eriksson, "Information Warfare: Hype or Reality?" *Nonproliferation Review* (Spring–Summer 1999): 58.

86. www.stratfor.com, "'I Love You' and the Problem of Cyberforce" (May 15, 2000): 3.

87. William E. Pohde, "What is Information Warfare?" *U.S. Naval Institute Proceedings* 122 (February 1996): 36–38.

88. "Information superiority" is the term used in the 1997 *National Military Strategy* and *Joint Vision 2010* to indicate "the capability to collect, process, and disseminate an uninterrupted flow of precise and reliable information, while exploiting or denying an adversary's ability to do the same." *National Military Strategy*, 18. "Knowledge superiority" was used in a U.S. Navy briefing to describe the objective of developing network-centric warfare capabilities.

89. Air Force Doctrine Document 2–5, *Information Operations* (August 5, 1998), i.

90. See, for example, Owens, *Lifting the Fog of War.*

91. Secretary of the Air Force F. Whitten Peters: "I think everyone has agreed that what we did in Kosovo was equivalent to a single Major Theater War." "Whit Peters on the Issues," *Air Force Magazine* 82 (October 1999): 47.

92. See Ralph Peters, *Fighting for the Future: Will America Triumph?* (Mechanicsburg, Pa.: Stackpole Books, 1999), 32–47; Caroline Davies, "Drinks, Drugs, and Terror —Cocktail That Turns Boys into Killers: Using Children in Combat Has Reached a Horrifying Scale in Africa," *Daily Telegraph* (London) (May 25, 2000): 4.

93. "In our lifetimes, this morally savage, unruly killer, not the trained, disciplined soldier, will be the type of enemy most frequently encountered by Euro-American militaries." Peters, *Fighting for the Future*, 48.

94. Testimony to the growing brutality of modern war comes from NGOs and relief agencies. Edmund Cairns, *A Safer Future: Reducing the Human Cost of War* (Oxford: Oxfam Publications, 1997), has sketched a future in which the majority of wars—fought primarily in the developing world—will focus on the civilian as target, will flout the existing laws of war, and will be fought over the distribution of resources within or between states.

95. "The U.S. Army will fight warriors far more often than it fights soldiers in the future." Peters, *Fighting for the Future*, 44.

96. Ignatieff, *Virtual War,* 210–12.

97. See Don Stauffer, "Electronic Warfare: Battles Without Bloodshed," *Futurist* 34 (January 2000): 23–26.

98. USCNS/21, *New World Coming,* 143.

99. See discussion in Anthony C. Zinni, "A Commander Reflects," *U.S. Naval Institute Proceedings* 126 (July 2000): 34–36.

100. Other sources include Robert F. Hahn II and Bonnie Jezior, "Urban Warfare and the Urban Warfighter of 2025," *Parameters* 29 (Summer 1999): 74–86.

101. The term "chaos in the littorals" is adopted from a joint U.S. Naval Institute–Armed Forces Communications and Electronics Association conference of that title held at San Diego, February 10–11, 2000.

102. Danzig, *The Big Three,* 42–49.

103. Ibid., 40–42.

104. Craig Covault, "Desert Storm Reinforces Military Space Direction," *Aviation Week and Space Technology* (April 8, 1991): 42; Steven J. Bruger, "Not Ready for the First Space War: What about the Second?" *Naval War College Review* 48 (Winter 1995): 73–83.

105. William L. Spacey II, *Does the United States Need Space-Based Weapons?* Cadre Paper 4 (Maxwell AFB, Ala.: Air University Press, September 1999), 1–7, 109; Randall G. Bowdish and Bruce Woodyard, "A Naval Concepts-Based Vision for Space," *U.S. Naval Institute Proceedings* 125 (January 1999): 50–53.

106. See John E. Hyten, *A Sea of Peace or a Theater of War: Dealing with the Inevitable Conflict in Space,* ACDIS Occasional Paper (Champaign: University of Illinois at Urbana-Champaign, April 2000).

107. USCNS 21, *New World Coming,* 143.

108. Spacey, *Does the United States Need Space-Based Weapons?* 107.

109. There are also other political constraints. See Kagan, "Star Wars in Real Life," 112–18.

110. Secretary of the Air Force Sheila E. Widnall, "The Space and Air Force of the Next Century," address to the National Security Forum, Maxwell Air Force Base, Alabama (May 29, 1997), at www.af.mil/news/speech/current/The _Space_and_Air_Force_of.html, quoted in Spacey, *Does the United States Need Space-Based Weapons?* 4.

111. Quoted in Spacey, *Does the United States Need Space-Based Weapons?* 4.

112. In terms of the current status of the United States, see Davis and Sweeney, *Strategic Paradigm 2025,* 286–88.

113. Seyom Brown has argued that gross imbalances in military power combined with inherently destabilizing deployments cause such competition. See Seyom Brown, *The Causes and Prevention of War,* 2nd edition (New York: St. Martin's Press, 1994), 94–98.

114. A similar approach (concerning Russia) was suggested earlier by Fred C. Ikle, "Comrades in Arms: The Case for a Russian-American Defense Community," *National Interest* 26 (Winter 1991): 22–32.

115. This is the basis behind the planning methodology known as competitive strategies. See Henry D. Sokolski, ed., *Prevailing in a Well-Armed World: Devising Competitive Strategies Against Weapons Proliferation* (Carlisle, Pa.: U.S. Army War College, Strategic Studies Institute, March 2000),

10–11. See also Khalilzad and Lesser, *Sources of Conflict in the 21st Century,* 19–20.

116. One proposed approach is to allow other powers to have their own geographic spheres of influence, as suggested in James Kurth, "American Strategy in the Global Era," *Naval War College Review* 53 (Winter 2000): 7–24.

117. Patrick M. Cronin, ed., *2015: Power and Progress* (Washington, D.C.: National Defense University Press, July 1996), 136–37.

118. See, for example, Paul Bracken, *Fire in the East* (New York: HarperCollins, 1999), 63–70.

119. This view is implied by Cronin: "While American military presence overseas would retain its value, the form and context of the presence must be adapted to the shifting parameters of conventional warfare." Cronin, *2015: Power and Progress,* 145.

120. "The Access Issue," 42–46.

121. U.S. Office of Naval Intelligence (ONI), *Challenges to Naval Expeditionary Warfare* (Washington, D.C.: ONI, 1997), 26–31.

122. A discussion of the force structure implications for the Army can be found in Davis and Sweeney, *Strategic Paradigm 2025,* 306–13.

123. See, for example, John Mueller, "The Escalating Irrelevance of Nuclear Weapons," in T. V. Paul, Richard J. Harknett, and James J. Wirtz, *The Absolute Weapon Revisited: Nuclear Arms and the Emerging International Order* (Ann Arbor: University of Michigan Press, 1998), 73–98.

124. Robert G. Joseph and Ronald F. Lehman II, project directors, *U.S. Nuclear Policy in the 21st Century, Final Report* (Washington, D.C.: National Defense University/ Lawrence Livermore National Laboratory, 1998), 1.13–1.16.

125. See Scott D. Sagan, "The Commitment Trap: Why the United States Should Not Use Nuclear Threats to Deter Biological and Chemical Weapons Attacks," *International Security* 24 (Spring 2000): 85–115.

126. See in Scott D. Sagan and Kenneth N. Waltz, *The Spread of Nuclear Weapons: A Debate* (New York: W. W. Norton, 1995).

127. "Traditional methods of deterrence have inherent limitations and tend to be ineffective in countering proliferation of WMD today." David W. Siegrist and Janice M. Graham, *Countering Biological Terrorism in the U.S.: An Understanding of Issues and Status* (Dobbs Ferry, N.Y.: Oceana Publications, 1999), 7, 18. An opposing view is implied by the discussion in Joseph and Lehman, *U.S. Nuclear Policy in the 21st Century,* 1.13, 2.40–2.41.

128. "For example, deterrence may prove difficult against religiously motivated terrorists who believe they are carrying out the will of their Supreme Being. The components of deterrence need to be reexamined, then refocused, with other more pertinent options added." Siegrist and Graham, *Countering Biological Terrorism in the U.S.,* 18.

129. "If their strategy can be beaten, terrorists can be defeated." Gray, "Combating Terrorism," 20.

130. Ibid., 22.

131. See Mark E. Kosnik, "The Military Response to Terrorism," *Naval War College Review* 53 (Spring 2000): 13–39.

THE PENTAGON'S NEW MAP

THOMAS P. M. BARNETT

Let me tell you why military engagement with Saddam Hussein's regime in Baghdad is not only necessary and inevitable, but good.

When the United States finally goes to war again in the Persian Gulf, it will not constitute a settling of old scores, or just an enforced disarmament of illegal weapons, or a distraction in the war on terror. Our next war in the Gulf will mark a historical tipping point—the moment when Washington takes real ownership of strategic security in the age of globalization.

That is why the public debate about this war has been so important: it forces Americans to come to terms with what I believe is the new security paradigm that shapes this age, namely, *disconnectedness defines danger.* Saddam Hussein's outlaw regime is dangerously disconnected from the globalizing world,

from its rule sets, its norms, and all the ties that bind countries together in mutually assured dependence.

The problem with most discussions of globalization is that too many experts treat it as a binary outcome: either it is great and sweeping the planet, or it is horrid and failing humanity everywhere. Neither view really works, because globalization as a historical process is simply too big and too complex for such summary judgments. Instead, this new world must be defined by where globalization has truly taken root and where it has not.

Show me where globalization is thick with network connectivity, financial transactions, liberal media flows, and collective security, and I will show you regions featuring stable governments, rising standards of living, and more deaths by suicide than murder. These

This essay has been edited and is reprinted from Esquire *(March 2003): 174–81.*

parts of the world I call the "Functioning Core," or "Core." But show me where globalization is thinning or just plain absent, and I will show you regions plagued by politically repressive regimes, widespread poverty and disease, routine mass murder, and—most important—the chronic conflicts that incubate the next generation of global terrorists. These parts of the world I call the "Non-Integrating Gap," or "Gap."

Globalization's "ozone hole" may have been out of sight and out of mind prior to September 11, but it has been hard to miss ever since. And measuring the reach of globalization is not an academic exercise to an eighteen-year-old marine sinking tent poles on its far side. So where do we schedule the U.S. military's next round of away games? The pattern that has emerged since the end of the cold war suggests a simple answer: in the Gap.

The reason I support going to war in Iraq is not simply that Saddam is a cutthroat Stalinist willing to kill anyone to stay in power, nor because that regime has clearly supported terrorist networks over the years. The real reason I support a war like this is that the resulting long-term military commitment will finally force America to deal with the entire Gap as a strategic threat environment.

For most countries, accommodating the emerging global rule set of democracy, transparency, and free trade is no mean feat, which is something most Americans find hard to understand. We tend to forget just how hard it has been to keep the United States together all these years, harmonizing our own, competing internal rule sets along the way—through a Civil War, a Great Depression, and the long struggles for racial and sexual equality that continue to this day. As far as most states are concerned, we are quite unrealistic in our expectation that they should adapt themselves quickly to globalization's very American-looking rule set.

But you have to be careful with that Darwinian pessimism, because it is a short jump from apologizing for globalization-as-forced-Americanization to insinuating—along racial or civilization lines—that "*those* people will simply never be like us." Just ten years ago, most experts were willing to write off poor Russia, declaring Slavs, in effect, genetically unfit for democracy and capitalism. Similar arguments resonated in most China-bashing during the 1990s, and you hear them today in the debates about the feasibility of imposing democracy on a post–Saddam Iraq —a sort of Muslims-are-from-Mars argument.

So how do we distinguish between who is really making it in globalization's Core and who remains trapped in the Gap? And how permanent is this dividing line?

Understanding that the line between the Core and Gap is constantly shifting, let me suggest that the direction of change is more critical than the degree. So, yes, Beijing is still ruled by a "Communist Party" whose ideological formula is 30 percent Marxist-Leninist and 70 percent *Sopranos,* but China just signed on to the World Trade Organization, and over the long run, that is far more important in securing the country's permanent Core status. Why? Because it forces China to harmonize its internal rule set with that of globalization—banking, tariffs, copyright protection, environmental standards. Of course, working to adjust your internal rule sets to globalization's evolving rule set offers no guarantee of success. As Argentina and Brazil have recently found out, following the rules (in Argentina's case, *sort of* following) does not mean you are panicproof, or bubbleproof, or even recessionproof. Trying to adapt to globalization does not mean bad things will never happen to you. Nor does it mean all your poor will immediately morph into stable middle class citizens. It just means your standard of living gets better over time.

In sum, it is always possible to fall off this bandwagon called "globalization." And when you do, bloodshed will follow. If you are lucky, so will American troops.

So what parts of the world can be considered functioning right now? North America, much of South America, the European Union, Putin's Russia, Japan, Asia's emerging economies (most notably China and India), Australia, New Zealand, and South Africa, which accounts for roughly four billion out of a global population of six billion.

Whom does that leave in the Gap? It would be easy to say "everyone else," but I want to offer you more proof than that and, by doing so, argue why I think the Gap is a long-term threat to more than just your pocketbook or conscience.

If we map out U.S. military responses since the end of the Cold War, we find an overwhelming concentration of activity in the regions of the world that are excluded from globalization's growing Core— namely, the Caribbean Rim, virtually all of Africa, the Balkans, the Caucasus, Central Asia, the Middle East, Southwest Asia, and much of Southeast Asia. That is roughly the remaining two billion of the world's population. Most have demographics skewed very young, and most are labeled "low income" or "low middle income" by the World Bank (i.e., less than $3,000 annual per capita).

If we draw a line around the majority of those military interventions, we have basically mapped the Non-Integrating Gap. Obviously, there are outliers excluded geographically by this simple approach, such as an Israel isolated in the Gap, a North Korea adrift within the Core, or a Philippines straddling the line. But looking at the data, it is hard to deny the essential logic of the picture: if a country is either losing out to globalization or rejecting much of the content flows associated with its advance, there is a far greater chance that the United States will end up sending forces at some point. Conversely, if a country is largely functioning within globalization, we tend not to have to send our forces there to restore order and thus to eradicate threats.

Now, that may seem like a tautology—in effect, defining any place that has not attracted U.S. military intervention in the last decade or so as "functioning within globalization" (and vice versa). But think about the larger point: ever since the end of World War II, this country has assumed that the real threats to its security resided in countries of roughly similar size, development, and wealth—in other words, other great powers like ourselves. During the Cold War, that other great power was the Soviet Union. When the big Red machine evaporated in the early 1990s, we flirted with concerns about a united Europe, a power-house Japan, and—most recently—a rising China.

What was interesting about all those scenarios is the assumption that only an advanced state can truly threaten us. The rest of the world? Those less-developed parts of the world have long been referred to in military plans as the "Lesser Includeds," meaning that if we built a military capable of handling a great power's military threat, it would always be sufficient for any minor scenarios we might have to engage in the less-advanced world.

That assumption was shattered by September 11. After all, we were not attacked by a nation or even an army but by a group of—in Thomas Friedman's vernacular—Super-Empowered Individuals willing to die for their cause. September 11 triggered a system perturbation that continues to reshape our government (the new Department of Homeland Security), our economy (the de facto security tax we all pay), and even our society (*Wave to the camera!*). More-over, it launched the global war on terrorism, the prism through which our government now views every bi-lateral security relationship we have across the world.

In many ways, the September 11 attacks did the U.S. national security establishment a huge favor by pulling us back from the abstract planning of future high-tech wars against "near peers" into the here-and-now threats to global order. By doing so, the dividing lines between Core and Gap were highlighted, and more important, the nature of the threat environment was thrown into stark relief.

Think about it: bin Laden and al Qaeda are pure products of the Gap—in effect, its most violent feed-back to the Core. They tell us how we are doing in exporting security to these lawless areas (not very well) and which states they would like to take "off line" from globalization and return to some seventh-century definition of the good life (any Gap state with a siz-able Muslim population, especially Saudi Arabia).

If you take this message from Osama and combine it with our military intervention record of the past decade, a simple security rule set emerges: *a country's potential to warrant a U.S. military response is inversely related to its globalization connectivity.* There is a good reason why al Qaeda was based first in Sudan and then later in Afghanistan: these are two of the most disconnected countries in the world. Look at the other places U.S. special operations forces have recently zeroed in on: northwestern Pakistan, Somalia, and Yemen. We are talking about the ends of the earth, as far as globalization is concerned.

But just as important as "getting them where they live" is stopping the ability of these terrorist networks to access the Core via the "seam states" that lie along the Gap's bloody boundaries. It is along this seam that the Core will seek to suppress bad things coming out of the Gap. Which are some of these classic seam states? Mexico, Brazil, South Africa, Morocco, Algeria, Greece, Turkey, Pakistan, Thailand, Malaysia, the Philippines, and Indonesia come readily to mind. But the United States will not be the only Core state working this issue. For example, Russia has its own war on terrorism in the Caucasus, China is working its western border with more vigor, and Australia was recently energized (or was it cowed?) by the Bali bombing.

If we step back for a minute and consider the broader implications of this new global map, then U.S. national security strategy would seem to be: (1) increase the Core's immune system capabilities for responding to September 11-like system perturbations; (2) Work the seam states to firewall the Core from the Gap's worst exports, such as terror, drugs, and pandemics; and, most important, (3) *shrink the Gap.* Notice I did not just say *mind the Gap.* The knee-jerk reaction of many Americans to September 11 is to say, "Let's get off our dependency on foreign oil, and then we won't have to deal with *those* people." The most naïve assumption underlying that dream is that reducing what little connectivity the Gap has with the Core will render it less dangerous to us over the long haul. Turning the Middle East into central Africa will not build a better world for my kids. We cannot simply will *those* people away.

The Middle East is the perfect place to start. Diplomacy cannot work in a region where the biggest sources of insecurity lie not between states but within them. What is most wrong about the Middle East is the lack of personal freedom and how that translates into dead-end lives for most of the population—especially for the young. Such states as Qatar and Jordan are ripe for perestroika-like leaps into better political futures, thanks to younger leaders who see the inevitability of such change. Iran is likewise waiting for the right Gorbachev to come along—if he has not already.

What stands in the path of this change? Fear. Fear of tradition unraveling. Fear of the mullah's disap-proval. Fear of being labeled a "bad" or "traitorous" Muslim state. Fear of becoming a target of radical groups and terrorist networks. But most of all, fear of being attacked from all sides for being different—the fear of becoming Israel.

The Middle East has long been a neighborhood of bullies eager to pick on the weak. Israel is still around because it has become—sadly—one of the toughest bullies on the block. The only thing that will change that nasty environment and open the flood-gates for change is if some external power steps in and plays Leviathan full-time. Taking down Saddam, the region's bully-in-chief, will force the United States into playing that role far more fully than it has over the past several decades, primarily because Iraq is the Yugoslavia of the Middle East—a crossroads of civilizations that has historically required a dictatorship to keep the peace. As baby-sitting jobs go, this one will be a doozy, making our lengthy efforts in postwar Germany and Japan look simple in retrospect.

But it is the right thing to do, and now is the right time to do it, and we are the only country that can. Freedom cannot blossom in the Middle East without security, and security is this country's most influential public-sector export. By that I do not mean arms exports, but basically, the attention paid by our military forces to any region's potential for mass violence. We are the only nation on earth capable of exporting security in a sustained fashion, and we have a very good track record of doing it.

Show me a part of the world that is secure in its peace and I will show you strong or strengthening ties between local militaries and the U.S. military. Show me regions where major war is inconceivable and I will show you permanent U.S. military bases and long-term security alliances. Show me the strongest investment relationships in the global economy and I will show you two postwar military occupations that remade Europe and Japan following World War II.

This country has successfully exported security to globalization's old Core (i.e., Western Europe, Northeast Asia) for half a century and to its emerging new Core (e.g., developing Asia) for a solid quarter-century following our mishandling of Vietnam. But our efforts in the Middle East have been inconsistent—in Africa, almost nonexistent. Until we begin the systematic, long-term export of security to the Gap, it will increasingly export its pain to the Core in the form of terrorism and other instabilities.

Naturally, it will take much more than the United States exporting security to shrink the Gap. Africa, for example, will need far more aid than the Core has offered in the past, and the integration of the Gap will ultimately depend more on private investment than anything the Core's public sector can offer. But it all has to begin with security, because free markets and democracy cannot flourish amid chronic conflict.

Making this effort means reshaping our military establishment to mirror image the challenge that we face. Think about it. Global war is not in the offing, primarily because our huge nuclear stockpile renders such war unthinkable—for anyone. Meanwhile, classic state-on-state wars are becoming fairly rare. So if the United States is in the process of "transforming" its military to meet the threats of tomorrow, what should it end up looking like? In my mind, we fight fire with fire. If we live in a world increasingly populated by Super-Empowered Individuals, we field a military of Super-Empowered Individuals.

This may sound like additional responsibility for an already overburdened military, but that is the wrong way of looking at it, for what we are dealing with here are problems of success—not failure. It is America's continued success in deterring global war and obsolescing state-on-state war that allows us to stick our noses into the far more difficult subnational conflicts and the dangerous transnational actors they spawn. I know most Americans do not want to hear this, but the real battlegrounds in the global war on terrorism are still *over there*. If gated communities and rent-a-cops were enough, September 11 never would have happened.

History is full of turning points like that terrible day, but no turning-back-points. We ignore the Gap's existence at our own peril, because it will not go away until we as a nation respond to the challenge of making globalization truly global.

RISING CHINA AND U.S. INTERESTS: INEVITABLE VS. CONTINGENT HAZARDS

DENNY ROY

China's rapid economic development raises the prospect of a serious People's Republic of China (PRC)–U.S. rivalry, with global ramifications comparable to last century's Cold War. How the United States and China manage their relationship will affect the fortunes of many states, not only in the Asia-Pacific region, but throughout the world. One crucial aspect of this matter is the potential danger a "rising challenger" might pose to the interests of the established superpower.[1] In recent years, the notion that a stronger China threatens the interests of the United States and some of its allies has become commonplace. In-depth assessments of this notion, however, are all too rare. This chapter attempts such an assessment.

The central argument here is that a stronger China potentially poses new types of hazards to U.S. interests. Some of these hazards are unavoidable

This essay has been edited and is reprinted from Denny Roy, "Rising China and U.S. Interests: Inevitable vs. Contingent Hazards," Orbis 47 (Winter 2003): 125–37, © 2003, with permission from the Foreign Policy Research Institute.

consequences of China's growth, regardless of Chinese intentions. In the post–Cold War era, in principle, the United States is inclined to oppose the rise of major new powers in regions of vital interest. It would like the international system to reflect its own and its close allies' preferences. A strong China therefore implies certain inevitable hazards to U.S. goals, and at a minimum, requires that the United States share leadership and rule-making responsibilities with a new, regional, great power and accept a diminution of its previously commanding influence. Nevertheless, such adjustments do not rule out a stable and cooperative Sino-U.S. relationship.

Serious problems will not emerge unless Beijing comes to have an adversarial relationship with Washington. The distinction between inevitable and contingent hazards highlights some difficult issues U.S. policymakers must face, including: (1) the impact of the United States' current policies toward China on China's future posture toward the United States; and (2) the possibility that U.S. concessions today might yield worthwhile dividends in the medium term.

INEVITABLE AND CONTINGENT HAZARDS

Official statements of U.S. interests in the Asia-Pacific region emphasize the goals of promoting democracy, supporting human rights, preventing conflict, and expanding opportunities for economic prosperity. These support America's unofficial goal, shared with all major nations, of amassing and maintaining as much influence as possible over its external political environment in order to bolster security and increase opportunities for prosperity. Although total control can never be achieved, even by a superpower, the more of it the better.

In a sense, the emergence of a new great power in an important region intrinsically harms U.S. interests, because relative American power and influence in that region must proportionately decline unless the United States expends more effort and resources to counteract the new player. In that case, Americans risk a diminution in their quality of life through reduced opportunities or a diversion of public funds from butter to guns. Yet the rise of a new regional power is less unwelcome if it brings expanded trade and investment opportunities and promises to contribute to the management of peace and stability. In either case, attempting to repress a rising power is unjustified in the absence of extraordinary hostility and a clear, compelling danger. In China's case, Washington has consistently stated that it welcomes a more prosperous China and one that supports the norms of the international community.[2] The abundant technical, educational, and administrative assistance China gains from America, engagement that indirectly abets China's rise to great power status, lends credence to these U.S. government statements.

China's rise implies certain inevitable hazards to U.S. interests that are not premised on any particular set of Chinese intentions. Even if its attitude toward the United States is comparatively benign, China's interests will never be perfectly aligned with America's. As China grows in power, its preferences will carry greater weight, and its influence on issues over which Beijing and Washington disagree will increase at American expense. Barring an extremely serious deterioration of Sino-U.S. relations, the United States has no reasonable choice but to accommodate this increase in Chinese influence over international affairs.

Although it is far too soon to talk about China's replacing the United States as the Asia-Pacific superpower, to the extent that China's capabilities in Asia relative to those of the United States increase, Asian countries will pay greater regard to Beijing's wishes. As the world's strongest country for the last half century, the United States has been the main sponsor and guarantor of a system of rules and values governing interstate relations. Various issues over the past decade have highlighted the Chinese government's disagreement with some of the rules of international relations that the United States supports. For example, China maintains a stricter, more traditional view of state sovereignty than the United States and some American allies do. Policies of the Western democracies are based on the premise that economic interdependence has weakened the power and authority of national governments and that certain events and activities within states may justify comment and, in some cases, even intervention by the international community. China is comparatively resistant to this premise, asserting the right and ability of the state to control affairs within its borders. Beijing has argued that the only legitimate international use of force is territorial self-defense and, therefore, that most American military action abroad is aggressive and destabilizing. Chinese government spokespersons characterize U.S. alliances in the Asia-Pacific region as Cold War anachronisms that undermine rather than strengthen regional security.[3] A stronger China could campaign more effectively for changes in the rules of the international system to reflect Beijing's preferences rather than Washington's. If realized, Beijing's principle of international relations would restrict some of the global influence the United States currently enjoys through its military and economic power.

By the same token, however, these principles would restrain a potential Chinese hegemon as well. The prospect of Chinese hegemony appears less ominous in light of Beijing's tradition of emphasizing the inviolability of national territory and "internal affairs" from foreign intrusion and the right of weaker countries to freedom from bullying by larger powers. It is not inconceivable, of course, that if China became Asia's dominant power, its focus might shift from a set of rules designed to protect the weak to one intended to maximize opportunities for the strong. But the abundant assurances Beijing has offered during the past decade have created expectations among neighbors, the Koreas and Southeast Asia, that China will keep its word. Otherwise Beijing risks losing their acquiescence to China's rise.

The growth of Chinese political, economic, and military power will inevitably displace some of America's present influence in Asia, regardless of Chinese intentions. But beyond this, the degree to which increased Chinese power endangers U.S. interests could vary greatly, depending on how Beijing seeks to employ this power. Here we move from the inevitable to the contingent.

Modernization of the People's Liberation Army Navy (PLAN) will increase its range and lethality. As it develops a greater capacity to venture into blue waters farther from the Chinese coast, which is clearly a goal of the military leadership, the PLAN's operational range will encompass important sea lines of communication (SLOCs), including the route traveled by oil tankers between the Strait of Malacca and Japan. This would place PLAN warships in a position to interdict shipping vital to the economic health of Japan and other Asia-Pacific countries. Beijing could conceivably attempt to impede shipping traffic in the context of a political dispute—for example, a flare-up of the Senkaku/Diaoyutai Islands issue.

Although absolute improvement in the PLAN's capabilities would inevitably accompany China's rise as a great power, a potential Chinese naval threat to international shipping should be considered a contingent threat for two reasons. First, an improved PLAN would not necessarily attain superiority over countervailing naval forces in the region, including those of the United States, Japan, and South Korea, especially if the latter combined forces. The navies of other countries will continue to improve along with the PLAN. Even in the future, the Chinese Navy's ability to cut SLOCs in the face of opposition by other Asia-Pacific countries is questionable. Second, such a hostile action by China, despite its own heavy reliance on international trade, presumes a serious crisis in Beijing's relations with the United States, which, as a player in Asia-Pacific security, would surely act to counter a threat to free navigation.

More generally, if China gained recognition as the dominant power in northeast and Southeast Asia, might Beijing impose an economic sphere of influence, demanding preferential treatment from its Asian trade and investment partners that squeezed out U.S. business and consequently restricted U.S. prosperity? Increased Chinese power and prestige would naturally work to China's advantage in regional trade. The desire of nearby countries to gain other benefits of associating with China would inevitably affect the outcome of particular business deals. This is a far cry, however, from Beijing's forcing its neighbors to reach deals with China on occasions when those neighbors would prefer to do business with the United States. It is natural for influence to accrue to great power status, even without coercion. The United States has long enjoyed the fringe benefits of superpowerdom. As an example, after receiving bids for the contract to replace the problem-plagued computerized combat system in its *Collins* class submarines, Australia recently selected the U.S. corporation Raytheon over the German firm STN Atlas,

even though a team of experts rated the German proposal superior on technical grounds. There was no apparent bullying by Washington. Rather, Canberra's decision fell in line with its desire for a closer military relationship with the United States, which can benefit Australia in many other areas because of America's power and presence throughout the Asia-Pacific.[4]

For now, an economic lockout scenario lacks motive as well as capability. There are few areas or sectors in which China and the United States are direct competitors. Most important, attempting to establish an exclusive trade bloc in East Asia would isolate China from the important American market. A more prosperous, developed China will continue to need American capital, advanced technology, and certain consumer goods. Demand for American services will increase. As the Chinese standard of living rises, arable land diminishes, and Chinese farmers find it difficult to withstand foreign competition; demand for U.S. agricultural products may increase as well. Thus the Chinese would do better to stay their present course of supporting a liberal international trade regime and preparing themselves to be efficient competitors.

Future Chinese proliferation of weapons of mass destruction (WMD) technology is best understood as a contingent hazard. This proliferation has served several purposes in the past, including revenue-raising, strengthening Pakistan's capability to counterbalance India, supporting anti-U.S. governments, and retaliating against U.S. policies of which Beijing disapproves. For the purposes of bringing in hard currency and strengthening Pakistan, a stronger China of the future is no more likely to proliferate WMD technology, and may be less so, than China today. Chinese transfers of WMD technology to other actors would not necessarily increase as China grows stronger. With a wealthier and more developed economy, China would feel less compelled to rely on politically incorrect means of earning cash, such as the sale of missiles and nuclear weapons components, which hurt China's international reputation and undermine the responsible image Beijing strives to cultivate.

Furthermore, there is a possible upside to China's evolving from a regional power into a great power with a global outlook: China might develop a greater interest in promoting peace and preventing destructive events in far-flung regions that otherwise have few direct consequences for China's immediate neighborhood. As China's capabilities relative to India grow, Beijing's need for a strong Pakistan decreases. This does not mean a stronger China will abandon its long-standing relationship with Islamabad, but the strategic rationale for WMD transfers to Pakistan will be no greater than in the past—unless the real target of such transfers is not India but the United States. Although Chinese WMD proliferation, for reasons other than raising revenue, is mainly a contingent hazard, it is a tool that a strong China could employ to imperil U.S. interests outside the

Asia-Pacific or as a bargaining chip to counter U.S. policies the Chinese find threatening (e.g., arms sales to Taiwan). As the determining factor is the character of Sino-U.S. relations, it can be anticipated that Chinese proliferation challenges will follow, rather than set, basic trends in that relationship.

A more powerful China would command greater deference from other states in Asia. This might translate into their acceptance of Chinese political demands to the detriment of U.S. interests. For example, although previously ambivalent toward the presence of U.S. troops in Asia, in recent years, China has clearly and consistently criticized American bases in South Korea and Japan. Japan generally tries to avoid offending Beijing when possible, and South Korea values its recently improved relations with the PRC. As China's political and economic weight increases, it might succeed in forcing one or both of these countries to evict U.S. military personnel. This scenario essentially relies on a prediction that Japan and South Korea could bandwagon with a stronger China. Alternatively, finding increased Chinese power and assertiveness threatening, Tokyo and Seoul could balance rather than bandwagon. In this case, they would seek to strengthen rather than reduce their defense ties with the United States.

China's nuclear weapons represent a partly inevitable but mostly contingent hazard for the United States. A stronger, wealthier China would have greater wherewithal to increase its arsenal of nuclear-armed intercontinental ballistic missiles and to increase their lethality through improvements in range, accuracy, and survivability. If China continues its rate of economic expansion, absolute growth in Chinese nuclear capabilities should be expected to increase. How great a danger improved Chinese nuclear forces would pose to American interests again depends on the state of Sino-U.S. relations. The nuclear arsenals of states with which the United States has friendly strategic relations (e.g., Britain, France) are not threatening; those of strategic competitors are. The political context matters more than the phenomenon itself. An improved Chinese nuclear weapons capability would be of little U.S. concern if the two countries were fully reconciled. However, Beijing's assumption that the United States is its most likely potential adversary will affect not only the targeting of China's nuclear force but also its features—including the number of warheads, the characteristics of the delivery system, and the doctrine governing the use of nuclear weapons during hostilities.

The complex Taiwan issue encompasses both inevitable and contingent hazards and both acceptable and unacceptable threats to U.S. interests. As China's relative political, economic, and military power increases, Beijing is in a stronger position to force Taiwan to submit to a settlement agreeable to China. However, numerous outcomes are possible, implying different levels of threat to American interests.

China-Taiwan reunification per se is not a serious threat to the United States. American interests would suffer negligibly, if at all, if reunification was voluntary and Taiwan's economy remained accessible to foreign businesses. Under the terms currently being offered by Beijing, Taiwan would retain its own armed forces, and Beijing would not place PLA units on the island, allaying the fear of Taiwan's becoming an "unsinkable aircraft carrier" for the PRC military. The easing of the tensions surrounding what is arguably Asia's most dangerous flashpoint would greatly reduce the chances of a military conflict that could easily drag in the United States.

Some reunification scenarios, however, would generate serious contingent threats. The worst case would be an unprovoked PRC military attack intended to seize and forcibly incorporate Taiwan. The immediate effects of such a conflict would include the disruption of trade in and through Northeast Asia. There would be longer-term negative consequences, whether or not the United States got involved. American intervention would bring not only the economic and military costs and risks of war with a large, nuclear-armed country, but also profound damage to Sino-U.S. relations likely to persist for decades. If Washington chose not to defend Taiwan from perceived PRC aggression or intervened unsuccessfully, the confidence of other Asian states in American reliability would decline, leading to a downturn in American regional leadership. A conflict in the Taiwan Strait might doom the U.S.–Japan alliance and set Tokyo on a course of military independence, either because Washington disappointed the Japanese by declining to intervene or because Tokyo disappointed the Americans by declining to allow satisfactory participation and support by the Japanese Self Defense Forces for the U.S. effort.

Some of the fears associated with a rising China are illusory. An example is the notion that the PLA will deny U.S. warships access to the Panama Canal based on the Hutchison Whampoa Company's control of the port facilities at both ends of the canal. Hutchison Whampoa is controlled by Hong Kong billionaire Li Ka-shing, who has past business links with the PLA. Should this threat materialize, airborne U.S. troops could quickly and easily seize control of the canal.

Another unlikely scenario that causes unnecessary fear is a clash between Chinese and U.S. armed forces in Korea. This encounter relies on the logic of the "power vacuum," which would presumably draw in both American forces from South Korea and PLA troops from the north following a collapse of the Pyongyang government. In such an event, with the hard lessons of 1950 in mind, the leadership of a combined U.S.–South Korean military operation in North Korea would ensure that the lead elements were South Korean rather than American personnel. China is cultivating good relations with South Korea and would be unlikely to risk a confrontation with Koreans occupying North Korea, especially in light of Beijing's public support for Korean reunification. The very notion of Beijing's sending the PLA into the Korean Peninsula, which, from the Chinese standpoint, is a drastic action fraught with political dangers, requires a stretch of the imagination. Moreover, the possibility of a North Korean military defeat, or "hard landing," which would result in the country's sudden occupation by troops not under Pyongyang's command, appears more remote now that Kim Jong Il's government has survived the privations of the 1990s, apparently remaining in firm control of a state apparatus that has always been extraordinarily strong. China has demonstrated a commitment to providing Pyongyang with advice and economic assistance in hopes of sustaining the present government. If this help failed to prevent a collapse of the Kim regime's authority, China's desire to prevent a U.S. ally from extending its territory up to the Chinese border might provide some rationale for intervention. This rationale is clearly overwhelmed, however, by Beijing's cordial relations with Seoul, the risk of war with the United States, the daunting prospect of taking over the administration of an alien and fiercely xenophobic society, and the upside for China of Korean unification—greatly increased pressure for U.S. forces to withdraw from South Korea and, in turn, Japan.

Although the dangers are sometimes exaggerated, the contingent hazards represent worrisome uncertainties, and this warrants avoiding an unnecessarily adversarial relationship with China. If relations between China and the United States were friendly, the harm done by a rising China to American international standing would be limited. Washington would have to accept more consultation, compromise, and shared leadership with Beijing and might face tougher competition in some sectors of the global marketplace. Increased Chinese demand for some American products and services and a greater Chinese contribution towards shouldering the burden of maintaining regional security would help offset these disadvantages. By contrast, an adversarial Sino-U.S. relationship would find Beijing using its growing strength in a purposeful and systematic assault on U.S. interests in Asia and elsewhere, as the PRC would tend to view U.S. interests as barriers to the achievement of Chinese goals. Unlike the first scenario, the second would constitute a serious challenge to U.S. interests, with the potential to develop into a new Cold War.

MINIMIZING THE HAZARDS

An important question that arises is whether present U.S. policy can shape the character of future Sino-U.S. relations or whether Chinese hostility to U.S. interests will grow naturally from the distribution of international power. Can the United States reduce the chances of confronting a strong, hostile China, and if so, how? The answer to these questions follow from one's basic assumptions about international politics. Three distinct theories bear on the future character of the Sino-U.S. relationship, each implying a different method of safeguarding U.S. interests.

The first theory accepts the Realist premise that intention follows capabilities. As countries grow stronger relative to other states in the system, they strive to gain greater control over their external environment to make themselves more secure. When two great powers compete for influence over the same geographic region, bilateral tensions result. From this standpoint, a China powerful enough to aspire to Asian hegemony will inevitably see the United States as a rival and potential enemy as long as the United States seeks to maintain its leadership in the western Pacific. Two big powers inhabiting the same Asia-Pacific region must unavoidably clash. This will occur even if the United States pursued a more conciliatory policy toward China. If blocking China's rise is not an option, the strategy recommendation consistent with this theory is to lay the groundwork for a network of political and economic arrangements, including alliances, that will deter China from using military force and thus preserve peace. Essentially, the strategy here is containment, although its implementation might range from subtle to blunt. Warnings of a "self-fulfilling prophecy," or making China an enemy by treating it as one, carry little weight if the expectation is that eventual Chinese hostility toward the United States is unavoidable.

A second theory assumes that a state's foreign relations are an extension of its domestic political system and culture. The clashes and affinities between different polities are the main drivers of international relations. According to this perspective, the character of the U.S. and Chinese political systems sets the tone for Sino-U.S. relations. Although the common Soviet enemy provided some scope for strategic coordination during the Cold War, relations between the PRC and the United States have been generally poor, due to the mutual perception of fundamental enmity between the two countries' politicoeconomic systems. The 1989 Tiananmen incident hardened America's belief that, despite moving toward liberalization in the economic sphere, the Chinese Communist Party (CCP) regime is stubbornly resistant to core U.S. political values. The trends of history and the experience of other Asian countries, however, suggest that China will move toward more thorough liberalization, political as well as economic. If China evolved toward a more democratic government at home and greater acceptance by its leaders of contemporary international values (including a more modern outlook on national sovereignty and the use of force to settle political disputes), the basic sources of tension in Sino-U.S. relations would disappear, and both countries could partake of the benefits of the "democratic peace" (the tendency of democracies not to go to war against one another). The bilateral relationship could be friendly even if China grew stronger. In this setting, the United States would be more likely to accept increased Chinese influence and leadership in the international community. The appropriate strategy, therefore, is "engagement": Americans should put their stock in Chinese liberalization, carefully encouraging the process, where possible, through trade, cultural interaction, technical and organizational advice, and educational exchanges.

A third theory presumes that the relationships between states are neither a function of the international power structure nor an interaction of domestic political systems but rather a social construction. Whether China and the United States are friends or enemies depends upon the two countries' interpretations of one another's policies. China's attempts to counter American activity both inside the region and elsewhere stem from the perception that the United States is hostile to the basic Chinese goals of economic development, national unity, and greater respect among its neighbors. If the United States changes policies that, in China's view, mark America as an enemy to vital Chinese interests, Chinese suspicions would subside. The two countries could then establish a permanently warm relationship, presuming Beijing conformed to its self-described vision of China as a great power contributing to regional peace and development while adhering to the Five Principles of Peaceful Coexistence.[5] This theory calls for a strategy that could be termed "conciliation." The premise is that China is not a "predator state" like Nazi Germany and would not respond to concessions with more aggressive challenges to the international status quo.

Although the three theories outlined above are simple conceptual archetypes, each of them influences U.S. policy toward China. Some of the basic building blocks of a potential containment strategy are already in place in the form of U.S. bases in the western Pacific and military cooperation agreements with Japan, South Korea, and Australia. Engagement is proceeding apace on several fronts. How large a role should a conciliation strategy play in the United States' China policy? A conciliation policy would be premised on the hope that if the Chinese were convinced from today onward that the United States harbored no particular hostility toward China, Chinese policies in the future would be less threatening to U.S. interests. The risk is that conciliation might invite an aggressive Chinese reaction rather than a response in kind. This risk is mitigated, however, by America's huge military edge over the PLA and by the likelihood that other states in the region would exhibit balancing behavior against a China that proved aggressive. China has a great distance yet to travel before it can effectively project power a significant distance from its borders.[6] If a strong China threatened its neighbors, they could be expected to join with the United States in a defensive coalition.

Unfortunately, the concessions the United States would have to make to overturn China's present perception of American intentions appear too drastic for Washington to contemplate.

WHAT CHINA WANTS FROM THE UNITED STATES

China's points of dissatisfaction with U.S. policy, essentially unchanged with the power transition from Jiang Zemin to Hu Jintao, may be organized in the shape of a pyramid. At the base are a host of specific issues that are not by themselves serious enough to significantly damage the relationship. They are symptomatic rather than determinate: if the United States and China had friendly relations, these issues would either be low-key or disappear altogether. Examples are bilateral trade disputes and what the Chinese interpret as U.S. attempts to militarily intimidate or harass China, such as the routine surveillance flights close to China's borders that led to the EP-3 incident in April 2001.

In the middle of the pyramid are weightier incidents and issues of broader import, including the bombing of the Chinese embassy in Belgrade in 1999; U.S.-backed U.N. intervention in various places around the globe against Chinese wishes; America's encouragement of Japan's taking a greater military role in the region; criticism of China's human rights record; support by some Americans for Tibetan independence; and the Bush administration's decision to build a missile defense system, which the Chinese are convinced is aimed at them.

It is at the top of the pyramid, however, where we find the two fundamental sources of Beijing's belief in U.S. hostility toward China. The first is America's lingering inability, despite normal official relations, to respect an authoritarian Chinese government that restricts many basic civil and political rights. The Chinese believe that Americans continue to support efforts to undermine the CCP regime through educational programs, foreign news reporting, funding for Chinese dissidents, and criticism intended to embarrass the Chinese government before the world. The second fundamental source of Sino-U.S. friction is Taiwan. As PRC officials have ceaselessly explained to the rest of the world, they consider themselves the rightful owners of Taiwan and expect outsiders to recognize that the resolution of the Taiwan question is an internal Chinese matter. In their view, U.S. support for Taiwan—including the dispatch of two U.S. aircraft carrier battle groups to the area during tensions in 1996 and continued U.S. arms sales—indicates a desire to keep China divided and weak, in direct opposition to China's most basic national aspirations.

Unlike the issues ranking lower in the pyramid, these pinnacle issues determine the character of the bilateral relationship. If the United States discontinues the policies of hostility toward the CCP regime and support for Taiwan's continued political separation from the mainland, China would have little reason based on U.S. behavior to consider America an adversary.

It is politically impossible, however, for the United States to yield on these two key issues. Neither the American public nor their officials are on the verge of a final reconciliation with the CCP. Prior to September 11, opinion polls indicated that Americans ranked China as the most unfriendly foreign country by a large margin.[7] Many U.S. politicians show little inclination to moderate their post-Tiananmen views of the Chinese government, despite the view of China hands that in the past decade, Chinese society and the private sector have grown steadily stronger relative to the state. To cite just one of many possible examples, the U.S. House of Representatives, at the urging of Christopher Smith (R-N.J.), passed a resolution in July 2001 condemning the Chinese government over an explosion at an elementary school in Jiangxi Province that killed 42 people, including 37 children. In violation of international conventions on child labor, students at the school were manufacturing fireworks, which accidentally detonated. The government tried to conceal the cause of the explosion, but Chinese reporters eventually revealed the unsavory facts.[8] Given America's values and historical self-image combined with the practices of partisan and electoral politics, it is difficult to imagine circumstances that would keep at least some U.S. politicians from leveling outspoken criticism against China over cases such as this. Ironically, modest loosening of political controls by the Chinese authorities, which represents progress toward liberalization, will probably result in intensified criticism from America in the short term, as the reportage of Chinese journalists provides more fodder for U.S. China-bashers.

Similarly, ideological and sentimental support for Taiwan has deep roots in American society. Despite the powerful attraction of trade with China, there is no foreseeable prospect of the United States' cutting off arms sales to Taiwan or of an American pledge not to intervene in the event of a Chinese attack on the island. Indeed, only dramatic political shifts on the other side of the Pacific Rim—that is, a peaceful resolution of the Taiwan question or liberalization of the Chinese government—could change or eliminate the American attitudes that make each of these two issues an obstacle to a friendly U.S. relationship with Beijing. Thus, there is no realistic possibility in the offing that the United States will take the steps that would give the Chinese reason to remove America from the position of chief potential adversary. Nor is Beijing prepared to make the major adjustments that could lead to a substantial warming of relations with the United States: renouncing the use of force against Taiwan or dramatically liberalizing the Chinese political system.

Although improving the quality of the bilateral relationship in the near term may be critically important for reducing threats to American interests in the medium term, seemingly immovable obstacles block the road. Both governments moved quickly to contain the political damage of the EP-3 incident. China's quick offer of official support for the post–September 11 campaign against terrorism, despite the ominous movement of U.S. military forces into Central Asia, apparently created a new area of potential common interest, although Chinese reservations about targeting Iraq showed that the scope for partnership here is limited. The current climate justifies hopes that a serious, respectful dialogue between Beijing and Washington could address the less

intractable security issues at the edges of the major bilateral obstacles and thus attempt to minimize the emergence of contingent hazards. As part of this dialog, America should seek to explain, among other things, why China need not feel threatened by the development of an antimissile defense system or by Japan's fulfilling the revised guidelines of its security relationship with the United States.

Whether Beijing's current antipathy toward the United States will persist, deepen, or wane as China grows stronger is critically important to U.S. grand strategy. And although strong economic relations and a number of common strategic goals provide a robust safety net, a substantial warming of the Sino-U.S. relationship is not likely. China's post-Jiang leadership is likely to continue to view the United States as its primary prospective enemy, and this premise will shape the PRC's outlook and policies, including the development of a modernizing PLA during the years immediately preceding China's expected arrival as a great power. For the United States, growing Chinese threats to American security and interests could be the cost of defending perceived interests today. This is potentially a poor bargain for America. Accommodating Beijing on the two key issues of Taiwan and the legitimacy of the CCP might do less harm than holding fast to present-day positions and thereby consolidating the long-term hostility of a rising China.

The United States often views adverse PRC policies as causes rather than symptoms of poor Sino-U.S. relations, leaving underexplored the possibility that some Chinese behavior is a reaction to perceived U.S. ill will. Beijing, of course, exhibits similar thinking. An aura of tragedy surrounds the Sino-U.S. relationship. Planning for a possible military conflict with the United States over Taiwan, for example, is clearly shaping the development of China's security policy. In turn, the perception of growing capabilities and possibly hostile intentions in China moves Washington to consider shifting additional U.S. naval assets to the western Pacific "to improve our forward-deterrent posture."[9] The world has room for both China and the United States to enjoy ample security and prosperity. Yet they appear locked on a course heading toward an outcome most people in both nations would prefer to avoid, one that entails diversion of resources towards a wasteful mutual antagonism.

NOTES

1. As Robert Gilpin explains, this scenario creates the risk of what he terms a "hegemonic war." Gilpin, *War and Change in World Politics* (Cambridge: Cambridge University Press, 1981).

2. For example, President Bush recently said "the United States is committed to helping China become part of the new international trading system so that the Chinese people can enjoy the better life that comes from economic choice and freedom," and that the United States has "a huge stake in the emergence of an economically open, politically stable and

secure China." Online at http://usinfo.state.gov/regional/ea/uschina/bush060l.htm.

3. See, for example, the Chinese government's White Paper on "China's National Defense in 2000," available online at www.ceip.org/files/projects/npp/resources/china-whitepaper.htm.

4. Robert Garran, "Navy Ties Up to Uncle Sam," *The Australian* (July 11, 2001): 1.

5. The Five Principles were put forward by Zhou Enlai in 1953 and written into China's constitution in 1982. They are mutual respect for sovereignty and territorial integrity, mutual nonaggression, noninterference in one another's internal affairs, equality and mutual benefit, and peaceful coexistence.

6. One careful and authoritative assessment is Bernard D. Cole and Paul H. B. Godwin, "Advanced Military Tech-nology and the PLA: Priorities and Capabilities for the 21st Century," in *The Chinese Armed Forces in the 21st Century,* ed. Larry M. Wortzel (Carlisle, Pa.: U.S. Army War College Strategic Studies Institute, 1999): 159–215.

7. In a 2000 Harris poll, 27 percent of respondents considered China an enemy. This was the highest percentage for any country the respondents named, with Russia a distant second at 14 percent. David R. Sands, "Americans See China as Least-Friendly Land," *Washington Times* (September 1, 2000): A13.

8. Online at http://lists.state.gov/archives/us-china.html.

9. Deputy Assistant Secretary of State Peter Brookes, quoted in John Pomfret, "In Fact and Tone, U.S. Expresses New Fondness for Taiwan," *Washington Post* (April 30, 2002): A12.

NEW BATTLE STATIONS?

KURT M. CAMPBELL AND CELESTE JOHNSON WARD

BASE FIDDLING

The Pentagon is now contemplating dramatic changes in where and how U.S. armed forces are based overseas. As Douglas Feith, undersecretary of defense for policy, described the process, "everything is going to move everywhere. . . . There is not going to be a place in the world where it's going to be the same as it used to be." Changes being considered include moving forces away from the Demilitarized Zone (DMZ) in South Korea and shifting large numbers of forces out of Germany. American defense planners want to create a global network of bare-boned facilities that could be expanded to meet crises as they arise. Taken together, the adjustments now under consideration—in where bases are located, in the arrangements Washington makes with host countries, in troop and ship deployments, and in theaters of operation—will constitute the most sweeping changes in the U.S. military posture abroad in half a century, greater even than the adjustments made after Vietnam and at the end of the Cold War.

Such an enormous transformation is necessary, American officials argue, because the way U.S. military assets overseas are currently configured does not address the nation's evolving security challenges. American forces should be moved closer to where threats are likely to arise. The military's flexibility and agility should also be improved, these officials say, by diversifying access points to crises and stationing troops in nations more likely to agree with U.S. policies. Such changes would have the side effect of reducing the friction caused by the large U.S. deployments in places such as Okinawa, Japan; Seoul, South Korea; and Germany.

If the planners get their way, the United States will shift people and assets from safe, secure, and comfortable rear-echelon facilities to jumping-off points closer to the flame, with all the attendant advantages and disadvantages such forward positions would imply. The shifts would have a compelling military logic. But they would also carry significant human, financial, and diplomatic costs. Because of the great size of the U.S. armed forces, any moves they make send ripples throughout local populations, economies, and security architectures. To ensure that the costs of changing to the new posture do not overwhelm the benefits, the Bush administration needs to carefully think the plans through, in all their dimensions. But to date, the military planning has advanced far beyond the supporting political and diplomatic process.

LILY PADS AND WARM BASES

As in a game of musical chairs, the position of U.S. forces abroad at any given time largely reflects where they happened to be when the last war stopped. Each strategic period thus begins with the infrastructure and deployments inherited from the last one. At the end of World War II, for example, the United States had bases around the globe left over from its fight

This essay has been edited and is reprinted from Foreign Affairs 82 *(September/October 2003): 95–103, by permission of* Foreign Affairs. *Copyright 2003 by the Council on Foreign Relations, Inc.*

against the Axis powers. Many of these bases were soon put to use for a different strategy; namely, hemming in the Soviet Union. Similarly, in the early 1990s, the U.S. global military posture reflected Cold War priorities but came to be used for the Clinton administration's national security strategy of "engagement and enlargement." The roughly 200,000 troops stationed in Europe and Asia, originally meant to limit Soviet ambitions, were, after an initial reduction, put to use to provide regional stability and help "shape" the international security environment.

In the post–September 11 world, the Pentagon has new objectives. U.S. forces are now responsible for fighting terrorism and curtailing the spread of weapons of mass destruction (WMDs), and so the Defense Department wants to change the U.S. basing posture accordingly. Some of the moves being contemplated reflect genuinely new thinking. For example, General James Jones, commander of the U.S. European Command, envisions creating a set of what he calls "lily pads": small, lightly staffed facilities for use as jumping-off points in a crisis. These "warm bases," as they have also been called, would be outfitted with the supplies and equipment to rapidly accommodate far larger forces. These small, expandable bases would be linked like spokes to a few large, heavy-infrastructure bases (such as Ramstein in Germany and Misawa and Yokosuka in Japan). At the margins, "virtual" bases would be established by negotiating a series of access rights with a wide range of states. Much more equipment would be prepositioned at land and sea, with an increased focus on specialized units for rapid base construction.

The Pentagon is already preparing a range of specific proposals for Asia, Europe, the Middle East, and the Persian Gulf. Already, Washington and Seoul have agreed to consolidate U.S. bases in South Korea, and then the Second Infantry Division and other supporting units will be moved south. The United States will increase its prepositioned equipment at air and sea hubs at the bottom of South Korea, so that forces can be rapidly reinforced in the event of a conflict. In Japan, the United States will likely seek to maintain most of its major air and sea bases as hubs, but it is considering moving some marines either out of Okinawa or to less-populated areas in the north of the island.

The U.S. air and naval presence in Asia will likely be increased, meanwhile, with Washington arranging for greater access, joint training, and other activities in such countries as the Philippines, Malaysia, and Singapore. This larger Asian deployment will be facilitated by the forward basing of bombers and attack or cruise missile submarines on the islands of Guam or Diego Garcia, along with the prepositioning of more equipment there. Access to naval facilities in Vietnam might also be sought at some point in the future. And the United States and India are steadily improving relations, including military-to-military consultations. In all likelihood, Indo-U.S. defense cooperation will expand and may lead to American access to South Asian bases, facilities, and training grounds.

Whereas the changes being made to the U.S. military posture in Asia are gradual, those contemplated for Europe are radical and abrupt. Reports are now widely circulating that, after its tour of duty in Iraq, the U.S. Army's First Armored Division will return to the United States rather than to Germany, where it has been based. Other U.S. units may be moved from Germany to bases in NATO's new Eastern European members. Poland, for example, has large training grounds and ranges not subject to civilian encroachment or heavy regulations that have bedeviled U.S. forces in Germany. And Bulgaria and Romania offer ports and airfields on the Black Sea, closer to potential areas of instability in the Caucasus, Central Asia, and the Middle East.

The U.S. European Command's responsibility extends to Africa, where enormous change is also in the offing. During the past several months, 1800 U.S. personnel have been deployed to Djibouti and have been given responsibility for counterterrorism planning and training in the Horn of Africa, and U.S. military planners contemplate a similar arrangement for western Africa.

In the Middle East, the United States will soon remove its forces from Saudi Arabia and transfer the major functions now performed at Prince Sultan Air Base to bases in Qatar. Other changes will depend on developments in Iraq and in the Israeli-Palestinian peace process but may also be forthcoming. And finally, new U.S. bases in Central Asia, established to assist the Afghanistan campaign, may end up serving longer-term aims, such as prosecuting the war on terrorism or, perhaps, checking a rising China.

IN WITH THE NEW

Behind the drive for change lies a complex mix of hard-nosed strategic assessments and political objectives. Pentagon officials believe that threats to U.S. security are likely to emerge from regions where there is a high risk of failed states, Islamic radicalism, drug trafficking, and other forms of volatility. Together, these regions form an arc of instability that bends from the triborder region of South America through most of Africa, the Balkans, the Caucasus, the Middle East, and central and Southeast Asia.

Many of the underlying concepts and objectives for changing the U.S. military posture have been identified in such documents as the Bush administration's 2002 *National Security Strategy,* the Defense Department's 2001 *Quadrennial Defense Review,* and speeches and remarks by the president and administration officials. These documents emphasize the need for military forces that are deployed to strike rapidly in unexpected places.

Another impetus for change is apprehension among U.S. officials about the reliability of traditional allies. Many in Washington find unsettling the signs of strategic drift in Berlin and Seoul and worry that policy disagreements could lead to crippling restrictions being placed on U.S. forces by host nations. In today's security environment, such officials believe, the United States cannot risk being denied unfettered access to key regions, and so these officials want to expand and diversify the list of places from which operations can be launched.

Other possible motivations might be at work as well. The plans bear the unmistakable imprint, for example, of Secretary of Defense Donald Rumsfeld, who has been determined to transform the way the U.S. military does business. And some analysts suspect that one of the aims of the new military posture is to encourage a radical redesign of the army's force structure. Early in the Bush administration, officials discussed eliminating at least one of the army's ten active divisions, and over the past three years, the army has borne the brunt of the administration's plans to transform the military into a lighter, more mobile, and more nimble force. To some defense reformers, tank divisions seem a glaring anachronism in the face of twenty-first-century threats. So it is no accident, in the view of some in uniform, that the units most affected by the new global reorientation of forces may be the army units currently based in Germany and South Korea.

WHAT PRICE FLEXIBILITY?

Military planning and the day-to-day management of global military operations are clearly the Pentagon's responsibility. But changes of the magnitude now envisioned would also have significant foreign policy implications, and so other parts of the U.S. government, not to mention the various allies in question, need to be included in the planning process. Such consultations do not seem to be taking place, however.

This is not to deny that changes may be needed in the global U.S. military footprint; indeed, many changes are long overdue. For example, it is hard to justify maintaining approximately 100,000 personnel and over 400 military facilities in Europe today, when the region faces no imminent threat. Similarly, the strategy and posture of U.S. forces in South Korea have not changed much for a decade, even as the rest of the U.S. military has been transformed. With the advent of greater speed and lethality, American troops no longer need to sit at the border in order to deter and, if necessary, halt, a North Korean attack. In general, the changes planned would offer U.S. forces overseas greater mobility and flexibility, allowing them to respond more effectively to the threats of the post–September 11 world.

Still, the most serious potential consequences of the contemplated shifts would not be military but political and diplomatic. Any change in U.S. overseas deployments, even on the margins, attracts enormous attention abroad and raises questions about Washington's intentions. The United States' foreign military presence remains a compelling symbol and bellwether of U.S. attitudes and approaches to foreign and defense policy, and so it is watched closely. Unless the changes that the Pentagon is contemplating are paired with a sustained and effective

diplomatic campaign, therefore, they could well increase foreign anxiety about and distrust of the United States.

A key premise behind the U.S. global footprint in the 1990s was that American forces helped maintain regional stability. The new posture, deliberately optimized for flexible war fighting, will be viewed as supporting a very different and more controversial strategy, one based on preemption and armed intervention. As the military analyst Andrew Bacevich of Boston University has observed, "the political purpose [of U.S. troops abroad] is [now] not so much to enhance stability, but to use U.S. forces as an instrument of political change."

The new posture would also represent a different kind of relationship with host states. In the past, U.S. forces were based in other countries to protect them from invasion or hostile action by others. The host and the United States shared the same risks and the same foe. Washington's new vision, however, hearkens back to U.S. policies of a century ago, when many host states served largely as staging points and "coaling stations" for operations elsewhere. Although it is still possible to argue that, under the proposed changes, the U.S. presence in foreign countries will serve local interests, and that fighting terrorism and containing the spread of WMDs will increase host countries' security, the link (at least for many foreign publics) may appear less clear, and this could pose problems down the road.

There are also practical considerations associated with the proposed deployments. Moving forces around is not a simple process and requires the negotiation of status-of-forces agreements with host nations. These agreements provide extraordinary legal guarantees to U.S. soldiers, essentially giving them local "get out of jail free" cards—as a result, as one might imagine, they prove very unpopular in many countries. Negotiating even modest revisions of existing agreements can sometimes take years, and getting a raft of new ones arranged in short order will be difficult.

A widely distributed U.S. global presence, finally, may lead to a widely distributed set of U.S. commitments and engagements. At the same time that the new posture would reflect and be designed to deal with a particular set of existing or foreseeable threats, it could also by itself generate new and unforeseen problems that would have to be dealt with in turn. Thus the proposed changes could increase the likelihood that the United States gets dragged into future local and regional conflicts, simply because its forces will already be on the ground.

DUE PROCESS

Given the sensitivity of the issues involved, several steps should be taken before and during the rollout of any new military posture. The first is ensuring that everything about the move is vetted carefully by all major relevant actors. Attention to process will not solve every problem, but it will certainly affect the receptivity of other countries to any changes. How such allies as South Korea and Japan respond, for example, will depend not just on the substance of the modifications themselves, but also on how well the United States consults with their governments, takes their reservations into account, and allays their various anxieties. In fact, rather than being seen as a routine obligation or a nuisance, consultations over the posture changes should be seen as an important opportunity to solidify, strengthen, and redefine those alliances for the future. In Europe, similarly, countries are likely to be more receptive to changes if they take place in the context of a revitalized NATO and a reinvestment in the Atlantic Alliance by the United States, rather than being seen as an expression of impatience or unconcern with "old Europe."

During the consultations, the United States should explain the purpose and rationale behind its actions, making it clear that the changes are global and not driven by any particular regional dynamic. Because of the timing, international observers will be prone to view the changes in the context of recent events, particularly the lead-up to and conduct of the war in Iraq. Without guidance from the United States, they will put their own spin on what is happening, which will not necessarily be accurate and could adversely affect other U.S. interests.

U.S. officials should also underscore repeatedly the fact that the United States has no intention of stepping back from its traditional security commitments. Getting the signals right will be critical to preempting unnecessary negative consequences. Despite much evidence to the contrary, some allies continue to worry about U.S. commitment and staying power and may read the new plans as an indicator of what the most powerful nation on earth thinks is important. They need to be assured that any moves are being driven by military concerns and do not reflect a significant change in diplomatic priorities.

The changes, moreover, should not be rushed or hyped, and they should be explained as evolutionary movements rather than radical departures. Particularly in delicate situations, such as on the Korean Peninsula, abruptness is unlikely to pay dividends. For that reason, in fact, the United States should consider delaying the movement of the Second Infantry Division out of the DMZ. It is true that there may never be an ideal time for such a change. But with the threat from North Korea unabated and perhaps even heightened recently, now would be an especially inopportune moment. Even though the move might increase the effectiveness of any military response to North Korean provocations, it would be a difficult sell in the region. Politics would inevitably overshadow strategic realities, and the result could be greater resentment of the United States in South Korea, greater concern in Japan, and greater anxiety throughout the region. When moves are ultimately made—as they should be—they should be done delicately and slowly, and with a close eye on regional perceptions and concerns.

The Bush administration's contemplated military redesign will be the first true overhaul of the United States' global military posture since it was gradually built up during the 1940s, 1950s, and 1960s. Washington's current forward positions are undergirded by an extremely complex set of legal, political, operational, and practical arrangements, some of which have evolved over decades and exist in delicate balance with one another and with various other aspects of American foreign policy. The Bush administration is now proposing to shift virtually every aspect of this armed presence in a sort of military "big bang." This is a bold and audacious proposition, especially given that there has not been a major push for such an overhaul either at home or abroad. Indeed, most Democrats and Republicans who follow defense-related issues, as well as most U.S. allies, have essentially supported maintaining the current posture while tinkering on the margins. So the stakes for this endeavor are high, and it is important that what is being proposed gets a thorough and reflective hearing.

Perhaps there is no good way to engineer changes of this magnitude without stirring up considerable controversy. But unlike during the Cold War, when most U.S. friends and allies shared a relatively common view about the dangers posed by Soviet adventurism, currently no international consensus exists about what the pressing threats are or how to deal with them. Major shifts now are therefore likely to be particularly unsettling and contentious.

All the changes outlined by the Pentagon have commonsensical explanations in terms of operational dynamics and military efficiencies, and the U.S. government should indeed gradually implement many of them over the years to come. But as it does so, it must take greater care than it has so far to avoid collateral damage to longstanding arrangements and relationships that have served the country well for decades and might continue to do so for decades to come. It makes no sense to gain marginal benefits for possible future operations at the cost of undermining close existing alliances or causing important countries to question their security ties to the United States—or, even worse, to consider other options, such as new military expenditures, new regional relationships, or the development of nuclear weapons. Borrowing from Clausewitz, military basing often involves politics by other means. The failure of Washington to understand that truth or to take it into account would be a grave mistake and could have lasting repercussions for the United States and the world.

PART II

AMERICAN DEFENSE
POLICY PROCESS

INTRODUCTION

COLLINS G. SHACKELFORD, JR.

Following the discussion in Part I of the context that shapes, inspires, and brings meaning to U.S. defense policy, Part II seeks to highlight elements that carry the reader beyond an introduction to U.S. government and traditional foreign policy studies. This part of *American Defense Policy* examines selected actors, organizations, and processes that illustrate how U.S. defense policy is an instrument of national security policy. It examines how various U.S. government elements approach the tasks of addressing the challenges of the twenty-first-century security environment. These tasks include the development of strategy, the calculus of ends and means of national power, the identification of issues, the specific policies and actions to execute strategy, and the allocation of limited resources—for example, dollars, and most precious of all, America's men and women in the armed forces.

The contemporary American defense policy process developed as institutions evolved and were shaped, not only by the values and context of their times, but also by such deliberate steps as the National Security Act of 1947 (P.L. 80-253), the 1948 Key West meetings to resolve issues relating to the functions of the three service departments and the Joint Chiefs of Staff, NSC-68, and amendments to the National Security Act that would create the Department of Defense, the position of chairman of the Joint Chiefs of Staff, and various defense agencies. The policy process would be further revised through a plethora of rules, reports, and other oversight activities of Congress, the Goldwater-Nichols Act of 1986, and directives from all elements of the executive branch of the U.S. government.[1]

The American defense policy process has wrestled with threats involving weapons for which nuclear yields are measured in megatons of TNT equivalent and lethal doses of chemical/biological agents are measured in micrograms and the size of individual particles (e.g., weaponized anthrax) in microns.[2] This process addresses contingencies and operations that range from the arctic to the tropics, from the deepest ocean trenches to geosynchronous orbits more than 20,000 miles above the surface of the Earth. American defense policy processes have faced challenges of national security by developing policies and programs that directly affect military/defense organizations, agencies, training, doctrine, weapons applications, weapons development, manpower issues (e.g., women in combat; the integration of African Americans; gays and lesbians in the armed forces), and a myriad of issues related to the Total Force.[3]

The processes associated with today's American defense policy, although never imagined by the Framers of the Constitution, have their roots in the words (and original debates) of the Constitution. Chapter 4 therefore seeks to bring forward the constitutional and legal elements associated with American defense policy processes. Like the values and contexts discussed in Part I, the Constitution has been a critical component to the nation's policy framework.

Richard Kohn provides the historical review of the Framers' context as they, and the states, addressed the issue of just what sort of military should be maintained in peacetime. In other words, what would be the government apparatus "to pay the Debts and provide for the Common Defense?" How did the Framers address the use of force in both the international and domestic context? What were the tensions between the centralization of the defense function at the national level and federal principles involving state militias? Kohn provides a succinct review of the issues and debates that serve as the origins of today's Total Force and the American defense policy process. As he stresses, the Framers' key tasks in this arena were, first, to give the government the means to defend itself and second, to make it more effective in the business of fighting. The Constitution, therefore, provides the basic framework for what develops over the history of the United States as the American defense policy process.

As noted by Kohn, this constitutional framework has proven to be quite durable through major international wars and domestic strife. And although this stability is notable and there has been no U.S. military uprising against the constitutional order, there have been challenges to the balance between the executive branch and Congress as they work toward a "common defense."

Louis Fisher provides a brief review and a march forward on the story of one such challenge to the constitutional framework; that is, war powers, as they evolved in the period since the Framers' debate and ratification of the Constitution in 1789. Fisher provides insights on the checks and balances among the three branches of government on the application and use of U.S. military forces. He captures the inherent tension between the executive branch and Congress through analyses of the use of force by the United States, especially during the Clinton administration. These summaries illustrate that tension that seeks a different balance between unilateral presidential decisions and congressional authorization. Fisher has argued for a balance that shifts toward Congress. He illustrates the importance of this shift by drawing on President Eisenhower's handling of the 1954 Indochina and Formosa crises. As explained by Fisher, President Eisenhower's judgement was perceptive when he realized that a commitment by the United States would have much greater impact if it represented the collective decision of the president and Congress. One must wonder if this is as appropriate a judgment when nonstate actors become the prominent physical threat to U.S. citizens and soldiers, or even if this was possible in the years after President Eisenhower, when nuclear missiles held Moscow and Washington leaders to decision times of 30 minutes or less.[4]

Beyond the Constitution's specific statements on the use of force, there is also a wide range of legal constraints captured by customary and positive law components of international law. Roger Barnett provides a review of their origins and the precepts of *jus ad bellum* and *jus in bello*. Their further codification is captured by a convention with states as signatories that provides a "Law of Armed Conflict" used by the U.S. military in the development of "Rules of Engagement."

Following this review of the constitutional and legal aspects that shape the American defense policy process, Chapter 5 highlights significant domestic policy actors and their respective roles. When one thinks of how the public views the issues and events that encompass American defense policy, one must appreciate that these views are filtered through the media, whether print, broadcast, or the worldwide web. Douglas Porch's article provides a critical review of the interactions—and inherent tensions—between the media and the U.S. military establishment as they each seek to advance their perspectives on the collection and dissemination of information.

The major components of the U.S. military establishment provide another set of policy actors. Sam Sarkesian, John Williams, and Stephen Cimbala provide a summary of the organizational structure and interactions among the Department of Defense, Joint Chiefs of Staff, and the services, as well as those between the executive branch and Congress. This is followed by James Locher's assessment of what could be considered the most significant reform of the U.S. defense establishment since World War II: the Goldwater-Nichols Department of Defense Reorganization Act of 1986. Catalyzed by such events as the failure of the Iranian hostage rescue mission and significant operational shortfalls among the services during the Grenada invasion, Congress undertook a contentious and somewhat lengthy effort that culminated in an act with eight specific objectives that include strengthening civilian oversight, enhancing the effectiveness of military operations, and improving DoD management. Locher's assessment suggests a balanced, but relatively positive scorecard for Goldwater-Nichols in producing a more unified military establishment. Yet as one views the emerging challenges of the twenty-first-century security environment, Locher's hope that "the act has provided the

tools and experience to enable a timely response" may well be a bit too optimistic.[5]

Chapter 5 concludes with a focus on the interagency process and the National Security Council, as rendered by the U.S. Commission on National Security in the 21st Century (USCNS/21). The commission's contribution emphasizes key domestic actors and their interactions, with particular focus on the interagency process.[6] The discussion includes both formal and less formal processes and interactions with elements of Congress. This final discussion on Congress provides a lead-in to the important dimension of resource allocation in U.S. defense policy processes.

Part II closes with Chapter 6, a look at the resource allocation processes associated with American defense policies. It is within this sequence of interactions between the Congress and a myriad of executive branch components that many of the "means" of U.S. military and security strategies are debated, refined, and funded. Although not a topic that receives significant coverage in courses on defense policy, the title of George Wilson's book, *This War Really Matters: Inside the Fight for Defense Dollars*, suggests it is a topic that deserves more coverage, especially when he reminds the reader that America is said to spend $500,000 a minute of American tax dollars on defense-related activities.[7] As captured by a slide used in various Pentagon briefings to characterize the challenges facing planners and programmers:

The PPBS [now PPBE System] *Problem*
When faced with a 20-year threat,
The government responds with a 15-year plan,
In a 6-year defense program,
Managed by 3-year personnel,
Attempting to develop a 2-year budget,
Which in reality is funded by a 1-year appropriation,
Which is typically 4–6 months late,
Actually formulated over a 3-day weekend,
And approved in a 1-hour decision briefing![8]

The chapter on resource allocation begins by focusing on the details of the national security resource allocation processes and actors. This analysis is provided by the USCNS/21 and expands the discussion introduced in Chapter 5 on the actions of both the executive branch and Congress. Moving from the processes between the branches of the U.S. government, Stuart Johnson's contribution takes the reader to the world of the Department of Defense's planning, programming, and budgeting system (formerly PPBS, now known as "PPBE System," as "execution" has been added). He argues for a process that shifts the focus of defense leaders away from the budgeting/execution phase of resource allocation to one more centered on "planning and idea generation." As one Pentagon observer remarked in the 1970s while working in the PPBS for the Air Staff, "When they told me the "P" for planning was silent, they weren't kidding." Stuart Johnson joins the call to invigorate this element of the PPBE System.

The resource allocation processes for American defense have weathered dramatic changes in the security environment. The excerpts from Eric Larson, David Orletsky, and Kristin Leuschner provide a summary of the three defense reviews that have helped shape the Department of Defense's transition away from a Cold War posture. They summarize the lessons from the Base Force (1989–90), Bottom-Up Review (1993), and the Quadrennial Defense Review (QDR 1997) that served as critical precursors for the QDR 2001 and the DoD effort to meet the imperative to "provide for the common defense." The final essay in Chapter 6 is by David Norquist. He brings to the discussion of resource allocation the perspective of one active in the process itself. Norquist seeks to answer the question: "Is the defense budget transformational?" He provides an assessment of a contemporary defense budget that highlights the difficulty of bringing about major changes required to meet the demands of a rapidly changing security environment. These difficulties are captured in Norquist's discussion of the distinction between modernization and transformation, at their most basic conceptualization. Norquist then discusses the "revolution in military affairs" that results from a transformation in which a radically new approach to warfare is implemented.

Although the demands of the times argue for a "revolution in military affairs" or true transformations of how the Department of Defense answers the call "for the common defense," Norquist points out a range of impediments to achieving a "transformational defense budget." They include obstacles to innovation (e.g., lack of vision), bureaucratic resistance, competition between legacy systems and those truly transformational, and changing requirements. Norquist concludes with a more optimistic assessment than some budget analysts, but he nonetheless highlights the challenges of providing the best defense resources in a dynamic security environment.[9]

Part II, with its focus on the processes of American defense policy, gives the reader a sense of how the U.S. government links shifting "means" to the ever-changing security environment. As captured by the National Defense Panel in 1997, "Only one thing is certain: the greatest danger lies in unwillingness or an inability to change our security posture in time to meet the challenges of the next century. The United States needs to launch a transformation strategy now that will enable it to meet a range of security challenges in 2010–2020."[10] This capacity of the U.S. military establishment to change, adapt, and transform to meet the challenges of a dynamic security environment depends upon the processes of American defense policy.

NOTES

The views expressed are the author's and in no way represent the opinions, standards, or policy of the U.S. Air Force Academy or the U.S. government.

1. See National Security Presidential Directive 1 (NSPD-1) at the Federation of American Scientists (FAS) website, www.fas.org/irp/offdocs/nspd/nspd-1.htm. The Library of Congress provides a useful summary of these executive level documents at www.loc.gov/rr/news/directives.html. For a detailed organizational history of the Unified Command Plan through the end of the Cold War, see Ronald H. Cole et al., *The History of the Unified Command Plan 1946–1993* (Washington, D.C.: Joint History Office, 1995).

2. The Stimpson Center in Washington, D.C. (www.stimson.org/?SN=CB2001112953#sources), Monterey Institute on Non-Proliferation (http://cns.miis.edu/index.htm), and the Federation of American Scientists (www.fas.org) provide summaries of the chemical and biological threats. The U.S. Department of Health and Human Services, Centers for Disease Control and Prevention offers an extensive array of facts on bioterrorism and chemical agents, toxins, and radiation emergencies at their "Emergency Preparedness & Response" website at www.bt.cdc.gov/index.asp.

3. The U.S. military consists of active and reserve components (RC). In 1973, the "Total Force" policy was institutionalized through the shift of various elements of the active force into the RC. The Total Force includes the active service members, RC, and National Guard. Over time, this Total Force policy has expanded to include military retirees, DoD civilian personnel, contractors, and host-nation support personnel. Both military campaigns against Iraq have involved significant call-ups of reserve and guard personnel. For details on how the U.S. military mobilizes the RC, see U.S. Joint Chiefs of Staff, *Joint Doctrine for Mobilization Planning,* Joint Pub 4-05 (Washington, D.C., June, 1995), available at www.dtic.mil/doctrine/jel/new_pubs/jp4_05.pdf. See Lawrence J. Korb, "Fixing the Mix," *Foreign Affairs* 83 (March/April 2004): 2–7, for contemporary commentary on the active component/RC mix as it is challenged with "winning the peace" simultaneously in Afghanistan and in Iraq.

4. Two products from the Congressional Research Service provide a thorough review of the war powers issues, recent congressional proposals for revisions/updates, and summaries of instances where the U.S. president deployed military forces and reported the deployment to Congress under the War Powers Resolution. See Richard F. Grimmett, *The War Powers Resolution: After Twenty-Eight Years* (Washington, D.C.: Congressional Research Service, Library of Congress, November 15, 2001) and *War Powers Resolution: Presidential Compliance* (Washington, D.C.: Congressional Research Service, Library of Congress, June 14, 2001).

5. For one such viewpoint that offers a less optimistic assessment, see Clark Murdock, et al, "Beyond Goldwater-Nichols: Defense Reform for a New Strategic Era" (Washington, D.C.: Center for Strategic and International Studies, March 2004).

6. The interagency process has become so important that beyond the traditional Professional Military Education institutions of the Joint Staff and Services, a specialized unit at the National Defense University has been established to focus on education and refinement of all aspects of the interagency process and its participants. For further details, see their website at www.ndu.edu/itea/.

7. George C. Wilson, *This War Really Matters: Inside the Fight for Defense Dollars* (Washington, D.C.: CQ Press, 1999).

8. A slightly shorter variation is found in Professor Sean O'Keefe's slide presentation on "Defense Resource Management Process," Maxwell School of Citizenship, Syracuse University, N.Y. (September 25, 2000).

9. See, for example, Steven M. Kosiak, *Analysis of the FY 2005 Defense Budget Request* (Washington, D.C.: Center for Strategic and Budgetary Assessment, 2004).

10. National Defense Panel, *Transforming Defense: National Security in the 21st Century* (Washington, D.C.: U.S. Government Printing Office, 1997), i.

CHAPTER 4

THE CONSTITUTIONAL AND LEGAL BASIS FOR AMERICAN DEFENSE AND NATIONAL SECURITY

THE CONSTITUTION AND NATIONAL SECURITY:
THE INTENT OF THE FRAMERS

RICHARD H. KOHN

Few issues in recent years have divided the field of constitutional jurisprudence more than the doctrine of original intent. The controversy is an old one, of course, extending back to the very beginning of government under the Constitution, when Americans immediately began arguing over the intentions of the framers and how closely to adhere to the exact text of the document, particularly where it was silent or ambiguous, or where its language was open to interpretation. In modern form, the controversy burst most dramatically into public view in 1985, when Attorney General of the United States Edwin Meese III, in a speech to the American Bar Association, criticized the U.S. Supreme Court for "mere policy choices rather than articulations of Constitutional principle," for "a greater allegiance to what the Court thinks constitutes sound public policy rather than a deference to what the Constitution, its text and intention, may demand." The role of the judiciary, asserted Meese, quoting Alexander Hamilton in *The Federalist Papers,* "was to serve as the 'bulwark of a limited constitution' . . . ; the judges were expected to resist any political effort to depart from the literal provisions of the Constitution. The standard of interpretation applied by the judiciary must focus on the text and the drafters' original intent." Only such an interpretation, in Meese's view, would "keep the powers created by the Constitution within the boundaries marked out by the Constitution." The Court should follow the example of the Administration of Ronald Reagan and use "the original meaning of constitutional provisions and statutes as the only reliable guide for judgment."[1]

The attorney general was quickly answered by Associate Justice of the Supreme Court William Brennan, Jr., in a speech at Georgetown University. "Like every text worth reading," the Constitution "is not crystalline. The phrasing is broad and the limitations of its provisions are not clearly marked. Its majestic generalities and ennobling pronouncements are both luminous and obscure. This ambiguity, of course, calls forth interpretation." For judges, argued Brennan, "constitutional interpretation is, for the most part, obligatory." They "cannot avoid a defini-

tive interpretation" either through inability or unwillingness to "penetrate the full meaning of the Constitution's provisions." This interpretation becomes "an order—supported by the full coercive power of the State." "The act of interpretation is, in a very real sense, the community's interpretation" and it must be "received as legitimate." Brennan rejected "The intentions of the Framers" as the standard of legitimacy, because it was "arrogant to pretend that from our vantage we can gauge accurately the intent of the Framers on application of principle to specific, contemporary questions." The "records" were too "sparse" or "ambiguous," the "Framers themselves did not agree." To Brennan, "our distance of two centuries cannot but work as a prism refracting all we perceive." The Constitution to him was "a structuring text, a blueprint for government." He and his fellow justices "read the Constitution in the only way that we can: as twentieth-century Americans. We look to the history of the time of framing and to the intervening history of interpretation. But the ultimate question must be: what do the words of the text mean in our time?" In Brennan's mind, "the genius of the Constitution rests not in any static meaning it might have had in a world that is dead and gone, but in the adaptability of its great principles to cope with current problems and current needs."[2]

Most historians have taken Brennan's view; their objection to "original intent" is the virtual impossibility of knowing for certain the intentions of the framers. To begin with, the documentary record of the Constitutional Convention and the state ratifying conventions was itself defective, as Justice Brennan argued. Only a partial fragment of those proceedings was recorded, and some of that, for reasons of partisanship or simple human error, is of questionable accuracy and reliability.[3] Knowing the intentions of any single person is difficult even for contemporaries—or for the individual involved—not to speak of scholars two centuries removed. For a group, the problem is compounded. At one time or another, over fifty men attended the convention and they varied enormously in their views.[4] Before the convention disbanded, thirteen left, some of whom proceeded to fight against

Richard H. Kohn, "The Constitution and National Security: The Intent of the Framers," in The United States Military under the Constitution of the United States, 1789–1989, *ed. Richard H. Kohn (New York: New York University Press, 1991), 61–94. Public domain.*

the Constitution. Three of the remaining forty-two refused to sign it, two becoming vocal opponents during the ratification struggle in their home states. Much of the Constitution, in truth, consisted of carefully crafted compromises approved in the convention by only the thinnest of majorities. Undoubtedly, the stances of these men were influenced by many factors: self-interest, the interests or needs of their states or section, religious scruple, ideology—or by any combination thereof. To this day, historians argue over their individual motives.[5] We do know that they were practical people of broad vision who, against great odds, undertook a rebellion and a revolution— and succeeded. For a generation, they adapted to meet the unexpected. The Constitution was itself such an adaptation, conceived during one of the most innovative eras in the history of government. Few of the framers believed it would last forever, and probably none of them liked it in its entirety. They made provisions for it to be changed, and judging by their own violent disagreements during the next thirty years over how it should be interpreted, it is unlikely that they expected future generations to adhere slavishly to their "original intent," even if it could be established beyond a reasonable doubt.[6] During the struggle over ratification, George Washington put it candidly: "I am not a blind Admirer (for I saw the Imperfections) . . . before it was handed to the Public; but I am fully persuaded that it is the *best that can be obtained at this Time*."[7]

Even if the framers' intentions are difficult to fathom, it is still important, quite beyond these years of bicentennial observance, to study the framers and their work. The Constitution is the fundamental charter of the U.S. government. It is the foundation that defines and determines how the country has defended itself for the past two centuries and defends itself today; it authorizes the institutions created for national security, the structure in which those institutions and their people operate, the process by which the institutions interact with each other, and the overall manner in which the nation is expected to prepare for, enter into, conduct, and end its military conflicts. Although the motives of the framers individually or collectively may remain uncertain, the document itself can be analyzed and explained by means of the conventional tools of historical analysis: what the Constitution says and why these words were written as they were. From the standpoint of security, the Constitution reaches beyond the issue of American defense, and for that reason alone is worth pondering. Ultimately, because Americans have been so distrustful of, and ambivalent toward, their military institutions, the Constitution addresses directly the age-old problem of how to protect liberty without, in the process, destroying it.

As they gathered in Philadelphia in the spring of 1787, the framers identified a number of threats to the new nation's interests and security, some general and some quite specific. Security was very much at the forefront of their concerns. Several actual or potential enemies lay on American borders. In Massachusetts, a rebellion had just been suppressed and in the view of Confederation Secretary of War Henry Knox, perhaps as many as one-fifth of the people of the New England states were as disaffected as the farmers who had risen up to protest against the burden of debt, worsening economic conditions, and the seacoast leadership of their region.[8] Knox spoke for many when he told George Washington, soon to be elected to chair the convention, that "our present federal government is indeed a name, a shadow, without power, or effect. We must either have a government, of the same materials, differently constructed, or we must have a government of events."[9] One of the fundamental goals of the Constitution was to remedy what the convention believed were deep, structural flaws in the ability of government under the Articles of Confederation to defend the United States; among them, the inability of the central government to mount and sustain military operations. At the opening of the substantive business of the convention, Governor Edmund Randolph of Virginia justified the plan of government he was offering by calling "The System of the present foederal Government . . . totally inadequate to the Peace, Safety and Security of the Confederation."[10] Noted another delegate, of Randolph's speech:

1. Congress unable to prevent war
2. Not able to support war
3. Not able to prevent internal sedition or rebellion.[11]

As Oliver Ellsworth of Connecticut began his speech to his state's ratifying convention, "A Union is necessary for the purposes of national defence. United, we are strong; divided we are weak. It is easy for hostile nations to sweep off a number of separate states one after another. . . . We must unite, in order to preserve peace among ourselves. . . . [A] parental hand over the whole . . . and nothing else, can restrain the unruly conduct of the members."[12]

As realists, the framers knew that war was possible at any time. They accepted war as natural to the world, an inevitable and almost normal part of international life, whether caused by economic competition, greed, dynastic quarrels, or other differences among states. "To judge from the history of mankind," wrote Alexander Hamilton, "the fiery and destructive passions of war reign in the human breast with much more powerful sway than the mild and beneficent sentiments of peace; and . . . to model our political systems upon speculations of lasting tranquillity is to calculate on the weaker springs of the human character."[13] The framers assumed that the United States, with its rich resources, its trade, and its population expanding into the interior of a vast continent abundant in raw materials, would be both a threat and a target for European nations.[14] More importantly, as a new nation and the first successful revolutionaries in modern times, Americans saw themselves as the only true repository of liberty left in a world of monarchies and tyranny. They saw themselves, and they thought that others viewed them, as a subversive threat to Europe's ancien régime.

The framers also believed the United States was endangered by centrifugal forces inherent in a weak central government. Perhaps the greatest danger lay in disunion. If instead of a single republic there emerged in North America a set of smaller states, European nations would certainly attempt to assert their control, or to play one state off against another. Or the states would drift apart and become rivals, competing for power, influence, trade, territory, or advantage, warring among themselves—in John Jay's words, "A prey to discord, jealousy, and mutual injuries, in short . . . *formidable only to each other.*"[15] It was by no means clear in 1787, and not in fact until after the Civil War some seventy-five years later, that there would be only one nation-state in the temperate zone of North America. Should the union fracture into thirteen independent nations or some combination of sovereign entities, Americans thought that Europe would be duplicated all over again, with shifting alliances and alignments, standing military forces, wars, and competition for domination. More importantly and more dangerous yet, independent states in North America would be vulnerable to penetration or subversion by European powers, to being drawn into the European power system, thus becoming tools for European states to reestablish their influence and threaten the liberty of Americans. As Hamilton put it, "*Divide et impera* [divide and command] must be the motto of every nation, that either hates, or fears us."[16] Therefore, in the view of those framers most concerned with security, part of the foreign danger was the internal threat to national integrity, which would destroy republican government. Thus, it was crucial to construct a union strong enough to prevent the re-creation of an essentially European international order in North America.[17]

At the same time that they saw broad and general dangers to the nation's security, Americans in the 1780s also identified more direct and specific threats. First were the British—close by in Canada, not necessarily willing to abide by the outcome of the war, eager to prevent American expansion, and continuing to protect their erstwhile allies, the Indians, by stopping expansion and aborting America's western imperial dreams. In Florida and Louisiana lay the Spanish—Catholic Spain—also unenthusiastic about American expansion into the Mississippi Valley, which would loosen Spain's tenuous hold on her own colonial territory. She, too, was conniving with Indians to halt American settlement, even attempting to suborn the settlers themselves in an effort to create an independent or puppet state between herself and the dynamic, expanding Americans. Both nations gave evidence of their intentions, the British by continuing to occupy strategically located forts on American soil, the Spanish by closing the mouth of the Mississippi River to American commerce. To the framers, weakness heightened the threat and the possibility of war. As James Wilson told the Pennsylvania ratifying convention, "we are still an inviting object to one

European power at least, and, if we cannot defend ourselves, the temptation may become too alluring to be resisted."[18]

From the sea there also came dangers, for as James Madison discerned, "almost every State will on one side or other, be a frontier."[19] The young nation was part of an Atlantic economy, its trade vulnerable, its access to markets and goods crucial to economic and material prosperity. On the one hand, the Atlantic posed a barrier to enemies, the crucial buffer that offered enough early warning of danger for Americans to mobilize for their defense. On the other hand, the Atlantic could act as a highway for invaders, as it did in 1776, when the British nearly shattered the rebellion by sending a massive fleet and an army to seize New York and strike inland. The realities of geography meant that strategic areas or regions could be invested and seized by any power that possessed the ships, men, matériel, and administrative capacity to mount such an undertaking. Because the United States was a maritime nation, some naval forces would be needed, if for nothing else than to protect American trade from pirates, as the country learned ruefully in the Mediterranean during the 1780s and 1790s. But the chief concern was the safety of American ports, not only the crucial nodes of the American economy, but the gateways through which the security and indeed the independence of the United States could be threatened. In early 1788, the historian David Ramsay instructed his fellow South Carolinians that "without money, without a navy, or the means of even supporting an army of our own citizens in the field, we lie at the mercy of every invader; our sea port towns may be laid under Contribution, and our country ravaged."[20]

The most specific threat—the one omnipresent in the minds of most Americans and certainly the framers of the Constitution—was the Indians, those native Americans with whom the Europeans had lived and warred for a century and a half, virtually from the beginning of settlement in the early 1600s. On both the northern and southern frontiers lay powerful tribes directly in the path of white expansion, some large and cohesive, like the Creek and Cherokee, others the remnants of eastern tribes driven out or displaced by earlier white encroachment. Some of the states had very special border problems, like Georgia, which at the very time of the constitutional debate was embroiled—"embarass'd," as a plantation manager lamented in early 1788— "with the indian war," which opened the state "to within thirty miles of Savannah" of being "ravaged by incursions of the Savages."[21] Even the opponents of the Constitution, such as the New York newspaper essayist "Brutus," whose objections to the military provisions were among the most sophisticated and informed, acknowledged the need "to raise and support a small number of troops to garrison the important frontier posts, and to guard arsenals."[22] Particularly in the Old Northwest, already by 1787 undergoing a boom of settlement, there existed a barrier of hostile tribes, aided and abetted by British agents. The British presence in the area underlined the weakness of American defense policy, for the Crown's troops and agents conspired with their Indian clients from forts on American territory, which remained in British hands until after Jay's Treaty in 1795.

The last, but also a highly important security problem, was the maintenance of internal order. As scholars have discovered in recent years, the mob was, in the eighteenth century, a fact of the political landscape; politics, like life, could be mean and raw, the streets mobilized to direct action by passion or design. Periodically the crowd rose up, frequently at times of stress or instability; Americans themselves had used the mob to great effect in the cities as the revolutionary movement formed and gathered momentum. Perceptive political leaders in the United States understood that once awakened, the monster might not easily be lulled back into somnolence. Twice in the two decades after the War for Independence —in western Massachusetts in 1786 and western Pennsylvania in 1794—insurrections broke out that were only ended by the mobilization of force. The threat was real and accepted generally by members of the Constitutional Convention, regardless of differences on other issues. "No government can be stable, which hangs on human inclination alone, unbiased by the fear of coercion," wrote Randolph shortly after the convention finished its work.[23] Echoed William Paterson of New Jersey, in presenting his small-states plan of union, "No government could be energetic on paper only, which was no more than a straw . . . there must be a small standing force to give every government weight."[24]

Although the framers believed that force was fundamental to government, they were less comfortable with its application in the process of governing civil society. "I confess . . . that I am at a loss to know whether any government can have sufficient energy to effect its own ends without the aid of a military power," wrote William Pierce of Georgia a few days after the convention disbanded. "Some of the greatest men differ in opinion about this point."[25] Earlier, at the height of fear about Shays's Rebellion, just before the convention assembled, George Washington endorsed "means of coercion in the Sovereign" to "enforce Obedience to the Ordinances of a Genl. Government; without which every thing else fails. . . . But the kind of coercion?"[26] Fellow Virginian George Mason, who refused to sign the Constitution, had no doubt. "What," he asked his colleagues, "would you use military force to compel the observance of a social compact?"[27] "This can never be accomplished— you can no more execute civil Regulations by Military Force than you can unite opposite Elements, than you can mingle Fire with Water."[28] Hamilton and Madison agreed, to the extent that force could not work as the foundation for government in a confederation of essentially independent states. "Force," asserted Hamilton, "may be understood [as] a *coertion of laws* or *coertion of arms.*"[29] Law could not operate on another sovereignty; each state could defy the central government and if that government resorted to force, "it amounts to a war between the parties," leaving "war and carnage" as the "only means" of compelling obedience.[30] But if the central government were national—able to "carry its agency to the persons of the citizens" without "intermediate legislations" and able to employ "the arm of the ordinary magistrate to execute its own resolutions" by means of "the Courts of Justice"—then law and force could operate together to compel compliance without tearing society apart.[31] Defiance would be a confrontation between individuals and government, not member states and a confederacy, and thus within the capacity of the courts, the marshalls, the *posse comitatus*, the militia, or finally, the regular army, to combat. Force then became functional as the last resort, left in the background and used only, as Madison told the Virginia ratifying convention, "when resistance to the laws required it," to prevent "society from being destroyed."[32]

Although all of these threats—of war and of the Confederation's weakness in war-making ability, of the Indians and of European incursion from land or sea, of disorder or rebellion—were quite real, most Americans at the same time were confident and optimistic about the security of their country. As a matter of military capability or potential, the nation was fundamentally strong. The United States had just defeated the greatest military power of the eighteenth-century world and become one of the few countries in history successfully to cast off the yoke of colonial subservience. With their geographic separation from Europe, their dispersed and independent-minded population, and their resources, Americans could not easily be subjugated. In a war of national existence, when the danger was obvious and the community mobilized, they had little to fear. The problem, as perceived in the 1780s, was structural: the Articles of Confederation. On the basis of the War for Independence and the years of peace afterward, it was not clear that the Confederation government could defend the United States, prepare the country for conflict, or on a continuing basis safeguard American borders and interests. In his "long and elaborate" opening statement to the convention, Edmund Randolph indicted the Confederation for a lengthy list of military deficiencies. Congress could not prevent invasion or stop individuals or states from starting wars. Without authority to send troops into a member state, Congress could not maintain internal order. Nor could Congress, without its own taxing or conscripting authority, raise money or men; instead, the government depended on requisitions to the states, which could choose to ignore or defy the requests with impunity. As James McHenry described Randolph's speech, "Imbecility of the Confederation . . . conspicuous when called upon to support a war. The journals of Congress a history of expedients."[33]

The framers knew that even during the War for Independence, with British armies operating on American soil, victory had been won by the very narrowest of margins. As veterans of the militia or

Continental Army, or of the wartime Congress or state governments, many members of the convention remembered vividly the war from first-hand experience.[34] There had been difficulties in fielding forces, raising money, and sustaining the effort, politically as well as militarily. American leadership had been uneven; arms and equipment had been lacking; and finances had been difficult to manage—and by the middle of the conflict, exhausted. War administration had never been sufficient to keep adequate forces raised, equipped, paid, or supplied. In the end, the struggle had been decided by the exhaustion of an enemy distracted by a Europe-wide coalition against her, an enemy that had lost the will to continue the effort and had decided to abandon a portion of her empire in order to preserve the rest. A few in the convention may even have understood that the alliances with European nations, particularly France, had provided the real margin of victory. For the Americans, then, the problem of defense was not a weakness of spirit or resources, or even the various threats that called into question the nation's security. The problem was the Articles of Confederation.

To begin with, the Articles recognized an association of states in which sovereignty was reserved to the states, not a national government of the people. The government could not act on its population. It could not enlist them, draft them, tax them, or coerce them, for it had no grant of authority or machinery to do so. The Confederation was, as the Articles read, a "league of friendship" in which "Each state retains it sovereignty, freedom and independence, and every Power, Jurisdiction and right which is not . . . expressly delegated to the United States, in Congress assembled."[35] The states retained the powers to tax and to raise forces. The Confederation could ask the states for men and money and appoint officers at the rank of general (not below), but only if Congress were virtually unanimous. On questions of troop and monetary requisitions, nine states had to be present and agree, and if a state was represented by only two delegates, as was often the case, and one did not vote in the affirmative, then that state could not be counted as consenting to the measure. Until 1781, there was not even a true war administration, with executive departments instead of committees to manage the business of finance, military and naval affairs, and foreign relations. One newspaper report described the problem as "the impotence of federal Government. . . . In short, they may DECLARE every thing, but can DO nothing."[36]

Although it was understood that this system was inefficient and dangerous in wartime, its weakness in peacetime had also come to be acknowledged. When offered a plan for a peacetime military establishment in 1783—to staff western forts, to patrol the interior and occupy American territory, to deter the Indians, and to guard leftover arms and stores—Congress could not even summon the will to decide whether it possessed such authority in peacetime, a point that bothered delegate James Madison at the time and one that remained a bone of contention throughout

the 1780s and into the debate over the Constitution.[37] In 1784, sectional and ideological divisions typical of American legislative bodies prevented Congress from asking for more than seven hundred militia from four states. Two of the states never acted at all, and the force created could hardly protect itself, much less the surveyors marking off western lands for sale or the people beginning to settle in the Ohio Valley. Twice in the 1780s, frontiersmen in Kentucky took matters into their own hands to attack Indian towns in what is today the states of Ohio and Indiana. The underpaid and underequipped First Regiment of the United States, poorly led and never large enough to accomplish its missions, could not fulfill even the most minimal national function. The troops "contribute nothing to the defence of the frontier inhabitants," wrote one observer. "They are rather prisoners in that country, than in possession of it."[38]

Likewise, Congress watched helplessly during the summer and fall of 1786 as Shays's Rebellion erupted in western Massachusetts and seemed to threaten similar outbursts elsewhere in New England and in the back countries of other regions. To many political leaders, the weakness of the Articles of Confederation was symbolized by the uprising of farmers protesting difficult economic conditions and the domination of eastern interests. "I believe it is not generally known on what a perilous tenure we held our freedom and independence at that period," claimed James Wilson in the Pennsylvania ratifying convention. "The flames of internal insurrection were ready to burst out in every quarter . . . and from one end to the other of the continent, we walked on ashes, concealing fire beneath our feet." Wilson could not conceive of a government "deprived of power to prepare for the defense and safety of our country" and he, like others of his persuasion, was not willing to entrust the function to militia, particularly when combating internal turmoil.[39] "Here is felt the imbecility, the futility, the nothingness of the federal powers," lamented a delegate sitting in Congress during the rebellion; "the U.S. have no troops, nor dare they call into action, what is called the only safeguard of a free government, the Militia of the State, it being composed of the very objects of the force."[40]

Thus it was clear to the framers of the Constitution that the Articles needed to be revised and the military powers of the central government strengthened. To a large degree, the country agreed with the men in the convention. The Comte de Moustier, who took up his duties as minister plenipotentiary from France just as the struggle over ratification was heading toward its climax, reported that the "insufficiency" of Congress "is generally recognized throughout the entire United States. . . . I think that it is impossible for the present form of Government to stand. Opinions are not in the least divided on the necessity of establishing another one," regardless of the "diversity of ideas" for change.[41] In fact, in the previous year, an unsuccessful effort had been mounted in Congress to revise the Articles.[42] For the framers, there was simply no alternative. The first function of government in their minds was defense—in Randolph's words, "A shield against foreign hostility, and a firm resort against domestic commotion."[43] When opponents during ratification attacked the Constitution for uniting in the government and in the legislative branch the powers of the purse and the sword—the ability to raise money and create armies—Federalists responded almost in rage that these powers defined government. "All governments have possessed these powers," Hamilton told the New York convention. "They would be monsters without them, and incapable of exertion."[44]

A second principle of the framers' thinking on defense policy was the necessity to centralize defense in the union and not rely on the states individually or in combination to see to the continent's security. For one thing, the burden would fall unevenly; for another, some states were more vulnerable than others. Most important, some were simply indispensable to the defense of the entire nation, like New York, with its deep and protected harbor, its navigable river leading far into the interior, and its strategic position adjacent to New England, Canada, and the middle states. The United States could not afford to entrust the common safety to a single member, no matter how well endowed, well intentioned, or willing at a given moment to shoulder the responsibility.[45]

Last of all, the framers believed, as a matter of common sense, that effective defense required preparation in peacetime. In a widely reprinted speech to a large audience in the Pennsylvania State House Yard less than three weeks after the Constitution was signed, James Wilson acknowledged the "popular declamation" against "standing armies in time of peace." But Wilson insisted that he did "not know a nation in the world, which has not found it necessary and useful to maintain the appearance of strength in a season of profound tranquillity."[46] The framers believed not only that the authority to prepare had to be spelled out clearly but also that some establishment in peacetime was needed regardless of the threat, merely to develop in the nation the expertise of military leadership and to keep alive the technical knowledge for combat. "War," wrote Hamilton, "like most other things is a science to be acquired and perfected by diligence, by perseverance, by time, and by practice."[47] And the framers certainly understood deterrence. James Madison put it most succinctly when he maintained in the Virginia ratifying convention that he "was no friend to naval or land armaments in time of peace; but if they be necessary, the calamity must be submitted to. Weakness will invite insults. A respectable government . . . will be a security. . . . The best way to avoid danger is to be in a capacity to withstand it."[48]

Thus when the Constitutional Convention convened in May 1787, the first task of the framers in the area of military affairs was to empower the government to possess a military establishment in peacetime. There must be no ambiguity on this point, as there had been in the Articles of Confederation. "Half

a dozen regiments from Canada or New Spain," Oliver Ellsworth wrote, "might lay whole provinces under contribution, while we were disputing who has power to pay and raise an army."[49] Thus the convention wrote into the Constitution a series of provisions designed to give Congress complete and comprehensive powers. In August, the Committee of Detail presented a draft from the various plans and resolutions of the Committee of the Whole. In the final document, of eighteen separate paragraphs listing Congress's powers (including the power "To make all Laws . . . necessary and proper for carrying into Execution the foregoing Powers"), fully eleven related explicitly to security:

To lay and collect Taxes . . . to pay the Debts and provide for the common Defence . . . ;

To borrow Money . . . ;

To Coin Money . . . ;

To define and punish Piracies . . . and Offences against the Law of Nations;

To declare War, grant Letters of Marque and Reprisal, and make Rules concerning Captures on Land and Water;

To raise and support Armies, but no Appropriation of Money to that Use shall be for a longer term than two Years;

To Provide and maintain a Navy;

To make Rules for the Government and Regulation of the land and naval Forces;

To provide for calling forth the Militia to execute the Laws of the Union, suppress Insurrections and repel Invasions;

To provide for organizing, arming, and disciplining, the Militia and for governing such Part of them as may be employed in the Service of the United States, reserving to the States respectively the Appointment of the Officers, and Authority of training the Militia according to the discipline prescribed by Congress;

To exercise exclusive Legislation in all Cases whatsoever, over . . . the Seat of the Government of the United States, and to exercise like Authority over all Places purchased by the Consent of the Legislature of the State in which the same shall be, for the Erection of Forts, Magazines, Arsenals, Dock-Yards, and other needful Buildings.[50]

On the provisions to possess peacetime armies and navies, there occurred no serious debate. The Committee of Detail's original version, "To raise armies," was amended to include the words "and support," which clarified and strengthened the grant of power to permit Congress to take whatever steps concerning pay, supplies, impressments, or other activity were needed to keep an army on foot, in peace or in war. The change was accepted without disagreement. Likewise, the committee's phrase "to build and equip fleets" became "to provide & maintain a navy," according to Madison "a more convenient definition of the power." But the broader language obviously implied a complete and permanent naval establishment. Elbridge Gerry of Massachusetts, the republican ideologue who had led the opposition to a military establishment in Congress in the 1780s, objected strongly on the grounds that "there was no check agst. standing armies in time of peace. . . . The people were jealous on this head" and he "could never consent to a power to keep up an indefinite number." Gerry proposed a limit of two or three thousand men. But only Luther Martin of Maryland agreed. The rest of the convention brushed the proposal aside. Charles Cotesworth Pinckney of South Carolina, who served eight years in the Continental Army, commanded at the regimental and brigade level, had been captured at Charleston in 1780, and had finished the war a brevet brigadier general, "asked whether no troops were ever to be raised until an attack should be made on us?" Dr. Hugh Williamson, North Carolina's surgeon general during the war, "reminded" Gerry of the "motion for limiting the appropriation of revenue as the best guard in this case." John Langdon, who as New Hampshire's agent for Marine during the war had managed privateers and built ships for the Continental Navy (then, as state speaker, had organized militia and even taken the field as a company commander), "saw no room for Mr. Gerry's distrust of the Representatives of the people." Finally, New Jersey's Jonathan Dayton, like Pinckney, an eight-year veteran of the Continental Army officer corps, repeated the principle that "preparations for war are generally made in peace; and a standing force of some sort may, for ought we know, become unavoidable."[51] Gerry's effort lost without even the need for a vote.

There was more debate on those powers that authorized support for military and naval forces. The power to tax and to manage the monetary system of course possessed a significance far beyond military affairs, but the framers also considered it essential for security—in Madison's words, "the sinew of that which is to be exerted in the national defence."[52] Pierce Butler of South Carolina reminded the convention "that money is strength" and recalled from reading in his youth "one of the remarks of Julius Caesar, who declared if he had but money he would find soldiers, and every thing necessary to carry on a war."[53] "The government should be able to command all the resources of the country," observed Ellsworth. "Wars have now become rather war[s] of the purse, than of the sword. Government must therefore command the whole power of the purse; otherwise a hostile nation may look into our Constitution, see what resources are in the power of government, and calculate to go a little beyond us. . . . A government which can command but half its resources is like a man with but one arm to defend himself."[54] The power to regulate the Army and Navy internally, and to control the territory on which military installations were built, were likewise necessary provisions, for the framers were constructing a system in which the states would have to administer civil and criminal justice, and land use. On the subject of a navy, Hamilton explained that "there must

be dock-yards and arsenals; and, for the defence of these, fortifications and probably garrisons," particularly "where naval establishments are in their infancy" without the ability "to protect its dock-yards by its fleets."[55]

Another way in which the framers empowered the government under the Constitution was to insert explicit language permitting the use of force in the two arenas thought most likely to require it: foreign war and domestic disorder. Congress would exercise the power to declare war and, with that, the authority to set policy in such areas as the defining of piracy and acts illegal under international law, the commissioning of private citizens to make war (particularly at sea—"letters of Marque and Reprisal"), and the making of "Rules concerning Captures on Land and Water."[56] In the eighteenth century, war had not yet become the exclusive domain of the state; many governments contracted out the business to private citizens or groups, or foreign units and mercenaries, and even military forces raised and commanded by sovereignties were known to profit—even become wealthy—by sharing in the booty captured on land and at sea. At the same time, Congress was empowered "to provide for calling forth the Militia to execute the Laws of the Union, to suppress Insurrections and repel Invasions," and, when doing so, to exercise overall authority "for governing such Part of them as may be employed in the Service of the United States."[57] In effect, the central government could command all the nation's military forces, even those of an area or state in rebellion. Thus, a state could not effectively resist.

Inherent in these war-making and military powers was the concept of centralization. At the same time that they empowered the national government, the framers severely limited the states in *their* powers, as a matter of principle and in order to centralize as completely as possible the defense function. Not only could the states have their militias seized and transferred to national control, and their citizen-soldiers subjected to discipline and to punishments for disobedience as defined by Congress, but the states were expressly prohibited "without the Consent of Congress . . . to keep troops or Ships of War in time of Peace, enter into any Agreement . . . with a foreign Power, or engage in War, unless actually invaded, or in such imminent Danger as will not admit a delay."[58] On these points, there occurred no recorded debate, but the language was adapted from the Articles of Confederation and designed, as it had been earlier, to put foreign policy, military power, and the determination of war and peace into the hands of the union and not one or more of the states individually. In this area, the Constitution merely clarified and strengthened the monopoly on war-making and foreign policy that the Articles had granted to the central government.

In the last broad area of empowering the government in military affairs—control over the militia—the framers disagreed strongly among themselves.

They believed in centralization but also in federalism. As Madison explained to Thomas Jefferson, one of the "great objects" to challenge the convention was "to draw a line of demarkation which would give the General Government every power requisite for general purposes, and leave to the States every power which might be most beneficially administered by them."[59] Madison thought that "The Militia ought certainly to be placed in some form or other under the authority which is entrusted with the general protection and defence," for "if resistance should be made to the execution of the laws," then "public force must be used" or "society would be destroyed."[60] The proper tool, if the *posse comitatus* was incapable, was militia: "the people ought unquestionably to be employed . . . rather than a standing army."[61] The problem was where to draw the line between state and national power over these state forces.[62]

That the militia needed reform all agreed. With the geographic separation from Europe and a deeply ingrained prejudice against standing armies, the American people would have no choice in a major conflict but to depend on themselves as citizens in arms for defense. Charles Pinckney put it this way in the convention: "as standing Armies are contrary to the Constitutions of most of the States, and the nature of Government, the only immediate aid and support that we can look up to, in case of necessity, is the Militia."[63] Yet the most knowledgeable of their military leaders had been enormously frustrated by militia during the War for Independence. Washington complained in 1776, "they come in you cannot tell how, go, you cannot tell when; and act, you Cannot tell where; consume your Provisions, exhaust your Stores, and leave you at last in a critical moment."[64] In 1783, when proposing plans for peacetime military institutions to meet the nation's security needs, the leadership of the Continental Army had been virtually unanimous in recommending the strengthening of the state forces. In 1786, Secretary of War Henry Knox had actually presented a detailed scheme for reorganization and reform. Essentially, the changes boiled down to three. First, make the separate militias uniform in organization, training, arms, and equipment, so that they could operate effectively together in battle. As James Wilson remarked to the Pennsylvania ratifying convention, "any gentleman who possesses military experience will inform you, that men without an uniformity of arms, accoutrements, and discipline are no more than a Mob in a Camp."[65] Second, improve the training by means of more frequent exercises in the field and enforce stiff fines on individuals for absence from muster or failure to possess the required arms and equipment. Last, reorganize the forces to separate out the youngest men for additional obligation and more realistic and frequent training, in order to create a force truly ready and usable in serious combat. Not all the framers endorsed the last, but virtually all of them agreed on the necessity for change. As Gouverneur Morris remembered a quarter of a century

later, "Those, who, during the Revolutionary storm, had confidential acquaintance with the conduct of affairs, knew that to rely on militia was to lean on a broken reed."[66]

The problem for the framers was how to achieve reform: to determine the degree of national authority to impose on state institutions. When Virginia's George Mason introduced the motion to give Congress the power "to make laws for the regulation and discipline of Militia of the several States reserving to the States the appointment of the Officers," the members immediately fell to squabbling. Mason, who normally opposed proposals to strengthen the national government and refused in the end to sign the Constitution

thought such a power necessary to be given to the Genl. Government. He hoped there would be no standing army in time of peace, unless it might be for a few garrisons. The Militia ought to be the more effectually prepared for the public defence. Thirteen States will never concur in any one system, if the disciplining . . . be left in their hands. If they will not give up the power over the whole, they probably will over a part as a select militia.

Earlier plans proposed to the convention had contained such a provision. Ellsworth of Connecticut, a strong nationalist on most other issues "thought the motion of Mr. Mason went too far." The "States . . . would pine away to nothing after such a sacrifice of power." Sherman agreed. Mason then withdrew his motion in favor of a weaker version: granting national authority over a portion to achieve a select militia. But his fellow southerners, Butler and Pinckney from South Carolina, wanted the stronger version, as did Madison. A few pressed for complete national authority. Gerry was outraged: "This [was] the last point remained to be surrendered. If . . . agreed . . . by the Convention, the plan will have as black a mark as was set on Cain." Even Delaware's John Dickinson, also a strong nationalist, admitted "that the States would never nor ought to give up all authority over the Militia."[67]

The logical solution was compromise, just as it was so often in the Convention: give the Congress and the states concurrent power similar to the concurrent taxing power. John Langdon warned about "the confusion of the different authorities on this subject," yet the disagreement was too intense.[68] The convention referred the problem to a committee of eleven, one delegate from each state, for rewording. Three days later, the committee recommended a clause allowing Congress "To make laws for organizing, arming, and disciplining the militia, and for governing such part of them as may be employed in the service of the United States, reserving to the States . . . the appointment of the Officers, and . . . training . . . according to the discipline prescribed" by the central government.[69] Again, a bitter fight erupted over the extent of national control. "To make laws for organizing, arming, and disciplining" granted too much power for Ellsworth, Jonathan Dayton,

Roger Sherman, and antinationalists Gerry and Luther Martin. Rufus King of Massachusetts tried to allay their fears by offering the committee's definitions: "Organizing" meant specifying the size and composition of the units and proportioning the officers and men; "arming" meant specifying the type, size, and caliber of weapons; and "disciplining" was "prescribing the manual exercise evolutions etc."[70] Gerry saw through such a narrow interpretation of the wording immediately, charging that it left "the States drill-sergeants."[71] Yet Gerry and the other opponents could not devise a substitute motion that could satisfy either ardent nationalists, who demanded uniformity and reform, or southerners, who wished their militias strengthened for future use on their open frontiers. The provision reported out by the committee of eleven passed with dissenting votes from Connecticut and Maryland only. At that point, Madison tried to restrict the states to the appointment of officers below the rank of general. Sherman "considered this as absolutely inadmissable."[72] Added Gerry, mixing anger with sarcasm, "Let us at once destroy the State Gov[ernmen]ts[,] have an Executive for life or hereditary, and a proper Senate, and then there would be some consistency in giving full powers to the Gen[era]l Gov[ernmen]t."[73] The convention rejected Madison's resolution, heeding Gerry's warning "ag[ain]st pushing the experiment too far."[74] Madison's effort indicated how strongly some wanted control of the militia shifted to the central government. "As the greatest danger is that of disunion of the States, it is necessary to guard agst it by sufficient powers to the Common Govt.," asserted the Virginian, "and as the greatest danger to liberty is from large standing armies, it is best to prevent them by an effectual provision for a good Militia."[75] But in the end, the compromise went as far as possible at the time and left the state militias a dual force, clearly under national control, if Congress asserted its power (as eventually it would early in the twentieth century) but never completely divorced from their state roots and orientation—even today, two hundred years after the Constitutional Convention wrestled with the issue.[76]

The framers of the Constitution thus succeeded in their first and primary task, that of empowering the new government to defend itself: to create and continue military forces in peacetime as well as in war; to control the state militias and thereby to possess a potential monopoly of military force in American society; to govern these forces, and purchase and maintain installations and stores of equipment; to make rules and laws for the operations of these forces; and, finally, to be able to use them in foreign or domestic conflict. The second task for the framers, and closely related, was to make this new government more effective in the business of fighting. Federalists often contended that these powers were not new but were mere clarifications and invigorations of powers possessed under the Articles of Confederation. The "proposed change does not enlarge these powers,"

insisted Madison; "it only substitutes a more effectual mode of administering them."[77] To a degree the argument was disingenuous. Nowhere in the Articles was an independent power to tax or to raise revenue (certainly a power crucial to security and to war-making) granted to the central government. And nowhere did the Articles explicitly authorize the government to raise armies in peacetime. But in a larger context, the Federalist argument had merit. Virtually every power assigned to Congress in the Constitution made the government more energetic and efficient in military affairs, as well as more capable and more powerful. The Constitution specified the circumstances under which the national government could take control of the state militias. The states were prohibited from having armies or navies or making war, or otherwise clogging the national war-making powers, unless permitted by Congress. And the framers took a number of steps, some large and others seemingly inconsequential, to clarify war-making powers and to ensure the government's effectiveness if the nation were embroiled in conflict.

An initial step was to charge those who held office to act positively to discharge their duty to perpetuate the Constitution and defend the nation. At the beginning of the preamble, where the purpose of the Constitution was set forth, the framers defined the obligation of government, among other things, to "insure domestic Tranquility" and "provide for the common defence." Lest there be doubt about individual responsibility, oaths of allegiance and fidelity were required, not only of the president, who had to swear or affirm before assuming office "to . . . preserve, protect and defend the Constitution," but for all other officers—in all three branches, elected and appointed, military and civilian, state and national—to "be bound by Oath or Affirmation, to support this Constitution."[78] Oaths stirred little comment in the convention. James Wilson "was never fond of oaths, considering them as left handed security only. A good Govt. did not need them. And a bad one could not or ought not to be supported."[79] But nationalists wanted state officials purposely charged to support the national government, and even Elbridge Gerry saw the benefit of tying "officers of the two Governments" into "the General System," as in cases of conflict in the past, state officials had "given a preference to State Govts."[80] Undoubtedly, the framers understood that an oath itself, in a broader sense, committed officeholders to the purposes of the Constitution—its structure, philosophy, and preservation. In the words of Associate Justice of the Supreme Court Joseph Story, one of the country's great nineteenth-century jurists, an oath "results from the plain right of society to require some guaranty from every officer, that he will be conscientious in the discharge of his duty. Oaths have a solemn obligation upon the minds of all reflecting men, and especially upon those, who feel a deep sense of accountability to a Supreme being."[81]

Two other provisions, one inserted after the powers of Congress and the other an entire section of one

Article, granted additional powers, especially in the area of internal security. The government could suspend "the Writ of Habeas Corpus" (literally translated, "having the body"), that ancient right of an individual not to be imprisoned or detained without being charged with a crime or without some evidence of wrongdoing. Under this provision, the government could incarcerate people without cause or hold them indefinitely "when in Cases of Rebellion or Invasion the public Safety may require it."[82] The Constitution also required that "the United States . . . guarantee to every State . . . a Republican Form of Government, and . . . protect each of them against Invasion, and . . . against domestic Violence." This "guarantee clause" was originally meant to empower the national government to intervene in the states if a rebellion was underway, not only to prevent conflict but also to avert revolution and the imposition of monarchical or aristocratic forms of government. For a generation, Americans had been concerned about insurrection and mob action to change government, and in the wake of Shays's Rebellion, even the threat of a monarchy. "If a Rebellion should be known to exist in the Empire, and the Genl. Govt. shd. be restrained from interposing to subdue it," protested Nathaniel Gorham of Massachusetts, then "an enterprising Citizen might erect the standard of Monarchy in a particular State, might gather together partizans from all quarters, might extend his views from State to State, and threaten to establish a tyranny over the whole, and the Genl. Govt. be compelled to remain an inactive witness of its own destruction."[83] In the convention, Randolph had argued for "republican government" as the "basis of our national union; and no state in it ought to have it in their power to change its government into a monarchy."[84] The convention had agreed. The final form, which used the wording of James Wilson, included a guarantee against foreign invasion. The national government gained not only the permission and the power but the responsibility to defend the political philosophy that underlay the entire structure of the Constitution, from foreign as well as internal threats.[85]

As important as these provisions were, the chief instrument to make the government more effective in war-making was a strong executive. Originally the framers gave Congress the power "to make war." But very quickly, and without much debate, they altered the wording to read "declare war," assigning to the legislative branch the responsibility to decide whether to engage in war and leaving to the executive the waging of it. The change was significant. In war, the power of government swelled enormously, for the very existence of society could hang in the balance. Government could impress people, seize property, suspend personal freedoms, decide the fate of cities or states—any of thousands of decisions arbitrarily affecting the lives and deaths of individuals and whole populations. As Madison explained to the convention, "in time of actual war, great discretionary powers are constantly given to the Executive Magistrate. Con-

stant apprehension of War, has the same tendency to render the head too large for the body."[86] No one person should hold such power and no country should be subject to such destiny without the gravest deliberation and the considered approval of the community at large. Furthermore, if the United States was to prosecute war successfully, the decision must have broad public support; only by placing the decision in the hands of the legislature—the branch closest to the people—could that support be manifested and thrown behind public policy.

Once decided, however, the conduct of war—the actual management of operations—must be concentrated in the hands of a guiding intelligence. This could not be the legislature, whose "proceedings," as Charles Pinckney noted, "were too slow."[87] The framers agreed with Pierce Butler: "vest the power in the President, who will have all the requisite qualities, and will not make war but when the Nation will support it."[88] Six months later in his Federalist essays, Hamilton defined "the administration of government . . . in its most precise signification" as "limited to executive details," to include the "actual conduct of foreign negotiations, the preparatory plans of finance, the application and disbursement of public monies, . . . the arrangement of the army and navy, the direction of the operations of war . . . and other matters of a like nature."[89] In Hamilton's mind, "the definition of good government" was "energy in the executive," defined as "first unity, second duration, thirdly an adequate provision for its support, fourthly competent power."[90] "Of all the cares or concerns of government, the direction of war most peculiarly demands those qualities which distinguish the exercise of power by a single hand." It "implies the direction of the common strength; and the power of . . . employing the common strength."[91]

By changing the language to give Congress the responsibility to determine on war, and by making the president (as the final text of the Constitution read) "Commander in Chief of the Army and Navy of the United States and of the Military of the several States, when called into the actual Service of the United States," the framers granted to the executive the power to conduct war. The office of commander-in-chief already possessed a century and a half of practice in Anglo-American understanding and a history that extended back even further. The office was a military post atop the chain of command, implying control of troops and units and ships, a part of executive power possessed by the colonial governors and their successors, the state governors "consonant to the precedents of the State constitutions," as Hamilton noted.[92] Washington had carried the title during the war. Direction of the military forces was one of the few powers of the British crown knowingly placed by the framers in the presidency, yet according to Hamilton in *Federalist* 69, although "nominally the same," it was "in substance much inferior," amounting "to nothing more than supreme command and direction of the military and naval forces, as first general and admiral of the Confederacy."[93]

Some in the convention did not want the president ever to take the field to command American forces in person, apparently fearing such presence might give him the personal hold over the armed forces that would permit their use against other branches of government, or even to overturn the Constitution itself. According to Luther Martin, the Maryland lawyer who helped to frame the Constitution but refused to sign it and worked feverishly to defeat its ratification, there were "objections" to the commander-in-chief clause in the convention, "and it was asked to be so far restrained, that he should not command in person; but this could not be obtained."[94] The framers apparently expected the President to delegate military administration and command to his civilian minister and to the armed forces, the officers of which he nominated to the Senate and, with its "Advice and Consent," appointed, just as he did "Ambassadors, other public Ministers and Consuls, Judges of the supreme court, and all other Officers of the United States."[95] His secretary of war, as Gouverneur Morris and Charles Pinckney suggested to the convention, would "superintend every thing relating to the War Department, such as the raising and equipping of troops, the care of military Stores—public fortifications, arsenals and the like—also in time of war to prepare & recommend plans of offence and Defence."[96] Generals would command troops, for in the eighteenth century, *general* was defined as "an officer in chief, to whom the prince has judged proper to intrust the command of his troops."[97] But even here, the power of appointing generals unsettled some of the framers. Sherman of Connecticut "contended" that the president "ought not" to appoint "general officers in the Army in time of peace. Herein lay the corruption in Great Britain. If the Executive can model the army, he may set up an absolute Government; taking advantage of the close of a war and an army commanded by his creatures."[98] But Sherman was brushed aside and the war-making character of the office was left intact.

By providing a strong presidency, the framers of the Constitution ensured that the new government could use its military power to prepare and defend the United States in peace and in war. Yet as they worked to empower the new government and make it more efficient at waging war, the framers continually wrestled with a far more delicate and dangerous dilemma: how to ensure that the set of institutions they were creating would not themselves pose a threat to the security of the country. This was the third great task: to check the military power, to make certain that those who would possess the tools of force would not use the power of coercion to overturn the Constitution and subvert republican government. The framers approached the problem on two levels, one substantive and the other political. On the one hand, they wanted to build into the system workable provisions to assure civilian control of the military and prevent an overthrow of the government or an undermining of constitutional process. On the other, whatever they devised, it would have to be perceived to be workable; the checks would have to persuade the American people, who would have to ratify the document, that a constitution that permitted armies and navies would not endanger the very liberties the institutions were meant to protect.

Few political principles were more widely known or more universally accepted in America during the 1780s than the danger of standing armies in peacetime. Because of its arms, its isolation from society, its discipline, and its loyalty and obedience to its commander, an army could not necessarily be controlled by law or constitution. An army represented the ultimate in power, capable, even if it did not attempt a coup on its own, of becoming the instrument by which others could terrorize a population, seize power, or perpetuate tyranny. For Americans, the threat of the standing army was deeply rooted in their political heritage. In the seventeenth century, England had endured a wrenching constitutional struggle over the control of its military forces, including a decade of military rule by Oliver Cromwell. In the aftermath, hostility to standing armies in peacetime became a central tenet of the radical Whig political philosophy that formed the intellectual foundations for the American revolution against Britain in the 1760s and 1770s. Through the lens of the English radical Whigs and their own reading of history, Americans fashioned the standing army into the universal tool of despotism, perhaps the single institution most dangerous to balanced government and personal liberty. When in the decade leading to American independence, the ministry in London shifted its forces from the frontiers to the seacoast to maintain order and enforce British authority, all the warnings of history and theory seemed to come true. The Boston Massacre in 1770, in which British soldiers killed several Americans, and the Intolerable Acts of 1774, one of which suspended civil government and put Massachusetts under the rule of the local military commander, made hatred of the standing army axiomatic in American politics. So strong was the tradition, so familiar were the warnings, and so powerful was the experience with Britain before the War for Independence that by the time of the Constitutional Convention, no American political leader could afford to ignore or even to question the danger of standing armies in peacetime.[99]

The framers possessed varied views of the subject. Rhetorically, they accepted the prejudice against a standing army. As Randolph told the Virginia ratifying convention, "there was not a member in the federal convention who did not feel indignation at such an institution."[100] Madison even proposed a clause in the Constitution condemning them, "as armies in time of peace are allowed on all hands to be an evil."[101] Such sentiments and statements were obligatory, however. Madison's language lost by a huge margin, with only two states in favor of it, even though the proposal was for show, a "discountenance" of armies without affecting "the essential power of the Govt. on that head."[102] A few of the framers—whether out of sympathy for aristocracy, worries about weak government, or fear that the democratic forces unleashed by the Revolution were loosening the bounds of deference that in their judgment underlay the social order—perhaps wanted an army for defense and internal control. "It is a well known fact," charged the knowledgeable Antifederalist essayist "Brutus," "that a number of those who had an agency in producing this system, and . . . will have a principle share in . . . government under it . . . are avowedly in favour of standing armies."[103] Hamilton and Gouverneur Morris fell into this category, but they also believed, along with others, that with oceans separating America from Europe, and the presence of an armed citizenry, no peacetime forces of any size would be necessary.[104] On the other extreme were a few, led by Elbridge Gerry and including George Mason, who believed the threat so substantial that they pressed for a numerical limit on the number of soldiers in peacetime, or a declaration against standing armies written into the document. The vast majority of framers fell somewhere in between, virtually unanimous that the government needed the power of creating a military establishment in peacetime, but conscious of the internal danger of military forces and certain that checks would be crucial not only to the proper functioning of American government in ages yet to come, but necessary to counter the accusations, sure to be leveled, that the Constitution was unacceptable because it permitted standing armies.

The very first step, and the most basic provision in the Constitution to control military power, was to place the authority to raise forces—to have an army—in Congress rather than the president, in the legislative branch elected by, and closest to, the people. Samuel Holden Parsons, a Connecticut lawyer and Continental Army officer who rose to the rank of major general, contrasted the Constitution with the British system, where the king possessed all of the powers of the sword, including raising the forces and war. There "the armies are *his* armies," wrote Parsons, "and their direction is solely by him without any control. The only security . . . against the ambition of a bad king, is the power to deny money. . . . Here the army . . . is the army of the people. It is they who raise and pay them; it is they who judge of the necessity of the measure." Parsons thought "we are safe . . . by Congress," for "a body of men raised by the legislature never did set up the legislative authority as the supreme head, independent of the people. . . . It is therefore *our* army . . . and not the sword . . . of a king."[105] When in the convention, Elbridge Gerry objected to the army provision, Langdon of New Hampshire "saw no room for Mr. Gerry's distrust of the Representatives of the people."[106] Federalists voiced this point repeatedly in the ratification debate: that the power was necessary, that the state constitutions always permitted the legislature to possess the power, that Parliament in Britain had the power to consent to armies, and that with the people opposed to armies—"jealous on this head" as Gerry said heatedly—Congress would be unlikely to authorize any but the most minimal military necessary.[107] As Sherman explained in a private letter, "the security is that the power is in the legislature who are the representatives of the people and can have no motive to keep up armies unnecessarily."[108]

A second check lay inherent in the structure of the legislature itself: bicameralism. Two separate chambers would have to agree independently on the need for an army and the resources for its support. So that this restraint would operate on a continuing basis, the framers inserted another stipulation—a third check—that "no Appropriation of Money" for an army "shall be for a longer Term than two Years."[109] Apparently suggested by George Mason, the idea was to force every new Congress to examine the need for an army and to certify its existence by appropriating the money, just as in England, an annual Mutiny Act and annual appropriations after the Glorious Revolution in 1689 authorized the Crown to have an army.[110] Thus no military force could exist, at least legally, in perpetuity: not by its own design, or by neglect, bureaucratic inertia, or obstructionism on the part of a minority in Congress, preventing the disbanding of the forces. "The Legislature . . . will be *obliged* . . . at least in every two years, to deliberate" on the subject, Hamilton reasoned in *Federalist* 26, "to come to a new resolution . . . by a formal vote in the face of their constituents." Because armies were controversial and "the spirit of party" would "infect all political bodies," there would be legislators "willing enough to arrange the measures and incriminate the views of the majority." So if an army were kept, the alarm would be continual, and as it took time and "progressive augmentations" to produce a force large enough "to menace" American liberties, the chances of a real threat were inconsequential.[111] Besides, as one essayist predicted, "Congress will always be cautious, and never keep one [an army] in pay, so numerous as to endanger their own safety or that of the people."[112]

If the first line of defense against a standing army was to entrust its existence to the representatives of the people, the second was that central check that permeated the entire Constitution: division of powers. The framers divided power over the military so that no one branch was fully in control. Congress created the Army, paid it, supplied it, made rules for its organization and governance, and otherwise determined its character and institutional structure. The president held the reins of command: as commander-in-chief, he sat astride the uniformed hierarchy "as first General and Admiral of the confederacy" (Hamilton's words), so that disobedience to his orders constituted mutiny, punishable by death.[113] In a very personal way, the framers blended control by both branches, by having the president commission all officers of the armed forces, but only after nominating them to the Senate, which had to approve not only the original appointment of all officers but also their promotion each time each officer rose a step in rank. If the Army as a whole revolted, then the militia could be mobilized to maintain or restore constitutional rule. Thus, the framers separated power over the military, just as they had in so many other areas of government. The two great powers, the purse and the sword, the latter the most direct threat to liberty, were separated but at the same time were shared by the two branches. Each, by exercising its authority over the armed forces, checked the other's capacity to use those forces against the state. Under the constitutional structure, no army could seize power or become the tool for a coup without shattering the Constitution and with it, legitimate government altogether.[114]

Should such an event occur, the framers believed in one final safeguard: the people in the form of the militia. To begin with, Americans were unlikely prospects for military adventures. "Regular troops, who are natives of a country, allied by friendship and blood to the other citizens, bred in the principles of republican liberty, and who have for years defended this country with their blood against a powerful invader, cannot be so generally corrupted . . . to enslave and murder their friends, and relations, brothers, sons and fathers," argued one observer; "in all probability a great part of this army would take part with the nation."[115] Even if an army could be marshaled, it would face hostile citizens armed and embodied in militia, ready to defend their liberties. In *Federalist* 46, Madison assailed as "the incoherent dreams of a delirious jealousy" the possibility that "the people and the States . . . should elect . . . men ready to betray both; that the traitors would "uniformly and systematically pursue some fixed plan" to swell the military; that all involved "should silently and patiently behold the gathering storm" and not act.[116] If it happened, the most the country would face was any army of "twenty-five or thirty thousand men. To these would be opposed a militia amounting to near half a million of citizens with arms in their hands . . . fighting for their common liberties, and united and conducted by governments possessing their affections and confidence." The very existence of the military, combined with the distance from potential enemies and the expenses and resources required, made a large army unnecessary and unlikely. As the country grew in ability to support troops, so too, would the size of the militia grow. Apprehensions of danger, which led to a larger army, would also cause the militia to be strengthened. However much some of the framers disdained the military prowess of the state forces, they accepted their value as an internal counterweight to standing armies. Precisely because he so feared armies, George Mason pressed the convention for national authority over the militia to effect its reform. And precisely because the militia served as a powerful check against an arbitrary and tyrannical national government, opponents of the Constitution worried that the new government's influence over the state forces would lead to their neglect, or worse yet, a concerted effort to enfeeble them in order to render the states impotent. That is the primary reason why opponents of the Constitution insisted, in ratifying conventions and afterwards, on amendments

to guarantee the right of citizens to bear arms. The final check on standing armies, in the minds both of the framers of the Constitution and opponents of the new system, was civil war.[117]

A government empowered to raise military and naval forces in peace as well as in war; a government more efficient and effective in the conduct of war and military operations; a government so constructed that its military forces could neither attempt nor become the instrument for a coup d'etat: these were the fundamental objectives of the framers of the Constitution in national security. In mid-September 1787, when they finished their work, not all of the framers were happy with the result. Gerry, for one, refused to sign, in part because of the lack of explicit checks on a standing army in peacetime. Yet most were satisfied that they had struck workable compromises between strengthening the central government and safeguarding American liberty, including the area of national defense. Nearly every framer was aware of the dilemma and most understood the balance to be delicate. But those who opposed the Constitution concluded that the document swung that balance too far, too dangerously, toward power for the government.

The public debate over the Constitution began before the document was published in September and lasted well into the summer of the next year. In that long, difficult, divisive struggle, the issues involving the military sparked an enormous debate and much vituperation. Antifederalist opponents focused most on the army and the militia clauses. The heart of their attack linked the two: if the framers were seeking a balance between liberty and security, out of ignorance, malevolence, or simple error, they had failed. The new government would have a standing army; the militias under its control would deteriorate out of neglect or by design; and at some future time, with no countervailing power and no possible physical restraints, that army would destroy the government.

Painstakingly, patiently, systematically, the framers of the Constitution and their political allies answered these arguments, all the while acknowledging the legitimacy of the concern. In the Virginia ratifying convention, Madison insisted that he was "no friend to naval or land armaments in time of peace, but if they be necessary, the calamity must be submitted to."[118] Yet the framers never quite succeeded in countering this criticism, partly because it was repeated so often and in such inflammatory terms, and partly because the principle resonated so sympathetically in American political understanding. That was why nearly every state ratifying convention proposed amendments to the Constitution that either warned against or limited standing armies, banned quartering of regulars in private homes, or suggested restrictions on federal power over, or guarantees to, the states. And that was why the Bill of Rights, when adopted in 1791, contained amendments guaranteeing to the people the right to bear arms and protections against quartering regulars in private homes.[119]

Thomas Jefferson and John Adams, two veteran leaders who observed the struggle from Paris and London, respectively, where they served as American ambassadors, were also bothered. Both had written on government, served in high political office during the war, and would administer the new government as vice president and president. "How do you like our new constitution?" Jefferson asked Adams. "I confess there are things in it which stagger all my disposition." The "President seems a bad edition of a Polish king. . . . [O]nce in office, & possessing the military force of the union, without either the aid or check of a council, he would not easily be dethroned." To Madison and others, Jefferson decried "the omission of a bill of rights" including "protection against standing armies."[120] Adams had different worries. "You are apprehensive of Monarchy; I, of Aristocracy," he replied to Jefferson.[121] In the end, both these titans of the epoch endorsed the plan of government despite their misgivings.

It would be easy from the distance of two centuries to question the depth of the framers' concern, or to dismiss the debate over the military sections of the Constitution as the overblown rhetoric of the first national political campaign in a young republic struggling to fashion a new system of government during an era of enormous political upheaval. The Constitution has survived wars for continental expansion and overseas empire, civil war, and world wars, and even the last four decades of a worldwide confrontation between economic and political systems, under the shadow of nuclear armageddon. Likewise, the Constitution has preserved internal order through times of rebellion, labor conflict, racial strife, wide swings of prosperity and depression, and even a civil war of unmatched ferocity that included the bloodiest fighting ever conducted on American soil. And through these turbulent two centuries, the American military has never made a single move to overthrow the government, nor has it scarcely ever even mentioned the subject, despite occasional episodes of real, and sometimes acute, civil-military tension.

Yet the fears were understandable in the late eighteenth century and, in historical perspective, still echo today. In his reasoned and incisive critique of the Constitution, the New York essayist "Brutus" observed that both Caesar and Cromwell ascended to power by means of legally constituted and properly authorized armies, and that a similar catastrophe may have been narrowly averted when Washington prevented a revolt by the officer corps at the end of the revolutionary war—and "no Country in the world had ever a more Patriotic army."[122] Since then, dozens of countries of every religious and cultural tradition have experienced military intervention, revolt, and coup, countries in every corner of the globe, at every stage of economic and political development, in peace and in war. Few nations on earth have lasted two centuries under one constitution, with civilian rule and civilian control of the military intact. The American Constitution, with its division of powers and authority, its checks and balances, has succeeded not only in defending the nation against all enemies foreign and domestic, but in upholding the liberty it was meant to preserve. No military force in the United States has ever risen up to challenge constitutional procedures or the Constitution itself, nor has any political leader, so far as is known, ever attempted to use military force against the Constitution. The unbroken record of subordination and loyalty by the American armed forces, under the Constitution of the United States, has been a blessing of the American political system, and the envy of nations the world over.

NOTES

The author states that the contents of this essay on the Constitution and national security are in the public domain [Ed.].

1. Edwin Meese III, "The Supreme Court of the United States: Bulwark of a Limited Constitution," *South Texas Law Review* 27 (1986): 464, 456–57, 465–66.

2. William J. Brennan, Jr., "The Constitution of the United States: Contemporary Ratification," ibid., 433–38.

3. See James H. Hutson, "The Creation of the Constitution: The Integrity of the Documentary Record," *Texas Law Review* 65 (1986): 1–39.

4. Isaac Kramnick, "The 'Great National Discussion': The Discourse of Politics in 1787," *William and Mary Quarterly*, 3d ser., 45 (1988): 4, makes this point.

5. The literature on the Constitution is enormous. For a review of recent work, see Richard B. Bernstein, "Charting the Bicentennial," *Columbia Law Review* 87 (1987): 1565–1624; Peter S. Onuf, "Reflections on the Founding: Constitutional Historiography in Bicentennial Perspective," ibid., 46 (1989): 341–75.

6. For the arguments on the framers' views of intent, see H. Jefferson Powell, "The Original Understanding of Original Intent," *Harvard Law Review* 98 (1985): 885–948; Charles A. Lofgren, "The Original Understanding of Original Intent," *Constitutional Commentary* 5 (1988): 77–113.

7. Extract of a Letter . . . , *Maryland Journal*, 1 Jan. 1788, Merrill Jensen, John P. Kaminski, Gaspare J. Saladino, et al., eds., *The Documentary History of the Ratification of the Constitution* (Madison, Wis.: University of Wisconsin Press, 1976) 15:137. A month after the convention ended, James Madison sent Thomas Jefferson a copy of the Constitution and recounted the major disagreements in the convention. Concluded Madison: "Adding . . . the natural diversity of human opinions on all new and complicated subjects, it is impossible to consider the degree of concord which ultimately prevailed as less than a miracle." 24 Oct., 1 Nov. 1787, ibid., 443. See also Washington to the Marquis de Lafayette, 7 Feb. 1789, ibid., 16: 70.

8. Knox to Washington, 17 Dec. 1786, George Washington Papers, Manuscript Division, Library of Congress. For recent interpretations of Shays's Rebellion, see David P. Szatmary, *Shays' Rebellion: The Making of an Agrarian Insurrection* (Amherst, Mass.: University of Massachusetts Press, 1980); Thomas P. Slaughter, *The Whiskey Rebellion: Frontier Epilogue to the American Revolution* (New York: Oxford University Press, 1986), 47–49.

9. Knox to Washington, 19 Mar. 1787, *Documentary History of the Constitution of the United States, 1787–1870* (5 vols., Washington, D.C.: U.S. Department of State, 1894–1905), 4:96.

10. John Lansing, Notes on Debates, 29 May 1787, James H. Hutson, ed., *Supplement to Max Farrand's The Records of the Federal Convention of 1787* (New Haven: Yale University Press, 1987), 26.

11. Gunning Bedford, Notes on Debates, 29 May 1787, ibid., 27.

12. Speech to the Conn. ratifying convention, 4 Jan. 1788, *Ratification,* 15: 244.

13. Federalist 34, *New York Packet,* 4 Jan. 1788, ibid., 261. See also Jay, Federalist 4, N.Y. *Independent Journal,* 7 Nov. 1787; Hamilton, Federalist 7, N.Y. *Independent Journal,* 17 Nov. 1787, ibid., 12: 568, 569, 14: 130–35; John Marshall, Speech in the Virginia ratifying convention, 10 June 1788, Jonathan Elliot, ed., *The Debates in the Several State Conventions, on the Adoption of the Federal Convention . . .* (Washington, D.C.: Taylor & Maurey, 1854), 3: 27. "That nations should make war against nations," wrote John Jay in 1783, "is less surprising than their living in uninterrupted peace and harmony." To Gouverneur Morris, 24 Sept. 1783, Henry P. Johnston, ed., *The Correspondence and Public Papers of John Jay* (New York: G. P. Putnam's Sons, 1890–1893), 3: 84.

14. See, in addition to the sources cited in note 13, "Extract of a letter from Wilmington, North Carolina, February 2," Charleston *City Gazette,* 11 Feb. 1788; and James Wilson, speech in the Pa. ratifying convention, 11 Dec. 1787, *Ratification,* 2: 583.

15. Federalist 5, N.Y. *Independent Journal,* 10 Nov. 1787, ibid., 14: 90. Hamilton listed the causes of wars among the states in Federalist 7, N.Y. *Independent Journal,* 17 Nov. 1787, ibid., 130–35. See also Edmund Randolph, "A Letter . . . ," published 10 Oct. 1787, ibid., 15: 130.

16. Federalist 7, N.Y. *Independent Journal,* 17 Nov. 1787, ibid., 14: 135.

17. For this line of reasoning, which was overwhelmingly nationalist in the 1780s and Federalist in the 1790s, see James Wilson, speech in the Pa. ratifying convention, 11 Dec. 1787; Madison, Hamilton, in Madison's notes, 29 June 1787, Max Farrand, ed., *The Records of the Federal Convention of 1787,* rev. ed. (New Haven: Yale University Press, 1937), 1: 464–65, 466–67; Jay, Federalist 5, N.Y. *Independent Journal,* 10 Nov. 1787, Hamilton, Federalist 8, *New York Packet,* 20 Nov. 1787, Madison, Federalist 41, N.Y. *Independent Journal,* 19 Jan. 1788, Wilson, *Ratification,* 2: 583, 14: 90–91, 143–45, 15: 421; Hamilton, Federalist 85, McLean edition, 29 May 1788, Jacob E. Cooke, ed., *The Federalist* (Middletown, Conn.: Wesleyan University Press, 1961), 588; Robert R. Livingston, speech in the N.Y. ratifying convention, 19 June 1788, Randolph, speech in the Va. ratifying convention, 6 June 1788, *Debates,* 2: 209, 3:75. Philip Schuyler, Hamilton's father-in-law, and a powerful New York nationalist, wrote privately, "I dread a dissolution of all union. Immediate quarrels between the states will ensue. These quarrels will beget armies, these armies a conqueror, and this conqueror may give as much a government as prevails at Constantinople." To Henry Van Schaack, 13 Mar. 1787, Henry C. Van Schaack, *The Life of Peter Van Schaack . . .* (New York: D. Appleton and Company, 1842), 154. As a corollary, the framers also believed that a major European war would inevitably draw in the United States, if it were weak. See Washington to Knox, 10 Jan. 1788, and "Philadelphiensis," VII (Benjamin Workman), Philadelphia *Independent Gazetteer,* 10 Jan. 1788, *Ratification,* 15: 330, 338.

18. 11 Dec. 1787, *Ratification,* 2: 583.

19. Federalist 14, *New York Packet,* 30 Nov. 1787, ibid., 14: 316.

20. "Civis," Charleston *Columbian Herald,* 4 Feb. 1788, ibid., 16: 26. See also "Z," Philadelphia *Freeman's Journal,* 16 May 1787, "Philadelphiensis," IV (Benjamin Workman), Philadelphia *Freeman's Journal,* 12 Dec. 1787, Hamilton, Federalist 24, N.Y. *Independent Journal,* 19 Dec. 1787, Madison, Federalist 41, N.Y. *Independent Journal,* 19 Jan. 1788, ibid., 13: 100, 14: 421, 15: 41, 43, 422–23. For an analysis of southern belief in the need for a navy, see French Vice Consul Gaspard Joseph Amand Ducher to Comte de la Luzerne, 2 Feb. 1788, ibid., 16: 14–15.

21. Phineas Miller to Samuel Ward, Jr., 10 Feb. 1788, ibid., 14: 104. See also Washington to Samuel Powell, 18 Jan. 1788, ibid., 15: 399.

22. "Brutus" X, *N.Y. Journal,* 24 Jan. 1788, ibid., 15: 465. The identity of "Brutus" remains unknown. See ibid., 13: 411.

23. "A Letter . . . ," 27 Dec. 1787, ibid., 15: 124.

24. 14 June 1787, *Records,* 1:246. See also James Wilson, speech to the Pa. ratifying convention, 11 Dec. 1787, Benjamin Rush, "Address to the People of the United States," Philadelphia *American Museum,* Jan. 1787, William Samuel Johnson, speech in the Conn. ratifying convention, 4 Jan. 1788, *Ratification,* 2: 577, 13: 46, 15: 248; Charles Pinckney, speech in the S.C. legislature, 16 Jan. 1788, *Debates,* 4: 260–61.

25. To St. George Tucker, 28 Sept. 1787, *Ratification,* 16: 446.

26. To Madison, 31 Mar. 1787, John C. Fitzpatrick, ed., *The Writings of George Washington . . .* (Washington, 1931–1944), 29: 190–91.

27. Robert Yates's notes, 20 June 1787, *Records,* 1: 346.

28. Rufus King's notes, 20 June 1787, ibid., 349.

29. Madison's notes, 18 June 1787, ibid., 284. See also Madison, Madison's notes, 31 May 1787, Madison to Washington, 18 Oct. 1787, ibid., 1: 54, 3: 131–32; Madison to Jefferson, 24 Oct. 1787, Julian P. Boyd et al., eds., *The Papers of Thomas Jefferson* (Princeton, 1950–), 13: 274.

30. Madison's notes, 18 June 1787, *Records,* 1: 285; Speech to the N.Y. ratifying convention, 20 June 1788, Harold C. Syrett et al., *The Papers of Alexander Hamilton* (New York, 1961–1987), 5: 19–20. See also Hamilton, Federalist 16, *New York Packet,* 4 Dec. 1787, Ellsworth, speech to the Conn. ratifying convention, 4 Jan. 1788, *Ratification,* 14: 339–43, 15: 245ff.

31. Federalist 16, *New York Packet,* 4 Dec. 1787, ibid., 14: 341. See also Federalist 15, N.Y. *Independent Journal,* 1 Dec. 1787, ibid., 328.

32. Madison, 14 June 1788, *Debates,* 3: 384. Antifederalist leader Richard Henry Lee expressed a somewhat similar view when he told John Lamb, an Antifederalist leader in New York, "Force and opinion seem to be the two ways

alone by which Men can be governed—the latter appears the most proper for a free people," 22 May 1788, John Lamb Papers, box 5, New York Historical Society, New York, N.Y. See also Lee to Edmund Pendleton, 26 May 1788, *Ratification,* 9: 879.

33. Lansing's notes, 29 May 1787, Hutson, ed., *Supplement to Records,* 26; McHenry's notes, 29 May 1787, *Records,* 1:25. McHenry appropriated Randolph's points in his speech to the Md. ratifying convention, 29 Nov. 1787, *Ratification,* 14: 279–80.

34. A recent compilation of the wartime service of the framers is Robert K. Wright, Jr., and Morris J. MacGregor, Jr., *Soldier-Statesmen of the Constitution* (Washington, D.C.: U.S. Government Printing Office, 1987).

35. "Articles of Confederation of the United States of America," 15 Nov. 1777, *Ratification,* 1: 86.

36. Baltimore *Maryland Gazette,* 22 May 1787, ibid., 13: 112.

37. See Richard H. Kohn, *Eagle and Sword: The Federalists and the Creation of the Military Establishment in America, 1783–1802* (New York: Free Press, 1975), 49–53; "Brutus" IX, *New York Journal,* 17 Jan. 1788, *Ratification,* 15: 397.

38. "A Citizen," *Maryland Journal,* 30 Jan. 1787, quoted in Kohn, *Eagle and Sword,* 72. For military affairs in the 1780s, see chapters 3 and 4 of ibid.

39. 11 Dec. 1787, *Ratification,* 2: 577.

40. Edward Carrington to the Governor of Virginia, 8 Dec. 1786, Edmund C. Burnett, ed., *Letters of the Members of the Continental Congress* (Washington, D.C.: Carnegie Institution, 1921–1938), 8: 517.

41. To Comte de Montmorin, 8 Feb. 1788, *Ratification,* 16: 82.

42. Thomas Rodney, Report of Debates in Congress, 3 May 1786, in George Bancroft, *History of the Formation of the Constitution of the United States of America,* 2d ed. (New York, D. Appleton and Company, 1882), 1: 500; Amendments to the Articles of Confederation proposed by a Grand Committee of Congress, 7 Aug. 1786, *Ratification,* 1: 163–68.

43. "Letter . . . ," 10 Oct. 1787, *Ratification,* 15: 123.

44. 27 June 1788, *Papers of Hamilton,* 5: 96. See also Wilson, speech to Pa. ratifying convention, 11 Dec. 1787, McHenry speech to the Md. ratifying convention, 29 Nov. 1787, Hamilton, Federalist 23, *New York Packet,* 18 Dec. 1787, Randolph, "Letter . . . ," 10 Oct. 1787, Ellsworth, speech to the Conn. ratifying convention, 4 Jan. 1788, Roger Sherman, "A Citizen of New Haven," *Connecticut Courant,* 7 June 1788, Madison, Federalist 41, 19 Jan. 1788, *Ratification,* 2: 578, 15: 4, 123, 244, 281, 419; Robert R. Livingston, James Madison, and William R. Davie, speeches to the N.Y., Va., and N.C. ratifying conventions, 23 June, 14 June, 24 July, 1788, *Debates,* 2: 279, 3: 4–13, 4: 17.

45. See, for example, Thomas McKean, speech to the Pa. ratifying convention, Jay, Federalist 4, N.Y. *Independent Journal,* 7 Nov. 1787, Hamilton, Federalist 25, *New York Packet,* 21 Dec. 1787, Randolph, "Letter . . . ," 10 Oct. 1787, *Ratification,* 2: 415, 13: 570, 15: 60–62, 124–25; Marshall and Madison speeches to the Va. ratifying convention, 14 June and 23 June 1788, *Debates,* 3: 419–21, 620–21.

46. 6 Oct. 1787, *Ratification,* 2: 169. See also Ellsworth, "Landholder V," *Connecticut Courant,* 3 Dec. 1787, ibid., 14: 336.

47. Federalist 25, *New York Packet,* 21 Dec. 1787, ibid., 15: 62.

48. 23 June 1788, *Debates,* 3: 309.

49. "Landholder V," 3 Dec. 1787, *Ratification,* 3: 481.

50. Article I, Section 8.

51. All questions are from Madison's notes, 18 Aug. 1787, *Records,* 2: 329–30.

52. Federalist 41, N.Y. *Independent Journal,* 19 Jan. 1788, *Ratification,* 15: 423.

53. Yates's notes, 11 June 1787, *Records,* 1: 204.

54. Speech to the Conn. ratifying convention, 7 Jan. 1788, *Ratification,* 3: 548. See also Randolph, Sherman, 29 May, 30 May 1787, McHenry's notes, Madison's notes, *Records,* 1: 25, 34; Wilson speech to Pa. ratifying convention, 11 Dec. 1787, Hamilton, Federalist 23, *New York Packet,* 18 Dec. 1787, Federalist 30, *New York Packet,* 28 Dec. 1787, *Ratification,* 2: 578, 15: 5, 161.

55. Federalist 24, N.Y. *Independent Journal,* 19 Dec. 1787, *Ratification,* 15: 43.

56. Article I, Section 8.

57. Idem.

58. Article I, Section 9.

59. 24 Oct., 1 Nov. 1787, *Ratification,* 13: 443.

60. Idem.; Madison to Washington, 16 Apr. 1787, Gaillard Hunt, ed., *The Writings of James Madison* (New York: G. P. Putnam's Sons, 1900–1910), 2: 347.

61. Speech to the Va. ratifying convention, 14 June 1788, *Debates,* 3: 378, 384.

62. This uncertainty was expressed best by Georgia delegate Abraham Baldwin, passing through his native Connecticut late in 1787. Baldwin told the President of Yale, Ezra Stiles (as recorded in Stiles's diary, 21 December 21, 1787) that the framers "were pretty unanimous" on "a firm foedral Governmt" which "shd comprehend all Things of common foedral Concern & wc individual States could not detrmn or enforce"—including "War & Armies." But "Jurisdictions & Govt of each state shd be left intire & preserved as inviolate as possible consistent with the coercive subordina for preservg the Union with Firmness." Merrill Jensen, John P. Kaminski, and Gaspare J. Saladino, ed., *The Documentary History of the Ratification of the Constitution* (Madison, Wis.: University of Wisconsin Press, 1976–), 15: 57.

63. "Observations . . . submitted to the Federal Convention," *Records,* 3: 118.

64. To the President of Congress, 20 Dec. 1776, *Writings of Washington,* 6: 403.

65. 11 Dec. 1787, *Ratification,* 2: 577–78.

66. To Moss Kent, 12 Jan. 1815, Gouverneur Morris Papers, Manuscript Division, Library of Congress. For a discussion of militia reform in this period, see Richard H. Kohn, "The Murder of the Militia System in the Aftermath of American Revolution," James Kirby Martin, ed., *The Human Dimensions of Nation Making: Essays on Colonial and Revolutionary America* (Madison, Wis.: University of Wisconsin Press, 1976), 304–22.

67. Madison's notes, 18 Aug. 1787, *Records,* 2: 326, 330–33.

68. All questions are from Madison's notes, 23 Aug. 1787, ibid., 384–88.

69. Madison's notes, 18 Aug. 1787, ibid., 331.

70. Convention Journal, 21 Aug. 1787, ibid., 352.

71. Madison's notes, 23 Aug. 1787, ibid., 384–85.

72. Ibid., 385.

73. Ibid., 388.

74. Idem.

75. Idem.

76. See Allan R. Millett, "The Constitution and the Citizen-Soldier," in Richard H. Kohn, ed., *The United States Military Under the Constitution of the United States, 1789–1989* (New York: New York University Press, 1991), 97–119.

77. Federalist 45, N.Y. *Independent Journal,* 26 Jan. 1788, *Ratification,* 15: 480.

78. Preamble; Article II, Section 1; Article VI.

79. Madison's notes, 23 July 1787, *Records,* 2: 87.

80. Ibid., 88.

81. *Commentaries on the Constitution,* 1833, in Philip B. Kurland and Ralph Lerner, eds., *The Founders' Constitution* (Chicago: University of Chicago Press, 1987), 4: 645. For more views on the purpose of oaths, see Madison, Federalist 44, *New York Packet,* 25 Jan. 1788, Jay, draft of Federalist 64, 5 Mar. 1788, *Ratification,* 15: 474, 16: 314.

82. Article I, Section 10.

83. Madison's notes, 18 July 1787, *Records,* 2: 48.

84. Yates's notes, 11 June 1787, ibid., 1: 206.

85. See William M. Wiecek, *The Guarantee Clause of the U.S. Constitution* (Ithaca: Cornell University Press, 1972), chapters 1 and 2.

86. Madison's notes, 29 June 1787, *Records,* 1: 465.

87. Madison's notes, 17 Aug. 1787, ibid., 2: 318. Charles Lofgren, "War-Making Under the Constitution: The Original Understanding," in Lofgren, *Government from Reflection and Choice: Constitutional Essays on War, Foreign Relations, and Federalism* (New York: Oxford University Press, 1986), 6–38, is the best analysis in print of the relative roles of Congress and the President in commencing war as the framers intended the division of authority. However, the issue has spawned an enormous literature over the past twenty years and is still contended heatedly in national politics. See, for example, "The Constitution in Danger: An Exchange," *The New York Review of Books,* 37 (May 17, 1990): 50–53.

88. Madison's notes, 17 Aug. 1787, *Records,* 2: 318.

89. Federalist 72, N.Y. *Independent Journal,* 19 Mar. 1788, *Ratification,* 16: 422.

90. Federalist 70, N.Y. *Independent Journal,* 15 Mar. 1788, ibid., 396.

91. Federalist 74, *New York Packet,* 25 Mar. 1788, ibid., 479.

92. Idem; David Gray Adler, "The President's War-Making Power," Thomas E. Cronin, ed., *Inventing the American Presidency* (Lawrence, Kans.: University of Kansas Press, 1989), 126–30; Willi Paul Adams, *The First American Constitutions: Republican Ideology and the Making of the State Constitutions in the Revolutionary Era* (Chapel Hill, N.C.: University of North Carolina Press, 1980), 274.

93. *New York Packet,* 14 Mar. 1788, *Ratification,* 16: 389; Lofgren, "War-Making Under the Constitution," 14–24.

94. "Genuine Information IX," Baltimore *Maryland Gazette,* 29 Jan. 1788, *Ratification,* 15: 493. New Jersey's ratifying convention proposed the limitation as an amendment to the Constitution. Ibid., 494, note 4. The fears on this point were not spelled out in detail, but by implication: that personal command would give a president the loyalty and control of an armed force enough to terrorize the country directly and mount a coup, whereas the delegation of command to another person, no matter how loyal, provided some check against an attempt. See William Paterson in Madison's notes, 14 June 1787, *Records,* 1: 244; Mason in the Va. ratifying convention, 18 June 1788, *Debates,* 3: 496; John Paul Jones to the Marquis de Lafayette, 14/26 June 1788, Papers of John Paul Jones, Manuscript Division, Library of Congress.

95. Article II, Section 2.

96. Madison's notes, 20 Aug. 1787, *Records,* 2: 343.

97. George Smith, *An Universal Military Dictionary* . . . (London: J. Milan, 1779), "General."

98. Madison's notes, 24 Aug. 1787, *Records,* 2: 405. For a somewhat different interpretation of the President's war-making power, see Leonard W. Levy, *Original Intent and the Framers' Constitution* (New York: Macmillan, 1988), 30–41.

99. For the origins of the prejudice against standing armies, see Kohn, *Eagle and Sword,* 1–6.

100. 14 June 1788, *Records,* 3: 319.

101. Madison's notes, 14 Sept. 1787, ibid., 2: 617.

102. Idem.

103. "Brutus," IX, *N.Y. Journal,* 17 Jan. 1788, *Ratification,* 15: 396.

104. Hamilton, Federalist 8, *New York Packet,* 20 Nov. 1787, Madison, Federalist 41, *N.Y. Journal,* 19 Jan. 1788, ibid., 14: 145–46; 15: 419–20; Morris to Moss Kent, 12 Jan. 1815, Morris Papers, Library of Congress.

105. Parsons to William Cushing, 11 Jan. 1788, *Ratification,* 3: 570.

106. Madison's notes, 18 Aug. 1787, *Records,* 2: 329.

107. Idem.

108. To ____, 8 Dec. 1787, Roger Sherman Papers, Yale University Library, New Haven, Conn. For Sherman's thinking, see "A Citizen of New Haven," *Connecticut Courant,* 7 Jan. 1788, "A Countryman II, III," *New Haven Gazette,* 22 Nov., 29 Nov. 1787, *Ratification,* 14: 173, 174, 296, 15: 281–82.

109. Article I, Section 8.

110. For the origin of this provision, see Mason, Paterson, Pinckney, Brearly, Gerry, and Sherman in Madison's notes, 18 Aug., 20 Aug., 5 Sept. 1787, Journal, 20 Aug., 5 Sept. 1787, *Records,* 2: 326–27, 327, 330, 334, 341, 505, 508, 509.

111. Federalist 26, N.Y. *Independent Journal,* 22 Dec. 1789, *Ratification,* 15: 8. For other statements by framers and Federalists, see Pelatiah Webster, *Remarks on the Address* . . . , 18 Oct. 1787, Tench Coxe, "An American Citizen I," 21 Oct. 1787, Hugh Williamson, speech at Edenton, N.C., *N.Y. Daily Advertiser,* 25 Feb. 1788, ibid., 13: 302, 435, 16: 204; Robert R. Livingston, Edmund Randolph, and James Iredell, speeches to the N.Y., Va., and N.C. ratifying conventions, 27 June 1788, 23 June 1788, 26 July 1788, *Debates,* 2: 345, 3: 600, 4: 96. "Marcus [Iredell]," 8 Jan. 1788, Griffith J. McRee, *Life and Correspondence of James Iredell* (New York: D. Appleton and Company, 1858), 2: 209–10; extract from a Philadelphia newspaper, *Massachu-*

setts Centinel, 3 Oct. 1787, "Candidus," *Providence Gazette,* 22 Dec. 1787; Noah Webster, "Examination . . . ," Oct. 1787, Paul Leicester Ford, ed., *Pamphlets on the Constitution . . .* (Brooklyn: NP, 1888), 50–51.

112. "Impartial," Philadelphia *American Museum* 2 (Oct. 1787), 2d ed. (1792), 377.

113. Federalist 68, *New York Packet,* 14 Mar. 1788, *Ratification,* 16: 389.

114. On the issue of dividing powers between the two branches, see Antonio de la Forest to Comte de Montmorin, 28 Sept. 1787, Madison to Jefferson, 24 Oct., 1 Nov. 1787, Madison, Federalist 38, 48, 51, *New York Packet,* 1 Feb. 1788, N.Y. *Independent Journal,* 25 Jan. 1788, 6 Feb. 1788, *Ratification,* 13: 259–60, 449, 15: 358, 16: 3–5, 43–44. For the issues of separation of powers, see Mason in Madison's notes, 6 June 1787, *Records,* 1: 139–40; Anonymous to Anonymous, [Apr. ?] 1788, Julian Parks Boyd, ed., "A North Carolina Citizen on the Federal Constitution, 1788," *North Carolina Historical Review* 16 (1939): 42; A Democratic Federalist [Tench Coxe?], Philadelphia *Independent Gazetteer,* 26 Nov. 1787, *Ratification,* 2: 298; Madison, speech in Va. ratifying convention, 14 June 1788, *Debates,* 3: 393–94. Federalists made the point that the President, although powerful, had vastly inferior military power in comparison to the British monarch, who had the ability not only to command the armed forces (including the militia at all times), and to regulate them, but also to declare war. See Hamilton in Federalist 69, *New York Packet,* 14 Mar. 1788, *Ratification,* 16: 388–89. Abraham Baldwin described to Ezra Stiles (Stiles's Diary, 21 Dec. 1787), the principles behind the Executive in the Constitution: "It appeared to be the Opin of Convention that he shd be a Character respectable by the Nations as well as by the foederal Empire. To this end that as much Power shd be given him as could be consistently with guardg against all possibility of his ascending in a Tract of years or Ages to Despotism & absolute Monarchy:—of which all were cautious. Nor did it appear that any Members in Convention had the least Idea of insidiously layg the Founda. of a future Monarchy like the European or Asiatic Monarchies either antient or modern. But were unanimously guarded & firm against every Thing of this ultimate Tendency. Accordingly they meant to give considerable Weight as supreme Executive, but fixt him dependant on

the States at large, and at all time impunishable." Ibid., 15: 57. See also Edmund Pendleton to Madison, 8 Oct. 1787, ibid., 13: 355.

115. Extract from a Philadelphia newspaper, *Massachusetts Centinel,* 3 Oct. 1787.

116. *New York Packet,* 29 Jan. 1788, *Ratification,* 15: 492.

117. For other statements about the militia, see Mason in Madison's notes, 14 Sept. 1787, *Records,* 2: 617; Madison and Mason, speeches in Va. ratifying convention, 14 June 1788, *Debates,* 3: 278–381; Mason to Jefferson, Boyd, et al., *Papers of Thomas Jefferson,* 13: 205; "The Republican," *Connecticut Courant,* 7 Jan. 1788; Hamilton, Federalist 28, N.Y. *Independent Journal,* 26 Dec. 1787, *Ratification,* 15: 104–5. For amendments, see "The Dissent of the Minority of the Pa. Convention," 18 Dec. 1787, ibid., 19; amendments proposed in the N.Y., Va., and N.C. ratifying conventions, 2 July 1788, 27 June 1788, 31 July 1788, *Debates,* 2: 406, 3: 659, 4: 235; "Agrippa" (James Winthrop), *Massachusetts Gazette,* 5 Feb. 1788; William Read Staples, *Rhode Island in the Continental Congress* (Providence, R.I.: Providence Press, 1870), 654–55.

118. 12 June 1788, *Debates,* 3: 309. See also Madison, Federalist 41, N.Y. *Independent Journal,* 19 Jan. 1788, *Ratification,* 15: 420

119. Kohn, *Eagle and Sword,* 83–86. For a bibliography on the Bill of Rights and a compilation of suggested amendments, see Gaspare J. Saladino, "The Bill of Rights: A Bibliographic Essay," and *"The Ratification of the New Federal Constitution . . .* (Richmond, 1788)," in Stephen L. Schechter and Richard B. Bernstein, eds., *Contexts of the Bill of Rights* (Albany, N.Y.: New York State Commission on the Bicentennial of the United States Constitution, 1990), 89–91, 114–16, 118–19, 127, 130, 134–35, 40, 142; Edward Dumbauld, *The Bill of Rights and What It Means Today* (Norman, Okla.: Oklahoma University Press, 1957), 173–205.

120. Jefferson to Adams, 13 Nov. 1787, to Madison, 20 Dec. 1787, *Ratification,* 14: 464, 482.

121. Adams to Jefferson, 6 Dec. 1787, Jefferson to William Smith, 2 Feb. 1788, Abigail Adams Smith to John Quincy Adams, 10 Feb. 1788, ibid., 14: 473, 500, 502.

122. "Brutus" X, *N.Y. Journal,* 24 Jan. 1788, ibid., 15: 462, 463. For the so-called Newburgh conspiracy, see Kohn, *Eagle and Sword,* chapter 2.

THE WAR POWER: NO CHECKS, NO BALANCE

LOUIS FISHER

Presidential war power has expanded dramatically in the past half-century, driven by major shifts in institutional positions: ambitious interpretations (and executions) of presidential power, acquiescence by the judiciary, and abdication by Congress. As a result, the fundamental characteristic of American government—the framers' reliance on checks and balances—has been abandoned in this area. We now have presidential wars, set in motion unilaterally by our chief executives and unrestrained either by judicial or legislative checks.

THE FRAMERS' CONSTITUTION

There can be little question about the framers' determination to prevent war making by a single person. They were well aware that British theorists, including John Locke and William Blackstone, had placed foreign affairs and the war power exclusively in the executive.[1] The framers repudiated that monarchical model of government in every respect. They made the subject of foreign affairs a power shared between Congress and the president, and they placed the power to initiate war solely in the hands of Congress.

There should be little doubt about the framers' intent in this area. At the Philadelphia Convention, Charles Pinckney said he was for "a vigorous Executive but was afraid the Executive powers of [the existing] Congress might extend to peace & war &c which would render the Executive a Monarchy, of the worst kind, towit an elective one." James Wilson supported a single executive but "did not consider the Prerogatives of the British Monarch as a proper guide in defining the Executive powers. Some of these prerogatives were of a Legislative nature. Among others that of war & peace &c." Edmund Randolph rejected any "motive to be governed by the British Governmt. as our prototype."[2] The framers recognized that in times of emergency, the president needed to exercise war powers of a defensive nature ("to repel sudden attacks"), but the power to mount an offensive war—to take the country from a state of peace to a state of war—was reserved solely to Congress.[3] When Pierce Butler recommended that the president be given the power to make war, the other delegates strongly objected. Roger Sherman said that the president "shd. be able to repel and not to commence war." Elbridge Gerry remarked that he "never expected to hear in a repub-

lic a motion to empower the Executive alone to declare war." George Mason agreed, noting that he was "agst giving the power of war to the Executive, because not [safely] to be trusted with it; . . . He was for clogging rather than facilitating war."[4]

These sentiments were echoed during the debates at the Pennsylvania ratifying convention. James Wilson assured his colleagues that the system of checks and balances "will not hurry us into war; it is calculated to guard against it. It will not be in the power of a single man, or a single body of men, to involve us in such distress; for the important power of declaring war is vested in the legislature at large."[5] The framers gave Congress the power to initiate war because they believed that presidents, in their search for fame and glory, would have an appetite for war.[6] In *Federalist* 4, John Jay issued this warning:

absolute monarchs will often make war when their nations are to get nothing by it, but for purposes and objects merely personal, such as a thirst for military glory, revenge for personal affronts, ambition, or private compacts to aggrandize or support their particular families or partisans. These and a variety of other motives, which affect only the mind of the sovereign, often lead him to engage in wars not sanctified by justice or the voice and interests of his people.[7]

Writing in 1793, James Madison expressed similar concerns. War, he said, was "the true nurse of executive aggrandizement." War multiplies the honors and emoluments of executive office: "The strongest passions and most dangerous weakness of the human breast; ambition, avarice, vanity, the honourable or venial love of fame, are all in conspiracy against the desire and duty of peace."[8] In a letter to Thomas Jefferson in 1798, Madison said that the Constitution "supposes, what the History of all Govts demonstrates, that the Ex. is the branch of power most interested in war, & most prone to it. It has accordingly with studied care, vested the question of war in the Legisl."[9]

The framers did not depend on good intentions or virtuous behavior within a single branch. Nor did they rely on abstract formulations of separation of powers. By the late 1780s, the concept of checks and balances had replaced separation of powers, which one contemporary pamphleteer called a "hackneyed principle" and a "trite maxim."[10] Instead of trying to artificially separate the powers of government, the framers looked to a sharing and partial intermixture of powers. Checks and balances required some over-

This essay has been edited and is reprinted from Congress and the Politics of Foreign Policy, *ed. Colton C. Campbell, Nicol C. Rae, and John F. Stack, Jr. (Upper Saddle River, N.J.: Prentice Hall, 2003), 1–21. Copyright © 2003. Reprinted by permission of Pearson Education, Inc., Upper Saddle River, N.J.*

lapping. The framers knew that the "danger of tyranny or injustice lurks in unchecked power, not in blended power."[11]

In *Federalist* 51, Madison argued that "the great security against a gradual concentration of the several powers in the same department, consists in giving to those who administer each department the necessary constitutional means and personal motives to resist encroachments of the others." Madison drove home his point with this axiom: "Ambition must be made to counteract ambition." Each branch would have to protect its own prerogatives. "The interest of the man must be connected to the constitutional rights of the place."[12]

IMPLEMENTING THE FRAMERS' DESIGN

For years, the framers' concept of the war power held sway. Presidents were entitled to use military force for defensive purposes. However, anything of an offensive nature—taking the country from a state of peace to a state of war—was reserved solely to Congress. That distinction was clearly understood by presidents and their executive officers. President George Washington restricted his military actions to defensive operations. His Secretary of War, Henry Knox, told territorial governors that military actions against hostile Indian forces were to be confined to "defensive measures" until Congress decided otherwise. Knox cautioned that Congress was "alone . . . competent to decide upon an offensive war."[13]

When President John Adams decided it was necessary to use military force against France in the Quasi-War of 1798, he never argued that he could do so singlehandedly. Instead, he came to Congress to seek authority by statute to increase the size of the military and reinforce the defense of ports and harbors. Under its exclusive power to "grant letters of Marque and Reprisal," Congress also authorized private citizens to provide vessels and other military assistance in the war against France. Alexander Hamilton, one of the strongest proponents of executive power, recognized that the Constitution vested in Congress the sole decision to make reprisals. Whatever power the president possessed to take defensive actions, any measure beyond that "must fall under the idea of *reprisals* & requires the sanction of that Department which is to declare or make war."[14]

President Thomas Jefferson acted unilaterally in 1801, when he dispatched a small squadron of frigates to the Mediterranean to protect against attacks by the Barbary pirates. Yet when Congress returned, he explained that he took no further action because he was "unauthorized by the Constitution, without the sanction of Congress, to go beyond the line of defense." It was up to Congress to authorize "measures of offense also."[15] Congress subsequently passed at least ten statutes authorizing Presidents Jefferson and Madison to take military actions against the Barbary pirates.[16] In 1805, when conflicts arose between the United States and Spain, Jefferson advised Congress about the situation and clearly identified the constitutional principles: "Congress alone is constitutionally invested with the power of changing our condition from peace to war."[17]

The actions of President James Polk illustrate that executive power can expand when the president moves troops into likely hostilities. Determined to gain from Mexico the territories known as Upper California and New Mexico, he moved U.S. troops into a disputed area and provoked a clash between American and Mexican troops. A bold move, but Polk never claimed that he could unilaterally take the country from a state of peace to a state of war. He knew that he had to come to Congress, explain the situation, and ask Congress to declare war, which it did.

President Abraham Lincoln is often described as a "military dictator." That is a misnomer. Although he took a number of extraordinary measures in the early months of the Civil War while Congress was in recess, he never argued that he possessed plenary power over war. Instead, he conceded that he might have exercised power that belonged to Congress, particularly when he suspended the writ of habeas corpus. For constitutional legitimacy, he looked to Congress. He notified the legislators that his actions, "whether strictly legal or not, were ventured upon under what appeared to be a popular demand and a public necessity, trusting then, as now, that Congress would readily ratify them."[18] The legislative debate on granting Lincoln retroactive authority for his actions rested on the assumption that his actions were illegal.[19] Congress subsequently passed legislation to legitimate what Lincoln had done.[20]

When one of Lincoln's actions was taken to the Supreme Court (seizing ships and their goods), the executive branch conceded the limits of presidential authority. Richard Henry Dana, Jr., representing the administration, told the Supreme Court that Lincoln's actions in responding to the Civil War had nothing to do with "the right *to initiate a war, as a voluntary act of sovereignty.* That is vested only in Congress."[21] Even in the midst of a national crisis unmatched in American experience, the executive branch understood the difference between a president's duty to take certain defensive actions and the constitutional authority reserved to Congress to mount an offensive war against other nations.

In addition to declaring war against England in 1812 and against Mexico in 1846, Congress also declared war against Spain in 1898 and issued declarations for World War I and World War II. Of course there were other presidential military actions that did not involve declared wars. On some occasions, the president used military force after Congress had passed *authorizations,* as with the Quasi-War against France and the actions against the Barbary pirates. There were also other military actions by presidents when Congress had neither declared nor authorized the use of force. However, these so-called life-and-property actions were relatively modest in scope and limited in duration. Edward S. Corwin accurately summed up these presidential initiatives as consisting largely of "fights with pirates, landings of small naval contingents on barbarous or semi-barbarous coasts, the dispatch of small bodies of troops to chase bandits or cattle rustlers across the Mexican border, and the like."[22] However one might describe these presidential actions, they cannot be considered legitimate precedents for President Truman's decision to involve the nation in war against North Korea or President Bill Clinton's actions in mounting an air war against Yugoslavia.

THE ROLE OF THE JUDICIARY

In describing judicial precedents before World War I, Christopher N. May asserted that the Supreme Court, "with one short-lived exception—refused to pass on the validity of laws adopted under the war powers of the Constitution."[23] He spoke of the "longstanding position that war powers legislation is not subject to judicial review," and claimed that the "notion that the war powers were exempt from judicial scrutiny had a long and distinguished lineage."[24] A more recent study, by Martin S. Sheffer, offers a similar view: "One must constantly remember that executive-legislative conflicts regarding questions of emergency, war, and peace, although raising many constitutional controversies, rarely find their way to the judiciary and, when they do, are rarely decided according to proper constitutional interpretation. For the most part, they are resolved . . . through political settlements agreed to by Congress and the President."[25] The courts, says Sheffer, "lie back, seeking to avoid having to rule on questions of the conduct of commander-in-chief [and war] powers, and when they are forced to rule, they usually uphold presidential action."[26]

In fact, the record is quite the opposite. Until recent decades, federal courts regularly took war power cases and decided them like other legal matters: analyzing the dispute in terms of statutory and constitutional authority and balancing governmental powers against individual rights. Courts did not lie back or shy away from war power disputes. A number of private citizens and private corporations took war power issues to the courts to have their case adjudicated, and the courts often decided against the president. Many of the early decisions were written by justices who had been members of the Constitutional Convention or participated in state ratifying conventions. Their opinions reflected the prevailing view that taking the country to war was a matter for Congress, not the president.

As a result of French interference with American shipping in the late eighteenth century, Congress suspended commercial intercourse with France and enacted a number of statutes to prepare for military operations. The Supreme Court decided three cases resulting from the Quasi-War, which lasted from 1798 to 1800. In *Bas v. Tingy* (1800), the Court decided a case involving a claim by Captain Tingy for compensation regarding the recapture from the French of a U.S. merchant ship belonging to Bas. Was Tingy entitled to compensation based on a 1798 act of Congress or a higher compensation based on a 1799 statute governing the recapture of ships from the "enemy"? In Justice Chase's language, "the whole controversy turns on . . . whether *France* was at that time an *enemy*? If *France* was an enemy, then the law [entitles Tingy] to one half of the value of the ship and cargo for salvage; but if *France* was not an enemy, then no more than one-eighth can be allowed."[27]

The Court did not flinch from this "war power" issue. It was asked to decide whether, in the absence of a formal declaration of war by Congress, the state of hostilities between the United States and France amounted to a war and entitled Tingy to a higher compensation. The Court ruled that the conflict amounted to war whether Congress decided to make a formal declaration or simply authorize military action, as it had done. War could be either declared ("perfect") or undeclared ("imperfect"). Thus the Court fully addressed the legal and constitutional issues.

In 1801, the Court again analyzed the question of undeclared but authorized wars. In *Talbot v. Seeman*, Chief Justice John Marshall had his first opportunity to address a war-related case. Talbot, captain of a U.S. ship of war, captured a merchant ship flying a French flag. The owner of the ship sued the captain in libel for the value of the ship. Deciding that the seizure had been legal, the Court ruled in favor of Talbot. To decide his rights, it was necessary to examine the relative situation between the United States and France at the time of the capture. Notice Marshall's language:

The whole powers of war being, by the constitution of the United States, vested in congress, the acts of that body can alone be resorted to as our guides in this inquiry. It is not denied, nor, in the course of the argument, has it been denied, that congress may authorize general hostilities, in which case the general laws of war apply to our situation; or partial hostilities, in which case the laws of war, so far as they actually apply to our situation, must be noticed. To determine the real situation of America in regard to France, the acts of congress are to be inspected.[28]

A third case from the Quasi-War involved a proclamation by President John Adams to seize ships sailing to and from French ports. Congress had only provided authority to seize ships sailing *to* a French port. Could a president, in time of war, exceed statutory authority and could such disputes be litigated in court? Not only did the Court take the case, it decided against the president. Chief Justice Marshall ruled that when national policy is defined by statute, presidential "instructions cannot change the nature of the transaction, or legalize an act which without those instructions would have been a plain trespass."[29]

The preeminence of congressional policy, once it has been expressed in a statute, appears again in an 1806 decision by a federal circuit court. Colonel William S. Smith, indicted under the Neutrality Act of 1794 for engaging in military action against Spain, claimed that his action "was begun, prepared, and set in foot with the knowledge and the approbation of the executive department of our government." The circuit court forcefully rejected his argument: "The president of the United States cannot control the statute, nor dispense with its execution, and still less can he authorize to do what the law forbids."[30] The court clearly understood the difference between the president's "defensive" power to resist invasion and the "the exclusive province" of Congress to undertake "offensive" military actions against foreign countries:

If, indeed, a foreign nation should invade the territories of the United States, it would I apprehend, be not only lawful for the president to resist such invasion, but also to carry hostilities into the enemy's own country; and for this plain reason, that a state of complete and absolute war actually exists between the two nations. In the case of invasion hostilities, there cannot be war on the one side and peace on the other. . . . There is a manifest distinction between our going to war with a nation at peace, and a war being made against us by an actual invasion, or a formal declaration. In the former case, it is the exclusive province of congress to change a state of peace into a state of war.[31]

The president, then, had no constitutional authority to initiate war. Does the president, the court asked, "possess the power of making war? That power is exclusively vested in congress."[32]

For the next 140 years—up to the Korean War decisions of the 1950s—federal courts accepted and decided a range of other war power issues. In 1814, the Supreme Court was faced with the question of whether property found on land at the commencement of hostilities against England in 1812 could be considered "enemy property" as a result of the declaration of war by Congress. To decide that issue, the Court found it necessary to look for any other legislative act that authorized the seizure. Concluding that the declaration of war did not contain authority for the seizure, the Court ruled that the seizure required a supplementary instruction from Congress.[33] When Congress by law delegates to the president power to "call forth the militia" to suppress insurrections and repel invasions, the Court recognizes that the judgment as to how to deal most effectively with such situations rests with the president, for he is carrying out discretionary authority committed to him by Congress.[34]

In several cases arising from the Mexican War, the Court emphasized that the president's power as commander-in-chief is exercised to carry out congressional policy and cannot go beyond it. For example, the president had no authority to annex territory to the United States by virtue of military conquest. The president had no independent authority to enlarge the boundaries of the United States, for that could be done "only by the treaty-making power or the legislative authority, and is not a part of the power conferred upon the President by the declaration of war."[35] In a separate ruling, the Court granted a U.S. civilian trader damages for the seizure of his property by an officer of the U.S. army. Orders of a superior officer could not justify an unlawful seizure.[36] In yet another lawsuit, the Court decided that neither the president nor any military officer had authority to establish a court in a conquered country to decide questions about the rights of the United States or of individuals in prize cases.[37]

In a controversial decision in 1860, a circuit court upheld presidential authority to bombard Greytown (San Juan del Norte), Nicaragua, in retaliation for an affront to an American diplomat.[38] The U.S. military response would be considered disproportionate today for several reasons. In 1868, Congress passed legislation stating that it shall be the duty of the president to use such means "not amounting to war" in obtaining the release of U.S. citizens deprived of liberty by a foreign government. That legislative policy remains as part of current law.[39] Moreover, most of the "life-and-property" actions of the nineteenth and early twentieth centuries would be condemned today, both under the nonintervention policy of the Organization of American States (OAS) and the U.N. Charter. The OAS Charter provides that the territory of a nation is inviolable and it "may not be the object, even temporarily, of military occupation or of other measures of force taken by another State, directly or indirectly, or any grounds whatsoever." Article 2(4) of the U.N. Charter proscribes "the threat or use of force against the territorial integrity or political independence of any state."

The Civil War ushered in a number of lawsuits, most of them accepted and decided by the federal courts. Regarding the president's authority to suspend the writ of habeas corpus, Chief Justice Taney sitting on circuit ruled that such authority belonged to Congress, not the president.[40] President Lincoln rebuffed this judicial limitation, but other cases involving suspension of the writ were decided, some in favor of the president and some against.[41] In 1863, the Court upheld President Lincoln's blockade of Southern ports and the seizing of neutral vessels in response to the rebellion of the South. In upholding Lincoln's action in this matter, the Court also regarded the power to initiate war as the exclusive province of the legislature. The president has "no power to initiate or declare a war either against a foreign nation or a domestic State."[42] During this period, the Court decided a number of cases concerning the authority of the president and the executive branch to operate military courts that infringed upon the responsibilities of civil courts.[43]

One of the few cases ducked by the Supreme Court is *Mississippi v. Johnson* (1867), which involved Mississippi's effort to enjoin President Andrew Johnson from using the military to implement two Reconstruction Acts. Writing for the Court, Chief Justice Chase held that the Court lacked jurisdiction to issue the injunction. The president's duties were "purely executive and political" and lay outside the scope of "judicial interference with the exercise of Executive discretion."[44] The Court saw it as a no-win situation. First, Johnson might refuse to comply with a court order. Second, if he complied with the injunction, he might face impeachment by Congress. Would the

Court then step in to support the president in opposition to the legislature?[45]

Courts have had to decide a number of cases to determine when war begins and when it ends,[46] the authority of U.S. military commanders to impose duties on goods coming from the United States into an occupied territory,[47] the right to damages to the owner of a vessel seized as enemy property,[48] and the actions of military authorities in making arrests without a warrant.[49] In the famous *Curtiss-Wright* decision of 1936, the Court decided whether Congress could delegate to the president authority to declare an arms embargo in South America.[50] In none of these cases did the courts draw back and refuse to decide a dispute because it involved some aspect of the war power.

During and after World War II, the Court decided a number of cases on whether Congress had too broadly delegated wartime economic power to the president, including mobilization of the resources of the business community, price-fixing authority, rent control, and determination and recovery of "excess profits."[51] The Court decided the cases involving military judgments to place a curfew on Japanese Americans and put them in detention centers.[52] In 1946, the Court reviewed—and rejected—the government's claim that the continuation of military rule in Hawaii was made necessary by prevailing circumstances.[53] In 1952, in a stunning 6-to-3 opinion, the Court decided that President Truman lacked constitutional authority to seize most of the nation's steel mills for prosecuting the war in Korea.[54] Although Truman consistently denied that the nation was at war, preferring to call the hostilities in Korea a "police action,"[55] federal judges had no problem in selecting the word "war" to decide clauses in life insurance cases. As one district judge noted: "We doubt very much if there is any question in the minds of the majority of the people of this country that the conflict now raging in Korea can be anything but war."[56] Prior to the Korean War, courts had also decided whether war exists within the meaning of life insurance claims.[57]

It was only with the Vietnam War cases that federal courts began to regularly duck war power cases. These cases were dismissed on the grounds that the issue was a political question, an unconsented suit against the United States, or that the plaintiffs lacked standing. For the first time in the nation's history, the courts were using the political question doctrine to avoid constitutional challenges regarding the war power.[58] From the administrations of Ronald Reagan to Bill Clinton, members of Congress brought war power cases to court, but they were routinely denied relief under doctrines that included nonjusticiability, mootness, ripeness, and standing. The most recent example is the suit brought by Representative Tom Campbell (R-Calif.) and twenty-five other members of the House against the war in Yugoslavia.

The judicial message in these cases has been consistent: if members want to challenge presidential war power, they must first use the institutional powers available to Congress as a whole, acting through a majority of its members rather than having a few legislators bring their dispute to the judiciary. Only after Congress acted against a president to create a true constitutional impasse would there be a basis for legislative standing.[59] Clearly the ball is in Congress's court, but legislators have muffed the opportunity for the past half-century.

THE ROLE OF CONGRESS

In 1945, while the Senate debated the U.N. Charter, President Harry Truman sent a cable to Senator Kenneth D. McKellar (D-Tenn.) defining executive power over war. At issue was a procedure that allowed the United Nations to use military force to deal with threats to peace, breaches of the peace, and acts of aggression. All U.N. members would make available to the Security Council, "on its call and in accordance with a special agreement," armed forces and other assistance for the purpose of maintaining international peace and security. Aware of this provision, Truman pledged that all agreements involving U.S. troop commitments to the United Nations would first have to be approved by both houses of Congress: "When any such agreement or agreements are negotiated it will be my purpose to ask the Congress for appropriate legislation to approve them."[60]

After the Senate approved the U.N. Charter, Congress passed legislation spelling out the conditions for U.S. participation in military actions authorized by the Security Council. Section 6 of the U.N. Participation Act of 1945 provides that agreements "shall be subject to the approval of the Congress by appropriate Act or joint resolution."[61] Truman's pledge and the unambiguous statutory language seemed to nail down a key principle: any U.S. military action pursuant to a Security Council directive would require joint action by the president and Congress.

Nevertheless, five years later, Truman took the country to war in Korea without ever seeking authority from Congress, and legislators offered few objections. How could Truman act militarily in Korea under the U.N. umbrella without obtaining congressional approval? The short answer is that he did not use the "special agreement" procedure that was the mechanism for assuring congressional control. In fact, no special agreement has ever been entered into by any country.

Truman met with congressional leaders at 11:30 A.M. on June 27, after the administration had already issued the orders for military intervention. In later meetings with congressional leaders, designed to give them briefings on developments in Korea, he never asked for congressional authority. Members of Congress seemed to have no recollection of, or regard for, the legislative history of the U.N. Charter and the specific language in the U.N. Participation Act. One of the few senators to challenge Truman's initiative was Arthur V. Watkins (R-Utah), who reminded his colleagues that during debate on the U.N. Charter "we were told time and time again . . . that nothing would take us into war under that pact without action by the Congress. The President could not do it."[62] No other senator developed that point. Instead, senators deferred to presidential leadership and decisiveness. Typical was the remark by Senator Estes Kefauver (D-Tenn.), who advised that "this is a time to close our ranks, to forget political considerations, and to stand behind the President in the vital decision he has made."[63] He might have added that it was time to forget constitutional, treaty, and statutory considerations. In the House, Representative Vito Marcantonio, a member of the American Labor Party from New York, offered one of the few constitutional critiques of Truman's action.[64]

Senate Majority Leader Scott W. Lucas (D-Ill.) saw no need for a congressional role. When Truman asked congressional leaders on July 3 whether he should present to Congress a joint resolution expressing approval of his action in Korea, Lucas counseled against it. He said that Truman "had very properly done what he had to without consulting the Congress." He told Truman that many legislators had suggested that the president "keep away from Congress and avoid debate." Lucas added that "if there should be a row in Congress that would not help abroad."[65] The fear of speaking with a divided voice meant that Congress would have no voice at all. However, whatever Lucas wanted to say in private or in public could not change the language and intent of the Constitution, the U.N. Charter, or the U.N. Participation Act. Lucas had no authority to alter those documents and neither did Truman.

The next step in congressional acquiescence was the Vietnam War. Based on sketchy and inconclusive information about two "attacks" by North Vietnam, Congress passed the Tonkin Gulf Resolution in August 1964. There was not a single dissenting voice in the House, and only two senators voted against the resolution, which carelessly transferred legislative power to the president by authorizing Lyndon Johnson to take "all necessary measures to repel any armed attack against the forces of the United States and to prevent further aggression." Neither house bothered to conduct independent investigations to verify Johnson's report of the two attacks. It is now well established that the second attack probably never occurred.[66]

Senator Frank F. Church (D-Idaho) acknowledged that independent legislative oversight was often necessary, but not here. He said there is a time "to question the route of the flag, and there is a time to rally around it, lest it be routed. This is the time for the latter course, and in our pursuit of it, a time for all of us to unify."[67] If lawmakers conclude there is no time to debate going to war, Congress becomes a cipher and the president an autocrat. Senator George D. Aiken (R-Vt.) did not believe that a legislator could afford to oppose the president for exercising the power "which we, under our form of government and through our legislative bodies, have delegated to his office."[68]

And yet no statute, and certainly no constitutional provision, had "delegated" the war power to the president. What was at stake was legislative abdication, not delegation.

On the House side, House Majority Leader Carl B. Albert (D-Okla.) urged legislators to set aside party differences and unite behind the president. House Minority Leader Charles Halleck (R-Ind.) offered similar reasons for supporting Johnson.[69] Representative Edwin R. Adair (R-Ind.) dismissed the concern that the Tonkin Gulf Resolution signaled an abdication by Congress of its constitutional duties over war and foreign affairs. Such issues were raised in committee "and we were given assurance that it was the attitude of the Executive that such was not the case, that we are not impairing our congressional prerogatives."[70]

Isn't that remarkable? Members of Congress, concerned that they might be abdicating their constitutional duties, are assured by executive officials that there is no problem. The framers expected the three branches to make independent judgments about their institutional prerogatives. They are not supposed to accept self-serving statements from officials who are in the process of encroaching upon the responsibilities of another branch.

That precise point was made in the National Commitments Resolution, which the Senate passed in 1969 (and has since ignored). In reporting this measure, the Senate Foreign Relations Committee stated that the Tonkin Gulf Resolution represented "the extreme point in the process of constitutional erosion that began in the first years of this century." In adopting the sweeping language of the Tonkin Gulf Resolution, Congress committed the error of "making a *personal* judgment as to how President Johnson would implement the resolution when it had a responsibility to make an *institutional* judgment, first, as to what any President would do with so great an acknowledgment of power, and, second, as to whether, under the Constitution, Congress had the right to grant or concede the authority in question."[71]

The National Commitments Resolution, which passed the Senate by a vote of 70 to 16, stated that a national commitment of U.S. armed forces results "only from affirmative action taken by the executive and legislative branches of the U.S. Government by means of a treaty, statute, or concurrent resolution of both Houses of Congress specifically providing for such commitment."[72] Of course a Senate resolution is not legally binding, but it is binding on the Senate as an institution. Nevertheless, senators have never complied with the language in this resolution. They have repeatedly accepted unilateral presidential military actions that are not sanctioned by treaties, statutes, or concurrent resolutions. The latter form of legislative action has never been legally binding, because they are not presented to the president for his signature or veto, and have little use as a result of the Supreme Court's decision in the legislative veto case of *INS v. Chadha* (1983).

The War Powers Resolution of 1973, enacted over President Nixon's veto, is generally treated as an effort at congressional "reassertion." In fact, by recognizing that the president may use armed force for up to ninety days without seeking or obtaining legislative authority, the resolution sanctions a scope of independent presidential power that would have astonished the framers. According to Section 2(a) of the resolution, the measure is intended to "fulfill the intent of the framers" and to "insure that the collective judgment of both the Congress and the President" will apply to the introduction of U.S. forces to foreign hostilities. The resolution has had no such effect. Instead, it violates the intent of the framers and does not in any sense ensure collective judgment. Presidents Reagan, Bush, and Clinton have made repeated use of military force without either seeking or obtaining authority from Congress. The resolution compromised basic institutional and constitutional prerogatives. A few legislators, led by Senator Thomas F. Eagleton (D-Mo.) recognized that the resolution—despite the hype surrounding it—was in fact a legislative sell-out and a surrender to presidential power.[73]

There were only five military operations under Presidents Gerald Ford and Jimmy Carter, and three of those actions were efforts by Ford to evacuate American citizens and foreign nationals from Southeast Asia. The other two uses of military force involved the rescue effort of the *Mayaguez* crew in 1975 and Carter's attempt to rescue American hostages in Iran in 1980. However, military activity accelerated during the Reagan, Bush, and Clinton administrations, and Congress did little to assert its supposedly coequal status.

President Reagan used military force against other countries a number of times: sending troops to Lebanon, invading Grenada, ordering air strikes against Libya, involving the nation in the Iran-Contra affair, and committing U.S. warships to the Persian Gulf in 1987. Not once did Reagan ask Congress for authority, either in advance or afterwards. With regard to Lebanon, Congress called on Reagan to trigger the sixty-to-ninety-day clock of the War Powers Resolution, but he refused. Congress then passed legislation on October 12, 1983, to activate the clock, but instead of limiting military force to ninety days, it authorized a period of eighteen months, obviously pushing the Lebanon issue beyond public debate in the 1984 elections. After the death of 241 U.S. Marines in a suicide bombing, Reagan pulled U.S. forces offshore and by March 30, 1984, terminated U.S. involvement. In response to the Grenada invasion, the House passed legislation to trigger the sixty-day clock and the Senate was poised to pass the same legislation. However, the administration's announcement that the operation would be concluded within sixty days prevented final enactment of the legislation.[74]

President George Bush invaded Panama in December 1989. A month later, in an address to Congress, he announced that American troops would be out of Panama by the end of February. Whether consciously or not, he appeared to be restricting himself to the sixty-to-ninety-day clock of the War Powers Resolution.[75] In August 1990, Bush made a larger commitment of U.S. troops, this time to Saudi Arabia after Iraq had invaded Kuwait. By November, Bush had increased the commitment to more than 500,000 troops, changing a defensive maneuver to an offensive capability. At no time did he or any other administration official acknowledge the need to come to Congress for authority to wage war against Iraq. The House Democratic Caucus, voting 177 to 37, adopted a resolution stating that the Constitution required Bush to first seek authorization from Congress.[76]

On January 8, 1991, with military action scheduled for a week away, Bush asked Congress to pass legislation "supporting" the use of American troops against Iraq. The next day he told reporters that he did not need a resolution from Congress. On January 12, Congress authorized Bush to take offensive actions against Iraq. In a separate vote on a nonbinding resolution, the House voted 302 to 131 for this language: "The Congress finds that the Constitution of the United States vests all power to declare war in the Congress of the United States. Any offensive action taken against Iraq must be explicitly approved by the Congress of the United States before such action may be initiated."[77]

In signing the bill, Bush continued to insist that he could have acted without congressional authority, explaining that his request for "congressional support did not, and my signing this resolution does not, constitute any change in the long-standing positions of the executive branch on either the President's constitutional authority to use the Armed Forces to defend vital U.S. interests or the constitutionality of the War Powers Resolution." Regardless of what he said in the signing statement, what governs legally is the language in the bill, not in his signing statement. Congress provided authority, not support.

Compared to military initiatives by Reagan and Bush, Clinton's eight years marked an extraordinary increase in the use of U.S. force against other countries. Clinton launched cruise missiles at Iraq in 1993 and 1996, ordered a four-day bombing in December 1998, and continued air strikes throughout 1999 and 2000. Under Clinton's term, the humanitarian venture started by Bush in Somalia turned into a military effort to remove the Somalia political figure, Mohamed Farah Aideed. Congress used its power of the purse to bring the military operation to a halt. Legislation in 1993 prohibited the use of any funds after March 31, 1994, for the operations of U.S. armed forces in Somalia unless the president requested an extension and received authority from Congress. The legislation permitted the use of funds after the cutoff date to protect American diplomatic facilities and American citizens.[78]

In 1994, Clinton was prepared to invade Haiti until a negotiating team led by former President Jimmy Carter settled the dispute peacefully. During 1993 and 1994, Congress considered a number of measures to restrict Clinton, but none was enacted into law. The legislative language ranged from binding limitations to nonbinding "sense of Congress" expressions. The latter typically gave Clinton total discretion to deploy American troops if he determined that military action was "vital" to U.S. national interests and there was insufficient time to seek and obtain congressional authorization. Legislators announced that Clinton, through his commander-in-chief powers, had full constitutional authority to order the invasion.[79] These legislators evidently interpreted presidential war authority as plenary and subject to no restrictions by the War Powers Resolution.

Clinton repeatedly intervened in the Balkans, using air strikes in 1994 against the Serbs, introducing 20,000 U.S. troops into Bosnia in 1995, and ordering an air war against Yugoslavia in 1999. At no time did he request authority from Congress. Initially he suggested that he would need "authority" from Congress for those operations, but that language was quickly replaced by the need for legislative "support."[80] Members of Congress debated a number of legislative provisions, but most of them were watered down to sense-of-Congress language. On October 20, 1993, the Senate voted 99 to 1 for these words: "It is the sense of Congress that none of the funds appropriated or otherwise made available by this Act should be available for the purposes of deploying U.S. Armed Forces to participate in the implementation of a peace settlement in Bosnia-Herzegovina, unless previously authorized by Congress." That language was later enacted into law, but it had no legally binding effect.[81] It was merely the "sense" of Congress.

In adopting that language, members of Congress demonstrated their awareness and support for constitutional principles, but they were never willing to enforce those principles. Instead, they regularly adopted statutory provisions that left the door totally open to presidential war initiatives. Clinton was satisfied in seeking authority not from Congress but from outside bodies, such as the United Nations and NATO. In ordering air strikes against the Serbs in 1994, he announced that he was operating through U.N. Security Council resolutions and NATO's military command: "The authority under which air strikes can proceed, NATO acting out of area pursuant to UN authority, requires the common agreement of our NATO allies."[82] In other words, Clinton would have to obtain approval from England, France, Italy, and other NATO allies, but not from Congress. Legislators did not challenge his authority to conduct air strikes in Bosnia.

Clinton's decision in 1995 to introduce ground forces into Bosnia provoked legislative action, but once again Congress was unable or unwilling to place checks on presidential power. The Senate debated "sense of the Senate" language to prohibit the use of funds to deploy U.S. troops to Bosnia and Herzegovina unless "Congress approves in advance the deployment of such forces." Not only did this language have no binding effect, but exceptions were made to allow Clinton to deploy U.S. ground forces if needed to evacuate U.S. peacekeeping forces from a "situation of imminent danger, to undertake emergency air rescue operations, or to provide for the airborne delivery of humanitarian supplies."[83] Several senators

agreed to support the provision only because it had no force of law.[84]

Senator Paul M. Simon (D-Ill.) explained that he would vote against the amendment, even though it was a sense of the Senate, "because foreign policy cannot be effective if Congress micromanages it." Sending 25,000 ground troops to Bosnia was micromanagement? What could have been a more fundamental issue for Congress, both in wielding the war power and in committing the power of the purse? Senator William S. Cohen (R-Maine) rejected Simon's position, noting that Clinton planned to deploy ground troops "to one of the most hostile regions in the world" and "without having any sort of defined plan presented to us."[85]

The House entered into a prolonged debate on the president's authority to commit ground troops to Bosnia. By a vote of 315 to 103, lawmakers passed a nonbinding resolution that U.S. troops should not be deployed without congressional approval. Ninety-three Democrats—nearly half of those in the House—joined 222 Republicans to support the resolution. As the months rolled by and the language shifted from nonbinding to legally binding, the margin of support declined to 242 to 171. Twelve Republicans voted against the second version. James B. Longley, Jr. (R-Maine) said he opposed sending American ground troops to Bosnia but deferred to presidential decisions: "I have to respect the authority of the Commander in Chief to conduct foreign policy. . . . I think there is no greater threat to American lives than a Congress that attempts to micromanage foreign policy. I have told the President that I would respect his authority as Commander in Chief."[86] First, the president's constitutional authority to "conduct foreign policy" does not include taking the nation to war. Second, respect for presidential authority should not be given a higher value than respect for constitutional limits. Third, presidential deployment of ground troops to Bosnia is not an issue of "micromanagement." Fourth, American lives are not threatened when Congress exercises its constitutional war power; they are threatened when presidents put American lives in harm's way.

Senate Majority Leader Robert J. Dole (R-Kans.) announced that Clinton had "the authority and the power under the Constitution to do what he feels should be done regardless of what Congress does."[87] Under this theory, no matter what Congress did in exercising its constitutional powers over war and peace, those legislative actions would be subordinated to what the president "felt" should be done. Congress would have no coequal (much less superior) power. There would be no checks and balance system, no tussling for power. In this substitution of autocracy for constitutional government, congressional challenges to presidential war initiatives became futile and useless. No matter how much lawmakers objected to presidential plans, they would have to swallow their reservations and stand to the side. A handful of senators spoke out in defense of congressional war prerogatives: Robert C. Byrd (D-W.Va.),

Russell D. Feingold (D-Wis.), Kay Bailey Hutchison (R-Tex.), James M. Inhofe (R-Okla.), and Jon L. Kyl (R-Ariz.).[88]

What the Senate finally did was to pass a bill providing "support" for American troops in Bosnia but expressing "reservations" about sending them there.[89] If senators thought it was a bad idea sending troops to Bosnia, it would have been consistent to block the deployment. But consistency was not a high value. More important was having it both ways. If things went well, Congress had not stood in the way. If things went poorly, it would be Clinton's fault. Either way, there would be no congressional accountability. On the same day as these Senate votes, the House failed by a vote of 210 to 218 to prohibit funds from being used to deploy troops to Bosnia. Clinton was able to send 20,000 troops to Bosnia without any legislative authority.

The next escalation of war was Clinton's decision in 1999 to bomb Yugoslavia. Although Congress was to be given no formal role in the use of force against the Serbs, legislatures in other NATO countries took votes to authorize military action in Yugoslavia. The Italian Parliament had to vote approval for the air strikes. The German Supreme Court ruled that the Bundestag, which had been dissolved with the election that ousted Chancellor Kohl, had to be recalled to approve deployment of German aircraft and troops to Kosovo. The U.S. Congress, supposedly the strongest legislature in the world, was content to watch from the back seat.

On March 11, 1999, the House voted to support U.S. armed forces as part of a NATO *peacekeeping* operation. That vote supported a peace agreement between Serbs and Kosovars, not military action. The Senate's vote on March 23 did support military air operations and missile strikes against Yugoslavia. However, that vote was on a concurrent resolution (S. Con. Res. 21), which passes both chambers but is not presented to the president. It therefore had no legal meaning.

On April 28, after the first month of bombing, the House took a series of votes on the war in Yugoslavia. It voted 249 to 180 to prohibit the use of appropriated funds for the deployment of U.S. ground forces unless first authorized by Congress. A motion to direct the removal of U.S. armed forces from Yugoslavia failed, 139 to 290. A resolution to declare a state of war between the United States and Yugoslavia fell, 2 to 427. A fourth vote, to authorize the air operations and missile strikes, lost on a tie vote, 213 to 213. Newspaper editorials and commentators derided the House of Representatives for taking multiple and supposedly conflicting votes. Nevertheless, the House articulated some basic values. It insisted that Congress authorize the introduction of ground troops and it refused to grant authority for the air strikes.

In contrast to the House, the Senate decided to duck the issue. Senator John S. McCain (R-Ariz.) offered a joint resolution to authorize Clinton to use "all necessary force and other means, in concert with U.S. allies, to accomplish U.S. and North Atlantic Treaty Organization objectives in the Federal Republic of Yugoslavia (Serbia and Montenegro)." That measure was tabled, 78 to 22. A few weeks later, the Senate tabled another amendment, this one by Senator Arlen Specter (R-Pa.) to direct the president to seek approval from Congress before introducing ground troops in Yugoslavia. Failure to obtain approval would deny the president funds to conduct the operation. His amendment was tabled, 52 to 48. An amendment by Senator Robert C. Smith (R-N.H.), to prohibit funding for military operations in Yugoslavia unless Congress enacted specific authorization, was tabled 77 to 21.[90] The Senate might just as well have considered one final motion: "Do we want to exercise our constitutional powers and participate in matters of war?" Tabled, 63 to 37.

OPTIONS FOR GEORGE W. BUSH

George W. Bush faces a number of key choices in the White House. He can accept and implement the big-presidency model adopted by most presidents over the past half century. Certainly he will be surrounded by aides who will urge him to press presidential power to the limit and not concede any territory or authority to Congress. It will be tempting to repeat one of the great constitutional clichés: "I didn't enter office to reduce the constitutional power of the presidency." No doubt presidential machismo —the display of virility—is the dominant model.[91]

Another model, faithful to constitutional principles, is available. It provides a sounder and healthier foundation for the presidency, the country, and world peace. After Truman had taken the nation to war against North Korea, Dwight D. Eisenhower concluded that his action was a serious mistake, both politically and constitutionally. Eisenhower thought that national commitments would be stronger if entered into jointly by both the executive and legislative branches. Toward that end, he asked Congress for specific authority to deal with national security crises. He stressed the importance of collective action by Congress and the president: "I deem it necessary to seek the cooperation of Congress. Only with that cooperation can we give the reassurance needed to deter aggression."[92]

In 1954, when Eisenhower was under pressure to intervene in Indochina to save beleaguered French troops, he refused to act unilaterally. He told reporters at a news conference: "There is going to be no involvement of America in war unless it is a result of the constitutional process that is placed upon Congress to declare it. Now, let us have that clear; and that is the answer."[93] Eisenhower told Secretary of State John Foster Dulles that in "the absence of some kind of arrangement getting support of Congress," it "would be completely unconstitutional & indefensible" to give any assistance to the French.[94]

Eisenhower's respect for constitutional principles is also evident in his handling of the Formosa crisis with China in 1954. A memorandum from Secretary Dulles stated that "it is doubtful that the issue can be exploited without Congressional approval."[95] Eisenhower said that any attack on airfields in China would require "Congressional authorization, since it would be war. If Congressional authorization were not obtained there would be logical grounds for impeachment. Whatever we do must be in a Constitutional manner."[96] When the situation in the Formosa Straits grew worse in 1955, Eisenhower did not turn for authority to the U.N. Security Council, as Truman had done. He urged Congress to pass appropriate legislation to authorize presidential action. That legislation, with strong majorities in each House, was enacted.[97]

In his memoirs, Eisenhower explained the choice between invoking executive prerogatives or seeking congressional authorization. On New Year's Day in 1957, he met with Secretary Dulles and congressional leaders of both parties to consider legislation leading to possible military action in the Middle East. House Majority Leader John W. McCormack (D-Mass.) asked Eisenhower whether he, as commander-in-chief, already possessed authority to carry out actions in the Middle East without waiting for congressional authorization. Eisenhower's reply demonstrates a profound understanding of the constitutional system. He told the congressional leaders that

greater effect could be had from a consensus of Executive and Legislative opinion, and I spoke earnestly of the desire of the Middle East countries to have reassurance now that the United States would stand ready to help. . . . Near the end of this meeting I reminded the legislators that the Constitution assumes that our two branches of government should get along together.[98]

Eisenhower's understanding of the war power was extremely perceptive. He knew that lawyers and policy advisers in the executive branch could always cite a multitude of precedents to justify unilateral presidential action. It was his seasoned judgment, however, that a commitment by the United States would have much greater impact on allies and enemies alike when it represented the collective judgment of the president and Congress. Singlehanded actions taken by the president, without the support of Congress and the people, can threaten national prestige and undermine the presidency. Eisenhower's position was sound then and it is sound now.

NOTES

1. Louis Fisher, *Congressional Abdication on War and Spending* (College Station, Tex.: Texas A&M University Press, 2000), 8.

2. Max Farrand, ed., *The Records of the Federal Convention of 1787* (New Haven: Yale University Press, 1937), 1: 64–66.

3. Ibid., 2: 318.

4. Ibid., 318–19.

5. Jonathan Elliot, ed., *The Debates in the Several State Conventions on the Adoption of the Federal Convention* (Washington, D.C.: J. B. Lippincott, 1836–1845), 2: 528. Similar comments were made by delegates to the North Carolina and South Carolina ratifying conventions.

Ibid., 4: 107, 287 (statements by James Iredell and Charles Pinckney).

6. William Michael Treanor, "Fame, the Founding, and the Power to Declare War," *Cornell Law Review* 82 (1997): 695.

7. Benjamin Fletcher Wright, ed., *The Federalist* (Cambridge, Mass.: Harvard University Press, 1961), 101.

8. Gaillard Hunt, ed., *The Writings of James Madison* (New York: G. P. Putnam & Sons, 1900–1910), 6: 174.

9. Ibid., 312.

10. M. J. C. Vile, *Constitutionalism and the Separation of Powers* (Oxford: Clarendon Press, 1967), 153.

11. Kenneth Culp Davis, *Administrative Law and Government* (St. Paul, Minn.: West, 1960), 54.

12. Wright, ed., *The Federalist,* 356.

13. Fisher, *Congressional Abdication of War and Spending,* 15–16.

14. Harold C. Syrett, ed., *The Papers of Alexander Hamilton* (New York: Columbia University Press, 1974), 21: 461–62 (emphasis in original).

15. James D. Richardson, ed., *A Compilation of the Messages and Papers of the Presidents* (New York: Bureau of National Literature, 1897–1925), 1: 315.

16. Louis Fisher, *Presidential War Power* (Lawrence, Kans.: University of Kansas Press, 1995), 26.

17. *Annals of Congress,* 9th Cong., 1st sess., 1805, p. 19.

18. Richardson, *A Compilation of the Messages and Papers,* 7: 3225.

19. *Congressional Globe,* 37th Cong., 1st sess., 1861, p. 393 (Senator Howe).

20. 12 Stat. 326 (1861).

21. *The Prize Cases,* 67 U.S. 635, 660 (1863) (emphasis in original).

22. Edward S. Corwin, "The President's Power," *The New Republic* (January 29, 1951): 16.

23. Christopher N. May, *In the Name of War: Judicial Review and the War Powers since 1918* (Cambridge, Mass.: Harvard University Press, 1989), vii.

24. Ibid., 1, 16.

25. Martin S. Sheffer, *The Judicial Development of Presidential War Powers* (Westport, Conn.: Praeger, 1999), ix.

26. Ibid., x.

27. 4 Dall. (4 U.S.) 37, 43 (1800) (emphasis in original).

28. 5 U.S. (1 Cranch) 1, 28 (1801) (emphasis added).

29. *Little v. Barreme,* 2 Cr. (6 U.S.) 170, 179 (1804).

30. *United States v. Smith,* 27 Fed. Cas. 1192, 1230 (C.C.N.Y. 1806) (No. 16,342).

31. Ibid.

32. Ibid.

33. *United States v. Brown,* 12 U.S. (8 Cr.) 110 (1814).

34. *Martin v. Mott,* 25 U.S. (12 Wheat.) 19, 28, 30 (1827).

35. *Fleming v. Page,* 50 U.S. (9 How.) 603, 614–15 (1850).

36. *Mitchell v. Harmony,* 54 U.S. (13 How.) 115 (1851).

37. *Jecker v. Montgomery,* 54 U.S. (13 How.) 498, 515 (1852).

38. *Durand v. Hollins,* 8 Fed. Cas. 111 (S.D.N.Y. 1860) (No. 4,186). See also *Perrin* v. *United States,* 4 Ct. Cl. 543 (1868).

39. 15 Stat. 224, sec. 3 (1868); 22 U.S.C. 1732 (1994).

40. *Ex parte Merryman,* 17 Fed. Cas. 144, 148 (C.C. Md. 1861) (No. 9,487).

41. *Ex parte Benedict,* 3 Fed. Cas. 159 (D.N.Y. 1862) (No. 1,292) (against the president); *Ex parte Field,* 9 Fed. Cas. 1 (C.C. Vt. 1862) (No. 4,761) (for presidential suspensions but against suspensions by the Department of War); In *re Dunn,* 8 Fed. Cas. 93 (S.D.N.Y. 1863) (No. 4,171) (upholding presidential suspensions); In *re Fagan,* 8 Fed. Cas. 947, 949 (D. Mass. 1863) (No. 4,604) (upholding president because of statutory authority).

42. *The Prize Cases,* 67 U.S. (2 Black) 635, 668 (1863).

43. *Dynes v. Hoover,* 61 U.S. (20 How.) 65 (1858); *Ex parte Vallandigham,* 68 U.S. (1 Wall.) 243. (1864); *Ex parte Milligan,* 71 U.S. (4 Wall.) 2 (1966); *Raymond v. Thomas,* 91 U.S. 712 (1876).

44. 71 U.S. (4 Wall.) 475, 499 (1867).

45. Ibid., 485.

46. For example, *United States v. Anderson* 76 U.S. (9 Wall.) 56 (1870); *United States v. Russel* (13 Wall.) 623 (1871); The Protector (12 Wall.) 700 (1872); *Hamilton v. Kentucky Distilleries Co.,* 251 U.S. 146 (1919); *Rupert v. Caffey,* 251 U.S. 264 (1920); *United States v. Standard Brewery,* 251 U.S. 210 (1920); *United States v. Cohen Grocery Co.,* 255 U.S. 81 (1921); *Commercial Trust Co. v. Miller,* 262 U.S. 51 (1923); *U.S. Trust Co. v. Miller,* 262 U.S. 58 (1923); *Ahrenfeldt v. Miller,* 262 U.S. 60 (1923); *Chastleton Corp. v. Sinclair,* 264 U.S. 543 (1924).

47. *Dooley v. United States,* 182 U.S. 222 (1901).

48. *Hijo v. United States,* 194 U.S. 315 (1904).

49. *Ex parte Orozco,* 201 F. 106 (W.D. Tex. 1912), dismissed, 229 U.S. 633 (1913).

50. *United States v. Curtiss-Wright Export Corp.,* 299 U.S. 304 (1936).

51. *United States v. Bethlehem Steel Corp.,* 315 U.S. 289 (1942); *Yakus v. United States,* 321 U.S. 414 (1944); *Bowles v. Willingham,* 321 U.S. 503 (1944); *Lichter v. United States,* 334 U.S. 742 (1948); *Woods v. Miller Co.,* 333 U.S. 138 (1948).

52. *Hirabayashi v. United States,* 320 U.S. 81 (1943); *Yasui v. United States,* 320 U.S. 115 (1943); and *Korematsu v. United States,* 323 U.S. 214 (1944).

53. *Duncan v. Kahanamoku,* 327 U.S. 304 (1946).

54. *Youngstown Co. v. Sawyer,* 343 U.S. 579 (1952).

55. *Public Papers of the Presidents of the United States, Harry S. Truman, 1945–1953* (Washington, D.C.: U.S. Government Printing Office, 1966) 179 Presidential News Conference June 29, 1950: 504; 191 Presidential News Conference, July 13, 1950: 522.

56. *Weissman v. Metropolitan Life Ins. Co.,* 112 F.Supp. 420, 425 (D. Cal. 1953). See also *Gagliormella v. Metropolitan Life Ins. Co.,* 122 F.Supp. 246, 250 (D. Mass. 1954); *Carius v. New York Life Insurance Co.,* 124 F.Supp. 388, 390 (D. Ill. 1954).

57. *New York Life Ins. Co. v. Durham,* 166 F.2d 874 (10th Cir. 1948); *New York Life Ins. Co. v. Bennion,* 158 F.2d 260, 264 (10th Cir. 1946).

58. Louis Fisher, "Litigating the War Power with *Campbell v. Clinton,*" *Presidential Studies Quarterly* 30 (September 2000): 564, 567–69.

59. Ibid., 569–74.

60. 91 *Congressional Record,* 8185 (1945).

61. 59 Stat. 621, sec. 6 (1945).

62. 96 *Congressional Record,* 9233 (1950).

63. Ibid.

64. Ibid., 9268.

65. *Foreign Relations of the United States* (Washington, D.C.: U.S. Government Printing Office, 1950), vol. 7, Korea, H. Doc. No. 82-264, vol. 7, 82d Cong., 1st Sess. (1976), pp. 287–88, 289–90, 291.

66. Fisher, *Congressional Abdication on War and Spending,* 54.

67. 110 *Congressional Record* 18421 (1964).

68. Ibid., 18457.

69. Ibid., 18542.

70. Ibid., 18543.

71. S. Rept. No. 129, 91st Cong., 1st (1969), 22–23 (emphasis in original).

72. 115 *Congressional Record,* 17245 (1969).

73. Fisher, *Congressional Abdication on War and Spending,* 65–67; Louis Fisher and David Gray Adler, "The War Powers Resolution: Time to Say Goodbye," *Political Science Quarterly* 113 (Spring 1998): 1–20.

74. Fisher, *Congressional Abdication on War and Spending,* 69.

75. Ibid., 74.

76. *Congressional Quarterly Almanac,* 1990, p. 742.

77. 137 *Congressional Record* 1034, 1049 (1991).

78. 107 Stat. 1476, sec. 8161(b)(B) (1993).

79. Fisher, *Congressional Abdication on War and Spending,* 84–88.

80. Ibid., 89–90.

81. *Congressional Record* 25479, 25485 (1993); 107 Stat. 1474, sec. 8146 (1993).

82. *Public Papers of the Presidents,* 1994, 1: 186.

83. 141 *Congressional Record* S14634 (daily ed. September 29, 1995).

84. Fisher, *Congressional Abdication on War and Spending,* 93.

85. 141 *Congressional Record* S14640 (daily ed. September 29, 1995).

86. Ibid., H13239.

87. Ibid., S17529.

88. Fisher, *Congressional Abdication on War and Spending,* 97.

89. 141 *Congressional Record* S18552 (daily ed. December 13, 1995).

90. Fisher, *Congressional Abdication on War and Spending,* 102–3.

91. Alexander DeConde, *Presidential Machismo: Executive Authority, Military Intervention, and Foreign Relations* (Boston: Northeastern University Press, 2000).

92. *Public Papers of the Presidents,* 1957, 11.

93. *Public Papers of the Presidents,* 1954, 306.

94. *Foreign Relations of the United States* (FRUS), 1952–1954, 13 (part 1), 1242.

95. Ibid., 14 (part 1), 611.

96. Ibid., 618

97. 69 Stat. 7 (1955).

98. Dwight D. Eisenhower, *Waging Peace* (Garden City, N.Y.: Doubleday, 1965), 179.

LEGAL CONSTRAINTS

ROGER W. BARNETT

The 1899 Hague Conference was the first at which the Japanese were present as international equals of the European and American powers which had hitherto engrossed the making of international law. But by what title had Japan got there? "We show ourselves at least your equals in scientific butchery, and at once we are admitted to your council tables as civilized men."—Richard Best

History is written by the victors. Thus, the heinous massacre that was Hiroshima has been handed down to us as a perfectly justified act of war.—Takashi Hiraoka, Mayor of Hiroshima

Operational and organizational constraints on the use of force may or may not be underwritten in law. Beyond those particular constraints, however, a developed body of international law has evolved to confine the use of force in a variety of ways. The historical roots of this body of law lie with notions of chivalry on the battlefield, a belief that all human activity should be bounded by the rule of law, a Western revulsion at the results of the use of force in past conflicts, concern that force be used only as a last resort, and the idea that wars and their battles are to be fought by certain groups of people, while others are to be exempt from their ravages. The centerpiece of the legal approach is that the use of force and its effects should be confined, as much as possible, to combatants. No direct and intentional harm should be visited upon noncombatants when force is used. Closely associated with an approach that seeks to detail the laws of armed conflict are efforts in arms control: for what better way to ensure against the use of force than to remove weapons from the hands of those who might be tempted to use them?

The pertinent laws are wide-ranging and complex. They provide an ever-thickening web of restraint. Moreover, activists are vigilant and eager to increase the strands of the web and to free it of its imperfections. Their agenda states clearly:

Any broadening of the interpretation of the right to resort to military force is fraught with danger. . . . Therefore international law must develop along the path of eliminating all loopholes in the legal regulation of the ban on the use of force. . . . Unilateral coercive military measures must disappear from international practice in the future. In this regard international law must become maximally clear and unambiguous in not permitting any broad interpretation of the right to rely on force.[1]

International law is both agreed and customary. As the former, it appears as international treaties, protocols, conventions, opinions of international courts and tribunals, and other documents to which a state is a party. As the latter, it derives from the practice of military and naval forces in the field, at sea, and in the air during hostilities. When such a practice attains a degree of regularity and is accompanied by the general conviction among nations that behavior in conformity with that practice is obligatory, it can be said to have become a rule of customary law *binding all nations*.[2]

It should be noted that a particular state need not agree with the particular tenet of customary law for it to be obligatory. It should also be noted that there is significant disagreement among nations as to what constitutes "the precise content of an accepted practice of armed conflict and to its status as a rule of law."[3] Moreover, both forms of international law involve relationships among sovereign states, not individuals or nonstate groups.

In the United States, all weapons under development must undergo a legal review,[4] as must the development of tactics, techniques, capabilities, and rules of engagement. All members of the U.S. armed services are required to be trained in the principles and rules of the law of war, the responsibility for which is assigned to the secretaries of the military departments.[5]

Despite an extended evolution, the law of armed conflict contains areas of disagreement and, regardless of efforts to eliminate it, permits a range of interpretation. Moreover, its application and enforcement have been uneven. Some states in the international system have chosen to comply, whereas others have flouted their international responsibility to uphold the laws. Responses to noncompliance have been anything but consistent:

When the Israelis bombed the Iraqi pre-operational nuclear reactor near Baghdad in 1981, world condemnation was rampant. Yet when the Coalition forces undertook precisely the same type of missions during the Gulf War, applause followed. When Argentina moved on the Falklands pointing to historical rationales over a century old, the act was not labeled aggression by the United Nations. When Iraqi forces invaded Kuwait citing twentieth century history and anticolonial motives, the United Nations not only branded the action aggression, but authorized the use of force to expel them. The world community accepted Tanzania's 1979

This essay has been edited and is reprinted from Asymmetrical Warfare: Today's Challenge to U.S. Military Power *(Washington, D.C.: Brassey's, 2003), 61–81, by permission of Brassey's.*

overthrow of Idi Amin's dictatorship in Uganda, but criticized Viet Nam's unseating of the at least as bloody Pol Pot regime the same year. The 1979 Soviet invasion of neighboring Afghanistan resulted in United Nations calls for withdrawal; four years later when the United States invaded Grenada, the United Nations remained silent.[6]

The law is grounded in just war theory, which is bifurcated into *jus ad bellum* and *jus in bello*. The former deals with questions having to do with the right to make war, whereas the latter is concerned with the conduct of war.

JUS AD BELLUM

Thomas Aquinas argued that three tests were necessary to justify the use of force, *jus ad bellum*. The first, "just cause," contended that the use of force must originate in a sound legal basis, either natural law or the law of nations. The purpose for this grounding was to put the use of force on a more rational basis than, for example, religious or ideological wars. The second, competent authority, meant that wars could be waged only by the initiation or with the consent of rulers. Ordinary citizens or nonauthoritative groups could not meet this test for *jus ad bellum*. The third, "right intention," meant that conquest or wanton destruction, for example, could not be justification for war making. The intention of the user of military force must be more noble and selfless. Justification for most asymmetrical uses of force—especially terrorism—would likely be trumped by all three tests.

Given this framework, the decision to make war was one that the sovereign was competent to make: the inherent right to wage war was one of the central tenets of sovereignty. "Since the end of the First World War," however, "we have witnessed a major departure from 'the sovereign right' idea and a return to a severely restricted legal right of States to resort to war."[7] In fact, today, *jus ad bellum* has been restricted exclusively to self-defense against armed aggression.[8] The Thomist tests: just cause, competent authority, and right intention have been narrowed to conform to the U.N. Charter's inherent right of self-defense, and nothing more. This constitutes one "right to rely on force" in the view of contemporary activists. A second, recent instance is that of "humanitarian intervention," such as was used in NATO's Kosovo action, Operation Allied Force, in 1999. The use of force in this case was not sanctioned by the United Nations, and in view of the Security Council veto, is unlikely to garner U.N. approval in the future. The tension arises from the incompatibility of humanitarian intervention and the principle of noninterference with the internal affairs of sovereign states, which is prohibited by the U.N. Charter.[9]

The universality of the United Nations—in which Taiwan is the only major state that is not a member, and its status as an independent state de facto is in question—has effectively answered the Thomist agenda: just cause is only in self-defense, competent authority is only the attacked state or the United Nations acting in a collective defense, and right intention is only to redress the aggression that provided the just cause.

Yet ambiguities persist despite such apparent pat answers. The United States, for example, has consistently reserved the right to act in anticipation of an attack. The U.S. argument hinges on the claim that it is not necessary, given the devastating impact of modern weapons, to absorb the first blow. One can conduct, in this view, "anticipatory self-defense," by striking an adversary that is preparing an attack. Agreement on this approach is far from universal, however. The U.N. Charter, considering only state actors, is also focused on an "armed attack." But that omits other methods of conducting warfare or most asymmetrical uses of force, such as terrorist attacks, computer hacking, or hostage taking.

Jus ad bellum also contained prudential tests, ones that have applicability when self-defense under the terms of the U.N. Charter is contemplated. Those tests were that the use of force would result in a preponderance of good over evil, that force would be used only as a last resort, that there would be a reasonable chance of success, and that peace be the expected outcome.

The first prudential test, the preponderance of good over evil, is also called the "proportionality of ends" test. It argues that the good ends served must not be outweighed by the harm caused by the application of force. In the Gulf War, for example, in applying this test, "Some targets were specifically avoided because the value of destruction of each target was outweighed by the potential risk to nearby civilians or, as in the case of certain archaeological and religious sites, to civilian objects."[10] It is clear that this test is one that military commanders ponder continually when they use force.[11]

Directed against unnecessary suffering or superfluous injury, and based on Protocol I Additional to the Geneva Conventions of 1949, the principle of proportionality has a more tightly focused meaning than might be expected. The proportionality rule prohibits attacks that "may be expected to cause incidental loss of civilian life, injury to civilians, damage to civilian objects, or a combination thereof, which would be excessive in relation to the concrete and direct military advantage anticipated."[12] Given this definition, if Saddam Hussein had attacked the coalition forces in the Gulf War with chemical weapons, it would have likely been deemed disproportionate to have responded with a nuclear weapon. But, viewed on a larger scale than the "direct military advantage anticipated," might a nuclear response have caused other owners of chemical weapons to reevaluate their need for them? What if, given the U.S. nuclear response to a chemical attack, many—or even all—others who possessed chemical weapons decided that they were not worth having? If, on a scale larger than the "direct military advantage anticipated," the prospects for the future employment of chemical weapons were substantially reduced, or perhaps even eliminated, might that provide a strong challenge to the narrow view of proportionality? On a less majestic scale, if the use of nuclear weapons by the United States had caused Saddam Hussein to sue immediately for peace, to quit Kuwait, and to come to terms, should that necessarily have been deemed "disproportionate"?[13]

The "last resort," or *ultima ratio,* test suggests that all other means to resolve the issue must be judged as ineffective before force can be used. Contrary to contemporary belief, there is no requirement to try other means first: diplomacy or trade policy, for example. Moreover, the test is one that is answered by logical, not by chronological ordering. Force might in fact be the first means employed by one who is convinced that no other method has a chance of being effective, and that time is of the essence. This is an important distinction: "last resort" does not equate to the exhaustion of all other means first. It implies that all others have been considered and rejected for good and sufficient reason. Nevertheless, this distinction goes unappreciated fully—or is ignored—by those who argue that last resort means that all other means must be exhausted first.

The third test is that the undertaking must have a reasonable prospect of success. This would appear to mean that there should be no gambling and no high risks assumed, and, if defeat looks certain, the correct choice would be to surrender. The requirement is not so stringent, however. In some cases, one has few options and is obliged to fight even against long odds. Yet the constraint is tangible: "The reasonable likelihood of success is a sine qua non of *jus ad bellum.* Human life is not to be hazarded lightly."[14]

The final test advises that, among a large agenda of potential ends, peace must be the one sought. Once again, there is latitude for interpretation here, beginning with the definition of the word "peace." Still it is a test and a goal of *jus ad bellum.*

In summary, considerations of the initial use of force are fundamentally constrained by the U.N. Charter and, at a greater level of specificity, by the four prudential tests. States that care deeply about international order will regulate their behavior to conform to these constraints, or at a minimum, seek to justify their behavior within their terms. Actors that have less of a stake in international order or justice will not be so constrained, will feel less need for justification, and might just view these constraints as points of weakness to be taken advantage of with asymmetrical acts.

JUS IN BELLO

Once war has begun, whether or not it is being waged in accordance with the tests of *jus ad bellum,* its conduct comes under the provisions of *jus in bello.* War, under this doctrine, cannot be waged indiscriminately or disproportionately. Those are the two principles governing *jus in bello.*[15]

Discrimination in war means that noncombatants cannot be attacked directly and deliberately. Because this is the case, a corollary would imply that military targets must not be located near obvious civilian and humanitarian structures—hospitals, historical monuments, and the like. Such measures as economic blockades, under this rubric, tend to be controversial.[16] If belligerents do not discriminate among combatants and noncombatants, they would seem to be in violation of the principle of discrimination. This and other humanitarian considerations explain why the economic sanctions imposed on Iraq by the United Nations in August of 1990 exempted medical supplies and certain foodstuffs.

If civilians cannot be deliberately attacked, how can one account for the large number of civilian casualties in Germany and Japan in the Second World War? Jointly with its European allies, the United States killed over 300,000 German civilians and, independently, a like number of Japanese civilians. Don't these constitute violations of the proscription on attacking civilians? Insofar as they resulted from targeting noncombatants, they clearly do.[17]

In fact, during this century, the proportion of civilian casualties imposed by armed conflict has increased from 1.5 percent in World War I to 90 percent in the 1980s.[18] However, the number of noncombatant deaths in wartime pales in comparison to the staggering totals of citizens who have been murdered by their own governments.

Perhaps 35 million people, of whom 25 million were civilians, have died as a direct consequence of military operations since 1900. . . . During the same period, however, at least 100 million human beings have been killed by police forces or their equivalent, almost never using heavy weapons but relying on hunger, exposure, barbed wire, and forced labor to kill the bulk, executing the rest by shooting them with small arms, by rolling over them with trucks (a favorite technique in China around 1950), by gassing them, or, as in the Cambodian holocaust of 1975–79, by smashing their skulls with wooden clubs.[19]

In time of war, however, the only justification that can condone attacks that jeopardize noncombatants is covered by the principle of "military necessity," which permits belligerents to apply force as required to achieve legitimate military objectives. Peacetime wanton killing can claim no such justification.

Nevertheless, "the effort, central to the laws of war to discriminate between the soldier and the civilian is full of moral ambiguity as well as practical difficulty."[20] Indeed, this is merely another case in which choices must be made and decisions taken based on incomplete—sometimes even false—information, and the consequences will be hotly debated, whichever way they turn out.

The principle of military necessity states that "only that degree and kind of force, not otherwise prohibited by the law of armed conflict, required for the partial or complete submission of the enemy with a minimum expenditure of time, life, and physical resources may be applied."[21] Rather than a justification for the use of force where it might otherwise be proscribed, *The Commander's Handbook on the Law of Naval Operations* describes this as a "*restraint* designed to limit the application of force in armed conflict to that which is in fact required to carry out a lawful military purpose."[22] The concept of military necessity, however, like so many others in the legal field, is open to subjective judgment and debate. One man's military necessity might be viewed as another's brutal crime.

If noncombatants cannot be deliberately attacked, what about mutual assured destruction, the doctrine of the superpowers during the Cold War, under which they held each other's civilian population hostage against aggression? Adam Roberts lends some insight:

Threatening the use of weapons or methods of warfare that would violate the traditional laws of war was seen as justified *if such threats prevented war altogether.* In particular, threats against cities or against centers of government, though they might be doubtful in laws-of-war terms, were perceived as offering a better basis for strategic stability than counter-force threats, with their notorious effects on strategic stability whether in peacetime or during crises.[23]

But the matter does not end there. Some believe that regardless of the ends (no war) the means (threatening megadeaths of civilians) were still immoral. Paul Ramsey argues in this regard, "Whatever is wrong to do is wrong also to threaten, if the latter means 'mean to do.' If aiming indiscriminately in actual acts of war (or in fight-the-war policies) is wrong, so also is threatening indiscriminately aimed action wrong to adopt in deter-the-war policies. . . . To put the point bluntly, if counter-population warfare is murder, then counter-population deterrent threats are murderous."[24] Yet Robert Pape counters by claiming that nuclear coercion relies on threats to noncombatants: "The threat to civilians implied by any use of nuclear weapons is likely to overwhelm their military impact. Accordingly, successful nuclear coercion rests on threats to civilians rather than against military vulnerabilities."[25]

The Vietnam War taught the United States that determining who was a civilian—and, accordingly, entitled to protection—and who was a combatant was not a simple matter. Deception operations by an adversary might also put noncombatants at risk. As James Turner Johnson notes, "This is the problem posed by Mao's dictum that guerillas should live among the populace like fish in the sea, and it is the problem posed by the PLO's habit of basing itself in the midst of civilian settlements."[26] But, deception is not invariably acceptable. There are perfidious means of deception that are patently impermissible, such as the improper use of a white flag of truce. Thus, Professor Johnson continues: "I believe that all these cases involve impermissible deception, and while there may be other variations of this practice, its distinguishing characteristic remains the obscuring of conditions that impose moral restraints on the use of force. Other forms of deception that do not undermine these restraints are permissible."[27]

Discriminating among combatants and noncombatants, never easy, is becoming more and more difficult over time.[28] Information warfare and space warfare are two new realms in which distinguishing between legitimate and illegitimate targets is increasingly difficult. The limiting case of determining who are and who are not combatants resides with terrorism. It lends a fine point to the question of the ends being insufficient to justify the means, for terrorism pivots on indiscriminate, unlawful targeting of innocents in order to influence the policies of others. Western legal tradition totally rules out terrorism, arguing that "if the only means at his disposal are the intentional harming of innocents . . . he must not fight."[29]

Discrimination means also that collateral damage must be avoided to the extent possible in the conduct of military operations. This also is not as simple as it might seem:

In each case, the extent of danger to the civilian population varies. It varies with the type of military objective attacked, the type of terrain, the type of weapons used, the kind of weather, and whether civilians are nearby. It also depends on the combatant's ability and mastery of bombardment techniques, the level of the conflict, and the type of resistance encountered during the attack.[30]

Disagreements rage on this issue every time military actions take place. In the Kosovo bombing, for example, "After a six-month investigation, including three weeks interviewing witnesses in Kosovo, the Human Rights Watch team determined that one-third of the number of lethal episodes and half the casualties could have been avoided if NATO nation forces had strictly followed the rules."[31] Yet "in practice, only 20 of the approximately 23,000 munitions expended by NATO in the 1999 Balkan air operations caused collateral damage or civilian casualties."[32] The subject of collateral damage is a vexing one; it can be determined neither unilaterally nor straightforwardly.

Proportionality as a principle of *jus in bello* argues that the costs of using force be warranted by the benefits obtained. It cautions against gratuitous or otherwise unnecessary harm and champions a minimum expenditure of time and assets to achieve one's objectives. Like discrimination, it requires some interpretation.

Proportionality does not imply "tit-for-tat." To respond to a single attack with three is not necessarily disproportionate. A proportionate attack might be described as what it takes to do the job, and no more. Proportionality does not require, even though it implies, balance or equality. The more unequal the response, either in the means used or in the intensity, however, the more difficult proportionality is either to determine or to assess. The U.S. air campaign in the Gulf War, for example, was labeled "illegally disproportionate," by at least one observer.[33]

On the face of it, the principle of proportionality seems to violate sound military practice. That is, should not the military commander prefer to win 25-0 rather than 14-12? Must one necessarily assume risks and casualties in order to comply with the requirements of proportionality? How great must those risks and casualties be? Yet, just as one would not employ a nuclear response to a minor conventional attack or destroy the entire adversary air force for a single attack on a warship, there are boundaries of proportionality, even if they tend to exist only in the eye of the beholder.

Another difficulty with proportionality arises from deterrence doctrine. Deterrence is said to work because a prospective aggressor calculates that his gains would not be worth the costs incurred. Does this not imply that the response he is encouraged to anticipate, the one that deters his acts, will be disproportionate? Logically, would not a credible disproportionate threat deter more reliably than a proportionate one? On the side of the deterrer, does it not encourage the issuance of disproportionate threats? One is reminded of Paul Ramsey's assertion quoted earlier: "Whatever is wrong to do is wrong also to threaten, if the latter means 'mean to do.'"[34] But is not the essential ingredient of deterrence the credibility factor—the "mean to do"?[35] All such questions must remain open, but all exert their asymmetrical constraints on the use of force.

LAW OF ARMED CONFLICT

The philosophical restraints of *jus ad bellum* and *jus in bello* have been codified and made more specific through a series of international agreements. With regard to the subject at hand, the use of force, the following are the most pertinent:

- 1907 Hague Convention[36]

  IV: Respecting the Laws and Customs of War on Land

  V: Respecting the Rights and Duties of Neutral Powers and Persons in Case of War on Land

  IX: Concerning Bombardment by Naval Forces in Time of War

- 1948 Convention on the Prevention and Punishment of the Crime of Genocide

- 1949 Geneva Conventions

- 1954 Hague Convention for the Protection of Cultural Property in the Event of Armed Conflict (the United States is not a party and is not bound)

International agreements such as these serve to make explicit the general arguments set forth earlier about the use of force. The Geneva Conventions alone contain over 400 detailed articles. The Annex to Hague IV, Article 25, for example, holds that "the attack or bombardment, by whatever means of towns, villages, dwellings, or buildings which are undefended is prohibited." This is clearly in keeping with the idea of protecting noncombatants and ensuring that unnecessary suffering and wanton destruction of property are avoided. Under the guidelines of military necessity, military objectives within towns can be attacked, with assurances that collateral damage not be excessive. Likewise, there is a prohibition on bombardment for the purpose of terrorizing the civilian population.

Medical facilities are specifically exempted from bombardment, as are buildings devoted to religion and the arts and historic monuments. Moreover, dams and other man-made restraints to floodwaters are protected if the potential for harm to noncombatants would be proportionally excessive. Of course, the misuse of such places for military purposes relieves them of their protected status during the period of misuse. The Hague provisions also contain restrictions on the employment of naval mines.

In addition, there are restraints on assassination. Hague IV "is construed as prohibiting assassination, proscription or outlawry of an enemy, or putting a price on an enemy's head, as well as offering a reward for an enemy 'dead or alive.'"[37] As a matter of U.S. national policy, assassination is forbidden by Executive Order 12333, but it is said not to apply in time of war, the distinction being made between assassination and targeting a state's wartime leaders.[38]

In view of these constraints, the widespread coalition attacks on the Iraqi civilian infrastructure in the Gulf War were challenged:

Electrical supply; civil communications; oil supply, storage, and refining; transportation means; and general governmental activity throughout the country were bombed. . . . But while the choice of the classes of these targets may not be in dispute, the necessity for attacking them, in terms of achieving the specific objectives of this war, and given its postulated duration, remains unclear.[39]

In addition, there has been a recent effort to render unlawful *any* use of nuclear weapons. Before the International Court of Justice,

countries arguing for the ban offered evidence of the horrors that nuclear weapons inflict. They said such weapons must be declared illegal because they violate the law of warfare as well as a host of human rights and environmental treaties. Countries with nuclear arms replied that their weapons are not inherently illegal and that their use may be banned only through negotiation—as with the conventions prohibiting chemical and biological weapons—and not by judicial order.[40]

The Court delivered its advisory opinion at the request of the General Assembly of the United Nations. In that opinion (which is not binding, unlike the judgments delivered by the Court in its ordinary jurisdiction) the Court stated that "the threat or use of nuclear weapons would generally be contrary to the rules of international law applicable in armed conflict."[41] Yet the Court qualified its advice by admitting that it "cannot reach a definitive conclusion as to the legality or illegality of the use of nuclear weapons by a State in an extreme circumstance of self-defense, in which its very survival would be at stake."[42]

U.S. military forces are guided in their conduct regarding the use of force by rules of engagement (ROE). ROE are promulgated by commanders to their subordinates in order to establish a framework under which the use of force might be initiated or prolonged. ROE exist at the national level, disseminated by the U.S. National Command Authority, and at each command level down to the tactical level. They provide means of additional control on the military actions of subordinate levels of command. Commanders can use ROE to fine-tune the actions of their subordinates in order to confine conflict to certain levels, geographic areas, or targets. ROE are "consistent with the law of armed conflict. . . . [and] often restrict combat operations far more than do the requirements of international law."[43] The inherent right of self-defense is strongly emphasized in U.S. rules of engagement. It should be noted that in multinational situations, the ROEs of participating states might differ, and the differences might be very radical. The degree of respect accorded to the ROEs of others is a matter of command relationships and negotiations among the participating states and constitutes an organizational constraint on the use of force.

Still, any use of force tends to have a political base, whether it is conducted by the rules or not. In the Vietnam War, for example,

in those instances in which U.S. attacks inadvertently hit prohibited targets, North Vietnam won the propaganda battle. International and American public opinion turned against the U.S. military by alleging that illegal American air strikes caused the damage, notwithstanding the fact that American air combat operations intentionally attacked only legitimate targets under strict rules of engagement.[44]

Thus, even ROE tend to be politically—and legally—rather than operationally based.

Finally, the prospect of being held accountable for "war crimes" casts a pall over considerations of the use of force. "The Nuremberg trials," wrote Bradd Hayes, "did underscore that military commanders have few, if any, defenses for carrying out illegal acts. . . . The principle of holding military commanders responsible for implementing illegal orders has a long history in United States law."[45] Criminal responsibility for violations of the law of war rests with those who order offenses committed or who "knew or should have known of the offense(s), had the means to prevent or halt them, and failed to do all which he was capable of doing to prevent the offenses or their recurrence."[46] The defense of superior orders—"I was only following the orders of my superior"—has long been disallowed. So military personnel have an obligation not to follow illegal orders of superiors, and they are responsible both for knowledge of illegal acts and those they *should have known about*. In an age where modern weapons permit launching an attack from a room in an air-conditioned building—or a ship or aircraft—thousands of miles away from its target, without seeing, or in any other way sensing, the target, these standards constitute a significant depressant to the legitimate use of force—one that will exert greater and greater leverage over time. Ultimately, they appear either to require long-range weaponeers not to launch their weapons in the absence of full knowledge of their targets; or, alternatively, these standards will be totally ignored and ineffective. Ignored and ineffective except, of course, when the victors impose them at the postwar war crime trials. It goes without saying that those who undertake asymmetrical acts of violence will be unaffected by such niceties.

ARMS CONTROL

Provisions in international law for the purpose of regulating conduct constitute one approach to controlling the use of armed force. Another is to impose direct constraints on the weapons and weapon systems themselves. Organized efforts to take weapons out of the hands of people in order to control their use extend back at least as far as the denunciation by the Church of the "homicidal and heinous use of catapults" in 1139.[47] The Hague Conferences of 1899 and 1907 represented the first formal multinational attempt to outlaw certain kinds of weapons.

Until 1987, it could be cogently argued that arms control had never succeeded in more than formalizing and sanctifying the status quo. Arms control agreements merely ratified or extended the current state of affairs: the Outer Space Treaty of 1967 (Treaty on Principles Governing the Activities of States in the Exploration and Use of Outer Space, including the Moon and Other Celestial Bodies), or the Limited Test Ban of 1963 (Treaty Banning Nuclear Weapon Tests in the Atmosphere, in Outer Space and under Water), for example.

Or they gave legal voice to what states had no intention of doing anyway:

- The Seabeds Treaty of 1971 (Treaty on the Prohibition of the Emplacement of Nuclear Weapons and Other Weapons of Mass Destruction on the Sea-Bed and the Ocean Floor and in the Subsoil Thereof)

- 1972 Bacteriological Weapons Convention (Convention on the Prohibition of the Development, Production, and Stockpiling of Bacteriological [Biological] and Toxin Weapons and on Their Destruction)

The year 1987 marked a watershed because, in this year, the Intermediate Nuclear Forces (INF) Treaty (Treaty between the United States and the Soviet Union on the Elimination of Their Intermediate-Range and Shorter-Range Missiles) accomplished what others had been unable to do: to alter the status quo, and to effect actual negotiated reductions in weapon systems.

Among its many goals, arms control has sought to reduce the risk of war, constrain arms competition (called "arms races" by the champions of arms control),[48] reduce unnecessary suffering, and depress the effects of military spending. It includes quantitative and qualitative measures, geographic controls, communications and administrative pacts, and confidence-building measures—often in combination. From the Declaration Respecting Expanding Bullets (known as the "Dum Dum Declaration") by the Hague Convention of 1899, through the so-called "Inhumane Weapons Convention" (Convention on Prohibitions or Restrictions on the Use of Certain Conventional Weapons Which May be Deemed to be Excessively Injurious or to Have Indiscriminate Effects [1981]) to the Chemical Weapons Convention, effective in 1997, arms control has sought in a myriad of ways to restrain the use of force. Most recently, land mines, laser weapons, child soldiers, and even small arms have been the focus of attention of arms control.

Although great amounts of energy have been devoted to the pursuit of arms control, its effects have been mixed. According to Louis Halle, in words penned before the watershed INF Treaty was concluded, but not without force and pertinence:

In no other organized endeavor of the nations of mankind has so much work been expended to so little effect as in the efforts to achieve arms control. We must suppose that there has been something fundamentally wrong at the conceptual level to account for so consistent a failure on so large a scale over so long a period.[49]

In the United States, formal arms control is undertaken as executive agreements or treaties. The Congress, through the Arms Control and Disarmament Act of 1961, has ensured that the president cannot independently pursue arms control. That act prohibits the president from taking action under any law to "obligate the United States to disarm or to reduce or to limit the . . . armaments of the United States except pursuant to the treaty making power of the President under the Constitution or unless authorized by further affirmative legislation by the Congress of the United States."[50]

In addition to the formal, positive constraints of arms control agreements, the United States has agreed to "negative security assurances." These arise in cases where the United States seeks arms control agreements from others, and assures them of its good intentions in order to secure their assent. With regard to the Nonproliferation Treaty, for example, the United States has pledged not to "use nuclear weapons against any non-nuclear-weapon State party to the Non-Proliferation Treaty or any comparable internationally binding commitment not to acquire nuclear explosive devices, except in the case of an attack on the United States, its territories or armed forces, or its allies."[51]

This is not the place to detail all the constraints that arms control has placed on the use of force.[52] For the decisionmaker or the war fighter, these constraints have the overall effect of removing options from the board. For potential adversaries, the constraints offer opportunities to their asymmetrical advantage. If, for example, there are no chemical weapons in the arsenal because they have been proscribed by prior agreement on arms control, then the option of retaliating against the use of chemical weapons in kind has been removed from the list of possible responses. Perhaps as important, they are not available to deter the use of chemicals. Other options, perforce, must be considered. Thus, when a prospective user of chemical weapons against a state that has none calculates the possible responses, it can rule out a response in kind, and try to determine the prospects of a stronger or a weaker response, and whether those prospects are tolerable. The credibility of a stronger deterrent response is thus brought under intense pressure, raising questions of necessity and proportionality to new heights.

The number and variety of constraints imposed on the use of military force by legal and arms control strictures are impressive. They affect not only the conduct of armed conflict, but training, organizing, and equipping for it as well. For the most part, they are additional to organizational and operational constraints, further increasing the overall burden on decisionmakers and war fighters. Moreover, it must be acknowledged that legal and arms control constraints affect only those who abide by them. To the extent that actors (states, groups, or individuals) proceed in disregard of legal and arms control norms, they are acting asymmetrically.

NOTES

1. Lori Fisler Damrosch and David J. Scheffer, eds., *Law and Force in the New International Order* (Boulder, Colo.: Westview Press, 1991), 20.

2. Department of the Navy, Office of the Chief of Naval Operations, *The Commander's Handbook on the Law of Naval Operations* NWP 1-14M, 5-2. Emphasis added.

3. Ibid., 5-3.

4. "The U.S. military has carried out legal reviews on its weapons systems since 1974, after many of the weapons it used in Vietnam were challenged under international law. . . . The United States is a leader in reviewing its *own* systems for compliance with international law. Although there is an international treaty signed by 155 nations calling for internal legal review, only about a dozen nations actually perform them." David Atkinson, "New Weapons Technologies Offer Complex Issues for Review," *Defense Daily* (September 1, 1999): 2.

5. U.S. Department of Defence Directive 5100.77, July 10, 1979.

6. Michael N. Schmitt, "The Resort to Force in International Law: Reflections on Positivist and Contextual Approaches," *Air Force Law Review* 37 (1994): 113–114. This excellent article contains an extended review of the issues.

7. G.I.A.D. Draper, "Wars of National Liberation and War Criminality," in *Restraints on War: Studies in the Limitation of Armed Conflict,* ed. Michael Howard (Oxford: Oxford University Press, 1979), 137.

8. "Nothing in the present Charter shall impair the inherent right of individual or collective self-defense if an

armed attack occurs against a Member of the United Nations, until the Security Council has taken measures necessary to maintain international peace and security." U.N. Charter, Article 51.

9. "Nothing contained in the present Charter shall authorize the United Nations to intervene in matters which are essentially within the domestic jurisdiction of any state or shall require the Members to submit such matters to settlement under the present Charter; but this principle shall not prejudice the application of enforcement measures under Chapter VII." U.N. Charter, Article 2(7).

10. U.S. Department of Defense, *Conduct of the Persian Gulf War: Final Report to Congress,* April 1992, O-10.

11. As another example: "According to a classified report now being prepared by the Air Force, not only did the air campaign conducted against Serbian emplacements in Bosnia last year destroy approximately 60 percent of the targets identified—about a 10 percent improvement over the Desert Storm campaign—it did so with no collateral damage." "NATO Air Forces Inflicted No Collateral Damage in Bosnian Air Campaign," *Inside the Air Force* (July 19, 1996), 1.

12. *Protocol Additional to the Geneva Conventions of 12 August 1949, and Relating to the Protection of Victims of International Armed Conflicts* (Protocol I), Article 57, Para. 2(a)(iii).

13. The report of the Persian Gulf War contains a passage that veers away from this "direct military advantage" test. It states, "It [proportionality] prohibits military action in which the negative effects (such as collateral civilian casualties) clearly outweigh the military gain. This balancing may be done on a target-by-target basis, as frequently was the case during Operation Desert Storm, but also may be weighed in overall terms against campaign objectives." U.S. Department of Defense, *Conduct of the Persian Gulf War,* O-10.

14. Paul Seabury and Angelo Codevilla, *War: Ends and Means* (New York: Basic Books, 1989), 220.

15. They are characterized slightly differently in the "General Principles of the Law of Armed Conflict" contained in the *Commander's Handbook on the Law of Naval Operations,* to wit:

1. Only that degree and kind of force, not otherwise prohibited by the law of armed conflict, required for the partial or complete submission of the enemy with a minimum expenditure of time, life, and physical resources may be applied. 2. The employment of any kind or degree of force not required for the purpose of the partial or complete submission of the enemy with a minimum expenditure of time, life, and physical resources, is prohibited. 3. Dishonorable (treacherous) means, dishonorable expedients, and dishonorable conduct during armed conflict are forbidden.

NWP 1-14M, 5-4 to 5-6.

16. See, for example, the discussion in *NWP* 1-14M, 8-4, footnote 15.

17. At the time, these attacks were justified as reprisals. Such attacks are now prohibited under Geneva Additional Protocol I (1977) Article 51 (6).

18. Robert O. Muller, "Introduction," in Eric Prokosch, *The Technology of Killing: A Military and Political*

History of Antipersonnel Weapons (London: Zed Books, 1995), ix.

19. Seabury and Codevilla, *War,* 6-7. See also Rudolph J. Rummel, *Death by Government* (New Brunswick, N.J.: Transaction Publishers, 1994).

20. Adam Roberts, "International Law and the Use of Force: Paper I," in *New Dimensions in International Security, Part II,* Adelphi Papers (London: Brassey's, Winter 1991–1992), 266: 63.

21. NWP 1-14M, 6-6.

22. Ibid. (emphasis in the original).

23. Roberts, "International Law," 55. Emphasis added.

24. Paul Ramsey, "A Political Ethics Context for Strategic Thinking," in *Strategic Thinking and Its Moral Implications,* ed. Morton A. Kaplan (Chicago: University of Chicago Center for Policy Study, 1973), 134–135.

25. Robert A. Pape, *Bombing to Win: Air Power and Coercion in War* (Ithaca, N.Y.: Cornell University Press, 1996), 10–11.

26. James Turner Johnson, "Just War Tradition and Low-Intensity Conflict," in *International Law Studies 1995: Legal and Moral Constraints on Low-Intensity Conflict,* ed. Alberto R. Coll, James S. Ord, and Stephen A. Rose (Newport, R.I.: Naval War College, 1995), 67: 167.

27. Ibid.

28. Colonel Charles J. Dunlap, Jr., has published a provocative article that opens challenges to the traditional considerations regarding noncombatants. See his "The End of Innocence: Rethinking Noncombatancy in the Post-Kosovo Era," *Strategic Review* 28 (Summer 2000): 9–17.

29. Seabury and Codevilla, *War,* 229.

30. U.S. Department of the Air Force, *An Introduction to Air Force Targeting,* AFP 200-17 (June 23, 1989), 37.

31. Elizabeth Becker, "Rights Group Says NATO Killed 500 Civilians in Kosovo War," *New York Times* (February 7, 2000): A10.

32. John A. Tirpak, "The State of Precision Engagement," *Air Force Magazine* 83 (March 2000): 24–25.

33. See Bruce Ross, "The Case for Targeting Leadership in War," *Naval War College Review* 46 (Winter 1993): 83.

34. Ramsey, "Political Ethics," 134–135.

35. In the seminal work on nuclear calculus, Herman Kahn posited: "If we want to have our strategic forces contribute to the deterrence of provocation, it must be credible. . . . Usually the most convincing way to look willing is to be willing." *On Thermonuclear War* (Princeton, N.J.: Princeton University Press, 1960), 287.

36. Hague III, Relative to the Opening of Hostilities, was rendered moot by the U.N. Charter.

37. Ross, "Case for Targeting Leadership," 80.

38. Ibid., 82.

39. William M. Arkin, Damian Durrant, and Marianne Cherni, *On Impact: Modern Warfare and the Environment. A Case Study of the Gulf War* (London: Greenpeace, 1991), 74.

40. Stephen Kinzer, "Word for Word/Anti-Nuclear Reaction; Refusing to Learn to Love the Bomb: Nations Take Their Case to Court," *New York Times* (January 14, 1996) (Lexis-Nexis, April 15, 1997).

41. Jennifer Scott, "World Court Says Nuclear Arms Illegal in War, But . . . ," *Reuters* (July 8, 1996) (Lexis-Nexis, April 15, 1997).

42. International Court of Justice, Legality of the Threat or Use of Nuclear Weapons, Advisory Opinion, July 8, 1996, Paragraph 96, www.peacenet.org.disarm/icjtxt.html (April 13, 1997).

43. NWP 1-14M, 4-5.

44. John G. Humphries, "Operations Law and the Rules of Engagement," *Airpower Journal* 6 (Fall 1992): 34.

45. Bradd C. Hayes, *Toward a Doctrine of Constraint*, Strategic Research Department Strategic Memorandum 9-94 (Newport, R.I.: Naval War College, 1994), 15.

46. U.S. Department of Defence, *Conduct of the Persian Gulf War*, O-25.

47. Yves Sandoz, "Preface," in Prokosch, *Technology of Killing*, xiii.

48. The works of Grant Hammond and Albert Wohl-stetter are pertinent in this regard. See Grant T. Hammond, *Plowshares into Swords: Arms Races in International Politics, 1840–1991* (Columbia, S.C.: University of South Carolina Press, 1993), and Albert J. Wohlstetter, *Legends of the Strategic Arms Race* (Washington, D.C.: U.S. Strategic Institute, 1975).

49. Louis J. Halle, *The Elements of International Strategy: A Primer for the Nuclear Age* (Lanham, Md.: University Press of America, 1984), 10: 73.

50. 22 USC § 2573 (1964).

51. *The Arms Control Reporter* (Brookline, Mass.: Institute for Defense and Disarmament Studies, 1991), 860-4.2.

52. A compilation of arms control treaties can be found at www.state.gov/www/global/arms/bureau_ac/treaties_ac.html.

CHAPTER 5

DOMESTIC POLICY ACTORS
AND THEIR ROLES

"NO BAD STORIES":
THE AMERICAN MEDIA-MILITARY RELATIONSHIP

DOUGLAS PORCH

The 1999 air war over Kosovo reignited a feud between the military and the news media that is generally believed to have been a permanent undercurrent of media-military relations since the Vietnam War. The events of September 11 and the subsequent declaration by President George W. Bush of a war on terrorism temporarily drove the feud underground. But soon the media began, albeit tentatively, to second-guess Pentagon strategy in Afghanistan. Indeed, the general consensus among military people, the press, and academics is that a cooperative working relationship between the press and the military that had been established in World War II collapsed in the 1960s. Although these groups disagree significantly on whether media criticism of U.S. policy and strategy contributed to America's defeat in Southeast Asia, the view that Vietnam was a turning point in media-military relations is widespread. "The War in Southeast Asia changed the fundamental contours of military-media relations," write a sociologist and a Pentagon reporter. "As in World War II, a group of young correspondents—David Halberstam, Neil Sheehan, Malcome Browne, Peter Arnett and Charley Mohr—who arrived in Vietnam in the early 1960s, became famous for their reporting. Unlike World War II, however, these reporters incurred the wrath of the official establishment for their contrary accounts of the war's progress."[1] Paradoxically, according to this view, media-military relations may have been better when censorship was in force, as in World War II.[2]

This essay will argue, however, that the strained relationship between the media and the U.S. military has nothing to do with censorship—for the simple reason that media-military relations have always been rocky, never more so than in World War II. The difference between World War II and Vietnam was not the presence of censorship but the absence of victory. In other conflicts, victory has erased memories of a troubled relationship; after Vietnam, the media was caught up in the quest for a scapegoat. Furthermore, the nebulous goals of the war on terrorism, the fact that it is likely to be a prolonged operation, and the inherent difficulties from a media perspective of covering a war fought from the air and in the shadows

virtually guarantee a degeneration of the relationship between two institutions with an inherent distrust of each other.

How then do we account for chronically poor media-military relations in America? The basic explanation is that the natures and goals of the two institutions are fundamentally in tension. For its part, the military, like most bureaucracies, prefers to do its business behind closed doors—all the more so because the nature of its business is so often shocking to the sensitivities of the public, on whose support it must rely. Therefore, the military inherently sees the media as a subversive, rather than a positive, element. The press, however, responds to the requirement of democracy to expose the actions of the government—including, especially, the military—to public scrutiny. Moreover, in recent years, the tendency to formulate U.S. foreign policy with little or no formal debate between the administration and the Congress has left a vacuum that the media has rushed to fill. Even were that not the case, however, the press has a responsibility to question the matching of policy to strategy.

Theoretically, this interaction of the press and military is mutually beneficial, for it could allow the two institutions to work symbiotically to build support for policy and to tell the military's story. Nevertheless, there is a shadow over media-military relations, which the legacy of the Vietnam War has darkened.

Finally, future trends are likely to make media-military relations more, rather than less, difficult. An increase in humanitarian operations, the reliance on air campaigns and stand-off weapons, the difficulties of covering a "terrorist war," the emergence of "information operations," and changes in the media environment pose severe challenges. Nevertheless, the two institutions must recognize that it is in the interests of both to make the relationship work.

FROM THE AMERICAN REVOLUTION TO VIETNAM

Poor media-military relations are in reality symptomatic of a deeper issue for civil-military relations in the United States. One of the sources of misunder-

Douglas Porch, "'No Bad Stories': The American Media-Military Relationship," Naval War College Review 55 (*Winter 2002*): 85–107. *Public domain.*

standings between the media and the military is the widely held perception among conservatives, both inside and outside the military, that the press was largely responsible for America's defeat in the Vietnam War. This "subversion" is held to have been a new departure in media-military relations, perpetrated by a new generation of skeptical "liberal" reporters, different from their predecessors.

In fact, however, the relationship between the media and the military did not suddenly collapse during the Vietnam War. Animosity between the two is as old as the foundations of the Republic itself. During the Revolution, George Washington complained that loyalist newspapers undermined patriotic morale, whereas patriotic ones lacked the most elementary notions of military secrecy. Soon afterward, officers sent by President John Adams to impose taxes on Pennsylvania farmers publicly flogged newspaper editors who criticized their actions. In 1814, during the New Orleans campaign, Andrew Jackson jailed and attempted to court-martial a local editor who had dared to publish an article without submitting it for censorship. The Mexican War of 1846 was the first in which papers competed to publish stories sent back by the newly invented telegraph and the Pony Express. This produced a nineteenth-century "CNN effect"; political leaders as well as the general public learned of developments from press stories that arrived before the official reports. The Associated Press was founded in 1848 to pool reporting resources, disseminate correspondence from soldiers at the front, and communicate the government's war goals to the public. Also in that war, the military published "camp newspapers," an early public-affairs attempt to keep up troop morale. The civilian press used them as sources "from the seat of the war."

During the Civil War, Abraham Lincoln realized early on that newspapers would be a key component in sustaining support in a deeply split North. In April 1861, the government took control of telegraph lines leading to Washington and in August, threatened court-martial should any of the 500 Northern journalists covering the war breach security. The noncombatant status of the 150 or so correspondents who reported from the front was seldom respected. General William T. Sherman, a firm believer in press censorship, blamed the Union defeat in the first battle of Bull Run on the publication of orders of battle in Washington and New York newspapers. Secretary of War Edwin M. Stanton seized newspapers that were too liberal with military information, while manipulating others into publishing false reports. This did not prevent "Copperhead" papers in the North from vehemently attacking Lincoln and the war.

Neither is press-driven policy a recent phenomenon. The "yellow journalism" promoted by rivals William Randolph Hearst and Joseph Pulitzer is often blamed for provoking the popular agitation that led to the Spanish-American War of 1898. Major General Nelson A. Miles replicated Stanton's manipulation of the press, deliberately misleading reporters about the location of his intended landing in Puerto Rico. The Espionage Act, which accompanied America's entry into World War I, followed by the Sedition Act of 1918, severely restricted the ability of the press to publish information on military operations or war production, let alone disparage the uniform and the flag. Woodrow Wilson established a Committee on Public Information that both regulated censorship and produced propaganda for the American cause. Credentialed war correspondents, sworn to tell the truth, reported from military camps well behind the lines in France. General John Pershing, commanding the American Expeditionary Force, accredited only thirty-one reporters and forbade even these to travel to the front lines.[3] Fear of a "stab in the back" lurked behind these measures; censorship was justified by the need "to keep up the spirit of the armies and people of our side."[4]

WORLD WAR II AND KOREA

World War II is often viewed as the golden age of media-military relations—a time when the country stood fully behind the war effort and the press reflected the patriotic mood. Civilian reporters were treated as part of "America's team," willingly acquiescing to press codes as a condition of accreditation by the War Department. The identities and movements of forces and material, production figures, casualties, and locations of archives and art treasures were forbidden to reporters; even weather forecasts and temperatures in major cities were censored. But the press accepted censorship with barely a murmur, and the reward for compliance was substantial—relatively free access to combat theaters.

Wearing the uniforms of officers, journalists joined press camps attached to and moving with combat forces. Print journalists, more or less embedded in units, wrote, often poignantly, of the horrors of battle and the suffering of the GIs. Twenty-seven reporters accompanied the D-Day assault in Normandy. The precursor of the modern press pool emerged among radio correspondents, serving as a "neutral voice" representative of all correspondents. Some servicemen who had been journalists before the war were made combat correspondents after basic training; their stories and photographs were released, after censorship, by the various service departments. Overall, the Office of War Information and the Office of Censorship exercised their control through persuasion, although the Espionage Act always lurked menacingly in the background.

Both pools and embedded reporters foreshadowed recent practice; many broader patterns now thought of as contemporary also emerged in World War II. In the first place, the press sometimes shaped policy and influenced strategy. For instance, descriptions of valiant Britain beneath the German blitz in the summer of 1940 helped to firm up the destroyers-for-bases arrangement and, ultimately, Lend-Lease. "Press and radio commentators were uniformly hostile, some passionately so," to the agreement General

Mark Clark struck in November 1942 with Vichy admiral Jean Darlan to halt the fighting between Vichy French and Allied troops in North Africa. "I have been called a Fascist and almost a Hitlerite," General Dwight Eisenhower, Clark's superior, complained.[5] Press criticism of the Darlan deal propelled the "unconditional surrender" policy adopted by the Casablanca Conference in January 1943. *Newsweek* continually pointed up the disparity between American goals in Europe and the resources available, as well as differences among the Allies over the future of Europe, reviving the arguments of congressional isolationists.[6]

The press also, as now, heavily influenced the fortunes of prominent commanders; even the most popular generals could be second-guessed. Drew Pearson was prepared to deflate the most exalted reputations in his syndicated column, "Washington Merry-Go-Round." In the opinion of Eisenhower's son John, the press came perilously close to ending Ike's career.[7] His decision in September 1943 to maintain Marshal Pietro Badoglio, one of Mussolini's ex-henchmen, and King Victor Emanuel in power in Italy was denounced by the *New York Times* as the continuation of military dictatorship supported by a puppet king.[8] After the Normandy breakout in August 1944, *Newsweek* allowed retired British general J. F. C. Fuller to criticize Ike for violating the principle of "concentration of force." Even in making Eisenhower its "Man of the Year" in December 1944, *Time* cautioned that Hitler's Ardennes offensive cast doubt on the Supreme Allied Commander's strategic judgement.[9]

It is often forgotten that some officers who received favorable press coverage assiduously cultivated reporters. "Without preaching or complaining, [Eisenhower] told [correspondents] frankly about what was going wrong, and made it possible for them to see the problems with their own eyes. He then counted on them to make the country aware of what was needed."[10] One correspondent who had expected to find Eisenhower "jumping all over the place issuing orders right and left" instead discovered a man "more like a big industrial executive who, on the day the plant is breaking production records, will show visitors around the mill as if he had nothing else to do."[11] In contrast, commanders whom reporters thought inadequately prepared were particular targets. The press, for instance, alerted the American public to shortcomings revealed by the Louisiana Maneuvers of August–September 1941.

Further, "investigative journalists" sought out opportunities to roast aloof or abusive commanders, like George S. Patton—who slapped and cursed soldiers hospitalized for shell shock. A "gentlemen's agreement" initially suppressed that incident, but in an egregious departure from journalistic ethics, war correspondents demanded that Eisenhower remove Patton, under threat of going public. When Eisenhower tried to compromise, Drew Pearson broke the story on his syndicated radio show. The subsequent public tempest was so violent that Secretary of War

Henry L. Stimson had to justify to the Senate Eisenhower's decision not to court-martial Patton. That incident, and others like it, demonstrated the high price political leaders had to pay to defend generals who offended norms of democratic behavior.[12]

In the Pacific, General Douglas MacArthur was notorious for pressuring reporters to file stories that reflected positively on him. However, he could not control reporters not accredited to his command. In January 1944, the *American Mercury* suggested that MacArthur's heroic image was a Republican-manufactured myth to use against Roosevelt. The Army War College library distributed the article to American servicemen all over the world; Republicans in the Senate blasted the War Department for carrying out a "smear." A blistered War Department subsequently prevented *Harper's Magazine* from publishing a second unflattering article; its editor objected, "This situation is intolerable in a free country." In the summer of 1944, the press publicized the fact that MacArthur was the only senior general allowed to have his wife in theater. It also reported, unfairly, that he made his headquarters in luxurious colonial mansions while his troops battled malaria.[13]

The surprise attack that opened the Korean War in 1950 found the military completely unprepared to handle the reporters who arrived to cover the panic and confusion of the war's early days. This inevitably provoked criticism that an uncensored press was giving information of use to the enemy and undermining the morale of U.N. forces. Local commanders responded with their own rules; ultimately the Overseas Press Club petitioned the Pentagon to replace this patchwork of "voluntary guidelines" with formal, standard ones. MacArthur (now supreme commander of U.N. forces in Korea) imposed formal censorship, forbidding reporters to criticize, among other things, military reverses, failures of U.S. equipment, or the South Korean government;[14] true to form, MacArthur also banned all articles critical of his leadership.[15] His successor, Matthew Ridgway, virtually barred the press from the armistice talks.

THE VIETNAM WAR AND ITS LEGACIES

Vietnam has been called the "first TV war," a test of the American public's tolerance for battle brought into its living rooms. Journalists were allowed practically unrestricted access, accompanying units and freely filing stories, photographs, and film. The idea that reporters opposed to the war used this freedom to publish negative stories that contributed significantly to the final defeat quickly became standard; it was espoused by Presidents Lyndon Johnson and Richard Nixon, as well as by the U.S. commander in Vietnam from 1964 to 1968, General William Westmoreland.

This explanation, however, has been discredited by numerous studies.[16] In fact, press coverage was generally favorable until the Tet offensive of 1968. As later became clear, that dramatic campaign was a military disaster for the North Vietnamese and Viet Cong; nonetheless, it blasted the credibility of claims by the White House and Westmoreland that the United States and South Vietnam were on the threshold of victory. The critical tone adopted by the press thereafter "confirm[ed] the widespread public view held well before Tet, that the people had been victims of a massive deception" and that the prospects for success were in fact doubtful.[17] Arguably, then, the press did not create public skepticism but simply reflected public concern about casualties and the lack of tangible progress. Certainly, neither the White House nor the military was honest with the press. Official briefings in Saigon—dismissed by the press as the "Five o'Clock Follies"—were remarkably uninformative, when not deceptive. However, coverage of the increasingly violent antiwar protests shored up support for the war, because it showed the peace movement in an unflattering light.

One cannot blame the press for asking searching questions about a poor policy-strategy match. That is its duty. Nevertheless, the impact of the Vietnam War on U.S. media-military relations has been profound. The press today regards the practically unrestricted access and uncensored reporting that it enjoyed in Vietnam as the norm, not a historical anomaly. The more superficial, or arrogant, of its members further believe that Vietnam confirmed and validated the power of the press to influence public opinion and, by extension, policy.

The military, for its part, saw proof of its longstanding suspicion that the press is an adversary and must be kept at arm's length during conflicts.[18] The Army in particular feels that a new, and distinctly destructive, press was born in Vietnam—skeptical of authority, liberal in political outlook, and invariably hostile to military values and missions. The mistake of Vietnam, many military people feel, was to give the media free rein, license that they used to subvert popular support. A piece of "military wisdom" emerged from Vietnam: "Real men don't talk to the press."[19]

THE ROOTS OF POOR MEDIA-MILITARY RELATIONS

If the poor media-military relations of today are not wholly a product of the Vietnam War but have existed throughout the nation's history, how does one account for them? First, the institutional cultures of the two communities are virtually antithetical. Whether or not the media have a liberal bias, it is certainly true that journalists see it as their role to expose abuses of power by large institutions and in the military arena, to publicize instances where democratic and military values clash. As a practical matter, however, the press is fragmented into many competing and self-regulating subgroups; there are no broad professional standards. "The great strength of American journalism is its amateur nature," insists one correspondent. "Anyone can become a reporter. This guarantees many different perspectives."[20] It also guarantees that journalists have a great deal of competition; each must not only collect information but package it in a form that will sell to the general public

—and therefore be blessed by editors—before other journalists do. Reporters are therefore under great pressure to bend, even break, rules in pursuit of a story—and a by-line.

If the world of the journalist is freewheeling and entrepreneurial, the task of managing violence imposes on the soldier an organization and attitude that is hierarchical and disciplined. The soldier is a team player in an institution with strict professional and ethical standards as well as rigorous, even ritualized, procedures. "The natural tendency of the military [is] to keep things under control," an Army public affairs officer observes.[21] The military man or woman particularly values loyalty and is deeply suspicious of, even offended by, the "publish and be damned" journalistic ethos. Furthermore, if recruitment, outlook, and technology make the Fourth Estate a heterogeneous institution—if it is an institution at all—a number of factors, especially the fact that soldiers, sailors, marines, and airmen live apart from civilian society, tend to impose insularity upon them and to homogenize their attitudes. The political outlook of military people tends to be conservative.[22]

Second, the goals of the two institutions are different. The journalist seeks to tell a story of such interest that the public will pay for it; every member of the military, however, is to pursue national objectives by fulfilling specific missions assigned by political leaders. Moreover, the mechanism by which the military performs its role is war, or the threat of war—and war is an awful thing, a job the military is understandably reluctant to perform in public. Military people typically believe that reporters, untutored in the fundamentals of the military profession, are psychologically unprepared to deal with the realities of combat. They fear that reporters, in quests for sensationalism rather than truth, may publish stories or images that breach security, cost lives, or undermine public support. For their part, reporters insist upon their professional obligation and constitutional duty to report the news. They consider the military's culture closed, its insistence on operational secrecy exaggerated, and its command climate a barrier to outside scrutiny.

These two dichotomies are in themselves the raw material for deterioration of the media-military relationship, but a third factor, some journalists argue, aggravates it—the increasingly haphazard way U.S. foreign policy is formulated. All parties concerned recognize, at least in theory, that media scrutiny is an aspect of a healthy civilian control of the military and also an exercise of free speech—both cornerstones of the Constitution, which military people are sworn to uphold. In that light, media activism becomes especially necessary when military operations are undertaken after only minimal public debate among elected officials. Many journalists argue that Washington seems to assume a public grant of virtual consent for the employment of military force whenever the president chooses, what one reporter calls a "fire-and-forget foreign policy."[23] They hold that the media have a charge to step into this policy vacuum, to supply the information and provide the deliberation that officials and politicians withhold and shirk—and even to shape policy. In retrospect, it seems hardly surprising that good will crumbled (as we will see) during the Kosovo conflict and appeared to be on shaky ground during the early stages of the assault on Afghanistan. The real question is why such deterioration was a surprise at the time; it had been foreshadowed in every American military involvement since Vietnam, especially in the Persian Gulf.

ATTEMPTS TO ESTABLISH A WORKING RELATIONSHIP

Warfare is a political act. Political leaders, in democracies at least, must inform the public about foreign policy goals; the military must convince the public that it can achieve those goals at an acceptable cost; and both must do so largely through the press. Press reports of success and progress strengthen and extend public support. The media also familiarize the public with the military and the complexity of its tasks. In short, the media offers the military a means to tell its story. The press, as we have seen, has its own incentives to report on military affairs, and it needs the military's cooperation to do so effectively. Therefore, both the media and the military have reasons to work with the other in a symbiotic relationship.

For the military's part, the necessary first step is to recognize that the press is a fact of life, a feature of the battlefield environment—"kind of like the rain," as one Marine put it. "If it rains, you operate wet."[24] Unfortunately, past attempts to establish effective, let alone harmonious, arrangements have foundered on hostility and distrust bordering sometimes on paranoia.

Press Pools

In the 1980s, the media and the Pentagon agreed on ground rules for cooperation. Each major command was issued public-affairs guidance acknowledging the right of the public and Congress to timely and accurate information about military operations, to the extent compatible with security. It set out precise rules on the accreditation of reporters, standards for stories, security reviews, and the support of media in combat zones.

The plans were first tested in Urgent Fury, the 1983 operation that rescued U.S. medical students on the island of Grenada. Two serious flaws quickly emerged. First, rather than integrating media affairs in its planning, the command simply handed off the press to a specialized corps of public affairs officers. Because these officers were themselves kept in the dark, they were unable to satisfy the press's curiosity about military goals, preparations, and progress. The second problem grew from the first—the military was logistically unresponsive to press needs, largely because the media had not been factored into operational planning. As a consequence, over 600 disgruntled reporters were marooned in comfortable exile on Barbados while the story played out, unseen and hence unreported, on Grenada.[25]

The resulting media outcry prodded the military to review its practices.[26] A commission was convened under Major General Winant Sidle, U.S. Army, to reconcile press access with operational security. The Sidle Commission's major accomplishment was the Department of Defense National Media Pool, created in 1985. Journalists nominated by the major news organizations and agreeing in advance to abide by security regulations and to share reports with nonpool reporters would be ready to move to the seat of war at a moment's notice. The Media Pool would operate as a group only until the "main body" of reporters appeared. Practice deployments in Central America suggested that the pool was logistically manageable, would produce a core of reporters versed in military affairs, and would ensure prompt coverage of events.

The pool was first mobilized operationally during Earnest Will, the reflagging of Kuwaiti merchant ships in 1987–88; it encountered problems that would become acute in subsequent deployments. The next opportunity came in December 1989, when U.S. troops were ordered into Panama. Unfortunately, that experience showed that old attitudes had not yet died. Secretary of Defense Richard Cheney—who held the media responsible for undermining public morale in Vietnam and "did not look on the press as an asset"—delayed calling out the pool.[27] The result was that nonpool reporters simply traveled to Panama on their own, to practice "four-wheel-drive journalism"; when the press pool was finally mobilized, its members, all specially prepared for the job, were fobbed off with briefings and not allowed to cover the action.[28]

If Panama did little to foster trust between the media and the military, the war in the Persian Gulf lifted matters to a new plateau of acrimony. At the outset of Desert Shield, things looked generally promising. Cheney quickly activated the seventeen-member Media Pool—only to learn that King Fahd of Saudi Arabia refused to grant visas to reporters. Some journalists simply flew to Bahrain and crossed the border into Saudi Arabia illegally—the "unilaterals," prowling on the margins of the conflict, in constant fear of expulsion by the U.S. military or the Saudi police.[29] When CNN began to broadcast from Baghdad, however, Fahd was persuaded to lift his ban. The pool got its initial briefing 5 days after the first U.S. troops deployed in Saudi Arabia in early August. It remained in existence for 3 weeks, even as the forces in Saudi Arabia were being swamped by 1,600 other reporters. In response to this massive media interest in the first large-scale military deployment since Vietnam, the military organized new, ad hoc press pools; accredited reporters who agreed to abide by security regulations and who would be escorted in small groups to visit military positions and be briefed by unit commanders. Noncompetitive ground rules made photographs, notes, and stories available to reporters not in the pools; the military would transmit the stories back to parent news organizations, using a communications facility in Dhahran.

Despite appearances of success, however, the pool system as practiced in the Gulf War had several problems. The primary issue was what seemed to journalists to amount to censorship and manipulation, arising from tight restrictions on all media travel. Press veterans of Vietnam were rapidly disabused of the notion that they would be free to flit about the war zone, then return to Dhahran to file stories. In fact, most reporters never saw the war; only 186 reporters ever joined the news pools, less than 10 percent of the journalists enrolled by the Central Command's Joint Information Bureau.

Also, journalists rapidly concluded that logistical support for the pools was low in the military's priorities, and that this was intentional. Requests to visit units were frequently rejected because of lack of transport (when not declined for security concerns). The system was cumbersome and unresponsive to breaking news. The military did not file pool products expeditiously. The media tours were "too canned." Ultimately, chafing under restrictions, journalists charged that delays and press-shy officers reflected a command mandate that there were to be "no bad stories."[30] Worse, from the press viewpoint, "when the war happened, we couldn't see it."[31] Veteran reporter Walter Cronkite later insisted that "the Pentagon's censorship policy" in the Persian Gulf "severely restricted the right of reporters and photographers to accompany our troops into action, as had been permitted in all our previous wars."[32] Two Australian scholars concluded that "the campaign to liberate Kuwait was perhaps the most underreported and media-managed conflict in history."[33]

The U.S. Marines—who perhaps realize more than the other services the value of the press—welcomed journalists, but ironically, even this openness backfired. The media later claimed that it had been unwittingly co-opted into an elaborate deception designed to draw attention to the Marine amphibious force off the coast—a force that the joint commander in chief, General Norman Schwarzkopf, did not intend to employ—so as to distract the Iraqis from the true objectives. The press charged that General Schwarzkopf had deceived it in other ways as well. One was the false impression given that precision, laser-guided ordnance dominated the air campaign. Another was exaggeration of the success of Patriot missiles in intercepting Iraqi Scuds (although these claims had been made in good faith). To such complaints, the military simply replied that it could not have allowed the media to reveal the coalition's true plans—especially not the "left hook" through the desert of southern Iraq into Kuwait.[34]

If it strained media-military relations, the pool system also—by its emphasis on collective effort and shared products—divided the journalistic fraternity itself. Journalists are competitors by nature, not team players. "[Competition] is their livelihood. They don't like the other guy's take on a story. [A public affairs officer] cannot tell other reporters what each is working on. That's death!"[35] Unable to compete freely for stories, reporters in the Gulf and their employers sought ways to circumvent the rules. The larger press organizations plotted to exclude members of smaller or independent ones from pools or groups selected for particular visits; certain nontraditional media in the field, like women's magazines, fought to be included. Reporters jostled to lobby public affairs officers or generals for priority. Such infighting, combined with arbitrary selection procedures for pool trips, sometimes pushed aside reporters experienced in military matters in favor of novices.[36] A few journalists evaded pool restrictions by becoming "pet journalists," willing to report favorably on a general or unit in return for access to the front.

Ultimately, in the view of media cognoscenti, the Gulf War pool system produced a mediocre product. It seemed to these veteran reporters an undifferentiated pap, distilled from the collective observations of the few journalists allowed into the field, rather than the creative perceptions of individual reporters free to fashion stories out of the raw drama they observed. They thought the journalistic quality of pool stories "depressing. . . . [A]bout one in ten has anything in it that's useful. . . . It's really pretty superficial stuff."[37]

Pools, therefore, are not popular with the press, which sees them as attempts to limit access to—and thereby censor, even manipulate—information. The immediate postwar result was the issuance of new guidelines declaring, "Open and independent reporting will be the principal means of coverage of U.S. military operations."[38] The directive retains the option of censorship—a clause that the media decided not to protest, believing that "security reviews" would soon become unenforceable, for reasons discussed below.

EMBEDDED MEDIA

The advent of operations other than war and journalists' objections to the pool system revived the concept of embedded media, an approach first used in World War II and Vietnam, applied in Haiti in 1994, and expanded for the Bosnia intervention the next year. In this arrangement, a reporter is assigned a unit, deploys with it, and lives with it throughout a lengthy period of operations. All in uniform are considered spokespersons for the military and for their missions. However, interviewers must nevertheless respect soldiers' privacy, as well as operational security. Rules also prohibit reporting on intelligence collection, special operations, or casualties.

Embedding reporters in units has much to offer both sides. These reporters, who usually bond with their units, are likely to appreciate the difficulties of the mission and tend to file favorable reports.[39] But the military cannot hope to mask bad policy or hide incompetence from such journalists. In general, living together breaks down media-military hostility, allows the press to blend into the operational landscape, and in turn, makes soldiers far less self-conscious about the presence of reporters—whom they often respect for sharing their dangers and hardships. The reporters get their stories, and the military gets free and generally favorable publicity for a job it performs with great credit. "I learn stuff every day with a unit," a veteran correspondent observes, "I've never been in a front line unit that didn't enjoy having reporters. . . . [They see it] as a sign that the American people are interested. The troops really love it. I was called 'our reporter.'"[40]

Embedding also attracts criticism, however. The media worry that reporters may identify too closely with their units and lose journalistic objectivity. For its part, the military dreads the off-the-record conversation or the minor or poorly understood event that produces an unflattering story. Loose lips sink not only ships but careers—and few officers who run afoul of the press today are likely to receive the sustained high-level support needed to save General Patton.[41] In Bosnia, reporter Tom Ricks once reported in print that an American battalion commander had told African-American troops in his command, by way of warning, that Croats are racists. The subsequent ruckus produced in the military what is called the "Ricks Rule"—that all conversations with journalists are off the record unless otherwise specified. Even that is considered weak protection against reportorial bad faith: "Any [public affairs officer] will tell you that there is no such thing as 'off the record.' There is no legal basis for it. There is only a thin journalist ethic."[42] Ricks himself argues, however, that the rule betrays unwillingness of seniors to support subordinates, and ultimately, distrust of civilian control of the military: "The amount of stuff I don't publish is astounding."[43]

KOSOVO AND THE FUTURE

The past decade has produced factors likely to make media-military relations more difficult than ever to manage. They include the advent of humanitarian operations, an increasing use by the United States of airpower and stand-off weapons, the war on terrorism, and the emergence of information operations. Furthermore, changing technological and institutional features of news coverage have outpaced formal attempts to order media-military relations. These factors first began to manifest themselves in the NATO attempt in 1999 to expel Yugoslav troops from the province of Kosovo.

Kosovo

Both the media and the U.S. military embarked upon NATO's bombing campaign with deep reservations. The media was profoundly skeptical of the undertaking, an attitude that got its dealings with the military off on the wrong foot.[44] Kosovo, the first war that NATO nations had fought since Desert Storm, was scripted in the same way, less the ground invasion. NATO's fundamental assumptions—that airpower alone was sufficient, that President Slobodan

Milosevic of Yugoslavia would bend to the alliance's will without a ground assault—had been debated only in private, within alliance councils and the U.S. executive branch. In agreement with broad sectors of expert and popular opinion, most correspondents believed that these assumptions amounted to wishful thinking. Most newsrooms sensed that the air strategy was simply the lowest common denominator available to an irresolute and deeply fractured alliance. Nor did NATO bolster its credibility with the press when its miscalculation of Milosevic's resolve became clear. Far from capitulating in a matter of days, if not hours, Milosevic remained defiant and intensified his torment of Kosovar Albanians. In the view of many journalists, neither the American nor the British peoples had an emotional investment in the conflict; both governments, the media concluded, would abandon the effort rather than undertake a ground invasion.[45]

Inevitably, then, the press was wary of information supplied by the military. Press conferences evoked the media's unhappy Gulf War memories of press pools, denial of access, obfuscation, and apparent manipulation; the press resolved not to be fooled twice. Because reporters had scant access to Kosovo, it could not see "ethnic cleansing." Nor could it effectively cover the air war.[46] NATO-supplied videos of precise strikes made the strikes appear to be extremely accurate—but so had they appeared during the Gulf War, when only a small percentage of the coalition air arsenals turned out to have been precision guided munitions. The fact that NATO aircraft were ordered to fly higher than 15,000 feet over Serbia and Kosovo seemed to confirm media pessimism over the ability of air strikes to prevent ethnic cleansing.[47]

Humanitarian Operations

On the surface, the advent of humanitarian operations has removed several sources of tension in media-military relations. Censorship is seldom an issue; operational security is not paramount, and the military is usually unable to deny the press access to the theater even if it wished to. In fact, humanitarian intervention has stood the traditional relationship between the American military and the press on its head. Unlike wartime, national survival is not at stake; the main effort is political, not military. The deployed force is only one of several organizations involved, and its mission is merely to facilitate the work of nongovernmental organizations (NGOs) and civilian governmental organizations, which have the primary tasks. "In the end, it is the NGOs' war to win or lose."[48] Therefore, press pools, if deployed, are merely temporary expedients, quickly abandoned. In fact, the media usually arrive before the military does; whereas in wartime, the military briefs reporters on the situation, in peace, operations reporters are usually better informed than the soldiers.[49]

Still, the tensions inherent in media-military relations do not dissipate at a stroke. On the contrary, they are complicated, particularly by the presence of nongovernmental organizations. Military commanders often believe the media have drawn them into operations that they view as dilutions of their true mission of fighting wars. The root problem seems to be that humanitarian operations typically lack high-level direction;[50] policy vacuums form, in which the media are susceptible to the influence of NGOs—which "are increasingly involving themselves directly in social, political, and even at times, military matters."[51] NGOs, the argument goes, depend for funding on publicity and accordingly solicit the media to disseminate pictures of starving children and desperate refugees, thereby generating pressure on the politicians, who in turn catapult soldiers into altruistic but poorly conceived missions.

Perhaps, as some correspondents believe, the isolation from the media of intervention forces, in their protected compounds, puts them at a distinct disadvantage in any battle with NGOs to sway public perceptions. Other observers are not so sure; because NGOs are frequently international, they lack drawing power for an American press corps focused on a national news market. Additionally, the media often find it difficult to understand a contradictory NGO culture that combines hard business attitudes with a "flaky-do-gooder" image.[52]

The Somalia intervention of 1992–95 began as an object lesson in media-military cooperation. The media were waiting on the beach when Navy SEALs landed as part of a signal to the Somali militias about the power of U.S. forces. However, relations soon went downhill. The media categorically refused thereafter to submit to military control. As the security situation deteriorated, the media images of starving Somalis were blamed for the decision to intervene in the first place, for contributing to mission creep, and finally, for undermining popular support by focusing on casualties. For the military, Somalia offered further proof of the media's power to inflict a "stab in the back," as in Vietnam.[53] The operation in Haiti in September 1994, however, saw a much more harmonious relationship. Ground rules were worked out in advance, and the press willingly complied with most of the military's operational security concerns. A Joint Information Bureau, set up by the intervention force in Port-au-Prince, processed requests from 1,300 journalists to visit units. No escort officers were requested or supplied. The only hint that media might be driving policy occurred when news reports caused the U.S. military to intervene to stop beatings of Aristide supporters by paramilitary forces loyal to deposed President Raoul Cedras.

AIR CAMPAIGNS AND THE MEDIA

Whatever progress was made during the humanitarian operations of the 1990s was disrupted, as we have seen, in Kosovo—in part because NATO chose to fight that war with airpower alone. From a media standpoint, the air campaign meant renewed dependence on the military for information. There are only three ways, all unsatisfactory, to cover an air war. A reporter can hitch a ride on an aircraft; this may give technical insights into *how* an air war is prosecuted, but a correspondent is unlikely to be able to gauge its effects from 15,000 feet in the air. The second option is to sit through military briefings and look at videos of precision strikes—that is, what the military wants the press to see. This leaves the third option, which is for reporters to cross the lines to get the other side's version.

The press received a particular incentive to elicit Serb and Russian accounts when NATO and Pentagon spokespersons and the supreme allied commander contradicted one another in their responses to the mistaken bombing of a convoy of refugee tractors near Djakovica on April 19, 1999. NATO "couldn't get its own story straight."[54] Collateral damage, rather than ethnic cleansing and the refugee crisis, threatened to become the central issue of the Kosovo conflict, undermining the moral credibility of, and hence public support for, the campaign. The problem was compounded by the fact that NATO's stand-off air campaign made the alliance look like a ponderous Goliath assaulting a nimble David—a problem repeated in Afghanistan.[55]

INFORMATION OPERATIONS

Information operations, an outgrowth of information warfare, emerge from the idea that instantaneous communications have revolutionized warfare. They have certainly revolutionized press coverage—with the result, some argue, that open media information is a more important dimension of information operations than familiar technical issues like cyber attack.[56] Kosovo focused attention on the role in conflict of media images; the view emerged that the will of a population to prosecute a conflict can be undermined by media-generated images, and therefore the media strategy must be an integral part of a campaign plan. "Public information is a battle space," it was argued, "that must be contested and controlled like any other."[57]

The room for improvement was obvious. A militarily weak Milosevic repeatedly forced the NATO allies onto the defensive by showcasing collateral damage caused by bombing. NATO's slow and sometimes inaccurate responses wounded its credibility. Its press offices were understaffed and lacked specialists able to monitor Yugoslavian media and anticipate propaganda ploys. NATO had no integrated, forceful public-relations/information campaign. Separate briefings in London, Washington, and Brussels often sent conflicting signals.

However, concentration on information operations is a potentially dangerous development in media-military—even civil-military—relations. It has led enthusiasts to view information as a commodity to be manipulated for operational advantage, rather than as a shared trust. (In any case, the concept is nothing new in war; in 1870, for instance, Otto von Bismarck edited the Ems dispatch to goad Louis Napoleon into declaring war on Prussia.) A new element was the press's willingness to go to the enemy for sources —as in Kosovo, and in Peter Arnett's famous broadcasts from Baghdad during the Gulf War—opening a channel for the enemy's own information operations. Osama bin Laden, and even the media-shy Taliban regime, discovered al Jazeera and the small, Pakistan-based Afghan Islamic News Agency to be useful vehicles for disseminating their messages in the Muslim world, messages that invariably found echoes in the Western news media. The perceived need to do so stems in part from the reluctance of the military to supply information, to impose "gray-outs" that leave the press hungry for material and instigate charges of secrecy and manipulation.

Some officials in the defense community itself argue that to treat information as a "battle space" has "dreadful implications," that mixing public affairs with information operations could do great harm.[58] BBC News set the gold standard for millions during World War II precisely in that, unlike its Axis competitors, it vowed to broadcast the bad news as well as the good. By manipulating media images for operational advantage, the military invites skepticism and hostility. The 1999 bombing of Serb television facilities suggests that in future conflicts, journalists may be regarded as military targets. Foreign governments may retaliate against Western reporters, closing off an important information channel. In the end, the public may become inoculated against government pronouncements of success, as during the Vietnam War, and withdraw its support.

Finally, to treat information as a battle space confuses operational success with strategic victory. If goals are clear, popular, and achievable at reasonable cost, no amount of media manipulation by either side will decide the issue. U.S. public support for the Kosovo conflict remained unshaken despite pictures of collateral damage, despite even the Chinese embassy bombing. The effectiveness of Serbian media ploys—such as posting its stories on the World Wide Web, in English—should not be exaggerated.[59]

Changes in the Media Environment

Two trends in the media world—one technological, the other market related—seem to offer contradictory indications about the future of media-military interaction. Technological advances are likely to make information increasingly available to the press and independent of military control. Market trends, however, suggest that the media's dependence on the military for sellable material will increase.

In future operations in which security risks are high, the military will no doubt insist on control of information; however, "security at the source" (that is, at the level of the individual service member) will necessarily become the rule, because media infrastructures, such as joint information bureaus, are already becoming irrelevant. Journalists can file directly from the field, anywhere on the globe, using cell phones, the Internet, and remote-area network data systems transmitting compressed video signals. Satellite, microwave, and fiber-optics systems are becoming miniaturized and increasingly mobile. Reporters have access to commercial satellite images that can reveal such things as troop deployments—making refusals for reasons of security to guide press pools to deployed units less credible and effective.[60] In fact, the security issue may soon be reversed: an enemy missile could home in on a reporter's signal. Commanders in the future may have to ask reporters willing to take that risk to move several hundred yards away from troop positions before relaying information.

The advances in technology, of course, cut both ways. Satellite imagery can easily be modified. Video images are—for the moment—more difficult to alter, but that will change. Manufactured videos and misleading stories can be posted on the Internet. The media itself should be the first line of defense, filtering this information to determine its credibility. But if journalists suspect that they are being censored, denied information, manipulated, or deceived by their own military, they may be more inclined to give the other side's version of events the benefit of the doubt.

Notwithstanding the media's new ability to collect and disseminate information independently, it is unlikely to go entirely its own way. A balance will probably be struck, not least because the long-term market trends are poor for foreign news coverage in general, and for military stories in particular. Today the media, although multinational in organization, must increasingly focus on regional niche markets. News is a business, and polls and focus groups inform editors that the priorities of the public are local news first, foreign news last. CNN, for instance, has begun regional production to feed "foreign" news to the markets where it is not foreign. In the United States, the international news most likely to be covered is that which produces the most dramatic footage or has an American connection. To obtain such material, the U.S. media needs the military; in that framework, the military itself is the story.

The media perceives that the American public suffers from "compassion fatigue." What sells a story is not the crisis but the fact that the military arrives to do something about it. "Unless U.S. troops are involved, it is difficult to convince an editor that a story is worthwhile."[61] In any case, there is strong marketing pressure on the media to conform to audience expectations; it is not in the interest even of an international news organization like CNN to show footage, or give its reporting a slant, that will offend the sensibilities of the American public. In fact, the criticism of the allegedly "liberal" American media after September 11 was that they became cheerleaders for the war on terrorism, "a knee-jerk pandering to the public," according to Australian journalist Carwyn James, "reflecting a mood of patriotism rather than informing viewers of the complex, sometimes harsh realities they need to know." For his part, CNN president Walter Isaacson confessed, "if you get on the wrong side of public opinion, you are going to get in trouble."[62] This creates a great initial advantage for the military—if, that is, it embraces rather than shuns the media.[63]

Indeed, ignorance and misinformation are far more dangerous for the military than is informed reporting, however critical in tone. But the media need help here. Because the press is fragmented, competitive, sometimes ignorant of military realities, and constantly whiplashed between the demands of the market and those of journalistic ethics, however defined, the quality of coverage of military events is inevitably uneven at best. Today, however, the situation is aggravated by the fact that newsrooms are no longer "old-boys networks," inclined to accept some of the military's more traditional ways as part of the journalistic landscape. The tendency of unprepared reporters, charging from crisis to crisis, unaware of the issues at stake or of how the military functions, is to frame complex matters in simplistic ways—or even to indulge in "gotcha" journalism (focusing on errors and misstatements). For its part, the military owes access to information both to Congress and the American people. Furthermore, it needs to get its story out—for the military will be competing with other groups, and enemies, eager to put their spin on events. To do this, it needs the media.

It will be impossible in the future to embargo news, as has sometimes been done in the past. An artificial news vacuum would be filled by on-line correspondents, NGOs, and even the enemy. The media gravitates toward the sources that are most obvious and available; tyrants and terrorists like Saddam, Milosevic, and bin Laden learned to welcome reporters. Future enemies can be expected to develop sophisticated media strategies to draw attention to, and assign external blame for, the suffering of their people; the possibilities available to them for distortion, manipulation, and disinformation are growing.[64] Therefore, it is imperative that the U.S. military establish a solid working relationship with the media, that it integrate them into its strategy—and not keep reporters at arm's length, as if they were hostile interlopers in a private domain.

NOTES

1. Charles C. Moskos and Thomas E. Ricks, "Reporting War When There Is No War: The Media and the Military in Peace and Humanitarian Operations," *Cantigny Conference Series, Special Report* (Chicago: Robert R. McCormick Tribune Foundations, 1996), 15–26. See also Frank A. Aukofer and William P. Lawrence, *America's Team: The Odd Couple—A Report on the Relationship between the Military and the Media* (Nashville, Tenn.: Freedom Forum First Amendment Center, 1995), p. 9; available on the World Wide Web at www.fac.org. Sixty-four percent of military officers surveyed agreed, strongly or "somewhat," that "news media coverage of the events in Vietnam harmed the war effort."

2. Charles C. Moskos, "The Media and the Military in Peace and Humanitarian Operations," in *Cantigny Conference Series, Special Report* (Chicago: Robert R. McCormick Tribune Foundation, 2000), 12, Table 1.

3. William Hammond, "The News Media and the Military," in *Encyclopedia of the American Military*, ed. John E. Jessup and Louise B. Ketz (New York: Scribner's, 1994), 3: 2095.

4. Lloyd J. Matthews, ed., *Newsmen and National Defense: Is Conflict Inevitable?* (Washington, D.C.: Brassey's, 1991), 8.

5. Stephen Ambrose, *Eisenhower: Soldier, General of the Army, President-Elect, 1890–1952* (New York: Simon & Schuster, 1983), 206.

6. David Eisenhower, *Eisenhower at War, 1943–1945* (New York: Vintage Books, 1987), 59–60.

7. Merle Miller, *Ike the Soldier: As They Knew Him* (New York: G. P. Putnam, 1987), 432.

8. Elena Agarossi, *A Nation Collapses: The Italian Surrender of September 1943* (Cambridge: Cambridge University Press, 2000), 68.

9. Eisenhower, *Eisenhower at War*, 600.

10. Ambrose, *Eisenhower*, 129.

11. Marquis Childs, *Eisenhower: Captive Hero* (New York: Harcourt, Brace, 1958), 79.

12. Eisenhower, *Eisenhower at War*, 219. For Patton's and Bill Mauldin's mutual antipathy—Patton was sure the "Willie and Joe" cartoonist was trying to "incite a goddamn mutiny," and Mauldin thought "the stupid bastard was crazy" —see Carlo D'Este, *Patton: A Genius for War* (New York: HarperCollins, 1995), 543, 694–95.

13. D. Clayton James, *The Years of MacArthur, 1941–1945* (Boston: Houghton Mifflin, 1975), 2: 413–16, 475–76, 493–95, 661, 871.

14. Michael Linfield, *Freedom under Fire: U.S. Civil Liberties in Times of War* (Boston: South End Press, 1990), 74.

15. Phillip Knightley, *The First Casualty: From the Crimea to Vietnam: The War Correspondent as Hero, Propagandist, and Myth Maker* (New York: Harcourt Brace Jovanovich, 1975), 337.

16. D. C. Hallin, *We Keep America on Top of the World: Television Journalism and the Public Sphere* (London: Routledge, 1994); C. A. Thayer, "Vietnam: A Critical Analysis," in *Defence and the Media in Time of Limited War*, ed. P. E. Young (London: Frank Cass, 1993), 89–115; W. M. Hammond, *Public Affairs: The Military and the Media, 1962–1968* (Washington, D.C.: Center of Military History, 1988); and *Public Affairs: The Military and the Media, 1968–1973* (Washington, D.C.: Center of Military History, 1996).

17. Peter Young and Peter Jesser, *The Media and the Military: From the Crimea to Desert Strike* (New York: St. Martin's Press, 1997), 91–92.

18. Lynn Gorman, "The Australian and the American Media: From Korea to Vietnam," *War and Society* (May 2000): 128.

19. General John Shalikashvili, U.S. Army, quoted in Aukofer and Lawrence, *America's Team*, 23–27.

20. Tom Ricks, interview with author, June 23, 2000. Charles Moskos cautions that one must not take the amateur nature of journalists too far. Journalists are professionals "in the sense that they are trained in their vocation, have a corporate self-identity, and serve in an institution that is a cornerstone of a democratic society." Moskos, "Media and the Military," 47.

21. John J. Fialka, *Hotel Warriors: Covering the Gulf War* (Baltimore: The Johns Hopkins University Press, 1991), 57.

22. Aukofer and Lawrence, *America's Team,* vii–viii.

23. Michael Ignatieff, *Virtual War: Kosovo and Beyond* (New York: Metropolitan Books, 2000), 177–80; and Ricks interview.

24. Fialka, *Hotel Warriors,* 27.

25. Publisher Larry Flynt unsuccessfully sued the U.S. Defense Department, claiming that denial of access to the battlefield on Grenada was a violation of First Amendment rights.

26. Joseph Metcalf, "The Press and Grenada: 1983," in "Defence and the Media in Time of Limited War," ed. Peter Young, special issue of *Small Wars and Insurgencies* 2 (December 1991): 169–70.

27. For Cheney's attitude, see Aukofer and Lawrence, *America's Team,* 5.

28. The press center was inadequately equipped, which delayed stories up to 4 days. On March 30, 1990, the Joint Chiefs of Staff issued new guidance for public affairs, requiring regional commanders-in-chief to coordinate all public affairs activities with the Assistant Secretary of Defense for Public Affairs, provide guidance for all public affairs activities, offer adequate communication and transport support, and ensure the implementation of all Defense public affairs policies and programs. For the up-to-date version, see *Doctrine for Public Affairs in Joint Operations,* Joint Publication 3-61 (Washington, D.C.: Joint Staff, May 14, 1997).

29. Peter de la Billiere, *Storm Command* (New York: HarperCollins, 1992), 64.

30. See Fialka, *Hotel Warriors.*

31. Carla Roberts of the *Wall Street Journal,* unpublished address to conference on "Partners or Partisans: NATO and the Media in Kosovo," U.S. Institute for Peace, Washington, D.C., April 4, 2000.

32. Letter to the editor, *New York Times* (May 16, 2000): A22.

33. Young and Jesser, *Media and Military,* 281.

34. For a summary of media and military attitudes in the Gulf War, see Aukofer and Lawrence, *America's Team,* 9–21.

35. Commander Robert Anderson, U.S. Navy, interview with author (July 6, 2000).

36. Fialka, *Hotel Warriors,* 41.

37. Ibid., 5.

38. *DOD Principles for News Media Coverage of DOD Operations* (Washington, D.C.: U.S. Defense Department, April 1992).

39. Barry E. Willey, "The Military-Media Connection: For Better or Worse," *Military Review* 78 (February 1999): 4–5.

40. Ricks interview.

41. General Mike Dugan was fired as chief of staff of the U.S. Air Force by Secretary of Defense Richard Cheney in September 1990, after a reporter allowed to fly back to Washington on Dugan's plane quoted him as saying that the Gulf War would consist of a massive air campaign targeting Saddam Hussein. Two years later, a reporter took exception to a comment by the commander of U.S. forces in the Pacific, Admiral Richard Macke, concerning an Okinawan rape case, ending the admiral's career.

42. Anderson interview.

43. Ricks interview.

44. Some believe that media skepticism was a predictable by-product of the military's tendency to view one conflict through the lens of another. If so, this phenomenon is hardly unique to the media—and Somalia remains the gold standard for those dubious of the benefits of humanitarian operations.

45. See Roberts, "Partners or Partisans," and Warren Strobel, *Late Breaking Foreign Policy: The News Media's Influence on Peace Operations* (Washington, D.C.: U.S. Institute for Peace, 1997).

46. Two hundred fifty reporters were allowed to fly in NATO aircraft and interview ground crews. This generated stories on the complexity of carrying out an air campaign but gave little insight into how well NATO's air strategy was working. Indeed, pictures of apparently unscathed Serbian tanks leaving Kosovo at the conclusion of the conflict gave the impression that the air campaign had been a complete shambles. Gary Pounder, "Opportunity Lost: Public Affairs, Information Operations, and the Air War against Serbia," *Aerospace Power Journal* 14 (Summer 2000): 70–71.

47. The media assumption was that high-altitude flying had been ordered to avoid casualties. It did, in fact, lessen the threat of surface-to-air missiles and antiaircraft artillery, but it also increased the accuracy of precision guided weapons, by affording more guidance time from a more stable controlling aircraft.

48. Chris Seiple, *The U.S. Military/NGO Relationship in Humanitarian Interventions* (Carlisle Barracks, Penn.: U.S. Army Peacekeeping Institute, 1996), 180.

49. Strobel, *Late Breaking Foreign Policy,* 10–15.

50. For the sources of military unease with peace operations, see John A. Gentry, "Complex Civil-Military Operations: A U.S. Military-Centric Perspective," *Naval War College Review* 53 (Autumn 2000): 57–76.

51. Scott Anderson, "What Ever Happened to Fred Cuny?" *New York Times Magazine* (February 18, 1996): 47.

52. Moskos, "Media and the Military," 33.

53. Veteran journalist Warren Strobel argues that it was not the casualties per se that provoked the military withdrawal from Somalia. Rather, the downing of a Blackhawk helicopter reignited a policy debate in Washington over the escalating goals and risks of the operation, a debate that had become dormant because of the good news to that point and apparently low costs. The media highlighted the true costs of the operation in a particularly dramatic way. Strobel, *Late Breaking Forein Policy,* 221.

54. Ricks interview.

55. Ignatieff, *Virtual War,* 162.

56. Carl H. Builder, *The Icarus Syndrome: The Role of Air Power Theory in the Evolution of the U.S. Air Force* (New Brunswick, N.J.: Transaction, 1996), 249.

57. Colonel Jack Ivy, U.S. Air Force, deputy director of the U.S. Air Force Public Affairs Center for Excellence,

Maxwell Air Force Base, Alabama, quoted in Pounder, "Opportunity Lost," 60.

58. One is Colonel P. J. Crowley, U.S. Air Force (Ret.), principal assistant secretary of defense for public affairs, quoted in Pounder, "Opportunity Lost," 60, 65.

59. A NATO spokesman points out that these events did impact public opinion in NATO countries where support for the war was soft, such as Germany, Italy, and Greece. Roberts, "Partners or Partisans."

60. Some of these technical developments are discussed in Young and Jesser, *Media and Military*, 12–14.

61. Based on unpublished comments by Scott Peterson and Daniel Benjamin, "News versus Snooze," conference held at the U.S. Institute for Peace, Washington, D.C., May 11, 2000.

62. Alessandra Stanley, "Opponents of the War Are Scarce on Television," *New York Times* (September 11, 2001): B4.

63. Young and Jesser, *Media and Military*, 14.

64. Peterson and Benjamin, "News versus Snooze."

THE MILITARY ESTABLISHMENT, THE PRESIDENT, AND CONGRESS

SAM C. SARKESIAN, JOHN ALLEN WILLIAMS, AND STEPHEN J. CIMBALA

The military establishment is a critical operational arm of the national security system. How it is organized and its relationship to the president and other political actors are necessary considerations in the study of national security policy. Furthermore, the education, socialization, and mind-sets of military professionals are important in shaping the military establishment and in determining its ability to pursue the goals of U.S. national security policy.

Since the end of World War II, the U.S. military establishment has gone through several important changes in organizational structure and notions of military professionalism. This process continued during the post–Cold War era, as it does today. The size of the military has been reduced, and it must reconcile itself to a variety of political and social forces that have affected its structure and missions. At the same time, it must adjust to an ill-defined security landscape. Aimed at making the military more responsive to prevailing threats and preparing it for future conflicts, these changes have made the conflict spectrum, as well as military organizations and professionalism, enormously complicated. Military success requires highly skilled and competent individuals at virtually all levels in the military hierarchy. This in turn has made the president and the national security establishment heavily dependent upon the military for sound advice.

The concept of national security has expanded to include military participation in humanitarian and peacekeeping missions and in combating international terrorism. As a result, military force has been used in missions and contingencies that are contrary to the views of the military establishment. All of this tends to dilute any notion that the president and Congress are captives of the military, as the use of force in the new era has become engulfed in civilian cultures and nontraditional missions. At the same time, the U.S. military is in the process of transformation—preparing for wars in the twenty-first century. This envisions changes in strategy, doctrine, and weaponry, among other factors.

THE COMMAND-AND-CONTROL STRUCTURE

The military establishment's focus of power shifted to the secretary of defense when that office was given control of the military departments; changes in 1986 further expanded the secretary's power, as well as that of the Joint Chiefs of Staff (JCS) chairman. These changes have had an impact on the development of strategy, the formulation of national security policy, and presidential control over the military establishment.

Several reference points need to be reviewed with respect to the structure of the Department of Defense. First, the secretaries of the military departments (Army, Navy, and Air Force) have no operational responsibilities; revisions to the National Security Act of 1947 downgraded their executive-department status to that of military departments (1949) and later removed them from the chain of command (1958). The primary responsibilities of the service secretaries are in administrative and logistical areas: manpower, procurement, weapons systems, service effectiveness, military welfare, and training responsibilities, among other duties. However, a strong personality in the service secretary's office can have a decided influence and political impact in shaping the posture and operational capability of the service.

Second, the role of the JCS chairman has been strengthened. Formerly, the JCS was a corporate body, and the chairman served principally as spokesman. In addition, the chairman had little control over who served on the joint staff from the services, whose commanders also rotated the chairman's functions among themselves in his absence. The chairman held a symbolic rather than a substantive position.

The 1986 Defense Reorganization Act (the Goldwater-Nichols Act) made the JCS chairman the primary military figure in the defense establishment. It gave him direct access to the president and assigned him responsibilities not only for strategic thinking but also for a range of other matters (including budget assessments and readiness evaluations), affording him a more direct relationship with the commanders-in-chief of specified and unified commands. He now has direct control over assignments to the joint staff. Also created by this legislation are several responsibilities assigned to the JCS vice chairman. The chairman no longer must accept joint staff members selected by the various services. In short, the chairman is now the most important member of the JCS, responsible only to the secretary of defense and the president.

Third, a new officer specialty was created by Congress.[1] This joint specialty provides for a lifetime career path for officers qualified as staff officers in joint staff positions. The objective is to have a pool of officers from all services qualified to serve on joint staffs. Although not intended to create a general staff corps on the old German army model, the program has lead to important changes within the profession and in the functioning of the joint staff. Education and experience in matters of joint staff responsibilities, as well as socialization processes, are likely to develop a staff mind-set on a long-term basis and inculcate some officers with a general staff mentality.

The chain of command and control of the operational arm of the military runs directly from the commander-in-chief to the secretary of defense to the JCS chairman to the commanders of the unified commands (see Figure 1).

UNIFIED COMMANDS

A unified command, as the name suggests, is a joint service operational responsibility. Until the 1986 Defense Reorganization Act, the commanders of unified commands had little control over what units were assigned to their command. This was the responsibility of the various services, whose component commanders had to depend on their own services for resources. The composition of forces was determined by each service. Thus unified commands reflected a mix of doctrines, equipment, and missions as determined by the services.

Now the commanders-in-chief of unified commands have been given more power in budget matters pertaining to their commands, hiring and firing authority over subordinate commanders, and direct access to the secretary of defense and JCS chairman, bypassing the respective services. The president, in turn, can give the JCS chairman primary responsibility for overseeing the activities of these commands. The 1986 Defense Reorganization Act established the JCS chairman as the spokesman for the commanders of the combatant commands, especially in operational requirements. Commanders now have the authority to act as real commanders, generally independent from the control of their respective services. The changes resulting from the 1986 act have had a positive impact on jointness and in the operational direction of the various commands.

It is also the case that in the new strategic environment, interservice rivalries have resurfaced as each service tries to protect its turf, not only in terms of missions but also budgets. In 2001, this remained a characteristic of the military establishment as each service attempted to prepare for twenty-first-century warfare and the new strategic landscape. Congress tried to override interservice squabbles and problems of command and control by imposing a strengthened secretary of defense and JCS chairman, as well as a strengthened command system, on the military establishment. But the problem of internal rivalries remains. In the past, the number of assistant secretaries of defense reflected the variety of matters under the responsibility of the secretary of defense. Indeed, the scope of activities and the amount of resources required to maintain and expand them created a vast managerial complex—too complex, according to some—that precluded an efficient military system.

The inherent rivalries leave the Defense Department vulnerable to politicization of its operational arms and hamper development of coherent policy and feasible options. Many of these plans were thrown into organizational disarray with Secretary of Defense Les Aspin's resignation (or firing) in December 1993, compounded by the withdrawal in January 1994 of retired Admiral Bobby R. Inman from consideration after he was nominated by President Clinton for the post. Deputy Secretary of Defense William Perry was nominated and confirmed as secretary of defense in February 1994, succeeded by former U.S. senator William Cohen in 1998. With the inauguration of George W. Bush in 2001, a new national security team was put into place and, with it, a new defense system under Secretary of Defense Donald Rumsfeld. This included a system designed to operate in several unconventional environments. In 2001, this included special attention to combating international terrorism. In spring 2002, it was announced that a new command would be established in the Department of Defense to coordinate North American defense forces.

In 1993, Secretary Aspin and the Clinton administration developed plans to reduce the number of

Figure 1
The Joint Chiefs of Staff and Unified Commands

The Joint Chiefs of Staff

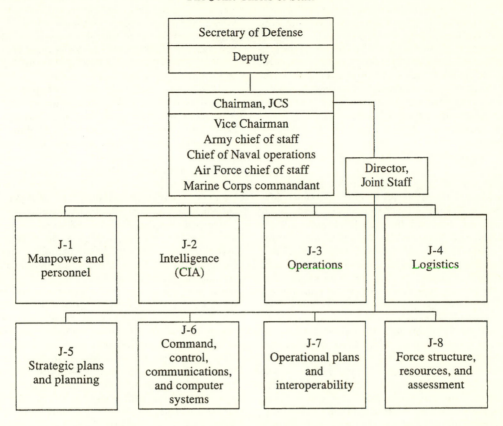

Unified Commands

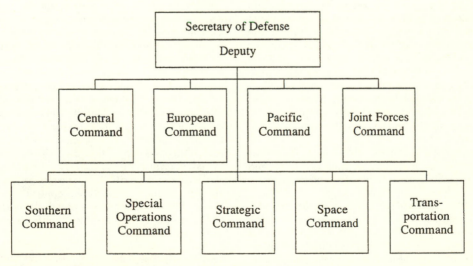

Source: William S. Cohen, *Annual Report to the President and the Congress* (2001), A-2. Available online at www.dtic.mil/execsec/adr2001.

assistant secretaries. "Under Mr. Aspin's plan, the traditional civilian Pentagon functions will be handled by four branches: weapons acquisition, personnel and readiness, the office of the Pentagon comptroller, and an office of national security policy."[2] The so-called Aspin Plan was abandoned by his successor, William Perry, in favor of a more traditional structure, which was adopted by Cohen. However, Secretary Rumsfield implemented plans to transform the military into a twenty-first-century force designed to respond to threats and potential threats. This encompasses changes in the military system that focus on doctrine, training, and weaponry, and incorporate information age technology.

CONGRESS: GUNS AND BUTTER

The role of Congress does not stop at legislation to restructure the military. Executive-legislative skirmishes over constitutional roles have already been discussed, but the division of authority over military appraisal and allocation also impact the formulation of strategy and its operational implementation. This is reflected in guns-and-butter issues: how much should be spent for defense, and how much for nondefense issues? The president may be the commander-in-chief, but Congress has the power of the purse. The weapons acquisition process, which obviously affects the military establishment's performance, is but one example. Congress allocates funds for research, development, and production.

All these struggles magnify the political dimension of the military establishment. Congressional hearings on strategy, resource allocation, and military performance strike at the heart of the military establishment, requiring operational commanders at all levels to become sensitive to the political nature of their responsibilities. The desire in Congress for more explicit military recommendations and more control over military commitments in contingencies short of war means that it struggles with the president, the secretary of defense, the JCS chairman, individual service chiefs, and a variety of high-level operational commanders. In 1993 and 1994, these struggles were especially visible over the reduction of the military and the shrinking defense budget. This continued in 2000 and into 2001—that is, until September 11. In the aftermath, budget allocations for defense increased.

Secretary William Cohen's 2001 Annual Report details information on the budget, manpower levels, and weaponry, among other things. The report states:

Like the three previous DoD budgets, the FY 2002 plan was developed largely based on the Department's May 1997 Quadrennial Defense Review [QDR]. The QDR detailed changes needed to address new global threats and opportunities and to make the best use of constrained resources . . . Over the long-term, DoD must fund the needed post–Cold War transformation of America's defense posture and modernize U.S. forces to ensure their future combat superiority.[3]

By 2000, the president and Congress had agreed to increase defense spending, although there was disagreement over the amount. This was compounded by disagreements within the Clinton administration and between the administration and Congress over force posture and strategy. In the aftermath of September 11, the existing budget proposals and allocations became almost irrelevant as Congress allocated more money to the Bush administration for defense and combating international terrorism.

Directly and indirectly, then, Congress has increased its role and linkage to the functioning and powers of the military establishment. Indeed, it can be said that Congress has become *part of* the military establishment. As such, it brings along a variety of political considerations, from personnel issues to base-closure decisions. Its judgments influence not only budget allocations but also the concept of vital interests, the structure of the military establishment, and the development of strategic options.

Civilians employed by the Department of Defense are an important element in the relationship between the military establishment and other political actors. In 1990, there were more than 1 million civilians working for the department, not counting the more than one million employed in defense-related industries. During the Clinton administration, there was a reduction in the number of civilians employed and in the money devoted to defense industries. By 2000, the number of civilians working for the Department of Defense had dropped to about 700,000. Those employed in defense-related industries had also been reduced.[4] To be sure, only a small part of this civilian component has a direct impact on national security policy and the functioning of the national command authority. Nonetheless, close links with the Department of Defense provide a channel for civilian attitudes and mind-sets to penetrate the military profession. Conversely, military attitudes and mind-sets penetrate the civilian component. This interpenetration is greatest at the higher levels, as all appointments at the assistant secretary level and above are political and normally civilian; a more noticeable degree of separation exists at lower levels, where civilians are rarely present in operational units.

Thus the dual influences in the military establishment simply confirm the long-standing norm that civilian control of the U.S. military is a well-established fact in law and reality. Equally important, the military profession has accepted this as a basic premise. Over the years, civilian rule has slowly but surely permeated weapons acquisition, force composition, strategic options, and command-and-control issues. It is in such areas that the president and the military establishment face some of the most serious opposition and disagreements.

FORCE RESTRUCTURING AND COMPOSITION

The relationship between the military and political leaders that evolved during the first years of the Clinton administration reshaped the military's com-

Table 2

The Restructuring of the Military, 1993–99

	1993	1999
Army active divisions	14	10
Navy aircraft carriers	13	11
Air Force fighter wings	16	13
Marine Corps active duty strength	182,000	174,000
Nuclear forces		
Submarines	22	18
Bombers	201	up to 184
Missiles	787	500

Source: Les Aspin, Secretary of Defense, *The Bottom-Up Review: Forces for a New Era* (Washington, D.C.: U.S. Department of Defense, September 1, 1993).

mand-and-control structure, force posture, and professionalism. A major part of this surfaced with Secretary of Defense Aspin's Bottom-Up Review.[5] This envisioned the restructuring and reduction of the military by the year 1999 as shown in Table 2.

In addition, there was a heavy reliance on reserve forces, with five-plus divisions for the Army, one aircraft carrier for the Navy, seven fighter wings in the Air Force Reserve, and 42,000 reserve personnel for the Marine Corps. There were several critics of the resulting Aspin Plan. For many, the force structure and force composition envisioned by the Bottom-Up Review was driven by budget considerations devoid of serious-strategic considerations.

Then–Chief of Staff of the Army General Gordon Sullivan and Lieutenant Colonel James Dubik wrote:

American political leaders expect the military to *contract* in both size and budget, *contribute* to domestic recovery, *participate* in global stability operations, and *retain* its capability to produce decisive victory in whatever circumstances they are employed—all at the same time. . . . International and domestic realities have resulted in the paradox of declining military resources and increasing military missions, a paradox that is stressing our armed forces. The stress is significant.[6]

All of these changes by the Clinton administration, combined with the president's efforts to lift the ban on homosexuals in the military and expand the role of women in combat, had a decided impact on the military profession, positive and negative. The negatives were reinforced by Clinton's avoidance of military service and his alleged antimilitary activities during the Vietnam War. This resulted in a gap in the relationship between the commander-in-chief and the military—a gap that many within the military believed had serious consequences for civil-military relations and professional status. For some, the military had become more of a social institution than a fighting institution. This was reinforced by those who challenged the use of the U.S. military in nation-building, peacekeeping, and humanitarian intervention.[7] How all this will change as a result of the war on terrorism remains to be seen.

THE WEINBERGER DOCTRINE

In the 1990s, professional concerns led to the resurfacing of the so-called "Weinberger Doctrine," later reinforced by the Powell Doctrine. Events in Somalia in 1993 seemed to confirm the relevance of these approaches. During the Somalia mission, the killing and wounding of U.S. soldiers in the failed attempt to capture the warlord Mohammed Farah Aideed led critics to point out that lack of clearly defined military objectives, inadequate support, and mission creep were fundamental causes of military failure.

The Weinberger Doctrine was established by the Secretary of Defense Caspar Weinberger in 1984 during the Reagan administration to spell out the conditions under which U.S. ground combat troops should be committed. The elements of this doctrine include:[8]

1. No overseas commitment of U.S. combat forces unless a vital national interest of the United States or an interest important to U.S. allies is threatened.

2. If U.S. forces are committed, there should be total support—resources and manpower to complete the mission.

3. If committed, U.S. forces must be given clearly defined political and military objectives, and the forces must be large enough to be able to achieve these objectives.

4. There must be a continual assessment between the commitment and capability of U.S. forces and the objectives, which must be adjusted, if necessary.

5. Before U.S. forces are committed, there must be reasonable assurance that Americans and their elected representatives support such commitment.

6. Commitment of U.S. forces to combat must be the last resort.

Later General Colin Powell spelled out his view on the use of force: "Have a clear military objective and stick to it. Use all the force necessary, and do not apologize for going in big if that is what it takes. Decisive force ends wars quickly and in the long run saves lives. Whatever threats we face in the future, I intend to make these rules the bedrock of my military counsel."[9]

The 1999 campaign in Kosovo against the Serbs and the Milosevic regime seemed to contradict the precepts of the Weinberger-Powell perspectives. The 78 day air campaign led to the end of the Serbian campaign against the Albanians in Kosovo. This was done without the commitment of ground troops. Yet critics argue that the air campaign was supported by the Kosovo Liberation Army, made up of Albanians armed and supported by outside sources, and by the pressure brought to bear by the Russians. In 2002, the issue of Kosovo remained unresolved, with no solution in sight. The fact is that the massive use of military force at the center of gravity of the adversary remains a clear military principle. How this can be applied to operations other than war, stability operations, and unconventional conflicts, including international terrorism, remains contentious.

THE MILITARY AND THE POLICY PROCESS

The structure of the Department of Defense and the nature and character of military professionalism are the primary determinants of the military's role in the national security policy process. That role has more to do with administrative and operational considerations than with the serious formulation of strategy, in which the military is in a distinctly secondary position.

The traditional professional posture rests partly on the premise that military personnel do not become involved in politics. Hence, because the policy process is inherently political, they are expected to keep their distance; and because formulation of strategy is in turn closely linked to the political process, they find themselves outside the formulation of strategy.

In addition, the joint perspective necessary for this process is difficult for military professionals to maintain, as career success typically runs through the respective services. Even the members of the JCS, with their dual role, tend first to their service responsibilities. The same is true of joint staff officers, and although their performance on the joint staff and their relative efficiency are determined by the JCS, service perspectives and career considerations tend to erode a joint perspective. Service parochialism and professional socialization instilled over a long career are difficult to overcome by assignment to a joint staff.

Another basic problem is that the role of the military in the policy process and formulation of strategy is affected by role conflict. The technology drive in the military, reflected in sophisticated battlefield weaponry, electronic warfare, and the evolution of an intricate organizational defense structure, has tended to shape the military establishment along the lines of civilian corporate and managerial systems. Furthermore, great effort within senior service schools has been made to develop officers capable of dealing with such complex conditions. As a consequence, military managership has become an important factor in career success and military efficiency. But not everyone agrees with this approach. Many military professionals and critics argue that the real need within the military services is for leaders and warriors. According to this view, emphasis on managership erodes the ability of the military services to successfully command and lead operational units in battle. Reliance on technology shifts the focus away from the psychological-

social dimensions of human behavior, thereby reducing competency in the art of leadership.[10]

Notwithstanding its coveted aloofness from politics, the military has been dragged into the fray on many fronts—weapons acquisition, budgets, and relations with Congress, among other things. Furthermore, contemporary conflicts, whether nuclear or unconventional in character, include important political considerations.[11] As some are inclined to argue, the military professional must begin functioning long before the opening salvos of war and operations other than war. Indeed, wars and conflicts in progress in the twenty-first century are characterized by inextricable political and military factors. Cases in point include the monitoring of the Iraqi military and the Kurds in northern Iraq, continuing involvement in Bosnia-Herzegovina and Kosovo, concern over political developments in Russia, and the China-Taiwan issue, among others. For military professionals to be successful, therefore, they must acquire political as well as military skills. At a minimum, military professionals must be able to deal with the political dimensions of conflict. In the twenty-first century, such considerations are no longer distinct from the operational environment.

However, the fear of many is that attention to politics not only detracts from developing military skills but also exposes the profession to politicization, which destroys professional integrity and autonomy. The only feasible posture, according to this view, is to maintain a clear separation between politics and the military profession. The traditional concept of civil-military relations and an apolitical military associated with democratic systems is based on this separatist view. Yet others argue that there is no such thing as an apolitical military—and the U.S. military is no exception. How these matters can be reconciled with the political character of conflicts and the military's role in a democracy remains a persisting dilemma for the military profession.

According to some, the military must inform the public as well as elected officials about their views regarding the military system and the use of force. The military profession cannot function as a "silent order of monks," as someone once put it.[12] "The military profession must adopt the doctrine of constructive political engagement, framing and building a judicious and artful involvement in the policy arena. A politics-savvy military profession is the basic ingredient for constructive political engagement."[13]

These characteristics of the military establishment do not allow simplistic views of its role in the national security policy process or in the formulation of strategy. On one hand, the views of the military cannot be ignored; on the other, the character of the military institution, the nature of the military profession, and the way the U.S. political system works preclude a lead role for the military. Research on the matters examined here reveals:

The combination of domestic and international issues promises to weigh heavily on the military profession and its strategic and doctrinal orientation. These issues strike at the core of the professional ethos. Even more challenging is that the military profession must be prepared to respond to a variety of national security challenges with diminished resources and considerably fewer personnel, and it must do so even in the face of skepticism within the body politic regarding issues of national security. Exacerbating all of this is that few politicians and academic commentators in the new era have had any real military experience. Although military experience is not the *sine qua non* for serious examination and analysis of national security and the military profession, without that experience it is difficult to design realistic national security policies or to understand the nature and character of the military profession.[14]

How the president and the national security establishment incorporate the military establishment into the policy process—while maintaining the character of the profession and not violating the norms and expectations of a democratic system—is a problem facing every president. The challenge surely cannot be met without an understanding of the character and nature of the military establishment and its professionals. The same holds true for anyone studying national security.[15]

Since the U.S. Constitution was approved, the evolution of power has placed the president in the dominant position in foreign affairs and national security. This remains the case even after passage of legislation, like the War Powers Resolution, designed to increase congressional power in these areas. Congress has an important role, but the nature of international security issues and the increasing complexity of international politics make it difficult for Congress to lead the nation or, for that matter, to check the president on policy initiatives, especially during a national crisis. In addition, presidential power has grown in response to increasingly complex U.S. economic and social systems, which have indirectly reinforced the president's power in national security policy.

In the post–Cold War era, the traditional notion of national security is being questioned, and as a consequence, presidential power in national security is undergoing change. Some observers see a stronger congressional role; others see a stronger presidential role. Given the uncertainty, it is small wonder that the powers of the president and Congress are being reexamined. It is too early to predict the long-term effects of the war on terrorism on this balance, but we expect that the president's role will be significantly strengthened, at least in the short term.

In any case, "presidents are not kings. To understand the power that they wield we must distinguish between foreign and domestic affairs and specifically what kind of power over what kind of issue and in what circumstances and against the opposition of which other centers of power."[16] Put simply, the exercise of presidential power is a function of the president's ability to understand the nature of the political process, his constitutional power, the international climate, and the power inherent in his own leadership

and skills as a politician. At the same time, Congress has increasingly reclaimed its share of responsibility.

THE PRESIDENTIAL POWER BASE

Several factors complicate the policymaking process, including the nature of the presidency, public expectations, and the demands of the international security environment. These all have philosophical, ideological, and political overtones. National security goes beyond a strong military and the ability to support it financially. It includes confidence in leadership, staying power, national will, political resolve, and agreement on national security goals. In today's strategic and political climate, it also includes some agreement on the meaning of national security.

The president faces potential opposition from several quarters. Although the president and Congress cooperate in many ways on national security matters, disagreements over policy diverge from the established procedure. Special interest groups, segments of the U.S. public, and allies may also oppose the president. Add to this disagreements within the administration and the national security establishment, and one can appreciate the extent of the problem, especially in the strategic landscape of the twenty-first century.

Aside from the Constitution, the institutional characteristics of Congress and the power of individual members create conflict. Constituencies, terms of office, and mind-sets all play a role. Incumbency strengthens the hand of many members of Congress. Incumbents perpetuate their power to ensure reelection, and few are defeated. Some members of the House of Representatives have been in office for more than 30 years. This has led some to view Congress as an institution of incumbents intent on maintaining office, overriding political party issues and categorizations.

The president can use several strategies to overcome opposition in Congress. Many are inherent to the office, whereas others depend on the effectiveness of presidential leadership style and techniques. Every president beginning with Dwight Eisenhower has used a congressional liaison staff to establish and maintain relations. It targets key members in both houses, especially potential allies. The staff keeps the president informed of congressional power clusters and the general mood and recommends tactics to develop support for presidential initiatives. Similarly, the staff keeps members informed about presidential initiatives.[17] Although the liaison staff is usually concerned with domestic issues, longer-range national security policy and defense issues are also important.

Other tactics for developing support include bargaining, threat and intimidation, and reward. For example, the attempts by Congress to invoke the War Powers Resolution over U.S. involvement in the Persian Gulf in 1987 was the focal point of much presidential maneuvering. This ultimately led to a compromise in which the president was simply expected to inform Congress of developments. The president must be cautious in following certain tactics, however, because Congress can react negatively to extreme pressure from the White House and can undermine the president's domestic and foreign agendas.

The president can decide that the best means to implement national security policy and strategy is to distance himself from Congress and provide minimum information. He can thereby maintain a degree of flexibility. The danger is that members of Congress, as well as the public, may perceive the president as isolated from major policy decisions and out of touch.

In a direct confrontation with Congress, the president can take his case to the people. In 1987, President Ronald Reagan used this tactic to develop support for financial aid to the contras opposing the Sandinista government in Nicaragua. Earlier, he took the case for Vietnam to the people, labeling U.S. involvement as a "noble cause" and honoring those who fought there. Other presidents have adopted this tactic when faced with congressional opposition to important presidential initiatives, as in 1993, when President Bill Clinton and First Lady Hillary Rodham Clinton sought to push through a health care reform package. Passage of the North American Free Trade Agreement (NAFTA) is another case in point. Here again, the president must be careful not to become overzealous. Congressional as well as public reaction to perceived inflexibility can undermine presidential initiatives; public backlash results if presidential policy fails to deliver.

In 1993 and 1994, U.S. national security strategy was not clear, and there was no clear strategic vision articulated by the Clinton administration.[18] This was seen in the apparently muddled response and misjudgments associated with U.S. involvement in Somalia, where eighteen U.S. soldiers were killed in an engagement in October 1993 (the subject of the popular film *Black Hawk Down*).[19]

The president has an advantage in dealing with Congress in the national security arena, however, because the sources of intelligence, the basis of policy and strategy skills, and the operational instruments are centered in his office. For example, the president's Cabinet, presidential advisers, national security staff, and the national security advisor are reinforcing powers. Even though expanded congressional staffs and their skills are important, the presidential power base—the Departments of Defense and State, the military advisory system, the Central Intelligence Agency, and the National Security Council and its staff—is dominant. Congress must rely on presidential sources for much of its information about national security.

Important exceptions include the Congressional Research Service, the committee system, and the congressional staffs, which have developed the ability to provide alternate approaches (e.g., to nuclear policy and defense budgets). However, much classified information remains the domain of the president, sometimes passed along to only a handful of members. Information leaks from Congress may cause the president to restrict congressional access to classified information, as President George W. Bush briefly considered in October 2001. Finally, nothing can substitute for face-to-face meetings between the president and other heads of state, or between the secretary of state and foreign ministers of other states, or for the knowledge that comes from liaisons with friendly intelligence agencies.

CONGRESS: THE LEGISLATIVE SYSTEM

The relationship between the chief executive and Congress has been described as an "invitation to struggle," as Benjamin Franklin said of democracy itself. The U.S. political system has a constitutional basis, with separation of powers among the branches of government and the resultant checks and balances. Although these characteristics are more pronounced in domestic politics and policy, they also play an important role in national security policy. To understand the congressional role in national security, we need to review the general features of the institution and the legislative process.

The Founders expected that Congress would dominate the political process. Although the president was given important powers in foreign affairs, participants at the Constitutional Convention wanted to ensure that he would not dominate the policymaking process. The president would have power to react in emergencies, but Congress would determine war policy. Furthermore, the power of Congress in the legislative process and budget matters was to provide an effective counterbalance to the president.

The scope of congressional responsibilities has increased, yet Congress is finding it more difficult to respond because of the cumbersome legislative process and the characteristics of the institution. As S. J. Deitchman concluded:

The Congress, representing diverse and often irreconcilable interests, is gaining long-term dominance over the Executive Branch.... Decision making in the interest of national security will become more difficult because the conflicts inherent in having a multiplicity of national-security decision-makers will have the effect of inhibiting, delaying, or distorting decisions that must be made in a world demanding increasing perceptiveness of international trends and more responsiveness and coherence in adapting to or attempting to influence them.[20]

Nevertheless, effective national security policy depends on congressional support and public acceptance. Because of the representative role of Congress and its power over the purse, no successful president can afford to disregard Congress, isolate himself from the legislative process, or distance himself from the leadership in Congress.

The organization and functioning of Congress rest primarily on the committee structure. In the normal course of the legislative process, a bill first goes to committees, with the chairs of committees and subcommittees exercising considerable power in determining its fate. Chairs are appointed by the majority party in each house, with seniority being critical to appointment. The internal power system of Congress does not rest solely with the committee structure, however. Congressional leadership positions, such as the Speaker of the House and the majority and minority leaders in both houses, carry power that generally exceeds that of committee chairs. Reforms in the 1970s placed final approval of leadership roles in the party caucus and eroded the disciplined party system as well as the authority of the party leadership. Combined with the committee structure and the power of individual members, these reforms have fragmented power within Congress.

Power in Congress thus derives from a mixture of sources: power over the purse, the status of the membership, relationships with colleagues, the party, and the formal leadership offices. As long as constituent support remains, members are powerful in their own right. Nonetheless, they can accomplish little by themselves; they are dependent upon colleagues to get things done. Every bill needs supporters, and this leads to constant interplay among internal forces seeking accommodation and compromise (or leading to confrontation). Thus even with internal power fragmentation, effective leadership in Congress is essential for the functioning of the legislative process.

CONGRESS AND THE EXECUTIVE: THE INVITATION TO STRUGGLE

Congress has a critical role in national security. According to Frederick Kaiser, "national security is not a simple set of well-integrated subject matters neatly arranged along a single, consistent policy continuum. . . . It is a complex set of diverse subject matters that cross into many different policy lines; these in turn raise different issues and concerns, institutional interests, and costs that affect congressional roles."[21]

At least two important distinctions need to be made as to the president and Congress. First, the institution of the presidency rests on one individual who heads a hierarchical branch of government. The center of power is clear, and the responsibility for executing the laws of the nation is focused on the president. There is little overt fragmentation of power or responsibility. In Congress, a different picture emerges. Not only is there considerable fragmentation of power within the institution; it is often difficult to place responsibility in any single member. Responsibility falls on Congress as an institution, making it possible for individual members to shift blame to the institution as a corporate body. This affords members a great deal of flexibility in taking political positions, and they can disclaim responsibility for any institutional outcome that is unacceptable to their constituencies.

Second, the president is the only nationally elected official (aside from the vice president, whose power is dependent on the president).[22] Thus only the president has a national constituency, with all that that suggests with respect to national security policy formulation. Individual members of the House of Representatives represent districts within states, many of which reflect narrow segments of the population. Furthermore, such districts can be dominated by one or two special interest groups. Senators, representing states, also reflect a small part of the total population. Even in states, the political power can rest with a handful of special interest groups.

Congress has attempted to overcome some of these disadvantages by referring to the corporate will of Congress. More often than not, this means little more than the will of a majority coalition—and if Congress is controlled by one party and the presidency by another party, the politics of the corporate will is relatively clear. The differing constituencies between the president and Congress not only reflect different power bases and interests; they create different policy mind-sets and the conditions of struggle over policy, programs, and budgets.

In his relationships with Congress and in trying to establish the necessary consensus and support for national security policies, the president must deal with a variety of power clusters within the institution. In the past, given party discipline and effective leadership in Congress, the executive could focus his attention on the Speaker of the House and the majority and minority leaders in both houses; today the president must also deal with other important members, especially key committee chairs. The increase in power clusters is especially pronounced in domestic policy, but it also affects national security policy. As some authorities conclude:

With more committees and subcommittees dealing with international issues; more staff and better information facilities at their disposal; more foreign travel by legislators and their aides; more groups, governments, and individuals trying to affect policy judgements, members of Congress, individually and collectively, have become less disposed to acquiesce in the president's initiatives. Some have even taken matters into their own hands.[23]

This was during President Reagan's second term in office. Congressman Stephen J. Solarz, for example, was directly involved in the Philippines as Ferdinand Marcos was deposed and replaced by a new government. In another example, Senator Christopher Dodd became the self-appointed spokesperson for the Daniel Ortega government in Nicaragua when he visited and dealt directly with Ortega. Before the dissolution of the Soviet Union, members of Congress also visited and met with Soviet President Mikhail Gorbachev. In 1993, Senator Bob Kerrey attempted to take the lead in establishing U.S. policy on POWs/MIAs in Southeast Asia, visiting North Vietnam in a highly publicized tour to give credence to his effort.

If the president loses popular support, or if his initiatives appear vacillating and ambiguous, Congress is more likely to take the lead. For example, following the killing of eighteen U.S. Army soldiers in

Somalia in late 1993, Congress set conditions for U.S. involvement there. Some observers noted the marginalization of the presidency in the matter. These are just a few examples of congressional usurpation of power in diplomatic and defense matters.

Nonetheless, the public looks to the president for leadership in national security policy. This is true also for most members of Congress, even though they debate and criticize policy. Part of this acquiescence stems from a recognition that it is difficult for Congress to lead; it is better postured to react and engage in oversight. Another factor is the tendency for Congress to be cautious in initiating national security policy for fear of being associated with failures or controversies that might affect their popularity with constituents. The safest position is to keep some distance from national security policy until it becomes clear whether it is succeeding or failing.

This allows the president some latitude in initiating national security policy, although policy failures are easily attributable to him. Equally important, the complexity of national security issues, the changed external power relationships, and the difficulty the United States faces in trying to control external situations all mean success is never assured. Failure is no longer a remote possibility. One can understand, therefore, the reluctance of members of Congress to become too closely associated, too soon, with presidential positions on national security, save for crises. In the international order of the twenty-first century, this reluctance is even more pronounced.

In summary, no president can ignore the congressional role in national security policy. Indeed, most successful policies depend on the bipartisan involvement of congressional leadership. Congress, sensitive to its responsibilities and protective of its prerogatives, demands an equal, if different, role in national security. Because there is ambiguity as to executive power in national security policy, the case is compelling for many members to be deeply involved. Ambiguity, shared power, institutional character, and the nature of national security policy thus create the basis for confrontation between the president and Congress.

THE PRESIDENT, CONGRESS, AND THE POLICY PROCESS

The president's ability to deal with Congress and to develop the support necessary for national security policy must be viewed from two dimensions: (1) the element of national security policy being considered; and (2) how the president's sources of strength can overcome the sources of conflict.

National security policy includes a range of subpolicies, from the defense budget and military manpower levels, to executive agreements and treaties, to covert operations. There is a degree of overlap between national security and foreign policy. This overlap has become considerable in the new strategic landscape, in which national security increasingly encompasses nonmilitary matters.

The president has a great deal of latitude in committing and deploying U.S. military forces, especially in the early stages of a crisis. Nevertheless, congressional oversight and budget power restrict the president in the long term. Congress, ever sensitive to negative reaction from constituents about U.S. force commitments, will make their reaction known to the president. To be sure, in short-term commitments for which success appears clear, as in the Gulf War, and even in longer-term commitments where there is a clear threat to the nation, as in the current war on terrorism, the president can enjoy popularity and support for his policies. But only the president will be blamed for any failure.

An essential part of the national security policy process is reflected in debates over the defense budget and the final shape of the national budget. The annual budget process focuses attention on general issues of national security. This does not involve serious discussion and debate over strategy, but there can be exceptions (e.g., the George W. Bush administration, which initially decided not to increase defense spending).[24] Yet budget debates are usually the most visible part of national security policy formulation, although specific events (e.g., September 11, the anthrax scare, Iran-contra, the Marines barracks bombing in Lebanon, the Gulf War, Somalia, Bosnia-Herzegovina) focus attention on specific issues that can lead to debate over national security policy. In 1993, Secretary of Defense Les Aspin's attempt to restructure the U.S. military drew criticism from Congress and other quarters and figured in defense budget debates and in national security policy in general.[25] In addition, some issues have gone beyond traditional national security notions (e.g., the Clinton administration's efforts to lift the ban on open homosexuality and to expand the role of women in the military). Such efforts can raise much criticism, with some observers linking issues to problems in national security policy.

Finally, some issues of U.S. national security may be a continual source of debate, but there is continuity in important aspects of U.S. policy, even in the new world order. The fight against terrorism, the close relationship with Western Europe, the concern over weapons proliferation, protection of freedom and nurturing of democratic systems, and control and reduction of nuclear weapons stockpiles will continue to be important priorities.

Well-established and accepted components of national security generally do not create controversial and difficult issues for the president. It is when the president wants to change direction, add a new dimension to established policy, undertake new initiatives, or fails to clarify national security policy that he faces opposition in Congress and among the public. In the past, national security included policies long understood by the U.S. public, such as the role in NATO and other security arrangements. But the end of the Cold War has thrown such relationships into disarray, even irrelevance. Questions are now being raised, for example, regarding the relevance of NATO now that the Soviet Union is no more. The George W. Bush administration clearly shares Bill Clinton's enthusiasm for expanding NATO.

In addition, recent developments have little to do with Cold War alliances. All of this has become more complicated in the twenty-first century, with its uncertain world order and altered strategic landscape.

LEADERSHIP AND POLICY

This study has stressed that the success of national security policy depends on the president's leadership and his relationship with Congress. The president has the key role, the constitutional authority, and much latitude in foreign and national security policy. His ability to build support in Congress, to control and direct the national security establishment, and to gain public acceptance of his policies is a direct function of his leadership style.

No single model of leadership is sufficient. Indeed, a variety of leadership approaches can establish a basis for legislative support, just as there are various tangible means by which the president can create and nurture congressional support.

Yet certain principles of leadership are essential in dealing effectively with Congress. These principles, and the way they are applied, must lead to the development of trust and confidence. This in turn evolves from the perceptions of members of Congress that the president is in control of the national security establishment, that his presence permeates that establishment, and that he clearly articulates a vision of U.S. strength and commitment. Furthermore, Congress must feel that the president's staff is knowledgeable, skilled, and supportive of his national security policy. Equally important, there must be mutual trust and confidence among the president and the national security staff, the military, and the intelligence establishment. Part of this evolves from the character, background, and experience of the commander-in-chief. In this respect, there is sometimes a decided gap between the president and the military.[26]

Much presidential strength is a function of personality and character. According to two prominent scholars:

The point to remember in assessing the presidential power and the ability of a given president to wield it effectively— or perhaps even abuse it—is that the style and character of the president himself is every bit as important as the inherent power of the institution. And when we talk about powers of the presidency, we must consider three factors: a president's sense of purpose; his political skills; and his character.[27]

And as James Q. Wilson concludes, "The public will judge the president not only in terms of what he accomplishes but also in terms of its perception of his character."[28] To understand the power that presidents wield, we must make some distinction between foreign and domestic affairs, specify the kind of power and the issue, identify the circumstances, and consider the opposition from other centers of power. We must also understand how well the president understands the political process itself, how deeply he feels about achieving the goals being sought, and how much political skill he brings to the job.

Trust and confidence between the executive and the legislature are strengthened by several procedures flowing out of the Oval Office. Members of Congress, especially the leadership, must feel that the president is sincere about consulting Congress and accepts the coequal status of Congress and the president. Furthermore, Congress must feel that the president is providing timely and useful information on matters of national security. This especially applies to covert operations and secret military movements, even though Congress initially is only a recipient of information and not an approving body.

Furthermore, the president must make himself reasonably accessible to members of Congress, especially to the leadership. Members become frustrated if ignored by the president and feel that such a situation damages their ability to deal with their own issues. In such an environment, confrontation and disagreement between Congress and the president are inevitable. The idea of consultation is engrained in the two institutions. Consultation can pave the way for support, provide the perception of congressional power, and become a symbolic tool for fulfilling congressional responsibility.

Even if the president does all these things, he will not be assured of success; but he will have the most favorable environment in which to pursue such goals. Leadership is the key to relationships with Congress, and leadership must begin with an understanding of the important role played by Congress as well as an appreciation for the human motivations of individual members.

CONCLUSION

The president cannot simply respond to popular passions of the moment; neither can he simply ingratiate himself with Congress. Such behavior can only lead to the erosion of executive credibility and project a picture of a weak leader. This can have serious negative effects on political will and can lead to the erosion of staying power in national security.

The president is ultimately responsible for the formulation and implementation of national security policy and strategy. For most elements of his policy, he is in a position to receive the support of Congress and the public. But there are elements of policy in which he may have to stand alone, taking credit for its success but assuming full responsibility for failure. How this plays out within the national security system depends on presidential leadership.

NOTES

1. A "specialty" is a primary or secondary career pattern for which officers may qualify by virtue of performance and education, among other considerations.

2. Michael R. Gordon, "Aspin Overhauls Pentagon to Bolster Policy Role," *New York Times* (January 28, 1993): A17. See also William Matthews, "Aspin Puts Stamp on Pentagon Hierarchy," *Army Times* (February 8, 1993): 6.

3. William S. Cohen, Secretary of Defense, *Report of the Secretary of Defense to the President and the Congress,* 2001, 243.

4. Ibid., Appendix C.

5. Les Aspin, *The Bottom-Up Review: Forces for a New Era* (Washington, D.C.: U.S. Department of Defense, September 1, 1993).

6. Gordon R. Sullivan and James M. Dubik, *Land Warfare in the 21st Century* (Carlisle Barracks, Penn.: Strategic Studies Institute, U.S. Army War College, February 1993).

7. See Gary T. Dempsey, with Roger W. Fontaine, *Fool's Errands: America's Recent Encounters with Nation Building* (Washington, D.C.: Cato Institute, 2001).

8. This summary is based on David T. Twining, "The Weinberger Doctrine and the Use of Force in the Contemporary Era," in *The Recourse to War: An Appraisal of the "Weinberger Doctrine,"* ed. Alan Ned Sabrosky and Robert L. Sloane (Carlisle Barracks, Penn.: Strategic Studies Institute, U.S. Army War College, 1988), 11–12. The Weinberger Doctrine appears in Department of Defense, *Report of the Secretary of Defense to the Congress for Fiscal Year 1987* (Washington, D.C.: U.S. Government Printing Office, February 5, 1986).

9. Colin Powell, with Joseph E. Persico, *My American Journey* (New York: Random House, 1995), 434.

10. Sam C. Sarkesian, "Who Serves?" *Social Science and Modern Society* 18 (March/April 1981): 57–60, and Sam C. Sarkesian, John Allen Williams, and Fred B. Bryant, *Soldiers, Society, and National Security* (Boulder: Lynne Rienner Publishers, 1995), 13–17.

11. Sam C. Sarkesian and Robert E. Connor, Jr., *The U.S. Military Profession into the Twenty-First Century* (London: Frank Cass, 1999), 169. See also Wesley K. Clark, *Waging Modern War: Bosnia, Kosovo, and the Future of Combat* (New York: Public Affairs, 2001).

12. Sam C. Sarkesian, "The U.S. Military Must Find Its Voice," *Orbis: A Journal of World Affairs* 42 (Summer 1998): 423–37.

13. Sarkesian and Connor, *U.S. Military Profession,* 169.

14. Sarkesian, Williams, and Bryant, *Soldiers,* 147.

15. There are any number of official documents dealing with issues of national security and the military, including defense budget issues. Among others, these include: the National Defense Panel, *Transforming Defense: National Security in the 21st Century* (Washington, D.C.: Report of the National Defense Panel, December 1997); Chairman, Joint Chiefs of Staff, *Joint Vision 2020* (Washington, D.C.: U.S. Government Printing Office, June 2000); *National Defense Budget Estimates for FY 1999* (Washington, D.C.: Office of the Undersecretary of Defense, March 1998); *Quadrennial Defense Review* (Washington, D.C.: Department of Defense, 1997); and Cohen, *Annual Report to the President and the Congress,* 2001.

16. Roger Hilsman, with Laura Gaughran and Patricia A. Weitsman, *The Politics of Policymaking in Defense and Foreign Affairs: Conceptual Models and Bureaucratic Politics,* third ed. (Englewood Cliffs, N.J.: Prentice-Hall, 1993), 145.

17. Richard A. Watson and Norman C. Thomas, *The Politics of the Presidency,* second ed. (Washington, D.C.: CQ Press, 1988), 257.

18. This was rectified somewhat later in his administration with the publishing of an annual National Security Strategy report. See, for example, *A National Security Strategy for a Global Age* (Washington, D.C.: December 2000).

19. Eighteen special operations personnel (sixteen Army Rangers and two members of the elite Delta Force) were killed on October 3 and 4, 1993, in an attempt to capture Somali warlord Mohammed Farah Aideed. He was a general in the Somali army and trained in the former Soviet Union. He was also a student of Mao Tse-tung and studied the strategic perspectives of Sun-tzu. Many of these matters have to do with guerrilla warfare, but in October 1993, Aideed's background and training were hardly noted by any spokesperson in the Clinton administration or by the media.

20. S. J. Deitchman, *Beyond the Thaw: A New National Strategy* (Boulder: Westview, 1991), 34.

21. Frederick M. Kaiser, "Congress and National Security Policy: Evolving and Varied Roles for a Shared Responsibility," in *Grand Strategy and the Decisionmaking Process,* ed. James C. Gaston (Washington, D.C.: National Defense University Press, 1991), 217.

22. The vice president's constitutional power as president of the Senate can be important if the Senate is evenly divided, as it was for a short time after the 2000 election.

23. George C. Edwards and Stephen J. Wayne, *Presidential Leadership: Politics and Policy Making* (New York: St. Martin's, 1985), 299.

24. See Tom Ricks, "Clinton's Pentagon Budget to Stand," *Washington Post* (February 7, 2001): 4. Any military leader who was surprised by this failed to read the tea leaves correctly. Their visceral dislike of Clinton personally and the Clinton-Gore military policies blinded them to the fact that the militarily hawkish Republicans were primarily *budget* hawks. If the military wanted to continue the status quo, only with more money, they should have hoped for a Gore victory.

25. Les Aspin, Secretary of Defense, "Bottom-Up Review," letter dated June 25, 1993, with enclosure on "Remarks" as prepared by Les Aspin, Secretary of Defense, at the National Defense University Graduation, Fort McNair, Washington, D.C., June 16, 1993. Also see Representative Les Aspin, "The New Security: A Bottom-up Approach to the Post–Cold War Era," U.S. House of Representatives, Armed Services Committee.

26. David Silverberg, "Clinton and the Military: Can the Gap Be Bridged?" *Armed Forces Journal International* 129 (October 1993): 53, 54, 57.

27. Erwin C. Hargraves and Roy Hoopes, *The Presidency: A Question of Power* (Boston: Little, Brown, 1975), 47.

28. James Q. Wilson, *American Government: Institutions and Policies,* fifth ed. (Lexington, Mass.: D. C. Heath, 1992), 338.

UNIFIED AT LAST

JAMES R. LOCHER III

Sound structure will permit the release of energies and of imagination now unduly constrained by the existing arrangements.—Defense Secretary James R. Schlesinger, 1983

Despite negative Pentagon attitudes, the Senate and House Armed Services Committees and other reorganization supporters had high expectations for the Goldwater-Nichols Act. Have results matched these expectations? Comparing the Department of Defense's performance since 1986 with congressional objectives provides a useful yardstick for assessing the act's contributions.

In reorganizing the Department of Defense, Congress' overarching concern centered on the excessive influence of the four services, which had inhibited the integration of their separate capabilities into effective joint fighting units. With its desire to balance joint and service interests as the backdrop, Congress declared nine purposes for the act: strengthen civilian authority; improve military advice; place clear responsibility on combatant commanders for accomplishment of assigned missions; ensure that the authority of combatant commanders is commensurate with their responsibility; increase attention to strategy formulation and contingency planning; provide for the more efficient use of resources; improve joint officer management; enhance the effectiveness of military operations; and improve DoD management.[1] Some objectives were more important than others. Congress gave priority to fixing problems in the department's operational dimension: military advice, responsibility and authority of combatant commanders, contingency planning, joint officer management, and the effectiveness of military operations.

Congress found numerous obstacles impeding effective civilian authority. Members agreed with John Kester's characterization of the secretary of defense: "His real authority is not as great as it seems, and his vast responsibilities are not in reality matched by commensurate powers."[2]

Congress saw the secretary's efforts being "seriously hampered by the absence of . . . independent military advice." Joint Chiefs of Staff (JCS) logrolling provided the secretary with watered-down advice. This forced the Office of the Secretary of Defense (OSD) to carry the entire burden of challenging the services on policies and programs. The Senate Armed Services Committee staff study assessed the outcome: "The natural consequence has been a heightening of civil-military disagreement, an isolation of OSD, a loss of information critical to effective decision-making, and, most importantly, a political weakening of the secretary of defense and his OSD staff. The overall result of interservice logrolling has been a highly undesirable lessening of civilian control of the military."[3]

Confusion concerning the roles of the military department secretaries ranked next on Congress' list of problems hampering the defense secretary's authority. The National Security Act of 1947 never defined the new secretary's relationship to the service secretaries. Bitter controversy over unification precluded clarification. The 1947 law preserved considerable independence for the civilian heads of the military departments. Subsequent amendments strengthened the defense secretary's power and staff, but they did not prescribe his relationship to the service secretaries. Not surprisingly, service secretaries energetically advocated parochial positions, frequently at the expense of their boss' broader agenda.

Three Goldwater-Nichols prescriptions were most important in addressing these problems. First, to leave no doubt as to the defense secretary's authority, report language declared, "The secretary has sole and ultimate power within the Department of Defense on any matter on which the secretary chooses to act."[4] Congress meant this to end claims by defense officials to jurisdictions independent of the secretary's authority.

Second, Congress envisioned that making the JCS chairman the principal military adviser would provide the secretary a military ally who shared a department-wide, nonparochial perspective. Capitol Hill foresaw this alliance ending the civil-military nature of Pentagon disputes.

Third, the law specified each service secretary's responsibility to the defense secretary. These provisions filled a void that had existed for nearly 40 years.

By empowering the secretary of defense to more effectively lead and manage the department, the Goldwater-Nichols Act achieved the objective of strengthening civilian authority. Disputes over the secretary's authority have ended; he is viewed as the ultimate power. Richard B. Cheney, the first defense secretary to fight a war under Goldwater-Nichols, found that "each service wants to do its own thing." He observed that "the Department of Defense is difficult enough to run without going back to a system that, in my mind, served to weaken the civilian

This essay has been edited and is reprinted from Victory on the Potomac (*College Station, Tex.: Texas A&M University Press, 2002*), 437–50, by permission of Texas A&M University Press.

authority of the secretary and the president. . . .
Goldwater-Nichols helped pull it together in a coherent fashion so that it functions much better . . . than
it ever did before."[5]

Despite Cheney's valid assertion, Goldwater-
Nichols's impact on civilian authority has received
more criticism than any other area. Critics claim that
the enhanced role of the JCS chairman and improved
Joint Staff capabilities have led "to the erosion of
civilian control of the military." These naysayers do
not suggest that the revitalized military is disobedient
or is making major decisions. They worry instead
about "the relative weight or influence of the military
in the decisions the government makes."[6]

There is no doubt that the Joint Staff now over-
shadows OSD, diminishing the civilian voice in the
decisionmaking process. Two trends have produced
this result: the improved quality of Joint Staff work
and a weaker performance by OSD. Ineffective leadership in a fast-paced environment and inattention to
personnel matters have contributed to OSD's decline. As worrisome as this imbalance may be, it does
not match the seriousness of the more overt challenges to civilian authority during the pre-Goldwater-
Nichols era. Then, the military often resisted the
authority of the defense secretary. As Cheney noted,
Goldwater-Nichols helped overcome that problem.
Now the concern is that officers are helping the secretary too much by providing better, more timely
information and more powerful ideas than do their
civilian counterparts.

The solution to this problem is not to weaken
military staff work but to improve civilian contributions. Changes in law are not needed to achieve this
outcome. The defense secretary already has sufficient authority to take the required actions. Creating
a dynamic leadership culture and building a highly
qualified civilian workforce are demanding, long-term
tasks. Of the failure to act, Eliot Cohen advised, "It
is the civilians, not the soldiers, who have abdicated
their responsibilities."[7]

Recalling pre-1986 military advice, General Colin
Powell, the first JCS chairman to fight a war under
Goldwater-Nichols, observed that "almost the only
way" previous chiefs reached agreement on advice
was "by scratching each other's back," while the Joint
Staff "spent thousands of man-hours pumping out
ponderous, least-common-denominator documents
that every chief would accept but few secretaries of
defense or presidents found useful." This partly explains "why the Joint Chiefs had never spoken out
with a clear voice to prevent the deepening morass
in Vietnam."[8]

In response to inadequate military advice, Congress crafted some of the Goldwater-Nichols Act's
most far-reaching provisions. The act made the JCS
chairman the principal military adviser, transferred
to him the duties previously performed by the corporate JCS, and added new duties. To assist the chairman, Congress created the position of vice chairman
as the second-ranking officer. Last, Congress gave
the chairman full authority over the Joint Staff.

A comprehensive assessment concluded that the
act "made a significant and positive contribution in
improving the quality of military advice," a judgment
shared by principal customers. Cheney said he regarded the chairman's uncompromised advice "a
significant improvement" over the "lowest common
denominator." Powell's successor as JCS chairman,
General John M. Shalikashvili, agreed, "We have been
able to provide far better, more focused advice."[9]

Former navy secretary John Lehman disagreed
with these assessments and the designation of the
JCS chairman as principal military adviser. Repeating his mid-1980s arguments, he said the chairman's role has "limited not only the scope of military
advice available to the political leadership, but also
the policy- and priority-setting roles of the service
chiefs and civilian service secretaries."[10]

Congress found pre-1986 operational chains of
command confused and cumbersome. The chain of
command roles of the defense secretary and JCS
were unclear. Despite removal of the military departments from the chain in 1958, service chiefs retained
de facto influence over combatant commands, increasing the confusion.

To achieve its objective of placing clear responsibility on combatant commanders, Capitol Hill
clarified the chain of command to each commander
and emphasized each commander's responsibility to
the president and secretary of defense for mission
performance. The Goldwater-Nichols Act directed
that the chain of command run from the president
to the secretary of defense to the combatant commander. The JCS, including the chairman, were explicitly removed.

Opinion is unanimous that this objective has been
achieved. Senior officials and officers have repeatedly cited the benefits of a clear, short operational
chain of command. Commenting on Operation Desert
Storm, General H. Norman Schwarzkopf stated,
"Goldwater-Nichols established very, very clear lines
of command authority and responsibilities over subordinate commanders, and that meant a much more
effective fighting force." Secretary of Defense Bill
Perry recalled that commentaries and after-action
reports were unanimous in attributing that war's
success "to the fundamental structural changes in
the chain of command brought about by Goldwater-
Nichols."[11]

Congress found the combatant commands weak,
unified in name only. They were loose confedera-
tions of powerful service components and forces.
The services used *Unified Action Armed Forces,*
which established policies for joint operations, to restrict the authority of the combatant commander and
give significant autonomy to his service component
commanders.

To correct this violation of command principles,
Congress modeled the law on the authority that the
military had traditionally given to a unit commander.
The Goldwater-Nichols Act empowered each combatant commander to give authoritative direction,
prescribe the chain of command, organize commands

and forces, employ forces, assign command functions to subordinate commanders, coordinate and approve aspects of administration and support, select and suspend subordinates, and convene courts-martial.

Service claims that the legislation would make warlords of the combatant commanders quickly ended as the soundness of balancing authority and responsibility at the combatant commander level—in line with military tradition—became apparent. Agreement is widespread that Goldwater-Nichols has ensured commensurate authority for combatant commanders. "This act," said Shalikashvili, "by providing both the responsibility and the authority needed by the CINCs [commander-in-chiefs], has made the combatant commanders vastly more capable of fulfilling their warfighting role."[12] Performance of these commands in operations and peacetime activities convincingly supports this judgment.

A minority view urges increased authority for combatant commanders through a greater resource-allocation role. Not wanting to divert these commands from their principal warfighting function, Congress intended that the JCS chairman and Joint Staff would represent their resource needs. To many observers, this approach continued to remain preferable to schemes that would require greater involvement by the commands. Recent JCS chairman General Henry H. Shelton agreed: "More involvement by the combatant commanders in resourcing would not be healthy. We want to keep them focused on warfighting."[13]

In formulating Goldwater-Nichols, the two Armed Services Committees determined that strategic and contingency planning in the Department of Defense were underemphasized and ineffective. Because strategic planning was often fiscally unconstrained, it was also unrealistic. Moreover, strategy and resource allocation were weakly linked. Contingency plans had limited utility in crises; often they were based on invalid political assumptions.

To highlight strategy making and contingency planning, Congress formulated four principal Goldwater-Nichols provisions. First, it directed the president to submit an annual report on national security strategy. Second, it instructed the JCS chairman to prepare fiscally constrained strategic plans. Third, the act required the defense secretary to provide written policy guidance, including political assumptions, for preparation and review of contingency plans. The fourth provision directed the under secretary of defense for policy to assist the secretary on contingency plans.

Prior to Goldwater-Nichols, the JCS had so jealously guarded nonnuclear contingency plans that the only civilian briefed on them was the defense secretary. Additional civilian access was denied to prevent civilian "meddling" in operational matters and leaks —civilians were not trusted with sensitive material. Alone, the secretary could not provide meaningful review or direction. The absence of rigorous civilian review led to plans based on unrealistic assumptions, sharply limiting their utility.[14]

Goldwater-Nichols increased attention to both strategy making and contingency planning. The quality of strategy documents has varied, but in every case, their value has been superior to those predating Goldwater-Nichols.

Contingency planning consists of two categories: deliberate plans and crisis action plans. Deliberate plans are prepared for all potential wars and major crises and updated every year or so. Crisis action plans respond to unexpected crises, such as the famine in Somalia in 1992. Improvements in contingency planning have occurred almost exclusively in the deliberate planning category. In 1996, Shalikashvili saw advances: "Our major war plans . . . are the best I have seen." Five years later, his successor, General Shelton, cited additional progress: "We have been able to better integrate the political-military, coalition, and interagency aspects into our plans." OSD eased into its oversight responsibilities, seeking to reassure a nervous joint system. A retired three-star general was hired to head the civilian review office, which was staffed by active-duty officers. A single civilian sat between the general and his staff. The office did not conduct its first contingency plan review until 1992; a year later, it had established a comprehensive review regime. Civilian involvement has increased, but military officers still dominate "civilian" review.[15]

For crisis action plans, progress on improving civilian review has been extremely limited. The joint chiefs have used traditional arguments of civilian meddling and untrustworthiness to deny access beyond the secretary, deputy secretary, and under secretary for policy. Occasionally, the price for the absence of rigorous civilian review is staggering: military planners failed to plan for postoperation law and order and restoration of government services in Operation Just Cause, the invasion of Panama in 1989. Lawlessness, looting, and slow recovery tarnished the operation's success. In modern conflicts and crises, policy and operations intertwine. The department's practice of separating them ignores the intent of Goldwater-Nichols, blocks essential collaboration between policy and operational planners, and will continue to produce unsatisfactory results.

Mid-1980s testimony before Congress revealed that the Department of Defense's ambiguous strategic goals gave service interests, not strategic needs, the dominant role in allocating resources. The lack of an independent military assessment of service programs and budgets also impaired the secretary of defense's resource management.

To achieve its objective of providing for more efficient use of resources. Congress turned to the JCS chairman for the lacking independent military perspective, assigning him six new resource-related duties. Two important ones were advising the secretary on combatant command priorities and assessing conformation of programs and budgets of the military departments and other defense components with strategic plans and combatant command priorities. The chairman was also empowered to recommend alternative programs and budgets.

The potential of resource-allocation reforms has been realized only once, when General Powell used his new resource advisory role in 1990 to formulate the Base Force. Reducing the Cold War force structure by 25 percent represented Department of Defense's most important and difficult resource issue since the passage of Goldwater-Nichols, so Powell's contribution was not insignificant. Besides this critical contribution, JCS chairmen have yet to provide definitive resource advice to defense secretaries.

The chairman has mechanisms for developing advice on resource allocation to best meet joint warfighting needs. Admiral William A. Owens, while serving as JCS vice chairman, instituted several innovative changes improving support by the Joint Requirements Oversight Council (JROC) for the formulation of resource advice. The council—consisting of the vice chairman and the four service vice chiefs—advises the chairman on requirements and acquisition. Owens introduced Joint Warfighting Capabilities Assessments (JWCAs), which cover such areas as sea, air, and space superiority and strategic mobility and sustainment, to assist the JROC in analyzing department-wide resource needs and priorities.

The JWCAs offer dramatic improvements in comparing service programs against mission requirements. Unfortunately, the JROC operates by consensus—just like the old JCS. At a time when the Department of Defense needs decisive priorities and tradeoffs, the JROC simply rubber-stamps service initiatives. Owens acknowledged that decisions still "squander enormous funds."[16]

Instead of informing the chairman's independent advice, the JROC prenegotiates in the old logrolling way. The military has come full circle to the wasteful, bad old days. Its approach could result in the services locking arms on major resource issues to politically overpower the defense secretary and Congress. When the JCS chairman permits these activities and surrenders his independent perspective, he abandons the intentions of Goldwater-Nichols. If such practices go uncorrected, Congress will need to act.

On joint officer issues, Congress concluded: "For the most part, military officers do not want to be assigned to joint duty; are pressured or monitored for loyalty by their services while serving on joint assignments; are not prepared by either education or experience to perform their joint duties; and serve for only a relatively short period once they have learned their jobs."[17] Because the Joint Staff and combatant command headquarters staffs are the preeminent military staffs, Capitol Hill found this situation intolerable.

Title IV of the Goldwater-Nichols Act established procedures for the selection, education, assignment, and promotion of joint-duty officers. Congress and the Pentagon fought the last Goldwater-Nichols battles over this title. The services resisted a joint-officer personnel system because the loss of absolute control over officer promotions and assignments would weaken their domination of the Pentagon.

Congress was equally determined to eliminate a system in which "joint thinkers are likely to be punished, and service promoters are likely to be rewarded."[18]

The joint-officer incentives, requirements, and standards prescribed by Goldwater-Nichols have significantly improved the performance of joint duty. Cheney judged that requiring joint duty "prior to moving into senior leadership positions turned out to be beneficial." He also felt that joint-officer policies made the Joint Staff "an absolutely vital part of the operation." Powell judged that the Joint Staff had "improved so dramatically" it had become "the premier military staff in the world." General Schwarzkopf commented that Goldwater-Nichols "changed dramatically" the quality of people "assigned to Central Command at all levels."[19]

These positive results were achieved despite the indifference of OSD, senior joint officers, and the Joint Staff, as well as efforts by the services to minimize title IV's impact. The JCS chairman at the time of Goldwater-Nichols's enactment, Admiral Crowe, later wrote of his unfavorable view of title IV: "The detailed legislation that mandated every aspect of the 'Joint Corps' from the selection process and the number of billets to promotional requirements was, I believed, a serious mistake that threatened a horrendous case of congressional micromanagement. In this instance the chiefs were unanimous in their opposition, and I agreed with them wholeheartedly." Not surprisingly, for many years, Joint Staff implementation reflected this sympathy toward service attitudes. "We probably have not advanced as far or as fast as we could have had more attention been directed toward joint officer management," admitted Shelton.[20]

The initiative of individual officers accounts for the success of the joint-officer provisions. Seeing joint duty as career enhancing, qualified officers vigorously pursue joint assignments.

Congress had hoped that the Department of Defense, after several years of implementing title IV, would develop a better approach to joint-officer management. That has not occurred. The Goldwater-Nichols objective of improving joint-officer management has been achieved, but the Pentagon still lacks a vision of its needs for joint officers and how to prepare and reward them.

For 40 years after World War II, service parochialism and independence denied the Department of Defense the unity of effort required to wage modern warfare. Congress found that the "operational deficiencies evident during the Vietnam War, the seizure of the *Pueblo,* the Iranian hostage rescue mission, and the incursion into Grenada were the result of the failure to adequately implement the concept of unified command."[21] To enhance the effectiveness of military operations, Congress' principal fix was to provide combatant commanders sufficient authority to ensure unity of command during operations and effective mission preparation. The Goldwater-Nichols Act also assigned to the JCS chairman responsibility for developing joint doctrine and joint training policies.

Overwhelming successes in Operations Just Cause in Panama and Desert Shield/Storm in the Persian Gulf region showed that the act had quickly unified American fighting forces. Of this improved performance, Powell said, "Goldwater-Nichols deserves much of the credit." Malcolm Forbes commented: "The extraordinary efficient, smooth way our military has functioned in the Gulf is a tribute to . . . the Goldwater-Nichols Reorganization Act, which shifted power from individual military services to officials responsible for coordinating them. . . . The extraordinary achievements of Secretary Cheney and Generals Powell and Schwarzkopf would not have been possible without Goldwater-Nichols." An article in *Washington Monthly* added, "Goldwater-Nichols helped ensure that this war had less interservice infighting, less deadly bureaucracy, fewer needless casualties, and more military cohesion than any major operation in decades."[22]

Speaking in 1996, Secretary Perry observed that Goldwater-Nichols "dramatically changed the way that America's forces operate by streamlining the command process and empowering the chairman of the Joint Chiefs of Staff and the unified commanders." It produced "the resounding success of our forces in Desert Storm, in Haiti, and . . . in Bosnia."[23]

Joint doctrine and training have experienced more modest progress, especially in the early years. In 1994, General Shalikashvili said: "While we have some joint doctrine, it is really in its infancy, at best. It is not well-vetted; it is not well-understood at all; and it is certainly not disseminated out there. And most certainly, it is almost *never* used by anyone." The JCS chairman, calling joint training "an embarrassment," said, "We have an awful long way to go to bring us into the 21st century." A year later, the Commission on Roles and Missions characterized the first generation of joint doctrine as "a compendium of competing and sometimes incompatible concepts (often developed by one 'lead' service)."[24] Attention has been given to these shortcomings, particularly joint training, which has benefited from establishment of the Joint Forces Command, Joint Training System, and Joint Warfighting Center.

The Joint Forces Command's role as the joint force integrator, trainer, provider, and experimenter has great potential for enhancing the effectiveness of military operations. To date, parochial attitudes by the services and some geographic unified commands and weak Joint Staff support have hamstrung the Joint Forces Command's progress. Inadequate resourcing has hindered the command's work. To carry the Department of Defense to the next level of jointness, Shelton argued, "The Joint Forces Command needs a funding line and acquisition authority." Shelton also believed that the department should use a joint budget account to fund all joint activities rather than continuing to rely on funding by service executive agents. Mike Donley asserted that the executive agent

system "has left the services with too much influence over joint funding priorities."[25]

Shelton recommended another dramatic change: "The next big step in jointness is to establish standing joint task forces and recognize that capability as a required core competency. We need to have the organization, training, and equipment that will allow us to move rapidly, have a common operational picture, and conduct rapid decisive operations as a joint force. That's a Ph.D. level of warfighting which you can't do with our current pickup team approach. We should designate four standing joint task force headquarters: East Coast, West Coast, Hawaii, and Europe."[26]

Despite the remaining work, improvements in joint warfighting capabilities have been swift and dramatic. In 1996, Senator Sam Nunn asserted, "The Pentagon's ability to prepare for and conduct joint operations has improved more in ten years—since passage of the Goldwater-Nichols Act—than in the entire period since the need for jointness was recognized by the creation of the Joint Army-Navy Board in 1903." Shalikashvili saw similar progress: "No other nation can match our ability to combine forces on the battlefield and fight jointly."[27] This was demonstrated at the small-unit level during the Afghanistan phase of the war on terrorism: Army Special Forces soldiers directed punishing Air Force and Navy air strikes.

A few critics, mostly retired Marines, have disputed these views. Retired Colonel Mackubin T. Owens, Jr., argued: "The contributions of the Goldwater-Nichols Act to the improved performance of the U.S. Armed Forces are marginal at best, and . . . the unintended consequences of the act may well create problems in the future that outweigh any current benefits." Retired Marine Lieutenant General Paul K. Van Riper warned: "The path to 'jointness' some are advocating has grave implications for national defense. . . . The organizational structures brought about by Goldwater-Nichols are not necessarily appropriate for the future."[28]

Many Goldwater-Nichols provisions helped improve the department's management. But, in adding this objective, Congress had in mind specific structural problems hindering sound management, including excessive supervisory spans of control, unnecessary staff layers and duplication of effort, continued growth in headquarters staffs, poor supervision of defense agencies, and an unclear division of work among defense components.

The secretary of defense's span of control especially concerned Congress. Forty-one officials and officers, excluding his deputy and personal staff, reported directly to him. To reduce this span, Goldwater-Nichols required the secretary to delegate the supervision of each defense agency and field activity to a senior civilian or the JCS chairman. The chairman's role as overseer of the combatant commands also lightened the secretary's supervisory burdens.

Other provisions consolidated certain functions in the military department secretariats, limited the number of service deputy and assistant chiefs of staff, reduced by 15 percent the number of personnel and general and flag officers in the military department headquarters, and reduced certain other staffs by 10 or 15 percent.

Yet such remedies were largely ineffective. The defense bureaucracy remains far too large. Duplication of effort continues. Defense agencies—some with expenditures larger than the biggest defense contractors—receive negligible guidance or oversight. The department still lacks a concept for the appropriate division of work among components.

Beyond the unfinished business of the Goldwater-Nichols Act, the Department of Defense faces other organizational challenges. The act's strengthening of the JCS, Joint Staff, and combatant commands has produced dramatic results in one of the department's two dimensions: warfighting. Reforms of business activities—performed principally by OSD, the military departments, and defense agencies—have been fewer and less successful. This dimension requires rigorous attention.

Secretary of Defense Bill Cohen attempted to provide this attention with his Defense Reform Initiative, launched in 1997. Cohen envisioned "igniting a revolution in business affairs within DoD that will bring to the department management techniques and business practices that have restored American corporations to leadership in the marketplace."[29]

But the Defense Reform Initiative has focused on the lesser challenges of Cohen's revolution. The department needs to elevate the initiative's sights to target major shortcomings. Of organizations like the Pentagon, business guru John Kotter wrote: "The typical twentieth-century organization has not operated well in a rapidly changing environment. Structure, systems, practices, and culture have often been more of a drag on change than a facilitator. If environmental volatility continues to increase, as most people now predict, the standard organization of the twentieth century will likely become a dinosaur."[30]

The Pentagon's change-resistant culture represents its greatest organizational weakness. Because of the Pentagon's immense success in wars cold and hot, it suffers from the "failure of success." It is an invincible giant who has fallen asleep. Given past successes, the Pentagon cannot break its embrace of past warfighting concepts and traditional weapon systems, as Secretary of Defense Donald Rumsfeld found in early 2001, during his troubled efforts to transform the military. This attachment leads to "preparing to fight the last war over again." Two business scholars observed, "Yesterday's winning formula ossifies into today's conventional wisdom before petrifying into tomorrow's tablets of stone."[31]

According to internal critics, long-range Pentagon plans "are not characterized by new operational concepts, or a new vision of how we might conduct military operations, or how we might respond to the wide array of possible future challenges." The department's plans for physical capital "largely continue the production of articles and polish ideas that triumphed during the Cold War."[32]

The Defense Department's change-resistant culture was less troubling during the relatively stable Cold War. But the twenty-first-century world is experiencing an unprecedented rate of change. Michael Hammer explains that "change is happening exponentially. It's not that every bit of additional knowledge adds a little more change to the world. But rather, because it interacts with all the other knowledge and experience that we already have in so many domains, it has a cumulative effect. That's why the rate of change has become so astounding."[33] To anticipate and adapt to change, the Department of Defense needs to employ the change-enabling techniques of successful American businesses, such as strategic visioning and a renewal process.

The Pentagon is choking on bureaucracy. The corporate headquarters totals thirty thousand, and staffs located within twenty-five miles of the Pentagon swell to 150,000. Each military department has two headquarters staffs (three in the navy)—one civilian and one military—sharing one mission. This duplicative structure, which originated in World War II, cannot be justified in a fast-paced environment. If the Department of Defense merged these staffs, it could greatly improve efficiency and effectiveness. There has been movement on this issue: in December, 2001, the Army and Air Force announced their intention to merge their two headquarters staffs.

The Pentagon's bureaucratic bloat creates enormous friction and increases time and energy expended on any given effort. As the pace and complexity of work have increased, the department has added staff rather than adopting new, efficient work practices. In particular, the Pentagon makes poor use of horizontal process teams—multifunctional groupings of experts given a single set of objectives and empowered to produce results. Businesses find that such teams produce better results with 30 percent of the effort. The Pentagon continues to rely on outmoded hierarchical approaches based on the archaic premise that "all wisdom resides at the top." Peter Senge notes that such approaches produce "massive institutional breakdown and massive failure of the centralized nervous system of hierarchical authoritarian institutions in the face of growing interdependence and accelerating change."[34]

The department's focus on inputs rather than outcomes further hinders its performance. The Pentagon is organized along functional lines, such as research and engineering, intelligence, and health affairs. Organization specialists understand that a functional structure leads to an input focus that hinders integration of diverse inputs to produce desired outcomes, such as mission capabilities. The input categories of the Future Years Defense Plan, the department's accounting system, reinforce these tendencies.

The department also faces organizational challenges in its external environment. The Pentagon must strengthen its ability to work with other government departments and agencies. Contemporary crises are complex. They have military, diplomatic, economic, law enforcement, technological, and information dimensions. As Senator Nunn said, "The old days of the Pentagon doing the entire mission are gone for good."[35] Successful peacetime preparation and crisis management require the effective integration of many, diverse capabilities and unity of effort across the government. This is especially true for homeland security, where weak cross-government coordination was painfully revealed by September 11. Two recent JCS chairmen, Generals Shalikashvili and Shelton, have recognized the need for better interagency harmonization. But the department is still too wedded to its traditional go-it-alone attitude. The need for improved national security planning and coordination across many departments and agencies has produced calls for a Goldwater-Nichols II to reform the interagency system.

The Pentagon must also learn how to work more effectively with international organizations like the United Nations and nongovernmental organizations like the Red Cross. Both will play significant roles in future crises and often interact with American military forces.

The Goldwater-Nichols Act ended a 45-year struggle to produce a unified military establishment. At the beginning of the twenty-first century, a new set of organizational changes is needed. Hopefully, the act has provided the tools and experience to enable a timely response by the Pentagon.

In the broad sweep of American military history, the post-Goldwater-Nichols era has been remarkable for the number and scope of significant DOD achievements and successes. Superb leadership played an important role, as did doctrine, training, education, and hardware developments. Nevertheless, a significant body of evidence and numerous assertions by senior officials and officers argue that the Goldwater-Nichols Act contributed enormously to these positive outcomes.

The act has attained most of the objectives established for it, helping to transform and revitalize the American military profession in the process. Goldwater-Nichols succeeded most in joint warfighting areas, to which Congress had given its highest priority. In some areas, act-inspired developments are still evolving and adding further luster to the legislation's achievements. In others, much remains to be done.

Secretary Perry used a historic yardstick to praise the legislation, calling the Goldwater-Nichols Act "perhaps the most important defense legislation since World War II." Admiral Owens saw the legislation in larger terms: "Goldwater-Nichols was the watershed event for the military since the second World War." In line with congressional expectations, the Goldwater-Nichols Act has profoundly improved the military's performance and warfighting capabilities. Even some critics have praised the act. In 1995, General John Wickham said, "It has achieved eighty percent of its objectives and will go down in history as a major contribution to the nation's security."[36] That is high praise from a former opponent.

NOTES

1. U.S. House of Representatives, *Goldwater-Nichols Department of Defense Reorganization Act of 1986: Conference Report [To accompany H.R. 3622]*, 99th Cong., 2d sess., Report 99-824, sec. 3.

2. John G. Kester, "The Office of the Secretary of Defense with a Strengthened Joint Staff System," in *Toward a More Effective Defense*, ed. Barry M. Blechman and William J. Lynn (Cambridge: Ballinger, 1985), 187.

3. U.S. Senate Committee on Armed Services, *Defense Organization: The Need for Change: Staff Report to the Committee on Armed Services*, 99th Cong., 1st sess., S. Prt. 99-86, Oct. 16, 1985, 620, 629.

4. *Goldwater-Nichols Department of Defense Reorganization Act*, Report 99-824, 101.

5. "About Fighting and Winning Wars—An Interview with Dick Cheney," *U.S. Naval Institute Proceedings* 122 (May 1996): 33.

6. Richard H. Kohn, "The Crisis in Military-Civilian Relations," *National Interest* (Spring 1994): 3–17.

7. Eliot A. Cohen, "What To Do about National Defense," *Commentary* 98 (November 1994): 21–32.

8. Colin Powell with Joseph E. Persico, *My American Journey* (New York: Random House, 1995), 410–11.

9. Christopher Allan Yuknis, "The Goldwater-Nichols Act of 1986—An Interim Assessment," in *Essays on Strategy X*, ed. Mary A. Sommerville (Washington, D.C.: National Defense University Press, 1993), 97; "About Fighting," 33; John M. Shalikashvili, "Goldwater-Nichols: Ten Years From Now," remarks, NDU Goldwater-Nichols Symposium, December 3, 1996, Washington, D.C.

10. John F. Lehman and Harvey Sicherman, "America's Military Problems and How to Fix Them," *Foreign Policy Research Institute WIRE: A Catalyst for Ideas* 9, no. 3 (February 2001), www.fpri.org.

11. U.S. Senate Committee on Armed Services, *Operation Desert Shield/Desert Storm: Hearings before the Committee on Armed Services*, 102d Cong., 1st sess., April 24, May 8, 9, 16, 21, June 4, 12, 20, 1991, 318; idem., *Nominations Before the Senate Armed Services Committee, First Session, 103rd Congress: Hearings before the Committee on Armed Services*, 103rd Cong., 1st sess., S. Hrg. 103-414, January–November 1993, 343.

12. Shalikashvili, "Goldwater-Nichols."

13. Henry H. Shelton, author interview, April 27, 2001.

14. Robert W. Komer, "Strategymaking in the Pentagon," in *Reorganizing America's Defense*, ed. Robert J. Art, Samuel P. Huntington, and Vincent Davis (Washington, D.C.: Pergamon-Brassey's, 1985), 215–17.

15. Shalikashvili, "Goldwater-Nichols"; Shelton interview; David Shilling and Christopher Lamb, author interview, May 21, 1999.

16. Bill Owens with Ed Offley, *Lifting the Fog of War* (New York: Farrar, Straus, & Giroux, 2000), 207.

17. U.S. Senate Armed Services Committee, *Defense Organization*, 242.

18. Ibid., 224.

19. "About Fighting," 33; "The Chairman as Principal Military Adviser: An Interview with Colin L. Powell," *Joint Force Quarterly* (Autumn 1996), 30; U.S. Senate Armed Services Committee, *Operation Desert Shield/Desert Storm*, 318.

20. William J. Crowe with David Chanoff, *Line of Fire*, (New York: Simon & Schuster, 1993), 158; Shelton interview.

21. U.S. Senate Armed Services Committee, *Defense Organization*, 7.

22. "The Chairman," 31; Malcolm S. Forbes, Jr., "Fact and Comment," *Forbes* (March 18, 1991): 23–24; Katherine Boo, "How Congress Won the War in the Gulf," *Washington Monthly* (October 1991): 31.

23. William J. Perry, speech honoring Senator Sam Nunn, the Pentagon, July 12, 1996, JRL, 2.

24. John M. Shalikashvili, remarks, Association of the United States Army Land Warfare Forum Breakfast, September 1, 1994, JRL; Commission on Roles and Missions of the Armed Forces, *Directions for Defense* (Washington, D.C.: U.S. Government Printing Office, 1995), 2–3.

25. Shelton interview; Michael B. Donley, "It's Time for DoD to Establish a Joint Budget," unpublished paper, May 2, 2001.

26. Shelton interview.

27. Sam Nunn, "Future Trends in Defense Organization," *Joint Force Quarterly* (Autumn 1996): 63; John M. Shalikashvili, "A Word from the Chairman," *Joint Force Quarterly* (Autumn–Winter 1994–95): 7.

28. Mackubin T. Owens, Jr., "Goldwater-Nichols: A Ten-Year Retrospective," *Marine Corps Gazette* (December 1996): 48–53; Paul K. Van Riper, "More on Innovations and Jointness," *Marine Corps Gazette* (March 1998): 55–57.

29. William S. Cohen, "Message from the Secretary," *Defense Reform Initiative: The Business Strategy for Defense in the 21st Century* (Washington, D.C.: U.S. Department of Defense, 1997), i.

30. John P. Kotter, *Leading Change* (Boston: Harvard Business School Press, 1996), 161.

31. Sumantra Ghoshal and Christopher A. Bartlett, "Changing the Role of Top Management: Beyond Structure to Processes," *Harvard Business Review* 73 (January–February 1995): 94.

32. U.S. Office of Net Assessment, *1996 Net Assessment Summer Study: Sustaining Innovation in the U.S. Military* (Washington, D.C.: U.S. Department of Defense, 1996), 2.

33. Michael Hammer, "Beyond the End of Management," in *Rethinking the Future*, ed. Rowan Gibson (London: Nicholas Brealey, 1997), 96.

34. Peter Senge, "Through the Eye of the Needle," in ibid., 125–26.

35. U.S. Commission on National Security/21st Century, *Seeking a National Strategy* (Washington, D.C.: U.S. Commission on National Security/21st Century, 2000), 14; Nunn, "Future Trends," 65.

36. Perry, speech honoring Sam Nunn, 2; Owens, "'Jointness' Is His Job." *Government Executive* (April 1995): 61; Wickham interview (May 9, 1995).

NATIONAL SECURITY STRATEGY AND POLICY DEVELOPMENT

U.S. COMMISSION ON NATIONAL SECURITY/21ST CENTURY

GENERAL

Apart from internal department and agency processes, overarching strategy and policy development involves several interagency subprocesses, including:

- The traditional interagency process as described in Presidential Decision Directive (PDD) 2 and overseen by the National Security Council (NSC) through the NSC staff;[1]

- The process for coordinating the development of economic policy directed by the National Economic Council (NEC); and

- The process of developing response strategies and policies through preparation of the Federal Response Plan (FRP) under the auspices of the Federal Emergency Management Agency (FEMA).

This section looks at each of these processes individually. It also examines how Congress influences policy and strategy development.

THE TRADITIONAL NATIONAL SECURITY INTERAGENCY PROCESS

The traditional interagency approach to national security problems occurs through a formal process that has its roots in the National Security Act of 1947.[2] Over the years, the process has varied in accordance with the wishes of the president and the strength of the assistant to the president for national security affairs (APNSA), who is often referred to as

U.S. Commission on National Security/21st Century, Road Map for National Security, *Volume 1:* Key Observations and Overarching Processes *(Washington, D.C.: U.S. Commission on National Security/21st Century, April 15, 2001), 4–33. Public domain.*

the national security advisor. The process itself is not codified in law below the full NSC, although much of the work and most of the decisions are made by various interagency committees below that level in accordance with presidential preferences.

BACKGROUND

Presidential Decision Directive 2

PDD-2, *Organization of the National Security Council,* establishes the Clinton administration's formal interagency structure and the processes for considering "national security policy issues requiring Presidential determination."[3] The document specifies interagency roles and responsibilities at multiple levels, and reflects the president's organizational preferences for dealing with "national security" *as the President defines that term.*[4] That is not unique. Because it reflects personal predilections, each administration's version of the national security interagency process is somewhat different and involves different players in the NSC system. Notwithstanding differences, the process has been evolutionary over time rather than revolutionary.[5]

Evolution of PDD-2

Administrations formalize their concepts of interagency processes and NSC responsibilities in authoritative documents, such as PDD-2. As a rule, each new administration builds on its predecessor's work. For instance, some perceive only minor differences between the Bush administration's National Security Directive 1 (NSD-1) and the Clinton administration's PDD-2.[6] There are some differences, however, in specific authorities that were delegated to the NSC/Principals Committee (PC) and the NSC/Deputies Committee (DC) to work *specific issues.* And NSD-1 creates specific functional and regional working groups, whereas the Clinton administration's PDD-2 omitted these groups.[7] NSD-1 appears to have been written to push decisions down and allow "the system" to work issues as much as possible at lower levels, while elevating decisions to the principals level later in the process. Overall, most decisions have been made at the same levels in the previous Bush and the Clinton administrations. In both administrations, over time, decisionmaking authority has migrated from the working groups to the NSC/DC, and occasionally the NSC/PC, although that trend may be more pronounced in the Clinton administration.

Because of their importance to national security, interagency process directives are generally published soon after an administration takes office. For example, the Clinton administration promulgated PDD-2 on January 20, 1993—Inauguration Day—whereas the Bush administration published NSD-1 in April of 1991—about three months into its tenure. (Interagency directives have been categorized in several different ways. In the Carter administration, they were titled "Presidential Directives" [PD], whereas the Reagan administration titled these documents

"National Security Decision Directives" [NSDD].[8] The Bush administration renamed them "National Security Directives," and NSD-1 and NSD-10 described its version of the interagency process.[9] The Clinton administration retitled them once again as "Presidential Decision Directives.") Formal processes are usually the basis for informal processes that develop almost as quickly.

Distinctions between Formal and Informal Processes

One expert describes the national security process as "an extension of the president's own concerns and interests."[10] Thus it is important to note that the president and his advisors do not always follow the formal processes reflected in documents to the letter. In fact, formal and informal processes coexist and complement each other. Often, informal processes are truncated versions of more formal arrangements and involve at least some of the same players. When informal processes arise, they often do so not because the formal process is not working properly, but because time constraints or participants' agendas suggest the need for something else. Careful review and comments by participants indicate that informal approaches based on formal processes are often an effective way to develop policy and strategy. In practice, the formal processes become reference points from which informal processes spring. Many important decisions are reached using informal processes; however, formal processes tend to be more rigorous and disciplined—when followed—and are better at ensuring all perspectives receive a hearing. If used properly, formal process can enhance participant trust in the system.

Informal processes often cut corners to speed up decisionmaking, but such shortcuts often "freeze out" some players. There is nothing in the research for this project that suggests this is inherently wrong; however, it is important for core participants to realize that truncating the involvement of lower-level staff experts—or entire departments or agencies—entails a certain amount of risk. A second significant point that affects current practices is that informal processes sometimes occur because technology makes them possible. For example, the ability to conduct secure teleconferencing almost at will can tempt decisionmakers to make decisions in near real time, without consulting staff experts who might frame issues more precisely and suggest a broader range of alternatives.

NSC COMPOSITION

Evolution of the NSC

Congress established the formal legal composition of the NSC in the National Security Act of 1947, and Congress has changed that composition several times.[11] The original law specified that, along with other individuals, the NSC would be composed of the president, the secretary of state, and the secretary of defense—the only members who have remained constant throughout. Two years later, in the National Security Act Amendments of 1949, Congress modified the original composition. This act removed the service secretaries and the chairman of the National Security Resources Board, added the vice president as a full member and designated the chairman of the Joint Chiefs of Staff (CJCS) and the director of Central Intelligence (DCI) as statutory advisors.[12] There have been other changes over the years, and a precedent for congressional action vis-à-vis the NSC is clearly established.

However, although Congress mandates membership in law, presidents usually add other individuals to the NSC to suit their needs and agendas. Furthermore, in the NSC system of committees, the president, not the Congress, decides membership and limits of authority. Thus, like the formal processes, the NSC membership and the membership of its committees have evolved to suit the needs of the president.

Current Membership

PDD-2 expanded NSC membership beyond that mandated by law in a way that reflected President Clinton's concept of a link between national security, economic, and domestic political matters. In addition to the statutory members (i.e., the president, the vice president, the secretary of state, and the secretary of defense) and the statutory advisors (i.e., DCI[13] and the CJCS), the Clinton NSC included:

the Secretary of the Treasury, the U.S. Representative to the United Nations, the Assistant to the President for National Security Affairs (APNSA), the Assistant to the President for Economic Policy, and the Chief of Staff to the President. The Attorney General shall be invited to attend meetings pertaining to his [sic] jurisdiction, including covert actions. The heads of other Executive departments and agencies, the special statutory advisors to the NSC, and other senior officials shall be invited to attend meetings of the NSC where appropriate.[14]

The Clinton NSC membership had parallels with that of the previous Bush administration. For the latter administration, the White House chief of staff and the APNSA joined the statutory members for NSC meetings. NSD-1 also states that the secretary of the treasury was to attend NSC meetings unless specifically asked not to do so. The document further specifies that the attorney general would be invited to attend when matters "pertaining to his jurisdiction, including covert actions" were discussed, and the heads of other executive branch agencies, the statutory advisors, and "other senior officials will be invited to attend meetings of the NSC where appropriate."[15] Supporting committees were essentially the same in terms of make-up and function for both administrations as outlined below, although PDD-2 is not as specific with respect to their duties as was NSD-1. In short, the primary differences between the Clinton and preceding Bush administrations'

interagency systems lie in application, not in membership or formal processes. Even the major informal processes were similar.[16]

NSC FUNCTIONS AND PURPOSES

The NSC and its supporting committees and groups serve as a forum to help presidents make and manage national security decisions.[17] Given the nature of the membership and the purpose as cited below, the Clinton administration apparently intended to use the NSC system of committees and working groups as a mechanism to integrate the elements of national power that the president believes are key. In the first substantive paragraph of PDD-2, President Clinton stated:

The NSC shall advise and assist me in integrating all aspects of national security policy as it affects the United States—domestic, foreign, military, intelligence, and economic (in conjunction with the National Economic Council). Along with its subordinate committees, the NSC shall be my principal means for coordinating executive departments and agencies in the development and implementation of national security policy.[18]

In other words, although it has not always been successful in doing so, the Clinton administration tried to use the NSC system of supporting committees and working groups to focus diverse elements of national power on questions of national security. To an extent, this is somewhat different than the approaches taken by earlier administrations, which, given the strategic environments of their times, often treated national security issues primarily as military and/or diplomatic questions.

It is noteworthy that although the NSC is established in law and by administration policy, its members rarely meet as the NSC. At present, the entire NSC per se as established by PDD-2 has not formally met since its inaugural meeting in 1993.[19] Instead, the principals and deputies committees, supported by interagency working groups, perform most of the interagency work, with the deputies handling the lion's share.

NSC COMMITTEES AND WORKING GROUPS

To assist the NSC in framing issues for the president and developing policy and strategy, PDD-2 establishes two formal committees and a series of formal working groups, in addition to the NSC staff and special advisors and emissaries. These are listed in the following paragraphs.

The NSC Principals Committee (NSC/PC)

The NSC/PC is chaired by the APNSA and is composed of the secretary of state, the secretary of defense,[20] the U.S. representative to the United Nations, the DCI, the CJCS, and the assistant to the president for economic policy, who is also the director of the National Economic Council (NEC) staff.

(The attorney general, the secretary of the treasury, and other executive department and agency heads may join the NSC/PC as required. See, for example, PDD-63 requirements for critical infrastructure protection, which uses the traditional interagency system, but expands membership, based on lead agency requirements.) In essence, the NSC/PC is the NSC without the president, vice president, and the secretary of the treasury and attorney general, unless invited, and the president's chief of staff.

The NSC Deputies Committee (NSC/DC)

The NSC/DC is chaired by the deputy assistant to the president for national security affairs (DAPNSA) and includes the under secretary of state for political affairs, the under secretary of defense for policy (USD[P]), the Deputy DCI, the Vice CJCS (VCJCS), and the assistant to the vice president for national security affairs.[21] The deputy assistant to the president for economic policy, who represents the NEC, and other executive branch officials may be invited to attend as necessary, and, when covert actions and other sensitive intelligence activities are discussed, a representative of the attorney general must attend.[22] In practice, the majority of interagency work, decisions, and coordination occur in the NSC/DC.

Interagency Working Groups (NSC/IWG)[23]

NSC/IWGs are established by the NSC/DC as appropriate and may be either permanent or ad hoc. During the Clinton administration, there have usually been about two dozen functional and/or geographic working groups at any one point. NSC/IWGs should be chaired by assistant secretaries, but sometimes are chaired by other individuals, including members of the NSC staff. Determination of lead departments and chairs is based on whether issues are primarily foreign policy and/or defense (Department of State [DoS] or defense [DoD]); economic (Department of Treasury or NEC); or intelligence, nonproliferation, arms control, and/or crisis management (NSC staff). The NSC/DC establishes guidelines for NSC/IWG operations, including designating participants.

The NSC Staff

The NSC staff is a combination of professional staff funded through the NSC budget (which is appropriated by Congress as part of the budget for the Executive Office of the president) and detailees from the executive branch departments, primarily State and Defense.[24] The staff is traditionally small, less than half the size of the Office of Management and Budget. In the previous Bush administration, it numbered 179, which the Clinton administration reduced to 151 initially (consistent with President Clinton's campaign promise to reduce White House staff); but by 1999, the number of personnel on the staff exceeded 200.

The politically appointed staff members were supplemented by a larger number of personnel seconded from executive branch departments, such as State and Defense. The theory behind this arrangement was that political appointees bring with them fresh ideas and an understanding of the administration's priorities that can be coupled with the experience of career civil servants and military officers who supplement the staff and who know how to get things done within government bureaucracies. Detailed staff members also bring with them a certain amount of loyalty to the department or agency to which they will eventually return, which can affect how they approach issues and decisions. Career civil servants and military officers also provide continuity when administrations change. Although they may eventually be replaced by the incoming APNSA, they usually serve throughout the transition period, when the national security decisionmaking apparatus may be especially vulnerable.

The staff is divided into administrative and substantive roles, depending on the president's requirements and the preferences and influence of the APNSA for whom they work. In policy and strategy development, the staff often plays a coordinating role as brokers of interagency agreements, but occasionally, it assumes the more substantive role of selecting options and making policy and strategy recommendations directly to the APNSA. The APNSA may take these staff recommendations directly to the president, bypassing the NSC and interagency process. However, to the extent that he/she does this, their image as an honest broker for the interagency community suffers. As members of the interagency perceive that the APNSA is not accurately representing their positions to the president, they may, themselves, begin to end run the interagency process, which, ultimately, will lead to policy and strategy development problems.

Its relatively small size and the large workload taxes the staff's capability with, as at least one author has pointed out, an adverse impact on the quality of decision packages.[25] Its small size and the press of daily business also limit its ability to oversee implementation and to engage in long-range planning, although the NSC staff has attempted both from time to time. In short, the staff seems to focus on current crises, which leaves little time for longer-range planning.

However, because it is small and organizationally flat, the staff is inherently flexible and often fills vacuums it detects in department and agency capabilities. As several staff members pointed out during interviews, small is often a virtue because it permits more rapid action, unencumbered by bureaucratic impediments. Those individuals interviewed indicated that, in their experience, the size of the staff and the nature of the processes made it especially effective, although this judgment is somewhat subjective. The deference shown the NSC staff by others in the NSC system is illustrated by the fact that papers and memoranda prepared by the staff usually receive preferential treatment, at least in the interagency working groups.

On occasion, tensions develop between the NSC staff, departments and agencies, and other members of the Executive Office of the president. Those with access to the president may suggest alternative approaches that are not always NSC staff preferences. Although this is sometimes frustrating to the staff, it is important that the president be able to acquire a range of views and options.[26]

Special Advisors and Emissaries

Special advisors and emissaries assist the president and the APNSA with particular problems. Although not part of the interagency process per se, these advisors are often experienced interagency players who know how to gain access to interagency resources when necessary. They are normally appointed for relatively long terms and are usually accountable to the president, not Congress or executive branch officials. An example of a special advisor is former Secretary of Defense Dr. William Perry, whom President Clinton designated to take the lead on improving relations with North Korea. Because special advisors and emissaries often report directly to the president, executive branch departments and agencies are sometimes uninformed about significant foreign policy issues.

THE FORMAL INTERAGENCY PROCESS

General

This section describes the formal PDD-2 prescribed interagency process for policy and strategy formulation.[27] Although it is formal in the sense that it is prescribed by the president, it lacks some of the traditional trappings associated with other formal processes. Specifically, unlike the resource allocation processes, for example (which have specific dates and a cycle of events leading to a well-defined product), the PDD-2 interagency process is more fluid and less regulated in terms of timelines, direction of movement, and products.[28] Apart from authorizing the NSC, the Congress does not oversee the interagency process—although Congress can influence it by holding hearings involving some of the participants or drafting legislation inter alia.

Products

Processes exist to generate products, including advice and decision packages. The interagency process must deal with a wide variety of issues that impact U.S. policy and strategy development, as well as implementation and resourcing. The nature of the products that result from the traditional interagency process depends on the level from which it is viewed. From the president's perspective, the interagency process produces decision options, introduces alternative views, makes decisions below the presidential level when appropriate, manages implementation of decisions, and assists in integrating "all aspects of national security policy."[29]

At the NSC/PC level, the process is designed to obtain presidential guidance and feedback, frame and refine issues, and produce policy and strategy options for NSC/PC deliberations and decisions and, when necessary, for consideration by the president. For the NSC/DC, the process provides a mechanism to obtain guidance from the president and the NSC/PC, identify and frame issues for action at the DC level or higher, and develop and manage policy and strategy. NSC/IWGs use the interagency process to identify, develop, and refine issues and options across several agencies.

Generating Policy and Strategy Issues

The interagency process permits issue development at different levels. Issues may originate with the president and be passed down through the NSC/PC and NSC/DC to the NSC/IWGs, with appropriate refinements and guidance at each level. Or NSC/IWGs may convince the NSC/DC that an issue merits consideration, thus surfacing it from the bottom up. Finally, issues may enter the interagency process from external processes, formal or informal (e.g., an issue raised at an informal meeting of the Secretaries of State and Defense with the APNSA that is subsequently passed to the NSC/DC for more detailed consideration or an issue that is raised by Congress during hearings).

Relationship with Other Processes

Although a separate process exists for crisis management (PDD-56) and infrastructure protection (PDD-63), the processes described in PDD-2 are interrelated with those and other procedures, and implementation depends upon actions and decisions taken under the authority of PDD-2. Sometimes the PDD-2 process is used in lieu of PDD-56 or PDD-63. For example, those individuals interviewed indicated that the process by which both Bosnia and Kosovo were managed resembled the PDD-2 approach more closely than the procedures in PDD-56. The PDD-2 process is also the model used by the NEC to develop economic and trade policy and strategies. Decisions made as a result of PDD-2 interagency deliberations often affect resourcing proposals made during preparation of the president's budget and are thus related to resourcing processes indirectly.

HOW THE PROCESS WORKS

Although interagency issues can originate from a number of sources, one way to illustrate it is to take a bottom-up approach. (Regardless of the approach taken—bottom-up or top-down—there are no fixed timelines that apply from one iteration to the next, and the process frequently does not flow linearly or sequentially.)

NSC/IWGs

These groups exist to conduct interagency studies, develop and refine issues and options, and coordinate implementation of decisions. As noted previously, the IWGs are established and chartered by the

NSC/DC and, in effect, work directly for the NSC/DC, which may specify frequency of meetings and membership. Assistant secretaries from the appropriate departments or NSC staff members chair NSC/IWGs. In the absence of detailed guidance from the NSC/DC, IWGs meet at the call of the chair, although IWG members often informally exert pressure to schedule meetings and shape agendas.

NSC/IWG members are supported by numerous intra- and interagency task groups and ad hoc committees, which are important not only for their substantive work, but for building consensus early in the process. Task group and committee membership often includes deputy assistant secretaries and action officers. For instance, a deputy assistant secretary of defense may chair a task group composed of members of his/her office, the Joint Staff, and the Department of State. This task group may provide information to an NSC/IWG for use during its deliberations. In addition to formalized task groups, action officers may informally discuss issues with counterparts in other departments and/or agencies and feed results back into IWGs.

Both IWGs and their supporting structures make some decisions that often are reflected in the types of assessments they do and the options they retain to pass on to the NSC/DC. Typically, the NSC/IWGs report out to the NSC/DC, which may accept, modify, or reject their recommendations. On occasion, usually during crises, members of the NSC/PC or NSC/DC may seek out individual members of an IWG for information, thus bypassing the formal process. For example, the USD(P) may converse directly with the deputy assistant secretary of defense for Near East and South Asian affairs to gain information he/she needs for NSC/DC deliberations without consulting the working group as a whole.[30]

The NSC/DC

The NSC/DC makes many of the decisions in the interagency process.[31] Its functions include providing guidance and direction to the NSC/IWGs, oversight of the interagency process, decisionmaking, and resolving interagency disputes. PDD-2 instructs the NSC/DC to "serve as the senior sub-cabinet forum for consideration of policy issues affecting national security." It also is charged to periodically review progress on "major foreign policy initiatives" and "existing policy directives," and for "day-to-day crisis management."[32]

The DAPNSA chairs the NSC/DC and has the authority to call meetings, determine the agenda, and ensure that appropriate papers are prepared.[33] He/she is enjoined to do this in consultation with other members; however, meetings are often held on short notice with minimum consultations or time for staffs to review the agenda and prepare briefing papers.[34]

The Deputies Committee is responsible for ensuring that issues are adequately analyzed, a full range of views is incorporated, appropriate options are identified, and relevant risks are assessed. Typically, the NSC/DC will establish and/or instruct an IWG, pass along the guidance it develops or receives from the NSC or NSC/PC, review IWG work, oversee necessary revisions, refine IWG packages, make decisions (or forward recommendations to the NSC/PC), and supervise implementation. When disputes between agencies arise, the NSC/DC attempts to resolve them at their level or, if that is not possible, passes them to the NSC/PC for resolution.

Informal meetings of selected DC members play an important role. These meetings are often freewheeling discussions in which rough decisions are made and then presented to the remainder of the DC for refinement and validation.

NSC/PC

The NSC/PC is the senior interagency forum short of the NSC. It examines issues and makes appropriate decisions, ratifies decisions made by the NSC/DC, and/or passes issues to the president for consideration. In the present example, issues and options developed initially at the NSC/IWG would be passed to the NSC/DC, where they would be refined once again, and passed to the NSC/PC for ratification or for the principals' decision.

When the NSC/PC reaches a decision (or ratifies a decision made by the NSC/DC), it passes the decision and applicable instructions to the NSC/DC for implementation. When necessary, the NSC/PC passes the decision package to the president for a decision, which, when obtained, is passed to the NSC/DC for implementation. Typically, issues passed to the president are those that the PC either cannot resolve or that are of such significance that a presidential decision is required (e.g., a foreign policy decision with major domestic political implications).[35]

The NSC

Although including much of the membership of the NSC/PC, the NSC is a separate body. Theoretically, the NSC/PC may pass issues to the NSC, which, according to PDD-2, advises the president on the appropriate course of action. In theory, the NSC meets "as required" and the APNSA determines the agenda, based on guidance from the president and in consultation with NSC members. In practice, the NSC has not met as a body during the Clinton administration except for its inaugural meeting.

SECURITY POLICY COORDINATION MECHANISMS

PDD-29, promulgated in September 1994, created several new entities to develop and coordinate national security policy. These are the Security Policy Board; the Security Policy Advisory Board; the Security Policy Forum; and the Overseas Security Policy Board.[36] The staff to support these entities operates under the auspices of the Security Policy Board and is funded by those activities that are members of the Board.

The Security Policy Board

This board, a successor organization to the Joint Security Executive Committee established by the secretary of defense and the DCI, reports to the president through the APNSA. It consists of the DCI, the deputy secretaries of defense, state, energy and commerce, the deputy attorney general, the VCJCS, and "one Deputy Secretary from a non-defense related agency [on an annual rotational basis] and one representative from the Office of Management and Budget and the NSC staff."[37]

The Board's purpose is to "consider, coordinate, and recommend" U.S. security policy directives, including procedures and practices.[38] It is enjoined to do this in consonance with the following principles:

1. Policies must realistically relate to threats but be flexible enough to accommodate changes that result from evolving threats;

2. Policies must be consistent and facilitate resource allocation;

3. Standards emanating from policies must be fair and ensure equitable treatment; and

4. Policies, practices, and procedures must be effective at affordable prices.

Consistent with these principles (and except for matters that are the responsibility of the secretary of state) the board proposes and reviews "legislative initiatives and executive orders pertaining to U.S. security policy, procedures, and practices."[39] The board is empowered to coordinate these matters across the interagency spectrum and to resolve conflicts. Although the board reports to the president through the APNSA and not through the NSC system, conflicts that the board cannot resolve are forwarded to the NSC/PC for resolution.

The Security Policy Advisory Board

The Advisory Board consists of five presidentially appointed members who act as an independent security policy forum. The Advisory Board must report to the president annually on how well the Security Policy Board and others have adhered to the four principles highlighted in the preceding paragraph. It is also enjoined to provide a "non-governmental and public interest perspective on security policy initiatives to the Security Policy Board and the intelligence community."[40]

The Security Policy Forum

The Security Policy Forum (originally an arm of the Joint Security Executive Committee before the latter became the Security Policy Board) is a subordinate element of the Security Policy Board. It has very broad interagency membership, and the Security Policy Board appoints the chair. Members include representatives from the Office of the Secretary of Defense; the Joint Staff; the military services; the Defense Intelligence Agency; and the NSA; the Central Intelligence Agency; the National Reconnaissance Office; the Coast Guard; the Departments of State, Commerce, Energy, Justice, Treasury, and Transportation; the Federal Bureau of Investigation; FEMA; the General Services Administration; the Defense Information Systems Agency/National Communications Systems; the Office of Personnel Management; the Information Security Oversight Office; the Nuclear Regulatory Commission; the National Aeronautics and Space Administration; the Office of Management and Budget; and "other agencies' representatives as invited."[41]

The forum exists to consider security issues raised by its members, the Security Policy Board, or others. As part of its consideration, it may develop policy initiatives and coordinate them, evaluate security policies and guide policy implementation, monitor security policies to ensure that they are equitable, and support national security goals.

PDD-29 empowers both the Security Policy Board and the Security Policy Forum to establish interagency working groups as necessary to carry out their functions.

The Overseas Security Policy Board

The board is empowered to "consider, develop, coordinate, and promote policies, standards, and agreements on overseas security operations."[42] This board is the successor to the Department of State's Overseas Security Policy Group and generally focuses on specific security matters. It reports to the president through the APNSA and is chaired by the director of the Diplomatic Security Service. Board members include representatives from the Departments of State (including the U.S. Agency for International Development), Defense (including the National Security Agency), Commerce, Justice (including the Federal Bureau of Investigation), Treasury, and Transportation; the Federal Aviation Administration; and the Office of Management and Budget.

INFORMAL INTERAGENCY PROCESSES

General

In *The Politics of U.S. Foreign Policy*, Jerel Rosati argues that, despite a reasonably effective national security decisionmaking structure, most presidents rely primarily on informal consultations with close advisors.[43] In a similar vein, Robert Hunter suggests that the manner in which the president deals with the interagency system is more important than formal structures.[44] Still another observer, Alexander George, notes that presidential personalities and learned behaviors often move them away from formal processes and into less structured methods where they feel more comfortable.[45] Each of these observers—and others—suggests that even though presidents have substantial control over the design and operation of formal national security processes, they tend to rely on informal mechanisms. (The widely circulated photo of John F. Kennedy in a tete-a-tete with his brother Robert Kennedy during the Cuban Missile crisis is a poignant example.)

As presidents invoke informal methods, interagency processes sometimes take similar courses, with informal systems often being abbreviated versions of more formal arrangements. When decision-makers abandon or modify processes or opt for a less formal approach, doing so is not of itself grounds for criticism or concluding that formal processes are ineffective. This section describes several important informal processes that reflect the formal interagency process and help participants satisfy policy and strategy development requirements.[46]

The Breakfast/Lunch Meetings

In both the previous Bush and Clinton administrations, the secretaries of defense and state and the national security advisor have held regular consultations over meals. The Cheney-Baker-Scowcroft (or CBS) breakfasts were an almost weekly activity, with formal agendas, information papers and talking points, and postbreakfast taskings. The Albright-Berger-Cohen (ABC) lunches of the Clinton administration are similar. The agenda is usually prepared by the NSC staff (in coordination with the staffs of the other participants) and distributed ahead of time. Staffs prepare briefing papers and talking points on those matters for which they have expertise. However, no staff attends the meetings as a rule. This guarantees confidentiality and perhaps a more open exchange, as participants cease to represent their bureaucracies and are free to advocate what they deem the best options.[47] Staffs depend on feedback from the principals. Officials interviewed believe these events serve an important function for surfacing and resolving issues quickly, although some acknowledged that feedback to staff was not always timely or complete.

Weekly Foreign Policy Breakfast

This informal event involves the ABC participants, plus the U.N. representative, the DCI, and the CJCS, all of whom are involved in the NSC. No staff attends, the gathering has no prepared agenda, and discussions are reportedly far ranging. Occasionally, taskings for staff result from these meetings.

Weekly Deputies Lunches

These are similar to the Foreign Policy Breakfasts except participants are members of the NSC/DC. (In Department of Defense's case, the deputy secretary of defense often attends instead of the USD(P), even though the deputy secretary is not part of the NSC/DC per PDD-2.)

The President–National Security Advisor Relationship

APNSAs hold unique positions. How extensively they are able to use their position to work around the formal process depends on the amount of influence they have with the president. Henry Kissinger and Zbigniew Brzezinski were perhaps the most influential, often appearing to ignore the interagency process altogether. President Reagan's series of advisors were less so, and the secretaries of state and defense

were more influential as a result. Brent Scowcroft and Samuel Berger appear to represent a middle-of-the-road approach. They are given credit by interagency participants for honestly expressing the views of other NSC members as well as their own, although both occasionally took NSC staff perspectives directly to the president without interagency consultation. The perception of the APNSA as an "honest broker" who adequately represents the opinions of others to the president is crucial to the APNSA's relationship with other interagency actors. To a considerable extent, his/her ability to present others' views is as important as the ability to function as a trusted advisor to the chief executive. The two abilities may be inseparable.

The APNSA's influence also depends on personality, bureaucratic skill, and whether they see their role as one of coordination or problem resolution. It also depends on how involved the president is in international affairs. Although many APNSAs have had daily audiences with the president, others have not. In the first Clinton administration, for example, Anthony Lake's ability to influence national security was reportedly limited in part because the president was focused on his domestic agenda and did not meet frequently with the APNSA.[48]

The importance of their personal relationship is perhaps more important than the processes by which the president and the APNSA interface. National security advisors, unlike the majority of NSC members, are neither elected officials nor appointed advisors with the advice and consent of the Senate. They are accountable to the president of course, but not to the American people (through Senate confirmation, for example), although they can and have made (or substantially influenced) decisions that affect the nation as a whole.

If they enjoy access to and influence with the president, their staffs tend to be more influential in the interagency process. This is especially true if the APNSA is seen as a spokesperson for administration positions. At the least, NSC staffs may introduce a certain amount of friction to the interagency process as they maneuver for position, or they may antagonize interagency interlocutors if they insist that only they know the mind of the president.[49] They may also take on more work than can be effectively handled, given the staff's relatively small size. That may require constant juggling, which leaves little time for planning or coordination. It can also result in decision packages that do not take advantage of the full range of expertise and options available in the interagency.

Importance of Personal Contacts

Action officers from different divisions and departments frequently hold informal discussions in a number of different venues to discuss substantive issues. Informal discussions also occur with members of the Congress and with their staffs (although in the main, members of Congress and staffers interviewed for this study claimed consultations were not as frequent as they would like). Sometimes these discussions evolve as staff members prepare issue papers for their principals in support of the formal process. Sometimes they occur as staffers try to build consensus for proposals or recommendations. Occasionally they develop when members of the executive branch disagree with administration policy and attempt to build support for change. Sometimes they occur as sidebars at hearings, conferences, meetings, or seminars.

The results and agreements reached through personal discussions are not always formally reported, but this networking is an important lubricant for the national security process at large. Participants in seminars and workshops report that the experience enables them to develop contacts that facilitate national security problem-solving beyond the immediate meeting. What transpires through these informal contacts mirrors in many respects formal constructs used by businesses to flatten organizations and improve information exchange between divisions without invoking a cumbersome hierarchy (e.g., integrated process or cross-functional teams).

Personality as an Informal Process Driver

Many interagency participants and observers note that personality figures prominently in successful policy and strategy development. The willingness of some participants to work closely together (or their unwillingness to do so), their desire to limit the number of people involved in decisionmaking (or their willingness to expand it), and the agendas they select to satisfy personal needs all impact on formal and informal processes. To the extent that requirements stemming from personality characteristics can be satisfied within the formal process, participants tend to stay within its confines. When these requirements are not satisfied by formal mechanisms, participants often modify formal processes or develop new, informal ones. Although they sometimes exclude important players, there are numerous indications that informal processes work—sometimes more effectively and expeditiously than formal ones.

OBSERVATIONS

Formal Process Value

All administrations have crafted formal interagency processes for dealing with traditional national security issues and problem solving. Although informal processes frequently replace portions of formal processes, formal approaches add discipline, serve as starting points for problem-solving regimes, provide mechanisms for effective information exchange, and offer problem solving continuity. As information is exchanged and a range of perspectives considered, formal processes help develop best-of-breed options and build consensus among those who must implement them. Formal processes are also especially valuable when introducing new factors into the traditional national security equation (e.g., economics) and as a road map for new process players. In judging the effectiveness of formal processes, the following attributes are important:

1. The extent to which the process provides for timely and accurate exchange of information;

2. The extent to which it permits development of an appropriate range of realistic and viable options;

3. The extent to which it discreetly accommodates consideration of all perspectives and positions, including dissenting opinions;

4. The extent to which it facilitates disciplined and systematic option assessment and evaluation;

5. Its capacity to identify risks (including political risks) and propose risk mitigation measures;

6. Its capacity to make realistic and timely decisions or recommendations in appropriate formats;

7. Its ability to effectively oversee implementation of decisions; and,

8. Its capacity to make rapid midcourse assessments and adjustments as required by situation or environmental changes.

Participants' judgements of process effectiveness vary also according to their perceptions of how well existing processes are likely to satisfy individual and organizational agendas. To the extent that formal processes do not satisfy their expectations in some way, they are inclined to use informal mechanisms.

Informal Process Value

Informal processes arise in each administration and supplement formal processes. They often emerge when key players believe that formal processes do not adequately satisfy their needs or will not do so quickly or discreetly enough. Some informal processes permit direct exchanges between the most senior participants with minimal staff involvement. This may allow participants at all levels to deal with issues from a best-value perspective instead of defending departmental turf in more formal discussions. Although often effective, informal processes can short circuit broader information exchanges and produce options that have not benefited from examination and refinement by staff. Carried to extremes, informal interagency processes can undermine thorough decisionmaking, complicate coordination across the interagency, lower staff morale produce one-sided recommendations, escalate decisionmaking to higher levels of the bureaucracy, and worst of all, produce bad decisions that are incapable of attaining stated objectives. In assessing informal process value, the need for discretion and speed must be weighed against the advantages of garnering additional information and options.

Integration of Nontraditional Elements

Despite language in PDD-2 to the effect that the interagency process will involve political and economic elements, the structure of NSC supporting committees does not reflect this intent in the Clinton administration. Neither the White House chief of staff's office, the president's political advisors, the Treasury, and/or the NEC[50] are represented on the NSC/PC or NSC/DC unless specifically invited. Although each entity is represented at the full NSC level, below that, council representation is apparently on a catch-as-catch-can basis. The implication is that, even though their participation would improve the value of national security policy and strategy, they remain less than full partners in both formal and informal processes below the top process level. (The national security advisor and the economic policy advisor do interact formally and informally, however, and they jointly staff the Office of Trade and International Economic Policy.)

The NSC Staff

The NSC staff is too small to adequately coordinate interagency matters, manage operations, conduct detailed analysis, and engage in long-term planning—all of which the staff occasionally attempts to do. To the extent that it takes on functions beyond traditional coordination, there is a danger that the quality of national security policy and strategy decisions may deteriorate. One illustration of the extent to which the staff has become increasingly involved in substantive matters—and perhaps has become overextended as a result—is the increased number of NSC/IWGs chaired by NSC staff. However, the staff can contribute in unique ways because of its closeness to the president and because its members are almost always experts in their fields. The Clinton NSC staff is a mix of academics and other individuals from outside government (who provide insight and innovation unfettered by bureaucratic agendas) and career military officers, civil servants, and Foreign Service officers borrowed from executive branch departments and agencies (who know how to make the bureaucracy work to implement solutions). The advantages to this approach are clear, although there is a risk that borrowed personnel may favor positions espoused by their parent organizations.

Managing the Interagency Process

The APNSA, assisted by the NSC staff, manages the formal interagency process for traditional national security applications, including developing agendas and chairing meetings. Always challenging, how well the process is managed has significant implications for the quality of interagency work and coordination, as well as for the amount of time and effort required to produce results.

Different administrations have employed different management techniques. During the previous Bush administration, for example, the national security advisor dealt with substantive matters, whereas his deputy was concerned with managing the staff and the interagency process. The "fetish for consensus building which tends to drive participants toward solutions acceptable to all but lacking in value" can complicate process management.[51] Consensus building is important, but when it becomes a primary objective, decision quality may suffer. Many interlocutors cited this, and excessive control by the NSC staff, for poor interagency coordination and performance in the past. The results of ineffective process management often include delayed decisions, requirements to rework analyses and recommendations, and frustration with efforts to produce amicable consensus instead of acknowledging differences and reaching best-value decisions. In short, ineffective interagency process management can drive officials at all levels toward informal processes.

THE ROLE OF CONGRESS IN POLICY AND STRATEGY DEVELOPMENT

BACKGROUND

There have been some common interests between the Congress and the executive branch with respect to national security in the past. However, the Congress, in accordance with its Constitutional responsibilities, has often challenged administration policies, strategies, and programs, and, in doing so, sets the stage for important debates. As one observer noted, "Congressional deference to the Executive's foreign policy was the exception" over the life of the Republic.[52] At a minimum, through hearings and legislation, the Congress ensures that the administration thinks through its policies and strategies during development. The Congress has vascillated between defining objectives and limits in a general sense to intervening in minute details and the organizational structure of executive branch departments.[53] When administrations establish partnerships and consult with the Congress, the legislative branch can be of great assistance, especially in building public support. Conversely, the Congress can help mobilize public opinion against administration activities, as it did during the Vietnam War.

Congressional interest in national security policies and strategies is rooted in a number of different areas. Programmatics certainly enter into some calculations, but so do large ethnic constituencies and their demands. And, as one member recently noted, sometimes the Congress becomes involved in policy and strategy development out of partisan political motives.[54] More importantly, members of Congress have Constitutional responsibilities with respect to national defense and foreign relations, and these duties are significant. Thus, the Congress is involved because their involvement is a responsibility in democratic governments and because by Constitutional design and custom "without Congressional support, the Executive cannot sustain long-term policies."[55]

Congressional involvement, although sometimes viewed with consternation by executive branch officials, can have a positive effect. This is especially true in cases in which the administration builds consultative relationships with key members on both sides of the aisle and with their staffs. This is not to imply that there will not be tensions between the two branches of government—tensions will occur under the best of circumstances and should. The trick is to make those tensions creative rather than disruptive.[56] As Senator Chuck Hagel recently put it, "policies must be relevant to challenges" and the Congress has a responsibility to help the executive branch come to grips with relevancy.[57] One veteran of the House Committee on International Relations believes the two branches work best together when the Congress is involved in development and formulation of policy and strategy, but leaves implementation to the administration.[58]

Building effective partnerships between the administration and the Congress has been accomplished numerous times in the past, but usually depends in large measure on administration willingness to share concepts with Congress in informal consultations and more formally in hearings and perhaps through other mechanisms.[59] In doing so, the president must play a leading role and "articulate a direction" in which policy and strategy should go.[60] By doing so, the administration can define boundaries and establish priorities for debate. For its part, Congress should, in the words of one observer, use its offices to "expose foreign policies to public view and debate . . . [and] as a whole . . . debate and authorize major foreign-policy moves."[61]

To some extent, the Congress does these things now, and the ways in which it influences national security policy and strategy formulation are described in the following paragraphs.

CONGRESSIONAL PROCESSES

Although the Congress does not participate directly in the internal administration processes described earlier, the Congress exerts influence over strategy and policy development in a number of ways. Formally, by holding hearings, committees can spotlight important strategic issues. Through the hearing process and subsequent reports, congressional committees can influence the administration's choice of strategic options by identifying those it supports and those it considers unacceptable. It can also produce committee and staff reports that spotlight issues and help focus public attention on strategic options and policies. This may push a strategy debate into the public eye, or it can influence a debate in favor of (or against) a specific proposal.

By constructing authorization bills and bills that regulate various aspects of national security (e.g., the organization or structure of agencies and departments, legal authorities, nominations for high office via the confirmation process), the Congress can affect the administration's strategic options and its resources to carry them out. By using the "power of the purse," the Congress can influence strategy development by the amount of funding it authorizes for various executive branch departments, agencies, organizations, programs, or activities. According to Hill

staffers, the most effective way to influence administration behavior and shape its actions is by placing restrictions on funding.[62] Through conferences to reconcile differences in House and Senate versions of authorization bills, members can influence one another's views.

The Constitutional responsibility for advice and consent grants Senate committees significant influence over various policy and strategy development issues via hearings and consideration of nominations and promotion to senior positions. The ability to delay or deny a president confirmation of a specific individual for high office—or to extract promises from the nominee or administration in return for a favorable recommendation—is a significant lever. Although these promises may not be legally binding, they serve as "hooks" for future debate. The Senate also conducts hearings on treaties and in doing so, shapes policy and strategy development by indicating the limits of acceptability.

In addition to these measures, if members who are powerful and well respected oppose certain concepts, the administration may discard some strategic options that are seen as politically risky in terms of obtaining Congressional approval. This is not to suggest that administrations are unwilling to challenge Congress on matters presidents believe are important: the evidence clearly indicates the opposite to be the case. However, during strategy development, administration officials are likely to take into consideration the prevailing sentiment on the Hill as reflected in a powerful member's pronouncements.[63] This is especially true of relevant committee chairs, given the committee's ability to influence structure and operating procedures or place limits on how funds can be expended for strategy implementation.

In a general sense, then, the Congress influences policy and strategy development by holding hearings introducing authorization and appropriations legislation, by exercising oversight of departments and agencies and conducting or directing investigations, and—in the case of the Senate—by approving administration appointments to senior positions and treaties.

NOTES

1. Although the term "National Security Council" (NSC) has specific meaning in law and practice, the term is sometimes used to denote the NSC staff. In this document, we use the term "NSC" to denote the National Security Council proper and "NSC staff" to refer to the staff.

2. The 1947 act created the NSC, whose staff oversees the traditional interagency process.

3. Although the language of PDD-2 suggests considerable presidential involvement, all but the most significant national security matters are dealt with by the NSC's committees and working groups, as described in subsequent paragraphs.

4. The White House, PDD-2, "Organization of the National Security Council," Washington, D.C., January 29, 1993. (Hereafter, PDD-2.)

5. The current Bush administration replaced PDD-2 with NSPD-1.

6. Some experts attribute these to the Clinton administration's favorable impression of the way their predecessor's model worked. See, for example, Vincent A. Augur, "The National Security Council System after the Cold War," in *U.S. Foreign Policy After the Cold War,* ed. Randall B. Ripley et al. (Pittsburgh: University of Pittsburgh Press, 1997).

7. Compare language in PDD-2 with NSD-1 ("National Security Council Organization"), dated April 17, 1989.

8. See NSDD-266 ("National Security Interagency Process") dated June 9, 1987 and NSDD-2 ("National Security Council Structure") dated January 12, 1982.

9. NSD-1 and NSD-10 ("Appointments to NSC Policy-Coordinating Committees"). NSD-1 includes many of the recommendations of the Tower Commission appointed by President Reagan in 1987 to review and make recommendations for improving the NSC system. Retired Air Force Lieutenant General Brent Scowcroft, President Bush's National Security Advisor, had been a member of the Tower Commission.

10. Augur, "National Security Council System," 67.

11. Public Law 253, cited as the "National Security Act of 1947," Title 1, Chapter 343, Sect. 101. "The Council shall be composed of the President; the Secretary of State; the Secretary of Defense . . . ; the Secretary of the Army . . . ; the Secretary of the Navy; the Secretary of the Air Force . . . ; the Chairman of the National Security Resources Board . . . ; and such of the following named officers as the President may designate from time to time: The Secretaries of the executive departments, the Chairman of the Munitions Board . . . , and the Chairman of the Research and Development Board."

12. Public Law 216, Sect. 3

13. The DCI is also the Director of the Central Intelligence Agency (CIA). His/her responsibilities include direction of the CIA, as well as management of the intelligence community, which consists of thirteen formal intelligence activities located throughout the government.

14. PDD-2, 1.

15. NSD-1, 1.

16. Of note, the current Bush administration released NSPD-1, which, in many ways, reverts the NSC back to the preceding Bush administration.

17. PDD-2, 1.

18. PDD-2, 1.

19. Interviews with NSC staff members.

20. PDD-2 provides that if the secretaries of state and defense cannot attend, their deputy secretaries or other designees may attend in their stead.

21. Note that even though it is known as the DC, the DoD and DoS representatives are under—not deputy—secretaries, although deputy secretaries from both departments sometimes attend.

22. When the NSC/DC is given responsibility for crisis management, it is redesignated as the DC/CM (i.e., crisis management). See the section on strategy and policy implementation and the discussion of PDD-56 therein.

23. As previously noted, the current Bush administration eliminated the term "Interagency Working Group" and replaced it with "Policy Coordination Committee." See NSPD-1.

24. Detailees normally serve in a nonreimbursable status—that is, their salaries continue to be paid by the departments and agencies from which they came.

25. Augur, "National Security Council System," 55–56.

26. NSC staff interviews.

27. This process may also be used for policy and strategy implementation, or it may devolve into the PDD-56 process.

28. "Products" in this case may be no more than one-page memoranda—far removed from the multivolumed *President's Budget,* for example.

29. PDD-2, 1. In cases in which the president is selectively involved in national security issues, the ability of the NSC/PC to function effectively (including making decisions) seems crucial.

30. Interviews with DoD staff members.

31. See, for example, Augur, "National Security Council System," 52–54, and interviews. The NSC staff has a larger volume of work than does the NSC/DC, but it is work that is done at a lower level and without the same decision-making authority or accountability requirements.

32. PDD-2, 2–3.

33. PDD-2, 3.

34. Interviews with DoD and DoS staff members.

35. Interviews with NEC staff indicate that, in the Clinton administration, the NSC/PC often defers to the president's political instincts and judgement for issues in which the PC envisions two or more solutions, each of which is satisfactory in itself but entails different levels of domestic political risk.

36. www.fas.org/irp/offdocs/pdd29.htm. (Note that the Security Policy Board, the Security Policy Advisory Board, and the Security Policy Forum were eliminated by the current Bush administration's NSPD-1, which specifically revoked PDD-29 and assigned the duties of these three entities to various Policy Coordination Committees. See NSPD-1, 6.)

37. www.fas.org/irp/offdocs/pdd29.htm, 2. (Hereafter pdd29.htm.)

38. pdd29.htm, 2.

39. pdd29.htm, 3.

40. pdd29.htm, 3.

41. pdd29.htm, 3.

42. pdd29.htm, 3.

43. Jerel A. Rosati, *The Politics of U.S. Foreign Policy* (New York: Harcourt Brace, 1993).

44. Robert Hunter, *Presidential Control of Foreign Policy* (New York: Praeger, 1982).

45. Alexander L. George, *Presidential Decisionmaking in Foreign Policy: The Effective Use of Information and Advice* (Boulder: Westview Press, 1980).

46. Note that the senior national security officials of the current Bush administration are also meeting weekly in informal sessions. However, these are often attended by the president or the vice president.

47. It is worth noting that "tank sessions" held by the Joint Chiefs of Staff, although part of a formal process, invoke a similar level of candor.

48. See Augur, "National Security Council System," for examples.

49. Several of those we interviewed indicated that they saw this as a problem with the current NSC staff.

Demonstrating this point conclusively would require a more complete analysis.

50. President Clinton created the NEC in 1993 to manage the interagency process for economic policy and to integrate economics into national security thinking in a more effective way. Six of its 18 members are also members of the NSC.

51. Augur, "National Security Council System," 61.

52. Robert B. Zoellick, "Congress and the Making of US Foreign Policy," *Survival* 41 (Winter 1999–2000): 21.

53. The recent congressionally directed reorganization of the Department of State, which folded several formerly independent activities into state under secretary offices, is one example.

54. Chuck Hagel, "Connecting Foreign Policy: Relevance, Challenge, and the Need for Leadership," remarks given at the Trilateral Commission Annual Meeting, March 1999. www.trilateral.org/annmtgs, 3.

55. Zoellick, "Congress," 23.

56. Lee H. Hamilton, "Congress and Foreign Policy," remarks given at the Trilateral Commission Annual Meeting, March 1999. www.trilateral.org/annmtgs.

57. Hagel, "Connecting Foreign Policy," 1.

58. Hamilton, "Congress and Foreign Policy," 1.

59. In his remarks to the Trilateral Commission, Lee Hamilton suggested establishing a standing consultative committee, which would meet periodically with the president and his key foreign policy advisors. Ibid., 3.

60. Zoellick, "Congress," 35.

61. Ibid., 37.

62. Interview with Senate Armed Services Committee staff.

63. For example, according to a former senator, when Senator Sam Nunn chaired the Senate Armed Services Committee, his reputation and ability to influence other senators on defense matters was such that administration officials considered how he would react to policy and strategy matters during formulation.

CHAPTER 6

THE RESOURCE ALLOCATION DIMENSION OF AMERICAN DEFENSE POLICY

NATIONAL SECURITY RESOURCE ALLOCATION

U.S. COMMISSION ON NATIONAL SECURITY/21ST CENTURY

GENERAL

The success of all national security processes and concepts ultimately depends on access to resources. Unless sufficient resources are available, development and implementation of policy and strategy are academic drills. All executive branch departments and a number of agencies participate in preparing the president's budget, which is then deliberated and approved by Congress, prior to being signed into law by the president.[1] The process by which the budget is conceptualized and prepared by the executive branch and deliberated and approved by Congress is interbranch.

OVERVIEW OF THE NATURE OF THE PROCESS

Because resources are finite and offsets (rather than plus-ups) are becoming more common, the preparation and deliberation process is often adversarial.

INTRADEPARTMENT

Precise processes used to link requirements to resources vary from department to department and they usually include a certain amount of tension. Within organizations, debates routinely occur over the shares each subelement will receive and whether a proponent's program is superior to an alternative proposed by someone else. (An example is the process by which the Programs Analysis and Evaluation [PA&E] Directorate in the Department of Defense presents alternatives to military service programs.[2] In these cases, the services usually view PA&E as meddlesome or uninformed.)

INTRA-EXECUTIVE BRANCH

Tensions can exist, too, when departments and agencies submit their budget requests to the Office of Management and Budget (OMB) for review. The director of OMB reviews department and agency budgets, listens to OMB staff recommendations, and then makes decisions that are often contrary to department and agency preferences, but are based on the director's understanding of the president's policies and priorities. When this occurs, it is sometimes necessary for the president to resolve disputes among his lieutenants. Because OMB is organized along *departmental* lines, it is difficult to examine and debate along *functional* lines (e.g., counter-terrorism, first response to weapons of mass destruction).

INTERBRANCH

Once the president's budget is submitted to the Congress, spirited debates often occur between members of Congress and administration officials testifying on behalf of the budget—and between members with different ideas of what is best for national security. An example of the latter is the deliberations and arm twisting concerning the purchase of additional B-2 bombers that occurred in the summer of 1997. Members often debate, too, whether funds marked for national security might be better spent on other needs. A case in point is the defeat of a June 1997 proposal to shift billions from the Department of Defense to fund highway infrastructure bills—a measure that was ultimately defeated in an early morning vote by the narrowest of margins. At the extremes, the Congress can hold up appropriations if it seeks to force the executive branch to handle matters differently.

Once Congress approves the budget and sends it to the White House, the president may veto it. If he does, the stage is set for what may become heated negotiations in an effort to reach a compromise.

TENSION AS A CREATIVE FORCE

Although competition between participants occasionally gets out of hand, more often these tensions are a positive, even creative force for finding the best alternatives. The fact that the budget share is often a zero-sum game ensures that participants will present alternatives, and that both original proposals and alternatives will be subjected to rigorous scrutiny. Consequently, decisionmakers in both the executive and legislative branches are presented with a range

U.S. Commission on National Security/21st Century, Road Map for National Security, *Volume 1:* Key Observations and Overarching Processes *(Washington, D.C.: U.S. Commission on National Security/21st Century, April 15, 2001),* 58–71. *Public domain.*

of options and supporting analysis, which should result in better decisions over the long term. Still, there is no shortage of parochialism in budget proceedings.

THE EXECUTIVE BRANCH—BUDGET PREPARATION PROCESS

PREPARATION OVERVIEW

Although particulars differ somewhat depending on the department, the overall preparation process is essentially the same. It may be summarized in terms of months:[3]

- January–March: president establishes general guidance

- March–May: OMB develops significant issues

- June: OMB provides budget preparation guidance[4]

- June–September: departments and agencies prepare budget requests

- September: departments and agencies submit budget requests

- September–October: OMB reviews budget submissions; prepares issues

- October–November: OMB director reviews and makes "passbacks"

- November–December: departments and agencies prepare appeals and the president makes decisions

- December–January: president's budget is prepared and approved

- January–February: president's budget is submitted to Congress

Note that these timeframes often change. For example, although the president's budget is supposed to be submitted to Congress no later than the first Monday in February, it sometimes arrives later. When administrations change, for instance, the new administration usually does not submit its budget until later in the spring, and the Congress does not object. Also, although OMB should provide budget preparation guidance by June for the budget to be submitted the following February, the formal guidance often is not provided until much later. According to DoD officials, sometimes it does not arrive until November. When this occurs, departments usually use informal channels to determine a funding range for use in budget preparation. Despite deviations, the schedule provides a useful reference for discussion.

Although described here in dispassionate terms, contention (and often acrimony) mark the resource allocation process at almost every step—between the executive branch and the Congress; among members of Congress and among their staffs; among departments and agencies and OMB; and between OMB

and NSC staff members. That most decisions are made at levels below the president should not be interpreted to mean that heated debates do not occur at those levels. Similarly, differences among members of the House and Senate and their staff over what share of the budget should go to national security and how much should be devoted to specific programs are often pronounced.

March–May

During this period, OMB analyzes the administration's goals and policies in light of changes in the strategic and political environments, and its success in obtaining funds for critical programs in the budget currently being executed (i.e., the budget that went into effect on October 1 of the previous calendar year).[5] The review includes programmatic initiatives, as well as Government Performance Reform Act initiatives and guidance from the president. As part of the review, OMB identifies issues requiring further investigation.

While OMB is conducting its review, departments and agencies usually begin to prepare initial budget request drafts. These are based on internal department guidance. For example, the Department of Defense may publish the Defense Planning Guidance (DPG)[6] and Defense Fiscal Guidance (FG) during this period, and the military services will have already begun to craft their proposed budgets, known as a Program Objective Memorandum (POM). Start points vary depending on department and agency tradition and culture, the size of the budget, and internal approval processes. According to OMB officials, for example, despite the size of its budget, the Department of Defense is among the most proficient departments in preparing budget requests because it has a long-range planning culture and a budget request approval system that is widely understood. Thus by June, the department has its own list of issues, and service POMs are close to completion. (Other departments and agencies have their own systems for preparing budget requests. These systems are no less effective than that used by the Department of Defense and are tailored to the culture and needs of the organization.)

June

Based on OMB's initial review (which is sometimes called the "spring issue review"), OMB develops a list of top-down issues that will be analyzed and reviewed during later stages of budget preparation. The OMB staff also provides guidance for budget preparation to executive branch organizations. This marks the formal beginning of budget request preparation.

June–September

During the summer, executive branch activities prepare their budget requests using OMB and department and agency guidance. Often, there are mid-session reviews with OMB, in which top lines, economic assumptions, and guidance may be changed. In most cases, formal OMB involvement with the departments is not great during this period, although there are informal conversations between OMB budget analysts and department personnel. However, because of the size and complexity of the Department of Defense's budget, OMB staff members are involved throughout the summer in the programming phase of that department's planning, programming, and budgeting system (PPBS). In fact, OMB staff participates in internal DoD issue reviews.[7] Thus, although information is continually exchanged between OMB and other departments, OMB's involvement in the DoD process is more extensive.

September

In September, departments and agencies submit their budget requests to OMB for review. The requests are bounded by OMB budget preparation instructions and top lines. Usually, OMB will use the month of September to review and analyze department budget requests prior to beginning "hearings" (see below). This review includes verification of figures, examination of supporting studies used by departments to justify some items, comparisons to the previous budget, extent of compliance with preparation guidance, and identification and analysis of a small number of additional issues. For example, in the case of the Department of Defense, the OMB staff reviews the department's budget to ensure that the figures are correct and that it is consistent with the president's defense and national security policies.[8] This is the norm for other departments and agencies as well.

As the review takes place, OMB staff members enter budget estimates into the budget preparation system (BSP), a computer program that tracks the overall budget preparation in near real time. This process is known as "scorekeeping." Inputs may change as a result of hearings, the director's review, or appeals. However, the initial inputs are the beginning of budget building at the top level.

September–October

Following budget request reviews, OMB conducts a series of hearings at which departments defend their requests. The hearing process begins with fact-finding analysis by OMB staff, who develop questions for departments to address during the hearings. The term "hearings" is somewhat misleading. Hearings may take the form of one-on-one meetings at the staff level, telephone and/or written inquiries, or they may involve relatively senior panels of OMB officials, including political appointees. The latter is usually the case if senior department officials are expected to be present.

Participants have described the hearings as animated. They allow departments to present and justify their budget requests and to present their side of the case with respect to OMB issues. Hearings are the best opportunity for departments to shape the president's budget, short of direct intervention by cabinet officers with the president. One observer notes that they provide an "opportunity for . . . agency representatives to make a dent in OMB decision-making."[9] Hearings also allow OMB to explain the president's policy in cases where such explanations are necessary.

If hearings involve formal meetings, they are usually held at OMB, except for those involving the Department of Defense. The procedure for DoD hearings centers on the department's internal issue review procedures. Beginning in the summer months and continuing into the fall, DoD and OMB staffs review the defense budget jointly. For other departments, the hearing process is usually shorter and may last hours or days. As a rule, both sides know the other's position prior to the hearings, and departments usually have the opportunity to review OMB issue papers in advance. At the conclusion of the hearings, unresolved issues are carried forward for the OMB director's review.

October–November

The OMB director's reviews for a particular department often begin while hearings are still ongoing for other departments. The entire review period can last 3 or 4 weeks. In preparation for the review, the OMB staff develops issue papers and briefings with budget recommendations. Issue papers include an executive summary; several alternatives, funding levels for each alternative, and the potential outcomes; legislation required for alternatives to be adopted; and stakeholder positions, including Congress, interest groups, other government organizations, and the general public. Issue papers end with recommendations.

Previous director reviews have been conducted in hearing format (in which staff present their case before the director and a panel of other senior OMB officials) and/or through issue books. When hearings are conducted for the director, the director and senior OMB staff members receive issue books prior to each session to acquaint them with substantive matters. During review sessions, the usual format is to begin with a budget overview, followed by a presentation of issue papers.[10] The director's review is closed except for OMB staff. The minutes of each session are closely held by OMB and are not usually released beyond the OMB staff. Departments do not attend director review sessions, and department views are presented to the director by the OMB staff. Because it is impossible to review the entire budget, director-level hearings focus on what have been described as "politically visible" issues—those items that have potentially significant policy impacts.[11]

As each review is completed, OMB decisions are forwarded to departments for incorporation into their final budget proposals. Decisions are known as "passbacks," which include the Director's decisions, as well as additional guidance and instructions as necessary. Once received by the department, passbacks are either accepted and included in the revised budget, or designated for appeal.

November–December

If a department elects to appeal the OMB director's decision(s), it prepares and presents its case during November and December. Technically, appeals are addressed to the president. However, they are often resolved before they reach that level, although this depends on the president's preferences. In cases of appeals on national security issues, the director of OMB, the president's national security advisor, the secretary of defense, the chairman of the Joint Chiefs of Staff, and others will often try to resolve appeals through compromise. When this is not possible, the appeal is passed to the president for decision. In these cases, the president may seek the advice of the same group, or he may elicit the opinions of others. Once the president decides, there is no further appeal. Interviews with OMB staff, with experience dating from the Nixon administration, indicate that the level of presidential involvement in the appeals process depends on the personality of the president. President Carter, for example, took an active role in deciding most appeals, whereas President Reagan was involved only in exceptional cases.

The OMB staff treats the appeals process seriously because appeals carry the weight of the cabinet secretary of the appealing department. Although lower levels of the bureaucracy may object to an OMB director's decision, it does not become an appeal without the consent of the department secretary. The OMB staff noted during interviews that because secretaries have a personal relationship with the president, it is in everyone's interest to resolve appeals before they reach the Oval Office.

December–January

Upon completion of the appeals process, decisions are included in the budget and final adjustments are made. These adjustments are based on the latest predictions and forecasts, including inflation and employment figures. The budget is then printed.

January–February

The president's budget is submitted to Congress prior to close of business on the first Monday in February, although presidents often provide budget highlights during the State of the Union Address in January. Once the budget is submitted, OMB reviews department testimony in support of the budget to ensure that it reflects the president's policies. It also exchanges information with the Congressional Budget Office (CBO) as appropriate to clarify specific issues. (OMB sources describe the relationship with CBO as constructive and valuable overall, although they acknowledge that there are disagreements and tensions.)

Once Congress begins its deliberations, OMB tracks the president's budget through the congressional process, assessing the impact of congressionally mandated changes (i.e., scorekeeping), and recommending shifts in approaches as necessary.

THE EXECUTIVE BRANCH—INFORMAL BUDGET PREPARATION PROCESS

The informal processes for budget preparation are based on personal relationships, for the most part. These include interaction between the OMB staff and department officials with responsibility for preparing budgets. In the case of some appeals, informal processes may involve interaction between a cabinet secretary and the president. An OMB interlocutor noted that part of the OMB staff's job is to know what is going on in the departments and agencies for which they have responsibility. Thus there are informal contacts between the OMB staff and the staffs of the departments. Although some staff contacts are more episodic than routine, in the case of the Department of Defense, contacts are continuous.

At more senior levels, clearly there are discussions between the president's key advisors, including the assistant for economic policy, and cabinet officials as part of the appeals process. Generally, the goal is to arrive at consensus solutions without involving the president. Achieving that goal requires informal interaction between principals to negotiate compromise solutions during the appeals process and at other times.

OMB participation in DoD program and budget reviews (and those of other departments to a lesser extent) is an informal process that is almost formal. As noted above, OMB is involved in DoD PPBS processes from the outset. It often attends program reviews and frequently uses these reviews in place of the hearings it holds for other departments.

THE LEGISLATIVE BRANCH—FORMAL BUDGET DELIBERATION AND APPROVAL PROCESS

There are three parallel budget processes that occur nearly simultaneously in the Congress. Although they formally begin when the president's budget arrives, in fact, members and staffs begin preparation months in advance. The three processes are the budget process, the authorization process, and the appropriations process. Each involves hearings, deliberations, and mark-ups (or amendments) of the president's budget and ultimately contributes to national security resourcing legislation.

There are timetables for these processes, but they are often ignored. Essentially, the goal is to produce the thirteen appropriations bills and to have them signed into law by the president prior to the beginning of the next fiscal year. Meeting interim milestones often does not seem to be a significant priority, and, as Congress makes its own rules, it can change them to suit its needs.

THE BUDGET PROCESS

Each house of Congress has a budget committee that produces a budget resolution that is voted on by the full chamber, and, when approved by both chambers, is binding on both houses unless the rules are changed.[12] The budget resolution sets ultimate ceilings on spending for authorizing and appropriating committees. In other words, it tells committees and subcommittees how much money they may authorize or appropriate. Authorizing committees, in turn, set specific "ceilings," whereas appropriating committees establish funding "floors." The budget resolution also tells these committees how much revenue can be expected and the current services budget (i.e., how much it will cost in the next year to do the same things that are done in the current year). The budget resolution is an internal congressional document that does not require the president's signature.

At the outset of the budget resolution preparation process, OMB presents the administration's case to the budget committees—usually in writing and in oral testimony. The committees may also receive alternative views, such as those provided by the CBO.[13] Unlike OMB, whose job it is to create the budget, the CBO reacts to that budget. It does so by analyzing it, making recommendations, and providing alternative economic estimates and forecasts. Simultaneously, other congressional committees review the president's budget and provide comments (views and estimates) approximately 6 weeks after it is received on the Hill.

The budget committee considers testimony and the views and estimates reports as it drafts the budget resolution, which, according to congressional rules, must be passed by April 15 annually. Once both chambers adopt the resolution, authorizing and appropriating committees conduct their markups and draft legislation to the top lines provided by the resolution (and the accompanying report) for their committees. In some years, there is no concurrent budget resolution. When that occurs, both the House and the Senate traditionally mark-up using the House budget figures.

The budget committees are also responsible under the Budget Act of 1974 for providing reconciliation instructions whenever an authorizing or appropriating committee exceeds the ceilings provided in the budget resolution. Essentially, reconciliation instructions tell the committees and subcommittees to take the necessary steps to bring revenues and expenditures into line through reconciliation legislation. The effect of reconciliation instructions is to keep committees from increasing spending for their areas of responsibility (and increasing the national debt) without finding corresponding offsets from other committees, which are usually unwilling to give up a portion of their share of the budget.

AUTHORIZING COMMITTEES

Each chamber has authorizing committees that have jurisdiction over the organization and structure, roles and responsibilities, and the amount of funding for activities that come within their jurisdictions. Authorizations set specific funding ceilings. These committees conduct hearings; they consider bills, res-

olutions, and reports; and they conduct or direct studies and reviews of matters over which they exercise oversight. Although the present discussion begins with the authorizing procedures, authorizing and appropriating committees actually conduct their work simultaneously.

By congressional rules, appropriations committees appropriate funds based on programs and amounts authorized by the authorizing committees. The authorizing committees establish ceilings on expenditures; the appropriating committees provide actual funding and may provide less than what is authorized. Rules also require that only authorizing committees are empowered by the Congress to draft legislative (or policy) language for inclusion in congressional bills. However, both rules are often violated. In fact, it is not uncommon for appropriating committees to complete their work before authorizing committees do, and legislative language is often included in appropriations bills.

The authorizing committees and their subcommittees formally begin work upon receipt of the president's budget, although they usually do not mark-up legislation until after the budget resolution is passed or the decision is made to use a particular set of budget assumptions in lieu of the budget resolution. Initially, authorizing committees conduct a series of hearings that involve department posture statements delivered by senior officials. These hearings are often wide ranging and do not necessarily focus on the president's budget. Frequently, authorizing hearings are vehicles for members to challenge administration policy, strategy, or ongoing initiatives.

Typically, the line-up for testimony is fairly deep. For example, the full House Armed Services Committee (HASC) will usually receive testimony from the secretary of defense, the deputy secretary, the under secretaries, some assistant secretaries (e.g., those for Command, Control, Communications, and Intelligence, Science, Technology, and Research), the service secretaries, the chairman of the Joint Chiefs of Staff, the vice chairman of the Joint Chiefs of Staff, the Joint Chiefs, and the Unified Command commanders-in-chief, among others. Subcommittees (which begin meeting before testimony before the full committee is complete) may ask for testimony from some of the same experts, and they often delve several layers deeper. For example, deputy assistant secretaries and functional subject matter experts at the action officer level may be called on to testify before authorizing subcommittees.

In addition to department officials and experts, committees and subcommittees routinely seek testimony from non-government expert witnesses. These include members of academia, industry officials, and former government officials.

Hearings occur according to the rules established by the committee or subcommittee chair, usually in conjunction with the ranking minority member of the committee or subcommittee. Committee majority and minority professional staffs prepare the agenda and furnish members with central themes and questions, as directed by the chair and the majority and minority staff directors. Professional staffs usually provide hearing packets to members a day or so before the hearings containing the agenda, lists of witnesses, suggested questions and themes, and witness' written testimony, if provided by the witnesses.

Members' personal staffs review these packets and prepare packets for members that correspond to the members' interests. For example, professional staff read-ahead packages are often broad, or reflect the interests of senior committee members. If a member has an interest that goes beyond the read-ahead package, his/her staff will provide the necessary information. Thus, if the service chiefs of staff are scheduled to give their posture statements, a member who is concerned about treatment of women in the military will most likely depend on his/her personal staff to prepare appropriate questions for use by the member.

The testimony season begins in February and continues into the summer. Toward the end of this process, subcommittees and committees will begin to mark-up proposed authorizing legislation. Committee and subcommittee "marks" are conducted according to rules promulgated by the chair. They are often closed to the public, and sometimes the number of staff members who can attend is also limited.

The mark-up is really a series of amendments and compromises that produces the version of the bill that will ultimately be voted on by the entire body and then sent to conference with the other chamber. Although marks always involve partisan efforts on behalf of particular programs, bipartisan cooperation is common, especially if the issue is one that affects a number of congressional districts. Examples of bipartisanship during 1997 mark-ups involving national security resourcing matters included agreements to authorize purchase of additional C-17, B-2, and F/A-18E/F aircraft. (This example also illustrates the fact that the Congress may require the administration to expend resources for items that the executive branch does not believe necessary, such as more C-130s.)

Once the mark-up is complete and the committee has voted on the amended version of the bill, the staff prepares reports and the final bill draft, which are sent to the floor for deliberation and vote. The bill is usually floor-managed by the committee chair or others designated by him/her. During floor deliberations, members may offer amendments, depending on the rules of debate and germaneness. Upon approval of each chamber's version of the authorization bill, a conference is scheduled to resolve differences between the House and Senate versions.

Conferences typically occur during the summer and fall, depending on when authorization bills are passed. Committee chairs and ranking members normally choose conference members, and conferences may be subdivided along subcommittee lines. Most compromises reached during conferences are worked out by the staff and approved by members. A few issues may require active member participation to resolve.

Compromises and amendments reached during conference are inserted into joint resolutions, and conference reports are published to reflect conference proceedings and agreements. When both houses pass the resolutions, they become the basis for appropriations and are sent to the president for signature.

APPROPRIATIONS COMMITTEES

Like authorizing committees, appropriations committees were created by congressional rules. There is no constitutional requirement for their existence. However, the Constitution does require that all expenditures of public funds be appropriated by law, and the appropriations committees were created to help Congress fulfill this obligation. (Until the 1860s, there were no separate authorization and appropriations committees; a single committee did both.) Appropriations committees establish funding floors.

Several premises should be understood. First, government departments and agencies cannot spend more money than Congress appropriates to them, nor can they reprogram funds for purposes other than that prescribed by authorization and appropriations bills and reports without approval. Second, according to congressional rules and customs, when specific amounts are specified in authorizing legislation, the appropriations committee and its subcommittees may not appropriate more money than the authorizing legislation allows, although they may appropriate less. Third, appropriations bills are law, and any policy or legislative provisions included in them are also law, despite internal congressional rules that prohibit the inclusion of policy language in appropriations. If legislative (or other) provisions are in conflict with authorizing provisions, the most recently passed bill has precedence—usually the appropriations bill. Fourth, appropriations bills can amend authorization bills under some circumstances.

The appropriating committees are responsible for reporting out the thirteen regular appropriations bills and usually at least one supplemental and one continuing resolution each year. Each regular appropriations bill consists of three major features: an enactment clause designating the fiscal year; specific account appropriations and account provisions; and provisions that apply generally.

Most of the appropriations committees' work is performed by thirteen subcommittees, each of which has responsibility for one of the regular appropriations measures. Although they have different titles, the actual jurisdictions of House and Senate appropriations subcommittees align almost exactly, and bills reported out by subcommittees are usually not changed substantively by the full committees.

Traditionally, appropriations bills originate in the House, but there is no legal requirement that they do so. As a rule, however, the House appropriations bills are produced first, then reviewed by the Senate. One effect of this procedure is that the Senate is usually faced with appropriations that are very close to the ceilings established in the concurrent budget resolution. Thus, much of what the Senate does falls into the category of shifting funds from one program or account to another rather than introducing new programs.

Although informal preparations begin much earlier, the House and Senate appropriations committees begin work formally when the president's budget arrives, even though the Senate does not usually conduct mark-ups until it receives the House version. The process—which involves hearings and investigations —is very similar to that used by the authorizing committees (although the specific procedural rules are different), and the appropriations subcommittees and authorizing committees often call many of the same witnesses.

Essentially, the thirteen appropriations subcommittees conduct hearings to verify estimates and costs and examine alternative approaches. They may also examine policy issues, often by agreement with the authorizing committees. In some respects, their interests overlap with those of the authorizing committees, although they may arrive at different conclusions.

Once appropriations bills have been marked-up and passed by the House, they are sent to the Senate, where the process is repeated. When the Senate passes its version, a conference is scheduled and differences between the versions are reconciled. Both chambers then pass the bill and it is sent to the president for signature. If the president approves the bill, it becomes law. If he vetoes it, it is returned to Congress for amendment or override. If he neither vetoes nor returns the bill within 10 days while Congress is still in session, the bill also becomes law without the president's signature; however, this method is rarely used.

THE LEGISLATIVE BRANCH— INFORMAL BUDGET DELIBERATION AND APPROVAL PROCESS

As is true of political processes in general, budget, authorization, and appropriations processes on the Hill involve compromise, much of which occurs informally. Agreements (crafted among members, among staffers, and sometimes between members and staffers) are based on personal relationships and common interests. Both are equally important, especially for bipartisan efforts. For example, in 1997 the chairman of the HASC,[14] the ranking member, and a small group of staffers put together a broad DoD reform initiative and presented it to the HASC as part of the mark-up.[15] Their efforts both to craft the initial proposal and to shepherd it through committee resulted in incorporating most of the provisions into the FY 1998 authorization bill.

Personal contacts are also important in bridging the gap between budget, authorizing, and appropriations committees. Although a few members of each committee may serve on one of the other committees, most exchanges of information and compromises occur through informal, personal contacts.

Although work on the budget formally begins when it arrives on the Hill, professional and personal staff informally track executive branch programs and budget preparation in the months prior. For example, if a program is of interest to a member, his/her personal staff (and depending on seniority of the member, committee professional staff) will employ informal contacts to provide updates and to attempt to influence preparation of the president's budget. These contacts may involve the department directly, or they may be based on information provided to the staff by contractors involved in production.

Another important informal process, although one of long standing, involves the intervention of outsiders in the budget process. Outsiders fall into two general categories: members who do not sit on committees with national security responsibilities, but who have national security interests; and lobbyists and political action groups.

The former group includes those who have both altruistic and constituent interests, but who serve on non-national security-related committees. For example, a member may have an electronics plant in his/her district that would benefit from more robust defense procurement funding. Or a member may feel strongly that defense spending will cut deeply into social programs.

In these cases and others, members are likely to seek out other members who sit on national security committees and enlist their assistance informally. This can occur on a larger scale in cases where state delegations tend to vote together on issues that affect members, as sometimes occurs with the California and Texas delegations in the House. Either method can be effective.

Lobbyists, political action groups, and private citizens can also interact informally with congressional processes. Members who have seats on the Armed Forces committees (and their staffs), for example, are often bombarded with information and appeals for help from these sources. Not infrequently, lobbyists are the only sources of information for members with respect to particular programs. In some cases, lobbyists work closely with members to develop coalitions of like-minded members for particular issues— almost as adjunct staff. This occurred, for example, when Congress debated buying nine additional B-2 bombers in 1997. In this instance, major contractors and their suppliers provided information to members on how other members were likely to vote and data on the number of workers in each district whose jobs might depend on additional production. Political action groups operate in similar ways. As was true in the case of member-to-member relations, these approaches are usually informal and often consist of telephone calls or drop-by visits.

Although prohibited by law from lobbying, the military services engage in similar practices. They often provide information and offer members the opportunity to visit bases or crisis areas. Each service has liaison officers on the Hill, and each has a flag or general officer as the senior congressional liaison. Calls to liaison offices by members or their staffs usually produce prompt responses. In some cases, they can result in the appearance of senior uniformed officers to personally explain service policies and positions. During congressional deliberations over appropriate methods for conducting basic training (single sex or co-ed), three-star representatives from each service made the rounds of key House members to state their service's case, and in the case of the Marine Corps, the commandant was personally involved. Other departments and agencies have similar liaison structures.

OBSERVATIONS

Links between Resource Allocation and National Security Strategy

The preparation and deliberation of resource allocation processes are characterized by a plethora of alternative approaches. The competition among alternatives at all levels, although time consuming, helps ensure that decisionmakers are provided with the best options from which to choose. In considering options, it is important to link them to strategy and policy goals. Reviews and hearings held by the departments and OMB help to do that during preparation, as do the witnesses summoned by Congress during its deliberations.

However, in general, there is no executive branch-wide national security document to which programs can be pinned. The national security strategy is too broad and general to serve as a planning and programming document that illuminates administration strategy and directs programming to ensure that strategic objectives are satisfied. This situation contrasts with the Department of Defense, which publishes the Defense Planning Guidance (DPG) that provides programming instructions for the services that are linked to DoD strategy. However, even the DPG often fails to list objectives—let alone prioritize them. As threats and challenges become more complex and responses require actions by different departments and agencies acting in concert, the absence of national-level planning guidance may prove detrimental.

The OMB–Department of Defense Link

An informal yet productive relationship exists between OMB and the Department of Defense. Essentially, OMB is involved in DoD budget preparation through staff interaction and OMB participation in DoD program reviews. This relationship, although sometimes adversarial, ensures that each side is aware of the other's perspective, and it offers the opportunity for issue clarification and resolution at the lowest level possible.

Yet this link, although effective and well developed, is department-focused, as are the links between OMB and other executive branch entities. Given this approach and OMB's organization, it is difficult to set up cross-functional reviews that involve more than one department. For example, determining spending for homeland security or counterproliferation efforts across the president's budget is cumbersome and time consuming.

Outsider Influence in Congressional Deliberations

Lobbyists and political action groups are a constant part of congressional budget deliberations. Sometimes they even act as auxiliary staff, providing analysis, data, and other forms of information to staff —especially personal staff members. Although this service has some value for staff who are usually not subject matter experts for most programs and who are pressed by other responsibilities, the information may not be objective. In essence, lobbyists and political action groups are advocates who are rewarded based on the success of their advocacy. Although they have the right to advocate, their efforts sometimes upset the value of the competition between alternatives that occurs during the budget preparation process.

NOTES

1. Under present law, the president's annual budget includes the next fiscal year's budget request and a projection for 4 years beyond that.

2. Although arguments within the Department of Defense occur over programs and alternatives, the amount of the defense budget that is allocated to each service has remained relatively stable over time. Critics point to more-or-less equal shares and observe that the arrangement precludes innovative approaches to national security.

3. Shelley Lynne Tomkin, *Inside OMB: Politics and Process in the President's Budget Office* (Armonk, N.Y.: M. E. Sharpe, 1998), and interviews with OMB and DoD officials. The Department of Defense operates on a year-to-year cycle, despite past attempts to move it to a 2-year cycle. Reasons for retaining the annual system include congressional resistance to the 2-year version.

4. In the case of the Department of Defense and some other departments, preparation guidance does not arrive until after budget preparation is under way.

5. When viewing the preparation cycle, it is important to keep in mind that it begins almost 18 months prior to the fiscal year for which the budget will be executed. For example, issues developed during the March–May timeframe in 2000 are for the budget that will be executed beginning on October 1, 2001 (FY 2002). Reform proposals that will

C B O role

require resources may be without them for as much as 2 years before the applicable budget is executed.

6. The DPG attempts to link planning and strategy to programming.

7. DoD officials view OMB participation as a generally positive event because it helps them explain their positions on programs and to gain OMB support. In the words of one senior, experienced DoD participant, having OMB sit in ensures that OMB knows exactly what it gets for its money, and exactly what capabilities it will lose when it cuts funding.

8. Interviews with OMB staff.

9. Tomkin, *Inside OMB,* 122.

10. Interviews with OMB staff.

11. Tomkin, *Inside OMB,* 128.

12. Budget committees are standing committees created by the Congressional Budget and Impoundment Control Act of 1974. Unlike most other congressional committees, the budget committees have no subcommittees.

13. The budget committees exercise oversight of the CBO.

14. The HASC was then known as the "House National Security Committee" (or HNSC).

15. This measure was originally H.R. 1777 and was informally referred to as the Spence-Dellums Resolution after the chair and ranking member of the committee.

THE NEW PPBS PROCESS TO ADVANCE TRANSFORMATION

STUART E. JOHNSON

The planning, programming, and budgeting system (PPBS) was developed by Secretary of Defense Robert McNamara in the early 1960s to manage DoD programs and resources. A key purpose was to rationalize investments in strategic nuclear delivery systems and to answer the pressing question, "How much is enough?" McNamara also used the PPBS to integrate the force plans of the three services. He held that, in the absence of such a system, each service developed its force program with only incidental attention to the other services. Consequently, the three programs were suboptimized—the resultant capabilities being less than the sum of the three parts.

McNamara had other objectives in developing this management tool. He sought to establish output metrics to measure the fulfillment of defense requirements. This proved difficult to do. In most cases, he had to settle for increased visibility of input measures—in particular, how much money was going into a program. Even achieving this proved challenging. Too often, he found that only the initial costs of a program were reported, and a bow wave of future costs was masked. To address this problem, he required that the full life-cycle cost of a major program be calculated and displayed.

Finally, McNamara intended to link force programming decisions to strategic assessments. The Five-Year Defense Program (FYDP) was established with ten major-force program (MFP) spending categories that cut across service competencies. The aim was to allow the secretary of defense and his staff to give strategic guidance to the military services and

then have a tool to measure the service responses in programmatic terms. The program review process would table alternative ways of fulfilling requirements. These would be developed, analyzed, and costed to allow the secretary of defense to make high-impact choices that cut across individual service programs.

The PPBS has undergone a number of changes over the past four decades, but the core elements and basic flow of the process endure. It has served the Department of Defense and the federal government well. Indeed, few other cabinet departments have a process in place that provides a systematic and relatively visible review of programs and resource allocations.

That said, the PPBS was designed in a much different security context than faces the United States today. In the early 1960s and for nearly three decades beyond, the nation faced global competition from a large, well-armed military power, the Soviet Union. Stability depended on an uneasy military equilibrium and the knowledge on both sides that conflict could result in catastrophic damage. This environment created an imperative to avoid mistakes. High priority was placed on a steady, evolutionary improvement in military forces to keep pace with a relatively well understood, steadily evolving adversary.

The PPBS was well suited to such a challenge. It forced defense planners in the military services and in the Office of the Secretary of Defense (OSD) to make choices and prioritize programs. Decisionmakers could get a fair degree of insight into the military capabilities that would be fielded in the near future.

Stuart E. Johnson, "The New PPBS Process to Advance Transformation," Defense Horizons 32 (Washington, D.C.: Center for Technology and National Security Policy, National Defense University, September 2003): 1–6. Public domain.

The risk of making a serious mistake and suffering its dangerous consequences was minimized. Moreover, this predictability allowed the Department of Defense to provide guidance in arms control negotiations in the 1970s and 1980s that was coupled to relative strengths and weaknesses of U.S. forces in relation to Soviet forces.

Today, the United States faces a different set of challenges. No country can confront the awesome military power of the United States head on. If a peer military competitor begins to emerge, there will be plenty of warning. Even the problem of defeating a regional aggressor in a classical cross-border invasion of a friend or ally continues to recede in likelihood and seriousness.

Threats to our security and to that of our allies have taken on a different character. The threats are more diffuse, harder to identify with certainty, and less tied to nation-states with powerful standing military forces. Threats for the foreseeable future are far more likely to arise from terrorists or rogue nations with access to weapons of mass destruction.

These threats are not "lesser included cases" that can be taken care of handily by large military formations configured for high-intensity conflict with a hostile nation-state or alliance. They are "different cases" that require a different response from forces organized and employed differently. Our forces, or a good part of them, need to transform, to find new ways of bringing highly focused military power to the battlefield promptly, from a long distance and with limited risk to themselves.

Managing transformation presents a challenge to a secretary of defense, whose primary management tool is the PPBS. The system was designed for a different time, security environment, and set of military challenges. The system is well suited to managing continuity, not change. It tends to impede transformation rather than encourage it.

Discarding the PPBS altogether is not feasible; the Department of Defense depends on it to administer the budget of a large and complex organization. That said, new elements can be incorporated into it to facilitate transformation. It is instructive to review obstacles to change, some of which already are under serious consideration by OSD.

THE PPBS CYCLE

The PPBS comprises several major stages:

- Quadrennial defense review (QDR): a strategic review of the security environment that reflects the defense priorities of the administration is prepared during the first year of each administration (including returning administrations).

- Defense planning guidance: prepared by OSD and issued to the military departments. This reflects the priorities of the secretary of defense and guides the military departments in preparing their proposed programs and budgets. It is targeted for submission in late spring.

- Program objective memoranda (POM): statements of the proposed program and activities of the military departments are submitted in the summer.

- Budget estimate submissions (BES): detailed estimates of the funding required to implement the program proposed in the POM submissions are delivered concurrently with them.

- Program and budget review: conducted by OSD staff and the joint staff to review the POM and determine whether they conform to the secretary's guidance, as expressed in the defense planning guidance (DPG). If there appears to be a disconnect, the staff will prepare an issue paper for review by senior DoD leadership. Their decisions are captured in program decision memoranda that may dictate a change in the department's program and budget.

- Budget submission: the draft budget submitted to the Office of Management and Budget (OMB) by mid-fall; it is incorporated into the budget submissions of other cabinet departments and sent to Congress in late January.

At this point, Congress holds hearings and reviews the budget, making its own revisions and finally sends it to the president for signing before the start of the new fiscal year (October 1).

The PPBS has a number of strengths, chief among them that it keeps track of a very large program and budget, and decisions involving large sums of money are relatively transparent. With determined leadership by senior DoD leaders, some change can be accommodated within the existing system. But the PPBS has shortcomings that transcend the capability or good will of the participants to overcome.

INDUSTRIAL AGE MANAGEMENT TOOL

The PPBS is an industrial age management tool that is ill suited to the information age. McNamara developed it to centralize control of DoD planning in OSD, despite the "Title 10" congressional requirement that the secretary of defense manage the department through the separate services. McNamara configured the PPBS based on the best management practices of a modern, large, industrial corporation that was in competition with similar corporations similarly operated, based on experience accumulated in the 1940s and 1950s. This led to a focus on three elements that provided savings and, presumably, a competitive edge: cost effectiveness, elimination of redundancy, and process management.

Cost effectiveness was chosen as a key (often the only) measure of merit in choosing among alternatives in the defense program. If there were a way to trim the cost of producing an end item or to substitute another, less expensive system to do the same job, the change would be adopted. Savings were also found by eliminating redundancy; most notably, in several strategic nuclear force programs. Finally, best practices of a large industrial corporation of the 1960s dictated a process to manage the development of a new product from engineering through getting the product to market. Likewise, the Department of Defense instituted a largely linear PPBS process to track the development of a weapon system from research and development through test and evaluation and initial production to full-scale production.

This process of centralized control came under considerable criticism from the armed services. In response, during the Nixon administration, Secretary of Defense Melvin Laird turned the process into more of a dialogue between OSD and the services. To decentralize the acquisition process while keeping it coherent, Deputy Secretary of Defense David Packard developed detailed guidelines for service procurement called the "5000 Series" of documents.

All these processes served the Department of Defense well during the Cold War, when deliberate, evolutionary improvement of forces sufficed. But forces today must react more quickly to a broad range of challenges that can change suddenly. Moreover, the military is being called on to execute types of missions it has never faced before. Evolutionary improvement of forces no longer suffices. The appropriate model for the services is a successful, information age management style.

Information age management, in contrast to industrial age management, looks for and cultivates the breakthrough concept. Instead of simply improving the existing product or service line, the successful corporation seeks entirely new ways of meeting market needs with emerging and existing technologies. This can mean a sharp departure from a company's customary way of doing business. A good example of a breakthrough concept occurred in the cable television industry. It invested heavily in fiber optics to achieve very-high-speed data transmission. When the market for cable television had largely become saturated, some companies recognized that a fiber-optic network also could provide high-speed Internet service. For a modest investment on the margin, they began to offer a bundled package of cable television and high-speed Internet service at a price below what competitors could offer separately.

In the same way, our PPBS process needs to have some capability to brainstorm and cultivate breakthrough concepts. Some of this can be done in the field. A good example was the use of Special Operations forces attached to Northern Alliance ground forces during Operation Enduring Freedom in Afghanistan. The Northern Alliance forces forced the Taliban and al Qaeda troops to concentrate; subsequently, Special Operations forces, using a global positioning system locator, transmitted coordinates of enemy positions to attack aircraft that struck those targets accurately and with devastating effect. This unique combination of close-up pressure on the enemy with precision, standoff firepower was a new way to employ proven technology and hastened the precipitous collapse of the Taliban government. The search for such breakthrough concepts must become part of the PPBS process.

PPBS SUITED TO STABLE STRATEGIC ENVIRONMENT

The PPBS process was designed to involve many players. This is a virtue for a system that aims at steady evolutionary improvement in forces; the multitude of participants maximizes continuity and minimizes risk. The problem is that such a system cannot respond to a dynamic strategic environment of the type that we have faced for a decade. The length of the cycle from concept to capability is simply too long.

A related issue is the focus of the PPBS process on major weapon systems. Although the procurement portion of the defense budget makes up only about 20 percent of the total, this part of the program gets the most scrutiny. This is to be expected: it is the part that is most visible and most amenable to analysis. Unfortunately, such focus on major weapon systems encourages evolutionary improvement of existing systems. The steady, low-risk improvement of the arsenal is out of place in a volatile strategic environment.

THE BURDEN OF REDUNDANCY

As the PPBS has evolved, the Department of Defense and Congress have imposed reporting requirements on participants. In all cases, there is a rationale for doing so, and in some cases, the process cannot run without them. In other cases, the reports are redundant, arrive out of phase with other activities in the PPBS cycle, and consume considerable staff time.

Consider an OSD analyst's role. The PPBS documents must be coordinated with multiple organizations within and sometimes outside the Pentagon—with unified and specified commands and defense agencies, to name two. The analyst also must keep an eye on overlapping reports that are being prepared by other divisions of OSD, by the joint staff, or by a service staff. Preparation and tracking of reports and meeting deadlines become confused with analysis and diminish the contribution staff can make to the important work of developing new options and strategic changes in direction.

A related problem is that preparing reports drains time and attention away from true planning. In most years, the planning phase has been thin or has been completed too late to serve as a useful framework for service programmers. The result has been that most of the attention is paid to the budgeting phase of the PPBS, at the expense of the planning and, to a lesser extent, the programming phases. The Department of Defense has instituted changes to the process to ameliorate this problem. In particular, a full DPG will be produced, and the services will be required to submit a full POM only biennially. The time freed up could be used to develop and put on the table innovative and transformational proposals.

THE DPG LACKS LEVERAGE ON SERVICE PLANS

The key tool available to the secretary of defense in giving guidance to the services on priorities to be reflected in their programs is the DPG. Ideally, the service programmers should be able to find in the DPG a planning framework to guide them as they build their POM. It has seldom worked. The DPG is usually too late and mostly too broad to provide a framework for service programmers or a metric against which service POM can be evaluated.

The service POMs are due to OSD in the summer. Naturally, the process of building the POM begins much sooner; it is at full throttle by the preceding fall. To provide an unambiguous framework for service programmers, the DPG would have to be signed out around the same time, and no later than October or November. This is seldom the case. Much more typical is a DPG that is issued half a year later—that is, only a month or two before the POMs are due to OSD.

The new process, which dictates a full DPG only every other year, will solve this problem on the off years and provide breathing room for OSD staff to complete the full DPG in good time during the years of the full PPBS cycle.

Ideally, the DPG should express the secretary's intent in output terms to give service POM builders clear direction to follow in their programming. In fact, much of the DPG is too broad in scope to be useful, in part because of the tyranny of consensus that rounds off the edges as the document is coordinated among multiple DoD offices with a stake in the document. Also, senior leaders do not focus on the front end of the PPBS process. Their energy, attention, and time typically (and understandably) are concentrated at the back end, when the deadline for submission of the DoD budget to OMB is pressing. This is not the optimum time allocation for senior leadership. Indeed, in the commercial world, such late engagement is a sign of a sick corporation: at the beginning and middle of a business process, the senior management gives scant time and attention. Only after a process or product has matured and is ready for production or marketing, and perhaps has run into trouble, does the senior leadership engage heavily. Hence, the bulk of their time is spent managing crises, trying to fix a program in the late stages, when their ability to influence the process is least.

ACTIONABLE RECOMMENDATIONS

The PPBS process serves an important administrative purpose in keeping an audit trail of a large and complex organization. But the secretary of defense needs that tool for an additional purpose: to manage the urgent process of transforming the armed forces to cope with a challenging, fluid strategic environment. The new resource allocation plan being implemented on a trial basis in the Department of Defense beginning this fiscal year provides important breathing room from the burden (and distraction) of repetitive report generation. How much these reforms will lead to more innovation and transformation in U.S. forces depends on how they are implemented and how the time freed up is used. A way ahead is outlined below. It builds on the restructured PPBS process for FY05–FY09 outlined below:

Year 1:

- POM and BES submissions are limited to change proposals that reflect specific secretary of defense guidance
- OSD staff works on the QDR and DPG

Year 2:

- QDR is issued
- DPG is issued
- POMs are submitted
- BESs are delivered
- The program and budget are reviewed

Year 3:

- The previous year's DPG is operative
- POM and BES submissions are limited to program change proposals as directed by the secretary of defense
- OSD staff works on the next DPG

Year 4:

- DPG is issued
- POMs are submitted
- BESs are delivered
- The program and budget are reviewed

SHIFT SENIOR-LEVEL ATTENTION TO PLANNING

Secretary of Defense Donald Rumsfeld has said, "I want to be around to watch the trains being loaded up at the beginning of this process, not wait till they finish their trip and are unloading." DoD leaders need not spend more time on the PPBS as a whole; they need to reallocate their time and to place proportionately more effort on the front end—the planning phase—and avoid the sick-corporation syndrome.

One way to shift leadership attention toward the front end of the process is for a few (perhaps three) small teams of half a dozen or so senior decision-makers to meet early in the planning phase to enrich their input to the planning of the PPBS. Each group could develop one or two transformational issues that could become an integral part of the DPG. Groups should meet for a limited time, which would encourage focus on high-impact transformational initiatives and avoid entanglement with details better handled by staffs. With leadership intent clear, staff could monitor execution of initiatives in the intervening months of that year's PPBS cycle.

Where would these initiatives come from? Transformation is the subject of a broad debate in the national security community, and there are plenty of ideas in circulation. Senior decisionmakers could select a high-leverage initiative from this pool, refine it, and articulate it in output terms. Because the leaders themselves are immersed in the critical issues facing the Department of Defense, they would have their own ideas of which initiatives could yield a high impact.

The key would be to ensure that each issue is high-leverage and expressed in output terms. An example might be: "Ensure that a team of up to 300 Special Operations troops can have an offshore platform in place within 30 days to conduct operations in hostile territory for at least 30 days." It would then be the job of the service staffs to include this requirement in their POMs and the job of OSD and the joint staff to monitor the process to ensure it is implemented.

REFLECTING THE SECRETARY'S INTENT

The DPG should express the intent of the secretary of defense through a clear statement of his priorities in output terms. Portions of the DPG do this, although not systematically. When the DPG does this, it gives service POM builders a framework to program against and OSD staff a clear standard for reviewing and evaluating the POMs. The two key words are "clear" and "output."

This is not a simple process. OSD staff would need guidance from the secretary to prepare the document with a precision that will resist the tyranny of consensus that too often comes from coordinating a document through myriad stakeholders. Once this intricate and difficult process has been completed, little is to be gained by repeating it the following year. Indeed, if written at the strategic level, the DPG should require only targeted changes in the following year.

The proposed cycle for an administration is outlined below. Many of the suggested changes track the procedures that the administration is instituting during the FY05–FY09 programming and budget cycle.

First year.   Make modest adjustments to the budget to be submitted to Congress. This is typical. Indeed, the press of time for Congress to conduct hearings and to mark up the budget prevents much more than this. The staff can use this year to conduct a QDR, as required by law. The DPG for the following year could be derived from the QDR almost concurrently, because most of the same decisionmakers are involved in preparing both reports. The DPG would have maximum utility if, as proposed by OSD, it were delivered by fall of the first year rather than late spring of the second year. This would give the services plenty of lead time, which is critical if they

are to adapt their second-year program to the new DPG. In addition, by fall of the first year, the new team has been in place for a while, and a group of senior leaders could meet to develop a handful of transformation initiatives that would become part of the programming for the second year POM.

Second year.   The QDR and DPG developed during the first year remain the operative guidance documents to the services as they build their POMs. The OSD staff could use the year to explore and analyze strategic issues with emphasis on transformation as directed by the senior OSD officials.

Third year.   The DPG remains operative, although amended by OSD leadership. The OSD staff uses the year to work on the next DPG that will be operative for the following year. A group of senior leaders could meet to develop a handful of transformation initiatives that would become part of the programming for the fourth year POM.

Fourth year.   The third-year DPG is the operative guidance document for service POM building. Again, the staff can use the time freed up to explore and analyze strategic transformational issues as directed by OSD leadership.

In sum, the service POM builders would have time to focus their programs in accordance with the intent of the secretary of defense, rather than scrambling around each year to make their programs conform to yet another (typically late-arriving) DPG.

RECAST THE FYDP

The FYDP was originally conceived in the 1960s to give the secretary of defense insight into how money was being allocated in major program areas across military departments. Ten MFPs were defined that expressed the principal missions the military needed to perform, and the departments were instructed to report their programs in these categories. This allowed the secretary to see how the objectives for each mission area were being funded, to identify duplications in effort among the services, or even to shift money among services if one service had a more cost-effective way of meeting an objective. It also allowed the secretary to make strategic choices (for example, shift money from one major program area to another—perhaps from strategic forces to general purpose forces) if the overall program were out of balance with the strategy. The FYDP was organized into the MFPs as shown below:

MFP 1: Strategic Forces

MFP 2: General Purpose Forces

MFP 3: Command, Control, Communications, and Space

MFP 4: Airlift and Sealift

MFP 5: Guard and Reserve Forces

MFP 6: Research and Development

MFP 7: Central Supply and Maintenance

MFP 8: Training, Medical, General Personnel Account

MFP 9: Administration and Associated Activities

MFP 10: Support to Other Nations

In the meantime, the strategic environment that the United States faces has changed dramatically, but the structure of the FYDP has not kept pace. In 1986, MFP 11 ("Special Operations Forces") was added at the direction of Congress as part of the Goldwater-Nichols Act. Other than that, the structure has changed little. With some change of categories, however, the FYDP can be made more amenable to focusing service programs on transformational initiatives. A candidate reconfiguring of the FYDP to reflect the current and emerging strategic environment is:

MFP 1: Joint Expeditionary Forces

MFP 2: Major Theater War Forces

MFP 3: Special Operations Forces

MFP 4: Mobility Forces

MFP 5: Forward Presence and International Activities

MFP 6: Strategic Nuclear Forces and Missile Defense

MFP 7: Command, Control, Communications, Computers, Intelligence, and Reconnaissance (C4ISR) Programs

MFP 8: Research and Development

MFP 9: Medical Programs

MFP 10: Central Supply, Maintenance, and Installations

MFP 11: Personnel, Training, and Development

The key change is to acknowledge that our forces are being called on increasingly to execute demanding joint expeditionary operations. These operations differ from a major theater war. They require prompt application of powerful military force in a highly precise, focused manner. This is a tall order, and getting it right will require a portion of our forces to be transformed. Separating those forces out of the present "General Purpose Forces" into the "Joint Expeditionary Forces" category would give the supporting programs extra visibility and a management tool for the secretary of defense to accelerate the transformation of these forces.

The strategic nuclear forces MFP could be expanded to include missile defense to underline the transformation of our strategy. This would emphasize the prominence of missile defense in our defense strategy and the decline in the centrality of strategic nuclear offensive forces.

More generally, warfighting functions are separated from general support functions to provide insight into the cost of support functions, which have grown disproportionately over the past decade. Med-

ical programs are separated to give them particular attention, because their costs are growing rapidly with no end in sight.

This configuration of MFPs could also serve as a template for writing the DPG. Providing policy guidance in a format that allowed the services to program against it in a straightforward manner would make their work and the program review process more efficient and effective.

INTEGRATE JOINTNESS INTO POM SUBMISSIONS

One of McNamara's aims in developing the PPBS was to ensure that the capabilities of the services were mutually enabling and synergistic. Every secretary of defense since has pursued this goal. Although progress has been made, there still is a long way to go. More importantly, the nature of war now and for years to come demands forces that can bring firepower to bear on the battlefield from every medium in a coordinated, seamless fashion. A seamlessly operating joint force cannot be assembled just before an operation; it must be equipped and trained to operate jointly months or years in advance. Building such a force is the aim of the proposed transformation.

Starting at the planning and programming phase, at least some elements of the PPBS, especially the programming, must be done jointly. This would be a painful process, but it would force close coordination among the service programmers. At the very least, it would make services aware of the details of one another's programs. At the very best, the resultant programs would incorporate interoperable design from the beginning. This would be a substantial step toward transforming the force.

The first step could be to direct an integrated, joint POM submission in the area of C4ISR programs. An interoperable C4ISR suite is critical to seamless operation of forces that will depend on strong information dominance over the enemy, a shared common operational picture, and targeting data. Chairman of the Joint Chiefs of Staff General Richard Myers has already proposed taking this step, acknowledging that it will be difficult but will yield a high payoff.

The next MFP that could be prepared jointly is the "Mobility Forces" MFP. This step should be far less difficult than preparing a joint C4ISR MFP submission. Following that, programs for "Forward Presence and International Activities" (which would include peacekeeping operations) could be prepared jointly. Finally—and critically—joint program preparation could be extended to the "Joint Expeditionary Forces" MFP.

REVIEW OPERATIONS AND MAINTENANCE

Operations and maintenance (O&M) has grown faster in absolute dollars and in percentage than the other major budget categories. Table 3 illustrates this growth.

Table 3

Budget Growth by Category (Billions of FY03 Dollars)

	FY99	FY03	Increase	Increase percentage
Military personnel	83.2	94.3	11.1	13.3
Operations and maintenance	114.2	150.2	41.2	37.8
Procurement	54.2	68.7	14.5	26.8
Research and development, testing and evaluation	40.9	53.8	12.9	31.5

The absolute dollar increase in O&M is greater by 50 percent than that of investment spending (procurement and research and development/testing and evaluation combined). Although there is no one-to-one correspondence between investment spending and force transformation, the process is supported by targeted investment in those technologies that enable force transformation: command, control, and communications; reconnaissance; surveillance; and precision strike, to name four. The causes of O&M growth are complex and need careful analysis, but the fact remains that growth can choke off investment needed to enable transformation.

Incentives need to be provided to put the brakes on the growth of the O&M budget. At present, there is very little incentive to save O&M costs; in fact, there are disincentives. As a unit approaches the end of a fiscal year, it often feels an imperative to accelerate O&M spending, lest it lose the surplus and receive a reduced allocation the following year. The most promising incentive is to allow a service or an installation to keep whatever O&M they can save and plow it back into improving the quality of its program. Although this would not roll back O&M spending substantially, it would provide a strong incentive to flatten off its growth.

INCENTIVES FOR TRANSFORMATION

Even though most senior DoD leaders believe that transformation is important, there are many competing priorities for resources, and there will never be enough money left over from core programs to fund transformation priorities. The problem is not a lack of good ideas; it is the lack of a budget incentive to make these programs a priority for the services. Some progress was made in the past budget cycle, when the services were asked to identify programs that were transformational, and those programs were given extra support in the program review.

This is a good start, but more can be done. One impediment to these initiatives is the difficulty of breaking into the programmatic priorities of the services. The key is to target funding incentives to the services to transition new equipment or processes with the understanding that, after a short time, the transformation programs would be integrated into the core service program. The Office of Force Transformation would be the appropriate OSD element for this function, and Joint Forces Command could be the cognizant military organization to review the candidates for this transition funding.

CONCLUSION

The PPBS is widely recognized as a barrier to transformation. Moving to a full PPBS cycle every other year will enable senior DoD leaders to shift their attention from the end of the process, where budgeting details dominate, to the beginning, where transformational initiatives can be introduced. This modest reform will give OSD and the services some breathing space that will enable them to innovate further. In a few years, the budget process might be sufficiently reformed that the Department of Defense can engage in wholesale transformation.

DEFENSE PLANNING IN A DECADE OF CHANGE

ERIC V. LARSON, DAVID T. ORLETSKY, AND KRISTIN LEUSCHNER

The post–Cold War era—which arguably can be dated to the fall of the Berlin Wall in November 1989—has been one of immense change, and one that created equally formidable challenges for defense planners. During this period, profound transformations took place in all key elements of the policymaking environment. These included changes in the shape of the international environment, the threats to U.S. interests, and U.S. national security and military strategy. Changes also occurred in the assignment of forces, in the patterns by which forces were employed abroad, and in U.S. military force structure and personnel levels. In addition, substantial reductions were made in defense budgets. These changes—which took place at different rates and at times moved in opposing directions—placed tremendous strain both on the machinery used for deliberative planning and on the policymakers who sought to strike a balance between strategy, forces, and resources. The result was a gap that widened rather than narrowed over the decade.

This report provides contextual historical background for the defense reviews of 2001, including a quadrennial defense review (QDR).[1] It focuses on how each of the three reviews conducted over the past decade addressed three key elements—strategy, forces, and resources—and describes the major assumptions, decisions, outcomes, planning, and execution associated with each.

THE BASE FORCE

ASSUMPTIONS, DECISIONS, AND OUTCOMES

The combination of favorable threat trends and adverse macroeconomic trends, including a deepening recession and the soaring budget deficit, and congressional calls for a "peace dividend" made it impossible for the new administration to protect the defense program after 1989.

In early 1989, the administration rejected the joint chiefs' proposal of 2 percent annual real growth and decided instead on a flat budget for one year (FY90) while the situation clarified, with modest real growth planned thereafter. Although it would not be until late 1990 that final budget levels were established, the base force and the administration's national security review in 1989 were both to be predicated on the assumption that a 25 percent reduction in force structure and a 10 percent reduction in defense resources were possible.

The revolution in the Soviet Union that had begun with General Secretary Mikhail Gorbachev's ascension led to a remarkable sequence of events, beginning with the fall of the Berlin Wall in November 1989 and culminating in the collapse of the Soviet Union in 1991—well after the public release of the base force.

The base force that was developed under Chairman of the Joint Chiefs of Staff (CJCS) Colin Powell benefited from earlier work by the joint staff and evolved in parallel with a larger administration review of national security and defense strategy: National Security Review 12. The aim of the base force was to provide a new military strategy and force structure for the post–Cold War era while setting a floor for force reductions. The floor was necessary in part to avoid creating the level of churning that might "break" the force, in part to secure the backing of the service chiefs, and later to hedge against the risks of a resurgent Soviet/Russian threat. For his part, Defense Secretary Richard Cheney's review of past defense drawdowns had animated a desire to avoid the sorts of problems wrought by the haphazard demobilizations that had followed World War II, Korea, and Vietnam. To accomplish his post–Cold War build-down in a manner that would ensure the health of the force, the secretary formed a strategic alliance with CJCS Powell that came at the price of recognizing the chairman's own constraints.

The base force—conceived as the minimum force necessary to defend and promote U.S. interests in the post–Cold War world—consisted of four force packages oriented toward strategic deterrence and defense (strategic forces), forward presence (Atlantic and Pacific forces), and crisis response and reinforcement (contingency forces).

The size of the force was to be determined primarily by regional needs and not on the basis of its capability to fight multiple major theater wars (MTWs); although the main conventional threat for the base force was the potential for major regional conflicts involving large-scale, mechanized cross-border aggression, the multiple-MTW construct that was to dominate defense planning for the remainder of the decade was an afterthought. The two-conflict case was simply one of a number of illustrative planning scenarios that were developed after the threat-based

This essay has been edited and is reprinted from Defense Planning in a Decade of Change: Lessons from the Base Force, Bottom-Up Review, and Quadrennial Defense Review, *MR-1387 (Santa Monica, Calif.: RAND Corporation, 2003), xiii–xxvi, 121–25, by permission of the RAND Corporation.*

planning environment collapsed to test the capabilities of the force. In fact, the two-simultaneous-conflict scenario was a case that Powell testified would put the base force "at the breaking point." Although flexible general-purpose forces were needed to address the entire "spectrum of threat,"[2] from humanitarian assistance and noncombatant evacuation operations to major regional conflicts, there is little evidence that substantial involvement in peacekeeping and other peace operations was anticipated during the development of the base force.

In 1990, as the base force was being finalized, pressures for defense spending reductions were given additional impetus by the federal deficit, which had ballooned in the final years of the 1980s, and by the possibility that crippling spending cuts would automatically be triggered under the Gramm-Rudman-Hollings antideficit laws. In the June 1990 budget summit, Secretary Cheney used the base force to illustrate the feasibility of a 25 percent smaller force that could provide approximately 10 percent in defense cuts. It was not until the October 1990 budget summit, however, that deficit and discretionary spending caps were finalized, resulting in deeper-than-expected cuts to defense budgets. The base force was presented with the next president's budget submission in early 1991.

Throughout the base force deliberations, the Air Force's principal aim was to preserve its modernization and acquisition programs while ensuring that the pace of reduction did not harm people or the future quality of the force. Accordingly, early in the process of defining the force, Air Force leaders accepted both the base force concept and the implication that U.S. Air Force's force structure would be further reduced, thus showing a willingness to trade force structure to maintain modernization. The number of tactical fighter wing equivalents would be reduced by about one-third, with most of the reductions coming from the active force. Strategic long-range bombers were also to be reduced, while the conventional capabilities of the bomber force were to be improved.

PLANNING AND EXECUTION

Although the base force set force structure targets for 1995 and 1997, the outcome of the 1992 presidential elections meant that the base force was actually implemented over only two years, FY92–FY93.

The base force's effort to adapt conventional forces to the post–Cold War world resulted both in force reductions and in modest changes to the allocation of resources among the services. These changes suggested a declining emphasis on land forces (the Army's share of DoD budget authority fell from 26.8 percent in 1990 to 24.3 percent in 1993) and an increasing emphasis on aerospace power (with the Air Force's share rising from 31.7 percent in 1990 to 32.9 percent in 1993).

Although few problems were encountered in realizing the planned 25 percent force structure and 20 percent active manpower reductions, policymakers had difficulty realizing the 20 percent reductions to reserve-component manpower, particularly to Army and Marine Corps reserves. This resulted in higher-than-anticipated reserve-component manpower levels and lower-than-expected savings. In the end, the rate at which civilian manpower fell over 1990–93 was greater than that for active- or reserve-component personnel and greater than had initially been planned.

Notwithstanding the Air Force leaders' hopes to trade force structure for modernization and acquisition, greater-than-expected budget cuts led to the reduction or termination of a number of high-priority Air Force modernization programs during the course of—or as a result of—the base force, including the B-2 (from 132 to 75 aircraft, and subsequently to 20 aircraft), the F-22 (from some 750 to 648 aircraft), and the C-17 (from 210 to 120 aircraft). Nevertheless, efforts to improve the conventional capabilities of long-range bombers and to expand capabilities for precision-guided munitions were begun as a result of the 1992 Bomber Roadmap and other initiatives.

To provide additional savings, the administration also pursued defense reform and infrastructure reductions through the Defense Management Review (DMR) and the Base Realignment and Closure (BRAC) Commission. The 1989 BRAC round identified 40 bases for closure, and the 1991 round envisioned closing another 50, for recurring annual savings of perhaps $2.5 billion to $3.0 billion a year. Nevertheless, by late 1992–93, concerns had arisen that not all of the anticipated $70 billion in savings from the DMR and BRAC rounds would be realized—a problem that the early Clinton administration faced. In fact, the percentage of Air Force total obligational authority devoted to infrastructure increased from 42 to 44 percent in 1990–93.

In addition to the difficulties encountered in reducing reserve-component military personnel and realizing savings from infrastructure reductions and defense reform, defense budgets continued to decline; each of the Bush administration's budget requests from FY 1990 to FY 1994 envisioned lower spending levels.[3] In the longer term, the problems were even more challenging. By December 1991, for example, the Congressional Budget Office was projecting that the base force could not be maintained and modernized in the 1993–97 period if Congress and the administration complied with the limits of the 1990 Budget Enforcement Act and that beyond 1997, shortfalls of $20 billion to $65 billion could be expected as policymakers sought to carry out necessary modernization.

Testimony suggests that base force policymakers expected that they would need to face these problems after 1992: Powell suggested that by 1995, a new base force, engendering additional cuts to force structure, might be necessary, and Secretary Cheney suggested that increases in real defense spending might be needed in the out years to cover modernization needs, including an anticipated procurement "bow wave."

THE BOTTOM-UP REVIEW

ASSUMPTIONS, DECISIONS, AND OUTCOMES

The 1993 *Report on the Bottom-Up Review* (BUR) was the second major force structure review of the decade that aimed to define a defense strategy, forces, and resources appropriate to the post–Cold War era.

Under the BUR, force structure and manpower reductions would accelerate and would surpass those planned in the "Cold War–minus"–sized base force, leading to a total reduction in forces of roughly one-third—a level well beyond the base force's planned 25 percent reduction, most of which had already been achieved by the end of FY93. Budgets would also fall beyond planned base force levels as a result of the BUR. Indeed, it appears that budget top lines were established before either force structure or strategy had been decided.

The aim of the BUR was to provide "a comprehensive review of the nation's defense strategy, force structure, modernization, infrastructure, and foundations." While embracing the base force's regionally focused strategy and emphasis on strategic deterrence, forward presence, and crisis response, the BUR redefined the meaning of engagement, giving increased rhetorical and policy importance to U.S. participation in multilateral peace and humanitarian operations and setting the stage for an increased operational tempo and rate of deployment, even as force and budgetary reductions continued.

During the 1992 presidential campaign, candidate Bill Clinton had argued that changes in the threat environment, taken together with the nation's poor economic circumstances, made possible a cut of approximately $60 billion in defense spending. By the time the FY94 budget was submitted in February 1993, the administration was planning force structure reductions to meet savings goals of $76 billion over FY94–FY97 and $112 billion over FY94–FY98; the $104 billion in cuts envisaged in the October 1993 BUR were only slightly smaller than those documented 6 months earlier in the president's budget. Put another way, the cuts to the defense top line planned in the FY94 budget were, within a few billion dollars in any given year, identical to those in the FY95 budget request that implemented the BUR. As a result, the strategy, force structure, modernization, and other initiatives described in the BUR were to be driven as much by the availability of resources as by the threats and opportunities in the emerging international environment and the administration's own normative foreign policy aims.

In carrying out the budget cuts, Clinton administration policymakers hoped to reduce defense spending without raising questions about their commitment to the nation's defense. The result was more modest cuts in force structure in the BUR than had been advocated by then–House Armed Services Committee Chairman Les Aspin in 1992, but deeper cuts in defense resources than had been advocated during the campaign. Another result was that a strategy was ultimately overlaid on a force structure that was justified in warfighting terms but would soon became preoccupied instead with operations in support of the administration's still-crystallizing strategy of "engagement and enlargement."

As described in the BUR, four "strategies" were considered, each of which identified a plausible mix of operations that future U.S. forces might need to conduct. After choosing—and then rejecting—the second strategy and force structure ("win-hold-win"), the BUR chose the force associated with a newly developed third strategy: the capability to win two nearly simultaneous major regional conflicts (MRCs). This force differed only slightly from the win-hold-win force but provided some additional capabilities for carrier-based naval presence operations, enhanced-readiness Army reserve-component forces, and a number of additional force enhancements (e.g., precision attack, strategic mobility) that aimed to improve the force's ability to underwrite two conflicts with a smaller force structure than the base force. This force was also smaller than that associated with a fourth strategy, which provided a capability for winning two nearly simultaneous MRCs *plus* conducting smaller operations. As was the case for the base force, the BUR force structure in part reflected Powell's negotiations with the service chiefs over force levels. Although the CJCS went to great pains to emphasize that the BUR force was designed for warfighting, the BUR also anticipated a high level of commitment to peace, humanitarian, and other operations. Accordingly, it laid down an elaborate logic to ensure the force's ability to disengage from peacetime operations and established several management oversight groups to monitor readiness and other risks that might result if this ambitious strategy were to be executed with smaller forces.

In the face of the additional anticipated budget cuts, the BUR undertook only selective modernization and generally sought to address key problems, such as the "bow wave" in the theater air program. The BUR also supported several so-called "new initiatives" that were directed toward improving U.S. capabilities in areas other than traditional warfighting. As described above, the BUR reported that it could support the strategy and force structure while realizing $104 billion in savings from the Bush baseline in nominal dollars; Office of the Secretary of Defense policymakers, however, are reported privately to have expected only some $17 billion in savings.

As it had with the base force, the Air Force embraced the new strategy and its emphasis on long-range aerospace power, including long-range conventional bombers, strategic mobility, enhanced surveillance and targeting, and precision-guided attack—even as Air Force leaders expressed disappointment that the BUR would fail to affect roles and missions and would instead result in a force they described as "Cold War-minus-minus." And as with the Base Force, the Air Force sought to trade force structure and end strength for continued modernization. Although Air Force commitments to contingency operations had already increased by the time of the BUR, the Air Force does not appear to have pressed the case that peacetime presence and contingency operations should also be considered in sizing the Air Force—an argument that the Navy had profitably used to justify a twelve-carrier force.

PLANNING AND EXECUTION

The BUR was implemented over four years via the FY95–FY98 budget submissions. Although the nominal strategy and force structure chosen in the BUR was predicated largely on the ability to fight and win two nearly simultaneous wars, it also implied higher levels of involvement in peace, humanitarian, and other smaller-scale operations than had the base force. The new strategy's heavy emphasis on peace operations resulted in commitments throughout the 1993–98 period that, from a historical perspective, were frequent, large, and of long duration. The evidence suggests that policymakers—including those in the Air Force—underestimated these demands, which, by some accounts, eventually amounted to the equivalent of one MTW's worth of forces. The result was growing congressional and other concern about the potential impact on warfighting of smaller-scale contingencies (SSCs).

The new strategy placed unprecedented demands on the Air Force in servicing peacetime contingency operations over this period while remaining ready for warfighting. Although the number of Air Force aircraft deployed to contingency operations in early 1990 had been nominal, it increased dramatically with the Iraqi invasion of Kuwait and the Gulf War in 1990–91 and then remained at a substantially higher level than before the war as a result of the need to sustain operations in northern and southern Iraq. Modest increases in the number of aircraft in contingency operations were seen thereafter as additional commitments accumulated, particularly in the Balkans. At any given time, more than 200 Air Force aircraft would typically be deployed throughout the 1993–98 period, although occasional peaks of 250 to 350 aircraft were also seen. With the force structure decisions taken in the BUR, however, the die had already been cast, resulting in a smaller force underwriting a more ambitious strategy and a fourfold increase in operational tempo over that prior to the fall of the Berlin Wall.

Although force structure goals were achieved relatively quickly, infrastructure reductions lagged; for example, the percentage of Air Force total obligational authority devoted to infrastructure fell from 44 percent in 1993 to 42 percent in 1998. And although the incremental costs of peace operations were only about $14.1 billion over FY94–FY98, the actual costs of the defense program turned out to be much higher than anticipated in the FY94 budget, the BUR, or the FY95 budget that implemented the BUR.[4] As a result of the imbalance between resources on the one hand and strategy and forces on the other, only some $15 billion of the $104 billion in anticipated savings reported by the BUR was realized —a level not significantly different from the $17 billion in savings that was privately said to be expected. Part of the difference was made up through emergency supplemental appropriations and by gradually increasing subsequent budgets to try to close the gap.

The resulting gaps had two principal results. First, despite the high priority and high levels of spending on operations and support (O&S) accounts, readiness problems emerged, many of them resource-related, while the risks associated with executing the national military strategy grew. Second, over the 1995–97 period, spending on modernization fell well below the levels planned in the FY94 (transition) and FY95 (BUR) budgets; instead, funds routinely "migrated" from investment accounts to O&S accounts, resulting in program stretch-outs and delays to planned modernization efforts.

In retrospect, then, it appears that the force chosen by the BUR was less suitable to the high levels of peacetime engagement in contingency operations that were actually observed in subsequent years than the force deemed capable of winning two nearly simultaneous MRCs *plus* conducting smaller operations. Furthermore, the failure to achieve most of the anticipated savings reported by the BUR suggests that the BUR force in fact required a base force–sized budget. In the end, the mismatch between a more ambitious strategy of engagement and the forces and resources that were declining at different rates made it impossible for the services to support the dual priorities of readiness and modernization during the years in which the BUR was implemented.

THE QUADRENNIAL DEFENSE REVIEW

ASSUMPTIONS, DECISIONS, AND OUTCOMES

The 1997 QDR considered the potential threats, strategy, force structure, readiness posture, military modernization programs, defense infrastructure, and other elements of the defense program needed for the 1997–2015 time frame and beyond.

The QDR was intended to provide a blueprint for a strategy-based, balanced, and affordable defense program. Lingering concerns about the deficit and the austere budgetary environment that resulted, however, placed continued constraints on defense resources, leading to the assumption of flat, $250 billion-a-year defense budgets. Equally important, the QDR aimed—within a flat budget and with only modest adjustments to force structure—to rebalance the defense program and budget to address some of the key problems that had developed during the BUR years, including the adverse effect of SSCs and the migration of funds from modernization (particularly procurement) accounts to operations accounts. The combination of budgetary constraints, Defense Secretary William Cohen's outsider status as the newest member of (and sole Republican in) the Clinton cabinet, and the dominant influence of the services in the review appear to have made it a foregone conclusion that the QDR would fail to challenge the status quo and would fall short of achieving the balance that was sought.

The QDR generally accepted the normative and other underpinnings of the BUR's strategy, reaffirmed the BUR's emphasis on two nearly simultaneous MTWs as the principal basis for force sizing, and posited that the United States might have to fight one or two MTWs over the 1997–2015 period. It also anticipated continued involvement over the same period in the kinds of SSCs that had been described in the BUR, including peace and humanitarian operations.

The QDR did make several important adjustments to the BUR strategy, however, two of which had substantive importance. First, it placed increased emphasis on the halt phase in MTWs. Second, it gave increased rhetorical recognition to the demands of SSCs and recognized the potential need to respond to multiple concurrent SSCs. Yet although it aimed to provide "strategic agility" (i.e., the capability to transition from global peacetime engagement to warfighting), the QDR did not advocate significant adjustments in force structure or resourcing to accommodate these demands. Finally, the QDR articulated a somewhat more cautious and nuanced employment doctrine than had the BUR, distinguishing among situations involving vital, important but not vital, and humanitarian interests, and identifying the sorts of responses appropriate to each.

The QDR rejected two straw men—a U.S. strategy of isolationism and one in which the United States would serve as "world policeman"—in favor of a strategy of engagement and a path that balanced current demands against an uncertain future. The result of the assessment was promoted as a more balanced strategy—dubbed "shape, respond, and prepare now"—that embraced both active engagement and crisis response options while also advocating increased resources for force modernization.

The QDR rejected a 10 percent cut in force structure because it would result in unacceptable risk, presumably both to warfighting capability and to the force's ability to engage in SSC operations. Accordingly, changes to force structure involved only modest reductions, as well as some restructuring. Among the most important of these changes was the decision to move one Air Force tactical fighter wing from the active to the reserve component, leaving slightly more than 20 tactical fighter wings in the force structure.

With force structure cuts essentially off the table, savings were to be achieved through manpower cuts. Secretary Cohen instructed the services to cut the equivalent of 150,000 active military personnel to provide $4 billion to $6 billion in recurring savings by FY03; the QDR reported the decision to further reduce active forces by 60,000, reserve forces by 55,000, and civilians by 80,000 personnel.

Finally, in a bow to the procurement spending goal that CJCS John Shalikashvili established in 1995, the QDR made a long-term commitment to achieve $60 billion a year in procurement spending by 2001—

a nominal level of procurement spending that was, in fact, less than what the chairman had originally specified.[5] Despite this, the QDR's modernization effort reflected the same response to the tight budgetary environment as the BUR—namely, to fund only "selective" modernization. In other words, to make the program affordable, the QDR made additional cuts to a number of acquisition programs and advocated additional savings through further infrastructure reduction and defense management reform.

Nevertheless, in many respects, the QDR presented the Air Force with important opportunities to promote the concepts and core competencies developed in its most recent strategic planning exercise. For example, the review emphasized rapid response and an early, decisive halt of cross-border aggression, which played to Air Force strengths in long-range precision strike and mobility. Similarly, the QDR's focus on reducing the stresses created by SSCs accented a number of post-BUR Air Force innovations, such as the air expeditionary force concept. Finally, the QDR strategy's rhetorical emphasis on preparing for an uncertain future played to a long-standing Air Force priority: investment in advanced technologies. However, Air Force leaders' hopes to use the QDR to challenge the status quo and to transform U.S. forces were reportedly dashed by CJCS Shalikashvili's message that there would be no "Billy Mitchells" in the QDR.

PLANNING AND EXECUTION

The QDR, together with its claim to have successfully balanced the defense program, was met with some skepticism both by Congress and many other observers. Nevertheless, rather than adjusting discretionary caps, the administration and Congress continued their previous pattern of reducing the resource gap through emergency supplementals and year-to-year increases.

In some respects, the new strategy elements of shaping and responding differed little from the BUR's strategy of engagement and enlargement: both relied heavily on forward presence and crisis-response capabilities, and both were concerned with ensuring stability in the near term in regions of vital interest. And although the QDR had anticipated continued participation in SSCs, actual U.S. participation in peace and other contingency operations turned out to be somewhat higher than anticipated. In February 1998, for example, CJCS Henry Shelton reported that 1997 had seen twenty major operations and many smaller ones, with an average of 43,000 service members per month participating in contingency operations.

Given the modest changes to force structure recommended by the QDR, it should come as little surprise that with only a few exceptions, force structure changes for major force elements were already in place in the FY01 president's budget and defense program.

Although the other services were expected to hit the QDR manpower targets by 2003, the manpower reductions programmed for the Air Force in the FY99 budget suggested that the Air Force would not achieve its targets by this date. The Air Force aimed to achieve its manpower reductions principally through aggressive competitive outsourcing of certain functions, the restructuring of combat forces, and the streamlining of headquarters. These plans encountered difficulties in their execution, however, resulting in a smaller personnel reduction than had been identified in the QDR and in a failure to realize all of the anticipated savings.

Evidence of readiness problems continued to accumulate in the wake of the QDR to the extent that, in the fall of 1998, the service chiefs reported that readiness problems were both more prevalent and more serious than had earlier been reported. The risks associated with executing the two-conflict strategy also increased over this period, with the risk associated with the second conflict now reported to be high, seemingly as a result of lower readiness levels for forces earmarked for the second MTW and shortfalls in strategic mobility. The result of these developments, which played out in late 1998 and early 1999, was a FY00 budget request that entailed the first real increase in defense resources in more than a decade: approximately $112 billion in additional resources, primarily to address readiness problems, was committed in the FY00 Future Years Defense Program, nearly restoring the funding that had been taken out in 1993–94.

Although the QDR sought to meet its $60 billion modernization goal by reducing excess facilities, closing additional bases, and realigning and streamlining infrastructure, additional rounds of BRAC were not authorized by Congress, and savings from defense reform efforts, although not insubstantial, were disappointing. The QDR's modest modernization goals appear to have been met, but the $60 billion target falls well short of the estimated $80 billion to $90 billion or more that is believed to be needed for recapitalization; funding for transformation of the force was even less generous and fell well below the $5 billion to $10 billion recommended by the National Defense Panel, which critiqued the QDR.

CONCLUSION

The three major defense strategy reviews of the past decade aimed to highlight the inputs (assumptions, threats, and domestic environments), outputs (decisions and other outcomes), and implementation experience of each review. After identifying some common features of the reviews, we offer some lessons regarding strategy, forces, and budgets, and we then close with some thoughts on how defense planning might be improved.

Stepping back from their details, the reviews appear to have shared at least three main features, each of which could benefit from additional scrutiny.

First, each assumed that the most important (and taxing) mission for conventional forces was halting and reversing cross-border aggression by large-scale mechanized forces. The experience in Kosovo suggests that adversaries have adapted to avoid Desert Storm–style outcomes, and the decline in mechanized forces worldwide raises questions about the continued utility of emphasizing this sort of scenario.

Second, each review in its own way treated presence and smaller-scale peace and other contingency operations as "lesser-included cases" that could successfully be managed by a force structure designed primarily for warfighting, and each assumed that these contingency operations would impose minimal costs and risks for warfighting. Recent experience suggests that these assumptions are true only when such operations are incidental and short-lived, as was the general pattern during much of the Cold War; by contrast, when such operations are large, tend to accumulate, and need to be sustained over time, they can, in fact, be quite taxing on warfighting capabilities, affecting readiness and increasing strategic risk.

Third, each review suffered from the absence of a bipartisan consensus on a post–Cold War foreign and defense policy, and this made the gaps that emerged between strategy, forces, and budgets particularly salient, arguably impeding their successful resolution. The new administration should consider how best to establish a shared vision of the nation's defense priorities, a better partnership with Congress, and a process for fuller consideration of defense funding needs.

We now turn to some lessons for strategy, forces, and budgets.

Regarding *strategy,* the historical record suggests that it is critically important to understand that changes in strategy—a regular feature of presidential transitions and defense reviews—can have a range of important ramifications. The change in normative aims and conception of engagement pursued by the Clinton administration and documented in the BUR, for example, underscored the importance of ethnic conflict and civil strife, promoted peace operations as a more important tool of U.S. policy, and had strong implications for the resulting pattern of U.S. force employment. Having failed to fit force structure and budgets to strategy, the resulting effects could and should have been better anticipated and resources realigned to mitigate or eliminate them.

Another critical result has to do with *force structure.* Table 4 shows that although there have been substantial reductions in force structure and manpower, only a modest amount of reshaping of the armed forces has actually taken place. Efforts to meaningfully modernize and transform the armed forces have been hampered by a high discount rate that has elevated current-day threats, force structure, and readiness concerns while effectively discounting longer-term needs, thus curtailing a more penetrating examination of roles, missions, and force restructuring.

With regard to *budgets,* there seems to have been a chronic reluctance to acknowledge what reasonable-risk versions of a strategy and force structure might

Table 4

Proposed Force Structure Changes: Base Force, BUR, and QDR

	FY90	1997 Base Force	1999 BUR Force	2003 QDR Force	FY01
Air Force					
TFWs (AC/RC)	24/12	15.3/11.3	13/7	12+[a]/8	12+/7+
Bombers (active)	228	181	184	187	181
Land-based ICBMs	1,000	550	550	550	550
Navy					
Aircraft carriers	15/1	12/1	11/1	11/1	12/0
Battle force ships	546	448	346	306	317
Marines					
Divisions (AC/RC)	3/1	3/1	3/1	3/1	3/1
Army					
Divisions (AC/RC)	18/10	12/8[b]	10/5+	10/8	10/8
End strength					
Active duty		2,070	1,626	1,418	1,360
Reserve		1,128	920	893	835

Note: AC, active components; RC, reserve components; TFW, tactical fighter wing–equivalent.
[a]The plus indicates a value between the number given and the next highest integer (e.g., 12+ signifies between 12 and 13 TFWs).
[b]Reserve component includes two cadre divisions.

really cost. Although the gaps between strategy, force structure, and resources are not unprecedented,[6] the tacit agreement of the executive and legislative branches to avoid debates over a higher defense topline, as well as fundamental issues of strategy and policy, may actually have impeded full disclosure and consideration of the problems that plagued the defense program for much of the decade. Instead, the reliance on modest year-to-year revisions that did not upset discretionary spending limits, coupled with the recurring exploitation of the loophole provided by emergency supplementals to mitigate particularly acute shortfalls, meant that the debates would occur only at the margin, and at a rhetorical level only. Failure to tackle these issues head-on may have retarded the recognition and remediation of the growing gaps between strategy, forces, and resources.

Shifting to the present, the new administration's defense review will wrestle with the same questions its predecessors faced: What are to be the nation's aims in the world? What are the main threats and opportunities it faces? What strategy and force structure will best serve the interests of the nation? What resources are needed to ensure low-to-moderate execution risk in that strategy, and capable and ready forces, both now and over the next 20 to 30 years?

In answering these questions, the new administration will be no more encumbered by the assumptions and decisions of the 1997 QDR than the incoming Clinton administration was by those of the base force. Nevertheless, the Department of Defense would profit from an assumption-based planning approach, in which signposts are established that can be used to gauge whether the key assumptions on which planning is predicated are still justified.[7]

These include assumptions about future threats, the likely frequency and mix of future missions, the adequacy of forces to undertake these missions, effects on overall readiness and strategic risk, and the availability of resources.

Such an approach is important by virtue of another great lesson of the past decade: that failure to recognize and respond promptly and effectively to emerging gaps and shortfalls can lead to the greatest and most protracted imbalances between strategy, forces, and resources.

NOTES

1. Section 118 of Title 10, U.S. Code, provides the statutory requirement for a QDR "during a year following a year evenly divisible by four."

2. Colin Powell, testimony before the House Armed Services Committee (February 6, 1992).

3. The Bush administration never formally submitted its FY94 budget request.

4. Office of the Secretary of Defense comptroller data were provided by the Joint Chiefs of Staff and include contingency operations in Southwest Asia, Bosnia, Haiti, Cuba, Rwanda, Somalia, and Kosovo. The incremental costs over the FY94–FY99 period were $20.1 billion.

5. In 1995, CJCS Shalikashvili had called for the annual procurement budget to reach $60 billion by FY98—the minimum level of procurement needed as determined by the Defense Program Projection, and originally conceived in terms of constant FY93 dollars. By the time of the QDR in 1997, the $60 billion had become a nominal dollar target that, accordingly, had lost some of its earlier purchasing power—all the more so as a result of its deferral from FY98 to FY01.

6. During the Cold War period, for example, airlift capacity remained well short of the 66 million ton miles/day that was the stated requirement for responding to a Soviet/Warsaw Pact attack across the inter-German border and a Soviet invasion of Iran. Current military airlift capacity is judged to be roughly 33 percent short of the requirement established in the DoD Mobility Requirements Study 05.

7. See James A. Dewar, Carl H. Builder, William M. Hix, and Morlie H. Levin, *Assumption-Based Planning: A Planning Tool for Very Uncertain Times,* MR-114-A (Santa Monica, Calif.: RAND Corporation, 1993).

THE DEFENSE BUDGET: IS IT TRANSFORMATIONAL?

DAVID L. NORQUIST

In the presidential campaign of 2000, George W. Bush often addressed the need to transform the armed forces. Once elected, he gave military transformation a central role in defense strategy. The administration presented its defense budget for fiscal year 2003 after 12 months of review. Did that budget support transformation? The initial reaction is mixed.

The Center for Strategic and Budgetary Assessments, which has been vocal in advocating transformation, registered its disappointment: "[The] new defense plan appears very similar to the defense plan this administration inherited. . . . Perhaps most questionable is the administration's decision to continue to move ahead with three new tactical fighter programs. . . . Likewise, the Crusader artillery system seems inconsistent with the goal of having an Army that is light enough to rapidly deploy."[1]

Some other supporters of modernization were more encouraged. The Lexington Institute was optimistic in part because it did not take the DoD budget as a break with the past: "Last year's trendy buzzword for what new management at the Pentagon would mean was 'transformation.' In the end they made the right choice, fully funding all three [tactical fighter] programs. . . . Even the Army's widely criticized Crusader howitzer program . . . turned out to be a major improvement necessary for the conduct of future land warfare."[2] But these critiques are focused on only a few programs that will neither bring about transformation nor prevent it.

THE LOST CRUSADER

Modernization is the process of fielding more advanced items of equipment that basically perform the same function as the matériel being replaced. Military innovation, or transformation, means profoundly changing equipment and its operational employment to create a radically new approach to warfare. The effect of implementing such change is a revolution in military affairs.

Modernization is sometimes mischaracterized as an obstacle to transformation, as happened in the case of the Pentagon announcement that the Crusader artillery program would be terminated. Press reports indicated that aborting this program was a test for transformation. It is not, because transformation can succeed with or without Crusader. The fate of Crusader is a choice between enhancing the firepower of Army heavy divisions and accelerating the transition to a future system. Transformation does not depend on this choice; it relies on designing equipment and doctrine for a future combat system.

To gauge the new defense budget, one must accept that invoking the term "transformation" as a byword—as opposed to "modernization" or "reform" —was a conscious choice. It ties administration policy to a school of thought that posits technology has dramatically changed the world and will lead to a revolution in military affairs.

For example, in the years between World Wars I and II, innovations such as the internal combustion engine and radio, combined with advances in doctrine, produced revolutionary combat units and ways of fighting. This revolution in military affairs produced the Blitzkrieg tactics used by German Panzer divisions and the strikes by carrier-based aircraft that rendered vulnerable any military force which relied on trench warfare and battleships.

The shift from the industrial to the information age, which radically altered the economy of the United States, has led many analysts to expect an equally profound change in the way we fight. The Tofflers describe how moving from an agrarian (first wave) society to an industrial (second wave) society has transformed the world. They believe the shift to an

David L. Norquist, "The Defense Budget: Is It Transformational?" Joint Force Quarterly 31 *(Summer 2002): 91–99.* *Public domain.*

information (third wave) society involves an equally exciting change: "A true revolution goes beyond [individual inventions] to change the game itself, including its rules, its equipment, the size and organization of the 'teams,' their training, doctrine, tactics, and just about everything else."[3] Or in other words, as the chairman of the Joint Chiefs of Staff has recently told Congress, "[Transformation] must extend beyond weapon systems and matériel to doctrine, organization, training and education, leadership, personnel, and facilities."

Transformation is a daunting task. Revolutions in military affairs are rare, and the military is traditionally poor at dramatic innovation. But it is against this ambitious goal of innovation that the defense budget should be judged.

The best way to determine the potential for success is past experience. What have been the pitfalls? Why did some nations succeed and others fail? Has the administration taken the right fiscal, political, and organizational steps to overcome obstacles? If so, it has succeeded in laying the groundwork for transformation. If not, it is likely to learn the lessons of history.

OBSTACLES TO INNOVATION

Sir Michael Howard observed, "I am tempted indeed to declare dogmatically that whatever doctrine the Armed Forces are working on now, they have got it wrong."[4] His sentiment is typical of those who have studied innovation and the evolution of doctrine. A more encouraging appraisal by someone who examined many cases of innovation concludes, "Peacetime innovations are possible, but the process is long."[5] There are valid reasons for such pessimism.

Major innovations are uncommon. Those policymakers with vision must grasp the relevance of changes in technology or the security environment and push for innovation. Decisionmakers must sort out the value of their proposals, which may be buried in more dubious ideas. In addition, military operations are complex. It is difficult to envision the effect of change in doctrine and technology without a prototype of the innovation for experimentation. But without a vision, it is hard to make a case for resources to develop technology. The history of aircraft carriers illustrates this problem.

By the end of World War I, the British had twelve carriers in service or under construction, more than all other countries combined; but 20 years later, the Royal Navy was still using them for reconnaissance, not airstrikes. A carrier could only carry twelve planes in the early 1920s. Britain believed that such a small force, although valuable as spotters to guide the fleet, would be insufficient to sink a battleship. Lack of vision contributed to poor technical progress. With only twelve aircraft, it was safer and easier to store planes below deck. But a clear deck made it less critical to develop arresting gear, catapults, and safety barriers. Absent that equipment, it was impossible to increase the number of aircraft aboard by storing

more planes on deck, and it prevented the fast launch and recovery procedures necessary to implement a massed airstrike without the planes running out of fuel. Moreover, for much of the interwar period, British carrier planes were built and operated not by the navy but the air force, which put a low priority on naval aviation. Thus the British experience derived from fleet maneuvers using aircraft carriers with a limited number of unimpressive planes. Rather than focusing on the offensive potential of carriers, the Royal Navy was more concerned about their vulnerability.

Although the United States, like Great Britain, originally used carriers as the eyes of the fleet, it was also studying their potential. The Naval War College, for instance, conducted a wargame in 1923 that assumed that carriers could deploy many more planes than was considered possible at the time. Students discovered that when the blue team used all its two hundred aircraft in a single strike, it crippled all red team carriers and sank a battleship. Rear Admiral William Moffett, the first chief of the Navy Bureau of Aeronautics, described the vision: "The function of a large carrier should be the same as that of a battleship . . . to deal destructive blows to enemy vessels. Its offensive value is too great to permit it to be ordinarily devoted to scouting."[6] The Navy conducted exercises in the interwar years that explored carrier-based airstrikes with mixed results. But Moffett, a former battleship commander, built support both inside and outside the service to continue work on this capability. The vision tested at Newport became a reality as both the number of carriers and their capabilities grew. As additional carriers entered the fleet, the Navy grouped them to increase the size of airstrikes. The final step in the innovation process occurred in 1943, when the multicarrier task force formally became part of naval doctrine.

SETTING GOALS

The Pentagon identified six transformational goals in presenting its budget: protecting bases of operation/homeland defense, denying enemies sanctuary, projecting power in denied areas, leveraging information technology, conducting effective information operations, and enhancing space operations. To meet these goals, the administration has initiated thirteen programs and accelerated twenty-two existing ones, such as hypervelocity missiles, unmanned aerial and underwater vehicles, high-energy lasers, the expanded global positioning system, the Army future combat system, the Navy DD (X) family of ships, and a high-capacity secure digital communications system.

Beyond pursuing specific systems, the Department of Defense has requested large budget increases for agencies and activities that focus on developing new technologies and prototypes; for example, $432 million (19 percent) for the Defense Advanced Research Projects Agency in FY03, added to the 14 percent increase in FY02. This agency is charged with demonstrating high-risk, high-payoff research with a working prototype. The Advanced Concepts Technology Demonstration program, which would convert more mature technologies into militarily useful prototypes, should increase by $79 million, or 65 percent, over 2 years.

In addition to technology, there is an increased focus on experimenting with new doctrine. Each service has wargames, battle labs, and field or fleet experiments to explore the implications of emerging technology on doctrine. To build on service programs, U.S. Joint Forces Command has an experimentation program for which another $33 million, or 51 percent, has been requested over the 2001 level. Most importantly, the new budget provides $20 million for a force transformation directorate within the Office of the Secretary of Defense to assume the leading role in evaluating the transformation activities of each military department. This approach avoids the problem that the Royal Navy experienced in the 1920s and 1930s by encouraging simultaneous development and experimentation to enable a variety of technologies, prototypes, and doctrines to contribute to transformation.

BUREAUCRATIC RESISTANCE

Once there are advocates for a potential innovation, the struggle shifts to finding support within the bureaucracy. However, militaries are complex organizations, and major change involves risk and uncertainty. Because the armed forces must respond to crises on short notice, their leaders are hesitant to make changes that sacrifice readiness. Meeting this challenge requires developing both a compelling case for change and a core group of supporters within the military.

The revolution in tank warfare died a bureaucratic death in the America between the wars. The U.S. Army was aware of the work of a British analyst, Captain B. H. Liddell Hart, who outlined the revolutionary potential of armored warfare. Military journals debated the possible impact of the tank. Nevertheless, the idea did not win the support of the service leadership.

The commander of the armor corps did not promote the development of independent armored divisions or the use of tanks for penetrating deep into enemy lines. Likewise, in a report released in 1919 on the lessons of World War I, the chief of staff of the U.S. Army concluded, "important as has been the effect of these mechanical developments and special services, their true value has been as auxiliaries to the Infantry. Nothing in this war has changed the fact that it is now, as always heretofore, the Infantry with rifle and bayonet that, in the final analysis, must bear the brunt of the assault and carry it on to victory."[7]

The National Defense Act of 1920 eliminated the tank corps, and its officers were assigned to other branches while the tanks and their development were left to the infantry. Former armor officers opposed the change but realized the cause was hopeless. As Dwight Eisenhower would recall, "In 1920 and 1921 George Patton and I publicly and earnestly expounded [ideas on armor] in the service journals of the day. The doctrine was so revolutionary . . . that we were threatened with court-martial."[8]

Within the Army, this revolutionary approach to war had no champion and no career path. Bureaucratic opposition and inertia smothered hope for this peacetime innovation. But the service changed its approach when it developed the air assault division.

In the early 1950s, the Army became concerned about the vulnerability of massed ground forces to nuclear, biological, or chemical attack. Although helicopter technology was still immature, leaders such as General James Gavin believed that air mobility could reduce this vulnerability. He appointed General Hamilton Howze, an armor officer, the first director of aviation. Howze turned to exercises to demonstrate the potential of helicopters and to begin developing tactics and doctrine.

Taking a cue from Moffett and naval aviation, the supporters of air mobility recruited mid-career officers into aviation. Howze recalled, "In order to get some real enthusiasts, people who would associate their lives and progress in the Army with aviation, we had to go outside of the current aviation ranks. I selected many of those people myself."[9]

Meanwhile, technical advances caught up with the bold ideas. Helicopters were becoming more reliable and more powerful. Both UH-1s and AH-1s had turbine engines. And within a few years, Vietnam provided the baptism by fire that solidified the place of the helicopter in Army force structure and warfighting doctrine.

LIMITED BY LEGACY?

When the budget for FY03 was unveiled, a lack of terminations in major programs caused many defense analysts to conclude that the services had stopped transformation. It would be more accurate to say that the battle was deferred.

The new budget funds the key modernization efforts in addition to the more revolutionary concepts while taking organizational steps to minimize the bureaucratic resistance that the new ideas will encounter when these options clash. For example, the administration has added $1.5 billion to the Air Force over the next 6 years for unmanned combat aerial vehicles. This approach means that these vehicles will enter production at the same time as the joint strike fighter. Future leaders of the Air Force will be in a position to make informed decisions on the mix of these two systems in light of their demonstrated, not merely theoretical, capabilities.

The proposed Navy budget provides for the acquisition of DDG–51 destroyers, but replaces the next generation of DD–21 land attack destroyer with research and development on new ships, technology, and fighting doctrine. In addition, the Pentagon is adding a billion dollars to convert four Trident nuclear submarines to a conventional strike mission, allowing the Navy to evaluate the combat value of a submerged long-range strike capability.

The Army budget would continue to fund upgrades to the existing heavy divisions, but there is no follow-on funding to develop a future heavy division. Instead, the budget accelerates the development of the future combat system, a family of manned and unmanned vehicles and weapon systems designed from the beginning to take advantage of the information revolution. In the meantime, the budget will also fund the fielding of medium-weight brigades, which combine existing equipment with new technologies and, most importantly, new organization and doctrine.

Although the Pentagon recently initiated studies to scale back several modernization programs, its approach raises a basic question. Does modernizing existing equipment or maintaining a legacy force structure prevent transformation? There is little historical evidence that it does. The United States spent five times more on battleship modernization than did the British before World War II, yet had more success in developing carriers. At the same time, Germany continued to focus heavily on training horse cavalry divisions, even as they experimented with armored warfare. Furthermore, even after developing tanks, Germany actually expanded its army to 120 infantry divisions. These units, operating on foot and often with horse-drawn artillery, did not prevent ten Panzer divisions from executing Blitzkrieg tactics.

STOCKING THE BUREAUCRACY

The struggle is about more than technology. It also involves people. When the secretary of defense created the Office of Force Transformation, he selected as its head retired Vice Admiral Arthur Cebrowski, the former commander of USS *Midway* and USS *America* battle groups. In addition to holding traditional commands, Cebrowski has a reputation for promoting innovative ship designs and warfighting concepts. And in selecting the next commander of U.S. Joint Forces Command, a position central to joint experimentation, the secretary turned to his senior military assistant, Vice Admiral Edmund Giambastiani. The decision to drive transformation is alive and well among senior leaders at the Pentagon: "I would hazard a guess that five years from now, looking back, we'll say that the single most transformational things we did were to select those people [the 4-star officers in charge of the major commands]. . . . They will then fashion their staffs and their key people, and they will be involved in the promotions of the people under them. And it'll affect the United States of America for the next decade and a half."[10]

The military undermines innovation when it prevents experimentation and the prototyping of ideas or when it opts to continue old ways after a new system is demonstrated. The proposal under the new plan provides time, resources, and leadership to demonstrate multiple technologies and related doctrine. When prototypes are used in exercises or conflicts—like the armed Predator unmanned aerial vehicle in Afghanistan—enthusiasm spreads. Users develop hands-on expertise and provide practical feedback. As the system evolves and greater capabilities are demonstrated, it becomes possible to design a revolutionary weapon system. Military decisions on the fate of such systems will determine whether transformation succeeds or fails. This approach relies on ensuring that the right individuals are in the right positions to make those decisions.

CHANGING REQUIREMENTS

Developing a new concept of warfare is inexpensive. Developing and fielding hardware to implement the concept is not. Therefore civilian leaders insist that the armed forces only pursue those systems that are compatible with expected security requirements. Unfortunately, innovations develop slowly, whereas national security requirements can change quickly.

Prospects for innovation in armored warfare prior to World War II were bright in Britain. The army had used tanks in World War I. Moreover, several forward-looking thinkers articulated the revolutionary potential of the tank. As Liddell Hart argued: "[Tanks] are not an extra arm or a mere aid to infantry, but are the modern form of heavy cavalry, and their correct tactical use is clear—to be concentrated and used in as large masses as possible for decisive manoeuvre against the flanks and communications of the enemy, which have been fixed by the infantry—themselves mechanised—and artillery."[11]

In August 1919, however, the War Cabinet formulated the ten year rule, stating that Britain would not be involved in a major war over the next decade and thus no expeditionary force would be needed. According to the civilian leadership, the army would focus on protecting the Empire. The tank was ill-suited to tropical climates or low-intensity conflict that London expected. Even in 1937, when war seemed likely, Prime Minister Neville Chamberlain pursued a policy of limited liability, in which the country would provide air and naval forces but rely on allies to furnish large armies. With the outbreak of World War II, the political leaders once again focused on the need for a modern army to fight a major land war in Europe. However, the delay in developing the equipment and doctrine for tank divisions put Britain at a distinct disadvantage compared with Germany, which had more consistently exploited armored vehicles.

In World War I, Germany planned to quickly defeat France and then turn on the Russians. Although this strategy failed, its security requirements remained the same. It was a land power faced with the possibility of a two-front war. The Versailles Treaty limited the Germans to seven infantry and three cavalry divisions and prohibited it from the production of tanks, yet these obstacles did not prevent the development of Panzer divisions.

General Hans von Seeckt, commander of the army from the end of World War I to 1926, saw mobility as a way to offset the small size of his forces: "In a few words then, the whole future of warfare appears to me to lie in the employment of mobile armies, relatively small but of high quality and rendered distinctly more effective by the addition of aircraft."[12] Although the focus was on preparing horse cavalry for this mission, he recognized that "motor transport is one of the most urgent questions of military organization."[13]

The Germans monitored the development of the tank in Great Britain throughout the 1920s and 1930s, and their journals discussed tactical problems with armored warfare. The government arranged in 1926 for the military to use a secret tank-training center in Kazan, Russia. In 1932, the army held maneuvers in Germany using tank battalions, even though its tanks were armored plates mounted on trucks. From this developed the concepts that would lead to the Panzer division. As General Heinz Guderian recalled:

My historical studies, the exercises carried out in England, and our own experiences with mock-ups had persuaded me that tanks would never be able to produce their full effect until the other weapons on whose support they must inevitably rely were brought up to their standard of speed and cross-country performance. . . . It would be wrong to include tanks in infantry divisions: what was needed were armoured divisions which would include all the supporting arms needed to allow the tanks to fight with full effect.[14]

Although the rise of the National Socialists in 1933 brought dramatic changes to Germany, the leaders realized that armor was consistent with their expansive goals. But the program was not without its problems. In maneuvers, tanks encountered maintenance failures, including XVI Panzer Corps under Guderian. In the invasion of Austria, "no less than 30 percent of his vehicles broke down or ran out of petrol . . . [while others] put the figures even higher, at 70 percent."[15] Despite these operational failures, the Versailles Treaty, and changes in leadership, Panzer divisions were promoted because they were consistent with German strategy.

CAPABILITIES-BASED PLANNING

According to the chairman of the Joint Chiefs of Staff, although the nation does not know who will threaten its interests, a capabilities-based strategy is focused on how a potential enemy might fight. It helps to identify the assets that the armed forces will need to deter and defeat a variety of threats.

The notion of two major regional conflicts (MRCs) —specifically, another Persian Gulf War and Korean conflict—became the measure by which the military was judged after Desert Storm in 1991. In the wake of September 11, some might argue that terrorism is the wave of the future, and the Bush administration concluded that the two-MRC scenario has outlived its usefulness. To avoid surprise, the Pentagon believes it is more important to demonstrate a breadth of capabilities than to focus exclusively on depth against one scenario.

As a result, the force planning requirements that drove budget development are no longer based on the two-MRC approach of the 1990s but on a broader, capabilities-based model. If a very specific strategic challenge were to arise, as Germany did in both World Wars, this change might dilute the military's focus. But the United States today is much closer to Great Britain's earlier experience, with global interests and a range of potential conflicts. Thus the shift away from the two-MRC focus is a sound approach to avoiding Britain's mistake with the 10-year rule.

EFFECTIVE INNOVATION

Another risk deserves attention. A nation may successfully pursue innovative ideas but still meet with disaster if enemy advances are more effective. For example, France built the Maginot Line along its border with Germany to protect its industries in Alsace-Lorraine. The defenses were a sophisticated set of bunkers, tunnels, and gun turrets, which represented a huge advance over the fortifications of World War I. The French halted the defenses on the Belgian border partly because of financial constraints but also as part of their strategy. By forcing Germany through Belgium, France believed they could guarantee both Belgian and British participation in the war. In addition, it hoped to avoid the devastation of another invasion of its territory.

While plans for the Maginot Line went forward, French tank doctrine stagnated. The basic field manual published in 1929 on armor warfare, *Instruction sur l'Emploi des Chars de Combat,* stated that tanks were "only a means of supplementary action temporarily set at the disposal of the infantry" and that they "considerably reinforce the action of the latter, but they do not replace it."[16] French armored units lacked mechanized support, thus preventing their use in breakthroughs. The 1937 manual rejected the exploitation mission.

France had 3,000 tanks and Germany had 2,400 in 1940. But the Germans structured their military to support Blitzkrieg. France was blinded to this revolution in warfare and was decisively defeated because of it. The sobering point is that the Maginot Line did what its planners expected. The Germans were forced to circumvent its defenses. It allowed France to concentrate its army on a narrow front. It ensured both Belgian and British participation in the war. Yet France still lost. It was not enough for Paris to try a new approach to war; it needed to be aware of German efforts and prepared to counter them.

THE NEW BUDGET

Because the United States has a high-tech economy, much of the debate on transformation is focused on information technology. The capabilities that the military is pursuing are generally designed to take advantage of information that can be moved and analyzed by computers. New technologies this makes possible include unmanned aerial vehicles and precision-guided munitions.

But it is conceivable that military transformation will be driven by different technologies, or perhaps by exploiting vulnerabilities in a force dependent on computers. To avoid creating a digital Maginot Line, it is critical to understand the technology and tactics that an enemy may pursue, such as weapons of mass destruction, ballistic missiles, cyberwarfare, and terrorism.

The DoD budget approaches this problem by directing resources toward a range of threats. Outlays for 2001 to 2003 contain $528 million (an increase of 130 percent) for additional research on chemical and biological defenses, $2,173 million (40 percent) for ballistic missile defense, and $262 million (51 percent) in equipment for U.S. Special Operations Command. Similar growth in spending was made for intelligence, information security, space, and homeland defense. Although it is impossible to eliminate the risk of surprise, the new defense budget provides sound levels of funding across various programs that should greatly reduce vulnerability.

Because the budget request for FY03 initially retained the Crusader and also declined to cut tactical fighter programs or reduce the number of carriers, critics quickly characterized the outcome as business as usual. It appeared that the bureaucracy had won and transformation had lost. This analysis was wrong. Proposals to scale back on these programs will be viewed as a make-or-break test for military transformation. But that analysis is wrong as well. The administration is taking steps to address obstacles that have prevented other nations in the past from transforming their militaries. That level of thoroughness is not simply good fortune; it is intentional.

A critical fight over military transformation did not occur with the development of the FY03 budget. It will unfold over the next 5 to 10 years, as the services acquire the next generation of matériel, as well as the doctrine and organization to operationalize them. To ensure that those future decisions actually transform the military, innovative technologies must become sufficiently mature, political and military leadership must foster innovation, and national security strategy must support a new approach to warfighting. The current defense budget certainly takes those steps. This is the path to transformation.

NOTES

1. Steven Kosiak, *2003 Defense Budget Request: Large Increase in Funding, Few Changes To Plans* (Washington, D.C.: Center for Strategic and Budgetary Assessments, 2002), 1.

2. Loren B. Thompson, "Did Rumsfeld Get it Right?" *San Diego Union-Tribune* (February 17, 2002).

3. Heidi Toffler and Alvin Toffler, *War and Anti-War* (Boston: Little, Brown, 1993), 29.

4. Michael Howard, "Military Science in the Age of Peace," *RUSI Journal* 19 (March 1974): 7.

5. Stephen Peter Rosen, *Winning the Next War* (Ithaca, N.Y.: Cornell University Press, 1991), 105.

6. Ibid., 70.

7. Walter Millis, ed., *American Military Thought* (Indianapolis, Ind.: Bobbs-Merrill, 1966), 355.

8. Wesley Yale et al., *Alternative to Armageddon* (New Brunswick, N.J.: Rutgers University Press, 1970), 76.

9. Rosen, *Winning the Next War,* 90.

10. The secretary of defense quoted by Vince Crawley in "New CINCs to Shape U.S. Military Policy for Decade," *Defense News* (February 25–March 3, 2002): 68.

11. B.H. Liddell Hart, *The Remaking of Modern Armies* (London: John Murray, 1927), 59.

12. Hans von Seeckt, *Thoughts of a Soldier* (London: Ernest Benn, 1930), 62.

13. Ibid., 84.

14. Heinz Guderian, *Panzer Leader* (London: Michael Joseph, 1952), 24.

15. Charles Messenger, *The Blitzkrieg Story* (New York: Charles Scribner's Sons, 1976), 118.

16. Barry R. Posen, *The Sources of Military Doctrine* (Ithaca, N.Y.: Cornell University Press, 1984), 131.

PART III

THE CHANGING INSTRUMENTS OF AMERICAN DEFENSE POLICY

INTRODUCTION

COLLINS G. SHACKELFORD, JR.

The instruments of American defense policy are continuously changing due to the U.S. government's efforts to address the challenges presented by the contemporary and future security environment. Ever Janus-faced, these efforts have domestic and external (international) components. Government efforts to adapt these instruments of American defense policy include the development of policies and defense programs that support the implementation of the national security and military strategies promulgated by the U.S. president and the chairman of the Joint Chiefs of Staff. These respective strategies seek to integrate a suite of national-level instruments to ensure the "common defense," as well as forge partnerships among state and nonstate actors.

Chapter 7, "Transformation in American Defense Policy," addresses several elements that were captured in the last edition with articles that spoke of the "Military Technical Revolution" (MTR), the "revolution in military affairs" (RMA), and the specter of "societal-level ideational conflicts waged in part through internetted modes of communication—and cyberwar at the military level."[1] These essays recognized that although the methods of warfare might have changed, the fog, friction, uncertainty, danger, and destruction remain inherent elements of war.[2] Since the previous edition, the Department of Defense has moved beyond the MTR and RMA and now seeks to embrace a somewhat broader sense of change captured in the term "transformation."

Today the debates on transformation can be seen in the press and the academic literature. To provide an introduction to this wide-ranging topic, this chapter draws first on Andy Krepinevich's essay, which expands on ideas he formulated while working for Andy Marshall in the DoD Office of Net Assessment.[3] Krepinevich sounds a cautionary note for those thinking that the U.S. asymmetric advantages in military power translate across the full spectrum of conflict operations. By developing the story of ten military revolutions that range from cavalry to computers, he draws inferences that suggest both promise and some peril. Based on his ten military revolutions, Krepinevich stresses the importance of innovation and adaptability as key attributes of competitive military organizations.

From the historical perspective, this chapter moves to Richard Kugler and Hans Binnendijk's exploration of the tensions between the evolutionary and revolutionary approaches to changes in the U.S. military. This debate has taken place both within and outside government. Drawing on their research, Kugler and Binnendijk offer a hybrid of the approaches that seems to capture the directions developed in the DoD Quadrennial Defense Review published in 2001.[4]

The concluding articles in Chapter 7 present a critique and response to DoD transformation. Frederick Kagan develops a critical analysis of the current direction of DoD transformation based on historical evidence, noting that America's competitors tend to catch up with whatever program America adopts to transform its armed forces. Kagan develops a case in favor of "redundancy" as a key attribute of the success of U.S. military forces. For example, when weather grounds aircraft, ground-based missiles or artillery can offer some compensation for that loss of firepower. Although redundancy may not be the most efficient means to field a full range of forces, it does provide a way to moderate the risk of single-point failures. Tom Hone, from the DoD Office of Force Transformation, replies that today's transformation efforts occur in a world where funds are relatively scarce. For him, transformation serves as a means to prevent the services from competing for resources to do the same job or perform the same mission.[5]

Transformation offers one avenue to explore the theme of the changing instruments of defense policy. Chapter 8, "Integrating Force and Other Policy Tools for a Comprehensive Defense," offers a second path. It explores the effort to integrate force into the wider range of instruments available to national leaders challenged by a dynamic security environment in which adjectives such as "anarchic," "cooperative," and "competitive" have prominent places in the lexicon of defense policy. Military power, with its associated technologies, organizations, doctrine, people, and strategies, must be congruent with the security environment to remain relevant to national leaders. The enduring elements of warfare—fog, friction, and uncertainty—suggest a context that will challenge even the best prepared military force. Such a force, as it contributes to the defense of the nation, must be viewed as one element in a suite of tools employed for the "common defense."

Robert Art provides a suitable beginning for exploring this challenge by developing a conceptual framework for examining the various uses of force. By discussing force in terms of four major functions—defense, deterrence, compellance, and "swaggering"—he offers an analytic framework to capture the full range of military behavior associated with a state. As he develops the discussion on these functions, one begins to appreciate the possible limits to the employment of military force. Reinforcing this appreciation of limits on military power, the chapter moves to Barry Posen's discussion of the command of the "commons." Posen admits that unipolarity and U.S. hegemony are not likely to diminish soon. He then develops the idea of a "commons," in which the U.S. military is dominant in the four dimensions of land, sea, air, and space. Yet even with this military dominance, he suggests that there are "contested areas" where the U.S. will be challenged by military resistance employing what other analysts describe as "asymmetric strategies." Given the inability of the U.S. military to dominate in these contested areas, Posen argues for a strategy not based on what he calls "primacy," but one more aligned with the concept of "selective engagement."[6] This approach seeks a less unilateral approach toward reaching foreign policy goals, assuming that policymakers need a more nuanced understanding of the U.S. military position to ensure that foreign and military policy are mutually supporting.[7]

The penultimate essay of this chapter turns to an area that has not been a cornerstone of American defense policy. Economic sanctions offer a complex and oftentimes ineffective option to national level decisionmakers. Yet the essay by Chantal de Jonge Oudraat offers a succinct review of the concept of sanctions and proposes an alternative strategy for economic sanctions, suggesting that they can be effective if part of a comprehensive coercive strategy, and if properly implemented.[8]

Richard Lacquement concludes the chapter with a reasoned discussion on a post–Cold War challenge to the U.S. military, peace operations and their myriad array of tasks that many observers say contradict the core functions of a military. Lacquement examines peace operations from the vantage point of reconstruction efforts in Iraq. Suddenly, stabilization operations and civil affairs are front and center in American defense policy. Drawing from the U.N. Brahimi Report and firsthand observations of the U.S. Army experience in Northern Iraq, Lacquement sketches the outlines of a revised approach as the United States accepts greater levels of responsibility in international peace operations.[9] He offers constructive recommendations that center on potential organizational changes to military, interagency, and civilian elements so as to better integrate their efforts during the post-conflict/combat phases of peace operations.

Chapter 9, "Preparing Future Defense Leaders," examines the changing instruments of American defense policy by turning to the development of defense leaders. As one reviews the challenges presented by the dynamic security environment and the array of potential strategies that might be employed to address that environment, the importance of those who develop and execute American defense policy becomes readily apparent. To expand on the words of Don Snider and Gayle Watkins, this group "is neither a public-sector bureaucracy manned by civil servants nor is it a business with employees."[10] Defense leaders are not limited to the highest levels of government, such as ranking civilian and military commanders who think at the strategic and theater-wide perspective.[11] Defense leaders also include young noncommissioned officers and lieutenants on the front line carrying through tasks that form the substance of American defense policy.[12]

These defense leaders, at whatever level, certainly draw on their life and professional experiences to guide them through uncertainty and new challenges. There is, however, another factor to this preparation of men and women as they advance to new levels of service. This factor is the education needed to develop individuals committed to public service in the name of the "common defense," service that will include operations that span a spectrum from humanitarian assistance to peace operations to combat. This chapter introduces the system of education that helps develop these leaders, now known as "professional military education" (PME). This system of education recognizes that in the armed services, each level of competence in the art of warfare must build on previous levels of education and experience.

If PME provides a framework, what then is the context within which this framework must operate? An answer to this question is provided in the essay by Joseph Collins. He reminds us that factors ranging from the international environment to the character of contemporary American society all shape the prevailing values and traditions of the armed forces. Collins then offers a range of recommendations that include an important role for PME and its traditional focus on strategy and leadership studies.

Next we delve into the 1997 study by the Center for Strategic and International Studies (CSIS) on PME. This reading provides a thorough introduction to the various levels of education that contribute to the development of American defense leaders. Beginning with entry-level programs—the service academies, Reserve Officer Training Corps (ROTC), and Officer Candidate School (OCS)—this report concludes with an examination of joint and individual senior service schools (SSS). This CSIS report highlights the challenges facing all levels of PME as it balances the imperative to advance the concept of military jointness, enlarge the professional competence of defense leaders, prepare these defense leaders "to confront complex ethical dilemmas," and enable them to face the demands of the twenty-first century.

It is exactly these demands of the twenty-first century that are at the center of the next essays in this chapter. The U.S. Army War College report "Educating International Security Practitioners" complements the CSIS study with a focus on how each level of education best prepares students to be national security professionals at their respective levels of service. The excerpts presented here are drawn from contributions by Brigadier General Daniel Kaufman and James Smith. Kaufman's focus is on the undergraduate level, whereas Smith examines the contributions of research centers and professional outreach programs. Each author has a unique perspective, but they share a common vision of the imperative to develop strategic leaders ready to outthink instead of merely attempting to outgun adversaries.[13] The chapter closes with Ervin Rokke's challenge to the war colleges to be agents for change within the services and the military's joint arenas. From the strategic context of military operations to the demands of the information age, he highlights the forces that drive change in professional military education. It is his argument that these institutions of professional military education must become more like civilian institutions of higher education so they will provide the intellectual capital needed for change in the armed forces.

Part III thus highlights the changing nature of military power. It begins with the concept of change in the means and manner of America's defense establishment. From the RMA to the current drive to "transform" defense, the United States seeks to address the challenges of the current security environment while simultaneously preparing for the future. The essential functions of force and alternatives for how force might be integrated with other elements of national power must be considered in this process. The education of military leaders at all levels becomes increasingly important as their responsibilities become more complex. Given the dynamic security environment presented in Part I, it is critical that America's changing instruments of military power, both hardware and flesh and blood, be prepared for the full range of challenges.

NOTES

The views expressed are the author's and in no way represent the opinions, standards, or policy of the U.S. Air Force Academy, or the U.S. government.

1. See, for example, John Arquilla and David Ronfeldt, "Cyberwar Is Coming," and Michael J. Mazarr with Jeffrey Shaffer and Benjamin Ederington, "The Military Technical Revolution," in *American Defense Policy,* ed. Peter L. Hays, Brenda J. Vallance, and Alan R. Van Tassel, 7th edition (Baltimore, Md.: The Johns Hopkins University Press, 1997), 566–80, 556–66.

2. See, for example, the September 12, 2001 interview with four distinguished retired military officers on "Reinventing War," *Foreign Policy* (November 2001): 31–47. Their forthright responses offer cautions on the use of military force but also highlight obstacles with the Bush admin-

istration's commitment to "transformation," misspent dollars in the defense budget, and "the military's technophobia."

3. An especially significant publication that began in the Department of Defense's Office of Net Assessment as a 1992 classified paper distributed to the services is now available absent a classified annex. See Andrew F. Krepinevich, Jr., *The Military-Technical Revolution: A Preliminary Assessment* (Washington, D.C.: Center for Strategic and Budgetary Assessment, 2002), available at www.csbaonline .org.

4. The 2001 *Quadrennial Defense Review* is available at www.defenselink.mil/pubs/qdr2001.pdf.

5. This complements arguments that the PPBE system, discussed in Part II, needs a more robust effort to link the planning and programming elements to lessen the overlap between capabilities and reduce inefficient redundancies across the services and throughout DoD agencies.

6. See, for example, Robert J. Art, *A Grand Strategy for America* (Ithaca, N.Y.: Cornell University Press, 2003). For the U.S. government's strategy, see the *National Security Strategy* (2002) and *National Military Strategy* (2004).

7. See also Rob de Wijk, "The Limits of Military Power," *Washington Quarterly* 25 (Winter 2002): 75–92, for a focused look at conceptual challenges facing traditional military forces as they adapt to a war on terrorism.

8. This essay is a credible extension of the concept of coercion that developed in Thomas C. Schelling, *Arms and Influence* (New Haven: Yale University Press, 1966), and Alexander L. George and William E. Simons, eds., *The Limits of Coercive Diplomacy,* 2nd edition (Boulder: Westview Press, 1994, originally 1971).

9. The U.N. Brahimi Report may be found at www .un.org/peace/reports/peace_operations/report.htm. For a comprehensive review of the report, see William J. Durch, Victoria K. Holt, Caroline R. Earle, and Moira K. Shanahan, *The Brahimi Report and the Future of UN Peace Operations* (Washington, D.C.: Henry L. Stimson Center, 2003), available at www.stimson.org.

10. Lloyd J. Matthews, ed., *The Future of the Army Profession* (New York: McGraw-Hill Primis, 2002), 3.

11. Such individuals are discussed in Eliot A. Cohen's widely cited work, synopsized in Chapter 10.

12. As captured in the words of Dwight D. Eisenhower, "The most terrible job in warfare is to be a second lieutenant leading a platoon when you are on the battlefield."

13. See also Leonard D. Holder, Jr., and Williamson Murray, "Prospects for Military Education, *Joint Force Quarterly* 18 (Spring 1998): 81–90; and Thomas J. Williams, "Strategic Leader Readiness and Competencies for Asymmetric Warfare," *Parameters* 33 (Summer 2003): 19–35.

CHAPTER 7

TRANSFORMATION IN AMERICAN DEFENSE POLICY

CAVALRY TO COMPUTER:
THE PATTERN OF MILITARY REVOLUTIONS

ANDREW F. KREPINEVICH

Over the next several decades, the world is destined to experience a revolution in the character of warfare. Indeed, the way in which the United States and its allies won a quick and overwhelming victory in the Gulf War suggests to many that we are already in the early stages of such a military revolution. But if so, there is much more to come.

As it progresses, this revolution will have profound consequences for global and regional military balances, and thus for U.S. defense planning. In the past, military revolutions have induced major changes in both the nature of the peacetime competition between states and their military organizations, and in the ways wars are deterred, fought, and resolved. By changing radically the nature of the military competition in peace and war, military revolutions have changed the "rules of the game." In so doing, they have often dramatically devalued formerly dominant elements of military power, including weaponry, weapons platforms, and doctrines. Military organizations that did not adapt in a rapidly changing, highly competitive environment have declined, often quite quickly.

What is a military revolution? It is what occurs when the application of new technologies to a significant number of military systems combines with innovative operational concepts and organizational adaptation in a way that fundamentally alters the character and conduct of conflict. It does so by producing a dramatic increase—often an order of magnitude or greater—in the combat potential and military effectiveness of armed forces.

Military revolutions comprise four elements: technological change, systems development, operational innovation, and organizational adaptation. Each of these elements is in itself a necessary, but not a sufficient, condition for realizing the large gains in military effectiveness that characterize military revolutions. In particular, although advances in technology typically underwrite a military revolution, they alone do not constitute the revolution. The phenomenon is much broader in scope and consequence than technological innovation, however dramatic the latter may be.

The transition from the Cold War period of warfare to a new military era that is now anticipated may take several decades—or it may arrive within the next 10 or 15 years. There is no common transition period from one military regime to another: the naval transition from wood and sail to the all-big-gun dreadnoughts with their steel hulls and turbine engines took roughly half a century; the emergence of nuclear weapons, ballistic missile delivery systems, and associated doctrine and organizational structures took roughly 15 years. The rate of transition is typically a function not only of the four elements noted above, but of the level of competition among the international system's major players and the strategies the competitors choose to pursue in exploiting the potential of the emerging military revolution.

It may be argued that with recent transition periods of 10 to 20 years, we are discussing a continuous military evolution rather than a revolution. But what is revolutionary is not the speed with which the entire shift from one military regime to another occurs, but rather the recognition, over some relatively brief period, that the character of conflict has changed dramatically, requiring equally dramatic—if not radical—changes in military doctrine and organizations. Just as water changes to ice only when the falling temperature reaches 32° Fahrenheit, at some critical point, the cumulative effects of technological advances and military innovation will invalidate former conceptual frameworks and demand a fundamental change in the accepted definitions and measurement of military effectiveness. When this occurs, military organizations will either move to adapt rapidly or find themselves at a severe competitive disadvantage.

TEN REVOLUTIONS

There appear to have been as many as ten military revolutions since the fourteenth century. The Hundred Years' War (1337–1453) spawned two of them. The first was the so-called "Infantry Revolution," which saw infantry displacing the dominant role of heavy cavalry on the battlefield.[1] During the period leading up to this military revolution, infantry typically employed tight formations of pole-arms and crossbowmen to protect the cavalry while it formed up for a charge. During the first half of the fourteenth

This essay has been edited and is reprinted from National Interest 37 *(Fall 1994): 30–42, by permission.*

century, however, the infantry—in the form of Swiss pikemen and English archers—emerged as a combat arm fully capable of winning battles, as was demonstrated at the battles of Laupen (1339) and Crecy (1346).[2] Following these engagements, major cavalry actions on the field of battle became increasingly rare.

Clifford Rogers cites several factors as responsible for the Infantry Revolution. One key factor was the development of the six-foot yew longbow, which gave archers a much enhanced ability to penetrate the armor of cavalrymen. It also gave archers both missile and range superiority over their adversaries. England, which developed a pool of yeoman archers over decades of warfare against the Scots and Welsh, established a significant competitive advantage over the formerly dominant army—that of the French—which failed to exploit the revolution until late in the fifteenth century.

But it was not the longbow alone that fueled the revolution. Once the ability of infantrymen to win battles was clearly established, tactical innovations followed. The English developed a tactical system based on integrating archers with dismounted men-at-arms. Interestingly, the dominance of infantry was given an additional boost by the fact that archers were far less expensive to equip and train than men-at-arms. Thus, Rogers points out, the tiny kingdom of Flanders, which was relatively quick in exploiting the revolution, was able to muster a larger army at Courtrai (1302) than the entire kingdom of France. Finally, the Infantry Revolution marked a sharp increase in casualties on the battlefield. Whereas formerly, it had been important to capture knights for the purpose of realizing a ransom, common infantrymen neither held that value, nor did they share knightly notions of chivalry. Battles thus became more sanguine affairs.

The Infantry Revolution was succeeded by the "Artillery Revolution," which dramatically altered war in the latter period of the Hundred Years' War. Although Roger Bacon's recipe for gunpowder dates back to 1267, cannons only began to appear on the European battlefield in significant numbers some 60 years later. Even then, almost a full century passed before artillery began to effect a military revolution. During this period, besieged cities typically surrendered due to a lack of supplies. In the 1420s, however, a major increase occurred in the number of besieged cities surrendering as a consequence of the besiegers' artillery fire fatally degrading the cities' defenses. In the span of a few decades, gunpowder artillery displaced the centuries-old dominance of the defense in siege warfare.

Several technological improvements underwrote the Artillery Revolution. One was the lengthening of gun barrels, which permitted substantial increases in accuracy and muzzle velocity, translating into an increase in range and destructive force (and also the rate of fire). Metallurgical breakthroughs reduced the cost of iron employed in fabricating gun barrels, reducing the overall cost of cannons by about a third.

Finally, the "corning" of gunpowder made artillery more powerful and cheaper to use.[3] As one Italian observer noted, artillery could now "do in a few hours what . . . used to take days."[4] Unlike the Infantry Revolution, the Artillery Revolution was expensive to exploit. As early as 1442, the French government was spending over twice as much on its artillery arm as on more traditional military equipment.[5]

A kind of snowball effect developed. The richer states could exploit the Artillery Revolution to subdue their weaker neighbors (or their own powerful regional nobles), which, in turn, increased the resources available to exploit their advantage further. This phenomenon was a significant factor in the growth of centralized authority in France and Spain. Along with the changes in technologies that spawned the great improvements in artillery and changes in siege warfare, new military organizational elements, such as artillery siege trains, were formed to cement the revolution. Once this occurred, defenders could no longer rely on castles for protection. This led to further changes in military organizations and operations, as the defenders now had to abandon their fortified castles and garrison units and move the contest into the field. And, as Francesco Guicciardini wrote, "whenever the open country was lost, the state was lost with it."

Military revolutions were not limited to land. The "Revolution of Sail and Shot" saw the character of conflict at sea change dramatically, as the great navies of the Western world moved from oar-driven galleys to sailing ships that could exploit the Artillery Revolution by mounting large guns. Galleys, being oar-driven, had to be relatively light, and, unlike ships propelled by sail, could not mount the heavy cannon that could shatter a ship's timbers, thus sinking enemy ships rather than merely discouraging boarding parties. Indeed, prior to the late fourteenth century, ship design had not improved significantly for two millennia, since the age of classical Greece. The French first mounted cannons on their sailing ships in 1494. But the death knell for the galley did not sound clearly until the Battle of Preveza, when Venetian galleasses won an overwhelming victory against Turkish galleys. The result was repeated at Lepanto in 1571.[6] By 1650, the warship had been transformed from a floating garrison of soldiers to an artillery platform.

The sixteenth century witnessed the onset of the "Fortress Revolution," which involved the construction of a new style of defensive fortification employing lower, thicker walls featuring bastions, crownworks, ravelins, and hornworks, all of which were part of a defensive fortification system known as the *trace italienne*. As Geoffrey Parker observes, "normally the capture of a stronghold defended by the *trace italienne* required months, if not years." Static defenses thus effected a kind of "comeback" against the Artillery Revolution. However, as with artillery, the new fortification system was terribly expensive, a fact that limited its application and left considerable opportunity for operations in the field.

This, in turn, shifted the focus back to infantry, where revolutionary developments permitted a new use of firepower: infantry moving beyond archers to the combination of artillery and musket fire on the battlefield, in what might be termed the "Gunpowder Revolution."

Muskets capable of piercing plate armor at a range of one hundred meters were introduced in the 1550s. The English abandoned longbows in the 1560s in favor of firearms. Finally, in the 1590s, the Dutch solved the problem of muskets' slow rate of fire through a tactical innovation that saw them abandon the tight squares of pikemen in favor of drawing up their forces in a series of long lines. These linear tactics allowed for a nearly continuous stream of fire, as one rank fired while the others retired to reload. Muskets were also attractive because they required little training in comparison to the years necessary to develop a competent archer (although linear tactics did require considerable drill). The large, tight squares of pikemen, which had proved so effective against cavalry, now became attractive targets for musket and artillery fire.

This revolution reached full flower in the campaigns of Gustavus Adolphus during the Thirty Years' War, which saw the melding of technology, military systems, operational concept, and new military organizations: a combination of pike, musketeers, cavalry, and a large rapid-firing artillery component utilizing linear tactics—what has been described as the Swedish military system—yielded stunning successes at Brietenfeld, Lutzen, Wittstock, Brietenfeld II, and Jankov.[7]

Linear tactics were perfected under the Prussian military system of Frederick the Great, who achieved significant improvements in the rate of fire, as well as major improvements in supply. But this refined system would be overturned by the "Napoleonic Revolution."

The French were the first to exploit the potential for a military revolution that had been building for several decades prior to Napoleon's rise to prominence. During this period, thanks to the emerging Industrial Revolution, the French standardized their artillery calibers, carriages, and equipment, and fabricated interchangeable parts. Other improvements in industrial processes allowed the French to reduce the weight of their cannon by 50 percent, thereby increasing their mobility while decreasing transport and manpower requirements dramatically.

The introduction of the *levée en masse* following the French Revolution helped to bring about another quantum leap in the size of field armies. Men proved much more willing to defend and fight for the nation than the crown. Consequently, France's revolutionary armies could endure privations and attack almost regardless of the cost in men (because they could call upon the total resources of the nation). In battle, the individual could be relied upon; skirmishers and individually aimed fire could be integrated to great effect into the rolling volleys of artillery and musketry. Furthermore, armies became

so large that they could now surround and isolate fortresses while retaining sufficient manpower to continue their advance and conduct field operations, thus largely negating the effects of the *trace italienne* and the Fortress Revolution.

The latter part of the eighteenth century also witnessed the creation of a new self-sufficient military organization—the division—and saw the growing importance of skirmishers in the form of light infantry, and cavalry as a reconnaissance, screening, and raiding force. A growing network of roads in Europe meant it was possible for an army to march in independent columns and yet concentrate quickly. Coordination was also improved through the availability of much more advanced cartographic surveys.

Napoleon's genius was to integrate the advances in technology, military systems, and military organizations (including his staff system) to realize a dramatic leap in military effectiveness over the military formations that existed only a short time before. Indeed, it took the other major military organizations of Europe at least a decade before they were able to compete effectively with the *Grande Armée* that Napoleon had fashioned to execute what one author has termed the "Napoleonic blitzkrieg."

Between the Napoleonic Wars and the American Civil War, the introduction of railroads and telegraphs and the widespread rifling of muskets and artillery again dramatically transformed the character of warfare—the way in which military forces are organized, equipped, and employed to achieve maximum military effectiveness. The result was the "Land Warfare Revolution." In the Civil War, both the Union and Confederate forces used their rail nets to enhance greatly their strategic mobility and their ability to sustain large armies in the field for what, in the war's final year, was continuous campaigning. Their exploitation of the telegraph facilitated the rapid transmission of information between the political and military leadership and their commanders in the field, as well as among the field commanders themselves. The telegraph also dramatically enhanced the ability of military leaders to mass their forces quickly at the point of decision and to coordinate widely dispersed operations far more effectively than had been possible during the Napoleonic era.

The effects of rifling, which improved the range and accuracy of musketry and artillery, were not as quickly appreciated by the American military. Union and Confederate generals who clung to the tactics of the Napoleonic era exposed their men to fearful slaughter, as at Fredericksburg, Spotsylvania, and Gettysburg. The introduction of repeating rifles in significant numbers late in the conflict enabled the individual soldier to increase substantially the volume, range, and accuracy of his fire over what had been possible only a generation or two earlier. One Confederate general is said to have observed that "had the Federal infantry been armed from the first with even the breechloaders available in 1861, the war would have been terminated within a year."[8] Still, both sides did adapt eventually.

The campaigns of 1864 and 1865 were marked by the proliferation of entrenchments and field fortifications. Indeed, by the time Sherman's men were marching from Atlanta to the sea in 1864, they lightened their packs by throwing away their bayonets—but they kept their shovels. Shelby Foote notes that the Confederate forces opposing Sherman had a saying that "Sherman's men march with a rifle in one hand and a spade in the other," while Union troops felt that "the rebs must carry their breastworks with them." Arguably, many of the major battles toward the war's end bore a greater resemblance to operations on the Western Front in the middle of World War I than they did to early Civil War battles like Shiloh or First Manassas.

Over the next 50 years, this new military regime matured. The increases in the volume, range, and accuracy of fires were further enhanced by improvements in artillery design and manufacturing and by the development of the machine gun. Again, military leaders who ignored or failed to see clearly the changes in warfare brought about by technological advances and who failed to adapt risked their men and their cause. This myopia was induced partly because no large-scale fighting occurred among the great powers of Europe between 1871 and 1914. World War I provides numerous examples of this phenomenon, as the military regime that began with the mid-nineteenth century revolution in land warfare reached full maturity. One recalls here the mutiny of the French Army after the futile and bloody Nivelle Offensive, the appalling casualties suffered by the British at the Somme and Passchendaele, and by the French and Germans at Verdun.

Just trailing this revolution in land warfare was the "Naval Revolution." The Revolution of Sail and Shot had long since matured. The wooden ships that were powered by the wind and armed with short-range cannon that had dominated war at sea had not changed appreciably since the sixteenth century. But over the course of a few decades of rapid change from the mid-1800s to the first years of the twentieth century, these vessels gave way to metal-hulled ships powered by turbine engines and armed with long-range rifled artillery, dramatically transforming the character of war at sea. As persistent challengers to British naval mastery, the French consistently led the way early in the Naval Revolution.[9] In 1846, they pioneered the adoption of steam propulsion and screw propellers on auxiliary ships. In 1851, they launched the *Napoleon,* the first high-speed, steam-powered ship of the line. And in the late 1850s, France began constructing the first seagoing ironclad fleet. The British, however, quickly responded to these French innovations, taking the lead in applying these technologies. The mature phase of this revolutionary period found Britain attempting to sustain its position against a new challenger, Imperial Germany, by launching the first all-big-gun battleship, *HMS Dreadnought,* in 1906. This period also saw the introduction of the submarine and the development of the torpedo. Indeed, the development of these two

instruments of war led to the introduction in World War I of entirely new military operations—the submarine strategic blockade and commerce raiding, and antisubmarine warfare.

Toward that war's end, however, new operational concepts were developed to mitigate the effects of the dominant military systems and operational concepts. On land, massed frontal assaults preceded by long artillery preparations gave way to brief artillery preparation fires, infiltration tactics, and the use of the light machine gun as the dominant weapon of the German storm trooper assault. At sea, Great Britain and the United States established elaborate convoy operations to counter the U-boat threat that had transformed the nature of commerce raiding.

World War I both represented the mature stage of one military epoch, and presaged the rise of the "Interwar Revolutions in Mechanization, Aviation, and Information." As the war progressed, the land forces of both the Allied and the Central powers found themselves employing new military systems based on dramatic advances in the fields of mechanization and radio. Following the war, improvements in internal combustion engines, aircraft design, and the exploitation of radio and radar made possible the Blitzkrieg, carrier aviation, modern amphibious warfare, and strategic aerial bombardment. Entirely new kinds of military formations appeared, such as the Panzer division, the carrier battlegroup, and the long-range bomber force. After a scant 20 years, the nature of conflict had changed dramatically, and those—like the British and the French—who failed to adapt suffered grievously.

Finally, in the mid-twentieth century, the "Nuclear Revolution" (especially after the coupling of nuclear warheads to ballistic missiles) brought the prospect of near-instantaneous and complete destruction of a state's economic and political fabric into the strategic equation. Here was a shift in technology so radical that it convinced nearly all observers that a fundamental change in the character of warfare was at hand. Indeed, in the eyes of some observers, once nuclear weapons were stockpiled in significant numbers by the superpowers, they could no longer be employed effectively. Their only utility was in deterring war. Nevertheless, one also sees here the emergence of very different warfighting doctrines and military organizations among nuclear states (e.g., the U.S. nuclear submarine force, Soviet Strategic Rocket Forces).

SEVEN LESSONS

Reflecting on this record extending over seven centuries, it is possible to make some general observations about the character of military revolutions.

First, and to reiterate a point made earlier, emerging technologies only make military revolutions possible. To realize their full potential, these technologies typically must be incorporated within new processes and executed by new organizational structures. In the cases outlined above, all major military organizations fairly rapidly gained access to the emerging technologies. Failure to realize a great increase in military effectiveness typically resulted not so much from ignoring technological change as from a failure to create new operational concepts and build new organizations.

Perhaps the clearest example of the importance of organizational innovation occurred early in World War II. On the Western front in 1940, British and French armored forces were roughly equal to the Germans' in size and quality. Both the allies and the Germans had modern aircraft and radios. In the interwar years, however, the German military had identified both the operational concept to best integrate these new military systems and the organization needed to activate that concept. The result was a major increase in military effectiveness and the acquisition of a decisive comparative advantage. Germany defeated the allied forces and conquered France in 6 weeks. That victory was primarily due to the *intellectual* breakthroughs that led to new operational concepts and the organizational flexibility that allowed them to exploit these concepts.

A second lesson is that the competitive advantages of a military revolution are increasingly short-lived. Military organizations typically recognize the potentially great penalties for failing to maintain their competitive position. In early periods of military revolution, it was possible to maintain dominance for a relatively long period (witness the sluggish response of France to the Infantry Revolution and that of much of Europe to the Napoleonic Revolution). But since the Napoleonic era, it has been true that if a major military organization is to derive an advantage by having first access to new technologies, it has to exploit those technologies quickly, before its major competitors copy or offset the advantage.

For example, the French innovations that sparked the nineteenth-century Naval Revolution stimulated a furious British response that matched and then exceeded the French effort. Although the British were loath to introduce radical changes in ship design, they felt compelled to when faced with the French initiative, and thus retained a major advantage. What gave Britain its competitive advantage was its economic strength, its ability to tap into that strength through its financial system, and its ability to concentrate its resources on a naval competition in a way that France, a continental power, never could. As the revolution matured, France's fleeting opportunities evaporated.

By the end of the Naval Revolution, the tables were again turned. When the British launched *HMS Dreadnought,* Germany quickly took up the British challenge, leading to the Anglo-German dreadnought arms race. Thus, the Royal Navy's lead in applying technologies to launch the first all-big-gun battleship designed to make all others "obsolete" produced only an ephemeral competitive advantage over Germany, and the other major navies of the world, which quickly constructed their own dreadnoughts.

Indeed, in the past two centuries, there do not seem to be any prolonged "monopolies" exercised by a single competitor in periods of military revolution. Fairly quickly, major powers who can afford the technology and who understand how to employ it have it if they want it. Of course, one is immediately led to ask the question: Is "fairly quickly" quickly enough? After all, Admiral Alfred von Tirpitz, who directed Germany's naval buildup, viewed with alarm the period from 1906, when Britain launched *Dreadnought,* to 1910, when Germany's naval building program was able to offset partially the British advantage. It may be that, although the period of competitive advantage appears to be fairly short, there is a potentially great advantage from being first, as the French discovered to their dismay and the Germans to their elation in the spring of 1940.

Having the initial competitive advantage in a period of military revolution—even if that advantage is considerable—is no guarantee of continued dominance, or even competitiveness. The list of military organizations that established an early lead, only to fall behind later, is long. Consider the history of the submarine: the French navy made much of the early progress in submarines in the late nineteenth century, but it was the Kaiser's navy that employed the new system to such devastating effect in World War I. In World War II, the United States quickly adopted many of Germany's innovations in mechanized airland operations and in submarine commerce raiding. Or take military aircraft: the Americans were in the forefront of aviation in the first years of the twentieth century, but by the time of their entry into World War I, they had fallen substantially behind many European states. Or tanks: an American tank designed in the 1920s was adapted by the Soviets in the process of developing the T-34, one of the most effective tanks to emerge during World War II. The U.S. Army, however, was equipped during the war primarily with the inferior Sherman tank.

Even though monopolies may be fleeting, they are real and often decisive in war. The early years of World War II—in some respects like the Napoleonic era revolution in land warfare during the late eighteenth century—demonstrate what can happen when only one power is innovative and adaptive. In the run-up to that war, Germany proved far more adept than France, Britain, and Soviet Russia at operational and organizational innovation on land. Although the Soviet Union, Great Britain, and the United States caught up to Germany's Blitzkrieg in the span of a few years, France was unable to adapt quickly enough in 1940 to avoid disaster, while Soviet Russia suffered enormous devastation at the hands of the German war machine.

A third lesson of history is that asymmetries in national objectives and strategic cultures, as well as limitations on resources and the potential number and strength of enemies, allow for niche, or specialist, competitors. This phenomenon seems to be characteristic of recent periods of military revolution, when technological change has been broadening and accelerating, offering a potentially rich menu of military innovation. Furthermore, the cost of competing imposes strong limitations on how a military organization will pursue the competition. Again, the best example of this phenomenon occurred during the Interwar Revolutions in Mechanization, Aviation, and Information. With one exception, the period was characterized by selective competition among the military organizations of the great powers. For example, for a time Germany, traditionally a land power, became dominant in mechanized air-land operations. Soviet Russia quickly joined that competition to survive. Japan, an island nation, competed in naval aviation and modern amphibious operations, whereas the British developed strong capabilities in strategic aerial bombardment, strategic defenses, and (arguably) modern amphibious operations. Only the United States had the resources to compete in every major area of the interwar military revolution (save strategic defenses, for which it had no need), while simultaneously positioning itself to exploit the coming military revolution in nuclear weapons. Clearly the level and sophistication of human and material assets, and the unique strategic circumstances faced by each competitor, shape how competitors approach and attempt to exploit the opportunities inherent in military revolutions.

Fourth, the historical record suggests that war and revolution in warfare are quite separate entities. True, it took the test of World War II to convince the world's major army organizations (and, one might add, much of the German army itself) that Germany's Blitzkrieg concept could produce great advantages for its practitioners. The war also convinced the U.S. Navy and the Imperial Japanese Navy that aircraft carriers would be the new centerpiece of battle fleets, and convinced everyone to recognize the revolution in naval warfare brought on by the use of submarines. But a confirming war is not essential for military organizations to seize opportunities. For instance, the revolution in naval warfare in the late nineteenth century, from wood, sail, and cannon to steel, turbines, and rifled guns, was widely accepted in the absence of war. The introduction of nuclear weapons is another obvious example of broad acceptance by military organizations that the competitive environment had changed radically.

Fifth, although most militaries will be quick to recognize a competitor's advantage, there are no certainties. Not even war will guarantee that all military organizations will recognize and exploit a military revolution, or understand a revolution in all its dimensions. Thus, in the American Civil War, both sides were relatively quick in exploiting the dramatic gains in strategic mobility and command, control, and communications made possible by the railroad and telegraph. But years passed before either side clearly realized how drastically the appearance of rifled guns and muskets in large numbers had invalidated the Napoleonic battlefield tactics. Again, despite the ex-

perience of World War I, the world's major naval powers tended to discount the effectiveness of strategic warfare conducted by submarines. And even after the German campaign in Poland alerted the world to the potential of the Blitzkrieg, the French army remained remarkably, indeed fatally, resistant to innovation.

More than anything else, it is perceptions of future contingencies and likely enemies that determine whether and when there is full exploitation of the advantages offered by the military revolution. Having a single enemy or challenger may ease a military organization's problem by making it more manageable. For instance, Britain had three major kinds of naval contingencies to prepare for in the interwar period: a war against a major continental power in Europe; a "small war" involving its imperial possessions; and a war against Japan. Conversely, the world's two other major maritime powers, the United States and Japan, saw one another as by far their most prominent challenger, and organized their naval forces around a single contingency—a Pacific War. As it turned out, the Americans and the Japanese exploited the revolution in naval aviation far more proficiently than did the British, in part because of their ability to focus more precisely. In competing during a period of military revolution, it is clearly advantageous to be able to identify not only the nature of future conflict but specific contingencies and competitors. But if that is not possible, a premium should be placed on possessing both sufficient organizational agility and resources to adapt quickly if or when the picture clarifies.

A sixth lesson is that technologies that underwrite a military revolution are often originally developed outside the military sector, and then "imported" and exploited for their military applications. Thus, in the early fourteenth century, the Artillery Revolution was fueled by the discovery that the method being used to cast church bells could also be used for casting artillery—so that, as Bernard Brodie observes, "the early founders, whose task had been to fashion bells which tolled the message of eternal peace . . . contributed unintentionally to the discovery of one of man's most terrible weapons." The development of the railroad and telegraph, which helped to effect the Revolution in Land Warfare, and the rise of the commercial automotive and aircraft industry which led to the Interwar Revolution, are other obvious examples. Indeed, all the military revolutions of the past two centuries are, in a real sense, spinoffs from the Industrial and Scientific Revolutions that have been central, defining processes of modern Western history.

That said, having a substantially inferior economic and industrial base need not be an absolute barrier to competition in a military revolution. During the interwar period, the Imperial Japanese Navy developed a first-rate naval aviation capability and modern amphibious forces, which they employed to devastating effect in the early months of their war with the

United States. The Japanese accomplished this with a gross national product (GNP) that was less than 20 percent (and perhaps closer to 10 percent) of that of the United States, its major naval competitor in the Pacific. Again, following World War II, the Soviet Union, despite a German invasion that destroyed much of its most productive areas, developed with relative speed a nuclear weapon strike force to rival that of the United States. This was accomplished even though the Soviet Union's GNP was much lower than that of the United States and it was burdened by war reconstruction costs and the maintenance of a far larger conventional military force. However, in neither case could this competitive posture be sustained indefinitely against a wealthier, equally determined rival.

In a sense, military revolutions may offer major opportunities for relatively small or "medium-sized" powers to steal a march on greater powers, or even for one great power to challenge an array of its peers. They do so by making it possible to substitute intellectual breakthroughs and organizational innovations for material resources. Examples are plentiful: Flanders exploiting the Infantry Revolution to challenge giant France; the Napoleonic Revolution that allowed France to challenge all of Europe; Germany's innovations (in mechanized air-land operations) during the Interwar Revolution against France, Britain, the Soviet Union, and the United States; and Japan exploiting the Interwar Revolution (in naval aviation) against the United States and Great Britain. Indeed, as Geoffrey Parker has argued, the West's global dominance from 1500 to 1800 is but an instance of this phenomenon writ large.

A seventh and last lesson is that a military revolution does not ineluctably imply a quantum leap in the cost of maintaining military forces. To take one example, the Infantry Revolution of the fourteenth century that replaced heavy cavalry with infantry archers and pikemen actually lowered the cost of maintaining forces. Also, the Nuclear Revolution has been comparatively cheap. Although the ability to employ such weapons to achieve political ends has been much debated, the fact remains that nuclear weapons appeared to offer those who possess them considerable "bang for the buck."[10]

THE CURRENT REVOLUTION

Where are we now? Some believe that a revolution in warfare has already occurred, and cite the recent Gulf War as evidence. American military operations in that war, however, do not meet the historical criteria for revolutionary change. The U.S. forces did not display any dramatic doctrinal changes in that war, nor any major new force structures or military organizations. One indication of how continuous with earlier practice the U.S. performance was is that during the U.S. "Linebacker" air operations in 1972, some nine thousand laser-guided bombs were dropped on Southeast Asia—roughly the same number as were

dropped during the Gulf War. We are in a military revolution—but in its early stages.

What the Gulf War did was show us a glimpse of the potential influence of this revolution on military effectiveness. The Gulf War may be seen as a "precursor war"—an indication of the revolutionary potential of emerging technologies and new military systems. In this respect, it may be similar to the battle of Cambrai that took place on the Western front in November 1917. There the British, for the first time, employed large numbers of planes and tanks in concert. They tried to integrate their operations, and those of the infantry and artillery, through the use of wireless communications. The British attack, spearheaded by nearly five hundred tanks, broke the German lines on a twelve kilometer front within hours.

This breakthrough was as surprising to the senior British leaders as the one-sided Desert Storm operation was to senior American commanders. Indeed, the British had made no plans to exploit such a rapid rupture of the German front. In retrospect, one also realizes that the potential for far greater success at Cambrai was compromised by the immaturity of the new technologies and systems employed (tank breakdowns; limitations on aircraft bomb loads; and on wireless range, portability, and reliability). To extend the analogy, we may be in the "early 1920s" with respect to this military revolution.

Where are we going? Although precise prediction is out of the question, it is possible to speculate with some confidence on the current revolution's general path and nature. It appears certain that it will involve great increases in the ability of military organizations to detect, identify, track, and engage with a high degree of precision and lethality far more targets, over a far greater area, in a far shorter period of time, than was possible in the Cold War era. (No doubt it will also lead to systems and operations designed to degrade or offset these capabilities.) This aspect of the revolution will probably involve an improved ability to understand target systems and their relationship to operational and strategic objectives. The leverage obtained from such a capability is potentially enormous, since knowing *which* subset of targets to strike out of the many identified will be crucial to the effective employment of large numbers of precision weapons.

Furthermore, the growing importance of simulations—from computer-assisted design and manufacturing, to individual training simulators, to simulations of complex military operations involving high levels of systems and architecture integration—may bring about a major increase in the ability of military organizations to extract the full potential of the human and material resources at their disposal.[11]

The transition rate to this revolution's mature stage will be a function of the level of military competition in the international system, the strategies for competition pursued by the competitors, and the four elements comprising a military revolution. It should also be appreciated that, as long as there are multiple competitors exploiting the potential of the emerging military revolution, the revolution itself will be likely to take several paths, if only because of the competitors' varying strategic goals, access to relevant resources, and strategic culture.

WHAT IT MEANS FOR US

Perhaps, as many believe, the United States and the world's other great powers have an opportunity unparalleled in this century to construct an international system that will provide a stable, enduring era of relative peace. Even if there is time and the opportunity is grasped, the question will remain: Will it last? Is it possible to avoid, or even forestall, a resumption of the great-power competition that has been a staple of the international system since the rise of nation-states? If history is any indicator, the United States will, at some point, find itself again in a military competition, in the midst of both a geopolitical and a military revolution. What can the world's dominant military power learn from the general lessons of the West's prior military revolutions?

First, the United States should anticipate that one or more competitors seeking to exploit the coming rapid and dramatic increases in military potential may soon arise. Remembering that monopolies are transient, the United States should ponder how to avoid such a competition, or how to postpone it for as long as possible. Or how to win it if necessary.

Second, continued American technological and operational leadership is by no means assured. During the Interwar Revolution, Great Britain held an initial dominant position in mechanized air-land and naval aviation operations that was quickly forfeited. Even when countries will not be able to compete in the full spectrum of military capabilities, some of them, by specializing, will become formidable niche competitors.

Third, it is by no means certain that competitors will follow the same path as the United States. Different security requirements and objectives, strategic cultures, geostrategic postures, and economic situations will likely lead the competitors in different directions. Although there are those who believe that, given our current advantage, this military revolution will only progress at a pace and direction that the United States decides to give it, history suggests that this is a dangerous delusion.

Fourth, it is not clear that the United States can rely on the cost of competition acting as an effective barrier to others. Although most military revolutions have raised the cost of "doing business," sometimes dramatically, there have been significant exceptions. In terms of direct and initial costs, the Nuclear Revolution is one of these exceptions, and, with proliferation very much at issue, this revolution is still with us. If much of the increase in military effectiveness in this emerging revolution stems from the so-called "Information Revolution," which has dramatically lowered the cost of information-related technologies,

competitors may find the barriers to competition relatively low. And given the history of military organizations' adapting technologies initially developed in the commercial sector, the United States' ability to restrict access to these technologies, in the manner it attempted with nuclear fission and missile technologies, may be marginal at best.

In summary, the lessons of earlier revolutions seem to contradict much of the conventional wisdom with respect to the United States' prospective competitive military position. In a revolutionary epoch, long-term U.S. military dominance is not preordained. Indeed, one could argue that the prospects for continued U.S. dominance would be greater in a military regime that was entering early maturity, rather than in its early, most dynamic stages. If America wants to avoid or delay a resumption of military competition, it will have to identify a strategy for that purpose and pursue it energetically. If a competition cannot be avoided, the United States will begin with strong competitive advantages in terms of technology and military systems. As we have seen, however, it is typically those military organizations that are highly innovative and adaptive that seem to compete best in periods of military revolution. In those terms, it has yet to be clearly demonstrated that the U.S. military should be sanguine regarding its ability to respond effectively to the challenge that this revolution will likely pose.

NOTES

1. Clifford J. Rogers, "The Military Revolutions of the Hundred Years' War," *The Journal of Military History* (April 1993): 241–78.

2. At the Battle of Crecy, for example, the French lost 1,542 knights and lords, and suffered over 10,000 casualties among crossbowmen and other support troops, whereas the English lost two knights, one squire, forty other men-at-arms and archers, and "a few dozen Welsh." Bernard Brodie and Fawn M. Brodie, *From Crossbow to H-Bomb* (Bloomington, Ind.: Indiana University Press, 1973), 39–40.

3. Corning involves mixing wet powder and allowing it to dry into kernels. It is purported to have been three times as powerful as the sifted form, and considerably less expensive. Other improvements included the introduction of the two-wheel gun carriage, trunnions, and iron cannonballs. See Rogers, "Military Revolutions," 269–71.

4. Francesco Guicciardini, *History of Italy* (New York: Washington Square Press, 1964), 153.

5. Rogers also notes that, although the technology and military weapon system had been perfected, when military organizations failed either to restructure effectively, whether through a lack of funds or organizational insight, they failed to achieve the benefits of a revolutionary increase in military effectiveness. For example, when the siege train was relatively weak, as was the case during the sieges of Guise (1424), Ferte-Bernard (1424), Torey Castle (1429), Chateau Gallard (1429), Laigny-sur-Marne (1432), and Harfleur (1440), the siege dragged on for from between 3 months to over a year.

6. Brodie and Brodie, *Crossbow to H-Bomb*, 64; and Geoffrey Parker, "The Western Way of War" (lecture presented at the Johns Hopkins SAIS, February 17, 1994), 87. Parker goes on to note that the galley, although displaced as the centerpiece of naval warfare, did manage to survive and even, on occasion, prevail into the eighteenth century.

7. Gustavus Adolphus actually increased marginally the ratio of pike to shot compared to the Dutch. However, he did it in such a way as to promote the integration of pike, shot, artillery, and cavalry into combined arms operations. See Michael Roberts, "The Military Revolution, 1560–1660," in *Essays in Swedish History* (London: Weidenfeld & Nicholson, 1967), 195–225; Geoffrey Parker also argues that a third military revolution (or perhaps more accurately, a third element of the military revolution) involved the radical increase in the size of armies that occurred in the latter part of the seventeenth century (between 1672 and 1710).

8. Brodie and Brodie, *Crossbow to H-Bomb,* 136. Shelby Foote observes that the Sharp repeating rifles employed by Union troops late in the war gave a cavalry force of 12,000 more firepower than an entire corps of infantry. See Shelby Foote, *The Civil War: A Narrative,* Vol. III (New York: Vintage Books, 1986), 872.

9. For a discussion of the early period of this revolution, see Bernard Brodie, *Sea Power in the Machine Age* (Princeton, N.J.: Princeton University Press, 1942), 48, 52,

66–68, 75–76, 195; Terrence R. Fehner, *National Responses to Technological Innovations in Weapon Systems, 1815 to the Present* (Rockville, Md.: History Associates, 1986), 7–14; and William H. McNeill, *The Pursuit of Power: Technology, Armed Force, and Society Since A.D. 1000* (Chicago: University of Chicago Press, 1982), 227–28, 239, 291–92.

10. Although this point is often made, its acceptance is far from universal. For example, the United States is just now beginning to face up to the enormous environmental costs associated with its nuclear weapons program. The cleanup costs are estimated to range from $150 billion to $200 billion over 30 years. The situation in the former Soviet states is considered to be far worse. See Government Accounting Office, *DoE Management: Consistent Cleanup Indemnification is Needed,* GAO/RCED-93-167 (Washington, D.C.: Government Accounting Office, July 1993). Still, it is not clear that long-term environmental costs will weigh heavily with the rulers of most of the countries that are now actively pursuing a nuclear capability.

11. For a more complete discussion, see Andrew F. Krepinevich, "La Révolution à Venir dans la Nature des Conflits: Une Perspective Americaine," in *Relflexions sur la Nature des Futurs Systèmes De Defense,* ed. Alain Baer (Paris: Ecole Polytechnique, November 1993); and Andrew F. Krepinevich, "Une Révolution dans les Conflits: une Perspective Americaine," *Defense Nationale* 50 (January 1994).

CHOOSING A STRATEGY

RICHARD L. KUGLER AND HANS BINNENDIJK

What strategy should guide the transformation of U.S. military forces in the years ahead? What basic philosophy, goals, and actions should animate the process of changing U.S. forces so that they are prepared for the future? These weighty questions require answers. Transformation is too important to be left to chance or to the vagaries of politics. It is a dynamic that can be pursued in more ways than one and that can succeed or fail. It definitely requires a guiding hand. To help shed light on this issue, we begin by exploring the nature of transformation and the U.S. historical experience with it. We then analyze key strategies for pursuing transformation and present a set of new operational concepts for carrying it out.

The Department of Defense intends to pursue transformation in meaningful ways, but a debate is raging over the best strategy for doing so. The debate is polarized between two quite different strategies:

one evolutionary, the other revolutionary. Focused mostly on the coming decade, the evolutionary "steady as you go" strategy proposes to transform in ways that, although important, are small in scope, slow-paced, and limited in vision. Although this strategy seeks to acquire weapons now emerging from the research and development (R&D) pipeline, it does not invest heavily in futurist technologies, and it proposes mostly modest changes to legacy force structures, platforms, and operations. By contrast, the revolutionary "leap ahead" strategy proposes to move in faster, bolder, and riskier ways. Focused mainly on 10 to 20 years from now and beyond, it wants to skip emerging weapons in favor of exotic technologies, while carrying out radical changes in U.S. forces and doctrines. A responsible case can be made for each strategy, but the tensions between them must be resolved if transformation is to unfold smoothly and not be ripped apart by two incompatible visions at war

Richard L. Kugler and Hans Binnendijk, "Choosing a Strategy," in Transforming the American Military, *ed. Hans Binnendijk (Washington, D.C.: National Defense University Press, 2002), 57–87. Public domain.*

with one another. Embracing one strategy at the expense of the other could leave the armed forces shortchanged in the future—either by not changing them enough or by changing them too much in the wrong ways.

Instead, we suggest that the United States should pursue a sensible blend of both strategies: a purposeful and measured transformation. This strategy aspires to keep U.S. forces highly ready and capable in the near term, to enhance their flexibility and adaptability in the midterm, and to guide their acquisition of new systems prudently in the long term. Although this strategy relies on emerging weapons to modernize U.S. forces, it urges vigorous experimentation with new technologies as they become available. It seeks ways to reorganize and reengineer traditional force structures so that they can perform joint operations more effectively in the information age. It also employs new operational concepts to guide the creation of future combat capabilities that meet the challenges ahead.

The transformation strategy that we urge is neither a slow crawl ahead nor a blind leap into the distant future but instead, a deliberate and well-planned march into the twenty-first century. It offers a way to balance continuity and change so that American forces remain superior in the coming years, while they gain the new capabilities needed to handle a widening spectrum of contingencies, missions in new geographic locations, and growing asymmetric threats. Above all, this strategy reflects awareness that transformation should be neither taken for granted nor pursued in simplistic ways. Because it is so vital, it demands careful analysis and wise judgment.

Modern military forces are complex institutions that can be thrown off kilter by imprudent meddling. Worse, they can be badly damaged if they are reshaped to fit some new, single-minded design that does not turn out as hoped. In transforming U.S. forces, the goal is to strengthen them for dealing with a complex and dangerous world, not simply to take chances in the mistaken belief that radical approaches are necessarily better than tried-and-true practices. New ideas should always be subjected to careful appraisals of their consequences—both good and bad—before they are adopted. If the dilemma is deciding whether to mimic a timid ostrich or an aggressive hawk, the answer is to behave like an owl, wisely seeking an intelligent blend of continuity and change, at a pace that is fast enough to be meaningful yet slow enough to be managed effectively. A purposeful and measured transformation is a strategy for an owl.

BRINGING TRANSFORMATION INTO FOCUS

The difficult challenge facing the Department of Defense is to pursue transformation while also attending to the rest of its agenda, which includes keeping the armed forces ready for near-term crises and balancing its investment priorities. Transformation is clearly important, but what exactly does it mean? Transformation is often used as a rallying cry to promote one particular theory of defense reform, but this is a misleading use of the term. Official DoD documents use the term in a generic sense rather than as an endorsement of any particular approach. The dictionary does likewise; it defines "transformation" as a substantial change in appearance, nature, or character. Changes of this sort can occur in more ways than one, but for a true transformation of a military to occur, it must be guided by coherent rules or concepts, and it must produce alterations in structures and functions that are major, not minor.

Normally, transformation occurs in response to new strategic conditions abroad or to changes bubbling up from within the military, or—as is the case today—to a combination of both. It involves a process of change that is more profound than normal, steady-state modernization, which occurs as new weapons and capabilities evolve in the natural course of events, with mostly incremental consequences. Rather than business as usual, transformation represents an effort to prepare military forces to be different than in the past and to wage war differently as well. Almost always, military forces are trying to improve themselves, but they seek to transform themselves only at widely spaced intervals, when new technologies and requirements make the step desirable, necessary, or unavoidable.

Some proponents interpret transformation mainly as a process of acquiring new weapons platforms to replace the tank, fighter plane, or aircraft carrier. Although some traditional platforms may need replacing or modification, this interpretation of transformation is too restrictive and serves one particular reform agenda. A military establishment might, in fact, retain its legacy platforms while changing in so many other areas (e.g., doctrine, organization, operations) that it emerges as heavily transformed. Indeed, this has been the common approach to transformation pursued by the U.S. military, which has undergone several waves of major changes in the past 60 years without switching platforms. A good example is the U.S. Navy. Two decades ago, it rejected calls for converting to small carriers or even replacing carriers with land-based aircraft for maritime missions. It was widely accused of a hidebound unwillingness to break free from the past, but it changed in so many other ways, including technology and doctrine, that it became transformed in warfighting capabilities.

In today's setting, transformation is aptly portrayed as a wide-ranging process of adjusting to the imperatives and opportunities of the information age. Such a transformation often begins with the arrival of new technologies, such as modern computers and information warfare systems, but it does not end there. Depending upon how far it is pursued, it can lead to changes throughout a military establishment; it might involve new platforms, but it is often carried out in a variety of different ways. To a degree, the process is driven by its own momentum, but military establishments have a wide range of choice in determining the breadth and pace of transformation. This discretion should be guided by a transformation strategy: it is important in determining how the process unfolds and critical to its effectiveness.

Transformation does not boil down to a choice between doing nothing and changing everything or between crawling ahead slowly and leaping forward at blinding speed. Transformation can be partial yet meaningful. For example, it might fully alter only 10 to 20 percent of the posture, while modestly changing most of the remainder, and can still produce a big improvement in combat capabilities. It could also be phased to unfold gradually, as a choreographed sequence of events, and to build on its achievements steadily as it unfolds. We argue for a purposeful and measured transformation anchored in such a vision of a careful, well-planned process. It starts with partial but pivotal changes and then expands to pursue broader departures as they prove their worth.

As Table 5 suggests, transformation can take place within three categories of "inputs" (that is, the combat forces and their assets) and a fourth category of "outputs" (the military capabilities and combat performance of the forces). Each has multiple important subcategories. Transformation might have a significant impact on some, most, or all of these categories and subcategories. The critical relationship is that between inputs and outputs: between force characteristics and battlefield performance. A big change

in one force characteristic, but not others, might produce little impact on battlefield performance. This transformation would be ranked as minor. By contrast, a large number of modest changes in multiple force characteristics could produce big changes in battlefield performance. This would be a truly major transformation, even though its surface manifestations might appear minor.

A partial, limited transformation could occur if a military force acquires new technologies (e.g., new command, control, communications, computers, intelligence, surveillance, and reconnaissance [C4ISR] systems; smart munitions) but does not change in other significant ways. A more ambitious transformation might replace old weapons with new weapons but not acquire different platforms. An example is buying new artillery tubes or jet fighters whose capabilities permit novel tactical uses.

The combination of new technologies and weapons might lead to new operational doctrines for employing forces on the battlefield but not produce major alterations in force structures and organizations, such as the mix of divisions and air wings. Alternatively, a military might alter its structures and doctrines but not its weapons. As a result of such changes, a military force might improve greatly in combat power and versatility, enough to transform what counts: its operational style, battlefield performance, and ability to win wars. Yet to the casual observer, its

Table 5

Components of Defense Transformation

Inputs: Transformation of force characteristics
Transformation of technologies and weapons
   Information systems and grids
   Technologies and subcomponents
   Legacy weapon systems
   New platforms
   Smart munitions
Transformation of force structures
   Combat force structures and organizations
   Logistic support and mobility
   Command structures and command, control, communications; computers;
      intelligence; surveillance; and reconnaissance systems
   Domestic infrastructure and bases
   Overseas presence, bases, and facilities assets
Transformation of force operations
   Networking of forces
   Joint doctrines
   Service doctrines
   Regional commander-in-chief's operation plan and campaign plans
   Interoperability with allies

Outputs: Transformation of capabilities and battlefield performance
Improved capacity for swift deployment
Improved firepower, maneuverability, survivability, sustainability
Better capacity to perform missions and operations, old and new
Capacity to support wider spectrum of strategies and contingencies
Improved adaptability: Capacity to perform strategic U-turns adeptly

---

outward appearance might not be much different from its predecessor.

A more profound transformation occurs when a military force employs new technologies and weapons to make major changes in platforms, such as replacing manned fighters with robot-piloted aircraft or heavy tanks with lightweight, wheeled vehicles; in force structures, such as replacing carrier battlegroups with patrol boats and submarines, or armored divisions with brigades that operate only deep-strike missiles and attack helicopters; or in operations. Such changes would greatly alter the force posture's internal characteristics, including its physical structure and outward appearances, as well as its battlefield performance. Sweeping changes of this sort, which occur infrequently, involve radically different technologies, forces, and approaches to warfighting and exemplify defense transformation at its most dramatic. But they are not the only type of transformation to occur or to be sought. The limited, partial transformations occur more often, but when they elevate military capabilities or alter the face of war, they are portentous developments in themselves.

Because any ambitious transformation, either partial or whole, cannot be carried out overnight, its timelines are important. A partial transformation is normally pursued in the near term and midterm, over a period of 5 to 10 years or so. This tends to be the case if it employs technologies and weapons that already exist or will be procured during this period and if it does not undertake significant alterations in force structures and platforms. It may set the stage for a bigger transformation later, or it might instead be self-contained. A wholesale transformation typically takes longer to carry out—15 to 20 years or more—and produces radically different forces that meet new strategic needs in the long haul. A key feature of a radical transformation is that it may deliberately bypass improvements in the near term and midterm to pursue long-term goals. Especially if resources are limited, partial changes in the midterm might not be a transitional step but, instead, a barrier to achieving bigger changes in the distant future.

The specific features of both partial and wholesale approaches are crucial in determining how the future is to unfold. Because these two approaches have different timelines, in theory, they can interlock together in supportive ways, with a partial transformation laying the foundation for bigger changes later, as new technologies emerge. Such complementarity is not, however, automatic or easily achieved. Indeed, partial and whole transformations can be competitive, with each consuming so many resources and energies that it stymies the other. This presents defense planners with hard choices. Complementarity must be deliberately sought by designing these two approaches to work together.

Regardless of whether the transformation is partial or whole, it is a means to an end, not an end in itself. Its success is measured by its capacity to produce better forces, greater capabilities, and higher performance, not by the extent to which it overturns past practices. As a result, it must be pursued with strategic goals and coordinated plans foremost in mind. No military establishment can expect to remain current in modern warfare by sticking its head in the sand like an ostrich, denying change in the hope that it will go away. But a full-scale hawkish transformation should be pursued only when it makes strategic sense, not in response to a mystical faith that radical change always begets big progress.

HISTORICAL LEGACY: TRANSFORMATION STRATEGIES IN THE INDUSTRIAL ERA

Nuclear Transformation: The First Two Decades of the Cold War

Shortly after World War II ended, the Cold War broke out. Because the conflict with the Soviet Union was initially political, the United States disarmed and also slowed the process of transforming its military forces with new technologies and doctrines. When the Korean War erupted in 1950, jet aircraft were used for the first time in large numbers, but otherwise, that conflict was waged with weapons, forces, and doctrines inherited from World War II. The big change came after the Korean armistice was signed, when the Eisenhower administration decided to nuclearize the American defense strategy. This effort was driven by three goals that reinforced one another: strengthening U.S. forces by equipping them with nuclear firepower, deterring Soviet aggression in Europe at a time when NATO conventional forces were too weak to halt a major attack, and buying security on the cheap because nuclear weapons were less expensive than conventional forces. The result was to propel the armed forces into a wholesale transformation driven by a single-minded design anchored in exciting new technologies and weapons systems. This ambitious effort was carried out in just a few years: never before had U.S. forces been changed so totally and quickly under a single organizing principle. This design concept proved short-lived, however; it produced the wrong forces for the new strategic circumstances that were to unfold in the 1960s.

To carry out its strategy of massive retaliation, the Eisenhower administration procured a large force of more than 2,000 nuclear-armed strategic bombers, with emphasis on the B-52. Later, it also started to deploy intercontinental ballistic missiles (ICBMs) and submarine-launched ballistic missiles (SLBMs), which were intended to supplement the bombers, not replace them. It authorized deployment of 7,000 tactical nuclear weapons to Europe to permit NATO to use rapid escalation to halt aggression. As a logical byproduct of this effort, it worked with the military services to reconfigure their conventional combat forces for nuclear war. The Air Force was especially nuclearized. Its new fighters of the 1950s were designed mostly to shoot down enemy nuclear bombers and to conduct tactical nuclear strikes in the enemy's rear areas. The Army was also affected; its new

Pentomic divisions were so tailored for nuclear operations that they could not mount much of a conventional defense. The Navy was similarly influenced, as its carriers, aircraft, and other combatants were redesigned for nuclear strike operations at sea or on land. The consequence was a gleaming new U.S. military posture, primed for nuclear war, but incapable of fighting serious conventional wars. The same was true for European forces in NATO.

Almost overnight, however, massive retaliation was invalidated as an all-purpose strategy when the Soviet Union surprised the West by making rapid progress nuclearizing its own strategy and forces. By the early 1960s, it was poised to begin procuring large numbers of ICBMs and SLBMs; it had already begun to deploy several hundred medium- and intermediate-range ballistic missiles targeted on Western Europe and to distribute 6,000 tactical nuclear warheads to its ground and air forces. The effect was to cast a bright spotlight on the Warsaw Pact's imposing superiority in the conventional war arena. The Soviet nuclear buildup meant that the United States and its allies became less able to deter conventional aggression by threatening nuclear escalation. The latter step now became too risky, because the Soviets were capable of retaliating with devastating nuclear counterblows. The Berlin crises and Cuban missile crisis exposed the dangers inherent in this situation. Alarmed, the Kennedy administration felt compelled to pursue a major rebuilding of U.S. conventional forces to deter nonnuclear attack and to broaden its options. All four services were suddenly instructed to reverse course by retailoring their forces, weapons, and doctrines for traditional warfare. In addition, the Kennedy administration had to initiate a bruising debate with the European allies to persuade them to abandon massive retaliation in favor of a new strategy of flexible response, one that mandated an expensive buildup of their own conventional forces. For both the United States and NATO, the 1960s were largely spent trying to recover from the setbacks of their nuclear transformation during the previous decade.

Because the reform process was far from complete by the mid-1960s, the United States fought the Vietnam War with forces that were halfway between a design for nuclear war and one for conventional war. For the most part, U.S. forces were well equipped and enjoyed major technological advantages over the enemy, yet they suffered from some liabilities of the past. For example, U.S. air forces were not well designed for conventional bombardment missions, and ground forces lacked special logistic assets for expeditionary operations. Smart munitions did not appear until late in the conflict. Many innovations had to be made as the war unfolded in the use of helicopters, forward air controllers, and sensors, for example. More important, forces from the four services were not well prepared for joint operations and often encountered trouble working together. Beyond this, overall U.S. military strategy was flawed. Victory could not be achieved through gradual escalation and sustained attrition warfare against a stubborn North Vietnamese enemy that refused to be driven from the battlefield. U.S. forces returned from Vietnam frustrated by their inability to translate sophisticated technology into decisive victory, but in the agonized political climate of the early 1970s, little was done to recover from the damage, much less to prepare for the future.

Building Modern Transformed Forces: The Past Quarter Century

In the mid- to late 1970s, heightened Cold War tensions helped propel U.S. military forces back along the path of rehabilitation and progress. Several factors combined together to accelerate the process. Key was the worried atmosphere that permeated the Department of Defense, which translated into a desire to improve U.S. forces in big ways. Senior civilians helped set the stage by urging innovation, and senior military officers, determined to recover from Vietnam, shared the sentiment. The Carter administration began to set strategic priorities by focusing on NATO and, later, on the Persian Gulf. The Reagan defense buildup of the 1980s provided the funds needed to fuel an ambitious effort to enlarge U.S. forces, improve their training and readiness, and procure new weapons. New technologies emerging from the R&D process enabled the U.S. military to modernize with an entirely new generation of weapon systems that were significantly better than their predecessors. The services began developing vigorous new doctrines for battlefield operations that promised to take full advantage of the weapons being procured. The result was a process of fast modernization and enhanced readiness that, by the late 1980s, had strengthened U.S. forces significantly. Although force structures and platforms did not change a great deal, major improvements were made in munitions and sensors, command and control systems, missiles and other technologies, doctrine, and operations.

Where the nuclear transformation of the 1950s had been driven by a single design, this transformation was quite different. Its guiding theme was better conventional forces, but its varied and broad-based efforts were driven by many different designs and theories, not all of them initially well coordinated with each other. A number of innovative ideas came from outside the services and even outside the Department of Defense. The four services were highly influential; each often marched to the beat of its own drummers, competing with the others while fighting off unwelcome challenges to its traditional structures, and yet responding to new technologies and doctrines emerging from within its ranks and elsewhere. Meanwhile, the defense industries produced new technologies and weapons at an often bewildering speed in ways that steadily broadened the range of operational choices available to the services, sometimes pushing them in unanticipated directions. A good example is the cruise missile, which appeared as new technology bubbled upward, rather than resulting from a new strategy imposed from the top down. By contrast, the new fighters and tanks were products of a strategic design, but when their capabilities became apparent, they were employed to create fresh, unanticipated doctrines.

Strenuous efforts were made in the Planning, Programming, and Budgeting System and the joint planning arena—by many authorities in the Office of Secretary of Defense, the joint staff, the services, and the regional military commands—to discipline this transformation and guide it in sound directions. But even so, its chief characteristic was pluralism in its ideas and organizations, reflecting the dynamics of economic markets and democratic politics, rather than control from the top by any single plan. Although this process was turbulent and confusing, it worked. It produced the best military forces in world history: transformed forces that were well aligned with new directions in defense strategy for the 1990s, not out of phase with them.

This process worked effectively, despite its lack of central control, because it was guided by a set of new operational concepts developed by the Pentagon and the armed services as the transformation was getting under way. These new concepts not only provided direction to each service but also imparted a sense of direction to joint planning and overall U.S. military strategy:

- "Power projection and rapid reinforcement" called for a better capacity to deploy U.S. forces swiftly to Europe, Asia, and the Persian Gulf

- "Maritime supremacy" called for the Navy to switch from defensive missions to offensive operations aimed at sweeping the seas of enemy blue-water navies

- "Expeditionary operations" encouraged the Marine Corps to evolve beyond amphibious assault to become a more flexible, multipurpose force

- "Multimission air operations" led the Air Force to broaden beyond air defense to pursue interdiction, close air support, and other contributions to the land battle

- "Operational art" led the Army to move away from linear defense toward mobile reserves, maneuver, and powerful counterattacks

- "AirLand battle" provided a concept for coordinating ground and air missions in attacking enemy forces

It is noteworthy that the successful transformation orchestrated by these concepts was carried out in the face of a determined Soviet buildup of its antiaccess and area-denial capabilities, aimed at preserving the Warsaw Pact predominance in Europe. The Soviet navy acquired a blue-water capacity with Backfire bombers, attack submarines, and missile-carrying surface combatants to challenge NATO for control of the North Atlantic. On the European continent, the Soviets created a huge force of theater missiles and tactical nuclear systems, 500 medium bombers, 4,200 combat aircraft, and nearly 100 heavily armed divisions capable of a Blitzkrieg offensive. Rather than respond to this threat by resorting to a standoff defense strategy from the sea, the United States and its European allies asserted their strategic interests by pursuing a stalwart forward defense of NATO borders. The result was a sustained peacetime competition between the two military alliances that saw NATO strengthen its position, ultimately checkmating the growing threat and establishing a robust defense posture. Had war erupted in the early 1970s, the Warsaw Pact would have been expected to win, but if it had occurred in the late 1980s, NATO would have acquitted itself far better and perhaps won the contest. This dramatic change in the force balance may well have played a major role in the Soviet Union's decision to throw in the towel in 1990. By any measure, the U.S. and NATO military buildup accomplished its political and strategic purposes.

Because U.S. defense strategy in the Cold War's final stages became increasingly global, a key strategic innovation was better strategic-mobility assets for rapid reinforcement. Largely a product of civilian leadership, the acquisition of better airlift, sealift, and prepositioning permitted faster power projection and overseas deployment from the United States, thereby contributing greatly to improved force balances in Europe and the Persian Gulf. The U.S. Navy, shaking off challenges to its traditional force structures, built new carriers, F-14 and F-18 fighters, Aegis defenses, cruise missiles, surface combatants, and submarines. As a result, it rebuffed the Soviet threat and emerged as dominating the North Atlantic and other seas as well. Meanwhile, the Marine Corps broadened beyond traditional amphibious assault missions to perform a wide variety of other ground and air operations. The Air Force acquisition of new F-15 and F-16 combat aircraft, the A-10 tank-buster, airborne warning and control systems (AWACs) and joint surveillance and target attack radar systems (JSTARS) command and control capabilities, improved avionics, smart munitions, and cruise missiles greatly enhanced its capacity to win the air battle, perform strategic bombardment against enemy rear areas, and contribute close air support to the ground battle. The Army's goal was to transform its infantry-heavy forces from the Vietnam era into a modern force of armored and mechanized units. Patriot missile batteries, which replaced the I-Hawk system, provided greatly improved air defense; improved artillery systems and better munitions significantly enhanced its ability to generate large volumes of accurate, lethal fires; Abrams tanks and Bradley infantry fighting vehicles provided the enhanced tactical mobility, survivability, and firepower to permit the Army to transition away from stationary linear defense to mobile maneuvers and mastery of the operational art. The combination of stronger air forces and ground forces greatly enhanced the capacity of the U.S. military not only to defend against strong attacks, but also to pursue offensive operations against them.

The transformation of U.S. forces was accompanied by efforts to upgrade allied forces in Europe and to strengthen alliance-wide interoperability. The acquisition of new combat aircraft and naval combatants contributed more to the growing combat power of NATO than is commonly realized. The U.S. improvements led the way by blending together continuity and change to create stronger forces with a growing capacity for joint operations. The extent of these gains in modern warfare was put on display in the Persian Gulf War in early 1991, when U.S. forces led a large, multinational coalition to inflict decisive defeat on a well-armed Iraqi adversary. The Desert Storm success was massive, but it was no accident, and 10 to 15 years earlier, it would not have been possible to such a degree. The same was true of the many other successful American crisis operations that occurred in the 1990s, including in Kosovo, where U.S. airpower won a war virtually on its own.

This U.S. military transformation was heavily influenced by new technologies and weapons, but it was anchored in efforts to make effective use of traditional force structures and platforms and in concerted attention to training, readiness, and skilled personnel. It focused on acquiring capabilities that were linked to well-understood operational concepts that reflected a clear understanding of modern war's political and military dynamics. Overall, it was not an impulsive effort, but instead, the culmination of a long, well-conceived, well-funded transformation lasting over a decade. Its positive impact on U.S. defense preparedness is the central military lesson of the Cold War's final climactic years.

MANAGING CHANGE: TRANSFORMATION FOR THE INFORMATION ERA

Today, the U.S. military stands on the brink of another transformation of special importance. In the early twenty-first century, warfare is in transition from the industrial age to the information age. Managing this transition effectively is vital to preserving American military superiority. The historical lessons of the past can be drawn upon to help illuminate the path ahead. Nonetheless, the transformation strategy chosen for the coming period must make sense for reasons of its own.

The imperatives of transformation are clearest when a military finds itself lacking modern weapons and facing strong enemies capable of defeating it in battle. The opposite situation exists today. The U.S. military is easily the world's strongest, armed with weapons and capabilities that far overshadow those of any potential rival. The challenge facing it, therefore, is not one of scrambling its way to the top, but of staying there. The absence of a clearly identified threat against which to counterbalance, or some other clear strategic guidepost to follow, means that the

United States will need to set its own relative standard regarding how its forces should change. Setting such standards is difficult because the future of defense technology and warfare is so obscure. Nobody doubts that major changes are in the wind. Several decades from now, U.S. forces will be very different from those of today. But in the coming 10 to 20 years, the proper mix will be hard to determine and will shift over time. For these reasons, crafting a sound transformation strategy requires making tough judgments about how the process of change should unfold.

STRATEGIC FRAMEWORK FOR TRANSFORMATION IN THE QUADRENNIAL DEFENSE REVIEW

A principal motive for transforming U.S. forces is to take advantage of the changes unfolding in military technology, doctrine, and weapon systems. Equally important, global security affairs are changing in ways that are rapidly altering future U.S. military requirements. Globalization is making the democratic community more prosperous and secure, especially in Europe, but also in Northeast Asia, the two geographic focal points of U.S. defense strategy during the Cold War. As the Pentagon's Quadrennial Defense Review (QDR) 2001 points out, however, globalization and other dynamics are creating a vast southern belt of instability that stretches from the Balkans and the Middle East to the East Asian littoral. There and elsewhere, the danger does not derive from any single threat, such as a new superpower rival, but rather from troubled economic conditions and chaotic security affairs, which combine to produce a diverse set of threats. One threat comes from regional rogues, such as Iraq, that are willing to pursue aggression against their neighbors. Another threat comes from terrorists, their sponsors, and the anti-Western ideologies motivating them. A third threat comes from the ongoing proliferation of weapons of mass destruction (WMDs) and lethal conventional weapons. A fourth comes from struggles over energy supplies and other natural resources, including water. A fifth springs from the upsurge of ethnic warfare in troubled states. A sixth threat might come from China, should it pursue geopolitical aims in ways that menace U.S. interests and regional stability.[1]

According to the QDR 2001, this multiplicity of dangers and threats means that the spectrum of operations facing U.S. forces is steadily widening. Although being prepared for major theater wars (MTWs) will remain important, contingencies at the lower end of the spectrum have been steadily increasing in recent years. These include ethnic wars, counterterrorist conflicts, limited crisis interventions, and peacekeeping. The future may also witness wars at the higher end of the spectrum, including against WMD-armed opponents, coalitions of countries opposed to the United States, or perhaps even China. The prospect of a widening spectrum of conflict, better-armed enemies, and operations in new, unfamiliar geographic locations promises to confront

U.S. forces with stressful demands and requirements unlike those faced since the Cold War ended. Whereas U.S. force operations during the Cold War were mostly positional and continental, they seem destined to become more mobile and littoral. Indeed, the U.S. overseas presence is likely to see its mission shift from local border defense of allies to serving as regional hubs of power projection in ways that interlock with forces deploying from the continental United States.

As the QDR 2001 reveals, the old preoccupation with being prepared to wage two concurrent MTWs is giving way to a more flexible construct. The new emphasis will be on maintaining multiple capabilities, not on dealing with single threats or contingencies. A new force-sizing standard apparently will call upon U.S. forces to be capable of conquering enemy territory in a single big MTW, while mounting a stalwart defense in a second regional conflict and carrying out multiple smaller-scale contingencies (SSCs). This standard and related calculations will likely generate requirements for forces similar in size to those of today, but with the capacity to operate successfully in a wider set of circumstances than was found in the regional wars in the Persian Gulf and Korea. Regional commanders-in-chief (CINCs) will be called upon to design a diverse set of operation plans, campaign plans, and strike packages so that they can handle the widening array of new challenges in their areas of operations. Forces stationed in the United States will need to become capable of deploying responsively to support these CINCs and their missions. Whereas earlier CINC force operations tended to be small or large, they will increasingly require medium-sized packages, whose mix of ground, naval, and air forces is tailored to the situation at hand.

The new U.S. defense strategy articulated by the QDR 2001 mandates that forces remain highly capable in the near term and beyond. U.S. forces will need to be well trained, highly ready, well equipped, sustainable, and able to carry out modern joint doctrine. To retain a sizable margin of superiority over adversaries, they will need to improve their capabilities in these areas as the future unfolds. They will probably not require a breakneck qualitative buildup akin to the Reagan era, but they will require the steady improvements that accompany robust modernization and preparedness efforts. The increase needed in any single year might not be large, but over the course of a decade or so, the total increase could be substantial—forces that are perhaps 25 to 50 percent stronger than they are now. Meeting this goal will require persistent efforts by the Department of Defense, adequate funding, and innovation.

As the QDR 2001 states, the future will require more than the steady amassing of greater combat capabilities in a technical and mechanical sense. It also will require that U.S. forces become highly adaptable, flexible, and agile. This will especially be the case in the midterm and beyond, when current global conditions could mutate in major ways. Rather than being rigidly fixed for a narrow set of contingencies and response patterns, U.S. forces will need to be able to operate in a wide set of crisis scenarios and to respond in diverse ways that change greatly from case to case. They will need to be able to react adroitly to surprising events, to shift gears abruptly, and to perform strategic U-turns gracefully. These characteristics necessitate that U.S. forces provide a flexible portfolio of assets and modular building blocks that can be combined and recombined to meet fluctuating situations and operational needs.

These emerging requirements, and the strategic conditions that generate them, mean that transformation cannot be single dimensional in its thinking. Only a few years ago, transformation was seen in mostly linear terms, as an exercise in balancing readiness, modernization, and futurist technological innovation. This agenda will remain important, but emerging global security conditions necessitate that the transformation also be carried out in ways that respond to new strategic challenges, missions, and international imperatives. The act of designing U.S. forces to handle changes that both bubble up from below and emerge from abroad greatly complicates how the transformation must be planned. Transformation, moreover, cannot focus on only one time frame or strategic goal; it must ensure that U.S. forces become steadily more capable from the near term onward, acquire greater flexibility and adaptability for the midterm, and absorb the exotic new technologies, weapons, and doctrines that will become available in the long term. Achieving all three of these goals necessitates a transformation strategy that is sophisticated, balanced, and multifaceted. The looming challenge will be to carry out this complex transformation with the resources that will be available, to set priorities in sensible ways, and to distribute shortfalls so that the risks in any single period, and in any functional area, are properly balanced.

"STEADY AS YOU GO" STRATEGY

A "steady as you go" transformation strategy would aim to achieve a slow, evolutionary march into the future. Inspired by the time-honored slogan, "If it ain't broke, don't fix it," it is anchored in the premise that because U.S. forces are already the world's best by a wide margin, they do not need a major facelift or overhaul. Instead, this strategy is based on the assumption that U.S. forces require only a gradual increase in capabilities that comes from steady-state modernization without big, hasty changes in platforms, structures, and operational concepts. Under this strategy, transformation will remain an element of DoD planning, but not the most important venture. Barring a major upsurge of new funds for acquisition, its pace will be similar to that of recent years. A decade or so from now, U.S. forces will be better armed than today, but their core features are likely to be mostly similar to now.

Although this strategy may not inspire visionaries, it has several advantages. It is manageable because it does not overburden the Department of Defense.

It allows U.S. forces to maintain their high readiness and to modernize gradually without subjecting them to an avalanche of difficult changes. It is prudent because it does not bet the future on risky, unproven ideas that could have negative unintended consequences. This strategy also is feasible because it can be carried out with the resources that realistically can be expected to be available. It will command the support of the military services and CINCs. It will allow the services to purchase significant numbers of new weapons now emerging from the R&D pipeline, thereby recapitalizing their rapidly aging inventory. This strategy provides room to adopt new ideas and technologies as the services verify their merits. It can be safely relied upon to deliver its goods. Provided future defense budgets are big enough to support both readiness and accelerated modernization, it will produce the steady but meaningful increases in capabilities that it offers.

The drawbacks of this strategy are equally obvious. By preserving U.S. forces mostly as they exist today, this strategy may suffice for the near term, but its suitability for the midterm and long term is suspect. Although it will elevate U.S. force capabilities in a technical and mechanical sense, it might not produce the gains in flexibility, adaptability, and agility that are needed for the midterm and beyond. It might not improve U.S. forces in the specific ways that will be mandated by growing adversary threats. For example, it might not adequately enhance their capacity to overpower antiaccess/area-denial threats. It runs the risk of perpetuating problems that are already evident with existing force structures, such as the Army's ponderous, slowly deploying formations. It might not robustly pursue joint operations, information-era networking, and new doctrines. It might overlook opportunities to strengthen U.S. forces through innovative programs and faster pursuit of exotic new technologies, weapons, and platforms that could become available in the long term.

Those who support this strategy assert that the Department of Defense and the services already have transformation well in hand and do not need to accelerate or greatly alter it. Critics deride this strategy as too stodgy, perpetuating industrial-era forces in the information era. Perhaps they are too harsh; this strategy can be pursued faster and more aggressively than a turtlelike crawl into the future. But transformation does require a powerful strategic vision and a coherent plan for making defense changes that are not only desirable but also necessary. U.S. forces cannot afford to stand pat or to act as though the coming era will reward business as usual. The "steady as you go" strategy suffers from the risk that it will neglect the future, not master it.

"Leap Ahead" Strategy

The "leap ahead" strategy is the polar opposite of "steady as you go." "Leap ahead" embodies revolutionary goals, bold agendas, fast progress, and big changes. Rather than focusing on the near term or midterm, it is occupied with radically transforming U.S. forces for the long term. Some of its proponents argue that U.S. forces should focus intently on just one or two new operational concepts; examples are standoff targeting and Asian littoral operations. Others go considerably further. They calculate that the coming 10 to 15 years will provide a strategic pause, a period of lessened international dangers that will enable U.S. strategy to focus on preparing to meet greatly enhanced threats in the distant future, including China's potential emergence as a military power and WMD proliferation to several regional rogues. Accordingly, they are willing to accept smaller forces and less modernization in the coming decade to fund new technologies and forces that can defeat future threats. An extreme version of this strategy calls for the Department of Defense to skip virtually the entire generation of weapons now emerging from the R&D pipeline, to release funds for speeding the march into the distant future. Such Pentagon perennials as the F-22, the Joint Strike Fighter, Crusader, Osprey, DD–21, and the new CVNX carrier could fall victim wholly or partly to this reprioritizing.

A centerpiece of "leap ahead" is a bigger R&D effort in such areas as ballistic missile defenses, information systems, space assets, and a host of exotic technologies. The strategy argues that traditional platforms are dinosaurs that will be extinct 2 or 3 decades from now. Accordingly, it calls for vigorous development of new platforms and force structures. For the Air Force, it would replace today's fighters with strategic bombers, unmanned combat aerial vehicles (UCAVs), and cruise missiles. For the Navy, it would replace today's big carriers and associated battlegroups with smaller carriers, arsenal ships, and submarines that fire many cruise missiles, mobile offshore bases, high-tech surface combatants, littoral ships, and fast patrol boats (such as those proposed as part of the Streetfighter concept). For the Army, it would bypass the Interim Force's mix of heavy, intermediate, and light units to accelerate conversion to a mobile, high-tech force based on ultralight forces and deep fires: an advanced version of the Objective Force now being pursued.

A main attraction of the "leap ahead" strategy is its innovativeness, creativity, and forward-looking mentality. It shakes off preoccupation with the near term to focus attention on the distant future, its new technologies, and its new forms of warfare. This strategy's attitude of being willing to upset applecarts and to accept high risks in pursuit of big payoffs is commonly portrayed as a healthy antidote to bureaucratic conservatism. By opening the door to an exciting new era of high-tech forces, "leap ahead" offers a path for the U.S. military to break away from the traditional practices of the past. Its emphasis on a few bold operational concepts offers a way to design future forces to wage war differently than now and to channel the acquisition of new technologies so that they combine together to produce integrated doctrines.

The drawbacks of this strategy become evident when its details are subjected to scrutiny. A major liability is that it may mortgage the near term and the midterm to invest in the distant future. What will happen to U.S. security if the future produces major conflicts and wars in the next 10 to 15 years, not a strategic pause of relative peace? Will U.S. forces possess the necessary capability and flexibility if the world remains dangerous in this period? If not, this strategy has potentially fatal flaws. This strategy also risks tearing the U.S. military apart to pursue ideas that may prove to be poorly conceived or simply infeasible. Some of its operational concepts may make sense, but only as contributions to a larger enterprise. As single-minded designs, they could leave the U.S. military less flexible and adaptable than it is today. This strategy's emphasis on exotic new technologies sounds appealing in principle, but many of them are unproven and untested. Indeed, a number are little more than glimmers in the eyes of scientists; they may prove to be infeasible or ineffective even if they are fully funded. This strategy could also leave the U.S. military in trouble in the distant future. How are the services to gauge technological directions if they do not acquire the weapons now emerging from the R&D pipeline, learn from their features, and make informed judgments about follow-on efforts? In addition, this strategy also suffers from imposing political problems. It is not likely to elicit the enthusiastic support of the services, which will be the institutions responsible for bringing it to fruition. If added atop the existing defense budget, its high costs could break the bank. If it is funded by imposing draconian cuts elsewhere, it could produce an unbalanced defense program, resulting in big losses of valuable capabilities in exchange for pursuing distant visions that could prove ephemeral.

Proponents praise this strategy for its daring vision. Critics regard it as an uncharted leap into the unknown, and perhaps into a bottomless void. The truth of the matter is hard to know without embracing the strategy to see if it works. But there are ample reasons for being skeptical of its sweeping formulations and alluring promises. Today's U.S. forces became the world's best not because they lurched ahead or embraced single-minded designs but because their improvements were carefully planned, tested, and evaluated as they became available. Nor did the Department of Defense lose sight of its multiple goals, its need for balanced forces, and its responsibility to protect national security across all time periods, not just the distant future. To the extent that these lessons apply in the future, the "leap ahead" strategy suffers by comparison. Parts of this strategy may make sense, but wholly buying into it is a different matter.

PURPOSEFUL AND
MEASURED TRANSFORMATION

Our preferred strategy aims for a sensible blend of "steady as you go" and "leap ahead" because this is the best way to pursue transformation safely and effectively. If carried out wisely, the preferred strategy is capable of eliciting the support of the services, achieving success with the budgets likely to be available, and accelerating effective reforms while keeping U.S. military strength intact. In balanced ways, this strategy strives to achieve all three key goals of keeping U.S. forces ready in the near term of 5 years, enhancing their flexibility and adaptability in the midterm of 6 to 15 years, and acquiring exotic new technologies especially for the long term. This strategy's key feature is its explicit focus on the midterm, which becomes not only a core planning concept in its own right but also a bridge for linking the near term with the long term.

By focusing on the midterm, this strategy provides targets and milestones for gauging how improvements in the near term and beyond can be orchestrated for steady improvement of U.S. military capabilities, flexibility, and adaptability. It provides a solid framework for gauging how long-term changes and new technologies can be pursued with firm standards and concrete goals. Under its guidance, long-term planning no longer involves a great leap from near-term capabilities into a hazy future. Rather it becomes a well-focused exercise for determining how to build upon midterm achievements to pursue the further improvements needed afterward. In essence, this strategy helps provide binoculars for seeing the future with enough clarity to know how to prepare.

Joint operations will be key to future defense strategy and missions, and thus one of this strategy's principal aims is to develop better forces and assets for this purpose. In modern warfare, each service requires contributions from the others to carry out its missions. Naval and marine amphibious forces are critical to securing access to littoral areas, so as to allow ground and air forces to deploy safely. They also provide fully one-third of U.S. tactical air power and deep-strike assets for intense combat once deployment is complete. Ground forces require help from air power to degrade enemy maneuver forces and logistic support, and air forces benefit when ground forces compel the enemy to mass its forces, thereby exposing them to air attack.

Equally important, joint operations generate greater combat power and battlefield effectiveness. They permit integrated campaigns that create maximum leverage and firepower through coordinated missions. Modern warfare places a high premium on swift, simultaneous missions carried out by multiple components, rather than the slower, sequential missions of the past. Speed and simultaneity by jointly operating forces are used to fracture the cohesion of enemy forces, disrupt their battlefield strategy, and leave them vulnerable to the effects of maneuver, fire, and shock action. These qualities have become vital to winning quickly and decisively, with few losses to American and allied forces. Creating a better capacity for joint operations can be pursued through such steps as acquiring new C4ISR systems, developing information networks, pursuing joint doctrines, and perhaps establishing joint task forces at key commands.

In its efforts to develop a better capability and adaptability for joint operations, this transformation strategy does not tear apart existing force structures on the premise that because they worked effectively in the past, they cannot work in the future. But neither does it stand still in this arena. Instead, it seeks to pursue a responsible, well-planned effort to reorganize and reengineer current structures to make them better attuned to the information age. It uses as a model the ways in which many U.S. business corporations have pursued reengineering of their structures and functions to compete more effectively. They have stripped away redundant management layers, abandoned unproductive enterprises, created interlocking information networks rather than hierarchical organizations, and focused organizational functions on profitable business outputs. Reengineering must be handled carefully to enhance existing practices rather than destroy them, but if carried out wisely, it can produce constructive innovations. U.S. military forces can profit from similar reorganization and reengineering to enhance their combat power, even in the years before new weapons and exotic technologies arrive on the scene.

Critics often say that the Army is the service that is most in need of such changes to replace its ponderous forces with streamlined combat and support units that can deploy swiftly and strike lethally in a joint setting. One idea, for example, is to replace the Army's existing corps of three divisions (105,000 soldiers) with a smaller corps of five to six brigade-sized combat groups totaling 65,000 troops. Similar thinking can also be applied to the Air Force, Navy, and Marines, and to the DoD domestic infrastructure. In the Navy, for example, reengineering might involve stationing Marine infantry units on carriers and configuring amphibious assault ships to operate as small aircraft carriers. Efforts to develop new ideas and experiment with them already are under way by the Joint Forces Command and the services. The issue is whether, and in what ways, these efforts should be accelerated or changed. A general guiding principle stands out. The services should not be hostile to change and innovation, but instead welcome it as the best way to prepare for the twenty-first–century of warfare. Clearly, they should not embrace new ideas for their own sake because new ideas are not necessarily good ideas. But they should experiment vigorously with attractive ideas and, when these ideas show merit, adopt them in a careful manner.

A purposeful and measured transformation also means that the U.S. military will need to modernize its weapon systems soon, not in the distant future. Many current weapons are still the world's best, but most were bought years ago and are anchored in technology developed in the 1970s. Many will soon be approaching the end of their useful lives, and some will shortly become either obsolete or too costly to maintain. Others will lose their competitive status on the battlefield as enemy forces acquire new technologies capable of shooting down U.S. aircraft, destroying U.S. tanks, and sinking U.S. ships. Critics

who argue that the coming generation of technologies should be skipped to pursue future exotic systems often fail to remember that the armed services have already skipped a generation because they procured few new weapons in the late 1980s and 1990s. The extended "procurement holiday" of that period forecloses another lengthy holiday to energize the R&D process for distant achievements. If such a holiday were taken, U.S. forces would find their capabilities increasingly eroding in the dangerous period ahead as they wait for exotic weapons that will become available only in the distant future.

Air modernization is the highest priority and most expensive program, but the ground and naval forces will need modernization as well. Critics often deride the new aircraft and other weapons now emerging from the R&D pipeline as merely legacy systems rather than as transformational platforms. But their capabilities are often so significantly advanced over existing models that they make the term "legacy" suspect. As past experience shows, there is nothing wrong with perpetuating legacy platforms if the result is to acquire new technologies and subcomponents that produce impressive capabilities that meet future requirements. The real issue is not whether these new aircraft and other weapons should be procured but instead whether enough of them can be bought with the funds likely to be available. Fiscal realities may conspire to slow the purchase of these new weapons, but this does not erode their military worthiness for the coming era.

In the view of this transformation strategy, the need to acquire new weapons emerging from the R&D pipeline does not negate the powerful reasons to consider alternative platforms and to pursue exotic technologies. Such new platforms as UCAVs, lightweight armored vehicles, and new naval combatants offer the potential to enhance U.S. combat capabilities, not as substitutes for legacy platforms but as complements to them. The same applies to such new technologies as robotics, new computer systems, ultrasmart munitions, hypervelocity missiles, electromagnetic rail guns, directed energy weapons, and nanotechnology. This transformation strategy calls for relevant new platforms and technologies to be funded, developed, tested, procured, and deployed as they mature, but they should not be acquired wholesale simply for their own sake. As they become available, they can be subjected to cost-effectiveness evaluation and integrated into the evolving force posture accordingly.

What kind of force posture will a purposeful and measured transformation likely produce in the midterm and somewhat beyond? In addition to being more capable and adaptable, the posture will be aligned with new U.S. defense strategy and future missions. It is likely to deploy similar manpower levels and combat formations as today, but it will have different internal characteristics. Perhaps 10 to 20 percent of the posture will be radically transformed to carry out demanding new operations in special areas (discussed below). It will possess ultrahigh-tech weapons, brand-new structures, sophisticated information systems and networks, and specialized capabilities. The remainder of the posture may be labeled "legacy forces," but they will be different from current forces in key ways. They will have reengineered structures, be equipped with new weapons and support assets, and be better tailored for joint operations. This, of course, is a snapshot of the posture at one point in time. The posture will be evolving continuously as the future unfolds, gradually incorporating more changes in structures, technologies, and weapons. But if this snapshot accurately portrays the midterm, it offers promise that U.S. forces will be significantly improved, still superior over opponents, able to win their wars, and transformed in the ways that count.

NEW OPERATIONAL GOALS TO GUIDE TRANSFORMATION

If a purposeful and measured transformation is to succeed, it must be guided by sound operational concepts that specify how U.S. forces should be prepared, deployed, and employed for combat missions and warfighting. A critical task is to evaluate new concepts to determine whether they fit sensibly into overall defense strategy and transformation goals, will actually produce their advertised capabilities in cost-effective ways, and can be blended together to provide wise guidance for building forces and allocating resources.

Joint Vision 2020 (*JV 2020*), a document produced by the joint staff in 2000, currently provides the main intellectual leadership for defense planning. Focused on joint forces for full-spectrum dominance, its core strategic concepts call for decisive force, power projection, overseas presence, and strategic agility. Based on this strategic architecture, *JV 2020*'s key operational concepts include information superiority, dominant maneuver, precision engagement, full-dimensional protection, and focused logistics. Within the military services, such concepts as rapid decisive operations and effects-based operations

have gained prominence as ways to help supplement *JV 2020*.[2]

Although *JV 2020* remains valid, recent defense reviews have produced a new set of operational concepts that are potential candidates for inclusion. Each of them is significant individually, but seen collectively, their importance grows. Many offer potent ideas for guiding transformation, acquiring new technologies, and creating new force structures. Virtually all of these concepts focus on keeping U.S. forces superior to future adversaries, mostly through acquiring new technologies and systems. They reflect presumptions that future adversaries will be stronger than now; will have access to information era systems; and will employ asymmetric strategies to help foil U.S. operations. In particular, they presume that future enemy forces will launch swiftly unfolding strikes to win quickly before U.S. forces can arrive on the scene. As a result, these concepts call upon U.S. forces to deploy swiftly and to win decisively, with minimum American and allied casualties. They thus seek to dominate future wars by controlling them, defeating enemy forces operationally and destroying them, occupying key territory, and producing favorable political outcomes.

The new operational concepts can be grouped into two categories (see Table 6). The first category provides concepts primarily for building transformed forces through new technologies and reengineering of structures. Owing to their general characteristics, such forces could be employed in combat in a variety of different ways. The second category provides guidance on more specific ways to employ these forces in crises and wars. All ten concepts can be considered goals of transformation.[3]

These new operational concepts are key to forging a purposeful and measured transformation because they provide a concrete sense of how future forces should operate and of the capabilities that will be needed. Their main thrust is to prepare high-tech combat forces, with advanced information networks and space assets, backed by strong mobility forces and lean logistic supply units. Their offensive measures

---

Table 6

Ten New Operational Concepts for Building and Employing Transformed Forces

Operational concepts for building transformed forces
  Joint response strike forces for early entry operations
  Enhanced information systems and space-based assets for force networking
  Accelerated deployment of theater missile defenses for force protection
  Realigned overseas presence and better mobility for swift power projection
  Interoperable allied forces for multilateral operations

Operational concepts for employing transformed forces
  Maritime littoral operations for projecting power ashore
  Standoff targeting and forcible entry for antiaccess/area-denial threats
  Enhanced tactical deep strikes for effective use of joint air assets
  Decisive close combat operations and deep maneuver for ground assets
  Deliberate and sustained operations

will create jointly operated forces from all services that can strike lethally at long range while dominating close engagements on the battlefield itself. Their defensive measures will help protect U.S. forces against new-era threats, especially WMDs and antiaccess/area-denial threats. Their emphasis on developing a wider network of bases and facilities, including along the Asian littoral, will help enable U.S. forces to operate in new geographic locations. The effect will be not only to create better capabilities in a technical sense but also to enhance adaptability, especially in contingencies at the medium-to-high end of the spectrum.

Nevertheless, these and other new operational concepts must be evaluated carefully to ensure that they make strategic sense, will produce new capabilities required by the armed services, and fit together to provide a coherent approach to warfighting. If they prove out, these concepts offer a new strategic vision for building and employing future U.S. forces, strengthened in many ways to carry out demanding missions through new-era joint operations. They will need appropriate weapons, technologies, and other assets for these new missions and operations, and therefore the transformation process must be accelerated. But this vision does not require a frantic leap into an uncharted future. It can be accomplished through a purposeful and measured transformation focused on the midterm that embodies a mixture of continuity and change through a combination of upgraded legacy forces and some ultrasophisticated forces.

This appealing vision of enhanced American technological prowess should not lose sight of equally important strategic judgments: that the Armed Forces must remain well trained and well led, that wars will remain contests of willpower, and that U.S. combat operations will always need to be guided by well-conceived political and military goals. Moreover, this vision has important global political implications that need to be recognized and handled wisely. The idea that the United States is assembling swift, high-tech strike forces backed by missile defenses will be welcomed by some countries, but it already is triggering apprehension in others, including allies and adversaries. Diplomacy will be needed to underscore that the United States is behaving responsibly, not like a rogue hyperpower with a unilateral agenda. Embedding American defense preparations in multilateral security ties, interoperability with allied forces, and partnership relations can help reduce apprehension. The larger point, of course, is that strongly transformed forces will help enhance the credibility of the United States abroad, strengthen its capacity to mold peacetime security affairs in ways that safeguard its interests, and defeat enemies that threaten the safety of the American people.

Notwithstanding their many attractive features, these concepts should not be viewed as a cure-all or as offering a stand-alone defense strategy. Although they mainly focus on wars at the high end of the spectrum, most of these concepts do not pay comparable attention to the lower end, where force improvements may also be needed. Their preoccupation with new technologies for strike operations, if carried too far, might risk overlooking the many other types of warfighting and the need for well-prepared forces that are ready in many ways. These concepts will need to be accompanied by measures in such mundane and often-neglected areas as logistic support, maintenance, and war reserves. Otherwise, they could create forces that possess glittering new technologies but lack the overall wherewithal to fight effectively.

These concepts and related transformation endeavors must be accompanied by a sound resource strategy and balanced investments. Adequate defense budgets will be needed: sustained increases that permit new ventures. Absent major reductions in other areas, nonetheless, fiscal constraints will be tight for many years, and priorities therefore must be set. None of these concepts offers a free lunch; all of them require investments in new capabilities. Fortunately, several of them are not very expensive. They can be carried out adequately with funding support that is consistent with foreseeable budgets. The exceptions are missile defense, space assets, and air modernization, all of which carry big price tags if pursued fully. In these and other costly programs, investment decisions will need to be made with a balanced focus on high-leverage payoffs and cost-effectiveness. Otherwise, spending on a few big-ticket concepts could leave the others starved for funds.

If savings must be found, the answer is not necessarily neglecting these concepts or slashing combat forces, which consume only one-third of the DoD budget. Equal or greater savings likely can be found by controlling the spiraling operations and maintenance (O&M) budget, trimming manpower across the Department of Defense, and reengineering domestic support structures. A great menace to affording transformation is the rising cost of the defense budget in other areas. DoD operating costs today (per capita spending for O&M and military manpower) are about 25 percent higher than they were a decade ago in constant dollars. Per capita spending on O&M today is fully 50 percent higher than a decade ago. Today, the annual O&M budget of about $125 billion is fully double the procurement budget, which stood at only about $62 billion for fiscal year 2002. In the 1980s, procurement spending was the same size as O&M budgets, not far smaller. Today's procurement budgets are far short of the amount needed to fund a major acquisition effort for transformation. Bigger procurement as well as research, development, test, and evaluation budgets are expected in the coming years. Unless ways can be found to stem the rising tide of operating costs and the domestic defense infrastructure, a successful transformation will be difficult to achieve, regardless of how many new concepts are created.

Even if adequate funds are available for transformation, the need for a coherent plan and program will not go away. The strength of these ten operational concepts lies not in their individual features, but in their capacity to work together to create a composite theory of force preparedness and employment doctrines. Any effort to pursue only a few concepts, while neglecting the others, could produce an unbalanced force incapable of the full-spectrum operations required by future strategic challenges. For example, preoccupation with missile defenses, standoff targeting, and littoral maritime operations could result in inadequate forces for direct crisis interventions. Likewise, an emphasis on forcible entry and deep strike, to the exclusion of close combat capabilities, could result in a lack of strong ground forces.

The armed services will be best served by investing wisely in a full set of valid new concepts in affordable, well-planned ways, while attending to the other aspects of defense preparedness. In the final analysis, a strong military posture will be marked by the capacity to perform many missions and operations

effectively, rather than a few superbly and others poorly. This is a central lesson of the past decades, during which the United States struggled hard to build its superior forces of today. It likely will prove to be the guiding beacon for building and using transformed forces for the twenty-first century.

NOTES

1. See U.S. Department of Defense, *Quadrennial Defense Review Report* (Washington, D.C.: U.S. Department of Defense, 2001).

2. See Joint Staff, *Joint Vision 2020* (Washington, D.C.: U.S. Government Printing Office, June 2000).

3. For more analysis, see Hans Binnendijk and Richard L. Kugler, *Adapting Forces to a New Era: Ten Transforming Concepts*, Defense Horizons 5 (Washington, D.C.: Center for Technology and National Security Policy, National Defense University, October 2001).

THE ART OF WAR

FREDERICK W. KAGAN

The American military today may be in the best position of any military in history. Its victories over Iraq and Afghanistan have transformed not merely the way the United States thinks about and conducts war, but the way the entire world sees violent conflict. American technological prowess and the skill of the professional American armed forces have opened a gap in capabilities between the United States and its closest competitors that many see as unbridgeable. Those triumphs, as well as the American people's perception of the threats that the United States faces, have also served dramatically to reduce the mutual mistrust and hostility that had separated the military from the public since the Vietnam War. Trusted by its people, emulated by its friends, feared by its foes, unequalled in capability and skill, the American military is in many respects at the height of its power. Properly handled, the U.S. armed forces might be able to maintain and even extend their preeminence into the distant future.

The challenges facing the military today, however, are no less daunting than the opportunities are promising. Most leaders and observers agree that the U.S. military will have to "transform" itself to maintain its lead, as well as to be able to meet the challenges of the present and the future for which it was not de-

signed. At the same time, the United States is engaged in a war on terrorism, in peacekeeping operations in Afghanistan, Bosnia, and Kosovo, and in a massive peacekeeping, counterinsurgency, counterterrorism, and reconstruction effort in Iraq. Tensions over nuclear proliferation remain high on the Korean peninsula and in Iran. Tensions also remain high over the cooperation of states like Syria in the war on terrorism and operations in Iraq.

These ongoing operations and threats have combined to stretch the U.S. armed forces beyond the breaking point. The Army has been compelled to deploy tens of thousands of soldiers for a full year at a time rather than the normal 6 months, to forego important training for those soldiers, and sometimes to send soldiers returning from one such deployment immediately into another. The National Guard and Reserves have been mobilized to an extent unprecedented since the 1970s, first for "homeland defense" in the wake of the September 11 attacks and now in support of operations in Iraq, the Balkans, and elsewhere. The strain on soldiers and their families is growing, morale is declining, and it is hard to believe that these trends will not begin to take a serious toll on recruitment and retention in the near future, potentially exacerbating the problem.

This essay has been edited and is reprinted from New Criterion 22 *(November 2003): 4–16, by permission of Encounter Books.*

The issues of transformation and military over-stretch are inextricably linked. The secretary of defense has adopted a vision of transformation that relies on high-technology weapons systems rather than on soldiers. He has continued to pursue this program, even as the armed forces have been stretched thinner and thinner. He has even resisted efforts by Congress to expand the military—a virtually unimaginable stance for a sitting secretary of defense—to preserve his program of military transformation. As a result, the United States is now attempting to transform its military in ways that hinder the conduct of current operations, even as those operations literally rip it apart. Worst of all, the current program of transformation turns its back on the approach that has brought America success so far, and flies in the face of the historical lessons about how to transform a military. If these problems remain unacknowledged and unaddressed, the United States may lose its predominance and endanger its security.

America achieved military dominance in 1991 with the collapse of the Soviet Union. Because no other state or group of states had been attempting to compete directly with the two superpowers, U.S. preeminence arrived unexpectedly and by default. The roots of the dominant position America holds today lie, therefore, in efforts American leaders made in the period from the late 1960s through the early 1980s to transform the military in order the better to face the U.S.S.R.

This first transformation had both a technological component and human element. In the 20 years from 1965 to 1985, America fielded a host of new weapons systems, created a global satellite constellation and advanced communications systems, and pioneered the development of entirely new technologies, such as stealth and precision-guided munitions (PGMs). In the midst of that technological transformation, a sociological transformation was also taking place within the armed forces. In the mid-1970s, the United States abandoned the draft and recruited an all-volunteer professional military. Current military theory focuses almost exclusively on the technological aspect of transformation, but the human element was at least as important in bringing the American armed forces to their current level of excellence.

Almost all of the main weapons systems American forces used in Iraq and Afghanistan were developed and fielded in the 1960s and 1970s. The Air Force used new concepts of aircraft design and took advantage of computerization to produce the first generation of "superfighters," including the F-15 and F-16, while the Navy developed its equivalent in the F-14. These aircraft, together with the F/A-18, fielded somewhat later, dominated the skies over Iraq and have led many of America's likeliest competitors to focus on air defense systems rather than on building their own aircraft with which to challenge the superfighters. Fear of the Soviet air defense systems, through which American bombers would have to penetrate to strike their targets, led to an intense program in stealth technology in the 1970s and 1980s. That program bore fruit in the form of the F-117 fighter and the B-2 bomber, used to great effect over Kosovo, Afghanistan, and Iraq.

The family of superfighters and other advanced aircraft designed in the 1960s and 1970s were intended to provide versatility and redundancy. Their designs reflected a determination to be the best at everything. The F-16 was designed to be the world's best dogfighter, able to achieve extremely high kill ratios with either its Sidewinder missiles or its guns. The F-15 is an air-superiority fighter that was always meant to rely on its superior missiles and missile control technology to defeat enemy aircraft before they got within anything like dogfighting range. The F-14 attempts to duplicate the better characteristics of both planes in a naval version—the F/A-18 is an improvement on the F-14, especially in the area of ground attack. Each plane overlaps the others in capabilities, but each is also designed to excel in a particular niche.

At the same time, the Air Force also fielded the A-10 ground attack aircraft. This ungainly, heavily armored plane with a 23 mm antitank gun in its snout was designed to be the best tank killer in the air. Its armor protects it from antiaircraft machine guns and allows it to fly low to the ground and slowly enough to identify and engage its targets directly. It was enormously effective in Iraq, filling a specific niche that directly supported the Army's missions, as well as the larger goal of destroying Iraq's armored forces. In short, it was not simply the development of PGMs that has made the U.S. Air Force the best in the world, but the quality of its aircraft across the board and in every specialty.

The current American Army is also the result of changes made in the 1970s designed to allow it to excel in many areas. In the wake of the Vietnam War, Army Chief of Staff Creighton Abrams was determined to revolutionize the Army's equipment by fielding a new generation of weapons systems, including the M1 "Abrams" Tank, the Bradley Infantry Fighting Vehicle, the Apache and Blackhawk helicopters, the Multiple-Launch Rocket System (MLRS), the Stinger surface-to-air missile, and the Patriot air defense system. These were the main weapons systems Army forces have used to such success in all of the post–Cold War conflicts.

The goal of this technological transformation was to provide balanced capabilities to the Army. The M1 tank is a case in point. It was better armored than any other vehicle in the world at the time, and remains incredibly hard to kill. Its 120 mm main gun, which fires depleted uranium antitank rounds, gave it unprecedented destructive power—there are virtually no vehicles in existence today that an M1 cannot destroy. The M1 can move at up to fifty miles per hour, an extremely high speed, considering the tank's seventy ton weight. The M1, therefore, offered superb offensive and defensive power and excellent tactical mobility.

It has proven remarkably versatile. In open maneuver warfare in the Iraqi desert, the M1 fulfilled its initial design goals. The Iraqis were unable to kill it even with direct hits from their T-72 tanks, and M1s killed almost every Iraqi vehicle they fired on with one shot. In 1991, as in 2003, American armored forces were able to move much faster than the Iraqis had expected.

The M1's defensive characteristics have also made it invaluable for a range of missions its designers had not foreseen. In peacekeeping operations in dangerous areas, such as Bosnia and Iraq, the M1's virtual invulnerability has been important in deterring attacks and keeping critical areas secure. The Bradley Infantry Fighting Vehicle has also proved invaluable in this regard. It is no accident that almost all of the casualties American forces in Iraq have taken (apart from friendly-fire incidents) were to soldiers who were either dismounted or riding in trucks or Humvees.

The willingness to accept redundancy and inefficiency in defense programs that characterized the Army and Air Force transformations around the 1970s reflected a larger willingness to balance the development of capabilities, sometimes different, sometimes similar, across the services. At the same time the Army was developing the Patriot antiaircraft missile, the Air Force was fielding the planes that convinced all of America's subsequent foes not even to try to fly. As the Army was planning a tank that was both nearly indestructible and indescribably lethal to enemy armored vehicles, the Air Force was fielding an aircraft specifically to kill enemy tanks. The examples of redundant development are legion.

The most recent wars have made the virtues of this redundancy manifest. On numerous occasions, including as recently as the 2003 Gulf War, weather conditions restricted the Air Force's ability to fly sorties against enemy armored concentrations. The ability of the tanks and Bradleys of the Third Infantry Division to survive encounters with those enemy armored forces saved American lives. The Patriot has proven largely unnecessary in its role as a system to shoot down enemy aircraft. Its transformation into a ballistic missile defense system, however, gave the coalition much greater confidence in its ability to handle Saddam Hussein's missiles during the last war. Redundancy in war can yield flexibility and security. It ensures that when one system fails for whatever unforeseen reason, another can take its place. It provides the ability to meet unexpected challenges. In military affairs, redundancy is a virtue.

Redundancy, of course, is expensive. During the Vietnam War and the Reagan build-up, the overriding threat of Soviet military power helped overcome America's traditional reluctance to spend money on its defense. Even Jimmy Carter, at the height of an economic recession that would cost him his presidency, felt obliged by the Soviet invasion of Afghanistan to begin the massive rearmament program that Ronald Reagan inherited and enlarged still further. The excellence of the American military in the 1990s owes a great deal to those days of open coffers.

The coffers inevitably closed with the fall of the Soviet Union. As Boris Yeltsin was attempting to forge a democratic Russian Federation on the ruins of the U.S.S.R., American defense officials and civilian experts were already talking of the "strategic pause" and the "peace dividend" that were supposed to follow that epochal event. Defense budgets dwindled and efficiency became the watchwod in the Pentagon and on Capitol Hill.

The focus on efficiency and economics led to an effort to adopt business practices into the work of the military. This effort has a long history. Robert McNamara, himself a retired Ford executive, attempted to bring business models into the Pentagon in the 1960s. He applied new metrics to the Vietnam conflict, centering on body counts. He introduced a "game-theory" approach to war in the form of "graduated pressure," in which military forces were explicitly used to send messages to the enemy, whose responses could then be predicted. In general, he preferred the advice of his "whiz kids," who understood the new way of thinking, to that of the professional military officers who clung to the "outdated" modes of conducting war. The results of this approach are well known.

Since then, the armed forces have adopted successively almost every major business fad—"total quality management," "velocity management," and "just-in-time logistics," among others. Efforts to reduce the defense budget in the 1990s to expand the "peace dividend" led Secretary of Defense William Cohen to announce a "revolution in business affairs" in the Pentagon, to parallel and support the "revolution in military affairs" that he sought to bring about by transforming the military. The goal was to make the Pentagon more efficient and to use the funds recouped by that efficiency to support transformation.

At the same time that Cohen and his successors were attempting to bring business models once again to the economic side of the Pentagon, others were attempting to replicate McNamara's attempts to bring business models into the conduct of war. Throughout the 1990s, a series of articles and books argued that the information revolution then sweeping the economy had an equivalent in the realm of war. Just as businesses had been forced to change their entire approaches to their work as a result of information technology, so, too, did armies. The "new economy," according to the wisdom of its advocates in the late 1990s, had its own new rules. Military thinkers like retired admirals William Owens and Arthur Cebrowski, among others, argued that war in the information age also had its own new rules. They argued further that the lessons of the new economy could be translated more or less directly to the business of waging war.

In *Network-Centric Warfare* (1999), a book central to the current U.S. program to transform its military, three defense analysts argued that the "information revolution" had fundamentally altered both business and war.[1] In the past, they claimed, success relied on the ability to move material objects around. Businesses that could produce items more rapidly and ship them faster and more cheaply succeeded; those that could not, failed. Similarly, armies succeeded by moving their forces to the decisive point and time and there concentrating them to defeat a similarly concentrated enemy.

The information revolution changed all that. Success in business now lay, they argued, in moving information around. Businesses that could acquire, disseminate, and analyze information would succeed; those that could not would fail. They described the reasons for Wal-Mart's success, pointing to its tightly integrated system for gathering information at the point of sale and disseminating that information not only to its own executives and other stores, but also to its suppliers.

Armies, the three defense analysts argued, now faced the same challenges. It was no longer necessary to concentrate forces—in fact, given the speed of events and the dangers of weapons of mass destruction, it had become dangerous. Instead, the successful army was the one that acquired the most exact possible knowledge of the enemy, analyzed that knowledge to determine which "nodes" to attack, and directed weapons systems launched from widely dispersed platforms to strike those nodes. It would not be necessary to move many forces around, only to ensure that they were within the thousand kilometer range of their proposed targets.

These proposals received powerful support when Donald Rumsfeld became secretary of defense in January 2001. Like McNamara, Rumsfeld came from the business community, and was determined to bring his business expertise to bear on the Pentagon bureaucracy. He believed enthusiastically in the Network-Centric Warfare (NCW) model then being propounded, and he went even further. Determined to transform the military in accord with NCW ideas, Rumsfeld was also determined to do it at the lowest possible cost. He adopted a business approach to that problem as well.

A business can improve its bottom line by focusing its resources on the few things it does very well and abandoning markets in which it is performing poorly. Efficiency is all in business, a fact reflected in the many mergers that have taken place during the recent economic downturn. By eliminating redundancy and focusing on the areas in which they can excel, companies can dramatically improve their competitive position in some markets, even at the cost, sometimes, of abandoning others. Rumsfeld has adopted this approach in the area of military transformation.

America's biggest lead, the "market" in which the United States has the best competitive advantage, now lies in the realm of long-range reconnaissance and strike capabilities. No other state or group of states can begin to match America's ability to identify a huge number of targets and to attack them from platforms thousands of miles away.

The advantage in this area is greater than that in others. The United States has the best ground forces in the world, but China has larger ground forces, Germany has excellent tanks, Russia has large amounts of artillery, and so forth. America has the greatest ability to move and supply large forces to distant theaters, but Britain, France, and Russia can project force halfway around the world as well. None of those states, however, can come close to matching America's ability to identify, track, and destroy targets from great distances.

Even if Rumsfeld had not been an enthusiastic supporter of NCW, it was only natural that his application of business principles to war would lead him to focus on America's capabilities with precision-guided munitions. This is currently the area of America's greatest competitive advantage. By directing funding into it, the United States can obtain an even greater competitive advantage—perhaps even the "lockout" that NCW advocates seek. In business, lockout occurs when one company attains such a predominant position that it cannot be challenged.

The watchwords for the Rumsfeld Pentagon have, therefore, been focus and efficiency. The Pentagon has repeatedly stated that all new weapons systems will be evaluated primarily on the degree to which they further the armed forces' ability to conduct NCW. Systems that bring other capabilities to the force have received less attention, less funding, and have sometimes been cancelled.

All of the services have participated in this race to a single goal. For example, the Navy now sells every new ship design on the basis of its ability to support NCW. The Air Force has focused most of its development in the past decade on upgrading its PGMs and the ability of its aircraft to carry and control them. It now attempts to justify the F-22 and the Joint Strike Fighter on the grounds that they will support NCW the better, although the evidence for that claim is sketchy at best.

The result of these service changes will be to homogenize the armed forces. No longer will each service bring unique capabilities to the table: all will now provide the same capability—the capability to identify and attack targets with PGMs at great distances. This homogenization will inevitably create redundancies that Rumsfeld's business model cannot tolerate in its search for efficiency. The secretary of defense recognized that fact early on. He cancelled the Crusader artillery system in part on the grounds that it did not provide capabilities different from those already provided by the air forces. He planned, prior to the Iraq war, to eliminate at least two and possibly as many as four of the Army's ten active duty combat divisions, because they, too, were becoming redundant as organizations that could identify and destroy enemy targets. Although the Joint Strike Fighter and the F-22 seem to be extremely redundant and do not really provide dramatically different capabilities, ironically, both systems have survived initial searches for efficiency on the grounds that they directly support the NCW concept.

The Rumsfeld vision of military transformation, therefore, is completely unbalanced. It will provide the United States with armed forces that do one thing only, even if they do it superbly well. They will be able to identify, track, and destroy enemy targets from thousands of miles away and at little or no risk to themselves. The suite of capabilities that the transformation of the 1970s and 1980s provided will be narrowed into a confined band of excellence. The business model that brought success to many companies in the 1990s will be adopted as the basis for this transformation, and all of America's future success will rest upon this one capability and the applicability of this single model. It is one of the most seductive and dangerous visions of modern times.

The Rumsfeld vision of military transformation suffers from a wide variety of flaws, some of which I have already considered in another forum.[2] One of the most significant flaws is the misunderstanding of the concept of the "revolution in military affairs" (RMA) that underlies this vision.

Although current documents mention RMA or the information revolution much more rarely these days, the concept remains central to present-day efforts to transform the military. All of the theoretical justifications for the current approach to transformation, written mostly at the turn of the millennium or just before, rely on this concept as their essential justification. The fact that it is slipping from current parlance reflects the reality that agencies responsible for transformation are focusing increasingly on the nuts-and-bolts aspects of their task and have stopped thinking seriously about the philosophical underpinnings and assumptions on which it is based.

The concept of RMA is a relatively new one in the history of military theory. Soviet military leaders coined it in the 1960s to describe the effects of mating thermonuclear weapons (hydrogen bombs) with intercontinental ballistic missiles (ICBMs). They argued that the unprecedented destructive power of thermonuclear weapons and the ability of ICBMs to penetrate even the densest air defense network created conditions for war so fundamentally different from those that had existed beforehand as to have brought about a revolution in the nature of war itself. Virtually overnight, many of the basic guidelines that had led previous commanders to success had become irrelevant, and new principles had to be sought.

The concept made its way slowly to the West, and really only came into vogue in the late 1980s to describe an entirely different revolution—the information revolution considered above. In the interim, however, military historians have taken up the concept with enthusiasm, many to support it, a few to attack it. "Revolutions in Military Affairs" now form an important part of syllabi at defense educational institutions, such as West Point and the National Defense University. Historians and military theorists have labeled everything from the advent of armored warfare to Napoleonic logistics and the development of the longbow as RMAs. Others have sought out the

absurdities of some of these arguments to assail the entire concept as meaningless. Whatever the merits of those assaults, however, they will fall on deaf ears in the Pentagon, where the RMA has become the critical concept underpinning American defense policy today.

In truth, the concept of RMAs is an important one for understanding the evolution of military development. In the course of military history, there have been a series of dramatic breaks in the way war is fought at the most basic level. Warfare changed dramatically from 1700 to 1760, from 1813 to 1863, from 1870 to 1915, from 1942 to 1991. Although many of the traditional guidelines to success continued to apply from one period to the next, many others also changed. In each change, there were elements of long-term evolution, which has led some to argue that the term *"revolution in military affairs"* is inappropriate. Yet the nature of war changes most rapidly when major wars are actually being fought, so that for all the theorizing and development that preceded them, the outbreak of the American Civil War in 1861, the Franco-Prussian War in 1870, World War I in 1914, and World War II in 1939, for instance, led to sudden and dramatic changes nevertheless.

The problem with the current vision of military transformation, therefore, is not that it relies on the concept of RMA, but that it does not properly understand that concept. Since the 1980s, advocates of an "American RMA" based on information technology have tended to define the term as an asymmetrical advantage that one state acquires over its opponents. They have sought to develop transformation programs to extend that asymmetrical advantage indefinitely into the future, so that the other states of the world would never catch up, and American preeminence (or "lockout") would be secured, to all intents and purposes, forever.

History does not support such an interpretation of this concept, however. In each of the periods in recent history in which one might see a fundamental change in the nature of war, it is true that one state usually began with a dramatic lead. Revolutionary France's ability in the 1790s to mobilize vast conscript armies and to sustain that mobilization for years gave France an important advantage over continental states unable to match such levels of mobilization. Prussia's early and enthusiastic development of a dense railroad net and of the general staff structure needed to plan for and control a railroad mobilization led directly to crushing victories over Austria in 1866 and France in 1871. The Nazis' creation of a technologically advanced and highly trained armored force, along with a significantly better armored warfare doctrine, led directly to the destruction of the Franco-British army in 1940.

In each case, however, we must also consider the sequel. Napoleonic France, Imperial Germany, and Nazi Germany all ultimately lost subsequent wars and were destroyed. The reasons for those failures are enlightening about the limitations of the current definition of revolution in military affairs.

Faced with the challenge of Revolutionary France, the other states of Europe were initially reluctant to make the social and political changes necessary to raise and maintain the large armies required to meet that challenge. Over years of sustained and unsuccessful warfare, however, France's enemies gradually changed their minds. Austria, Prussia, and Russia all eventually mobilized large forces. In Russia's case, the army went from around 250,000 individuals at the end of the eighteenth century to about 850,000 in 1815, a level at which it remained until an even more dramatic increase during the Crimean War. The mobilization and support of such large armies caused problems for all of the states of Europe, and led, in part, to the revolutionary disturbances that wracked the continent following Napoleon's final fall. The leaders of those states, however, ultimately accepted such costs to enable them to successfully adapt to the new requirements of war. They were thereby able to defeat Napoleon.

The Germans went through a similar process twice. Their advantages in railway mobilization in 1866 and 1870 had been greatly reduced by 1914. France and Russia had spent fortunes upgrading their own railway systems and had developed general staff structures able to match the Germans' planning abilities. As a result, the German mobilization in 1914 was matched by equally skillful French and Russian mobilizations, the German war plan broke down, and Germany was ultimately crushed under the weight of superior allied forces. Germany's enemies had successfully adopted the methods that had led Germany to success in the mid-nineteenth century, and they then turned those methods against the Germans during World War I.

Hitler faced a kindred problem. The techniques that generated his initial successes against the French and the British, who had both developed inappropriate armored doctrines and tanks largely unsuitable for the sort of rapid mobile warfare the Germans fought, did not lead subsequently to victory against the Soviets. Problems of planning and confused objectives, among other things, vitiated initial German successes in 1941, and allowed the Soviets time to recover. When they did recover, the Soviets began to implement an armored warfare doctrine superior to the one the Germans had been using and to build tanks excellently designed to support that doctrine. Beginning with their victory at Stalingrad in late 1942, the Soviets conducted a virtually unbroken march to the west that resulted in the capture of Berlin in May 1945.

Even the "nuclear revolution" itself, the change in warfare that had led to the coining of the acronym "RMA," saw a similarly rapid balance. The United States and the Soviet Union fielded thermonuclear-tipped ICBMs at virtually the same time, and throughout the Cold War, each advance by one side in this area was matched almost immediately by the other.

It goes without saying that each of these examples had much more complexity than can be explored in this essay. Napoleon's adversaries made many changes to their armies other than simply increasing their size, including incorporating and improving on other aspects of Napoleonic warfare that had brought Bonaparte his early successes. Germany's Schlieffen Plan failed in 1914 not simply because the French mobilized well, but also because Schlieffen's successor had altered it in important ways. Hitler's invasion of the Soviet Union failed partly because of Hitler's inappropriate interference in the operation and his insistence on trying to achieve all of his ultimate objectives simultaneously, among other things.

The issues identified in this essay, however, were central parts of the explanations for the outcome of all of these conflicts. If the allies in 1813, the French and Russians in 1914, and the Soviets in 1942 had not successfully adopted the critical features of the new military thinking that had brought their enemies victory, it is most unlikely that the other factors contributing to their success would have saved them from defeat. The key point is that the failings of Napoleon and the Germans would have been irrelevant if they had retained the asymmetrical advantages with which they had started. Their inability to react perfectly when they had lost those advantages was what led them to defeat.

History so far, therefore, has been very clear that asymmetrical advantages gained by one state do not normally last very long. Technology and technique inevitably spread. Other states acquire either similar or counteracting capabilities. The final victors of each new "revolutionary" epoch have not usually been the states that initiated the revolution, but those that responded best once the technologies and techniques had become common property.

History also shows that the initial successes those "revolutionary" states achieved have tended to breed arrogance and overconfidence, hindering their ability to respond as other states began to match their capabilities. Napoleonic France, Imperial Germany, and Nazi Germany all ossified in their techniques after the initial victories, and lost to enemies who, forced by defeat, built on their own advances more successfully.

The search for an indefinite American asymmetrical advantage, therefore, requires not merely a revolution in military affairs: it also requires a fundamental revolution in human affairs of a sort never seen before. It requires that America continue to change its armed forces so rapidly and successfully that no other state can ever catch up—indeed, that no other state in the world even try.

This unrealistic requirement is central to the current vision of military transformation. As, according to this vision, American armed forces will only be able to do one thing—strike targets precisely from great distances away—they will succeed only on two conditions. First, they will always have to fight wars in which striking targets precisely from great distances will lead directly to victory, and second, they will always have to fight enemies incapable of either matching that skill or of preventing the United States from using it. The precise weapons will always have to get through, their effects will always have to be decisive, and no enemy will ever be able to fire them effectively at American forces.

History suggests that these conditions will not be met for very long. But transformation enthusiasts today argue that the United States is in a unique position and that the rules really have changed. It is worth considering in some detail, therefore, whether or not it is likely that the United States will be able to retain its asymmetric advantages for decades to come.

The first question in this debate concerns the proliferation of the technology the United States now relies on to maintain this advantage. The situation in this regard is both promising and alarming. On the one hand, American technological superiority rests primarily on computerization. PGMs are precisely guided because of the computer chips in their guidance systems and the communications systems that allow them to home in on either global positioning system coordinates or laser designators. The ability of American forces to identify, track, and strike targets also relies on such computer chips, and on the satellites that support the communications systems. The proliferation of microprocessors and satellites, therefore, could start an adversary on the road to challenging American technological preeminence.

It hardly needs stating that computerization is a revolution racing throughout the world, not just in America, or even that most microprocessors these days are made outside of the United States. The American satellite constellation is the most sophisticated and dense of any, but many states have the ability to launch satellites themselves or to hire private companies to launch them. The real American advantage in this regard results from two things: money and time.

Building the current satellite constellation was exorbitantly expensive. The United States probably would not have undertaken it initially but for the fear of the Soviet Union. The development of PGMs and building large numbers of them was also extremely expensive. Very few states in the world today have the economic resources necessary even to begin such massive programs, let alone see them rapidly through to conclusion.

The very age of the American systems, moreover, is also an asset. The United States has had time not merely to computerize all of its major weapons systems and the weapons they fire, but to develop dense computer networks that connect them. That networking is an important part of America's technological advantage today, and it is not something that any would-be adversary could easily or rapidly replicate. Despite the ready proliferation of the technologies themselves, therefore, it would seem, after all, that the United States should expect to maintain its current technological lead for a considerable time.

Several factors militate against this happy conclusion. For one thing, few, if any, of America's enemies will have the vast resource-stretching responsibilities that America has. They will be concerned only with their own region of the world and will focus their efforts on developing communications and target tracking systems only over a small portion of the globe. They will not need a dense global satellite constellation or the ability to project power over thousands of miles. The costs to them of developing systems comparable to America's, but only in a restricted geographic area, will accordingly be much smaller than the price that the United States has had to pay to achieve that capability everywhere.

Then, too, other states can reap the benefits of modern communications systems without bearing the expensive burden of basic scientific research and development. Microprocessors, satellites, encrypted laser communications systems, cell phone systems, and the whole host of technologies that form the basis of American military superiority are now the property of the world. It will not cost America's enemies anything like what it cost the United States to develop its capabilities, either in money or in time. Because technology inevitably becomes less expensive as it proliferates and as time goes on, moreover, the situation for America's would-be adversaries will only improve in this regard.

Moreover, just as many European states drastically improved their railway networks in the nineteenth century, so now, many states are improving their satellite constellations and are naturally networking government and economic computer systems to support economic growth today. They are thereby also laying the groundwork for a rapid development of the military advantages that flow from those communications and networking capabilities. Many of the technologies that have led in the past to American success are now latent in every aspect of modern economic life, and this fact will reduce both the cost and the time required for a potential adversary to "revolutionize" its armed forces to match those of the United States.

Note that technology is only part of the story of America's success. The way the U.S. military has integrated the technology into its professional, highly-trained armed forces has been at least as important as the quality of the technology itself. In this area, too, the United States has had an advantage since the mid-1970s, because most of America's likely enemies retained conscript militaries unable to match America's troops in skill, educational level, or experience. Even this advantage, however, is evaporating.

The first Gulf War started a global trend toward transforming large conscript armies into smaller professional forces. The second one has accelerated that trend. The Russians have struggled toward this goal, with only limited success, for a decade. The French abandoned their conscript military, whose traditions harked back to the Revolution of 1789. Even the Chinese have recently announced that they would reduce their military and concentrate on developing a smaller, more professional and highly qualified force. The United States made the transition and garnered the advantages of that transition in about 15 years. It remains to be seen how long it will take the rest of the world to do so.

When America's enemies have developed the technology and trained the people who will use it, they will also have to develop the doctrines and techniques to make it effective. In this regard, they have the most significant advantage of all. Much of America's tested doctrine has been published; much can be deduced from the CNN coverage of America's most recent wars. Once again, America's enemies can start from the position of proven success that the U.S. armed forces achieved, and build from there.

The real advantage of potential U.S. adversaries in this area, however, results from the fact that they will be developing armed forces specifically designed to fight an enemy with the same capabilities. America's military has not done so. American military doctrine continues to foresee fighting enemies lacking any significant capacity to deploy PGMs, who are lacking dense satellite constellations and communications systems and without the ability to strike targets precisely at great distances. It is one of the more troubling lessons of the history of new military technology that the states that pioneer the new technologies and techniques generally fail to adapt successfully to the situation in which all major states have the same technologies and techniques. It remains to be seen whether America will do any better than its predecessors in this regard.

The problems identified above are nearly all inherent in any program of military transformation. They are not unique to Rumsfeld's vision. History suggests that whatever program the United States adopts to transform its armed forces, America's enemies will tend to catch up and level the playing field. The problem with the current program is that it relies on maintaining an overwhelming advantage in a single area of military performance indefinitely. The failure to contemplate having to fight creditable opponents and the imbalance of the effort to transform the military both create serious risks and vulnerabilities for American armed forces in the future.

The solution is to refocus America's efforts at transforming its military on a program designed to produce balanced capabilities and to defeat a comparably armed and capable enemy. In the first instance, that will mean rebalancing the efforts to remake the ground and the air services. Right now, the initiative is primarily reliant on air- or sea-launched weapons. Advocates of this approach point out that it is cheaper and safer—cheaper because maintaining large ground forces divisions is costly, and safer because it obviates the need to put America's young men and women in harm's way. This is one of the main reasons that Rumsfeld and others have repeatedly advocated cutting the size of the Army and transferring the funds saved thereby into the purchase of advanced munitions, communications, and targeting systems for the Air Force and Navy.

It is easy to show the consequences of this approach in Iraq. Armies do more than destroy targets. They hold ground passively. They provide critical police functions. They can still conduct counterguerrilla

operations much more effectively than air-launched munitions. For a country engaged in nation-building, counterinsurgency, and counterterrorism, there is no escape from the need to have a large and capable army, and America is suffering badly now from having an army that is too small.

It is not simply that current operations require significant ground forces, however, or even that the conditions that drive that requirement are likely to persist for some considerable time. The real reason to maintain a robust army that does more than simply add sophisticated launchers to the targeting mix is that it greatly complicates the enemy's ability to respond to America's movements and capabilities.

If the enemy knows that all that will be faced is a barrage of PGMs, that adversary will find countermeasures—digging too deeply for the weapons to penetrate, jamming or blinding U.S. reconnaissance assets, or the like. If the enemy must face advancing American ground forces as well as PGM strikes, however, the possible reactions are much more limited. Enemy forces will have to be concentrated to a much greater extent to ensure that they can face an American ground attack. It will not be sufficient to blind American satellites or disrupt computer networks if the American ground forces rolling forward can see enemy soldiers through their viewing prisms and kill them with their own weapons. Deeply dug bunkers may still protect vital command and control centers and weapons, but the importance of that fact will be greatly diminished when American soldiers have control of the enemy country above ground.

Recent history repeatedly highlights the importance of this fact. In 1991, Saddam Hussein withstood 39 days of devastating aerial attacks and remained undaunted. After 3 days of a coordinated air-ground campaign, he made peace. In 1998, he withstood another barrage of cruise missile attacks following his expulsion of weapons inspectors, and did not change his policy in the least. In 2003, he had prepared himself and his country for yet another drawn-out bombing campaign, and was stunned not by the "shock and awe" of the air campaign, but by the incredibly rapid ground offensive spearheaded by the 3rd Infantry Division, the 101st Air Assault Division, and the 1st Marine Division.

Throughout the history of airpower, evidence abounds that unbalanced attacks are much less successful than balanced attacks. German strategic bombing of Great Britain in World Wars I and II failed to bring that country to the peace table. Allied strategic bombing in World War II was equally ineffective, until it was combined with a massive ground campaign in Germany, or the threat of a massive invasion of the Japanese home islands. Strategic bombing directed at North Vietnam, unaccompanied by any meaningful threat of a ground invasion, failed completely to achieve its purpose.

The advocates of such bombing attacks are always ready to explain that if they had been given a little more time, a few more bombs, fewer political restrictions, and so forth, they would have brought the enemy to his knees without the need for ground forces. That assertion has never been proven. Even in Afghanistan, Bosnia, and Kosovo, ground forces or the threat of their use played the decisive role in bringing the enemy to surrender. In Afghanistan and Bosnia, the United States relied on local forces to supply the ground troops, which helped convince the hostile regimes to give in, but also left the United States politically beholden to its allies and unable to achieve its political aims as a result. During the Kosovo operation, Slobodan Milosevic withstood the American air attack right up until it became clear that a ground attack might follow—and then he surrendered.

In this world, anything is possible. The United States might win a future war relying solely on airpower, for the first time in history, with no American or local ground forces involved and no meaningful threat of their deployment. That possibility cannot be excluded. The Rumsfeld vision of military transformation, however, does not pursue that as a possibility: it relies on it as a certainty. By focusing all of America's defense resources on the single medium of airpower, Rumsfeld is betting America's future security on the conviction that the U.S. armed forces will be able to do *every time* what no military to date has *ever* been able to do. In doing so, he is greatly simplifying the task of those preparing to fight the United States by presenting them with only one threat to defeat.

A sound program of military transformation would proceed in exactly the opposite way. It would recognize the value of America's technological advantage in the area of PGMs. It would continue to enlarge and enhance them, much as Rumsfeld currently proposes. But it would not do so at the expense of the unique capabilities that ground forces bring to bear. It would focus, instead, on developing the capabilities of ground forces that are distinct from the capabilities provided by airpower. Ground forces can seize and hold terrain, separate hostile groups, and comb through urban areas with infinitely greater precision and distinction between combatant and noncombatant than can airpower. They can present the enemy with unacceptable situations simply by occupying a given piece of land, forcing the enemy to take actions that reveal intentions and expose the enemy to destruction. And it goes without saying that only ground forces can execute the peacemaking, peacekeeping, and reconstruction activities that have been essential to success in most of the wars America has fought in the past hundred years.

Above all, the United States must avoid the search for "efficiency" in military affairs. Redundancy is inherently a virtue in war. America's leaders should intentionally design systems with overlapping capabilities, spread across the services, and should intentionally support weapons that do not directly contribute to the overarching vision of war that they are pursuing. America should continue to try to build armed forces that are the best in every category and have the latent capabilities to meet challenges that cannot now even be imagined.

NOTE

1. David S. Alberts, John J. Garstka, and Frederick P. Stein, *Network Centric Warfare: Developing and Leveraging Information Superiority* (Washington, D.C.: U.S. Department of Defense C4ISR Cooperative Research Program, 1999).

2. See Frederick W. Kagan, "War and Aftermath," *Policy Review* 120 (August–September 2003): 3–27.

UNDERSTANDING TRANSFORMATION

TOM HONE

KAGAN'S ARGUMENT

Kagan's basic argument is that "the current program of transformation turns its back on the approach that had [sic] brought America success so far, and flies in the face of the historical lessons about how to transform a military." The successful approach that Kagan praises is one he calls "redundancy," and it means the development of multiple systems to carry out the same or related military missions.

For example, in the 1991 war against the forces of Iraq that had invaded and occupied Kuwait, the

Note: Frederick W. Kagan, a professor at the U.S. Military Academy at West Point, has written several essays critical of DoD transformation efforts. The present essay is a commentary on Kagan's article that appeared on the *Wall Street Journal's* OpinionJournal website in November 2003.

Tom Hone, "Understanding Transformation," Transformation Trends (*Washington, D.C.: Office of Force Transformation, U.S. Department of Defense, January 16, 2004). Public domain.*

Army's Multiple-Launch Rocket System barrages could strike the enemy's rear areas even if the weather prohibited air strikes. The Army also fielded Patriot and other antiaircraft systems to protect coalition ground forces in case Iraqi attack aircraft slipped through the coalition's combat air patrols. Penetrating Baghdad's air defenses was a mission given to both the Air Force's F-117 stealth attack aircraft and the Navy's Tomahawk cruise missiles. This is what Kagan calls "redundancy."

He goes on to argue that the critics of redundancy asserted that this duplication of mission capability was inefficient in cost terms. He admits that overlapping mission capabilities were indeed inefficient in cost terms, but also claims that, "In military affairs, redundancy is a virtue." It is a virtue because it reduces risk. As he says, "The willingness to accept redundancy and inefficiency in defense programs [of] the 1970s reflected a larger willingness to balance the development of capabilities . . . across the services." In his view, therefore, the forces produced in the 1970s and early 1980s were better able to deal with conflicts because they did not depend for their success on just one type or set of capabilities. If one approach (such as bombing from the air) did not work, then another (using the Army's aviation and organic artillery) could meet the mission need.

As Kagan also acknowledges, redundancy "is expensive," and he argues that the Defense Department, after the Cold War ended, turned to the American business community for ideas on how to field an effective force at the lowest reasonable cost. This effort to get more military power for less money led first the Clinton administration and then the Bush administration to turn to "Network-Centric Warfare." This new approach to warfare was embraced as a "revolution in military affairs" (RMA) that would solve the dilemma of how to field a powerful military on a peacetime budget.

According to Kagan, RMA had two parts. The most obvious was an emphasis on developing and fielding "long-range reconnaissance and strike capabilities." The second part was to purchase these capabilities by eliminating the redundancy that Kagan says was so valuable in earlier conflicts. As he says, the "watchwords for the Rumsfeld Pentagon have, therefore, been focus and efficiency," and "All of the services have participated in this race to a single goal," which is that all new weapons must be compatible with the Network-Centric approach to war.

Kagan strongly criticizes this approach: "The Rumsfeld vision of military transformation . . . is completely unbalanced. It will provide the U.S. with armed forces that do one thing only, even if they do it superbly well." Kagan does not pull his punches: "this single model . . . is one of the most seductive and dangerous visions of modern times."

But why is this "single model" so dangerous? Kagan provides several answers. First, he goes over some history to show that past RMAs have given the nations or forces that developed them only a temporary advantage. The British developed tanks in World War I, for example, but were defeated by the German Army's successful use of tanks, aircraft, and radio communication in 1940. In 1945, the United States detonated the world's first nuclear weapon. The Soviet Union "caught up" in 1949. Kagan's point is that this action-reaction cycle is inevitable, so that any effort by the United States to "freeze" other nations out of the market for long-range strike will inevitably fail. The key technologies will spread, says Kagan, and therefore any attempt to base U.S. military capabilities on them alone will not achieve the goal of staying ahead militarily. As he says, asymmetrical advantages "gained by one state do not normally last very long."

But his criticism is stronger than this. As he notes, "The search for an indefinite American 'asymmetrical advantage' . . . requires not merely a revolution in military affairs; it also requires a fundamental revolution in human affairs of a sort never seen before. It requires that America continue to change her armed forces so rapidly and successfully that no other state can ever catch up—indeed, that no other state in the world even try." Then comes his major criticism: "This unrealistic requirement is central to the current vision of military transformation."

As he says, the problem "with the current program is that it relies on maintaining an overwhelming advantage in a single area of military performance indefinitely." This, Kagan argues, is too risky. It invites defeat by opponents who become adept at guerilla wars and at terror. He points to recent events in Iraq as evidence of his claim that "armies do more than destroy targets," and that, in cases such as Iraq, "there is no escape from the need to have a large and capable army." Having the ability to attack an enemy with precision munitions is not enough.

His criticism of Secretary of Defense Rumsfeld is direct and harsh: "By focusing all of America's defense resources on the single medium of air power [coupled with PGMs], Mr. Rumsfeld is betting America's future security on the conviction that the U.S. armed forces will be able to do *every time* [emphasis in original] what no military to date has *ever* [emphasis in original] been able to do. In doing so, he is greatly simplifying the task of those preparing to fight the U.S. by presenting them with only one threat to defeat."

Kagan's recommended solution to this problem is straightforward: "A sound program of military transformation would proceed in exactly the opposite way. . . . It would focus . . . on developing the capabilities of ground forces that are distinct from the capabilities provided by air power." It would also "avoid the search for 'efficiency' in military affairs. Redundancy is inherently a virtue in war. America's leaders should intentionally design systems with overlapping capabilities, spread across the services, and should intentionally support weapons that do not directly contribute to the overarching vision of war that they are pursuing."

KAGAN'S ARGUMENT CRITICIZED

The problem with Kagan's critique is that he does not understand transformation. Transformation is not just about embracing new technology. Transformation is certainly not about just gaining a military advantage through the coupling of air systems (manned and unmanned) and precision weapons. Instead, transformation is an effort to provoke the military and civilian leaders of the nation to ask themselves some tough questions and then to find the right, albeit challenging, answers.

One question is this: Why did U.S. ground forces assaulting Baghdad have to find out what sort of enemy units they faced by using the traditional technique of coming to grips with the enemy? The Army calls this "movement to contact." Why should our soldiers—fighting on behalf of the richest, most technologically advanced country on the planet—have to do this? Why can't the nation's resources be used to provide soldiers at the tactical level with a picture of what is in front of them? And why can't our ground, sea, and air forces share a common battlefield "picture" that shows where they are and where the enemy is located?

Here is another question: Why can't the United States provide for its postconflict forces a system that allows them to disperse crowds or mobs without killing a lot of people who do not (at that moment at least) deserve to die? Small arms, tanks, machine guns, and grenades are good for killing and wounding the enemy. If the United States is to intervene in places to remove brutal dictators or to stop genocide, then why can't our forces have the tools to handle the inevitable crowds effectively?

Here is yet a third question: If the prompt use or show of force is often enough to keep a relatively small outbreak of violence from becoming something much larger and more destructive, then why can't U.S. forces move quickly to the places, worldwide, where such outbreaks occur and then operate with the support of other U.S. forces, even if they are not right next to the forces that have deployed? Put another way, why can't this country overcome the problem of not being able to combine the capabilities of widely dispersed forces?

Here is my last question: Why can't this productive and innovative nation combine intelligence with operations so that it is the enemy who is surprised and ambushed, and not U.S. forces? Why can't U.S. forces be both agile and immediately alert to the dangers they face?

Would anyone claim that trying to answer these questions is a waste of time and effort? I seriously doubt it. Yet these are precisely the sorts of questions that "transformation," which Kagan does not like, is striving to answer.

Or turn the clock back, as Kagan does, but select a different example. Put yourself in General Eisenhower's shoes after the Normandy invasion in June 1944. Wouldn't you like to defeat Germany in the West before winter sets in? Of course. But why can't you? For a number of significant reasons. One is that your air forces have essentially primitive weapons—unguided bombs dropped from high-altitude bombers or fast flying, low-altitude attack planes. The bombs are not all that accurate. As a result, heavy bombers

(B-17s and B-24s) trying to support ground offensives often miss their targets. Sometimes they even bomb Allied forces by mistake. Moreover, this lack of accuracy means that Allied bombers have to return again and again to targets within Germany to achieve anything close to the desired effects.

A problem worse than bomber accuracy is logistics. Through the summer and early fall of 1944, the Allied armies in northern France and Belgium depended on two ports for supplies, and both were no farther east than the initial Normandy landing beaches. As a result, the Allied offensive against the German armies in France began to slow down because of a lack of supplies. Logistics slowed down the offensive that had routed the German armies in northern France, and a slowed offensive gave the Germans more time to retreat and regroup. General Eisenhower wanted a rapid advance across a broad front. His logistics organization could not sustain such an offensive.

Another problem for you if you are in Eisenhower's place is intelligence. You badly need to know where the effective German divisions are and when they plan to move by road or by rail. You have an advantage in the air, and you want to be able to use it before the weather covers the front with rain, clouds, and fog. But to use your aviation and limited ground forces effectively, you need to be able to locate the enemy. Your intelligence is effective, but not effective enough.

As supreme Allied commander, you face many other problems, but what if you could have solutions to those just mentioned? What if your air forces had precision munitions? What if your logisticians had more ports, larger transport aircraft, and better means of moving supplies from ports and supply dumps to the front? What if you did not even have supply dumps, but could supply units with what they needed when they needed it? What if your intelligence organization could pinpoint the location of enemy formations and anticipate their movements?

If you could just have these things, you could avoid having to halt offensives for lack of supplies. You could isolate German armies from their support by using your superior air forces. You could use your airborne artillery (those B-17s and B-24s) to smash enemy positions and formations. You would know where these targets are, and your aircraft would have weapons accurate enough to hit them—even in darkness and through clouds. Finally, your intelligence would warn you of efforts like the German Ardennes counteroffensive in the winter of 1944. In short, you could win the war earlier, with many fewer casualties.

This is what transformation is about. It says, "Take traditional military problems and ask what can be done to solve them." Is the enemy hiding under cover or beneath storms? Then develop systems that can find the enemy and strike him. Is the enemy trying to hold his units together with electronic communications? Then identify those communications and disrupt or manipulate them. Is the enemy planning a phased operation? If so, then put it out of phase.

The emphasis on cost-effectiveness in transformation is necessary because the funds for national defense are limited. *There will never be enough funds to cover all the legitimate needs*. With funds relatively scarce, the Department of Defense must maximize the capabilities it offers to the president at the lowest reasonable cost. That can be (and is being) done by investing in sensors and in other means of gathering information. With adequate information—including the identification and location of key targets—the forces of the United States can maximize their combat potential while not taking an undue share of the nation's human and material resources.

What Kagan does is to set up a "straw man" and then demolish it. He reduces transformation to RMA, and then he goes even further and reduces RMA to using only aviation to attack key targets with precision munitions. In so doing, he ignores what both "RMA" and "transformation" mean. Transformation is much broader than RMA, and RMA itself has emphasized sensors and communications far more than Kagan's essay suggests.

Moreover, he is just wrong to claim that the many redundant systems produced in the past were a planned effort to reduce risk through deliberate duplication and overlap. There was indeed redundancy, and redundancy of the type he describes and praises is indeed a means of reducing risk, but a lot of the redundancy of the past was the result of a lack of coordination among the services or the consequence of a requirements process that forced supporters of a new system to round up allies by inflating formal system requirements. There were no "good old days." The funds have always been short, and therefore the competition for them has always been great. Now, however, there are some sensible military standards that the secretary of defense can apply to the many requests for scarce resources.

The standards are in the service and Joint Forces Command (JFCOM) transformation roadmaps. That is where you go to find the future. That is where you find answers to the really hard questions, such as "Why can't U.S. soldiers and Marines see into urban complexes to locate the enemies waiting there to ambush them?" Secretary Rumsfeld is trying to convince the services to stop competing for resources to do the same job or perform the same mission. His technique is to direct the services and JFCOM to actively participate in the defense planning process by developing coherent, consistent roadmaps that will eventually lead to forces that have the capabilities required to support the national security strategy of the United States. Another way of putting this is to say that Secretary Rumsfeld wants a force that is deliberately and not accidentally relevant to the nation's security needs.

The services and JFCOM have responded to the secretary's direction and taken his emphasis on transformation seriously. Does this mean that Kagan is correct when he asserts that the Department of Defense is trying to achieve an unattainable aim—the "locking out" of potential military challengers from the "marketplace" of military progress? No. What the Defense Department is trying to do is change the way those in this vast organization think about defense. Transformation is about thinking and behaving as much as it is about science, technology, and development. It is not about getting from here to there in a material sense. Instead, it is about regarding combat and conflict in a new way—a way that takes advantage of the great potential of the American people and the economic, technical, and scientific institutions they create and support. These are the traits manifested in the people that volunteer to make up this nation's military.

Kagan is right to say that redundancy can be and has sometimes been "a virtue in war." But a lot of that redundancy he praises was not created to reduce risk in wartime. It just happened that way. It was accidental. Transformation is about making those virtues deliberate.

CHAPTER 8

INTEGRATING FORCE AND OTHER POLICY TOOLS FOR A COMPREHENSIVE DEFENSE

TO WHAT ENDS MILITARY POWER?

ROBERT J. ART

It is vital to think carefully and precisely about the uses and limits of military power. That is the purpose of this essay. It is intended as a backdrop for policy debates, not a prescription of specific policies. It consciously eschews elaborate detail on the requisite military forces for scenarios *a . . . n* and focuses instead on what military power has and has not done, can and cannot do. Every model of how the world works has policy implications. But not every policy is based on a clear view of how the world works. What, then, are the uses to which military power can be put?

WHAT ARE THE USES OF FORCE?

The goals that states pursue range widely and vary considerably from case to case. Military power is more useful for realizing some goals than others, although it is generally considered of some use by most states for all of the goals that they hold. If we attempt, however, to be descriptively accurate, to enumerate all of the purposes for which states use force, we shall simply end up with a bewildering list. Descriptive accuracy is not a virtue per se for analysis. In fact, descriptive accuracy is generally bought at the cost of analytical utility. (A concept that is descriptively accurate is usually analytically useless.) Therefore, rather than compile an exhaustive list of such purposes, I have selected four categories that themselves analytically exhaust the functions that force can serve: defense, deterrence, compellence, and "swaggering"[1] (see Table 7).

Not all four functions are necessarily well or equally served by a given military posture. In fact, usually only the great powers have the wherewithal to develop military forces that can serve more than two functions at once. Even then, this is achieved only vis-à-vis smaller powers, not the other great ones. The measure of the capabilities of a state's military forces must be made relative to those of another state, not with reference to some absolute scale. A state that can compel another state can also defend against it and usually deter it. A state that can defend against another state cannot thereby automatically deter or compel it. A state can deter another state without having the ability to either defend against or

compel it. A state that can swagger vis-à-vis another may or may not be able to perform any of the other three functions relative to it. Where feasible, defense is the goal that all states aim for first. If defense is not possible, deterrence is generally the next priority. Swaggering is the function most difficult to pin down analytically; deterrence, the one whose achievement is the most difficult to demonstrate; compellence, the easiest to demonstrate but among the hardest to achieve. The following discussion develops these points more fully.

The "defensive" use of force is the deployment of military power so as to be able to do two things—to ward off an attack and to minimize damage to oneself if attacked. For defensive purposes, a state will direct its forces against those of a potential or actual attacker, but not against the unarmed population of an attacker. For defensive purposes, a state can deploy its forces in place prior to an attack, use them after an attack has occurred to repel it, or strike first if it believes that an attack upon it is imminent or inevitable. The defensive use of force can thus involve both peaceful and physical employment and both repellent (second) strikes and offensive (first) strikes.[2] If a state strikes first when it believes an attack upon it is imminent, it is launching a preemptive blow. Preemptive and preventive blows are undertaken when a state calculates, first, that others plan to attack it and, second, that to delay in striking offensively is against its interests. A state preempts to wrest the advantage of the first strike from an opponent. A state launches a preventive attack because it believes that others will attack it when the balance of forces turns in their favor and therefore attacks while the balance of forces is in its favor. In both cases, it is better to strike first than to be struck first. The major distinction between preemption and prevention is the calculation about when an opponent's attack will occur. For preemption, it is a matter of hours, days, or even a few weeks at the most; for prevention, months or even a few years. In the case of preemption, the state has almost no control over the timing of its attack; in the case of prevention, the state can in a more leisurely way contemplate the timing of its attack. For both cases, it is the belief in the certainty of war

This essay has been edited and is reprinted from International Security 4 (Spring 1980): 3–35. © 1980 by the President and Fellows of Harvard College and the Massachusetts Institute of Technology.

Table 7

The Purposes of Force

Type	Purpose	Mode	Targets	Characteristics
Defensive	Fend off attacks and/or reduce damage of an attack	Peaceful and physical	Primarily military Secondarily industrial	Defensive preparations can have dissuasion value; defensive preparations can look aggressive; first strikes can be taken for defense.
Deterrent	Prevent adversary from initiating an action	Peaceful	Primarily civilian Secondarily industrial Tertiary military	Threats of retaliation made so as not to have to be carried out; second strike preparations can be viewed as first strike preparations.
Compellent	Compel adversary to stop doing something or start doing something	Peaceful and physical	Civilian, industrial, and military with no clear ranking	Easy to recognize but hard to achieve; compellent actions can be justified on defensive grounds.
Swaggering	Enhance prestige	Peaceful	None	Difficult to describe because of instrumental and irrational nature; swaggering can be threatening.

that governs the offensive, defensive attack. For both cases, the maxim, "the best defense is a good offense," makes good sense.

The "deterrent" use of force is the deployment of military power so as to be able to prevent an adversary from doing something that the state does not want its adversary to do and that he might otherwise be tempted to do by threatening unacceptable punishment if he does it. Deterrence is thus the threat of retaliation. Its purpose is to prevent something undesirable from happening. The threat of punishment is directed at the adversary's population and/or industrial infrastructure. The effectiveness of the threat depends upon a state's ability to convince a potential adversary that it has both the will and power to punish severely if the undesirable action in question is undertaken. Deterrence therefore employs force peacefully. It is the threat to resort to force in order to punish that is the essence of deterrence. If the threat has to be carried out, deterrence, by definition, has failed. A deterrent threat is made precisely with the intent that it will not have to be carried out. Threats are made to prevent actions from being undertaken. If the threat has to be implemented, the action has already been undertaken. Hence deterrence can be judged successful only if the retaliatory threats have not been implemented.

Deterrence and defense are alike in that both are intended to protect the state or its closest allies from physical attacks. The purpose of both is dissuasion—persuading others not to undertake actions harmful to oneself. The defensive use of force dissuades by convincing an adversary that it cannot conquer one's military forces. The deterrent use of force dissuades by convincing the adversary that its population and territory will suffer terrible damage if it initiates the undesirable action. Defense dissuades by presenting an unvanquishable military force. Deterrence dissuades by presenting the certainty of retaliatory devastation.

Defense is possible without deterrence, and deterrence is possible without defense. A state can have the military wherewithall to repel an invasion without also being able to threaten devastation to the invader's population or territory. Similarly, a state can have the wherewithall credibly to threaten an adversary with such devastation and yet be unable to repel his invading force. Defense, therefore, does not necessarily buy deterrence, nor deterrence defense. A state that can defend itself from attack, moreover, will have little need to develop the wherewithall to deter. If physical attacks can be repelled or if the damage from them drastically minimized, the incentive to develop a retaliatory capability is low. A state that cannot defend itself, however, will try to develop an effective deterrent, if possible. No state will leave its population and territory open to attack if it has the means to redress the situation. Whether a given state can defend or deter or do both vis-à-vis another depends upon two factors: (1) the quantitative balance of forces between it and its adversary; and (2) the qualitative balance of forces, that is, whether the extant military technology favors the offense or the defense. These two factors are situation-specific and therefore require careful analysis of the case at hand.

The "compellent" use of force is the deployment of military power so as to be able either to stop an adversary from doing something that it has already undertaken or to get the adversary to do something not yet undertaken. Compellence, in Schelling's words, "involves initiating an action . . . that can cease, or become harmless, only if the opponent responds."[3] Compellence can employ force either physically or peacefully. A state can start actually harming another with physical destruction until the latter abides by the former's wishes. Or, a state can take actions against another that do not cause physical harm but that require the latter to pay some type of significant price until it changes its behavior. America's bombing of North Vietnam in early 1965 was an example of physical compellence; Tirpitz's building of a German fleet aimed against England's in the two decades before World War I, an example of peaceful compellence. In the first case, the United States started bombing North Vietnam to compel it to stop assisting the Vietcong forces in South Vietnam. In the second case, Germany built a battlefleet that in an engagement threatened to cripple England's to compel the latter to make a general political settlement advantageous to Germany. In both cases, one state initiated some type of action against another precisely to be able to stop it—to bargain the action away for the desired response from the "put upon" state.

The distinction between compellence and deterrence is one between the active and passive use of force. The success of a deterrent threat is measured by its not having to be used. The success of a compellent action is measured by how closely and quickly the adversary conforms to one's stipulated wishes. In the case of successful deterrence, one is trying to demonstrate a negative, to show why something did not happen. It can never be clear whether one's actions were crucial to, or irrelevant to, why another state chose not to do something. In the case of successful compellence, the clear sequence of actions and reactions lends a compelling plausibility to the centrality of one's actions. Fig. 2 illustrates the distinction. In successful compellence, state B can claim that its pressure deflected state A from its course of action. In successful deterrence, state B has no change in state A's behavior to point to, but instead must resort to claiming that its threats were responsible for the continuity in A's behavior. State A may have changed its behavior for reasons other than state B's compellent action. State A may have continued with its same behavior for reasons other than state B's deterrent threat. Proving the importance of B's influence on A for either case is not easy, but it is more plausible to claim that B influenced A when there is a change in A's behavior than when there is not. Explaining why something did not happen is more difficult than explaining why something did.

Compellence may be easier to demonstrate than deterrence, but it is harder to achieve. Schelling argues that compellent actions tend to be vaguer in their objectives than deterrent threats and for that reason, more difficult to attain.[4] If an adversary has a hard time understanding what it is that one wishes

Figure 2
Compellence and Deterrence

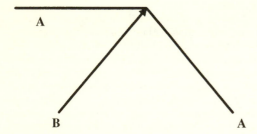

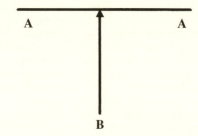

Compellence	**Deterrence**
1. A is doing something that B cannot tolerate	1. A is presently not doing anything that B finds intolerable
2. B initiates action against A to compel it to stop its intolerable actions	2. B tells A that if A changes its behavior and does something intolerable, B will inflict punishment
3. A stops its intolerable actions and B stops its (or both cease simultaneously)	3. A continues not to do anything B finds intolerable

it to do, its compliance with one's wishes is made more difficult. There is, however, no inherent reason why a compellent action must be vaguer than a deterrent threat with regard to how clearly the adversary understands what is wanted. "Do not attack me" is not any clearer in its ultimate meaning than "stop attacking my friend." A state can be as confused or as clear about what it wishes to prevent as it can be about what it wishes to stop. The clarity, or lack of it, of the objectives of compellent actions and deterrent threats does not vary according to whether the given action is compellent or deterrent in nature, but rather according to a welter of particularities associated with the given action. Some objectives, for example, are inherently clearer and hence easier to perceive than others. Some statesmen communicate more clearly than others. Some states have more power to bring to bear for a given objective than others. It is the specifics of a given situation, not any intrinsic difference between compellence and deterrence, that determines the clarity with which an objective is perceived.

We must, therefore, look elsewhere for the reason why compellence is comparatively harder to achieve than deterrence. It lies, not in what one asks another to do, but in *how* one asks. With deterrence, state B asks something of state A in this fashion: "do not take action *X;* for if you do, I will bash you over the head with this club." With compellence, state B asks something of state A in this fashion: "I am now going to bash you over the head with this club and will continue to do so until you do what I want." In the former case, state A can easily deny with great plausibility any intention of having planned to take action *X*. In the latter case, state A cannot deny either that it is engaged in a given course of action or that it is being subjected to pressure by state B. If they are to be successful, compellent actions require a state to alter its behavior in a manner quite visible to all in response to an equally visible forceful initiative taken by another state. In contrast to compellent actions, deterrent threats are both easier to appear to have ignored or easier to acquiesce to without great loss of face. In contrast to deterrent threats, compellent actions more directly engage the prestige and the passions of the put-upon state. Less prestige is lost in not doing something than in clearly altering behavior due to pressure from another. In the case of compellence, a state has publicly committed its prestige and resources to a given line of conduct that it is now asked to give up. This is not so for deterrence. Thus, compellence is intrinsically harder to attain than deterrence, not because its objectives are vaguer, but because it demands more humiliation from the compelled state.

The fourth purpose to which military power can be put is the most difficult to be precise about. "Swaggering" is in part a residual category, the deployment of military power for purposes other than defense, deterrence, or compellence. Force is not aimed directly at dissuading another state from attacking, at repelling attacks, or at compelling it to do something

specific. The objectives for swaggering are more diffuse, ill-defined, and problematic than that. Swaggering almost always involves only the peaceful use of force and is expressed usually in one of two ways: displaying one's military might at military exercises and national demonstrations and buying or building the era's most prestigious weapons. The swagger use of force is the most egoistic: it aims to enhance the national pride of a people or to satisfy the personal ambitions of its ruler. A state or statesman swaggers to look and feel more powerful and important, to be taken seriously by others in the councils of international decisionmaking, or to enhance the nation's image in the eyes of others. If its image is enhanced, the nation's defense, deterrent, and compellent capabilities may also be enhanced; but swaggering is not undertaken solely or even primarily for these specific purposes. Swaggering is pursued because it offers to bring prestige "on the cheap," and because of the fundamental yearning of states and statesmen for respect and prestige. Swaggering is more something to be enjoyed for itself than to be employed for a specific, rational end.

And yet the instrumental role of swaggering cannot be totally discounted because of the fundamental relation between force and foreign policy that obtains in an anarchic environment. Because there is a connection between the military might that a nation is thought to possess and the success that it achieves in attaining its objectives, the enhancement of a state's stature in the eyes of others can always be justified on realpolitik lines. If swaggering causes other states to take one's interests more seriously into account, then the general interests of the state will benefit. Even in its instrumental role, however, swaggering is undertaken less for any given end than for all ends. The swaggering function of military power is thus simultaneously the most comprehensive and the most diffuse, the most versatile in its effects and the least focused in its immediate aims, the most instrumental in the long run and the least instrumental in the short run, easy to justify on hard-headed grounds and often undertaken on emotional grounds. Swaggering mixes the rational and irrational more than the other three functions of military power and, for that reason, remains both pervasive in international relations and elusive to describe.

Defense, deterrence, compellence, and swaggering—these are the four general purposes for which force can be employed. Discriminating among them analytically, however, is easier than applying them in practice. This is due to two factors. First, we need to know the motives behind an act to judge its purpose; but the problem is that motives cannot be readily inferred from actions because several motives can be served by the same action. But neither can one readily infer the motives of a state from what it publicly or officially proclaims them to be. Such statements should not necessarily be taken at face value because of the role that bluff and dissimulation play in statecraft. Such statements are also often concocted with domestic, not foreign, audiences in mind, or else are deliberate exercises in studied ambiguity. Motives are important in interpreting actions, but neither actions nor words always clearly delineate motives.

It is, moreover, especially difficult to distinguish defensive from compellent actions and deterrent from swaggering ones unless we know the reasons for which they were undertaken. Peaceful defensive preparations often look largely the same as peaceful compellent ones. Defensive attacks are nearly indistinguishable from compellent ones. Is the state that attacks first the defender or the compeller? Deterrence and swaggering both involve the acquisition and display of an era's prestigious weapons. Are such weapons acquired to enhance prestige or to dissuade an attack?

Consider the following example. Germany launched an attack upon France and Russia at the end of July 1914 and thereby began World War I. There are two schools of thought as to why Germany did this. One holds that its motives were aggressive—territorial aggrandizement, economic gain, and elevation to the status of a world empire. Another holds that its motives were preventive and hence defensive. Germany struck first because it feared encirclement, slow strangulation, and then inevitable attack by its two powerful neighbors, foes whom it felt were daily increasing their military might faster than it was. Germany struck while it had the chance to win.

It is not a simple matter to decide which school is the more correct because both can marshall evidence to build a powerful case. Assume for the moment, though, that the second is closer to the truth. There are then two possibilities to consider: (1) Germany launched an attack because it *was* the case that its foes were planning to attack eventually, and Germany had the evidence to prove it; or (2) Germany felt it had reasonable evidence of its foes' *intent* to attack eventually, but in fact the evidence was wrong because it misperceived their intent from their actions. If the first was the case, then we must ask: how responsible was Germany's diplomacy in the 15 years before 1914, aggressive and blundering as it was, in breeding hostility in its neighbors? Germany attacked in the knowledge that they would eventually have struck, but if its 15-year diplomatic record was a significant factor in causing them to lay these plans, must we conclude that Germany in 1914 was merely acting defensively? Must we confine our judgment about the defensive or aggressive nature of the act to the month or even the year in which it occurred? If not, how many years back in history do we go to make a judgment? If the second possibility was the case, then we must ask: if Germany attacked in the belief, mistakenly as it turns out, that it would be attacked, must we conclude that Germany was acting defensively? Must we confine our judgment about the defensive or aggressive nature of the act simply to Germany's beliefs about others' intent, without reference to their actual intent?

It is not easy to answer these questions. Fortunately, we do not have to. Asking them is enough because it illustrates that an assessment of the *legitimacy* of a state's motives in using force is integral to the task of determining what its motives are. One cannot, that is, specify motives without at the same time making judgments about their legitimacy. The root cause of this need lies in the nature of state action. In anarchy, every state is a valid judge of the legitimacy of its goals because there is no supranational authority to enforce agreed-upon rules. Because of the lack of universal standards, we are forced to examine each case within its given context and to make individual judgments about the meaning of the particulars. When individual judgment is exercised, individuals may well differ. Definitive answers are more likely to be the exception rather than the rule.

Where does all of this leave us? Our four categories tell us what are the four possible purposes for which states can employ military power. The attributes of each alert us to the types of evidence for which to search. But because the context of an action is crucial to judge its ultimate purpose, these four categories cannot be applied mindlessly and ahistorically. Each state's purpose in using force in a given instance must fall into one of these four categories. We know a priori what the possibilities are. Determining which possibility is an exercise in judgment, an exercise that depends as much upon the particulars of the given case as it does upon the general features of the given category.

WHAT ARE THE LIMITS TO THE USE OF FORCE?

There are inherent limits to what force can accomplish. Military power can be used to conquer the territory of another nation, but not to conquer the minds of its inhabitants. Military power is a necessary ingredient for political power, but is no substitute for political support and political leadership. Military power can create the necessary political preconditions for an economy to prosper, but cannot substitute for the industry of a people or for a sound trade and monetary policy.[5] First and foremost, a state uses its military power to check, deter, or defend against the forces of another nation. With greater difficulty, it may try to compel others, but compellence, as we have seen, is difficult to achieve. Force can easily be used to maim and kill, but only with greater difficulty and with great expenditure of effort, to rule and pacify. Nuclear weapons can maim and kill more swiftly and with greater ease than can conventional weapons, but they do not thereby automatically enable one nation to rule or pacify another, nor to bring political harmony to its populace. The effectiveness with which military functions can be discharged does not translate directly into the effectiveness with which political functions can be performed. If that were the case, then military power alone would be sufficient to conduct a successful foreign policy. But that, clearly, is not the case. If one nation possesses a military edge over another, it is in a stronger bargaining position than it would otherwise be. But it still has to bargain, and it is here that diplomatic and political skills and economic resources come into play. In international relations, superior military strength means enhanced resources with which to bargain but does not guarantee outright control. As Kenneth Waltz has succinctly put it: "Inability to exercise *political* control over others does not indicate military weakness."[6]

Even for the greatest of nations, moreover, military power is always in short supply. Great powers have great ambitions and, consequently, need to ration their military power among competing goals. Smaller powers have great needs and little wherewithal to satisfy them and, consequently, must carefully husband their military power for their most pressing needs. For the great and small alike, there are, in addition, always opportunity costs in the exercise of military power. Except in those situations in which a nation is fighting for its very existence, there are always good reasons for limiting the amount of force actually applied to achieve a given goal. Thus, military power is a necessary ingredient for political and economic success in international relations, but not the sole ingredient. No matter how militarily powerful a nation is, force cannot achieve those things for which only political skill and economic industry are suited. In an anarchic world, it is better to be militarily strong than weak. But such strength alone, especially when there are other strong powers, is not a panacea.

WHAT IS THE FUTURE OF FORCE?

If the past be any guide to the future, then military power will remain central to the course of international relations. Those states that do not have the ability to field large forces (e.g., Denmark) or those that choose to field forces far smaller than their economies can bear (e.g., Japan) will pay the price. Both will find themselves with less control over their own fate than would otherwise be the case. Those states that field powerful military forces will find themselves in greater control, but also that their great military power can produce unintended effects and that such power is not a solution to all their problems. For both the strong and the weak, however, as long as anarchy obtains, force will remain the final arbiter to resolve the disputes that arise among them. As has always been the case, most disputes will be settled short of the physical use of force. But as long as the physical use of force remains a viable option, military power will vitally affect the manner in which all states deal with one another in peacetime.

The efficacy of force endures. It must. For in anarchy, force and politics are connected. By itself, military power guarantees neither survival nor prosperity. But it is almost always the essential ingredient for both. Because resort to force is the ultimate card of all states, the seriousness of a state's intentions is conveyed fundamentally by its having a credible military posture. Without it, a state's diplomacy generally lacks effectiveness. Force need not be physically used to be politically useful. Threats need not be made overtly to be communicated. The mere presence of a credible military option is often sufficient to make the point. It is the capability to resort to military force if all else fails that serves as the most effective brake against having to do so. Lurking behind the scenes, unstated but explicit, lies the military muscle that gives meaning to the posturings of the diplomats. Diplomacy is the striking of compromises by parties with differing perspectives and clashing interests. The ultimate ability of each to resort to force disciplines the diplomats. Precisely because each knows that all can come to blows if they do not strike compromises do the diplomats engage in the hard work necessary to construct them. There is truth to the old adage: "The best way to keep the peace is first to prepare for war."

NOTES

1. The term "compellence" was coined by Thomas C. Schelling, *Arms and Influence* (New Haven: Yale University Press, 1966). Part of my discussion of compellence and deterrence draws upon his as it appears in Chapter 2 (pages 69–86) of his volume, but, as will be made clear below, I disagree with some of his conclusions.

2. Military power can be used in one of two modes—"physically" and "peacefully." The physical use of force refers to its actual employment against an adversary, usually but not always in a mutual exchange of blows. The peaceful use of force refers either to an explicit threat to resort to force, or to the implicit threat to use it that is communicated simply by a state's having it available for use. The physical use of force means that one nation is literally engaged in harming, destroying, or crippling those possessions that another nation holds dear, including its military forces. The peaceful use of force is referred to as such because, although force is "used" in the sense that it is employed explicitly or implicitly for the assistance it is thought to render in achieving a given goal, it does not result in any physical destruction of another nation's valued possessions. There is obviously a gray area between these two modes of use—the one in which a nation prepares (i.e., mobilizes or moves) its military forces for use against another nation but has not yet committed them to inflicting damage.

3. Schelling, *Arms and Influence,* 72.

4. Ibid., 72–73.

5. For a brilliant sketch of the role that American military power played in creating the political conditions conducive to economic and monetary expansion, see Robert Gilpin, *U.S. Power and the Multinationals* (New York: Basic Books, 1975), 99–112.

6. Kenneth N. Waltz, "National Force, International Structure, and the World Balance of Power," *Journal of International Affairs* 21 (1967): 215–31. Reprinted in part in *International Politics,* ed. Robert Art and Robert Jervis (Boston: Little, Brown, 1973), 252.

COMMAND OF THE COMMONS:
THE MILITARY FOUNDATIONS OF U.S. HEGEMONY

BARRY R. POSEN

Since the end of the Cold War, scholars, commentators, and practitioners of foreign policy have debated what structure of world power would follow the bipolar U.S.-Soviet competition, and what U.S. foreign policy would replace containment. Those who hypothesized a long "unipolar moment" of extraordinary U.S. power have proven more prescient than those who expected the relatively quick emergence of a multipolar world.[1] Experts who recommended a policy of "primacy"—essentially hegemony —to consolidate, exploit, and expand the U.S. advantage have carried the day against those who argued for a more restrained U.S. foreign policy.[2] One can argue that the jury is still out, the "moment" will soon pass, and the policy of hegemony enabled by great power will be fleeting. But the evidence does not support such predictions. Unipolarity and U.S. hegemony will likely be around for some time, although observers do suggest that the United States could hasten its own slide from the pinnacle through indiscipline or hyperactivity.[3]

The new debate on U.S. grand strategy is essentially about which variant of a hegemonic strategy the United States should pursue. The strategy proposed by President George W. Bush is, in caricature, unilateral, nationalistic, and oriented largely around the U.S. advantage in physical power, especially military power.[4] This is "primacy" as it was originally conceived. The last years of Bill Clinton's administration saw the emergence of a strategy that also depended heavily on military power, but was more multilateral and liberal and more concerned with international legitimacy. It aimed to preserve the dominant U.S. global position, including its military position, which was understood to be an essential underpinning of global activism.[5] That strategy has recently been elaborated, formalized, and defended under the rubric of "selective engagement" by Robert Art.[6] Although this is too big an argument to settle solely on the basis of a military analysis, the understanding of U.S. military power developed below suggests that selective engagement is likely to prove more sustainable than primacy.

One pillar of U.S. hegemony is the vast military power of the United States. A staple of the U.S. debate about the size of the post–Cold War defense budget is the observation that the United States spends more than virtually all of the world's other major military powers combined, most of which are U.S. allies.[7] Observers of the actual capabilities that this effort produces can focus on a favorite aspect of U.S. superiority to make the point that the United States sits comfortably atop the military food chain, and is likely to remain there. This essay takes a slightly different approach. Below I argue that the United States enjoys command of the commons— command of the sea, space, and air. I discuss how command of the commons supports a hegemonic grand strategy. I explain why it seems implausible that a challenge to this command could arise in the near-to-medium term. Then I review the arenas of military action where adversaries continue to be able to fight U.S. forces with some hope of success—the "contested zones." I argue that in the near-to-medium term, the United States will not be able to establish command in these arenas. The interrelationship between U.S. command of the commons and the persistence of the contested zones suggests that the United States can probably pursue a policy of selective engagement but not one of primacy.

I purposefully eschew discussing U.S. military power in light of the metrics of the current and previous administrations. The Clinton administration planned to be able to fight two nearly simultaneous major theater wars; the Bush administration's emerging, and even more demanding, metric is the "4-2-1" principle—that is, deter in four places, counterattack in two, and if necessary, go to the enemy's capital in one of the two.[8] These metrics obscure the foundations of U.S. military power—that is, all the difficult and expensive things that the United States does to create the conditions that permit it to even consider one, two, or four campaigns.[9]

COMMAND OF THE COMMONS

The U.S. military currently possesses command of the global commons. Command of the commons is analogous to command of the sea, or in Paul Kennedy's words, it is analogous to "naval mastery."[10] The "commons," in the case of the sea and space, are areas that belong to no one state and that provide access to much of the globe.[11] Airspace does technically belong to the countries below it, but there are few countries that can deny their airspace above 15,000 feet to U.S. warplanes. Command does not mean that other states cannot use the commons in peacetime. Nor does it mean that others cannot ac-

This essay has been edited and is reprinted from International Security 28 (Summer 2003): 5–46. © 2003 by the President and Fellows of Harvard College and the Massachusetts Institute of Technology.

quire military assets that can move through or even exploit them when unhindered by the United States. Command means that the United States gets vastly more military use out of the sea, space, and air than do other states; that it can credibly threaten to deny their use to others; and that others would lose a military contest for the commons if they attempted to deny them to the United States. Having lost such a contest, they could not mount another effort for a very long time, and the United States would preserve, restore, and consolidate its hold after such a fight.[12]

Command of the commons is the key military enabler of the U.S. global power position. It allows the United States to exploit more fully other sources of power, including its own economic and military might, as well as the economic and military might of its allies. Command of the commons also helps the United States to weaken its adversaries by restricting their access to economic, military, and political assistance. Command of the commons has permitted the United States to wage war on short notice even where it has had little permanent military presence. This was true of the 1991 Persian Gulf War, the 1993 intervention in Somalia, and the 2001 action in Afghanistan.

Command of the commons provides the United States with more useful military potential for a hegemonic foreign policy than any other offshore power has ever had. When nineteenth-century Britain had command of the sea, its timely power projection capability ended at the maximum range of the Royal Navy's shipboard guns. The Royal Navy could deliver an army many places around the globe, but the army's journey inland was usually difficult and slow; without such a journey, Britain's ability to influence events was limited. As the nineteenth century unfolded, the industrialization of the continental powers, improvements in land transportation, and the development of coastal warfare technologies, such as the torpedo and mine, reduced the strategic leverage provided by command of the sea.[13]

The United States enjoys the same command of the sea that Britain once did, and it can also move large and heavy forces around the globe. But command of space allows the United States to see across the surface of the world's land masses and to gather vast amounts of information. At least on the matter of medium-to-large-scale military developments, the United States can locate and identify military targets with considerable fidelity and communicate this information to offensive forces in a timely fashion. Air power, ashore and afloat, can reach targets deep inland; and with modern precision-guided weaponry, it can often hit and destroy those targets. U.S. forces can even more easily do great damage to a state's transportation and communications networks, as well as its economic infrastructure. When U.S. ground forces do venture inland, they do so against a weakened adversary; they also have decent intelligence, good maps, and remarkable knowledge of their own position from moment to moment. Moreover, they can call on a great reserve of responsive, accurate, air-delivered firepower, which permits the ground forces considerable freedom of action. Political, economic, and technological changes since the 1980s have thus partially reversed the rise of land power relative to sea power that occurred in the late nineteenth century and helped to erode Britain's formal and informal empire.

The Sources of Command

What are the sources of U.S. command of the commons? One obvious source is the general U.S. superiority in economic resources. According to the Central Intelligence Agency, the United States produces 23 percent of gross world product (GWP); it has more than twice as many resources under the control of a single political authority as either of the next two most potent economic powers—Japan with 7 percent of GWP and China with 10 percent.[14] With 3.5 percent of U.S. gross domestic product devoted to defense (nearly 1 percent of GWP), the U.S. military can undertake larger projects than any other military in the world. The specific weapons and platforms needed to secure and exploit command of the commons are expensive. They depend on a huge scientific and industrial base for their design and production. In 2001, the U.S. Department of Defense budgeted nearly as much money for military research and development as Germany and France together budgeted for their entire military efforts.[15] The military exploitation of information technology, a field where the U.S. military excels, is a key element. The systems needed to command the commons require significant skills in systems integration and the management of large-scale industrial projects, at which the U.S. defense industry excels. The development of new weapons and tactics depends on decades of expensively accumulated technological and tactical experience embodied in the institutional memory of public and private military research and development organizations.[16] Finally, the military personnel needed to run these systems are among the most highly skilled and highly trained in the world. The barriers to entry to a state seeking the military capabilities to fight for the commons are very high.

Command of the Sea

U.S. nuclear attack submarines (SSNs) are perhaps the key assets of U.S. open-ocean antisubmarine warfare (ASW) capability, which, in turn, is the key to maintaining command of the sea.[17] During the Cold War, the Soviet Union challenged U.S. command of the sea with its large force of SSNs. The U.S. Navy quietly won the "third battle of the Atlantic," although the Soviet successes in quieting their nuclear submarines in the 1980s would have necessitated another expensive and difficult round of technological competition had the Cold War not ended.[18] At more than $1 billion each (more than $2 billion each for the new U.S. SSN), modern nuclear submarines are prohibitively expensive for most states.

Aside from the United States, Britain, China, France, and Russia are the only other countries that can build them, and China is scarcely able.[19] Several partially built nuclear attack submarines remained in Russian yards in the late 1990s, but no new ones have been laid down.[20] Perhaps twenty to thirty Russian nuclear attack submarines remain in service.[21] Currently, the U.S. Navy has fifty-four SSNs in service and four under construction. It plans to build roughly two new boats every 3 years. It also has a program to convert four Ohio-class Trident ballistic missile submarines into nonnuclear cruise missile–carrying submarines for land attack. The U.S. Navy also dominates the surface of the oceans, with twelve aircraft carriers (nine of them nuclear powered) capable of launching high-performance aircraft.[22] The Soviet Union was just building its first true aircraft carrier when its political system collapsed. Aside from France, which has one, no other country has any nuclear-powered aircraft carriers. At $5 billion apiece for a single U.S. Nimitz-class nuclear-powered aircraft carrier, this is no surprise.[23] Moreover, the U.S. Navy operates for the Marine Corps a fleet of a dozen large helicopter/vertical-short take-off and landing carriers, each almost twice the size of the Royal Navy's comparable (three-ship) Invincible class. To protect its aircraft carriers and amphibious assets, the U.S. Navy has commissioned thirty-seven Arleigh Burke–class destroyers since 1991—billion-dollar multimission platforms capable of antiair, antisubmarine, and land-attack missions in high-threat environments.[24] This vessel is surely the most capable surface combatant in the world.

COMMAND OF SPACE

Although the United States is not yet committed to actual combat in or from space, it spends vast amounts on reconnaissance, navigation, and communications satellites.[25] These satellites provide a standing infrastructure to conduct military operations around the globe. According to General Michael Ryan, the chief of staff of the U.S. Air Force, the United States had 100 military satellites and 150 commercial satellites in space in 2001, nearly half of all the active satellites in space.[26] According to Air Force Lieutenant General T. Michael Moseley, air component commander in the U.S.-led invasion of Iraq in March 2003, more than fifty satellites supported land, sea, and air operations in every aspect of the campaign.[27] Secretary of Defense Donald Rumsfeld plans to emphasize the military exploitation of space, and has set the military the mission of "space control."[28] For FY02–FY07, the Pentagon plans to spend $165 billion on space-related activities.[29]

Other states can and do use space for military and civilian purposes. Although there is concern that some commercial satellites have military utility for reconnaissance and communications, many belong to U.S. companies or U.S. allies, and full exploitation of their capabilities by U.S. enemies can be severely disrupted.[30] The NAVSTAR/global positioning system (GPS) constellation of satellites, designed and operated by the U.S. military but now widely utilized for civilian purposes, permits highly precise navigation and weapons guidance anywhere in the world. Full exploitation of GPS by other military and civilian users is permitted electronically by the United States, but this permission is also electronically revocable.[31] It will not be easy for others to produce a comparable system, although the European Union intends to try. GPS cost $4.2 billion (in 1979 prices) to bring to completion, significantly more money than was originally projected.[32]

The dependence of the United States on satellites to project its conventional military power does make the satellites an attractive target for future U.S. adversaries.[33] But all satellites are not equally vulnerable; low earth orbit satellites seem more vulnerable to more types of attack than do high earth orbit satellites.[34] Many of the tactics that a weaker competitor might use against the United States would probably not be usable more than once—use of space mines, for example, or so-called "microsatellites" as long-duration orbital interceptors. The U.S. military does have some insurance against the loss of satellite capabilities in its fleet of reconnaissance aircraft and unmanned aerial vehicles. A challenge by another country could do some damage to U.S. satellite capabilities and complicate military operations for some time. The United States would then need to put a new generation of more resilient satellites in orbit. One estimate suggests that the exploitation of almost every known method to enhance satellite survivability would roughly double the unit cost.[35]

The United States has had a number of antisatellite research and development programs under way for many years, and some are said to have produced experimental devices that have military utility.[36] The planned U.S. ballistic missile defense system will also have some antisatellite capability. U.S. conventional military capabilities for precision attack, even without the support of its full panoply of space assets, are not trivial. It is quite likely that an opponent's own satellites, and its ground stations and bases for attacking U.S. satellites, would quickly come under sustained attack. The most plausible outcome of a war over space is that the United States would, after a period of difficulty, rebuild its space assets. The fight would not only leave the adversary devoid of space capability, but would also cause the United States to insist on the permanent antisatellite disarmament of the challenger, which it would try to enforce. Finally, the United States would probably assert some special interest in policing space.

COMMAND OF THE AIR

An electronic flying circus of specialized attack, jamming, and electronic intelligence aircraft allows the U.S. military to achieve the "suppression of enemy air defenses" (SEAD); limit the effectiveness of enemy radars, surface-to-air missiles (SAMs) and fighters; and achieve the relatively safe exploitation of enemy skies above 15,000 feet.[37] Cheap and simple air defense weapons, such as antiaircraft guns and shoulder-fired lightweight SAMs, are largely ineffective at these altitudes. Yet at these altitudes, aircraft can deliver precision-guided munitions with great accuracy and lethality, if targets have been properly located and identified. The ability of the U.S. military to satisfy the latter two conditions varies with the nature of the targets, the operational circumstances, and the available reconnaissance and command and control assets (as discussed below), so precision-guided munitions are not a solution to every problem. The United States has devoted increasing effort to modern aerial reconnaissance capabilities, including both aircraft and drones, which have improved in particular the military's ability to employ air power against ground forces, but these assets still do not provide perfect, instantaneous information.[38] Confidence in the quality of their intelligence and the lethality and responsiveness of their air power permitted U.S. commanders to dispatch relatively small numbers of ground forces deep into Iraq in the early days of the 2003 war, without much concern for counterattacks by large Iraqi army units.[39]

The U.S. military maintains a vast stockpile of precision-guided munitions and is adding to it. As of 1995, the Pentagon had purchased nearly 120,000 air-launched precision-guided weapons for land and naval attack at a cost of $18 billion.[40] Some twenty thousand of these weapons were high-speed anti-radiation missiles, designed to home in on the radar emissions of ground-based SAM systems, a key weapon for the SEAD campaign. Thousands of these bombs and missiles were launched in Kosovo, Afghanistan, and Iraq, but tens of thousands more have been ordered.[41]

The capability for precision attack at great range gives the United States an ability to do significant damage to the infrastructure and the forces of an adversary, while that adversary can do little to harm U.S. forces.[42] Air power alone may not be able to determine the outcome of all wars, but it is a very significant asset. Moreover, U.S. air power has proven particularly devastating to mechanized ground forces operating offensively, as was discovered in the only Iraqi mechanized offensive in Desert Storm, the battle of al-Khafji, in which coalition air forces pummeled three advancing Iraqi divisions.[43] The United States can provide unparalleled assistance to any state that fears a conventional invasion, making it a very valuable ally.

The Infrastructure of Command

Two important Cold War legacies contribute to U.S. command of the commons—bases and command structure. Although the United States has reduced the number of its forces stationed abroad since the Cold War ended and has abandoned bases in some places (e.g., Panama, the Philippines), on the whole, the U.S. Cold War base structure remains intact.[44] Expansion of NATO has given the United States access to additional bases in eastern and southern Europe. These bases provide important stepping stones around the world. The Pentagon has also improved the U.S. military's access in key regions. After the 1991 Gulf War, the United States developed a network of air base, port, and command and control facilities throughout the Persian Gulf, and cycled troops and aircraft through these bases. This base structure allowed the United States to attack Iraq successfully in 2003, despite the unwillingness of long-time NATO ally Turkey to permit the use of its territory to add a northern thrust to the effort. Although U.S. leaders were disappointed by Turkey's stance, it is noteworthy that sufficient bases were available in any case. After September 11, the U.S. government negotiated access to former Soviet air bases in the now independent states of Kyrgyzstan, Tajikistan, and Uzbekistan.[45]

The U.S. military has taken a number of other steps to improve its ability to send large forces across great distances. Munitions, support equipment, and combat equipment are prepositioned around the world, ashore and afloat. For example, the equivalent of three and one-third divisions' (ten brigades') worth of army and marine equipment was prepositioned at key spots in Asia, Europe, and the Persian Gulf during the 1990s. Perhaps five brigades of this equipment were employed in March 2003. In a crisis, troops fly to designated airfield-port combinations to marry up with this equipment. Since 1991, the United States has built a fleet of twenty large, medium-speed, roll-on/roll-off military transport ships, to facilitate the movement of military matériel. Each ship can carry nearly one thousand military vehicles and can offload this equipment at austere ports, if necessary.[46] These ships were extensively employed in the mobilization for the war to topple the Iraqi Ba'ath regime. Similarly, the United States has modernized its fleet of long-range airlift aircraft; ninety C-17s of the 180 on order have been delivered.[47] These aircraft are capable of carrying tank-sized cargos into relatively mediocre airfields. They, in turn, are supported by a fleet of aerial tankers. Finally, it is easy to forget that since World War II, the U.S. Marine Corps has specialized in putting large ground and air forces ashore against opposition. The Marine Corps alone has as many personnel as the combined land and air forces of the United Kingdom, and the U.S. Navy operates almost forty special-purpose combat ships for amphibious operations, roughly the same number of major surface combatants as the entire Royal Navy.[48]

Finally, all this capability is tied together by a seldom-mentioned Cold War legacy: the Unified Command Plan through which the U.S. military organizes the entire world for war. The U.S. military divides the world into both functional and regional commands. In most cases, the regional command elements are based in the theaters in which they would fight. PACOM is based in Hawaii and oversees U.S. forces in the Pacific. EUCOM, based in Europe, manages U.S. forces committed to NATO. CENTCOM oversees the Persian Gulf and Indian Ocean, but does so formally from Florida. Also in Florida, SOUTHCOM oversees Central and South America. These commands are each led by a four-star commander-in-chief (formerly referred to as a "CINC," pronounced "sink," they are now called "combatant commanders"). These are large multifunction military headquarters, to which are often attached significant operational forces. They engage in military diplomacy among the countries in their command and arrange joint exercises. They integrate the products of U.S. command of space with the permissive conditions of command of the air and sea, to develop responsive war plans that can generate significant combat power in the far corners of the world on relatively short notice. That the geographical commands were barely touched by the passing of the Cold War is mute testimony to the quiet consensus among the foreign and security policy elite that emerged soon after the passing of the Soviet Union: the United States would hold on to its accidental hegemony.[49]

Maintaining Command

U.S. command of the commons is the result of a Cold War legacy of both capabilities and bases, married to the disparity in overall economic power between the United States and its potential challengers. This disparity permits the United States to sustain a level of defense expenditure that dwarfs the spending of any of the world's other consequential powers. If grand strategists wish to pursue an activist global foreign policy, then they must preserve command of the commons. What then must the United States do? In the very long term, if a country comes to rival the United States in economic and technological capacity, it will be difficult to prevent a challenge, although it may be possible to out-compete the challenger. But in the short and medium terms, a successful challenge can be made highly impractical. In the short term, there is not much any other country can do to challenge the United States. In the medium term, through careful attention and resource allocation, the United States should be able to stay comfortably ahead of possible challengers. Indeed, some of the more grandiose aspirations of the Pentagon may be realized: Pentagon documents in the early 1990s talked about deterring any effort to build a capability to challenge the United States.[50] The first full statement of the grand strategy of the administration of George W. Bush also declares, "our forces will be strong enough to dissuade potential adversaries from pursuing a military build-up in hopes of surpassing, or equaling, the power of the United States."[51] This objective goes well beyond the traditional U.S. goal of deterring attacks. Yet it

may be possible to create barriers to entry into the global military power club that are so high as to seem insurmountable.

Maintaining Command at Sea

Although the United States does not face a significant naval challenge to its supremacy in the open ocean, it should nevertheless preserve a scientific and technical capability to resume a sustained, large-scale, open-ocean antisubmarine warfare contest. Similarly, although the United States may not need the numbers of SSNs that it had during the Cold War, or even that it has today, it must nevertheless remain on the cutting edge of SSN design and production.

Maintaining Command in Space

In space, the United States has a more complicated political-military task. It benefits from the fact that those states capable of space activities have eschewed putting weapons in space. The United States has made the same decision, on the assumption that if it did, so would others. Ultimately, the United States has more to lose than to gain from such a competition. The military does need to work aggressively on techniques to harden, hide, and maneuver satellites in case an adversary does try to interfere. An ability quickly to reconstitute some space capabilities should also be maintained, as should alternative reconnaissance means—aircraft and drones. The United States should also maintain some counteroffensive capabilities for purposes of deterrence and defense. The United States can leverage its long-range conventional attack capabilities to deny others the free use of space if they attack U.S. assets, and to reduce their offensive capabilities—mainly through direct and electronic attacks on an adversary's space launch, ground control, and tracking facilities. The United States should also maintain some antisatellite weapons research and development programs.

Maintaining Command of the Air

Perhaps the most contested element of U.S. command of the commons is command of the air. Here, the air force buys weapons as if the principal challenge is adversary fighter aircraft. The U.S. Air Force, Navy, and Marine advantage in air-to-air combat is nearly overwhelming, however. It will be easier for others to challenge U.S. access above 15,000 feet with ground-based SAMs of advanced design. The late–Cold War Soviet designs, and their follow-on systems, the so-called "double-digit" SAMs (with the SA-10 the best known and most lethal system) can offer real resistance to the U.S. military.[52] Fortunately for the United States, these systems are expensive, and Russian manufacturers sell only to those who can pay cash. China has purchased a significant number from Russia, and other countries will likely follow.[53] U.S. SEAD capabilities do not seem to be keeping up with this threat, much less staying ahead of it. The Pentagon needs to put more effort into SEAD if it hopes to retain command of the air.

Command of the commons is the military foundation of U.S. political preeminence. It is the key enabler of the hegemonic foreign policy that the United States has pursued since the end of the Cold War. The military capabilities required to secure command of the commons are the strong suit of the United States. They leverage science, technology, and economic resources. They rely on highly trained, highly skilled, and increasingly highly paid military personnel. On the whole, the U.S. military advantage at sea, in the air, and in space will be very difficult to challenge—let alone overcome. Command is further secured by the worldwide U.S. base structure and the ability of U.S. diplomacy to leverage other sources of U.S. power to secure additional bases and over-flight rights as needed.

Command of the commons is so much a part of U.S. military power that it is seldom explicitly acknowledged, under this rubric or any other. And far too little attention is paid to the strategic exploitation of command of the commons. For example, many U.S. defense policy documents in recent years allude to the need for speed of deployment to distant theaters of operations and speed of decision in the theater contingency.[54] Among other things, this has caused the U.S. Army to become obsessed with "lightening" itself, to better travel by air and to limit its logistics tail in the theater. This interest in speed seems misplaced. It underexploits the possibilities provided by command of the commons—the ability of the United States to muster great power; to militarily, economically, and politically isolate and weaken its adversaries; and to probe, study, and map the dimensions of the adversary to better target U.S. military power when it is applied. Full exploitation of command of the commons is rendered doubly necessary by the real problems presented, once U.S. forces get close to the adversary. Below 15,000 feet, within several hundred kilometers of the shore, and on the land, a contested zone awaits them. The U.S. military hopes that it can achieve the same degree of dominance in this zone as it has in the commons, although this is unlikely to happen.

THE CONTESTED ZONE

The closer U.S. military forces get to enemy-held territory, the more competitive the enemy will be. This arises from a combination of political, physical, and technological facts. These facts combine to create a "contested zone"—arenas of conventional combat where weak adversaries have a good chance of doing real damage to U.S. forces. The Iranians, Serbs, Somalis, and the still unidentified hard cases encountered in Operation Anaconda in Afghanistan have demonstrated that it is possible to fight the U.S. military. Only the Somalis can claim anything like a victory, but the others have imposed costs, preserved at least some of their forces, and often lived to tell the tale—to one another. These countries or entities have been small, resource poor, and often militarily "backward." They offer cautionary tales. The success of the 2003 U.S. campaign against the Ba'ath regime in Iraq should not blind observers to the inherent difficulty of fighting in contested zones.

Most of the adversaries that the United States has encountered since 1990 have come to understand U.S. military strengths and have worked to neutralize them. The U.S. military often uses the term "asymmetric" threats to encompass an adversary's use of weapons of mass destruction, terrorism, or any mode of conventional warfare that takes into account U.S. strengths. This category is a kind of trap: smart enemies get a special term, but by subtraction, many are expected to be stupid. This is unlikely to prove true; in any case, it is a dangerous way to think about war.

The essential facts are as follows. First, local actors generally have strong political interests in the stakes of a war—interests that may exceed those of the United States. Their willingness to suffer is therefore often greater. Second, however small the local actors are, they usually have one resource in more plentiful supply than the all-volunteer U.S. military —males of fighting age. Although young men are no longer the most important ingredient of land warfare, they do remain critical, particularly in cities, jungles, and mountains. Third, local actors usually have some kind of "home-court advantage." Just as the U.S. military has built up an institutional memory over decades that has helped it to preserve command of the commons, local actors have often built up a similar institutional memory about their own arenas. They have intimate knowledge of the terrain and the meteorology and may have spent years adapting their military tactics to these factors. This advantage is magnified because the local actors are often on the defense, which permits their military engineers to disperse, harden, and camouflage their forces, logistics, and command and control. Fourth, foreign soldiers have studied how the U.S. military makes war. The Cold War saw a great deal of foreign military education as a tool of political penetration by both the U.S. and Soviet blocs. Potential adversaries have been taught Western tactics and the use of Western weaponry. There are even reports that those who have fought the U.S. forces share information on their experiences. Fifth, the weaponry of the close fight—on land, in the air at low altitudes, and at sea in the so-called "littorals"—is much less expensive than that required for combat in the commons. A great deal of useful weaponry was left over from the Cold War, especially Warsaw Pact designs, which are particularly cheap. Demand for weaponry has diminished greatly since the Cold War ended, so there is plenty of manufacturing capability looking for markets.[55] Moreover, the diffusion of economic and technological capabilities in the civil sector is paralleled in the military sector. New manufacturers are emerging, who themselves will seek export markets. Finally, weaponry for close-range combat is also being continuously refined. Old weapons are becoming more lethal because of better ammunition. New versions of old weapons are also more lethal and survivable. Because these weapons are relatively inexpensive, even some of the newer versions will find their way into the hands of smaller and poorer states.

Taken together, these mutually reinforcing factors create a contested zone. In this zone, encounters between U.S. and local forces may result in fierce battles. This is not a prediction of U.S. defeat. The United States will be able to win wars in the contested zone, as it did in Afghanistan in 2002 and Iraq in 2003. It is a prediction of adversity. It is a prediction of a zone in which the U.S. military will require clever strategies and adroit tactics. It is a zone in which the U.S. military must think carefully and candidly about its own strengths and weaknesses, and how to leverage the former and buffer the latter.

LIMITS TO AIR POWER

Although U.S. aircraft possess significant potential destructive capacity, clever defenders can make it difficult to realize this potential. A combination of large numbers of inexpensive, low-altitude air defense weapons; small numbers of intelligently organized and operated medium-altitude weapons; and systematic efforts at camouflage, protection, and concealment have permitted ground forces to survive the onslaught of modern U.S. air power under some circumstances.

Inexpensive weaponry drives U.S. fighters to high altitudes, where their effectiveness against ground forces is reduced. Below 15,000 feet, expensive tactical fighter aircraft are vulnerable to inexpensive weaponry—light-to-medium automatic cannon (antiaircraft artillery [AAA]) and relatively small and inexpensive short-range SAMs (mainly portable infrared-guided systems similar to the U.S. Stinger). Although some kinds of decoys work against some of the low-altitude SAMs, the effectiveness of AAA is essentially a function of how many weapons the adversary possesses, their location relative to important targets, and how much ammunition they are able and willing to expend. AAA is best thought of as a kind of aerial minefield. Vast numbers of AAA weapons were built during the Cold War, especially by the Warsaw Pact, but also in the West. They seem not to wear out.[56] The majority of U.S. aircraft and helicopters lost in the Vietnam War were brought down by AAA.[57] Although coalition aircraft losses in the 1991 Persian Gulf War were very low, AAA and short-range infrared SAMs caused 71 percent of the attrition.[58] Currently, the U.S. military reports only seven aircraft lost to enemy fire in the 2003 war—six attack helicopters and an A-10. It is likely that all were victims of short-range air defense weapons.[59] In the only major success for Iraqi air defenses, twenty-seven of thirty-five U.S. Army attack helicopters were damaged and one was lost in a single

raid—all to AAA.[60] Even in South Vietnam, where North Vietnamese and Vietcong units had no radars for early warning, these weapons brought down 1,700 helicopters and aircraft between 1961 and 1968.[61] Generally, it is now the strategy of U.S. and Western air forces to fly above 15,000 feet to avoid AAA. This reduces losses, but it also significantly reduces a pilot's ability to locate enemy forces on the ground, to distinguish targets from decoys, to distinguish undamaged targets from damaged ones, and more generally, to develop a feel for the ground situation. A mobile adversary, with some knowledge of camouflage and deception, operating in favorable terrain, can exploit these problems. Thus inexpensive and simple air defense weapons help to protect ground forces even when they do not down many aircraft.

Operations above 15,000 feet can be further complicated by an integrated air defense system (IADS), which combines a communications system, early warning radars and signals intelligence collection devices, and medium-to-high-altitude SAM systems, as well as AAA.[62] An IADS does not have to shoot down many aircraft to lend assistance to ground forces. As discussed earlier, U.S. aircraft leverage technological advantages to suppress these integrated air defenses by jamming their radars and communications, by targeting SAMs with radar homing missiles, and by attacking communications nodes. More often than not, direct attacks on SAMs cause the gunners to shut down their radars, which makes the SAMs ineffective. At the same time, it usually ensures that the radar homing missiles fail to destroy the launchers—hence the term "SEAD" (suppression of enemy air defenses). Since 1972, both the Israeli air force and the U.S. air forces have proven this tactic, but it comes at a cost. It is safe to enter enemy airspace only when a host of expensive and scarce special assets are assembled.

Although the United States can command enemy airspace when it musters its SEAD capabilities, it cannot do so without them, and thus an adversary gets three benefits.[63] First, the scarcity of suppression assets slows the overall rate of U.S. attack to the rate at which they can be assembled and organized.[64] Second, it is not safe to remain in airspace that is defended by an IADS, because it is difficult to sustain enough pressure to keep the defender's radars "off the air" for more than a short time. Finally, it seems that suppression operations generate lots of patterned activity—much of it emitting electronic signals. A dense network of reasonably good radars and passive electronic intelligence capabilities can develop a picture of such patterned activities and thus provide early warning of U.S. attacks. Married to a decent communications system, the adversary's forces in the field can be alerted to take cover.[65] The defender may not shoot down many U.S. or other Western aircraft with this system; indeed, the harder it tries, the more likely it is to suffer destruction. But by playing a game of cat and mouse, the defender can survive and achieve its minimum objective—it can ration U.S. attacks and gain useful early warning of those attacks. If patient, the defender may from time to time encounter tactical situations where it can score a kill.

In 1999, the Serb army demonstrated that AAA at low altitudes and a well-constructed, if obsolescent, IADS at medium-to-high altitudes can offer powerful assistance to an adversary ground force as it attempts to survive the attacks of U.S. air forces. NATO did little damage against Serb field forces in Kosovo in 1999.[66] It was no doubt discouraging to the adversary's air defense troops that they shot down so few U.S. aircraft. Nevertheless, when air defenses successfully defend key assets, they have done their job. Serbian forces presented a large array of small mobile targets. The adversary could easily camouflage tanks, tracks, and guns and could also offer a wide variety of decoys to attract the attention of U.S. pilots. Serbia's mobile SAMs also largely survived U.S. attempts to destroy them, so the United States was forced to continue mounting elaborate suppression operations, providing the Serbs with useful early warning.

There were obvious limits to Serbian success. Large, fixed transportation targets (e.g., bridges) and economic infrastructure targets (e.g., power stations) cannot be moved and they cannot easily be camouflaged. Only truly modern SAMs can possibly defend such targets from high-altitude aircraft armed with precision-guided munitions. In the end, it was the U.S. ability and demonstrated willingness to destroy Serbia's infrastructure and economy that coerced Slobodan Milosevic into accepting a deal that satisfied NATO's war aims, but that deviated in important ways from NATO's original demands. The cautionary lesson is that a well-operated, if obsolescent, IADS can defend a ground force skilled at camouflage and deception.[67]

Iraqi air defenses and ground forces were apparently less successful at this game in 2003 than the Serbs were in 1999. Information is still limited, but several explanations seem plausible. First, Iraqi air defenses were in very poor shape on March 19, when the war officially began. The Iraqi air defense system was badly damaged in the 1991 war, damaged further during 11 years of engagements with U.S. and other Western air forces in the northern and southern no-fly zones, and largely prevented from replacing its losses or improving its technology by the 12-year arms embargo. Existing Iraqi SAMs also seem to have been in disrepair, perhaps due to their age, the embargo, or operator incompetence.[68] Second, it appears that Iraqi SAM operators were more aggressive in the early days of the war than was sensible, giving U.S. and British pilots excellent engagement opportunities. Third, Iraqi ground forces appear not to have enjoyed as much success at cover, concealment, and camouflage as did the Serbs. The terrain south of Baghdad may not have been favorable to such tactics, although opportunities did exist and much Iraqi equipment survived U.S. and British air attacks.[69] Perhaps as important, Iraqi forces had to concentrate and sometimes chose to maneuver en masse to try to meet U.S. ground attacks, creating better targets for U.S. aircraft.[70] Serb ground forces faced neither the necessity to concentrate nor the temptation to maneuver on a large scale because they faced no risk of a NATO ground attack.

The 1999 Kosovo war may provide other lessons as well. Militaries that have fought, or think they might fight, the United States now exchange lessons and technology. Serbs and Iraqis discussed tactics before the war in Kosovo began.[71] Iraq sought commercial communications technology to increase the resilience of its air defense communications network.[72] This assistance seems to have come from Chinese firms, which suggests that Serb, Iraqi, and Chinese air defense experts have compared notes.[73] Serbia's mobile SA-6s largely survived NATO attacks, but its immobile SA-3s fared poorly.[74] Formerly immobile, obsolescent Iraqi SA-3 missiles turned up in domestically built mobile versions on the backs of trucks prior to the 2003 war.[75] That Iraq did not profit from its contacts with Serbia does not undermine the central point—past and potential U.S. adversaries may exchange information. The Iraqis themselves demonstrated in the 1991 Gulf War that mobility pays: although coalition forces chased Iraqi truck-mounted Scud surface-to-surface missiles all over the desert, it seems clear that none were destroyed during that war.[76] Scuds made no appearance in the 2003 war, but Iraq did possess many smaller, short-range tactical ballistic missiles. Although these were priority targets for U.S. forces because of their presumed ability to deliver chemical weapons, many of these systems survived attack. Indeed, on April 7, 2003, after nearly 19 days of combat, a missile struck the headquarters of the Second Brigade of the 3rd Infantry Division, just south of Baghdad.[77]

THE LIGHT INFANTRY CHALLENGE

The 1991 and 2003 Gulf Wars strongly suggest that there are few, if any, ground forces in the world that can challenge the U.S. Army in tank warfare in open country. But there are other possible ground fights—in cities, mountains, jungles, and marshes. And the United States needs to be cognizant of some of the difficulties that may lie ahead. The first is sheer numbers. The two remaining designated members of the "axis of evil," Iran and North Korea, have conscript armies: together, these two countries have thirteen million males between the ages of eighteen and thirty-two.[78] They do not train all these men for war; the training their soldiers get is almost certainly uneven; and for local political reasons, some of these young men would not necessarily fight. But this total does give some idea of the potentials: these men are an important military resource. This pattern can be expected elsewhere. The world's population is expected to grow from six billion to eight billion by 2025, with most of that growth in the developing world.[79] Moreover, ground troops should have no trouble finding infantry weapons. According to one study, there are perhaps 250 million military and police small arms in the world, including mortars and shoulder-fired antitank weapons.[80]

U.S. strategists must also be cognizant of the significant police problem that would arise in the event the United States tried to conquer and politically reorganize some of these populous countries. The historical record suggests that stability operations require between two and twenty soldiers and/or policemen per thousand individuals, depending on the level of political instability.[81] The low figure is consistent with average U.S. police presence; the high figure with the height of the Troubles in Northern Ireland. Prior to the commencement of hostilities against Iraq in March 2003, many experts warned that the postwar occupation of the country could require significant troops. General Eric Shinseki, then chief of staff of the U.S. Army, estimated before the Congress in late February 2003, that several hundred thousand troops would be required for several years to occupy Iraq with its twenty-two million people. Undersecretary of Defense Paul Wolfowitz derided this estimate.[82] By the end of April 2003, Pentagon planners were projecting that a force of 125,000 would be needed for at least a year.[83] As of early June, plans to withdraw troops of the hardworking 3rd Infantry Division, which spearheaded the drive to Baghdad, had been shelved due to the deteriorating security situation, leaving 128,000 U.S. Army troops in Iraq and 45,000 more in Kuwait performing logistics functions. Perhaps another 30,000 U.S. Marines and British troops were also in Iraq. One unnamed U.S. Army officer averred that he has not seen the army so stretched in his thirty-one years of military service.[84] Yet with nearly 160,000 troops in Iraq, Major General Tim Cross, the British deputy head of Reconstruction and Humanitarian Assistance, agreed that there were too few troops to keep order.[85]

U.S. military personnel, however, have almost become too expensive to hire. The Department of Defense completed a detailed study in summer 2002 suggesting that the military services cut ninety thousand uniformed personnel.[86] It considered asking the army to cut one of its ten active divisions. At the time, the U.S. defense budget was going up, and the United States was already heavily engaged in the war on terror. The U.S. government had defined this war broadly, and the Pentagon civilian leadership favored extending it to Iraq. The demand for U.S. personnel would likely rise. Yet the sheer expense of uniformed personnel caused the Defense Department to briefly consider reducing the size of the armed forces.[87] This suggests that the United States must avoid lengthy military operations that require a large number of ground troops.

It is tempting to believe that heavily armed, high-technology ground forces can easily defeat large numbers of enemy infantry. But two vignettes, one from Somalia and the other from Afghanistan, suggest a different lesson. Elite U.S. Special Operations forces suffered high casualties in a mission gone awry in Mogadishu in 1993.[88] They were in part a victim of their own mistakes. But Somali gunmen fought with courage, and some skill, and were assisted by the urban environment. They clearly had "gone to school" on U.S. forces in preceding weeks, learning their patterns and tactics.[89] Their local intelligence apparatus may have provided some warning of the U.S. raids, and a crude communications system allowed them to mobilize and coordinate the movement of their forces.[90] The Somalis reportedly altered simple, Soviet-pattern RPG-7 antitank rockets to make them more effective weapons against U.S. helicopters.[91] Some observers suggest that al Qaeda taught them this trick. Soviet AK-47 assault rifles, RPG-7 antitank rocket launchers, and ammunition for both appear to have been plentiful. And no wonder—millions of AK-47s had been manufactured and could be had for as little as $200 apiece in Somalia.[92] The Somalis did, however, suffer grievous casualties, perhaps thirty times the eighteen U.S. dead.[93] The Somalis may be among the most individually courageous fighters U.S. soldiers have encountered since the North Vietnamese. But even better prepared and better armed urban infantry combatants do exist, as the Russians discovered in Grozny in 1995.

In recent years, the U.S. military has been working assiduously to improve its urban combat capability, but soldiers still expect fights against competent defenders in cities to be costly and difficult.[94] A military rule of thumb is that it takes one company, one day, and 30–40 percent casualties to take one well-defended city block, which would usually be defended by a platoon one-third its strength.[95] It is generally believed that casualties of this magnitude would render a unit combat ineffective for some period. After two fights of this kind, it would likely take months to rebuild the unit's combat power—even if the infantry replacements could be found, which seems difficult, given the U.S. voluntary recruitment system. The entire U.S. active Army has only about sixty infantry battalions (180 companies), so it would be stressed if it stumbled into a major, extended, urban campaign against an army of even modest size. Saddam Hussein's regime did not prepare to wage such a campaign in Baghdad in 2003, allowing its best units to be destroyed outside of the city.[96] But Iraqi infantry experienced their only successes in smaller cities across southern Iraq, most notably in an-Nasiriya, where they fought bloody battles with the U.S. Marines.[97] The marines suffered more than half of the U.S. casualties in the war, although they provided about one-third of the ground forces. Their commander, Lieutenant General James Conway, explained this anomaly as follows: "The forces that we had come up against were pretty much in the villages and towns along the single avenues of approach that we had that led into Baghdad. It was close-quarter fighting, in some cases hand-to-hand fighting."[98]

Captured documents from al Qaeda training bases in Afghanistan show how competent infantry can be trained with relatively low-technology techniques.[99] Al Qaeda trainers, many of whom appear to have served in regular forces, gathered tactical manuals from various armies. They distilled the information from these manuals into a syllabus. They lectured from the syllabus and insisted that each aspirant take copious notes, in effect copying a manual for himself. All procedures appear then to have been carefully drilled in the field. Bases were decorated with large training posters on various subjects.

Operation Anaconda (March 2–18, 2002) provides a sense of the success of this training, although it is unclear whether the adversary consisted entirely of al Qaeda troops trained in Afghanistan.[100] Given the obvious skill of the defenders, it may be that these were the instructors, and not the troops, waging the fight. The adversary proved extremely skillful at camouflage; a motorized column of Afghan allies was ambushed at close range.[101] U.S. forces, although supported by reconnaissance and intelligence assets of all kinds, probably located not more than half of al Qaeda's prepared positions in the Shah-e-Kot valley.[102] In at least one case, U.S. Special Forces helicopters landed practically on top of some of these positions, and were quickly shot up with heavy machine gun and rocket-propelled grenade (RPG) fire.[103] One Chinook transport helicopter was destroyed and another severely damaged. Every U.S. attack helicopter supporting the operation was peppered with bullet holes; four of seven AH-64s were damaged so severely that they ceased to fly sorties.[104] U.S. infantry were often brought under accurate mortar fire, which produced most of the two dozen U.S. casualties on the first day of the fight.[105] After several days of combat, many al Qaeda troops withdrew under cover of poor weather.[106] Few bodies were discovered in the valley, although U.S. officers believe that many al Qaeda were killed and obliterated by powerful bombs. As far as one can tell, al Qaeda waged this fight with the ubiquitous Soviet-pattern AK-47 assault rifle, RPG-7 shoulder-fired antitank grenade launcher, PKM medium machine gun, 12.7-millimeter DShK heavy machine gun, and 82-millimeter medium mortar. (There were no reliable reports of infrared-guided short-range air defense missiles fired, although a good many of them seem to have been found in Afghanistan.) Pictures of caches in Afghan caves often show crates of ammunition for these weapons stacked floor to ceiling.[107] It is important to note that better ammunition for existing Warsaw Pact–pattern infantry weapons will surely appear. Sophisticated, lightweight fire control systems, which can radically increase the lethality of such weapons, have also been designed. In addition, new generations of affordable infantry weapons will start reaching potential adversaries. Even in the Anaconda battle, night-vision devices were reportedly found in abandoned enemy positions.[108] If true, an important U.S. technical and tactical advantage has already waned. In short, large numbers of males of military age, favorable terrain, solid training, and plentiful basic infantry weapons can produce significant challenges for the U.S. military.

LITTORAL COMBAT

Since the Cold War ended, the U.S. Navy has been keen to show that it is relevant to the problems of the day. Thus early in the 1990s, it began to reorient itself toward affecting military matters ashore, insofar as it barely had any enemies left at sea. Its first public statements about this project were *From the Sea* and *Forward . . . From the Sea*.[109] The chief of naval operations reemphasized the navy's mission close to the adversary's shore as part of his *Sea Power 21* concept.[110] Although the Navy leadership understands that combat in the littorals is a different kind of mission from its past specialization, and that this requires different assets and skills, not much progress has been made in the past decade.[111]

A properly constructed sea-denial capability in littoral combat combines several elements: bottom mines; diesel electric submarines; small, fast, surface attack craft; surveillance radars; passive electronic intelligence collectors; long-range, mobile, land-based SAMs; and long-range, mobile, land-based antiship missiles. Aircraft and helicopters also play important roles. These systems are inexpensive relative to the cost of U.S. warships and aircraft. There are a number of militaries worldwide with expertise in littoral combat.[112] Germany, Israel, Sweden, and perhaps South Korea are probably the best in terms of combining the most modern relevant technology and weaponry with good training and appropriate tactics. (Only Germany and Sweden have organized themselves to fight a superpower navy, however.) China, Iran, North Korea, and Taiwan have all developed a considerable littoral capability, although each suffers some shortfalls. In recent years, no great power has actually fought a first-class littoral navy, but there are examples of how damaging the various elements of littoral warfare can be.

Naval mines are very lethal and difficult to find and eliminate.[113] Iraq nearly blew the U.S. cruiser *Princeton* in half during Desert Storm with two modern bottom mines.[114] A more primitive Iraqi moored contact mine badly damaged and nearly sank the amphibious landing ship LPH *Tripoli* in the same engagement. In 1987 a $1,500, World War I–design, Iranian floating mine nearly sank the U.S. frigate *Samuel Roberts*.[115] Iraq still possessed some naval mines in the 2003 war, but few were deployed. Nevertheless, it took nearly a week for a combined force of British, U.S., and Australian mine-hunting units to clear the channel to the port of Umm Qasr of what was subsequently discovered to have been a total of eleven mines. It was learned, however, that the Iraqis had been preparing to lay another seventy-six mines as the war began, and commanders were very relieved that the outbreak of the war forestalled this action.[116]

Mobile land-based antiship missiles might prove as difficult to find as mobile Scuds or mobile SAMs. An improvised, land-based French-built Exocet badly damaged a British destroyer during the 1982 Falklands

War.[117] Land-based Iranian Silkworm antiship missiles, of Chinese manufacture, damaged two tankers at a Kuwaiti oil terminal in 1987, from nearly 80 kilometers away.[118] Similar missiles were fired by Iraq in the same area in the 2003 war, although no shipping was hit and no serious damage was done. Iraqi antiship missiles instead struck a harborside shopping mall in Kuwait City on March 29, and then struck near Umm Qasr on April 1. U.S. and British ground and air forces had been in southern Iraq for more than a week, yet these systems had eluded detection.[119] Antiship missiles fired from surface vessels and aircraft have damaged or sunk several large naval vessels. Two Exocets fired from an Iraqi aircraft nearly sank the U.S. frigate *Stark* in 1987, killing thirty-seven sailors.[120] Air-launched Exocets sank the British destroyer *Sheffield* and the container ship *Atlantic Conveyor* in the 1982 Falklands War.[121] U.S. ship-launched Harpoons sank two Iranian ships in Operation Praying Mantis in April 1988. Two Iranian ships managed to fire missiles in the same engagement, but neither was successful.[122]

Although they did not prove lethal against large ships, lightly armed (Swedish-built) Iranian Boghammer speedboats proved a nuisance in the Persian Gulf during the 1980–88 Iraq-Iran War. Their main mission was machine gun and rocket attacks on ships trading with the Gulf states, especially Kuwait, which provided the money that fueled Saddam Hussein's war machine. Because the shallow waters of the northern Gulf were considered too dangerous for large warships, due to mines and presumably land-based antiship missiles, the U.S. Navy built two floating bases aboard large, leased, commercial barges and used them for Special Operations helicopters and patrol boats to deal with this threat.[123] They did this successfully, although at some risk. The use of a small motorboat by suicide bombers against the U.S. destroyer *Cole* on October 14, 2000, has added a new dimension to this threat. Moreover, much more sophisticated fast-attack aircraft can be built.[124] Major navies now feel compelled to devise new weaponry to counter these cheap, nimble, and potentially deadly attackers. In a recent U.S. wargame, a defending "red force" navy consisting of small boats and some aircraft, attacked the simulated U.S. Navy task force entering the Persian Gulf and sent much of it to the bottom.[125]

Finally, although modern diesel electric submarines have not sunk any major surface combatants of late, they have proven extremely difficult to catch. Hunting for diesel electric submarines in coastal waters is rendered difficult by the poor acoustical transmission properties of shallow water and the background noise of coastal traffic. When running on its battery, a diesel electric submarine is naturally very quiet. When recharging the battery, its diesel sounds much like any other diesel in coastal waters. Its snorkel may generate a heat and radar signature, which ASW aircraft could exploit, but not if they can in turn be engaged by SAMs based afloat or ashore.

A German-designed Argentine submarine made several unsuccessful attacks against British aircraft carriers during the Falklands War. Large quantities of ASW munitions were used against it, without scoring a hit.[126] When the Iranians took their first Soviet-designed Kilo-class submarine out for its maiden voyage several years ago, the U.S. Navy is said to have quickly lost track of it.[127]

Treated separately, these weapons are not only annoying but also potentially deadly. Deployed together, they produce synergies that can be difficult to crack. These synergies become even more deadly when the "terrain" favors the defense (i.e., in constricted waters such as the Persian Gulf). Bottom mines are difficult enough to find and disable when one is not liable to attack. If the minefield is covered by fire, if it lies within the lethal range of shore-based antiship missiles, the work could be impossible. A maximum effort by a task force of heavily armed surface vessels may with difficulty defend mine hunters working close to shore against antiship missile attack, but this will surely produce a signature that will attract the attention of surveillance assets ashore and perhaps draw the combined attention of surface, subsurface, and land-based assets.[128] The point here is not that the U.S. Navy could not ultimately take a competent littoral defense force apart. It probably could. The point is that it could take time, and may impose considerable costs.

Thus far, the United States has been fortunate in that it has encountered adversaries with perhaps only one of these three capabilities—air, land, or sea. And even when the adversary has had one of these specializations, it has not necessarily been the best of breed. Serbian air defense troops were extremely good, but their best weaponry was at least a generation old, maybe older. The Somalis fought with great tenacity and, candidly, drove the United States from the country. But they were neither as well armed nor as well trained as the al Qaeda troops in the Shah-e-Kot valley during Operation Anaconda in Afghanistan. The al Qaeda troops were still not as well armed as some adversaries that U.S. forces might encounter, and there were probably not more than a few hundred of them in the fight. Finally, the U.S. Navy's littoral engagements in the Persian Gulf have been fought under fortuitous conditions. Iraq did not take littoral warfare especially seriously. The Iranian navy suffered because it had lost many of its officers in the 1979 revolution and arguably had never fully focused on the littoral mission. The shah of Iran had delusions of grandeur and sought a blue water navy.

One cannot predict whether the United States will encounter an adversary with the full panoply of capabilities that make possible the contested zone, and the United States need not take up the challenge if it is presented with such an array. A decade from now, however, it seems plausible that China and Iran will have mastered a range of air, sea, and land combat capabilities. U.S. Naval authorities are already nervous about Iran's capabilities.[129] North Korea is probably quite good in the arena of close, ground combat, but only mediocre in the realm of air defense and littoral warfare.[130] Russia will probably be the source of most of the best antiaircraft systems sold around the world to possible U.S. adversaries, although China will surely enter that market as its systems improve. Russia will also produce and sell deadly weapons for littoral warfare. It is likely that Russia itself will remain a master of antiair warfare, will develop (or arguably redevelop) mastery in littoral warfare, but will have problems generating land power, especially infantry power.

IMPLICATIONS

Military strategy that fully exploits command of the commons is not complicated in principle. From time to time, even a policy of selective engagement may necessitate offensive engagements; indeed, they may necessitate fights in the contested zone. The main point is that time is usually on the side of the United States. U.S. military power resides mainly in North America, where it is largely safe from attack. Command of the sea allows the United States to marshal its capabilities—and those of its allies—from around the globe to create a massive local material superiority.

Command of the commons also permits the isolation of the adversary from sources of political and military support, further increasing the U.S. margin of superiority and allowing the passage of time to work in favor of the United States. This is especially useful against adversaries who depend on exports and imports. U.S. allies have large numbers of good, small-to-medium, naval surface combatants, especially appropriate for maintaining a blockade.[131] These ships play important roles in the worldwide war on terror.[132] They played important roles in the isolation of Iraq, which was under economic embargo from 1990. Although Iraq illegally exported some oil and illegally imported some weapons and military technology between 1990 and 2003, its military capability suffered greatly in these years. It failed to modernize in any significant way and was prevented from recovering its ability to invade its neighbors. The erosion of Iraq's conventional combat power contributed to U.S. confidence as it considered an invasion of Iraq in the autumn of 2002. Once the third Persian Gulf War began in March 2003, it rapidly became clear that Iraqi conventional weapons had on the whole not improved since 1991. Iraqi tactics improved slightly, in part because U.S. forces could not avoid the contested zones. Over the past decade, the U.S. Navy and allied navies quietly helped to starve Iraq's army and air force. Had they not done so, U.S. casualties in the 2003 war in Iraq would surely have been higher.

Command of space allows the close study of the adversary and the tailoring of U.S. capabilities to fight that enemy, and command of the air permits a careful wearing away of the adversary's remaining strengths. There is little that an adversary can do to erode U.S. military capabilities or political will unless the United States engages on the enemy's terms. But the United States does not need to be in any rush to launch attacks into enemy-held real estate. Instead, it can probe an adversary's defenses, eliciting the information that U.S. forces need. U.S. probes can also lure the adversary into using up some of its scarce and difficult-to-replace imported munitions. At the appropriate time, if necessary, quantitatively and qualitatively superior U.S. and allied forces can directly challenge the much-weakened adversary. The fight may still prove difficult, but the United States will have significantly buffered itself against the perils of the contested zone.

In land warfare, U.S. military capabilities are particularly lethal when defending against adversaries who have to move forward large amounts of heavy military equipment and supplies over long distances. Command of space and of the air permit the United States to exact an immense toll on advancing ground forces and the air forces that support them. This means that the United States should have a good chance of deterring regional aggressors and successfully defending against them in the event that deterrence fails, if it has some forces in the theater and is permitted to mobilize more forces in a timely fashion. Command of the sea helps the United States keep forces forward deployed, even in politically sensitive areas, and reinforce those forces quickly. Rapid response still, however, depends on good political relations with the threatened party. On the whole, states worry more about proximate threats than they do about distant ones. But the tremendous power projection capability of the United States can appear to be a proximate threat if U.S. policy seems domineering. So command of the commons will provide more influence and prove more militarily lethal, if others can be convinced that the United States is more interested in constraining regional aggressors than achieving regional dominance.

Command of the commons and the enduring contested zones mean that allies remain useful—more useful than current U.S. strategic discourse would suggest. The allies provide the formal and informal bases that are the crucial stepping stones for U.S. power to transit the globe. The military power of these allies contributes modestly to maintenance and exploitation of command of the commons, but can contribute significantly to the close fights and their aftermath. The NATO allies, for example, have great expertise in sea mine clearance and possess many mine hunters; Britain and France together have nearly half again as many mine-hunting vessels as the U.S. Navy.[133] Several of the allies have good ground forces, and perhaps most critically, good infantry that seem able to tolerate at least moderate casualties. The British Army and Royal Marines have forty-three infantry battalions—all professionals—nearly half as many as the United States; France has another twenty.[134] Given the relative scarcity of U.S. infantry, allied ground forces are also particularly useful in the postconflict peace-enforcement missions necessary to secure the fruits of any battlefield victory.

IMPLICATIONS FOR GRAND STRATEGY

The nature and scope of U.S. military power should affect U.S. grand strategy choices. U.S. military power is very great; if it were not, no hegemonic policy would be practical, but that does not mean that every hegemonic policy is practical. Today, there is little dispute within the U.S. foreign policy elite about the fact of great U.S. power, or the wisdom of an essentially hegemonic foreign policy. Even before the September 11 terrorist attacks, the foreign policy debate had narrowed to a dispute between primacy and selective engagement; between a nationalist, unilateralist version of hegemony and a liberal, multilateral version of hegemony. U.S. command of the commons provides an impressive foundation for selective engagement. It is not adequate for a policy of primacy.

Primacy, in particular, depends on vast, omnicapable military power, which is why the Bush administration pushes a military agenda that aims self-confidently to master the "contested zones."[135] President Bush and his advisers believe that the United States need not tolerate plausible threats to its safety from outside its borders. These threats are to be eliminated. Insofar as preventive war is difficult to sell abroad, this policy therefore requires the ability to act alone militarily—a unilateral global offensive capability. The effort to achieve such a capability will cause unease around the world and make it increasingly difficult for the United States to find allies; it may cause others to ally against the United States. As they do, the costs of sustaining U.S. military preeminence will grow. Perhaps the first problem that primacy will create for U.S. command of the commons is greater difficulty in sustaining, improving, and expanding the global base structure that the United States presently enjoys.

Current Pentagon civilian leaders understand that they do not yet have the military to implement their policy. They hope to create it. For political, demographic, and technological reasons, the close fights in the contested zones are likely to remain difficult—especially when the adversary is fighting largely in defense of its own country. Senior civilian and military planners in the Pentagon seem to believe that, somehow, the technological leverage enjoyed in the commanded zone can be made to apply equally well in the contested zone, if only the Pentagon spends enough money. This seems a chimera. Although one doubts that the United States would lose many fights in the contested zones, the costs in lost U.S., allied, and civilian lives of one or more such fights could be great enough to produce significant political problems at home and abroad for an activist U.S. foreign policy of any kind.

Selective engagement aims above all to create conditions conducive to great power peace on the assumption that many other benefits flow from this blessing, the foremost being U.S. security. In return for their cooperation, others get U.S. protection. Command of the commons makes this offer of protection credible. Their cooperation, in turn, makes the protection easy for the United States to deliver. Great powers typically chafe at such dependency relationships, so U.S. diplomacy must be particularly adroit to sustain their willingness to cooperate. Command of the commons gives the United States a tremendous capability to harm others. Marrying that capability to a conservative policy of selective engagement helps make U.S. military power appear less threatening and more tolerable.

Command of the commons creates additional collective goods for U.S. allies. These collective goods help connect U.S. military power to seemingly prosaic welfare concerns. U.S. military power underwrites world trade, travel, global telecommunications, and commercial remote sensing, which all depend on peace and order in the commons. Those nations most involved in these activities, those who profit most from globalization, seem to understand that they benefit from the U.S. military position—which may help explain why the world's consequential powers have grudgingly supported U.S. hegemony.

There is little question that the United States is today the greatest military power on the planet and the most potent global power since the dawn of the age of sail. This military power is both a consequence and a cause of the current skewed distribution of power in the world. If the United States were not the dominant economic and technological power, it would not be the dominant military power. The fact of U.S. military dominance is also a consequence of choices—the choice to spend vast sums on armaments and the choice of how to spend those sums. Nevertheless, the immense U.S. military effort has not produced military omnipotence, and it probably cannot. Policymakers need a more nuanced understanding of the favorable U.S. military position to exploit it fully and to ensure that foreign and military policy are mutually supporting.

NOTES

I thank Robert Art, Owen Coté, Etienne de Durand, Harvey Sapolsky, and the anonymous reviewers for their comments on earlier drafts of this essay. Previous versions were presented at the U.S. Naval War College Current Strategy Forum, the Weatherhead Center Talloires Conference "The Future of U.S. Foreign Policy," the Institut Français des Relations Internationales, the Centre for Defence Studies at King's College, and the European University Institute. An earlier version of this article, entitled "La Maîtrise des espaces, fondement de l'hégémonie des Etats-Unis," appears in *Politique étrangère* (Spring 2003): 41–56.

1. The most comprehensive analysis of the extraordinary relative power position of the United States is William C. Wohlforth, "The Stability of a Unipolar World," *International Security* 24 (Summer 1999): 5–41.

2. Barry R. Posen and Andrew L. Ross, "Competing Visions of U.S. Grand Strategy," *International Security* 21

(Winter 1996): 5–53, summarizes the initial phase of the post–Cold War U.S. grand strategy debate. In that article, we discussed a policy called "primacy," a then-popular term in U.S. foreign policy discourse. Primacy is one type of hegemony. A distinction should be made between a description of the structure of world politics—that is, the distribution of power among states—and the policies of a particular nation-state. The United States has more power in the world than any other state, and by a substantial margin. See Wohlforth, "The Stability of a Unipolar World." This has become clear over the past decade. Thus it is reasonable to describe the world as "unipolar." Although this much power sorely tempts a state to practice a hegemonic foreign and security policy—that is, to further expand and consolidate its power position and to organize the world according to its own preferences—this is not inevitable. In terms of its potential capabilities, the United States has been a great power for at least a century, but it has followed foreign policies of varying activism. The U.S. national security elite (Democratic and Republican) did, however, settle on a policy of hegemony sometime in the late 1990s. The people of the United States did not play a significant role in this decision, so questions remained about how much they would pay to support this policy. The attacks of September 11 and the subsequent war on terror have provided an important foundation of domestic political support for a hegemonic foreign policy. Debates between Democrats and Republicans now focus on the modalities of hegemony—whether the United States should work through multilateral institutions to exercise and increase its power or work outside them.

3. Stephen G. Brooks and William C. Wohlforth, "American Primacy," *Foreign Affairs* 81 (July 2002): 20–33.

4. George W. Bush, *The National Security Strategy of the United States of America* (Washington, D.C.: White House, September 20, 2002), 30. To be fair, Bush's *National Security Strategy of the United States of America* contains many allusions to alliances, cooperation, liberal values, and economic and political development. Nevertheless, the oldest and most powerful U.S. allies—the Europeans—are hardly mentioned in the document. Even allowing for the need for stern language to mobilize public support for the war on terror, the document has a martial tone—and is strongly committed to a wide variety of proactive uses of force. Also, the document has a vaguely nationalist flavor: "The U.S. national security strategy will be based on a distinctly American internationalism that reflects the union of our values and our national interests." Perhaps to drive home this point, the document devotes an entire paragraph to disassociating the United States from the International Criminal Court.

5. Posen and Ross, "Competing Visions of U.S. Grand Strategy," 44–50, dubbed this strategy "selective (but cooperative) primacy."

6. Robert J. Art, *A Grand Strategy for America* (Ithaca, N.Y.: Cornell University Press, 2003). In the mid-1990s, most proponents of selective engagement had in mind a less ambitious strategy than Art now proposes. Formerly, the criteria for selective engagement were clear: does an international problem promise significantly to increase or decrease the odds of great power war? Now the purpose of the strategy is to retain U.S. alliances and presence in Europe,

East Asia, and the Persian Gulf "to help mold the political, military, and economic configurations of these regions so as to make them more congenial to America's interests." Included in the goals of the strategy are protection of the United States from grand terror attack, stopping the proliferation of weapons of mass destruction (nuclear, chemical, and biological), preserving peace and stability in Eurasia, securing access to oil, maintaining international economic openness, spreading democracy, protecting human rights, and avoiding severe climate change. Art does propose priorities among these objectives. See ibid., 223–48.

7. According to the Center for Defense Information, the FY03 budget request of $396 billion "is more than the combined spending of the next 25 nations." See www.cdi.org/issues/wme.

8. U.S. Department of Defense, *Quadrennial Defense Review Report* (Washington, D.C.: U.S. Department of Defense, September 30, 2001), 20–21.

9. This article does not review three military theoretical terms that have absorbed much attention over the past decade: the "revolution in military affairs," "Network-Centric Warfare," and "military transformation." To do so would require a major digression. I am trying to build an understanding of the overall U.S. military position and its strategic implications on the basis of a small number of empirical observations about familiar categories of conventional military activity.

10. Paul M. Kennedy, *The Rise and Fall of British Naval Mastery* (London: Macmillan, 1983 [first published in 1976 by Allen Lane]). Kennedy distinguishes "naval mastery" from temporary, local naval superiority, or local command of the sea:

> By . . . the term "naval mastery," however, there is meant here something stronger, more exclusive and wider-ranging; namely a situation in which a country has so developed its maritime strength that it is superior to any rival power, and that its predominance is or could be exerted far outside its home waters, with the result that it is extremely difficult for other, lesser states to undertake maritime operations or trade without at least its tacit consent. It does *not* necessarily imply a superiority over all other navies combined, nor does it mean that this country could not temporarily lose local command of the sea; but it does assume the possession of an overall maritime power such that small-scale defeats overseas would soon be reversed by the dispatch of naval forces sufficient to eradicate the enemy's challenge. Generally speaking, naval mastery is also taken to imply that the nation achieving it will usually be very favourably endowed with many fleet bases, a large merchant marine, considerable national wealth, etc., all of which indicates influence at a global rather than a purely regional level.

Ibid., 9 (emphasis added).

11. Alfred Thayer Mahan called the sea "a wide common." Ibid., 2.

12. As is the case with much analysis of conventional military issues, for the sake of analytic simplicity, I do not treat the implications of the proliferation of weapons of mass destruction. Insofar as the main accomplishment of weapons of mass destruction is to increase significantly the

costs and risks of any hegemonic foreign policy, the proliferation of these weapons for U.S. grand strategy should be considered independently of a treatment of their narrow tactical military utility. That said, broadly speaking, the limited diffusion of these kinds of weapons would likely make the contested zone even more contested before they affect command of the commons.

13. Ibid., 177–202.

14. I calculated these percentages from the country entries in Central Intelligence Agency, *The World Factbook, 2001* (Washington, D.C.: U.S. Central Intelligence Agency, 2001). The purchasing power parity method used by the Central Intelligence Agency creates an exaggerated impression of China's current economic and technological capability. Measured by currency exchange rates, the United States had 29.5 percent of GWP in 1999, Japan had 14 percent, and China had only 3.4 percent. See "World Gross Domestic Product by Region," *International Energy Outlook, 2002,* Report DOE/EIA-0484 (Washington, D.C.: Energy Information Administration, 2002), Table A3, Appendix A.

15. International Institute for Strategic Studies [IISS], *The Military Balance, 2002–2003* (London: IISS, 2002), 241, 252–53. My colleague Harvey Sapolsky called this to my attention.

16. Harvey M. Sapolsky, Eugene Gholz, and Allen Kaufman, "Security Lessons from the Cold War," *Foreign Affairs* 78 (July 1999): 77–89.

17. The actual wartime missions of SSNs in the canonical major regional contingencies—aside from lobbing a few conventional cruise missiles and collecting electronic intelligence close to shore—are murky at best.

18. Owen R. Coté, Jr., *The Third Battle: Innovation in the U.S. Navy's Silent Cold War Struggle with Soviet Submarines* (Newport, R.I.: Naval War College, 2003), 69–78.

19. Construction of a new Chinese nuclear attack submarine has been delayed many times, and one is not expected to be completed until 2005. France does not have a nuclear attack submarine under construction, but it has a program planned for the 2010s. Britain has ordered three new nuclear attack submarines, and one is currently under construction. See A.D. Baker III, "World Navies in Review," *Naval Institute Proceedings* 128 (March 2002): 33–36.

20. A. D. Baker III, "World Navies in Review," *Naval Institute Proceedings* 125 (March 1999): 3–4. According to Baker, "Submarine construction in Russia had all but halted by the fall of 1998." At the time, there were four incomplete Akula-class nuclear attack submarines and one incomplete new-design attack submarine in Russian yards. See also Baker, "World Navies in Review" (March 2002), 35–36. One of the Akulas was finally commissioned at the end of 2001. One more may yet be completed.

21. IISS, *Military Balance, 2002–2003,* 113, suggests twenty-two. Baker, "World Navies in Review" (March 2002), suggests about thirty. I count Oscar-class cruise missile submarines as attack submarines.

22. For figures on the U.S. Navy and Marine Corps, see IISS, *Military Balance, 2002–2003,* 18–21.

23. For costs of current U.S. warships, see Office of the Comptroller, U.S. Department of Defense, "Shipbuilding and Conversion," *National Defense Budget Estimates for the Amended FY 2002 Budget (Green Book), Procurement*

Programs (P1) (Washington, D.C.: U.S. Department of Defense, 2002), n. 17–18.

24. See www.globalsecurity.org/military/systems/ship/ddg-51-unit.htm.

25. The Pentagon has been hinting for some time that it would like to put weapons into space both for antisatellite attacks and for attacks on terrestrial targets. Many independent space policy analysts oppose this because the United States gets more out of space than any other state. They acknowledge that this makes U.S. space assets an attractive target, but they argue that hardening satellites, ground stations, and the links between them makes more sense than starting an expensive arms competition in space. Implicitly, they also rely on deterrence—the superior ability of the U.S. military to damage an adversary's ground stations, links, and missile launch facilities, as well as to retaliate with nascent U.S. antisatellite systems against the other side's satellites. See, for example, Theresa Hitchens, *Weapons in Space: Silver Bullet or Russian Roulette* (Washington, D.C.: Center for Defense Information, April 19, 2002); Michael Krepon with Christopher Clary, *Space Assurance or Space Dominance? The Case against Weaponizing Space* (Washington, D.C.: Henry L. Stimson Center, 2003), 58–86; and Charles V. Pena and Edward L. Hudgins, *Should the United States "Weaponize" Space?* Policy Analysis 427 (Washington D.C.: Cato Institute, March 18, 2002), 5–10.

26. Vernon Loeb, "Air Force's Chief Backs Space Arms," *Washington Post* (August 2, 2001): 17.

27. Jim Garamone, "Coalition Air Forces Make Ground Gains Possible," American Forces Press Service (April 5, 2003), www.defenselink.mil/new/APR2003/n04052003_200304053.html.

28. According to U.S. Department of Defense, *Quadrennial Defense Review Report* (2001), "The ability of the United States to access and utilize space is a vital national security interest." Moreover, "the mission of space control is to ensure the freedom of action in space for the United States and its allies and, when directed, to deny such freedom of action to adversaries." According to the report, "Ensuring freedom of access to space and protecting U.S. national security interests are key priorities that must be reflected in future investment decisions." Ibid., 45.

29. U.S. General Accounting Office, *Military Space Operations: Planning, Funding, and Acquisition Challenges Facing Efforts to Strengthen Space Control,* GAO-02-738 (Washington, D.C.: U.S. General Accounting Office, September 2002), 3. It appears that U.S. military spending on space has nearly doubled since 1998, when it was estimated at $14 billion. See John Pike, "American Control of Outer Space in the Third Millennium" (November 1998), www.fas.org/spp/eprint/space9811.htm.

30. Pike, "American Control of Outer Space."

31. The United States formerly corrupted the GPS satellite signals to reduce the accuracy that a nonmilitary user terminal could achieve. On May 1, 2000, President Clinton ended this policy due to the vast commercial possibilities of highly accurate positional information. At that time, the U.S. government believed that it could employ new techniques to jam the GPS signals regionally in a way that would prevent an adversary from exploiting them, but not dilute the accuracy elsewhere. See Bill Clinton, "Improving the Civilian Global Positioning System (GPS)"

(May 1, 2000), www.ngs.noaa.gov/FGCS/info/sans_SA/docs/statement.html.

32. This is the cost of the development and deployment of the system, and the acquisition of sufficient satellites (118), to achieve and sustain a twenty-four satellite array. By 1997, $3 billion had been spent on "user equipment," the military terminals that calculate location on the basis of the satellites' signals. See U.S. Department of Defense, "Systems Acquisition Review Program Acquisition Cost Summary as of June 30, 1997." See also U.S. General Accounting Office, *Navstar Should Improve the Effectiveness of Military Missions—Cost Has Increased,* PSAD-80-91 (Washington, D.C.: U.S. General Accounting Office, February 15, 1980), 14. The European Union has decided to produce a competing system to GPS, called "Galileo." It is estimated that 3 billion euros will be required to buy and operate thirty satellites. European advocates of Galileo explicitly argue that Europe must have its own satellite navigation systems or lose its "autonomy in defense." See Dee Ann Divis, "Military Role for Galileo Emerges," *GPS World* 13 (May 2002): 10.

33. Tom Wilson (Space Commission staff member), "Threats to United States Space Capabilities," prepared for the *Report of the Commission to Assess United States National Security Space Management and Organization* (Washington, D.C.: U.S. Government Printing Office, January 11, 2001). Secretary of Defense Donald Rumsfeld chaired this commission.

34. A technically competent country with limited resources may be able to develop a capability to damage or destroy U.S. reconnaissance satellites in low earth orbit. See Allen Thomson, "Satellite Vulnerability: A Post–Cold War Issue," *Space Policy* 11 (February 1995): 19–30.

35. This is based on my simple addition of the maximum estimated cost increases associated with hardening satellites, providing them the capability for autonomous operations, giving them some onboard attack reporting capability, making them maneuverable, supplying them with decoys, and providing them with some self defense capability. See Wilson, "Threats to United States Space Capabilities," 6.

36. Pike, "American Control of Outer Space in the Third Millennium."

37. Barry R. Posen, *Inadvertent Escalation: Conventional War and Nuclear Risks* (Ithaca, N.Y.: Cornell University Press, 1992), 51–55. For a detailed description of a suppression operation, see Barry D. Watts and Thomas A. Keaney, *Effects and Effectiveness: Gulf War Air Power Survey,* Volume 2, Part 2 (Washington, D.C.: U.S. Government Printing Office, 1993), 130–45.

38. During Desert Storm, the United States employed one experimental joint surveillance target attack radar system (JSTARS) aircraft, a late Cold War project to develop an airborne surveillance radar capable of tracking the movements of large enemy ground forces at ranges of hundreds of kilometers. The U.S. Air Force has fifteen such aircraft. Similarly, U.S. forces employed few, if any, reconnaissance drones in Desert Storm; the U.S. Air Force now operates both high- and low-altitude reconnaissance drones. Under the right conditions, drones allow U.S. forces to get a close and persistent look at enemy ground forces. For current U.S. Air Force holdings, see IISS, *Military Balance, 2002–2003,* 22–23.

39. James Conway, "First Marine Expeditionary Force Commander Live Briefing from Iraq," U.S. Department of Defense news transcript (May 30, 2003), www.defenselink.mil/transcripts/2003/tr20030530-0229.html.

40. U.S. General Accounting Office, *Weapons Acquisition: Precision-Guided Munitions in Inventory, Production, and Development,* GAO/NSIAD-95-95 (Washington, D.C.: U.S. Government Accounting Office, June 1995), 12.

41. The U.S. military says that it needs 200,000 GPS satellite-guided bombs, the joint direct attack munition (JDAM)—seven thousand of which were used in the Afghan War. Six thousand five hundred JDAMs were used in the Iraq war. See T. Michael Moseley, commander, United States Central Command Air Forces, "Operation Iraqi Freedom —By the Numbers," Assessment and Analysis Division, USCENTAF (April 30, 2003), 3, www.iraqcrisis.co.uk/downloads/resources/uscentaf_oif_report_30apr2003.pdf. Boeing is producing this weapon at the rate of two thousand per month, and the military wants to increase production to 2,800 per month. See Nick Cook, "Second-Source JDAM Production Line Moves Closer," *Jane's Defense Weekly* (October 16, 2002): 5.

42. Daryl G. Press, "The Myth of Air Power in the Persian Gulf War and the Future of Warfare," *International Security* 26 (Fall 2001): 5–44, carefully and convincingly demonstrates that despite weeks of bombing, Iraqi mechanized ground forces in Kuwait and southern Iraq were still largely intact when the United States opened its ground attack. Perhaps 40 percent of Iraqi fighting vehicles were destroyed or immobilized by the air campaign, prior to the start of ground operations. Nevertheless, once the coalition ground operation began, Iraqi mechanized units managed to maneuver in the desert, in spite of U.S. command of the air. They did not suffer much damage from U.S. fixed-wing air attacks during the ground campaign. These forces were destroyed or enveloped by U.S. and allied mechanized ground forces. It should be noted, however, that army and marine attack helicopters destroyed much Iraqi armor.

43. Ibid., 12; and Michael R. Gordon and Bernard E. Trainor, *The Generals' War: The Inside Story of the Conflict in the Gulf* (Boston: Little, Brown, 1995), 267–88.

44. The United States currently has military installations in three dozen foreign countries or special territories. See Office of the Deputy Undersecretary of Defense (Installations and Environment), Department of Defense, "Summary," *Base Structure Report (A Summary of DoD's Real Property Inventory), Fiscal Year 2002 Baseline,* www.defenselink.mil/news/Jun2002/basestructure2002.pdf. This report counts only installations in which the United States has actually invested federal dollars. Missing from the list are Kuwait and Saudi Arabia, so a peculiar definition of U.S. base must guide the report. Unfortunately, comparable time series data do not exist to permit comparison to the last days of the Cold War. Secretary of Defense William S. Cohen noted in 1997 that although the Department of Defense had reduced active-duty military forces by 32 percent, it had reduced its domestic and overseas base structure by only 26 percent. See William S. Cohen, *Report of the Quadrennial Defense Review* (Washington, D.C.: Department of Defense, May 1997). The vast majority of overseas installations that were either reduced or closed, 878 out of 952, were in Europe. See Department of Defense, "Additional

U.S. Overseas Bases to End Operations," Department of Defense news release, April 27, 1995. From 1988 to 1997, the number of U.S. troops stationed abroad (on land) dropped from 480,000 to 210,000; 80 percent of the reduction came in Europe. See William S. Cohen, *Annual Report to the President and the Congress, 2000* (Washington, D.C.: U.S. Department of Defense, 2000), C-2.

45. Other post–Cold War allies offering overflight, port, or actual basing contributions to the war on terrorism include, among others, Albania, Bulgaria, the Czech Republic, Djibouti, Estonia, Ethiopia, Latvia, Lithuania, Pakistan, and Slovakia. See U.S. Department of Defense, *International Contributions to the War against Terrorism,* fact sheet, June 7, 2002. See also William M. Arkin, "Military Bases Boost Capability but Fuel Anger," *Los Angeles Times* (January 6, 2002): A1, noting that U.S. military personnel were working at thirteen new locations in nine countries in support of the war on terror.

46. Military Sealift Command, U.S. Navy, fact sheet, "Large, Medium-Speed, Roll-on/Roll-off Ships (LMSRs)," October 2002. Thirty-three ships of various types, including nine of the LMSRs, are employed to preposition equipment, ammunition, and fuel. See also Military Sealift Command, U.S. Navy, fact sheet, "Afloat Prepositioning Force," April 2003. A total of eighty-seven dry cargo ships of various kinds, including eleven LMSRs and many other roll-on/roll-off ships are based in the United States.

47. "Boeing and U.S. Air Force Sign $9.7 Billion C-17 Contract," news release, Boeing Corporation, August 15, 2002, www.boeing.com/news/releases/2002/q3/nr_020815m.html. This follow-on procurement contract added sixty C-17 Globemaster III transport aircraft to the 120 already on order.

48. IISS, *The Military Balance, 2002–2003,* 18–21, 60–63. It is worth noting that Britain and France are the only two countries in the world, aside from the United States, with any global power projection capability.

49. Ronald H. Cole, Walter S. Poole, James F. Schnabel, Robert J. Watson, and Willard J. Webb, *The History of the Unified Command Plan, 1946–1993* (Washington, D.C.: Joint History Office, Office of the Chairman of the Joint Chiefs of Staff, 1995), www.dtic.mil/doctrine/jel/history/ucp.pdf; see especially pages 107–17.

50. George H. W. Bush's administration reportedly issued draft defense planning guidance to the Pentagon in March 1992 with this objective. "Excerpts from Pentagon's Plan: 'Prevent the Emergence of a New Rival,'" *New York Times* (March 8, 1992): 14. For reportage, see Patrick E. Tyler, "U.S. Strategy Plan Calls for Insuring No Rivals Develop," *New York Times* (March 8, 1992): 1, 14; and Barton Gellman, "The U.S. Aims to Remain First among Equals," *Washington Post National Weekly Edition* (March 16–22, 1992): 19. For examples of contemporary commentary, see Leslie Gelb, "They're Kidding," *New York Times* (March 9, 1992): A17; James Chace, "The Pentagon's Superpower Fantasy," *New York Times* (March 16, 1992): 17; and Charles Krauthammer, "What's Wrong with the 'Pentagon Paper'?" *Washington Post* (March 13, 1992): A25.

51. Bush, *The National Security Strategy of the United States of America,* 30. According to *Report of the Quadrennial Defense Review* (2001), 12, "Well targeted strategy and

policy can therefore dissuade other countries from initiating future military competitions"; see also ibid., 36.

52. Owen R. Coté, Jr., "The Future of the Trident Force" (Cambridge, Mass.: Massachusetts Institute of Technology Security Studies Program, May 2002), 25–29, discusses air defense suppression generally, and the significant problems posed by the SA-10, specifically. See also Owen R. Coté, Jr., "'Buying . . . From the Sea': A Defense Budget for a Maritime Strategy," in *Holding the Line: U.S. Defense Alternatives for the Early Twenty-first Century,* ed. Cindy Williams (Cambridge, Mass.: MIT Press, 2001), 146–50.

53. IISS, *The Military Balance, 2002–2003,* 148, credits China with 144 SA-10s. This implies perhaps a dozen batteries. "SA-10" is a NATO designation; Russia calls the weapon "S-300." See Federation of American Scientists, "SA-10 Grumble," www.fas.org/nuke/guide/russia/airdef/s-300pmu.htm.

54. The *Quadrennial Defense Review Report* (2001) seems to be preoccupied with swiftness: for example, the Department of Defense seeks forces to "swiftly defeat aggression in overlapping major conflicts" (p. 17); "The focus will be on the ability to act quickly. U.S. forces will remain capable of swiftly defeating attack against U.S. allies and friends in any two theaters of operation in overlapping time frames" (p. 21); and "One of the goals of reorienting the global posture is to render forward forces capable of swiftly defeating an adversary's military and political objectives with only modest reinforcement" (p. 25; repeated on p. 26).

55. Daniel Williams and Nicholas Wood, "Iraq Finds Ready Arms Sellers from Baltic Sea to Bosnia," *International Herald Tribune* (November 21, 2002).

56. Prior to the start of the third Gulf War in March 2003, Iraq was reported to have had three thousand antiaircraft guns. Many of Iraq's air defense duels with U.S. aircraft in the no-fly zones during the preceding decade depended on AAA. Iraq did not shoot down any Western aircraft before the war, but U.S. airmen nevertheless viewed these guns as a serious threat: "For years, the Iraqis used antiaircraft artillery (AAA), unguided rockets, and surface-to-air missiles against coalition aircraft in both the northern and southern no-fly zones. In fact, they started firing at our aircraft in 1992, and over the last three years Iraqi AAA has fired at coalition aircraft over 1,000 times, launched 600 rockets and fired nearly 60 SAMs." Secretary of Defense Donald H. Rumsfeld and Gen. Richard Myers, chairman, Joint Chiefs of Staff, news briefing, September 30, 2002. See IISS, *The Military Balance, 2002–2003,* 106, for Iraq's AAA inventory.

57. Kenneth P. Werrell, *Archie, Flak, AAA, and SAM: A Short Operational History of Ground-Based Air Defense* (Maxwell Air Force Base, Ala.: Air University Press, 1988), 102. According to Werrell, "Between 1965 and 1973 flak engaged one-fourth of all flights over North Vietnam and accounted for 66% of U.S. aircraft losses over the North."

58. Thomas A. Keaney and Eliot A. Cohen, *Gulf War Air Power Survey Summary Report* (Washington, D.C.: U.S. Government Printing Office, 1993), 61–62. Thirty-eight aircraft were lost, and forty-eight were damaged. In explaining these low losses, Keaney and Cohen note: "although some crews initially tried NATO-style low-level ingress tactics during the first few nights of Desert Storm, the sheer

volume and ubiquity of barrage antiaircraft artillery, combined with the ability of Stinger-class infrared SAMs to be effective up to 12,000–15,000 feet, quickly persuaded most everyone on the Coalition side to abandon low altitude, especially for weapon release." See also U.S. General Accounting Office, *Operation Desert Storm: Evaluation of the Air Campaign,* GAO/NSIAD-97-134 (Washington, D.C.: U.S. General Accounting Office, June 1997), 94. Fourteen aircraft were destroyed or damaged by radar SAMs, twenty-eight by infrared SAMS, and thirty-three by AAA. AAA was much more likely than the other systems to damage rather than destroy a successfully engaged target.

59. Moseley, "Operation Iraqi Freedom—By the Numbers."

60. Rowan Scarborough, "Apache Operation a Lesson in Defeat," *Washington Times* (April 22, 2003): 1. This was apparently a clever Iraqi ambush. An Iraqi observer watched the helicopters take off and used a cell phone to alert some air defense units. On a prearranged signal, the local power grid was turned off for a few seconds to alert the rest. See William Scott Wallace, U.S. Army, "Fifth Corps Commander Live Briefing from Baghdad," U.S. Department of Defense news transcript (May 7, 2003), www.defenselink.mil/transcripts/2003/tr20030507-0157html.

61. Between 1961 and 1968, 1,709 U.S. aircraft were lost over South Vietnam, of which 63 percent were helicopters and the rest fixed-wing aircraft. During this period, AAA was the only air defense weapon available to the communists in the South. Werrell, *Archie, Flak, AAA, and SAM,* 112.

62. Passive electronic intelligence collection consists of radio receivers that track both radio and radar emissions. Without information on the precise content of coded communications, such systems may still develop an understanding of certain patterns of communications that are associated with certain kinds of operations. Occasional lapses in communications security may provide the actual content of communications to the receiver. Radio direction finding can provide indications of where certain patterns of electronic emissions occur, and where they are going. These can be cross-referenced with what radars may observe. The reports of spies and observers can also be integrated with this information. Over time, a competent adversary may build up a picture of U.S. procedures and tactics, which can prove invaluable. It is likely that this is how the Serbs were able to shoot down a U.S. F-117 stealth fighter in 1999. Because the Serbs destroyed so few U.S. aircraft, the magnitude of this particular achievement is underappreciated.

63. Some believe that the advent of stealth obviates this statement, but that does not seem to be the case. Stealth aircraft missions are generally planned to benefit from air defense suppression, although it appears that these missions rely on somewhat less direct suppressive support than do conventional bombing missions. Little more can be said, as the tactics of stealth missions are highly classified.

64. See Timothy L. Thomas, "Kosovo and the Current Myth of Information Superiority," *Parameters* 30 (Spring 2000): 14–29. Relying on accounts by Admiral James Ellis, commander-in-chief of Allied Forces Southern Europe during the Kosovo war, Thomas reports the Serbian strategy: "To prevent its air defense assets from being neutralized,

the Serbian armed forces turned their assets on only as needed. They therefore presented a 'constant but dormant' threat. This resulted in NATO using its most strained assets (e.g., JSTARS, AWACS, or airborne warning and control system) to conduct additional searches for air defense assets and forced NATO aircraft to fly above 15,000 feet, making it difficult for them to hit their targets. Ellis noted that NATO achieved little damage to the Serbian integrated air defense system." Ibid., 8 (web version).

65. As Thomas notes, "their [Serbian] offsets included deception, disinformation, camouflage, the clever use of radar, spies within NATO, helicopter movement NATO couldn't detect, and the exploitation of NATO's operational templating of information dominance activities (e.g., satellites, reconnaissance flights). See ibid., 3, 9 (web version).

66. On Serbia's air and ground strategies, as well as Serbia's tactical successes, see Barry R. Posen, "The War for Kosovo: Serbia's Political-Military Strategy," *International Security* 24 (Spring 2000): 54–66.

67. For a collection of deception tactics and countermeasures that the Serbs are said to have employed, see "Tactics Employed by the Yugoslav Army to Limit NATO Air Strikes' Effectiveness," Associated Press (November 18, 2002). Daryl Press notes that even in the deserts of Kuwait and southern Iraq, U.S. fighter aircraft experienced difficulties attacking a dug-in, camouflaged, ground force. See Press, "The Myth of Air Power in the Persian Gulf War," 40–42. As of this writing, insufficient information has emerged to determine the effectiveness of these techniques in the U.S.-led war with Iraq that began in March 2003.

68. T. Michael Moseley, "Coalition Forces Air Component Command Briefing," U.S. Department of Defense news transcript (April 5, 2003), www.defenselink.mil/news/Apr2003/t04052003_t405mose.html, alludes to enforcement of the no-fly zones as an opportunity to degrade the Iraqi air defense system. He reports that after the first 3 or 4 days of the war, his flyers were able to switch from suppression to destruction of Iraqi air defenses, which suggests that the defenders suffered heavy losses in the early days, perhaps because they turned their radars on too often. Finally, he said that "every time they move one of those things [a SAM or radar] they have a tendency to break something on them," which suggests unreliable and/or poorly maintained equipment. After the conventional phase of the war ended, an Iraqi air defense officer, General Ghanem Abdullah Azawi, declared: "There has been practically no air defense since 1991. Nobody rebuilt it. We didn't receive any new weapons." Quoted in William Branigin, "A Brief Bitter War for Iraq's Military Officers: Self-Deception a Factor in Defeat," *Washington Post* (April 27, 2003): A25.

69. One journalist who toured Iraqi defenses south of Baghdad either in late March or early April reports that Iraqi units were well dispersed, dug in, and camouflaged. He saw some damaged equipment but more that had survived. Robert Fisk, "Saddam's Masters of Concealment Dig In, Ready for Battle," *Independent* (April 3, 2003): 1. On April 5, U.S. troops "found herds of tanks abandoned by the Iraqi Army and Republican Guard" in Karbala. See Jim Dwyer, "In Karbala, G.I.'s Find Forsaken Iraqi Armor and Pockets of Resistance," *New York Times* (April 6, 2003): B4. One postwar report suggests that "fewer than 100 Republican

Guard tanks were knocked out in the battles around Baghdad, so coalition officers say hundreds of modern T-72 main battle tanks and BMP infantry fighting vehicles are still to be found." Tim Ripley, "Building a New Iraqi Army," *Jane's Defence Weekly* (April 16, 2003): 3. Other journalists toured the same area after the end of conventional fighting and reported the existence of vast, but entirely unused, prepared defensive positions and the destruction of many reasonably well-camouflaged Iraqi combat vehicles, although they kept no count. They note little evidence of dead Iraqi soldiers and suggest that many units melted away. Terry McCarthy, "What Ever Happened to the Republican Guard?" *Time* (May 12, 2003): 24–28. On the whole, it seems that large quantities of Iraqi armored vehicles and weapons survived concentrated Western air attacks, but Iraqi troops abandoned their equipment. One cannot know if better-led, more tactically proficient, and more politically committed troops would have found ways to employ this surviving equipment to offer stronger resistance to U.S. ground forces.

70. William M. Arkin, "Speed Kills," *Los Angeles Times* (June 1, 2003): M1, suggests that the Iraqis suffered grievous damage when they tried to maneuver under cover of a late-March sandstorm. More generally, a U.S. Marine noncommissioned officer declared, "Every time they try to move their tanks even 100 yards, they get it from our aircraft. We are everywhere." See Matthew Fisher, "Skirmishes in Baghdad: Marines Blow Up Scores of Abandoned Iraqi Tanks and Armoured Vehicles," *Times Colonist* (Victoria, Canada) (April 7, 2003): A5.

71. Philip Shenon, "The Iraqi Connection: Serbs Seek Iraqi Help for Defense, Britain Says," *New York Times* (April 1, 1999): A16. This appears to have been two-way commerce. Until very recently, many companies in the former Yugoslavia apparently exported military equipment to Iraq in violation of the U.N. arms embargo. See Williams and Wood, "Iraq Finds Ready Arms Sellers from Baltic Sea to Bosnia."

72. A fiber-optic network was reportedly added to Iraq's air defense command and control system. See IISS, *The Military Balance, 2002–2003*, 98.

73. Andrew Koch and Michael Sirak, "Iraqi Air Defences under Strain," *Jane's Defence Weekly* (February 28, 2001): 2. The article also notes that although some Serbs have reportedly helped Iraq militarily over the years, others reportedly provided intelligence about Iraq to the United States and Britain.

74. Department of Defense, news briefing, June 10, 1999. See the slide "Air Defense BDA," www.defenselink .mil/news/Jun1999/990610-J-0000K-008.jpg.

75. IISS, *The Military Balance 2002–2003*, 98.

76. For reviews of the evidence supporting this point, see William Rosenau, *Special Operations Forces and Elusive Enemy Ground Targets: Lessons from Vietnam and the Persian Gulf War*, MR-1408-AF (Santa Monica, Calif.: RAND, 2001), 40–44; and "The Great Scud Hunt: An Assessment," Centre for Defence and International Security Studies, Lancaster University, 1996, www.cdiss.org/ scudnt6.htm.

77. Two soldiers and two journalists were killed, fifteen soldiers were wounded, and seventeen military vehicles were destroyed. Steven Lee Myers, "A Nation at War: Third Infantry Division; Iraqi Missile Strike Kills Four at Tactical Operations Center," *New York Times* (April 8, 2003): B3.

78. IISS, *The Military Balance, 2002–2003*, 103–5, 153–54, 279, 299. Nearly ten million are in Iran, which conscripts perhaps only 125,000 of its 950,000 eligible males annually. North Korea appears to conscript virtually all of its eligible males.

79. U.S. Commission on National Security/21st Century, *New World Coming: American Security in the 21st Century, Supporting Research and Analysis* (Washington, D.C.: U.S. Commission on National Security/21st Century, September 15, 1999), 40.

80. Alexander Higgins, "UN-Backed Study Estimates 639 Million Small Arms in World," Associated Press (June 24, 2002); see also "Red Flags and Buicks: Global Firearm Stockpiles," chapter summary, *Small Arms Survey* (2002), www.smallarmssurveyorg/Yearbook/EngPRkitCH2_11.06.02 .pdf.

81. James T. Quinlivan, "Force Requirements in Stability Operations," *Parameters* 25 (Winter 1995): 61.

82. Eric Schmitt, "Pentagon Contradicts General on Iraq Occupation Force's Size," *New York Times* (February 28, 2003): 1.

83. Tom Squitieri, "Postwar Force Could Be 125,000," *USA Today* (April 28, 2003): 1.

84. Bradley Graham, "Iraq Stabilization Impinges on Army Rotation, Rebuilding," *Washington Post* (June 6, 2003): A21.

85. "'Too Few Troops' in Iraq," *BBC News* (May 26, 2003), http://news.bbc.co.uk/go/pr/fr/-/2/hi/middle_east/ 2938176.stm.

86. Tom Bowman, "Pentagon to Consider Large-Scale Troop Cuts," *Baltimore Sun* (July 10, 2001): 1A. A reduction of almost ninety thousand soldiers, sailors, airmen, and marines is contemplated because "with personnel eating up a significant portion of the defense budget, and with Rumsfeld and his aides eager to harness the latest technology and weaponry, the Pentagon has begun to focus on cutting jobs among the 1.4 million people on active duty." See also Robert S. Dudney, "Hyperextension," *Air Force Magazine* (August 2002): 2, noting Secretary of Defense Rumsfeld's reluctance to add manpower, which he considered to be "enormously expensive."

87. The final defense authorization for FY03 approved a modest increase in the size of the U.S. active force.

88. Mark Bowden, *Black Hawk Down: A Story of Modern War* (New York: Atlantic Monthly Press, 1999), is the source for what follows.

89. Ibid., 21.

90. Ibid., 31, 230.

91. Ibid., 110–11. The RPG-7, intended as a point-detonated antitank projectile, reportedly also has a time fuse to ensure that it will explode somewhere in the midst of the enemy in the event that the shooter misses his target. The Somalis may have somehow shortened the time setting on this fuse, to cause the projectile to burst in the air at relatively short range—essentially turning it into a medium-caliber AAA round. Alternatively, the Somalis may simply have learned the range at which this explosion would normally occur and fired at least some of their RPGs at helicopters at the appropriate range.

92. Ibid., 109.

93. Ibid., 333.

94. The 1968 Battle for Hue in South Vietnam offers a cautionary tale that is much studied by the U.S. military. Hue was not a particularly large city, with 140,000 people on sixteen square kilometers, although its heavy stone construction provided excellent defensive positions. It took 25 days for eleven South Vietnamese and three U.S. Marine Corps infantry battalions, with vastly superior firepower, to evict sixteen to eighteen Vietcong and North Vietnamese infantry battalions from the city. U.S. Army units assisted with critical supporting attacks outside the city. The U.S. and South Vietnamese troops suffered six hundred killed and 3,800 wounded and missing to do so, and the fighting destroyed much of the city. Estimates of communist dead range from one thousand to five thousand, out of a force of perhaps 12,000. See Abbott Associates, *Modern Experience in City Combat,* Technical Memorandum 5–87, AD-A180 999 (Aberdeen, Md.: U.S. Army Human Engineering Laboratory, 1987), 67–68. Casualty estimates are from Jack Shulimson, Leonard A. Blasiol, Charles R. Smith, and Captain David Dawson, *U.S. Marines in Vietnam: The Defining Year, 1968* (Washington, D.C.: History and Museums Division, Headquarters, U.S. Marine Corps, 1997), 213.

95. Barry R. Posen, "Urban Operations: Tactical Realities and Strategic Ambiguities," in *Soldiers in Cities: Military Operations on Urban Terrain,* ed. Michael C. Desch (Carlisle, Pa.: Strategic Studies Institute, U.S. Army War College, 2001), 153–54. See also *Combined Arms Operations in Urban Terrain,* FM 3–06. 11 (Washington, D.C.: Headquarters, Department of the Army, February 28, 2002), secs. 4-13, 4-37, 5-12.

96. According to General Alaa Abdelkadeer, a Republican Guard officer interviewed after the war, the Iraqis had discussed the details of an urban defense of Baghdad before the war, "but none of this was carried out." Robert Collier, "Iraqi Military Plans Were Simplistic, Poorly Coordinated," *San Francisco Chronicle* (May 25, 2003): A19.

97. Peter Baker, "A 'Turkey Shoot,' but with Marines as the Targets," *Washington Post* (March 28, 2003): A1; Dexter Filkins and Michael Wilson, "A Nation At War: The Southern Front; Marines, Battling in Streets, Seek Control of City in South," *New York Times* (March 25, 2003): A1; John Roberts, "On the Scene: A Formidable Foe" (March 26, 2003), www.cbsnews.com/stories/200 . . . 6/iraq/scene/printable546258.shtml; and Andrew North, "Nasiriya, 0941 GMT," in "Reporters' Log: War in Iraq," *BBC News* (March 31, 2003), www.bbc.co.uk/reporters.

98. Conway, "First Marine Expeditionary Force Briefing."

99. Anthony Davis, "The Afghan Files: Al-Qaeda Documents from Kabul," *Jane's Intelligence Review* 14 (February 2002): 16. Davis visited Kabul shortly after its fall and collected many al Qaeda documents. According to Davis, "much of the literature also underlines the extent to which al-Qaeda was a highly organized military undertaking as well as a committed terrorist network. Detailed training manuals and student notebooks indicate that theoretical and on-the-job training involved not only small arms and assault rifles but a range of heavier weapons, including 12.7 millimeter machine guns, AGS-17 automatic grenade launchers, mortars, and even 107 mm BM-1 and BM-12 rocket systems." Ibid., 18.

100. The section that follows relies largely on journalistic accounts of the battle. I have supplemented these accounts with some information gleaned in private conversations with U.S. military officers. See also the excellent study by Stephen Biddle, *Afghanistan and the Future of Warfare: Implications for Army and Defense Policy* (Carlisle, Pa.: U.S. Army Strategic Studies Institute, U.S. Army War College, November 2002), 28–37.

101. Richard T. Cooper, "The Untold War: Fierce Fight in Afghan Valley Tests U.S. Soldiers and Strategy," *Los Angeles Times* (March 24, 2002): 1.

102. In the case of one communications bunker, an army intelligence specialist noted: "you wouldn't see it unless you looked directly on it. Predator wouldn't have been able to see it." The bunker contained a radio set up with "low probability of intercept techniques," which would have made it very difficult for U.S. electronic intelligence assets to detect its presence. See Thomas E. Ricks, "In Mop Up, U.S. Finds 'Impressive' Remnants of Fallen Foe," *Washington Post* (March 20, 2002): 1.

103. Cooper, "The Untold War," 1; see also U.S. Department of Defense, "Background Briefing on the Report of the Battle of Takur Ghar," May 24, 2002.

104. According to one reporter, "Five [AH-64] Apaches were present at the start of the battle, a sixth arrived later that morning and a seventh flew up from Kandahar to join the fight that afternoon. None of the helicopters was shot down, but four were so badly damaged they were knocked out of the fight. The fire the Apaches braved was so intense that when the day was over, 27 of the 28 rotor blades among the seven helicopters sported bullet holes, said Lt. Col. James M. Marye, the commander of the 7th Battalion, 101st Aviation Regiment." Sean D. Naylor, "In Shah-E-Kot, Apaches Save the Day—and Their Reputation," *Army Times* (March 25, 2002): 15.

105. Sean D. Naylor, "What We Learned from Afghanistan," *Army Times* (July 29, 2002): 10. It appears to me that a problem with al Qaeda mortar fuses saved some American lives; Soviet shells with point-detonated fuses occasionally bored into the mud without exploding. Western time or proximity fuses would not have had this problem and would have produced a more lethal explosion.

106. Walter Pincus, "Attacks on U.S. Forces May Persist, CIA, DIA Chiefs Warn of Afghan Insurgency Threat," *Washington Post* (March 20, 2002): 1. The director of the Central Intelligence Agency, George Tenet, testified to Congress, "There are many, many points of exit that people in small numbers can get out. We're frustrated that people did get away." Ibid., 1.

107. Ricks, "In Mop Up, U.S. Finds 'Impressive' Remnants of Fallen Foe" reports "sheaves of rocket-propelled grenades." Commenting on the lessons of the 2003 Iraq war, Colonel Mike Hiemstra, director of the Center for Army Lessons Learned, notes, "The Proliferation of rocket-propelled grenades [RPGs] across the world continues to be huge." See "More 'Must-Have' Answers Needed," *Jane's Defence Weekly* (April 30, 2003): 25. The RPG was widely used by the Iraqis in the 2003 war; it seems to have been their only effective antiarmor weapon.

108. Ibid., and Cooper, "The Untold War," 1, report night-vision devices being found in two separate al Qaeda positions.

109. U.S. Department of the Navy, . . . *From the Sea, Preparing the Naval Service for the 21st Century*, White Paper (Washington, D.C.: U.S. Department of the Navy, September 1992). See also *Forward . . . from the Sea*, U.S. Naval Institute Proceedings (Washington, D.C.: U.S. Department of the Navy, December 1994), 46–49.

110. Vern Clark, U.S. Navy, "Sea Power 21 Series—Part I," *U.S. Naval Institute Proceedings* 128:196 (October 2002). The Pentagon recognizes the special problems of littoral warfare: "Anti-ship cruise missiles, advanced diesel submarines, and advanced mines could threaten the ability of U.S. naval and amphibious forces to operate in littoral waters," *Quadrennial Defense Review Report* (2001), 31; see also page 43. Recognition is not the same as solution, however. They recognized the problem in 1992: "Some littoral threats . . . tax the capabilities of our current systems and force structure. Mastery of the littoral should not be presumed. It does not derive directly from command of the high seas. It is an objective which requires our focused skills and resources." U.S. Department of the Navy, *Forward . . . From the Sea*, 4. Yet progress has been slow. According to the General Accounting Office, the Navy, "does not have a means for effectively breaching enemy sea mines in the surf zone; detecting and neutralizing enemy submarines in shallow water; defending its ships against cruise missiles, or providing adequate fire support for Marine Corps amphibious landings and combat operations ashore." U.S. General Accounting Office, *Navy Acquisitions: Improved Littoral War-Fighting Capabilities Needed*, GAO/NSIAD-01-493 (Washington, D.C.: U.S. General Accounting Office, May 2001), 2.

111. The problem of inexpensive technology complicating great power naval operations in the littorals is not new. This was a key fact of late nineteenth- and early twentieth-century naval life, which ended the practice of the "close blockade." See Kennedy, *The Rise and Fall of British Naval Mastery*, 199–200.

112. This is my personal assessment. For suggestive, supporting material, see the various country entries in IISS, *The Military Balance, 2002–2003*.

113. See Gregory K. Hartmann and Scott C. Truver, *Weapons That Wait: Mine Warfare in the U.S. Navy* (Annapolis, Md.: Naval Institute Press, 1991), 254–62. These authors note that naval mine warfare has usually proven to be very cost effective. During World War II, U.S. forces damaged or sank five to nine Japanese ships per $1 million of mine warfare expenditure. Ibid., 236–37. See also "Appendix A: Mine Threat Overview," in Jay L. Johnson and James L. Jones, *U.S. Naval Mine Warfare Plan, Programs for the New Millennium*, 4th ed. (Washington, D.C.: U.S. Department of the Navy, 2000).

114. The mine was an Italian-manufactured "Manta," which cost perhaps $10,000. Edward J. Marolda and Robert J. Schneller, Jr., *Shield and Sword: The United States Navy and the Persian Gulf War* (Washington, D.C.: Naval Historical Center, Department of the Navy, 1998), 267.

115. Ibid., 37.

116. "Minister of State for the Armed Forces and the First Sea Lord Admiral Sir Alan West: Press Conference at the Ministry of Defence," London (April 11, 2003), www.operations.mod.uk/telic/press_11april.htm.

117. Max Hastings and Simon Jenkins, *The Battle for the Falklands* (New York: W. W. Norton, 1983), 296–97.

118. Robert W. Love, *A History of the U.S. Navy, 1942–1991* (Harrisburg, Pa.: Stackpole, 1992), 784.

119. Paul Lewis and Steward Penney, "Timeline: Week Two," *Flight International* (April 8, 2003): 11.

120. Marolda and Schneller, *Shield and Sword*, 36.

121. Hastings and Jenkins, *Battle for the Falklands*, 153–56, 227–28.

122. Love, *A History of the U.S. Navy*, 787–89.

123. David B. Crist, "Joint Special Operations in Support of Earnest Will," *Joint Forces Quarterly* 29 (Autumn/Winter 2001): 15–22. Crist notes some forty-three attacks in 1986, though only one actually sank a ship.

124. Richard Scott, "UK Plans to Counter Threat of Terrorists at Sea," *Jane's Defence Weekly* (June 19, 2002): 8. According to Scott, "Staff in the UK Ministry of Defence's Directorate Equipment Capability . . . have identified a significant gap in the capability of ships to adequately defend themselves against fast attack craft (FACS) fast inshore attack craft (FIACS), and acknowledge a capability upgrade as an urgent priority." Ibid. In an act of perhaps unintentional irony, the second story on the same page of the magazine is "Taiwan to Launch Prototype Stealth PCFG," or fast-attack missile patrol boat. If Taiwan can build stealthy small craft, then so can many other small and middle-sized countries, and the threat can be expected to grow.

125. Robert Burns, "Ex-General Says Wargames Were Rigged," Associated Press (August 16, 2002).

126. John Morgan, "Anti-Submarine Warfare: A Phoenix for the Future," *Undersea Warfare* 1 (Fall 1998), www.chinfo.navy.mil/navpalib/cno/n87/usw/autumn98/anti.htm. Morgan warns (ibid.):

Finally, ASW is hard. The *San Luis* operated in the vicinity of the British task force for more than a month and was a constant concern to Royal Navy commanders. Despite the deployment of five nuclear attack submarines, twenty-four-hour-per-day airborne ASW operations, and expenditures of precious time, energy, and ordnance, the British never once detected the Argentine submarine. The near-shore regional/littoral operating environment poses a very challenging ASW problem. We will need enhanced capabilities to root modern diesel, air-independent, and nuclear submarines out of the 'mud' of noisy, contact-dense environments typical of the littoral, and be ready as well to detect, localize, and engage submarines in deep water and Arctic environments.

127. I have heard this from several U.S. naval officers. Iran apparently began operating its first Kilo submarine in 1993. At the time, Vice Admiral Henry Chiles, commander of the Atlantic Fleet's submarine force did not consider the Iranians to be a "serious military threat." He did expect that "a year from now I think they'll have a greatly improved military capability." Quoted in Robert Burns, "Admiral Calls Iranian Subs a Potential Threat to U.S. Interests," Associated Press (August 4, 1993).

128. Iraq's naval tactics were not adept during Operation Desert Storm: "Fortunately for the allies, the Iraqis had failed to activate many of the weapons, and chose not to

cover the minefields with aircraft, naval vessels, artillery, or missiles. More expertly laid and defended mines would have sunk ships and killed sailors and marines." Marolda and Schneller, *Shield and Sword,* 267.

129. "U.S. Alarmed by Growing Iranian Might: U.S. Navy Commander," Agence France-Presse (February 4, 1996). Vice Admiral Scott Redd, then commander of the U.S. Fifth Fleet, declared, "Iran now poses a threat to navigation and aircraft flying over the Gulf." Referring to then new Iranian sea-launched antiship missiles he noted, "From a military point of view, I have to warn of the new threat, which is represented by Iran's ability to launch missiles from all directions and not only from its shores." Ibid.

130. North Korea exports several vessels designed for coastal operations, including miniature submarines. It has sold several such vessels to Iran. See Bill Gertz, "N. Korea Delivers Semi-submersible Gunships to Iran," *Washington Times* (December 16, 2002): A3.

131. Britain, France, Germany, and Italy together operate ninety-nine destroyers and frigates. The U.S. Navy operates 117 cruisers, destroyers, and frigates. European surface combatants are smaller and less capable than those of the U.S. Navy, but they permit the surveillance and control of a great deal of additional sea space. Moreover, these navies either possess significant littoral combat experience, such as Britain, or build some of the world's most lethal littoral weapons, such as France (antiship missiles) and Italy (bottom mines). IISS, *The Military Balance, 2002–2003,* country entries.

132. Michael R. Gordon, "Threats and Responses: Allies —German and Spanish Navies Take on Major Role Near Horn of Africa," *New York Times* (December 15, 2002): 36. Task Force 150 is an eight ship flotilla conducting patrols in the Indian Ocean in search of al Qaeda operatives. Its first commander was German, and its second was Spanish. This is part of a larger multinational operation in the region, which includes ships from Australia, Canada, France, Germany, Greece, Italy, Japan, the Netherlands, Spain, the United Kingdom, and the United States. "Greece Contributes Frigate to Anti-Terrorism Campaign," Xinhua News Agency (March 12, 2002).

133. IISS, *The Military Balance, 2002–2003,* country entries.

134. Ibid.

135. The Pentagon has set the goals of "defeating anti-access and area denial threats," and "denying enemies sanctuary by providing persistent surveillance, tracking, and rapid engagement with high-volume precision strikes . . . against critical mobile and fixed targets at various ranges and in all weather and terrains." *Quadrennial Defense Review Report* (2001), 30. Moreover, "Likely enemies of the United States and its allies will rely on sanctuaries—such as remote terrain, hidden bunkers, or civilian 'shields'—for protection. The capability to find and strike protected enemy forces while limiting collateral damage will improve the deterrent power of the United States and give the president increased options for response if deterrence fails." Ibid., 44.

MAKING ECONOMIC SANCTIONS WORK

CHANTAL DE JONGE OUDRAAT

The U.N. Security Council has increasingly imposed economic sanctions to prevent, manage, or resolve violent conflict. Such sanctions have often entailed tremendous economic costs to the target countries, but have failed to change the political behavior of their leaders. Moreover, they have had unintended social and humanitarian effects, leading many commentators to question their morality as a policy instrument.[1] Notwithstanding these problems, for many policymakers, sanctions remain attractive as an apparently inexpensive and low-risk way of showing concern and taking action short of military force.[2] It is therefore important to develop a better understanding of the way economic sanctions work in order to make them more effective and to limit their harmful humanitarian consequences.

The scholarly literature on sanctions is abundant and, on balance, sceptical.[3] Most scholars and analysts have, however, paid too much attention to the outcomes of sanctions regimes, and too little to the conditions under which they are imposed, the development of sanction strategies, and problems of implementation. They have also tended to study economic sanctions in isolation, independent of other coercive policy instruments; notably, the actual use of force. In fact, economic sanctions, although certainly no panacea, can be effective if they are part of comprehensive coercive strategies that include the

This essay has been edited and is reprinted from Chantal de Jonge Oudraat, "Making Economic Sanctions Work," Survival *42:3 (Autumn 2000): 105–27, by permission of Oxford University Press.*

use of force and are implemented properly. Many sanctions regimes in the 1990s failed because they did not meet these two key conditions.

THE TRACK RECORD

The theory behind sanctions is that they will produce economic deprivation, triggering public anger and politically significant protest. The latter, in turn, will lead to changes in the behavior of troublemaking elites or their removal from power. Sanctions can be comprehensive, partial, or targeted against individual corporations or people. They may encompass a multitude of services and goods or be limited to specific services (e.g., air traffic) and strategic goods (e.g., oil). Embargoes limit and ban exports to the target; boycotts limit and ban imports from the target.

The objective of sanctions imposed by the United Nations under Chapter VII of its Charter is "to maintain or restore international peace and security." The Security Council has significant latitude in defining threats to "international peace and security" and has shown great creativity in doing so. Indeed, it has increasingly deemed internal conflicts and gross violations of human rights to be justifications for international action. Since the end of the Cold War, the Security Council has imposed comprehensive economic sanctions four times, partial sanctions six times, targeted financial measures twice, and arms embargoes eleven times. Between 1945 and 1988, sanctions of any type were imposed only twice (see Table 8).

Comprehensive Economic Sanctions

Comprehensive economic sanctions were adopted against Iraq in 1990; against the Federal Republic of Yugoslavia (FRY)—that is, Serbia and Montenegro—in 1992; against the military junta in Haiti in 1994; and, again in 1994, against the Bosnian Serbs. The results have been mixed.

Iraq

The sanctions against Iraq were imposed because of its invasion and illegal occupation of Kuwait in August 1990.[4] However, they did not have the desired effect—Iraqi withdrawal from Kuwait—so in January 1991, a coalition of states led by the United States used military force to expel Iraqi forces. Subsequently, sanctions remained in place to force Iraqi compliance with the cease-fire resolution; in particular, its disarmament provisions.

In economic terms, Iraq was a good candidate for sanctions. Its economy was weak following the 8-year war with Iran in the 1980s, it was dependent on trade (oil exports accounted for more than 95 percent of the country's foreign-currency exchange receipts and 60 percent of its gross domestic product [GDP]), and its level of foreign debt was high. In political terms, however, the country was less vulnerable. Its mainly rural population lived under a strict and repressive authoritarian regime, which did not tolerate political opposition. That Iraqi President Saddam Hussein had little regard for his people had been demonstrated dramatically in March 1988, when Halabja, a town 260 kilometers northeast of Baghdad, was attacked with chemical weapons. More than five thousand people were killed, and many more seriously injured.

U.N. sanctions have now been in effect for over 10 years, and implementation of the sanction regime has been relatively good. These measures have been very effective in terms of their economic impact. Iraq's GDP in 1993, at $10 billion, was close to its 1960s levels. The annual value of imports fell from $11.5 billion in 1980 to $0.5 billion in 1996 and over the same period, exports plummeted from $28.3 billion to $0.5 billion.[5] However, sanctions have been less effective from a political point of view. Saddam remains in charge in Baghdad, and has not shelved plans to develop weapons of mass destruction. Moreover, the sanctions regime has had grave humanitarian consequences, which have undercut their legitimacy. Child mortality has more than doubled, malnutrition is rampant in the south and center of the country, and the proportion of low-birth-weight babies rose from 4 percent in 1994 to approximately 25 percent in 1997.[6] Exemptions for medicine and food, as well as the Oil for Food Program adopted by the Security Council in August 1991, have not prevented the Iraqi population from suffering. Under the terms of the program, revenues from the sale of Iraqi oil could be used to pay for food and medicines.[7] However, until December 1996, Baghdad refused to accept these conditions, and frequently ordered insufficient food and medicines, hoarded them in warehouses, illegally reexported humanitarian supplies, or simply stopped oil exports. The apparent strategy was to increase the misery of the Iraqi people, thereby putting pressure on the Security Council to lift sanctions altogether. To an extent, this worked. By the end of 1999, China, France, and Russia in particular were lobbying for an end to sanctions. In December 1999, the Security Council committed itself to suspending sanctions if Iraq accepted a new weapons monitoring and verification system.[8] Little headway was made in the months that followed, and negotiations on such a system stalled. Meanwhile, the humanitarian situation in Iraq continued to deteriorate.

The postwar sanctions, unlike their pre-war counterparts, were not integrated into a comprehensive coercive strategy.[9] After the war, outside powers were not willing to mount a sustained military operation to support the coercive sanction effort.[10] By limiting their options in this way, they may have managed to keep Iraq from developing new weapons programs, but this came at heavy moral costs and at the expense of the Iraqi population.

The FRY and the Bosnian Serbs

In May 1992, in response to the FRY's involvement in the war in Bosnia-Herzegovina, the Security Council imposed full trade sanctions, a freeze on the FRY government's financial assets, a ban on maritime and air traffic, and a ban on participation in

Table 8

U.N. Security Council Sanctions, 1945–2000

Country	Type of sanction	Date imposed [I] Date lifted [L]	Enabling UNSC resolution
Southern Rhodesia	Comprehensive economic sanctions	I Dec 16, 1966	232 (1966)
		L Dec 21, 1979	460 (1979)
South Africa	Arms embargo	I Nov 4, 1977	418 (1977)
		L May 25, 1994	919 (1994)
Iraq	Comprehensive economic sanctions	I Aug 6, 1990	661 (1990)[a]
Republics of the Former Yugoslavia	Arms embargo	I Sep 25, 1991	713 (1991)[b]
		L Jun 18, 1996	1021 (1995)
FRY	Comprehensive economic sanctions	I May 30, 1992	757 (1992)[c]
		L Nov 22, 1995	1022 (1995)[d]
FRY	Arms embargo	I Mar 31, 1998	1160 (1998)
Bosnian Serbs	Comprehensive economic sanctions	I Sep 23, 1994	942 (1994)
		L Oct 1, 1996	1074 (1996)
Somalia	Arms embargo	I Jan 23, 1992	733 (1992)
Libya	Arms embargo	I Mar 31, 1992	
	Partial economic sanctions	L Apr 5, 1999	748 (1992)[e]
Liberia	Arms embargo	I Nov 19, 1992	788 (1992)
Haiti	Arms embargo	I Jun 16, 1993	841 (1993)
	Partial economic sanctions	L Aug 27, 1993	861 (1993)
Haiti	Arms embargo	I Oct 18, 1993	873 (1993)
	Partial economic sanctions		
Haiti	Comprehensive economic sanctions	I May 21, 1994	917 (1994)
		L Oct 16, 1994	944 (1994)
UNITA (Angola)	Arms embargo	I Sep 15, 1993	864 (1993)[f]
	Partial economic sanctions		
UNITA (Angola)	Targeted financial sanctions	I Jun 12, 1998	1173 (1998)
Rwanda	Arms embargo	I May 17, 1994	918 (1994)[g]
		L Aug 16, 1995	1011 (1995)[h]
Sudan	Partial economic sanctions	I May 10, 1996	1054 (1996)[i]
Sierra Leone	Arms embargo	I Oct 8, 1997	1132 (1997)
	Partial economic sanctions	L Jun 5, 1998	1171 (1998)[j]
Sierra Leone	Partial economic sanctions	I Jul 5, 2000	1306 (2000)
Taliban (Afghanistan)	Targeted financial sanctions	I Nov 15, 1999	1267 (1999)
	Partial economic sanctions		
Eritrea/Ethiopia	Arms embargo	I May 17, 2000	1298 (2000)

Source: Use of Sanctions under Chapter VII of the UN Charter (March 31, 2000), www.un.org/News/ossg/sanction.htm.

[a]For subsequent resolutions, see Office of the Spokesman for the Secretary-General (OSSG), *Use of Sanctions under Chapter VII of the UN Charter.*

[b]See also UNSC Res. 727 (1992), January 8, 1992, which reaffirms that the arms embargo applies to all republics of the former Yugoslavia.

[c]See also UNSC Res. 787 (1992), November 16, 1992; and UNSC Res. 820 (1993), April 17, 1993, which strengthened sanctions. UNSC 943 (1994), September 23, 1994, suspended certain sanctions.

[d]Sanctions were suspended in November 1995, and lifted on October 1, 1996. See UNSC Res. 1074, October 1, 1996.

[e]See also UNSC Res. 883 (1993), November 11, 1993, which tightened sanctions. Sanctions were suspended on April 5, 1999. See U.N. Security Council Presidential Statement, S/PRST/1999/10, April 8, 1999.

[f]See also UNSC Res. 1127 (1997), August 28, 1997; and UNSC Res. 1130 (1997), September 29, 1997, which strengthened the sanction regime.

[g]UNSC Res. 997 (1995), June 9, 1995, affirmed that the prohibition on the sale and supply of arms also applied to persons in states neighboring Rwanda.

[h]The sale and supply of arms to nongovernmental forces remained prohibited.

[i]See also UNSC Res. 1070 (1996), August 16, 1996, which foreshadowed an air embargo on Sudan. This embargo never went into effect because of the expected humanitarian consequences.

[j]The arms embargo remained in place for members of the former military junta and the RUF.

international sporting and cultural events. Belgrade's diplomatic status was also downgraded.[11]

Like Iraq, the FRY's economy was vulnerable to sanctions. In the early 1990s, it was in the midst of a difficult transition from centralized to market-based arrangements. Unemployment and inflation had been rising since 1981. Foreign borrowing had become more difficult, and had been made conditional on the implementation of economic reforms. Finally, the dissolution of Yugoslavia in 1991 imposed heavy costs. The former republics of Yugoslavia had been economically interdependent; in particular, they had relied heavily on one another for food, energy supplies, and manufactured goods. The FRY produced only 20 percent of the fuel it needed, and depended on imports from China, Russia, Iran, and Romania for most of the rest.[12] Although private citizens had substantial foreign-currency reserves, these helped to mitigate the effect of sanctions only in their initial stages.[13]

As in Iraq, however, the political conditions for imposing sanctions were less than ideal. The country's communist apparatus was still largely in place, and Serbian leader Slobodan Milosevic controlled the police forces and media. The army was loyal to him, and the political opposition was weak. Finally, Serbia was a predominantly rural state and had been susceptible to strong nationalist appeals and ethnic scapegoating since the late 1980s. Rather than blaming Milosevic for their hardship, the Serbs could be expected to "rally around the flag" and blame the United Nations instead.

And indeed, initially, sanctions had little effect on the war in Bosnia; in 1992, systematic forced expulsions of civilians took place in the eastern, northern and northwestern parts of the country. In response to these actions, including numerous reports of sanction violations, the Security Council decided in November 1992 to strengthen the sanctions regime and decreed that the transhipment through the FRY of petroleum, coal, steel, and other products was prohibited.[14] In addition, the European Union and the Conference for Security and Cooperation in Europe (CSCE) started a program to help neighboring states to implement, monitor, and enforce the sanctions regimes.[15]

Meanwhile, diplomatic efforts to negotiate a truce made some headway. On April 17, 1993, the Security Council formally endorsed the comprehensive peace plan for Bosnia presented by U.N. negotiator Cyrus Vance and his EU counterpart, David Owen. At the same time, the Security Council threatened the FRY with tougher sanctions if the plan was not accepted by all parties within 9 days.[16] Responding to this threat, Milosevic endorsed the plan on April 25. However, the Bosnian Serbs continued to oppose it, and consequently, the more drastic sanctions went into effect the following day. On May 2, Radovan Karadzic, the Bosnian-Serb leader, pressured by Milosevic, agreed to put the plan to a popular vote later that month.

At the time, Owen was convinced that Milosevic had given up the idea of forming a "Greater Serbia,"

and believed that the threat of more stringent sanctions, as well as a threat to use force, had been instrumental in bringing about a change in Milosevic's position and had persuaded him to lean on Karadzic. Owen had hinted repeatedly that if the Serbs did not accept the plan, Western countries would contemplate using force, and the sanctions resolution of April 1993 had explicitly authorized states to do so to enforce the sanctions regime. Owen believed that Belgrade would not have objected if the Vance-Owen plan had been imposed on the Bosnian Serbs militarily.[17] However, the Clinton administration's reservations about the plan, along with dissent among the Western allies, made such a course impossible.[18] Washington had made it clear that U.S. troops would only be available if all parties consented to the Vance-Owen plan. The Europeans, in turn, were unwilling to impose the plan on the Bosnian Serbs without U.S. support. The timid Western reaction to the Serb assaults on Srebrenica in April 1993 drove this point home.[19] In addition, the debate in early May 1993 between the United States and Europe over "lift and strike" (the U.S. proposal to lift the arms embargo on the Bosnian government and to strike Bosnian-Serb targets from the air) showed the Bosnian Serbs that none of the Western powers had much stomach for forceful military action. Not surprisingly, they rejected the Vance-Owen plan on May 16, 1993. Ultimately, the effect of sanctions helped to harden Milosevic's position, and he quickly reestablished full relations with the Bosnian Serbs.[20] This was the first missed opportunity to end the war in Bosnia. Disagreements among the Western allies had undercut the threat of more stringent economic sanctions, as well as the threat to use force.

The second missed opportunity for the effective use of sanctions came in 1994. In July, the Contact Group (comprising France, Germany, Russia, Britain, and the United States) presented a new peace plan linked to a partial lifting of U.N. sanctions. Again, the Western powers had foreshadowed the possible use of military force. Again, Milosevic gave his support to the proposal. He also threatened to sever political and economic ties with the Bosnian Serbs if they rejected it. The promise of a partial lifting of sanctions was alluring. Moreover, the active involvement of the United States in the Contact Group and the creation of the Bosnian/Muslim-Croat Federation now made the threat of force more credible. Even so, the Bosnian Serbs rejected the plan on August 3. The following day, Milosevic, as promised, broke off economic and political relations with them. His reward, however, was limited, consisting of lifting the ban on all civilian flights to and from Belgrade, the reintroduction of a ferry service to Italy, and lifting the ban on participation in international sporting events and cultural exchanges. Meanwhile, the Security Council imposed sanctions on the Bosnian Serbs, prohibiting all economic contact and ordering states to refrain from holding talks with the Bosnian-Serb leadership.[21]

However, the Western allies soon revealed themselves to be as feeble as before. The U.S. backpedaled on its threats to launch military strikes and, before long, the Western coalition was again at loggerheads over "lift and strike." Unsurprisingly, under these conditions, the border between the FRY and the Serb-controlled areas in Bosnia remained extremely porous. Moreover, Milosevic continued to support the Bosnian-Serb military leadership. It is arguable that a more substantial suspension of sanctions at this point would have led Milosevic to take a firmer line with the Bosnian Serbs. Although a suspension might have been morally difficult for the Western states, this strategy, coupled with direct military action against the Bosnian Serbs, was adopted in 1995.

Most observers agree that, after 1993, the sanction regime was relatively well implemented. But there is little consensus on the political effectiveness of the sanctions against the FRY. Some observers view them as remarkably successful; others believe that they had no impact whatsoever.[22] Whatever the case, there were surely missed opportunities. Had the threat of more stringent sanctions been supported by a credible threat of military action, the war in Bosnia might have ended in 1993 or 1994. Eventually, after the fall of Srebrenica in August 1995, the United States held direct talks with Milosevic. Washington convinced him that, unless he agreed to the peace plan that the United States had put on the table, military force would be used. This, coupled with the material effect of sanctions, appears to have been what moved Milosevic to put pressure on the Bosnian Serbs to stop the war. Economic sanctions combined with the threat of military force—not the long-term effects of sanctions alone—was the key to changing Milosevic's behavior.

Haiti

The U.N. Security Council threatened Haiti with an oil and arms embargo in June 1993 to return to power the country's democratically elected president, Jean-Bertrand Aristide, who had been ousted by a military coup in September 1991.[23] All economic indicators, including Haiti's extreme dependence on outside oil supplies and on the United States for most of its trade, led many observers to believe that the junta would respond to economic pressure.[24] Indeed, 2 days before sanctions were to take effect, it agreed to enter into negotiations with Aristide. In July, an agreement was reached allowing for the creation of a new government, the deployment of U.N. peacekeepers, and the return of Aristide.[25] But delays in implementation led to the unraveling of the agreement. By October, the Haitian military and its supporters had stocked up supplies and mustered enough confidence to defy the Security Council and prevent U.N. peacekeepers from deploying in Haiti.[26]

Sanctions were reimposed, and U.N. member-states were authorized to enforce them with a naval blockade.[27] In December 1993, the Security Council warned the Haitian military to implement the July agreement or face stronger sanctions. But because of divisions among Security Council members, the deadline of January 15, 1994, passed without any action. Although in May 1994, the Security Council at last approved a total trade ban (except for medical supplies and foodstuffs), the strengthened sanctions had little effect on the military regime. In July 1994, the junta expelled all U.N. officers. Faced with this new act of hostility, the Security Council authorized a military operation to depose the regime.[28] U.S. troops landed on September 19, 1994, Aristide was returned to power on October 15, and sanctions were lifted soon after.[29] Since then, Haiti has struggled to keep violence under control, install a democratic regime, and resuscitate its economy.

As with the FRY, there were missed opportunities in Haiti. The weak reaction of the United Nations and the United States to rising violence in the latter half of 1993 prolonged the life of the junta and the suffering of the Haitian people. As with Iraq, although Haiti's economy was vulnerable to sanctions, the brutal nature of the country's military regime, which was unconcerned about the suffering of the country's poor, should have given outside countries pause. Conversely, the humanitarian effects of sanctions were considerable, and could have been easily foreseen. Haiti was the poorest country in the Western hemisphere.[30] More than 70 percent of its people lived in abject poverty and had no ready access to safe drinking water or medical care. Sanctions, even though not well-implemented, accelerated the economy's decline, penalizing Aristide and his supporters more than the ruling elites.[31]

In contrast to the Iraqi and Yugoslav cases, the sanctions against Haiti were poorly implemented. The military and the ruling elite managed to obtain most basic goods, and quite a few not-so-basic ones. Many states considered implementing and enforcing the sanctions regime to be a U.S. problem, and made little effort to do it themselves. Although mounting a naval blockade or closing the Haitian-Dominican border presented few technical or resource problems for the United States, it did pose political ones. Consequent delays gave Haiti's rulers opportunities to set up alternative supply routes and to establish networks for the illegal trade in drugs and other contraband.

Ultimately, however, the case of Haiti shows that economic sanctions can be effective if all coercive options—including the use of military force—remain open.[32] Once the credibility of enforcing powers is compromised, threatening to use sanctions is no longer sufficient. At that point, sanctions have to be complemented by military action.

PARTIAL AND TARGETED SANCTIONS

The U.N. Security Council imposed partial economic sanctions against Libya in 1992, the National Union for the Total Independence of Angola (UNITA) in 1993, Sudan in 1996, Sierra Leone in 1997 and 2000, and the Taliban in Afghanistan in 1999. Only in the cases of UNITA and Sierra Leone, however, was the general objective to stop civil strife.[33]

UNITA in Angola

An arms and oil embargo was imposed on UNITA in 1993, following Jonas Savimbi's refusal to honor the results of U.N.-supervised elections and the rebel group's return to war.[34] Despite repeatedly threatening to impose additional sanctions, the Security Council did nothing until 1997, when travel and diplomatic sanctions were imposed.[35] Fighting nonetheless escalated in 1998, prompting the Security Council in June to freeze UNITA's financial assets, ban all financial transactions with the group, and prohibit the trade of Angolan diamonds not certified by the government. Travel restrictions on UNITA officials were also tightened.[36]

The implementation and enforcement of these measures were, however, dismal. Guerrilla groups are not particularly vulnerable to normal trade sanctions, mainly because they do not engage in normal trade. In addition, independent rebel groups generally withstand economic or political pressures well: they have a high economic pain threshold and their members are generally well motivated. Most importantly, UNITA had access to diamonds, which enabled it to keep its military campaign alive. The bulk of UNITA's assets are in the form of rough diamonds, which are sold as needed. Estimates of UNITA's earnings from diamond sales between January 1993 and December 1998 range from $2.3 billion to $3.7 billion.[37] These revenues enabled UNITA to build a highly mobile and well-armed army of 35,000 soldiers. Neighboring countries—Burkina Faso, Namibia, Rwanda, South Africa, and Zambia—helped UNITA to smuggle its diamonds out of Angola and provided safe havens for the group's diamond transactions.[38] The group also made significant amounts of money from landing fees for aircraft bringing in food, medicines, and other commodities. In 1996–97, when commercial activity in Angola was at its peak, it may have earned as much as $5 million a month in this way.[39]

Individual, targeted financial sanctions are, in theory, an attractive alternative to a comprehensive or partial approach because they offer the prospect of avoiding costs to neighboring countries, as well as minimizing the impact on innocent people. Their failure against UNITA, however, demonstrates the myriad problems associated with them. The true ownership of assets can be concealed in many ways; assets can be swiftly transferred to circumvent sanctions and many countries have neither the technology nor the domestic legislation to monitor financial transactions. Moreover, Internet banking has opened up new ways to move money around—ways that experts on sanctions and money laundering have only just begun to analyze. Many of the techniques for making targeted financial sanctions work borrow from traditional techniques for detecting money laundering. These techniques are progressing, yet there remains a wide variety of effective laundering methods.

Given the ineffectiveness of sanctions in changing UNITA's behavior, the Security Council decided in 1999 to adopt a different strategy and shifted its focus to the "sanction-busters." It commissioned a report on violations and hoped to induce better third-party compliance through a "naming-and-shaming" campaign. The report, published in March 2000, broke with past U.N. practice and openly accused individuals, including acting and former heads of state, of violating the sanctions regime.[40] Within the United Nations, the report received a reserved welcome, and it remains to be seen whether it will have concrete results.[41]

Sierra Leone

In May 1997, the Armed Forces Revolutionary Council (AFRC) overthrew the civilian government of Ahmed Kabbah. Five months later, the U.N. Security Council imposed an oil and an arms embargo against Sierra Leone, along with travel restrictions on members of the junta, and authorized the Nigerian-led Military Observer Group (ECOMOG) of the Economic Community of West African States (ECOWAS) to enforce these measures, by force if necessary.[42] Initially, sanctions seemed to have a positive effect. Only 15 days after they were imposed, the junta accepted an agreement that called for the restoration of the elected civilian government and the demobilization of Sierra Leone's armed forces and rebel groups. However, as in Haiti, junta leaders failed to implement the agreement. In February 1998, ECOMOG troops toppled the military regime, and Kabbah was returned to power. The sanctions against AFRC members remained in place, as did measures against the Revolutionary United Front (RUF), a rebel group that had sided with it. These had little effect. In October, the RUF launched a major offensive, seizing the capital, Freetown, in January 1999. Although Nigerian troops reinstalled the civilian government, much of the country remained in rebel hands.

Under international pressure, from the United States in particular, Kabbah and RUF leader Foday Sankoh negotiated an agreement in July 1999. A government of national unity was established, the rebels were given amnesty, and the United Nations was invited to oversee the agreement's implementation. In May 2000, however, it unraveled. Like Savimbi in Angola, Sankoh cornered a substantial part of Sierra Leone's diamond trade. The Sierra Leone government is estimated to have lost between $200 million and $300 million annually to smuggling, mainly by the RUF.[43] Until his capture in May, Sankoh had secured the cooperation of Liberian President Charles Taylor, and most of the RUF's "conflict diamonds" passed through Liberia, which sold false certificates to hide their origin. Since the mid-1990s, Liberia has exported some 31 million carats—more than 200 years' worth of its national diamond-mining capacity.[44] In July 2000, after several hundred U.N. peacekeepers had been taken hostage, the Security Council imposed a boycott on rough diamonds from Sierra Leone.[45] But without monitoring and enforcement mechanisms, these sanctions are likely to have little effect.

Partial and targeted sanctions in Angola and Sierra Leone failed because they were stand-alone measures, not part of a coercive strategy, and because of poor implementation. An energetic response from the United Nations and outside powers to the first signs of defiance may well have led to very different outcomes in both countries. Half-measures, however, stood no chance of success.

ARMS EMBARGOES

Arms embargoes are a special kind of economic sanction. Their primary objective is not to inflict economic pain, but to deny access to weapons, thereby inducing military stalemates and preventing conflicts from escalating. They are also intended to limit third-party involvement in conflicts. Arms embargoes have been imposed eleven times since 1991; in most cases, as elements of larger economic-sanctions regimes. Only in Somalia, Liberia, and Rwanda, and in the FRY in 1998 and Ethiopia and Eritrea two years later, did the U.N. Security Council impose stand-alone arms embargoes.

Imposing arms embargoes when conflicts are active is often seen as a logical first step toward halting violence. This can, however, have unintended effects, particularly in cases of internal conflict. Embargoes tend to favor the warring factions that have access to government military ordnance and industries, while making it more difficult for others to organize and defend themselves. They can thus favor one side over the other, rather than pushing both toward a military stalemate and a political settlement.[46] The blanket arms embargo imposed in September 1991 on all the republics of the former Yugoslavia greatly favored the Serbs and, in the Bosnian conflict, was extremely costly for the Bosnian Muslims. Having become more attentive to these unintended effects, the Security Council decided not to impose an arms embargo on Burundi and Sudan in 1996, or on Afghanistan in 1999. As with other forms of sanctions, implementation and third-party compliance is also a problem. Internal conflicts are usually fought with small arms and light weapons—mortars, machine guns, rifles, machetes, and the like. The international trade in weapons such as these is difficult to regulate and verify, especially since much of it is conducted on the black market.[47]

FRAMING A SANCTIONS STRATEGY

A sound sanctions strategy should contain three elements. It must assess the target's strengths and weaknesses, so as to determine how effective sanctions will be; determine how sanctions should be imposed, and what form they should take; and stipulate the conditions under which sanctions should be lifted.

ASSESSING THE TARGET

The effectiveness of coercive efforts, including sanctions, largely depends on the economic and political characteristics of the target (see Table 9). These will dictate whether it is able to withstand economic pressure and devise counter-threats and actions that could neutralize the effects of sanctions.

Three economic characteristics of a sanctions target are particularly important:

- The type of economy, including its nature (market or centralized), level of development, and general health;[48]

- Export and import dependencies; and

- The volume of overseas assets.

The economic impact of sanctions depends on how quickly the target economy can adjust to them. This differs from one economic system to the next. Market economies are generally more vulnerable to economic sanctions than are centrally planned ones, because in market economies, the allocation and distribution of resources are dependent on external price signals instead of on decisions by central

Table 9

Vulnerability to Sanctions

More vulnerable	Less vulnerable
Economic characteristics	
Market economy	Centralized economy
Highly developed economy	Underdeveloped economy
Weak economy	Healthy economy
High dependence on exports and imports	Low dependence on exports and imports
High dependence on international capital markets	Low dependence on international capital markets
Social and political characteristics	
Industrial society	Rural society
Ethnically mixed	Ethnically homogenous
Internally fragmented	Internally cohesive
Democratic regime	Authoritarian regime
Strong political opposition	Weak political opposition

authorities. (In the FRY, for example, Milosevic could ease the impact of sanctions by instructing state enterprises to keep underemployed workers on the payroll.) Developing and rural economies, because they are generally more labor-intensive than capital-intensive, are also less vulnerable to sanctions. Depressed economies or those in recession are more vulnerable than robust and expansionist economies. That said, outside powers should be careful about imposing sanctions on developing or troubled economies. Sanctions aggravate existing developmental problems and can easily result in humanitarian crises. Moreover, imposing sanctions in cases such as these may give political elites convenient excuses for the dire state of their countries' economies.

Foreign trade is another good indicator of economic vulnerability. Countries that are highly reliant on trade with a limited number of partners are especially vulnerable. Haiti, because of its dependence on the United States, was thus considered a good candidate for sanctions. This vulnerability increases if exports or imports consist of raw materials or industrial goods, as opposed to small consumer goods. The former are more important to keeping economies going, whereas it is more difficult to smuggle raw materials (except diamonds) across borders. The presence of such strategic resources as oil or gas may make targets less vulnerable to sanctions, particularly if they are relatively self-reliant in other sectors. But if the export of strategic resources is their main source of income, as in Iraq, sanctions may have a sharp impact.

Finally, it is important to measure the volume of the target's overseas assets. For countries that are heavily reliant on foreign banks or international financial institutions, financial sanctions are a promising choice. The importance of foreign investment and remittances from nationals abroad is also a good indicator of a target's economic vulnerability. If financial transactions like remittances are not covered by a sanctions regime, they may enable targeted countries to weather the impact of sanctions, as occurred in the FRY.

The key social and political characteristics of a target are:

- The type of society, including its nature (industrial or rural), ethnic and religious make-up, and the degree of internal cohesion;

- The nature of the regime; and

- The strength of the opposition.

Industrialized societies, which have sizeable middle classes of business people and retailers, are more sensitive to economic sanctions than are rural societies. These middle classes are likely to push for negotiations and compromise. Moreover, group cohesion tends to be weaker in industrialized societies than in rural ones.[49] The level of a society's cohesion is also influenced by its ethnic and religious make-up. An ethnically or religiously homogenous country will be more cohesive than an ethnically or religiously mixed one.

The political character of the regime will also influence whether sanctions will succeed. Authoritarian regimes are generally less vulnerable than democratic ones, because they are usually better able to control their political opponents. Indeed, the existence of a political opposition is often cited as one of the critical conditions for the success of sanctions, as one of the principal aims is to bolster political opposition to a regime. The FRY case, however, suggests that imposing comprehensive sanctions when the opposition is weak is counterproductive. Ruling elites may depict their domestic opponents as traitors, thus amplify existing jingoistic attitudes. This strategy, in turn, insulates the political leadership from criticism and allows it to draw strength from its defiance of outside forces.

When a country is in the midst of a civil war, sanctions will often have asymmetric effects because different groups will almost always have different vulnerabilities. Identifying the strengths and weaknesses of these groups, including the varying effects sanctions may have on them, is essential to avoid hurting the "good guys," as happened in Haiti. If a country's political system has collapsed, it is hard to identify a target for sanctions. In such cases, they may be inadvisable.

DETERMINING TACTICS

Once the target's strengths and weaknesses are properly assessed and outside powers have determined that sanctions can be used to bring about political change, these powers should decide which tactics are likely to be most effective: a swift and crushing blow or a gradual tightening of the screws. Two schools of thought dominate the debate on sanction tactics. One theory maintains that sanctions are most effective when they are imposed immediately and comprehensively. Those who subscribe to this line of thinking argue that sanctions should be imposed early in a crisis, because gradual imposition gives the target time to adjust; for example, by stockpiling supplies, finding alternative trade routes, and partners, and moving financial assets.[50]

The other school of thought contends that sanctions are most effective when imposed gradually and incrementally. Proponents argue that comprehensive sanctions are the economic equivalent of wars of attrition, which will almost inevitably cause people to resist and rally behind the regime. Moreover, they argue that sanctions are instruments through which parties may be brought to the negotiating table. Comprehensive sanctions may have a greater impact than partial sanctions on a target's economy, but this does not necessarily translate into changes in political behavior. On the contrary, such sanctions may solidify the target's positions.[51]

Both schools of thought are valid some of the time: again, the political and economic characteristics of a target are the keys to determining which road to choose. Partial sanctions may be sufficient when target economies are extremely vulnerable or when dealing with weak economies. In such cases, comprehensive sanctions may easily lead to a humanitarian emergency. Partial measures may also be sufficient when dealing with countries that have democratic regimes; strong political oppositions; and industrialized, atomized societies. Conversely, centralized economies, authoritarian regimes, rural societies, and countries with weak political oppositions and no trade or capital-market dependencies should probably be hit immediately with comprehensive sanctions. Outside powers should also more readily consider threatening to use force in such cases.

In determining whether to strike quickly and hard or slowly and softly, outside powers should consider the seriousness of the situation at hand. Sanctions should be proportional to the objective: the more ambitious the goal, the stronger the sanctions regime. However, when outside powers confront gross violations of human rights or genocide, they may want to forego sanctions altogether, and intervene militarily. In all cases, the threat of force should remain on the table.

LIFTING SANCTIONS

Finally, outside powers need to formulate the conditions under which sanctions should be lifted or abandoned. These exit *strategies* should not be confused with exit *schedules*. Efficacious exit strategies will identify the conditions under which sanctions can be lifted, without imposing rigid, artificial deadlines. Sanctions may be lifted either because the behavior that led to their imposition has changed or because they have demonstrably failed to bring the desired changes about.[52]

Because comprehensive sanctions often have devastating humanitarian implications, they are politically and morally difficult to sustain and, if kept in place for too long, they can have untoward effects. In other words, sanctions tend to become less effective the longer they are maintained. The target has time to adapt, increasing its self-sufficiency and reducing its dependence on the outside world. It may also develop new links with states not fully participating in the sanction regime. Finally, the humanitarian situation in a targeted country may become explosive, which may make it difficult to justify continuing sanctions.

If imposing sanctions has no immediate effect, two alternatives should be considered. First, the outside powers can promise to lift some elements of the sanction regime if the target starts engaging in "good" behavior. That said, lifting sanctions before all conditions are met might be tricky, as was shown in Haiti, when the U.N. Security Council decided to lift sanctions before Aristide had been restored to power. The Haitian military took advantage of this opportunity to stockpile strategic goods and, once resupplied, resumed its defiance of the Security Council. A "carrot-and-stick" approach thus requires accurate and timely assessments of the target's aspirations and intentions.

The second alternative is to increase the pressure on the target by threatening to use military force. The threat may have to be made early if the target is not particularly vulnerable economically or politically. The cases of Haiti and the FRY suggest that the threat to use force makes sanctions more effective by giving credibility and gravity to the coercive effort.

ADDRESSING IMPLEMENTATION PROBLEMS

A sound sanctions strategy is essential to the eventual success of a sanctions regime. But however good the strategy, the measures must be fully implemented on the ground if they are to remain effective and credible. Every sanction regime has suffered from implementation problems. Four in particular stand out.

The first is that sanctions regimes have been interpreted differently by different states. Although U.N. sanctions are supposed to be imposed collectively, implementing them is left to individual countries, which invariably have to adopt national legislation to do so. The language of most U.N. sanction resolutions is often the result of compromises, with vague and ambiguous wording.[53] Thus the interpretation of sanction resolutions will often vary from state to state, which leads to uneven implementation. Although most U.N. sanctions regimes have Sanctions Committees, tasked with examining and promulgating guidelines to facilitate implementation, such interpretative guidance is not binding on U.N. members. Giving the committees interpretative authority could enhance the implementation of sanctions regimes. In addition, a single Sanctions Committee could be established, which would deal with all U.N. sanctions regimes.[54]

The second problem is that states monitor sanctions differently. Few have the expertise or resources needed to establish or maintain efficient monitoring mechanisms.[55] International organizations can be helpful when it comes to monitoring sanctions regimes. The sanctions regime against the FRY benefited from unprecedented international arrangements designed to assist states—the FRY's neighbors in particular—to implement and monitor the measures decreed by the Security Council.[56] Unfortunately, most U.N. sanctions regimes do not have the resources they need for effective monitoring. Unlike the European Union, the United Nations is not able to deploy several hundred people in the field. Plans to strengthen U.N. capacities in this area surface regularly, but the United Nations has not been provided with sufficient resources to really address these problems.[57]

The third problem concerns noncompliance and enforcement. Although the Security Council can decide to impose economic sanctions, it has no way of forcing or encouraging recalcitrant states to adhere to them unless it imposes sanctions on these states as well. Moreover, targeted states or organizations may engage in countermeasures, making the cost of compliance too high for third parties. The FRY, for example, threatened neighboring countries with countermeasures, making them extremely wary of enforcing the sanction regime.[58] Handling enforcement problems is generally left to individual states but, because sanction resolutions rarely include provisions that specify penalties for violations, there is little uniformity. Harmonizing national legislation in this area (with U.N. guidance) would prevent individual and corporate sanction-busters from simply moving from one country to another to avoid prosecution and punishment. Experience with recent sanctions regimes has also pointed to the desirability of establishing national sanction-implementation offices, which would coordinate monitoring and enforcement at the national and international levels.[59] Such coordination is particularly important with respect to targeted financial sanctions.

The fourth problem concerns cost. Sanctions often carry with them substantial negative effects for third-party states. Without compensation, these countries may not be sufficiently motivated to implement and enforce the regime in question. Article 50 of the U.N. Charter gives states the right to consult with the Security Council if they suffer unduly from sanctions imposed on other countries. Until 1990, the Security Council received only four such requests and took action in only two of these cases.[60] However, the Iraqi sanctions regime imposed in 1990 triggered requests for assistance from twenty-one states, which estimated their total losses at more than $30 billion.[61] This prompted then-U.N. Secretary-General Boutros Boutros-Ghali to urge the Security Council to devise measures to insulate states from the unintended negative effects of sanctions regimes.[62] Boutros-Ghali subsequently proposed establishing a body to assess the likely impact of sanctions on both the target country and others before they are imposed; to monitor their implementation; to measure their effects, which would enable the Security Council to maximize their impact while minimizing collateral damage; to ensure the delivery of humanitarian assistance to vulnerable groups; and to evaluate claims submitted by states under Article 50.[63]

Many countries opposed the plan on the grounds that the Security Council would become paralyzed if it had to guarantee compensation to states for collateral damage before deciding on sanctions.[64] Moreover, they argued, in situations in which the maintenance or restoration of international peace and security were at stake, the Security Council had to be able to act swiftly. This would make prior consultations difficult, if not impossible.[65] Opponents also raised questions about the methodology to be employed to assess the losses of affected countries. Boutros-Ghali argued that, because decisions to impose sanctions are taken collectively, their costs should also be borne collectively, just as the cost of peacekeeping is met by all U.N. members.[66] Until now, compensation for third parties has been handled on an ad hoc, case-by-case basis.[67] Although this will probably continue for some time, sanctions regimes would be more effective if third parties suffering collateral damage were compensated for it.

CONCLUSION

The track record of U.N. sanctions regimes has been mixed. Neither comprehensive nor partial sanctions has succeeded in stopping civil strife in the countries that they have targeted. Targeted financial sanctions, although attractive in theory, remain extremely difficult to implement, requiring monitoring and enforcement capabilities that most countries do not possess and that may be too expensive for them to acquire. In addition, many sanctions regimes have had secondary and unintended consequences. Comprehensive—and even partial or selective—sanctions risk sparking humanitarian crises in target countries. Arms embargoes may keep victims defenceless, and air-traffic restrictions may impede the delivery of humanitarian relief. These difficulties notwithstanding, the missed opportunities in the FRY and Haiti, and even to some extent in Sierra Leone, show that sanctions can bring about political change —if certain conditions are met. The misapplication of this policy instrument in the 1990s should not lead us to remove sanctions from our policy repertory. Two conditions need to be met for them to be effective.

First, sanctions need to be part of a comprehensive coercive strategy that includes the threat and use of military force. Thus, sanctions should be seen as part of a coercive continuum. A sound coercive strategy will guide outside powers on when and how to impose sanctions, when and how to step up coercive pressure, and when to change instruments. Knowledge of the target is essential. Because of their potentially serious social, economic, and political effects, sanctions should not stay in place for long periods. Thus, the parties imposing sanctions must consider early on what course they will take should sanctions fail.

Second, sanctions need to be implemented and complied with by third parties, and monitoring and enforcement mechanisms need to be put in place. Imposing sanctions, like using force, requires resources. Neighboring countries might need to be compensated for economic losses, and they might need assistance in setting up monitoring and enforcement mechanisms. Most importantly, to ensure third-party compliance, a broad international consensus on the use of coercive action needs to be built. An interested supporting party has to take the lead in defining the precise objectives that the sanctions seek to achieve, and keeping the relevant international actors focused on them. In the case of Iraq, the United States has played such a role. In the FRY and Haiti, the United States hesitated and the sanctions efforts faltered.

If outside powers are not willing to consider using military force, they should not contemplate imposing economic sanctions. Sanctions should only be considered if the problem is serious enough to ultimately warrant the use of force. Coercion is a serious business, especially when it has devastating humanitarian consequences—as economic sanctions generally do. States should go down this road only if they are prepared to meet the costs of coercion, and only if they are determined to see the process through.

NOTES

1. See, for example, Joy Gordon, "A Peaceful, Silent, Deadly Remedy: The Ethics of Economic Sanctions," *Ethics and International Affairs* 13 (1999): 123–50; John and Karl Mueller, "Sanctions of Mass Destruction," *Foreign Affairs* 78 (May 1999): 43–53; Thomas G. Weiss, David Cortright, George Lopez, and Larry Minear, *Political Gain and Civilian Pain: Humanitarian Impacts of Economic Sanctions* (Lanham, Md.: Rowman and Littlefield, 1997); and Patrick Clawson, "Sanctions as Punishment, Enforcement, and Prelude to Further Action," *Ethics and International Affairs* 7 (1993): 17–37.

2. Part of the popularity of sanctions stems from the fact that, although international law substantially constrains the use of force, there is no major legal impediment to imposing sanctions. The U.N. Charter does not contain a specific prohibition and does not prohibit states from imposing sanctions unilaterally.

3. For a very sceptical view, see Robert Pape, "Why Economic Sanctions Do Not Work," *International Security* 22 (Autumn 1997): 90–136. On sanctions more generally, see David Cortright and George A. Lopez, eds., *The Sanctions Decade: Assessing UN Strategies in the 1990s* (Boulder, Colo.: Lynne Rienner, 2000); Margaret Doxey, *United Sanctions: Current Policy Issues* (Halifax, Nova Scotia: Centre for Foreign Policy Studies, Dalhousie University, June 1999); Richard N. Haass, ed., *Economic Sanctions and American Diplomacy* (New York: Council on Foreign Relations, 1998); and Gary Clyde Hufbauer, Jeffrey J. Schott, and Kimberly Ann Elliot, *Economic Sanctions Reconsidered: History and Current Policy,* second edition (Washington, D.C.: Institute for International Economies, 1990).

4. Iraq invaded Kuwait on August 2, 1990. The Security Council voted on multilateral sanctions on August 6. It barred all imports from, and exports to, Iraq, except medical supplies, foodstuffs, and other items of humanitarian need. See UNSC Res. 661 (1990). See also UNSC Res. 665 (1991), August 25, 1991, which authorized enforcement of Resolution 661 (1990) in the form of a naval blockade.

5. See Sarah Graham-Brown, *Sanctioning Saddam: The Politics of Intervention in Iraq* (London: I. B. Tauris, 1999), 161.

6. Ibid.; Beth Osborne Daponte and Richard Garfield, "The Effect of Economic Sanctions on the Mortality of Iraqi Children Prior to the 1991 Persian Gulf War," *American Journal of Public Health* 90 (April 2000): 546–52. Osborne Daponte and Garfield estimate that child mortality quadrupled between September and December 1990.

7. See UNSC Res. 706 (1991), August 15, 1991. See also UNSC Res. 712 (1991), September 19, 1991; UNSC Res. 778 (1992), October 2, 1992; and UNSC Res. 986 (1995), April 14, 1995. The last of these resolutions established new rules for the Oil for Food Program, and authorized the sale of Iraqi oil up to the value of $1 billion every 3 months. In February 1998, this amount was raised to $5.25 billion every 6 months. See UNSC Res. 1153 (1998), February 20, 1998. In December 1999, the ceiling on oil exports was removed. See UNSC Res. 1284 (1999), December 17, 1999.

8. Ibid.

9. In this context, it may be recalled that, shortly after the Iraqi invasion of Kuwait in 1990, President George H. W. Bush realized that economic sanctions alone would not dislodge Iraqi forces and so began a massive deployment of military forces in the Gulf. See Lawrence Freedman and Efraim Karsh, *The Gulf Conflict 1990–1991: Diplomacy and War in the New World Order* (Princeton, N.J.: Princeton University Press, 1993), 203, 209.

10. The United States regularly launched limited air strikes against Iraq, but these fell short of a sustained military campaign and were only partially supported by U.S. allies.

11. See UNSC Res. 757 (1992), May 30, 1992.

12. See Susan L. Woodward, *Balkan Tragedy: Chaos and Dissolution after the Cold War* (Washington, D.C.: The Brookings Institution, 1995); and Carol J. Williams, "Defiant Serbia Moves to Avert Gas Shortages," *Los Angeles Times* (June 2, 1992): A4.

13. The National Bank of Yugoslavia had an estimated $1.8–2.2 billion in overseas assets. Private assets held in different offshore banking centres were believed to total between $3.3 billion and $5 billion. See Vojin Dimitrijevic and Jelena Pejic, "UN Sanctions against Yugoslavia: Two Years Later," *The United Nations in the New World Order: The World Organization at Fifty,* ed. Dimitris Bourantonis and Jarrod Wiener (New York: St. Martin's Press, 1995), 146.

14. See UNSC Res. 787 (1992), November 16, 1992.

15. Sanction Assistance Missions were set up in October 1992 in Hungary, Romania, and Bulgaria; in Macedonia in November 1992; and in Croatia, Ukraine, and Albania in early 1993.

16. See UNSC Res. 820 (1993), April 17, 1993.

17. See David Owen, *Balkan Odyssey* (New York: Harcourt Brace, 1995), 159.

18. On U.S. policy see, for example, Bert Wayne, *The Reluctant Superpower: United States' Policy in Bosnia, 1991–95* (New York: St. Martin's Press, 1997).

19. In response to persistent Bosnian Serb attacks on the Muslim enclave of Srebrenica, Western powers decided to make Srebrenica nominally a safe area. However, they failed to deploy sufficient military forces to provide genuine security.

20. Owen believed that Milosevic had been insufficiently rewarded when he threw his support behind the Vance-Owen plan. According to Owen, this lack of international encouragement made Milosevic renege on his pledge to cut off the Bosnian Serbs in May 1993. See Owen, *Balkan Odyssey,* 297–98.

21. See UNSC Res. 942 (1994), September 23, 1994.

22. John Stremlau argues in *Sharpening International Sanctions: Toward a Stronger Role for the United Nations* (New York: Carnegie Corporation of New York, November 1996) that sanctions were effective; Woodward, *Balkan Tragedy,* believes they were not.

23. See UNSC Res. 841 (1993), June 16, 1993. Initial efforts, including a call for sanctions by the Organisation of American States to restore Aristide to power, failed.

24. Seventy-five percent of Haitian exports went to the United States, and 60 percent of imports came from there.

25. For details of the agreement, see James Morell, *The Governors Island Accord on Haiti* (Washington, D.C.: Washington Center for International Policy, International Policy Report, September 1993).

26. The Haitian military had staged an unfriendly reception for the USS *Harlan County*, which transported the first batch of U.N. peacekeepers. Banners warned that the deployment of U.N. troops would result in another Somalia, where days earlier, U.S. soldiers had been killed, prompting President Bill Clinton to announce that all U.S. troops would withdraw from Somalia. The Haitian military evidently hoped to scare off the United States, and managed to do so.

27. See UNSC Res. 873 (1993), October 13, 1993; and UNSC Res. 875 (1993), October 16, 1993.

28. See UNSC Res. 940 (1994), July 31, 1994.

29. See UNSC Res. 944 (1994), September 29, 1994.

30. Haiti had the lowest life expectancy (48 years), the highest infant mortality rate (124 per 1,000), and the highest illiteracy rate (between 63 percent and 90 percent). Some 70 percent of Haitian children suffered from malnutrition, and 35 percent were seriously malnourished.

31. Between 1992 and 1993, Haiti's GDP fell by almost 20 percent. By 1994, over thirty thousand people had lost their jobs, and unemployment was between 65 percent and 80 percent. Meanwhile, the production of food crops declined and food prices soared.

32. Some analysts have argued that sanctions in Haiti were a failure because they were not comprehensive and were imposed gradually. See, for example, Elizabeth Rogers, "Economic Sanctions and Internal Conflict," in *The International Dimensions of Internal Conflict,* ed. Michael E. Brown (Cambridge, Mass.: MIT Press, 1996), 424. However, the track record in Haiti was uneven because outside powers—the United States in particular—hesitated in their policy towards the junta.

33. Sanctions were imposed on Libya, Sudan, and the Taliban because of their support for terrorist groups and their refusal to extradite alleged terrorists. For details, see Cortright and Lopez, *The Sanctions Decade.*

34. See UNSC Res. 864 (1993), September 15, 1993.

35. See UNSC Res. 1127 (1997), August 28, 1997; UNSC Res. 1130 (1997), September 29, 1997; and UNSC Res. 1135 (1997), October 29, 1997.

36. See UNSC Res. 1173 (1998), June 12, 1998; UNSC Res. 1149 (1998), January 27, 1998; UNSC Res. 1157 (1998), March 20, 1998; and UNSC Res. 1164 (1998), April 29, 1998.

37. See "Angola II, Deadly Diamonds: UNITA's New Armour Financed by a Web of Deals from Luzamba to Antwerp," *Africa Confidential* 40:8 (April 16, 1999): 6–7. See also Blaine Harden, "Africa's Gems: Warfare's Best Friend," *New York Times* (April 6, 2000): A1. It has been estimated that, in February 1999 alone, UNITA sold diamonds worth $32 million. See "Angola II, Deadly Diamonds."

38. See *Report of the Panel of Experts on Violations of Security Council Sanctions Against UNITA,* S/2000/203 (New York: United Nations, March 10, 2000).

39. Ibid.

40. Ibid.

41. See James Bone, "UN Notebook: Has Angola Sanctions Panel 'Gone Awry'?" *UN Wire* (April 11, 2000), www.unfoundation.org. See also "Angola/UN Name and Shame," *Africa Confidential* 41:6 (March 17, 2000): 8.

42. See UNSC Res. 1132 (1997), October 8, 1997. The Security Council had imposed a restricted sanction regime only after prodding from ECOWAS, which had imposed comprehensive economic sanctions in August 1997. The Security Council feared that sanctions could easily create a humanitarian disaster in Sierra Leone. Shortly after the sanctions were imposed, the United Nations dispatched an assessment team to measure the humanitarian effects of sanctions. See *Inter-Agency Assessment Mission to Sierra Leone: Interim Report* (New York: U.N. Office for the Coordinator of Humanitarian Affairs [OCHA], February 1998).

43. See Douglas Farah, "Diamonds Are a Rebel's Best Friend: Mining of Gems Helps Sierra Leone Militia Stall Peace Process," *Washington Post* (April 17, 2000): A12.

44. See Harden, "Africa's Gems."

45. See UNSC Res. 1306 (2000), July 5, 2000.

46. See Joanna Spear, "Arms Limitations, Confidence Building Measures, and Internal Conflict," in *The International Dimensions of Internal Conflict,* ed. Michael E. Brown (Cambridge, Mass.: MIT Press, 1996), 393.

47. Ibid., 377–410.

48. The level of development of a country can be measured in different ways. Economic indicators include per capita income; growth rate; and the size of the manufacturing, services, and agricultural sectors. Social indicators include life expectancy, infant mortality, and access to health services and potable water.

49. Lewis Coser, *The Functions of Social Conflict* (New York: The Free Press/Macmillan, 1964), 87–94. Coser has argued that, when group cohesion is strong, external pressure reinforces this cohesion and the willingness to resist this pressure. When group cohesion is weak, external pressure leads to apathy and disintegration, and hence a diminished capacity to resist outside pressure.

50. See, for example, Hufbauer, Schott, and Elliot, *Economic Sanctions Reconsidered;* Kimberly Ann Elliot, "Factors Affecting the Success of Sanctions," in *Economic Sanctions: Panacea or Peacebuilding in a Post–Cold War World?* ed. David Cortright and George Lopez (Boulder: Westview Press, 1995), 51–60; Rogers, "Economic Sanctions and Internal Conflicts," 413; *Preventing Deadly Conflict: Final Report* (New York: The Carnegie Corporation of New York, December 1997), 54; and U.S. Department of State, Inter-Agency Task Force on Serbian Sanctions, "UN Sanctions Against Belgrade: Lessons Learned for Future Regimes," in *The Report of the Copenhagen Round Table on UN Sanctions: The Case of the Former Yugoslavia, Copenhagen 24–25 June 1996 and Annexes* (Brussels: Sanctions Assistance Missions Communications Centre, European Commission, 1996), 327.

51. See, for example, Ivan Eland, "Think Small," *Bulletin of the Atomic Scientists* (November 1993): 36–40; Ivan Eland, "Economic Sanctions as Tools of Foreign Policy," in *Economic Sanctions: Panacea or Peacebuilding in a Post–Cold War World?* ed. David Cortright and George Lopez (Boulder: Westview Press, 1995), 29–42; and James McDermott, Ivan Eland, and Bruce Kutnick, *Economic Sanctions: Effectiveness as Tools of Foreign Policy,* GAO/

NSIAD-92-106 (Washington, D.C.: U.S. General Accounting Office, February 1992). See also Cortright and Lopez, *The Sanctions Decade.*

52. The importance of exit or termination strategies has been recognised within the United Nations, but such strategies have not in practice been adopted. See, for example, *United Nations Sanctions as a Toll of Peaceful Settlement of Disputes: Non-Paper Submitted by Australia and the Netherlands,* A/50/322 (New York: United Nations, August 3, 1995).

53. Many authors have argued that the Security Council should adopt standardized texts for its sanctions resolutions. This would also facilitate efforts to develop national legislation for sanctions regimes. See Cortright and Lopez, *The Sanctions Decade,* 234.

54. See Michael P. Scharf and Joshua L. Dorosin, "Interpreting UN Sanctions: The Rulings and Role of the Yugoslavia Sanctions Committee," *Brooklyn Journal of International Law* 19:3 (December 1993): 826. Scharf and Dorosin have called for the creation of a single comprehensive Sanctions Committee, which would deal with all U.N. sanctions regimes and be composed of legal experts chosen by the Security Council members for fixed periods. They also propose that the Sanctions Committee make its decision by vote rather than by consensus, and authorize oral and written presentations for the purposes of interpretation by states other than Security Council members. See also Lloyd Dumas, "A Proposal for a New United Nations Council on Economic Sanctions," in *Economic Sanctions: Panacea or Peacebuilding in a Post–Cold War World?* ed. David Cortright and George Lopez (Boulder: Westview Press, 1995), 187–99.

55. For example, only twelve countries have laws enabling them to enforce financial sanctions. See Cortright and Lopez, *The Sanctions Decade,* 234.

56. These arrangements involved a variety of international organisations: the United Nations, the Organisation for Security and Cooperation in Europe, the European Union, NATO, the Western European Union, and the International Conference on the Former Yugoslavia. They covered maritime traffic and land-border control posts, as well as river traffic.

57. In April 2000, the Security Council decided to set up, independently of the U.N. Sanction Committee, a dedicated five-strong group of experts to collect information and investigate leads concerning violations of the sanctions regime imposed on UNITA. See UNSC Res. 1295 (2000), April 18, 2000.

58. For example, in January 1993, five Yugoslav tugboats carrying petroleum products to the FRY threatened to blow up their barges if they were not allowed to proceed. Faced with the possibility of a major ecological disaster, the Romanian and Bulgarian authorities let the convoys pass. The following month, when the Romanian government stopped a Yugoslav convoy of nineteen barges, the FRY brought navigation on the Danube to a standstill and threatened to blow up the levee at Parahovo. See U.S. General Accounting Office, *Serbia-Montenegro: Implementation of UN Economic Sanctions,* GAO/NSIAD-93-174 (Washington, D.C.: U.S. General Accounting Office, April 1993), 15; and U.N. documents S/25182 and S/25189, January 27, 1993; and S/25373, March 5, 1993.

59. See, for example, *Final Report of the Commission of Inquiry on the Rwandan Arms Embargo,* S/1996/195, March 14, 1996, para. 77–79. See also the *Report of the Panel of Experts on Violations of Security Council Sanctions Against UNITA,* S/2000/203, March 10, 2000.

60. For details, see the *Report of the UN Secretary-General on the Question of Special Economic Problems of States as a Result of Sanctions Imposed Under Chapter VII of the United Nations,* S/26705 or A/48/573, November 8, 1993, paras. 5–23.

61. Ibid., paras 24–25.

62. See *Report of the UN Secretary-General, An Agenda For Peace,* S/24111 or A/47/277, June 17, 1992, para. 41.

63. See *Position Paper of the UN Secretary-General on the Occasion of the Fiftieth Anniversary of the United Nations, Supplement to An Agenda for Peace,* S/1995/1 or A/50/60, January 3, 1995, paras. 73–76.

64. See *Report of the UN Secretary-General on the Question of Special Economic Problems,* para. 140.

65. See *Report of the Special Committee on the Charter of the UN on Implementation of the Provisions of the Charter of the United Nations Related to Assistance to Third States Affected by the Application of Sanctions under Chapter VII of the Charter,* A/50/361, August 22, 1995, para. 7.

66. This argument is developed in *Supplement to an Agenda for Peace;* and in *Implementation of the Provisions of the Charter of the United Nations Related to Assistance to Third States.*

67. Cortright and Lopez, *The Sanctions Decade,* 230. Cortright and Lopez suggest that special donor conferences should be convened to raise money when imposing sanctions.

BUILDING PEACE IN THE WAKE OF WAR:
APPROPRIATE ROLES FOR ARMED FORCES AND CIVILIANS

RICHARD A. LACQUEMENT, JR.

The military, probably since Vietnam . . . became more and more saddled with conflict resolution . . . peacekeeping, humanitarian efforts, nation building. The military has resisted this. They don't like it. They're not trained for it. But there's no one else to do it and it continues to be the mission that confronts us. Now either we legitimize it for the military . . . or we find other agencies of government to pick up that slack. It can't be dumped on a military that is not trained, equipped or organized for that mission.[1]—General (ret.) Anthony Zinni

Warfighting is indisputably the primary task for the armed forces but, just as warfare takes place on a spectrum of political activity, units and individuals primarily engaged in warfare cannot expect their realms of activity to be neatly separated from political activities.[2] As the recent situations in Afghanistan and Iraq illustrate, winning major battles is not sufficient for winning the peace and accomplishing all major policy objectives. Moreover, Afghanistan and Iraq are but the most recent of several operations that have engaged United States armed forces in complicated postconflict[3] situations that involve humanitarian aid and reconstruction amidst continued threats of organized violence.[4] Given the continuing need for security, there are very good, logical reasons for the American armed forces to participate in postconflict operations. In the chaos surrounding the end of conflict, civilian agencies often face severe demands with limited security or logistical structures.

Generous funding and expert competence place the American military at a significant advantage compared to many other national entities. With a very large labor force and an organization built to withstand significant disruption at the hands of armed opponents, the military has a remarkable capacity to provide basic human needs. This is a very attractive

capacity that offers potential solutions to a host of problems. But civilian leaders should understand that there are costs to using the armed forces in secondary missions. The appropriate professional expertise and jurisdictions of the armed forces are a useful way to clarify this.[5] This essay analyzes appropriate military and civilian roles in postconflict situations. It lays out the context of postconflict situations and briefly summarizes civilian and military roles, related interagency challenges, and some of the problems associated with military participation in postconflict situations. Responding to General Zinni's challenge, the essay ends by providing policy recommendations to legitimize and improve the military's role in postconflict operations and also suggesting improvements for civilian government agencies to pick up some of the slack.

POSTCONFLICT CONTEXT: CIVILIAN AND MILITARY

In theory, it is easy to stipulate a simple division of labor between military forces and civilians. The military's primary task is preparedness for war or other major, organized violence. Military professional expertise is commonly understood as "the management of violence."[6] The armed forces can be summed up as organizations adept at "killing people and breaking things." The armed forces are a state's tool for warfighting. Civilians are responsible for virtually all other aspects of societal organization and functioning. This includes basic societal systems to support politics, governance, economics, education, public works, information media, health and medical, and law enforcement.[7]

Fig. 3 illustrates a simple view of postconflict activities. Such a division is much easier declared than realized. The intervening aspects include the nature of the security environment, the fungible nature of many military capabilities, and the availability of capabilities in civilian agencies (local, national, or international).

There are many demands that arise in the wake of conflict that are likely to involve military units. The most obvious is the need to establish a secure environment in the conflict area. Addressing experiences in East Timor, Australian Major General Michael Smith noted that in complex peace operations where combat remains a real possibility, security must be provided by military forces that have strong warfighting proficiency with constabulary-type skills added.[8] In situations where there is still armed resistance, even if there is general agreement to support a peaceful settlement, the presence of combat forces is crit-

---

PEACE OPERATIONS: A broad term that encompasses peacekeeping operations and peace enforcement operations conducted in support of diplomatic efforts to establish and maintain peace.

PEACEKEEPING: Military operations undertaken with the consent of all major parties to a dispute, designed to monitor and facilitate implementation of an agreement (ceasefire, truce, or other such agreement) and support diplomatic efforts to reach a long-term political settlement.

Source: U.S. Joint Chiefs of Staff, *Joint Doctrine Encyclopedia* (Washington, D.C.: U.S. Department of Defense, July 1997), 578.

Figure 3
Postconflict Activities

Activities include:

Significant Military Involvement

- **Transition to civil authorities**
- **Support of truce negotiations**
- **Civil affairs support to reestablish a civil government**
- **Psychological operations to foster continued peaceful relations**
- **Continuing logistic support from engineering and transport units**

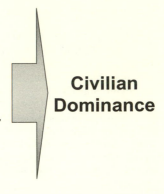

Civilian Dominance

Source: U.S. Joint Chiefs of Staff, Joint Pub 3-07, *Joint Doctrine for Military Operations Other Than War* (Washington, D.C.: U.S. Department of Defense, June 16, 1995), IV-12.

ical to deterring resistance forces or, if need be, to defeat them. Aerial surveillance, intelligence networks, and patrolling—foot, vehicle, and aerial—are all important components of an active presence to deter, suppress, or defeat organized attacks.

Following a war or major armed conflict, other key security tasks include disarmament, demobilization, and reintegration of the organizations and individuals that were engaged in battle. Violent conflict usually includes a heightened degree of mobilization by belligerent populations. In the wake of war, there is the need to deal with militarized forces in the area—defeated and victorious—whose justification has been overcome by events. This can include the organized, armed opponents of states as well as various unconventional resistance groups. In Iraq, for example, the issue of the former regime's military and other security personnel is particularly acute. Following major combat operations that deposed the Saddam Hussein regime and installed the Coalition Provisional Authority (CPA), the Iraqi military was one of many former-regime institutions that Ambassador Bremer dissolved.[9] During major combat operations, vast quantities of arms and ammunition were seized. Many Iraqi fighters were killed and several thousand were captured. But of the estimated 400,000 soldiers at the beginning of the war, the vast majority simply stopped fighting and melted away into the population. Following major combat operations, there have been tremendous efforts to manage the impact of this massive demobilization (referred to by some observers as "self-demobilization"). This includes addressing the economic and social disruption of a huge, suddenly unemployed work force (and the families they support) and establishing control over the vast quantities of arms and ammunition that the security forces had at their disposal. There are

also feelings of disappointment, embarrassment, and even humiliation among many individuals because of the defeat they suffered.[10]

In East Timor, Australian and U.N. forces encountered similar problems with reintegrating into society the militias that unsuccessfully opposed independence, as well as the successful resistance movement (Falintil). After 24 years fighting for independence, the end of the conflict made wartime force levels unnecessary. Although a few of the fighters were incorporated into new security organizations, many former fighters were disarmed and forced to find a new role in society.[11] As in East Timor, Kurdish Iraqi fighters (also known as "Peshmerga"), who fought with the American-led coalition, were no longer needed in the same quantity as before the fall of Saddam's regime.[12]

The displacement or defeat of groups providing security has a major impact on local power structures. The end of a violent conflict engenders local social and economic shockwaves that extend well beyond military forces. The disruptions of conflict extend dramatically to the civil societies of the affected regions. Especially in wars with unlimited aims, in which the goal is "overthrow the enemy—to render him politically harmless or militarily impotent,"[13] the defeat of armed forces is often closely matched by disruption to the basic governing structure. Hence, even as military forces find one of their primary tasks resolved (defeat of an enemy's armed forces) the secondary effects on civil society are just beginning to emerge. In the wake of war, civil unrest is likely to follow. Hence, there is critical need for attention to the myriad tasks of civil order and rudimentary functions of governance that extend to realms beyond military professional expertise. These are tasks more appropriate to civilian experts in national government, international organizations, and nongovernmental organizations with fields of expertise like public administration, public works, legal and judiciary systems, health, economic development, and education.

CIVILIAN AND MILITARY ROLES AND INTERAGENCY CHALLENGES

The context of postconflict stability operations is one that demands much from soldiers and civilians. Even when command authority is clear, the situations require a complex blend of military and civilian skills. The environment is one in which fundamental local security arrangements and the routine functions of daily civil society have been severely disrupted, if not destroyed. This puts soldiers and civilians from outside the area in a complex problem-solving situation. The ambiguities of cause, effect, and intention make solutions difficult. Dealing with remaining armed threats requires great sensitivity and the capacity to judge subtle aspects of intentions and cultural differences.

The postconflict situations in Afghanistan and Iraq are teaching Americans many of the same lessons others have learned. For example, many of the challenges the United States has encountered were experienced recently by the United Nations in missions undertaken after the Cold War. A very thorough and thoughtful effort to learn from experiences during the 1990s was the August 2000 report to the secretary general of the United Nations on Peacekeeping (known as the Brahimi report).[14]

The report is a candid look at problems of U.N. peacekeeping missions in the 1990s. Several of these missions had proven particularly daunting for the United Nations, due to the ambiguous nature of local consent and the severe disruptions created by extended and often intensely violent conflicts.[15] Many of the missions were hampered from the start by broad mandates without sufficient resources. Uncoordinated efforts of bureaus within the United Nations provided additional obstacles to mission effectiveness.[16] Separate bureaucratic channels for economic development, humanitarian aid, political affairs, and security led to poorly organized efforts. Short-term expedients were often decoupled from long-term, sustainable programs. The organizational framework for strategic thinking, planning, and integration was not very robust. Within particular missions as well as across different missions, lessons to improve UN performance were poorly shared.[17]

The Brahimi report suggested important improvements to fix many of the problems. The United Nations has done much to implement the recommendations of the Brahimi report. The planning and initial execution of the U.N. mission in Liberia, for example, is a very self-conscious effort on the part of the United Nations to use the lessons and guidance of the Brahimi report to organize and execute a mission in a manner more likely to yield long-term success.[18]

Similar challenges of interagency planning and coordination have confronted the United States and its coalition partners in Afghanistan and Iraq. Reading through the Brahimi report with the situations in Afghanistan and Iraq in mind, it is not hard to substitute U.S. interagency problems for the United Nations' problems—particularly the well-documented tensions between the U.S. State and Defense Departments in dealing with Iraq.[19] Given many of the difficulties encountered during endeavors to establish effective postconflict civilian and military operations, the Brahimi report appears to be a prescient set of warnings as well as a useful template. Well resourced and planned combat operations to overthrow the Taliban and the Hussein regime have been followed by less well-prepared efforts to manage postconflict stabilization. Although significant military forces have remained after each conflict, the civilian capacity to plan and execute humanitarian, development, governance, and civil society–building activities has been limited. Furthermore, although there are significant military resources in each country, in neither country has coalition military power been able to achieve complete security. Significant, persistent armed resistance remains in each case, and there are areas of each country where coalition control is tenuous or nonexistent.[20] This is important both in terms of the immediate security threat of remaining resistance forces and as an impediment to more effective peace-building activities by civilians.

In summary, recent postconflict situations have highlighted thorny complexities for both military and civilian organizations. Such challenges have been encountered by the civilian and military agencies of the United Nations, NATO, the United States, and many other individual states. One clear general lesson emerges: it is unrealistic to create separate, discrete civil and military realms in such complex and fluid environments. The paramount imperative is to have robust, coherent civil-military cooperation and coordination.

WHAT CAN THE AMERICAN ARMED FORCES DO?

It used to be a very set-piece war that we [U.S. armed forces] fought. More and more we are aware that we are involved in full-spectrum operations. A single force may indeed find itself, as they did in Iraq, in the middle of a fight while doing peacekeeping operations and stability operations. We believe that is going to be an element of the future. . . . The ability to transition rapidly from war fighting to [stability and support] operations is a very, very difficult thing for us.[21]

There is a divide between the roles that military units can play in postconflict situations and the professional justification for the roles that they should play. As noted, the American military is a very large, labor-intensive organization of amazing variety and complexity that makes it very attractive for many tasks.[22] However, the reason that the military has such a highly diverse and articulated force structure is so that it can function in the violent crush of combat without excessive dependence on external resources.

The American military can feed itself, generate its own electricity, make its own potable water, protect itself through a variety of passive and active measures, move itself within a theater, provide shelter for its personnel, deliver its own fuel, communicate globally, provide health care for its soldiers, and provide administrative support for a vast network of units and individuals. It has a flexible organizational structure run by a well-educated body of leaders with a clear hierarchy. As an integral element of its military capacity, the U.S. armed forces are almost completely self-sufficient and can be segmented, moved, and connected in a myriad of combinations and permutations of autonomous, self-sustaining communities.[23] These communities are designed to take care of themselves while they generate and apply combat power. It is no surprise, however, that military units can use the skills they possess for operating their own communities (ranging from the equivalent of small towns to medium-sized cities) to encompass some of the most basic life-support systems of local civilian communities wherever they operate. Of course, the American military forces can only sustain themselves via the national umbilical cord of strategic sealift and airlift that connects them to the American homeland and its vast support base.

There are few military forces in the world that can match all of the capabilities of the U.S. military; however, there are many national military forces that can provide at least some of those capabilities. Through a variety of supranational organizations, such as NATO and the United Nations, international forces can be designed to provide similar capabilities.[24]

Military organizations have learned these tasks as the imperatives of war evolved over the centuries. To avoid the uncertainties and fluctuations of living off the land (and the costs in local support so readily attendant), the American military forces have developed a very complicated but effective way to provide basic needs internally. This extends to training and individual equipment that permit soldiers to take care of themselves in different environments and varying degrees of privation.

Iraq provides a fascinating example of the many roles within the capacity of the American armed forces. After major combat operations,[25] indeed, even during the latter stages of major combat operations, coalition forces became involved in providing basic

Figure 4
Range of Military Operations

Military Operations			General U.S. Goals	Examples
C O M B A T		War	Fight and Win	Large-Scale Combat Operations Attack/Defend/Blockade
	N O N C O M B A T	Military Operations Other Than War	Deter War and Resolve Conflict	Peace Enforcement Counterterrorism Show of Force/Raid/Strike Peacekeeping/NEO Nation Assistance Counterinsurgency
			Promote Peace and Support U.S. Civil Authorities	Freedom of Navigation Counterdrug Humanitarian Assistance Protection of Shipping U.S. Civil Support

Source: U.S. Joint Chiefs of Staff, Joint Pub 3-07, *Joint Doctrine for Military Operations Other Than War* (Washington, D.C.: U.S. Department of Defense, June 16, 1995), I-2.

services and support to the local population. As the conflict in Iraq continues, albeit at a lower, but persistent level of violence, forces on the ground find themselves engaged in a conflict with organized, armed resistance while devoting a large portion of their effort to getting life back to normal for the Iraqi people and preparing to transfer governing authority to a new Iraqi government.[26] The ability to win over or at least neutralize the Iraqi population is a critical security requirement for the armed forces and therefore is an important part of the overall mission.[27]

Direct security missions for coalition armed forces include patroling, raids, searches, checkpoint operations, and the training of local police and security forces. In providing for the basics of life, military forces in Iraq are directly involved in many activities. Armed forces have been involved in the opening and control of national borders to support the delivery of humanitarian aid and commerce. They have also engaged in construction and reconstruction of buildings, bridges, roads, and other infrastructure. Coalition armed forces have helped to reconstruct power and water systems. Coalition forces have assisted in the distribution and security of fuel supplies (benzene and propane). The forces have helped to clean up neighborhoods, establish sports programs for youth, reopen schools, establish or reestablish communication systems, establish information networks (newspaper, TV, community meetings), establish local government, reestablish the banking system, clear mines and unexploded ordnance, dig wells, repair irrigation systems, build houses, establish a judicial system (to include detention, administrative processing, courts, and prisons), and generate local employment both directly (local hires to perform services for the armed forces) and indirectly (through support for various projects).[28]

In postconflict stability operations, some military specialties gain in prominence and value. Such specialties include military police, engineers, psychological operations, public affairs, and legal personnel. Within the U.S. and many other armed forces, the units and individuals with these specialties were integrated, trained, and structured for war. However, these specialties, with minor adjustments, are particularly well suited to the demands of postconflict operations by supporting local communities in addition to the military units to which they are assigned.

One element of the military that is mainly structured and trained for stability operations is civil affairs. The U.S. military has a large number of civil affairs soldiers, most of whom are assigned to the reserves.[29] Civil affairs soldiers are explicitly intended for liaison and assistance with civilian communities in foreign lands. They conduct liaison with local residents, civilian government agencies (U.S. and international), and nongovernmental organizations (NGOs):

The focus of CA [civil affairs] is to engage the civil component of the operational environment by assessing, monitoring, protecting, reinforcing, establishing, and transitioning

The CPA shall exercise powers of government temporarily in order to provide for the effective administration of Iraq during the period of transitional administration, to restore conditions of security and stability, to create conditions in which the Iraqi people can freely determine their own political future, including by advancing efforts to restore and establish national and local institutions for representative governance and facilitating economic recovery and sustainable reconstruction and development.

Source: L. Paul Bremer, CPA Regulation Number 1, May 16, 2003.

—both actively and passively—political, economic, and information (social and cultural) institutions and capabilities to achieve U.S. national goals and objectives at the strategic, operational, and tactical levels of operation both abroad and at home.[30]

Civil affairs units should be understood as enablers.[31] They can be enablers for their military superiors to exercise higher-order governing functions (city, province, or national leadership). They can be enablers to integrate the efforts of government and bureaucratic specialists within the local community with experts from other American or international governmental organizations (e.g., U.S. State Department, United Nations, European Union) and NGOs (e.g., contractors specialized in governance issues such as the Research Triangle Institute).

Another area in which military personnel frequently provide a service generally associated with civilians is in the training of civilian police. Again, as with other missions, the point is that there are military police that are readily deployable as part of military units. Although they are structured and intended for different purposes, their compatibility with civilian style policing is very close. For Americans in particular, the absence of a national police force or paramilitary force means that there is little capacity for police training that the national government can tap into.[32] Furthermore, at the American state and local level, police forces tend to have very little spare capacity that could be sent to a foreign crisis area. Hence, in postconflict environments, military police are frequently called upon to assume responsibility for local police duties.

NEGATIVE EFFECTS OF POSTCONFLICT MILITARY ACTIONS

Although there are many valuable capabilities, there are several difficulties in using American and other external armed forces in the conduct of many aspects of postconflict operations. These difficulties commonly include negative effects on local governance and legitimacy, on the local population, on civilian organizations, and on the external military units themselves.

NEGATIVE EFFECTS ON LOCAL GOVERNANCE AND LEGITIMACY

Peace and stability are very vague political objectives. More specifically, the objective is usually the acceptance by the local population of a new governing structure, based on substitution for a previous, unacceptable one or by the displacement of an external governing power in favor of greater local autonomy. In this and many similar cases, long-term stability depends on the legitimate acceptance by the local population of a new governing structure with the ability to provide an acceptable quality of life. Armed forces may provide security, but security does not define the mission in its totality. Providing security from violent attack is a necessary but not sufficient condition for achieving lasting, stable peace. To the degree that foreign armed forces are perceived as sustaining the position of a local party, the legitimacy of that party may be compromised. This may jeopardize the prospects of stable, sustainable peace. External military forces may be needed to provide immediate security in the aftermath of war, but may compromise the legitimacy and sovereignty of local government. Moreover, because upholding peace may sometimes require long-term commitment to stay and uphold a new regime, the focus on an "exit strategy" may be counterproductive.[33]

"The manner in which US forces terminate their involvement may influence the perception of the legitimacy of the entire operation, and . . . requires careful planning."[34] It is thus valuable for military forces to try to ensure the effectiveness and legitimacy of local efforts to move forward and to forestall problems that might arise from too strong an identification of military forces with local control.

NEGATIVE EFFECTS ON THE LOCAL POPULATION

There are several ways that the presence of armed forces can have unintended negative consequences on the local population, despite the most benign intentions. This includes programs undertaken by the military to serve its short-term interests that are not necessarily in the community's long-term interests.

Social distortions are an example of difficulties that can arise from contact between individuals of dissimilar cultures and backgrounds. This can be amplified by the distance that naturally exists between civilians and members of the military. Misunderstandings related to local customs are common. They can affect both the legitimacy of the mission and the effectiveness of any local structures endorsed by the outside power. Such distortions include cultural norms of interaction between men and women, difficulties with basic communication due to language barriers, and differing norms of common courtesy. Common courtesy problems can range from the relatively simple and mundane, such as maintaining

eye contact and politely handling simple offers of hospitality, to the very important customs related to dealing with deaths or injuries to noncombatants. Problems can include gestures or actions that may be taken as an affront although not intended as such (e.g., showing the soles of one's shoes to Somalis—a sign of disrespect—as occurred when troop-carrying Blackhawk helicopters flew over population centers).

Economic distortions are also a common problem. Foreign military forces and civilian workers, particularly those from the United Nations or high-paying industrialized countries, can create significant problems in less economically developed areas. In East Timor, well-paid U.N. peacekeepers and U.N. employees created a major economic boom in their immediate vicinity. Paid according to the higher standards of living of their native countries or the lofty scales of the United Nations and other major international organizations, these foreigners were very wealthy relative to the locals among whom they worked. The wealth effects they introduced through interaction with the local community created major distortions. This included the hiring of locals for jobs such as drivers and translators. It also included purchases in the local economy to support the international workers (from such basic items as food, fuel, lodging, and simple amenities to larger, more expensive items, such as vehicles, office equipment, and TVs).[35] These transient communities of soldiers, international civil servants, and nongovernmental employees create markets and demands that may not survive their departure.[36] In economically depressed locations with very high unemployment, the effect is likely to be particularly pronounced. For example, in some missions, there have been reports of local professionals, such as medical doctors and professors, taking work as translators or drivers with the United Nations and other international groups for the high pay, thereby depriving the local community of valuable professional skills and services.

A related factor is the diverging interests of armed forces, which may simply be interested in winning local acquiescence just for the time that the forces are in the area. This might be accomplished by providing lavish salaries, expensive projects, and maybe even providing valued goods to keep people happy while military forces are in the area. This may work as an expedient but is likely to exacerbate or create problems of long-term sustainability.

NEGATIVE EFFECTS FOR CIVILIAN ORGANIZATIONS

Military actions and presence can also complicate the operations of civilian governmental and nongovernmental activities. The main manifestation of this is compromised neutrality, impartiality, or independence; that is, the ability to separate military and civilian efforts. In a contentious situation, one of the considerations is that military, humanitarian, and development workers from outside may be perceived as working in concert. If military and civilian workers are seen operating together or in close coordination, the neutrality of the civilian workers may come into question. For many NGOs, local perceptions of their neutrality, impartiality, and independence are critical components of their security and hence their ability to operate freely throughout an area.[37] Even being seen entering the military compounds of armed forces that have taken sides in a particular conflict (or are perceived to have done so) could compromise the perceived neutrality of the NGO.

In a benign, traditional peacekeeping mission, in which all parties consent to the presence of military forces in the role of peacekeepers, the problem of military and civilians working closely together is largely inconsequential. In unstable postconflict situations where there are still parties hostile to outside intervention, all outsiders are at some risk of being perceived as parties to the dispute. Particularly with regard to forcible regime change or efforts to impose new governing structures against the wishes of at least some parties, there is a chance that any effort to stabilize or improve the lives of local residents may diminish the legitimacy and acceptance of the governing arrangements they support. Hence, disruption of even humanitarian and development projects is likely to be an extension of the conflict for political control.[38]

Reflecting concerns over this problem, U.N. missions are provided guidance that the military should not be used for nonmilitary missions except in very highly circumscribed situations—and then only as an expedient until the mission can be assumed by civilians. In this formulation, the military should only undertake nonmilitary activities as a last resort and under the supervision of civilians to ensure that they are integrated into the long-term reconstruction framework.[39] This guideline is a useful distinction, but as with the general distinction between civilian and military realms, a difficult one to realize in practice.

Negative Effects on the Military

Engaging in activities that do not contribute directly to warfighting skills imposes an important cost on the readiness of the armed forces to perform their first and foremost responsibility to fight and win wars. Hence, the significance of a particular assignment must be measured in terms of degraded readiness to perform this task.

Waging war is a very difficult and complex undertaking. When armed forces are not engaged in war, the efforts to train, prepare, and equip for war require vast commitments of time and resources. There is almost always more that units and individuals can do to be better prepared. There are many ways to slip—to develop skills in a suboptimal manner and thereby reduce warfighting readiness. In situations short of war, the presence of soldiers and units ready for war is an important element in deterring hostile forces or defeating them if necessary. Troop visibility in supporting a local population is important for community relations, but it also places more stress on soldiers' training by stripping them of force protection and surprise relative to an enemy.[40]

There are two important ways to perceive the costs of this dynamic. The first is that the military units are usually not optimized for the postconflict stability tasks they are often asked to support and therefore may be ineffective or inefficient at taking on a mission for which they are not prepared. Second, if they are needed for combat, the armed forces engaged in peace operations may not be fully ready and may require refresher training or reorientation.[41]

Focus on an exit strategy for armed forces is another aspect that can be problematic. The difficulty comes when the focus is on how quickly to remove military forces, whether or not the overall objectives for the mission have been accomplished in an enduring fashion. A poor way to approach the issue is one in which military forces seek to accomplish minimal objectives that permit them to withdraw in good order, regardless of the effect on the community they leave behind. The departure of the military forces may uncover underlying problems that have been held in abeyance. There may be circumstances in which the military forces have been ostensibly successful in suppressing violent conflict while they are present, in a way that proves ephemeral once they depart.

POLICY RECOMMENDATIONS

Fundamentally, the complex nature of postconflict situations reflects tremendous civilian and military overlap in the endeavor to achieve overarching political objectives. Therefore effective solutions must include efforts to improve both military and civilian capacity. The first step is to better conceptualize and clarify appropriate military and civilian roles and responsibilities. Flowing from these roles are recommendations for better organizational structures and processes to enhance postconflict stability operations.

Clarify Roles and Rationales

The armed forces are unique assets that society relies on for one of its most fundamental needs: security. Opportunity costs of alternate uses of the armed forces are rightfully measured in relation to the primary task to secure the society. Although there are several ways that war-trained armed forces can prove valuable in other contexts, civilian leaders should be particularly sensitive to alternative sources for meeting such needs. The armed forces' best exit strategy will be to transition tasks with which they were temporarily entrusted back to civilians—who may be from U.S. government agencies, international organizations, NGOs, or the local population itself.

Professions are defined by the expertise that they provide to their clients, as well as by the jurisdictions in which they apply this expertise.[42] I have argued elsewhere that the quintessential expertise of American military professionals "is the development, operation, and leadership of a human organization, a profession, whose primary expertise is the application of coercive force on behalf of the American people."[43] The jurisdictions in which a profession practices are determined as part of competition within a system of professions.[44] For the U.S. military, the most important jurisdiction for the application of this expertise is war. But war is not the only possible jurisdiction. Outside of war, there are various degrees to which professional military expertise can provide valuable service on behalf of important national objectives.[45]

In the market sector, professions compete for clients (consumers) and can choose not to compete in sectors that offer no rewards or that compromise other values. For the American military, negotiations take place with the executive and legislative civilian leadership of the constitutional government. Military leaders have less choice over whether to accept jurisdictions or missions, for they must do whatever their sole client (American society, represented by its civilian leaders) dictates. Jurisdictions engender potential requirements for the armed forces and their professional leaders. Resource constraints on personnel, equipment, and budget limit the capacity of the armed forces. Important assessments of the appropriate allocations of limited resources must accompany negotiations between civilian and military leaders to determine the appropriate jurisdictions for the military. Although civilian leaders make the final decisions, military leaders should provide professional advice and expertise to help shape the decisions.

Military forces provide capacity for the organized use of violence or coercive force unmatched by any other organization. Nonetheless, in the wake of a major war (e.g., in Iraq) and other chaotic postconflict situations, armed forces are among the few elements capable of providing basic services and coherent, organized response. In situations in which local institutions and governing capabilities are displaced or destroyed by the preceding military campaign, armed forces entering an area become the focal point of organized efforts for recovery. International law and basic human decency require the military to assume key responsibilities in addressing immediate problems and the basic needs of the local population.[46] However, the armed forces are not expert in civil governance and the myriad associated tasks. There are compelling reasons why the military should be better prepared for these tasks as an expedient. But, this should go hand in hand with improvements in civilian capacity to help relieve the armed forces and minimize the time and scope of such expedients.

IMPROVE MILITARY CAPACITY FOR STABILITY OPERATIONS

Military forces often find themselves in the position of meeting immediate needs of local populations in the wake of major armed conflict. Since the preconditions of addressing other basic human needs is generally predicated on the achievement of at least a modicum of security, it stands to reason that military forces that provide the secure environment will also be rapidly and of necessity deeply intertwined with the initial efforts to deliver humanitarian needs and basic communal services. It is also easy to make the connection between rudimentary elements of sustainable life for a local population and security for the authorities whose task is to improve the community's quality of life. Unsurprisingly, armed forces in these circumstances see the provision of an acceptable quality of life to the native population as a way to enhance their local acceptance and forestall violent opposition. This links efforts for community outreach and support to fundamental security concerns. The problem is the degree to which such forces, optimized for the demands of violent conflict, are appropriately tailored to meet the complex demands of humanitarian assistance and sustainable local governance. Recognizing the necessary but different demands of the postconflict environment, the armed forces should be better trained and organized for such operations.[47]

Logical extrapolations of dispersed and rapidly executed military operations suggest that, much like in Iraq, the quick defeat of an enemy will lead to an equally swift transition of control over territory to the successful military forces. The defeat or displacement of opposing armed forces will often go hand in hand with destruction of the local governing arrangements they sustained. Governance and control will therefore devolve into new local hands or to the successful military forces themselves. Fighting and winning military campaigns is thus only part of achieving many political objectives.[48] This means that military leaders must be aware of the political and social shockwaves their actions send through the societies in which they operate. This does not mean that the military should become expert in the myriad, complex tasks of governance; however, it does suggest that the armed forces must understand these complex situations. The armed forces have difficulty addressing circumstances for which they are not trained or organized. This demands greater effort before such operations to ensure rapid, favorable exploitation of military capabilities in the wake of armed conflict.

Elements of relevant military reform should include improved professional education to emphasize follow-through from successful warfare to postconflict stability, commensurate with national political objectives. The emphasis on this critical transitional stage should also be accompanied by greater awareness of the overlapping and intertwined nature of military and civilian responsibilities. This requires less emphasis on idealized divisions of labor that clearly separate civilian and military spheres and more emphasis on the coordination and mutual support between military and civilian leaders and their organizations.

In other words, parts of the force should be optimized for peace operations, to include the demands of postconflict transition. The natural bridge between military and civilian efforts within the current force structure is the civil affairs units. Within the current force structure, however, civil affairs units are small and very diverse. The expertise of the various teams is uneven and the depth of the teams is shallow. Civil affairs units provide assessment and liaison capacity. To execute major civil rehabilitation, they rely on more robust military forces or civilian organizations.

The capabilities and effectiveness of the soldiers and teams that support civil affairs units would be enhanced by dedicating portions of the active force to peace and stability operations. Brigade-sized elements associated with civil affairs units and comprised of engineers, military police, legal personnel, and command and control elements should be devoted to priority training and preparation for the complex demands of stability operations. My recommendation is that each regional combatant command have at least one brigade (approximately five thousand soldiers) structurally optimized for stability operations. Officers and other leaders of these units should be specially trained and developed for such assignments. This does not mean creating a separate service or new personnel specialties. The soldiers and units proposed may be required to support other military missions, to include combat, which means that they will always need to be soldiers ready to undertake or support warfighting. Nonetheless, rather than the current tendency to take units optimized for combat and then to cobble them together and reorient them for the complexities of peace operations as a temporary diversion, my recommendation is to reverse the emphasis and increase the effectiveness of a portion of the force for peace and stability operations that, in extreme situations (e.g., when all other combat optimized forces are tapped out) can step in with some retraining and modest reorientation to perform more traditional combat or combat support roles. The alignment with a regional combatant command is designed to allow greater concentration of regional specialists and linguists to support the particular command.

IMPROVE CIVILIAN CAPACITY FOR STABILITY OPERATIONS

We do not just need armed forces better trained for the complex civil governance tasks of postconflict situations. We also need better civilian capacity for rapid deployment and integration into postconflict stability operations. More robust leadership and coordination mechanisms are needed to harness the capacity of military organizations to sustainable programs. Such programs should be able to continue after military forces depart.

What this suggests is the need for more members of civilian agencies that can be deployed to work in postconflict situations on short notice, most likely in conjunction with American military forces. Much like the State Department political advisors at higher military commands, as well as the more independent USAID disaster assistance response teams (DART), government agencies involved in economic development, humanitarian assistance, civil-society building,

governance, and other basic functions need to have the capacity to deploy personnel either in conjunction with military forces or separately. A natural fit would appear to be the placement of civilian governmental personnel within civil affairs units. To effectively integrate members of civilian agencies with military units, there should be habitual relationships and training.[49]

Although the need for such civilian capacity is clear for a particular crisis, one significant difficulty is to justify the personnel strength and training that appears unrelated to peacetime needs. This recommendation implies the creation and maintenance of excess personnel and organizational capacity relative to routine, peacetime needs to provide capabilities for immediate foreign deployment in the event of a crisis. Personnel should have appropriate security screening and language training. When not deployed with their affiliated combatant command, they can provide depth within their parent agency. Such deployable capacity would be appropriate for the State Department (USAID, as well as a pool of Foreign Service Officers), the Justice Department (judiciary, as well as law enforcement elements), Treasury, Commerce, other economic agencies, and even agencies involved in urban development, social services, disaster assistance, and health—in short, agencies associated with the stewardship of domestic civil society.

REFORM THE NATIONAL SECURITY PROCESS

The need for greater integration of civilian and military management of stability operations extends to the interagency process at the highest levels:

> How a force starts will largely determine the culture of the whole operation, and it is far more difficult to pick up the pieces from a bad start than it is to continue to operate effectively and improve. This emphasized the need for thorough planning and preparation and a high level of readiness to enable forces to respond quickly and decisively.[50]

The origin of the recent difficulties in Iraq was not in the capacity of the military forces to deal with the situation but with the civilian authority to harness and use this capacity in a coherent, sustainable manner. In this regard, administration critics are on solid ground to claim that the postwar planning was inadequate to the task.[51] A former U.S. Ambassador to Saudi Arabia compared the situation in Iraq to "a badly managed Pentagon-operated theme park."[52] Moreover, since the postwar planning was largely given to the Pentagon, postwar preparations took an understandable lesser priority to the exigencies of the war plan. This also reflects a fundamental shortsightedness, excessive compartmentalization, and misguided reliance on the assumption that postconflict planning could somehow catch up to the effects of military action. More troublingly, there is evidence that the State Department did a lot of work on these issues well before the war but that their efforts were heavily discounted or ignored by the Pentagon leadership that took over postwar planning responsibilities.[53] Interagency planning and coordination simply did not extend far enough into the operation. In Iraq, there were major disconnects between military and civilian organizations. The civilian organizational structure did not mirror the military structure, nor did it mirror the governing structure of the country in which it would operate.[54]

The sloppiness of the manner in which the United States has managed the postconflict situations in both Afghanistan and Iraq points up a need for re-assessment within the U.S. government akin to what the military services faced in the mid-1980s and what the United Nations has faced since the end of the Cold War. Military forces have proven to be very capable in performing tasks in support of postconflict situations. Nonetheless, the United States appears to have encountered many problems in its most recent postconflict situation similar to those identified in the Brahimi report. Logically, the U.S. National Security Council would appear to be the mechanism for reconciling such competing values. A more systematic effort to explore integration of national functions is warranted.

The 1986 Goldwater-Nichols Act provides a useful model for approaching U.S. government reorganization to meet national security needs of the current era. Just as the Goldwater-Nichols Act helped to reform the military and the Department of Defense for national defense, a similar effort to better integrate the functions of economic development, diplomacy (to include public diplomacy), and security would improve American capacity to deal with the complex issues of peace-building in the wake of major conflict. Along these lines, the Brahimi report provides a useful template of how the United Nations responded to similar challenges in postconflict effectiveness amongst its agencies.

CONCLUSION

You will take every step in your power to preserve tranquility and order in the city and give security to individuals of every class and description—restraining as far as possible, till the restoration of civil government, every species of persecution, insult, or abuse, either from the soldiery to the inhabitants or among each other.[55]

We need candid, well-grounded debates and forthright negotiations between military and civilian leaders about the appropriate roles for the armed forces on behalf of the nation. To be sure, the American military will faithfully execute the missions they receive from their civilian masters. However, the extensive demands that stretch the capacity of the American armed forces require important decisions about the use of finite national capabilities. Civilian leaders must reconcile American military expertise and core competence with expedient or secondary tasks for which civilians are or should be better organized. The extensive scope of recent military involvement in stability and support operations in part reflects the lack of capacity outside the military to

handle such complex and important tasks. To have a coherent professional exit strategy for the armed forces requires a coherent entrance or hand-off strategy for other agencies of the civil government or local community. The military needs to undertake realistic training and structural adaptations to better handle its roles in transition from violent conflict to the complicated amelioration of social, economic, and political concerns that are inextricably tied to security concerns. Fundamentally, however, the tasks of creating and sustaining a well-functioning civil society are the appropriate realm of civilians inside and outside the government. To build successful peace in the wake of war will require improvements on the part of both military and civilian organizations. The most salient aspect of the postconflict transition from military operations to civil governance is the recognition that this is an environment of overlapping and shared responsibility for both military and civilian leaders that does not permit an easy division of labor. Successful achievement of overarching political objectives will require close postconflict cooperation between civilian and military organizations.

Clausewitz wisely noted that "no one starts a war —or rather, no one in his senses ought to do so— without first being clear in his mind what he intends to achieve by that war and how he intends to conduct it." Although referring specifically to war, the caution is equally sound with respect to the use of military forces in the immediate aftermath of war. Uppermost in focus must be the political objectives for which the armed forces are employed. Although these objectives are frequently less concrete and extend beyond the operational objectives of combat, the military is likely to play a role just as critical—if not more so—in the immediate aftermath of war. Along with appropriate civilian leaders and agencies, the armed forces are crucial to shaping the conditions of peace that can make durable the results of war. Just as war is the continuation of politics, the use of military forces must be integrated as part of the political continuum in the wake of war.

NOTES

The views expressed in this paper are those of the author and do not necessarily reflect the official policy or position of the Department of the Army, Department of the Navy, Department of Defense, or U.S. Government.

I thank Damon Coletta, Bradford Lee, and Karl Walling for their valuable comments on earlier drafts of this essay. I also thank the U.S. Air Force Academy Institute of National Security Studies for generous funding assistance to support this project.

1. *News Hour With Jim Lehrer,* PBS TV, September 30, 2003, interview with Retired General Anthony Zinni.

2. This theme is interwoven through the classic by Carl von Clausewitz, *On War* (Princeton: Princeton University Press, 1976).

3. I have used the term "postconflict" to encompass the larger set of situations following major violent events that include conventional, interstate wars, civil wars,

insurgencies, rebellions, and other instances of violent conflict. The term "postwar" is an equally suitable and virtually equivalent term; however, the tendency of some to perceive war as a particular legal state of affairs would be too narrow to capture the array of situations this study attempts to address.

4. Recent, similar missions in postconflict situations included El Salvador, Somalia, Bosnia, and Kosovo.

5. See Don Snider and Gayle Watkins, eds., *The Future of the Army Profession* (New York: McGraw-Hill, 2002), and Richard Lacquement, *Army Professional Expertise and Jurisdictions* (Carlisle, Pa.: Strategic Studies Institute, October 2003).

6. The phrase has been used by many authors but was first introduced by Harold D. Lasswell, "The Garrison State," *The American Journal of Sociology* 46:4 (January 1941): 455–68.

7. For distinctions between civilian and military activities, see Samuel Huntington, *The Soldier and the State: The Theory and Politics of Civil-Military Relations* (Cambridge, Mass.: Harvard University Press, 1957), especially chapter 4. Also see Morris Janowitz, *The Professional Soldier* (New York: Free Press, 1971), especially the prologue and Chapter 1.

8. Michael G. Smith with Moreen Dee, *Peacekeeping in East Timor: The Path to Independence,* International Peace Academy Occasional Paper Series (Boulder, Colo.: Lynne Rienner, 2003), 130.

9. See L. Paul Bremer, CPA Order 2, *Dissolution of Entities,* May 23, 2003, www.cpa-iraq.org/regulations/CPAORD2.pdf.

10. Within a few weeks after major fighting, large demonstrations among unemployed former military members prompted the promulgation of a policy for monthly payments to former members of the Iraqi military (retirees were already receiving payments under the perpetuation of the pension system). See CPA Order 2 dissolving the Iraqi Army (among other organizations) and CPA statement by Senior Ministry of Defense advisor Walt Slocombe, June 24, 2003, establishing payments for former Iraqi soldiers. There were no provisions for the tens of thousands of Kurdish fighters (Peshmerga) who cooperated with the coalition in the effort to unseat Saddam Hussein.

11. Smith, *Peacekeeping in East Timor,* 79–82.

12. Although the threat from Saddam's army is gone, this is still a very problematic issue for the future composition and organization of Iraqi security forces. In negotiations for the interim Iraqi Constitution signed in March 2004, the status of Kurdish Peshmerga fighters is one of the major unresolved issues.

13. Clausewitz, *On War,* 69.

14. United Nations, "Report of the Panel on United Nations Peace Operations," A/55/305–S/2000/809, August 21, 2000 (hereafter referred to as the "Brahimi report").

15. Missions included U.N. efforts in El Salvador, Cambodia, Haiti, Sierra Leone, East Timor, and the Balkans.

16. Brahimi report and interviews with U.N. personnel.

17. Ibid.

18. Interviews with U.N. personnel.

19. For a detailed description of the postwar planning efforts for Operation Iraqi Freedom, see James Fallows, "Blind into Baghdad," *Atlantic* (January 2004): 53–74.

20. This appears to be true in the mountainous areas of Afghanistan that border Pakistan (which, on the Pakistani side, are also generally beyond the effective control of the Pakistani government). Coalition forces appear to have tenuous control over portions of Baghdad and parts of the region known as the Sunni Triangle in Iraq.

21. Assistant Deputy Chief of Staff for Developments at the U.S. Army Training and Doctrine Command (TRADOC) Brigadier General Philip Coker, as quoted by Kim Burger, "US Army and Support Operations: Caught off Guard?" *Jane's Defence Weekly* (October 1, 2003): 25.

22. This is mainly a commentary on the capabilities of the U.S. Army and the Marines, although the Navy and the Air Force can play some roles in postconflict stability operations. The most important caveat is that to the degree that such missions are still dangerous and require the presence of capable, robust warfighting forces, there will be a need to maintain attack aviation readily available. The sustained availability of close air support aircraft will be a necessary complement to ground combat forces. For any tasks, the need for strategic and theater air and sea lift are also likely to create sustained demands on the naval and aerial assets devoted to Transportation Command. Additionally, the Air Force and Navy have engineer units with skills that can be profitably employed in reconstruction and repair efforts. With respect to the Army and Marines, the Army's mission for sustained land combat (as opposed to the Marine's charter for expeditionary combat) means that the Army is the service that maintains the dominant capacity for logistics and support on land within a theater of operations. Fuel handling, supply operations, engineering, civil affairs, command and control, and a myriad of other functions derive from the Army's role in being prepared to seize and control territory. Because people live on land, it is natural and unsurprising that the service that operates on land is the one most likely to assume the expedient missions in support of the people on land in postconflict environments.

23. By American military doctrinal definitions, "joint" refers to "activities, operations, organizations, etc., in which elements of two or more Military Departments participate" and "combined" refers to operations "between two or more forces or agencies of two or more allies." Definitions are from *DOD Dictionary of Military Terms,* www.dtic.mil/doctrine/jel/doddict/index.html.

24. Of course, these multinational organizations and the military units they create have many elements of friction and inefficiency inherent in the amalgam of diverse and independent national elements.

25. President Bush very deliberately used the phrase concerning the end of "major combat operations" as a way of suggesting that the most intense fighting of Operation Iraqi Freedom had ended without using language that would declare the war over. I will use this commonly accepted reference to distinguish between the major offensive operations of March and April 2003 versus the persistent violence or insurgency since the coalition assumed control of Iraq.

26. For a statement of coalition aims, there are many official documents and statements. Two representative descriptions of U.S. and coalition efforts are President Bush's statement upon signing the Emergency Supplemental Appropriations Act for Defense and for the Reconstruction of

Iraq and Afghanistan, November 6, 2003; and the Coalition Provisional Authority Regulation Number 1. Both documents are available at the CPA web site, www.cpa-iraq.org/index.html.

27. The mission statement of the coalition armed forces (known as Combined Joint Task Force 7 [CJTF 7]) is (as of January 2004):

> CJTF-7 conducts offensive operations to defeat remaining noncompliant forces and neutralize destabilizing influences in the Area of Operations (AO) to create a secure environment in direct support of the Coalition Provisional Authority (CPA). Concurrently, conducts stability operations which support the establishment of government and economic development to set the conditions for a transfer of operations to designated follow on military or civilian authorities.

Understanding of the armed forces efforts in Iraq is also based on the author's observations and experiences in Mosul, northern Iraq, June to August 2003, where he was assigned to the 101st Airborne Division (Air Assault) as a special assistant to the commanding general.

28. Based on the author's observations and experiences. This information was captured in briefings provided to visitors to the 101st Division sector. See also Michael R. Gordon, "101st Airborne Scores Success in Northern Iraq: A Reconstruction Effort Is Led by the Military," *New York Times* (September 4, 2003): A1.

29. Of the approximately ten thousand civil affairs soldiers in the U.S. Army, 96 percent are in the reserves. A key reason for keeping a large number of civil affairs billets in the reserves is to have functional teams of individuals who bring experience in their particular function from their civilian lives. For example, lawyers or local government administrators for the administrative and legal teams, and individuals with experience in local management and utilities for public works teams. For organization of civil affairs teams, see Department of the Army, *FM 41-10, Civil Affairs Operations* (Washington, D.C.: U.S. Department of the Army, 2000), especially Chapter 3. However, these are not fixed requirements and there is great unevenness in the match between individual experience in the civilian world and the demands of civil affairs in a particular mission. For example, just because someone was part of a department of an American federal, state, or local agency does not mean that they are necessarily well suited to the demands of a city or national administration in Iraq, Afghanistan, or some other country. Moreover, the generally junior rank and youth of American soldiers in civil affairs units may qualify them well for lower-level administrative tasks and coordination, but not for the higher-order tasks of significant population centers (cities, governorates, or countries). Comparable relevant skills for such tasks more likely equate to those of managers and civil service leaders in city, state, or federal government in the United States. In short, Civil Affairs units provide useful skills and valuable diversity for important governing functions; however, they are not well structured to meet the demands commonly placed upon them to provide effective governance support in unstable circumstances.

30. U.S. Department of the Army, *FM 3-05.401: Civil Affairs Tactics, Techniques and Procedures* (Washington, D.C.: U.S. Department of the Army, September 2003), 1-1.

31. Civil affairs units have many specialties distributed among several teams but very little depth. A typical functional team has three individuals (usually an officer, an NCO, and one soldier). A battalion of one hundred to two hundred soldiers has one lieutenant colonel commander. What this provides is a capacity for assessment and some moderate assistance to a local community; however, it is very short on capacity to undertake projects independently. Its greatest advantage is in combination with larger military units—brigade or larger—because these have more robust leadership and labor capabilities. Furthermore, although civil affairs personnel are soldiers and are trained in fundamental combat skills and self-protection, they are not designed to respond to significant military attacks and therefore rely heavily on combat units to provide force protection in dangerous environments. This includes reliance on combat forces to provide general security in an area, as well as direct support for Civil Affairs teams operating in particular locations.

32. The U.S. Federal Bureau of Investigation can and has provided limited support to U.S. military operations abroad; however the bureau is not designed or structured for such duties. In other countries, national police or paramilitary forces (such as the Italian Carbinieri and French Gendarmes) do provide national deployment capability.

33. My thanks to Karl Walling for his insights and comments on this point.

34. *Joint Pub 3-07*, IV-12 to IV-13.

35. An example of this includes the effect of U.S. military presence and economic efforts on the price of cement, a critical building material, in Iraq. See Hugh Pope, "U.S. Buying Power Leaves Iraqis Short of Key Building Materials," *Wall Street Journal* (November 12, 2003): A16.

36. For a treatment of this phenomenon, see Mark Lee, "The Internationals," *Atlantic* (July 2001): 35–36.

37. Antonio Donini, Symposium at the Naval War College, Newport, R.I., January 26, 2004.

38. Antonio Donini, Norah Miland, and Karin Wermester, eds., *Nation-Building Unraveled? Aid, Peace and Justice in Afghanistan* (Bloomfield, Conn.: Kumarian Press, 2004).

39. From interviews with U.N. DPKO members as well as from the U.N. memo, "General Guidance for Interaction between United Nations Personnel and Military Actors in the Context of the Crisis in Iraq," March 21, 2003.

40. Other examples of differing uses of forces include the reorientation of engineers from their focus on mobility (the breaching of obstacles and support for the maneuver of combat forces) and countermobility (the creation of obstacles and other barriers to slow or halt enemy maneuver) to reconstruction and infrastructure projects on behalf of local populations. At the other end of the spectrum, logistics units intended primarily to support the operations of combat and combat support forces can easily use the same skills for effective logistics on behalf of humanitarian assistance or reconstruction missions.

41. An example of this is the predeployment need to prepare a force for the differing demands of peace operations as well as the need, upon redeployment, to reorient and retrain for major war.

42. Andrew Abbott, *The System of Professions: An Essay on the Division of Expert Labor* (Chicago: University of Chicago Press, 1988).

43. Lacquement, *Army Professional Expertise and Jurisdictions,* and Richard Lacquement, "Understanding Professional Expertise and Jurisdiction," *Military Review* (March 2003): 61–65. See also Snider and Watkins, *The Future of the Army Profession.*

44. Abbott, *The System of Professions,* 33.

45. Lacquement, "Understanding Professional Expertise and Jurisdiction," 65.

46. 1949 Geneva Convention; in particular, the sections related to treatment of noncombatants and the responsibilities of occupying forces. A full-text copy is available at www.unhchr.ch/html/menu3/b/91.htm.

47. For a similar argument along these lines, see Nadia Schadlow, "War and the Art of Governance," *Parameters* 33 (Autumn 2003): 85–94.

48. Useful treatments of this point include Frederick W. Kagan, "War and Aftermath," *Policy Review* 120 (August 2003), available at www.policyreview.org/aug03/kagan.html; and Fallows, "Blind into Baghdad."

49. Basic individual self-defense and common task training should also be part of the preparation for *any* civilians likely to operate in a combat zone.

50. Smith, *Peacekeeping in East Timor,* 153–54.

51. Among many accounts, some of the most thoughtful and comprehensive include the PBS TV *Frontline* series, "Truth, War and Consequences," October 9, 2003 (video and text from the program at www.pbs.org/wgbh/pages/frontline/shows/truth/) and David Rieff, "Blueprint for a Mess," *New York Times Magazine* (November 2, 2003): 28–38.

52. Afzal Khan, "Mideast Experts See Complicated Process for Stabilizing Iraq" U.S. Department of State Information Program, October 3, 2003, Internet, http://usinfo.state.gov.

53. Reiff, "Blueprint for a Mess" and Fallows, "Blind into Baghdad."

54. ORHA (later renamed the Coalition Provisional Authority—CPA) was originally created with a central headquarters and three regional offices. It was later expanded to four regional offices. The previous Iraqi government had been organized with a central government and eighteen governorates. There were no regional governing structures. For the regional CPA organizations, there were no natural regional governing structures with which to create parallel interactions.

55. George Washington, quoted in *FM 3-05.401: Civil Affairs Tactics, Techniques and Procedures,* 1-1.

CHAPTER 9

PREPARING FUTURE
DEFENSE LEADERS

THE COMPLEX CONTEXT OF AMERICAN MILITARY CULTURE: A PRACTITIONER'S VIEW

JOSEPH J. COLLINS

Military culture—the prevailing values, norms, philosophies, customs, and traditions of the armed forces—has always had a significant impact on operational effectiveness.[1] But even culture has a context. As strong an actor as culture is, it is also acted upon by other forces. As Edgar Schein of the Massachusetts Institute of Technology has noted:

Changes in the environment will produce stresses and strains inside the group, forcing new learning and adaptation. At the same time, new members coming into the group will bring in new beliefs and assumptions that will influence currently held assumptions. To some degree . . . there is constant pressure on any given culture to evolve and grow.[2]

For military culture, evolution poses polar dangers, both of which have been the object of much speculation in recent newspaper and journal articles. On the one hand, military culture may evolve too far, causing the force to become "civilianized" and less than ready for the rigors of combat. On the other hand, given the functional imperative of combat readiness, an isolated military fixated on its own norms and traditions could lose sight of the values of the society it is sworn to defend and end up at loggerheads with its political masters. Where American military culture lies between these two extremes is an open question. To answer it, one must first examine the complex context within which today's American military culture has evolved, including pressures from the international environment, the decisions made by the nation's leadership to deal with that environment, and pressures from within American society itself.

PRESSURES ON TODAY'S FORCE: THE INTERNATIONAL ENVIRONMENT AND MANAGEMENT DECISIONS

After the Cold War, the United States encountered not the end of history, but a new disorder, featuring ethnic conflicts, failed states, and humanitarian disasters. Complicating matters was the strategy that the United States adopted at the end of the Bush administration, a strategy that, as codified in the spring of 1997, tasked the armed forces not only to "deter and fight" wars, but to shape the environment to prevent wars—in effect, legitimizing the peace operations and humanitarian activities that have become its common missions.[3]

From 1993 to 1997, this new approach resulted in more than forty largely successful military operations, a pace of operations roughly three to four times that during the Cold War. At the same time, a relatively high percentage of U.S. forces remain forward deployed, with a hundred thousand troops in Europe, another hundred thousand in East Asia, and a task force averaging about twenty thousand personnel in the Persian Gulf area. Service officials say that half of the Navy is at sea at any one time, with one-third forward deployed. In 1996, the Army and the Marine Corps noted that their average member was deployed or otherwise spent about 140 days a year away from his or her home station. The Air Force has noted a quadrupling of personnel deployed away from their bases since the end of the Cold War. Moreover, the pace of training in all of the services is only slightly less than it was during the Cold War. This frantic pace of training, operations, and deployments has not bypassed U.S. reserve components, whose person-day contributions to active missions increased from 900,000 in 1986 to 6 million in 1993 and an astounding 13.2 million in 1997.[4]

Complicating the pace of operations, a significant forward presence, and the high level of training is the 36 percent reduction of the active force from its maximum Cold War strength. Concurrently, the defense budget has declined nearly 40 percent. To maintain this breakneck pace of activities at the lowest possible cost, modernization has been severely underfunded by as much as $20 billion a year. Since 1994, advocates of more funding for modernization have argued for an increase from roughly $40 billion to more than $60 billion a year in procurement spending, a target that will not be reached until FY01. Moreover, those in favor of transforming the armed forces so that they can adapt to the revolution in military affairs claim that an additional $5–10 billion yearly is needed, above the $60 billion already programmed.[5]

We are fast approaching the day when it will be difficult to brag about our matériel readiness. For example, in 1998, the Air Force operations deputy,

This essay has been edited and is reprinted from Washington Quarterly 21 *(Autumn 1998): 213–28. © 1998 by the Center for Strategic and International Studies (CSIS) and the Massachusetts Institute of Technology.*

Lieutenant General Patrick K. Gamble, said that in a few years, 78 percent of the Air Force's six thousand airplanes would be more than 20 years old.[6] The other service operations deputies had similar tales of woe, unanimously bemoaning the failure to deal with the central reality that the vast majority of military systems—from tanks and trucks to fighter aircraft—were purchased during the first 6 years of the Reagan administration. In effect, the United States is facing a huge bow wave of unmet modernization expenditures, which, if it hits head on, may well capsize the ship.

In the Pentagon, this may look like a budget problem; but in the field, it means older, less reliable equipment, more time in the motor pool or maintenance bay, and the channeling of scarce local assets to keep equipment ready for the next deployment or major training exercise. Fudging maintenance procedures, cannibalizing equipment, and falsifying readiness reports are also not out of the question.

The effects of aging equipment are also felt in the field in terms of confidence in our military capabilities. For example, in an Army-wide survey of more than fifteen thousand soldiers, noncommissioned officers, and junior officers, 41 percent described the condition of the equipment in their unit as "poor," a less than ringing endorsement of matériel readiness.[7] Compounding this problem is the growing hollowness in selected military units, especially the Army's five second-line divisions. For example, 30–40 percent of infantry squads in two divisions had minimal or no personnel assigned to them; in another division, 40 percent of the squads were either empty or not combat ready.[8] To another question in an Army-wide survey about whether they would feel good going into combat with their company tomorrow, more than 40 percent of the soldiers, noncommissioned officers, and officers surveyed said that they would not.[9] Given problems in matériel and personnel readiness, these uncertain responses are relatively easy to understand.

SOCIETAL PRESSURES ON TODAY'S FORCE

It is important to remember that pressures emanating from the international environment and governmental attempts to cope with that environment both affect a force that is, on the average, 57 percent married. The pressures on our 1.4 million active service men and women are, to some extent, shared by their 2.2 million family members.[10]

Also affecting military culture and the organizational climate are a series of factors that has its origin in American society. In effect, our all volunteer, mostly family-oriented force—whose pay never seems able to keep up with civilian wage scales—is feeling pressure from a civilian-military value gap, the attraction of a booming economy, and the normal "three-way strife" that comes from the gender, race, and ethnic issues that have migrated from civil society into the military.

It has become axiomatic: we live in an information age, and that fact is changing how we work, how we think about work, and how we make war. The totality of changes implied by this simple set of facts is enormous. At least two implications are clear. First, many military occupational specialties will become increasingly technical; tomorrow's force will require even better educated troopers than it has today. Military service could become even more like a job and less like an adventure.[11] The warrior ethic, the essence of traditional military virtues, which is said to be more frequently found in the combat elements of each service, could come to seem alien to an ever greater number of service men and women. Second, in today's fluid job market, devotion to large, hierarchical institutions may well become unusual, making it harder for young soldiers, sailors, airmen, and marines to form lasting bonds with their services.

Much of what we know about the gap between civilian and military values has been unfairly put on the shoulders of "Generation X," Americans born between 1965 and 1977 who make up nearly 70 percent of the armed forces. All in all, while the prevailing attitudes of Generation X-ers may not be ideal for military service, the success of today's force in a number of challenging operations shows that the Generation X volunteer and his or her younger siblings can become highly skilled service men and women, once they are recruited into the service from the booming economy.

However, even if Generation X is not itself the origin of the gap between military and civilian value systems, there nevertheless exists a real split between society and the military. Andrew Bacevich, a scholar and a former army officer, outlined the conservative view of the gap between the systems:

Traditional military professionalism—rooted in the ideal of the warrior as the embodiment of soldierly virtue—has also become an anachronism. It celebrates the group rather than the individual. It cherishes virtues such as self-sacrifice, self-denial, and physical courage that are increasingly alien to the larger culture. It clings to a warrior spirit that is deeply and perhaps irreducibly masculine. In short, orthodox notions of what is meant to be a soldier clash head-on with the imperatives of political correctness.[12]

He concludes that military officers have been slow to understand the attack on military culture and even slower to mount a defense of their culture, an important measure of operational effectiveness.

Part of the civil-military cultural gap stems from the inherent difference between typically individualistic, liberty-based civic values—which are tolerant of materialism, excessive individualism, and alternative life styles—and military values, which are built around such codes as the Army's "Duty, Honor, Country," or the Navy's "Honor, Courage, and Commitment." The study of American military culture in the twenty-first century by the Center for Strategic and International Studies lists the core military values as self-sacrifice, discipline, obedience to legitimate authority, physical and moral courage, a merit-based rewards system, and loyalty to and respect for comrades, unit, and nation. None of these is standard fare in the land of plenty. On the practical level, the armed forces have successfully bridged this cultural gap with training and socialization, but some writers, such as Tom Ricks, have written eloquently of the dysfunctional aspects of having a military that may believe that it is morally superior to its parent society.[13]

In the future, it is possible that this gap will shrink. Indeed, particularly (but not exclusively) in conservative circles, there has been a movement to return to basic values, suggesting that civilian values may be starting to shift in a direction that may be inherently more compatible with military culture.[14] At the same time, however, there is perhaps a more dangerous gap to worry about, one that is a natural outgrowth of the all volunteer force, which is now beyond its thirtieth birthday.

This gap might be called the "understanding gap." Before the adoption of an all volunteer force, the draft kept Americans familiar with military issues and lessened the tendency toward separatism within the military. Especially during times of large wars—such as World War II, the Korean War, and the Vietnam War—the nation generated large numbers of veterans who returned to civilian life familiar with military affairs. Today, not even a major conflict such as Desert Storm in 1991 could generate a significant number of new veterans who would then be returned to civilian life. Moreover, the clock is ticking for our current pool of veterans. While there are still 25.6 million veterans, they are largely senior citizens. The median age of a Vietnam veteran is more than 50 years, and his or her counterparts from the Korean War (median age: 66 years) and World War II (median age: 75 years) are well into their Social Security years.[15] All in all, the general public and much of the civilian elite is losing its capacity to relate on a personal level to what is happening in the military. Career military people may be similarly losing touch with the civilian world, although in the officer ranks, this is somewhat mitigated by the ubiquity of graduate schooling in civilian institutions and the numerical dominance of officers commissioned through the Reserve Officers' Training Corps in civilian colleges, as opposed to military academy graduates.[16]

The legislative and executive branches of the federal government are not immune to the effect of the graying of veterans. Although about half of U.S. senators are veterans, only about one-third of the younger House members have served in uniform. By many accounts, seats on the Senate Armed Services Committee and the House National Security Committee are no longer highly sought after.[17] In short, the military finds itself not only isolated from American society as a whole, but also isolated from the very leaders to whom it must turn for programmatic decisions in times of crisis.

A final source of pressure on American military culture is racial, ethnic, and gender-related strife. Volumes have been written on gender issues and associated adjustment problems in the male-dominated

military services. Much has been made of the effect of women on the warrior ethic, the divisive issue of sexual harassment, and the tradeoffs entailed by either mixed or single-sex basic training. Although military officials have from time to time been guilty of displays of political incorrectness,[18] what is often overlooked is the superior job performance of the vast majority of women in the service, as well as their excellent record on operations and deployments. Moreover, the addition of women to the volunteer pool—whatever its effects on the warrior ethic—has also kept recruit quality high. Indeed, if women were unavailable for service, one wonders whether the all volunteer force would be able to survive.

The former Chairman of the Joint Chiefs, General Henry H. Shelton, the former commander of the Special Operations Command and officer who exudes the warrior spirit, was recently questioned on this issue:

I was asked if . . . women were worth all the trouble they seem to cause the services. I must admit I was somewhat taken aback by the direction of the question. But my response was equally direct. The fact of the matter is that we simply could not do our mission today without the women who volunteer to serve their country. We need their talent, we need their numbers, and we need their leadership. There simply is no alternative.[19]

Most senior military personnel managers cannot imagine how they would recruit an all male force of the same size and quality (measured by such indicators as high school diplomas and upper-level mental categories) as the gender-integrated force that exists today. Indeed, given the recruiting problems discussed below, the presence of large numbers of women in the force may be even more essential in the future.

One final point: although the services have done well on racial integration and equal opportunity, one Army-wide survey on sexual harassment found that soldiers believe by a more than two-to-one ratio that ethnic or racial discrimination was more prevalent than sexual harassment in their unit.[20] Clearly, for all of their progress the services have not solved racial and ethnic problems in the force, despite very little recent coverage of these issues.

EFFECTS ON MILITARY CULTURE

In World War II, British wags noted that there were only three problems with American forces in England: "they were overpaid, oversexed, and over here." Today, America's all volunteer, mostly married force is overworked, underpaid, and "over there," performing relatively unfamiliar missions all over the world in the name of a public that respects its men and women in uniform but pays little attention to their problems. The effect of these pressures on the force and, potentially, on military culture are many.

First and foremost, the environmental pressures and management decisions have left many members of the force asking a few basic questions. Troops and officers—and even a few generals—have trouble separating what is important from what is essential. During the Cold War, men and women in uniform knew what the mission was and what being combat ready meant. Even if you had to move from the Fulda Gap to the Iraqi border to ply your trade, the expectations were still quite clear. Today there are a welter of missions and a degree of confusion over the purpose. If you are keeping a tenuous peace by walking patrols in Bosnia, you may feel put upon by being taken to Hungary for a tank gunnery exercise. The opposite may also be true. You may feel cheated by being taken off combat alert in the 82nd Airborne Division to spend a few months peacekeeping in the Sinai. Indeed, in the army's sexual harassment survey, 32 percent of the men and 55 percent of the women surveyed did not agree that the army's main focus should be on warfighting.[21] Part of that answer may result from shifting values and varied perspectives among the different types of units and between the genders, but part of it also stems from changes in what units are doing today or preparing to do in the months to come.

Still, the international environment and our strategic responses to it have been destabilizing for all ranks. For some troops, the new emphasis on peace operations over clear-cut combat operations is unsettling and antithetical to the traditional American way of war. As Andrew Bacevich writes:

The immediate purpose on which those soldiers embark bear small resemblance to high-minded crusades. Their task is not the lofty one of saving the world from totalitarianism but the necessary one of staving off disorder. As a result, their efforts will seldom yield the satisfaction of clear-cut victory. Nor will they culminate in the lasting peace . . . held up as the great object of American participation in world affairs. . . . Policing the imperium is a task for which there is no end in sight.[22]

An awesome burden falls on the shoulders of officers and noncommissioned officers, which is magnified many times over by a military culture that lionizes the role of the leaders and the unit commanders. However, leadership also has a context and is not simply an independent variable. By all accounts, leadership in the armed forces today may well be in need of improvement. Among the most common complaints from the field are: "up or out" officers must succeed in every assignment; stressed units and their commanders are afforded little freedom to fail; "zero defects" thinking and careerist behaviors are the rule. The public has also seen many—too many —cases of "sick" leaders who have fallen victim to the same diseases, such as sexual harassment, that they were supposed to cure in the first place.[23]

There is disturbing evidence that far too many leaders are not measuring up. For example, about 45 percent of the respondents in an Army-wide survey said their leaders "were more interested in looking good than being good." Only half of the respondents believed that their noncommissioned officers "would lead well in combat."[24] Even fewer of the respondents, a mere 40 percent, thought that their officers "would lead well in combat." A renowned leadership expert, a retired general officer with extensive troop experience, noted that "anecdotes about poor leadership, particularly at the field grade and general officer levels, are too persistent to ignore."[25]

RELIEVING THE PRESSURE

All of the factors noted above, individually but especially in combination, put intense pressure on the people in the military, the organizational climate of its units, and military culture. Although the armed forces have been in worse shape—during and right after Vietnam, for example—today's force is in a serious predicament. Even if the internal value structures that underpin military culture are largely intact, and the armed forces remain in the public's mind the most widely respected institution in the country, one cannot counsel complacency.[26] Without prompt and significant corrective measures, the culture will erode, the force will fail, and men and women in uniform may die. This will not happen tomorrow. But without corrective measures, it is a virtual certainty within a few years.

One recommendation concerns the training and educational institutions of the armed forces. These are not just places for communicating skills and concepts; they are the armed forces' mechanisms to communicate and reinforce its culture. If the services fail to treat these institutions as a top priority, they will weaken the culture that they are supposed to reinforce.

For example, the problems of the Aberdeen Proving Ground came about partly as a result of regarding that important training institution as "overhead" and assigning the minimum number of officers and senior noncommissioned officers to the staff and faculty there. In the Army, it is no secret that for regular officers, duty with recruiting units, the reserve components, or in basic or advanced individual training units has traditionally been looked down upon and is not a job for the best and brightest. At Aberdeen, the Army and America got less than they paid for, but they could have avoided the problems altogether if more and better officers and noncommissioned officers had been assigned to that critical mission. More attention to institutional training and the critical role of core values is needed. On this issue, all of the services should follow the example of the Marine Corps, whose commandant and his generals have made improving basic training a top priority.

In a similar vein, the services should reemphasize the critical role of culture, leadership, and ethics in their staff college and war college–level curricula. Just as the renaissance of the post-Vietnam army owed much to studies in leadership and strategy offered at the U.S. Army War College, today's armed forces would benefit from a professional military education at institutions that focus on these important subjects. Additionally, crimes by officers and noncommissioned officers remind us that culture-related institutions must continually emphasize the importance of ethical behavior. As a recent study on professional military education by the Center for Strategic and International Studies noted:

A string of recent misbehaviors . . . has caused some observers to wonder whether the uniformed services have lost their ethical direction. . . . If the ethical compass of the uniformed services is wavering or is seen to be, it must fall largely on the senior leadership and the PME [professional military education] system to recalibrate it, putting dynamic changes into a rational ethical context for officers.[27]

Another recommendation is for the armed forces to find ways to lower the pace of routine operations and training without downgrading the importance of peace operations or other activities designed to contribute to conflict prevention. Some good things have already happened in this area. For example, the services are more closely monitoring the effects of repetitive deployments on service members and their families. In 1997, citing waste and the tempo of operations, the outgoing chairman of the Joint Chiefs, General John Shalikashvili, reduced participation in joint training exercises by up to 25 percent and recommended to the chiefs that they follow suit in their own services.[28] Routine deployments to show the flag could also be reduced with little harm to national security.

To maintain a quality force, the nation must put more money into the defense budget to support modernization. At the same time, it must add funds for salaries, benefits, and housing for the men and women in uniform who constitute the keystone of our national security. For those living on the civilian economy far from a military installation, the extra pay will not come soon enough. A warning lies in the words of a sergeant major from the U.S. Southern Command, recently transplanted from Panama to Florida. He said about the life of his troops in the moderately expensive Miami area: "We are having big problems. . . . We have staff sergeants on food stamps. That's a damn shame. That really bothers my heart. These are people responsible for 10 to 40 men's lives, who can't afford to keep their families here."[29]

The current line is that we will be able to afford a higher degree of modernization and a better quality of life for the troops once management improvements and infrastructure reductions are taken care of. This has been said for years, and the public has always come away disappointed.

However, if an increase in the defense budget is not forthcoming, the secretary of defense will have to consider reducing the strength of the active armed forces. This measure will free up funds for modernization and improvements in the quality of life, but it may leave the United States short of forces in a major crisis while exacerbating deployment stress on today's men and women in uniform.

Finally, the armed forces, in league with the Veterans of Foreign Wars, the American Legion, and the service and military retiree associations, must work harder to create a dialog with the American people on civil-military concerns. This should be an important task for both active units, which have the most resources, and reserve units, which hold the keys to the communities in which they serve. "Telling the military story" should be a secondary specialty of every soldier, sailor, airman, and marine.

In the end, the armed forces must remain America's armed forces, but they must not do so at the expense of the military virtues that are needed to buttress operational effectiveness. Thankfully, the importance of monitoring the degree of evolution that military culture is undergoing has not escaped the view of our military leadership. As General Shelton, a chairman of the Joint Chiefs, noted:

Few issues can have greater significance for our armed forces, or for the nation, than how the military interacts with the society it serves and from which it is drawn. The values that define us as an institution dedicated to selfless service will remain the foundation of who we are, and what we do. Yet we must evolve and adapt to remain part of, and not apart from, the society we defend and protect.

NOTES

1. This definition is the one used as a working definition in a major study being prepared by the Center for Strategic and International Studies, "American Military Culture in the Twenty-First Century." This study will establish by more scientific methods, including a survey of fifteen thousand men and women in uniform, the state of the cultural and organizational climates in the armed forces today and ways of maintaining their future effectiveness. The findings in this essay should be considered preliminary in nature, a practitioner's view of causes and effects based on personal study and observation over the course of a military career spanning nearly 28 years. For a definition of culture, see also Edgar Schein, "Organizational Culture," *American Psychologist* 45 (February 1990): 111. Schein divides culture into observable artifacts, values, and basic underlying assumptions.

2. Schein, "Organizational Culture," 116.

3. William S. Cohen, *Report of the Quadrennial Defense Review* (QDR) (Washington, D.C.: U.S. Department of Defense, May 1997), 8–18.

4. John Shalikashvili, "The United States Armed Forces: A Prospectus," a speech to the Council on Foreign Relations, published in *National Security Studies Quarterly* 3 (Winter 1997): 98–100. See also Pat Towell, "Strain Showing as Military Tries to Do More with Less," *Congressional Quarterly Weekly Report* 56 (April 25, 1998): 1081–83. Data on the reserve forces come from a presentation by Major General James A. Andrews, U.S. Air Force, of the Office of the Assistant Secretary of Defense for Reserve Affairs, to the Cantigny Conference on "Citizens and Soldiers: The Responsibilities of Service in Twenty-First Century Democracies," Chicago, May 1, 1998.

5. See, for example, National Defense Panel, *Transforming Defense: National Security in the Twenty-First Century* (Washington, D.C.: National Defense Panel, December 1997), vii.

6. Ernest Blazar, "Inside the Ring," *Washington Times* (March 19, 1998): 10.

7. Headquarters, Department of the Army, *The Secretary of the Army's Senior Review Panel on Sexual Harassment,* Vol. 2 (Washington, D.C.: U.S. Department of the Army), A-30, question 83. In May 1998, the Senate Armed Services Committee also expressed its concerns about readiness and aging equipment. See George C. Wilson, "Cohen Finding It Difficult to Take the Hill for Clinton," *Legislate News Service* (May 15, 1998).

8. U.S. General Accounting Office data as cited in Ernest Blazar, "Inside the Ring," *Washington Times* (April 6, 1998): 8. For reports of Secretary of Defense Cohen's concerns on readiness, see Jon Anderson, "Cohen Takes Aim at Readiness," *European Stars and Stripes* (May 5, 1998): 1.

9. Department of the Army, *Review Panel on Sexual Harassment,* A-29, question 78.

10. U.S. Department of Defense, *Defense '97: Almanac* 5 (Fall 1997): 17–22; and other unpublished Department of Defense statistics provided to the author.

11. One interesting five-part newspaper series on the U.S. Army concludes that the transition has already taken place. F. Richard Ciccone et al., "Today's Army: Less an Adventure than a Job," *Chicago Tribune* (April 19, 1998): 1.

12. Andrew Bacevich, "Tradition Abandoned: America's Military in a New Era," *National Interest* 48 (Summer 1997): 22.

13. For a popular view that regards the gap as ominous, see Tom Ricks, "The Widening Gap between the Military and Society," *Atlantic* (July 1997): 66–78.

14. Various movements led by Colin Powell and others have centered on youth and the educational system, but there have been books and other movements, such as the Promise Keepers, that have addressed the issue as one of values and ethics. For one literary example, see the highly popular book by William Bennett, ed., *The Book of Virtues* (New York: Touchstone, 1996).

15. Unpublished statistics from the Department of Veteran Affairs, autumn 1997.

16. Some analysts see improvements in officers' civilian education as a source of greater military influence in defense decisionmaking. See Christopher Gibson and Don Snider, "Examining Post-War Civil-Military Relations: A New Institutionalist Approach," a working paper prepared for Harvard University's Olin Foundation, September 1996. As a veteran of Pentagon tours before and after the Goldwater-Nichols reforms, I agree that this phenomenon has had an influence on the internal civil-military balance in the Pentagon. However, the Goldwater-Nichols reforms set up procedures and powers to secure better and stronger military advice, which is bound to yield more influence. Compounding both of these phenomena, the Joint Staff—which gained from both better educated staff officers as well as from increased power through Goldwater-Nichols—has become the preeminent strategic and operational staff in the Pentagon.

17. Conversations with congressional staffers, April 1998.

18. For an extreme case of political correctness in the Air National Guard, see Matt Labash, "Pulling the Wings Off the Warriors," *Weekly Standard* (May 18, 1998): 22–30.

19. General Henry H. Shelton's remarks to the Defense Advisory Committee on women in the military, unpublished typescript, Reston, Virginia (April 24, 1998), 4.

20. Department of the Army, *Review Panel on Sexual Harassment,* A-29, questions 76, 77.

21. Department of the Army, *Review Panel on Sexual Harassment,* A-31, question 88.

22. Andrew Bacevich, "Tradition Abandoned," 20.

23. For an exhaustive list of crimes, misdemeanors, and the like, see Gregory Forster, "Confronting the Crisis in Civil-Military Relations," *Washington Quarterly* 20 (Autumn 1997): 21–23.

24. Department of the Army, *Review Panel on Sexual Harassment,* A-21, A-25, A-26, questions 38, 54, 61.

25. Walter F. Ulmer, Jr., "Military Leadership into the 21st Century: Another 'Bridge Too Far?'" *Parameters* 28 (Spring 1988): 6.

26. See the report on the Hart and Teeter polls in the *Washington Post* (March 24, 1997): 17; and material from the Council on Excellence in Government at www.excelgov.org.

27. Center for Strategic and International Studies Study Group on Professional Military Education, *PME: An Asset for Peace and Progress* (Washington, D.C.: Center for Strategic and International Studies Study, 1997), 8.

28. Remarks by General John M. Shalikashvili in his farewell policy speech to the National Press Club, September 24, 1997.

29. Christopher Marquis, "Miami's Costs Shock Southcom Soldiers," *Miami Herald* (May 11, 1998): 1.

PROFESSIONAL MILITARY EDUCATION:
AN ASSET FOR PEACE AND PROGRESS

CENTER FOR STRATEGIC AND INTERNATIONAL STUDIES STUDY GROUP ON PROFESSIONAL MILITARY EDUCATION

During a commencement address at the U.S. Military Academy, Secretary of Defense William J. Perry described a painting that hangs in a Pentagon corridor outside his office. A young serviceman is depicted praying with his family before leaving on an overseas deployment. Beneath the painting is the passage from Isaiah in which the Lord asks, "Whom shall I send? And who will go for us?" And Isaiah responds, "Here I am. Send me."

"At this critical point in our history, your nation has asked: 'Whom shall I send? Who will go for us?'" Perry told the assembled cadets of the West Point Class of 1996. "And you have answered: 'Here I am. Send me.' Your nation is grateful."

No one knows better than a secretary of defense how much will be asked of the young officers now entering service in the U.S. military. They represent the human capital that will sustain the global leadership of the United States and secure its role as the world's sole remaining superpower into the twenty-first century. The demands placed upon these officers, and the myriad challenges they will confront, have rarely been higher.

Since the end of the Cold War, for example, the rate at which the United States has sent its service members on deployments has increased by more than 300 percent. In 1996 alone, the nation deployed forces to operations in Bosnia, Haiti, Kuwait, Macedonia, Palestine, the Sinai, Turkey, the Western Sahara, northern Iraq, and the Taiwan Straits. Operations spanned the spectrum from disaster relief and peacekeeping to deadly combat.

By delivering that message at West Point, the secretary of defense underscored the critical role of the professional military schools in preparing officers to meet these increasingly complex challenges and cope with revolutionary changes in the military profession. Indeed, along with the Reserve Officer Training Corps (ROTC) and Officer Candidate School (OCS), the service academies represent a first, critical step in the long journey of the education of military officers.

That journey will span their entire careers, and include steps up a steep pyramid of learning known as professional military education (PME). Milestones along the way are likely to include primary education at officers' basic and advanced warfare specialty schools to prepare young officers for early command; intermediate education at the command and general staff colleges, in which promising majors and lieutenant commanders will redirect their gaze from small unit tactics to the operational level of modern warfare; senior education at the prestigious war colleges, in which the services groom their future leadership by immersing select lieutenant colonels, commanders, and full colonels in the study of theater-level operations, grand strategy, national security policy, and the intricacies of the civil-military relationship; and special courses for general and flag-rank officers, including the National Defense University's Capstone course and the Air University's Joint Flag Officer Warfighting Course.

An overwhelming majority of senior officers who aspire to the pinnacle of command will also acquire advanced civilian degrees to expand the breadth of their knowledge, or postgraduate degrees from such graduate-level military institutions as the U.S. Naval Postgraduate School, the Air Force Institute of Technology, or the Uniformed Services University of the Health Sciences.

The armed services cannot rely on "lateral entry" job applicants to fulfill their need for well-rounded military officers at each rank. Each level of competence in the art of warfare builds on previous levels of education and experience. Virtually all must work their way up from the bottom. In concert with an extensive training regime and an officer's operational experience, PME thus provides an essential framework on which the armed services mold the hierarchy of leadership.

With the end of the Cold War and subsequent reductions in U.S. military forces, however, it is natural to search for efficiencies and potential savings in all aspects of military operations. For many Americans, the threat of full-scale war now seems remote. Logic might also tempt an organization that has reduced its manpower by roughly one-third—while dramatically consolidating its force structure and number of worldwide bases—to consider commensurate reductions in enrollment at its educational institutions. A number of scandals in recent years also have raised questions about the tenor of ethical instruction and the overall educational environment in military schools, especially at the service academies.

This essay has been edited and is reprinted from Professional Military Education: An Asset for Peace and Progress *(Washington, D.C.: Center for Strategic and International Studies Press, 1997), ix–xi, 13–17, 21–25, 27–32, 38–39, 41–44, 51–55, 64, by permission of CSIS Press.*

The Center for Strategic and International Studies (CSIS) Panel on Professional Military Education was determined from the outset to address all of these issues. Part of the task we saw as descriptive. As the all volunteer military that was established in 1973 matures and now shrinks, the number of Americans who have direct experience serving in the military continues to decline. Policymakers in Washington increasingly must wrestle with the difficult decisions regarding the military education system without the benefit of personal military experience to inform them.

This report attempts to fill in some of the blanks on how the PME system works, including answering such basic questions as: With the end of the Cold War, what savings can realistically be expected from the PME system? What challenges still confront today's military forces? What are the unique demands of the military profession that dictate a tailored, formal, and continuing education to prepare officers to shoulder the progressive burdens and responsibilities of rank?

The panel also sought to assess the services' progress in implementing the Skelton Panel reforms of 1989, named in honor of Representative Ike Skelton, former chairman of the House Armed Services Committee's Panel on Military Education. The much-needed Skelton Panel reforms—a product of the first comprehensive congressional review of PME in the 200-year history of the Congress—flowed out of the landmark Goldwater–Nichols reforms. The Skelton Panel reforms focused primarily on strengthening the commitment of the armed services to "joint" military education, providing a more professional and highly qualified faculty, and increasing academic rigor in professional military schools. The accepted judgement of the Skelton Panel reforms is that no single military service will ever fight a war on its own. Modern technology leads to dominance on the battlefield only if the Army, Navy, Air Force, and Marine Corps can operate as a joint force.

Today, some argue that OCS and the ROTC can be substituted for the academies and that the advanced military education institutions can be eliminated. Eliminating the finest PME system in the world would be shortsighted in the extreme and would jeopardize our future as a nation. Our military education system needs to be reformed and enriched, not reduced or abolished. If we are to keep the standards of OCS and the ROTC (both of which have contributed so significantly to the success of our active forces, reserves, and National Guard), then we must have the professional base of education and training that only the service academies provide. At a time when there is such serious discussion of the crisis in the U.S. education system—it would be folly to weaken or abandon the academies.

The panel addresses specific areas in which we feel the PME system must improve to meet rapidly evolving challenges. Although the military education institutions have made great progress since the 1989 Skelton Panel reforms, more must be done to incul-cate a truly joint culture at all strata of the military profession. A series of recent controversies, meanwhile, suggests that service members are confronting increasingly complex ethical dilemmas for which they are inadequately prepared. The service schools and colleges must also do more to help the officer corps adapt to the rapid technological advances of the information age.

Can leadership and character really be taught? Can values be instilled? Plato was convinced they could. He set up his academy, which endured for centuries, not only to teach philosophy—that is, the love of wisdom—but also to build values and leadership. Our service academies have attempted for more than 100 years to teach leadership and character.

In today's armed services, the concern of General Edward C. Meyer, former Army chief of staff, about a "hollowing out" of military forces in the 1970s involves more than just readiness. It can involve a hollow spirit, a hollow quality of life, and, perhaps most dangerously, a hollow leadership. Military history repeatedly teaches us that it is better to have a small force that is well led than a force strong in numbers but weak in leadership. We must neither mute nor dilute the profession of arms.

This report suggests that steps in the right direction have been taken and are being taken, but that changing times require more attention and adjustment of the PME system. The human factor involves competence, leadership, and character. Our military institutions, long the finest in the world, try to teach all three. In our democracy, power relates to all three.

THE NEED FOR PME

In the lean years of the 1920s and 1930s following World War I, the U.S. military chose to invest heavily in education. That effort paid incalculable dividends when the services were forced to manage an enormous expansion and mobilization in preparation for World War II, with the command and general staff colleges and war colleges yielding the crop of U.S. officers that included Army Generals Dwight D. Eisenhower, George C. Marshall, Matthew B. Ridgway, Omar N. Bradley, Douglas A. MacArthur, Maxwell Taylor, George Patton, Joseph Stillwell, and Lucian Truscott; Marine Generals Alexander A. Vandegrift and Oliver P. Smith; Admirals Earnest King, Chester Nimitz, William F. Halsey, Raymond Spruance; and Army Air Corps Generals Hap Arnold and Hoyt Vandenberg.

No one suggests that the command and general staff and war colleges correctly anticipated the full impact of shifting strategic alliances and technological advancements during the 1920s and 1930s. They did, however, give students a common tactical language and an accepted methodology for solving problems.

"The Army Command and General Staff College unquestionably made a critical contribution to the winning of World War II, as virtually all its students attest," writes Charles E. Kirkpatrick.[1] "A graduate could function effectively on any Army staff, a price-less element of commonality in a largely citizen-soldier Army."

At the more senior war colleges, students prac-ticed and refined U.S. plans for a possible war against Japan and Germany. At the U.S. Naval War College, for example, the U.S. fleet crossed the Pacific to do battle with Japan's Imperial Navy 127 times in war games. By 1934, the Naval War College was advising the Office of the Chief of Naval Operations to plan for a 4-year conflict that would involve the progressive seizure of island bases in the Marshalls, Carolinas, and/or the Mariannas.

"The [war college] courses were so thorough that, after the start of World War II, nothing that happened in the Pacific was strange or unexpected except the kamikazes," remarked Admiral Chester W. Nimitz, a Naval War College graduate and commander-in-chief of the Pacific theater during World War II. Af-ter the Allied victory, no less a personage than British Prime Minister Winston Churchill posited that World War II was won in the U.S. war colleges in the 1920s and 1930s.

In the period following the trauma of Vietnam, the services once again relied heavily on their edu-cational institutions to help cope with change and to right a badly foundering military. At each step in the PME pyramid, agonizing self-appraisals were conducted into a military culture that had been cor-rupted during the war by the corrosive effect of body counts, careerism, racial tensions, rampant drug use, and impending political defeat in a war the American public no longer supported.

The service academies subsequently struggled to adjust to the antiauthoritarian generation that came of age in the 1960s and to such societal changes as the introduction of the first female cadets and mid-shipmen in 1976. Many young officers who served in Vietnam returned to the service academies as in-structors, grappling with these issues firsthand while trying to reconnect with a generation that would prove critical to the eventual success of the all volunteer force.

In sometimes brutally frank assessments, such as the Army War College's seminal 1970 *Study on Mil-itary Professionalism*,[2] the war colleges castigated the senior leadership for instituting a system of statis-tical measures (e.g., body counts, pacification charts) that, during the Vietnam conflict, were allowed to become ends in themselves. All of the schools also struggled with the strategic implications of a military that was turning its focus from the jungles of South-east Asia to deterring the Soviet Union and Warsaw Pact on the plains of Europe. Throughout this dif-ficult period, the armed services retained the proto-typical American belief in education and higher learning as the prime means to betterment for both organizations and individuals.

The end result was the education and advance-ment of a generation of officers who contributed sig-nificantly to winning the Cold War and to leading one of the most lopsided victories in U.S. history in the Persian Gulf War. In the example of such leaders as Generals Colin Powell and H. Norman Schwarzkopf —graduates of the National War College and Army War College, respectively—the country saw that an institution that had once been derided as a hotbed of antiintellectualism had become, by a number of qualitative and quantitative measures, the brightest and most highly educated force the United States had ever fielded.

Partly as the result of such enlistment incentives as the Montgomery G.I. Bill of 1984, which rewards enlistees for their initial tour of duty with significant stipends toward a college education, the standards were raised dramatically for the enlisted ranks as well. In 1980, for example, only 68 percent of enlisted per-sonnel had graduated from high school. Today, that figure stands at more than 95 percent, the highest level ever for the U.S. military. According to the Pen-tagon, the number of recruits scoring in the top two categories on the military's standard intelligence test doubled during the 1980s.

The officer corps has adjusted to the intellectual demands placed on it by a brighter and more inquis-itive rank-and-file with a renewed emphasis on PME and advanced academic degrees. "Whether you're talking about a general or a lieutenant, military lead-ers today are challenged by bright, capable soldiers who ask tough questions," said Representative Ike Skelton. "Gone are the days when a General Custer could tell his soldiers to get on their horses and ride without ever having to explain why. Maybe he *should* have had to explain."

In addition to adjusting to better-educated per-sonnel, today's officers are challenged by the demands of understanding and commanding the more tech-nologically advanced instruments of modern warfare. Toward this end, the service academies allow distin-guished graduates to pursue some graduate scholar-ship programs for study immediately following gradu-ation. The academies have been well represented in the more renowned programs, including the Rhodes, Marshall, Truman, Fulbright, and Guggenheim schol-arships. Each year, the academies send more than a hundred graduates directly to advanced programs. On a much larger scale, all of the services actively sup-port advanced degree programs for their officers. The Air Force and Navy have institutionalized their needs in the Air Force Institute of Technology (AFIT) and the Naval Postgraduate School, respectively. The AFIT Graduate School of Engineering is the thirty-eighth largest producer of advanced engineering degrees in the United States. In 1996, AFIT admit-ted 247 officers in residence and sponsored 244 in civilian universities. The Naval Postgraduate School admitted 498 officers in residence and sent 142 to civilian schools. Each year, the Army sends between four hundred and five hundred officers to civilian advanced degree programs. The services place a high value on the advanced education of their officer corps, particularly in the technical fields.

Graduate education in civilian institutions greatly benefits both the military profession and the society it serves. First, the officers benefit from the analytical skills and critical judgment found in civilian schools as contrasted with the traditional military practices and perspectives. Second, officers profit from their exposure to the diverse views of the society they serve. Conversely, society gains insight and understanding of the military and the professionalism of the officer corps. In 1973, only 24 percent of all officers had earned advanced degrees; by 1996, that number had increased to 38 percent. Another, more striking difference is that, in 1973, only 35 percent of lieutenant colonels and 46 percent of colonels in the Air Force had earned advanced degrees, compared with 90 percent of lieutenant colonels and 98 percent of colonels in 1996. According to a study by the Center for Creative Leadership in Greensboro, North Carolina, over 80 percent of Army officers selected for promotion to brigadier general have earned advanced degrees, compared with approximately 20 percent of their contemporaries in the corporate world. After giving intelligence quotient tests to more than 160 new brigadier generals, the Center for Creative Leadership also found that officers scored in the ninety-second percentile of the population, again ranking above corporate executives with comparable responsibilities.

The result is a command-level cadre of officers conversant in economics, international affairs, and the applied sciences, as well as in military strategy and tactics. Officers like General John Galvin, a professor and author with a master's degree in English literature who oversaw the peaceful deconstruction of the Berlin Wall as the former supreme allied commander in Europe. Or General Colin Powell, who earned a master's degree in business administration at the George Washington University before serving as national security adviser and then as chairman of the Joint Chiefs of Staff, managing successful combat operations in *Just Cause* and *Desert Storm*. Or General Wesley Clark, a Rhodes Scholar and presently commander-in-chief of Southern Command. Or Admiral James R. Stark, who earned his doctorate between commands and went on to become commandant of the Naval War College.

"Churchill said that World War II was won in the classrooms of U.S. military schools in the 1920s and 1930s," said retired General Edward C. "Shy" Meyer, CSIS Study Group panel member and former Army chief of staff. "And I think Desert Storm and the Cold War were won in the military classrooms and training centers during the 1970s and 1980s."

Today at the war colleges, the performance of Powell, Schwarzkopf, and the leaders of more recent peacekeeping deployments have been added to the annals of great battles and successful operations that students and martial scholars study and deconstruct. Those students then will graduate to command their own units, and thus the mantle of leadership is passed along through the PME system.

"I'm convinced that through the nation's war colleges and command and general staff schools, there is a linkage of leadership that passes down through history, from the great captains of the past such as General Omar Bradley, Admiral Chester Nimitz, and General Dwight Eisenhower, to the military leaders of today," said Representative Skelton.

After serving out a career in the military, many of those officers will continue to rise to the upper ranks of leadership in the U.S. government, following in the footsteps of President Eisenhower and former Secretary of State George C. Marshall, upon whose plan Europe was rebuilt in the aftermath of World War II. More recently, military leaders who have helped shape the country's fortunes as civilians include retired Lieutenant General Brent Scowcroft, national security adviser to two presidents; retired Admiral William J. Crowe, ambassador to the United Kingdom; retired General Barry McCaffrey, presently director of the Office of National Drug Control Policy; and retired Lieutenant General Julius W. Becton, a former director of the Federal Energy Management Agency, noted college president, and chief executive officer of the beleaguered Washington, D.C., public school system. In such leaders, the country continues to reap dividends from its investment in PME.

"For most men, the matter of learning is one of personal preference. But for [military] officers, the obligation to learn, to grow in their profession, is clearly a public duty," said the late General Omar N. Bradley.

PRECOMMISSIONING PME

Newly minted officers enter the active duty ranks through one of three primary paths, each of which represents an essential piece of the overall fabric of the U.S. officer corps. Officer Candidate Schools (OCS) or Officer Training Schools (OTS) are 13- to 14-week programs designed primarily to fill gaps in the officer corps, especially during mobilizations in response to a national emergency. ROTC has 2- and 4-year programs in military instruction designed to supplement the undergraduate curriculum at civilian colleges and universities.

The service academies—the U.S. Military Academy at West Point, New York; the U.S. Naval Academy at Annapolis, Maryland; and the U.S. Air Force Academy at Colorado Springs, Colorado—all offer intense 4-year programs of undergraduate study, military education and drill, organized athletics, and immersion into the military's ethic and culture.

Officer Candidate Schools/ Officer Training Schools

OCS and OTS can trace their origins back to two voluntary camps for undergraduate college students held just prior to World War I. Similar training camps eventually produced most of the officers for that conflict, and were expanded into OCS and OTS prior to World War II. Since that time, OCS and OTS have continued to provide the services with a high-intensity crash course for commissioning officers, especially in response to national emergencies and large-scale mobilizations.

By providing superior enlisted personnel and non-commissioned officers an avenue of entry into the officer corps, OCS also continues the military tradition of the battlefield commission for service members who have proved themselves in the enlisted ranks. Those selected for the Army's 14-week OCS course thus do not have to possess a college bachelor's degree. The philosophy is slightly different for the Navy OCS and Air Force OTS, which fill special requirements in the officer corps and generally demand a college degree. The Marine Corps OCS has programs for both college graduates and noncommissioned officers, and, in fact, OCS supplies the bulk of new Marine Corps officers.

Many OCS and OTS graduates commissioned as reserve officers compete for and win regular commissions and serve the country with distinction for full military careers—and beyond. General John W. Vessey began his Army service in the enlisted ranks but eventually became chairman of the Joint Chiefs of Staff. Retired three-star General Charles W. Dyke, now president of his own corporation, was selected as a private first class for Infantry OCS at Fort Benning, Georgia, and then went on to become 9th Corps commander headquartered in Japan. General Dyke's OCS classmate, retired Colonel William J. Taylor, a college dropout who enlisted in the Army, went first through 9 years of night school while serving in tank units and then through additional years of full-time graduate civilian schooling fully funded by the Army to earn his doctorate and become a professor and director of national security studies at West Point. Says Taylor, now senior vice president at CSIS: "Immediately after commissioning, I went to the Army Armor Officer Basic Course at Fort Knox, where I was placed in contact for the first time with peers from West Point. They became my role models in many ways, setting standards I was determined to achieve."

Reserve Officer Training Corps

Of the three avenues of accession, the ROTC has provided the armed services with the single largest pool of military officers for many years. In 1995, for example, 6,400 active duty officers were commissioned from ROTC programs, compared with 3,070 graduates from the service academies and 2,700 through OCS.

The military's heavy reliance on the ROTC for the bulk of its future officers and the presence of military officers and ROTC programs on hundreds of college campuses across the country represent one of the most critical and enduring bonds that link the all volunteer U.S. military with the American society from which it must draw its strength and, ultimately, its direction.

The roots of the ROTC program can be traced back to the mid-1800s, at which time its primary purpose was to provide officers for the reserve forces. Congress formalized the ROTC in 1916 in response to a lack of sufficient numbers of officers to conduct even the punitive expedition into Mexico that year. Every major conflict since that time has reinforced the fact that, during a mobilization, the country needs the ready pool of military officers—which only the ROTC can supply. To date, more than one million men and women have received their commissions through the ROTC.

Although the ROTC always supplemented the service academies in preparing students for commissioned service, the requirement of the Cold War for a large, standing military increased its importance in filling the active duty officer ranks. In 1964, Congress passed the ROTC Vitalization Act, which established 2- and 4-year scholarships and increased compensation for cadets. By enticing new officers into service from a much broader range of socioeconomic and geographical backgrounds, the ROTC helped shape the armed services into a more egalitarian force, highlighting the critical role the program plays in making the U.S. military a more accurate reflection of the American society it serves.

That influence is evident in the gradual loosening of the grip service academy graduates once held on the top ranks of the military hierarchy. In 1964, for example, fully 100 percent of the Army's four-star generals and 95 percent of its three-star generals were service academy graduates. By 1989, those percentages had dropped to 64 and 33, respectively. In fact, none of the last three Army officers to become chairman of the Joint Chiefs of Staff, the top uniformed position in the country, has been an academy graduate. In addition to OCS alumnus General Vessey, the preeminence of ROTC alumni Generals Colin Powell and John Shalikashvili should serve as encouragement to graduates from diverse commissioning sources.

Today's ROTC participants will supplement their undergraduate education with studies on basic soldiering skills, military history and organization, the principles of war, military ethics, and leadership development. For most participants, the instruction by carefully selected military officers will represent their first direct exposure to the unique culture and warrior ethic of their chosen branch of service. During at least one summer, ROTC cadets and midshipmen spend 4–6 weeks at a summer training camp. After completing both their undergraduate degrees and ROTC requirements, scholarship students are committed to serving in either the active duty or reserves, typically for 8 years.

As many experts have noted, each ROTC class that joins the active duty ranks strengthens the bond between American society at large and the professional U.S. military. "Because its graduates are so representative of the entire nation, ROTC is perhaps the most visible sign of the implied contract which exists between our society and its military forces," said Don Snider, a CSIS panel member and presently Olin Chair in National Security Studies at the U.S. Military Academy. "Especially in an all-volunteer force, ROTC represents a key foundation of the civil-military structure."

Just as society reaps benefits from investments in PME even after a service member leaves uniform, so too does value accrue from investments in ROTC programs. "I regard the military as an honorable and valuable career, whether for three years or thirty. ROTC plays a very important role in that career process," said D. M. Reid, senior vice president of the Xerox Corporation. "ROTC puts young men and women on a fast track faster, building their confidence early, developing their management skills early, and testing their leadership abilities early. That's good for the country."

As historians have noted, however, that critical relationship between the military and the country's youth is not without the tensions that surface from time to time on college campuses. During the Vietnam War, for example, a significant number of university faculties pressured their administrations to banish ROTC programs from their campuses. More recently, the controversy surrounding the military's general prohibition against the service of persons known to be homosexual led a number of prestigious schools to challenge the presence of ROTC programs on their campuses, including Dartmouth and the University of California. Harvard has cited the military's policy on homosexuals as the reason for its exclusion of an ROTC program from campus. Such controversies help explain why the services view the ROTC as a critical but not wholly reliable source of officer accessions.

Considering the drawdown in forces and budgets, the services also have been forced to cut their ROTC programs and scholarships. The need for ROTC-produced Army lieutenants has decreased from 8,200 in 1989, for example, to 4,500 in 1995, with a further reduction to 3,800 expected by 1998. Funding for Army ROTC will decrease from $159.1 million in FY92 to an estimated $128.8 million (in inflation-adjusted 1992 dollars) by FY01. As part of that reduction, the Army has been working to phase out fifty ROTC detachments across the country, closing eighteen in 1995 alone.

As the services reduce their ROTC programs, great care should be taken to ensure that the remaining pool continues to reflect the country's broad diversity. The ROTC has been particularly successful, for example, at the country's historically black colleges. ROTC graduates from these schools help the services ensure that, to the extent possible, the officer corps will reflect the broad diversity in the enlisted ranks.

Even though it will be tempting for the services to absorb cuts in the ROTC by eliminating their most expensive programs—specifically, programs at Ivy League or other elite schools—some experts believe such a strategy would prove short-sighted as well. "If they look only at a cost-analysis chart, the services could decide to eliminate ROTC programs at many of the more competitive campuses," said Charles Moskos, a panel member, leading military sociologist and professor of sociology at Northwestern University, and chairman of the Inter-University Seminar on Armed Forces and Society:

Though hard to quantify, however, there are tremendous benefits to both Princeton and the U.S. military of having an ROTC program on that campus, which may produce a disproportionate number of the nation's future civilian leaders. There's also evidence to suggest that the American people will only accept significant casualties in a future conflict when all socio-economic groups are suffering somewhat equally, and that means including elites in the military.

On reading the final draft of this report, panelist Samuel Williamson, president and vice chancellor of the University of the South, wrote, "The need to retain the ROTC programs at our best civilian institutions cannot be overstressed."

THE SERVICE ACADEMIES

The idea for a federally chartered and funded military academy to prepare students for the profession of arms can be traced back almost as far as the birth of the United States. The oldest academy, West Point, was established in 1802 during the administration of President Thomas Jefferson. Considering the focus on a core curriculum heavy in mathematics and engineering, a large number of early graduates became civil engineers and helped pave the way for the expansion of the young republic. Almost since their inception, the academies have provided the armed services with a core cadre of high achievers, many of whom have risen to the top ranks of military leadership and have stepped forward to guide U.S. armed forces in times of national crises.

From the moment they are mustered into formation at the beginning of the intense summer training session that precedes their freshman year at each of the service academies, students know they are in for an educational experience unlike any other. The next 6 weeks represent a rigorous indoctrination into a regime of military drill and study in preparation for an austere, extremely fast-paced, and stressful 4 years. Time management itself becomes a defining challenge for cadets and midshipmen, who must divide their energies among demanding academic courses, military drill, physical education, and organized athletics. Summers are devoted to training camps or are spent in the field with active-duty units.

Each of the service academies thus represents a crucible in which many future officers are fully immersed for the first time in the traditions, demands, and culture of the U.S. military. Some youths will find the spartan lifestyle and the warrior ethic onerous, and they will leave. Others will respond to the call to duty and sacrifice in service of a higher purpose.

"Though this is an institution of higher learning, it's not really like a college campus," a female cadet at West Point told the panel. "It's more of a carefully structured leadership environment. For four years, everything you learn is aimed at making you a better leader down the road." A senior male cadet responded similarly: "When you first arrive at the Academy, you don't understand why they make you shout out minutes, or cut the cake a certain way, or read the newspaper every day. There are times early on when you are so stressed out wondering why, why, why?" He went on: "Standing back, however, I now see that everything we do here has a purpose, even the tedious things I hated doing at the time. It's about building teamwork and camaraderie with your classmates."

Today, the service academies still represent a critical magnet for attracting and molding some of the country's most promising students. With 75 percent of academy appointments made by Congress, the student body also reflects the geographic and socioeconomic breadth of the country itself. This is significant, especially because the ROTC tends to be underrepresented in the Northeast. The military schools themselves consistently rate among the best in the United States. In 1994, for example, *Barron's Profile of American Colleges* rated all three academies in its "Most Competitive" category.

Few would argue that the service academies entice some of the brightest and most highly sought-after high school graduates in the country into the military. For example, the SAT scores at West Point and the Naval Academy for the class of 1993 averaged 1,213 and 1,241 (out of a possible 1,600), respectively—higher than comparative averages at such schools as Vanderbilt and the University of California at Berkeley.

By targeting and attracting some of the highest-achieving women and minority students in the country, the academies also have been critical in shaping an officer corps more reflective of the diversity in the enlisted ranks (30–40 percent minority and 5–13 percent female), a key goal of each of the services. From 1989 to 1992, for example, West Point set goals of recruiting 7–9 percent black students, 4–6 percent Hispanic, 2–3 percent Asians/Pacific Islanders/Native Americans, and 10–15 percent women.

As the armed services struggle to cope with the technological change heralded by the information age, they will have to use the service academies—with core curricula heavy in science, math, and engineering—to supply the top military technicians of the future. The percentage of Naval Academy graduates who serve as nuclear-qualified submariners, for example, is significantly higher than it is for ROTC graduates (37 percent versus 28 percent for ROTC and 28 percent for OCS); and in the Army, 53 percent of officers in the field of operation research and systems analysis are West Point graduates, as are 34 percent of those involved in research and development.

It is this ability to attract some of the brightest young Americans and inspire them to careers in the military that many senior officers view as the most essential contribution of the service academies. "As you look at this radically changing world in new ways, you realize that a very high-quality education system remains critical to attracting and developing the kinds of young people we need," said Admiral William Owens, the recently retired vice chairman of the Joint Chiefs of Staff and a panel adviser. "We can't start slicing into educational institutions such as the service academies, because they are the crown jewels in terms of our ability to face a revolutionary future."

The services are convinced that each graduating academy class represents a core cadre of extremely bright young officers fully steeped in the military culture of selfless duty, honor, and sacrifice, conversant in academic backgrounds relevant to a high-technology military, and reflective of the diversity apparent in the enlisted ranks. Around that assured cadre of young standardbearers who can rally others by their example, the services believe they will have a better chance of assembling a rounded officer corps for the future.

"The service academies have more than paid for themselves in leadership and on the battlefield. There's no bar chart, pie chart, or graph that will show that," claimed Representative Ike Skelton. "We need these schools as an anchor for each service, to set the standards for all officers."

Ethics, Morality, and the Honor Code

Considering the extraordinary power they wield in a free society—and the unique responsibility to prepare service members to use violence, if so commanded, in the service of the nation—the armed services necessarily place tremendous emphasis on virtues such as truth, honor, and selfless duty. Helping establish and reinforce that ethos remains a prime function of the PME system.

From their first day at a service academy, for example, cadets and midshipmen are indoctrinated in the traditional military values of duty, honor, and integrity. Each of them signs an honor pledge promising not to lie, cheat, or steal. As military officers they accept a strict moral code that condemns drunkenness, adultery, and other such "conduct unbecoming an officer."

It is largely for this reason that the public holds the service academies to a higher standard, an exalted expectation that the academies themselves encourage. The reputation of the academies, however, has been undermined in recent years by a string of scandals, including incidents of cheating, drug abuse, theft, and sexual harassment. Although it is not clear that the incidence of such misconduct actually has risen in any quantitative sense, the scandals have caused many observers to wonder whether the ethical compass at the academies is wavering from true north.

Finding an answer to that question, or identifying a common thread connecting the various incidents, is not easy. It is worth noting, however, that all armed forces are a mirror image of the societies they serve, reflecting their strengths and sometimes magnifying their weaknesses. The weakness evident in a number of the recent scandals at the service academies, say administrators, is a growing moral relativism.

"If you look at American society in general, you increasingly see an attitude that as long as you don't break the law and go to jail, whatever you're doing is OK," said Admiral Charles Larson, superintendent at the Naval Academy. "When Americans make a mistake, they tend to hire a lawyer to try and get them off, rather than stand up for what is right and honorable. So now we realize we have to construct that ethical foundation, so that everyone understands our values."

In recent years, the Naval Academy alone has endured scandals involving cheating, drugs, and sexual harassment; its officials even uncovered evidence of student involvement in a car theft ring and a murder. The school's response has been to develop a detailed, 4-year character development program based on the West Point model that reinforces fundamental ethics. Naval Academy officials consider the program their top priority.

In response to sexual harassment complaints, the Naval Academy also has devoted roughly half its character development curriculum to human relations courses. Each company of midshipmen also elects a human education resource officer, who receives extra training in counseling, conflict resolution, and diversity.

As part of its reforms in response to Tailhook—a scandal in which a small number of naval aviators closed ranks to thwart investigations into 140 complaints of sexual harassment at a Las Vegas convention—the Naval Academy also has begun stressing in mandatory ethics courses that an officer owes a greater allegiance to the service and its ideals than to class or shipmates. "What you find is that the tough ethical choices are not between good and evil, but rather between two goods: in this case, between loyalty and truth," said Larson. "And certainly a weakness in the past was that we probably put too much weight on classmate and shipmate loyalty, and not enough on higher loyalties."

To clarify an officer's responsibilities, the Naval Academy now teaches a hierarchy of loyalties: to the Constitution, the country, the Navy, the ship and the shipmate, and finally, to self. "And as you go down that hierarchy, the loyalty should always be to the higher standard," said Larson, who notes that virtually all of the recent scandals were first revealed by midshipmen reporting violations through the honor system. "We teach that if your shipmate or classmate violates our ethics and values, then he's betrayed you, and thus no longer deserves your blind loyalty."

The challenge of constructing a sound ethical foundation is not, of course, limited to the Naval Academy. The Air Force Academy has adopted a similar character development program. Administrators at West Point have found it necessary to reemphasize ethics throughout the curriculum as well, beginning with a cadet's first days on campus.

"It's generally accepted here that the people who walk through our gates and report that first summer are coming from a society that has more diverse views on basic values than in the past," said Colonel Anthony Hartle, vice dean at West Point. "That doesn't mean we lower our expectations, but it does mean we have to make certain values clear that perhaps we didn't have to emphasize as much in the past."

That emphasis permeates a cadet's 4-year experience at West Point, from the signing of the Cadet Honor Code and the taking of 50 hours of substantive instruction in honor and ethics to serving on Cadet Honor Education Teams and on Honor Boards that decide the academic fate of fellow cadets charged with misdeeds, which can range from plagiarism to outright lying or cheating. Out of an average of 120 investigations into wrongdoing launched at West Point each year, roughly forty will result in an Honor Board hearing. Punishments range from reprimands to suspensions and even expulsions.

"Sitting on an honor board is where the Honor Code ceases to be lip service and becomes real. I learned more about honor sitting on one board than in 35 hours in class," one West Point cadet told panel members. "The whole experience forces you to examine how dear you really hold these values. Enough to sit in judgment of someone else? For many of us, sitting on an honor board is the defining moment of our cadet careers."

The extent to which the ideals of duty and honor permeate the service academy environment is also revealed in the comments of a cadet who transferred from another college after having served an enlisted tour. "The immersion into such a stressful environment, with a code that you can cling to, has had an incredible effect on me," the cadet told the panel. "When I was at my first college, I cheated and lied. Now I can never imagine lying either here or in my military career. I've come to understand this as a code of conduct that I will always strive toward."

As noted in several reports, a number of recent misconduct incidents have involved sexual harassment. The panel on military education thus strongly supports two major steps that West Point has adopted to limit instances of sexual harassment or abuse of cadets by upper classmen and instill a sensitivity toward classmates from different ethnic, racial, or gender groups.

In 1990, West Point, under Superintendent David Palmer, officially abandoned the old Fourth Class Plebe System that had existed at the Academy for 150 years, which included a level of institutionalized hazing of subordinates, especially of the freshmen (or "plebe") class. Freshmen no longer are required to sit at attention and shout at mess, nor are they to be yelled at in a demeaning manner by upperclassmen. Upperclassmen also have abandoned the practice of stopping any plebe for extracurricular grilling and punishment; disciplinary action now is limited to a plebe's direct chain of command.

In place of the old system, the academy, under Superintendent Howard Graves from 1991 to 1995, substituted the Cadet Leader Development System. It emphasizes the development of each class, rather than the focusing of all three upper classes on the plebes. The principles of the new system, spelled out in a handbook given to all cadets, are based on the emerging science of leader development. One of its main points is a greater respect for the dignity of all subordinates and consideration for others, including the freshmen class.

One failing of the old system, say experts, was that it created significant potential for abuse and harassment of anyone who stood out from the crowd, including minorities and women. "A byproduct of the old plebe system was that it could result in an insensitivity to subordinates in general, and that is just less tolerated today than in the past, not only in the Army but in American society," said retired Lieutenant General Walt Ulmer, a panel member, former commandant of West Point, and former president of the Center for Creative Leadership.

"A lot of people thought we changed the 4th Class System because of concerns female cadets couldn't take it, but in fact our major concern was that the upper class cadets were practicing inappropriate leadership that would never be tolerated in today's Army," said Don Snider, panel member and Olin Chair in National Security Studies at West Point. "Why practice a model of leadership for three years that is inappropriate in the Army?"

Officials at both the Naval Academy and Air Force Academy say they have followed West Point's lead, substituting a leader development program for the old Fourth Class Plebe System. In addition to severely limiting the excesses of the old system, West Point officials also have begun requiring a program that includes more than 60 hours of instruction in Consideration of Others. The approach highlights the need for officers who have a basic respect for human dignity and a commitment to treating people fairly, especially subordinates. "I think it's important to emphasize consideration for others, because we tend to forget sometimes that just because everyone looks the same in their uniform, we're not the same," a female West Point Cadet told Panel members:

With the majority of the campus being male, for instance, there can be a tendency toward rowdiness. It's important to keep an eye on the line where that becomes rudeness. So while in the past it may have been easy to ignore conflicts arising from issues of gender or race, now people speak out more about behavior that bothers them.

Duty Obligation, Faculty, Joint Approach

Both through its appointment authority and direct oversight via Boards of Visitors panels, Congress has taken an active hand in guiding the service academies since their founding, and recent legislation and reforms have continued that tradition. In the past few years, Congress has made its concerns evident in such areas as the length of active duty obligation assumed by graduates and the types of commission they receive; the correct mix of civilian and military faculty at the academies; and what some perceive as the undue influence of varsity athletics, and concerns that athletic competition between the academies may lead to a parochial mindset at odds with the joint culture promoted by the 1986 Goldwater-Nichols reforms and by the Joint Chiefs of Staff.

Intent on seeing the services maximize the country's considerable investment in the service academies, in 1989, Congress raised from 5 to 6 the number of years service academy graduates must serve on active duty, beginning with the class of 1996. Because the active duty obligation was reduced back to 5 years by the 1996 National Defense Authorization Act, however, no academy class actually incurred a 6-year obligation.

Although the free education and monetary allowance granted by the academies represent a significant enticement, service academy leaders were concerned about the extension's effect on recruitment. It is worth remembering, they note, that young men and women contemplate the service academy experience from the perspective of teenagers. Looking beyond their personal horizons as far as 10 years into the future may have been daunting. Academy leaders were particularly worried that the extension would hurt recruitment of highly qualified women and minority students, who are aggressively recruited by other institutions of higher education.

In the FY92 National Defense Authorization, Congress also ordered that all officers commissioned after September 30, 1996, receive reserve commissions, reversing the practice of automatically granting academy and some exemplary ROTC graduates regular commissions. Especially during a military drawdown, proponents of the move argued that it would level the playing field between academy and ROTC graduates.

Proponents of granting regular commissions to service academy graduates generally see the practice as recognition of the extra effort required during the attainment of a 4-year academy education. As noted in a recent Congressional Research Service report on the academies, Congress virtually has eliminated the distinction between regular and reserve commissions over the past few years in terms of tenure or as protection from a reduction in force. Nevertheless, if legislation more closely equates the service academies with the ROTC, some fear it will represent the opening round toward the elimination of the traditional academy system.

In 1993, Congress also passed legislation calling for West Point and the Air Force Academy to increase their civilian faculty, to bring the faculty mix in line with the Naval Academy, which has an approximate even split between civilian and military instructors. The move follows criticisms by a number of civilian academic associations that uniformed instructors (which in 1991 accounted for 97 percent of the faculty at both West Point and the Air Force Academy) generally did not have doctoral degrees, the basic educational qualification for faculty at civilian colleges. Others have argued that increasing the number of civilian faculty would broaden the viewpoints expressed at the service academies and combat any insularity that could result from inbreeding a purely military faculty.

Although both West Point and the Air Force Academy have begun increasing the proportion of civilians on their faculties with an aim to reach 25 percent by 2002, academy leaders are deeply ambivalent about moving toward an evenly split or preponderantly civilian faculty. Doctorates may be essential to civilian colleges that put great emphasis on research and a "publish-or-perish" philosophy, they argue, but the service academy experience puts far greater weight on mentoring and role models.

Military instructors are rated high for their accessibility to students and willingness to provide instruction and support in athletics and leadership development well beyond the confines of an 8-hour day. For students who may have had little exposure to the military culture, carefully selected uniformed instructors also serve as critical role models and offer an ideal toward which students intent on a career in the military can strive.

Most agree that the service academies should play a role in creating a joint culture. The Goldwater-Nichols Act and Skelton Panel reforms largely have been a success, with interservice coordination and cooperation at all-time highs. The services must do more, however, to instill a deep and abiding devotion to a joint culture even at the precommissioning level. "The goal is that every student should be sufficiently exposed to another service to grasp the idea that they are a member of the U.S. armed forces first, and a member of their specific service second," said Dr. Adam Yarmolinsky, a PME Steering Committee member and regents professor of public policy at the University of Maryland. "That will require them to spend time at another service academy at some point in their undergraduate education."

INTERMEDIATE-LEVEL PME: COMMAND AND GENERAL STAFF COLLEGES

The intermediate command and general staff colleges trace their roots back to the 1800s, when the industrial revolution began to reshape the conduct of warfare forever. Dramatically more lethal weapons could be mass produced. Railroads were capable of moving incredible loads of war material and troops over greater distances in shorter periods of time. Ironclad ships proclaimed the ascendance of steam over sail. A nascent telegraph system heralded a new age of "instant" communication. All of these advancements conspired to make war a complex science and warfighting a profession requiring intensive study by devoted practitioners.

As the bellwether of this change, the Civil War convinced many military leaders of the need to establish an education system for mid-career officers. The Army's School of Application for Infantry and Cavalry was established in 1881 at Fort Leavenworth, Kansas, becoming the forerunner for the Army's Command and General Staff College. The Naval War College followed in 1884 at Newport, Rhode Island, sprouting a College of Naval Command and Staff in 1923 for intermediate-level officers. In 1920, the Marine Corps established the Field Officer Course, which grew into the Marine Corps Command and Staff College at Quantico, Virginia. In 1926, the Air Corps Tactical School was founded at Maxwell Field, Alabama, and eventually evolved into the Air Command and General Staff College and the Air War College. In 1946, the Armed Forces Staff College

was founded at Norfolk, Virginia, to provide a joint education counterpart to the service staff colleges.

Today, each of the intermediate service colleges offers selected mid-grade officers—generally majors and lieutenant commanders with more than 11 years of service—a chance to step out of the field and the realm of small-unit tactics and into an academic environment for 10 months to study the larger operational sphere of warfare. Having mastered field command and small-unit tactics, students prepare themselves to command larger units, such as battalions, brigades, or air squadrons, and to serve as principal staff at higher-echelon headquarters, including division, air wing, battle group, and corps. The intermediate service schools must satisfy the first of two phases of the Program for Joint Education, so students also become familiar with multiservice forces used in joint and combined operations.

The focus at the intermediate service colleges includes both the tactical and operational levels of warfare, with the core curriculum including study in both micro- and macro-level military operations. At the Army Command and General Staff College, for example, students study the history and theory of war, leadership and command principles, military law, and the resourcing and logistics necessary to support joint-service operations. Their counterparts at the College of Naval Command and Staff explore the employment of maritime forces in support of joint operations. At the Marine Corps Command and Staff College, the focus is on amphibious operations and employment of Marine air-ground task forces, and the Air Command and Staff College highlights the integration of the air component into joint operations. All of the schools emphasize the role of professional ethics in military command and operations.

Although it makes up a part of the National Defense University, the intermediate-level Armed Forces Staff College (AFSC) occupies a unique niche in the PME system. Officially established in 1946, the AFSC was designed from the outset to focus officers on the demands of the joint arena. Uniformed leaders in World War II had noticed the need for such an education during complex multiservice and coalition operations. "There is a need for a school which will conduct short courses in joint staff technique and procedure in theaters and joint overseas operations," said General Dwight D. Eisenhower in a 1946 memorandum on the AFSC.

After the Skelton Panel reforms of 1989, the AFSC course was designated as the second phase of the Program for Joint Education. For 12 weeks, officers work in seminars whose participants are evenly divided among the services. The need to depend on one another's service-specific expertise to solve problems typical to a joint operation helps participants grow as a multiservice team. Outside of a real-world operation, AFSC officials believe no other experience or educational institution challenges young officers to design, deploy, and sustain a joint military force. The final exam at the AFSC is a simulated

3-week war game that pits seminar teams against an opposing force in a real-world scenario.

Because the intermediate staff colleges provide the foundation for an officer's expertise in his or her service's core capabilities, increasing the joint curriculum and study will cause natural tensions. Considering the overarching importance of instilling a joint culture at every PME level, however, the panel is convinced by arguments made by the chairman's Panel on Joint Professional Military Education that more should be done to make the intermediate service colleges the primary source of comprehensive joint military education. Graduates of the intermediate staff colleges eventually should be prepared for most joint assignments.

SENIOR PME

THE SENIOR SERVICE COLLEGES

The senior service colleges are the wellspring from which the services draw their future leadership. The student body represents carefully selected officers at the lieutenant colonel/colonel or commander/captain level (16–22 years of service). Because most attendees have completed successful command tours in major units, the focus at the war colleges is on the strategic level of warfare.

For 10 months, students learn not only about the integration of their service into joint operations and multinational warfare, they also study the role of the military as one instrument of national security among a pantheon that includes political, diplomatic, intelligence, and economic structures. The critical civil-military relationship is explored in depth, as officers learn their role in a hierarchy of national command in which ultimate authority rests with senior political leaders. Graduates eventually will assume high-level command, staff, and policy responsibilities in the national security arena.

In keeping with their emphasis on the theater level of warfare and decisionmaking in the macro-realm of national security strategy, the war colleges strive to create officers who know *how* to think as opposed to *what* to think. Real-world case studies are the preferred method of instruction, and officers are encouraged to offer creative solutions and "out-of-the-box" thinking in response to demanding problems and scenarios. There are rarely right or wrong answers, only reasoned judgments and sound analyses. The aim is to produce mentally agile officers capable of thinking creatively in response to complex problems, often in dangerous and uncertain environments.

The influences of the war colleges are evident in the upper ranks of the military today. In Bosnia, for example, many U.N. officials and Western diplomatic personnel have remarked on the fact that the U.S. officers in command of the NATO Implementation Force frequently offer the most creative approaches to problems that have civilian managers throwing up their hands in frustration. "Their [military officers'] organizational and management skills make us look like kids selling lemonade on a Sunday afternoon," a Western ambassador in Bosnia told one reporter for the *Washington Post*.

The need for institutions of advanced military education for more senior officers can be traced back to the 1800s and the dawn of the industrial revolution. The College of Naval Warfare was established in 1884 at Newport, Rhode Island. The Army War College followed in 1903, later moving to its present home at Carlisle Barracks, Pennsylvania. As mentioned earlier, war college graduates were judged by many experts as critical to turning the tide in World War II. When the Air Force became a separate service in 1947, the Air War College evolved from the Army Air Forces University at Maxwell Air Force Base in Alabama. In 1990, the Marine Corps War College was founded at Quantico, Virginia.

The National War College—part of the National Defense University at Fort McNair in Washington, D.C.—grew directly out of the experiences of World War II. From its founding, the school has focused on the integration of all military services into the greater scheme of national security. Students are drawn from all quarters of the national security apparatus, from military officers to career foreign service officers. The emphasis is on grand strategy and the use of the military as a tool of statecraft in both wartime and peace. Graduates receive a master's degree in national security strategy and qualify for completion of both phases of the Program for Joint Education. Studies show that 36 percent of the student body will go on to achieve general or flag rank status.

As is the case with all the schools with phase two accreditation in the Program for Joint Education, the student body of the National War College is essentially split among the services (25 percent each Army, Air Force, naval services, and government civilian). Officers at these schools thus form close personal relationships with one another and their counterparts in other services that can become critical in future crises. Students form into teams for intramural softball, for example, to cement these relationships and promote teamwork. During the tense initial months of *Desert Shield*, Chairman of the Joint Chiefs of Staff General Colin Powell was delighted to discover that both the air component and Army component commanders during the crisis—General Chuck Horner and General John Yeosock, respectively—were former softball teammates and fellow students in the National War College class of 1976.

Besides the war college, the National Defense University also operates the Industrial College of the Armed Forces (ICAF). A successor of the Army Industrial College established in 1924, the ICAF was founded in the recognition that modern wars would be won or lost largely on the effective mobilization of the industrial base. Today this joint school prepares a specially selected group of military officers and government civilians for senior positions managing industrial capability and natural resources in support of national security strategy. The emphasis is on the unique demands of resourcing a national security strategy in a democracy, especially in a post–Cold War environment with rapidly declining defense budgets and a shrinking industrial base.

Although former ICAF graduate General Dwight D. Eisenhower drew on the expertise gained at the school and his wartime experiences to warn of the power of the "military-industrial complex," the former supreme allied commander also knew that this "arsenal of democracy" was instrumental in winning World War II.

Each of the senior service colleges also serve as critical research laboratories and archives of specialized knowledge and core competitiveness for their respective services. It is for this very reason that suggestions to consolidate the war colleges miss the point. To cite just a few examples, the Army War College's Strategic Studies Institute conducts regular analyses of innovative warfighting concepts for the Office of the Deputy Chief of Staff for Operations and Plans, and the Center for Strategic Leadership conducts war games and simulations. The Naval War College's Center for Naval Warfare Studies, meanwhile, offers the Global Game series, which places members from all strata of the national command authority in the largest and most comprehensive war game in the world. The Air University offers a College of Aerospace Doctrine, Research, and Education to test new theories on the application of air power.

The senior service colleges provide critical continuing education for select officers who are about to accept high-level command and staff responsibilities. Because there is a clear, de facto link between education and advancement in rank in today's military, acceptance to a war college also serves as a key milestone in an officer's career, enhancing his or her reputation and status within the military organization.

FELLOWSHIPS

Each year, the services assign selected officers to 1-year fellowships at graduate schools, in civilian think tanks, in high-level Department of Defense study groups, or in other government departments and agencies. The assignment to a fellowship is in lieu of a senior service college and is considered the equivalent to that level of military education. The intent of this program is to allow in-depth study of specific issues and exposure to high-level policy and decisionmaking. Each program has a different focus, but all are intended to expose the selected officers to nationally and internationally known academicians and policy analysts, leaders of industry, and senior government officials.

The hands-on experience obtained in these fellowships cannot be replicated in the classroom. The direct exposure and involvement in how policy is analyzed, shaped, implemented, and evaluated is invaluable in preparing officers to move up into the policy-related levels of their respective services, or in preparing them to work with other governmental and civilian organizations.

Examples of the organizations to which officers are assigned are the U.S. Congress, CSIS, the Brookings Institution, the Council on Foreign Relations, the Kennedy School of Government at Harvard University, the Foreign Service Institute, the Rand Corporation, the Chief of Naval Operations Strategic Studies Group, the Mershon Center, and the Fletcher School of Law and Diplomacy.

These fellowships complement the total PME packages for the services by offering a unique opportunity for future leaders to gain critical understanding of U.S. national security policy and process. Additionally, the organizations involved gain an empirical understanding of the uniformed services and current operational considerations. The combined benefit of these fellowship programs is significant for the selected officers, their services, and the U.S. national security policy community.

CAPSTONE

One of the final steps in the military's pyramid of professional education is Capstone, a 6-week course for all officers nominated to general or flag rank. Originally created as a voluntary program in 1982, the Capstone course became mandatory as a result of the Skelton Panel reforms of 1989. Taught at the National Defense University, the course emphasizes the military's role as only one arrow in the quiver of national security strategy. Participants are typically briefed by members of Congress, the Department of State, members of the National Security Council, the chairman of the Joint Chiefs of Staff, and representatives of the national media. Field trips are also made to visit commanders-in-chief at geographic commands around the world.

Strategic issues are stressed in Capstone, as are the relationships between senior military leaders and other members of the national security apparatus at home and abroad. National Defense University officials believe the ease that former graduates have shown briefing the media during real-world crises in recent years, for example, is partially the result of their Capstone exposure. "The officers we get are typically good already at briefing other military types, but we try and teach them about briefing civilians who don't have the same depth of understanding of military matters," said one Capstone director.

CONCLUSION

The institutions of PME have made great progress since the 1989 Skelton Panel reforms, yet more must be done to inculcate a truly joint culture at all strata of the military profession, to prepare the country's military leaders to confront increasingly complex ethical dilemmas, and to help the officer corps adapt to the rapid technological advances of the information age.

In these times of military downsizing, the history of the interwar period of the 1920s and 1930s should teach us that the armed services should not cut education to mirror cuts in force structure. On the contrary, the greater the cuts in force structure, the more vital the PME system. The country must prepare its officers to think smarter, not richer. The CSIS study panel is convinced that the senior congressional and military leadership understands this and, with attention to the recommendations in this report, will be able to meet the many challenges the country faces in maintaining comparative military advantages in strategy, force structure, doctrine, and training over those who would challenge the country's security interests in the new millennium. U.S.

officers of character, leadership, and values, properly trained in their rapidly changing profession of arms, would offer no less.

NOTES

1. Charles E. Kirkpatrick, "Filling the Gaps: Reevaluating Officer Education in the Inter-War Army, 1920–1940," paper presented at the American Military Institute Annual Conference, Virginia Military Institute, April 14, 1989.

2. *Study on Military Professionalism* (Carlisle Barracks, Pa.: U.S. Army War College, June 30, 1970).

MILITARY UNDERGRADUATE SECURITY EDUCATION FOR THE NEW MILLENNIUM

DANIEL J. KAUFMAN

Whatever one might think about the nature of the post–Cold War international environment, one conclusion seems certain: the demands placed on the leaders of the nation's military services have grown in scope and complexity. These demands extend well beyond the traditional service responsibilities for fielding well-trained and equipped forces to carry out combat or other types of operations. Today, service members are engaged in a host of activities that range from teaching military officers in the nations of the former Soviet Union the role of the military in a democracy to [combat operations in] Iraq.

The brief history of the post–Cold War period has reinforced the need for military officers who are not only technically and tactically proficient, but well versed in strategy, culture, information systems, and decisionmaking as well. How will the military services acquire such leaders? What should newly commissioned officers know about national security affairs? The purpose of this essay is to examine the role and desired nature of national security undergraduate education, focusing on the programs of the three major service academies.

The military services of the United States acquire their newly commissioned officers from one of three sources: Officer Candidate Schools, the Reserve Officer Training Corps (ROTC), or the service academies. (A very small number of officers—usually specialists, such as doctors—receive a direct commission.) Officer Candidate Schools are 13- to 14-week programs designed primarily to fill shortfalls in

the officer corps, particularly during mobilizations in response to a national emergency. ROTC consists of 2- to 4-year programs in military instruction designed to supplement the undergraduate curriculum in civilian colleges and universities. The majority of new officers who enter the services each year are commissioned through ROTC. The service academies —the U.S. Military Academy at West Point, New York; the U.S. Naval Academy at Annapolis, Maryland; and the U.S. Air Force Academy at Colorado Springs, Colorado—are 4-year undergraduate degree-granting programs that include an intense program of military training and professional development in addition to the academic curriculum. Each academy provides approximately nine hundred to a thousand commissioned officers to its respective service each year. The focus of this essay is on the national security education programs at the service academies. Every ROTC program requires the study of military science; however, curricular requirements and content, to include those in security studies, are determined by the individual school.

NATIONAL SECURITY EDUCATION AT THE UNDERGRADUATE LEVEL: PURPOSE, FOCUS, AND SCOPE

It seems clear that a national security education program at the undergraduate level is necessary for all three services. In fact, one could make a compelling argument that such a program is one of the

Daniel J. Kaufman, "Military Undergraduate Security Education for the New Millennium," in Educating International Security Practitioners: Preparing to Face the Demands of the 21st Century International Security Environment, *James M. Smith, Daniel J. Kaufman, Robert H. Dorff, and Linda P. Brady (Carlisle Barracks, Pa.: U.S. Army War College, 2001), 7–20. Public domain.*

reasons why West Point and its sister academies should continue to exist. If any undergraduates, anywhere, should study national security, it is surely cadets and midshipmen at the federally funded service academies.

The United States retains interests throughout the world, and threats to those interests have not disappeared with the collapse of the Soviet Union. In some measure, traditional threats remain. There are still states that oppose U.S. national interests in important regions of the world. The proliferation of modern military weaponry and the possible spread of weapons of mass destruction have raised the potential costs of regional conflict. On another level, the threats have become more diffuse, harder to define, and much more difficult to protect the citizenry against than they were during the Cold War. The spectrum of conflict is broader today, the risks more immediate, if less destructive. Chances that the world will be destroyed because of a superpower nuclear exchange have diminished dramatically, but the chances that a city in the United States may face attack by a nuclear, biological, or chemical weapon at the hands of a rogue state or a substate actor, domestic or foreign, have increased even more dramatically. Concern for the protection of human rights has led the United States into areas of admittedly less than vital national interest, and this "moral imperative," as well as the responsibilities of leadership, promise no early reprieve from such engagements.

The purpose of an undergraduate education in national security studies should then be clear: to prepare graduates of the service academies for positions of responsibility in both operational and policy-making assignments. Service academy graduates will oversee the implementation of U.S. national security policy, develop the future capabilities that the defense of the United States and its allies will require, and contribute to the formulation of national security policy. Consequently, it is imperative that newly commissioned officers understand current U.S. national interests and those of our allies, the threats to those interests, and the constraints on our ability to meet those threats. Taking all of these factors into account, officers must be able to contribute to the development of national security strategy, now and for the future.

Any security education program should ensure that young officers understand the history of U.S. national security policy and the principles that have driven U.S. strategic choices in the past. They should be able to derive the theories and principles that will form the foundation for the future national security policy of the United States. The scope of this education should, in the words of West Point's Olin Pro-

fessor of National Security Studies retired General George Joulwan, "prepare them for challenges facing officers from the rank of Lieutenant to Lieutenant General." Those are the responsibilities that they will confront, from graduation day to the day some few of them retire as senior members of the Department of Defense, other executive branch agencies, and even the U.S. Congress.

EDUCATING FUTURE LEADERS: FOUNDATIONS FOR A LIFETIME OF SERVICE

An officer is an expert with specialized knowledge and skill in the direction, operation, and control of an organization whose primary function is the application of violence. However, officer expertise is much broader and more comprehensive than the act of warfighting itself, and it is fostered through a continuous process of development. Just as law at its border merges into history, politics, economics, sociology, and psychology, so also does military expertise. Beyond these borders, military knowledge has frontiers on the natural sciences of chemistry, physics, and biology. An officer must understand the profession's relationship to these many other fields. Therefore, professional military education must begin with a broad, liberal, cultural background, which for the American officer traditionally has been the baccalaureate degree.

Undergraduate education is necessarily foundational in many respects. The academic programs at the three service academies provide not only a broad liberal education, they also prepare graduates for the professional environments in which all of them will serve. They do so by combining an extensive core curriculum with a majors program that supports study in depth of a chosen discipline. Although the details of the core curricula at the three academies differ slightly, the purpose is the same: to provide the intellectual foundation needed to carry out the responsibilities of a commissioned officer in the decades ahead.

In the end, commissioned officers who lead the nation's military services in the twenty-first century will need to be facile with technology and comfortable with uncertainty and change. They will need to be attuned to the role culture plays in determining the structure and dynamics of the international system. Finally, they must be accomplished players in the fragmented decisionmaking environment that defines American pluralism. The educational programs at the service academies are designed to produce just such leaders for the nation, now and in the future.

EDUCATING INTERNATIONAL SECURITY PRACTITIONERS: THE ROLE OF RESEARCH CENTERS AND PROFESSIONAL OUTREACH PROGRAMS

JAMES M. SMITH

INTERNATIONAL SECURITY IN A TIME OF TRANSITION

The world has changed! And so must our concepts and mechanisms of international security. Already we have witnessed decreasing national security allocations and emphasis—political, economic, and military—accompanied by significant force downsizing. We see international security practitioners refocusing to address a wider range of issues and conflicts in dozens of countries, many of which we had never paid any detailed attention to before. Combining these reduced resources and the widened plate of challenges, we see practitioners taking on roles of greatly increased responsibility, often at an age and experience level much lower than in at least the recent past.

As a result, the importance of education, research, and outreach—always important—has increased greatly. We must begin to understand and address the multitude of ambiguities and asymmetries if we are to out-think, as opposed to being forced solely to attempt to outgun, our rivals and adversaries. At base, if we are truly to shape this changing environment, to respond to its current and emerging difficulties and prepare for its future challenges, we—meaning all of the wide range of international security practitioners within and outside of government—must first understand it. Thus, research must define the questions and find and chart the answers. And outreach education must share the results of that research across the entire network of interested parties.

This essay, then, lays out the details of those roles for international security research and outreach education today and into the near- to mid-term future. It begins with a brief description of the three worlds, past, present, and future, in which research and outreach education must today reside. Then it details traditional roles of research and outreach education, emphasizing how they continue to apply or how they must be adapted for today's era of transition. It offers some current examples of ongoing security research and outreach within the Department of Defense. And, finally, it offers some recommendations for international security research and outreach education as we step forward on to this uncharted path.

TODAY'S THREE WORLDS OF INTERNATIONAL SECURITY

International security research and outreach today occupy three worlds; the past, the present, and the future. Each must be addressed in designing and conducting research and outreach education programs. Which aspects of the past international security environment and of our policy, strategy, and organizational and force structures remain relevant and necessary today? How must—or should—they be modified to fit the current and projected worlds? What is new, different, and demanding of new forms and norms of strategy and structure? And who is and will be central players in the emerging international security arena? What skills, knowledge, and capabilities are needed to address the emerging insecurities? These are all questions that must be asked and answered as we prepare for evolving and emerging roles as practitioners within this transitioning environment. We step into the unknown and uncomfortable arena grounded in all three worlds; past, present, and future.

The recent past, the Cold War, had become almost comfortable, at least in retrospect, with its foundation in "knowns" and its resulting air of general predictability. The central threat was well known, and it emanated from a single source with a fairly predictable scope. Our response strategy was continuous for almost half a century under the umbrella of containment. Our response structure—military, political, and economic—evolved within the bounds of containment and the Soviet threat. And our national and alliance organizations that managed the U.S. and NATO dimensions of the response were established and became experienced, based upon the dictates of late 1940s' structural guidelines. In short, the Cold War could be characterized by words such as "continuity," "evolution," and "structure." But that chain has now been broken.

The current era is one of transition, and transitions are, by their very nature, characterized by uncertainty, searching, and a heightened level of danger from possible misinterpretations and miscalculations of an as-yet not fully defined, diverse world. This is indeed the era of "new world disorder." The threat

---

James M. Smith, "Educating International Security Practitioners: The Role of Research Centers and Professional Outreach Programs," in Educating International Security Practitioners: Preparing to Face the Demands of the 21st Century International Security Environment, *James M. Smith, Daniel J. Kaufman, Robert H. Dorff, and Linda P. Brady (Carlisle Barracks, Pa.: U.S. Army War College, 2001), 41–53. Public domain.*

today has multiple faces; it spans the entire threat spectrum from "slingshots to nukes," and its center of gravity has shifted down that spectrum at least to some significant degree. This raises very real questions as to the efficacy of strategic hallmarks, such as the triad deterrent force, the applicability of nuclear deterrence itself to a range of threats—limited nuclear and nonnuclear—and from a range of sources, including states, failed states, and nonstates. All of this raises crosscutting pressures on the proper balance of response tools—economic, political, military, and informational—and on the preferred balance of capabilities within the military itself. Do we continue to develop and procure high-end systems for a real but less likely strategic threat, or do we instead put our effort into forces and capabilities best suited to "operations other than war?" And who best to make these decisions and adjustments: the Cold War national and NATO decision structure, or a reformed cast of players with a new agenda? In a few words, then, today's international security environment is one characterized by the terms "disorder," "ambiguity," and "tension."

If today's environment is one of disorder and ambiguity, the future has been characterized as projecting that condition forward into dynamic uncertainty. International security researchers and policymakers have already made several attempts to capture the trends and foreseeable outputs of the transition at various future periods. For example, the Joint Chiefs of Staff, as an extension of their *Joint Vision* process, outlined trends in the international security environment and their military implications for the year 2010 in their *Concept for Future Joint Operations;*[1] the *Report of the Quadrennial Defense Review* (QDR) projects those global trends and military implications forward to 2015;[2] the National Defense Panel (NDP) projects the security environment and its implications forward to 2020;[3] and both the Air Force and the Army have made projections of the 2025 security environment.[4] The subsequent Commission on National Security (CNS) comprehensive strategy and organization review is also forecasting the international security environment to 2025.[5] Key findings of the QDR, NDP, and CNS projections are depicted at Tables 10 and 11.

Table 10

Projections of the International Security Environment

	QDR 2015	NDP 2020	CNS 2025
Population growth		X	X
Migration to resources	X	X	X
Economic unrest		X	X
Ethnic unrest		X	X
Regional unrest	X	X	X
Interdependence		X	X
Economic blocs form		Possible	X
Nonstate actors rise		X	X
Failed states	X	X	
Regional peer emerges	X		Possible
Global peer emerges	Perhaps after 2025		Unlikely by 2025
Regional blocs emerge	Possible		Possible

Note: An X entry indicates that the topic was addressed and is seen as a likely event.

Table 11

Military Characteristics, 2015–25

	QDR 2015	NDP 2020	CNS 2025
Technological advances		X	X
Proliferation of weapons	X	X	X
Proliferation of delivery	X		X
Proliferation of information	X	X	X
Asymmetrical threats	X	X	X
Homeland threats	X	X	X
Mountain, jungle, urban		X	
Operations from continental United States		X	X
Importance of information/space		X	X
Essence of war unchanged			X

Note: An X entry indicates that the topic was addressed and is seen as a likely event.

These forecasts predict an international security environment characterized by population growth and migration to critical resources, all in a continuing arena of economic and ethnic unrest that could well be exacerbated by this migration. This foretells continuing regional unrest in the developing world. Another characteristic of world regions is likely to be continuing and increasing economic interdependence, creating powerful economic blocs as supranational international security actors. Potential threats and potential coalition partners both could arise from the following four categories of primary security players: nonstate actors, failed and failing states, regionally powerful states (with one or two perhaps aspiring to the status of global peer competitor to the United States), and regional blocs of greater or lesser power and cohesion. Finally, the forecasts emphasize that advances in technologies and proliferation of those technologies—weapons, delivery systems, and information—will likely lead adversaries to respond to continuing U.S. military superiority via asymmetrical responses, including attacks using weapons of mass destruction on our forward-deployed forces or on the U.S. homeland. Besides the potential for fighting attacks at home, the forecasts see increasing security operations in mountains, jungles, or urban environments, and with the increasing requirement for operations from continental United States (CONUS) bases. Both space and the infosphere are also seen as increasing realms of security activities.

As is evident from these projections, then, the future international security environment is still, largely, a hazy picture. It promises a whole new world superimposed upon the skeleton of a lingering past. Threats could emanate from emerging peers, certainly from failed and rogue states, and as asymmetries from states and nonstates as well. Just as the threats remain hazy, only thin threads of a response strategy—one with changed concepts of deterrence and compellence, for instance—appear. Without a clear strategy to face an uncertain range of threats, no firm structure can be decided. What we can do today is prepare general capabilities in a range of functional areas, old and new, all in the context of significant resource limitations. And just as the threat and response are unclear, also elusive is a clear concept of a decision structure to address them—and this in an era when the experience base in the whole range of security is shrinking both in the government and the public. The future, then, offers up a whole slate of questions and requirements and sets a steep agenda for international security research and outreach education.

INTERNATIONAL SECURITY RESEARCH AND OUTREACH FOR A TIME OF TRANSITION

Against the backdrop of these three worlds and within the transition between them, international security research and professional outreach education have several roles to play. These roles relate to interpreting any continuing relevance of the past, fostering realistic understanding of today's international security environment, and informing efforts to shape its future development. This essay briefly traces several roles of research and outreach, and then fits them to the three worlds they must each address.

RESEARCH ROLES

Clarify Ambiguity

The forecasts reviewed above all represent efforts to at least structure future uncertainty. Research must challenge such forecasts, their assumptions, methodologies, and predictions to validate or to refute, even replace, their findings before we go too far along the paths they might indicate. This effort, to the extent that it produces a forecast in which there is confidence, also provides a basis for extending forecast efforts more deeply and broadly into the future. Conversely, as none of the existing forecasts are "complete" beyond the comfortably foreseeable, the effort spawns multiple follow-on efforts to either expand the scope or the time projection of the existing forecasts.

Define Security Dimensions/Components

Validating and extending forecasts of the international security environment requires the identification, definition, and examination of new or additional environmental characteristics. In some cases, this entails expanding the context of our conception of the environment to incorporate aspects whose present-day and future security roles we had previously undervalued. In others, it entails defining security roles and impacts of components of the international environment that had previously not been seen as having security implications. Many of these emerging security components have little or no Cold War security foundations, so research is vital to understanding their contemporary and future play as contributors to international security.

For example, we have become fairly comfortable with at least recognizing that there are economic and environmental dimensions to security.[6] However, we have yet to fully integrate these dimensions, and we have not yet fully sorted out the potentially central roles that international governmental organizations (IGOs) and nongovernmental organizations (NGOs) play in these and other security realms, nor have we even really begun to address the real and potential impact of international criminal organizations (ICOs) and international terrorist organizations (ITOs).[7]

Create and Extend Knowledge

Research has always sought to create new understanding or extend known elements into new realms. Today's research, as it addresses the uncertainty of the present and seeks to clarify at least the context of the future, can and must be even more attuned to pushing us "outside the box" of the known and comfortable and into the discomfort of ambiguity. Again, the key mechanisms here are clarifying, extending the context, testing, and refining theory as a guide.

For example, we in the military have become fairly knowledgeable about nuclear weapons and can extend much of that knowledge to new nuclear actors and possible uses. However, we are not as knowledgeable about chemical and biological weapons, agents, dispersal systems, or the transportation and detection of these components. We need to fully define their threat and shape our response based on realistic scientific and strategic knowledge.

Develop, Test, Extend, Adapt Theory to Reinforce, Refute, or Refine It

A central role of research is always to challenge and apply theory toward greater explanatory powers. Today, however, this role is crucial. It may be, in fact, dangerous to blindly extend Cold War theory to the present day and the future international security environment without testing and validation. We must demonstrate the continuing applicability of past theory before extending it to the present and future. And we must seek to adapt, develop, and begin to validate new threads of theory to help us navigate the foggy paths into uncertainty.

Examples here must begin with deterrence: we think that we understood the deterrent relationship between the United States and the Soviet Union, but does that even begin to extend to states holding much smaller nuclear arsenals? What about rogue states without "rational" regard for norms of interstate behavior? Furthermore, is there any relevance at all for nonstate holders of nuclear weapons? And ultimately, regardless of actor, does nuclear deterrence extend to deter attacks employing chemical, biological, or other weapons of mass destruction? These are but a few of the issues concerning deterrence that remain to be resolved. And deterrence is only one arena of security theory that demands reevaluation today.

Inform Policy

Research is seldom conducted solely for its own sake. Particularly in the realm of international security affairs, research has traditionally sought to inform, critique, or direct policy. This role, too, is reinforced today. Policy can either muddle into the mist, or it can proceed on a more certain course directed by expanded theory and knowledge. Research cannot be purely academic here—the tasks are too immense, the stakes too high, and the international security research community too small to allow such a luxury. Academics can (and must) adapt their designs to incorporate the related and legitimate questions of policymakers to help shape a more secure future.

Research agencies need to institute innovative, cross-disciplinary collaboration networks to address the full scope and range of new and altered, often expanded, challenges. This mixing of expertise and perspectives can provide a better foundation for the development of policy options and for eventual policy decisions. And it can adapt those more theoretical or academic approaches to the new set of problems and issues toward practical policy relevance.

Fit to Three Worlds

International security research, then, must today reach back to understand the details, dynamics, and mechanisms of Cold War security to determine whether and how those characteristics translate into the current environment. It must detail the present to identify, define, and relate all of today's relevant players and components—to map as much of the present environment as possible as a guide into uncertainty. And it must project the past and present into the future as a framework upon which to hang developments as they occur—to allow us to flesh out the context and content of unfolding events toward greater understanding and more rational policy action. Research must help us address the *what, why, how,* and *so what* questions of the current and future international security environments. And professional outreach education must pass on the results of that research, the answers to those questions, and the new, expanded questions that are raised, to the critical *who* involved in international security policy practice today.

OUTREACH ROLES

Educate Direct Participants

Professional outreach education is vital today as a means of informing and educating direct participants in the international security policymaking process. The top priority is to fully support the education of participants. Behind that task, many of today's participants, even a majority in key branches and offices, have little or no prior experience in security fields. For example, according to the Retired Officer's Association, only 31 percent of the elected members of the House of Representatives in the 106th Congress that assumed office in January 1999 had served in the armed forces, active or reserve. Only 25 percent of the House freshmen had any military experience. Even in the 106th Senate, only 43 percent had ever worn a uniform, and not one of the 1999 freshman class of the Senate had any military experience. As recently as the 103rd Congress, 41 percent of the House and 60 percent of the Senate had military experience. As the postdraft, post-Vietnam generation rises to prominence in government, the trend is clear. Furthermore, very few of the congressional staffers who develop the policy options and recommend policy decisions to the elected members have direct military or other security experience. Well-founded security policy demands active outreach and education efforts here.

Inform/Educate Interested/Knowledgeable Public

The situation described above for elected officials is also reflected among the most engaged and otherwise knowledgeable segments of the population outside of government. Since the end of the draft in 1972, the number of Americans with direct security experience and detailed knowledge has steadily declined. Active policy players must be educated, just as is the case for elected officials; otherwise, they will engage in the policy debate with only the most superficial knowledge of the substance of the international security environment, that perhaps from a skim of the front page of the daily newspaper.

Outreach efforts must include publication and dissemination of, particularly, the results of the new research directions outlined above. One possible innovation here is to provide educational materials for both outreach and more traditional education programs by packaging related research results into texts that focus on the new, expanded security environment. Another idea would be to replace the traditional security conference—of which there are many both in government and the broader academic and consultant/business communities each year—and conference report, normally sent only to conference participants, with book conferences designed to package finished papers into texts and outreach materials. The interested public is a ready audience, but they need authoritative materials.

Shape Government/Public Support/Consensus

The outreach education efforts covered above are central not just to educating direct and peripheral policy participants, but also to forging wider understanding, consensus, and support for government security policy. This is indeed a steep challenge, when few in the wider public can even identify Bosnia or Kosovo on a world map, let alone intelligently discuss the complexity of the situations there. Yet wider knowledge and consensus support are absolutely essential to the types of long-term, sophisticated policy efforts that such situations dictate, and policy without consensus backing is problematic at best. International security practitioners must, then, deliberately reach out to inform, as a vehicle toward understanding and eventual consensus.

Toward this end, the texts and educational materials cited above should be disseminated as widely as possible both inside and outside the knowledgeable and interested community. Copies should be distributed to research libraries and made available to civilian educational institutions. And today, these materials, as well as the screened and cleared results of security research, should be posted on the Internet. A Cold War era senior government official recently stated at a security forum that nothing of value would be found on the Internet since the "good" materials were all classified. I do not believe that, today, this is or necessarily should be true—encouraging innovative thinking in nontraditional arenas and encouraging outreach and understanding across communities requires communication. The Internet is becoming a—if not the—primary means of communication to many segments of society, and prudent dissemination of security information via the Internet should be part of the outreach effort.

Network (Foster Policy Community)

A critical component of security policymaking across the Cold War era was an active, effective, inter-branch and transsocietal policy community. This network of specialists was able to remain engaged on policy debate and development regardless of the personalities or parties in power in the executive and legislative branches of government. With the decline in security experience in the government today and with the shrinkage of the nongovernmental security sector, security practitioners must consciously work to foster what remains of the old policy community. They must simultaneously reach out to extend the network's reach to new agencies and individuals, particularly those from the sectors representing the new dimensions of security policy. This effort, like the one to build public consensus and support, is a legitimate educational challenge to security practitioners, for only with knowledge can there be effective policy debate.

Invigorating this network requires active and targeted outreach, focusing around the new and expanded players both within government and the interdisciplinary civilian communities, where needed expertise lies. It must be active outreach to foster involvement and contribution. It must also engage a new generation of rising security specialists to ensure the continued vitality of the community. Internships and research assistantships and mentoring, faculty workshops to inform and engage, and development of seminar materials as outlined above are all ways to revitalize and extend this community.

Identify Areas for Further Research

Finally, as the circle of interested and able participants grows to include a full representation of the emerging security community and as the debate widens and deepens, new questions will be raised and existing beliefs and actions subjected to new challenges. This full debate will strengthen policy while it also raises new questions and poses new requirements for the international security research community.

What is needed are true workshops, aimed at exploring new and innovative approaches, to replace a singular reliance on formal conferences and theoretical paper presentations. We must realize that the audience is as important as those at the front table, and that in this uncertain world, none of us has a monopoly on truth or even superior knowledge. For example, the young graduate student who is fully comfortable with a new set of technologies can bring fresh light on unseen solution sets in many cases. We cannot afford to overlook this potential contribution —indeed, we must actively seek it out and provide arenas conducive to wider interaction.

Fit to Three Worlds

As with research, professional security outreach efforts must first identify and engage those individuals and sectors from the Cold War policy community that remain central to today's security policy debate. They must also identify, inform, and engage emerging players and the representatives of new agencies and sectors—the newly identified security components—

to energize today's policy debate toward policy consensus and action. This is a true challenge, given the few current practitioners with requisite experience in international security issues or policy. And this effort to extend knowledge, widen and deepen debate, and energize a true security issue network is a key component to effective security understanding and policy formulation into the future.

This, then, completes the circle. Research clarifies ambiguity, identifies and defines new security components, and challenges theory to inform policy debate and decisionmaking. Security practitioners then disseminate the results of that research via professional outreach education aimed at informing, fostering, rebuilding, and extending the policy community. This engaged community, through informed debate, then identifies new areas and raises new questions for research. The circle continues to turn, and both policy and the degree of security it seeks are advanced. International security research and professional outreach education represent a continuing and vital requirement for today and tomorrow.

INTERNATIONAL SECURITY RESEARCH AND OUTREACH INTO THE EARLY 21ST CENTURY

Is there, then, a continuing need for international security research and professional outreach efforts into the post–Cold War era? The clear answer is that international security research and outreach are perhaps more important today than they were even at the height of the Cold War. The stakes, in the presence of widely available destructive capabilities and the absence of effective systemic checks to the threat or even use of those capabilities, remain extremely high. And the true extent and nature of the threat beyond weapons of mass destruction has become more complex, varied, and ambiguous. So security research must also widen and deepen to provide a map into the fog and friction of potential war and "other than war." Furthermore, security outreach education must transmit the results of that research to inform policy efforts to shape and respond in this insecure world.

To whom should these efforts be directed? The efforts must target a wider range of practitioners as the scope of what we consider "security" continues to broaden. It must attract and recruit researchers with greater interdisciplinary capabilities and focus from a shrinking pool of ready participants, and it must disseminate the results of the new research via active outreach to extend and inform an engaged policy community. The participants and observers require active outreach as their direct security experience continues to decline, and building understanding and consensus behind security policy efforts takes on ever greater importance.

What skills are appropriate to the present and future practitioners in the field of international security? The skills required of today's and tomorrow's international security practitioners are technical, informational, and human, and represent an expanded set of disciplines and dimensions. As the range of technical components of security expands, the technical requirements of research and outreach also increase. Furthermore, as the security world becomes more tied to the infosphere, informational skills and focus take on greater salience. But we must never lose sight of the fact that security remains, at base, a human pursuit in a human world. It has already been noted that the widening scope of security involves an expanded scope of practitioners, and it involves them directly and in significant ways earlier in their experience. Some would say that what is needed is a cadre of technocrats capable of critical thought, those with detailed expertise yet also with the ability to face undefined decisions quickly and wisely. Security policy and strategy are more complex, and the skill set of practitioners in this realm must enable them to face that challenge.

And what should be the focus of international security research and professional outreach efforts? The resultant focus, scope, content of the research and outreach effort must then be broader, deeper, and more interdisciplinary than it was in the past. It must address a wider range of technical areas in new and as-yet ill-defined ways, and it must provide a basis for understanding among an uniformed, inexperienced audience. Nuclear physics, chemistry, biology, sociology, psychology, agriculture, environmental engineering, economics, history, international law, and a range of languages and regional studies are only a few of the areas indicated for expanded roles in security research today.

What methodologies are appropriate to this international security research and outreach effort? Again, this new and changing world requires methods and theories both from the past and from emerging disciplines and areas. The old must be challenged and validated, and the new demonstrated to apply. Security today is a field open to innovative and imaginative approaches, and traditional practitioners must be receptive to these new approaches. The range of disciplines involved in today's security research itself indicates a wide range and unique mix of methods of inquiry, and the interdisciplinary, technical content of security policy demands a mix and emphasis on multiple means of presenting and disseminating information to the policy community.

Finally, what is the place of international security research and professional outreach education in academia today? Even as the scholarly world continues to retreat from the field of international security in the post–Cold War era, the field demands full participation in security research and outreach. The "new world disorder" presents a true challenge to the academic community to engage this field as a legitimate research area—one that offers a real opportunity to contribute meaningfully to policy and security now and into the future. Outreach must include a deliberate effort to bridge government and academia, to link inquiry and policy in addressing the uncertainties and complexities we all face.

International security research and professional outreach education then must link past, present, and future, bridge disciplines and communities in an expanded inquiry into wider fields of ambiguity, and inform less-experienced practitioners toward active debate and policymaking. It must provide a validated context to the security environment and policy efforts to address it. It must establish a framework to at least structure uncertainty so that we can navigate the future with some level of confidence, asking more of the right questions and adding knowledge to steer our way across dangerous shoals. In short, it must identify and inform the many possibilities, pitfalls, and options as we embark into a dim and foggy future. That is the challenge today: to engage, explain, shape, and respond, together as a government, academic, and citizen team, in the face of uncertainty and danger.

NOTES

1. Joint Chiefs of Staff, *Concept for Future Joint Operations* (Washington, D.C.: Joint Chiefs of Staff, 1997), 8–10.

2. Office of the Secretary of Defense, *Report of the Quadrennial Defense Review* (Washington, D.C.: Office of the Secretary of Defense, May 1997), 3–5.

3. National Defense Panel, *Transforming Defense: National Security in the 21st Century* (Washington, D.C.: National Defense Panel, December 1997), 5–17.

4. Ronald R. Fogleman and Sheila E. Widnall, *Global Engagement* (Washington, D.C.: Department of the Air Force, 1996), 1–5; Robert H. Scales, Jr., *America's Army: Preparing for Tomorrow's Security Challenges,* Issue Paper 2 (Carlisle, Pa.: U.S. Army War College, Strategic Studies Institute, November 1998), 1–6.

5. U.S. Commission on National Security/21st Century, *New World Coming: American Security in the 21st Century* (Washington, D.C.: U.S. Commission on National Security/21st Century, September 15, 1999). This initial report forecasts the environment, whereas subsequent reports consider organization and strategy to address that environment.

6. President Bush called economic security coequal to military security and included environmental security as a significant component of that economic dimension in his 1991 national security strategy statement. The Clinton national security strategy statements maintain the emphasis on economic security while elevating environmental security to an individual component having both economic and military dimensions. See James M. Smith, "U.S. National Security Strategy and National Military Strategy in the Post–Cold War World: Continuity and Change," in *Introduction to Joint and Multilateral Operations,* ed. James E. Schlagheck and James M. Smith (New York: American Heritage, 1998), for a broader discussion of the evolution of the national security strategy statements.

7. An example of an IGO is the United Nations; an NGO, the Red Cross; of ICOs, illicit drug cartels; and of an ITO, al Qaeda.

MILITARY EDUCATION FOR THE NEW AGE

ERVIN J. ROKKE

During his transition from Princeton University to the White House, Woodrow Wilson is alleged to have said that academic politics are the worst kind because the stakes are so low. As any dean with curriculum revision experience will attest, Wilson had a point. Squaring curricula with student needs at the expense of faculty interests is a complex task.

The stakes clearly have changed, however, at least in the context of professional military education (PME) at the war colleges. Not only has the post–Cold War era placed new substantive and pedagogical requirements on military educators, but new demands on the relationship between PME institutions and the policy community as well. Adapting to this change is the basic challenge confronting the war colleges today.

The issue is straightforward: either the war colleges become agents for change within the individual services and joint arena or they become anachronisms. Whatever the nature of academic politics, the downside is irrelevancy at best and demise at worst. Five major factors contribute to this phenomenon.

FACTORS FOR CHANGE

INTERNATIONAL POLITICS

Historians and political scientists hold that the international system changes when new answers emerge to three fundamental questions: Who are the major players? What can they do to one another? What do they wish to do to one another? The unexpected end of the Cold War was only the latest watershed in the world order. One classic example of an earlier watershed is the French Revolution, which spawned a new player (democratic France), a new

Ervin J. Rokke, "Military Education for the New Age," Joint Force Quarterly 9 *(Autumn 1995): 18–23. Public domain.*

capability (a citizen army), and new intentions (liberty, equality, and fraternity). Similar transitions occurred with the Congress of Vienna (1815), German unification (1870), Treaty of Versailles (1919), and agreements following World War II.

From the perspective of war college curricula, it is useful to examine the ongoing post–Cold War transition against the backdrop of past changes. In each instance, the results were not readily apparent. The answers to questions concerning players, capabilities, and intentions are no more likely to surface quickly or clearly today than in previous realignments of the international system. Assessments made in the democratic atmosphere of Paris circa 1789 did not foresee an autocratic Napoleon on the horizon. Similarly, most internationalist projections made at Versailles following World War I failed to predict a global depression or a resurgent Germany.

The first requirement, then, for the curricula at war colleges is to ensure that students do not presume to know who their future opponents or coalition partners will be. This appreciation for uncertainty is the beginning of wisdom in the post–Cold War era. But underscoring uncertainty is not the same thing as saying that everything is up for grabs. On the contrary, it means that the war colleges must delve into what is known but is frequently neglected in the defense establishment. For example, students must understand more than their predecessors did about economics, technologies, and diverse cultures to make sound judgments. This perspective brings into question several major tenets of defense policy that were prevalent in a bipolar world. Although it offers few clear-cut policy prescriptions, it is essential to appreciating the security implications of a world order in flux.

TECHNOLOGY

Advances in technology are hardly new phenomena. Stirrups, gunpowder, the steam engine, radio, stealth, and other innovations dramatically changed the nature of warfare. Curricula are replete with cases of how such advances were treated by institutions and individuals wedded to more traditional approaches.[1] Recently, however, breakthroughs related to warfare have occurred with greater frequency, more substantial impact on quality versus quantity tradeoffs, and increased organizational implications.

A former director of the Defense Intelligence Agency, Lieutenant General James Clapper, has raised an excellent case of the accelerating impact of technology on quality-quantity tradeoffs.[2] During World War II, some 9,000 bombs dropped by more than 1,500 B-17 bomber sorties were required to destroy a 6,000 square foot target. In Vietnam, the destruction of a similar target took only 176 bombs delivered by 88 F-4 fighter sorties. During the Gulf War, one bomb carried by an F-117 fighter-bomber did the job. This is not to imply that a single 2,000 pound bomb can today destroy every 6,000 square foot target. Advances in guidance system technology, however, have

made a qualitative improvement in weapon effectiveness. Technological advances by ground and naval forces also resulted in impressive warfighting efficiencies during Desert Storm.

Equally important for PME are the organizational, structural, and budgetary implications of accelerated technological breakthroughs. The price of improved technology is high, particularly if applied to such systems as the stealthy F-117 aircraft. Indeed, given the tradeoff between a new item of equipment representing a breakthrough in sophistication as opposed to just a better, simpler item, some defense experts argue for the latter.[3] Whatever the ambiguity of quality-quantity tradeoffs, however, the organizational impact of increasingly expensive high-tech items is clear. As the cost and operational complexity of systems increase substantially, the organizational response is centralization. In the case of the evolution from photographic reconnaissance aircraft to satellites, the focal point of operations and control moves from the battlefield to Washington.

INFORMATION

Perhaps no single factor has as much potential as the information explosion for changing the way in which military organizations function, both during peace and in war. The widespread adoption of information technologies in the latter part of the twentieth century has set the stage for a social transformation of historic magnitude by making unprecedented amounts of information instantaneously available in easy-to-use forms at ever-diminishing cost. The emerging information highway, which extends from earth to geosynchronous orbit, will certainly alter society, to say nothing of conflict. Worldwide 24-hour connectivity and sensors and hardware needed to support information processing are already in place. So are stand-off weapons that can be launched from almost anywhere and strike targets with accuracies measured in fractions of yards.

To date, the best thinking on innovative applications for information age technologies has been done by the staff of the Office of Net Assessment under Andrew Marshall at the Pentagon. They have recast functional areas associated with traditional service expertise into precision strike, dominating maneuver, space warfare, and information warfare. Moreover, they suggest that the potential for a revolution in military affairs (RMA) exists in a zone where these new warfare areas intersect and offer a new construct that demonstrates the military potential afforded by information. The vice chairman, Admiral William Owens, has with similar logic advanced a vision of a two-hundred square nautical mile battlefield box about which virtually everything is known on a near real-time basis and within which all targets can be hit using standoff weapons.[4]

Not surprisingly, debates about whether RMA notions are fact or fiction provide grist for the mill in many PME seminars. But information age issues go far beyond procedures for waging war to the heart of military organization. Cheap microchips and break-throughs in communications have made huge amounts of information available and created pressure for decentralization and flat organizational structures. Bluntly stated, vertical organizational structures long associated with the military, along with the central-ization resulting in part from high-tech and costly equipment, are not optimal for the information age. When tank, ship, and aircraft operators can di-rectly receive much of the information they need to fight, at least some higher headquarters will become extraneous.

JOINTNESS/COALITION WARFARE

Consistent with the Goldwater-Nichols Act, the increasingly prominent combatant commanders-in-chief have responsibility for command and con-trol in warfare. To support them, the services have made major improvements in collaboration and inter-operability. Jointness is in. Outstanding professionals are now assigned to positions on joint staffs, and a succession of Joint Task Force exercises and deploy-ments has proven that the armed forces are capable of functioning within multiservice command struc-tures. Even service monopolies on developing re-quirements have been redressed by the Joint Re-quirements Oversight Council, overseen by the vice chairman.

As the services become more familiar with joint responsibilities and work more effectively together, we are also finding that the likelihood of the United States fighting alone is becoming remote. Experi-ences such as the Gulf War, former Yugoslavia, and other recent crises suggest that alliances and well-greased multinational command chains are insuffi-cient, if not outmoded. Ad hoc alliances and coalitions are the norm, and the United Nations is increasingly involved in humanitarian and peace operations.

Coordinating strategy and tactics to include rules of engagement—as well as the distribution of intelli-gence to coalition partners with both varying capac-ities for information and differing levels of security access—are tasks that war college graduates face. The problem becomes more complex as tensions arise between the centralizing tendencies of jointness and the decentralizing, multiple chain of command biases of coalition warfare.

ECOLOGY

Perhaps less known but significant in their impact on security are environmental phenomena. Although this area has received little attention in PME, it is drawing increasing emphasis worldwide. It embraces climate change, ozone depletion, deforestation, bio-diversity loss, and air and water pollution. Recent examples include the 1989 conflict between Senegal and Mauritania, which was sparked by a scarcity of water and arable land, and the mass migration from Rwanda, which became a crisis of epic proportions

because of the lack of potable water. In short, eco-logical developments could well affect the circum-stances under which the armed forces are used as well as how they are used. Clearly this new challenge is relevant to PME—although it has gone largely unaddressed.

And so it is that various factors, from international politics and ecology through technology and infor-mation, are moving doctrine, organization, and op-erations in new and often conflicting directions. As General Wayne Downing, commander-in-chief of U.S. Special Operations Command, told students attending the School of Information Warfare and Strategy, "In the information age, the very nature of war is changing."[5]

IMPERATIVES FOR PME

The central task of war colleges is to prepare stu-dents to succeed across a broad spectrum of national security challenges. The impact of these institutions is, in large part, a function of how well their gradu-ates perform. We are in the business of equipping leaders to deal with the security environment of the twenty-first century. The unpredictable nature of the ongoing process of change makes this more akin to a floating craps game than an exact science. Never-theless, it is a game in which we all must play. As the chairman, General John Shalikashvili, observed, "The unexpected has become the routine; we need people who are comfortable in an uncertain world."[6] In this game, the role of war colleges is to make the odds better for graduates. And those odds can be shortened by doing everything possible to convey an under-standing of the emerging security environment, as well as teaching students to recognize and deal with the unexpected. This is the PME challenge.

Managing change is what national security is all about. War colleges must equip leaders to assume this critical responsibility. We must give graduates the tools to function comfortably in a world in which rapid change is the norm. To do so, however, PME needs to strengthen the capability to affect the full spectrum of national security policies by embracing added roles for PME, and we must revise curricula and supplement the substance of what we teach.

Like most institutions of higher learning, war colleges can become ivory towers divorced from the world that they serve. If they are to help align mili-tary culture with the technological, environmental, and geopolitical revolutions, they must be fully in tune with national security processes that stimulate and implement change. This goes beyond policy formu-lation and includes technology insertion, doctrine de-velopment, planning and budgeting, and training.

How can PME institutions do this? First, they should be "present at the creation" to ensure an en-vironment that encourages new thought and rewards rather than punishes innovation. Similarly, they must follow organizational processes for change. War-gaming, policy-relevant research, and faculty participation in ad hoc commissions are classic examples. Each war college has a research institute to connect its parent institution with the activities of the national security community.

Second, PME institutions have a responsibility to expose ideas, new as well as old, to the critical light of academe. Wargames and simulation exercises work well. So do informal, off the record discussions between students and visiting lecturers from the policy arena. Each senior PME institution enjoys special relationships with individuals sympathetic to the military and who literally try out new ideas on faculty and students. More of these exchanges are needed with policymakers and leaders who are not instinctively sympathetic to military culture.

Finally, PME institutions have a duty to be harbingers of change. Classes and seminars are common ways for disseminating innovative ideas. So are professional journals. Less developed, but with greater potential, are options associated with the information highway. Without a home page and a routine means for distributing the best of faculty and student research, a war college is simply not doing its job in the information age. In brief, PME can and must play a central role as an agent in altering that greatest barrier to meaningful change—our traditional culture.

ADAPTING CURRICULA

In the classroom, as in headquarters or war zones, the basis for innovation lies in critical thinking about capabilities, concepts, and organizations relevant to current and future needs. As in the past, military innovators in the information age must develop an appreciation for what exists, as well as analytic skills for critiquing the status quo. It is not a choice between notions of modern warfare and more abstract theories of coercion. Unfortunately, for already tight curricula and busy students, it is a combination of both.

Indeed, because of the complexity of joint and combined operations, curricula must deal with the doctrine and capabilities of multiple nations and services. Moreover, blurred boundaries among military, diplomatic, economic, and psychological tools require unprecedented sensitivity for what policy types call the "interagency process." In sum, developing PME curricula—like our security environment itself—is of necessity an exercise in risk limitation. There simply is not the time to cover all contingencies. The most one can do is prepare for dealing with uncertainty.

The classic approach to this dilemma is a balance among academic disciplines, the interests and backgrounds of students, and the demands of theory and practice. Like a classic liberal education, war college curricula must cover a range of academic disciplines that include basic and engineering sciences, as well as humanities and the social sciences.

What, then, is different about curricular requirements today? For a start, the balance of PME has shifted with the advent of the revolution in information technology. Whereas military strategists in past revolutions, such as that brought on by nuclear weapons, tended to be civilian thinkers with humanities and social science backgrounds, the current revolutionary force puts a higher premium on basic and engineering sciences. Historical perspective and an appreciation of bureaucratic politics remain vital, but an adequate intellectual framework in the information age requires some understanding of the ones and zeroes being passed around in such incredible quantities. In short, the center of mass at the war colleges must move toward more technical academic disciplines.

To conclude, there is a current revolution in PME that parallels the RMA. In both cases, core functions and procedures are undergoing fundamental changes. In both cases, we are seeing disparate rates of progress among the constituent parts. And in both cases, we are facing difficult resource tradeoffs between traditional approaches on the one hand and information age alternatives on the other.

PME institutions must assume the role played by first-class research universities. We have a duty to mobilize our institutions to expand knowledge through research, educate practitioners, and serve as catalysts for change through outreach. The war colleges must provide the intellectual capital for changing the existing paradigm.

The stakes are high in the RMA and PME. Significant obstacles and inertia must be overcome. The RMA has the potential to alter priorities among service capabilities. Similarly, the revolution in PME—challenging curricula and teaching methods—has the potential to transform war colleges into innovative centers that spawn and foster new concepts of warfare. In the final analysis, both revolutions demand changes in culture. Because PME shapes and promotes service and joint cultures, it would be difficult if not impossible for the RMA to succeed without a corresponding revolution in war college curricula. This places a major burden on those of us involved in PME and requires that we move ahead with the revolution.

NOTES

1. A classic example is found in Edward L. Katzenbach, Jr., "Tradition and Technological Change," in *American Defense Policy,* 5th edition, ed. John F. Reichart and Steven R. Sturm (Baltimore: The Johns Hopkins University Press, 1982), 638–51; also see Stephen P. Rosen, *Winning the Next War: Innovation and the Modern Military* (Ithaca, N.Y.: Cornell University Press, 1991).

2. James R. Clapper, presentation at the National War College, February 9, 1995.

3. See Jack N. Merritt and Pierre M. Sprey, "Negative Marginal Returns in Weapons Acquisition," in *American Defense Policy,* 3rd edition, ed. Richard G. Head and Ervin J.

Rokke (Baltimore: The Johns Hopkins University Press, 1973), 486–95.

4. William A. Owens, speech to the Retired Officers Association, Des Moines, Iowa, July 1, 1995.

5. Wayne A. Downing, presentation at the School of Information Warfare and Strategy, National Defense University, August 16, 1995.

6. John M. Shalikashvili, presentation at the National Defense University, August 18, 1995.

PART IV

CONTEMPORARY PERSPECTIVES
ON DEFENSE POLICY

INTRODUCTION

DAMON V. COLETTA

The previous parts in this book introduced the values and institutional processes that produce defense policy. This part discusses policy outputs. In a sense, Part IV is the culmination of the entire book—the international and domestic environment, American policymakers, and policy instruments interact to produce specific policies designed to advance American interests, policies that are usually controversial. The policy areas most central to American defense policy, covered in this section, are civil-military relations, conventional forces, nuclear policy, missile defense, and homeland security necessitated by the threat of terrorism.

From the collapse of the Soviet Union in 1990 until the attacks of September 11, 2001, American defense policies were formulated without clear strategic direction. Although the 1991 Gulf War demonstrated the combat capabilities of the American military, in subsequent years the military was used increasingly for peacemaking, maintaining regional stability, and "shaping the environment." Often, in such places as Somalia, Bosnia, and Kosovo, the mission of the military was ambiguous. The Pentagon took on such assignments only reluctantly, fearful that there was no clear exit strategy.

September 11 brought new direction to American defense policy. Since September 11, the Bush administration has sought dramatic reformulation of American policies to engage in the contemporary global struggle, not another world war or cold war, but an unprecedented war on terror. Many of the regional issues in Europe, Asia, Africa, and Latin America that engaged policymakers in the twentieth century remain, but now they are seen through the lens of a more focused global strategy centered on protecting the American homeland. Prodigious efforts have been made to implement the National Security Strategy, including a previously unimaginable $470 billion defense budget projected for 2007.[1] Along with increased funding has come a new willingness to use the American military in combat operations throughout the world, with or without the consent of key allies.

Despite the clear strategic direction, many defense policy issues remain highly contested. For example, what lessons do recent wars provide? Does Kosovo demonstrate that air power alone can win wars? Does Afghanistan or Iraq provide a new model of warfighting that will apply to future conflicts? Questions on nuclear policy inspire further debate. In a world no longer ruled by Mutual Assured Destruction but endangered by the proliferation of weapons of mass destruction, should the United States deploy low-yield nuclear weapons that can penetrate bunkers and destroy enemy weapons before the latter are used? When Americans fear further catastrophic terrorist attacks on their own soil, how can the military play a role in homeland security without taking over law enforcement duties or violating the civil rights and liberties of Americans? High-stakes contests about future force structure also spill over into civil-military debates that shape when and how the United States uses force.[2] The chapters that follow take on these issues clearly and forcefully.

In Chapter 10 on civil-military relations, Eliot Cohen reviews the major schools of thought on American civil-military relations, with special attention to Samuel Huntington's objective control, or what he terms the "normal theory."[3] Cohen acknowledges that professional expertise distinguishes military commanders from their civilian leaders and that this logical specialization creates the potential for debilitating micromanagement by politicians. He nevertheless presses leaders, especially under the fluid circumstances of wartime, to probe their military commanders with challenging questions about their assumptions and plans. To reap the benefits of Cohen's interrogative method, parties must respect one another across the civil-military divide. The essay by Peter Feaver and Richard Kohn and that by Marybeth Ulrich address the causes, consequences, and prescriptions for civil-military friction. Summarizing results from surveys taken by the Triangle Institute for Security Studies, Feaver and Kohn lay out the ideological and policy dimensions of the gap dividing military and civilian elites. Ulrich brings together notions of the gap and mission requirements after September 11 to derive a list of best practices for officers immersed in the modern dynamics of civil-military relations.

Chapter 11, on conventional forces, brings our attention to substantive policy dilemmas. Keeping in mind the military's tasks to organize, train, equip, and plan, the essays here focus on the utility and limitations of air, sea, and land forces as instruments of national power. Anthony Cordesman's analysis of the air and missile campaign in Kosovo examines both the accomplishments and the myths surrounding this recent and controversial application of U.S. airpower to suppress ethnic conflict in the former Yugoslavia. In the aftermath of September 11, Clark Murdock describes how the Navy is reexamining the role of sea power, both in projecting force against terrorist bases overseas and in regulating the increasing volume of sea commerce in a globalizing world. Stephen Biddle peers inside the stunningly swift campaign to remove al Qaeda terrorists and the Taliban regime from Afghanistan. Special Forces in that conflict indeed grew beards, rode horses, and employed lasers to designate targets for Air Force bombers, but the detailed record of ground engagements indicates that more conventional Army skills will still be necessary to succeed in future warfare.

At the other end of the spectrum, given the success of space-dependent platforms for navigation, communication and reconnaissance, all the services are considering greater investment in the frontier beyond land, sea and air. Karl Mueller lays out the main lines of debate on the weaponization of space, suggesting that a deliberate approach—rather than a complete ban or a headlong rush to new offensive capability—is most likely to garner political support in the near term. Finally, Chairman of the Joint Chiefs Richard Meyers provides a concise articulation of the U.S. military's new global vision to address the war on terror alongside more traditional responsibilities. The shift to a global perspective has special implications for the roles and responsibilities of regional combatant commanders who have executed the warfighting operations in their assigned areas since the Goldwater-Nichols Act.

Accompanying the changes in conventional thinking, American nuclear policy has also undergone dramatic reevaluation.[4] The threat from the massive nuclear arsenals of the Soviet Union has declined. Meanwhile, the potential for a rogue state or terrorist network to marry missile technology, or unconventional means of delivery, with a crude warhead seems to be growing. This threat is especially difficult to ignore after the al Qaeda group demonstrated technological savvy, a willingness to cause mass casualties, and utter contempt for the classical logic of deterrence.

Chapter 12, on nuclear policy and missile defense, leads off with two concise presentations by Michael Levi and James Kitfield, which sketch the public debate on the prudence of developing new nuclear weapons. The chapter then covers the controversy over missile defense. Although nuclear warheads are not openly proposed for enhancing the efficiency of national missile defense, missile defense is closely related to nuclear issues because the most dangerous threat tracked by such systems is still a nuclear warhead.[5] In terms of current thinking, biological weapons must survive impact and find a host, whereas chemical weapons must maintain a lethal level of concentration. Consequently, in missile mode, neither option could kill or destroy as effectively as a nuclear device. In any case, the Missile Defense Agency in the Pentagon seeks the capacity to destroy incoming projectiles before they arrive at their target regardless of whether the warhead is biological, chemical, or nuclear.[6] Bob Schaffer, a former congressman from Colorado, explains why investment in a space-based missile defense is needed today. Philip Coyle of the Arms Control Association provides a technology review of current designs, concluding that national missile defense has some distance to go before it will effectively blunt an attack.

After September 11 and the subsequent launching of the war on terror, the need to protect America's home soil took top priority. Early Americans were indeed called upon to defend Pennsylvania, New York, and Washington from foreign attack in the eighteenth and early nineteenth centuries, but today, both the nature of the task and the foe have changed dramatically. On the morning of the terrorist attacks, some of America's minutemen were flying F-16 fighters from the District of Columbia Air National Guard, a descendant of the state militias that preceded even the first Continental Army and American independence. A few minutes, however, was not enough warning to execute all the required procedures developed in the intervening years by a standing, professional military. When the National Guard fighters answered an alarm to protect the capital against a possible renegade airliner, they went without ammunition, without the appropriate protocols to communicate with the Air Force fighters that were at that moment racing to the scene, and without rules of engagement for attacking commercial airplanes carrying tens if not hundreds of innocent civilians.[7]

This vignette from September 11 illustrates some of the problems addressed in Chapter 13 on homeland security and the threat of terrorism. Bruce Hoffman assesses how characteristics of the terrorist threat have changed with the rise of global networks, such as al Qaeda. Jeffrey Norwitz and Mark Sawyer take stock in their essays of novel demands on American defense policy, focusing on how the military is forging new relationships with civilian agencies in law enforcement and intelligence.[8] The two essays can only give a flavor for the immensely complicated task of establishing a federal Department of Homeland Security and coordinating it with the efforts of the U.S. military's Northern Command, as well as with local agencies.[9] The men and women who responded nearly instantaneously on September 11 wore not just the insignia of a National Guard squadron but also the insignias of police officers, firemen, medical workers, and many other civilian services. Richard Kohn, who has also written on civil-military relations and the U.S. Constitution in this volume, evaluates legal and political implications resulting from the expansion of U.S. military operations within the American homeland.

The ironic turns of American defense policy today do not end with images of the world's greatest economic and military power feverishly reorganizing itself against a new type of menace, one that bypasses high-tech defense screens and feeds off what are normally considered societal strengths, such as political openness and advanced infrastructure.[10] Given the international environment of 1796, President George Washington's policy for homeland security was to avoid the entanglements of permanent alliances. Today's environment is much different.

After September 11, national security critically depends upon how successfully the United States follows a different course, strengthening alliances and nurturing partnerships, not just among law enforcement, intelligence and civil transportation, but among militaries (some democratic and some not) as well.[11] However, for this policy to work, the exercise of American power must be seen as legitimate by the nations of the world. Keener appreciation for the staying power afforded by international legitimacy may yet emerge as the next big development in American defense policy.[12]

NOTES

The views expressed are the author's and in no way represent the opinions, standards, or policy of the U.S. Air Force Academy or the U.S. government.

1. Quoted in Burkard Schmitt, *Defense Expenditure* (Paris: European Union Institute for Security Studies, November 24, 2003), 3.

2. Peter Feaver and Christopher Gelpi, *Choosing Your Battles: American Civil-Military Relations and the Use of Force* (Princeton, N.J.: Princeton University Press, 2004).

3. This article is based on Cohen's award-winning book *Supreme Command: Soldiers, Statesmen, and Leadership in Wartime* (New York: Free Press, 2002).

4. A special Department of Defense briefing and unclassified excerpts from the Nuclear Posture Review may be found at www.globalsecurity.org/wmd/library/policy/dod/npr.htm.

5. The 1972 agreement between the Soviet Union and the United States to suspend deployment and future development of antiballistic missile (ABM) defenses was intended to make the world safer for offensive nuclear warheads, thus demonstrating both sides' political commitment to the stabilizing properties of mutual assured destruction. In 2001, however, the United States argued that relations had improved between the United States and Russia and that the graver threat was from offensive missiles fired by nonstate actors or rogue states. American developments in missile defense are thus highly conditioned by America's unilateral withdrawal from the ABM Treaty, a onetime centerpiece of nuclear weapons policy.

6. See the Missile Defense Agency website at www.acq.osd.mil/bmdo/.

7. William Scott, "F-16 Pilots Considered Ramming Flight 93," *Aviation Week and Space Technology* 157 (September 9, 2002): 7.

8. For another major area—transportation—in which military organizations need to interface with civilian agencies, see Stephen Flynn, "America the Vulnerable," *Foreign Affairs* 81 (January 2002): 60–74.

9. Home pages for the Department of Homeland Security and Northern Command are at www.dhs.gov/dhspublic/ and www.northcom.mil/.

10. Richard Betts, "The Soft Underbelly of American Primacy: Tactical Advantages of Terror," *Political Science Quarterly* 117:1 (2002): 19–36.

11. Colin Powell, "A Strategy of Partnerships," *Foreign Affairs* 83 (January 2004): 22–34.

12. See, for instance, Robert Kagan, "A Tougher War for U.S. Is One of Legitimacy," *New York Times* (January 24, 2004): B7.

CHAPTER 10

CIVIL-MILITARY ISSUES IN A COMPLEX WORLD

SUPREME COMMAND IN THE TWENTY-FIRST CENTURY

ELIOT A. COHEN

The term "supreme command" figures in a book by the same title that is too rarely read today: a memoir of World War II by Maurice Hankey.[1] A small, neat, bald man, Hankey was a former Royal Marine officer and model civil servant known to two generations of British politicians as "the man of secrets." From 1912 to 1938, he served as the secretary to the Committee on Imperial Defence and the Cabinet, a position which gave him a unique perspective on supreme command. Ironically, this man of secrets struggled with the censors to get his sober memoir published. The tale told by Hankey is that of supreme command as bureaucratic process—interwoven political and military decisionmaking at top levels of government. The British, masters of the art of committee work, established the modern pattern of supreme command in the Committee on Imperial Defence, which was a rough model for the National Security Council in the United States in 1947.

Supreme command as bureaucratic process consists of three elements. The development of specialized and trained military staffs began in the nineteenth and matured in the twentieth centuries. As late as the interwar period, some American war plans called for Washington-based staffs to sally forth into the field or establish command posts at sea, but by the outbreak of World War II, those ideas were understood to be impractical, if not downright dangerous. War is a complex bureaucratic effort that requires evaluating intelligence reports, managing the flow of matériel, and preparing strategic and operational plans that look out 6 months to a year or more. Thus supreme command as process requires modern strategic command posts as centers of activity in the White House and Pentagon when war breaks out.

The second aspect of contemporary supreme command, standing committees to coordinate the work of the military and later of government agencies, was primarily a result of World War II, although the practice did not spread to some regions of the world until the end of the century. Although the war gave birth to both the Joint Chiefs of Staff and a permanent secretariat to support them, it took nearly 40 years for the Joint Staff to assume its current form. Similarly, the National Security Council and its web of committees and multilevel working groups did not mature for decades and continues to evolve today with the organization of a Department of Homeland Security.

Finally, communication from the field to the center of government has progressed from the use by Abraham Lincoln of the telegraph office in the War Department as the first situation room to the live video feeds to presidential airborne or buried command posts of today. As world politics reacted to instantaneous television coverage, so did the requirement for supreme command. Despite fear of overcentralized decisionmaking, the impulse to pull more information to the highest level persists and does not appear to lag behind technological advances in the civilian sector.

However, supreme command is not only a set of extremely vital mechanisms, procedures, and innovations, but a more fundamental phenomenon. In this sense, it consists of the relationship between civilian leaders and military commanders; it is civil-military relations at the top in wartime, and as such, involves problems as old as war itself. To paraphrase Winston Churchill, the story of supreme command is one of reciprocal complaints by politicians and generals. In the United States, politicians fret over military options while soldiers complain about micromanagement, interference, and ambiguous guidance.

THE NORMAL THEORY AND UNEQUAL DIALOG

Implicit in this latter set of complaints (the former gain scant attention) is a common view of what a healthy civil-military relationship should look like —that is, what one might call the normal theory of civil-military relations. This theory holds that there should be a division of labor between soldiers and statesmen. Political leaders should develop objectives, provide resources, set broad parameters for action, and select a commander—then step back, and intervene only to replace him should he fail at his task. But this almost never happens, and military history contains an unending account of resentments voiced by generals about political interference. Livy

---

Eliot A. Cohen, "Supreme Command in the 21st Century," Joint Force Quarterly 31 *(Summer 2002): 48–54. Public domain.*

captures this approach in the irritable speech of a general about to embark for the Third Macedonian War in 68 B.C.:

Generals should receive advice, in the first place from the experts who are both specially skilled in military matters and have learned from experience; secondly, from those who are on the scene of action, who see the terrain, the enemy, the fitness of the occasion, who are sharers in the danger, as it were, aboard the same vessel.

Thus, if there is anyone who is confident that he can advise me as to the best advantage of the state in this campaign which I am about to conduct, let him not refuse his services to the state, but come with me into Macedonia. . . . If anyone is reluctant to do this and prefers the leisure of the city to the hardships of campaigning, let him not steer the ship from on shore. The city itself provides enough subjects for conversation; let him confine his garrulity to these; and let him be aware that I shall be satisfied with the advice originating in camp.[2]

Legislators level the same criticism on behalf of military leaders, although they usually reproach only members of the executive who represent the opposition party. Thus a Republican senator holding hearings on the conduct of the Kosovo conflict by the Clinton administration opined:

I firmly believe in the need for civilian control of the military in a democratic society, but I also believe we can effectively adhere to this critical principle by clearly outlining political objectives and then, within the boundaries of those objectives, allowing the military commanders to design a strategy in order to assure the achievement of those objectives.[3]

The normal theory is alive and well.

Yet the finest democratic war statesmen of the past did not act in accord with the dictates of this theory. They prodded, nagged, bullied, questioned, and harassed subordinates, although they rarely issued direct orders or overruled them. They invariably excited the irritation and even anger of talented military subordinates. William Tecumseh Sherman refused in cold fury to shake hands with Secretary of War Edwin Stanton at a parade celebrating the end of the Civil War; Chief of the Imperial General Staff and Chairman of the Chiefs of Staff Field Marshal Alan Brooke ranted at Winston Churchill in his published diaries in a manner that at times verged on hysteria. Nonetheless, the fruit of this style of civilian leadership—which respected military professionalism but never merely deferred to it—was victory.

Moreover, popular myth notwithstanding, the military failures of modern democracies have not resulted from micromanagement or interference, but the reverse. Lyndon Johnson and Robert McNamara did select targets in North Vietnam, but never questioned the assumptions of search and destroy operations. They repeatedly wrote something approaching blank checks for manpower and matériel for Vietnam and paid little attention to command arrangements devised by the military for conducting that conflict. For years they put up with generals whose profes-

sional qualities seem remarkably dim—William Westmoreland, for example, lasted 4 years in command. Abraham Lincoln, who could decide that an officer was incapable in a matter of months, would not have abided that. In a similar vein, disaster resulted between 1967 and 1973, when Israeli political leaders accepted the nearly reckless assumptions of their military advisers on the capabilities of the Arab states.

First and foremost, active control entails what can be called an "unequal dialog" between civilian politicians and senior officers. Most great political leaders rarely give orders to generals and insist that they obey: rather, they abide by Churchill's dictum that "it is always right to probe." They expect and even welcome blunt disagreement among the military and civilians in the privacy of a council chamber, but require solidarity and obedience outside. Indeed, during World War II, American generals and admirals failed to realize just how much British civilian and military leaders were at odds. This style of supreme command does not admit to principled boundaries between civilian and military authority. Rather, it recognizes that, depending on circumstances, civilians can find themselves involved in decisions that might appear to be none of their affair. It is, however, an approach to supreme command that varies in intensity of oversight and control: if it is meddling, it is selective meddling.

The unequal dialog is necessary for three reasons that are constant through history. The first is the profoundly political nature of war. When Clausewitz stated that *"war is only a branch of political activity . . . it is in no sense autonomous,"*[4] he made a radical and correct claim. Much in war, even seemingly tactical details, may have political consequences. Churchill found himself presiding over decisions on increasing the speed of transatlantic convoys by two knots. The issue confronting the Royal Navy was tradeoffs between greater risks of exclusion from faster convoys and greater safety for those in them. At a time when every shipload contributed to the survival of Britain, the question of what risks were acceptable became political, as did decisions on what kinds of weapons to use, what sort of collateral damage to inflict, and what level of casualties to accept. The only issue is whether politicians rely on the assessments by generals or their own judgment, which, in all likelihood, is better; but, in any case, political leaders are ultimately responsible. For example, if joint planners make decisions (rather than recommendations) on what kind of forces are acceptable to another nation, or what kinds of losses the American public can put up with, they are making choices for which they are neither particularly qualified nor ultimately responsible.

Active civilian control also appears because of a peculiar aspect of military professionalism: uncertainty. Generals and admirals often disagree vehemently on operational and tactical choices, and the stakes are sometimes too high for civilians to merely put faith in the senior officer present. The stakes have not been sufficiently high in recent wars to demand civilian intervention, but the potential remains. During World War I, Georges Clemenceau was compelled to arbitrate between his two senior generals, Ferdinand Foch and Philippe Pétain, over doctrine for defensive warfare. That case involved only one service: rivalries today among services and their perspectives on joint warfare rarely allow one to speak of a single view on the conduct of operations.

Finally, the uncomfortable truth is that those who often rise to the top in peacetime may be unsuited for high command in war. They may be too narrow, indecisive, or tolerant, or they may be insufficiently callous or merely unlucky. In the heat of war, politicians must reshuffle or relieve senior officers. That is a hard judgment to make: not all defeated generals are incompetent and not all victorious ones are able. Successful wartime statesmen create winning military establishments by forming sound judgments on character and personality. It is very different to determine whether a surgeon or engineer is professionally qualified. And only through intense dialog can civilian leaders hope to evaluate the quality of military subordinates.

The norm for healthy civil-military relations at the top of government, then, is tension and what often looks like interference, because civilians do things that can indicate a lack of confidence in their commanders. The resulting friction is real. One should note parenthetically that not every instance of civil-military comity indicates a healthy relationship. Recall that General Westmoreland wrote of the president, "I have never known a more thoughtful and considerate man than Lyndon B. Johnson," an indication that both men failed to manage their relationship.[5] A bland pleasantness in civil-military relations may also mean that civilians are evading their responsibilities or that soldiers have succumbed to the courtier mentality rather than that true harmony exists.

THE AGE OF GLOBAL PREDOMINANCE

The unequal dialog between soldier and politician is more important than ever because of the role of America in the world, the way it conducts foreign policy, and the complexities in the use of force.

French officials and writers refer to the United States as a "hyperpuissance"—hyperpower. Americans shy away from that term, and most object to "global hegemon" or "imperial preeminence." "Sole surviving superpower" or "indispensable nation" have a better ring to them because both of these terms imply a status derived from fortuitous circumstance rather than aspiration, or benevolence and not domination. And yet when national political leaders speak, it is unconsciously in the tones of a hyperpower. Foreign leaders are told what the United States expects of them and informed when the president is disappointed in their performance. More to the point, American power floods the planet to a greater extent than was the case even in 1945. Cold War alliances and attendant commitments remain intact, even if diminished. Meanwhile, American soldiers, sailors, marines, and airmen implement foreign policy in every corner of the globe—overturning regimes in Afghanistan, building bases in Central Asia, patrolling the Persian Gulf, throwing a protective shield around Taiwan, and chasing terrorists in the Philippines. Behind this force with its weaknesses—aging weapons and unneeded facilities—is an establishment fueled by a budget rising to nearly $400 billion a year, something like seven or eight times as much as the next largest potentially hostile power, China, and two and a half times the combined spending of its NATO allies.

Furthermore, U.S. foreign policy had become increasingly militarized in a number of ways even prior to September 11. Theater or combatant commanders, whose powers were greatly enhanced by the Goldwater-Nichols Act, led to dominance by the Pentagon in the daily conduct of foreign affairs. The Department of Defense can do things: it can move people and matériel, and it can staff problems more effectively than can other parts of the bureaucracy. Unified commands have resources and geographical prominence that surpass the capabilities of regionally oriented assistant secretaries in Foggy Bottom or ambassadors abroad.

Not surprisingly, theater commanders have been thrust to the fore in making foreign policy. The struggle of General Wesley Clark with the Pentagon (including the secretary of defense) over intervention in Kosovo in 1999 demonstrates what can result. No matter what one thinks about the outcome, it is clear that Clark was a semi-independent actor who negotiated with European nations as well as Washington and sought to impose solutions (e.g., blocking the Russian advance on Pristina Airport) in the face of opposition from both allies and parts of his own government.

Unified commanders have become proconsuls, and it should come as no surprise that they move easily in the realm of diplomacy—sometimes formally. A former general is secretary of state; in the last administration, two important diplomatic posts, Great Britain and China, were held by retired flag officers; and when the president recently needed a special envoy to the Middle East, he turned to a retired four-star general. There is nothing sinister in the rising influence and participation of active duty and retired officers in foreign affairs. It reflects their experience and abilities. But with the gradual extension of the roles of military officers in policymaking has come an unhealthily blurred outlook. When generals, active or retired, speak out on national security issues, they now do so less as military experts than as members of a broader policy elite. Pronouncements by senior officers on China, Yugoslavia, or the Persian Gulf contain considerably more on politics than on military operations.

Active civilian control can always breed resentment, and the situation today is no exception. Surely the present secretary of defense is one of the more assertive in recent memory, particularly (as far as one can tell) in terms of managing the actual conduct of operations. Yet stepping back, it is admittedly difficult for civilians to get their way in anything from major changes in acquisition programs to options for military activities that involve something less than a massive use of force. The problems are exacerbated by the slow pace with which administrations are staffed, the relative weakness of the Office of the Secretary of Defense compared to the Joint Staff, and the demands of a political system that keeps senior civilians on a treadmill of congressional hearings and periodic reports. But they also reflect the stability of a system that has in many instances shifted the terms of reference in civil-military relations from a question of military means and political ends to policy in a much broader sense.

THE FUTURE OF SUPREME COMMAND

The process of supreme command in the United States works well. We have an elaborate National Security Council system, with both the organization and technology (in particular, video teleconferencing) to make sound decisions on using force. To insiders, no doubt, the government often looks chaotic and incoherent, but by comparison with decisionmaking elsewhere, it is sound. There is tinkering to be done, and any system only works as well as those who administer it. Nonetheless, the problems of supreme command as process are largely solved.

Supreme command as relationship is always difficult. This situation is partly a result of the inevitable friction between those who are products of closed, hierarchical, rigid organizations and those with different backgrounds—in politics, business, law, or academe—who have nominal and sometimes real authority over them. These intrinsic difficulties are exacerbated in two ways.

First, the use of force abroad will increasingly put civil-military relations under pressure. There will be very few clean wars of the kind the American public thought was waged in 1991 against Iraq—a conflict won in a cathartic burst of violence followed by declarations of victory and parades at home. Future wars will be—and the current war is—ambiguous, openended, and inconclusive; they will require missions that the military does not like, and include different types of military governance. This prospect by itself will generate a great deal of friction. Compounding the issue will be contending views of warfighting within the armed forces, among which civilians must choose. In Afghanistan, civilian leaders observed and were drawn by applications of force that combined Special Operations Forces and long-range airpower, differing significantly from the conventional means used in the Persian Gulf. The rising influence of the special operations, space, long-range strike, and other communities will compete with advocates of more traditional platforms and outlooks, such as heavy armor and aircraft carriers. This will lead to a struggle not merely among services but within them. As civil-

ians select military leaders, they will favor some interests over others and find themselves caught up not only in debates over priorities, but over approaches to warfare. The ill feeling engendered by canceling the Crusader artillery system is only a foretaste of such tension.

Furthermore, even the resources of the United States will be taxed by attacking terrorists, dominating the Persian Gulf, and dealing with China while maintaining older commitments in areas like the Korean peninsula and Europe. In most recent major conflicts—Vietnam, the Persian Gulf, and the former Yugoslavia—America was flush with resources: the only question was choosing how much to project into a theater. As the demands of global predominance stretch the military, however, the time will come when civilian and military leaders find themselves compelled to accept real risks of a kind not seen since World War II. It is sobering to remember that by 1945, the Army had deployed all of its eighty-nine divisions overseas, and all but two were committed in combat. It was, as one historian put it, a photofinish, which may have been a "surprisingly accurate forecast," or equally likely "an uncommonly lucky gamble."[6]

Such choices would be more manageable were it not for the second and larger problem of supreme command and a widespread unwillingness to talk or even to think about it seriously. Administrations always will deny that civil-military tension exists even as tenacious reporters uncover it. In public, soldiers and statesmen praise one another and stoutly maintain that they think and act in harmony, even as something quite different goes on behind the scenes. In fact, a careful reading of memoirs and press interviews after the event shows the normal difficulty of such relationships—as the artfully written reminiscence by Colin Powell, *My American Journey,* reveals. Such understandable and sometimes necessary disingenuousness must not obscure the truth or change expectations about difficult times at the top when the nation goes to war.

The issue of civil-military relations has been exacerbated by a willful misreading of recent events. Simplistic and often erroneous interpretations of supreme command in both Vietnam and the Persian Gulf—the former supposedly representing a cautionary tale of interference, meddling, and overweening subjugation of military judgment, and the latter offering an exemplary case of clear objectives, delegation, and civilian detachment—are extremely harmful. Both interpretations miss the mark: Vietnam for reasons already noted—in particular, the strange detachment of civilians; and the Persian Gulf War because of the reality of political control (like compelling U.S. Central Command to throw assets at mobile missile launchers) and the deplorable consequences of absence in others (especially politicians who lacked involvement in negotiating the armistice).

Worst of all is the nearly irresistible temptation of political and military leaders (and for that matter, journalists and pundits) to preach the normal theory of civil-military relations even when they must know in their hearts that it simply does not work. And yet platitudes on "letting the military do their job" and "not interfering" persist, with the result that military leaders are surprised and resentful when it happens, and civilian leaders sometimes at a loss to know precisely what role to play. The unequal dialog in war requires a great deal of forbearance, mutual understanding, and good judgment. Even then it breeds friction and discontent. But that dialog will never occur if military education fails to prepare officers for it and civilians deceive themselves and others about its utility. The nation looks ahead toward a century that will be less brutal, but which promises no diminution of strategic difficulties. Whether we will successfully navigate the perils that lie ahead depends in no small measure on the skill with which that unequal dialog is conducted.

NOTES

This essay is based on the author's book, *Supreme Command: Soldiers, Statesmen, and Leadership in Wartime* (New York: Free Press, 2002).

1. Maurice Hankey, *Supreme Command*, 2 vols. (London: George Allen and Unwin, 1960). On the issue of supreme command, see Peter D. Feaver and Richard H. Kohn, eds., *Soldiers and Civilians: The Civil-Military Gap and American National Security* (Cambridge, Mass.: MIT Press, 2001); Dana Priest, "A Four-Star Foreign Policy?" *Washington Post* (September 28, 2000): A1 (see also subsequent articles "Engagement In 10 Time Zones" [September 29, 2000] and "Standing Up to State and Congress" [September 30, 2000]); and Aleksandr A. Svechin, *Strategy* (Minneapolis: East View, 1992).

2. Livy, *Histories*, Book XLIII, translated by Alfred C. Schlesinger (Cambridge, Mass.: Harvard University Press, 1951), Vol. XIII: 159–63.

3. Remarks of Senator Gordon Smith, "The War in Kosovo and a Postwar Analysis," U.S. Senate, Committee on Foreign Relations, 106th Cong. 1st sess., September 28 and October 6, 1999 (Washington, D.C.: U.S. Government Printing Office, 2000), 77.

4. Carl von Clausewitz, *On War*, edited and translated by Michael Howard and Peter Paret (Princeton, N.J.: Princeton University Press, 1989), 605. Emphasis in original.

5. William Westmoreland, *A Soldier Reports* (New York: Doubleday, 1976), 307.

6. Maurice Matloff, "The 90-Division Gamble," in *Command Decision*, ed. Kent Roberts Greenfield (Washington, D.C.: U.S. Government Printing Office, 1960), 381.

THE GAP: SOLDIERS, CIVILIANS, AND THEIR MUTUAL MISUNDERSTANDING

PETER D. FEAVER AND RICHARD H. KOHN

In a 1997 speech at Yale University, Secretary of Defense William Cohen claimed to see "a chasm developing between the military and civilian worlds, where the civilian world doesn't fully grasp the mission of the military, and the military doesn't understand why the memories of our citizens and civilian policy makers are so short, or why the criticism is so quick and so unrelenting." Cohen was voicing an age-old concern about America's relations with its military, one echoed in recent years by policymakers who fear that, absent an urgent threat to the nation's security, a democratic society will not nurture and support an adequate military, and that the military's loyalty to civilian authority will diminish accordingly.

The question at the end of the 1990s was said to be a "cultural" one: Has a gap in values between the armed forces and civilian society widened to the point of threatening the effectiveness of the military and impeding civil-military cooperation? To answer this question, we directed a comprehensive study, The Project on the Gap Between the Military and Civilian Society, sponsored by the Triangle Institute for Security Studies (TISS)—a consortium of faculty from Duke University, the University of North Carolina at Chapel Hill, and North Carolina State University—with a grant from the Smith Richardson Foundation. Specifically, the project sought to answer three questions: What is the character of the civil-military gap today? What factors are shaping it? What are the implications for military effectiveness and civil-military cooperation?

To assess these questions, we, in cooperation with roughly two dozen experts, surveyed some 4,900 Americans drawn from three groups: military officers identified for promotion or advancement, influential civilians, and the general public.[1] The questions we

This essay has been edited and is reprinted from National Interest *61 (Fall 2000): 29–37.*

posed addressed many topics: defense and foreign policy, social and moral issues, and the relations between civilian policymakers and military officers. Our team then analyzed the answers and combined them with other political, sociological, and historical studies to draw conclusions and offer specific recommendations.

We discovered that, although the concerns of the secretary of defense and others should not be exaggerated, numerous schisms and disturbing trends have emerged in recent years, which, if not addressed, may further undermine civil-military cooperation and in certain circumstances, harm military effectiveness.

NOT A NEW CONCERN

Concerns about a troublesome divide between the armed forces and the society they serve are hardly new and in fact go back to the beginning of the Republic. Writing in the 1950s, Samuel Huntington argued that the divide could best be bridged by civilian society tolerating, if not embracing, the conservative values that animate military culture. Huntington also suggested that politicians allow the armed forces a substantial degree of cultural autonomy. Countering this argument, the sociologist Morris Janowitz argued that in a democracy, military culture necessarily adapts to changes in civilian society, adjusting to the needs and dictates of its civilian masters.[2] The end of the Cold War and the extraordinary changes in American foreign and defense policy that resulted have revived the debate.

The contemporary heirs of Janowitz see the all volunteer military as drifting too far away from the norms of American society, thereby posing problems for civilian control. They make four principal assertions. First, the military has grown out of step ideologically with the public, showing itself to be inordinately right-wing politically, and much more religious (and fundamentalist) than America as a whole, having a strong and almost exclusive identification with the Republican Party. Second, the military has become increasingly alienated from, disgusted with, and sometimes even explicitly hostile to, civilian culture. Third, the armed forces have resisted change, particularly the integration of women and homosexuals into their ranks, and have generally proved reluctant to carry out constabulary missions. Fourth, civilian control and military effectiveness will both suffer as the military—seeking ways to operate without effective civilian oversight and alienated from the society around it—loses the respect and support of that society.

By contrast, the heirs of Huntington argue that a degenerate civilian culture has strayed so far from traditional values that it intends to eradicate healthy and functional civil-military differences, particularly in the areas of gender, sexual orientation, and discipline. This camp, too, makes four key claims. First, its members assert that the military is divorced in values from a political and cultural elite that is itself alienated from the general public. Second, it believes this civilian elite to be ignorant of, and even hostile to, the armed forces—eager to employ the military as a laboratory for social change, even at the cost of crippling its warfighting capacity. Third, it discounts the specter of eroding civilian control because it sees a military so thoroughly inculcated with an ethos of subordination that there is now too much civilian control, the effect of which has been to stifle the military's ability to function effectively. Fourth, because support for the military among the general public remains sturdy, any gap in values is inconsequential. The problem, if anything, is with the civilian elite.

The debate has been lively (and inside the Beltway, sometimes quite vicious), but it has rested on very thin evidence—competing anecdotes and claims and counterclaims about the nature of civilian and military attitudes. Absent has been a body of systematic data exploring opinions, values, perspectives, and attitudes inside the military compared with those held by civilian elites and the general public. Our project provides some answers.

THE REAL GAP

The military officers in our survey are indeed much more conservative than the civilian elite, but not more conservative than the general public.[3] On social values, the military diverges from both the elite and the public, fitting somewhere between the two—considerably more conservative than the former but not as conservative as the latter. On the issue of personal and political freedoms, for example, the military responses were unambiguously on the side of civil liberty. Very strong majorities of the officers we surveyed responded that they opposed removing from public libraries antireligious books (89 percent), procommunist books (94 percent) or prohomosexuality books (82 percent)—higher support for free speech than one would find in a random sample of the public at large. Intriguingly, one of the largest gaps between our military sample and that of the general public concerns views on human nature. On the classic question of whether most people can be trusted, a strong majority in both our elite samples—civilian (60 percent) and military (65 percent)—responded affirmatively, but an equally strong majority of our mass sample responded that "you can't be too careful." Still, military officers express great pessimism about the moral health of civilian society and strongly believe that society would be better off if it adopted military mores. Although civilian elites share such pessimism, they strongly disagree that the military has a role to play in civic renewal.

Military officers are more "religious" than civilian elites, although not as dramatically as some have claimed. If "religious" is measured by the frequency of attending religious services or of engaging in religious activity, the difference is slight. For instance, roughly comparable percentages of officers and civilian elites report that they pray anywhere from several times a day to once a week (roughly a fifth in all instances). The opinion divide is somewhat greater if the gauge is taken to be the degree to which faith plays a role in everyday life. Servicemen are more likely than civilian elites to agree that "the Bible is the inspired word of God, true, and to be taken word for word" (18 versus 11 percent); more likely to agree that "the Bible is the inspired word of God, true, but not to be taken word for word" (48 versus 34 percent); and less likely to agree that "the Bible is a book of myths and legends" (3 versus 7 percent). In any case, the differences are not strikingly large. Except for a larger proportion of Roman Catholics and a smaller proportion of Jews, religious identification in the armed forces is congruent with that of the broader American population.

Despite common assumptions to the contrary, civilian elites, although having relatively little personal connection with the military, do not express a great deal of hostility to the warrior culture. Only 7 percent (compared with 1 percent of servicemen) believe that a so-called "social engineering role"—that is, redressing historical discrimination—is a "very important" role for the military, although somewhat more (23 percent versus 14 percent of the military) say it is at least "important." However, on the question of whether the cultural gap hurts military effectiveness, roughly a third of civilian elites who have never served in the military think so, and, interestingly, slightly more than a third of the military agrees. Elite civilians do not have an inflated view (relative to the military) of the military's ability to perform effectively in constabulary missions, although they are somewhat more eager to use the military for humanitarian operations. The military officers we surveyed criticized the quality of political leadership and expressed a pervasive hostility toward the media; yet at the same time, both rising officers and the rank and file possess more trust and confidence in government institutions than do their civilian counterparts.

The officers we surveyed also express little dissatisfaction (about the same as the public and civilian elites) with the current extent of gender integration in the military, although they oppose expanding combat roles for women. But by a very large margin (76 percent), the military officers we surveyed oppose gays and lesbians serving openly, an idea that more than 50 percent of both the civilian elites and the mass public favor.[4]

Although officers still consider themselves to be neutral servants of the state, the officer corps has developed a more distinctive partisan affinity. Over the last generation, the percentage of officers that identifies itself as independent (or specifies no party affiliation) has gone from a plurality (46 percent) to a minority (27 percent), and the percentage that identifies itself as Republican has nearly doubled (from 33 percent to 64 percent).[5] Although elite civilians and the mass public are split about evenly, for every Democrat in our sample of officers, there are eight Republicans. Their political views are not,

however, the "hard right" Republican positions some observers expected to see.

WHAT FACTORS SHAPE THE GAP?

Most students of these issues, no matter what side they take in the debate, assert the following: the media are hostile to the military and portray it negatively, encouraging civilian hostility toward it; popular culture (e.g., films, novels) caricatures and disparages the military; the media influence civilian attitudes toward the use of force (the "CNN effect"); the gap between military personnel and civilians is widening, due to such factors as the decline in veterans as a percentage of civilian society, the downsizing of the armed forces since the Cold War, and the self-selection of the all volunteer force; and professional military education is the key arena in which the professional values and norms of the officer are shaped, and, hence, where civil-military concerns should be addressed.

Our team's findings challenge many of these assumptions. The media play a complex role in shaping civilian and military perspectives. But contrary to views widely held among elite military officers, the major daily newspapers do not generally portray the armed forces in a harsh light. Content analyses over a period of 6 months discovered ratios of positive to negative stories in excess of two to one.[6] Although popular fiction and film do stereotype both the military and civilian society, the effect is not uniform. Some action thrillers (e.g., *Executive Orders, Rules of Engagement*) have depicted tough realists in uniform with higher moral standards, greater loyalty, and more competence than civilians—and have disparaged politicians, political institutions, and a hedonistic and greedy civilian culture. High-brow fiction and film (*Catch-22*, Stanley Kubrick's war films) tend to do the reverse.[7]

Our military and civilian samples did differ in background, suggesting that demographics may partly exacerbate differences between the two groups. The up-and-coming officers in our sample were disproportionately male, white, Catholic, and highly educated. Nevertheless, differences of opinion persist even when demographic factors are controlled, suggesting that the military may selectively attract and promote a certain profile of officer that accounts for some of these differences. Thus, opinion gaps between officers and civilian elites are narrower at the lowest ranks than at the more senior levels. Numerous factors have contributed to the "Republicanization" of the officer corps. They include the fallout from Vietnam, Democrats abandoning the military and Republicans embracing it, an increase during the 1980s in the proportion of young people identifying themselves as Republican and expressing an interest in joining the military, and the Reagan-era military build-up.[8] Finally, the curricula at military academies and war colleges fail to provide officers with a coherent understanding of American society, its culture, and the tradition of American civil-military relations. In some cases, military education accentuates civil-military differences.[9]

THE STAKES

Unquestionably, this gap in viewpoints affects national defense, but not always in the way observers of civil-military relations seem to believe. So far, the defense budget has not been hurt by the gap and the divide does not appear to be the principal factor driving the current crisis of recruiting and retaining people in uniform.[10] Yet even though much is made of the public's respect for and confidence in the military, this confidence is brittle and shallow, and may not endure.[11] Personal connections to the military among civilians are declining. And because the gap in opinion tracks closely with the presence of such contacts, support for national defense could diminish in the future.

For the first 75 years of the twentieth century, there was always a higher percentage of veterans in Congress than in the comparable age cohort in the general population. This "veteran's advantage" preceded the introduction of the draft but began to decline with the end of conscription. Indeed, beginning in the mid-1990s, the percentage of veterans in Congress has dropped below that in the population at large. Thus far, this has not affected congressional voting patterns, but, if the general gap is indicative, the change in veterans' representation will diminish congressional understanding of the military and may affect agenda-setting and support.[12]

The experience gap is partly counterbalanced by the military's significance as an institution in American society, which remains very high. The material presence of the military remains strong; it consumes a large, if shrinking, portion of the gross domestic product (GDP); its reach is geographically distributed in rough proportion to regional population share (although sparse in the Midwest); and it is prominent on the public stage and especially in the media.[13] There are trends, however—such as the downsizing of the armed forces, which reduces social connections to the military—that will inevitably diminish its institutional presence.

Emerging professional norms within the officer corps promise more friction in civil-military relations. The principle of civilian control is well entrenched in the United States, but the military officers we surveyed showed some reluctance to accept one of its basic premises; namely, that civilian leaders have a right to be wrong. Contrary to the traditional understanding of civilian control, a majority of elite military officers today believes that it is proper for the military to insist rather than merely to advise (or even advocate in private) on key matters, particularly those involving the use of force—for instance, "setting rules of engagement," developing an "exit strategy," and "deciding what kinds of military units (e.g., air versus naval, heavy versus light) will be used to ac-

complish all tasks." Most likely a result of the Vietnam debacle—which the military still blames on civilian micromanagement, failed strategies, and "go along" military leaders—this assertiveness has already caused friction among policymakers and will continue to do so. It may lead in some instances to unprofessional behavior. Many military officers we briefed disagree with our interpretation of this finding. Ironically, many of them invoked a reading of *Dereliction of Duty*, H. R. McMaster's widely read and influential analysis of civil-military relations under President Johnson and Secretary McNamara, to justify a norm that military officers ought to insist that their advice be followed, and resign in protest if the senior civilian leadership seems to be pursuing a reckless policy.[14]

The so-called "Republicanization of the force" finding has received considerable attention and in some cases has been misunderstood. Although we discovered a remarkably high percentage of partisan association, we did not ask other questions on our survey about partisanship and therefore have no systematic evidence of a correlation between party identification and intensity of partisan activity. But there is anecdotal evidence that the old taboos are weakening: senior officers, for example, have identified their party affiliation in talks with junior subordinates or written letters to the editor critiquing one party or another. To dismiss this partisan gap with the explanation that the military is simply "identifying with the GOP out of self-interest" is to miss the point entirely. Developing a partisan identity harms the U.S. military and national defense. Viewed as "just another interest group," the armed forces would lose public and financial support. Uniformed advice would be less trusted by the civilian leadership, and, eventually, military professionalism would deteriorate.

Another of our findings is that the presence of veterans in the national political elite has a profound effect on the use of force in American foreign policy. At least since 1816, the greater the presence of veterans in this elite, the less likely the United States has been to initiate the use of force in the international arena.[15] This effect is statistically stronger than many other factors known to influence the use of force. The trend of declining veterans in the national political elite suggests, all other things being equal, a continuing high rate of military involvement in conflicts in the coming years.

Finally, the notion that the American public is unusually casualty shy—widely believed by policymakers, civilian elites, and military officers—is sheer myth. The American public will accept casualties if they are deemed necessary to accomplish a mission that has its support. Concerning the constabulary interventions that have become a staple of the post–Cold War era, the public is much more accepting of casualties than the military officers we surveyed.[16] The military's casualty aversion is not a mere expression of self-preservation, but is more likely grounded in a lack of confidence in the political leadership, or a belief by senior officers that casualties will spell failure, no matter what the outcome of the operation.

IMPLICATIONS

Three main critiques have been offered by those who think that the civil-military gap is much ado about nothing. First, divides of this sort have been around since the beginning of the Republic. Second, the principal challenges facing national security today are recruiting, retention, modernization, organization, and the growing mismatch between military missions and the resources devoted to defense—none of which is chiefly caused by this gap. Third, such divergences do not really matter because, at the highest policy levels, civilian and military elites have "fused"—that is, suppressed their differences to cooperate and work together amicably.[17]

But the gap and the tensions related to it are real, and they may have serious and lasting consequences for U.S. national security—consequences that could shackle future administrations. To begin with, the post–Cold War era is the first period in American history in which a large professional military has been maintained in peacetime. The lack of an urgent and immediate threat to the nation's existence, of the kind that during the Cold War forced military and civilian elites to reconcile their differences, may now foster a much higher level of civil-military conflict.[18] And if, as we foresee, support for the armed forces and understanding of their needs diminish, they will be less capable and effective.

Then, too, although the gap is not the principal cause of recruiting and retention problems, it is likely to exacerbate them in the future. The public's respect and admiration for the military no longer translates into a willingness to join the armed forces. The narrowing of personal connections to the military means that recruiters today must persuade doubtful prospects with less help from family and friends who have served themselves. Moreover, because expressions of support for the armed forces derive partly from personal connections to them, the reservoir of public confidence may shrink as the war generations die off.

Finally, the fusion between civilian and soldier at the most senior policymaking levels will not compensate for the distrust of civilians expressed in the lower ranks of the services. In fact, the divergence of opinion between the senior and junior ranks has created a troubling divide within the officer corps itself. In suggesting that the military has a responsibility not merely to advise but to insist on policy, field grade officers believe that their leaders, under certain circumstances, should resist civilian direction or resign in protest. In our follow-on exchanges with hundreds of military officers, a two-part rationale has been offered: civilian leaders are increasingly ignorant about military matters and so cannot be trusted to make wise decisions; and, in any case, the greatest disasters in U.S. history (Vietnam being the exemplar) could have been averted had senior officers spoken out against misguided, even duplicitous, politicians.[19] Mid-level officers who endorse this thesis express frustration with their senior leaders for not resisting more vigorously political pressure and perceived civilian mismanagement. Many complain about readiness, gender integration, and declining standards of discipline and training. Nearly half of the officers we surveyed said they would leave the service if "senior uniformed leadership [did] not stand up for what is right in military policy."[20]

The implications for civil-military cooperation, civilian control, and indeed, American democracy, are profound. The seniormost military officers we briefed understand that civil-military relations in a democracy do not and cannot operate this way. "The mid-level officers seem to think," one told us, "that we can 'insist' on things in the Oval Office. That is not how it works at that level." The military advises and even advocates strongly in private, but, once a decision is made, its duty is to execute official policy. In the U.S. military, there is no tradition of resignation in protest of dubious or unwise policies. In fact, the American military rejected individual and mass resignation—which can be indistinguishable from mutiny—at Newburgh, New York in 1783, when dissident officers tried to sway the army to march on Congress or go on strike, and were only dissuaded by a dramatic confrontation with their commander, George Washington. Union officers could not say in 1862, "We signed on to save the Union, not to free the slaves; we quit." George C. Marshall did not consider resigning in 1942 over the decision to invade North Africa, which he opposed. Resignation accompanied by protest undermines civilian control by giving a whip to the military ("do it our way or else")—and, paradoxically, leads to an *increase* in the politicization of the force. For if civilians fear a resignation in the event of a serious policy dispute, they will vet the military leadership for pliability and compliance and promote only "yes-men."

To address these troubling trends, the Department of Defense must undertake a series of initiatives to improve civilian understanding of military affairs. Secretary of Defense Cohen's recent "Public Outreach Initiative" website is a good but modest step. The Marine Corps' new "One Year Out" program, which places promising officers in civilian work places, should be expanded to more officers and broadened to the other services. The Reserve Officer Training Corps (ROTC) must be expanded without regard to "yield" until such time as the entire officer accession process can be revised. Congress should fund expanded outreach to the media and community leaders through such programs as the joint Civilian Orientation Course and through cooperation with Hollywood. Tinkering with the civilian side will fail, however, unless accompanied by change on the military side, and the place to begin is officer education. Civil-military relations need thorough coverage at every level, from Academy and ROTC through Staff and War College and flag officer short courses.

For the longer term, systemic change will be needed, particularly a review from the ground up of the military and civilian personnel systems, to assure the quantity and quality of people in national defense. The way we recruit, promote, and manage the precious human resources of the armed forces has changed remarkably little over the past half century, and the system has in any event been a response to two world wars and the Cold War—an industrial age system now trying to field an information age force. Likewise, the quality of civilian policymakers has too long been neglected. And, because national defense spending depends so heavily on professional and personal relationships among the uniformed and civilian leaderships, future administrations should institutionalize procedures for team-building between political appointees and their military counterparts and subordinates.

Ultimately, however, responsibility for the relationship, as with everything else in military affairs, lies with civilians: partly Congress, but especially the commander-in-chief. In the upcoming presidential election, the American public should judge its politicians accordingly—and in the coming years, hold them accountable for their stewardship of the nation's security.

NOTES

1. For greater detail on the project, see our website, www.poh.duke.edu/civmil.

2. Huntington, *The Soldier and the State: The Theory and Politics of Civil-Military Relations* (Cambridge, Mass.: Harvard University Press, 1957); Janowitz, *The Professional Soldier: A Social and Political Portrait* (Glencoe, Ill.: Free Press, 1960).

3. Ole R. Holsti, "A Widening Gap between the U.S. Military and Civilian Society? Some Further Evidence, 1998–99," TISS project paper; James Davis, "The Brass and the Mass," TISS project paper.

4. Laura Miller and John Allen Williams, "Combat Effectiveness vs. Civil Rights?" TISS project paper.

5. Ole R. Holsti, "A Widening Gap between the U.S. Military and Civilian Society? Some Evidence, 1976–1996," *International Security* (Winter 1998): 11; Holsti, "A Widening Gap," TISS project paper.

6. Krista Wiegand and David Paletz, "The Elite Media and the Military-Civilian Culture Gap," TISS project paper.

7. Howard Harper, "Reaching and Reflecting Audiences in Fiction and Film," TISS project paper.

8. Michael Desch, "Explaining the Gap," TISS project paper; David Segal, Peter Freedman-Doan, Jerald Bach-

man, and Patrick O'Malley, "Attitudes of Entry-Level Enlisted Personnel," TISS project paper.

9. Don M. Snider, Robert F. Priest, and Felisa Lewis, "The Influence of Professional Military Education," TISS project paper; Judith Stiehm, "Civil-Military Relations in War College Curricula," TISS project paper.

10. Benjamin Fordham, "The Civil-Military Gap and Peacetime Military Policy," TISS project paper.

11. Paul Gronke and Peter Feaver, "Uncertain Confidence," TISS project paper.

12. William Bianco with Jamie Markham, "Vanishing Veterans," TISS project paper.

13. James Burk, "The Military's Presence in American Society, 1950–2000," TISS project paper.

14. The book argues that the civilians lied to the service chiefs and misrepresented their views to Congress and the public—and the chiefs went along with it, thus contributing to a disastrous military strategy. Officers interpret the book as saying that the chiefs ought to have resisted the strategy and to have resigned over it—a rendering congruent with the "received wisdom" in the officer corps for the past quarter century. According to the author, the book does not argue that the Joint Chiefs of Staff (JCS) should have insisted that the administration follow its advice, but, rather, that the JCS failed to give its best military advice to the national command authority. H. R. McMaster, *Dereliction of Duty: Lyndon Johnson, Robert McNamara, the Joint Chiefs of Staff, and the Lies that Led to Vietnam* (New York: HarperCollins, 1997).

15. Peter Feaver and Christopher Gelpi, "Civilian Hawks and Military Doves," TISS project paper.

16. Feaver and Gelpi, "The Civil-Military Gap and Casualty Aversion," TISS project paper; Cori Dauber, "The Role of Visual Imagery in Casualty Shyness," TISS project paper.

17. David W. Tarr and Peter J. Roman, "The Military Leadership, Professionalism, and the Policy-Making Process," TISS project paper.

18. Russell F. Weigley, "The American Civil-Military Gap," TISS project paper.

19. In contrast, Eliot Cohen has argued that the success of democracies at war has involved effective questioning, oversight, and on occasion, intervention by civilian leaders into the technical aspects of military affairs. Cohen, "The Unequal Dialogue," TISS project paper.

20. This is much higher than the opposition expressed with regard to other hot-button issues about which officers have strong views: slightly more than a quarter said they would leave if "homosexuals were allowed to serve openly in the military," and only 6 percent said they would leave if "women were allowed to serve in ground combat units."

INFUSING CIVIL-MILITARY RELATIONS NORMS IN THE OFFICER CORPS

MARYBETH PETERSON ULRICH

INTRODUCTION

The backdrop of American military professionalism is the American political system. The heart of the American political system is embodied in the democratic institutions established in the Constitution. The Constitution's division of powers and authority, along with its system of checks and balances, "has succeeded not only in defending the nation against all enemies foreign and domestic, but in upholding the liberty it was meant to preserve."[1] George Washington in his farewell address noted that the American political system was based on "the right of people to make and to alter their constitutions of government"[2] and that adherence to the constitution is a sacred obligation of all until it is changed "by an explicit and authentic act of the whole people. The very idea of the power and the right of the people to establish government presupposes the duty of every individual to obey the established government."[3]

The American founders chose to establish a republic as the best way to uphold liberty and ensure the security of its citizens. "A Republic, by which I mean a Government in which the scheme of representation takes place, opens a different prospect, and promises the cure for which we are seeking."[4] In a republic, the fate of the democratic citizenry is entrusted to "the medium of a chosen body of citizens, whose wisdom may best discern the true interest of their country, and whose patriotism and love of justice will be least likely to sacrifice it to temporary or partial considerations."[5] Representative democracy entrusts the management of governmental affairs to those elected by virtue of their demonstrated aptitude or desire to take on the burden of being responsible for the "people's business."

Most of democratic theory is focused on ensuring that these political agents remain accountable to the polity. The founders' preference for republican democracy was rooted not in the belief that a system based on a "scheme of representation" and shared powers would produce the most efficient outcomes, but in the confidence that such democratic processes embodied the best chance for the preservation of liberty.[6]

Civil-military relations in a democracy are a special application of representative democracy with the unique concern that designated political agents control designated military agents.[7] Acceptance of civilian supremacy and control by an obedient military has been the core principle of the American tradition of civil-military relations.[8] U.S. military officers take an oath to uphold the democratic institutions that form the very fabric of the American way of life. Their client is American society, which has entrusted the officer corps with the mission of preserving the nation's values and national purpose. Ultimately, every act of the American military professional is connected to these realities—he or she is in service to the citizens of a democratic state who bestow their trust and treasure with the primary expectation that their state and its democratic nature will be preserved.

A military professional cannot operate independently from the state or the society he or she serves. Whether the service is to an authoritarian or democratic state or to something in between, the service is embedded in a societal context that forms the basis for a set of relationships. These civil-military relations reflect the absence or presence of democratic institutions and the nature of the particular national security system in place to formulate and implement national security policy.

This essay seeks to spark a dialog on the current state of civil-military norms within the U.S. military profession. A framework laying out key principles to consider when exercising professional judgment in this area is presented. Underlying the framework is the assumption that the character of a democratic state's civil-military relations has implications for the quality of its national security policy, the preservation of the democratic values on which the state was founded, and the relationship between the democracy's citizens and the military. A crucial factor in this process is the development of a brand of professionalism within the officer corps that is consistent with these underlying principles.

DEMOCRATIC MILITARY PROFESSIONALISM

The military profession is unique because of the distinct function that society has entrusted to it; that is, to direct, operate, and control an organization whose primary function is the threat or use of deadly military might against enemy forces or targets that the political leadership designates. Military professionals in all political systems share a mandate to be as competent as possible in their functional areas of responsibility in order to defend the political ends

This essay has been edited and is reprinted from The Future of the Army Profession, *ed. Lloyd J. Matthews (New York: McGraw-Hill Primis, 2002), 245–70. Reproduced with permission of the McGraw-Hill Companies.*

of their respective states.[9] However, military professionals in service to democratic states face the added burden of maximizing functional competency without undermining the state's democratic character. These military professionals must practice a brand of professionalism that takes this burden into account.

Samuel Huntington in his classic work, *The Soldier and the State,* posited that there is an inherent tension between the state exercising its responsibility to provide for the security of its democratic polity and militaries established to fulfill this function. Indeed, the requirement to balance the functional imperative (providing for the national defense) with the societal imperative (preserving and protecting democratic values)[10] calls for the development of democratic military professionals.[11] Officers comfortable with their roles as democratic military professionals will be better equipped to navigate the complex terrain of civil-military relations.

The Nature of National Security Communities in Democratic States

Democratic military professionals do not pursue their responsibilities to the state in isolation. They are part of a broader national security community comprised of national security professionals[12] from both the civilian and military spheres; other societal actors, such as journalists and academics, who contribute intellectual capital and foster debate; legislative bodies with constitutional responsibilities to oversee and provide resources for national security policy; and, finally, the public at large, to whom all of the above are ultimately responsible. National security policy is the product of the overlapping participation of all members of a state's national security community.

National security professionals, however, have a unique role because they are charged with the responsibility to formulate and execute national security policy within the prescribed bounds of a democratic policymaking process. These officials, who may come from both the civilian and military spheres, have diverse functions requiring mutual cooperation in order to make and carry out policy.[13] Each national security professional's "home sphere" emphasizes different areas of competence. The civilian national security professional's career will be characterized by greater experience at the strategic and political levels, whereas the military national security professional may be more rooted in technical expertise and operational knowledge related to the use of force. To craft effective national security policy, civilian and military national security professionals must develop overlapping areas of competence.

Scholars and practitioners alike recognize that the lines separating the competencies of military professionals and political leaders have become increasingly blurred. There is no clear threshold between peace and war marking the point at which political and military leaders hand off responsibility.[14] A strategic environment replete with military operations other than war, coalition partners, nongovernmental actors, and tenuous public support has resulted in an ambiguity of roles across the civilian and military spheres. Even if clear lines between peace and war could be drawn, the era when war was regarded mainly as the business of soldiers and international politics the exclusive domain of diplomats has long since passed.[15] The existence of a core group of national security professionals, comprised of capable and respected colleagues with overlapping competencies in political and military affairs, is instrumental in achieving balanced civil-military relations and effective national security policy outcomes.

Implications for Democratic Military Professionals

Democratic military professionals must understand the breadth and depth of their participation in the national security process. They must recognize that, although participation in a national security community is often a collaborative process requiring the expertise and inputs of various actors, there are distinct differences in responsibilities stemming from one's constitutional role in the process. These differences may dictate certain limits on the various legitimate actors in the process. Although national security in democracies is conducted within the context of civil-military relationships, these civil-military relations necessarily have a specific structure that channels participants' competencies and responsibilities to maximize security at the least cost to democratic principles.

The scope of this essay is limited to the development of a set of comprehensive norms for military professionals in their civil-military relations. Implications for other members of the national security community will emerge throughout this essay, but my charge is to improve the quality of participation of democratic military professionals in the national security policymaking process. My focus is on officers' political-social expertise, which includes behaviors related to their participation in the process as policy collaborators and in their participation in the political process in general.

A starting assumption is that professional development programs in the civilian and military spheres, as well as the conventional wisdom extant in society at large, inadequately address officers' political-social expertise. Studies reviewing the curricula at the precommissioning and senior service college levels of professional military education reveal that fundamental principles related to civil-military norms are poorly understood at the undergraduate level.[16] Furthermore, 20-plus intervening years of professional socialization to include attendance at a senior service college do not equip future senior military leaders with a thorough understanding of civil-military norms sufficient to navigate the ambiguities of "advice," "advocacy," "insistence," and "political participation."[17]

Even in the most advanced democracies, such as the United States, participants in the national security process are continuously engaged in improving the competencies required to adequately exercise their national security responsibilities. When an area of competence is underdeveloped or the competency levels are not sufficiently balanced across the civilian and military spheres, the achievement of both the functional and societal imperatives is threatened.

FIRST PRINCIPLES FOR MILITARY PROFESSIONALS IN SERVICE TO DEMOCRATIC STATES

My professional experience as a cadet, officer, and civilian scholar with 21 years of socialization to the military profession informs me that there is no commonly accepted theoretical framework on which to evaluate various civil-military behaviors. Cadets' and officers' understandings vary widely regarding what they regard as professional civil-military relations norms. Meanwhile, military professionals at various stages of development observe a confusing range of behaviors, illustrating the profession's failure to espouse a particular set of civil-military relations norms.

The specific recommendations that follow as each specific issue area is explored in this essay are rooted in a conceptual framework founded on two fundamental theoretical concepts that govern civil-military relations in democratic states. The first part of the framework examines the match-up between the competencies and responsibilities of actors from the civilian and military spheres who participate in the national security process. The second key piece of the framework stems from Samuel Huntington's contention that "military institutions of any society are shaped by two forces: a functional imperative stemming from the threats to the society's security and a societal imperative arising from the social forces, ideologies, and institutions dominant within the society."[18] This competition for preeminence between societal and functional imperatives is a primary source of tension in civil-military relations.

This conceptual framework governing democratic civil-military relations serves as the underlying theoretical basis to guide officers through the maze of civil-military issues that confront them throughout their careers. The competency-responsibility match-up and the balancing of the societal and functional imperatives will underpin the recommendations that follow for the development of civil-military norms for military professionals across the relevant issue areas.

ISSUE AREA ONE: THE ROLE OF MILITARY PROFESSIONALS IN THE POLICYMAKING PROCESS

A fundamental concept guiding national security professionals as they carry out their respective national security duties is that each position carries unique competencies and responsibilities. Distinctions between competencies and responsibilities are related to the nature of the position and the con-stitutional authority on which it is based. National security outcomes are optimized when civil-military relations are in balance; that is, when participants maximize their respective competencies and appropriately channel these competencies through their respective responsibilities. Conversely, suboptimal policy outcomes are often the result of an imbalance between participants' competencies and their decisionmaking responsibilities. Such conditions often result in strained civil-military relationships.

It may periodically, or even frequently, be the case that military professionals perceive that their competence or expertise in a given issue area is superior to that of civilian authorities with the responsibility to make policy decisions. Military professionals may perceive that civilian decisionmakers have set aside or discounted their expert advice in favor of counsel from national security professionals within the civilian sphere. Military professionals may perceive that the resultant policy outcome is poor. Indeed, the policy outcome *may be* poor as a result of such an imbalance between competencies and responsibilities in the national security community.

However, democratic civil-military relations are characterized by military professionals who tolerate such occasional poor policymaking outcomes to preserve the fundamental long-term interest of upholding the democratic character of the state. Military institutions in service to democratic societies should espouse as a fundamental norm of civil-military relations that the profession's first obligation is to do no harm to the state's democratic institutions. Usurping or undermining the decisionmaking authority of civilian decisionmakers is a clear violation of the responsibilities inherent in each actor's constitutional role.

An officer's oath is to "support and defend the Constitution of the United States against all enemies, foreign and domestic." An officer's allegiance, therefore, is not just to the state, but to the democratic character of the state as embodied in the institutions established in the Constitution. Professional judgment in this area depends on having in place a system of officer professional development that encourages the incorporation of democratic values in an officer's overall set of internal values and the cultivation of a sense of duty, honor, and professional obligation that links the special requirements of service to a democratic state to an officer's overall professionalism.[19]

Table 12 highlights the variations possible across the key factors of competence and responsibility, illustrating which variations deviate from first principles of civil-military democratic norms. The ideal match-up maximizes competence *and* responsibility, so as to get both the benefits of effective policy and compliance with norms of national security decisionmaking in a democracy. This option is found in quadrant 1 of Table 12. In this scenario, national security professionals pool their respective expertise in a collaborative process that culminates with the appropriate national security professional in the civilian sphere making the national security decision.

Table 12

Competence-Responsibility Match-Up

4. High competence + low degree of appropriately exercised responsibility = effective but undemocratic policy outcomes

1. High competence + high degree of appropriately exercised responsibility = effective and democratic policy outcomes

3. Low competence + low degree of appropriately exercised responsibility = ineffective and undemocratic policy outcomes

2. Low competence + high degree of appropriately exercised responsibility = ineffective and democratic policy outcomes

Competence   Responsibility ⟶

George C. Marshall's service at the highest levels of government from 1939 to 1950 epitomized the civil-military norms operating in option 1. As chief of staff of the Army, secretary of state, and secretary of defense, Marshall was the standardbearer for a generation of officers that unwaveringly accepted the concept of civilian control. Indeed, professional judgment in this respect was so firm that American military leaders consciously and quietly accepted a not inconsiderable number of policy decisions at variance with their professional strategic judgment. These instances ranged from the decision to support a strategy to hold the Philippines in 1941 despite the perceived lack of military means to do so, to acquiescence in the decision to invade North Africa in 1942 despite their concerns that such a diversion of military resources would dangerously prolong the initiation of a decisive cross-channel invasion.[20] Whether these military leaders exploited the limits of dissent within democratic policymaking processes will be addressed further in the next section. The relevant point here is that American military professionalism operative in the World War II era did not tolerate behaviors that threatened the democratic character of national security policy outcomes.

Perceived deficiencies in competency on the civilian side were not, however, completely ignored. At times when Marshall or his staff perceived strategic competence to be lacking in the political leadership, he encouraged his staff to see such instances as opportunities as opposed to liabilities. For instance, he viewed President Franklin Roosevelt's shortfalls as a strategic thinker as an opportunity to educate the president on how he could best support the war effort.[21]

Marshall's frankness coupled with his unquestioning acceptance of civilian authority gained him the full confidence of Roosevelt. Roosevelt repeatedly offered Marshall command roles in the war, which were never accepted due to each man's understanding that Marshall's contribution as expert adviser and honest broker in Washington was irreplaceable.[22] Marshall's rock-solid sense of duty, selflessness, and honesty were also highly prized assets in his service to President Harry Truman as secretary of state. Truman remarked, "He was a man you could count on

to be truthful in every way, and when you find somebody like that, you have to hang on to them."[23]

Marshall possessed the ability to refrain both from capitalizing on his popularity to prevail in the policymaking process and from spending his enormous political capital to further his ambition or advance his personal judgments. Such restraint is evidence that he understood the distinct responsibility that civilian political leaders had in the decisionmaking process. Such behavior also ensured that he was never viewed as a competitor in the national security decisionmaking process, but as a trusted source of counsel able to accept the rejection of his professional advice on one occasion in order not to compromise his status as an objective adviser in the next.

In option 1, civil-military tension is low due to the trust between expert military adviser and civilian policymaker. Political objectives are communicated to democratic military professionals, who in turn apply their strategic expertise to help shape the policy through particular applications of the military instrument of power. Having participated in forging the military dimensions of the policy, the military professionals are far more likely to embrace the policy. The resultant policy is characterized by the combined expertise of national security professionals from both the civilian and military spheres, the democratic accountability inherent in the civilian policymaker's position, and democratic institutions undiminished by officers intent on pressing their policy preferences beyond the bounds of the policymaking process.

The next best choice is found in option 2 of Table 12. In this scenario, competency is lower, but decisions are at least made within the norms of democratic national security decisionmaking. The short-term policy decision may be ineffective, but no long-term damage has been inflicted on democratic institutions. This is the option that democratic military professionals may find the most difficult to carry out, particularly if the competence deficit is perceived to be present in the civilian sphere.

Examples of civil-military relations characterized by option 2 can be found in states in the process of democratic transition from authoritarian rule. Democratic institutions are not yet fully developed, and competencies across the civilian and military national security spheres are uneven. Often the military possesses the lion's share of strategic expertise, but this expertise may be lacking in its appreciation of the broader political issues at play in strategy formulation.

The postcommunist states of Central and Eastern Europe a decade into their transitions from authoritarian rule had largely mastered the task of subordinating their military institutions to civilian rule. However, in many respects, national security policy outcomes remained ineffective due to the dearth of national security professionals with expertise in both political and military strategic competencies. Defense ministries and general staffs have been unable to develop national security planning processes that effectively set priorities, coordinate resources to focus on the achievement of the stated objectives, and ensure that the means allocated to defense are optimized. The political leadership, however, may often lack the interest, expertise, or both that are necessary to direct the overall formulation of national security policy. What has been particularly lacking is the ability of the political leadership to provide a strategic vision that can serve as the basis of a national security strategy and a national military strategy.

As a result, the actual capabilities of postcommunist armed forces are low. Progress has been slow, to be sure, but democratic institutions have not suffered from the intervention or overreach of military leaders in search of short-term gains for their institutions. Over time, competency in both spheres has grown. The political leaderships have assumed a heightened role in the national security planning process, and national security institutions have begun to respond to the demands for more rational defense planning. Real collaboration in the national security policymaking process is beginning to take place, with the potential to effect positive change in defense capabilities.

Although the particular circumstances of democratizing states have been highlighted to illustrate the dynamics of option 2, insufficient expertise channeled responsibly can at times plague even consolidated democracies. In option 2, the trust between the military and political leadership will not be as high as what is possible within more collaborative conditions of policymaking. Indeed, respect between the two spheres may be low due to the perceived incompetence that each sphere attributes to the other. The lack of expertise within the policymaking process will inevitably lead to substandard decisions that will adversely affect the military's ability to carry out the functional imperative of providing the state with effective national security. However, the societal imperative maintains its hold within the officer corps' professionalism. Democratic decisionmaking processes and institutions remain intact, so that when a balance of competencies across the civilian and military spheres is either achieved or restored, an outcome with the characteristics of option 1 is possible.

The worst outcome is represented in option 3 of Table 12. Decisions characterized as reflecting low

competencies that are then inappropriately channeled to circumvent democratic processes will result in poor policy outcomes that simultaneously harm democratic institutions. This particular choice should be a rare phenomenon in advanced democracies with developed national security communities. This outcome may, however, be common in states with both weak democratic institutions and unprofessional military forces.

Military rule is characteristic of option 3 of the table. Pakistan is an example of a state that has been plagued since its establishment in 1947 with questionable competencies on both the civilian and military sides, as manifested in chronically poor governance, weak democratic institutions, and unprofessional military forces in terms of their lack of restraint toward undermining civilian governments. The Pakistani army has overthrown a legitimately constituted government four times in Pakistan's 52-year history, which has severely strained the political stability and viability of democracy in the country.[24] The most recent takeover, in October 1999, posed particular challenges for the international community because it was the first time that nuclear weapons came under control of a military regime. During periods of military crisis, the caution, deliberation, and accountability that contribute to sustaining stability in democracies may be lacking in such contexts. Option 3 represents the worst outcome because the lack of competence inevitably leads to poor policy outputs coupled with the undermining or elimination of democratic processes.

Finally, option 4 of Table 12 represents an outcome that threatens advanced democracies with unbalanced civil-military relations. Overall national security competence may be high, but it may reside more dominantly in one sphere or the other. Military leaders may perceive that their professional judgment necessarily points to a particular policy decision. The political leadership, not concurring with this judgment, may select a different course of action. Such a mismatch of competence as perceived by the military, who lack responsibility for decisionmaking, may tempt military professionals to exert various aspects of their informal power in order to prevail in short-term policy decisions.

The post–Cold War era in U.S. civil-military relations has featured a series of incidents that one civil-military relations scholar, Peter Feaver, has called military "shirking"—that is, various degrees of military noncompliance in the face of the political leadership's desired policy preferences.[25] These incidents include the military's reluctance to embrace the Somalia, Bosnia, and Haiti missions, the resistance to President Bill Clinton's initiative to allow homosexuals to serve openly in the military, and efforts to resist dramatic changes in the military services' roles, missions, and force structure in the strategic reviews of the Clinton and George W. Bush administrations.[26]

Noncompliance may take various forms. One technique in the post–Cold War era has been to present only a limited range of options for the use of the military instrument of power, with each known to be unacceptable to the political leadership. When advising the administration of the elder George Bush on courses of action available for a potential Balkan intervention to achieve the political objective of reining in the violence in 1991, Chairman of the Joint Chiefs of Staff Colin Powell put the price tag at 250,000 troops.[27] This calculation, however, was based on assumptions interjected by Powell himself into the policymaking process; namely, that victory must be decisive and that overwhelming force must be used (the so-called "Powell Doctrine"). This preference for decisive force was incompatible with the political leadership's search for a course of action that could employ limited force to achieve limited political objectives. The military's actions, in this case, delayed action on a top-priority U.S. foreign policy initiative until conditions met the military's terms.[28] Other methods of military shirking include manipulating the defense bureaucracy to shape outcomes more in line with preferred policy ends and expending political capital in such a way that undermines the responsibility of the political leadership to implement their preferred policy end.[29]

Option 4 may also negatively affect the role of the military profession in affairs of state. The role of the military institution as a trusted policy collaborator that possesses expertise unique to the military profession may be compromised if option 4 is repeatedly chosen. Civilian policymakers may come to view the military actors in the national security community as competitors in the decisionmaking process, more concerned with promoting their own institutional interests than the national interest as discerned by civilian decisionmakers. Furthermore, a collaborative policymaking environment is impossible to achieve when either side works to intimidate the other. Fear on the part of the political leadership and lack of respect on the part of the military as an institution characterized civil-military relations in the Clinton administration. It was reported that President Clinton was more intimidated by the military than by any other political force. According to a former senior National Security Council official, "I don't think there was any doubt that he was out-and-out afraid of them."[30] But such fear-induced victories come at the cost of democratic institutions, because the national security actor who has inappropriately made or influenced policy is neither directly nor indirectly accountable to society at large via the ballot box.

Recommended Civil-Military Norm: The military profession's first obligation is to do no harm to the state's democratic institutions and the democratic policymaking processes that they establish. The civilian political leadership sets political objectives that the military supports in good faith. The military leadership should apply its expertise without shirking or taking actions that, in effect, have a determinative effect on policy outcomes. Military professionals must develop a clear sense of the distinction between national security competency and the responsibility to

exercise competency through distinct roles in the national security policymaking process.

The incorporation of such a principle does not mean that low levels of competency in either the civilian or military spheres are acceptable as a permanent condition of the civil-military relationship. Indeed, living with the result of ineffective short-term policy decisions resulting from low competency levels should inspire both sides to redouble efforts to close competency gaps. This could involve military and civilian actors in reassessing their national security competencies internally, with each side also identifying strategies to imbue their counterparts with either the military or political competencies that are lacking.

ISSUE AREA TWO: CIVIL-MILITARY NORMS VIS-À-VIS DISSENT

An issue area closely related to civil-military norms in the policymaking process is the problem of dealing with dissent. Dissent is normally considered to issue only from the military sphere, because the ultimate power over decisionmaking in a democracy lies with the civilian leadership. However, disagreement is a regular visitor to any collaborative decisionmaking process. Norms should exist in both spheres to encourage healthy debate while recognizing that disparate responsibilities mandate ultimate deference to the civilian decisionmaker.

Civilian policymakers should encourage military professionals to offer their best advice and not punish military participants who work within the established bounds of dissent in democratic national security decisionmaking processes. History is rife with examples of military professionals whose professional expertise was not advanced with sufficient candor and vigor within the bounds of collaborative decisionmaking to influence civilian leaders' national security decisions. H. R. McMaster's *Dereliction of Duty*, a widely read book among the current generation of American military officers, makes the argument that although the Joint Chiefs recognized that the graduated pressure strategy in Vietnam was fundamentally flawed, they did not vigorously express their professional judgment in the policymaking process. As a result, McMasters contends, that strategy was set without the best advice of the president's principal military advisers.[31] More recently, congressional leaders chastised the joint chiefs for continuing to support the fiscal 1999 defense budget instead of forthrightly advocating a budget that adequately ensured the readiness of the armed forces.[32]

Military professionals in service to democratic states should muster all of their national security expertise relevant to the achievement of a particular political objective that the civilian leadership sets forth. This is especially true when more strictly military competencies are at stake, such as judgments related to evaluating risks to soldiers and the tactical conduct of ongoing operations.[33] Civilian decisionmakers rightfully expect that military professionals under their command be forthright and thorough, yet ultimately compliant to civilians with regard to the determination of national political objectives and the ways to achieve them.

Policy advocacy has its place within the bounded limits of a collaborative policymaking process, but advocacy actions counter to the civilian leadership's known preferences may begin to usurp the civilian leader's distinct responsibilities. For instance, efforts to influence the terms of debate in public forums while national security professionals are still at odds in intragovernmental discussions may shift the military professional's status from objective expert to suspect competitor. Such actions both poison a collaborative decisionmaking environment that is critical to the achievement of optimal national security outcomes and demonstrate a willingness to overlook distinctions in responsibility across the civilian and military spheres to achieve short-term political gain.

Resignation in protest is often discussed as an acceptable means of dissent that permits policy advocacy to spill beyond the normal channels of discourse between military and civilian actors in the national security policymaking process. Resignation, however, may not be the panacea that those in favor of a more assertive role for military leaders in the policymaking process sometimes suggest. Military leaders should consider both the positive and negative consequences of resignation before resorting to this action. First, resignation is the extreme method of dissent. The intent is to publicly express disagreement with the responsible political leaders, thus pitting the resigning actor's political capital against the policymaker's. A resignation followed by news media outbursts aimed at advancing institutional interests over national interests may harm the objective status of the military profession in the democratic political process.

On the positive side, resignation represents a clear withdrawal from future participation in the policymaking process and consequently removes the threat that the resigning actor may continue to undermine the role of the political leadership within the official system. The possibility of playing the role of "competitor" vis-à-vis the elected political leadership in the policymaking process is diminished, although a competitor role could be assumed outside government in retirement.

Recommended Civil-Military Norm: Military participants in the national security policymaking process should expect a decisionmaking climate that encourages a full exchange of expertise across the military and civilian spheres. Military professionals, furthermore, should have the expectation that their professional judgment will be heard in policy deliberations. However, military participants must develop the professional judgment to recognize when the bounds of the policymaking process have been breached. When acts of dissent take them outside these bounds, military leaders must acknowledge that they have gone beyond the limits of their roles in terms of offering advice and have begun to carry out behaviors that directly challenge the role of political leaders with the responsibility to make policy.

ISSUE AREA THREE: CIVIL-MILITARY NORMS AND PARTISAN POLITICS

Much attention has been paid in recent years to the increasing willingness of U.S. officers to label themselves as conservative Republicans. Although Morris Janowitz's research in the 1950s documented military officers' self-identification as political conservatives,[34] partisan identification as conservative Republicans is a development of more recent decades. Despite Janowitz's finding that most officers of the pre-1960s were moderately conservative,[35] the ideological gradations within the two parties were such that these officers could have found a home in either the Democratic or Republican party at the time. Most officers of that era, however, chose not to profess a particular party affiliation.

Ole Holsti's research has contributed empirical data to the ongoing professional and scholarly dialog concerning the growing gap between U.S. society and its military with regard to party identification. Using survey data resident in the Foreign Policy Leadership Project database, Holsti showed that between 1976 and 1996, the proportion of officers who identified themselves as Republicans doubled from one-third to two-thirds.[36] Tom Ricks's interviews with junior officers led him to conclude, "Today's junior officer seems to assume that to be an officer is to be a Republican."[37]

Ideological self-identification also points to a rise in professed conservatism in the officer corps. Holsti's data show that the ratio of conservatives to liberals in the officer corps went from four to one in 1976 to twenty-three to one in 1996.[38] The shift is due to the decline in the self-identification of officers admitting to be liberals of any variety—even moderate liberals. In 1996, only 3 percent of the officers surveyed reported an ideological self-identification as somewhat liberal or very liberal, whereas 73 percent reported that they were somewhat conservative or very conservative.[39]

Although it may be reasonable to expect the ratio of conservatives to liberals in a culturally conservative, hierarchical institution such as the U.S. military to be something less than a mirror of American society, a twenty-three to one conservative to liberal ratio as evident in Holsti's data may begin to raise questions about whether the military reflects the society it serves. By way of contrast, the data gathered in the 1999 Triangle Institute for Security Studies (TISS) survey revealed that civilian elites self-identified more evenly between conservatives and liberals, with 32 percent reporting that they were either somewhat conservative or very conservative and 37.5 percent weighing in as either very liberal or somewhat liberal (in contrast, only 4.4 percent of the officers in the 1999 survey reported an ideological self-identification as somewhat liberal or very liberal).[40]

To fulfill its primary obligation to its client, society must grant the military the legitimacy to carry out its solemn function. Legitimacy is enhanced when the military institution is perceived to be "of society" in terms of being composed of a representative cross-section of the population. The alternative outcome is to increasingly become a distinct group representing only limited demographic characteristics and attitudes of the society at large. As the perception grows that the military's political ideology is dramatically divergent from the society it serves, the parallel assumption will grow that the military is an institution apart from the society it serves. How an officer votes should remain an officer's prerogative in a democracy, but as the ideological gap between the military and society at large grows, it may become more difficult for soldiers to conduct their professional affairs in an ideologically neutral way.

Military sociologists who study organizational culture break military socialization into two dimensions —anticipatory and secondary. Anticipatory military socialization encompasses individuals who self-select to belong to the military, thus implying a fit between organizational and personal worldviews.[41] Secondary military socialization takes into account the organization's role in instilling a worldview in its members.[42]

The effects of a growing perception in society that the military is a haven for politically conservative youths will only skew the self-selection rates among politically conservative youths further. Accession policies should be examined to ensure that measures are in place to recruit a more politically diverse element of the citizenry to serve society as military professionals. Such moves as enhancing Reserve Officer Training Corps (ROTC) programs in Ivy League schools or in traditionally African American colleges may help to balance out anticipatory socialization trends. Within the secondary socialization process, over which the military has more direct control, there should be a return to the fundamental principle that Morris Janowitz espoused in his classic work, *The Professional Soldier.* He advocated imbuing within military professionals an ethic of civil service that would view detachment from partisanship as a critical element for assuring society of the military professional's partisan neutrality.[43] Incorporating the principle of nonpartisanship as part of an officer's professional code (rather than relying on a mere tradition, which is always subject to erosion) could help restore balance in U.S. civil-military relations.

The profession must take note that a long-term erosion of the American military's tradition of political neutrality, which tradition has its roots in the advent of the professionalization of the American military led by Generals William Tecumseh Sherman and Emory Upton (as well as Rear Admiral Stephen Luce) in the decades following the Civil War, has since taken place.[44] This now-visible trend has profound implications for the profession and its ability

to serve society. Certainly, the icons of the profession noted above would be distressed to learn that many officers today regard membership in a particular political party to be a defining element of officership.

The American military at present needs to reinforce the professional norm that it can serve any political party in a principled fashion. Principled professionalism is not determined by the congruity of a particular party's agenda with an individual soldier's principles, but by adherence to the norms of principled officership. *The United States Military Academy Strategic Vision—2010* lays out eight principles of officership to guide officers in carrying out the responsibility that society entrusts to them. One of these key principles is subordination. The guidelines demand that "officers strictly obey the principle that the military is subject to civilian authority and do not involve themselves or their subordinates in domestic politics or policy beyond the exercise of the basic rights of citizenship. Military officers render candid and forthright professional judgments and advice and eschew the public advocate's role."[45] Soldiers must be equally comfortable serving either party that society chooses to govern.

Advancing civil-military norms related to officers' political activities must balance officers' constitutional rights to participate in the political process with necessary limits stemming from the military profession's unique responsibility to society. Thus far in this essay, I have advocated the development of a collaborative national security policymaking environment that draws on the strengths of each component of the state's national security community. This is at odds with a vision that some civil-military relations theorists espouse; that is, those who focus on the primacy of civilian control achieved on the basis of two distinct, nonoverlapping civilian and military spheres, with the military sphere clearly subordinate to the civilian sphere.[46]

In contrast, the collaborative vision of national security policymaking rejects the notion that military professionals obediently execute the demands of the civilian government as apolitical beings somehow immune from the politics of conflict and distant from the political process itself. National security professionals from both the civilian and military spheres must be participants in the national security decision-making process if competencies from both spheres are to be sufficiently leveraged.

Indeed, the very concept espoused here of the national security professional as a military officer schooled in the political context of military policy requires the participation of at least some military professionals in civilian graduate programs to master many of the competencies shared by civilian national security professionals.[47] There are, however, important distinctions to be made between possessing a certain degree of political expertise in order to serve in a policy collaboration role, on the one hand, and using political-military expertise as the basis for abusing the limited responsibility of national security professionals within the military sphere in the decision-making process, on the other.

Perhaps the most contentious area of this debate concerns norms governing policy advocacy that may stem from individual political preferences. The terms of this debate often revolve around whether military members' identities are thought to be rooted in their rights as citizens or in membership in a profession with circumscribed rights stemming from the unique obligation of the profession to society. "The mythic tradition of the citizen-soldier is dead," declared defense specialists Elliott Abrams and Andrew Bacevich.[48] The nature of modern war has spurred the gradual evolution of military forces comprised of volunteers whose military service is not a compulsory, transitory departure from civilian life, but rather a compensated choice to make military service their lives' callings.[49] Today, soldiers consciously decide to depart civilian life to serve society in the military profession. In doing so, these all volunteer force members are more beholden to professional norms than were their conscripted forbears.

Those more approving of partisan behavior argue that "soldiers in uniform are, after all, citizens, and so long as they obey orders they retain the rights of expression of their counterparts in the civilian world—and most certainly so the moment they doff the uniform."[50] Although this position is possibly valid from a purely legal perspective, it ignores the impact that such political behavior can have on the profession's ability to perform its primary function in society.[51] Society cannot be adequately served by a military profession that refuses to subordinate its individual and institutional interests to the greater national interest, or that is perceived to take sides in the political process.[52]

There was a general perception in the 2000 presidential election that "the military" supported Republican candidate George W. Bush. This did not stem from any specific mass actions by active duty military personnel or participation in overt campaigning, but resulted primarily from a manifestation of self-identification among military personnel, reported widely in the news media, that the Republican party and its presidential candidate were the "best fit" for the military culture.[53]

There still seems to be a consensus within the U.S. military profession that the "tradition of an apolitical military is critical to our democratic system."[54] According to a Marine brigadier general survey response, "The military is held in high esteem by the American public because we remain neutral and nonpartisan. Once the institution is seen as 'looking out for itself' instead of looking out for the country, we risk losing the trust of the American people."[55]

The problem is defining and clarifying professional norms regarding what acts are unacceptably "political." Involvement in a collaborative policy-making process in accordance with the norms laid out above constitutes engagement in politics, but in a manner that is consistent with the military professional's advisory and expert role. However, expressions of partisan preferences that could be perceived as speaking for the profession itself fall outside professional norms. Both budding professionals and seasoned veterans have difficulty distinguishing between legitimate participation in the national security process and behaviors that are gradually steering the profession away from its apolitical roots toward partisanship.

Recommended Civil-Military Norm: Principled officership requires adherence to an ethic of nonpartisanship. Military professionals must be comfortable serving any political party that prevails in the democratic political process. The demands of principled officership must carry the day, even if they entail limitations on officers' liberties as citizens. Officers should consider the impact that their public profession of political beliefs has on their subordinates and on the relationship of the profession to society at large. Association of the military profession with any single political party undercuts the legitimacy on which the military depends to serve society.

ISSUE AREA FOUR: CIVIL-MILITARY NORMS AND RETIRED OFFICERS

The development of professional norms governing the political activities of retired officers, especially retired general officers, is intrinsically linked to the goal of keeping partisanship out of the active ranks. As one active duty two-star Marine officer noted, "my concern is the effect of a retired general officer's commitment to a political party immediately after retirement on junior officers. Rather than the junior officer taking time to be fully informed on the current issues, there may be a tendency to blindly follow a senior that they admire for his/her service accomplishments."[56]

Another important consideration is the effect that retired officers' actions have on public perceptions of the military as an institutional actor in the political process. As one active duty four-star officer put it, "constitutional rights are not the issue. Judgment is. The public doesn't distinguish between the active duty general [officer] and retired general [officer]. As a result, the entire military is politicized. If a retired general officer elects to run for office and enter the process that is fine—but not otherwise."[57]

In a domestic political environment in which the civil-military gap is growing, such distinctions will be increasingly difficult to make. Indeed, one could argue that the Bush campaign's attempt to line up retired general officers of celebrity status to support candidate Bush and to participate directly in the campaign through the Republican convention and on the campaign trail was an attempt to create the impression in the public's mind that "the military" was behind Bush. If asked to identify general officers of the U.S. military, probably few Americans could name a general officer on active duty, but many could likely recall the names Colin Powell and H. Norman Schwarzkopf from their association with the successful outcome of the Gulf War.

Although these individual retired officers may justify their involvement in the Bush campaign as merely the exercise of their rights as private citizens, their individual decisions may by themselves—or certainly in the aggregate—begin to look like an institutional preference. But is it in the best interests of the profession as a whole to be perceived to hold partisan preferences and to publicly advocate them as a participant in the political process? Such a development necessarily has a negative impact on the profession's retention of its nonpartisan tradition, which has been an essential element of forging effective national security policy.

The profession would be well served if retired officers paused to consider the impact of their individual actions on the profession and on the military's retention of a nonpartisan stance. Professional self-policing in lieu of strict legal restrictions on retired officers' free speech rights is the only feasible course of action in this issue area. Attempts to legally regulate such political activities would be frustrated in the courts and might run counter to the goal of infusing in emergent military professionals a sense of responsibility, even later in retirement, to protect the profession's capacity to serve society. Instead, the preferred method is to turn to the profession's internal capacity to educate officers on their responsibility in this area and to foster professional judgment as well as expected standards of behavior.

Most retired officers, especially retired general officers, expect to be treated as members of the profession in retirement. Although retired officers may eagerly shed the various restrictions that governed their lives on active duty, it is customary to refer to a retired officer by his or her rank. Many retired officers pursue second careers in the defense industry. It is not unusual for these officers, especially those of higher rank, to include their rank on their business cards. Anecdotal testimony of active duty officers in the field as buttressed by my own experience indicates that such retirees working as contractors and collaborating with active duty personnel are often bestowed great deference in the workplace due to the weight that their active duty rank still wields.[58] In addition, norms of protocol call for affording former senior officers particular courtesies commensurate with their active duty rank.

Andrew Abbott in his seminal book, *The System of Professions,* singled out the mastery of a body of abstract knowledge as the definitive characteristic of a profession.[59] In the same vein, Huntington characterizes a professional as having acquired a body of expertise through prolonged education enhanced through experience. Once these standards of professional competence are gained, they "are capable of general application irrespective of time and place."[60] In the military profession, rank is a measure of professional competence, with the most expert members at least notionally being awarded the highest ranks. The military profession is unique because it requires its most expert members to retire at the peak of their professional competence to make room for the next

generation of senior leaders. It is not surprising, then, that in retirement senior officers are often sought out to share their expertise to shape policy decisions or to advise active officers. As the masters of abstract knowledge, still of great utility to the current generation of active senior leaders and to society in general, military officers are essentially professionals for life.

Corporateness is another essential element of professionalism that carries into retirement. The common bonds of shared professional competence, social associations, and continued interaction with the profession through professional organizations, as well as access to various exclusive amenities (e.g., medical care, Post Exchange shopping, commissary privileges, and access to most post services), connect retired officers with the active force for life.

More uncertain in its applicability to retired officers is responsibility. What ongoing responsibilities do retired officers have to the military profession? Huntington argued that "the principal responsibility of the military officer is to the state."[61] Furthermore, Huntington continues, "His responsibility to the state is the responsibility of the expert adviser. . . . He cannot impose decisions upon his client which have implications beyond his special competence."[62] With regard to the continuing service to society as a military expert, a four-star active duty officer commented, "Upon retirement, general officers have all the rights of citizens not otherwise in government. However, should they endorse a political party or candidate their usefulness to their service or DoD as a military expert becomes compromised!"[63]

Finally, although an explicit legal code[64] may regulate some aspects of this responsibility to society, "to a larger extent, the officer's code is expressed in custom, tradition, and the continuing spirit of the profession."[65] To the extent that a retired officer remains a member of the military profession, commitment to some continuing responsibility to society must remain.

On all three counts, expertise evinced in the mastery of abstract knowledge, corporateness, and responsibility, retired officers retain important aspects of the professionalism ascribed to serving officers. The active forces and society grant retired officers qualified authority to continue as members of the military profession. However, "authority often confers obligation."[66] The question at hand is what are the limits of this professional obligation and who sets them?

Abbott offers a framework to settle jurisdictional conflict across and within professions.[67] One potential application of this framework to the conflict between the professional obligations of active and retired officers is to consider the work of retirees as a profession within a profession. As the current stewards of national security accountable and subordinate to the political leadership, active duty senior leaders set the professional norms. These current senior leaders can establish a constructive requirement for retired officers to reflect on the adverse impact the unrestrained exercise of their political rights could have on the profession and its ability to participate neutrally in the political process and to serve society.

Such professional regulation would, in effect, subordinate the retiree sphere of military professionals under the active strategic leadership in professional areas that have a continuing impact on the military profession. This will require the renegotiation of jurisdictional boundaries within the profession that both recognizes retirees as members of the profession and obligates them to adhere to a set of professional norms aimed at preserving the military profession's ability to perform its exclusive function within society. A self-regulating profession develops norms in the formative educational and training experiences of its new members and continuously enforces such standards as new members progress to greater positions of responsibility in the profession.

Recommended Civil-Military Norm: Retired officers have a continuing responsibility to serve the military profession. Although such professional responsibilities are more limited than those of the currently serving senior leadership, some degree of professional obligation remains. Active duty senior leaders as the stewards of professional norms should set the expectation that retirees consider the impact of their individual and mass actions on the profession. Useful guidelines in this area include considering the impact particular activities could have on the active serving force, contemplating whether individual choices could be perceived as institutional positions, and finally, exercising judgment regarding the degree to which the expression of partisan preferences affects the military institution's capacity to be perceived as nonpartisan in the policymaking process.

Issue Area Five: Balancing the Functional and Societal Imperatives

In the literature on civil-military relations, the functional imperative to provide for the national defense and the societal imperative to preserve and protect the democratic processes of the republic are often presented as competing and implicitly incompatible obligations.[68] It is important to consider analytical frameworks that do not assume that these imperatives are always in opposition and to reflect on contexts in which they may be mutually reinforcing.[69]

Military professionals in service to democratic states, as noted at the beginning of this essay, must be as functionally competent as possible to secure the national security interests of the state. Additionally, they are simultaneously charged with performing this function within the societal context of liberal democracy. Their responsibility is to defend the state while concurrently appreciating that the pursuit of national security is affected by national values, national character, and the ideology of the state.

Developing norms in this issue area is inextricably linked to the desired professional judgment associated with the first two issue areas identified

in this essay. These civil-military norms focused on the military professional's role in the policymaking process. Mastering the "first principle" inherent in the responsibilities-competencies match-up is key to grasping the mandate to balance the functional and societal imperatives.

The history of American civil-military relations is replete with examples of the military institution battling with its civilian masters over the incorporation of societal values in the military. The integration of blacks and women both came amid protests from within the military profession that such changes would harm the institution's ability to perform its function.

In the case of President Harry S. Truman's initiative to integrate the armed forces through Executive Order 8981, Truman used his executive powers to make a first move toward enacting the broader civil rights agenda that he campaigned on in 1948. The desegregation order came the same day that he issued an executive order calling for fair employment within the federal government.[70] Both moves were aimed at correcting what Truman considered to be glaring injustices incompatible with national values.[71] Chief of Staff of the Army General Omar Bradley opposed the president's desire for instant integration of the armed forces, arguing it "would be hazardous for [the United States] to employ the Army deliberately as an instrument of social reform."[72] Resistance was also rooted in postwar political realities that made the Army reluctant to alienate powerful Southern legislators and the large portion of its own officer corps that hailed from Southern states.[73] In the end, integration under General Bradley was slow and gradual. Ironically, the functional imperative demanding that sufficient manpower be available to effectively man the units being sent to Korea spurred Bradley's successor, General J. Lawton Collins, to fully comply with the integration order.[74]

A crucial barrier to giving women the same opportunities to advance through the officer ranks as men was removed in 1975 with President Gerald Ford's signing of Public Law 94-106, which called for the admittance of women to the service academies in 1976. Clinging to tradition and citing an inevitable dilution of the nation's ability to produce combat leaders, the Army, Navy, and Air Force stood united in their opposition to the congressional pressure to open the academies' doors to women.[75] But such a stance was out of sync with various compelling forces at work within the societal imperative. First, indications of society's readiness to embrace the concept of equal opportunities for women was evident in Congress' passage of the Equal Rights Amendment in March 1972.[76] Second, congressional sentiment to admit women to the academies had been brewing for several years due to the frustrations of individual members of Congress from both parties to have their female nominees admitted. Additionally, lawsuits were crawling through the legal system on behalf of women applicants.[77] The congressional hearings pitted the functional imperative against the societal imperative. The services' arguments against encroachment on its professional autonomy clashed with the congressional will to integrate. Ultimately, women were admitted with the passage of amendments to DoD legislation pending in both the House and the Senate without much congressional opposition.[78]

Democratic military professionals must develop the judgment required to distinguish between "social engineering" and legitimate evolutions of professional practices reflective of the democratic values of the state. Professional autonomy in a democracy does not mean that the profession can regulate itself in ways that are incompatible with democratic values. Many armies in service to authoritarian societies, such as those that characterized the former Soviet bloc, may have had long traditions of abusing conscripts, keeping their internal operations secret from the public, and excluding undesired elements of the society from its ranks. But when democratic institutions began to take root, the newly empowered democratic civilian leaders—increasingly accountable to the newly empowered democratic citizenry—demanded change. The shift in the political system sparked inevitable changes in the form of military professionalism practiced in the state.[79]

Ideally, military institutions that are attuned to the discrepancies between professional norms and democratic norms will anticipate the inevitability of externally driven change. Such proactive behavior affords the military profession the opportunity to autonomously incorporate changes more on its own terms. The next barrier to fall is likely to be the open integration of gays into the military. Recent surveys show that societal attitudes are well ahead of the military on this issue. The 1999 TISS study reported that although 75 percent of military leaders are opposed to integrating gays, 57 percent of the public and 54 percent of civilian leaders are in favor of doing so.[80] The right configuration of societal forces and the political support of a Democratic Congress and/or a Democratic president may ultimately compel the change. Arguments that such a change will erode the functional imperative will likely be advanced again, but just as with the previous instances of integrating blacks and women, the institution will likely adapt without significant damage to its functional capabilities. Such a result, however, depends on the military institution setting the appropriate conditions within the profession for the change to succeed.

Recommended Civil-Military Norm: Tension between the functional and societal imperatives is a constant feature of civil-military relations in a democracy. Military professionals in service to democratic states must recognize that their jurisdiction over the profession is limited in that it is inherently connected to societal values and the realities of civilian control, leaving ultimate control over the profession in the hands of their constitutional overseers. It is in the best interest of the military to foster the development of professionals who are engaged with their societies. Officers must stay abreast of societal forces and their reflection in the preferences of those empowered with civilian control—the president and Congress. Such engagement will allow the profession to better manage civilian-driven change and improve the prospects to retain professional standards of good order and discipline essential to the functional imperative. Military institutions that fail to anticipate societal-driven change will inevitably succumb to the realities of the system of democratic political control, which allows civilians vested with the appropriate authority to demand that democratic values prevail. Military professionals must carefully distinguish between their responsibilities to objectively advise on the potential adverse impact of societal-driven change and their professional inclination to thwart initiatives that threaten to alter the status quo of military culture.

ISSUE AREA SIX: MAINTAINING LINKAGES WITH DEMOCRATIC SOCIETY AT LARGE

Finally, much attention in recent years has been paid to the existence of a "civil-military gap." Tom Ricks set off a debate with his July 1997 cover story in *The Atlantic Monthly* detailing his conclusions based on field interviews of young Marines who felt alienated from their former friends and family upon their return home from boot camp.[81] There was a certain hostility toward civilian society evident in the soldiers' reaction to the undisciplined and perceived immorality of their civilian peers' behaviors and lifestyles. Ricks's book, *Making the Corps* (1997), elaborated on his findings, sparking great interest in whether the military was no longer "of" society, but was becoming "separate" from society. Ricks's observations, combined with the concurrent work of Holsti and other observers documenting the shift in military officers' party identification with conservative Republicanism, has led to concerns that "instead of viewing themselves as the representatives of society . . . officers believe they are a unique element within society."[82]

Social scientists have been busy at work examining whether the civil-military gap and its various manifestations exist, and determining the consequences and implications of the gap if it does exist. As James Burk has noted, "They [journalists, policymakers, and scholars studying the gap] ask whether there is a fundamental difference between the military and civilian society and reflect concern about the difficulty of establishing an effective working relationship between the two so both may flourish."[83] This observation hearkens back to the principle laid out at the onset of this essay—that national security depends on the effective collaboration of the entire national security community, which commits its separate competencies to the task, yet recognizes the distinct responsibilities of each within the democratic framework.

Recommended Civil-Military Norm: Military professionals must recognize the importance of fostering links with society to ensure that the military never becomes an entity separate from society, but remains always of society. Respect for American democratic institutions that allows for various manifestations of behavior in the civilian community that may be incompatible with military service but quite appropriate within a free citizenry should also be fostered. Although military professionals properly may not want to exchange their value system with that of some elements of society, they should be taught to respect the process by which such divergences occur. Even though societal imperatives may at times be viewed as "antifunctional" because they emanate from societal forces rather than security needs, armed forces in service to a democracy must reflect to some degree the culture of the society they are sworn to defend.[84]

CONCLUSION

In this essay, I have argued that, at present, the military profession in the United States does not subscribe to a single set of civil-military norms that regulate its participation in the policymaking process, the general political process, and even its relationship with the society it is charged to serve. Maintaining balanced civil-military relations that will best serve a democratic state's national security needs is a high-maintenance proposition, but essential to the achievement of high-quality national security policy outcomes. Infusing enlightened professional norms in this area would be a major contribution toward keeping U.S. civil-military relations on track toward correcting some troubling trends.

Specific recommendations for each issue area have been discussed throughout this essay. Common principles link the specific recommendations. The adoption of a coherent set of civil-military norms depends on the profession's acceptance of two key principles. The first is that although there may be overlapping competencies regarding the political leadership's and military participants' expert knowledge relevant to national security, there are distinct differences in the responsibility and authority of each in the political system. The second principle evident across the issue areas is the military professional's obligation to balance the functional and societal imperatives. Principled officership must include the realization that the profession's service takes place within the context of a society with a particular set of political and social values and within a specific democratic political system with unique processes of civilian control.

All levels of professional military education must focus on equipping officers at every stage of their professional development with a set of guiding principles that will ultimately result in the establishment of a shared set of civil-military norms within the American military profession. Such measures will enable officers to sort out the ambiguities inherent in collaborating in the national security policymaking process, participating in a democratic polity, and re-maining an entity that is "of" and not "separate from" the society it serves.

NOTES

The views and opinions expressed in this essay are those of the author and are not necessarily those of the Department of the Army or any other U.S. government entity.

1. Richard H. Kohn, "The Constitution and National Security: The Intent of the Framers," in *The United States Military under the Constitution of the United States,* ed. Richard H. Kohn (New York: New York University Press, 1991), 87.

2. George Washington, "George Washington, Excerpt from 'Farewell Address' (1796)," in *100 Key Documents in American Democracy,* ed. Peter B. Levy (Westport, Conn.: Praeger, 1999), 70.

3. Ibid.

4. James Madison, "The Federalist No. 10," in *The Federalist,* ed. Jacobe E. Cooke (Hanover, N.H.: Wesleyan University Press, 1961), 62.

5. Ibid.

6. Joseph A. Schumpeter, *Capitalism, Socialism, and Democracy* (New York: Harper & Brothers, 1950), 253.

7. Peter D. Feaver, "The Civil-Military Problematique: Huntington, Janowitz, and the Question of Civilian Control," *Armed Forces and Society* 23 (Winter 1996): 155.

8. Russell F. Weigley, "The American Military and the Principle of Civilian Control from McClellan to Powell," *Journal of Military History,* Special Issue 57 (October 1993): 27.

9. Marybeth Peterson Ulrich, *Democratizing Communist Militaries: The Cases of the Czech and Russian Armed Forces* (Ann Arbor, Mich.: University of Michigan Press, 2000), 10.

10. Samuel P. Huntington, *The Soldier and the State* (Cambridge, Mass.: Harvard University Press, 1957), 2.

11. Ulrich, *Democratizing Communist Militaries,* 10–11, 116–53.

12. I attribute the idea that a distinct form of professionalism exists in "national security professionalism" to Peter J. Roman and David W. Tarr. These scholars created this concept as a distinct form of military professionalism related to military professionals' expertise in foreign and security policy as it is carried out across the government. I have adapted the concept to apply to both civilian and military participants in the national security process. See Peter J. Roman and David W. Tarr, "Military Professionalism and Policymaking: Is There a Civil-Military Gap at the Top? If So, Does It Matter?" in *Soldiers and Civilians: The Civil-Military Gap and American National Security,* ed. Peter D. Feaver and Richard H. Kohn (Cambridge, Mass.: Belfer Center for Science and International Affairs, 2001), 409–11.

13. Recognition that civilian and military officials often have overlapping roles in the policymaking process is found in Christopher P. Gibson and Don M. Snider, "Civil-Military Relations and the Potential to Influence: A Look at the National Security Decision-Making Process," *Armed Forces and Society* 25 (Winter 1999): 193–218.

14. Richard A. Chilcoat, "Strategic Art: The New Discipline for 21st Century Leaders," *U.S. Army War College*

Guide to Strategy (Carlisle Barracks, Pa.: U.S. Army War College, 2000), 205.

15. Edward H. Carr, *The Twenty Years' Crisis: 1919–1939* (New York: Harper & Row, 1946), 1.

16. See Don M. Snider, Robert F. Priest, and Felisa Lewis, "Civilian-Military Gap and Professional Military Education at the Pre-Commissioning Level," *Armed Forces and Society* 27 (Winter 2001): 249–72.

17. See Judith Hicks Stiehm, "Civil-Military Relations in War College Curricula," *Armed Forces and Society* 27 (Winter 2001): 284–92. TISS survey data discussed in this article indicate that professional military education curricula need to clarify the distinctions between behavior that is advisory or advocative in nature—that is, merely offering counsel versus recommending in a pleading fashion. Officers' views on the appropriateness of "insisting" were also probed in the study. "Insisting" characterizes behaviors beyond counseling or forcefully recommending to include actions that demand vehemently and persistently. A significant number of officers surveyed replied that insistent behaviors were at times appropriate in civil-military relations. Finally, the term "political" is often unclear to officers. To many officers, "political" tends to have a pejorative quality and is applied to anything pertaining to conflict among participants in democratic policymaking processes. A better understanding of the American political process and the legitimate role that officers play as participant-citizens and as contributors in policymaking could improve officers' comfort with processes that form the fabric of American political life.

18. Huntington, 2.

19. I attribute this insight to Lieutenant Colonel John "Paul" Gardner, U.S. Army War College, Class of 2001.

20. Weigley, "The American Military and the Principle of Civilian Control," 42–46.

21. Forrest C. Pogue, "Marshall on Civil-Military Relationships," in *The United States Military under the Constitution of the United States, 1789–1878,* ed. Richard H. Kohn (New York: New York University Press, 1991), 205–6.

22. Ibid., 206.

23. David McCullough, *Truman* (New York: Simon & Schuster, 1992), 534.

24. Gaurav Kampani, "The Military Coup in Pakistan: Implications for Nuclear Stability in South Asia," *CNS Reports* (Monterey, Calif.: Center for Nonproliferation Studies, October 1999); available at http://cns.miis.edu/pubs/reports/gaurav.htm.

25. Peter D. Feaver, "Crisis as Shirking: An Agency Theory Explanation of the Souring of American Civil-Military Relations," *Armed Forces and Society* 24 (Spring 1998): 407–34.

26. On resistance to force structure changes, see "Revolt of the Generals," *Inside the Ring* (August 10, 2001), available at www.gertzfile.com/gertzfile/ring081001.html.

27. David Halberstam, "Clinton and the Generals," *Vanity Fair* (September 2001): 230–46.

28. Michael C. Desch, *Civilian Control of the Military* (Baltimore: The Johns Hopkins University Press, 1999), 32.

29. Ibid.

30. A former Clinton administration National Security Council official quoted in Halberstam, "Clinton and the Generals," 230.

31. H. R. McMasters, *Dereliction of Duty* (New York: Harper, 1997), 327–28.

32. George C. Wilson, *This War Really Matters: Inside the Fight for Defense Dollars* (Washington, D.C.: Congressional Quarterly Press, 2000), chap. 6.

33. John W. Peabody, *The "Crisis" in American Civil-Military Relations: A Search for Balance between Military Professionals and Civilian Leaders,* Strategy Research Project (Carlisle Barracks, Pa.: U.S. Army War College, 2001), 23.

34. Morris Janowitz, *The Professional Soldier* (New York: The Free Press, 1971), 236–41. Janowitz's data stem from a 1954 survey of Pentagon staff officers. He readily admits that the survey question posed asked only for a response based on general political orientation—neither party identification nor the specific content of the conservatism was provided.

35. Ibid., 238. Of those surveyed, 45.3 percent reported that they were a little on the conservative side. An almost equal number of respondents, 21.6 percent and 23.1 percent, reported that they were conservative or a little on the liberal side, respectively.

36. Ole R. Holsti, "A Widening Gap between the U.S. Military and Civilian Society?" *International Security* 23 (Winter 1998): 11.

37. Thomas E. Ricks, "Is American Military Professionalism Declining?" *Proceedings* (July 1998), available at http://proquest.umi.com.

38. Ibid.

39. Ole R. Holsti, "A Widening Gap between the U.S. Military and Civilian Society?" 13.

40. Ole R. Holsti, "Of Chasms and Convergences: Attitudes and Beliefs of Civilians and Military Elites at the Start of a New Millennium," in *Soldiers and Civilians: The Civil-Military Gap and American National Security,* ed. Peter D. Feaver and Richard H. Kohn (Cambridge, Mass.: Belfer Center for Science and International Affairs, 2001), 33.

41. "Worldview" is the term that Winslow used in her study. In this context, worldview refers to political ideology.

42. Donna Winslow, *Army Culture,* Report published in fulfillment of U.S. Army Research Institute Contract No. DASW01-98-M-1868 (Washington, D.C.: U.S. Department of the Army, 2000), 13.

43. Morris Janowitz, *The Professional Soldier* (New York: The Free Press, 1971), 233.

44. Huntington, *The Soldier and the State,* 230–31.

45. *United States Military Academy Strategic Vision–2010* (West Point, N.Y.: Office of Policy, Planning, and Analysis, July 1, 2000), 7–8.

46. See Huntington, *The Soldier and the State;* and Desch, *Civilian Control of the Military.*

47. For an extensive treatment of civilian and military competencies as factors influencing the contrasting power of military professionals and civilian policymakers in the policymaking process, see Gibson and Snider, "Civil-Military Relations and the Potential to Influence," 193–218.

48. Elliott Abrams and Andrew J. Bacevich, "A Symposium on Citizenship and Military Service," *Parameters* 31 (Summer 2001): 19.

49. Eliot A. Cohen, "Twilight of the Citizen-Soldier," *Parameters* 31 (Summer 2001); this argument runs throughout the article.

50. Ibid, 28. Cohen presents but vehemently disagrees with this perspective.

51. The courts are increasingly supporting this position. See Lloyd J. Matthews, "The Army Officer and the First Amendment," *Army* (January 1998): 25–34; and Lloyd J. Matthews, "The Voorhees Court-Martial," *Army* (September 1998): 17–23.

52. Note again the principles of officership required for service in the 21st century in *United States Military Academy Strategic Vision—2010.*

53. See Steven Lee Myers, "The 2000 Campaign: The Convention; Pentagon Taking Opportunity for Show," *New York Times* (July 28, 2000): A15; Richard H. Kohn, "General Elections; The Brass Shouldn't Do Endorsements," *Washington Post* (September 19, 2000): A23; Steven Lee Myers, "The 2000 Campaign: Support for the Military; Military Backs Ex-Guard Pilot Over Pvt. Gore," *New York Times* (September 21, 2000): A1; "Nonpartisan Military Best," *Omaha World Herald* (October 16, 2000): 6; David Wood, *Newhouse News Service,* "E-day Attack; Military Set to Invade the Polls; Observers Worry about Surge in Partisan Politics," *Times Picayune* (October 20, 2000): 5; David Wood, "Military Breaks Ranks with Non-Partisan Tradition; Many in Service Turn to Bush, Reject Political Correctness," *Plain Dealer* (October 22, 2000): 16A. See also Holsti, "Of Chasms and Convergences," 31–32.

54. Comment of an active duty Army general officer in response to the *U.S. Army War College Survey: Retired Generals and Partisan Politics* (October 2000). Survey was conducted by U.S. Army War College student, Lieutenant Colonel William R. Becker, as part of his Strategy Research Project, *Retired Generals and Partisan Politics: Is a Time Out Required?* (Carlisle Barracks, Pa.: U.S. Army War College, April 2000), 30.

55. Comment of a Marine one-star general in response to the *U.S. Army War College Survey: Retired Generals and Partisan Politics* (October 2000). See Becker, *Retired Generals and Partisan Politics,* 37.

56. Comments of a Marine two-star officer in response to the *U.S. Army War College Survey: Retired Generals and Partisan Politics* (October 2000). See Becker, *Retired Generals and Partisan Politics,* 41.

57. Comments of an active-duty four-star officer in response to the *U.S. Army War College Survey: Retired Generals and Partisan Politics* (October 2000). See Becker, *Retired Generals and Partisan Politics,* 47.

58. Interviews with Army War College students regarding their experience in the field with retired general officers working with active units as contractors, Carlisle Barracks, Penn., August 2001. During my own field research in Central and Eastern Europe (CEE) in July 2001, I encountered several retired U.S. general officers working as contractors for CEE governments or representing a particular defense corporation whose employment or access was based on active duty expertise and/or reputation.

59. Andrew Abbott, *The System of Professions: An Essay on the Division of Expert Labor* (Chicago, Ill.: University of Chicago Press, 1988), 102.

60. Huntington, *The Soldier and the State,* 8.

61. Ibid., 16.

62. Ibid.

63. Becker, *Retired Generals and Partisan Politics,* 47.

64. See *Joint Ethics Regulation (JER)* 2-304 (November 2, 1994), 29, for a description of restrictions placed on retirees with regard to capitalizing on their retired military status. Additionally, sections 672, 675, and 688 of *Title 10, United States Code* detail the authority to recall retirees to active duty.

65. Ibid.

66. Abbott, *The System of Professions,* 60.

67. See Abbott, *The System of Professions,* 69–89. Abbott offers five "settlements" that can be applied to jurisdictional disputes: (1) the claim to full and final jurisdiction; (2) the subordination of one profession to another; (3) division of labor that splits jurisdictional areas into two interdependent parts; (4) allow one profession an advisory role vis-à-vis another; (5) divide jurisdictions not according to content of work, but according to the nature of the client.

68. For a more in-depth discussion of this conflict and its impact on military culture, see John Hillen, "Must U.S. Military Culture Reform?" *Orbis* 43 (Winter 1999): 43–57.

69. James Burk, "The Military's Presence in American Society, 1950–2000," in *Soldiers and Civilians,* ed. Peter D. Feaver and Richard H. Kohn (Cambridge, Mass.: Belfer Center for Science and International Affairs, 2001), 247–74.

70. Robert H. Ferrell, *Harry S. Truman: A Life* (Columbia, Mo.: University of Missouri Press, 1994), 298.

71. McCullough, *Truman,* 588–89.

72. Omar N. Bradley, *A General's Life* (New York: Simon & Schuster, 1983), 485.

73. Leo Bogart, *Project Clear: Social Research and the Desegregation of the United States Army* (New Brunswick, N.J.: Transaction, 1992), xxi–xxii.

74. Ferrell, *Harry S. Truman,* 588–89.

75. Jeanne Holm, *Women in the Military* (Novato, Calif.: Presidio, 1993), 307.

76. Ibid., 264.

77. Ibid., 305–12.

78. The House amendment passed 303–96 and the Senate amendment was accepted without a roll call vote. Ibid., 310.

79. Ulrich, *Democratizing Communist Militaries,* 11.

80. Peter D. Feaver and Richard H. Kohn, *Project on the Gap between the Military and Civilian Society: Digest of Findings and Studies* (Chapel Hill, N.C.: Triangle Institute of Security Studies, October 1999). These findings are also reported in Feaver and Kohn, *Soldiers and Civilians.*

81. Thomas E. Ricks, "The Widening Gap between the Military and Society," *Atlantic* (July 1997): 66–78.

82. Conclusion of Major Robert A. Newton who conducted a survey of Marine officers in 1995, as quoted in Ricks, "The Widening Gap Between the Military and Society."

83. James Burk, "The Military's Presence in American Society," 247.

84. Hillen, "Must U.S. Military Culture Reform?" 45.

CHAPTER 11

CONVENTIONAL FORCES

THE STRATEGIC IMPACT AND MILITARY EFFECTIVENESS OF THE AIR AND MISSILE CAMPAIGN

ANTHONY H. CORDESMAN

The success of the air and missile campaign in Kosovo has already led some advocates of air and missile power to talk about the war as evidence that air and missile power can win a victory without a ground campaign. It has led others to speculate that air and missile power is now so decisive that it should be given a larger share of military budgets and force postures relative to ground and naval forces.[1]

There is no doubt that the air and missile campaign in Kosovo demonstrated the steadily improving effectiveness and lethality of air and missile power. There is no doubt that steady and important advances are taking place in targeting and intelligence, battle management, all-weather offensive combat, weapons lethality, long-range attack capability, precision guided munitions, the precise launch of unguided ordnance, beyond-visual-range air combat, air defense suppression, and stealth and penetration capability. The air and missile war in Kosovo is clearly a validation of these trends, as well as of the importance of technology in reshaping the nature of war.

THE SPECIAL CONDITIONS OF THE WAR IN KOSOVO

At the same time, the growing importance of air and missile power has been characteristic of virtually every war since World War I, and it is far from clear that Kosovo says anything truly new or unique about the value of air and missile power per se. To begin with, it is important to consider the special conditions that shape the air and missile war in Kosovo:

- Serbia was a small power with limited air and surface-to-air missile assets, and had no re-supply during the war.

- Serbia had no military allies, and was surrounded on all sides by nations friendly to NATO—although Supreme Headquarters Allied Powers Europe sources reported on June 30 that two hundred Russians were present in Serbia in some capacity, that at least two were killed by the Kosovo Liberation Army (KLA),

and that some form of Russian presence existed in the Serbia forces used in the attack on Mount Pastrik.

- NATO fought a limited war that did not threaten the survival of the Serbian regime and military forces.

- NATO accepted a situation in which Serbia could carry out massive ethnic cleansing—the key threat that NATO initiated the war to prevent.

- NATO also did not really win through air and missile power alone, and could not prevent the need for a land phase involving the deployment of major peacekeeping forces with a risk of an extended presence of half a decade or more and a continuing risk of low-intensity conflict.

MORE THAN AIR POWER LED TO NATO'S VICTORY

One must be careful about giving air and missile power more credit than it is really due. Jointness was critical to the operation in providing both land and sea-based air and missile power. Serbia was forced to withdraw from Kosovo for a variety of reasons other than the effectiveness of air and missile power:

- Serbia suffered from acute economic weakness at the start of the war.

- Serbia alienated most of the world by its ethnic cleansing activities and lost all meaningful outside political support. Once Russia joined NATO in pressing for a peace settlement, Serbia had no hope of outside aid or that the world would tolerate ethnic cleansing.

- The total failure of Serbian forces to defeat the KLA in the planned 5–6 days, and Serbia's inability to defeat the ground operations of the KLA without exposing its forces to devastating air attack.

- The presence of a substantial NATO ground force already in the region, and the deployment of Task Force Hawk and the growing political debate in NATO over the need for a ground option created the growing possibility that NATO would pursue a ground option if NATO air and missile power did not achieve decisive results.

As discussed later, there is also some evidence that the Serbian leadership was aware that NATO had secretly prepared a ground invasion option, and that it faced a very real threat of a major NATO invasion in the fall of 1999.

THE RELEVANCE OF KOSOVO TO OTHER WARS

The "iron law" of military history is that no past war is ever a completely valid model of the next conflict. This may be particularly true of Kosovo. It is very unlikely that the air and missile war in Kosovo will be a model for future wars; the tactics and technologies used would not have decisively reversed or altered the outcome of many other wars fought since World War II.

The United States alone has used military force well over 240 times since World War II. Without going through the list of cases, it is doubtful that the improvements in air and missile power reflected in Kosovo would materially have changed the outcome of most cases. The success of coalition air and missile power during the air phase of the Gulf War is almost certainly a far more important watershed in the role of air and missile power than is Kosovo, and involved a far more serious enemy and set of tactical problems.

Consider the following cases—which involve both the kind of major regional contingencies that are the focus of U.S. strategy and the kind of low-intensity conflicts and peacemaking missions that seem to have become typical of post–Cold War military deployments:

- *Vietnam:* Improvements in air and missile power might have forced an earlier cease-fire and led to an earlier U.S. withdrawal. Air power could not have altered the fact that South Vietnam was politically a "failed state."

- *Beirut and Lebanon after 1982:* A highly political and asymmetric war involving low-intensity combat in which no combination of the U.S. edge in land, air, and sea power could have been decisive.

- *The Liberation of Kuwait in 1991:* Air power made a massive contribution to victory, but could not have liberated Kuwait without a massive land component.

- *Somalia in 1992–93:* A highly political and asymmetric war involving low-intensity combat in which neither the U.S. edge in land or air and missile power could have been decisive.

- *Iraq since 1991:* Air power has been used repeatedly to contain Saddam Hussein, and with considerable success, but the regime remains intact.

- *The Defense of Kuwait in 1999:* Air power might or might not be able to prevent a sudden Iraqi surprise attack on Kuwait, the seizure of Kuwait City, and holding the Kuwaitis for ransom. U.S. Central Command experts seem to feel it could not halt an all-out Iraqi advance.

- *Korea in 1999:* Air power would have no chance of decisively defeating a North Korean advance without a massive land component.

- *Counterproliferation in 2000 and Beyond:* Air power has a very uncertain capability to deter a threat with extensive missile forces and weapons of mass destruction unless it is armed *with* weapons of mass destruction. There are no current prospects that air and missile power can replace a land-oriented, on-the-scene body like the U.N. Special Commission in the counterproliferation mission.

- *Counterterrorism, Low-Intensity Combat, and Peacemaking in 2000 and Beyond:* The advances taking place in air and missile power are best suited to the defeat of exposed enemy forces in regular wars. Like other aspects of the revolution in military affairs, they have uncertain advantage in highly political asymmetric wars.

As a minor historical aside, it is also worth pointing out that NATO's use of air and missile power in Kosovo was not the first victory of such power in war without a major land component. This is true even if one ignores the impact of Serbia's inability to defeat the ground operations of the KLA without exposing its forces to devastating air attack, and that Serbia's decision to accept NATO's terms was probably influenced by the growing prospect that NATO would pursue a ground option if NATO air and missile power did not achieve decisive results.

The first decisive use of air and missile power to defeat a significant ground power without the use of extensive land forces was almost unquestionably the Royal Air Force's (RAF) defeat of the advance of the Saudi Ikhwan on Transjordan in August 1922. (If one objects to the presence of a few British armored cars in the conflict, it would then be the RAF's defeat of advance of the Saudi Ikhwan on Iraq at the "battle" of Busaiya in October 1927.) If one picks the right war or battle, air and missile power has been "decisive" ever since the days of the biplane—for nearly 80 years.

ROB PETER TO PRAISE PAUL?

No analyst can deny that the outcome of the air and missile war in Kosovo is an important further argument to fund strong, combat-ready air forces and to continue to fund major advances in the technology of air combat and the deployment of air combat systems. It is not, however, a reason for arguing for major tradeoffs in the funding given air and missile power relative to other combat elements or for re-defining "jointness." Not only was airpower not de-cisive in Kosovo, tradeoffs that weaken land and sea power put a steadily heavier burden on air and mis-sile power and create added pressures to use it in missions where air and missile power alone may not be able to do the job.

This is not a practical option for an America that is attempting to remain the "world's only superpower" while spending some $20–30 billion less a year than is needed to maintain its current force structure, maintain its current rate of commitments, and mod-ernize to maintain and reinforce its technical edge. Military cannibalism is not a solution to the problems of underfunding and overdeployment. It is interest-ing to note that both Secretary Cohen and General Shelton rejected the idea of air-oriented tradeoffs during the same press conference given on June 10 to praise the performance of NATO air and missile power during the war:

Questioner: Mr. Secretary and Mr. Chairman, I'd like to ask you both, given the success of this air-war and the fact that there's extreme political reluctance in both this coun-try and in Europe to bloody ground troops in combat any more, are ground troops in combat—is this going to be the way that the West fights wars in the future? Will ground combat troops become somewhat superfluous? And will Army budgets suffer to the Air Force because of this?

Secretary Cohen: Let me speak as Secretary of Defense, that we will continue to use ground forces wherever they are required in the best possible military campaign that can be devised, under the most optimum circumstances. We are not afraid to use, in any case, a ground component to a military campaign. We have ground forces that are cur-rently deployed in South Korea. We have ground forces that are deployed in Southwest Asia. There's never any hesitancy on the part of this Department or this President to use those forces when the circumstances dictate.

As we've indicated so many times before, under this scenario, at least, we were constrained because we had to have consensus. We were not about to take unilateral action. We had to have a consensus of NATO. NATO had one consensus—which was for the application of air power. There was no consensus for the application of ground forces in a non-permissive environment. So ordinarily you would say you would always have a plan for both air and sea and ground. Under this particular circumstance, the consensus was for the application of air power as the Chairman has laid out in a phased campaign. It ultimately proved to be successful.

You saw just a few weeks ago once the element of whether ground forces would go into a non-permissive environment, you certainly saw some question of division within the alliance itself. Had that taken place at the very beginning, we would have seen Milosevic carrying out his campaign of ethnic terror and purging at the same time that NATO countries would have been still debating the issue

of who would participate and who would not. So we think, under the circumstances, this was the best of a series of bad options, but this was the best option under the circum-stance, and ultimately has proved successful.

Questioner: Will the Army suffer and the Air Force ben-efit from what—smart weapons? I would ask the Chairman.

Secretary Cohen: The answer is no. The Army will not suffer as a result of this. The Army's in the process of re-shaping itself, modernizing, acquiring the kind of equipment that will be necessary for the Army to function as a superior force in the 21st century. This is not a zero-sum game. This is not a situation where the Air Force with its superb per-formance will result in diminishing the Army's resources. We have one military and it's fully integrated and it is joint, and where the ground force is required the ground force will go. Where the Air Force is required, it will go as well. Presumably, we'll operate for the most part fully integrated and joint. This was a unique situation.

General Shelton: One of the great strengths of our armed forces are the complementary capabilities that are brought, that we have within the services that enable us to cover the entire spectrum of conflict. We've got the world's greatest Air Force, Army, Navy, Marine Corps, Coast Guard today, and we're able then to apply the forces that we need and do it in a joint environment to enable us to carry it out.

It would be a mistake to ever take any of those off the table. Depending on what you're asked to do to meet the political objectives, either of NATO or of the United States if we're acting unilaterally, requires you to have those types of capabilities if you're going to have global responsibilities, and you've got to have global power, and you've got to have the complementary capabilities of each of the services.

STRATEGIC LIMITS ON IMPACT OF AIR POWER IN KOSOVO: LESSONS FOR THE FUTURE?

There are other reasons to be cautious about generalizing the lessons of the air and missile war in Kosovo. The air and missile campaign in Kosovo involved constraints that made it impossible to use air and missile power with maximum effectiveness. NATO's air and missile campaign began with twelve major grand strategic, and tactical limitations that make much of the debate over the broader lessons of this air and missile campaign somewhat moot. The outcome of the air and missile campaign was heavily affected by these initial political and conceptual limits, and the resulting Rules of Engagement (ROE).

No one can now determine what would have happened if:

- *NATO and key NATO member-country polit-ical leaders had not repeatedly publicly ruled out a ground option and had not signaled Ser-bia that it had freedom of action in Kosovo.* Regardless of whether NATO would have used such an option, NATO failed to preserve an im-portant political and strategic lever that might have contributed to an earlier termination of the conflict. Although strategic ambiguity is not an ideal lesson for every conflict, it is often a powerful tool. In this case, NATO politics meant that NATO's leaders spent more time during much of the crisis trying to reassure their own peoples than they did in trying to influence the enemy, although it is possible that their secret efforts to prepare for a ground option did eventually help terminate the conflict.

- *Enough air and missile power had been assembled at the start of the campaign to approach "decisive force."* During the first 38 days of the Gulf War, allied air forces flew nearly 100,000 sorties, dropped around 226,000 munitions, and struck some 1,200 targets. In a similar period in Kosovo, they flew about 12,000 sorties and fired about 4,000 bombs and missiles at 230 sites.[2] At the end of the air and missile campaign in Kosovo, NATO had expended some 23,000 air munitions and 329 cruise missiles. The coalition had claimed to have destroyed 40 percent of Iraq's tanks in the Kuwait theater of operations, 32 percent of its armored personnel carriers, and 48 percent of its artillery. In contrast, NATO claimed to have hit less than 15 percent of the tanks and armored personnel carriers in Kosovo. The coalition had also completed the deployment of some 700,000 troops for the liberation of Kuwait versus NATO's deployment of around 20,000 peacekeepers.

- *NATO had entered the air and missile war having planned for an option other than the success of the initial negotiations or Serbian acceptance of these terms after a limited number of strikes.* NATO went to war without serious planning for key options or readiness for a major war.

- *NATO had planned from the start to deal with the risk of a dramatic increase in ethnic cleansing and ethnic warfare, rather than adapting to the reality of these events once air strikes began.* NATO threatened war without having a clear contingency plan to deal with the very problem that led it to threaten air strikes in the first place.

- *NATO had immediately escalated to strategic bombing of Serbia when massive ethnic cleansing began, and had been willing to attack targets vital to the functioning of civilian life.* NATO's strategic bombing campaign did not reply to ethnic cleansing in kind.[3]

- *NATO had begun the war with a full targeting plan geared to all possible contingencies, supported by the proper in-theater intelligence and reconnaissance assets, and taking the problems of collateral damage fully into account.*[4]

- *NATO had been willing to take added casualties and losses in return for added effectiveness.*

- *NATO had given military effectiveness more priority relative to the risk of inflicting collateral damage.*

- *NATO had prepared a clear plan for a psyops and political warfare campaign when the campaign began, and had struck to deprive Milosevic of his main propaganda instruments like radio and TV transmitters at the start, and had been prepared to beam in its own "truth" message.* Serbia was able to maintain control over Serbia's media and the information available to most of its population throughout the war, and often out propagandized NATO in the world media. NATO never achieved information parity, much less information dominance, in any political sense of the term.

- *NATO had realistically planned for the technical limits of air and missile power in bad weather and against a highly political target base like the mix of Serbian refugees and Kosovar refugees in Kosovo.*

- *The AH-64s and multiple-launch rocket systems had been predeployed and combat ready, or had been committed once they were combat ready.*

- *NATO had planned to deal with the refugee problem in humanitarian terms by creating military safe havens.*

This mix of limitations severely weakened the impact of the air and missile campaign during the initial weeks of the war, and several of these limitations continued to have a major impact throughout the campaign. Many of these limitations also reflect what seems to be a continuing U.S. and Western inability to understand the risks inherent in threatening military action. It is easy to use terms like "peace making" but they are simply polite new ways of describing the nineteenth-century concept of "just war." The result of threatening force can easily lead to worst-case scenarios, and to wars that have to be fought to a grim conclusion.

Put differently, the need to avoid or minimize the kind of limitations placed on air power in Kosovo constitute one of the major lessons of the war. Major powers like the United States and NATO cannot afford to plan for success under conditions that cripple military effectiveness. If they threaten to use force, they must be prepared to use it with the strength and decisiveness required, and they must plan for worst cases.

The mix of political and financial costs and risks inherent in deploying inadequate forces offset any savings in far too many cases to make this an acceptable policy. It may not be possible to avoid a wide range of political constraints in most contingencies, but the risk and probable military impact of such constraints needs far more explicit analysis, and any such tradeoffs should be made only after very careful consideration.

"SHOCK AND AWE" OR "LIMITS AND RESTRAINT"

There is a strong case to be made for the use of decisive force even when moral and ethical factors are fully taken into account. The morality of war cannot be summarized in a sound bite or the kind of catch phrase that belongs in a fortune cookie. It also cannot be defined in terms of an effort to minimize short-term casualties, equipment losses, and collateral damage. Limiting military action in the short term can extend the overall length and intensity of war, increase casualties, and create conditions that make it more difficult to reach a stable outcome and a lasting peace. It can mean failing to protect an ally or to serve the humanitarian goal that is the purpose of fighting in the first place. Inadequate force is often as likely to produce the wrong strategic and moral outcome as excessive force.

NATO was not prepared to deal with these realities when it negotiated with the Serbs or began the bombing campaign. It was not prepared to use decisive force in either political or military terms. The end result was thousands of dead and over 1.5 million refugees.

NATO did end the air and missile campaign with a military victory, but virtually all Serbian ethnic cleansing occurred during the course of the air and missile campaign. Although some wartime estimates of mass killings and the hardships suffered by the Kosovar Albanians in Kosovo may be exaggerated, it still seems clear that ethnic cleansing reached the point by mid-May where it affected so much of the Kosovar Albanian population. It also seems clear that at least 80 percent of the people NATO attempted to protect suffered grievously during the war. NATO totally failed to meet its initial goal of putting an "immediate end to ethnic cleansing" unless immediate is defined as 11 weeks.

NATO's restraint meant that it was not prepared to deal with the asymmetric nature of the war. It did not seek to use air and missile power decisively to force an end to ethnic cleansing. It gave the Serbs de facto strategic sanctuaries, and its slow pattern of escalation in some ways taught the Serbs to accept the damage done by air and missile power where a sudden massive use of air and missile power might have led to far more immediate results. Gradual escalation tends to fail, or to make escalation the norm, where shock and decisive force can sometimes produce far more prompt results. There are no rules to history, but if force is worth using at all, the early use of decisive force is generally best.

It is also important to note that public opinion tended to shift against the war toward the end of the campaign, and that there were growing pressures to put an end to the fighting. Western public opinion had not been prepared for a long conflict or for a ground option because it was not politically convenient for NATO's political leaders to discuss these options in the short term. It is far from clear that the United States, NATO, or other peacemakers are prepared for longer and more frustrating conflicts in the future, or ones with higher losses. The U.S. withdrawals from Lebanon and Somalia are cases in point. Furthermore, the factors that tend to limit the United States' and NATO's willingness to use force decisively are the same kind of factors that act to prolong conflicts and make their outcome uncertain.[5]

The practical problem for NATO, the United States, and the West is whether it is possible for the West's political leaders to deal with these issues in ways that will permit the use of decisive force. If they do not, the kind of limitations NATO faced during the air and missile campaign in Kosovo are part of a pattern of growing political limitations on the ways in which Western democracies can wage war.

It may well be that the advances in warfighting capability that make up the revolution in military affairs have a self-canceling backlash by creating a steadily growing set of political limitations on the ways in which wars can be fought, and steadily growing demands to minimize friendly and hostile casualties and collateral damage. One of the ironies of the advances in modern air and missile power, and modern military technology of all kinds, is that it may be impossible to use it to achieve "shock and awe" in all but the most drastic contingencies, and that real-world military plans and doctrine must be based on "limits and restraint."

NOTES

1. These speculators did not include the chief of staff of the U.S. Air Force or senior officers in the Air Staff, who stressed the need for joint operations. For a balanced view of Kosovo pro-air enthusiasts, see Air Marshall Sir John Walker, "Air Power for Coercion," *Royal United Services Institute Journal* (September 1999): 13–19. Good descriptions of how the U.S. Air Force is approaching the future development of air power and of its emphasis on joint operations can be found in Bryan Bender, "USAF: The Strategic Vision," *Jane's Defense Weekly* (September 8, 1999): 8–36; and Major General Bruce Carlson, "Juggling Air Dominance," *Armed Forces Journal International* (September 1999): 50–56.

2. See the comments on these problems by Lieutenant General Michael Short, NATO's joint force air component commander in the Balkans, in John A. Tirpak, "Short's View of the Air Campaign," *Air Force Magazine* (September 1999): 43–47. The impact of the rapid assembly and deployment of forces is also raised in a Russian analysis of the lessons of the war. See A. B. Krasnov, "Aviation in the Yugoslavian Conflict," *Soviet Military Thought,* MTR-No 005 (September 1, 1999).

3. Tirpak, "Short's View of the Air Campaign."

4. The problems in targeting are also raised by Colonel A. B. Krasnov in a Russian analysis of the lessons of the war. See Krasnov, "Aviation in the Yugoslavian Conflict."

5. A number of these issues is raised in Edward N. Luttwak, "Give War a Chance," *Foreign Affairs* 78 (July 1999): 36–44.

THE NAVY IN AN ANTI-ACCESS WORLD

CLARK A. MURDOCK

The proliferation of anti-access (or area-denial) systems and strategies has been identified as a key military feature of globalization. The *Quadrennial Defense Review Report* (*QDR Report*) identifies the antiaccess challenge—"Projecting and sustaining U.S. forces in distant anti-access or area-denial environments, and defeat anti-access threats"—as one of the six critical "emerging strategic and operational challenges" that will focus and drive the transformation of the U.S. military:[1]

Future adversaries could have the means to render ineffective much of our current ability to project military power overseas. Saturation attacks with ballistic and cruise missiles could deny or delay U.S. military access to overseas bases, airfields and ports. Advanced air defense systems could deny access to hostile airspace to all but extremely low-observable aircraft. Military and commercial space capabilities, over-the-horizon radars, and low-observable unmanned aerial vehicles could give potential adversaries the means to conduct wide-area surveillance and track and target American forces and assets. Anti-ship cruise missiles, advanced diesel submarines, and advanced mines could threaten the ability of U.S. naval and amphibious forces to operate in littoral waters. *New approaches for projecting power must be developed to meet these threats.*[2]

In the past, the Department of Defense has been somewhat in denial about the anti-access challenge. Many of these capabilities are, in fact, already part of the current threat environment. But the *QDR Report's* full embrace of the imperative to change is a significant step forward.

After first analyzing the general nature of the U.S. power projection versus anti-access competition, this essay addresses how the U.S. Navy should meet the anti-access challenge.

PROJECTING POWER AND PRESENCE INTO ANTI-ACCESS ENVIRONMENTS

How the United States projects power and presence into an antiaccess environment will be central to the global security dynamic for at least 2 decades.[3] All grand strategies—such as balance of power, containment, and deterrence—depend both on capability and will. That the United States has the capability to project power into any regional theater is beyond question. What is at issue is America's willingness to do so. The question of *what* constitutes unacceptable losses to Americans in the pursuit of *what kinds* of interests has been tested by regional aggressors and would-be hegemons.

Americans clearly will support high-intensity military operations (such as Operations Desert Storm and Allied Force) of important regional interests as long as casualties are minimal and the campaign is successful. In the immediate wake of the September 11, 2001, terrorist attacks on the World Trade Center and the Pentagon, 83 percent of those polled by *The Washington Post* backed military action against the perpetrators, even if it led to war, and two-thirds of the respondents favored going to war even if it should prove a long one with large numbers of U.S. military casualties—including 45 percent who "strongly supported" it.[4] However, just as clearly (considering Somalia), Americans will not support an inconclusive or ineffective military operation involving casualties "disproportionate" to minor U.S. interests.

In both Operations Desert Storm and Allied Force, U.S. opponents tried to inflict casualties on American forces but failed, largely because the United States refused to engage in a manner that exposed U.S. and allied forces to significant losses. In the Gulf War, ground forces were not committed until Iraqi forces were decimated by the air campaign. In Allied Force, the air campaign was conducted beyond the effective range of Serbian air defenses. The results were minimal or no allied military casualties, even at the cost of longer campaigns (no one envisioned a 78-day air campaign against Serbia) or at the expense of more ambitious political objectives (such as the removal of Saddam Hussein from power).

In light of American (and coalition) successes, the offense-defense competition between the United States and its potential regional opponents has turned asymmetric. The United States can now project power and employ force at politically acceptable costs to the president. Unable to directly defend against superior U.S. conventional forces, potential opponents are acquiring anti-access capabilities (in the case of China, advanced conventional capabilities; in other cases, biological and chemical weapons and their means of delivery) to increase their ability to inflict higher casualties on U.S. power projection forces. The United States, in turn, must increase the survivability of its forces in the face of increasing anti-access threats. Reducing the vulnerability of U.S. power projection forces is not only intrinsically worthy—after all, the lives of young American men and

Clark A. Murdock, "The Navy in an Anitaccess World," in Globalization and Maritime Power, *ed. Sam J. Tangredi (Washington, D.C.: National Defense University Press, 2002), 473–85. Public domain.*

women are at stake—but is also critical to America's global role. Although many (including myself) believe the American aversion to casualties has been overstated, why test it? Once an adversary discovers what the actual American tolerance is (i.e., what kinds of costs Americans will accept for what kinds of interests), the limits of U.S. power will have been defined. From a strategic perspective, it is sensible to maintain strategic ambiguity about the real limits to U.S. power.

The ability of the United States to ensure that U.S. power projection forces remain highly survivable even as anti-access capabilities grow and proliferate will ultimately dissuade potential opponents from further efforts. The vulnerability of U.S. forces to anti-access attacks increases as they come in closer to engage the enemy. The U.S. capability to defeat large-scale aggression should reside largely in forces capable of operating initially from beyond adversary killing zones. If U.S. power projection forces have to come deep into the theater to engage, the United States, in effect, is putting its center of gravity (American casualties) into the adversary's wheelhouse. For the next couple of decades, "highly survivable" means standoff and (good) stealth.

Future large-scale military campaigns will be phased campaigns; the United States will fight at a distance until it is safe to close. Improving standoff, force protection, and forcible entry capabilities will shorten the time required before land forces can close, but large forces deployed deep in the theater during peacetime will remain too vulnerable to surprise attacks. U.S. power projection forces must work patiently from the outside in, as they first punish aggression and take down adversary anti-access capability before closing with the enemy.

Deploying some forces forward in critical areas, however, is essential as an expression of U.S. commitment and willingness to protect its regional interests. "Trip-wires" helped contain the Soviet Union during the Cold War and will constrain would-be hegemons in the twenty-first century. Forward deployed forces also can serve as a casus belli; Americans will support fighting anyone who kills many Americans, regardless of how important U.S. interests in the region are. "Deter forward" is not the same thing as "defend forward."

The presence of U.S. forces in a region (unless they are just passing through) sends a message to everyone in the region that U.S. interests are of such importance that it may use military force to defend or advance them. The act of deploying forces forward during peacetime also signals an awareness (on the part of the United States) that its interests in the region are being threatened. If there is no threat, why send military forces? This message, if credible, should reassure friends and allies and deter potential threats to those interests. U.S. forward presence makes the United States a global power. It reassures allies and friends; it sends a message to potential aggressors; and it positions the United States for rapid response

to smaller-scale contingencies and humanitarian relief missions. U.S. presence forces are there to be *seen* and to deal with lesser contingencies. They address the "will" side of the U.S. deterrent against large-scale aggression.

U.S. presence forces should not be shaped for defending forward against large-scale aggression. Requiring forward stationed and deployed forces to defeat large-scale aggression with minimum reinforcement ensures that a regional aggressor will have many lucrative anti-access targets to hit at the outset of the conflict. The potential payoff (to the aggressor) would be twofold. First, it would send a message to the American people: "Are U.S. interests here worth these kinds of costs?" Second, it could disable U.S. forces to defeat the aggressor's subsequent attack. Much in the same way that Saddam Hussein was criticized (in rogue state circles) for giving the United States 5 months to build up its forces in Southwest Asia, Slobodan Milosevic was criticized for not attacking the twenty-plus bases from which the coalition mounted Operation Allied Force. The next regional aggressor is likely to attack U.S. assets in the theater early in the conflict to test the will of the United States to intervene. Because large forward deployed forces in peacetime will always be vulnerable to surprise attacks, the United States should not have its ability to defeat large-scale aggression within range of the enemy. U.S. presence forces should raise the bar for large-scale aggression but not tempt potential aggressors into believing that it could disable through preemption the main portion of America's capability for defeating large-scale aggression.

U.S. power projection forces, however, must be highly lethal and highly survivable, capable of frustrating an aggressor's plans and inflicting great pain. These forces address the "capability" side of the deterrent against large-scale aggression. Conducting rapid global strike strictly from the continental United States (CONUS), however, makes it too difficult to mass the fires needed to halt aggression. U.S. power projection capabilities would be greatly enhanced if the United States could operate from robust, heavily defended, assured access bases on the periphery of a regional theater. The United States would initially wage standoff war from these periphery bases and then use them as staging areas for follow-on forces. For example, bombers operating from Guam, western Australia, and Diego Garcia could cover the vast Asian theater. Defending these periphery bases from missile attacks would be critical but much easier than defending closer-in bases from heavier anti-access attacks.

Neither presence nor power projection in an anti-access world should be viewed as lesser-included cases of one another. Moving more Air Force firepower into standoff systems could begin a division of labor among the military services across the spectrum of conflict. Although naval standoff systems (missile-carrying ships and submarines) are an important global strike asset, the Navy-Marine team is critical to global presence and more than capable of handling challenging smaller-scale contingencies. Air Force standoff forces and strategically mobile, CONUS-based Army maneuver forces should be optimized for the high end of the spectrum, although lighter Army-Air Force forces provide an important land-based element of global presence. In the mid-term, space provides the global surveillance that enables all U.S. forces, but in the long term will provide silver bullet global strike assets. Greater role specialization from the services will be necessary to ensure that the U.S. military as a whole can project power and presence effectively and affordably in the twenty-first century.

THE EMERGING QDR CONSTRUCT

At first blush, the QDR construct for forward presence seems inconsistent with the argument made here that U.S. presence forces should be shaped for handling lesser contingencies, not for defending forward against large-scale aggression. In describing how the U.S. military global posture would be reoriented to meet new challenges (including the anti-access one), the *QDR Report* states that one of its goals is "to render forward forces capable of defeating an adversary's military and political objectives with only modest reinforcement."[5] The *QDR Report,* however, envisions new forms of forward presence that would include "immediately employable supplement[s]" to forward deployed and stationed forces:[6]

A reorientation of the [military global] posture must take account of new challenges, *such as antiaccess and area denial threats.* New combinations of immediately employable forward stationed and deployed forces; globally available reconnaissance, strike, command and control assets; information operations capabilities; and rapidly deployable, highly lethal forces that may have to come from outside a theater of operations have the potential to be a significant force multiplier for forward stationed forces, including forcible entry forces.[7]

An earlier draft version of the *QDR Report* expressed the need for new forms of forward presence in even stronger terms. Although the stronger verbiage was excised from the final report and does not necessarily reflect official DoD policy, it does indicate that significant segments of the Department of Defense are sympathetic to the argument that new forms of forward presence are indeed needed. According to the earlier draft, "in an information age that enables rapid, networked operations," forward forces can be augmented by immediately employable supplemental forces (that are either globally distributed or CONUS-based) and are capable of creating strategic and operational effects "almost instantly both from within as well as from beyond a theater."[8] The draft continued by implying that no longer would DoD measure "forward presence in terms of the troops, naval tonnage, and the number of aircraft visible to the eye in any given theater" but

that new measures of effectiveness were needed for these "new forms of forward presence."[9]

The final *QDR Report* clearly recognizes that the ability of the U.S. military to project firepower rapidly, massively, and precisely into a theater is growing. In its effort to increase the deterrent impact of its forward forces, it has effectively broadened the definition of forward presence (what I call "presence forces") to include rapidly deployable forces. Broadening the definition of "presence forces" is exactly right; potential aggressors must understand that the United States has an immediately employable force to frustrate their aggression. U.S. forward forces should be capable of handling conflicts short of major aggression—a carrier battlegroup or amphibious ready group represents a substantial capability—but the capability to defeat large-scale aggression is increasingly resident in U.S. rapidly deployable power projection forces, of which naval forward presence forces are but one part.

THE NAVY IN AN ANTI-ACCESS WORLD

In its 2000 *Strategic Planning Guidance,* the Navy identified "combat-credible forward presence" as its "enduring contribution" to the Nation.[10] According to this document, "sea-based, self-contained and self-sustaining" naval expeditionary forces project power and influence through the means of "Knowledge Superiority and Forward Presence," defined as:

Knowledge Superiority is the ability to achieve a real-time, shared understanding of the battlespace at all levels through a network which provides the rapid accumulation of all information that is needed—and the dissemination of that information to the commander as the knowledge needed—to make a timely and informed decision inside any potential adversary's sensor and engagement timeline.

Forward Presence is being physically present with combat credible forces to Deter Aggression, Enhance Regional Stability, Protect and Promote U.S. interests, Improve Interoperability, and Provide Timely Initial Crisis Response where our national interests dictate.[11]

The issue, as I have often debated with Navy officers, is "combat credible" to do what? Even though the Navy often says that it is the Army and the Air Force that win the nation's wars, the Navy dearly wants a part of the action:

At the other end [that is, high end] of the spectrum, on-station naval expeditionary forces can provide timely and powerful sea-based response through the full range of amphibious and precision strike operations. . . . Ultimately, naval expeditionary forces, capable of direct and decisive influence through maritime power projection, are the nation's essential first responders and shape the early phases of hostilities to set the conditions for victory.[12]

The Navy enables its war-winning sister services by providing them "assured access" to the forward bases and ports they require. This is a commitment that even the Navy recognizes as flying into the face of the anti-access threat:

In order to assure U.S. access forward, naval forces will be required to counter a host of threats: sea and land mines, cruise missiles, submarines, chemical and biological weapons, space-based sensors, and information warfare. Maintaining our ability to assure access and project power in light of these threats will be increasingly vital and remains one of our most important priorities.[13]

"Knocking down the anti-access door" (as one Navy briefing expressed it) in order to give the Air Force and Navy access to close-in bases and ports early in the conflict makes little strategic sense. After noting the widespread proliferation of anti-access capabilities, driven by the need of lesser powers to focus military investments, Owen Cote states flatly, "Fixed targets on the surface will be indefensible if within range of an opponent's likely arsenal of precision TBMs [tactical ballistic missiles] and cruise missiles, for as long as the supply of those weapons last."[14] Gaining access to indefensible bases is not how to fight large-scale aggression.

This is bad news for the Army and Air Force. The news for the Navy is not much better. Cote continues, "Even mobile targets will be at much greater risk of prompt destruction if the opponent retains access to wide-area battlefield surveillance assets."[15] As Steven Kosiak, Andrew Krepinevich, and Michael Vickers observed, today's anti-access threat to naval forces—"a mix of diesel submarines, sophisticated anti-ship mines, land- and sea-based high-speed anti-ship cruise missiles, and land-based aircraft and ballistic missiles"—is tough, but the future threat is even worse:

It is also possible to envision new forms of extended-range blockade in which an adversary employs maritime forces (e.g., submarines and mines) in combination with land- (e.g., aircraft, cruise and ballistic missiles, UAVs [unmanned aerial vehicles] and UCAVs [unmanned combat aerial vehicles]) and space-based systems. Such an adversary would employ extended-range scouting systems to identify slow-moving maritime craft movement, while extended-range strike forces engage the target. One suspects that this form of blockade is likely to emerge initially at choke points . . . or be focused on a few ports . . . [but] it does not require a huge leap in imagination to envision how an enemy's blockade capabilities might be brought to bear against critical targets in more open waters, as the means for conducting extended-range reconnaissance proliferate and mature, along with the means to conduct attacks at ever greater ranges.[16]

This is far from a benign threat environment.

The Navy excelled at defending itself when it was a blue-water navy, but it must now fight in the littorals, where it is not only easier for adversaries to acquire surface ships as targets, but they are within range of a greater array of land- and sea-based capabilities as well. The proliferating threats to naval surface vessels—from SS-N-22 Sunburn antiship cruise missiles to sophisticated naval mines—is rapidly reducing the survivability delta between bases that move at zero knots per hour to those that move at twenty-five knots per hour. Everything forward is becoming a biological and chemical weapons magnet. Although the Navy is investing in active and passive defenses, increasing global transparency and the proliferation of anti-access capabilities is outpacing the force protection capabilities of U.S. power projection forces, including naval surface vessels. The Navy needs a new paradigm for projecting presence and power in an antiaccess world.

PROJECTING NAVAL PRESENCE

The growing vulnerability of naval presence does not mean that virtual presence is the answer. One cannot do gunboat diplomacy without a gunboat. From a purely military perspective, the United States can see who is doing what to whom and hurt them badly without being there. But drawing a line in the sand and threatening to wreak havoc from the skies if a regional rogue crosses that line invites failure; it passes the initiative to the aggressor and stresses our will or resolve to carry out threats. Being there does not always solve the "will" problem—consider U.S. "air occupations" of Bosnia-Herzegovina in 1992 and of northern Iraq in 1996—but it can help. The United States has global interests, but it is hard to advance these interests without a global presence.

The primary purpose for deploying U.S. forces in a region during peacetime is political: their very presence signals that the United States is a power in that region and intends to remain so. The more continuous the presence in a particular region is, the stronger the message. For example, U.S. forces stationed permanently in Japan and Korea leave no room for ambiguity: the United States will defend Japan and Korea if attacked. Less permanent forms of presence, rotational deployments, and temporary deployments for exercises and training leave more room for miscalculation, which can be offset by continuity of the deployments.

The *QDR Report* notes that Asia, which "contains a volatile mix of both rising and declining regional powers," is "gradually emerging as a region susceptible to large-scale military competition."[17] The vast distances of the Asian theater put a premium on naval forward presence, in part because the U.S. Navy budget includes funds for its presence operations. The Air Force and Army, however, not only must fund the extra resources required for rotational or temporary deployments but also must suffer the vagaries of the military airlift system. But even the Navy finds it difficult to "show the flag" anywhere (except in Japan) in the huge Asian theater on a continuous basis. Naval forward presence forces spend far too much time crossing oceans that no one covets. The carrier is widely viewed as the flagship of U.S. forward presence, and its presence in Asia should be increased.

Homeporting a second carrier in Asia, perhaps in northern or western Australia, would greatly enhance the U.S. presence in Asia.[18] Not only would homeporting a second carrier significantly enhance carrier time forward,[19] establishing a new permanent installation in Asia, but it also would signal clearly and loudly that the United States was in Asia to stay. As an alternative, the United States should consider ending the requirement for a continuous presence of a carrier in the Mediterranean. Europe is both a small theater and hosts several U.S. Army and Air Force units. The U.S. commitment to European security is not in doubt; the U.S. commitment to Asian security is. The *QDR Report* calls for the Navy to "increase its aircraft carrier battlegroup presence in the Western Pacific and . . . explore options for homeporting an additional three to four surface combatants, and guided cruise missile submarines (SSGNs), near that area."[20] That is a good start. As Asia's importance rises, U.S. interests will grow, as should the U.S. naval presence.

As argued previously, U.S. naval presence forces should be shaped largely for smaller-scale contingencies and humanitarian relief missions, not for defeating large-scale aggressions. This does not mean that the Navy will need less force protection. As symbols of American military might, U.S. Navy assets will always be a favorite target for terrorist attacks, as seen most recently in the 2000 attack on the USS *Cole.* U.S. involvement in smaller-scale contingencies will always carry the risk of reprisal attacks. The Navy's improving force protection capabilities should be increasingly capable of defense against small-scale attacks.

Although the *QDR Report* eschews "shaping" and "engagement," terms favored by the previous administration, there is no downgrading of the importance of U.S. forward presence that plays a key role in three of the four Defense Policy Goals—assuring allies and friends, deterring threats to U.S. interests, and defeating aggression if deterrence fails (dissuading future military competition is the fourth goal).[21] The *QDR Report,* however, maintains that:

U.S. military will promote security cooperation with allies and friendly nations. A primary objective of U.S. security cooperation will be to help allies and friends create favorable balances of military power in critical areas of the world to deter aggression and coercion. Security cooperation will serve as an important means for linking [DoD] strategic direction with those of its allies and friends.[22]

The Department of Defense will focus its peacetime overseas activities on security cooperation to help create favorable balances of military power in critical areas of the world and to deter aggression and coercion. A particular aim of DoD security cooperation efforts will be to ensure access, interoperability, and intelligence cooperation, while expanding the range of preconflict options available to counter coercive threats, deter aggression, or favorably prosecute war on U.S. terms.[23]

Being there still matters immensely, but Secretary of Defense Donald Rumsfeld prefers a focus on "security cooperation," not engagement for engagement's sake.

In addition to being prepared for a wide variety of potential missions short of large-scale aggression, U.S. naval forces deployed forward will contribute significantly in several important areas.

Prewar Situational Awareness. In line with its embrace of "Knowledge Superiority" as one of its two "means" (the other is forward presence), the Navy is investing heavily in the command, control, communications, computers, and intelligence (C4I) capabilities that enable Network-Centric warfare. Although the Navy focuses on how the knowledge gained from its forward presence will help it conduct its missions, the Navy recognizes, as stated in the *2000 Strategic Planning Guidance,* that the "U.S. Armed Forces . . . will benefit from a regional knowledge base that is built and enhanced by day-to-day naval presence, familiarity with forward operating environments, and foreign-area expertise."[24] Previously acquired "close-in" knowledge is, in fact, more valuable when the fight against large-scale aggression begins at stand-off ranges.

Sea-Based Theater Missile Defense. U.S. power projection forces should operate initially from robust, heavily defended bases on the periphery of contested theaters. Defending these periphery bases will be much easier than defending close-in bases and ports from much heavier anti-access attacks. But in some instances, the United States will want to defend an ally or friend against missile attack, even if the scale of attack threatens to overwhelm U.S. defenses. Sea-based TMD will play a critical role in these scenarios.

Antiterrorist Operations. In the wake of the horrific attacks of September 11, the United States has committed itself to a war against global terrorism that will probably have no end. New concepts of operations for attacking terrorists will require new mixes of capabilities—special operations forces, UAVs, distributed sensor networks, and so on—that can be hosted on forward deployed naval assets that can operate autonomously from international waters. The U.S. Marine Corps announced within 2 weeks of the attack that it would reactivate the 4th Marine Expeditionary Brigade as a specialized counterterrorism unit of 4,800 personnel, which would include the existing Chemical/Biological Incident Response Force Marines.[25] The urgency of the campaign against terrorism will undoubtedly fuel a major growth in sea-based antiterrorist capabilities.

In short, there is no lack of critical missions for U.S. naval presence forces. In fact, what the United States needs is more naval forward presence in more places. This is what a global power needs to stay a global power.

NAVAL POWER PROJECTION

In confronting large-scale aggression, U.S. power projection forces must initially fight from a distance, as they first punish aggression and take down an adversary's anti-access capability before closing with the enemy. The Navy, of course, already has substantial standoff capability in its conventional missile-carrying submarines and surface ships. The Navy's Tomahawk cruise missile has been prominently featured in several campaigns and retaliatory raids. The Navy is also planning to convert four Trident ballistic missile submarines to conventional missile carriers, which will greatly augment the Navy's stand-off capabilities (particularly if the nuclear-powered cruise missile attack submarines retain the same crew rotation policy they did as nuclear-powered ballistic missile submarines). Naval standoff capabilities have proven particularly useful early in a conflict in attacks on the enemy's integrated air defenses. The Navy, however, should accelerate its acquisition of a land-attack missile to give it a prompt target kill capability.

Navy carriers and amphibious ready groups also project power, but they have to deploy deep into the theater to apply force against land targets. Modernizing with the planned Joint Strike Fighter helps somewhat, but its range (at nine hundred miles, two hundred more than the Air Force's range) is too short for severe anti-access environments, and it is not stealthy enough for advanced surface-to-air missile environments. In future large-scale campaigns, naval surface vessels are simply too valuable and too vulnerable to risk forward early in the conflict. That is probably true even for the notion of a Streetfighter warship, which would be a smaller, faster, presumably more expendable ship. For a casualty-adverse America, however, there is no such thing as an expendable ship, and in the event of an actual large-scale war, the United States, in the same manner it rejected an amphibious attack in the Persian Gulf War, will be reluctant to bring naval surface ships forward into the teeth of an adversary's still functioning antiaccess capability.

Navy carriers and amphibious vehicles, however, will be in the force for decades. The introduction of new technologies—intelligence, surveillance, and reconnaissance UAVs, particularly a stealthy variant; combat UAVs; unmanned underwater vehicles; and smaller and cheaper land-attack missiles—could significantly increase their standoff capability, although it would come at the expense of shorter-range capabilities. The Navy's introduction of its Cooperative Engagement Capability will greatly increase the ability of its fleet to fight as a distributed network, making it much easier to integrate new longer-range assets.

FINAL THOUGHT

The U.S. Navy will have to change to meet the challenges of an anti-access environment, but less profoundly than its sister services. It does not need forward bases and ports from which to operate. The Navy, which embraced the presence role in the 1993 Bottom-Up Review (BUR), will remain the Nation's premier presence force. Its role in high-intensity conflict has been declining, but most of the demand for the Nation's military forces has been in areas where the Navy and Marines excel—peacetime overseas activities (now focused on security cooperation), smaller-scale contingencies, and humanitarian relief missions. In 1993, the BUR used presence as a force structure justifier for the first time. But in 2001, the QDR Report said that the Department of Defense will now use smaller-scale contingencies as a force-planning tool, not as lesser included cases of its war-fighting capabilities.

The anti-access world provides serious challenges to the Navy at the high end of the spectrum of conflict, even as the demand for its capabilities on the lower end seems to be growing.[26] Conducting the forward presence mission as if it were our primary response to high-intensity conflict is a recipe for disaster, both for the naval forces involved and our nation.

NOTES

1. U.S. Department of Defense, *Quadrennial Defense Review Report* (Washington, D.C.: U.S. Department of Defense, September 30, 2001), 30 (the document is hereafter referred to as *QDR Report*). The other critical challenges include protecting the U.S. homeland, forces abroad, allies, and friends from nuclear, biological, and chemical weapons and their means of delivery; ensuring information security and conducting effective information operations; providing persistent surveillance and rapid engagement with high-volume precision strike against all targets under all conditions; enhancing the capability and survivability of space assets; and developing an interoperable, joint Command, Control, Communications, Computers, Intelligence, Surveillance, and Reconaissance architecture.

2. Ibid., 31. Emphasis added.

3. Many of the ideas in this section were first explored in Clark A. Murdock, *Projecting Power and Presence into 21st Century Asia* (Washington, D.C.: DFI-International Paper, 2001). Office of the Secretary of Defense, Office of Net Assessment, supported the project for which that paper was written.

4. *Washington Post* (September 29, 2001): A14.

5. *QDR Report*, 25. In a much earlier draft, the force planning paradigm for "deterring forward" used the phrase "with minimum reinforcement" instead of "only modest reinforcement," a requirement sufficiently stringent that one Office of the Secretary of Defense office maintained that the U.S. Navy would need thirty-six carriers to meet it.

6. Ibid., 26.

7. Unreleased earlier draft of *QDR Report* (early September 2001), 38. Emphasis added.

8. Ibid., 39.

9. Ibid.

10. U.S. Navy Chief of Naval Operations, *Navy Strategic Planning Guidance with Long Range Planning Objectives* (Washington, D.C.: U.S. Department of the Navy, April 2000), 36.

11. Ibid., 19–21.

12. Ibid., 20.

13. Ibid., 27.

14. Owen R. Cote, Jr., "Buying ' . . . From the Sea': A Defense Budget for a Maritime Strategy," in *Holding the Line: U.S. Defense Alternatives for the Early 21st Century*, ed. Cindy Williams (Cambridge, Mass.: MIT Press, 2001), 156.

15. Ibid.

16. Steven Kosiak, Andrew Krepinevich, and Michael Vickers, *A Strategy for a Long Peace* (Washington, D.C.: Center for Strategic and Budgetary Assessments, January 2001), 36.

17. *QDR Report,* 4.

18. Homeporting a second carrier in Guam would also increase naval presence in Asia, but not quite as much as a port in Australia (Guam is still more than a thousand miles from the theater). Moreover, the political statement made by basing a carrier in Australia would be much stronger for both the United States and Australia.

19. Cote observes that today's twelve-carrier force with one homeport abroad provides 2.5 carrier battlegroups (CVBGs) forward at any one time, whereas an eleven-carrier force with two homeports abroad would provide between 3.5 and 4 CVBGs forward at any one time. See Cote, "Buying ' . . . From the Sea,'" 177.

20. *QDR Report,* 27. The Marine Corps was also told to "develop plans to shift some of its afloat prepositioned equipment from the Mediterranean toward the Indian Ocean and Persian Gulf" and to "explore the feasibility of conducting training for littoral warfare in the Western Pacific."

21. Ibid., iii–iv.

22. Ibid., 11.

23. Ibid., 20.

24. U.S. Navy Chief of Naval Operations, *Navy Strategic Planning Guidance,* 22.

25. Joshua S. Higgins, "Anti-Terrorism Unit Set For Activation" (October 17, 2001), at www.usmc.mil/marinelink/mcn2000.nsf/. Article reference number 200110221060.

26. For a discussion and redefinition of the concept of the "spectrum of conflict," see Sam J. Tangredi, "Assessing New Missions," in *Transforming America's Military,* ed. Hans Binnendijk (Washington, D.C.: National Defense University Press, 2002), 3–30.

AFGHANISTAN AND THE FUTURE OF WARFARE

STEPHEN BIDDLE

WHAT'S NEW?

America's novel use of Special Operations forces (SOF), precision weapons, and indigenous allies has attracted widespread attention since its debut in Afghanistan, proving both influential and controversial. Many believe it was responsible for the Taliban's sudden collapse. They see the "Afghan model" as warfare's future and think it should become the new template for U.S. defense planning. Others, however, see Afghanistan as an anomaly—a nonrepeatable product of local conditions. Both camps are wrong. The Afghan campaign does indeed offer important clues to the future of warfare, but not the ones most people think—because the war itself was not fought the way most people think.

Both sides in the debate assume that the Afghan campaign was waged at standoff ranges, with precision weapons annihilating enemies at a distance, before they could close with U.S. commandos or indigenous allies. For proponents of the Afghan model, this is what gives the model its broad utility: with SOF-guided bombs doing the real killing at a distance, even ragtag local militias will suffice as allies. All they have to do is screen U.S. commandos from occasional hostile survivors and occupy abandoned ground later on. America can thus defeat rogues at global distances with few U.S. casualties and little danger of appearing to be a conquering power. For Afghan model detractors, conversely, it is the apparent ability to annihilate from afar that makes the campaign seem so anomalous and a product of idiosyncratic local factors.

Yet the war was not purely a standoff affair. Contrary to popular belief, there was plenty of close combat in Afghanistan. Although they were initially taken by surprise, Taliban fighters quickly adapted to American methods and adopted countermeasures that allowed many of them to elude American surveillance and survive U.S. airstrikes. These surviving, actively resisting Taliban fighters had to be overcome by surprisingly traditional close-quarters fighting.

Interviews with a broad range of key American participants in the war, along with close analysis of available official documentation on the war effort and personal inspection of its battlefields, lead to the conclusion that the war as a whole was much more orthodox, and much less revolutionary, than most now believe.[1] Precision airpower was indeed necessary for turning a stalemated civil war into a Taliban collapse in a few weeks, but it was far from sufficient. Although much was truly new in Afghanistan, much was not, and as the continuities were at least as important to the outcome as were the novelties, the war's lessons for strategic and defense policy are different from what either camp in the current debate now asserts.

Stephen Biddle, "Afghanistan and the Future of Warfare," Foreign Affairs 82 *(March/April 2003): 31–46. Public domain.*

ONE THING AFTER ANOTHER

The Afghan campaign began the night of October 7, 2001, with a program of airstrikes aimed initially at destroying the Taliban's limited air defenses and communications infrastructure. Early air attacks produced few results, however, because the country had little fixed infrastructure to destroy. By October 15, SOF teams designated to make contact with the major Northern Alliance warlords had been inserted. A three-part campaign followed, divided roughly into a northern phase revolving around control of the city of Mazar-i-Sharif, a southern phase centered on the city of Kandahar, and subsequent battles against Taliban and al Qaeda forces at Tora Bora and during Operation Anaconda in the Shah-i-Kot Valley.

The fight for Mazar-i-Sharif began when Gen. Abdul Rashid Dostum, supported by American SOF, took the village of Bishqab on the banks of the Dar-ye Suf south of Mazar on October 21. This was followed by engagements at Cobaki, Chapchall, and Oimetan over the next few days as Dostum fought his way up the river valley. The key battle came when Dostum's troops overran hostile forces occupying old Soviet-built defensive positions at the hamlet of Bai Beche on November 5. Shortly thereafter, General Muhammed Atta's forces and their accompanying SOF captured Ac'capruk on the Balkh River, and the door swung open for a rapid advance to Mazar, which fell to Atta and Dostum's troops on November 10. The fall of Mazar unhinged the Taliban position in northern Afghanistan. Kabul fell without a fight on November 13, and after a 12-day siege, a force of some five thousand Taliban and al Qaeda survivors, encircled in the city of Kunduz, surrendered on November 26.

With the fall of Kabul and Kunduz, attention shifted to the Taliban's stronghold of Kandahar in the south. SOF teams and Hamid Karzai's allied Afghan forces advanced on the city from the north; Gul Agha Shirzai's allied Afghans and supporting SOF advanced from the south. After a series of battles, on the night of December 6, Mullah Muhammad Omar and the rest of the senior Taliban leadership fled the city and went into hiding, ending Taliban rule in Afghanistan.

Allied forces, meanwhile, tracked a group of al Qaeda survivors thought to include Osama bin Laden to a series of redoubts in the White Mountains near Tora Bora. These redoubts were taken in a 16-day battle ending on December 17, but many al Qaeda defenders escaped death or capture and fled across the border into Pakistan.

In March 2002, a second concentration of al Qaeda holdouts was finally identified in the Shah-i-Kot Valley east of Gardez. In Operation Anaconda, Western and allied Afghan forces descended on these al Qaeda defenders, killing many, dispersing the rest, and bringing to a close the major combat operations in the country to date.

PREY TO PRECISION

Early on, the war went mostly the way Afghan model proponents assume. The new model took the Taliban

by surprise, and their initial dispositions were poorly chosen for this kind of warfare.[2] They typically deployed on exposed ridgelines with little effort at camouflage or concealment. Their entrenchments were haphazard, lacking overhead cover for infantry positions or proper emplacements for combat vehicles. As a result, their positions could often be identified from extraordinary distances. And once located, their poor entrenchment and exposed movements made them easy prey for precision weapons.

The result was slaughter. At Bishqab, for example, U.S. SOF pinpointed Taliban targets at ranges of more than eight kilometers. Skeptical Northern Alliance commanders peered through their binoculars at Taliban positions that had stymied them for years and were astounded to see the defenses suddenly vaporized by direct hits from two-thousand-pound bombs. At Cobaki, Taliban observation posts were easily spotted at 1,500–2,000 meters and annihilated by precision bombing. At Zard Kammar, Taliban defenses were wiped out from more than a kilometer and a half away. At Ac'capruk, exposed Taliban combat vehicles and heavy weapons on hillsides west of the Balkh River were spotted from SOF observation posts on the Koh-i-Almortak ridgeline some four to five kilometers distant and were obliterated by American air strikes.

The Taliban fighters were not the only ones surprised by these results. Some allied Afghans initially thought the lasers U.S. SOF used to designate bombing targets were actually death rays, because they apparently caused defenses to vanish whenever caught in their cross hairs. Both sides, however, learned fast. Within days of the first SOF-directed air strikes, American commandos were already reporting that Taliban vehicles in their sectors had been smeared with mud to camouflage them. By November 5, the Taliban forces were making aggressive use of overhead cover and concealment. In the fighting north of Kandahar and along Highway 4 south of the city in December, al Qaeda defenses were well camouflaged, dispersed, and making use of natural terrain for expedient cover. This pattern continued through Operation Anaconda in March, by which time, al Qaeda forces were practicing systematic communications security, dispersal, camouflage discipline, use of cover and concealment, and exploitation of dummy fighting positions to draw fire and attention from their real positions. The Taliban did not just passively suffer under American attack; they adapted their methods to try to reduce their vulnerability. And as they did, the war changed character.

NOW YOU SEE THEM, NOW YOU DON'T

Among the more important changes was the increasing difficulty U.S. forces experienced in finding targets for precision attack. At Bai Beche from November 2 through November 5, for example, a mostly al Qaeda defensive force occupied an old, formerly Soviet system of deliberate entrenchments. With proper cover and concealment, the defenders were able to prevent American commandos from locating the entirety of their individual fighting positions, many of which could not be singled out for precision attack.

By the time of the December fighting along Highway 4, even less information was available. In fact, concealed al Qaeda defenses among a series of culverts and in burned-out vehicles along the roadside remained wholly undetected until their fire drove back an allied advance. An al Qaeda counterattack in the same sector using a system of wadis, or dry valleys, for cover approached undetected to within one hundred or two hundred meters of allied and American SOF positions along the highway before opening fire.

At the village of Sayed Slim Kalay north of Kandahar between December 2 and December 4, concealed al Qaeda defenders likewise remained undetected until they fired on unsuspecting U.S. and allied attackers. An al Qaeda counterattack using local terrain for cover maneuvered into small-arms range of friendly defenders before being driven back.

During Operation Anaconda in March 2002, an intensive prebattle reconnaissance effort focused every available surveillance and target-acquisition system on a tiny, one-hundred-square-kilometer battlefield. Yet fewer than half of all the al Qaeda positions ultimately identified on this battlefield were discovered prior to ground contact. In fact, most fire received by U.S. forces during Anaconda came from initially unseen, unanticipated defenders.

How could such surprise be possible in an era of persistent reconnaissance drones, airborne radars, satellite surveillance, thermal imaging, and hypersensitive electronic eavesdropping equipment? The answer is that the earth's surface remains an extremely complex environment with an abundance of natural and manmade cover available for those militaries capable of exploiting it.

Objective Ginger on the Anaconda battlefield illustrates this problem. Overhanging rock concealed troops from overhead surveillance systems. In principle, one might hope to observe resupply movement or al Qaeda patrols into or out of such positions, or to overhear radio communications from their occupants. Al Qaeda fighters wearing the flowing robes of local herdsmen and traveling in small parties among the mountains, however, are nearly impossible to distinguish at a distance from the noncombatants who tend goats or travel through such areas routinely. And defenders able to operate under radio silence by communicating using runners, landlines, or other nonbroadcast means can reduce signal intercepts to a level that makes identifying specific fighting positions very difficult. Against such targets, it is far from clear that any surveillance technology coming any time soon will ensure reliable targeting from stand-off distances.

This problem is not unique to Afghanistan. Militarily exploitable cover is commonplace in almost any likely theater of war. For targets who observe radio silence, as al Qaeda now does, foliage degrades all existing sensor technologies; urban areas provide overhead cover, create background clutter, and make it difficult to distinguish military targets from innocent civilians. And both foliage and urban cover are widely available. More than 26 percent of Somalia's land area is wooded or urban, as is more than 20 percent of Sudan's, 34 percent of Georgia's, and 46 percent of that in the Philippines. In most countries, the central geostrategic objectives are urban areas. Even where the bulk of the national land area is open desert (as in Iraq), the cities are both the key terrain and an ample source of cover (Baghdad alone covers more than three hundred square kilometers). The natural complexity of such surfaces offers any opponent with the necessary skills, training, and adaptability a multitude of opportunities to thwart even modern remote surveillance systems. Against such opponents, remote surveillance will still detect some targets, and remote sensors remain crucial assets, but the only sure means to identify targets is direct ground contact. A ground force whose advance threatens objectives that the enemy cannot sacrifice and thus must defend compels the enemy to give away its locations by firing on its attackers. Skilled attackers can eventually locate any defensive position by observing the source of the fire directed at them—and this, in fact, is how the majority of the al Qaeda positions discovered during Operation Anaconda were found.

DIE ANOTHER DAY

Just as enemy targets became harder to find once the Taliban adapted to the new model, the ones that were found also became tougher to kill. At Bai Beche, although the entrenched defenders could not all be located individually, American commandos knew the defensive system's extent and thus called for heavy bombing across the entire position for more than 2 days. Yet even after this extensive effort, enough defenders survived to thwart the initial attack.

At the Qala-e-Gangi fortress west of Mazar-i-Sharif, an uprising by Taliban prisoners was driven underground by fire from Western and allied Afghan troops on the parapets surrounding the bullpen area where the prisoners had been held. The renegades were quickly isolated in a handful of small underground chambers whose locations and perimeter were well known. These hideouts were then pounded by allied airpower; entire ammunition payloads of multiple AC-130 Spectre gunships and no fewer than seven 2,000-pound satellite-guided bombs were expended against this tiny area. Yet the defenders survived and continued to resist; they succumbed only to the medieval technology of flooding the chambers with cold water.

During Operation Anaconda, well-prepared al Qaeda positions survived repeated aerial attack by U.S. precision munitions. On Objective Ginger on March 4, for example, American troops inadvertently disembarked from their assault helicopters almost on top of an unseen al Qaeda position; after being pinned down for much of the day, they were extracted that night. They then spent much of the next 10 days fighting their way back toward the Ginger hilltop from more secure landing zones well to the north. In the meantime, American aircraft pounded the hill. Yet in spite of more than a week of sustained heavy bombing, al Qaeda positions on Ginger survived to fire on U.S. infantry when the latter finally reached and overran the objective. One dug-in al Qaeda command post was found surrounded by no fewer than five 2,000-pound bomb craters. Still, its garrison survived and resisted until overrun.

This does not mean that precision firepower is not extremely lethal, or that even well-dug-in al Qaeda defenders did not suffer heavy losses from precision engagements. But the evidence does indicate that a combination of cover and concealment can allow defenders, although battered, to survive modern firepower in sufficient numbers to mount serious resistance.

Nor was Afghanistan the first time that properly prepared defenses have survived massive firepower, precise or otherwise. French defenses at Verdun in 1916 endured a 2-day German artillery barrage equal to about 1,200 tons of explosives—in nuclear parlance, more than a kiloton, or more explosive power than the W48 tactical nuclear warhead—yet enough of the entrenched defenders survived this maelstrom to halt the German assault. In 1917, German defenses at Messines absorbed more than a kiloton of explosive power per mile of frontage but were still able to halt the ensuing British offensive. German positions in the village of Cassino on March 15, 1944, were struck by three hundred tons of bombs in a single day but defeated the associated Allied infantry advance. On July 18, 1944, more than 4,500 Allied aircraft, three corps' worth of artillery, and naval gunfire from two Royal Navy cruisers and the monitor *Roberts* deposited more than 8,700 tons of explosives—more than eight kilotons of firepower—on just seven kilometers of German frontage in less than 3 hours in Operation Goodwood. Yet the entrenched Germans halted the subsequent British armored advance, destroying more than one-third of all the British armor on the continent in the process.

Firepower on such scales is tremendously destructive, and each of these defenders suffered heavily under the barrages. But these examples show that even fantastic volumes of firepower alone cannot annihilate defenses outright. Today's precision allows crushing firepower to be delivered using vastly fewer platforms, but to expect precision to accomplish what literally nuclear-scale fires have failed to attain in the past is to ask too much of new technology. Although the village of Cassino was struck by far less accurate weapons than were aimed at the al Qaeda defenders of Objective Ginger, this tiny Italian hamlet was still hit with the equivalent of more than three hundred 2,000-pound satellite-guided bombs. Such devastating force was more than enough to reduce every building in the village to rubble—but not enough to exterminate its defenders. The problem at Verdun, Messines, or Cassino or in Operation Goodwood was not an inability to turn defenses into crater fields or reduce specific buildings to rubble due to lack of precision. The problem was and remains that resolute defenders can survive even within crater fields and rubble piles to mount serious resistance. In the past, firepower has been critical, but against resolute, well-prepared defenders, it has rarely been sufficient; taken together, Bai Beche, Qala-e-Gangi, and Operation Anaconda suggest that it is not now, either.

TOO CLOSE FOR COMFORT

As enemy forces adapted, their decreasing vulnerability to standoff attack meant an increasing burden of close combat. Little of this fighting represented guerrilla warfare. At least through Anaconda in March, the Taliban sought to take and hold ground in very orthodox ways: they tried to defend key geographic objectives, not harass their enemies with hit-and-run tactics. These defenses, however, were sufficiently covered and concealed to allow important fractions of them to survive American air attack. The resulting ground combat was neither trivial nor wholly one-sided: many battles were close calls, with either initial reverses, serious casualties, or both.

At Bai Beche on November 5, for example, the dug-in al Qaeda defenders refused to withdraw after more than 2 days of heavy American bombing. To dislodge them, Northern Alliance troops were ordered to charge the position. Their first attempt was driven back. On observing this reverse, the attached American SOF began calling in renewed airstrikes in anticipation of a second assault. In the process, however, an SOF warning order to the Northern Alliance cavalry to prepare for another push was mistaken by the cavalry as a command to launch the assault, with the result that the cavalry began its attack much sooner than intended. The surprised Americans watched the Afghan cavalry break cover and begin its advance just as a series of laser-guided bombs had been released from American aircraft in response to the SOF calls for air support. The SOF commander reported that he was convinced they had just caused a friendly fire incident: the bomb release and the cavalry advance were much too close together for official doctrinal limits, and the air strike would never have been ordered if the SOF had known that the cavalry was just then jumping off for the second assault. As it happened, the bombs landed only seconds before the cavalry arrived. In fact, the cavalry galloped through the enormous cloud of smoke and dust that was still hanging in the air after the explosions, emerging behind the enemy defenses before the garrison even knew what was happening. The defenders, seeing Northern Alliance cavalry to their rear, abandoned their positions in an attempt to avoid encirclement.

The result was an important victory—in fact, the victory that turned the tide in the north. But the battle involved serious close combat (cavalry overrunning prepared, actively resisting defenses), and the outcome was a very close call. The assault profited from an extremely tight integration of movement with suppressive fire—far tighter even than either the cavalry or its supporting SOF would ever have dared arrange deliberately. Luck thus played an important role in the outcome. The Northern Alliance might well have carried the position eventually, even without the good fortune of an extraordinary integration of fire and movement. This battle was clearly crucial, and the cavalry would presumably have redoubled its efforts if the second attempt had failed. Still, the outcome involved an important element of serendipity.

Nor was Bai Beche unique in demanding hard fighting at close quarters. As noted above, al Qaeda counterattackers came within small-arms range of U.S. and allied forces before being driven back at Sayed Slim Kalay and at Highway 4. At Kunduz in late November, al Qaeda counterattackers penetrated allied positions deeply enough to compel supporting American SOF teams to withdraw at least three times to avoid being overrun. During Operation Anaconda, allied forces associated with General Mohammed Zia and supported by American SOF were assigned to drive al Qaeda defenders from the "Tri-cities" area (the villages of Shirkankeyl, Babakuhl, and Marzak); they were instead pinned down under hostile fire from prepared defenses on the surrounding mountainsides and eventually withdrew after they proved unable to advance. Only after the al Qaeda defenders pulled back under joint, multinational attack by allied airpower, Western infantry, and multinational SOF were Zia's troops able to enter the Tri-cities and adjoining ridgelines. Then at Tora Bora, massive American bombing proved insufficient to compensate for allied Afghan unwillingness to close with dug-in al Qaeda defenders in the cave complexes of the White Mountains. This ground force hesitancy probably allowed bin Laden and his lieutenants to escape into neighboring Pakistan.

Among these examples, the fighting along Highway 4 in December is particularly instructive. The American-allied Afghans here were divided between two factions. The first, commanded by Haji Gul Alai, were very capable troops by Afghan standards. They used terrain for cover and concealment, maintained good intervals between elements in the advance, moved by alternate bounds, exploited suppressive fire to cover moving elements' exposure, and were able to exploit the effects of American airstrikes by coordinating their movement with the bombing, unlike many other Afghan factions. The second faction, by contrast, was much less skilled: the attached SOF commander characterized it as "an armed mob —just villagers given weapons." These troops' tactics consisted of exposed, bunched-up movement in the open, with no attempt to use terrain to reduce their exposure, and little ability to employ supporting or suppressive fire. At the Arghestan Bridge on December 5, this second faction launched an assault on a dug-in al Qaeda position south of the Kandahar airport. Driven back repeatedly, it proved unable to take the position, in spite of U.S. air support. Only after these troops were withdrawn and Haji Gul Alai's forces took over the assault the following day could the al Qaeda positions be taken.

Of course, the alliance ultimately prevailed militarily and succeeded in driving the Taliban from power.

Precision American airpower was undoubtedly a precondition for this victory—together with its SOF spotters, it turned a stalemated civil war into a dramatic battlefield victory for America and its allies. Although precision bombing was necessary, however, it was not sufficient. It could annihilate poorly prepared fighting positions, and it could inflict heavy losses on even well-disposed defenses. But it could not destroy the entirety of properly prepared positions by itself. And unless such positions are all but annihilated, even a handful of surviving, actively resisting defenders with modern automatic weapons can slaughter unsophisticated indigenous allies whose idea of tactics is to walk forward bunched up in the open. To overcome skilled, resolute defenders who have adopted the standard countermeasures to high-firepower airstrikes still requires close combat by friendly ground forces whose own skills enable them to use local cover and their own suppressive fire to advance against hostile survivors with modern weapons.

By and large, America's main Afghan allies in this war either enjoyed such fundamental skills or profited from accidentally tight coordination of their movement and American firepower (as at Bai Beche), or both. The anti-Taliban fighters were not always the motley assortment of militiamen they are sometimes said to have been. Enough of them were capable of modern military tactics to allow them to exploit the great potential of precision airpower when it is integrated with ground maneuver.

But not all of America's allies in this war were up to the job. Although the typical combat units on each side were about equally matched (as the stalled preintervention battle lines implied), the quality of troops on both sides in Afghanistan was actually quite uneven—and this diversity offers a couple of valuable opportunities to observe instances of unequally skilled forces in combat. In such unequal fights as the first day at Arghestan Bridge and the assault on the Tri-cities during Anaconda, the results suggest that where indigenous allies are outdone tactically, American airpower and SOF support alone may not be enough to turn the tide. In Afghanistan, the Northern and Southern Alliances, eventually combined with the American and Canadian troops that fought during Anaconda, together provided significant ground forces that ultimately shouldered an essential load of old-fashioned close combat against surviving, actively resisting opponents. Even with twenty-first-century firepower, without this essential close-combat capability, the outcome in Afghanistan could easily have been very different.

THE MORE THINGS CHANGE

So what does this analysis tell us about the future of warfare? The answer is that Afghanistan, at least, suggests a future much more like the past than most observers now believe. Precision firepower did not simply annihilate well-prepared opponents at standoff range in Afghanistan. To overcome skilled, resolute opposition required both precision firepower and skilled ground maneuver; neither alone was sufficient.

But this is hardly news. Since at least 1918, all great-power militaries have understood the importance of combining fire and maneuver. The synergy between these elements lies at the heart of all successful twentieth-century tactical systems; it is hardly a product of twenty-first-century technology.

Of course, this is not to suggest that nothing has changed since 1918. In particular, fire support's form has changed dramatically since then—and the increases in firepower's range, precision, and round-for-round lethality have obviously been dramatic in recent years. The increasing lethality of standoff precision engagement has made the combination of fire and movement much more powerful where both elements are present. Tight integration of laser-guided bombs with skilled ground maneuver is far more effective today than was cooperation between seventy-seven-mm field guns and German *Stosstruppen* in 1918. This important development has greatly increased America's real military power relative to that of any plausible foe.

But what new technology has not done is allow militaries to succeed using either fire or maneuver alone. The maneuver elements in Afghanistan were not always American, but success turned on the proficiency of forces, whether Western or Afghan, in executing a demanding system of integrated fire and maneuver—much as it has for the past 90 years. This underlying continuity is at least as significant for the future of warfare as the accompanying extraordinary technological change in the form that firepower has taken.

In short, Afghanistan was neither a revolution nor a fluke. The Afghan model will not always work as it did in Afghanistan because the United States will not always enjoy allies who match up so well against their enemies. But where they do, the model should be roughly as lethal as it was in Afghanistan. The model is thus at once oversold by its proponents and undersold by its detractors. It can work under some important preconditions, but those preconditions will not always be met. In Iraq, for example, the lack of a credible, trained opposition bodes ill for an Afghan-style campaign without major American ground forces.

Even more broadly, we should be wary of suggestions that precision weapons have so revolutionized warfare that either the American military or American foreign policy can now be radically restructured. Some now argue that the revolutionary potential of precision weapons, teamed with SOF and indigenous allies, can underwrite a neoimperial American foreign policy, in which the Afghan model enables cheap but effective military intervention on a potentially global scale. Other experts would redesign the military to shift it away from expensive, labor-intensive close combat capability and toward reliance on standoff precision engagement, with corresponding deep cuts in conventional ground forces. Interpretations of the Afghan campaign as a triumph of new technology that made conquerors of a ragtag militia fuel such proposals and reinforce the general perception of military revolution, with the concomitant need for transformational responses from American policymakers. Yet the war's actual conduct offers little support for such claims. An American military dependent on standoff precision would fare well where its allies were up to the job, but it would fail badly elsewhere. In a world of diverse military organizations and few certainties about where or when the United States may need to fight, such a restructuring would be very risky. And as the Afghan model will sometimes allow interventions at little cost in American lives, but sometimes not, a neoimperial foreign policy requires, among other things, a willingness to accept real costs in critical theaters.

What the Afghan war ultimately shows is that even today, continuity in the nature of war is at least as important as change. To ignore the continuity and focus exclusively on the change risks serious error and fundamental misunderstanding of this war's true meaning for the future—which is neither as transformational nor as idiosyncratic as many have asserted.

NOTES

The views expressed in this essay are the author's and do not necessarily reflect those of the U.S. Army War College's Strategic Studies Institute.

1. For complete documentation and a more detailed account of the campaign, see Stephen Biddle, *Afghanistan and the Future of Warfare: Implications for Army and Defense Policy* (Carlisle, Pa.: U.S. Army War College Strategic Studies Institute, 2002).

2. America's opponents were not a unitary or monolithic military. Their three main components—indigenous Afghan Taliban, foreign allies who fought for the Taliban regime, and the subset of these trained in al Qaeda's infamous camps—had very different military properties and combat performance, with al Qaeda proving most capable and Afghan Taliban least. Throughout this article, "Taliban" refers collectively to any hostile forces; "Afghan Taliban" refers to the indigenous Afghan component; "foreign Taliban" refers to all non-Afghan components; and "al Qaeda" refers exclusively to forces trained in bin Laden's camps and associated with his organization.

TOTEM AND TABOO: DEPOLARIZING THE SPACE WEAPONIZATION DEBATE

KARL P. MUELLER

Should the United States place weapons in space? This question, long neglected in most discussions about U.S. defense policy except where it touched upon arguments about ballistic missile defenses and Cold War nuclear stability, is now at last becoming the subject of active and serious debate in the United States and abroad. Many factors are contributing to this trend, including the growing economic and military importance of satellites, renewed U.S. interest in national missile defense, and the work of the Space Commission chaired by Donald Rumsfeld prior to his appointment as secretary of defense.[1]

The U.S. policy debate about space weaponization is often portrayed as a fight pitting idealistic arms control enthusiasts who oppose all weapons against warmongering militarists who never saw a weapon they did not like. Although there are indeed people who do fit one or the other of these stereotypes,[2] most serious opponents and advocates of space weaponization do not. Moreover, positions on this question do not always fall along a simple left-to-right or liberal-to-realist continuum, so these caricatures fail to capture the key elements of the debate, even when treated as polar extremes between which more moderate opinions are possible.

This essay seeks to describe the principal schools of thought regarding space weapons (this term will be used in its widest possible sense for the sake of simplicity) in a way that better corresponds to reality, suggesting a roadmap to the debate that distinguishes among six different positions regarding the question of whether and when the United States ought to build space weapons. To do this, the preliminary problems of defining and characterizing space weapons and space weaponization are first addressed. Following the subsequent discussion of weaponization perspectives, the questions of whether space weaponization is inevitable, and whether this matters, are examined; the essay then returns to the subject of how all participants in the weaponization debate might move beyond their current polarization to make greater progress towards developing sound policy in this increasingly important arena.

WHAT IS SPACE WEAPONIZATION?

Space weaponization is a subset of space militarization. If one envisions a continuum running from space systems not being used for any militarily useful purposes at all, to satellites providing services to support terrestrial military operations (from the late 1950s for the United States), to satellites being integral parts of terrestrial weapon systems (from the 1990s), and finally, to weapons themselves being deployed in space, weaponization occurs when the upper range of the spectrum is reached. At its most extreme, space weaponization would include the deployment in quantity of a full range of space weapons, including satellite-based systems for ballistic missile defense (BMD), ground- and space-based antisatellite weapons (ASATs), and a variety of space-to-Earth weapons (STEWs), and these would play a central role in any type of military operations conducted by their owners.

However, space militarization is not a simple linear path along which a phase change occurs at some fixed point and space suddenly becomes weaponized. Instead, there are a number of intermediate steps along the way, and how politically significant each will be is not only unclear, but must necessarily be unclear prior to the event because it is a matter of social construction. For example, both the United States and the Soviet Union developed and tested rudimentary ASAT systems during the Cold War.[3] Some observers insist that this means space has already been weaponized, rendering the subject of this discussion irrelevant, but this is clearly a fallacious argument: we have not yet crossed the principal space weaponization threshold, precisely because almost everyone believes that we have not.

Thus there is no single definition of "space weapons" that is appropriate in every context.[4] Instead, there are a number of dimensions of weaponization along which a given development may resemble more or less closely an idealized version of space weaponization. For each dimension, it is possible to identify a number of steps on the ladder, ranging from qualities that do not look very much like those of a "space weapon" to ones that seem quite extreme. However, in exactly what order the steps should be placed is not always apparent, as will be discussed below. At least six of these dimensions are worth considering in some detail, although others could certainly be identified as well.

BASING

The most basic dimensions are where the weapon is based and what sort of targets it can attack. The basing dimension ranges from purely terrestrial weapons, such as land-based ASAT lasers or terrestrial weapons for attacking space launch and support facilities, to

This essay has been edited and is reprinted from Astropolitics 1 (Spring 2003): 4–28.

true space-based weapons, satellite weapons platforms placed in orbit for the long term well before a crisis or conflict. Intermediate steps along this continuum include direct ascent ASATs (which are launched into space but not into orbit); suborbital weapons, including ballistic missiles (which travel through space en route to their targets but do not linger there); and launch-on-demand orbital weapons (which are deployed into space only when needed, thus perhaps avoiding crossing the weaponization threshold during peacetime). Somewhere along this continuum fall weapons such as today's global positioning system (GPS)–guided munitions, in which a terrestrial weapon depends upon space systems to operate; in some respects, a satellite-guided bomb or cruise missile is thus very much a space weapon, although policymakers and the public clearly do not consider the deployment of such weapons to constitute space weaponization.

POTENTIAL TARGETS

Two features of the targets that candidate space weapons could attack are important: their location and their nature. Target locations include the land and sea surface, objects aloft in the atmosphere, and objects (satellites and suborbital projectiles) in orbital space, where it is important also to distinguish among different orbital altitudes, especially low-, medium-, and geosynchronous Earth orbit (LEO, MEO and GEO, respectively).[5] Among space-based weapons, the ability to attack terrestrial targets ("space force application," in U.S. military doctrine) is usually taken to be a more extreme form of weaponization than being able to attack other space vehicles, although a case can be made that the former actually represents far less of a departure from current military capabilities than does the latter, and therefore this conventional intuition should be reversed. The types of targets that can be attacked is a fairly straightforward matter, relating to how hard, small, fast, agile, distant, and stealthy a target the weapon is capable of striking. To this list could be added the question of how many targets could be attacked, either in total or during a particular window of opportunity, particularly for the rare weapon system that cannot simply be scaled up to increase the number of targets it can strike.

Together, the basing and target location variables, along with the attack mechanisms discussed below, define the major categories of space (or not-quite-space) weapons.[6] The hierarchy of "space weaponness" among them can be ambiguous—for example, is deploying a direct ascent ASAT a more limited or more extreme step toward weaponization than deploying a space-based laser for BMD? In general, it can be said that space-to-space weapons and STEWs are generally considered to be space weapons, that terrestrial ASATs sometimes (but not always) are,[7] and that terrestrial and purely suborbital systems (including intercontinental ballistic missiles [ICBMs]) for striking terrestrial targets usually are not.

Muddled as this picture can be, it is further complicated by the fact that some weapons have the ability (often termed "residual capabilities") to attack secondary targets. For example, nuclear-tipped antiballistic missiles and even short-range ballistic missiles can potentially be employed as powerful ASAT weapons. This does not make a Scud missile a space weapon for most political purposes, but it would certainly have to be taken into account in any arms control effort to prohibit the possession of ASATs. Much the same is true of the limited but potentially significant antisatellite capabilities of the U.S. Space Shuttle and many other space systems designed to perform purely nonviolent functions.

ATTACK MECHANISM

Space weapons can employ a wide range of mechanisms to affect their targets. The most obvious are conventional explosive, kinetic energy, and directed energy (e.g., laser, radio frequency) weapons, which together occupy the middle range of this continuum and clearly qualify as weapons. Above these are nuclear weapons (and perhaps biological and chemical weapons, although the latter are especially unlikely for space weapons employment), the only category of weapon whose deployment in space is proscribed by international law or treaty.[8]

More interesting in political terms is the other end of the spectrum: devices or techniques that could have weaponlike effects but whose status as weapons is ambiguous. These include such things as electronic jamming of communications and telemetry, barriers with which to shade satellite solar panels or obstruct the view of space-based sensors, and space "special forces" capabilities, including direct human or mechanical interference with or sabotage of satellites in orbit.[9]

The remaining dimensions are less significant with respect to defining whether a system is a space weapon, and thus whether deploying it would constitute space weaponization. However, they might potentially be very important in determining the political significance of the deployment of such a weapon.

WEAPON EFFECTS

Weapon effects are an obvious and a relatively simple matter: does the weapon destroy, damage, or merely disrupt the activities of the target,[10] and to what degree of severity? If less than destruction, how long lasting are the effects, will they abate on their own, and/or how easily can they be repaired or circumvented? Finally, will the effects cost lives, either directly or indirectly, or only damage property or cause other economic harm?

DISCRIMINATION

The extent to which the effects of a weapon can be confined to its intended target is also likely to play an important part in shaping perceptions of the system, with more discriminate weapons appearing on the whole to be less objectionable, if not necessarily less weaponlike.[11] This is most obvious, perhaps, with respect to the creation of orbital debris by kinetic energy ASATs and the widespread damage that would be produced by using exoatmospheric nuclear detonations for antisatellite purposes or to inflict electromagnetic pulse damage against terrestrial targets. At the lower end of the damage scale, a device to deny GPS signals to a narrow area or certain categories of receivers would be more discriminate than one that produced a similarly disruptive effect over a broad region. For STEWs, of course, traditional concerns about discrimination and collateral damage in weapons effects would apply.

POTENTIAL UTILITY

Finally, the scenarios in which a weapon would or would not be effective or useful are likely to affect the political implications of developing it. A weapon that would be powerful if used in a first strike but highly vulnerable to preemption by an enemy who struck first would probably create more furor or discontent than one that would work well on the strategic defensive. Because of the relative visibility of satellites and the predictability of their orbits, many space-based weapons would tend toward the offensive end of the scale rather than the defensive, but a variety of factors would enter into this equation. Similarly, weapons that could be deployed or employed without detection (or anonymously) would likely offer more to an aggressor than ones whose use and ownership would be obvious. Clearly, if a weapon is effective only against a certain class of targets, say long-range ballistic missiles, this would have a considerable effect on how it was perceived, depending in large part on which states expected to possess such targets. Similarly, whether a system would be capable of attacking many targets or only a few (a major consideration for missile defense systems in particular[12]) would likely have considerable importance in determining the scenarios in which it would or would not be valuable.

Together, all of these factors would shape the political impact of any particular decision to develop or deploy space weapons, potentially including, but not limited to, whether the action in question would or would not be considered to constitute the profound violation of the current space sanctuary norm with which many space weaponization discussions are primarily concerned.

SIX PERSPECTIVES ON SPACE WEAPONIZATION

As the introduction to this essay suggested, the space weaponization debate often appears at first glance to be as a classical confrontation between hawks and doves.[13] The former, now apparently in the ascendancy within the U.S. government under the George W. Bush administration, are said to believe that space weapons should and will be deployed more or less as soon as they can be, and that the United States must lead the way down this path lest another state do so in our place. The other side of the debate is typically portrayed, at least by their opponents, as starry-eyed arms control enthusiasts who believe space should be preserved as a sanctuary free of weapons; in fact, this was the preferred policy of the U.S. government during most of the space age, albeit usually for reasons that had little to do with idealism, although the Clinton administration was more conspicuous in its reluctance to develop space weapons than its predecessors.

Like any good cartoon, this image contains a considerable amount of truth. However, it is too simple a picture on which to base serious analysis of what is actually a far more complicated debate. There are in fact a variety of positions on both sides of the weaponization question, which the following discussion groups into a taxonomy of six basic perspectives, three of which favor a space sanctuary and three of which envision and advocate U.S.-led space weaponization, at least under certain circumstances.[14] Each of these schools of thought is at least internally consistent, although they are not all of equal intellectual merit. However, it is important to note that these categories are ideal types, and are not mutually exclusive: it is entirely possible, and even common, for individuals in the real world to hold beliefs that fall into more than one of these camps, which the reader should bear in mind throughout the discussion that follows.[15]

SANCTUARY IDEALISTS

The perspective most categorically opposed to space weaponization can aptly be labeled "sanctuary idealism."[16] Perhaps the most widely held of all the perspectives, especially outside of the United States, sanctuary idealism opposes the spread of weapons or warfare into any new realm (with outer space being the most prominent one not yet weaponized) and the deployment of new types of weapons; typically, sanctuary idealists also at least nominally favor the elimination of some or all of the types of weapons that already exist, although this is of limited relevance to the space weaponization debate.

The reasons for this policy preference vary among the idealists, but may range from aesthetic, moral, or philosophical distaste for contaminating unpolluted territory with engines of war, to more instrumental fears that opening new arenas to military competition will drain scarce resources from peaceful uses or will increase the level of animosity and distrust among nations. Most typically, sanctuary idealism is based on two central political premises. The first is that weapons are necessary for—and tend, through arms races, to be a cause of—war, so the absence of space weapons prevents space warfare, whereas their presence would not only make war in and from space possible, but would in fact encourage it. The second principle is that minimizing the amount and the extent of warfare is intrinsically desirable. Similar themes have underlain some earlier arms control advocacy, such as the effort before and after the First World War to prohibit the use of aircraft as instruments of war.

Thus, unlike the strands of space sanctuary theory discussed below, sanctuary idealist arguments are not for the most part related to the specific characteristics of space weapons, either individually or in general, or to the physical nature of orbital space. The logic of the idealist approach applies more or less similarly to other types of weapons that might be banned (e.g., chemical weapons, landmines) and to other places from which weapons might be prohibited (e.g., Antarctica, the deep seabed, regional nuclear-free zones). However, space weapons are a natural focus for such arms limitation advocacy, because averting the development of new weapons appears far easier than does reversing the status quo after new weapons have been deployed and integrated into military operations.

Sanctuary idealists generally advocate some variation on the same policy theme as other sanctuary proponents: the United States should work to keep orbital space free of weapons. This might be pursued through negotiating an international agreement to ban space weapons, as China and Russia have occasionally proposed in the past. Even without such an agreement, most sanctuary idealists would argue that the United States should continue to exercise unilateral restraint in the development, or at least the deployment, of space weapons to reduce the incentives for other states to build their own; some sanctuary idealists also contend that the example the United States would set by unilaterally eschewing space weaponization would give significant political and moral encouragement for other states to do the same. However, although space sanctuary proponents believe that the potential costs and risks of actually weaponizing space would be high, even sanctuary idealism is compatible with "space control" measures such as improving U.S. space tracking capabilities or hardening U.S. satellites to make them less vulnerable. None of the major schools of thought sees merit in American vulnerability to attack in space, although they may differ widely with regard to choosing the best ways to avert it.

Sanctuary Internationalists

Whereas the idealists oppose new weapons and weapons in new places in general, "sanctuary internationalists" oppose space weapons in particular because of their potentially harmful effects on international stability. Drawing in part on theories about the effects of offensive advantage and the security dilemma,[17] this perspective argues that the nature of space weapons makes them far better suited to offensive than to defensive warfare: weapons in orbit can strike quickly and with little warning, but are themselves vulnerable to attack because they move predictably, cannot remain over friendly territory, and are difficult to conceal. Thus, both the owners of space weapons and their enemies would have incentives to strike first in a crisis.[18] These theories predict that in addition to encouraging preemptive attacks and preventive wars, if states were to shift their military investments from terrestrial to space weapons, the growing advantage of the offense would tend to produce other pathological political effects, heightening international tensions and further reducing stability.[19]

Sanctuary internationalism also warns of the potential coupling between space weaponization and nuclear instability, on several levels. First, and perhaps least seriously in the current global environment, opponents of space-based BMD, like generations of BMD critics before them, fear that such systems would weaken the deterrent potency of major powers' second-strike nuclear forces. Second, sanctuary advocates are concerned that antisatellite warfare could contribute to nuclear instability by disabling space-based ballistic missile launch detection systems, reducing strategic warning, and potentially allowing states to launch missile attacks anonymously and thus with the hope of avoiding retaliation. Third, they note that conventional space weapons, such as kinetic energy projectiles launched from orbit, might have considerable utility in their own right as part of a first strike against an enemy's nuclear capabilities. Finally, they argue that space weaponization might encourage nuclear proliferation, because states facing threats from space weapons but lacking the ability to respond in kind or to neutralize the danger would be likely to seek asymmetric means to shore up their security, among which the acquisition of nuclear weapons might be attractive.

For the sanctuary internationalist, the undesirability of space weaponization would depend on the particular shape it took. Some space weapons would tend to be more destabilizing than others: the more a specific set of technologies and deployment choices creates a situation in which space weapons are valuable to an aggressor but vulnerable to preemption, the more malignant the stability implications of space weaponization would be, and some space weapons might even enhance stability. However, as most possible space weapons would combine a high degree of first strike utility and vulnerability relative to most terrestrial weapons, and because space weapons without destabilizing characteristics might help pave the way for space weapons with them, sanctuary internationalists are inclined to oppose space weaponization in general, although they would tend strongly to embrace other, stabilizing means of reducing vulnerability to attack in or from space. Finally, they would not necessarily favor the United States responding to another state's deployment of space weapons by doing the same: depending on the scenario, an American response in kind might either enhance or reduce overall stability.

SANCTUARY NATIONALISTS

The third sanctuary perspective is grounded in the tradition of classical realism. "Sanctuary nationalists" oppose space weaponization not because it would weaken global stability but because they believe that although space weaponization might enhance American military capabilities in absolute terms, it would weaken the power and security of the United States relative to the rest of the world. Many of their arguments cluster around the theme that it is the United States, as both the dominant world power and the preeminent spacefaring state, which has the most to lose from space weaponization.[20]

First, and most visibly, the United States derives the greatest advantage from the space sanctuary status quo. The U.S. military, government and commercial sectors have led the world in exploiting the potential of satellites and space technology for a host of vital functions, with satellites being particularly indispensable for U.S. military operations. If satellites were subjected to substantial threat of attack or interference, it would be a greater hardship for the United States than for any other major country.

Second, the United States enjoys an unrivaled ability to project military power around the world. Although space weapons would further increase its expeditionary military capabilities, their benefits would be only marginal in the vast majority of scenarios. However, effective space weapons might greatly enhance the military capabilities of other states, which currently have little capability to attack the United States and whose military inferiority is due in no small part to the U.S. advantage in space capabilities. Moreover, although the United States would enjoy a large initial lead over its rivals in a space weapons competition, it already has a huge advantage in the other dimensions of military power, and there is little reason to believe that rivals would find it harder to challenge U.S. preeminence in space power than in sea or airpower.

Third, sanctuary nationalists argue that the dynamics of alliance formation and maintenance imply that if the United States leads the way in space weaponization, it would not only antagonize rivals and enemies, but would also tend to weaken the system of security ties between the United States and its large and powerful bloc of allies. The potentially oppressive proximity and omnipresence of American weapons in orbit might not actually encourage other states to align against an apparent assertion of U.S. hegemony, but would at least make them less comfortable and cooperative with American dominance in international politics.[21] Even in the absence of such balancing behavior, a shift in U.S. military strategy toward greater autonomy from allies and coalition partners, which is one of the principal selling points of STEWs, would tend to weaken existing security relationships and increase the burden of defense on U.S. national resources.

Some sanctuary nationalists also contend that a shift to space weapons as the key currency of military power would weaken the global military dominance of the United States by making its currently overwhelming advantage in power projection through air and naval power obsolescent. Much as Britain's naval superiority was undermined when steam replaced sail, and again when pre-Dreadnought battleships were replaced by their steam turbine-driven, all-big-gun successors, the slate would be wiped clean, and states that had previously lagged behind in the old technology would be able to compete in the new one from something closer to a neutral start.[22]

Thus sanctuary nationalists do not think that U.S. space weapons would be intrinsically bad, but instead that their eventual costs would greatly outweigh their benefits, particularly insofar as U.S. space weaponization would lead to other states building their own space weapons. Although sanctuary nationalists are likely to doubt that U.S. restraint in space weaponization would set a compelling moral example for other states to follow, or that arms control agreements would be a powerful barrier to weaponization, they maintain that other states would be more likely to embark on space weaponization if the United States does so first, for two reasons. The more obvious of these is that U.S. space weapons would give other countries more valuable and threatening targets to attack in and from space, creating greater incentives for ASAT and even STEW development.

The other reason is more subtle: a belief that by leading the way in space weaponization, the United States would not only encourage other states to follow suit and shield them from any political stigma that might be associated with being the first state to weaponize space, but would actually make it easier for them to do so. By serving as the technological trailblazer, and paying the costs of developing new technologies, the United States would reduce the technological and cost barriers for the states that followed. Such "advantages of backwardness," well-recognized in economists' studies of the product cycle, are consistently visible in the development of military technologies, including aircraft, missiles, and nuclear weapons.[23]

The prescription that emerges from nationalist sanctuary theory is that the United States should avoid taking actions that will motivate or facilitate adversaries' development of space weapons or cause other effects that would tend to reduce U.S. military advantages over other states. In general, this would point toward avoiding space weaponization, whether through multilateral regimes or unilateral restraint—either one conditional on the actions of other countries—or other means. However, as for the internationalists, the specific features of potential space weapons would affect whether and to what extent the development in question would endanger U.S. security. To take one example, some but not all of the effects that nationalists seek to avoid would probably be less serious if the United States built suborbital rather than long-term orbital space weapons.

SPACE RACERS

Of the three proweaponization perspectives, the one that generally appears least extreme, although it is not necessarily the one that shares the most common ground with space sanctuary theory, is that of the "space racers." These are more or less reluctant space weaponization advocates, and may accept that sanctuary is desirable in the abstract, but who believe that space weaponization is inevitable and that this makes it imperative for the United States to lead the way in the development and deployment of space weapons.[24] The space racer perspective is shared by many experts, including academic theorists who are attracted to restraint in armament but pessimistic about its prospects, and military leaders who are reluctant to see defense resources diverted from other areas into space weapons, but who are similarly skeptical about the chances of avoiding this.[25] Because the thesis that space weaponization is inevitable is tied to many of the proweaponization perspectives, the next section will examine it in some detail, and the present discussion will focus simply on its implications.

For space racers, the most important consideration with respect to space weapons is that the United States should not allow other countries to surpass, or even to rival, it in this arena of military competition. Being the leading space power may offer significant military advantage, or it could simply be an important source of national prestige and international political influence.[26] In either case, the United States must keep ahead of the pack, and in the end, must be the first state to weaponize space; for even if that is unpleasant, it will surely be better than being the second state to do so. Moreover, if weaponization is inevitable and if leading the way is imperative, any political costs associated with being the first state to violate the sanctuary of space will have to be paid sooner or later, and delaying it will not avert having to pay the price.

According to this perspective, the correct time for the United States to weaponize space will depend at least in part on the behavior, capabilities, and intentions of other countries. If the threat of a rival state weaponizing space were remote, the United States would have the option of moving relatively slowly down this path, as long as it carried out sufficient research and development efforts to remain squarely in the forefront of this dormant arms competition. Many space racers are far from sanguine about the prospect of space weaponization by other states, especially in light of China's rapidly advancing space program, and anticipate that it will not be very long before the United States is compelled to deploy weapons in space. Other see the threat of space weapons rivals as less imminent, but in either case, the space racer perspective is essentially threat based.

Although it can be described as the most "middle of the road" approach to space weaponization policy —or perhaps because of this—the space racer perspective is arguably also the least intellectually satisfy-

ing. Its central weakness, although it is not necessarily a fatal one, is the contention that space weapons will be so irresistible that states will not be able to refrain from building them, and so powerful that it would be catastrophic for another state to build them before we do, yet not so attractive that the United States should build them as fast as possible in the absence of a military space challenger. Most sanctuary theories reject the first or the second (or both) of these propositions; the other two proweaponization perspectives accept these but reject the third.

SPACE CONTROLLERS

In the U.S. military space community, the dominant attitude regarding weaponization is probably what has become known as the "space control" perspective. Space controllers believe that space will necessarily be an important arena of future conflict due to the great military benefits that space systems will provide to states that operate them. Some military missions, such as boost-phase ICBM defense against large adversaries, can feasibly be conducted only from space, and the ever-increasing importance of satellites for communications, targeting, and other essential military functions will make both attacking enemy satellites and defending one's own satellites (for which space controllers believe that space weapons will be required) a matter of leading strategic priority. In addition, as the relevant technologies improve, STEWs will become a potent military instrument.

Space controllers may accept the proposition that weaponizing space will be politically costly— although many in this camp tend to ignore such political variables in their enthusiasm for the development of American spacepower,[27] not all do—but in addition to agreeing with the space racers that any such costs will have to be borne sooner or later, they believe that these will be outweighed by the benefits of any space weapons that are militarily worth deploying. Moreover, they are highly skeptical of the suggestion that U.S. restraint in space weapons development would significantly reduce other states' inclination to weaponize space as soon as doing so appears to be militarily advantageous to them, and of the prospects for negotiating feasible limitations on space weapons.

For space controllers, the right time for the United States to weaponize space will be as soon as doing so appears to be useful, whether or not other states are moving in the direction of doing the same. The key criterion for such a decision will not be a comparison of potential U.S. space weapon capabilities with those of rival states, but a comparison of future U.S. military capabilities with and without the potential space weapons. From the space controllers' perspective, space racers seem to lack the courage of their own convictions: if space weapons will enhance the nation's power, the United States should not squander the opportunity to develop them while waiting for a challenger to appear on the horizon.

SPACE HEGEMONISTS

Finally, at the most proweaponization end of the spectrum, are the "space hegemonists." Whereas space controllers believe that space will be an important arena of conflict in the future, space hegemonists argue that space will be *the* critical battlefield, the "ultimate high ground." In the tradition of Mahan and Douhet, space hegemonists believe that he who controls space will control the world.[28] In the words of then-Senator Bob Smith, the most prominent if not the most persuasive spokesman for this perspective, concerted American development of space weapons "will buy generations of security that all the ships, tanks, and airplanes in the world will not provide.... With credible offensive and defensive space control, we will deter and dissuade our adversaries, reassure our allies, and guard our nation's growing reliance on global commerce. Without it, we will become vulnerable beyond our wildest dreams."[29]

With respect to the development of space weapons themselves, space hegemonists differ from space controllers only in matters of degree. Whereas the controllers favor deployment of weapons as soon as it is militarily advantageous, the hegemonists tend to advocate an even more aggressive weaponization program, with little consideration of the possibility that space weapons might not prove to be the optimal solution to most military problems. Space controllers tend to envision space weapons complementing terrestrial weapons, as well as offering unique capabilities that would be impossible or difficult to provide without them; space hegemonists are more inclined to envision space weapons as supplanting most terrestrial weapons and dominating the traditional battlefields, as well as the new ones in space, in a genuinely transformational revolution in military affairs.[30]

Where the space hegemonists stand out most fundamentally from other weaponization advocates is on the political dimension, where controlling space becomes controlling the world. One explanation for how this is to occur, as Smith has suggested, is that overwhelming U.S. spacepower will be unassailable, so that the rest of the world will not challenge American hegemony. Either they will perceive it to be benign, or they will be so intimidated by it that defiance of the United States will appear pointless. The weakness of this argument lies in the tension between believing that there are rival states strong enough to become the space hegemon if the United States fails to do so, and believing that these same rivals are too weak or too meek to develop dangerous space capabilities in the face of U.S. spacepower.

The other scenario, couched in less optimistic realpolitik terms, is that space weapons will be so powerful that the United States must exploit its current lead in space technology to seize control of the high ground and actively deny its use by unfriendly states.[31] According to this point of view, rival powers will indeed have incentives to challenge U.S. dominance in space, and because the United States will not be able to afford to have its control of space contested, it will need to quash any such challenges before military space races develop, including preemptively destroying any space vehicles launching without U.S. authorization and any terrestrial ASAT weapons that unfriendly states might build. This vision of the future represents the core elements of the other proweaponization perspectives being carried to their logical extreme: if space weapons are too powerful not to build, they must also be too powerful to allow our potential enemies to possess.

IS SPACE WEAPONIZATION INEVITABLE?

As discussed above, the belief that space weaponization is, or is not, inevitable looms large for several of the major perspectives. It is most central for the space racers, for it is the expectation of inevitable weaponization that drives them into the proweaponization camp. The other proweaponization perspectives are not based on such an inevitability belief, but their adherents routinely invoke it as an argument against a sanctuary approach. For their part, all three of the sanctuary perspectives presume that weaponization is avoidable, or at least that American actions can affect how soon and in what form it occurs. Therefore the following discussion briefly examines the four principal arguments for the thesis that space weaponization is inevitable.[32]

Specifically, the question here is whether there is good reason to believe with certainty that space weapons will be built and deployed to a substantial degree in the near-to-medium term—say, the next 50 years, regardless of the behavior of the United States.[33] There are four prominent arguments that hold that this is true: human nature predestines weaponization, historical analogies with the sea and air prophesy it, the growing economic importance of satellites mandates it, and the military utility of space weapons will make not building them strategically irrational. This section considers each of these propositions in turn, arguing that the first three are thought provoking but ultimately weak, whereas the last is more powerful but less than conclusive.

HUMAN NATURE

The simplest inevitability argument is that warfare and armaments are intrinsically uncontrollable because people are warlike: weapons and warfare abhor a vacuum, and will spread wherever humanity goes.[34] This assertion is often accompanied by arguments that arms control never works, although it is possible to argue more narrowly that only space arms control is infeasible.[35]

This generalization is not far from the truth, yet it is far enough from truth that it can and should be considered invalid. For example, although the long-standing success of the 1957 Antarctic Treaty's proscription of military bases in Antarctica, often cited as an example of an effective sanctuary regime, would be far more impressive if the signatory powers actually had strong incentives to establish bases on that continent, it still flies in the face of the idea that weaponization must always follow wherever people go (the argument that space weapons in particular will have military utility too great to resist is a different proposition from the contention that weapons always spread everywhere). Similarly, some types of weapons have fallen into disrepute over the past century. Although they have not yet disappeared, it could be argued that chemical and biological weapons have been shunned by all but renegade states and terrorists, and antipersonnel land mines are following in their wake. Many states that could easily have developed nuclear weapons have opted not to do so, in some cases in spite of apparently very good military reasons to go nuclear.[36] Perhaps most strikingly of all, even among space weapons advocates, one does not find voices arguing that the placement of nuclear weapons in orbit is inevitable based on the rule that weapons always spread. The fact that this has not happened is due to many factors other than the 1967 Outer Space Treaty's prohibition on such weaponization, but if some weapons do not necessarily follow wherever people go, the idea that a law of human nature requires that others will do so should not be seriously embraced as a basis for national policy.

HISTORICAL ANALOGIES

The second argument that space must inevitably be weaponized is that the evolution of sea and airpower reveal a striking historical pattern leading inexorably in this direction, which the exploitation of space is also following. According to an influential recent commander of U.S. Space Command, for example:

If we examine the evolutionary development of the aircraft, we see uncanny parallels to the current evolution of spacecraft. . . . The potential of aircraft was not recognized immediately. Their initial use was confined to observation. . . . Until one day the full advantage of applying force from the air was realized and the rest is history. So too with the business of space. . . . [Military] space operations, like the land, sea, and air operations that evolved before them, will expand [into] the budding new missions already included in the charter of U.S. Space Command of space control and force application as they become more and more critical to our national security interests.[37]

The parallels between the early days of space flight and especially, the early development of aerial flight are indeed striking, at least at first glance. Yet on closer examination, it is clear that the spread of weapons into the three previous environments into which human activity has so expanded—the seas, the air, and the undersea world—has been far from identical, raising serious doubts about the soundness of drawing such deterministic analogies when predicting the future of military space exploitation.[38]

Sea Power

The first new realm into which human enterprise expanded was the surface of the oceans and other bodies of water, initially along the coasts and later onto the high seas. Maritime transport offered many advantages over land-bound alternatives, especially prior to the invention of the railroad, and armed conflict followed commerce onto the seas. Navies soon developed to protect merchant vessels from pirates and other enemies, to prey on enemy shipping and to attack or defend coastlines and sea lanes.

In spite of the intuitive similarities between seafaring and spacefaring, however, there is one fundamental difference between them which makes the sea-space analogy very weak: ships primarily transport goods and people, whereas spacecraft (with only minor exceptions) are built to collect, relay, or transmit information. This means that space piracy is not a problem, so space navies are not required to suppress it, while "commerce raiding" threats to space systems can be ameliorated by building redundant, distributed systems of satellites; for merchant shipping, this is obviously not an option. It also means that whatever threats may be posed by enemy space systems, invasion is very low on the list. In short, satellites have more in common with lighthouses than with oceangoing ships, and space commerce resembles telegraphy or terrestrial radio more than it does maritime trade.[39] This does not mean that nothing we know about sea power can be applied to space, or that space strategists should not study the works of Julian Corbett and Alfred Thayer Mahan. However, there is little reason to conclude from the evolution of naval forces either that the weaponization of space is inevitable, or that it is not.

Air Power

The parallels between military use of the air and of space are far more impressive. Both balloons and airplanes were used for military observation soon after they were invented, and because aerial observation was so powerful in the First World War, armed aircraft were soon employed as interceptors and then as escorts. Airplanes and airships were also used for bombing even before the dawn of air-to-air combat, and by 1918, virtually every modern military air mission had been undertaken or proposed.[40] Serious commercial exploitation of the air came only later. In space, strategic reconnaissance was the purpose of most early satellites, and intelligence collection remains the most well-known military space application;[41] it was the value of being able to destroy enemy surveillance satellites that drove the ASAT programs in both the United States and the Soviet Union.[42]

However, the evolution of air and space power has not been as similar as space weapons advocates' analogies often suggest. For example, less than a decade elapsed between the Wright brothers' first flight and the first aerial combat missions, whereas in the fifth decade after *Sputnik,* space remains un-weaponized. Of course, the occurrence of a major war in the 1910s had much to do with the rapid evolution of airpower, and spacepower might look very different today if the Third World War had broken out in the 1960s, but with no major wars now on the horizon, this caveat hardly makes the parallel between the two cases look like a strong basis for space policy in the early twenty-first century. In fact, both superpowers did develop antisatellite interceptors, but then abandoned their ASAT programs, something utterly without precedent in the history of airpower that casts further doubt on the soundness of the air-space analogy. Naturally, it would be foolish to conclude from the history of the past 50 years that space will definitely not be weaponized during the next 50, but it would also be reckless to deduce the opposite from the history of flight between 1903 and 1915.

Submarine Power

Space weaponization advocates rarely mention the third new environment into which human activity has expanded: the undersea world. In this case, although there are many similarities between submarine and space operations, the two weaponization histories have little in common. Warfare was the sole purpose of the first generations of subsurface vessels, joined only much later and on a vastly more limited scale by scientific research, while submarines have so far been of virtually no commercial significance. This says little about what the future of spacepower will look like, but it provides one more reason to be skeptical about the proposition that weapons spread into new environments according to a consistent and deterministic pattern.

It is also worth noting that one of the most striking commonalities among the three historical precedents is rarely if ever predicted to hold true for space as well. Nuclear weapons were deployed in each of these environments by all the major nuclear powers more or less as soon as each was capable of doing so. Yet not only has this failed to happen in space, but those who make analogical arguments for the inevitability of space weaponization conspicuously fail to claim that the nuclearization of space will occur in the future, raising doubts about the extent to which even its supporters actually believe in these assertions.

ECONOMIC VULNERABILITY

The third inevitability argument is that as space systems become more and more economically important to the United States, these assets will naturally become attractive targets of attack for rival states, terrorists, and other enemies, and therefore it will be necessary to place weapons in space in order to protect them.[43] American industry, commerce, and civil society do indeed depend increasingly heavily on space systems for communications, navigation, weather prediction, and many other functions.[44] However, it is far from clear that attacking U.S. commercial space assets would automatically appear worthwhile to an enemy seeking ways to hurt the United States, or that protecting them would necessarily require weapons in space.

In the abstract, it is apparent that an enemy seeking to harm or to intimidate the United States might want to attack important satellites, potentially causing disruption of the services they provide, destroying expensive pieces of American infrastructure, and possibly even causing significant damage to the U.S. economy. However, an enemy that wanted to achieve such a result against the United States could do so far more easily by attacking something other than satellites in orbit, and unlike satellites, most of these targets can be attacked without first developing or acquiring specialized weapons for one exotic target set.[45] Attacking satellites is certainly possible, but crippling or destroying a small object hundreds of miles overhead moving at 17,000 miles per hour (to say nothing of satellites at far higher altitudes, where most communications and navigation satellites reside) is considerably more challenging than doing comparable damage to targets such as ships, airliners, bridges, dams, pipelines, computer networks, office buildings—the list could go on almost indefinitely.[46] That such targets are not attacked on a regular basis is due mainly to the relatively small numbers and limited capabilities of serious terrorist enemies, not to any great degree of protection for these assets. Increased defensive measures since September 11 have done little to alter the relative difficulties of attacking space and terrestrial targets. Moreover, if an enemy did want to disrupt the use of American satellites, attacking their ground control stations and launch facilities might well be more effective than striking satellites in orbit, as well as much easier.

If an adversary did wish to attack U.S. satellites rather than something else to hurt the United States,[47] space-based lasers or kinetic energy weapons would be useful for defense against direct ascent ASATs or "space mines" that were detected before attacking, but they would provide no protection against attacks by ground-based lasers or covert mines already positioned near their targets, against electronic jamming or against attacks on the infrastructure that supports satellites.[48] Instead, the greatest improvements in the security of valuable U.S. space assets might be achieved by making satellites less vulnerable to attack and especially, by making them individually less valuable through the construction of satellite systems that are more distributed and redundant, with more, smaller satellites doing the same jobs as fewer, large, expensive ones.[49] The ultimate goal would be for the communications and other satellite infrastructures to become like the U.S. interstate highway system: economically vital, but not worth attacking because its resilience means that none of its individual components is critical.

MILITARY ADVANTAGE

The best argument for the proposition that space weaponization is inevitable is that the military utility of space weapons will soon be so great that even if the United States chooses not to build space weapons, other countries will certainly do so, in large part because of the great and still growing degree to which U.S. military operations depend upon what has traditionally been known as "space force enhancement": the use of satellites to provide a vast array of services, including communications, reconnaissance, navigation, and missile launch warning, without which American military power would be greatly diminished. This parallels the argument that the importance of satellites to the U.S. economy will make them an irresistible target, except that military and intelligence satellites are far more indispensable, and successful attacks against a relatively small number of them could have a considerable military impact, for example by concealing preparations for an invasion or by disrupting U.S. operations at a critical juncture.[50] Rivals of the United States might also find STEWs to be a very attractive way to counter US advantages in military power projection.

This is a reasonable argument, but to conclude for this reason that space weaponization is inevitable, rather than merely possible or likely, is unwarranted, for several reasons. There is no question that space systems are critical to U.S. military capabilities. An enemy that attacked them might be able to impair U.S. military operations very seriously, but although this ranks high among threats that concern U.S. strategists, it need not follow that enemies of the United States will do so, or will invest in the weapons required to do so. The U.S. armed forces possess many important vulnerabilities that adversaries have opted not to attack in past conflicts, typically due to resource limitations, a desire to avoid escalation, or fear of the reaction of third party audiences. For example, during Operation Allied Force in 1999, Serbia apparently did not attempt to mount special forces attacks against key NATO airbases in Italy or to use man-portable missiles to shoot down aircraft operating from them, although such an action could have profoundly disrupted the alliance's bombing campaign.[51] Moreover, it is quite possible that if a potential enemy did want to develop the ability to attack U.S. space systems, it would choose to do so in ways that would not involve weaponizing space— such as investing in computer network attack capabilities, nonspace weapons to attack the terrestrial elements of space systems, or ASAT capabilities that are not weapons in the conventional sense—and against which the logical defensive countermeasures would not involve deploying U.S. space weapons. For military as well as commercial satellites, a transition to redundant networks of satellites would do much to reduce their vulnerability, perhaps together with supplementing satellite platforms for some military functions with new types of terrestrial systems, such as high endurance unmanned aerial vehicles (UAVs).[52]

In the end, most of the inevitability arguments are weak. Even the best one, that space weapons will provide irresistible military advantages for those who employ them, is plausible but not decisive, and many of those who assert it probably harbor exaggerated expectations about the capabilities that space weapons will offer. In spite of the many people who apparently believe the inevitability thesis to be true, there is good reason for prudent policymakers to assume that the weaponization of space is not in fact predestined and that U.S. military space policy is one of the factors, although not the only one, that will shape the likelihood of space weaponization by other countries.

INEVITABILITY VS. PRIMACY AND URGENCY

The prominence of the inevitability question in debates about space weaponization is not surprising, but too often, it distracts attention from two far more important issues: whether it is in fact desirable and important for the United States to be the first country to weaponize space and/or for weaponization to occur sooner rather than later. If so, an aggressive effort to develop space weapons may be called for even if weaponization is not strictly inevitable. If not, a space sanctuary strategy may be appropriate for the United States even if it is certain that space will eventually be weaponized.

For space racers, primacy is what matters most, because they believe that the first state to deploy space weapons will have a great, and perhaps insurmountable, advantage over its rivals, although they may not in fact be eager to see the disappearance of the existing space sanctuary. Knowing simply that weaponization is inevitable is of little value from this perspective, although having a reasonable idea of when it would occur would be important. For many more ardent weaponization advocates, in contrast, the right time to deploy space weapons is immediately, or at least as soon as possible, regardless of what other countries may be likely to do later on. Thus, although they often make inevitability arguments, these are essentially tangential to the real basis of their policy prescriptions. Finally, for space sanctuary advocates who fear that weaponization will cause international instability or will erode U.S. hegemony and who doubt that a rival could in fact establish a decisive lead over the United States by taking the first step in a space weapons race, averting the deployment of at least some types of space weapons as long as possible appears desirable, even if they are only temporarily delayed.

BEYOND TOTEM OR TABOO

The polarization of the space weaponization debate—treating a complex, multidimensional policy question as a simple all-or-nothing choice, in which weaponization advocacy and opposition take on extreme, almost theological qualities—produces several seriously malignant consequences. The most obvious of these is that it discourages real dialog among those who favor alternative military space policies. Many of the participants in the debate appear to be interested only in preaching to their fellow believers, treating their adversaries' arguments so dismissively that they cannot possibly change the minds of those who view the issues differently from themselves. The marketplace of ideas breaks down when contending camps turn inward from healthy competition to mercantilist isolationism.

But this extreme polarization also harms the interests of the individual camps themselves. Weaponization opponents who treat space weapons as an absolute taboo risk squandering opportunities to establish potentially worthwhile restraints on space weapons development, deployment, or use that fall short of complete prohibition. They also preclude the possibility of supporting forms of weaponization that might enhance global stability or further their ultimate policy objectives in other ways. Of course, it can be argued that compromise will invite predation by one's adversaries, so that supporting benign weaponization would backfire over the long run, but such a position should be based on open and rational debate of its merits, not on doctrinaire faith that more arms control is always better than less, or that armament and security are incompatible.

Conversely, spacepower advocates who make space weapons their totem distract both themselves and others from the fact that many, even most, of the important space policy measures that are needed now and in the near future do not involve building space weapons per se. Better space tracking networks, systems to detect attacks against satellites, passive defenses, and more effective exploitation of space-dependent terrestrial weapons, such as satellite-guided munitions, all promise to dramatically enhance U.S. spacepower—and U.S. national security. Becoming "shooters" might make it easier for space operators to win full citizenship rights alongside pilots in officer's club bars, but in the end, with or without space weapons, they will need to make the rest of the armed forces understand that today all U.S. airmen, sailors, soldiers, and Marines are "space warriors."

Beyond calling for moderation and taking the views of others seriously, what can be done to make the space weaponization debate more intelligent and productive? A good place to start would be for all sides in the debate to acknowledge four simple but important truths about space weaponization that are often overlooked in polemical arguments about the subject.

First, space weaponization is inherently political, a fact that space weapons advocates sometimes seek to ignore—although, happily, this is gradually becoming less common. This is not a question simply, or even primarily, of science and engineering. Whether space weapons will make the United States more powerful or secure, or less, depends on political variables: how other countries will react to them, what resources we will have to redirect to build them, and so on. Military capability can be measured in static,

absolute terms, but power is relative and dynamic. Moreover, the effects that weaponization would have on international politics, and even what actions would be considered to constitute weaponization, depend on subjective and perhaps malleable perceptions, both of space weapons and of American military power.

Second, however, the military and technical details of space weapons do matter a great deal, although weaponization opponents—and enthusiasts as well—often paint their arguments with too broad a brush. Although all satellites do share certain important properties, the specific features of particular space weapons must be taken into account when assessing their strategic, and even their broader political, implications. This became second nature during Cold War debates over nuclear weapons and strategic defenses, when the minutiae of warhead accuracy, basing modes, and command and control systems were in the forefront of most nuclear policy discussions, and even ardent doves could couch their arguments in the language of throw weights and equivalent megatonnage.[53] Space weapons (like conventional weapons more generally) are a far more complicated and diverse subject, and require much effort and attention to debate satisfactorily, yet surprisingly little work has yet been done to describe and analyze them in adequate detail.[54]

Third, because of the previous point, many participants on both sides of the space weaponization debate harbor what are likely to be quite unrealistic expectations about the capabilities of space weapons, and to a lesser extent, about their costs.[55] It is seductively easy to speak in general and often glib terms about global reach, the importance of holding the high ground, and revolutions in military affairs, but it is important to develop and debate a more nuanced understanding of the ways in which space weapons truly are and are not likely to alter the strategic landscape if they are built.

Finally, everyone involved in the debate should remain aware that their arguments are necessarily based on educated speculation, not certainty. This is particularly true with respect to the political implications of weaponization. Would U.S. STEWs cause other states to be more or less friendly toward the United States, for example? Theorists on all sides of the debate offer answers to this question. These should be evaluated against relevant historical experience, for there is evidence that can shed light on the question, and some of these arguments appear better than others on careful consideration. However, at the end of the day, a considerable degree of intellectual humility is in order: nobody actually *knows* with confidence what will happen if and when space is weaponized—and what shape weaponization takes, and what happens between now and then, will certainly affect its consequences.

These are burdensome calls to action. It is more work to develop analyses and recommendations about policy that are well informed by the physical and social sciences than it is to offer ones that are not. However, as in debates about nuclear weapons and strategy during the Cold War, this is an area of policy that is too important to be guided by anything less.

NOTES

This essay is based on a paper originally presented in the Ballistic Missile Defense and Weaponization of Space series at the Elliot School of International Affairs, George Washington University, Washington, D.C. I thank Thomas Ehrhard, Peter Hays, Theresa Hitchens, John Logsdon, and Michael V. Smith for their many helpful comments and suggestions. The opinions expressed here do not reflect the views of RAND or any agency of the U.S. Government.

1. On the last, formally named The Commission to Assess United States National Security Space Management and Organization, see Peter L. Hays and Karl P. Mueller, "Going Boldly—Where? The USAF, Aerospace Integration, and the U.S. Space Commission," *Aerospace Power Journal* 15 (Spring 2001): 34–49.

2. See Sigmund Freud, *Totem and Taboo: Some Points of Agreement between the Mental Lives of Savages and Neurotics,* trans. James Strachey (New York: Norton, 1950 [1913]), 199–200.

3. For the history and details of these programs, see Paul B. Stares, *The Militarization of Space: U.S. Policy, 1945–1984* (Ithaca, N.Y.: Cornell University Press, 1985).

4. See, for example, Bob Preston et al., *Space Weapons, Earth Wars*, Rand MR-1209-AF (Santa Monica, Calif.: RAND, 2002), 23.

5. To this list could be added potential systems for destroying or diverting interplanetary objects threatening to collide with the Earth, some of which might have secondary military capabilities. For an overview of orbital characteristics, see, for example, *Joint Publication 3-14: Joint Doctrine for Space Operations* (Washington, D.C.: U.S. Department of Defense, August 9, 2002), Appendix F. In general, attacking a satellite in MEO or GEO is far more difficult than attacking one in LEO due to the longer ranges involved.

6. For technological details, see *New World Vistas: Air and Space Power for the 21st Century,* Space Applications Volume (Washington, D.C.: U.S. Air Force Scientific Advisory Board, 1995); William L. Spacy II, *Does the United States Need Space-Based Weapons?* (Maxwell Air Force Base, Ala.: Air University Press, 1999); Preston et al., *Space Weapons, Earth Wars,* especially chap. 3; Ashton B. Carter, "Satellites and Anti-Satellites: The Limits of the Possible," *International Security* 10 (Spring 1986): 46–98; U.S. Congress, Office of Technology Assessment (OTA), *Anti-Satellite Weapons, Countermeasures, and Arms Control* (1985), reprinted in *Strategic Defenses* (Princeton, N.J.: Princeton University Press, 1986).

7. See, for example, Karl P. Mueller, "Is the Weaponization of Space Inevitable?" paper presented at the International Studies Association Annual Convention, New Orleans, La., March 27, 2002.

8. Under the terms of the 1967 Outer Space Treaty, which prohibits the placement of weapons of mass destruction in space. The 1972 ABM treaty also prohibited space-based weapons that could be used for BMD, at least according to most interpretations, until the United States withdrew from the treaty in 2002.

9. See, for example, Simon P. Worden, "Space Control in the 21st Century," in *Spacepower for a New Millennium,* ed. Peter L. Hays et al. (New York: McGraw-Hill, 2000), 225–38.

10. U.S. military doctrine classifies space control effects into a hierarchy of five alliterative categories (deception, disruption, denial, degradation, and destruction); see *Joint Publication 3-14,* IV-6 to IV-8.

11. This generalization might be offset in certain cases by more discriminate weapons appearing to be more useful for aggressive purposes.

12. See Preston et al., *Space Weapons, Earth Wars,* Appendix A.

13. For example, James Oberg, *Space Power Theory* (Washington, D.C.: U.S. Government Printing Office, 1999), 146–47.

14. The most widely used such typology at present is that provided in David E. Lupton, *On Space Warfare: A Space Power Doctrine* (Maxwell Air Force Base, Ala.: Air University Press, 1988), more recently summarized and updated in Hays et al., *Spacepower,* 3–4. Lupton describes four categories of policy preferences, which he calls Sanctuary, Survivability, Control, and High Ground, but defines these primarily in terms of the relationship between space systems and the strategic nuclear balance, which limits the utility of his framework for understanding the current weaponization debate (e.g., he characterizes his Sanctuary school as favoring vulnerable space systems, which makes it little more than a straw man). However, my discussion of proweaponization perspectives does draw heavily on the more useful parts of his framework.

15. This is equally true of many of the citations in the following discussion. The fact that an example is used below to illustrate an argument from one of these perspectives should not be taken to imply that everything in the cited work, or in other works by the same author, falls into the same category as they are defined here.

16. The "idealist" label is not intended to imply that this perspective is unrealistic, but rather that it is guided by larger normative principles, in keeping with the classical idealist tradition in international political theory.

17. For example, Robert Jervis, "Cooperation Under the Security Dilemma," *World Politics* 30 (January 1978): 167–214; Steven E. Miller, Sean M. Lynn-Jones, and Stephen Van Evera, eds., *Military Strategy and the Origins of the First World War* (Princeton, N.J.: Princeton University Press, 1991); Sean M. Lynn-Jones, "Offense-Defense Theory and Its Critics," *Security Studies* 4 (Summer 1995): 660–91.

18. Bruce M. DeBlois, "Space Sanctuary: A Viable National Strategy," *Air Power Journal* 12 (Winter 1998): 42–44, 52. In fact, different types of space weapons would vary greatly in their ability to strike quickly; see Preston et al., *Space Weapons, Earth Wars.*

19. For further discussion, see Stephen Van Evera, "Offense, Defense, and the Causes of War," *International Security* 22 (Spring 1998): 5–43.

20. See David W. Ziegler, *Safe Heavens: Military Strategy and Space Sanctuary Thought* (Maxwell Air Force Base, Ala.: Air University Press, 1998); Karl P. Mueller, "Space Weapons and U.S. Security: The Dangers of Fortifying the High Frontier," paper presented at the American Political Science Association Annual Meeting, Boston, Mass., Sep-

tember 6, 1998; Charles S. Robb, "Star Wars II," *Washington Quarterly* 22 (Winter 1999): 81–86.

21. The key presentation of these arguments is Stephen M. Walt, *The Origins of Alliances* (Ithaca, N.Y.: Cornell University Press, 1987); they are challenged in Randall L. Schweller, *Deadly Imbalances: Tripolarity and Hitler's Strategy of World Conquest* (New York: Columbia University Press, 1998). For the proposition that the United States won the Cold War because it was a relatively unthreatening superpower, see John Lewis Gaddis, *We Now Know: Rethinking Cold War History* (New York: Oxford University Press, 1997).

22. On the Royal Navy, see, among others, Paul M. Kennedy, *The Rise and Fall of British Naval Mastery* (Atlantic Highlands, N.J.: Ashfield Press, 1983 [1976]), especially pages 205–37; Mueller, "Space Weapons and U.S. Security," 13–15; DeBlois, "Space Sanctuary," 51.

23. See Robert Gilpin, *War and Change in World Politics* (Cambridge: Cambridge University Press, 1981), 176–79; Alexander Gerschenkron, "The Advantages of Backwardness," in *Economic Backwardness in Comparative Perspective* (Cambridge, Mass.: Harvard University Press, 1962), 5–11. However, following a technological trailblazer, especially one with greater resources, does not necessarily guarantee the ability to catch up with or surpass it, as demonstrated, for example, by the U.S.-Soviet competition in submarine and antisubmarine warfare capabilities.

24. For example, Commander-in-Chief, U.S. Space Command General Ralph Eberhart, speech to the Unified Aerospace Power in the New Millennium conference, Alexandria, Va., February 8, 2001; James H. Hughes, "Warfare in Space," *Journal of Social, Political and Economic Studies* Monograph Series 28 (2000): 7–10.

25. "The logic essentially boils down to a belief that weapons in space are an inevitability. Since weaponization of space is inevitable, the United States, as the country with the historical opportunity to be the first to field them, would be foolish not to do so. And should it not afford itself of the opportunity, it will likely find itself hostage to the state that does," Oberg, *Space Power Theory*, 147.

26. This is analogous to arguments of reluctant nuclear arms racers in the 1970s and 1980s that having a larger nuclear arsenal than one's adversary might be militarily irrelevant in a world of mutual assured destruction, yet still be important because of the political effect of appearing to be the dominant nuclear power. See Charles L. Glaser, "Why Do Strategists Disagree about the Requirements of Strategic Nuclear Deterrence?" in *Nuclear Arguments,* ed. Lynn Eden and Steven E. Miller (Ithaca, N.Y.: Cornell University Press, 1989), 109–71.

27. A prominent example is the strong and unconditional recommendation in U.S. Air Force Scientific Advisory Board, *New World Vistas,* 164, that "the Air Force should broaden the use of space to include direct force projection against surface, airborne, and space targets," even though the study included no analysis at all of the potential consequences of pursuing such a policy.

28. This geopolitical argument is made preeminently in Everett C. Dolman, *Astropolitik: Classical Geopolitics in the Space Age* (London: Frank Cass, 2001).

29. Bob Smith, "The Challenge of Spacepower," *Airpower Journal* 13 (Spring 1999): 33.

30. For example, U.S. Air Force Scientific Advisory Board, *New World Vistas,* xviii: "In the next two decades, new technologies will allow the fielding of space-based weapons of devastating effectiveness to be used to deliver energy and mass as force projection in tactical and strategic conflict. This can be done rapidly, continuously, and with surgical precision, minimizing exposure of friendly forces."

31. Dolman, *Astropolitik.*

32. For a more detailed examination of this issue, see Mueller, "Is the Weaponization of Space Inevitable?"

33. It is possible to argue that weaponization is inevitable because the United States will certainly build such weapons for reasons internal to itself, but this is not a useful meaning of "inevitability" when seeking to guide U.S. policy.

34. See Michael V. Smith, "Ten Propositions About Spacepower," Master's thesis, School of Advanced Airpower Studies, June 2000, Proposition 10; Oberg, *Space Power Theory,* 147–49; General Chuck Horner, in Tom Clancy and Chuck Horner, *Every Man a Tiger* (New York: Putnam, 1999); Commisson to Assess U.S. National Security Space Management, *Report of the Commission to Assess United States National Security Space Management and Organization* (Washington, D.C.: Commisson to Assess U.S. National Security Space Management, 2001), 100.

35. For an example of the former, see Steven Lambakis, *On the Edge of Earth: The Future of American Space Power* (Lexington: University of Kentucky Press, 2001). For a sober overview of arms control issues related to space weapons, see Peter L. Hays, *United States Military Space: Into the Twenty-First Century* (Maxwell Air Force Base, Ala.: Air University Press, 2002), 49–114.

36. See Mitchell Reiss, *Without the Bomb: The Politics of Nuclear Nonproliferation* (New York: Columbia University Press, 1988) and *Bridled Ambition: Why Countries Constrain Their Nuclear Capabilities* (Washington, D.C.: Woodrow Wilson Center Press, 1995).

37. General Howell M. Estes III, commander, Air Force Space Command, speech to the Air Force Association Annual Symposium, Los Angeles, October 18, 1996 (some ellipses in the original), at www.spacecom.af.mil/usspace/. See also Thomas D. Bell, *Weaponization of Space: Understanding Strategic and Technological Inevitabilities*, Occasional Paper 6 (Maxwell Air Force Base, Ala.: Center for Strategy and Technology, U.S. Air War College, 1999), 16–20; Lambakis, *On the Edge of Earth,* 140–41; Air Force Chief of Staff General Michael Ryan, keynote address to the Unified Aerospace Power in the New Millennium conference, Alexandria, Va., February 8, 2001.

38. Regarding the dangers of faulty analogical reasoning in general, see Richard E. Neustadt and Ernest R. May, *Thinking in Time* (New York: Free Press, 1986); and Yuen Foong Khong, *Analogies at War* (Princeton, N.J.: Princeton University Press, 1992). One could potentially argue that cyberspace represents a fifth environment worth considering in this context. The shape of the weaponization story for this case would depend on exactly how one defined the arena in question, and what constitutes a weapon within it. Again, some interesting parallels with the development of space technology would appear, and the overall pattern would not correspond to that of any of the other four cases.

39. As space travel expands beyond earth orbit into interplanetary space, where the transportation of material goods may finally become one of its major functions, the parallels between sea and space power may become more pronounced.

40. For discussion of this evolution, see Lee Kennett, *The First Air War, 1914–1918* (New York: Free Press, 1990). An analogy can also be drawn between airborne spotters enhancing the effectiveness of artillery in the First World War and contemporary use of GPS guidance for aerial munitions.

41. On the evolution of satellite reconnaissance, see William E. Burrows, *Deep Black: Space Espionage and National Security* (New York: Random House, 1986); Jeffrey T. Richelson, *America's Secret Eyes in Space* (New York: Harper & Row, 1990) and *A Century of Spies: Intelligence in the Twentieth Century* (New York: Oxford University Press, 1995). On the evolution of the U.S. and Soviet space programs, see Walter A. McDougall, . . . *The Heavens and the Earth: A Political History of the Space Age* (New York: Basic Books, 1985).

42. Of course, there are important physical differences between air and space warfare, such as air being territorial whereas low Earth orbital space is not, but these do not in themselves prevent drawing parallels between the evolution of air and spacepower. See Bruce DeBlois, " Ascendant Realms: Characteristics of Airpower and Space Power," in *Paths of Heaven: The Evolution of Airpower Theory,* ed. Phillip S. Meilinger (Maxwell Air Force Base, Ala.: Air University Press, 1997), 529–78; Michael Smith, "Ten Propositions about Spacepower," especially pages 43–50.

43. Bell, *Weaponization of Space,* 6–7; Oberg, *Space Power Theory,* 147; Thomas S. Moorman, Jr., "The Explosion of Commercial Space and the Implications for National Security," *Air Power Journal* 13 (Spring 1999): 19. Worden, "Space Control," provides one of the more sophisticated versions of this argument.

44. Although this is true in the aggregate, it is less true than most analysts expected it to be a few years ago, and more true in some functional areas than in others. Most notably, the satellite communications boom of the 1990s has substantially leveled off due to the growth of long-distance fiber-optic cable networks, and the anticipated rise of commercial satellite telephone networks has been overtaken by advances in terrestrial cellular telephony; see Barry D. Watts, *The Military Use of Space: A Diagnostic Assessment* (Washington, D.C.: Center for Strategic and Budgetary Assessments, 2001), 49–56, and Hays, *U.S. Military Space,* 8–18.

45. A partial exception to this generalization might be the possibility of detonating an exoatmospheric nuclear explosion, which would not only destroy nearby satellites but also energize the Van Allen radiation belts, drastically reducing the lifespan of all unhardened satellites orbiting at the affected altitudes. Such an attack—which would be of dubious short-term military value—might appear to be a way to use a single nuclear weapon to produce massive economic damage without causing many human casualties (at

least directly). However, it presumably would not be a way to use a nuclear weapon free from fear of retaliation.

46. It is not particularly difficult compared to building, launching, and operating satellites, however. The relative difficulty of attacking satellites in orbit is even more pronounced for nonstate terrorist organizations, which are unlikely to be even remotely as capable of conducting ASAT attacks against satellites as they are of striking a wide range of terrestrial economic targets.

47. It remains difficult to envision a motive for such a course of action, however. Although attacking satellites might provide an opportunity to cause economic harm without directly injuring anyone, there are plenty of terrestrial targets where this would also be true. Satellites might be attacked more covertly than most terrestrial targets (though the opposite is more likely to be true), but terrorists or other coercers would have to reveal their actions to achieve their goals, and any concerted antisatellite campaign for economic warfare purposes would quickly become visible to the victim.

48. Spacy, *Does the United States Need Space-Based Weapons?* 25–26, 33–37. Terrestrial ASAT lasers could be counterattacked by STEWs, but would also be vulnerable to attack by other means.

49. Robert B. Giffen, *U.S. Space System Survivability: Strategic Alternatives for the 1990s,* National Security Affairs Monograph Series 82-4 (Washington, D.C.: National Defense University Press, 1982); Ziegler, *Safe Havens,* 30.

50. The greatest damage might be achieved by disabling a large part of the GPS satellite network, which would have a wide array of devastating military (and also economic) effects, especially now that many U.S. weapons are guided to their targets by GPS signals, but this would be difficult to achieve because the GPS constellation is large, hardened, and operates in relatively high altitude orbits.

51. Many other examples will spring to mind upon contemplating the matter, but I am reluctant to compile target lists for potential enemies.

52. Ziegler, *Safe Havens,* 28–29.

53. See Karl Mueller, "Strategic Airpower and Nuclear Strategy: New Theory for a Not-Quite-So-New Apocalypse," in *The Paths of Heaven: The Evolution of Airpower Theory,* ed. Phillip S. Meilinger (Maxwell Air Force Base, Ala.: Air University Press, 1997), 279–320.

54. Notable recent exceptions include Preston et al., *Space Weapons, Earth Wars;* and Spacy, *Does the United States Need Space-Based Weapons?*

55. It is widely accepted among military space professionals that such expectations, along with many other popular beliefs about space operations, are also powerfully and unrealistically shaped by the portrayals of space warfare in movies and television. This is by no means a new or surprising pattern: expectations about air warfare both before and after the First World War had much to do with the works of H. G. Wells and other authors of speculative fiction; see, for example, Michael Paris, *Winged Warfare: The Literature and Theory of Aerial Warfare in Britain, 1859–1917* (Manchester: Manchester University Press, 1992).

SHIFT TO A GLOBAL PERSPECTIVE

RICHARD B. MYERS

In ancient India, six blind men encountered an elephant for the first time and quickly began to squabble about the nature of elephants.

The first blind man bumped into the elephant's side and declared that the beast was like a wall.

The second, discovering the ear, concluded it was like a fan.

The third blind man came across the tail and thought the elephant to be very much like a rope.

The fourth, encountering the elephant's leg, was sure the animal resembled a tree.

Finding the tusk, the fifth blind man proclaimed the elephant to be like a spear.

And the sixth, grasping the elephant's trunk, concluded the giant pachyderm most resembled a snake.

We all know from the ancient Oriental story of the six blind men and the elephant that how we perceive something determines our understanding of it and, by implication, our response to it. With that in mind, the U.S. military must shift from a regional to a global view of our security environment to better understand and respond. In the past, America's security needs were served adequately by having its uniformed leaders in Washington maintain the global vision, while the majority of U.S. military organizations maintained a regional or functional focus. However, to provide effectively for the nation's defense in the twenty-first century, we must all come to understand and appreciate the global perspective. Examining trends in the global security environment and the ways in which the U.S. military has organized to deal with past challenges provides the foundation for understanding the implications for America's armed forces today, as we transform our military into one that is ready to effectively provide missile defense, information operations (IO), space operations, and other capabilities that do not respect our traditional regional boundaries.

TRENDS IN THE GLOBAL SECURITY ENVIRONMENT

During the last decade of the twentieth century, we witnessed dramatic shifts in the global security environment. Revolutionary technological advances and monumental political changes rendered our world safer in some ways, although less predictable and arguably less stable. While students of international affairs debated the broader meaning and impact of globalization, defense professionals worked to understand the security implications of these global trends.

Technological changes since 1990 have occurred at an extraordinary pace. Consider for a moment where you were and what you were doing as the Berlin Wall came down. How many people at that time owned a cellular phone or a personal computer, had logged on to the Internet, or knew what a global positioning satellite system was? Whereas television news coverage of the Vietnam War took 36–48 hours to reach American viewers, stories of the Gulf War were broadcast around the world instantaneously. During the Gulf War, Cable News Network was unique in providing continuous coverage of global news. Now, several major networks in the United States cover global events as they happen—24 hours a day, 365 days a year—not to mention the variety of international news programs produced and broadcast by foreign broadcast corporations. Al Jazeera provides programming that shapes perceptions of the United States in much of the Arabic-speaking world. Imagery satellites capable of better than one-meter resolution were at one time the sole purview of superpowers but are now operated by companies in the United States and Europe for the benefit of whoever is willing to pay for the images. In August 2002, commercial satellite images of airfields in the Horn of Africa were broadcast around the world, allegedly showing potential staging areas for attacks against Iraq. For those who missed the news, the satellite photographs were available on the Internet.

Political changes in the 1990s were no less staggering. As a fighter pilot, I spent the first 25 years of my Air Force career studying Soviet fighter aircraft that NATO would have to confront in deadly combat if the Cold War ever heated up. Now, Soviet fighters that could be seen in the West only in classified photos are performing at air shows over America's heartland. Today, officers from the former Soviet Union attend professional military education at our staff colleges and war colleges, and three former Warsaw Pact members have joined NATO. The end of the Cold War lowered the threat of nuclear Armageddon and brought an end to many of the proxy wars through which the two sides struggled to exert their influence. But the Cold War imposed a certain element of stability and predictability to international affairs that no longer exists. Alarming numbers of customers—both state and nonstate actors—seek to acquire weapons of mass destruction and the means to deliver them, including long-range ballistic missiles. In short, the technological and political changes that have improved our quality of life and brought us

---

Richard B. Myers, "*Shift to a Global Perspective,*" Air and Space Power Journal *17 (Fall 2003): 5–10. Public domain.*

all closer together can also be perverted to empower those who would do us harm.

HISTORICAL CONTEXT

As we chart our way ahead, we do not begin with a clean sheet of paper. We must first know how we arrived at our current way of organizing for national security to understand why we are better off organizing functionally or globally for some mission areas rather than relying entirely on regional combatant commands. At the same time, we should appreciate, not abandon, the value of regional expertise in implementing our national security strategy and national military strategy.

The experiences of the Second World War and early Cold War helped dispel lingering illusions about America's security and its proclivity for isolationism; those experiences drew America's new international responsibilities into tighter focus. Responding to America's changed role in the world, Congress passed the National Security Act of 1947, creating the National Security Council, the Central Intelligence Agency, and the Department of Defense. While Congress legislated the overarching security structure, President Harry Truman established the first Unified Command Plan (UCP), which established our regional and functional combatant commands. Among these newly created commands were the U.S. European Command (USEUCOM), U.S. Pacific Command (USPACOM), U.S. Atlantic Command (USLANTCOM), and Strategic Air Command (SAC). The containment policy our armed forces helped to support was a global one, but, arguably, little need existed for our regional commanders to focus globally. In any case, the regional commanders lacked the technological means needed to gain and maintain a global perspective.

The first UCPs merely codified the command structures that existed at the end of the Second World War. What had once been General Dwight Eisenhower's command became USEUCOM; General Douglas MacArthur's command became Far East Command; and Admiral Chester Nimitz's command became USPACOM. Other regional commands had responsibility for Alaska, for the Caribbean, and for guarding the northeastern air approaches to the United States, but vast areas of the world remained unassigned to any combatant command.[1] When our first combatant commands were established, the service chiefs played an active role in the commands and served as the Joint Chiefs of Staff's (JCS) executive agents in overseeing the commands.

From the outset of the Cold War, regional commands focused on their regions while the JCS kept a global perspective. Although this arrangement served the nation well enough to see us through the Cold War, signs of trouble appeared as early as 1951, when President Truman dismissed General MacArthur in the midst of the Korean War. After serving as chief of staff of the Army in the 1930s, MacArthur lived in Asia until his dismissal. He first served as military advisor to the Philippine government and then was made commander of U.S. troops in the Southwest Pacific area during the Second World War. After the war, MacArthur became military governor of Japan, overseeing its occupation and reconstruction. With the outbreak of the Korean War, General MacArthur's Far East Command provided the U.S. underpinning to the war effort of the United Nations. In response to MacArthur's protest against limited objectives in the Korean War—"no substitute for victory"[2]—Gen Omar Bradley, chairman of the JCS, informed Congress that he and the joint chiefs unanimously agreed that in the global struggle against communism, a wider war in Asia represented "the wrong war, at the wrong place, at the wrong time, and with the wrong enemy."[3] Although partly a clash over the utility of limited objectives in war, the disagreement largely reflected the two sides' differing perspectives —MacArthur's Asia-centric regional view and the joint chief's global outlook, which had to account for Europe as well as Asia.

In the 56 years since the first UCP, our combatant command structure has been expanded geographically and empowered legally, The Goldwater-Nichols Act of 1986 strengthened the role of our combatant commands, and with UCP 2002, the last remaining unassigned regions of the world—Russia, the Caspian Sea, Antarctica, and the countries of North America—were finally placed within our combatant commanders' areas of responsibility (AOR). Now, the entire globe is encompassed within the AORs of our five regional combatant commands—USEUCOM, USPACOM, U.S. Central Command (USCENTCOM), U.S. Northern Command (USNORTHCOM), and U.S. Southern Command (USSOUTHCOM).

In addition to regional combatant commands, the United States has had functional combatant commands since the inception of the UCP. In fact, SAC was technically the first, formally becoming a combatant command just 2 weeks before USPACOM, USEUCOM, and USLANTCOM did so. Still, today's functional, unified combatant commands are relatively recent creations that began with the establishment of U.S. Space Command (USSPACECOM) in 1985.[4] In the 15 years that followed, successive administrations established U.S. Special Operations Command (USSOCOM), U.S. Transportation Command (USTRANSCOM), U.S. Strategic Command (USSTRATCOM), and U.S. Joint Forces Command (USJFCOM). The rise of these functional commands highlights the reality that some military missions or responsibilities can be better fulfilled by carving out functions from our regional commands' responsibilities than by having the functions dispersed among the regional commands.

The newly established USSTRATCOM—formed by joining its capabilities and resources with those of USSPACECOM—is taking on some missions that have been unassigned previously and that overlap the responsibilities of our regional combatant commands. USSTRATCOM's nuclear focus broadened considerably with the latest Nuclear Posture Review

(NPR), signed by the secretary of defense in December 2001. In addition to specifying the road ahead for America's nuclear arsenal, the 2001 NPR introduced a new strategic triad. The old triad of intercontinental ballistic missiles, long-range bombers, and submarine-launched ballistic missiles has given way to a triad of strategic offensive capabilities, strategic defenses, and the infrastructure and research and development needed to sustain America's strategic capabilities. Strategic offensive capabilities include nonnuclear—even nonkinetic—strikes, as well as the traditional employment of nuclear force. As described in the NPR, the new triad is enabled by command and control (C2), intelligence, and planning capabilities. The president's decision to join USSPACECOM and USSTRATCOM to form a new U.S. Strategic Command was a major step in fulfilling the vision for a new strategic triad. Despite the familiar name of the new command, it is as different from the former USSTRATCOM as it is from the former USSPACECOM. It is an entirely new command—and greater than the sum of its two predecessors. Obviously, the new USSTRATCOM will have global responsibilities, and its commander and staff must have a global perspective for dealing with threats to U.S. security.

USSOCOM has also been given new responsibilities and a greater role in the global war on terrorism. The very phrase "global war on terrorism" highlights the global approach needed for dealing with the problem of terrorism. At the first DoD press conference of 2003, the secretary of defense announced the change of focus at USSOCOM, pointing out that "Special Operations Command will function as both a supported and a supporting command."[5] In the past, USSOCOM, with very few exceptions, has been the supporting command to our regional combatant commands. Obviously, terrorist networks today have a global presence, with members and cells around the world, and we can no longer adequately counter the scourge of terrorism by relying solely on regional strategies. We also need a global approach to the problem.

IMPLICATIONS FOR THE U.S. MILITARY

The establishment of a new USSTRATCOM and an expanded role for USSOCOM does not come at the expense of our regional combatant commands. This is not a zero-sum equation. Our regional combatant commands provide essential regional expertise; they represent an enduring basis for U.S. presence around the globe; they are the keys to successful theater security cooperation with our allies and friends; and they form the basis for pursuing multinational interoperability and military coalitions. In both peace and war, our regional combatant commands give direction to and exert C2 over U.S. military activities around the world. The challenge for our armed forces today is to balance these regional responsibilities with the need to address missions that are global in nature.

Whether we divide our combatant commanders' responsibilities and authorities along functional lines and address them on a global basis or we choose to deal with them along regional lines, we create seams—discontinuities where one command's responsibilities end and another's begin. These are unavoidable, unless we take the impractical step of making one commander responsible for everything, everywhere, all the time. However, seams can become vulnerabilities that our adversaries might exploit. Therefore, when organizing our combatant commands, we strive to place seams where it makes the most sense to place them—where they provide us the greatest effectiveness and efficiencies and present our adversaries with the least opportunity to do us harm.

Missions that cross all regional boundaries require a global approach. One of those is computer network defense. Electrons do not respect geographic boundaries, and requiring each of our geographic commands to plan independently for protecting computer networks would create unacceptable seams. Thus we assigned the lead for computer network defense to USSPACECOM in 1999. This assignment of a global mission to a commander with a global perspective was a precursor of the new missions assigned to the new USSTRATCOM.

Many inherently global military mission areas are of increasing importance to our security and cannot be addressed well from a regional perspective. Such inherently global areas include (1) integration of missile defense across AORs; (2) certain elements of IO; (3) space operations; (4) global strike operations; (5) certain intelligence, surveillance, and reconnaissance (ISR) activities associated with global strike, missile defense, IO, and space operations; and (6) counterterrorism. Missile defense is a responsibility of all of our regional combatant commands. However, no such command, including the newly established USNORTHCOM, is more suited than any other to integrate missile defense operations across AORs in support of the president's stated goal of providing protection for deployed U.S. forces, allies, and friends. When missiles in a distant theater can be used against targets *anywhere* on the globe, the United States needs global ISR and global C2 to integrate its missile defense capabilities—which, by the way, include offensive capabilities to preempt or prevent missile attacks. We cannot afford to think of missile defense merely in terms of actively intercepting missiles after launch.

Similarly, certain elements of IO require a global perspective and better integration of our nation's capabilities. Although IO should become a core warfighting capability of all our combatant commands, certain IO activities could create effects of such magnitude that focusing on regional consequences would become unnecessarily restrictive and ultimately unhelpful. Even when the effects of IO are limited to a single AOR, we will need a global perspective to ensure that theater IO is compatible with IO in other AORs. A global perspective will often provide the essential starting point for success, whether we are attempting to get a message across to an audience that spans more than one theater, conducting electronic warfare (EW) activities to inhibit long-distance communications, performing computer network operations, or carrying out military deception programs. Even within a single theater, USSTRATCOM will add value to the regional combatant commands by integrating efforts previously stovepiped in different organizations (e.g., C2 warfare, psychological operations [PSYOP], EW, and computer network attack [CNA]).

Space operations present another military mission area requiring a global perspective rather than a regional focus. Given the vital role space operations play in global communications, one cannot always determine precisely where space operations end and IO begins. In the past, the supported-supporting relationships between regional combatant commands and USSPACECOM were predominantly one way, with the latter supporting the regional commands. In the future, we are much more likely to see regional commands supporting the new USSTRATCOM to ensure the success of military operations taking place in space. This change in roles will require our regional combatant commands to develop a deeper appreciation for the global perspective of America's security needs.

Given the nature of threats facing America in the twenty-first century, including such fleeting targets as mobile ballistic missiles or leaders of terrorist networks, we must develop the ability to take appropriate military action rapidly, anywhere on the globe. The instruments of such action include today's long-range bombers, shipborne weapon systems, and special forces, but we will need new global capabilities in the future. Regional combatant commands could play either supported or supporting roles in global strike operations, depending on the scenario and weapon systems involved. However, one need look no farther than our current global war on terrorism to appreciate the need for a global perspective in planning for and prosecuting global military operations.

We will need global ISR activities for gathering indications and warning data and for otherwise enabling global strike, space operations, certain elements of IO, and integrated missile defense. Moreover, we need global C2 capabilities to enable integrated global missile defense, facilitate global strike, integrate regional operations with global operations, and integrate regional operations in one AOR with those of another. Knitting together various regionally focused ISR activities is unlikely to yield a coherent global perspective. Simply put, we cannot obtain a relevant global perspective without ISR activities that, to some degree, are globally coordinated and directed—a function performed by the Defense Intelligence Agency. The new factor is that, given the low-density/high-demand nature of many of our ISR resources, regional combatant commands are more likely than before to be required to conduct ISR activities in support of global operations tasked to USSOCOM or USSTRATCOM.

CONCLUSION

Often, discussions about the need to shift from a regional focus to a global perspective lead to debates about supported-supporting relationships. Inevitably, someone will make the claim that functional combatant commands should always support regional combatant commands. Implied, if not stated, is the belief that conducting operations or executing missions is the sole purview of regional combatant commands, and that no functional combatant command should conduct operations in a regional combatant commander's AOR. Such hard-and-fast rules have never existed, and supported-supporting relationships continue to depend on the situation and mission objectives. That is why supported-supporting relationships are spelled out in planning orders, deployment orders, execution orders, the Joint Strategic Capabilities Plan, operations plans, and concept plans. Moreover, the term "supported" does not imply sole responsibility for execution. A supporting combatant commander can execute or conduct operations in support of the supported commander—something USTRANSCOM does every day. Ultimately, our combatant commanders support the president and secretary of defense in the pursuit of American security, and the array of possible command relations between combatant commanders should not be constrained unnecessarily. To the extent we can harness the ability to observe and operate globally, without self-imposed artificial limitations, we will generate new military capabilities to add to the ones we have today, thereby yielding a greater number of military options from which the president can choose.

The president and secretary of defense must maintain a global perspective, and so must the military officials charged with supporting them. Communications from the president and secretary of defense to the combatant commanders normally pass through the chairman of the JCS, but the joint chiefs and the chairman are not in the chain of command. If ever a time existed when our nation's security could be adequately provided for by having uniformed leaders in Washington maintain a global perspective while commands around the world focus exclusively on their regions, that time has long since passed into history. To fulfill faithfully the "commander's intent" from the president on down, combatant-command staffs, service staffs, the Joint Staff, and U.S. officials serving on allied staffs must appreciate our commander-in-chief's perspective—a global one. If we attempt to do otherwise, we will surely end up like the six blind men of the ancient Eastern parable in their first encounter with an elephant, endlessly disputing the nature of something we fail to perceive fully. By shifting our view from a regional to a global perspective, we will better comprehend and respond to America's security needs in the twenty-first century.

NOTES

1. Ronald H. Cole et al., *The History of the Unified Command Plan, 1946–1993* (Washington, D.C.: Joint History Office, February 1995), 11–15.

2. General Douglas MacArthur, speech before Congress, April 19, 1951, reproduced in Douglas MacArthur, *Reminiscences* (New York: McGraw-Hill, 1964), 459.

3. General Omar Bradley, testimony to Congress, May 15, 1951, cited in Omar N. Bradley and Clay Blair, Jr., *A General's Life: An Autobiography* (New York: Simon & Schuster, 1983), 640.

4. Prior to the formation of USSPACECOM in 1985, purely functional combatant commands tended to be specified commands (i.e., all of their forces came from a single service). SAC was an example of a specified command. The last specified command, U.S. Forces Command (USFORSCOM), became the Army component to USLANTCOM in 1993 (USLANTCOM became U.S. Joint Forces Command [USJFCOM] in 1999).

5. Secretary of Defense Donald H. Rumsfeld, transcript of a DoD press conference, the Pentagon, Washington, D.C. (January 7, 2003). See Elizabeth G. Book, "Rumsfeld: Special Operations Command Slated for Growth," *National Defense* (February 2003), at www. nationaldefensemagazine .org/article.cfm?Id=1033.

CHAPTER 12

NUCLEAR POLICY AND
MISSILE DEFENSE

THE CASE AGAINST NEW NUCLEAR WEAPONS

MICHAEL A. LEVI

Does the United States need nuclear bombs to destroy enemy bunkers and chemical or biological weapons? For some people, the answer is clear. Strong proponents of nuclear weapons speak of the need to give the president every possible military option, and the Bush administration's 2002 Nuclear Posture Review reflects this affirmative response. On the other side, committed opponents maintain that no potential military capability could justify designing—let alone building or using—new nuclear bombs. For both camps, the details of the proposed weapons are irrelevant.

Yet neither of the simple arguments for or against new nuclear weapons is broadly accepted. The United States does not develop every possible weapon simply to provide the president with all options; policymakers have, for example, judged the military value of chemical weapons insufficient to outweigh the political benefits of forgoing them. However, the nation has never rejected nuclear use outright and has always reserved the possibility of using tactical nuclear weapons. Indeed, until the end of the Cold War, such weapons were central to U.S. military thinking.

Despite their disagreements, the people engaged in debate over new nuclear weapons have tacitly agreed on one thing: that these weapons would deliver substantial military benefits. Thus they have cast the dilemma over new nuclear weapons as one of military necessity versus diplomatic restraint. But this is a false tension: new nuclear weapons would, in fact, produce few important military advances. Yet their development would severely undercut U.S. authority in its fight against proliferation.

Advocates of new tactical nuclear weapons have tended to focus shortsightedly on simple destructive power. In particular, most arguments for bunker busting nuclear weapons ignore the difficulty of locating threatening bunkers in the first place. During the Gulf War of 1991, military planners painstakingly assessed the potential consequences of bombing Iraqi chemical weapons facilities, debating nuclear and nonnuclear weapons, as well as the option of leaving the bunkers alone. Ultimately, the military used conventional weapons to bomb every known facility. Subsequently, however, international weapons inspectors,

aided by Iraqi defectors, discovered that those targets had been the mere tip of a vast Iraqi system for producing and storing weapons of mass destruction. Had the military used nuclear weapons to bomb all known chemical facilities during the Gulf War, the United States would have made barely a dent in Iraq's deadly capability while incurring massive political backlash as people died from the accompanying nuclear fallout.

The challenge of finding hidden targets is the norm, not an exception. In Afghanistan, U.S. efforts to eliminate the Taliban and al Qaeda were hindered by the difficulty of tracking down their underground hideouts. Intelligence technology, which relied heavily on detecting mechanical equipment, power lines, and communications systems to identify hidden facilities, floundered in the face of a backward enemy who employed none of the technologies being searched for. Osama bin Laden is still alive not because the United States lacked powerful weaponry, but because U.S. intelligence could not find him in the caves of Tora Bora.

Still, an inability to locate all enemy weapons stockpiles and underground leadership targets is not an argument for leaving alone those that can be found. But proponents of nuclear weapons have overstated the capability of the nuclear option even in cases for which targets can be located, while underestimating nonnuclear potential. In particular, proponents have contended that nuclear weapons are needed to compensate for difficulties in precisely locating underground targets; that they are needed to neutralize chemical and biological agents and thus prevent their deadly use; and that only with nuclear weapons will there be no "safe havens" (no depth below which enemies are safe). However, each of these arguments can be debunked, as illustrated in the following examples.

INADEQUATE INTELLIGENCE

Libya has been suspected of producing chemical weapons at its Tarhunah complex, located sixty kilometers southeast of the capital city of Tripoli and hidden in tunnels and bunkers under roughly twenty meters of earth. The problem is that U.S. analysts

This essay has been edited and is reprinted from Issues in Science and Technology *(Spring 2003): 63–68, by permission.* Copyright © *2003 by the University of Texas at Dallas, Richardson, Texas.*

have not been able to produce an exact blueprint of the underground chambers. This lack of precision leads some observers to argue that, although the facility is, in theory, shallow enough to be destroyed with conventional arms, uncertainty concerning its location may require the large destructive radius of a nuclear weapon to compensate.

A nuclear weapon detonated at or near the surface produces a large crater and sends a massive shockwave into the ground. Underground facilities within this crater are destroyed, as are facilities slightly outside the zone by strong stresses that rupture the earth. Based on the intelligence community's knowledge (even given its uncertainty) about the Tarhunah facility, it is apparent that a five-kiloton earth-penetrating nuclear weapon could destroy it. This attack would produce a moderate amount of nuclear fallout, the precise nature of which would depend on whether the weapon was detonated inside the facility or in the surrounding earth. To be conservative, military planners would have to assume the latter. Such a blast would kill every human being within approximately fifteen square kilometers, according to calculations by Robert Nelson of Princeton University. Although this zone would not reach Tripoli, concerns about fallout would require medical monitoring for civilians as far as twenty kilometers downwind from the facility. U.S. troops in the zone would have to halt operations or risk being exposed to fallout. Troops could not enter the immediate facility area to inspect damage or collect intelligence, even with protective gear, which is ineffective against nuclear fallout.

Alternatively, there are a number of nonnuclear approaches that are already available or could be developed for destroying or neutralizing this type of complex. If the main bunker could be more precisely located, then a single earth-penetrating conventional bomb could reach it. A missile the length of the current GBU-28 penetrator, modified to strike the surface at twice the GBU-28's current impact speed, could smash through the cover of earth and reinforced concrete and destroy the facility with conventional explosives. This suggests that the military should focus on improving intelligence capabilities, particularly the ability to precisely map underground targets that have already been located, rather than on devising ever more powerful weapons.

Even if the facility cannot be precisely localized, several conventional penetrator missiles used simultaneously could mimic the effect of a small nuclear weapon. One scenario would be to mount multiple sorties to cover the entire suspected facility area. In a more sophisticated approach, the military is now developing a "small-diameter bomb" that packs several penetrating missiles into the payload of a single aircraft—essentially, an underground version of the ubiquitous cluster bomb. Extending the small-diameter concept to missiles the length of the GBU-28 would enable simultaneous delivery of as many as twenty-four penetrating missiles, at least several of which could be expected to penetrate the facility.

Still other options are available. If the facility were operating, then conventional electromagnetic pulse weapons—recently added to the U.S. arsenal—might be applied to destroy or disable equipment inside. Because an electromagnetic pulse can easily travel down a bunker's power and ventilation ducts, equipment inside would be vulnerable to attack. Such weapons could be delivered by cruise missile.

In an indirect approach to rendering the facility useless, cruise missiles could be used to temporarily block its entrances. It also would be possible to establish a "no-personnel zone" or "no-vehicle zone" around the facility. A range of intelligence assets, such as spy satellites, would be trained on the area surrounding the complex, and any attempt to move material into or out of the facility would be stopped. Although the facility itself might continue to produce weapons, those weapons could not be removed and used on the battlefield. These approaches would be limited by the need to continually devote assets to a single facility or to mount repeated attacks; if there were many simultaneous targets of concern, the method might not prove feasible.

In each case of applying conventional weapons, collateral damage due to chemical dispersal would be minimal outside the facility. Inside, chemical agents would be dispersed, but U.S. troops inspecting the area could mitigate the dangers from these by wearing protective gear.

AGENT DEFEAT

Proponents of nuclear weapons for attacking stockpiles of chemical and biological agents, called "agent defeat weapons," typically argue that the biological or chemical fallout produced by a conventional explosive attack can be more deadly than the fallout produced by a nuclear weapon. This argument misses two crucial points: in many cases, nonnuclear agent defeat payloads can avoid spreading chemical and biological fallout; and the fallout from a nuclear attack, although perhaps less extensive than the potential biological or chemical fallout, is still prohibitive.

Consider a hypothetical example from Iraq, which is suspected of retaining stockpiles of weaponized anthrax and is known to use hardened bunkers extensively. A typical bunker might be twenty meters in height and cover an area measuring four hundred square meters, have walls that are five meters thick and a roof of reinforced concrete, and be buried under five meters of earth. Built during the absence of U.N. weapons inspections, the bunker's existence has become known to U.S. intelligence through satellite imagery captured during its construction. It is believed to contain several tons of anthrax in storage barrels, although in the absence of a continuing ground presence, this cannot be confirmed.

A twenty-ton penetrating nuclear weapon (if it were developed) detonated at the floor of the facility would incinerate its contents, preventing the dispersal of anthrax. But it would also spread nuclear fallout. Deaths from acute radiation poisoning would be expected as far us one kilometer downwind. People nearer than four kilometers downwind would, if not evacuated quickly, receive a radiation dose greater than that received by a nuclear worker during an entire year.

Nonnuclear payloads might, however, spread less collateral damage while avoiding political problems. A penetrating bomb carrying a fragmenting warhead and incendiary materials could be used. The warhead would break the anthrax out of any exposed containers, and the heat from the incendiary materials would neutralize the anthrax. Containers that were heavily shielded might not break open, but although the anthrax would not be destroyed, neither would it be released. The bunker would remain intact.

Alternatively, a penetrating bomb carrying submunitions and neutralizing chemicals could be used. The submunitions would spread throughout the bunker and release the anthrax from its containers, even if it were stored behind barriers, and the neutralizing chemicals would render the anthrax inert. The bunker would probably remain intact, although it could be breached if it had been poorly constructed.

U.S. planners may not want to directly attack the bunker. Instead, a watch could be placed on the facility using satellite imagery coupled with armed unmanned aerial vehicles. Anyone or anything attempting to enter or leave the bunker would be destroyed, making the anthrax inside unusable.

DEEP BURIAL

Among proponents of new nuclear weapons, the most consistent error is the assumption that they would be silver bullets, leaving no underground facilities invulnerable to their effects. But such is not the case. Even the two-megaton B-83 bomb, the highest-yield weapon in the U.S. arsenal, would leave unscathed any facilities buried under more than two hundred meters of hard rock. In contrast, functional defeat approaches—sealing off entrances rather than directly destroying the bunker—have no depth limitations.

To better understand this, consider North Korea's Kumchangri underground complex, which was once suspected of housing illicit nuclear weapons activities. The depth of the facility, built into the side of a mountain, is not publicly known, but its main chamber may quite possibly be deeper than two hundred meters, putting it out of the range of even megaton-sized, earth-penetrating nuclear weapons. Even if the facility were only 150 meters underground, a one-megaton penetrating nuclear weapon would be required to destroy it, and the resulting nuclear fallout would have enormous consequences. If the wind were blowing southwest, then the North Korean capital of Pyongyang, eighty miles away, would have to be evacuated within hours of detonation to prevent the death of more than 50 percent of its residents from radiation poisoning. If the wind were blowing north or northwest, then residents of several large cities in China would have to be evacuated immedi-

ately. And if the wind were blowing south, then residents of several large cities in South Korea, as well as U.S. troops stationed in the demilitarized zone, would have to be evacuated within hours to avoid numerous radiation deaths.

Alternatively, regardless of the facility's depth, military planners could seek to disable rather than destroy the facility. Cruise missiles could be used to collapse entrances to the bunker. Entrances, however, might be reopened quickly, requiring repeated sorties to keep the facility closed. Thermobaric weapons, which debuted in Afghanistan, could be used to send high-pressure shockwaves down the tunnels, possibly destroying equipment inside the facility.

An "information umbrella" approach also might be applied. The United States, possibly together with allies, would declare that no North Korean vehicles would be allowed to come near the facility. This curfew would be monitored using surveillance assets, and any vehicle attempting to enter or leave the facility would be destroyed.

MISGUIDED FEDERAL EFFORTS

Despite the limitations of nuclear capabilities, some policymakers are marching ahead. For the past year, Congress has been focused on a new weapon system called the "robust nuclear earth penetrator" (RNEP), a modification of either the B-61 or B-83 bomb that would have improved earth-penetration ability. The Department of Energy, in its 2003 budget request, asked for funding to begin a 3-year, $45 million "feasibility and engineering" project that would include "paper studies" of the RNEP and might possibly "proceed beyond the mere paper stage and include a combination of component and subassembly test and simulation," according to John Gordon, then the administrator of the DoE's National Nuclear Security Administration.

This effort would be misguided. Misunderstanding of weapons technology and engineering has consistently marked congressional debate over the RNEP, and any further discussion first requires setting the record straight. Some observers have incorrectly characterized the RNEP as a low-yield "mininuke," implying that it is more usable than other nuclear weapons. But as Representative Curt Weldon pointed out correctly during House debate, the RNEP is not a mininuke—indeed, it is a very large, clumsy weapon.

Yet confronted with the observation that nuclear weapons are militarily useless, many people embrace this as a virtue, arguing that these weapons are for deterrence, not for warfighting. Their claim, however, is based on dubious deterrence arguments left over from the Cold War. At the core of this claim is the contention that deterrence works only when the United States threatens what the enemy values most; that many enemies are so foreign that it is impossible to reliably judge what they value; and that the United States therefore must be able to robustly threaten every asset of theirs.

This argument is not compelling. Consider, for example, the recent debate over the value of deterrence in confronting Iraq, in which analysts and politicians split into two camps. One faction claimed that Saddam Hussein is fundamentally undeterrable, and thus the United States must disarm him. The other argued that Saddam is rational and deterrable, and thus the United States should not attack. No camp argued that it is impossible to deter Saddam only because the United States currently has no earth-penetrating nuclear weapons that place his underground bunkers at risk—and that Iraq therefore should be attacked.

Some proponents of the RNEP have sought to dodge detailed debate over its utility, arguing that without the proposed feasibility study, it is impossible to determine whether the weapon would be useful. But to understand what a feasibility study can and cannot accomplish, consider one of the leading RNEP proposals: modifying the two-megaton B-83 bomb to add ground-penetrating capability. Using basic physics, it is possible to estimate the weapon's potential penetration depth and, in turn, place upper and lower bounds on fallout hazards and destructive capability. Indeed, many people, including myself, have made such estimates—and doing so certainly does not require a multiyear, multimillion-dollar feasibility study.

The proposed study would build on these basic calculations, looking more carefully at engineering limitations and narrowing the basic estimates. For example, laboratory scientists might conclude that, although it may be scientifically possible to build a missile capable of achieving an impact speed of nine hundred meters per second, it would be impossible to engineer the missile to withstand such an impact shock. This failure would reduce the estimate of earth penetration, decreasing the projected destructive potential while increasing the expected fallout hazard.

Given preliminary scientific estimates, military and political decisionmakers—before initiating the research project—should be able to come to one of three conclusions regarding the RNEP. First, either its maximum destructive capability is too small, or the minimum fallout hazard too large, to make further development worthwhile. In this case, the proposed study is unnecessary.

Second, its minimum destructive capability is large enough, and the maximum fallout hazard small enough, to warrant development. In this case, the argument for a feasibility study as a preliminary step is a ruse; the more honest position would be to immediately endorse full development and deployment of the new weapon.

Third, depending on where within the preliminary estimates the destructive capability and fallout hazards fall, the weapon may or may not be useful. In this case, a feasibility study would be essential to refining the estimates and making a decision on proceeding.

The third possibility, however, is unlikely. The fallout hazard that such a bomb would produce is enormous. It could quickly kill people hundreds of kilometers downwind and would contaminate cities even farther away. There are only two reasonable conclusions from this exercise: either one can decide that this is excessive collateral damage and oppose the RNEP, or one can decide that no collateral damage is excessive for this mission and support the RNEP. To claim a need for further engineering study of the robust nuclear earth penetrator is disingenuous.

BROADER DISCUSSION NEEDED

Although many people now maintain that the military has little interest in tactical nuclear weapons, policymakers continue to contemplate developing and deploying them. This will, unfortunately, remain the natural state unless political decisionmakers force a change. Although designers of nuclear weapons have a built-in imperative to seek nuclear solutions to military problems, there is little to be gained by the uniformed military from pushing back. It falls to Congress to actively solicit the advice of military thinkers on the utility or lack thereof of new tactical nuclear weapons.

To date, only the Senate Committee on Foreign Relations has devoted substantial hearing time to tactical nuclear weapons. But these weapons have not only political but military liabilities. To explore these issues, the House and Senate Armed Services Committees should convene hearings on the robust nuclear earth penetrator and on tactical nuclear weapons more broadly. The committee should solicit input from retired military officers and from individuals who have spent time understanding both the nuclear and nonnuclear options. Only by making direct comparisons will policymakers be able to find agreement on a way forward.

THE PROS AND CONS OF NEW NUCLEAR WEAPONS

JAMES KITFIELD

Even as antinuke demonstrators were organizing protests around the country to commemorate the early-August anniversaries of the U.S. bombings of Hiroshima and Nagasaki in 1945, the U.S. Strategic Command held a little-publicized meeting of senior Bush administration officials on August 6 and 7 to advance plans for a new generation of nuclear arms. Proponents of the plan argue that the United States needs to tailor smaller, bunker-buster nukes to threaten underground nuclear facilities that may be built by such nations as North Korea and Iran. Opponents counter that manufacturing a new generation of nuclear weapons will deal a severe blow to the international arms control regime and break down the firewall separating nuclear and conventional arms, leading to greater nuclear proliferation and the increased possibility of a nuclear war. What both sides agree on, however, is that nuclear proliferation is emerging as the single greatest threat to U.S. national security, and that America is at a crossroads in determining how to deal with it.

In recent interviews, *National Journal* correspondent James Kitfield spoke with leading voices on both sides of the argument. C. Paul Robinson is director of Sandia National Laboratories, one of the nation's three primary nuclear weapons labs, and a former chief negotiator at the U.S.-U.S.S.R. Nuclear Testing Talks in Geneva during the 1980s. Joseph Cirincione is director of the Non-Proliferation Project at the Carnegie Endowment for International Peace in Washington, D.C., and a coauthor of *Deadly Arsenals: Tracking Weapons of Mass Destruction.* The following are edited excerpts of their separate interviews.

NJ: The one point of agreement that emerges in the debate about the Bush administration's 2002 Nuclear Posture Review is that the fundamental equation of nuclear deterrence has been forever altered by the dissolution of the Soviet Union, the proliferation of nuclear technology, and the September 11, 2001, terrorist attacks. Is that a fair assumption?

Robinson: Deterrence has changed dramatically since the end of the Cold War, and we're still sorting out what that means for our nuclear posture and the future. As Russia becomes more of a friend than an enemy, we are no longer confronted with a nation that threatens our very existence. I spent many sleepless nights during the Cold War worrying about stability matrixes and first-strike, "use-them-or-lose-them" calculations. That kind of Armageddon scenario is now a distant worry.

I still worry, however, about the proliferation of nuclear materials and technologies from Russia, because in many respects it's a Third World nation now, and in the Third World everything is for sale. I regret that as a nation we haven't been bolder in developing a Marshall Plan for Russia that would help it reach at least a minimum level of prosperity, which is the best antidote to that kind of proliferation. That problem is related, in turn, to what I believe is our greatest emerging threat—rogue states armed with nuclear or other weapons of mass destruction.

NJ: Given such seismic events as the dissolution of the Soviet Union and the September 11 terror attacks, doesn't it make sense to reevaluate our strategic ability to deter aggression?

Cirincione: Absolutely, and we should be taking a new look at our deterrence posture. But it's important for people to understand that this is not what the Bush administration is doing. The January 2002 Nuclear Posture Review directed the Departments of Energy and Defense to begin development of new nuclear weapons, and to formulate new policies to accommodate such weapons. As a result, the nuclear weapons labs have reestablished advanced-warhead concept teams to explore modifications of existing weapons, and to develop low-yield weapons and nuclear earth-penetrators that can be used against hardened targets. So the Bush administration has already decided that we need new nuclear weapons, and they are now going ahead implementing policies to reach that goal step by step. They understand that this is a very controversial decision, however, so they have adopted "salami" tactics—they are slicing off a little bit at a time.

NJ: Are the labs developing new nuclear weapons?

Robinson: That depends on how you define "new." If we take a warhead off the shelf that we designed and tested in the past, and then put it on a new delivery vehicle, is that a new nuclear weapon? We will probably have to manufacture new copies because we produced only a few originally, but it is not a new design, nor will we need to test it. I can categorically state that no one is proposing returning to nuclear testing.

The main point is that the world is not static. Over the past decade, nations have gone to school on our conventional military capabilities, and many of them have adopted a strategy of moving their high-value targets out of our reach by locating them in deeply buried tunnels and inside mountains. If you want to know who the main culprits are, just look at which nations are buying these huge tunnel-boring machines. You'll find that North Korea, Iran, Syria, and Libya have all built a lot of underground facilities. We keep having to relearn this lesson that the world is not stupid, and potential adversaries will constantly take actions to better their strategic position and counter our strengths. I would argue that the United States must respond by maintaining a robust deterrent against whatever is hidden in those underground facilities.

NJ: Does the United States need a low-yield, nuclear bunker-buster to hold an enemy's underground facilities at risk?

Cirincione: This argument that we need mininukes as earth penetrators is based on a lie. Every independent study done on this issue has concluded that for any target buried more than fifty yards underground, you would still need a very large nuclear warhead. Mininukes of a kiloton or less just don't get the job done. The big nukes you would need in order to reach a truly deep underground bunker, meanwhile, would kick up so much dirt that you would have a major problem with radioactive fallout.

More to the point, there are multiple ways of attacking underground facilities using conventional weapons that would be more effective. With repeated precision strikes using conventional earth-penetrating bombs, you can bore deeper and deeper until you reach your target. You could use high-temperature thermobaric weapons that have the advantage of destroying biological and chemical agents and pathogens. You could use precision-strike or Special Operations forces to seal the exit and entrance tunnels to an underground facility.

NJ: Are there viable conventional alternatives to nuclear bunker-busters?

Robinson: Our primary focus is still to accomplish this with conventional weapons, and we work hard on that problem. Nuclear weapons remain a blunt instrument of last resort. We've conducted more than four thousand penetrator tests at Sandia since the 1960s, however, and we have a lot of data on the problem. Basically our tests show that conventional penetrators don't work very well. In the aftermath of the bombing campaign against Serbia, for instance, we discovered that we did very little to no damage against buried targets.

So if we can find ways to strike these buried targets with conventional weapons, we will. If we can't, however, we need to look at what can be accomplished with a nuclear earth-penetrator that causes the least possible amount of collateral damage. That leads you away from two-stage, thermonuclear weapons to smaller-yield, lighter weapons with high reliability. A national command authority confronted in a crisis with the prospect of killing forty thousand people with a thermonuclear weapon in order to take out a bunker is probably going to decide not to. If we could design a bunker-buster that would kill an estimated two thousand to three thousand people, on the other hand, the answer would probably be yes if

the situation was critical. Those are the weapons the Bush administration gave us the OK to begin researching about a year ago, because our scientists felt handcuffed by restrictions that were in place at the time.

NJ: Would rogue nations be deterred from acquiring weapons of mass destruction, or building underground bunkers, if they knew their facilities could be reached by nuclear earth-penetrators?

Cirincione: The Bush administration has adopted this arrogant attitude that the United States can take the dramatic step of developing these weapons, and there will be no international repercussions or imitators. If the most powerful nation the world has ever known says it needs a new class of nuclear weapon to defend itself against weapons of mass destruction, however, why don't other countries also need them? Why doesn't Iran, which has actually been attacked by chemical weapons?

The real danger of this concept is that it blurs the lines between nuclear and conventional weapons, making nukes just another tool in the toolbox that could be used for tactical battlefield purposes. In that sense, this argument is less about deterrence than war fighting. We already have plenty of doomsday weapons in our arsenal if all we're trying to do is scare people. They are planning on using these weapons. And if the United States were to use them, it would cross a threshold that has not been breached since the Truman administration. That in turn would encourage other nations to develop and use nuclear weapons in a similar manner. That's not in the United States' national security interests. Given that we have never accepted a nuclear weapon into our arsenal without testing—with the exception of the Hiroshima bomb—the path the Bush administration is on also greatly increases the likelihood that the United States will return to nuclear testing, which would be a terrible blow to the nonproliferation regime.

NJ: Will developing a nuclear bunker-buster likely lead to new testing?

Robinson: I don't think we will need new testing, because the warhead we are talking about has already been tested. As I said earlier, we would need to start production of new warheads again.

I continue to abide by my statements that we're a long way from going back to nuclear tests. Having said that, I helped write the safeguards that were written into the Comprehensive Test Ban Treaty ratification protocols, which essentially stated that the president of the United States would withdraw from the treaty and return to testing if a serious problem developed in the U.S. nuclear arsenal that required testing for a solution. The point I'm making is, the United States has been willing to abide by these treaties only as long as they do not conflict with our essential security posture.

NJ: How do you respond to arms control experts who charge that remanufacturing a new class of nuclear bunker-busters violates the Nonproliferation Treaty [NPT], which commits the United States to "pursue negotiations in good faith on effective measures relating to the cessation of the nuclear arms race" and "to nuclear disarmament?"

Robinson: I was in the Reagan administration when we debated what exactly was meant by Article VI of the NPT, and it seems to me that the end state of total nuclear disarmament that the treaty envisions will occur around the same time that the lamb lies down with the lion. And I always argued that even at that point, the lamb still won't get much sleep.

In truth, I believe that the NPT was intended more as a confidence-building measure than as a real arms control treaty that we were willing to bet our country's survival on. We would never have negotiated an arms control treaty with the ridiculous verification inspections by the International Atomic Energy Agency [IAEA] prescribed in the NPT, which missed the programs in Iraq and Iran and even Israel. Where has the IAEA spent the most money in terms of inspections? In Germany, Canada, and Japan. Why? Because it is a confidence-building measure among friendly countries eager to prove they are not violating it. It was never set up to catch cheaters. That's why I disagree with people who infer that the NPT is a real arms control treaty. It's not.

NJ: Is the NPT more a gentlemen's agreement than an arms control treaty?

Cirincione: That's just nonsense. President Bush just negotiated a treaty on strategic nuclear weapons with Moscow that has no verification regime, yet he still insists that it's vital to our national security. The NPT was the beginning of what became a comprehensive, interlocking network of treaties, agreements, and enforcement mechanisms designed to stop the proliferation of not only nuclear weapons, but also chemical and biological weapons. It established a legal and diplomatic framework for a nonnuclear future, and it has worked. Instead of the twenty to twenty-five nuclear nations that President John F. Kennedy predicted, we now have eight worldwide. That's still eight too many, but that's not a bad track record.

As the nuclear states continue to move toward ever-smaller arsenals as called for in the NPT, we will continue to devalue nuclear weapons globally. That's the whole crux of the matter: Given our overwhelming conventional military superiority, the United States is more secure in a world where nuclear weapons are devalued and dwindling as opposed to a world where we and others are developing new nuclear weapons for new uses.

Now, there are certainly enforcement problems with the nonproliferation regime, as there are with all international and national laws. Does that automatically mean the laws are useless? No, it means we need to get better at enforcement and adapting them to new circumstances. There's no question that we need to toughen IAEA inspections and to take a fresh look at some of the fundamental tenets of the nonproliferation regime. Some people in the Bush administration think the first thing you do in such a circumstance is tear down the bridge you're standing on. I argue instead that we need to strengthen the bridge.

NJ: Do you credit the NPT for slowing the march of nuclear proliferation?

Robinson: I think the North Atlantic Treaty extending our nuclear umbrella to our European allies did much more to prevent nations from going nuclear than the NPT, and will do more in the future as more Eastern European nations join NATO. That's why I argue that we should also extend that umbrella further from Japan to encompass Southeast Asian nations such as South Korea, Thailand, Singapore, and the Philippines.

NJ: Do you ever worry that the United States' aggressive strategy of preemption, coupled with our overwhelming conventional military capability, might convince some nations that nuclear weapons are their only deterrent against us?

Robinson: The National Security Strategy lays out very carefully the conditions that might prompt preemption, which are basically limited to those instances when the threat of many American deaths is imminent and you have the nexus of rogue states with weapons of mass destruction and links to terrorists. Having said that, a friend of mine recently pointed out that the United States was not deterred from going to war by Iraq's supposed arsenal of chemical and biological weapons. We haven't responded nearly as quickly to North Korea's announcement that it has nuclear weapons. Some people could draw the lesson that the United States can be deterred by nuclear weapons, but not by chemical or biological ones. I can't argue with that conclusion.

THE UNITED STATES NEEDS SPACE-BASED MISSILE DEFENSE

BOB SCHAFFER

MAKING LONG-RANGE NUCLEAR MISSILES OBSOLETE

Thank you, Ambassador Cooper. Good afternoon ladies and gentlemen. I have been a long-time admirer of Ambassador Hank Cooper since before I went to Congress in 1996. As a member of Congress, I relied on the ambassador's judgment and vision for guidance when considering questions of America's defense against those who would threaten our liberty.

The district I represented, up until January of this year, in Congress was essentially the entire eastern half of Colorado—very rural. Consequently, the committees to which I was assigned in Congress had to do with agriculture, natural resources, and education. I served on no committees that had direct involvement with national defense, foreign affairs, or military preparedness.

But as one who represented a constituency of broad interests, I endeavored to learn as much as I could about national defense. And the more I learned about the very real threat America faces with respect to long-range missile attack, the more I became convinced that there are not enough leaders in Congress paying attention to this vital national security concern.

As Ambassador Cooper mentioned, my interest led me around the world, meeting with parliamentarians and defense leaders of other nations. I made eight trips to Russia, as many to Ukraine, and others to Asia, Central Asia, and Europe.

Since September 11th, America has been focused on combating terrorism in Afghanistan, Iraq, and elsewhere. We have been reorienting our national defense to address the weakness exploited by the terrorists who killed Americans on American soil, and toward protecting Americans abroad from similar potential attacks. This, of course, is necessary and exactly what we should be doing.

America is not focused enough on conventional threats.

Let me explain my concern for national security through an analogy of home security. As homeowners, we put the toughest lock, where, on the front door, right? Well, the burglars have figured out how to get in through the windows. In response, we are now fortifying our windows, doubling them up, and locking down the smaller points of access. This makes perfect sense.

However, my friends, we are leaving the front door wide open to conventional attack from poten-

tial threats far more sophisticated and direct than the terrorists of rogue nations. We can't forget that countries like China still maintain arsenals of long-range ballistic missiles targeted at American cities like the one we're in right now. From their current launch sites, these missiles are just a half-an-hour away from their American targets. Once launched, we have no defense against them.

GOOD LEADERSHIP IS ESSENTIAL

As a suggestion, I was asked to speak on what it will take for us to build the effective defenses we need, to defend us from the increasing threat and proliferation of ballistic missiles of all types, whether short-range, intermediate-range, and long-range, capable of attacking our homes and cities.

Two words will do: Good leadership.

In one way, the current Bush administration has displayed good leadership in its missile defense program. It has exerted the will to deploy a missile defense as seen in its decisions to withdraw from the 1972 ABM [Antiballistic Missile] Treaty, deploy a National Missile Defense system, and increase funding.

As a result of President Bush's leadership, the 1972 ABM Treaty resides in the dustbin of history. As a result of President Bush's leadership, the United States stands on the verge of deploying a National Missile Defense system, which is expected to reach initial operation in the next few years.

It may be helpful to review some highlights of the National Missile Defense program, if only to point out how Americans not only have the desire to defend themselves from ballistic missile attack, they also have the commitment and ability to build a defense. Highlights include how:

- In early September, Northrop Grumman submitted a bid to compete for the Missile Defense Agency's Targets and Countermeasures prime integration program, valued at more than $1 billion for an initial 4-year program. The Bush administration takes the issue of mid-course-phase decoys and countermeasures seriously.

- In August this year, progress was reported on the construction of a $900 million sea-based X-band radar, which will be home ported at Adak, Alaska, in the Aleutian Islands superceding earlier plans to build a ground-based X-band radar on Shemya Island, also in the

This essay has been edited and is reprinted from Vital Speeches of the Day *(October 15, 2003): 28–32, by permission.*

Aleutians. This sea-based X-band radar will be self-propelled, using a semisubmersible oil rig being modified at shipyards in Brownsville and Corpus Christi. The radar will weigh fifty thousand tons and be 390 feet long and 250 feet high. Scheduled to begin operation in 2005, this sea-based, X-band radar will hand off ballistic missile tracking information to interceptors located at Fort Greely, Alaska, and Vandenberg Air Force Base.

- Also in August, Orbital Sciences Corporation test launched from Vandenberg a prototype of the three-stage booster to be used in the ground-based interceptor for our National Missile Defense system.

President Bush's plan calls for deploying by 2004, four ground-based interceptors at Vandenberg, and six ground-based interceptors at Fort Greely, increasing the number of ground-based interceptors deployed at Fort Greely to a total of twenty by the end of 2005. Contracts have been let for pouring concrete for the missile silos at Fort Greely, and for refurbishing existing missile silos at Vandenberg Air Force Base. In June 2002, for example, it was reported how a contract for $325 million was issued to build six underground missile silos at Fort Greely.

These are significant steps to our deployment of a National Missile Defense. The deployment of X-band radar, development of a booster for the ground-based interceptor, testing of the kinetic kill vehicle, and fielding of interceptors are coming together.

INTELLIGENT DESIGN

But good leadership involves more than the will to deploy a defense. While the will to deploy a missile defense is a key ingredient, an ingredient missing from the preceding Clinton administration, which believed in the ABM Treaty as the cornerstone of arms control, good leadership also needs to point the way of how to build an effective defense. Building an effective defense requires more than spending money. It requires an intelligent design.

Speaking of money, Congress and the Bush administration have recognized the importance of funding missile defense. For example, in June of this year, the House Appropriations Committee approved a budget of about $8.9 billion for missile defense, an increase of about $1.3 billion. Real money is being spent.

Congress has shown increasing willingness to fund a missile defense, and for good reason. Not only has the threat of ballistic missile attack increased from China's buildup of ballistic missiles of all types, but the proliferation of ballistic missiles continues to increase. The proliferation of ballistic missiles poses a grave threat internationally. India and Pakistan look at each other in terms of increasing numbers of ballistic missiles, some of which are presumably armed with nuclear weapons.

Japan is losing any sense of complacency over the increasing ballistic missile threat it faces, as it was reported in June how North Korea has fielded between 160 and 170 intermediate-range Nodong missiles that can reach nearly all of Japan. In June, it was also reported how Japan, in response to this hostile buildup of ballistic missiles by North Korea, requested an additional $1.2 billion for the next fiscal year to deploy a two-layer missile defense system, consisting of PAC-3 missiles produced under license, and upgrading its four Aegis destroyers to deploy the SM-3 interceptor.

From our experience in Iraq, we know that the PAC-3 missile works very well, both as an interceptor of short-range ballistic missiles and of aircraft, using hit-to-kill technology based on radar guidance. PAC-3 performed with a high probability of intercept, unlike the earlier improved PAC-2, which, although successful from a strategic viewpoint in the 1991 Gulf War, was essentially jury-rigged for its mission of intercepting Scuds.

The Navy's SM-3 ballistic missile interceptor has proved itself positively, achieving three interceptions out of four attempts. The fourth interception test in June 2003, while unsuccessful, demonstrated the ability of naval ships to share target cuing information as the firing of the SM-3 from the USS *Lake Erie* was reportedly cued from another ship uprange. The test failure of the SM-3 evidently occurred when one of the cells of its solid-fuel Divert and Attitude Control System failed to ignite—a problem of quality control rather than of the underlying technology.

The United Sates has over 20 years of experience in testing hit-to-kill technology for missile defense, achieving its first successful interception of an ICBM [intercontinental ballistic missile] target in the June 1984 Homing Overlay Experiment. The time has come to deploy hit-to-kill technology in an effective defense.

But building an effective missile defense requires an intelligent design. It requires the same elements of good strategy that have always formed an essential part of military victory, whether victory through a policy of peace through strength, or a policy of determination to achieve victory and lasting peace.

An effective defense requires good position. No small part of military strategy is devoted to the maneuver and positioning of troops. Good position, good location, holding the high ground, whether the top of a hill or a mountain top, being able to look down and fire at an approaching enemy, is a key element of military strategy. For this reason, U.S. military strategy emphasizes air superiority, the high ground of combined air, land, and sea operations. There is also the high ground of space, which U.S. military forces recognize as vital to the operation of our intelligence, communications, reconnaissance, and navigation systems, which rely heavily on satellites.

Building an effective missile defense also requires good position. But this position isn't found on the ground: it is found in space, where the ballistic missile operates. Building an effective missile defense requires a strategy that deploys a missile defense in the high ground of space. Good leadership would deploy a missile defense in space. Good leadership would point the way to space.

Both the Strategic Defense Initiative of the 1980s and early 1990s and Project Defender of the late 1950s and early 1960s pointed the way to space, recognizing the inherent advantages of deploying a missile defense in space. The earlier Project Argus nuclear test shots in 1958 and Starfish 1962 also pointed to space. Dr. Nicholas Christofilos from Lawrence Livermore realized space provides a position with global coverage against ballistic missile threats.

The strategic advantages of deploying a missile defense in space are considerable. Global coverage, the capability for boost-phase interception, the use of robotics minimizing operational costs, and the potential of high-energy lasers and particle beams led these earlier missile defense programs to emphasize the development of defenses based in space.

Even the Clinton administration was aware of the advantages that accrue from deployment of a missile defense in space, as seen in its decision to complete the termination of the Brilliant Pebbles program for deploying a space-based interceptor defense, and attempt to terminate the Space Based Laser.

Believing in the ABM Treaty as the cornerstone of arms control, the Clinton administration was not interested in building effective defenses. While Brilliant Pebbles had been approved for acquisition in 1991, it was subsequently opposed by key Democrats in Congress, who sought a technological regression, unwilling to change the strategy of Mutual Assured Destruction embodied in the ABM Treaty.

TECHNOLOGICAL LEADERSHIP AND SPACE SUPERIORITY

Building an effective missile defense requires the United States to deploy its kinetic kill interceptors in space like Brilliant Pebbles, not in underground concrete missile silos. An intelligent design would utilize the advantages that deployment in space offers in providing global coverage, boost-phase interception, the use of robotics, minimal operational cost, and the ability to use high-energy lasers for boost-phase interception and active discrimination of decoys.

There is a third ingredient for building an effective missile defense. This ingredient is technological leadership, including the ability to manage programs involving technology to produce timely results. Good leadership needs to manage the effort to build a missile defense effectively, to produce timely results rather than create an endless cycle of studies, delays, testing, and indecision.

In the past, the United States has exhibited bursts of technological leadership, including President Reagan's Strategic Defense Initiative, which supported a vast program of research and development for missile defense technology. We need to remember those times and examples of technology leadership to build an effective missile defense.

Good leadership involves more than creating program momentum by funding a single program with more dollars. It includes the ability to manage technology and lead a fundamentally strong program to completion and success. It includes the ability to concurrently manage technology development programs with acquisition, to allow for improvements in current acquisition and the development of second- and third-generation defenses.

It includes the ability to concurrently manage a variety of technology programs, pursuing at the same time different avenues of basing and technology, recognizing the wealth of ideas and technology developed under the Strategic Defense Initiative, giving the United States the ability to construct a missile defense in multiple layers. It includes the ability to match an intelligent design for building an effective missile defense with the pursuit of technology, seeking a technological momentum designed to defeat the ballistic missile. It includes an understanding of how the strategy of Mutual Assured Destruction, which was behind the ABM Treaty, was designed to restrain the use and development of technology.

Notably, space not only offers a position of advantage for deploying a missile defense, it stimulates the development of new technology.

Technological leadership includes the ability to resolve problems. Highlights of where technological leadership has been lacking in the current program for building a missile defense include:

- The termination in 2001 of the Navy Area Wide defense program, which would have provided Aegis cruisers and destroyers with a defense against short-range ballistic missiles and aircraft like PAC-3.

- While the proposed SM-2 Block VI-A interceptor for Navy Area Wide would have relied on a blast fragmentation warhead rather than hit-to-kill, differentiating it from PAC-3, its program termination may be viewed with disappointment.

- The termination in 2001 and 2002 of the Space Based Laser program, which would have provided a very effective boost phase defense against ballistic missiles of all types: short, intermediate, and long-range.

Notably, the Space Based Laser program successfully demonstrated its end-to-end beam generation and training back in 1997. From that point on, the program's next step was to test a scalable high-energy laser in space. Presumably, the termination of the Space Based Laser program came as a result of opposition in the Senate to the deployment of missile defenses in space. Apparently lacking in the current administration was an understanding of the advantages of technological readiness of the Space Based Laser—unwilling to overcome apparent political opposition at a time when most Americans support missile defenses.

Technological leadership also includes the ability to communicate the advantages of technology, as well as the ability to develop it. While the current administration has demonstrated its commitment to fund a missile defense and support the deployment of a ground-based defense and has withdrawn from the ABM Treaty, it has yet to support a design to build an effective defense, much less insist on technological leadership.

America's current plans include a virtual technological regression in any planning for a space-based interceptor defense—unwilling or unable to use past technology developed for Brilliant Pebbles.

Unwilling or unable to use Brilliant Pebbles technology for space-based interceptors, the current administration and the Congress have been unwilling or unable to employ technological advances that have occurred in:

- The increasing use of robotics, including autonomous operation and data fusing and joint decisionmaking between independently operating robots, which NASA [National Aeronautics and Space Administration] has developed for missions on Mars.

- The development and increasing use of photonic or fiber optics for sensors, communications, and computer processing, which provide a means to defend against electromagnetic pulse.

- The development of three-dimensional computer chips, allowing for the integration of different processes, whether computer processing, communications, processing of sensor data, or active response within the same chip.

These advances in photonics and computer chips, combined with continuing advances in nanotechnology, including Micro Electro Mechanical Systems or MEMS, could potentially allow for the development of kinetic kill vehicles smaller than Brilliant Pebbles, which were essentially based on late 1980s technology. Instead of building kinetic kill vehicles that weigh in the tens of kilograms, the United States could potentially be building kinetic kill vehicles that weigh under a kilogram, perhaps in the tens of grams,

approaching the theoretical limits for kinetic kill vehicles suggested by Lowell Wood at Lawrence Livermore when he proposed the idea of Genius Sand as an advance generation Brilliant Pebbles.

America's defense planners seem to have a striking aversion to the development of advanced technology systems, especially those taking advantage of deployment in space, as seen not only in its termination of the Space Based Laser, but its very low level of funding for the development of a system of space-based relay mirrors that could utilize a high-energy laser to strike at targets around the world. This system of relay mirrors, suggested in the Strategic Defense Initiative as a way to take advantage of high-energy laser technology that was ground-based or air-based, is being funded at a level of around $1 million, when it should be funded at the billion-dollar level.

The state of U.S. technological leadership is also seen by Pentagon planning to deploy a system of optical communication satellites, in other words, satellites using laser communications, which would provide much needed bandwidth and high security. These had been proposed in the early 1980s, and the Air Force had performed some early demonstrations. More than 20 years after this exciting concept was proposed, the Pentagon is finally planning to spend hundreds of millions of dollars to develop a satellite laser communications system. This comes after the European Union successfully demonstrated the use of laser communications with its Artemis satellite.

I was asked to speak about what it will take for us to build the effective defenses we need. Good leadership is the answer. Three key ingredients to good leadership include not only the will to build a defense, but an intelligent design and technological leadership. Over the past 3 years, our country has clearly demonstrated its will to build a missile defense. I strongly suggest to you that we still need an intelligent design and technological leadership to build an effective defense.

NOTE

Speech delivered to the Council for National Policy, Colorado Springs, Colorado, September 26, 2003.

IS MISSILE DEFENSE ON TARGET?

PHILIP E. COYLE

The clock is ticking. Last December, President George W. Bush announced plans to begin deployment of a strategic nationwide missile defense system at Fort Greely, Alaska, by September 30, 2004. With less than a year left before that deadline, it is clear that the president's decision has drastically changed the priorities in the missile defense program and lowered the bar on the acceptable standards for an effective military system.

If the Bush administration's now anemic testing schedule continues on track, the United States is set to deploy a missile defense system that is simply not up to the job. The ground-based midcourse defense (GMD) system, as it is now called, has not shown that it can hit anything other than missiles whose trajectory and targets have been preprogrammed by missile defense contractors to eliminate the surprise or uncertainty of battle. Nor has it proven that it can hit a tumbling target, perform at night, or find ways to counter the decoys and countermeasures that a real enemy would use to throw a defense off track. Tests so far have all been conducted at unrealistically low speeds and altitudes, and it is not clear that the system will be able to track and identify the warhead it is supposed to destroy.

Such criticism is not partisan in nature. Bush's new testing schedule lacks not only the comprehensive tests planned by the Clinton administration, but even the testing objectives of Bush's first 2 years. Indeed, the Pentagon's current missile defense plan marks a radical shift from a half-century of military testing carried out under Republican and Democratic administrations alike.

After Bush's announcement, the missile defense program's priorities immediately switched from challenging and necessary testing to building facilities at Fort Greely and hauling hardware and equipment to Alaska. Since construction began on June 15, 2002, 550 acres have been cleared, at least 620,000 cubic yards of dirt have been removed, eleven buildings have been built, and twenty-five others refurbished. Six missile silos are to be completed by next February, ten more by the end of 2005, and as many as forty in the years to come. Yet the ability of the missile defense system to carry out its required tasks has barely inched forward.

BEFORE THE DEPLOYMENT DECISION

As envisioned, the GMD system is meant to consist of a set of silo-based interceptors, beginning with six at Fort Greely and four at Vandenberg Air Force Base in California. These interceptors are to carry infrared detectors capable of discriminating enemy warheads from decoys. The system is slated to include a mobile, sea-based, X-band radar, as well as fixed early warning radars at Shemya, at the end of the Aleutian chain, and at Beale Air Force Base near Sacramento, and warning radars in England and Greenland. It also is to use satellites with infrared detectors capable of distinguishing between launches of peaceful rockets and intercontinental ballistic missiles (ICBMs) and discriminating enemy warheads from decoys. Finally, the GMD system is supposed to have a complex battle management command and control system that includes a network of satellites and ground elements extending from Washington, D.C., to Alaska, including Cheyenne Mountain in Colorado and sites in California.

In developing a schedule to develop and test the components needed for this system, the president began with a system inherited from his predecessor. The GMD system has more than a passing resemblance to the National Missile Defense (NMD) system planned by President Bill Clinton to protect the United States from attack by long-range ballistic missiles. However, the GMD system is now only the centerpiece of the larger Bush Ballistic Missile Defense System (BMDS), a "layered" system intended to be capable of shooting down missiles in all phases of their flight—boost, midcourse, and terminal—and from platforms based on land, at sea, in aircraft, and in space.

During the first 2 years of the Bush administration, the Pentagon carried out a testing program that did not depart radically from its predecessor. To be sure, there were some changes. The Bush administration has conducted five flight intercept tests of the GMD system, as opposed to three flight intercept tests of the NMD system in the final 2 years of the Clinton administration. However, all of the flight intercept tests attempted in the first 2 years of the Bush administration were quite similar to tests during the Clinton years and did not push the state of the art as strongly as tests either planned or accomplished during the Clinton administration.

The Bush administration has shown some political wisdom in following a cautious script. Year after year, delays in the development program had stretched out the planned milestones, and mounting technical difficulties had shown that this program was no different than any other high-technology military development. It would not be surprising if it took a decade or more to develop an effective military capability.

This essay has been edited and is reprinted from Arms Control Today 33 *(October 2003): 7–14, by permission.*

Only 6 days before the president's deployment decision, the program had experienced yet another dramatic failure, when an interceptor "kill vehicle" failed to separate from its rocket booster. To the people doing the actual work, the last thing they expected was an order from the president to move the schedule for deployment to the left.

TESTING NOT ACCELERATED

Bush administration officials such as Lieutenant General Ronald Kadish, the head of the Missile Defense Agency (MDA), have sought to calm concerns expressed by Congress and the press by saying that the Pentagon would rev up the pace of testing to meet the president's goals. Yet overall, the pace of flight intercept tests and, most importantly the rate of successful flight intercept tests, has stayed about the same. Since the inception of flight intercept tests in October 1999, five successful intercepts have been carried out in eight attempts. That is a rate of about one success every 10 months. At that pace, it could take 10 or 15 years before the GMD system could pass the twenty or thirty developmental tests required before realistic operational testing could be conducted. Developmental tests, especially in the early years of a program, may be heavily scripted with unrealistic or artificial limitations. Operational testing, however, must be realistic, with the systems operated by real soldiers, sailors, airmen, or Marines, as they would be in battle.

Yet intent on deploying the system in time for the 2004 presidential elections, the Bush administration has sought to act as if the necessary milestones were unnecessary obstacles. Just look at how the Pentagon dealt with problems caused by the unreliable surrogate booster rocket used in the first eight flight intercept tests, as well as delays in the operational, production version needed to launch the "kill vehicle" to collide with incoming missiles in space: it simply cancelled nearly half of the intercept flight tests it had initially outlined. Unable to make the system square with the usual Pentagon definitions of military capable programs, the Department of Defense has dumbed down the requirements for a military effective program. Incapable of having key components such as an eagle-eyed X-band radar and flight sensors in place for the "deployment date," the Pentagon is ready to place the system on operational status even without the parts needed for it to be effective.

The problems began with the booster rockets. Booster development and testing alone has taken about 3 more years than planned. At one point in the schedule, booster development and testing were to have been completed in 2000, but that slipped to 2001 and now 2003. In the meantime, a surrogate rocket booster, a modified Minuteman ICBM used in all of the flight intercept tests, has been the direct cause of three major failures. So program officials saw little benefit in risking high-profile future tests on that booster. Pentagon officials are now counting on new prototypes from Lockheed Martin and Orbital Sciences Corporation. Both booster designs are likely to have only one intercept attempt each before they are deployed next fall as part of the GMD system.

Pentagon officials were able to celebrate a rare success in August, when Orbital Sciences successfully launched its booster carrying a mock kill vehicle. The Lockheed Martin design is awaiting a similar test as this article goes to press. But because of the absence of an effective booster, the testing of the overall GMD system has been set back.

Equally significant, some of the remaining flight intercept tests are gradually being downscaled from full flight intercept tests to "radar characterization" tests and other simulations that do not require the interceptor actually to hit its target. For example, two flight intercept tests planned to have been in the remaining months before deployment have been cancelled and replaced by nonintercept, radar characterization tests. Nor is much progress being demonstrated in the ability of the system to discriminate between actual enemy warheads and decoys and countermeasures.

Not only does the lack of stressing flight intercept tests undermine military effectiveness, it also weakens public accountability. Given MDA policy to classify information about these tests, it is difficult for Congress or the press to track, let alone confront, the agency's claims based on nonflight intercept tests, ground tests, or other simulations that do not involve the clear test of whether an interceptor hits its target.

EFFECTIVENESS STANDARDS

Last December, Secretary of Defense Donald Rumsfeld acknowledged that missile defenses would not be very good at first. The capability would not be defined by the classic military phrase "Interim Operational Capability"—namely something new with proven warfighting worth—but rather capability, as Rumsfeld put it, "with a small 'c'." Nevertheless, he said, even at first this new missile defense would be "better than nothing."

The president's decision to deploy missile defenses is a remarkable example of a new procurement philosophy at the Pentagon called "capability-based acquisition," which means the opposite of what it sounds like. The priority is on acquisition and deployment, not demonstrated, effective warfighting capability. In a sign of the times, last January, Joint Chiefs Chairman General Richard Myers circulated a new draft Instruction on the Joint Capabilities Integration and Development System that officially eliminates military requirements, replaces them with "capabilities," and talks about "crafting capabilities within the art of the possible."

In addition to speaking of capability-based acquisition, U.S. defense officials also talk in terms of spiral development or evolutionary acquisition. These terms are used more or less interchangeably and, except for the fact that they all describe an interactive approach for building capability, no one in the Pentagon seems to know what they really mean or how to implement them in practice.

The term "spiral development" originates with Professor Barry Boehm, director of the University of Southern California's Center for Software Engineering. In Boehm's model, rigorous testing is needed at each loop in the developmental process.[1] In the Defense Department, however, spiral development is seen as a way to avoid testing and to cut corners.

The traditional Defense Department approach—sometimes called "fly before buy"—is to wait to procure a new military system until it has successfully demonstrated that it can work in realistic operational tests designed to simulate real-world conditions. For major defense acquisition systems, the law prohibits full-rate production until the system has been through realistic operational testing and the results are reported to the secretary of defense and the U.S. Congress. If the added military utility turns out to be only marginal, such systems are usually cancelled.

But major military development programs can take decades and, in an attempt to speed the process, capability-based acquisition was conceived. Capability-based acquisition aims to streamline the process drastically by shortening development time and deciding to fund marginal improvements to military value that might not have been considered worthy of funding in the past.

However, as the president's missile defense decision shows, capability-based acquisition can mean buying new equipment that has not been through realistic operational testing and that offers little or no demonstrated military utility. Neither the GMD system, to be deployed near Fort Greely in Alaska, nor its sea-based adjuncts, to be deployed on Navy ships, has gotten far in its developmental testing; and neither has begun, let alone completed, more stressing and realistic operational tests. That is why the development and testing for both these systems—over the next 2 years and both before and after initial deployment in 2004—will be so important.

The shift to capability-based acquisition leads to confusion all the way around. For example, a recent General Accounting Office report[2] on the readiness of technology to support missile defense evaluated those technologies against a lesser standard than would be required actually to defend the United States from a realistic threat.

Rumsfeld cites the Predator Unmanned Aerial Vehicle as an example of this "capability-based" approach. In one sense it is not, because the Predator went through realistic operational testing more than 2 years ago. In another sense, however, the Predator is an ideal example of capability-based acquisition, in that it did not meet its military requirements in those tests, was found to be not effective and not suitable, and yet proved its worth in the wars in Afghanistan and in Iraq.[3] The Predator brings a new type of reconnaissance to the battlefield, and although that capability falls short of what its military users wanted and still want, it is much "better than nothing."

Of course, such judgments are relative. The current version of the Predator costs only about $3.5 million apiece, whereas the GMD system is estimated to cost at least $70 billion, although no one knows what the final bill will be.

THE PAC-3 MISSILE

However, the Patriot Advanced Capability 3 (PAC-3) illustrates a more traditional defense procurement cycle. Finished with a first phase of both developmental and operational testing, it is in low-rate production and was deployed in limited numbers in the Persian Gulf for use in the war in Iraq. Although it appeared to be doing well in developmental tests—hitting ten out of eleven targets—those early tests involved the usual artificialities of preplanned intercepts. In more realistic operational tests conducted last year, the PAC-3 hit only three targets out of seven tries, or less than 45 percent.

Even more critically, none of those tests included Scud missiles, its intended targets. Nor did any of the Patriot's successes in the recent war come against Scuds. If Saddam Hussein had the faster and longer-range Scud missiles, he never used them. So, the performance of the PAC-3 against Scuds has still not been demonstrated in combat and has not been tested at home. Otherwise, the results in Iraq so far appear to be consistent with the results from operational testing.

Recognizing that the PAC-3 requires further testing, the president's budget request for FY04 lays out another twenty-three new flight intercept tests to be conducted beginning in 2003 through 2006. The first of these will be developmental tests with more realistic operational tests to follow.

Yet proponents of missile defense have cited the "successes" of Patriot missiles in Iraq as proof that strategic missile defense can work as well. But if the Patriot turns out to have significant effectiveness, it will be mostly because of a firing doctrine that shoots two or three Patriot missiles at each incoming target. No tests of the GMD system have been conducted involving either multiple incoming targets nor multiple attempts to kill a single target. Also, an ICBM travels farther, faster, and at higher altitudes than such short-range tactical missiles as Scuds and may carry decoys and countermeasures.

Assuming the Bush administration goes ahead with deployment, following only one or two more flight intercept tests, what kind of system will we have?

At a Space and Missile Defense Conference last August, Major General John Holly, GMD program director, reportedly said the GMD system would initially have 70 percent of its required capability. Such a claim misleads Congress and the American taxpayer. In 2004, 70 percent of the major system elements required to find and discriminate targets will not be operational, and the GMD system will not have demonstrated the capability to shoot down 70 percent of enemy missiles launched toward the United States. For the GMD system to work in 2004, it requires the MDA getting advance notice from the enemy—say, North Korea. This is because the GMD system has never been tested without enemy target information being provided—and preprogrammed into the system—well in advance of interceptor launch and without an element of surprise. North Korea would probably not be so obliging.

TARGET DISCRIMINATION

Since the Union of Concerned Scientists Report on Countermeasures[4] was published in April 2000, the most persistent criticism of the GMD program is that it has not demonstrated that it can deal with even relatively simple countermeasures. Early tests included between one and three balloons that did not resemble the target reentry vehicle in signature, motion, or shape. Tests need to be done with decoys that resemble the target reentry vehicle in convincing ways. To be believable, the GMD program must demonstrate that when a decoy actually resembles the target reentry vehicle in some way, the Exoatmospheric Kill Vehicle (EKV) can still tell the difference. To do this, at the very least, the GMD program needs the combined capabilities of high-quality X-band radars, heat-sensing missile discriminating satellites, and interceptors with target discrimination capabilities as well. Problems continue in all three areas, meaning that if a "capability-based system" is deployed in 2004, it will have essentially no real capability.

X-BAND RADAR

During the Clinton administration, Lieutenant General Kadish told Congress that establishing an X-band radar on Shemya in Alaska was "the long pole in the tent" for the then-NMD system—that is, the X-band radar was pacing the overall deployment schedule. The X-band radar is needed to provide essential target tracking and countermeasures discrimination information to the interceptor missiles.

The Bush administration decided not to request funding for an X-band radar at Shemya and instead has let new contracts for a self-propelled, floating X-band radar to be deployed on a modified oil-drilling platform. The floating radar can engage a wider variety of missile flight test trajectories than a fixed radar at Shemya. But construction of the sea-based radar is not expected to be finished until 2005 and then must undergo 7 months of testing and be towed around South America to the Pacific Ocean because the huge platform will not fit through the Panama Canal.

SPACE-BASED INFRARED SATELLITES

The Space-Based Infrared Satellite (SBIRS) program has had two parts: SBIRS-high and SBIRS-low.

SBIRS-high is a replacement for the Defense Support Program (DSP) missile launch warning satellites, the first of which were deployed in the early 1970s. Over the years, at least twenty-three DSP satellites have been launched. SBIRS-high has fallen years behind schedule, and its cost estimate has increased from $4.1 billion to $8.5 billion with no satellites as yet launched.

SBIRS-low, a constellation of up to thirty satellites in low-Earth orbit, was to track and characterize enemy missiles and discriminate decoys from the target reentry vehicle in the target cluster for the GMD system. SBIRS-low has also fallen years behind schedule, and cost estimates have increased from about $10 billion to $23 billion. In 2002 the SBIRS-low program was restructured and renamed the Space Tracking and Surveillance System (STSS). The new name implies that the original discrimination objectives of SBIRS-low may not be met by STSS. Also, fewer satellites are being studied, and there is no official cost estimate for STSS. The MDA is studying STSS constellations of various sizes, for example nine, eighteen, or twenty-seven satellites, and the best way to obtain early test results from the first one or two satellites in orbit. But no operational testing is now slated until at least 2007.

Ironically, Bush's June 2002 abrogation of the 1972 U.S.-Russian Anti-Ballistic Missile (ABM) Treaty has raised questions over whether STSS should be built as planned. Without the constraints of the ABM Treaty, the United States can now deploy land- or sea-based missile-tracking radar systems close to perceived enemy countries, such as North Korea. The ABM Treaty did not permit forward-based missile tracking radars of this sort.

At a Senate hearing on April 9, 2003, MDA head Lieutenant General Kadish said the Pentagon was "rethinking the overall sensor requirements for a system without a treaty restriction." He further added that "there is a major debate inside the community over whether we should have space sensors or terrestrial-based radars or a combination of both, based on affordability reasons and a whole host of other technical issues." Such a debate, although welcome technically, means that the basic architecture of which STSS might be a part is undetermined and that a combined network of radars and infrared sensors on land, at sea, and in space certainly will not be operational in 2004, if this decade.

INTERCEPTOR TARGET DISCRIMINATION CAPABILITY

Because tests have not been done with decoys that resemble the target reentry vehicle in convincing ways, the interceptors have not yet been stressed to show that they can deal with such countermeasures. A tumbling target presents discrimination challenges in relation to other objects in the target cluster that may also be tumbling, such as the bus.

The last flight intercept attempt, IFT-10, which failed because the EKV did not separate from the booster, was to have been the first nighttime test, designed to show that GMD interceptors can discriminate objects under different lighting conditions. All of the previous flight intercept tests were conducted in daylight. Because IFT-10 failed for other reasons, nothing was learned about nighttime discrimination in this test. Surprisingly, the MDA may go ahead with deployment in 2004 without trying to repeat a nighttime test. Agency officials have said only that the possibility that one of two remaining flight intercept tests before deployment may be conducted at night is under consideration.

All of the flight intercept tests so far have included both a C-band beacon and a global positioning system (GPS) transponder on the target reentry vehicle. The interceptor's flight path is formulated using data derived from the C-band beacon onboard the target because there is no radar to track the target early in its flight. To be credible, the ground-based interceptor must eventually show that it can hit a target with no targeting aids onboard the target reentry vehicle.

All of the flight intercept tests so far have provided target information, such as its velocity and trajectory, to the interceptor before the intercept attempt. In actual combat, all of this information probably would not be available before interceptor launch. Tests need to be done that show that, if some or all of this advanced information is missing before launch, the interceptor can still successfully perform its mission.

In a recent report, the General Accounting Office also stated that the upgrade of the early warning radar at Shemya, called "Cobra Dane," as well as that of another early warning radar in California, will not be completed by October 2004. That will push even further into the future testing to demonstrate that these radars can process and communicate needed information in real time to other elements of the GMD system.

Without the discrimination capabilities of an X-band radar, SBIRS-high and STSS (SBIRS-low) or a combined land/sea/space radar network, along with interceptor missiles with demonstrated discrimination capability, the GMD system to be deployed in 2004 will not have the major elements needed to be operationally effective and would appear to be just for show.

BEYOND INITIAL
DEFENSIVE OPERATIONS

Even before the Bush administration has demonstrated that the initial GMD system works properly, it is planning even more ambitious deployments. According to the Pentagon, there will be significant "block upgrades" every 2 years through 2014.

In fact, in its budget request for FY04, the MDA describes its GMD program as part of "an integrated and evolutionary [BMDS] of initial modest capability." The agency explains that "while there is only one BMDS, there is no final or fixed missile defense architecture."

Adding another complication, administration officials have also said that they intend to build a "layered" system, capable of intercepting enemy missiles in all phases of flight—boost, midcourse, and terminal—and from platforms on land, at sea, from aircraft, and from space. The idea is that, if the interceptors in one layer miss their targets, the interceptors in subsequent layers will not.

The first step would be the deployment of as many as twenty missile interceptors to be placed on three Navy ships. Initially, the interceptors would be used only to guard against short- and medium-range missiles, as their interceptors will be too slow to be effective against the faster long-range missiles.

Pentagon officials acknowledge that such a sea-based system will not initially play a role in defending against long-range missiles. But they will be putting elements of the system in place beginning in 2005. The interceptors have scored three hits in four early intercept tests to date. Although the development of more powerful ship-based interceptors will take many years, the Pentagon still sees a useful role for ships in protecting against long-range missile threats. MDA officials would like the ships to serve as platforms for high-power phased-array radar systems that can be moved close to trouble spots, such as North Korea. That would allow them to help track an enemy ICBM early in its flight and relay that information to the battle command and control center or to a strategic missile interceptor in flight. Fifteen ships are to be upgraded with such advanced radar systems by the end of 2005.

CONCLUSION

Now, with only a year to go, the pressure is on. But difficulties in the development program and delays in the major elements of the GMD system have made it clear that, if anything is deployed next fall, it will be more of a scarecrow than a realistic or effective missile defense capability.

Accordingly, the president's decision to deploy the GMD system in Alaska by the end of FY04 has changed everything but changed nothing. To be sure, it has reordered the priorities for engineers and scientists working in the program, as well as curtailed realistic flight intercept testing and progress in target discrimination. It also has changed the standards of effectiveness that the program must achieve and has led to massive construction at Fort Greely.

The president's decision has also served to illustrate the problems with a capability-based approach to testing. As it is being implemented for missile defense, the new emphasis on capability-based acquisition means buying new equipment that has not been through realistic operational testing and that will have little or no demonstrated military utility in 2004. The Pentagon's most successful development programs, such as the satellite- and laser-guided precision weapons demonstrated in Iraq, continue to rely on rigorous testing. This includes the Patriot program, which is vastly improved since 1991 but is still imperfect. Moreover, the successes with the Patriot missile in Iraq against relatively slow, low-flying, short-range missiles do not mean that missile defense against ICBMs will quickly follow. The concepts may seem similar, but the missions and technical challenges are completely different.

So a choice must be made: Rumsfeld can either meet a political imperative by October 2004 or build a missile defense system that works. But the technical and operational challenges of an effective missile defense system are such that the Pentagon cannot do both.

NOTES

1. B. W. Boehm, "A Spiral Model of Software Development and Enhancement," *IEEE Computer* (May 1988): 61–72.

2. U.S. General Accounting Office, "Additional Knowledge Needed in Developing Systems for Intercepting Long-Range Missiles," AO 03-600 (Washington, D.C.: U.S. General Accounting Office, August 2003).

3. The military users wanted the Predator to be able to fly in less than ideal weather and at night, to provide reliable communications, to be able to complete flights without having to abort, and to meet its maintenance requirements so as not to add substantially to the burdens U.S. troops already face overseas. Also, the military users wanted better discrimination from the Predator's sensors. For example, in operational tests, the infrared sensor on the Predator only achieved a 5 percent probability of recognizing a tank, such as a Russian T-72 or U.S. M1A1 tank, compared with the desired, objective probability of 90 percent. The Predator also was unable to locate targets as accurately as required.

4. Andrew M. Sessler, et al., "Countermeasures: A Technical Evaluation of the Operational Effectiveness of the Planned U.S. National Missile Defense System" (Cambridge, Mass.: Union of Concerned Scientists/Massachusetts Institute of Technology, April 2000).

CHAPTER 13

HOMELAND SECURITY AND THE THREAT OF TERRORISM

RETHINKING TERRORISM AND COUNTERTERRORISM SINCE SEPTEMBER 11

BRUCE HOFFMAN

A few hours after the first American air strikes against Afghanistan began on October 7, 2001, a pre-recorded videotape was broadcast around the world. A tall, skinny man with a long, scraggly beard, wearing a camouflage fatigue jacket and the headdress of a desert tribesman, with an AK-47 assault rifle at his side, stood before a rocky backdrop. In measured, yet defiant, language, Osama bin Laden again declared war on the United States. Only a few weeks before, his statement would likely have been dismissed as the inflated rhetoric of a saber-rattling braggart. But with the World Trade Center now laid to waste, the Pentagon heavily damaged, and the wreckage of a fourth hijacked passenger aircraft strewn across a field in rural Pennsylvania, bin Laden's declaration was regarded with a preternatural seriousness that would previously have been unimaginable. How bin Laden achieved this feat, and the light his accomplishment sheds on understanding the extent to which terrorism has changed and, in turn, how our responses must change as well, is the subject of this essay.

THE SEPTEMBER 11 ATTACKS BY THE NUMBERS

The enormity and sheer scale of the simultaneous suicide attacks on September 11 eclipsed anything previously seen in terrorism. Among the most significant characteristics of the operation were its ambitious scope and dimensions; impressive coordination and synchronization; and the unswerving dedication and determination of the nineteen aircraft hijackers, who willingly and wantonly killed themselves, the passengers, and crews of the four aircraft they commandeered and the approximately three thousand persons working at or visiting both the World Trade Center and the Pentagon.

Indeed, in lethality terms alone, the September 11 attacks are without precedent. For example, since 1968, the year credited with marking the advent of modern, international terrorism, one feature of international terrorism has remained constant despite variations in the number of attacks from year to year. Almost without exception,[1] the United States has annually led the list of countries whose citizens and property were most frequently attacked by terrorists.[2] But, until September 11, over the preceding 33 years, a total of no more than perhaps one thousand Americans had been killed by terrorists either overseas or even within the United States itself. In less than 90 minutes that day, nearly three times that number were killed.[3] To put those uniquely tragic events in context, during the entirety of the twentieth century, no more than fourteen terrorist operations killed more than one hundred persons at any one time.[4] Or, viewed from still another perspective, until the attacks on the World Trade Center and Pentagon, no single terrorist operation had ever killed more than five hundred persons at one time.[5] Whatever the metric, therefore, the attacks that day were unparalleled in their severity and lethal ambitions.

Significantly, too, from a purely terrorist operational perspective, *spectacular* simultaneous attacks—using far more prosaic and arguably conventional means of attack (e.g., car bombs)—are relatively uncommon. For reasons not well understood, terrorists typically have not undertaken coordinated operations. This was doubtless less of a choice than a reflection of the logistical and other organizational hurdles and constraints that all but the most sophisticated terrorist groups are unable to overcome. Indeed, this was one reason why we were so galvanized by the synchronized attacks on the American embassies in Nairobi and Dar-es-Salaam 3 years ago. The orchestration of that operation, coupled with its unusually high death and casualty tolls, stood out in a way that, until September 11, few other terrorist attacks had. During the 1990s, perhaps only one other terrorist operation evidenced those same characteristics of coordination and high lethality: the series of attacks that occurred in Bombay in March 1993, when ten coordinated car bombings rocked the city, killing nearly three hundred people and wounding more than seven hundred others.[6] Apart from the attacks on the same morning in October 1983 of the U.S. Marine barracks in Beirut (241 persons were killed) and a nearby French paratroop headquarters (where sixty soldiers perished); the 1981 hijacking of three Venezuelan passenger jets by a mixed com-

This essay has been edited and is reprinted from Studies in Conflict and Terrorism 25:5 (2002): 303–16, *by permission of Taylor & Francis, Inc., www.routledge-ny.com. Copyright © 2002 Bruce Hoffman.*

mando of Salvadoran leftists and Puerto Rican *independistas;* and the dramatic 1970 hijacking of four commercial aircraft by the Popular Front for the Liberation of Palestine (PFLP), two of which were brought to and then dramatically blown up at Dawson's Field in Jordan, there have been few successfully executed, simultaneous terrorist spectaculars.[7]

Finally, the September 11 attacks not only showed a level of patience and detailed planning rarely seen among terrorist movements today, but the hijackers stunned the world with their determination to kill themselves as well as their victims. Suicide attacks differ from other terrorist operations precisely because the perpetrator's own death is a requirement for the attack's success.[8] This dimension of terrorist operations, however, arguably remains poorly understood. In no aspect of the September 11 attacks is this clearer than in the debate over whether all nineteen of the hijackers knew they were on a suicide mission or whether only the four persons actually flying the aircraft into their targets did. It is a debate that underscores the poverty of our understanding of bin Laden, terrorism motivated by a religious imperative in particular, and the concept of martyrdom.

The so-called *"Jihad Manual,"* discovered by British police in March 2000 on the hard drive of an al Qaeda member's computer, is explicit about operational security (OPSEC) in the section that discusses tradecraft. For reasons of operational security, it states, only the leaders of an attack should know all the details of the operation and these should only be revealed to the rest of the unit at the last possible moment.[9] Schooled in this tradecraft, the nineteen hijackers doubtless understood that they were on a one-way mission from the time they were dispatched to the United States. Indeed, the video tape of bin Laden and his chief lieutenant, Dr. Ayman Zawahiri, recently broadcast by the Arabic television news station al Jazeera, contains footage of one of the hijackers acknowledging his impending martyrdom in an allusion to the forthcoming September 11 attacks.

The phenomenon of martyrdom terrorism in Islam has of course long been discussed and examined. The act itself can be traced back to the Assassins, an off-shoot of the Shia Ismaili movement, who some 700 years ago waged a protracted struggle against the European Crusaders' attempted conquest of the Holy Land. The Assassins embraced an ethos of self-sacrifice, in which martyrdom was regarded as a sacramental act—a highly desirable aspiration and divine duty commanded by religious text and communicated by clerical authorities—that is evident today. An important additional motivation then as now was the promise that the martyr would feel no pain in the commission of his sacred act and would then ascend immediately to a glorious heaven, described as a place replete with "rivers of milk and wine . . . lakes of honey, and the services of 72 virgins," where the martyr will see the face of Allah and later be joined by seventy chosen relatives.[10] The last will and testament of Muhammad Atta, the ringleader of the September 11 hijackers, along with a "primer"

for martyrs that he wrote, entitled, "The Sky Smiles, My Young Son," clearly evidences such beliefs.[11]

Equally as misunderstood is the attention focused on the hijackers' relatively high levels of education, socioeconomic status, and stable family ties.[12] In point of fact, contrary to popular belief and misconception, suicide terrorists are not exclusively derived from the ranks of the mentally unstable, economically bereft, or abject, isolated loners. In the more sophisticated and competent terrorist groups, such as the Liberation Tigers of Tamil Eelam (LTTE, or Tamil Tigers), it is precisely the most battle-hardened, skilled, and dedicated cadre who enthusiastically volunteer to commit suicide attacks.[13] Observations of the patterns of recent suicide attacks in Israel and on the West Bank and Gaza similarly reveal that the bombers are not exclusively drawn from the maw of poverty, but have included two sons of millionaires. Finally, in the context of the ongoing Palestinian-Israeli conflict, suicide attacks—once one of the more infrequent (though albeit dramatic, and attention-riveting, tactics)—are clearly increasing in frequency, if not severity, assuming new and more lethal forms.

WHERE THE UNITED STATES WENT WRONG IN FAILING TO PREDICT THE SEPTEMBER 11 ATTACKS

Most importantly, the United States was perhaps lulled into believing that mass, simultaneous attacks in general and those of such devastating potential as seen in New York and Washington, D.C., on September 11 were likely beyond the capabilities of most terrorists—including those directly connected to, or associated with, Osama bin Laden. The tragic events of that September day demonstrate how profoundly misplaced such assumptions were. In this respect, the significance of past successes (e.g., in largely foiling a series of planned terrorist operations against American targets between the August 1998 embassy bombings to the November 2000 attack on the USS *Cole,* including more than sixty instances when credible evidence of impending attack forced the temporary closure of American embassies and consulates around the world) and the terrorists' own incompetence and propensity for mistakes (e.g., Ahmad Ressam's bungled attempt to enter the United States from Canada in December 1999) were perhaps overestimated. Both impressive and disturbing is the likelihood that there was considerable overlap in the planning for these attacks and the one in November 2000 against the USS *Cole* in Aden, thus suggesting al Qaeda's operational and organizational capability to coordinate major, multiple attacks at one time.[14]

Attention was also arguably focused too exclusively either on the low-end threat posed by car and truck bombs against buildings or the more exotic high-end threats, against entire societies, involving biological or chemical weapons or cyberattacks. The implicit assumptions of much of American planning scenarios on mass casualty attacks were that they would involve germ or chemical agents or result from widespread electronic attacks on critical infrastructure. It was therefore presumed that any conventional or less-extensive incident could be addressed simply by planning for the most catastrophic threat. This left a painfully vulnerable gap in antiterrorism defenses where a traditional and long-proven tactic —like airline hijacking—was neglected in favor of other, less conventional threats and where the consequences of using an aircraft as a suicide weapon seem to have been ignored. In retrospect, it was not the 1995 sarin nerve gas attack on the Tokyo subway and the nine attempts to use bioweapons by Aum that should have been the dominant influence on our counterterrorist thinking, but a 1986 hijacking of a TWA flight in Karachi, where the terrorists' intention was reported to have been to crash it into the center of Tel Aviv, and the 1994 hijacking in Algiers of an Air France passenger plane by terrorists belonging to the Armed Islamic Group (GIA), who similarly planned to crash the fuel-laden aircraft with its passengers into the heart of Paris. The lesson, accordingly, is not that there need be unrealistic omniscience, but rather that there is a need to be able to respond across a broad technological spectrum of potential adversarial attacks.

We also had long consoled ourselves—and had only recently began to question and debate the notion—that terrorists were more interested in publicity than killing and therefore had neither the need nor the interest in annihilating large numbers of people.[15] For decades, there was widespread acceptance of the observation made famous by Brian Jenkins in 1975 that, "Terrorists want a lot of people watching and a lot of people listening and not a lot of people dead."[16] Although entirely germane to the forms of terrorism that existed in prior decades, for too long this antiquated notion was adhered to. On September 11, bin Laden wiped the slate clean of the conventional wisdom on terrorists and terrorism and, by doing so, ushered in a new era of conflict.

Finally, before September 11, the United States arguably lacked the political will to sustain a long and determined counterterrorism campaign. The record of inchoate, unsustained previous efforts effectively retarded significant progress against this menace. The carnage and shock of the September 11 attacks laid bare America's vulnerability and too belatedly resulted in a sea change in national attitudes and accompanying political will to combat terrorism systematically, globally, and, most importantly, without respite.[17]

TERRORISM'S CEO

The cardinal rule of warfare, "know your enemy," was also violated. The United States failed to understand and comprehend Osama bin Laden: his vision, his capabilities, his financial resources, and acumen, as well as his organizational skills. The broad outline of bin Laden's curriculum vitae is by now well known: remarkably, it attracted minimal interest and understanding in most quarters prior to September 11.[18]

The scion of a porter turned construction magnate, whose prowess at making money was perhaps matched only by his countless progeny and devout religious piety, the young Osama pursued studies not in theology (despite his issuance of fatwas, or Islamic religious edicts), but in business and management sciences. Bin Laden is a graduate of Saudi Arabia's prestigious King Abdul-Aziz University, where in 1981, he obtained a degree in economics and public administration. He subsequently cut his teeth in the family business, later applying the corporate management techniques learned both in the classroom and on the job to transform the terrorist movement he founded, al Qaeda, into the world's preeminent terrorist organization.[19]

Bin Laden achieved this by cleverly combining the technological munificence of modernity with a rigidly puritanical explication of age-old tradition and religious practice. He is also the quintessential product of the 1990s and globalism. Bin Laden the terrorism CEO could not have existed—and thrived —in any other era. He was able to overcome the relative geographical isolation caused by his expulsion from the Sudan to Afghanistan, engineered by the United States in 1996, by virtue of the invention of the satellite telephone. With this most emblematic technological artifice of 1990s global technology, bin Laden was therefore able to communicate with his minions in real time around the world.[20] Al Qaeda operatives, moreover, routinely made use of the latest technology themselves: encrypting messages on Apple PowerMacs or Toshiba laptop computers, communicating via e-mail or on Internet bulletin boards, using satellite telephones and cell phones themselves, and, when traveling by air, often flying first class.[21] This "grafting of entirely modern sensibilities and techniques to the most radical interpretation of holy war," Peter Bergen compellingly explains in *Holy War, Inc.,* "is the hallmark of bin Laden's network."[22]

For bin Laden, the weapons of modern terrorism critically are not only the guns and bombs that they have long been, but the minicam, videotape, television, and the Internet. The professionally produced and edited 2-hour al Qaeda recruitment videotape that bin Laden circulated throughout the Middle East during the summer of 2001—which, according to Bergen, also subtly presaged the September 11 attacks —is exactly such an example of bin Laden's nimble exploitation of "twenty-first-century communications and weapons technology in the service of the most extreme, retrograde reading of holy war."[23] The tape, with its graphic footage of infidels attacking Muslims in Chechnya, Kashmir, Iraq, Israel, Lebanon, Indonesia, and Egypt; children starving under the yoke of U.N. economic sanctions in Iraq; and most vexatiously, the accursed presence of "Crusader" military forces in the holy land of Arabia, was subsequently converted to CD-ROM and DVD formats for ease in copying onto computers and loading onto the World Wide Web for still wider, global dissemination. An even more stunning illustration of his communications acumen and clever manipulation of media was the prerecorded, preproduced, B-roll, or video clip, that bin Laden had queued and ready for broadcast within hours of the commencement of the American air strikes on Afghanistan on Sunday, October 7.

In addition to his adroit marrying of technology to religion and of harnessing the munificence of modernity and the West as a weapon to be wielded against his very enemies, bin Laden has demonstrated uncommon patience, planning, and attention to detail. According to testimony presented at the trial of three of the 1998 East Africa embassy bombers in Federal District Court in New York last year by a former bin Laden lieutenant, Ali Muhammad,[24] planning for the attack on the Nairobi facility commenced nearly 5 years before the operation was executed. Muhammad also testified that bin Laden himself studied a surveillance photograph of the embassy compound, pointing to the spot in front of the building where he said the truck bomb should be positioned. Attention has already been drawn to al Qaeda's ability to commence planning of another operation before the latest one has been executed, as evidenced in the case of the embassy bombings and the attack 27 months later on the USS *Cole*. Clearly, when necessary, bin Laden devotes specific attention—perhaps even to the extent of micromanaging—various key aspects of al Qaeda "spectaculars." In the famous "home movie"/videotape discovered in an al Qaeda safe house in Afghanistan that was released by the U.S. government in December 2001, bin Laden is seen discussing various intimate details of the September 11 attack. At one point, bin Laden explains how "we calculated in advance the number of casualties from the enemy, who would be killed based on the position of the tower. We calculated that the floors that would be hit would be three or four floors. I was the most optimistic of them all . . . due to my experience in this field," alluding to his knowledge of construction techniques gleaned from his time with the family business.[25] Bin Laden also knew that Muhammad Atta was the operation's leader[26] and states that he and his closest lieutenants "had notification [of the attack] since the previous Thursday that the event would take place that day [September 11]."[27]

The portrait of bin Laden that thus emerges is richer, more complex, and more accurate than the simple caricature of a hate-filled, mindless fanatic. "All men dream: but not equally," T. E. Lawrence, the legendary Lawrence of Arabia, wrote. "Those who dream by night in the dusty recesses of their minds wake in the day to find that it was vanity: but the dreamers of the day are dangerous men, for they may act their dream with open eyes, to make it possible."[28] Bin Laden is indeed one of the dangerous men that Lawrence described. At a time when the forces of globalization, coupled with economic determinism, seemed to have submerged the role of the individual charismatic leader of men beneath far more powerful, impersonal forces, bin Laden has cleverly cast himself as a David against the American Goliath: one man standing up to the world's sole remaining superpower and able to challenge its might and directly threaten its citizens.

Indeed, in an age arguably devoid of ideological leadership, when these impersonal forces are thought to have erased the ability of a single man to affect the course of history, bin Laden—despite all efforts—managed to taunt and strike at the United States for years even before September 11. His effective melding of the strands of religious fervor, Muslim piety, and a profound sense of grievance into a powerful ideological force stands—however invidious and repugnant—as a towering accomplishment. In his own inimitable way, bin Laden cast this struggle as precisely the "clash of civilizations" that America and its coalition partners have labored so hard to negate. "This is a matter of religion and creed; it is not what Bush and Blair maintain, that it is a war against terrorism," he declared in a videotaped speech broadcast over al Jazeera television on November 3, 2001. "There is no way to forget the hostility between us and the infidels. It is ideological, so Muslims have to ally themselves with Muslims."[29]

Bin Laden, though, is perhaps best viewed as a "terrorist CEO": essentially having applied business administration and modern management techniques to the running of a transnational terrorist organization. Indeed, what bin Laden apparently has done is to implement for al Qaeda the same type of effective organizational framework or management approach adapted by corporate executives throughout much of the industrialized world. Just as large, multinational business conglomerates moved during the 1990s to flatter, more linear, and networked structures, bin Laden did the same with al Qaeda.

Additionally, he defined a flexible strategy for the group that functions at multiple levels, using both top-down and bottom-up approaches. On the one hand, bin Laden has functioned like the president or CEO of a large multinational corporation: defining specific goals and aims, issuing orders, and ensuring their implementation. This mostly applies to the al Qaeda "spectaculars": those high-visibility, usually high-value and high-casualty operations like September 11, the attack on the USS *Cole*, and the East Africa embassy bombings. On the other hand, he has operated as a venture capitalist: soliciting ideas from below, encouraging creative approaches and "out of the box" thinking, and providing funding to those proposals he thinks promising. Al Qaeda, unlike many other terrorist organizations, therefore, deliberately has no one, set modus operandi, making it all the more formidable. Instead, bin Laden encourages his followers to mix and match approaches: employing different tactics and different means of operational styles as needed. At least four different levels of al Qaeda operational styles can be identified:

1. *The professional cadre.* This is the most dedicated, committed, and professional element of al Qaeda: the persons entrusted with only the most important and high-value attacks—

in other words, the "spectaculars." These are the terrorist teams that are predetermined and carefully selected, are provided with very specific targeting instructions, and who are generously funded (e.g., to the extent that during the days preceding the September 11 attacks, Atta and his confederates were sending money back to their paymasters in the United Arab Emirates and elsewhere).

2. *The trained amateurs.* At the next level down are the trained amateurs. These are individuals much like Ahmed Ressam, who was arrested in December 1999 at Port Angeles, Washington, shortly after he had entered the United States from Canada. Ressam, for example, had some prior background in terrorism, having belonged to Algeria's GIA. After being recruited into al Qaeda, he was provided with a modicum of basic terrorist training in Afghanistan. In contrast to the professional cadre, however, Ressam was given open-ended targeting instructions before being dispatched to North America. All he was told was to attack some target in the United States that involved commercial aviation. Ressam confessed that he chose Los Angeles International Airport because at one time, he had passed through there and was at least vaguely familiar with it. Also, unlike the well-funded professionals, Ressam was given only $12,000 in "seed money" and instructed to raise the rest of his operational funds from petty thievery—for example, swiping cell phones and laptops around his adopted home of Montreal. He was also told to recruit members for his terrorist cell from among the expatriate Muslim communities in Canada and the United States. In sum, this was a distinctly more amateurish level of al Qaeda operations than the professional cadre deployed on September 11; Ressam clearly was far less steeled, determined, and dedicated than the hijackers proved themselves to be. Ressam, of course, panicked when he was confronted by a Border Patrol agent immediately upon entering the United States. By comparison, nine of the nineteen hijackers were stopped and subjected to greater scrutiny and screening by airport personnel on September 11. Unlike Ressam, they stuck to their cover stories, did not lose their nerve and, despite having aroused suspicion, were still allowed to board. Richard Reid, the individual who attempted to blow up an American Airlines passenger plane en route from Paris to Miami with an explosive device concealed in his shoe, is another example of the trained amateur. It should be emphasized, however, that as inept or even moronic as these individuals might appear, their ability to be lucky even once and then to inflict incalculable pain and destruction should not be lightly dismissed. As

distinctly second-tier al Qaeda operatives, they are likely seen by their masters as expendable: having neither the investment in training nor the requisite personal skills that the less numerous, but more professional, first-team al Qaeda cadre have.

3. *The local walk-ins.* These are local groups of Islamic radicals who come up with a terrorist attack idea on their own and then attempt to obtain funding from al Qaeda for it. This operational level plays to bin Laden's self-conception as a venture capitalist. An example of the local walk-in is the group of Islamic radicals in Jordan who, observing that American and Israeli tourists often stay at the Radison Hotel in Amman, proposed, and were funded by al Qaeda, to attack the tourists on the eve of the millennium. Another example is the cell of Islamic militants who were arrested in Milan in October 2001 after wiretaps placed by Italian authorities revealed discussions of attacks on American interests being planned in the expectation that al Qaeda would fund them.

4. *Like-minded insurgents, guerrillas, and terrorists.* This level embraces existing insurgent or terrorist groups who, over the years, have benefited from bin Laden's largesse and/or spiritual guidance; received training in Afghanistan from al Qaeda; or have been provided with arms, matériel, and other assistance by the organization. These activities reflect bin Laden's "revolutionary philanthropy": that is, the aid he provides to Islamic groups as part of furthering the cause of global jihad. Among the recipients of this assistance have been insurgent forces in Uzbekistan and Indonesia, Chechnya, and the Philippines, Bosnia, and Kashmir. This philanthropy is meant not only hopefully to create a jihad "critical mass" out of these geographically scattered, disparate movements, but also to facilitate a quid pro quo situation, in which al Qaeda operatives can call on the logistical services and manpower resources provided locally by these groups.

Underpinning these operational levels is bin Laden's vision, self-perpetuating mythology and skilled acumen at effective communications. His message is simple. According to bin Laden's propaganda, the United States is a hegemonic, status quo power; opposing change and propping up corrupt and reprobate regimes that would not exist but for American backing. Bin Laden also believes that the United States is risk and casualty averse and therefore cannot bear the pain or suffer the losses inflicted by terrorist attack. Americans and the American military, moreover, are regarded by bin Laden and his minions as cowards: cowards who only fight with high-tech, airborne-delivered munitions. The Red Army, he has observed, at least fought the mujahedin in Afghanistan on the ground; America, bin Laden has maintained, only fights from the air with cruise missiles and bombs. In this respect, bin Laden has often argued that terrorism works—especially against America. He cites the withdrawal of the U.S. Marines, following the 1983 barracks bombing, from the multinational force deployed to Beirut and how the deaths of eighteen U.S. Army Rangers (an account of which is described in the bestselling book by Mark Bowden, *Black Hawk Down*, and a film of the same title)—a far smaller number—prompted the precipitous U.S. withdrawal from Somalia a decade later.[30]

Finally, it should never be forgotten that some 20 years ago, bin Laden consciously sought to make his own mark in life as a patron of jihad—holy war. In the early 1980s, he was drawn to Afghanistan, where he helped to rally—and even more critically, fund—the Muslim guerrilla forces resisting that country's Soviet invaders. Their success in repelling one of the world's two superpowers had a lasting impact on bin Laden. To his mind, Russia's defeat in Afghanistan set in motion the chain of events that resulted in the collapse of the U.S.S.R. and the demise of communism. It is this same self-confidence coupled with an abiding sense of divinely ordained historical inevitability that has convinced bin Laden that he and his fighters cannot but triumph in the struggle against America. Indeed, he has often described the United States as a "paper tiger" on the verge of financial ruin and total collapse—with the force of Islam poised to push America over the precipice.

Remarkably, given his mind-set, bin Laden would likely cling to the same presumptions despite the destruction of the Taliban and liberation of Afghanistan during this first phase of the war against terrorism. To him and his followers, the United States is doing even more now than before to promote global stability (in their view, to preserve the status quo) and ensure the longevity of precisely those morally bankrupt regimes in places like Egypt, Saudi Arabia, the Gulf, Pakistan, and Uzbekistan, which bin Laden and his followers despise. In bin Laden's perception of the war in Afghanistan, most of the fighting has been done by the Northern Alliance—the equivalent of the native levies of imperial times; although instead of being led by British officers as in the past, they are now guided by U.S. military Special Operations personnel. Moreover, for bin Laden—like guerrillas and terrorists everywhere—not losing is winning. To his mind, even if terrorism did not work on September 11 in dealing the knockout blow to American resolve that bin Laden hoped to achieve, he can still persuasively claim to have been responsible for having a seismic effect on the United States, if not the entire world. Whatever else, bin Laden is one of the few persons who can argue that they have changed the course of history. The United States, in his view, remains fundamentally corrupt and weak, on the verge of collapse, as bin Laden crowed in the videotape released last year about the "trillions of dollars" of economic losses caused by the September 11 attacks. More recently, Ahmed Omar Sheikh, the chief

suspect in the killing of American journalist, Daniel Pearl, echoed this same point. While being led out of a Pakistani court in March, he exhorted anyone listening to "sell your dollars, because America will be finished soon."[31]

Today, added to this fundamental enmity is now the even more potent and powerful motivation of revenge for the destruction of the Taliban and America's "war on Islam." To bin Laden and his followers, despite overwhelming evidence to the contrary, the United States is probably still regarded as a "paper tiger," a favorite phrase of bin Laden's, whose collapse can be attained provided al Qaeda survives the current onslaught in Afghanistan in some form or another. Indeed, although weakened, al Qaeda has not been destroyed and at least some of its capability to inflict pain, albeit at a greatly diminished level from September 11, likely still remains intact. In this respect, the multiyear time lag of all prior al Qaeda spectaculars is fundamentally disquieting, because it suggests that some monumental operation might have already been set in motion just prior to September 11.

FUTURE THREATS AND POTENTIALITIES

Rather than asking what could or could not happen, it might be more profitable to focus on understanding what has not happened, for the light this inquiry can shed on possible future al Qaeda attacks. This approach actually remains among the most understudied and, in turn, conspicuous lacunae of terrorism studies. Many academic terrorism analyses—when they venture into the realm of future possibilities at all—do so only tepidly. In the main, they are self-limited to mostly lurid hypotheses of worst-case scenarios, almost exclusively involving chemical, biological, radiological or nuclear weapons (CBRN), as opposed to trying to understand why—with the exception of September 11—terrorists have only rarely realized their true killing potential.

Among the key unanswered questions are:

- Why haven't terrorists regularly used man-portable surface-to-air missiles (SAMs/MANPADS) to attack civil aviation?

- Why haven't terrorists employed such simpler and more easily obtainable weapons like rocket-propelled grenades (RPGs) to attack civil aviation by targeting planes while taking off or landing?

- Why haven't terrorists used unmanned drones or one-person ultralight or microlight aircraft to attack heavily defended targets from the air that are too difficult to gain access to on the ground?

- Why haven't terrorists engaged in mass simultaneous attacks with very basic conventional weapons, such as car bombs, more often?

- Why haven't terrorists used tactics of massive disruption—both mass transit and electronic (cyber)—more often?

- Why haven't terrorists perpetrated more maritime attacks, especially against cruise ships loaded with holidaymakers or cargo vessels carrying hazardous materials (e.g., liquefied natural gas)?

- Why haven't terrorists engaged in agricultural or livestock terrorism (which is far easier and more effective than against humans) using biological agents?

- Why haven't terrorists exploited the immense psychological potential of limited, discrete use of CBRN weapons and cyberattacks more often?

- Why haven't terrorists targeted industrial or chemical plants with conventional explosives in hopes of replicating a Bhopol with thousands dead or permanently injured?

- And, finally, why—again with the exception of September 11—do terrorists generally seem to lack the rich imaginations of Hollywood movie producers, thriller writers, and others?

Alarmingly, many of these tactics and weapons have, in fact, already been used by terrorists—and often with considerable success. The 1998 downing of a civilian Lion Air flight from Jaffna to Colombo by Tamil Tigers using a Russian-manufactured SA-14 is a case in point. The aforementioned series of car bombings that convulsed Bombay in 1993 is another. The IRA's effective paralyzing of road and rail-commuting traffic around London in 1997 and 1998 is one more as were the similar tactics used by the Japanese Middle Core to shut down commuting in Tokyo a decade earlier. And in 1997, the Tamil Tigers launched one of the few documented cyberterrorist attacks when they shut down the servers and e-mail capabilities of the Sri Lanka embassies in Seoul, Washington, D.C., and Ottawa. As these examples illustrate, terrorists retain an enormous capability to inflict pain and suffering without resorting to mass destruction or mass casualties on the order of the September 11 attacks. This middle range, between worst-case scenario and more likely means of attack is where the United States remains dangerously vulnerable. Terrorists seek constantly to identify vulnerabilities and exploit gaps in U.S. defenses. It was precisely the identification of this vulnerability in the middle range of America's pain threshold that led to the events of that tragic day.

CONCLUSION

Terrorism is perhaps best viewed as the archetypal shark in the water. It must constantly move forward to survive and indeed to succeed. Although survival entails obviating the governmental countermeasures designed to unearth and destroy the ter-

rorists and their organization, success is dependent on overcoming the defenses and physical security barriers designed to thwart attack. In these respects, the necessity for change to stay one step ahead of the counterterrorism curve compels terrorists to change—adjusting and adapting their tactics, modus operandi, and sometimes even their weapons systems as needed.[32] The better, more determined, and more sophisticated terrorists will therefore always find a way to carry on their struggle.

The loss of physical sanctuaries—the most long-standing effect that the U.S.-led war on terrorism is likely to achieve—will signal only the death knell of terrorism as it has been known. In a new era of terrorism, "virtual" attacks from "virtual sanctuaries," involving anonymous cyberassaults, may become more appealing for a new generation of terrorists unable to absorb the means and methods of conventional assault techniques as they once did in capacious training camps. Indeed, the attraction for such attacks will likely grow as American society itself becomes ever more dependent on electronic means of commerce and communication. One lesson from last October's anthrax cases and the immense disruption it caused the U.S. Postal Service may be to impel more rapidly than might otherwise have been the case the use of electronic banking and other online commercial activities. The attraction, therefore, for a terrorist group to bring down a system that is likely to become increasingly dependent on electronic means of communication and commerce cannot be dismissed. Indeed, Zawahiri once scolded his followers for not paying greater attention to the fears and phobias of their enemy, in that instance, Americans' intense preoccupation with the threat of bioterrorism. The next great challenge from terrorism may therefore be in cyberspace.

Similarly, the attraction to employ more exotic, however crude, weapons, such as low-level biological and chemical agents may also increase. Although these materials might be far removed from the heinous capabilities of true weapons of mass destruction (WMD), another lesson from last October's anthrax exposure incidents was that terrorists do not have to kill three thousand people to create panic and foment fear and insecurity: five persons dying in mysterious circumstances is quite effective at unnerving an entire nation.

This essay has discussed and hypothesized about terrorism. What, in conclusion, should be done about it? How should it be viewed? First, it should be recognized that terrorism is, always has been, and always will be instrumental: planned, purposeful, and premeditated. The challenge that analysts face is in identifying and understanding the rationale and "inner logic"[33] that motivates terrorists and animates terrorism. It is easier to dismiss terrorists as irrational homicidal maniacs than to comprehend the depth of their frustration, the core of their aims and motivations, and to appreciate how these considerations affect their choice of tactics and targets. To effectively fight terrorism, a better understanding of terrorists and terrorism must be gained than has been the case in the past.

Second, it must be recognized that terrorism is fundamentally a form of psychological warfare. This is not to say that people do not tragically die or that assets and property are not wantonly destroyed. It is, however, important to note that terrorism is designed, as it has always been, to have profound psychological repercussions on a target audience. Fear and intimidation are precisely the terrorists' timeless stock-in-trade. Significantly, terrorism is also designed to undermine confidence in government and leadership and to rent the fabric of trust that bonds society. It is used to create unbridled fear, dark insecurity, and reverberating panic. Terrorists seek to elicit an irrational, emotional response. Countermeasures therefore must be at once designed to blunt that threat but also to utilize the full range of means that can be brought to bear in countering terrorism: psychological as well as physical, diplomatic as well as military, economic as well as persuasion.

Third, the United States and all democratic countries that value personal freedom and fundamental civil liberties will remain vulnerable to terrorism. The fundamental asymmetry of the inability to protect all targets all the time against all possible attacks ensures that terrorism will continue to remain attractive to our enemies. In this respect, both political leaders and the American public must have realistic expectations of what can and cannot be achieved in the war on terrorism and, indeed, the vulnerabilities that exist inherently in any open and democratic society.

Fourth, the enmity felt in many places throughout the world toward the United States will likely not diminish. America is invariably seen as a hegemonic, status quo power, and even more so as the world's lone superpower. Diplomatic efforts, particularly involving renewed public diplomacy activities, are therefore needed at least to effect and influence successor generations of would-be terrorists, even if the current generation has already been missed.

Finally, terrorism is a perennial, ceaseless struggle. Although a war against terrorism may be needed to sustain the political and popular will that has often been missing in the past, war by definition implies finality. The struggle against terrorism, however, is never-ending. Terrorism has existed for 2,000 years and owes its survival to an ability to adapt and adjust to challenges and countermeasures and to continue to identify and exploit its opponent's vulnerabilities. For success against terrorism, efforts must be as tireless, innovative, and dynamic as those of the opponent.

NOTES

1. The lone exception was 1995, when a major increase in nonlethal terrorist attacks against property in Germany and Turkey by the Kurdistan Workers' Party (PKK) not only moved the United States to the number two position but is also credited with accounting for that year's dramatic rise in the total number of incidents from 322 to 440. See Office of the Coordinator for Counterterrorism, *Patterns of Global Terrorism 1999*, Publication 10321 (Washington, D.C.: U.S. Department of State, April 1996), 1.

2. Several factors can account for this phenomenon, in addition to America's position as the sole remaining superpower and leader of the free world. These include the geographical scope and diversity of America's overseas business interests, the number of Americans traveling or working abroad, and the many U.S. military bases around the world.

3. See "Timetables of the Hijacked Flights," in *Inside 9-11: What Really Happened,* reporters, writers, and editors of *Der Spiegel* magazine (New York: St. Martin's, 2002), 261–62.

4. Brian M. Jenkins, "The Organization Men: Anatomy of a Terrorist Attack," in *How Did This Happen? Terrorism and the New War,* ed. James F. Hoge, Jr., and Gideon Rose (New York: Public Affairs, 2001), 5.

5. Some 440 persons perished in a 1978 fire deliberately set by terrorists at a movie theater in Abadan, Iran.

6. Celia W. Dugger, "Victims of '93 Bombay Terror Wary of U.S. Motives," *New York Times* (September 24, 2001): A3.

7. Several other potentially high-lethality simultaneous attacks during the 1980s were averted. These include a 1985 plot by Sikh separatists in India and Canada to simultaneously bomb three aircraft while inflight (one succeeded: the downing of an Air India flight while en route from Montreal to London, in which 329 persons were killed); a Palestinian plot to bomb two separate Pan Am flights in 1982, and perhaps the most infamous and ambitious of all pre-September 11th incidents: Ramzi Ahmed Yousef's "Bojinka" plan to bring down twelve American airliners over the Pacific. See Jenkins, "The Organization Men," 6.

8. See Yoram Schweitzer, "Suicide Terrorism: Development and Main Characteristics," in *Countering Suicide Terrorism: An International Conference,* The International Policy Institute for Counter-Terrorism at the Interdisciplinary Center Herzliya (Jerusalem: Gefen, 2001), 76.

9. See bin Laden's comments about this on the videotape released by the U.S. government in November 2001, a verbatim transcript of which is reproduced in ibid., 313–21.

10. "Wedded to Death in a Blaze of Glory—Profile: The Suicide Bomber," *Sunday Times* (London) (March 10, 1996); and Christopher Walker, "Palestinian 'Was Duped into Being Suicide Bomber'," *Times* (London) (March 27, 1997).

11. See *Inside 9-11,* 304–13.

12. See, for example, Jenkins, "The Organization Men," 8.

13. See in particular the work of Dr. Rohan Gunaratna of St. Andrews University in this area and specifically his "Suicide Terrorism in Sri Lanka and India," in *Countering Suicide Terrorism,* 97–104.

14. It is now believed that planning for the attack on an American warship in Aden harbor commenced some 2 to 3 weeks before the August 1998 attacks on the East Africa embassies. Discussion with U.S. Naval Intelligence Service agent investigating the USS *Cole* attack (December 2001).

15. See Steven Simon and Daniel Benjamin, "America and the New Terrorism," *Survival* 42 (Spring 2000): 59–75; and Olivier Roy, Bruce Hoffman, Reuven Paz, Steven Simon and Daniel Benjamin, "America and the New Terrorism: An Exchange," *Survival* 42 (Summer 2000): 156–72. Simon and Benjamin aver that I had become "too closely bound to the academic fashion of the moment" (page 171). As I told both Simon and Benjamin after September 11, their observation was indeed correct.

16. Brian Michael Jenkins, "International Terrorism: A New Mode of Conflict," in *International Terrorism and World Security,* ed. David Carlton and Carlo Schaerf (London: Croom Helm, 1975), 15.

17. See, for example, the discussion of two former members of the U.S. National Security Staff, Daniel Benjamin and Steven Simon, on the effects of the al-Shifa on the Clinton Administration and its counterterrorism policy after the August 1998 embassy bombings. Daniel Benjamin and Steven Simon, "A Failure of Intelligence?" in *Striking Terror: America's New War,* ed. Robert B. Silvers and Barbara Epstein (New York: New York Review of Books, 2002), 279–99.

18. It should be noted that on many occasions, the Director of Central Intelligence, George Tenent, warned in congressional testimony and elsewhere of the profound and growing threat posed by bin Laden and al Qaeda to U.S. national security.

19. See Peter L. Bergen, *Holy War, Inc.: Inside the Secret World of Osama bin Laden* (New York: Free Press, 2001), 14–15.

20. Bruce Hoffman, "Terrorism's CEO: An On-Line Interview with Peter Bergen, author of *Holy War, Inc.*" (January 2002) at www.theatlantic.com.

21. Bergen, *Holy War, Inc.*, 28.

22. Ibid., 28.

23. Ibid., 27.

24. Ali Muhammad, a former major in the Egyptian Army, enlisted in the U.S. Army, where he served as a noncommissioned officer at Fort Bragg, North Carolina, teaching U.S. Special Forces about Middle Eastern culture and politics. Muhammad, among other al Qaeda operatives, like Wadi el-Hoge, demonstrates how al Qaeda found the United States a comfortable and unthreatening operational environment. See Hoffman, "Terrorism's CEO," www.theatlantic.com/unbound/interviews/int2002-01-09.html.

25. *Inside 9-11,* 317.

26. Ibid., 319.

27. Ibid., 317.

28. T. E. Lawrence, *Seven Pillars of Wisdom* (Harmondsworth: Penguin Books, 1977), 23.

29. Neil MacFarquhar with Jim Rutenberg, "Bin Laden, in a Taped Speech, Says Attacks in Afghanistan Are a War against Islam," *New York Times* (November 4, 2001): B2.

29. Mark Bowden, *Black Hawk Down: A Story of Modern War* (New York: Atlantic Monthly Press, 1999).

31. Raymond Bonner, "Suspect in Killing of Reporter Is Brash and Threatening in a Pakistani Court," *New York Times* (March 13, 2002): A14.

32. Bruce Hoffman, *Inside Terrorism* (London and New York: Orion and Columbia University Press, 1998), 180–83.

33. My colleague at St. Andrews University, Dr. Magnus Ranstorp's, formulation.

COMBATING TERRORISM: WITH A HELMET OR A BADGE?

JEFFREY H. NORWITZ

Washington, D.C.: In a surprise development that has the Justice Department spinning, Saudi dissident and wanted terrorist Osama bin Laden appeared today at Washington, D.C., police headquarters accompanied by a team of defense lawyers. His attorneys told stunned police officials that bin Laden wished to surrender to law enforcement authorities. Bin Laden, who has been chased all over the world following his 1998 federal indictment for the dual embassy bombings in Africa as well as his alleged involvement for September 11 terrorist attacks, said he'd been hiding in Iranian caves ever since American military assaults on Afghanistan. He decided to turn himself in rather than continue to evade U.S. Special Forces who "wanted him dead—not alive." His defense team refused to reveal how bin Laden, on the FBI's ten-most-wanted-list, managed to make his way into the country undetected. They demanded safety for their client while in detention and, assuming bin Laden would not be afforded bail, insisted on his right to a speedy trial. A Justice Department lawyer who requested anonymity told reporters that in the coming weeks, bin Laden's lawyers will probably move for full discovery of all evidence, testimony, witness identities, and details of the prosecution case. Additionally, anticipating that some of the evidence is classified, bin Laden's defense team may move to be given security clearances as well as for their defendant, so he*

This essay has been edited and is reprinted from Journal of Homeland Security *(August 2002), www.homelandsecurity.org/journal. Copyright © Jeffrey H. Norwitz.*

can assist in his own defense. Exercising due process provisions, bin Laden's defense team can be expected to force the prosecution to reveal sensitive criminal and intelligence leads or risk dismissal of charges. Furthermore, through the process of voir dire, designed to elicit information about prospective jurors so attorneys can challenge members to find the most receptive audience, Justice lawyers are afraid that the Defense will try to shape the jury with members who are amenable to bin Laden's cause.[1] In one nightmarish scenario that has the attorney general scrambling, the accused terrorist and murderer of over five thousand people may claim it is impossible to receive a fair trial, and challenge the justice system to relocate the trial where the population has no preconceived ideas about the September 11 attack, if that is even possible. If not, the Defense has a good foundation for appealing any conviction based on "an inability to receive a fair trial." According to an experienced attorney with the Justice Department, "This case will bounce from one judicial stage to another until the concept of justice becomes secondary to procedure. A trial court is simply not suited for dealing with this sort of legal quandary posed by prosecuting such a defendant." Initial defense efforts to suppress evidence are already scheduled for pretrial motions next month.

How prepared are we for such a development? Is this the way the American public expects terrorists to be handled? Is this the sort of "war" that President Bush envisioned? A war of words, semantics, legal parsing of statutory phrases and Constitutional rights granted to a murderous zealot who despises the very nation that grants him these rights? It is time to consider very carefully how this nation goes about waging war on terrorism. Which is it? Is terrorism a crime to be fought with search warrants and jurisprudence, or is it an act of war, as President Bush has affirmed? If criminalists with a badge are the warriors, then the battlefield will look very much like this fictitious account.

The American public was galvanized by the events of September 11. Military members mourned lost Pentagon comrades but became resolute, as the president said, "I have a message for our military: Be ready."[2] Meanwhile, our leaders in Washington demonstrated bipartisanship and genuine unity in the face of the largest terrorist attack ever on United States' soil. Indeed, the word "war" became commonplace in media and government lexicon, and citizens, political leaders, and the military became energized.

Curiously, as talk of military mobilization permeated the media, we heard of Herculean law enforcement efforts by thousands of federal, state, and local officers to gather physical evidence, execute search warrants, and run thousands of leads seeking to establish criminal culpability for this atrocity. This essay will examine old paradigms about terrorism and offer a perspective on how criminal approaches have not grasped the nature of this war.

WORDS HAVE MEANING

When viewed legally, terrorism will always be a crime, regardless if the act is a murder, hijacking, kidnapping, or bombing. Within legal vernacular, terrorist crimes have "elements of the offense," each of which must be proven beyond a reasonable doubt; venue must be established to determine the appropriate court to hear the case; finally, if convicted, a defendant will be sentenced in accordance with precedent, and appeals can run their course as well. As viewed through a political lens, terrorism is a tool of nonstate or state actors, driven by religious or political ideation designed to manipulate governments and politics through violence. Consequently, terrorism can be dealt with either as a crime or as an attack on the body politic. Because defeating terrorism is clearly in our national interest, all elements of power (diplomatic, economic, and military) ought to be employed.

In defining the nature of war, Clausewitz held, "war is not a mere act of policy but a continuation of political activity by other means." Terrorism is political activity and the terrorist has chosen to make a political statement using violence. To further clarify what war is, consider Clausewitz's observation, "The political objective is the goal, war is the means of reaching it, and means can never be considered in isolation from their purpose."[3] In other words, war is a means toward a political end and, correspondingly, terrorism is war.

Differing definitions confuse the question of whether terrorism is a crime or an act of war. The Defense Department defines terrorism as "The *calculated* [emphasis added] use of violence or threat of violence to inculcate fear; intended to coerce; or to intimidate governments or societies in the pursuit of goals that are generally political, religious, or ideological."[4] In contrast, the Justice Department's definition includes "the *unlawful use* [emphasis added] of force or violence against persons or property to intimidate or coerce a government, the civilian population, or any segment thereof, in furtherance of political objectives."[5] Words mean something and the differences are striking.

The Defense Department regards terrorism as a "calculated" act. The identity of the actor is irrelevant. It could just as well be an individual or a nation-state. Additionally, there is no suggestion of illegality —just that the act be purposeful as opposed to an accident, and intended to intimidate or coerce governance. Implicit in the Justice Department's definition of terrorism is the concept of illegality, which clearly empowers Justice, via the Federal Bureau of Investigation (FBI), to take the lead in a terrorist incident. Thereafter, the best forensic science and investigative resources are secured enabling leads to be disseminated and results analyzed among countless law enforcement agencies. But consider for a moment the statutory guidelines, jurisdictional limitations, and laws of jurisprudence that must be adhered to in the legal rubric.

Because the objective of a criminal investigation is successful prosecution, all law enforcement effort must withstand judicial scrutiny at trial. Provisions of Articles IV, V, and VI of the U.S. Constitution, as well as the Bill of Rights, offer powerful protections against law enforcement excess that, by extension, applies to international terrorists operating on our soil. Moreover, every decision made by investigators will be reviewed for compliance with legal precedent from countless prior decisions with mindnumbing attention to detail. Any procedural error, intentional or otherwise, will be cause for suppression of evidence or testimony. And what about differing legal structures between allied nations in countering terrorism? Evidence obtained by one nation's police may not meet the standards for admissibility into the court system of a partnered nation. Likewise, will admissions of guilt be universally accepted in all courts regardless of which police conducted the questioning? Even if a conviction is obtained, the criminal justice system still will go over everything on appeal with the threat of a reversal of the first verdict. Is this the way we want to wage war on terrorists? Not according to a recent commission's findings.

FEDERAL COMMISSION FINDINGS

The National Commission on Terrorism was established by Congress in 1999 with the appointment of ten commissioners (all eminently qualified), who, after a series of hearings and international visits, produced a report relative to new and emerging threats of international terrorism.[6] One of the commission's recommendations was to "pursue a more aggressive strategy against terrorism." Critical analysis was given to the question of whether terrorism should best be handled as a criminal matter, suggesting a new paradigm which would give Defense a much greater leadership role in the event of a catastrophic terrorist attack. The members of the commission held that law enforcement tools were not adequate to address international terrorism. According to the commission:

Law enforcement is designed to put individuals behind bars, but is not a particularly useful tool for addressing actions by states. The Pan Am 103 case demonstrates the advantages and limitations of the law enforcement approach to achieve national security objectives. The effort to seek extradition of the two intelligence operatives implicated most directly in the bombing gained international support for economic sanctions that a more political approach may have failed to achieve. The sanctions and the resulting isolation of Libya may have contributed to the reduction of Libya's terrorist activities. On the other hand, prosecuting and punishing the two low-level operatives for an act almost certainly directed by Qaddafi is a hollow victory, particularly if the trial results in his implicit exoneration.

As it happened, only one of the Libyan defendants acting on behalf of the state intelligence service was convicted and the other freed without implication of Qaddafi himself—a hollow victory indeed.[7]

In yet another example of apparent ineptitude of a police response to terrorism, research by *The Christian Science Monitor* disclosed that in the 6 months following September 11, criminalists in the United States and Europe arrested nearly 1,400 people in connection with the attacks but they charged only one. Moreover, no al Qaeda cells have been uncovered in the United States.[8] Recent revelation of the May 8 Chicago arrest of New York–born Jose Padilla (also known as Abdullah al Muhajir) for his part in planning a possible bombing attack on behalf of al Qaeda is evidence of the value of militarily obtained intelligence employed to intercept a terrorist attack. Indeed, Padilla is being treated as an "enemy combatant" by the Justice Department and sent to a military jail in South Carolina.[9]

The most recent government statistics concerning criminal prosecutions of terrorism cases are more encouraging; however, are they meaningful? In the 12 months following September 2001, federal prosecutors charged 1,208 defendants with a variety of crimes they concluded were related to terrorism or internal security. There were only 115 such crimes in the 12 months prior to September 11. Yet, the median prison term before September 11 was 21 months, whereas subsequently the prison sentence was 2 months.[10] Why the decrease in punishment at a time when terrorism is such a high priority? Perhaps the answer can be found by looking at the Justice Department's expanded definition of terrorism-related prosecutions, which include identity theft and immigration matters. Although a false ID case may occasionally be of great significance, these kinds of matters have never before been classified as terrorism. The soaring number of prosecutions and the declining length of sentences merely reflect a shift in what kinds of behavior the government considers under terrorism and internal security laws.[11]

While distinguishing terrorism as a crime or an act of war, Stephen Gale, a counterterrorism expert who teaches at the University of Pennsylvania, points out, "if you think someone is going to take out your electrical grid, in a criminal investigation you arrest him. In a war you shoot first and ask questions later."[12] Michael Clarke, head of the Centre for Defense Studies at London University observes, "Terrorism poses a fundamental challenge to the legal system. Terrorists often do nothing indictable till they commit the act. Ninety percent of the time sleepers are absolutely legal, so you can't do anything about them even if you know who they are. Terrorism challenges our categories of what is legal and what is illegal."[13]

The National Commission on Terrorism's findings highlighted unrecognized Pentagon organizational and resource strengths as they relate to terrorism:

The U.S. Government's plans for a catastrophic terrorist attack on the United States do not employ the full range of the Department of Defense's (DoD's) capabilities for managing large operations. Additionally, the interagency coordination and cooperation required to integrate the DoD properly into counterterrorism planning has not been accomplished. The DoD's ability to command and control vast resources for dangerous, unstructured situations is unmatched by any other department or agency. According to current plans, DoD is limited to supporting the agencies that are currently designated as having the lead in a terrorism crisis . . . FBI and FEMA. But, when a catastrophe is directly related to an armed conflict overseas, the President may want to designate DoD as a lead federal agency.

Missing from the commission's report, but of equal significance, is the Department of Defense's ability to compile worldwide intelligence from an array of sources unavailable to civilian law enforcement. Moreover, given the military intelligence community's system of satisfying diverse intelligence requirements, the infrastructure to do the same with terrorism is a DoD strength—and without the dilemma of testimonial scrutiny at a later time. Does that mean that military operations are free from legal constraint? Of course not.

MILITARY LIMITED

There is an ethos in America, rooted in our birth as a nation, that standing armies are a threat to governments, unless they are at war. Whig politics of the early American Colonies held that when conflict is finished, so should be the standing army. Whigs believed that a standing military force in time of peace was a threat to liberty.[14] Evolution and compromise obviously modified that dismal view of standing armies; however, the framers of the Constitution still wanted to limit the military's authority over the population, and our citizenry today holds that protection dear. Three documents with presidential or Congressional authorship seek to ensure legal limits of military power.

The Posse Comitatus Act is codified in law under 18 U.S.C. 1385 and explicitly prohibits, unless with presidential intervention, using the armed forces to execute laws upon the citizenry.[15] Executive Order 12333 (U.S. Intelligence Activities), provides presidential endorsement to the limits of all intelligence activity, military and otherwise. The purpose of EO 12333 is to balance constitutional protections against the need for timely and accurate information about the activities, capabilities, plans, and intentions of foreign powers, organizations, and persons.[16] Furthermore, EO 12333 provides succinct, specific, and strong language relative to what DoD agencies may and may not do concerning intelligence activities. Last, Presidential Decision Directive 39 (U.S. Policy on Counterterrorism) lays out roles and missions for federal agencies, including the Department of Defense.[17]

As the bulwark of protection for citizens against military abuse, these three documents provide a tremendous check-and-balance on what our armed forces can do domestically in performing Homeland Security missions. In contrast to fears of rampant military disregard for legal framework and citizens' rights, our courts are very attuned to permissible conduct, and so are today's military commanding officers and service personnel. Presently, the Pentagon has already embraced urban warfare in training and doctrine resulting in exemplary skills dealing with such a challenging environment.[18] If there are legal limits on the military's activity at home, what sort of guidelines exist for military operations on foreign soil?

The legalities of employing U.S. armed forces in foreign countries to battle terrorism are complex. Military operations abroad must complement, and be coordinated with, the strategic use of diplomatic and economic elements of national power. Likewise, if force is envisioned where casualties and property destruction are likely, the Law of Armed Conflict will limit military action to that which is necessary, reasonable, and justified.[19]

Armed conflict is not the end of law. It is in fact the beginning of a different legal status as it relates to how belligerents behave. Two legal terms underscore the dimension to which the Law of Armed Conflict is codified. *Jus ad bellum* is the law that defines whether the conflict has a legal basis to happen in the first place. *Jus in bello* is the law that outlines what actions in war are legal in and of themselves. Clearly, war is not the absence of legal restraint, nor does war condone uncontrolled maniacal behavior. War crimes tribunals are evidence that the world will not stand for unconstrained military devastation. Any suggestion of unbridled American military vigilantes, ranging the globe on vendettas, is unsupportable.

AMERICAN PERCEPTIONS

The American public has long held that terrorism was something which happened elsewhere. Former Secretary of State George Shultz theorized that our nation's threat was "99 percent overseas" and empirical data suggested this to be true.[20] When one looks at statistics for the 1970s and 1980s, international terrorist incidents varied annually from the middle four hundred to more than six hundred events. Occurrences lessened in the late 1980s; however, following the Gulf War, the number rose to over 560. By 1996, international terrorist incidents diminished to less than three hundred a year.[21]

While the world experienced a statistical rollercoaster of terrorist incidents, the number of domestic episodes remained startlingly low. America's premier law enforcement community of federal, state, and local authorities was touted as having halted terrorism at our borders and with that apparent achievement, law enforcement also took on the responsibility of consequence response in the event of a rogue attack. The Federal Emergency Management Agency (FEMA) seemed the likely candidate for coordination of national assets, and local and state agencies looked to FEMA for direction. Naturally, FEMA turned to the Army for resources, training, and actual response capability, seeing the Army as possessing the greatest disaster response, which, not surprisingly, replicated the mayhem of warfare. Meanwhile, many Americans developed an artificial sense that somehow, our guardian oceans would keep harm from our shores, as historically was the case. Terrorism experts, however, warned this sense of safety was fictional because of broadened economic globalization and ease of world travel. September 11 proved them correct.

Nevertheless, what worked in the past seemed adequate to ensure domestic tranquility, especially in light of competing demands for scarce federal resources. The Pentagon was committed elsewhere, and terrorism remained the domain of law enforcement. Americans expected terrorism to remain an overseas dilemma, and the public expected police to be the key protector of the homeland.

WHAT IS OUR EXPERIENCE?

How did our country come to deal with terrorism this way? Upon assuming office, President Reagan was deeply affected by the Carter administration's struggle against international terrorism and as a result, was determined to deploy the traditional elements of national power to defeat the terrorist menace. Economic measures, diplomatic mechanisms, and military force were the tools that supported Reagan's strategy. During the early Reagan years, terrorism became synonymous with warfare, particularly after 241 Marines and other servicemen were killed in Beirut by a terrorist truck bomb on October 23, 1983.[22]

Despite early military victories, such as airstrikes against Libya and the capture of Abu al Abbas, responsible for the *Achille Lauro* hijacking, other driving factors undermined America's military assault on terrorism. Reagan's use of military force against terrorists was curtailed when it appeared we had traded weapons for hostages during Iran-Contra, thereafter diminishing our credibility with other nations as a consequence of our deal with Tehran. Accordingly, military strategies became almost impossible to execute because of reduced international support and, as a consequence, American counterterrorist emphasis returned to a law enforcement and judicial one. Military involvement in counterterrorism dwindled as criminalists took over. Yet, one dilemma remained: the lack of intelligence haunted the battle against terrorism and, indeed, continues today.

Good intelligence is the cornerstone for dealing effectively with terrorism, and the U.S. intelligence community, heavily dependent on superb technical collection means, is almost omniscient. Unfortunately, terrorists do not tend to be vulnerable to technical collection, owing to their disparate, celllike nature and veiled operational profile, thereby thwarting photographic and signals exploitation. Human intelligence collection (HUMINT) is the most effective source but also the most difficult to obtain. Frequently, terrorist cells have familial foundations and are extremely difficult to penetrate. Unfortunately, American HUMINT capabilities were severely diminished during the 1970s and 1980s when, responding to public outcry about the sometimes "dirty" nature of recruiting intelligence operatives, the Central Intelligence Agency (CIA) changed vetting practices disallowing its agents to enlist sources with dubious backgrounds.[23] Furthermore, would intelligence agents be required to testify as to how they obtained information? For instance, would techniques of handling clandestine sources be subject to judicial scrutiny and rules of evidence admissibility? How could a legal case be prosecuted when "chain-of-custody," a judicial requirement to establish "authenticity" of evidence, cannot be demonstrated for bomb making gear supplied by a double agent? If law enforcement captured a terrorist, would they face their accuser and have the benefit of legal representation? Lastly, the rise of "leaderless resistance," a concept of independent action encouraging unitary but coordinated violence, has also severely limited American counterterrorist efforts.[24]

By 1990, with the fight against terrorism returned to the law enforcement world, the military went back about its business of fighting and winning the nation's wars, and also being relegated to a "supporting" role in counterterrorism. However, the paradigm of FBI-led primacy in the fight against terrorism took a new shift on September 21, 2001 when President Bush addressed Congress and the American people to explain a new war on terrorism. According to the president and congressional sentiment, the military seemed again to be the tool of choice.

PRESENT DRIVING FORCES

Released just 7 months before the terrorist attack of September 11, The U.S. Commission on National Security/21st Century, popularly called the "Hart-Rudman Commission," after its chairs, issued their report, *Road Map for National Security: Imperative for Change*. In it, the commission made some startlingly prophetic observations about the preparedness of the United States to deal with a catastrophic terrorist attack. One of the key findings is related to "organizational realignment," in a subchapter of the same title. Therein is suggested the creation of the National Homeland Security Agency, with cabinet-level status and direct responsibility to the president. The commission's findings included minimizing the Justice Department and FBI's leadership role in homeland defense and increasing Defense's profile across the range of mission tasks.[25]

Likewise, increased priority of homeland security is reflected in the Quadrennial Defense Review (QDR) Report, which lays out the DoD vision for future force structure and strategy. The QDR "restores the defense of the United States as the Department's primary mission."[26] Furthermore, the Pentagon acknowledges that preparing for homeland security will impact organization and structure of future forces, as well as redefined expectations of reserve and active components. Indeed, the newly issued Unified Command Plan established Northern Command (NORTHCOM) as a separate combatant command to provide a more coordinated approach for military support to homeland defense civil authorities.[27] As a road map for national military strategy, the QDR points out, "the U.S. military will be prepared to respond in a decisive manner to acts of international terrorism committed on U.S. territory or the territory of an ally." The Department of Defense's vision for the future unequivocally includes the war on terrorism.

On War, Clausewitz's seminal work, states war is successfully waged only when there is a synergy between the government, the military, and the will of the people. Support of all three is necessary for victory.[28] Likewise, Clausewitz observes that organized warfare between great powers has a construct which can be studied, albeit sometimes clouded by fog and friction of battle. He also comments on the fortunes of a war against the likes of modern terrorists, suggesting that poor political understanding and a constrained military policy will play into the hands of an enemy without rules or moral limitations. As if predicting the difficulty of facing terrorism, Clausewitz observed, "woe to the government, which, relying on half-hearted politics and a shackled military policy, meets a foe who, like the untamed elements, knows no law other than his own power."[29]

Colin Gray, professor of International Politics and director of the Centre for Strategic Studies at the University of Reading, England, supports the idea that terrorists are enemy soldiers and not criminals, but he points out, "If we redefine what the concept and the legal idea of 'war' encompasses, then so also will we have to redefine who can wage it legitimately."[30] Indeed, the matter of militarily captured terrorists in Afghanistan challenged our concept of war-time prisoners and whether they could be questioned about terrorist activity. If interrogated as prisoners of war, must they be afforded self-incrimination protections? The American Bar Association, Task Force on Terrorism and the Law, recently concluded that the actions of September 11 were acts of war, although because noncombatant civilians were attacked, the perpetrators violated the law of armed conflict, forfeiting Hague Convention protections.[31] At the same time, Pentagon doctrine states that captured terrorists are not afforded "prisoner of war" protection because terrorists act outside the laws of war.[32] As we redefine notions about crime and war while rethinking strategies to fight terrorism, there are some key areas for consideration.

A NEW PARADIGM IS NECESSARY

America must remove impediments, real and perceived, to DoD involvement in homeland security. First, we must reflect on the original purpose of the Posse Comitatus Act, with a long view toward broadening the use of armed forces in traditional law enforcement roles. Only the military can truly deal with catastrophic events, such as biological and chemical attack, as well as radiological release and consequence management. Furthermore, the organic capability for superb military investigation, intelligence analysis, and fact-finding can be an invaluable augmentation to state and local authority during a calamity. This may need to include questioning of civilians and perhaps collection of information relevant to tracking terrorists. Furthermore, the possibility that this material may have evidentiary value, cannot be discounted.

According to John R. Brinkerhoff, a retired Army officer and former FEMA associate director and Office of the Secretary of Defense (OSD) senior career executive, the Posse Comitatus Act has been grossly misinterpreted as preventing the military services from acting as a national police force. Brinkerhoff points out that Posse Comitatus was passed in 1878 when, reacting to southern sheriffs and U.S. marshals pressing Army troops into their service without Washington's approval, Congress voted to restrict the ability of U.S. marshals and local constabulary to conscript military personnel into their posses.[33] In passing the Posse Comitatus Act, Congress conceded the use of military troops for police actions when authorized by the president or Congress. Brinkerhoff offers that an erroneous interpretation has resulted from a general Pentagon desire to avoid domestic unrest quagmires. He adds that much of the twisting of Posse Comitatus was by persons averse to any role for military forces in law enforcement including the military itself.

It now appears that to fully engage our armed forces to defeat terrorism, we must rethink Posse Comitatus. It is not a rigid proscription on use of the military to enforce or execute laws. Rather, when so ordered by the president, the military can support civilian authorities in a wide array of enforcement missions where it is uniquely trained and equipped. Why continue to craft strategies that require states to shoulder additional burden owing to Posse Comitatus because, when strictly construed, it is no obstacle to armed forces and civilian partnership in domestic security? Rethinking policy and practice regarding Posse Comitatus should be a priority for the new Department of Homeland Security as it creates linkages to the Pentagon's NORTHCOM in the coming heretofore criminal justice–constrained battle against terrorism.[34]

Second, "preemption" is a term which has drawn considerable attention, particularly in the president's rhetoric, and deserves consideration in the quiver of weapons against terrorism. When thought of in a criminal context, police can frustrate unlawful schemes only within a legally consistent framework of probable cause, elements of the offense, legally obtainable evidence, reasonable expectation of privacy, hearsay, and entrapment. Preemption, as envisaged by the Law of Armed Conflict, has none of these constraints and therefore finds fertile ground as a military option. Along these lines, P. H. Liotta offers that terrorists can be expected to practice chaos as a strategy. "We will practice preemption against those who seek to harm our vital interests and our way of life. Military forces will increasingly be in the business of shooting archers, and not just catching arrows. That is to say that we cannot just wait for chaos provocations to occur before we react."[35] According to Liotta, however, our execution of military options must be tempered with a clear understanding of the nature of the enemy and how, if misapplied, military force may play right into the hands of terrorists who will practice chaos as a strategy.

The White House recently released the *National Strategy For Combating Terrorism,* which conveys the four-point methodology of defeat, deny, diminish, and defend in a war against terrorist organizations of global reach. The national strategy brings to bear "direct or indirect use of diplomatic, economic, information, law enforcement, military, financial, intelligence and other instruments of national power."[36] Clearly, the war on terrorism is emerging from the sterile impartiality of the court room to reflect dynamic new challenges.

The March 1, CIA-orchestrated, predawn seizure of Khalid Shaikh Mohammed, al Qaeda's chief of operations and suspected mastermind behind September 11, from a house in Rawalpindi, Pakistan, illustrates what cooperation between intelligence, military, and law enforcement authorities can achieve in the terror war. Mr. Mohammed was quickly spirited out of Pakistan to an undisclosed location, presumably for interrogation by CIA specialists, as his knowledge, as well as information gathered at his capture sight, is time perishable. Considerations of evidence admissibility or prosecutorial strategy are moot because Mr. Mohammed is not envisaged to face a jury of his peers.

Reminiscent of the case against Jose Padilla, who was planning new attacks in the United States, Mr. Mohammed will not be afforded legal counsel. In a nine-page legal affidavit concerning Padilla, Vice Admiral Lowell E. Jacoby, director of the Defense Intelligence Agency, asserted that more than one hundred terrorist attacks have been thwarted due to the interrogation of enemy combatants captured by counterterrorist efforts. In recommending against Padilla talking to a lawyer Jacoby said, "I also firmly believe that providing Padilla access to counsel risks loss of a critical intelligence resource, resulting in a grave and direct threat to national security."[37]

The conundrum of legal process in the terror war is also playing itself out in Portland, Oregon, where, in an ongoing criminal prosecution of five defendants charged with conspiring to assist al Qaeda, the defense is challenging the FBI's use of expanded surveillance power under the USA Patriot Act.[38] Regardless of the Oregon court's decision, this legal maneuver underscores the controversy over methods when terrorists are pursued with prosecution as an objective or when they are considered combatants rather than defendants, as in the case of Khalid Shaikh Mohammed.

CONCLUSIONS

Considering the challenges and new risks that America is facing, "We are going to have to invent new ideas about what war is, and that will have far-reaching implications for the legal system," says Stephen Gale.[39] According to some experts, the inevitability of another terrorist attack in the United States is undeniable.[40]

NOTES

Revision of article originally published August 2002. The views expressed in this article are those of the author and do not reflect the official policy of the Naval Criminal Investigative Service, Naval War College, the Department of Defense or the U.S. government.

1. More information about voir dire can be found at www.jri-inc.com/voirdire.htm.

2. George W. Bush, "Address to a Joint Session of Congress" (September 12, 2001), at www.thedailycamera .com/news/terror/sept01/21atext.html.

3. The late professor Michael Handel authored three books on Clausewitz. As a professor of strategy at the U.S. Naval War College, Handel established a matchless reputation as an expert on theories of war, and Clausewitz in particular. Carl von Clausewitz, quoted in Michael I. Handel, *Masters of War,* 3rd ed. (London: Frank Cass, 2001), 68.

4. Definition of terrorism in accordance with U.S. Department of Defense Directive 2000.12, *DoD Antiterrorism/ Force Protection (AT/FP) Program* (April 13, 1999), at www.dtic.mil/whs/directives/corres/text/d200012p.txt.

5. Definition of terrorism in accordance with "Organization of the Department of Justice," *Code of Federal Regulations, Title 28—Judicial Administration* (Washington, D.C.: U.S. General Services Administration, National Archives and Records Service, Office of the Federal Register, July 1, 2001), chap. I, 51–52, at www.access.gpo.gov/nara/ cfr/waisidx_01/28cfr0_01.html.

6. The members of the commission were L. Paul Bremer III, Maurice Sonnenberg, Richard K. Betts, Wayne A. Dowling, Jane Harman, Fred C. Ikle, Juliette N. Kayyem, John F. Lewis, Jr., Gardner Peckham, and R. James Woolsey. See Report of the National Commission on Terrorism, *Countering the Changing Threat of International Terrorism* (Washington, D.C., 1999) at www.fas.org/irp/threat/ commission.html.

7. Information about the Pan Am 103 trial and conviction is available on the World Wide Web (February 15, 2002) at www.geocities.com/CapitolHill/5260/verdict.html.

8. Peter Ford, "Legal War on Terror Lacks Weapons," *Christian Science Monitor* (March 27, 2002) at www .csmonitor.com/2002/0327/p01s04-woeu.htm.

9. Initial release of information on this case can be read at "Transcript of the Attorney General John Ashcroft Regarding the Transfer of Abdullah Al Muhajir to the Department of Defense as an Enemy Combatant" (June 10, 2002) at www.usdoj.gov/ag/speeches/2002/061002agtranscripts.htm.

10. Statistical analysis and reports concerning criminal prosecutions of terrorism and national security cases is studied by the Transactional Records Access Clearinghouse, a research organization associated with Syracuse University. Their report entitled *Criminal Enforcement against Terrorists and Spies in the Year after the 9/11 Attacks* is available at http://trac.syr.edu/tracreports/terrorism/fy2002 .html.

11. Ibid.

12. Stephen Gale, quoted in Ford, "Legal War on Terror Lacks Weapons."

13. The term "sleepers" is a reference to persons who quietly reside in a community and go unnoticed to intelligence or law enforcement but in fact have criminal or terrorist objectives and are waiting for an opportunity or higher direction to execute a preplanned mission. Sleeper agents are very difficult to detect and harder to prosecute due to the benign nature of their lives. See Michael Clarke, quoted in Peter Ford, "Legal War on Terror Lacks Weapons."

14. In the sixteenth century, a British political faction known as "Whigs" drew on certain ideas of Niccolo Machiavelli, believing that any army powerful enough to defend a state would also have the power to overthrow it. The danger, according to Machiavelli, was especially acute in time of peace, when the army's usefulness was finished. Therefore, the concept of standing armies was challenged by Machiavelli, and by Whigs who found his philosophies attractive. This became central to their political thought and influenced early American colonial politics, as well as the crafting of our Constitution and Bill of Rights. See Jeffrey H. Norwitz, "What was the Whig Vision for Military Service?" Unpublished research paper (Newport, R.I.: U.S. Naval War College, 2001).

15. An excellent treatment of Posse Comitatus is contained in Thomas R. Lujan, "Legal Aspects of Domestic Employment of the Army," *Parameters* (Autumn 1997), which is available at http://carlisle-www.army.mil/usawc/Parameters/97autumn/lujan.htm. The Posse Comitatus Act itself is available at http://law2.house.gov/usc.htm.

16. President Ronald Reagan, Executive Order 12333, "United States Intelligence Activities, 1981," at www.archives.gov/federal_register/codification/executive_order/12333.html.

17. President William J. Clinton, Decision Directive 39, "U.S. Policy on Counterterrorism, 1995." PDD-39 is classified SECRET. A redacted version is available at www.fas.org/irp/offdocs/pdd39.htm.

18. One example of innovative training in the area of urban operations is The Center for Emerging Threats and Opportunities (CETO), a Marine Corps–Potomac Institute for Policy Studies partnership dedicated to exploring innovative ways to deal with nontraditional threats to national security. More information about CETO is available at www.defenselink.mil/news/Jul2001/p07232001_p143-01.html.

19. The Yale Law School provides an extensive reference resource concerning the Law of Armed Conflict at www.yale.edu/lawweb/avalon/lawofwar/lawwar.htm.

20. George Shultz, quoted in Douglas Menarchik, "Organizing to Combat 21st Century Terrorism," in *The Terrorism Threat and U.S. Government Response*, ed. James M. Smith and William C. Thomas (Colorado Springs: U.S. Air Force Institute for National Security Studies, 2001), 222.

21. U.S. Department of State, *Patterns of Global Terrorism* (Washington, D.C.: 2001), as well as earlier annual reports, are available at www.state.gov/s/ct/rls/pgtrpt/.

22. More information about the Marine barracks bombing is available at www.beirut-memorial.org/.

23. An outstanding treatment of the challenges of human source intelligence and specifically the recruitment of questionable sources was authored by retired Admiral Stansfield Turner; Turner reviews his controversial tenure as director of the CIA and the problems of operating a secret intelligence organization in a democratic society. See Stansfield Turner, *Secrecy and Democracy—The CIA in Transition* (Boston: Houghton Mifflin, 1985).

24. The concept of Leaderless Resistance was proposed by Ulius Louis Amoss in 1962. In 1983, Louis Beam expounded on Amoss's idea in a quarterly journal entitled *The Seditionist*, wherein he wrote essays proposing the overthrow of the American government. Leaderless Resistance is a system based upon the cell organization, but does not have any central control or direction. Utilizing the Leaderless Resistance concept, all individuals and groups operate independently of each other, and never report to a central headquarters or single leader for direction or instruction. Beam's essay is available at www.louisbeam.com/leaderless.htm.

25. The commission's suggestion of a cabinet-level agency to deal with Homeland Security included some of the earliest deliberation reflected in the president's recent proposed Department of Homeland Security. See The U.S. Commission on National Security/21st Century, *Road Map for National Security: Imperative for Change* (Washington, D.C.: U.S. Commission on National Security/21st Century, 2001), 10–29.

26. U.S. Department of Defense, *Quadrennial Defense Review Report* (Washington, D.C.: U.S. Department of Defense, 2001). A copy and analysis of the QDR is available at www.comw.org/qdr/.

27. More information about Northern Command (NORTHCOM) is available at www.defenselink.mil/specials/unifiedcommand/.

28. Handel, *Masters of War*, 102.

29. Ibid., 121.

30. Colin S. Gray, "Thinking Asymmetrically in Times of Terror," *Parameters* (Spring 2002), available at http://carlisle-www.army.mil/usawc/parameters/02spring/gray.htm.

31. American Bar Association Task Force on Terrorism and the Law, "Report and Recommendations on Military Commissions" (January 4, 2002) at www.abanet.org/leadership/military.pdf.

32. Joint doctrine states that "by definition, terrorists do not meet the four requirements necessary for combatant status (wear uniforms or other distinctive insignia, carry arms openly, be under command of a person responsible for group actions, and conduct their operations in accordance with laws of war). . . . For this reason, captured terrorists are not afforded the protection from criminal prosecution attendant to prisoner of war status." See Joint Chiefs of Staff, *Joint Tactics, Techniques and Procedures for Antiterrorism*, Publication 3-07.2 (Washington D.C.: U.S. Department of Defense, March 17, 1998), available at www.fas.org/irp/doddir/dod/jp3_07_2.pdf.

33. An excellent treatment and analysis of Posse Comitatus and its history is found in John R. Brinkerhoff, "The Posse Comitatus Act and Homeland Security" (Analytic Services Inc., 2002), available at www.homelanddefense.org/journal/articles/brinkerhoffpc.doc.

34. The Department of Homeland Security is fully defined and discussed at www.whitehouse.gov/deptofhomeland/book.pdf, as well as its own website at www.dhs.gov/dhspublic/.

35. Dr. Peter Liotta, Professor of Strategy at the U.S. Naval War College, writes about the emergence of "adversaries who . . . will increasingly look for innovative ways to 'attack' without attacking directly the brick wall of American military predominance. The chaos strategist thus targets the American national security decision making process and, potentially the American people, rather than American military force, in order to prevail. Such a strategist seeks to induce decision paralysis." Liotta applies this concept to the war on terrorism and offers insightful analysis for American defense planners. See Peter H. Liotta, "Chaos as Strategy," *Parameters* (Summer 2002), available at http://carlisle-www.army.mil/usawc/parameters/02summer/liotta.htm.

36. The White House, *National Strategy for Combating Terrorism* (Washington, D.C.: White House, February 2003), 15, available at www.whitehouse.gov/news/releases/2003/02/counter_terrorism/counter_terrorism_strategy.pdf.

37. Vice Admiral Lowell E. Jacoby, quoted in Richard Serrano and Greg Miller, "100 Terrorist Attacks Thwarted U.S. Says," *Los Angeles Times* (January 11, 2003), available at www.latimes.com/news/nationworld/nation/la-na-padilla 11jan11,0,4645248.story?coll=la-home-headlines.

38. The USA Patriot Act is available at http://news .findlaw.com/cnn/docs/terrorism/hr3162.pdf; additional analysis and review of the Act is available at www.ala .org/washoff/patriot.html.

39. Stephen Gale, quoted in Ford, "Legal War on Terror Lacks Weapons."

40. According to a *Washington Post* article, "In response to a senator's question about the gravity of the threat, one CIA intelligence official said there is a 100 percent chance of another attack should the United States strike Afghanistan." See Susan Schmidt and Bob Woodward, "FBI, CIA Warns Congress of More Attacks if U.S. Strikes Afghanistan," *Washington Post* (October 5, 2001): A01. According to a CBS News poll on April 3, 2002, 74 percent of questioned Americans thought that another terrorist attack was likely. See poll at http://cbsnewyork.com/mideast/StoryFolder/story_337275743_html.

CONNECTING THE DOTS: THE CHALLENGE OF IMPROVING THE CREATION AND SHARING OF KNOWLEDGE ABOUT TERRORISTS

MARK SAWYER

On September 11, al Qaeda executed horrific attacks against the United States, and instantaneously, the use of the term "connect the dots" exploded across the airways to describe what pundits said did not happen in the Intelligence Community prior to the attacks. It is universally accepted that the process by which the United States analyzes terrorist threats needs to be improved. Improving the system requires an understanding of what the process needs to be.

"Connect the dots" is a useful term, and a useful point of departure, but only if we understand what we are really talking about: how do you recognize, collect, and share dots, connect dots, and share the knowledge created by the connection? Connecting the dots —the centerpiece—is just one aspect. The analytic process and the quality of the analysts are but a bright spot in the picture. How to get the right data to the analysts (sharing data) and how to best use their analyses (sharing intelligence) are the key questions.

My intent is not to discuss the intelligence cycle[1] per se but to discuss aspects of the cycle that need to be understood to improve terrorist threat analysis. There are three components of the process:

1. Identification, collection, and sharing of data (or dots);

2. Creating knowledge (or connecting the dots); and

3. Sharing the created knowledge.

For the sake of discussion, I assume that the process is national, owned and run by the federal government, with state and local governments and the private sector as partners. A secondary assumption is that all the analysis is done at the federal level.

BACKGROUND

In the immediate aftermath of September 11, the use of the phrase "connect the dots" was tied to traditional forms of foreign intelligence.[2] But it soon became apparent that the need to secure the United States involved understanding more than just traditional foreign intelligence about terrorists and their activities. Information about terrorists from law enforcement and nonintelligence sources is equally important. Securing America also involves understanding the potential targets and their vulnerabilities and mitigating these vulnerabilities with protective actions.

The *National Strategy for Homeland Security* defines homeland security as "a concerted national effort to prevent terrorist attacks within the United States, reduce America's vulnerability to terrorism, and minimize the damage and recover from attacks that do occur."[3] The strategy highlighted the new structures needed: "Today, no government entity is responsible for analyzing terrorist threats to the homeland, mapping those threats against our vulnerabilities, and taking protective action."[4] The strategy says that the Department of Homeland Security—only a proposal before Congress at the time the strategy was released—would perform this function.

According to the strategy, the Department of Homeland Security would perform comprehensive vulnerability assessments for critical infrastructure and key assets. The rationale for the department to merge intelligence and information analysis and vulnerability assessments is so that it can "focus on longer-term protective measures, such as the setting of priorities for critical infrastructure protection and 'target hardening'." The Department of Homeland Security would also provide warnings to the nation and "would serve as the primary provider of threat information to state and local public safety agencies and to private sector owners of key targets, thereby minimizing confusion, gaps and duplication."[5] To accomplish these tasks, the position of under secretary for Information Analysis and Infrastructure Protection in the Department of Homeland Security was created. The under secretary was given the following responsibility:

To access, receive, and analyze law enforcement information, intelligence information, and other information from agencies of the Federal Government, State and local government agencies (including law enforcement agencies), and private sector entities, and to integrate such information in order to—

(A) identify and assess the nature and scope of terrorist threats to the homeland;

(B) detect and identify threats of terrorism against the United States; and

(C) understand such threats in light of actual and potential vulnerabilities of the homeland.[6]

On May 1, 2003, the Terrorist Threat Integration Center was established. The center "will serve as a hub for terrorist threat–related information collected domestically or abroad."[7] As described by a White House fact sheet, the Terrorist Threat Integration Center will fuse and analyze all-source information related to terrorism and provide terrorist threat assessments for our national leadership. It is made up of elements of the following: the Department of Homeland Security, the Federal Bureau of Investigation (FBI) Counterterrorism Division, the director of Central Intelligence's Counterterrorism Center, the Department of Defense, the Department of State, and the Intelligence Community.[8]

It is still unclear what the respective roles are of the under secretary for Information Analysis and Infrastructure Protection and the Terrorist Threat Integration Center. The Homeland Security Act gave the responsibility for all-source terrorist threat analysis to the Department of Homeland Security, whereas the Terrorist Threat Integration Center places this responsibility with the director of Central Intelligence. Several leading members of Congress have expressed concern that congressional direction has not been followed, and that the Terrorist Threat Integration Center, in its current form, perpetuates past mistakes by subjecting it to the authority of the director of Central Intelligence.[9]

IDENTIFYING, COLLECTING, AND SHARING DATA

WHAT IS A DOT?

The object of identifying, collecting, and sharing data is to provide raw material to the analyst. The first question that must be addressed is: What is a dot? This question is most easily and best answered in retrospect: a dot is any piece of data that is relevant to gaining knowledge of a terrorist group, threat, or attack. However, the question is much harder to answer in anticipation, before a specific act occurs, a terrorist group is identified, or a threat is recognized.

So how do you recognize a dot? There are several ways. One way is to evaluate each new potential dot against existing knowledge or context. You have a "story," and you compare the potential dot to the story to see whether it is related. It could be related negatively (it casts doubt on a part of the story, but it is still related) or positively (it advances the story). A second way is to consider a set of potential dots together and attempt to determine linkages. A third, intermediate, step, to decrease the set of potential dots, is to build templates of normal behavior—dots would be outside normal behavior. Alternatively, templates of terrorist behavior are built, and dots are consistent with that behavior. Dots are not self-evident; data must be determined to be a dot. The answer to the question "What is a dot?" is in essence an analytic function. Indeed, the identification of a dot is most likely to be performed in the analysis and production phase of the intelligence cycle. Yet the understanding of the analyst, derived from experience in determining what dots are, needs to inform the collection and sharing of data (potential dots).

HOW ARE DOTS COLLECTED AND SHARED?

As dots are not self-evident, how do you decide what data to collect? An unavoidable risk is that some specific dots will never be collected. A second risk is that many potential—although in the end, not actual—dots will be collected and will make the system less efficient. The best way to manage these risks is to identify data sets for which the potential for dots is highest. The data domains where dots are most likely to be found include traditional foreign intelligence data, domestic intelligence data,[10] law enforcement data, critical infrastructure, key asset and major event situational awareness data, personal data held by private companies, and citizen observations. Once specific data has been identified as a potential dot, it must be provided to analysts in an understandable form.

Traditional Foreign Intelligence Data

For traditional foreign intelligence, a mature system exists that identifies where potential dots are, and various methods exist to collect the data and forward it to analysts. This system is formal, and the collection, processing, and exploitation are, for the most part, predetermined. For the other domains, this process has not yet been established. Furthermore, there may be legal impediments to collection in other domains. Yet even foreign intelligence data collection and sharing could be improved. First, the sets of data in which traditional foreign intelligence is collected could be expanded to include more open-source data—experts, media, and the Internet.[11] Second, there is a problem with sharing data between members of the Intelligence Community.[12] Senator Susan Collins quoted administration officials as saying that the sharing that does occur between the FBI and the Central Intelligence Agency (CIA) is done by "brute force," meaning that costly workarounds enforced by the intercession of senior leadership have ensured sharing instead of its being part of normal procedure.[13]

Domestic Intelligence and Law Enforcement Data

Domestic intelligence and law enforcement data are similar but different. The hope is that law enforcement data would contain domestic intelligence. However, the determination of whether law enforcement data is domestic intelligence is not usually made until it is analyzed. Moreover, the collection and transmittal of this data to analysts is not institutionalized; in some cases, it does not occur.

At the federal level, the FBI is the agency responsible for terrorism-related domestic intelligence and law enforcement. There have been two main criticisms of the FBI concerning the collection and sharing of data.[14] The first is that the FBI, by mission, training, and culture, has focused on building case files of data to be used in court, to the exclusion of other data that may show trends or patterns.[15] The second criticism is that the FBI, because of antiquated information systems and business processes, does not have a full understanding of the information in its possession, nor does it have the ability to search or share the information.[16] There have been no mechanisms for the FBI to share its data with analysts. One of the thrusts of the FBI's transformation has been the creation of a "corps of reports officers." FBI Director Mueller has said that these officers "will be responsible for identifying, extracting and collecting intelligence from FBI investigations and sharing that information throughout the FBI and to other law enforcement and intelligence agencies."[17] On March 28, 2003, the FBI announced that it had deployed a nationwide computer network called "Trilogy." This network will allow the use of the Virtual Case File application by the end of 2003.[18]

Locally, data may exist in law enforcement, but again, it is unsharable. There is no mechanism in place to capture this data and provide it electronically to analysts across the nation.[19] The sniper attacks in the Washington, D.C., area in autumn 2002 provide examples of the deficiencies in how law enforcement currently collects and shares crime-related data. There were issues with collecting and sharing ballistics data and fingerprints found at crime scenes. Additionally, not all criminal warrants are shared across the nation. The source of these problems is both funding (the cost of collecting and analyzing these data at the local level and the cost of joining national systems) and operating procedures (judgments made that certain crime-related data are not worth collecting and sharing).[20] These same types of issues impact the collection and sharing of law enforcement data with utility for domestic intelligence.

Beyond the details of crimes, the observations of approximately 708,000 sworn[21] state and local law enforcement officers[22] can be the source of much domestic intelligence. However, one must determine how these observations are to be collected and which observations should be shared. There is a need for state and local officers to be trained in identifying what data need to be shared. The USA Patriot Act requires the Department of Justice to provide training to state and local officials in identifying and handling foreign intelligence found during the course of their investigations.[23] It is uncertain whether this type of training is occurring. There are individual efforts by the FBI's Joint Terrorism Task Forces[24] to train state and local law enforcement officers in what is foreign intelligence,[25] but these efforts seem to be piecemeal. The FBI has produced and distributed nationwide training CDs that provide an introduction to international and domestic terrorism.[26]

State and local law enforcement officials have additional concerns about collecting and sharing information with the FBI. There is always the concern that the FBI will come in and take over the case. Law enforcement metrics are all based on arrests and convictions, and when the FBI takes over a case, this will not show any results for the state or local entity. Another issue is the one-way flow of information—to the FBI.

Critical Infrastructure, Key Asset, and Major Event Situational Awareness Data

Collecting and sharing data that provide an understanding of the operating status of critical infrastructure, key assets, and major events will allow for the detection of anomalous changes in operations and activities. Furthermore, it will provide an understanding of potential targets of terrorist activities to allow better interpretation of data that may point to terrorist targeting of critical infrastructure, key assets, and major events. However, there are four significant challenges to collecting and sharing these data:

1. Determining what data most easily convey the status of these entities;

2. Assesing potential risk to private entities of sharing proprietary and other "private" data— there are risks of disclosure to competitors and of liability;[27]

3. Displaying the data to make them understandable in a systematic way; and

4. Ensuring that all the data flows are timely.

Personal Data and Public Observations

Personal data held by private companies, along with public observations, may provide insight into anomalies in people's behavior that may indicate terrorist behavior. However, there are challenges in collecting and sharing data. First, there have been privacy and civil liberties objections raised to the government's access to this data. Both the Terrorism Information Awareness program being developed by the Defense Advanced Research Projects Agency and the Computer Assisted Passenger Prescreening System (CAPPS II) being developed by the Transportation Security Administration, which are developing software and tools to make sense of large sets of data and to enable the discovery of relationships between data, have run into congressional opposition.[28]

Second, in the United States, there is no concerted campaign to make the public more aware and to encourage people to report suspicious activities. In the United Kingdom, by contrast, the public was enlisted in the fight against the Irish Republican Army through several campaigns.[29] More recently, after many Australians died in the Bali terrorist bombing, the Australian government launched a national terrorism awareness advertising campaign asking people to "be alert but not alarmed" and to report anything suspicious via a toll-free tip line.[30] This was followed up with a mailing to each household, telling Australians how to recognize and report suspicious behavior and containing information on how to protect themselves in the event of an emergency.[31] The one U.S. effort attempting to enlist private citizens who are in the same places on a regular basis and therefore could notice people and activities out of the ordinary, Operation TIPS (Terrorist Information and Prevention System), was prohibited in the Homeland Security Act of 2002 in reaction to privacy and civil liberties objections.[32]

The data sources examined for potentially useful data need to be expanded, requiring the creation of processes to collect and share data from new domains. In addition to the problems discussed above, these processes require automated information management. As it is, there is an overload of data from the existing domains. To greatly expand the amount of data without increasing the ability to process the data would make things more difficult. Automated information management would allow for the winnowing of data from the set to be forwarded to the analyst.[33] Yet this process must be informed by analysts' insights and experience. Additionally, the sharing process must be nonlinear. The process must focus on data that are most likely to be dots while preserving all the data. The preserved data need to be periodically reexamined in light of advances in the understanding of the story, as developed through analysis, to see whether new dots can be discerned.

CREATING KNOWLEDGE

Once dots have been successfully collected and shared, analysts still must discern meaning. Just as dots are more easily identified in retrospect, so are patterns.[34] The goal of analysis in this process is to create the most perfect knowledge about terrorist threats and attacks. Although there are several improvements that should be made in this part of the process, the underlying skill and expertise of the analysis pool is good, and the analytic methodology used is sound. The major problems are due to too few experienced analysts, because of the time it takes to season a person and the language and subject matter expertise required. The FBI, in particular, has challenges in this area. The FBI has been criticized not only for not knowing what data it has and not being able to collect and share these data, but also for not having the necessary analytic capability. There are three reasons for this: First, the number-one mission of the FBI has been to build court cases, not analyze trends for prediction purposes. Second, the number of analysts is small. Third, the FBI's culture has focused on the special agent; everyone else is a second-class citizen.[35] The FBI has recognized these deficiencies and is working to improve its analytic capability in terms of both quality and the number of analysts.[36]

Analysis in general could be improved through the better use of collaboration. Although most advocates of more collaboration focus on the sharing of data (dots), the key to analysis is people. A dot may be a dot to one person but not to another.[37] The process of analysis needs to ensure not only that data are shared but also that analysts' insights and experience are shared. The interaction of people with different experiences, data, thought patterns, and knowledge is the basis for true collaboration. An important insight may not unlock the puzzle for one analyst, but it may be the piece for another to do so. It is the iterative process of sharing knowledge, thoughts, and ideas that produces results. Collaboration needs to be a process whereby individuals build on one another's work.

A second change that could improve analysis is to create competition. During debate over the creation of the Department of Homeland Security and, in particular, the position of under secretary of Homeland Security for Information Analysis and Infrastructure Protection, Tom Ridge, then head of the Office of

Homeland Security, stated that a "second set of eyes" would improve overall analysis. Many objected, including Senators Carl Levin and Ron Wyden. They argued that competitive analysis would dissuade people who own the data from sharing the data with their competitors.[38] This debate has continued with the role of the Terrorist Threat Integration Center in relation to the under secretary of Homeland Security for Information Analysis and Infrastructure Protection and the director of Central Intelligence's Counterterrorism Center. Senator Levin argued at a congressional hearing that it is important that one entity analyze foreign intelligence and that another analyze domestic intelligence so that responsibility is not confused.[39]

Although creating the knowledge (the analysis part of the process) is the bright spot, there is room for improvement. It is well understood that the FBI, the agency tasked to perform domestic intelligence, needs to improve its analytic capability. The FBI has recognized this problem and has undertaken a program to ameliorate it, but because culture plays such a strong role in the deficiency, the FBI has a difficult task ahead.

SHARING THE
CREATED KNOWLEDGE

Once knowledge has been created, it needs to be shared with those who can act on it. In late 2002, the Gilmore Commission, as well as the Independent Task Force sponsored by the Council on Foreign Relations and chaired by former Senators Gary Hart and Warren Rudman, reported that state and local law enforcement still was not receiving adequate threat information from the federal government. The Hart-Rudman Report used particularly damning words: "When it comes to combating terrorism, the police officers on the beat are effectively operating deaf, dumb, and blind." The report stated that watch lists were still not available to state and local law enforcement and warned that while these issues get sorted out, "known terrorists will be free to move about to plan and execute their attacks."[40]

In testimony before Congress in October 2002, Comptroller General of the United States David Walker summed up the difficulties with information sharing in the United States:

State and local officials continue to be frustrated by difficulties in the communication and sharing of threat information among all levels of government. Some of the problems they cited include: limited access to information because of security clearance issues, the absence of a systematic top-down and bottom-up information exchange, and uncertainties regarding the appropriate response to a heightened alert from the new homeland security advisory system.[41]

Former Baltimore Police Commissioner Edward Norris stated empathically that the federal government is the impediment to intelligence sharing among local, state, and federal agencies. He said he had requested several times that the FBI provide a full briefing on all Baltimore-based terrorism investigations but never received one.[42]

Efforts are under way to improve the dissemination of knowledge about terrorism and terrorists. The Joint Terrorism Task Forces have helped provide some level of sharing, but, as they are currently operated, they leave much to be desired.[43] In some metropolitan areas, they have created a group of haves (local police departments with a member on the task force) and the have-nots.[44] Also, even with Top Secret clearances, state and local members of the task forces do not have access to all the information that the federal members do.[45] U.S. Army, Pacific has established a task force in Hawaii focused on force protection. The Army has created a secure web page for state and local law enforcement and political decisionmakers. It posts a newsletter on the site, providing important information. The purpose is to share DoD information with these entities as part of providing force protection for DoD personnel and installations.[46]

The challenge in disseminating intelligence concerning the terrorist threat is impacted by four major issues:

1. Identifying the dissemination requirements;

2. Safeguarding information;

3. Determining which federal agency is responsible for disseminating information to state and local governments, the private sector, and the American people; and

4. Communicating what state and local government, the private sector, and the public should do, based on this intelligence.

DISSEMINATION REQUIREMENTS

The most important issue for improving the sharing of terrorist threat analysis is to determine what information needs to be shared, to whom, and in what timeline. I have not been able to find a process that defines the requirements for this type of sharing. The National Strategy for the Physical Protection of Critical Infrastructures and Key Assets, released in February 2003, calls for defining requirements for information sharing and establishing mechanisms to share the required information.[47] Who will produce this requirements analysis, when it will be completed, and what will be the quality of the results?

The foundation of that requirements analysis will be an understanding of the potential customer sets. There are four basic levels of officials who have a need for information developed from connecting the dots, and each has different information needs. Additionally, within each level, officials have different responsibilities—law enforcement, fire service, emergency medical services, and the like—that require different information. At the top level are the decisionmakers. For the most part, these are the executives of the various political jurisdictions—the president, governors, county executives, and mayors. Additionally, at the federal level, this would include cabinet members and members of Congress. Next are the top-level operational heads and agency chiefs, such as the commanders of the military's combatant commands; the director of the FBI; the heads of emergency services of states, counties, and towns; chiefs of police, emergency medical services, and fire departments; sheriffs; heads of the state, big city, and big county public health departments; and executives of companies involved in critical infrastructure. The next level is the on-scene tactical commanders of public safety (police, fire, and emergency medical services) personnel, hospital chiefs, and plant and facility managers. The last level is the frontline operators, such as police, fire, emergency medical services, doctors, nurses, and private security.

SAFEGUARDING INFORMATION

A major impediment to sharing analyses and information is the safeguarding of sensitive information. In the area of foreign intelligence, losing sources and methods can create long-term gaps in our knowledge, not to mention loss of life. In law enforcement, an investigation may be compromised before key evidence can be collected, resulting in the inability to prosecute and win a criminal case. Safeguarding is achieved by providing access to classified information only to those people cleared to receive the information and with a need to know.[48]

The FBI estimates that granting a Secret clearance takes an average of 9 weeks; a Top Secret clearance takes 9 months. Many law enforcement veterans are upset that despite having spent 20 or 30 years in law enforcement, they still need to be checked out by the FBI before they are granted a clearance. Some law enforcement executives have not requested clearance because of the process involved. The FBI reports that 1,000 law enforcement executives and 1,200 officers have received clearances since September 11. The officers received their clearances for their work with Joint Terrorism Task Forces. Another four hundred law enforcement executives were being processed for clearances.[49]

What can be done to expand the pool of individuals with whom information can be shared? There are two ways. The first is to clear more people. This is the tack taken by Senator John Edwards in the Antiterrorism Intelligence Distribution Act of 2003. This bill states that its purpose "is to ensure that sufficient numbers of appropriate personnel of State and local governments, including personnel of law enforcement, rescue, fire, health, and other first responder agencies, receive security clearances for access to classified information of the Federal Government." The bill requires that 180 days after its enactment, the state and local officials identified will have received their clearances.[50]

A second method is to reclassify information to a lower level. Stephen Cambone, the under secretary of Defense for Intelligence, said to Congress in regard to sharing information from the Terrorist Threat Integration Center:

The key to it is going to be to separate the information from the sources. And that's something that we need to learn to do. It is unfortunate that we oftentimes lend the credibility of the information to the source. And so therefore, you tend to send the sourcing along with the information as a way of validating the information. But once you've done that, of course, you can't disseminate the information very far because it puts the source at risk. So one of the interesting cultural changes we are about to undergo . . . is to separate the collection from the analysis. And if we can learn to do that—and they are struggling to learn to do it—I think then that flow of information will be easier.[51]

This change may only provide some measure of improvement because of the risk that some sources and methods may be lost or that some essential information may be left out during the process. The separation of collection from analysis would require a great cultural change on the part of many intelligence and law enforcement officials.

An issue that impacts both the sharing of data and knowledge is the perception of unequal partnership between the federal government and state and local governments. This stems for the most part from the one-way information flow caused by the fact that even though state and local data will be unclassified (although sensitive), it will form part of a classified analysis, which then cannot be shared with the people who contributed the data. After analysis, after a determination is made that law enforcement data (for this is the essence of the complaint) is domestic intelligence, it is likely to be considered more sensitive, perhaps even classified, and therefore not as easily shared downward.

WHO DISSEMINATES TO STATE AND LOCAL GOVERNMENT?

It is unclear which department or entity will be the main federal point of contact with state and local government, private entities, and the public. The National Strategy for Homeland Security states that the Department of Homeland Security would be the main communicant. In March 2002, Homeland Security Presidential Directive 3, which created the familiar color-based Homeland Security Advisory System, made the U.S. attorney general responsible for the system. The Homeland Security Act of 2002 gave this responsibility to the Department of Homeland Security. Homeland Security Presidential Directive 5, signed on February 28, 2003, modified Directive 3 to assign responsibility for the advisory system to the Department of Homeland Security. As modified, Directive 3 states:

The Secretary of Homeland Security shall ensure, consistent with the safety of the Nation, that State and local government officials and law enforcement authorities are provided the most relevant and timely information. The Secretary of Homeland Security shall be responsible for identifying any other information developed in the threat assessment process that would be useful to State and local officials and others and conveying it to them as permitted consistent with the constraints of classification. The Secretary of Homeland Security shall establish a process and a system for conveying relevant information to Federal, State, and local government officials, law enforcement authorities, and the private sector expeditiously.

At the same time, the president recognized that the Department of Homeland Security does not have the capability, required by the last sentence, to share the information. This paragraph was added: "At the request of the Secretary of Homeland Security, the Department of Justice shall permit and facilitate the use of delivery systems administered or managed by the Department of Justice for the purposes of delivering threat information pursuant to the Homeland Security Advisory System."[52] Despite the seemingly clear language in the legislation and the presidential directives, it is not hard to believe that the FBI would want to continue being the main communicant with law enforcement. Furthermore, is it possible for threat and protective measures to be separated from investigation at the federal level, where the Department of Homeland Security is in charge of the former and the FBI the latter? An additional consideration in this question is the role the Terrorist Threat Integration Center will have in communicating threats outside of the federal government.

DISSEMINATING ACTIONS TO TAKE IN RESPONSE TO THE TERRORIST THREAT

A final issue is what role the Department of Homeland Security plays in recommending or providing protective measures. The department is supposed to map the threat against vulnerabilities and "recommend measures necessary to protect the key resources and critical infrastructure of the United States in coordination with other agencies of the Federal Government and in cooperation with State and local government agencies and authorities, the private sector, and other entities."[53] How specific will these be, and how long will it take to produce the playbook —the measures that should be taken, given the intersection of specific threats and vulnerabilities? Furthermore, what role does the Department of Homeland Security have in ensuring that these recommendations are adopted? The language concerning protective measures, as originally proposed by the president, stated that the duties of the secretary of Homeland Security would include *taking or seeking to effect* necessary measures to protect the key resources and critical infrastructures in the United States, in coordination with other executive agencies and in cooperation with State and local government personnel, agencies, and authorities, the private sector, and other entities" (emphasis added).[54] But this language was weakened by Congress so that the secretary is to recommend action rather than take it.

Sharing the created knowledge about homeland security with the entities that can use the knowledge and in a form that they can act on is impeded by traditional constructs concerning intelligence. Traditional classification policy is an impediment to sharing, yet changes to the policy must balance the risk of losing sources and methods. Understanding the differences in the customer set and then determining what their specific needs are (as opposed to an attitude that says, "we need everything") may be able to put a finite scope to the issue and allow for more easily arrived-at solutions.

CONCLUSION

Since September 11, much has been done to improve the creation and sharing of knowledge about terrorists and terrorist threats. A Department of Homeland Security with an under secretary for Information Analysis and Infrastructure Protection was created, a Terrorist Threat Integration Center was established, and the FBI has embarked on a transformation to improve its ability to produce intelligence. The process to connect the dots is being improved, yet much more can and should be done.

The improvement will need to focus on process and technology as well as culture. A significant reason that improvement is not as far along as it should be, nearly 2 years after September 11, is a lack of leadership. Clarity of responsibility and authority is needed, followed by holding individuals accountable for fulfilling their responsibilities. Only leadership and accountability will enable the changes in culture required to successfully provide the intelligence needed to secure the nation.

NOTES

The views expressed in this essay are those of the author. They do not necessarily reflect the views of the ANSER Institute for Homeland Security or its clients.

1. The intelligence cycle is planning and direction, collection, processing and exploitation, analysis and production, and dissemination. See the U.S. Intelligence Community web page.

2. I use the term "traditional" forms of foreign intelligence because any intelligence about an international terrorist is, by definition, foreign intelligence. According to section 3 of the National Security Act of 1947 as amended (50 USC 401a), "foreign intelligence" means "information relating to the capabilities, intentions, or activities, of foreign governments or elements thereof, foreign organizations, or foreign persons, or international terrorist activities."

3. George W. Bush, *The National Strategy for Homeland Security*, June 2002.

4. Ibid.

5. Ibid.

6. The Homeland Security Act of 2002, Public Law 107-296, section 201.

7. Director of Central Intelligence, "Terrorist Threat

Integration Center Begins Operations" (Washington, D.C.: Director of Central Intelligence, May 1, 2003).

8. Ibid. White House fact sheet, "Strengthening Intelligence to Better Protect America" (Washington, D.C.: White House, January 28, 2003).

9. Representative Christopher Cox, Chairman of the House Select Committee on Homeland Security; Representative Jim Turner, its ranking member; Senator Thad Cochran, chairman of the Senate Homeland Security Appropriations Subcommittee; and Senator Joseph Lieberman, ranking member of the Senate Government Affairs Committee, ranking member of the Senate Armed Services Committee, and senior member of the Senate Government Affairs Committee—among others—have stated concerns about the creation of the Terrorist Threat Integration Center. Much of the concern centered on the fact that Terrorist Threat Integration Center functions were given to the Department of Homeland Security and that this situation causes confusion over the roles of the center and the department. See House Select Committee on Homeland Security, "New Terror Intel Center No Substitute for Homeland Security Department Role" (May 2, 2003); "Hearing of the Homeland Security Subcommittee of the Senate Appropriations Committee, Subject: Fiscal Year 2004 Budget Request for the Department of Homeland Security" (Washington, D.C.: Federal News Service via Nexis, April 30, 2003), the exchange between Senator Cochran and Secretary of Homeland Security Tom Ridge; Senator Joseph Lieberman, "Lieberman Pursues Aggressive Homeland Security Oversight Appeals to Bush to Better Manage Intelligence Information" (April 29, 2003); and a letter to President Bush from Senator Lieberman concerning the Terrorist Threat Integration Center (April 29, 2003).

10. In this essay, "domestic intelligence" means foreign intelligence collected domestically about people in the United States.

11. For a theory of open-source intelligence that has a commercial bent, see Robert D. Steele and Mark M. Lowenthal, "Open Source Intelligence: Private Sector Capabilities to Support DoD Policy, Acquisition, and Operations," Defense Daily Network at www.defensedaily/index.html. Steele founded Open Source Solutions and is a major advocate for open-source intelligence and for government funding of commercial open-source intelligence providers. Lowenthal was, until recently, president of OSS USA and is now assistant director of Central Intelligence for Analysis and Production.

12. The Intelligence Community is made up of the Central Intelligence Agency, the National Security Agency, the National Imagery and Mapping Agency, the National Reconnaissance Office, the Defense Intelligence Agency, and the intelligence elements of the Army, Navy, Marine Corps, Air Force, Coast Guard, Department of State, Department of the Treasury, Department of Energy, Federal Bureau of Investigation, and Department of Homeland Security.

13. *Findings of the Final Report of the Senate Select Committee on Intelligence and the House Permanent Select Committee on Intelligence Joint Inquiry Into the Terrorist Attacks of September 11, 2001* (Washington, D.C.: U.S. Government Printing Office, December 10, 2002), 7–8,

Finding 9; and "Transcript of Senate Government Affairs Committee Hearing," Federal Document Clearing House Political Transcripts via Nexis (February 26, 2003), statement by Sentor Susan Collins.

14. Senator Richard Shelby, the vice chair of the Senate Intelligence Committee in the 107th Congress, wrote a minority report to the Joint Intelligence Committee investigation of September 11. In it, he strongly criticized the Intelligence Community and, in particular, the FBI for their performance in sharing data and in analysis. He said the FBI was a law enforcement agency and not an intelligence agency and that it was "dysfunctional." See Richard Shelby, "September 11 and the Imperative of Reform in the U.S. Intelligence Community: Additional Views of Senator Richard C. Shelby, Vice Chairman, Senate Select Committee on Intelligence" (Washington, D.C.: U.S. Government Printing Office, December 10, 2002), 7–8 (Executive Summary), 61–76 (Part IV, Domestic Intelligence).

15. Ibid., 62–71.

16. Ibid., 64.

17. White House, "Strengthening Intelligence to Better Protect America." Statement for the record of Robert S. Mueller III, director of the Federal Bureau of Investigation, on the war on terrorism, before the Senate Select Committee on Intelligence (February 11, 2003).

18. FBI press release, "FBI Completes Deployment of State-of-the-Art Network" (March 28, 2003).

19. Major John Skinner, commanding officer of the Baltimore Police Department's Criminal Intelligence Division, made the point at a homeland security conference that all the potential data is within the police departments, but it is not being linked. The 2003 Government Conference on Emerging Technologies: Defending America Together, 8–10 January 2003, Las Vegas, Nev.

20. David M. Halbfinger and Jayson Blair, "Holes in System Hid Links in Sniper Attacks," *New York Times* (November 29, 2002): A1.

21. "Sworn" means empowered to make arrests.

22. U.S. Department of Justice, Office of Justice Programs, Bureau of Justice Statistics, "Census of State and Local Law Enforcement Agencies, 2000," NCJ 194066 (Washington, D.C.: U.S. Department of Justice, October 2002). These are full-time sworn personnel. There are an additional 42,800 part-time sworn personnel. Of the 708,000, 75 percent were assigned to patrol or investigation duties.

23. USA Patriot Act, Public Law 107-56, section 908, requires the attorney general to "provide appropriate training to . . . officials of State and local government who encounter, or may encounter in the course of a terrorist event, foreign intelligence in the performance of their duties." The training is to assist these officials in both identifying foreign intelligence and utilizing foreign intelligence.

24. Beginning in 1980, the FBI created Joint Terrorism Task Forces in its field offices. The task forces ensure interagency liaison and communications and combine federal, state, and local law enforcement resources. All assigned task force members have Top Secret clearances, giving them access to the information developed during the course of an investigation. Each task force has a chief information officer to oversee information sharing between participants in the task force. Plans call for sixty-six task forces. See FBI,

statement for the record of Kathleen McChesney before the House Government Reform Committee (November 13, 2001); FBI, statement for the record of Robert Jordan before the Senate Judiciary Committee, Subcommittee on Administrative Oversight and the Courts (April 17, 2002); and (for the number of task forces) FBI, opening oral statement of Pasquale J. D'Amuro on "Consolidating Intelligence Analysis: A Review of the President's Proposal to Create a Terrorist Threat Integration Center," Senate Government Affairs Committee (February 26, 2003). Also see Police Executive Research Forum, "Protecting Your Community From Terrorism: The Strategies for Local Law Enforcement Series," vol. 1 (Washington, D.C.: Office of Community Oriented Policing Services, U.S. Department of Justice, March 2003), "Improving Local-Federal Partnerships," chapter 4, for FBI and state and local law enforcement's views on Joint Terrorism Task Forces (available at www.cops.usdoj.gov/Default.asp?Item=1361).

25. Author's conversations with FBI officials and ibid., 44.

26. Ibid., 72.

27. There is disagreement concerning the need for further exemption from the Freedom of Information Act and from antitrust laws. In response to Freedom of Information Act concerns, section 214 of the Homeland Security Act of 2002 provides protection for information voluntarily provided to the Department of Homeland Security. The Department of Homeland Security has published a regulation for comment that would provide this protection for information voluntarily provided to any federal department or agency; see *Federal Register* 68 (April 15, 2003): 18523–29. For a broad overview of the issues (before the Homeland Security Act of 2002) see U.S. Government Printing Office, H.R. 4246, "The Cyber Security Information Act of 2000: An Examination of Issues Involving Public-Private Partnerships for Critical infrastructure," hearing before the House Government Reform Committee, Subcommittee on Government Management, Information, and Technology, serial no. 106-223 (Washington, D.C.: U.S. Government Printing Office, June 22, 2000); see also U.S. Government Accounting Office, "Homeland Security: Information Sharing Responsibilities, Challenges, and Key Management Issues," testimony before the House Government Reform Committee, GAO-03-715T (Washington, D.C.: U.S. Government Accounting Office, May 8, 2003), 23–24.

28. Despite only producing tools and software, these programs have raised a fear that the government will "data mine" on a large scale the many commercial systems that hold data on individuals; see division M, section 111, the Consolidated Appropriations Resolution, 2003, Public Law 108-7; the report required by that section is discussed in U.S. Defense Advanced Projects Agency, "Report to Congress Regarding the Terrorism Information Awareness Program" (Washington, D.C.: U.S. Defense Advanced Projects Agency, May 20, 2003). For CAPPS II, see Robert O'Harrow, Jr., "Aviation ID System Stirs Doubts; Senate Panel Wants Data on Impact on Passenger Privacy," *Washington Post* (March 14, 2003): A16, and Joe Sharkey, "A Safer Sky or Welcome to Flight 1984?" *New York Times* (March 11, 2003): C9. An overview of both the Terrorism Information Awareness and CAPPS II is in the hearing of the House Government Reform Committee, Subcommittee on Tech-

nology, Information Policy, Intergovernmental Relations and the Census [addressing whether factual data analysis can strengthen national security] (Washington, D.C.: Federal News Service via Nexis, May 6, 2003).

29. The United Kingdom had several public awareness campaigns, covered in Philip Webster, "Blast Leads to Security Review at All Key Events; IRA Attack on Inglis Barracks," *London Times* (via Nexis, August 2, 1988); Mark Bradley, "Public Urged to Help Beat Bombers," Press Association via Nexis (October 29, 1996); and Mark Bradley, "Police Launch Anti-Terrorist Ad Campaign," Associated Press Worldstream (October 29, 1996).

30. Mike Corder, "Government to Run Counterterrorism Advertisements to 'Reassure' Australians," Associated Press Worldstream via Nexis (December 26, 2002).

31. "Australia Sends Anti-Terror Kits to Every Household," Agence France-Presse via Nexis (February 3, 2003).

32. Homeland Security Act of 2002, section 880.

33. The development of tools to do this has been opposed on privacy and civil liberties grounds.

34. For a discussion of intelligence failures and hindsight, see Malcolm Gladwell, "Connecting the Dots: The Paradoxes of Intelligence Reform," *New Yorker* 79 (March 10, 2003): 83–89. Gladwell asks a key question in analyzing the performance of the Intelligence Community in regard to September 11: "Was this pattern obvious *before the* attack?" He discusses research conducted by psychologist Baruch Fischhoff, specifically an experiment concerning people's estimates of how successful President Richard Nixon's trip to China would be before he made the trip, compared to their recollection of their estimate after the trip. He says that people's recollection of their estimate was more positive after reading news accounts of the trip. Stating that Fischhoff calls this "creeping determinism," Gladwell quotes Fischhoff, "The occurrence of an event increases its reconstructed probability and makes it less surprising than it would have been had the original probability been remembered."

35. See Michael Bromwich, "The Hard Work of Transforming the F.B.I.," *New York Times* (June 2, 2002); and Shelby, "September 11 and the Imperative of Reform," 62–71.

36. See FBI, testimony of Robert S. Mueller on Joint Intelligence Committee Inquiry before the Senate Select Committee on Intelligence and the House Permanent Select Committee on Intelligence (October 17, 2002).

37. Lowell Jacoby, statement for the record for the Joint 9/11 Inquiry House Permanent Select Committee on Intelligence and Senate Select Committee on Intelligence, *Congressional Reports: Joint Inquiry into Intelligence Community Activities before and after the Terrorist Attacks of September 11, 2001* (Washington, D.C.: U.S. Government Printing Office, October 1, 2002), 3–4.

38. See, in the joint hearing of the House and Senate Select Intelligence Committees, Federal News Service via Nexis (October 3, 2002), the exchange between Senators Dewine and Lee Hamilton, and retired General William Odom; in the hearing of the Senate Governmental Affairs Committee, Federal News Service via Nexis (June 27, 2002), the exchange between Senator Joseph Lieberman and William Webster; and in the hearing of the Senate Governmental Affairs Committee, Federal News Service via Nexis

(June 20, 2002), the exchange between Senator Joseph Lieberman and Tom Ridge.

39. "Transcript of Senate Government Affairs Committee Hearing," FDCH Political Transcripts via Nexis (February 26, 2003).

40. Independent Task Force Sponsored by the Council on Foreign Relations, "America—Still Unprepared, Still in Danger," Report (New York: Council on Foreign Relations, December 2002), 13; "Fourth Annual Report of the Advisory Panel to Assess Domestic Response Capabilities for Terrorism Involving Weapons of Mass Destruction" (Arlington, Va.: RAND, December 2002), 29, available at www.rand.org/nsrd/terrpanel/terror4.pdf.

41. David Walker, "Homeland Security: Information Sharing Activities Face Continued Management Challenges," testimony before the Senate Select Committee on Intelligence and the House Permanent Select Committee on Intelligence, GAO-02-1122T (Washington, D.C.: U.S. Government Accounting Office, October 1, 2002), 7.

42. Edward Norris, statement before the Joint 9/11 Inquiry Select Committees on Intelligence, *Congressional Reports: Joint Inquiry into Intelligence Community Activities.*

43. Police Executive Research Forum, "Protecting Your Community From Terrorism," vol. 1, chapter 4, for FBI, state, and local law enforcement's views on Joint Terrorism Task Forces.

44. Author's conversation with local law enforcement official.

45. Police Executive Research Forum, "Protecting Your Community From Terrorism," vol. 1, page 16.

46. Craig B. Whelden, "Hawaii's Homeland Security," *Military Review* 82 (May 2002): 2–7.

47. George W. Bush, *National Strategy for the Physical Protection of Critical Infrastructure and Key Assets* (Washington, D.C.: White House, February 2003), 26–27.

48. "Clearing" someone means investigating the person's background to determine suitability and trustworthiness. "Need to know" means a requirement for the information in order to perform duties.

49. Scott Dodd, "Police Say Security Clearances Unwieldy; Full Background Checks Required for FBI Data," *Charlotte Observer* via Nexis (March 7, 2003); also Police Executive Research Forum, "Protecting Your Community From Terrorism," vol. 1, chapter 3, for FBI and state and local law enforcement's views on security clearances. There seems to be a great misunderstanding of the security clearance process.

50. Antiterrorism Intelligence Distribution Act of 2003, S. 266, introduced in the Senate by Senator John Edwards on January 30, 2003.

51. Stephen [appears as Steven] Cambone, "Hearing of the Senate Armed Services Committee," Federal News Service, via Nexis (February 27, 2003).

52. George W. Bush, Homeland Security Presidential Directive 3, "Homeland Security Advisory System" (March 12, 2002); and George W. Bush, Homeland Security Presidential Directive 5, "Management of Domestic Incidents" (February 28, 2003).

53. Homeland Security Act of 2002, section 201(d)(6).

54. George W. Bush, draft Homeland Security Bill, section 201(5), sent to Congress on June 18, 2002.

USING THE MILITARY AT HOME: YESTERDAY, TODAY, AND TOMORROW

RICHARD H. KOHN

Today the United States is undergoing a great transformation in national security thinking and priorities. Between the end of the Cold War in 1989 and the collapse of the Soviet Union in 1991, the country began to abandon the policy of containment and the strategy of deterrence that had governed American relations with the rest of the world for over 4 decades. For only the fourth time in its national history, the United States has been changing its national security policies and reconfiguring its military institutions to adapt to a new role in world politics.[1] Once again, for a variety of reasons—not least because of technolo-gies Americans themselves pioneered—defense of the American homeland has become central to national security. Protecting the American people inside the United States is the most significant and perplexing of the changes underway in national defense. What should be—must be—the role of the military in homeland defense?

HISTORICAL EXPERIENCE

Until the middle of the twentieth century, safeguarding the continental United States and American

This essay has been edited and is reprinted from Chicago Journal of International Law 4 *(Spring 2003): 165–92. Reproduced with permission.*

territories overseas was the primary mission of the American military. The very first American military forces, the colonial militias, came into existence precisely for the purpose of homeland defense, adapted from the citizen military forces of early modern England, which themselves had been formed for defense against invasion in the absence of a standing army. In North America, beginning in the second quarter of the seventeenth century, colonial governments required the service of the able-bodied white male population to muster periodically, keep arms, train, and embody not only for defense but for offensive expeditions against hostile Indian tribes. In the eighteenth century, during the wars between England and France for imperial domination, the threat metastasized into the combined invasion of French and sometimes Spanish forces from the sea, as well as on land. The scale and scope of these conflicts forced the colonies to depend on British military forces, and on occasion, to fully mobilize the human and material resources of their own populations. So focused on defense were these militia forces that they were almost always restricted by law to service within the colony of origin. At the same time, volunteers or men drafted from the units were used for offensive expeditions to attack Indian tribes, or to seize the seaports, cities, or fortifications of other European powers in the new world.[2]

During the nineteenth century, these local militias —either in the form of the enrolled units (the entire militia of a colony or state), a group of individual volunteers, drafted individuals, or through the concept of a citizen's obligation to serve when required— formed the basis of American military power. After the Civil War, with the creation of state national guards (volunteer militia), the militias began their transformation into the warfighting reserves of the regular armed forces.[3] Beginning in the 1970s, the reserves became even more closely aligned with the regulars in the "Total Force" policy;[4] some ground units were assigned to fill out regular Army divisions to make them ready for combat, and some support functions like Civil Affairs migrated almost entirely into the reserve components.[5] In the case of the Air Force, reserve forces grew increasingly integrated into virtually all combat and support operations of the regulars over a generation's time.[6] In the 1990s, National Guard and reserve ground forces began to supplement regular Army forces in peacekeeping and peace enforcement duties overseas, an unprecedented use of reserves in constabulary duties, in addition to their other duties.[7] The Guard and Reserve leadership grasped every mission available to prove the military importance of reserve forces and to acquire the most resources and the most modern weapons possible.[8] The regulars, stretched thin after the Cold War by numerous foreign interventions and peacekeeping operations, welcomed the relief from the stresses that a high operational tempo had placed on their personnel and equipment.[9] Yet throughout the twentieth century, the National Guard remained state forces, no matter how closely monitored, trained,

organized, or shaped by the federal government, or how completely focused they became on warfighting in doctrine, organization, training, and weapons.[10]

Furthermore, going back to the beginning of American history, American military forces, both militia and regular, fulfilled internal domestic functions as well; particularly, the maintenance of order when local and state law enforcement institutions proved inadequate. The framers of the Constitution agreed, as one put it after the Constitutional Convention, that "no government can be stable, which hangs on human inclination alone, unbiased by the fear of coercion."[11] Although they disagreed about the extent to which government depended on military power to keep order and enforce its will, they were agreed that regular forces must remain in the background. "Force," according to Alexander Hamilton, "may be understood [as] a *coertion of laws* or *coertion of arms*."[12] For the normal functioning of society, law would compel obedience and keep order. If that were to fail, then the power of the community would act in the form of police or sheriffs forces, or in extremity, the militia. If that failed, then the regular forces would be called out as the last resort: "when resistance to the laws required it," James Madison told the Virginia ratifying convention, to prevent "society from being destroyed."[13] As far as the internal use of military power was concerned, the Constitution favored very specifically militia rather than regulars. Congress' power read: "To provide for calling forth the Militia to execute the Laws of the Union" and "suppress Insurrections."[14]

Militias have been used throughout American history to keep order and to enforce the laws. State forces suppressed rebellions in western Pennsylvania in 1794 and in Rhode Island in 1841; intervened in coal mine strikes in Pennsylvania and Colorado early in the twentieth century, and in a famous textile strike in Lawrence, Massachusetts, in 1912; mobilized to stop a lynching in Mississippi in 1904, to quarantine Arizona against California cattle with hoof-and-mouth disease in the early 1920s, and to stop violence in the longshoreman's strike in San Francisco in 1934. In the decade from 1886 to 1895 alone, a time of intense industrial strife, state governors called out the Guard over three hundred times.[15] In the South, an additional militia role developed, adapted from sugar plantations in Barbados in the seventeenth-century Caribbean: to police slavery through the prevention of insurrection, regulation of slave movement and gatherings, and the apprehension of runaway slaves by means of regular patrols in towns and the countryside—practices that lasted more than a century and a half to the end of the Civil War, and that continued illegally against African Americans by the Ku Klux Klan and other terrorist or vigilante groups during Reconstruction.[16]

The regular armed forces, created in the 1780s and 1790s after American Independence, fulfilled similar missions of homeland defense and internal order. For more than a century, the Army garrisoned frontier and seacoast forts to occupy American territory, control strategic points of transportation and communication, and prevent or slow invasions of more populated areas.[17] Until its modernization at the end of the nineteenth century and the adoption of doctrines emphasizing command of the sea and the destruction of invading forces in fleet actions, the Navy focused on harassment of hostile forces, raiding enemy commercial shipping, and the defense of American coasts and harbors. Even the new fleet strategy was predicated on stopping enemy forces from invading the United States. As late as the eve of World War II, with hemispheric defense the basis of American war planning, even such offensive forces as the strategic bomber fleets being planned by the Army Air Corps were being justified to Congress and the American people as defenses that could attack enemy fleets heading for North America.[18] Only during and after the Cold War did American strategy call for defending the country and advancing American interests by positioning forces abroad and going on the offensive. Even then, a sizable slice of American military power—strategic nuclear forces, air defenses, portions of the National Guard and reserves —was configured deliberately to prevent attack on American soil or respond to it in some way.

Moreover, the regular armed forces have always fulfilled internal, constabulary functions, even in the twentieth century after they had recast themselves into warfighting organizations designed to combat the military establishments of the great powers.[19] The Army explored the West, enforced Jefferson's embargo laws (or tried to), mapped and surveyed railroad routes, implemented government policy toward the Indians, enforced federal law over the Mormons, captured fugitive slaves, intervened to restore order during the era of industrial and labor strife into the 1920s, restored order during race riots, dispersed Bonus marchers in the nation's capital in 1932, ran Civilian Conservation Corps camps, guarded interned Japanese Americans during World War II, fought forest fires, dredged rivers and harbors, built dams and flood control systems, and fed and sheltered Americans displaced by fires, floods, and earthquakes. Disaster assistance became "so commonplace" that "by the 1960s," according to one historian, "few seasons passed without some involvement in flood, hurricane, tornado, blizzard, or other form of help for civilians in emergencies."[20] The Navy mapped and charted coastal areas and distant seas, chased pirates, suppressed the slave trade, negotiated foreign agreements, safeguarded Americans and their interests overseas, promoted and protected American commerce, and fostered scientific research. Marines guarded diplomats and the U.S. mails,[21] suppressed riots, fought fires, and, like the other services, engaged in disaster relief. The Air Force has provided search and rescue, aerial photography, humanitarian airlift, medical evacuation, and disaster relief throughout its history.[22]

Many of these internal roles receded into the background after World War II because the armed forces (including the National Guard and reserves) became absorbed by foreign warfighting, preparing to intervene abroad or to wage limited wars as part of the Cold War. Nation-building and exploration were no longer necessary or desirable because they distracted the armed forces from the capacity to win high-tech, high-tempo military conflicts against foreign adversaries, particularly Soviet and Warsaw Pact forces. After World War II, industrial strife diminished, and except for some notable instances of racial conflict— either urban riots or southern resistance to school desegregation—violence and disorder on a scale that overpowered local and state law enforcement institutions declined in frequency.

Yet the armed forces never quite succeeded in evading some domestic functions. Since World War II, the National Guard has been activated innumerable times by state governors or by the President to quell riots, enforce racial integration, prevent looting in the wake of natural disasters, or for other purposes of internal order. Disaster assistance, fighting forest fires, keeping order, coping with anti–Vietnam War violence, and many other internal activities involved the American military episodically throughout the last half of the twentieth century. Army units manned antiaircraft missile defenses around American cities in the 1950s and 1960s while squadrons of air defense fighters maintained readiness to intercept Soviet bombers. Regular Army units at Ft. Lewis, Washington, were even pressed into the hunt for "D.B. Cooper," the legendary criminal who hijacked a jetliner over the Northwest, parachuted out of it, and disappeared with the $200,000 ransom he extorted out of the Federal Bureau of Investigation (FBI).[23] Ground forces were still called upon to cope with race riots and resistance to school desegregation in Arkansas, Mississippi, and Alabama, and to support other state and federal organizations in times of need. Beginning in the late 1980s, the Army and Air Force were pressed into service to assist in the "war" on drugs, interdicting shipments headed for American shores, and in some instances, to assist in the effort to halt illegal immigration along the border with Mexico.[24] On the eve of September 11, the reserve forces had just begun to consider reevaluating their roles and missions. The regular forces, although under great pressure by the new Bush administration to "transform," had done little to alter their doctrine, weapons, or organization to meet the challenges of the twenty-first-century security environment. Neither regulars nor reserves had even begun to seriously contemplate homeland defense, a term hardly known to the armed forces of the United States when the airplanes struck the Pentagon and felled two of the three tallest buildings in the country on September 11.[25]

SINCE SEPTEMBER 11

The attacks of September 11 quickly forced the military establishment to think anew and act on the internal role that had so declined in relative importance. Air National Guard and regular Air Force fighter planes scrambled to intercept the hijacked airliners heading for the Pentagon and over Pennsylvania. Even in the reduced level of threat before that tragic day, the North American Aerospace Defense Command (NORAD) operated air defense fighters regularly assigned and on alert to protect American air space, but with almost no concept of defense against terrorists using aircraft as weapons of destruction and no intention of flying regular interceptor patrols over American cities, which became routine for months after, and continues intermittently, albeit with reduced numbers of sorties. "Operation Noble Eagle isn't an operation," Secretary of the Air Force James Roche informed an audience during the increased homeland defense threat level of Code Orange in February 2003. "Ladies and gentlemen, it's our future. It's never going away!"[26]

From the beginning of the crisis on September 11, the armed forces rushed to support the state and local agencies responding to the disaster—as armed forces have been doing for most of American history. According to the Bush administration's National Strategy for Homeland Security issued in July 2002, "New Jersey and New York guardsmen and Navy and Marine Corps reservists provided medical personnel to care for the injured, military police to assist local law enforcement officials, key asset protection, transportation, communications, logistics, and a myriad of other functions to support recovery efforts in New York City."[27] In Washington, D.C., Maryland Guardsmen sent military police for security at the Pentagon. Nationwide, over seven thousand National Guard began patrolling 429 commercial airports and soon, Guardsmen began supplementing Customs Service and Immigration Service officers at U.S. borders. At West Point, the need to protect the installation 24 hours a day, 7 days a week, so overwhelmed the Military Academy's local security details that the faculty— even one general—took turns as gate guards until the National Guard could be put in place.[28] Between September 11, 2001, and early February 2003, some 170,000 Guardsmen and reservists were activated at one time or another to supplement border security, protect airports, guard military bases and such civilian installations as power plants and bridges, protect the population at special sporting or civic events, and for other purposes of homeland defense.[29] For the first time, Army reservists were to guard U.S. Air Force bases.[30] As the armed forces mobilized and deployed for a campaign against Iraq, the numbers exceeded 150,000 by mid-February 2003, and may reach as high as 250,000 people on active duty.[31] The secretary of defense ordered a change in the missions of the regulars and reserves: the active duty regular forces were to concentrate on overseas missions, including those that had in recent years been migrating to the reserves, and reserve forces were to focus on defense inside the United States. As the Pentagon's "transformation" chief, retired Navy Vice Admiral Arthur Cebrowski, put it, the "post-9/11 reality" is "that we need a new way to rebalance our overseas interests and our concern for homeland security."[32]

The Coast Guard, the nation's fifth armed service, formed in 1915 from a merger of the Revenue Cutter and Life Saving Services, underwent a metamorphosis. From a law enforcement institution operating under the Transportation Department devoted to catching smugglers, enforcing fisheries statutes, interdicting illegal drugs, and providing maritime safety services to Americans on coasts, lakes, and inland waterways, the Coast Guard almost overnight became an antiterrorist force charged with security for the nation's ports and sea frontiers. Now it is part of the new Department of Homeland Security. Its aged fleet of aircraft, ships, and boats will be replaced or upgraded as quickly as possible, a recapitalization of at least $17 billion over the next 2 decades, "the largest contract for new assets ever awarded in Coast Guard history."[33]

Since September 11, the White House and the Department of Justice have used the military establishment to incarcerate and interrogate suspected terrorists and "enemy combatants" and keep them beyond the reach of the civilian judicial system, even if they are American citizens, to collect intelligence and prevent future attacks. The threat to try terrorists in military commissions under the authority of an Executive Order that severely restricted the individual rights of the detainees, seemed at the time it was issued (barely 2 months after September 11) grounded as much in expediency as necessity.[34] Repudiated by a committee of the American Bar Association, the Executive Order was softened by rules governing its implementation drawn up by the Pentagon.[35] At the same time, the government designated prisoners captured in Afghanistan and Pakistan as "unlawful enemy combatants" outside the provisions of the Geneva Convention on prisoners of war.[36] They have been incarcerated at the Marine Corps base at Guantanamo, Cuba, precisely because that facility is beyond the reach of American courts. That detention has since been essentially sanctioned by two U.S. District Courts.[37] Two American citizens held in Navy prisons in Norfolk, Virginia, and Charleston, South Carolina, since April and June of 2002, have not been charged with crimes nor have they been allowed access to legal representation, an apparent violation of their constitutional rights. Efforts to allow them access to legal counsel have been opposed by the government and rebuffed by the judiciary, without any declaration or admission of the suspension of the right of habeas corpus by either Congress or the executive branch. This legal limbo was expressly sought by the government for the purposes of domestic security and intelligence collection but condemned by the American Bar Association.[38]

Perhaps the greatest change in the armed forces after September 11 occurred not in operations or deployments or the use of military legal institutions, but in organizational changes inside the Department of Defense. Because intelligence is so critical to preventing terrorism, the department has a new undersecretary for Intelligence, a role to be filled by Stephen Cambone, Secretary Rumsfeld's most trusted lieutenant for "transformation." A new assistant secretary for Homeland Defense has also come into existence to coordinate planning and activities inside the Office of the Secretary. Most importantly, in response to a recommendation by the Joint Chiefs of Staff, the secretary of defense revised the Unified Command Plan, the document governing the organization and responsibilities of the nation's military forces worldwide, to create a command in North America to protect the United States. Northern Command will "consolidate . . . existing missions that were previously executed by other military organizations. The command's mission is homeland defense and civil support, specifically . . . to deter, prevent, and defeat threats and aggression aimed at the United States, its territories, and interests . . . including consequence management operations" with whatever forces are "assigned . . . by the President."[39] Northern Command's head (dual-hatted as NORAD commander), Air Force General Ralph Eberhart, not only plans and prepares operations to help civilian "first responders" after an attack, but also engages in military operations on and over "the continental United States, Alaska, Canada, Mexico, and the surrounding water out to approximately 500 nautical miles" including "the Gulf of Mexico, Puerto Rico and the U.S. Virgin Islands."[40]

What seemed to be major but essentially bureaucratic alterations represented in reality a transformation of American national security thinking: a greater concern about domestic safety than foreign attack, about internal threats than external war, about the murder of American citizens in large numbers and the harming of American institutions, installations, landmarks, and physical and electronic infrastructure at home rather than war with foreign nations. "Defending our Nation against its enemies is the first and fundamental commitment of the Federal Government," the President declared in issuing his first National Security Strategy, a year after September 11. "Today, that task has changed dramatically. Enemies in the past needed great armies and great industrial capabilities to endanger America. Now, shadowy networks of individuals can bring great chaos and suffering to our shores . . . turn[ing] the power of modern technologies against us. . . . The gravest danger our Nation faces lies at the crossroads of radicalism and technology."[41]

THE FUTURE

The danger posed by the use of the regular military forces internally is dual: on the one hand, impairing military effectiveness in the primary task of the regulars today, warfighting overseas; and on the other hand, undermining civil liberty (as has happened in past wars) by using regular troops for law enforcement, to try or incarcerate American citizens, to gather intelligence, or to suppress dissent or antiwar protest.

On the surface, there seems little ground for worry. The creation of a civilian cabinet Department of Homeland Security charged with overall responsibility for preventing and dealing with the consequences of further attacks suggests that the military would not assume inappropriate authority over the population even in catastrophic circumstances. Expressing sensitivity about using the military at home, The National Homeland Security Strategy issued in the summer of 2002 listed only limited roles for the armed forces internally:

1. Conventional military activities in those "extraordinary" situations "such as combat air patrols or maritime defense operations" in which the military "would take the lead in defending people" and American "territory" with support "by other agencies";

2. "Responding" to "emergencies such as . . . an attack or . . . forest fires, floods, tornadoes, or other catastrophes," for which the Defense Department would react "quickly to provide capabilities that other agencies do not have"; and

3. "Limited scope" situations "where other agencies have the lead—for example, security at a special event like the recent Olympics."[42]

The Defense Department has shunned a wider role for the military in law enforcement. "Frankly I don't think the American people want to see the military performing a domestic law enforcement function," Deputy Secretary of Defense Paul Wofowitz has stated. Although there would be much "close handing off of information both ways" among the Defense Department, the intelligence agencies, and the FBI, "when it comes to doing a wiretap on a domestic suspect, I don't think people want the Defense Department doing that."[43] Likewise, General Eberhart voiced genuine sensitivity to civil liberties: "We also understand Civics 101," he told a reporter. "I really don't think . . . the military will be doing things that should be done by other agencies."[44] The Northern Command's website contains explicit pages on "Limitations" and "Operating with the Law."[45]

Yet the behavior of the Bush administration in the fight against terrorism is anything but reassuring. The conservative columnist George Will, listing some of the radical changes inherent in many administration foreign and domestic policies and proposals, observed that "America has a president unusually comfortable contemplating, and pushing, change."[46] Attorney General John Ashcroft, in a single statement at a National Security Council meeting the day after September 11, altered the primary mission of the Justice Department and the FBI from law enforcement to antiterrorism—without comment from the president.[47] "The president had made clear to Ashcroft in an earlier conversation that he wanted to make sure an attack like the ones on the Pentagon and World Trade Center never happened again," reported the Washington Post's Bob Woodward. "It was essential to think unconventionally. Now, Ashcroft was saying, the focus of the FBI and the Justice

Department should change from prosecution to prevention, a radical shift in priorities."[48]

The administration apparently presumed that protecting an open society against a ruthless, formless, suicidal enemy bent on killing large numbers of Americans required new thinking and unprecedented measures—and perhaps heretofore unacceptable new methods. Ashcroft, acting and often speaking for the administration, has demonstrated a limited sensitivity to civil liberties and, despite rhetoric to the contrary, scant regard for traditional legal safeguards. Outgoing House Majority Leader Dick Armey "said he thought Mr. Ashcroft and the Justice Department were 'out of control.'"[49] A scholar of the history of the attorney general's office put it this way: "The terrorist attacks have energized Ashcroft in a remarkable way, resonating with his sincere belief that there is evil in the world."[50]

Furthermore, the administration is the most secretive seen in Washington in decades: "a sea change in government openness," according to a reporter who consulted "dozens of experts."[51] A November 5, 2001, Executive Order restricted the release of presidential documents from previous administrations, angering not only historians and journalists but many in Congress, including some in the president's own party.[52] A November 13, 2001, Executive Order authorized military commissions for the purpose of trying enemy combatants in secret.[53] The administration has closed immigration court proceedings to the public and chosen to keep secret the names of thousands of immigrants swept up after September 11 and the names of the prisoners designated "unlawful enemy combatants" incarcerated at Guantanamo and in Bagram, Afghanistan. The attorney general established an interagency task force to reconsider punishments for leaking classified information, the first such review in 2 decades.[54] The administration has kept all sorts of information away from Congress, including activating a "shadow" government of civil servants at "secret underground sites outside Washington to ensure that the federal government could survive a devastating terrorist attack on the nation's capital."[55] At one point, after leaks on Capitol Hill, the president threatened to share classified information only with the heads of the committees involved in national security—to the dismay and sometimes outrage of lawmakers, including Republicans.[56]

Surveillance of American citizens and immigrants has expanded enormously, but not as much as the administration wished. Two weeks after the terrorist attacks in New York and Washington, D.C., the attorney general suggested in a White House meeting that Americans spy on each other: "We want to convey the message that you're likely to be detected if you're doing something wrong."[57] This Terrorism Information and Prevention System (TIPS), described by the Administration as "a nationwide program to help thousands of American truck drivers, letter carriers, train conductors, ship captains, and utility workers report potential terrorist activity,"[58] appeared so intrusive that Congress actually prohibited it.[59] A program of surveillance targeted at "hundreds of mostly young, mostly Muslim men" was instituted to find al Qaeda sleeper agents planted inside the United States.[60] The government won broad authority to use the permission of the Foreign Intelligence Surveillance Court to institute wiretaps and other undercover investigations against suspects, and to use the information gathered thereby in criminal proceedings, thus erasing a barrier protecting the Fourth Amendment guarantee against "unreasonable searches" and warrants without "probable cause."[61] According to one recent analysis, "from New York City to Seattle, police officials are looking to do away with rules that block them from spying on people and groups without evidence that a crime has been committed," and "at the same time, federal and local police agencies are looking for systematic, high-tech ways to root out terrorists before they strike."[62] One Defense Department program provoked national attention and much anxiety: the Total Information Awareness (TIA) research effort at the Defense Advanced Research Projects Agency. TIA would sift thousands of disparate databases to detect suspicious activity in an effort to anticipate terrorist behavior. The system would "mine" computer records generated by Americans' private behavior—credit card charges, phone usage, travel behavior, medical data, e-mail messages, and other evidence of personal behaviors—with such vast implications for privacy and opportunity for government abuse (acknowledged by a panel of computer scientists and policy experts who reviewed the system for the Pentagon) that Congress prohibited further development without regular reporting to, and oversight from, Capitol Hill.[63] Similarly the government, according to one report, plans to require "Internet service providers to help build a centralized system to enable broad monitoring of the Internet and, potentially, surveillance of its users."[64]

Immediately after September 11, the administration proposed legislation to expand authority to monitor voice and e-mail messages, broaden the definition of terrorism, punish people who even unknowingly support or harbor terrorists, intensify attacks on money laundering that could support terrorism, break down the barriers between intelligence gathering and criminal investigations, allow the government authority to detain immigrant suspects indefinitely or expel them without court review, and permit other heretofore prohibited or unprecedented police powers. The administration hurried its proposals through the House and Senate a month after September 11, and when both chambers balked at the extremity of some of the provisions, the administration attacked the Democrats and intensified the pressure. In spite of these tactics, Congress insisted on limitations on the new government authority and sunset provisions for the more intrusive or authoritarian powers.[65] Yet in early 2003, the administration apparently intended to return to the Congress requesting further expansion of police powers, provisions for secret arrests and detentions, exceptions from judicial oversight, and other changes that invade civil liberties, to prosecute the war on terrorism more aggressively.[66]

If, then, the Bush Administration tilts decidedly in favor of security over liberty to prosecute what top officials see as an extremely difficult, ambiguous war against a suicidal enemy with no "center of gravity," an enemy clearly capable of using the American legal system and the openness of American society to its advantage, it is likely that the military will be used internally, perhaps in ways that threaten civil liberties or diminish the warfighting effectiveness of the regular armed forces. And it is likely that the American people will support such expedients.[67]

The dangers are threefold.

First, the federal government might turn to the regular armed forces because they are handy, convenient, and superficially at least, effective—and because the civilian agencies involved in homeland defense at various levels of government are not being funded adequately. The concern is not the ordinary conduct of the war at home. The use of a military surveillance system to help local law enforcement catch the Washington, D.C., area sniper in the fall of 2002 drew little criticism. Nor did calling up the National Guard to patrol airports or protect military installations, or supplement the Border Patrol. In fact, reorienting and reordering the National Guard to focus primarily on homeland security would be returning it to its traditional role; the hundreds of thousands of soldiers in the Guard, embedded in 3,100 communities, are the appropriate pool of military people to prepare for domestic attack.[68] They already possess the links with local responders—in some cases, they *are* the local responders in civilian life (a duplication that would have to be prohibited): the fire, police, emergency medical, public health, and other people who provide security and would react to minimize the damage and begin reconstruction after a terrorist attack. Other internal military missions, such as missile defense and cyber defense, could be assigned to the Guard or reserves. The danger in developing capabilities in the regular forces for homeland use is that those capabilities would be most effective in civilian agencies, in the National Guard, or down at the state and local levels that will respond first to a terrorist attack. One example is the Marine Corps's Chemical and Biological Incident Response Force, developed in the mid-1990s in part to help civilian society.[69] One of a number of such organizations in the armed services and scattered across the federal government, the force would likely be useless unless it arrived at the scene within an hour.[70] Experts know that responding to a chemical or biological attack will first occur at the local level, that speed will be critical, and that state and local emergency services, police, fire, public health, and government people need the training, equipment, practice, and staffing if lives are to be saved and panic avoided.[71] Another example: should the Army really be training federal executives to deal with the issues facing them in terrorist attacks just because the federal executives are ineligible for the Justice Department program offered to state and local officials?[72] The dangers of using or relying on the military are many: the duplication and waste of resources, the ineffectiveness of the effort, and the diversion of money, people, and focus from traditional responsibilities, which can diminish the warfighting effectiveness of a military establishment already strained by a broad range of missions and commitments.[73]

A second danger is that the military establishment will be pressed into service temporarily on a substantial scale for disaster response should the United States be struck with one or more weapons of mass destruction, or some massive disruption of our cyber networks that causes multiple or sequential natural or human disasters—and that the "temporary" would last for a very long time. The United States remains, 18 months after September 11, enormously vulnerable to attacks on its trade, ports, transportation and cyber systems, power plants, chemical industry (some 850,000 "facilities that work with hazardous or extremely hazardous substances"), landmarks, and other sites.[74] In the year before the attacks, "489 million people, 127 million cars and 211,000 boats passed through our border inspection systems," wrote a Coast Guard commander who studied the problem and reported to the U.S. Commission on National Security/ 21st Century.[75] Little or no additional federal support has reached the two million local firefighter, emergency service, and law enforcement first responders who would have to deal with a chemical or biological attack in their communities.[76] Nor has the public health system—federal, state, and local— been adequately improved, expanded, or reformed to deal with mass casualties.[77] Judging from the response of the government to September 11 and the possibility of mass panic in the event of future attacks— the reaction to the anthrax and the Washington, D.C., area snipers—one can easily imagine enormous pressure for the use of military forces immediately after a successful attack. A large outbreak of smallpox might require huge areas to be quarantined, with checkpoints controlling the movement of the population, requiring numbers of people that only the military could provide. "Depending on the extent of the outbreak, a quarantine could remain in place—potentially in multiple U.S. cities or regions simultaneously—for weeks, months or even years."[78] "The United States may have to declare martial law someday . . . in the case of a devastating attack with weapons of mass destruction causing tens of thousands of casualties," retired Army General Wayne A. Downing speculated at the end of 2002, some 6 months after leaving the White House as deputy national security adviser for counterterrorism.[79] Northern Command's head, General Eberhart, agrees: "There may be situations if we ever got into a major chemical biological nuclear attack problem where we may, in fact, be in charge," but only if "it's become so bad that the lead federal agency in working with the state governors say . . . 'we give up.' . . . And then the president and the secretary of defense . . . decide, 'yes, that is appropriate.'"[80] Assaults on the food supply, water, or energy resources could provoke a massive deployment of available people for response, recovery, and protection, so the possibilities of an incident involving the military establishment are significant. Even if tens of thousands are not pressed into service, the need for some of the specialized units—medical, chem-bio, police, civil administration, and the like—might prove enormously disruptive to military operations abroad. That is the value of Northern Command: to plan for such an event and to begin to think through the coordination with local and state authorities. Thinking about the very worst catastrophe—the explosion of nuclear weapons in American cities—goes back several years at least. In December 2002, at the recommendation of a commission created 4 years earlier "to advise the president and Congress on domestic response to terrorism involving weapons of mass destruction," discussions began "among various federal agencies" to "delineate a role for U.S. troops, should local and state law enforcement authorities become overwhelmed" by an attack using smallpox.[81] This same commission concluded that it was nowhere clear, even after the creation of the Department of Homeland Security, "which Federal agency" would be "in charge" of the federal response to various kinds of attacks, and "who is in charge is especially problematic when it comes to a bioterrorism attack."[82]

The very planning of such responses with the thousands of federal, state, county, and local public and private agencies and institutions by Northern Command contains inherent dangers. Military staffs are among the most effective planning organizations in American society. Their processes and perspectives—their unstated assumptions—could begin to influence the procedures and operations of state and local law enforcement agencies, fire departments, emergency services providers, public health organizations, and governmental agencies: militarizing them enough to harm the performance of their normal responsibilities. In the past 2 decades, the military model has already invaded the American criminal justice system to an unprecedented degree: the dramatic rise in numbers of SWAT teams; increased cooperation between the military and police; "boot camps" in the correctional system; the language, concepts, and mentality.[83] American foreign relations likewise have increasingly come to be influenced by military concerns, understandings, and the military itself, in ways unlike the era of the Cold War and quite beyond the demands of a "war on terrorism": a reliance on military commands to manage many regional relationships or bilateral relations; the threat or use of force to achieve American aims; the subordination of other interests to security beyond the dictates of the war on terrorism.[84] An inadvertent militarization of domestic society[85]—quite beyond the uneven and diffuse ways in which the military has come to pervade American civic life and culture after 5 decades of world and cold wars—arising indirectly, but unnecessarily, from the demands of homeland security,

although unforeseen, is possible. And lurking in the background, there is always the possibility that military operations on American soil will result in collateral damage and unintended violence and death, unless the regular military devotes considerable time to training for a homeland role, with the resulting degradation of its conventional warfighting capability.

A third danger is the increasing blurring of the line between military and civilian functions, in part because of convenience and in part because the struggle against terrorism is likely to last indefinitely. In many respects, the "war on terrorism" is no war at all, but a concerted (and hopefully coordinated) national and international effort involving law enforcement, policing, diplomacy, economic initiatives, and military operations to protect the United States against radical Islamic terrorists. There has been no mobilization, no continuous combat, no sudden heating up of the economy or rise in prices, no raising of taxes, no call to sacrifice, no major interruption or upheaval of civilian life—the kinds of experiences common to other wars in American history. In fact, just the opposite has occurred. Americans were asked to "go back to normal" after September 11, to travel and spend, and were given no precise definition of the enemy, no explicit articulation of a strategy to win the war, nor a description of what victory would be, how the war would be waged, and when and how it might end. Instead the government has repeated consistently that this war will last indefinitely, and that it might involve combat at home. One of the government's most senior, experienced counterterrorism experts casts doubt on the "war" paradigm: "I am disturbed by how often I hear references to 'as long as the emergency lasts' or 'as long as the war on terrorism is going on.' . . . What we are doing has an indefinite run."[86]

The greatest worry is the gradual transformation of military forces into adjuncts of the law enforcement, domestic intelligence, and prosecutorial functions that have heretofore been strictly civilian. This has happened before—during almost every war since the mid-nineteenth century, with harm to American civil liberties and to the relationship between the armed forces and the American people. During the Civil War, the federal government used the Army to arrest, try, and imprison thousands of citizens for disloyalty, many of them Northerners, and some for statements or speeches that seemed to many at the time to be legitimate dissent or opposition to the Lincoln administration and its policies. Others were arrested on suspicion of profiteering, fraud, corruption, or otherwise shady dealings relating to the government, and there were documented cases of torture in the prisons.[87] During World War I, some 2,300 of over six thousand enemy aliens arrested by the Justice Department were "interned by the military as dangerous to the national security."[88] The Army and Navy participated in government censorship of telegraph and cable messages, newspapers, radio, and public speech. The Army broke strikes, raided labor meetings and union headquarters, and harassed and suppressed radical labor groups, often acting in the role of local law enforcement—arresting and detaining suspects—as well as keeping order. In Seattle, the Office of Naval Intelligence actually arrested Wobblies (members of the International Workers of the World) on the docks and ships. Military Intelligence, which was, in the words of an Army history, "consciously antiradical and antilabor," created over five hundred units nationwide to spy on workers in war production plants in an attempt to prevent sabotage.[89] The Army connected not only with federal, state, and local law enforcement, but with private patriotic and vigilante groups watching aliens and radicals in what the history called a "machinery of repression" that, in the end, acted to suppress dissent as well as guarantee the security of the homefront.[90] During the 1920s and 1930s, the War Department maintained and updated plans to protect the country from domestic unrest and internal revolution fomented by radicals, leftists, and pacifists, on whom military intelligence collected information.[91] During World War II, the Army advocated and then carried out the evacuation of Japanese Americans from the West Coast to "relocation centers" run by the civilian War Relocation Authority.[92] During the Cold War, the Army gathered intelligence on civilian groups thought to be radical or subversive, including civil rights and peace organizations. During the Vietnam War, Army surveillance increased dramatically in size and scope: spying on antiwar protests, investigating unrest on college campuses, monitoring racial turmoil in American cities, and scrutinizing political dissent.[93]

The use of the military internally to support African American voting during Reconstruction influenced Congress, with the approval of the Army, to pass the Posse Comitatus Act in 1878, to keep the regular Army from being used to enforce the laws. The military establishment valued this separation, not wishing to be diverted from its focus on war or to be perceived as the tool of one set of Americans against another. Thus the armed forces resisted eroding these restrictions in the 1980s to help interdict the importation of narcotics in the war on drugs.[94] And the military continues to be troubled by the tendency. As one student of the problem concluded 4 years before September 11, "in recent years, Congress and the public have seen the military as a panacea for domestic problems."[95] "Civilian law enforcement requires the cognizance of individual rights and seeks to protect those rights, even if the person being protected is a bad actor. Prior to the use of force, police officers attempt to de-escalate a situation" and "are trained to use lesser forms of force when possible." However, "soldiers" emphasize "deadly force." "Escalation is the rule" and "in an encounter with a person identified with the enemy, soldiers need not be cognizant of individual rights, and the use of deadly force is authorized without any aggressive or bad act by that person."[96]

The larger principle is this: that regular armed forces need to face outward, against American enemies, rather than inward, where a military force can become an institution acting on behalf of one part of the community against another. That corrodes the morale of the forces, harms recruiting, reduces readiness, undermines the support of the country for the armed forces, and ultimately drives a wedge between the military and society. Temporarily reinforcing civilian agencies in border control or with drug interdiction, or to provide security for the Olympics or sporting events like the Super Bowl seem, on the surface, functional and helpful. For nearly 2 decades, regular military forces, including Special Forces, have been aiding border control authorities along the Texas-Mexico border and law enforcement organizations nationwide since the early 1990s. But when Marines inadvertently killed an innocent teenage goat herder in 1997, ground reconnaissance along the border ceased.[97] Yet today, that same border with Mexico presents a special challenge for keeping terrorists out of the United States.[98] Both the chairman of the Senate Armed Forces Committee and General Eberhart of Northern Command have called for a review of the Posse Comitatus Act limitations on domestic uses of the armed forces.[99] In January 2003, Undersecretary of Defense Edward "Pete" Aldridge asked the Defense Science Board to review "what specific roles and missions" the military should possess in homeland defense. Citing the great resources the military possesses, Aldridge pointed out the "many . . . systems engineering, technical capabilities, relevant technologies, logistics expertise and modeling and simulation capabilities needed for effective homeland security."[100]

The problem in the end is not likely to arise from the military itself. Over a century of concern about the use of regular forces internally, and over a decade of discussion about the negative impact on war-fighting capabilities and civil liberties, have made the uniformed leadership extremely wary of altering the boundaries separating military and civil functions in law enforcement and domestic operations.[101] Memories of using the Army against labor and radical groups in World War I and to spy on antiwar protests during the Vietnam War have dimmed but remain alive in institutional understanding. The danger lies in public pressure exerted on the political leadership to act, and in turn, a tendency to use the military because it has the resources and the organizational effectiveness to accomplish what the American public might demand.

The United States has experience with a national security state and its excesses during World War I, World War II, and the Cold War. Although the domestic threat lies more in civilian counterintelligence, the use of the military lies constantly in the background, particularly for those nightmares—the endless "what ifs" in our imaginations—of one or more catastrophes involving weapons of mass destruction, the results of which overwhelm not only temporary civilian responders, but "consequence management" over the long term, and the patience and willingness of the American people to balance security with liberty.[102] Significantly, the courts, normally the bulwark of liberty in American society, have consistently deferred to the military in the operation of the system of military justice, and to the other branches and particularly the executive branch on civil liberties in wartime, permitting infringements during war that, under other circumstances, would not be allowed.[103] The Supreme Court under William Rehnquist has gone further, adopting a doctrine that designates the military "a society apart from civilian society," superior morally and culturally, and essentially exempt from civilian judicial oversight.[104] Under this doctrine, civilian control would be left exclusively to executive and legislative branches that might, under future circumstances and without regard for traditional constitutional and legal safeguards, give power and authority to the military inside the United States, over American citizens. It is this blurring of boundaries—the militarization of internal security and the possible use of the military domestically—that poses the greatest danger.

Over 2 centuries ago, as the Constitutional Convention was concluding its work and the members were signing the document, the aged scientist, diplomat, and political leader Benjamin Franklin remarked that throughout the convention's work, he had speculated whether a sun carved on the back of the president's chair was rising or setting. "But now at length I have the happiness to know that it is a rising and not a setting Sun."[105] At the same time, Franklin sensed the fragility of the experiment. Accosted outside the hall by a local woman, "Well, Doctor, what have we got, a republic or a monarchy?" "A republic," Franklin responded, "if you can keep it."[106]

NOTES

Portions of this article were included in lectures to the National Security Studies Decision Making Seminar, Johns Hopkins University School of Advanced International Studies, Baltimore, Maryland; the History and Strategy Roundtable, National War College, Washington, D.C.; the National Security Law Course, Duke University Law School, Durham, North Carolina; and the National Security Management Course, Maxwell School of Citizenship and Public Affairs, Syracuse University, Syracuse, New York. The author thanks Michael Allsep, Andrew J. Bacevich, Peter D. Feaver, Abigail A. Kohn, Lynne H. Kohn, Jonathan Luric, Erik Riker-Coleman, and Scott Silliman for assistance and advice.

1. Previous transition periods were the 1780s to early 1800s, when the United States created national military policies and institutions to replace the military and naval direction and forces Britain had provided its colonies, and to create the nineteenth-century constabulary military establishment; the 1800s to the early twentieth century, when the Navy and Army modernized their weapons, organizations, and doctrines to change from constabularies into warfighting institutions planning and preparing in peacetime for mobilization and warfare; and the late 1940s to the early 1950s, when the United States reorganized the government for national security, adopted containment and deterrence as its foreign policy and military strategy, and constructed a large standing military establishment partly deployed overseas, ready for limited or general war, and stationed in Europe and the Far East. For short, comprehensive interpretations of the American military experience, see John Shy, "The American Military Experience: History and Learning," in *A People Numerous and Armed: Reflections on the Military Struggle for American Independence,* revised edition (Ann Arbor: University of Michigan Press, 1990), 265; C. Vann Woodward, *The Future of the Past* (Oxford: Oxford University Press, 1989), chapter 4. The effort to reorganize the military establishment in the 1990s can be followed in a series of reviews conducted on the Department of Defense. See Les Aspin, U.S. Department of Defense, *Report on the Bottom-Up Review* (Washington, D.C.: U.S. Department of Defense, 1993), portions available at www.fas.org/man/docs/bur/index.html; Commission on Roles and Missions of the Armed Forces, *Directions for Defense: Report of the Commission on Roles and Missions of the Armed Forces,* Executive Summary ES-1-ES-9 (Washington, D.C.: Commission, 1995), available at www.fas.org/man/docs/corm95/di1062.html; William S. Cohen, U.S. Department of Defense, *Report of the Quadrennial Defense Review* (Washington, D.C.: U.S. Department of Defense, 1997), available at www.defenselink.mil/pubs/qdr/index.tml; National Defense Panel, *Transforming Defense: National Security in the 21st Century* (Washington, D.C.: U.S. Department of Defense, 1997), available at www.dtic.mil/ndp/FullDoc2.pdf; U.S. Commission on National Security/21st Century, *Road Map for National Security: Imperative for Change: The Phase III Report of the U.S. Commission on National Security/21st Century* (Washington, D.C.: U.S. Commission on National Security/21st Century, 2001), available at www.nssg.gov/PhaseIIIFR.pdf.

2. For surveys of the militia and colonial wars, see John K. Mahon, *History of the Militia and the National Guard* (New York: Macmillan, 1983), 6–34; Douglas Edward Leach, *Arms for Empire: A Military History of the British Colonies in North America, 1607–1763* (New York: Macmillan, 1973). For examples of the extent of mobilization of the population during the colonial period, see Fred Anderson, *A People's Army: Massachusetts Soldiers and Society in the Seven Years' War* (Chapel Hill, N.C.: University of North Carolina Press, 1984); Harold E. Selesky, *War and Society in Colonial Connecticut* (New Haven: Yale University Press, 1990).

3. See Mahon, *History of the Militia and the National Guard,* 110. For a general discussion, see also ibid., 108–24.

4. See ibid., 253–56, 265; Richard B. Crossland and James T. Currie, *Twice the Citizen: A History of the United States Army Reserve, 1908–1983* (Office of the Chief, Army Reserve, 1984), 211–17; Charles Joseph Gross, *Prelude to the Total Force: The Air National Guard, 1943–1969* (U.S. Air Force Office of Air Force History, 1985), 3, 166–72; Gerald T. Cantwell, *Citizen Airmen: A History of the Air Force Reserve, 1946–1994* (Air Force History and Museums Program, 1997), 249–57.

5. Gary Hart, *The Minuteman: Restoring an Army of the People* (Free Press, 1998), 140–43.

6. See Mahon, *History of the Militia and the National Guard,* 254. For a general discussion, see also Gross, *Prelude to the Total Force;* Cantwell, *Citizen Airmen.*

7. See David T. Fautua, "How the Guard and Reserve Will Fight in 2025," *Parameters* (Spring 1999): 127, 129; David T. Fautua, "Army Citizen-Soldiers: Active, Guard, and Reserve Leaders Remain Silent About Overuse of Reserve Components," *Armed Forces Journal International* (Sept 2000): 72; Joshua Kucera, "U.S. Bosnia Force Now Made Up Only of Guard, Reserve Units," *Pittsburgh Post-Gazette* (December 8, 2002): A10; Faye Fiore, "A County That's in Fatigues: In Alabama, One Place Will Sacrifice like No Other if War Comes; Police, Teachers, Even a Mayor, Are Set to Deploy, Leaving Critical Gaps," *Los Angeles Times* (January 21, 2003): A1; Karen Serivo, "Report Says National Guard Strained by New Demands," *National Journal Congressional Daily* (February 19, 2003).

8. See Fautua, "Army Citizen-Soldiers," 74.

9. See ibid., 72; Kucera, "U.S. Bosnia Force," A10.

10. See Fautua, "How the Guard and Reserve Will Fight," 130–31. For a general discussion, see also Mahon, *History of the Militia and the National Guard;* Gross, *Prelude to the Total Force;* Cantwell, *Citizen Airmen.*

11. Quotation is from the original documents, as noted in a more extended analysis in Richard H. Kohn, "The Constitution and National Security: The Intent of the Framers," in *The United States Military under the Constitution of the United States, 1789–1989,* ed. Richard H. Kohn (New York: New York University Press, 1991), 61, 67 (quoting Edmund Randolph).

12. Ibid.

13. Ibid.

14. U.S. Constitution, art. I, §8, cl 15.

15. For short overviews of the use of the militia domestically, see Robert W. Coakley, "Federal Use of Militia and the National Guard in Civil Disturbances: The Whiskey Rebellion to Little Rock," in *Bayonets in the Streets: The Use of Troops in Civil Disturbances,* ed. Robin Higham (Lawrence, Kans.: Kansas University Press, 1969), 17; Clarence C. Clendenen, "Super Police: The National Guard as a Law-Enforcement Agency in the Twentieth Century," in ibid., 85.

16. Sally E. Hadden, *Slave Patrols: Law and Violence in Virginia and the Carolinas* (Cambridge, Mass.: Harvard University Press, 2001), 12–13, 16–24, 30–32, 35–47, 206–20.

17. The deployment of the Army can be conveniently viewed in Francis Paul Prucha, *A Guide to the Military Posts of the United State 1789–1895* (State Historical Society of Wisconsin, 1964), 6–7, 9, 11, 13, 15, 17, 22, 27, 29, 31, 33, 35. See also Emanuel Raymond Lewis, *Seacoast Fortifications of the United States: An Introductory History* (Washington, D.C.: Smithsonian Institution Press, 1970); Robert B. Roberts, *Encyclopedia of Historic Forts: The Military, Pioneer, and Trading Posts of the United States* (New York: Macmillan, 1988).

18. For interwar planning, see Louis Morton, "Germany First: The Basic Concept of Allied Strategy in World War II," in *Command Decisions,* ed. Kent Roberts Greenfield (U.S. Department of the Army Office of the Chief of Military History, 1960), 11; Edward S. Miller, *War Plan Orange: The U.S. Strategy to Defeat Japan, 1897–1945* (U.S. Naval Institute, 1991); David E. Johnson, *Fast Tanks and Heavy Bombers: Innovation in the U.S. Army, 1917–1945* (Ithaca, N.Y.: Cornell University Press, 1998), chapter 11;

Mark A. Stoler, *Allies and Adversaries: The Joint Chiefs of Staff, the Grand Alliance, and U.S. Strategy in World War II* (Chapel Hill, N.C.: University of North Carolina Press, 2000), chapters 1, 2.

19. For a recent overview of the military's historical role in providing a broad array of functions all in the name of homeland defense, see John S. Brown, "Defending the Homeland: An Historical Perspective," *Joint Force Quarterly* (Summer 2002): 10.

20. B. Franklin Cooling, "The Army and Flood and Disaster Relief," in *The United States Army in Peacetime: Essays in Honor of the Bicentennial, 1775–1975,* ed. Robin Higham and Carol Brandt (Military Affairs/Aerospace Historian, 1975), 61, 73.

21. For a brief note on the Marines' defense against mail robberies, see Edwin Howard Simmons, *The United States Marines: A History,* 3rd edition (U.S. Naval Institute, 1998), 112.

22. For a historical look at some of the internal constabulary roles played by the various branches of the armed forces, consider Russell F. Weigley, *History of the United States Army,* enlarged edition (Bloomington, Ind.: University of Indiana Press, 1984); Simmons, *The United States Marines;* Kenneth J. Hagan, ed., *In Peace and War: Interpretations of American Naval History, 1775–1978* (Westport, Conn.: Greenwood Press, 1978); Kenneth J. Hagan and William R. Roberts, eds., *Against All Enemies: Interpretations of American Military History From Colonial Times to the Present* (Westport, Conn.: Greenwood Press, 1986); Clayton D. Laurie and Ronald H. Cole, *The Role of Federal Military Forces in Domestic Disorders, 1877–1945* (U.S. Army Center of Military History, 1997); Maurer Maurer, *Aviation in the U.S. Army, 1919–1939* (U.S. Air Force Office of Air Force History, 1987), 131–48, 299–317, 422–26, 443–44.

23. E-mail from Andrew J. Bacevich, director, Center for International Relations, Boston University, to author (February 27, 2003; on file with author). Bacevich was stationed at Ft. Lewis at the time and participated in the search; Sam Skolnik, "30 Years Ago, D. B. Cooper's Night Leap Began a Legend," *Seattle Post-Intelligencer* (November 22, 2001): A1.

24. See Matthew Carlton Hammond, "The Posse Comitatus Act: A Principle in Need of Renewal," *Washington University Law Quarterly* 75 (1997), 953–54, 972; Charles J. Dunlap, Jr., "The Thick Green Line: The Growing Involvement of Military Forces in Domestic Law Enforcement," in *Militarizing the American Criminal Justice System: The Changing Roles of the Armed Forces and the Police,* ed. Peter B. Kraska (Boston: Northeastern University Press, 2001), 29, 31–32.

25. For a sense of the debate over homeland defense before September 11, see Aaron Weiss, "When Terror Strikes, Who Should Respond?" *Parameters* (Autumn 2001): 117. The author was a member of a seminar in Maclean, Virginia, organized by Booz Allen Hamilton for the Department of Defense's Reserve Forces Policy Board, *Seminar on the National Guard and Reserves in the 21st Century: Recommendations for the Total Force Policy—2025* (September 5, 2001). The author was also a member of the National Security Study Group, a collection of national security scholars and practitioners that assisted the U.S.

Commission on National Security/21st Century (the "Hart-Rudman Commission"), which recommended in March 2001 the creation of a cabinet department for homeland defense. See U.S. Commission on National Security/21st Century, *Road Map for National Security*, 10–29.

26. "The Sound of Freedom: Everlasting," *Inside the Pentagon* (February 20, 2003).

27. Office of Homeland Security, *National Strategy for Homeland Security* 44 (July 2002), available at www.whitehouse.gov/homeland/book/nat_strat_hls.pdf.

28. E-mail from Captain Kevin Clark, instructor, U.S. Military Academy, West Point, to author (March 29, 2003; on file with author).

29. In its early 2003 budget document, the administration listed "8,000 National Guard at baggage screening checkpoints at 420 major airports." George W. Bush, *Securing the Homeland, Strengthening the Nation* (2002), 4, available at www.whitehouse.gov/homeland/homeland_security_book.pdf. See also Daniel J. Shanahan, "*The Army's Role in Homeland Security*," in *Transformation Concepts for National Security in the 21st Century*, ed. Williamson Murray (Strategic Studies Institute, 2002), 285, 295–98.

30. Bill Gertz and Rowan Scarborough, "Inside the Ring," *Washington Times* (December 13, 2002): A7.

31. To see the speed of the buildup in February 2003, compare "National Guard and Reservists Now on Duty Exceed 110,000," *Miami Herald* (February 6, 2003): 20A; Thomas E. Ricks and Vernon Loeb, "Unrivaled Military Feels Strains of Unending War: For U.S. Forces, a Technological Revolution and a Constant Call to Do More," *Washington Post* (February 16, 2003): A1. See also Sydney J. Freedberg, Jr., "Weekend Warriors No More," *National Journal* 34 (June 8, 2002): 1690. Reserve components make up 47 percent of the entire military establishment; for the Army, reserve components actually outnumber the regulars, 550,000 to 480,000. Michael Kilian, "Reserves Turning into Active Force: Iraq War Would Add to Civilian Burden," *Chicago Tribune* (November 20, 2002): 1-1.

32. Vince Crawley, "Changing of the Guard: Revised Missions, Chain-of-Command Pattern Emerging," *Army Times* (November 25, 2002): 23.

33. Jacquelyn Zettles, "Interview with the Commandant," *Coast Guard Magazine* (August 2002): 10. For a review of the new ships and aircraft, see ibid., 30–57; Renae Merle, "For The Coast Guard Fleet, a $15 Billion Upgrade: Agency's Profile, and Its Duties, Have Grown since Sept. 11," *Washington Post* (June 25, 2002): A3. "We were always involved in homeland defense," said the commander of the 14th Coast Guard District in Hawaii, Rear Admiral Ralph Utley. "But on Sept. 10 it only took up 2 percent of our time. By Sept. 12, it was up to 58 percent": Gregg K. Kakesako, "9/11 Changed Coast Guard: The Terrorist Attacks Force a Shift in Priorities from Rescues to Maritime and Harbor Security," *Honolulu Star-Bulletin* (September 8, 2002). Nationally, the change in the "port security mission" was from "1–2 percent of daily operations to between 50–60 percent today [February 2002]," Bush, *Securing the Homeland*, 18. See also *The Coast Guard & Homeland Security: A New America*, CD-ROM video, enclosed in a letter from Rear Admiral K.J. Eldridge, assistant commandant for governmental and public affairs, U.S. Coast Guard, to author (February 21, 2003; on file with author). A short history of the Coast Guard can be found in John Whiteclay Chambers II et al., eds., *The Oxford Companion to American Military History* (Oxford: Oxford Universty Press, 1999), 144–46.

34. See "Detention, Treatment, and Trial of Certain Non-Citizens in the War Against Terrorism," 66 Fed. Reg. 57833 (2001); "President Bush's Order on the Trial of Terrorists by Military Commission," *New York Times* (November 14, 2001): B8. For early reaction, see William Safire, "Kangaroo Courts," *New York Times* (November 26, 2001): A17; Susan Schmidt and Bradley Graham, "Military Trial Plans Nearly Done; Bush to Decide Which Detainees Will Be Tried by Tribunals," *Washington Post* (November 18, 2001): A10; George Lardner, Jr., "Legal Scholars Criticize Wording of Bush Order: Accused Can Be Detained Indefinitely," *Washington Post* (December 3, 2001): A10; Hearing on Department of Justice Oversight: Preserving Our Freedoms while Defending against Terrorism before the Senate Committee on the Judiciary, 107th Cong., 1st Sess. (November 28, 2001), statement of Scott L. Silliman, executive director, Center on Law, Ethics, and National Security, Duke University School of Law, available at http://judiciary.senate.gov/testimony.cfm?id=126&wit_id70; Jeanne Cummings, "White House Counsel's Methods Outrage Military Legal Experts," *Wall Street Journal* (November 26, 2002): A4.

35. John Mintz, "U.S. Adds Legal Rights in Tribunals; New Rules Also Allow Leeway on Evidence," *Washington Post* (March 21, 2002): A1; Jess Bravin, "U.S. Prepares Tribunal System to Prosecute Alleged Terrorists," *Wall Street Journal* (December 10, 2002): A8; Jess Bravin, "Crimes Qualifying for Military Tribunals Are Set," *Wall Street Journal* (February 28, 2003): A2.

36. See *Geneva Convention Relative to the Protection of Prisoners of War*, 6 UST 3316 (1956).

37. See American Bar Association, Task Force on Treatment of Enemy Combatants, Criminal Justice Section, Section of Individual Rights and Responsibilities, *Report to the House of Delegates* (February 2003), 3n8, available at www.abanet.org/leadership/recommendations03/109.pdf; Paisley Dodds, "U.S. Defends Guantanamo Detentions," *AP Online* (January 17, 2003); Armstrong Starkey, "The Prisoners," *Historically Speaking* 4 (November 2002), 32–33.

38. See American Bar Association, *Report to the House of Delegates*, 1. (Resolutions approved by the Association's House of Delegates call for "meaningful judicial review of their status" such as to accommodate the needs of the detainee and the requirement of national security, for legal representation "in connection with the opportunity for such review," and for "Congress, in coordination with the Executive Branch, to establish clear standards and procedures governing the designation and treatment of U.S. citizens and other[s] . . . detained . . . as 'enemy combatants.'"). For the most recent court ruling, see Neil A. Lewis, "The Courts: Detention Upheld in Combatant Case," *New York Times* (January 9, 2003): A1; *Hamdi v. Rumsfeld*, 316 F3d 450 (4th Cir 2003); Anthony Lewis, "Marbury v. Madison v. Ashcroft," *New York Times* (February 24, 2003): A17. Contrast with a defense of the government position in Ruth Wedgwood, "Rule of Law: Lawyers at War," *Wall Street Journal* (February 18, 2003): A22. See also Deborah R. Finn, Ruth Wedgwood, and Stewart Baker, Muhammed Saleem, and Suzanne Evans, Letters to the Editor, "Balancing Liberty and Security," *New York Times* (February 27, 2003): A30.

39. U.S. Northern Command, *Who We Are—Mission,* available at www.northcom.mil/index.cfm?fuseaction=s.whoweare&section=3. For the new intelligence position, see Thomas Duffy, "New DoD Intel Directorate Will Have Broad Policy, Program Influence," *Inside the Pentagon* (March 27, 2003). For Northern Command and its background, see Bruce M. Lawlor, "Military Support of Civil Authorities—A New Focus for a New Millennium," *Journal of Homeland Security* (October 2000, updated September 2001), available at www.homeandsecurity.org/journal/articles/Lawlor.htm (Lawlor, an Army major general with a law degree, was the first commanding general of "Joint Task Force–Civil Support," a headquarters begun in October 1999 to command "Department of Defense consequence-management forces in support of a civilian lead federal agency following a weapon of mass destruction incident in the United States, its territories, or its possessions." Currently he is chief of staff to Tom Ridge, the head of the Department of Homeland Security.); Bradley Graham, "Military Favors a Homeland Command; Forces May Shift to Patrolling U.S.," *Washington Post* (November 21, 2001): A1; Thomas E. Ricks, "Northern Command to Defend the U.S.: Pentagon Reveals Shift in Structure," *Washington Post* (April 18, 2002): A8; News Call, "Pentagon Realigus Military Structure: U.S. Northern Command Will Be Activated in October," *Army Magazine* (June 2002), available at www.ausa.org/www/armymag.nsf/(news)/20026?OpenDocument; Elaine M. Grossman, "Defense Officials Close to Naming New Homeland Security Command," *Inside the Pentagon* (December 6, 2002); Elaine M. Grossman, "Rumsfeld Envisions New Command Responsible for Homeland Security," *Inside the Pentagon* (January 17, 2002); "DoD to Establish Permanent Homeland Security Organization; Cambone Leads Transition Team," *InsideDefense.com* (March 12, 2002).

40. U.S. Northern Command, *Who We Are—Homefront,* available at www.northcom.mil/index.cfm?fuseaction=s.whoweare&section=4.

41. Preface to *The National Security Strategy of the United States of America* (September 2002), available at www.whitehouse.gov/nsc/nss.pdf.

42. Bush, *National Strategy for Homeland Security,* 25.

43. Timothy Dodson, "Face to Face: A Conversation with Paul Wolfowitz: I Don't Think the One Problem Can Wait on the Other," *Sun-Sentinel* (Fort Lauderdale) (November 24, 2002): 5F.

44. Philip Shenon and Eric Schmitt, "The Military: Meeting Daily, U.S. Nerve Center Prepares for Terrorists," *New York Times* (December 27, 2002): A14. See also Eric Schmitt and Philip Shenon, "Domestic Defense: General Sees Scant Evidence of Close Threat in U.S.," *New York Times* (December 13, 2002): A26.

45. See U.S. Northern Command, *Who We Are—Limitations,* available at www.northcom.mil/index.cfm?fuseaction=s.whoweare&section=9; U.S. Northern Command, *Who We Are—Operating With the Law,* available at www.northcom.mil/index.cfm?fuseaction=s.whoweare&section=10.

46. George Will, "Boldly Redeploying the Troops," *News & Observer* (Raleigh) (February 13, 2003): A17.

47. Bob Woodward, *Bush at War* (New York: Simon & Schuster, 2002), 42.

48. Ibid.

49. Eric Lichtblau and Adam Liptak, "On Terror, Spying and Guns, Ashcroft Expands Reach," *New York Times* (March 15, 2003): A1.

50. Adam Liptak, "Under Ashcroft, Judicial Power Flows Back to Washington," *New York Times* (February 16, 2003): 4-5 (quoting Nancy Baker, associate professor of government at New Mexico State University). See also Anthony Lewis, "Taking Our Liberties," *New York Times* (March 9, 2002): A15; James A. Barnes et al., "Grading the Cabinet," *National Journal* (January 25, 2003): 232, 234: "What Attorney General John D. Ashcroft describes as the Justice Department's 'wartime reorganization and mobilization' has dramatically shifted its focus from fighting crime in the streets to preventing another 9/11.... Ashcroft's aggressive tactics fit the desire within the White House to rewrite the rule book if that's what it takes to fight the domestic war on terrorism." For an indication of Ashcroft's response to the criticism, see Kevin Johnson, "Ashcroft Defends Anti-Terror Tactics; Prosecutors Told to Be 'Unrelenting'," *USA Today* (October 2, 2002): A12. For an overall assessment of Ashcroft's leadership, see Lichtblau and Liptak, "On Terror, Spying and Guns, Ashcroft Expands Reach," A1.

51. Adam Clymer, "Government Openness at Issue as Bush Holds Onto Records," *New York Times* (January 3, 2003): A1. See also Lewis, "Taking Our Liberties," A15. In 2001, the number of document "classification actions . . . increased by 44 percent," Information Security Oversight Office, *2001 Report to The President* (September 2002), 2, available at www.fas.org/sgp/isoo/2001rpt.pdf.

52. Executive Order 13233, "Further Implementation of the Presidential Records Act," 66 Fed Reg 56025 (2001), reprinted in "Source Material: Executive Order 13233," *Presidential Studies Quarterly* (2002): 185 (including the responses of the American Political Science Association and the American Historical Association); Martha Joynt Kumar, "Executive Order 13233: Further Implementation of the Presidential Records Act," *Presidential Studies Quarterly* 32 (2002): 194–209. See also Clymer, "Government Openness," A1; Stanley I. Kutler, "Presidency: An Executive Order Richard Nixon Would Love," *Washington Spectator,* reprinted in *History News Network* (January 3, 2002), available at www.historynewsnetwork.org/articles/article.html?id=494; David E. Rosenbaum, "Top Secret: When Government Doesn't Tell," *New York Times* (February 3, 2002): 4-1; Bruce Craig, "Bush Issues New Secrecy Executive Order," *NCH Washington Update* 9 (March 27, 2003): 13.

53. "Detention, Treatment, and Trial of Certain Non-Citizens in the War Against Terrorism."

54. Jerry Seper, "Ashcroft Creates Interagency Force on Security Leaks; Some Urge Making It a Felony," *Washington Times* (December 16, 2001): A3. See also Jack Nelson, *U.S. Government Secrecy and the Current Crackdown on Leaks,* Joan Shorenstein Center on the Press, Politics and Public Policy, Working Paper 2003-1 (Harvard, 2002), available at www.ksg.harvard.edu/presspol/publications/Nelson.pdf.

55. Amy Goldstein and Juliet Eilperin, "Congress Not Advised of Shadow Government; Bush Calls Security, 'Serious Business'," *Washington Post* (March 2, 2002): A1.

56. Laurence McQuillan, "For Bush Secrecy Is a Matter of Loyalty," *USA Today* (March 14, 2002): A1. See also

Steve Chapman, "Executive Secrecy in the War on Terror: How Can We Judge Whether President Bush and John Aschcroft Have Acted Responsibly When They Refuse to Put All of the Cards on the Table?" *Chicago Tribune* (August 18, 2002): 2-9; James G. Lakely, "GOP Veterans Rap Secrecy on Defense Issues; Senators "Furious" With Rumsfeld," *Washington Times* (January 14, 2003): A1; Robert D. Novak, "Disaffected Troops," *Washington Post* (January 13, 2003): A21.

57. Woodward, *Bush at War,* 169.

58. Bush, *National Strategy for Homeland Security,* 12.

59. Gail Russell Chaddock, "Security Act to Pervade Daily Lives," *Christian Science Monitor* (November 21, 2002): 1.

60. Philip Shenon and David Johnston, "The Investigation: Seeking Terrorist Plots, the F.B.I. Is Tracking Hundreds of Muslims," *New York Times* (October 6, 2002): 1-1.

61. Dan Eggen, "Broad U.S. Wiretap Powers Upheld; Secret Court Lifts Baron Terror Suspect Surveillance," *Washington Post* (November 19, 2002): A1; Linda Greenhouse, "Opponents Lose Challenge to Government's Broader Use of Wiretaps to Fight Terrorism," *New York Times* (March 25, 2003): A12; U.S. Constitution, Amendment IV.

62. Michael Moss and Ford Fessenden, "New Tools for Domestic Spying, and Qualms," *New York Times* (December 10, 2002): A1.

63. See John Markoff, "Intelligence: Pentagon Plans a Computer System that Would Peek at Personal Data of Americans," *New York Times* (November 9, 2002): A12; J. Michael Waller, "The Nation: Homeland Security: Fears Mount Over 'Total' Spy System," *Insight* (December 24, 2002), available at www.insightmag.com/news/338890.html; Dan Eggen and Robert O'Harrow, Jr., "Surveillance Plan Worries GOP Senator," *Washington Post* (January 22, 2003): A13; William Safire, "Privacy Invasion Curtailed," *New York Times* (February 13, 2003): A41; Audrey Hudson, "'Supersnoop' Scheme Blocked Pending Review by Congress; Privacy Issues Cited in Pentagon TIA Project," *Washington Times* (February 13, 2003): A1.

64. John Markoff and John Schwartz, "Electronic Surveillance: Bush Administration to Propose System for Wide Monitoring of Internet," *New York Times* (December 20, 2002): A22.

65. For detailed summaries of the USA Patriot Act of 2001, see Elizabeth A. Palmer and Keith Perine, "Provisions of the Anti-Terrorism Bill," *CQ Weekly* 329 (Feb 2, 2002): 329; *Bill Summary and Status for the 107th Congress,* HR 3162, 107th Cong., 1st Sess., available online at http://thomas.loc.gov/cgi-bin/bdquery/z?d107:HR03162: @@@L&summ2=m& (visited April 6, 2003). See also Neil A. Lewis and Robert Pear, "Negotiators Back Scaled-Down Bill to Battle Terror; Speaker Seeks a House Vote Soon— Wiretap Powers to Grow," *New York Times* (October 2, 2001): A1; Neil A. Lewis and Robin Toner, "Democrats in Senate Are Pressured on Terror Bill," *New York Times* (October 3, 2001): B8; Neil A. Lewis and Robert Pear, "Legislation: Terror Laws Near Votes in House and Senate," *New York Times* (October 5, 2001): B8; Robin Toner and Neil A. Lewis, "Congress: House Passes Terrorism Bill Much Like Senate's, but with 5-Year Limit," *New York Times* (October 13, 2001): B6; Adam Clymer, "Antiterrorism Bill Passes; U.S. Gets Expanded Powers; Bush Set to Sign; Measure

Provides Tools White House Sought, with Some Limits," *New York Times* (October 26, 2001): A1; Timothy Lynch, "Breaking the Vicious Cycle: Preserving Our Liberties while Fighting Terrorism," *Policy Analysis* (Cato Institute 2002): 443.

66. See Charles Lane, "U.S. May Seek Wider Anti-Terror Powers," *Washington Post* (February 8, 2003): A1; Adam Clymer, "Domestic Security: Justice Dept. Draft on Wider Powers Draws Quick Criticism," *New York Times* (February 8, 2003): A10; Gene R. Nichol, "Ashcroft Wants Even More," *News & Observer* (Raleigh) (February 20, 2003): A15. The administration also intends to try to make the USA Patriot Act's changes permanent. See Eric Lichtblau, "Republicans Want Terrorism Law Made Permanent," *New York Times* (April 9, 2003): B1.

67. For the willingness of the American public, even people traditionally sensitive to civil liberties, "to give up some of their personal freedoms in order to make the country safe from terrorist attacks," see Laurie Goodstein, "Civil Liberties: Jewish Groups Endorse Tough Security Laws," *New York Times* (January 3, 2002): A14. Michael Ratner provides a catalog of the Bush administration's invasions of, and threats to, civil rights and liberties in *Moving toward a Police State or Have We Arrived?: Secret Military Tribunals, Mass Arrests and Disappearances, Wiretapping & Torture* (2002), available at www.humanrightsnow.org/policestate.htm.

68. Bill Miller, "National Guard Awaits Niche in Homeland Security Plan; White House's Caution Chafes Against Those Urging Action," *Washington Post* (August 11, 2002): A12. A call for the redirection of the National Guard was in the original Phase III Hart-Rudman Commission report, *Road Map for National Security,* 25–26, and is also in Gary Hart, Warren B. Rudman, and Stephen E. Flynn, *America Still Unprepared—America Still in Danger: Report of an Independent Task Force Sponsored by the Council on Foreign Relations* (Council on Foreign Relations, 2002), 34–36, available at www.cfr.org/pdf/Homeland_Security_TF.pdf.

69. See Kwame Holman, *The NewsHour with Jim Lehrer: Focus: Guarding the Homeland,* PBS television broadcast (September 27, 2002); *Chemical/Biological Incident Response Force (CBIRF),* GlobalSecurity.Org, available at www.globalsecurity.org/military/agency/usmc/cbirf.htm.

70. See Amy E. Smithson and Leslie-Anne Levy, *Ataxia: The Chemical and Biological Terrorism Threat and the U.S. Response* xiv, Stimson Center Report No. 35 (2000), available at www.stimson.org/?SN-CH20020111235; Holman, *The NewsHour with Jim Lehrer: Focus: Guarding the Homeland.*

71. Smithson and Levy, *Ataxia,* 113. For additional information on training and equipment programs, an assessment of frontline readiness, and for recommendations on how to prepare for chemical and biological terrorist threats, see ibid., 288–303 and chapters 5–6.

72. Jason Peckenpaugh, *Course Offers Anti-Terrorism Training for Federal Executives,* GovExec.com (February 19, 2003), available at www.govexec.com/dailyfed/0203/021903dp1.htm.

73. For an example of how stretched one service is to deal with multiple commitments and a campaign in Iraq, see Elaine M. Grossman, "Air Chief Reaches Deeper to Find Forces for Multiple Warfronts," *Inside the Pentagon*

(February 20, 2003). See also Press Release, United States Department of Defense, "National Guard and Reserve Mobilized as of November 27, 2002" (November 27, 2002), available at www.defenselink.mil/news/Nov2002/b11272002_bt603-02.html. During the Afghan campaign, some 83,000 of the 1.25 million Guard/Reserves were on active duty. See Kilian, "Reserves Turning into Active Force." See also "Making Headlines This Week: Debate Swells Over Sending Unarmed Troops to Guard U.S. Borders," *Inside the Air Force* (March 8, 2002); Hearing on Combating Terrorism: Protecting the United States Part II before the Subcommittee on National Security, Veterans Affairs, and International Relations of the House Committee on Government Reform, Rep. 107-156, 107th Cong., 2d Sess. 118 (2002) (statement of Peter Verga, Special Assistant for Homeland Security).

74. The figure for chemical industry sites comes from Smithson and Levy, *Ataxia*, xiv. For general analysis of national vulnerabilities, see ibid., throughout; Hart, Rudman, and Flynn, *America Still Unprepared*; Gilmore Commission, *Fourth Annual Report to the President and the Congress of the Advisory Panel to Assess Domestic Response Capabilities for Terrorism Involving Weapons of Mass Destruction: IV. Implementing The National Strategy* (2002), available at www.rand.org/nsrd/terrpanel/terror4.pdf. See also James Dao, "Gaps in Security: Report Finds U.S. Unprepared for Next Terrorist Attack," *New York Times* (October 25, 2002): A15; Philip Shenon, "Domestic Security: Ridge Discovers Size of Home Security Task," *New York Times* (March 3, 2002): A1; Richard Pérez-Peña, "A Security Blanket, but with No Guarantees," *New York Times* (March 23, 2003): A1.

75. Stephen E. Flynn, "Safer Borders," *New York Times* (October 1, 2001): A23. See also Jamie Dettmer, "Special Report: Tighter Security in Store for Seaports," *Insight* (February 25, 2002), available online at www.insightmag.com/news/174891.html (visited March 8, 2003); Hans Binnendijk et al., "The Virtual Border: Countering Seaborne Container Terrorism," *Defense Horizons* 16 (2002), available online at www.ndu.edu/inss/DefHor/DH16/DH16.pdf (visited March 20, 2003).

76. The President's 2003 budget submitted in February 2002 called for an additional $3.5 billion, more than a tenfold increase in federal monies, but a year later the money had just been appropriated. Bush, *Securing the Homeland*, 10–11; Philip Shenon, "Threats and Responses: Local Governments; Antiterror Money Stalls in Congress," *New York Times* (February 13, 2003): A1; Daniel Benjamin and Steven Simon, "The Worst Defense," *New York Times* (February 20, 2003): A31; Philip Shenon, "Domestic Security: In Reversal, White House Concedes That Counterterrorism Budget Is Too Meager," *New York Times* (February 27, 2003): A14; Philip Shenon, "Bush Administration to Seek Emergency Money to Protect against Terrorist Attacks in U.S.," *New York Times* (March 20, 2003): A22.

77. See American Political Network, "Bioterrorism Preparedness: States Not Ready for Potential Attack, Report," *American Health Line* (November 4, 2002): 7 (describing the lack of preparedness of state health authorities for mass causalities in the event of a bioterrorist attack).

78. Elaine M. Grossman, "U.S. Officials Mull a Military Role in Enforcing Smallpox Quarantine," *Inside the Pentagon* (December 19, 2002). Grossman notes other experts

who believe a massive vaccination program quickly instituted after an attack would be likely to make a quarantine regimen unnecessary. See also Sheryl Gay Stolberg and Judith Miller, "BioTerrorism: Many Worry That Nation Is Still Highly Vulnerable to Germ Attack," *New York Times* (September 9, 2002): A16. For the possibility of panic, see David Wood, "America Is Vulnerable to Panic in Terror Attack, Experts Say," *Newhouse News Service* (August 20, 2002). For a hint of the problems involved in quarantine—the need for military involvement and the great dangers to lives and civil liberties—see Smithson and Levy, *Ataxia*, 268–70.

79. Quoted in Barton Gellman, "In U.S., Terrorism's Peril Undiminished: Nation Struggles on Offense and Defense, and Officials Still Expect New Attacks," *Washington Post* (December 24, 2002): A1.

80. Holman, *The NewsHour with Jim Lehrer: Focus: Guarding the Homeland*. For the full interview, see Interview by Dan Sagalyn with Air Force General Ralph Eberhart, Online NewsHour (September 24, 2002), available at www.pbs.org/newshour/terrorism/ata/eberhart.html.

81. Grossman, "U.S. Officials Mull a Military Role in Enforcing Smallpox Quarantine."

82. Gilmore Commission, *Fourth Annual Report to the President and the Congress,* iv.

83. See Dunlap, "The Thick Green Line," 32.

84. See, for example, David Halberstam, *War in a Time of Peace: Bush, Clinton, and the Generals* (New York: Scribner, 2001); Richard H. Kohn, "The Erosion of Civilian Control of the Military in the United States Today," *Naval War College Review* 60 (Summer 2002): 60; Andrew J. Bacevich, *American Empire: The Realities & Consequences of U.S. Diplomacy* (Cambridge, Mass.: Harvard University Press, 2002); Dana Priest, *The Mission* (New York: Norton, 2003). For an argument that this trend is much broader than foreign policy alone and extends back almost three generations, see Michael S. Sherry, *In the Shadow of War: The United States since the 1930s* (New Haven: Yale University Press, 1995).

85. My use of the term "militarization" follows Sherry's: "the process by which war and national security became consuming anxieties and provided the memories, models, and metaphors that shaped broad areas of national life." Sherry, *In the Shadow of War,* xi. My use includes the "caveats" he applies to the concept, including a certain blurriness and a "varied and changing rather than uniform historical process" embracing "varied, even discordant, phenomena." Ibid., xi–xii.

86. Paul Pillar, as quoted in Steve I Hirsch, "The War against Terror Will Be Indefinite," *National Journal* 254 (January 26, 2002). The Chairman of the Joint Chiefs of Staff expressed similar views about the conflict being indefinite. Bradley Graham, "General to Troops: Sit Tight: In Qatar, Myers Says No End in Sight to War on Terrorism," *Washington Post* (December 21, 2002): A18. For the debate over whether the struggle against terrorism is or should be a "war," see Donald H. Rumsfeld, "A New Kind of War," *New York Times* (September 27, 2001): A21; Richard H. Kohn, "A War like No Other," *OAH Newsletter* 29 (November 2001), available at www.oah.org/pubs/nl/2001nov/kohn.html; Michael Howard, "What's in a Name? How to Fight Terrorism," *Foreign Affairs* 81 (January 2002): 8;

William M. Arkin, "September 11 and Wars of the World," presentation at the U.S. Naval War College, Newport, R.I., September 25, 2002, available online at www.salon.com/news/feature/2002/10/11/arkin/print.html (visited March 20, 2003); Eliot A. Cohen, "World War IV," *Wall Street Journal* (November 20, 2001): A18; R. James Woolsey, "World War IV," address at Restoration Weekend, Center for the Study of Popular Culture (November 16, 2002), in Front-PageMagazine.com (November 22, 2002), available online at www.frontpagemag.com/articles/Printable.asp?ID=4718 (visited March 2, 2003).

87. See Mark E. Neely, Jr., *The Fate of Liberty: Abraham Lincoln and Civil Liberties* (Oxford: Oxford University Press, 1991), 94–103, 109–12.

88. Paul L. Murphy, *World War I and the Origin of Civil Liberties in the United States* (New York: Norton, 1979), 74n4.

89. Laurie and Cole, *The Role of Federal Military Forces,* 233, 253.

90. Ibid., 234. For a general discussion, see ibid., chap. 10; William Preston, Jr., *Aliens and Dissenters: Federal Suppression of Radicals, 1903–1933* (Cambridge, Mass.: Harvard University Press, 1963), 105–17, 161, 244–46; Joan M. Jensen, *Army Surveillance in America, 1775–1980* (New Haven: Yale University Press, 1991), 131–77.

91. Jensen, *Army Surveillance,* chap. 9; Laurie and Cole, *The Role of Federal Military Forces,* chap. 14.

92. See Stetson Conn, "The Decision to Evacuate the Japanese From the Pacific Coast," in Greenfield, ed., *Command Decisions,* 125; Jacobus tenBrock, Edward N. Barnhart, and Floyd W. Matson, *Prejudice, War and the Constitution* (Berkeley: University of California Press, 1970); Roger Daniels, *The Decision to Relocate the Japanese Americans* (Krieger, 1985); John Joel Culley, "Enemy Alien Control in the United States During World War II: A Survey," in *Alien Justice: Wartime Internment in Australia and North America,* eds. Kay Saunders and Roger Daniels (Brisbane, Australia: Queensland, 2000), 138; Sandra C. Taylor, "From Incarceration to Freedom: Japanese-Americans and the Departure From the Concentration Camps," in Saunders and Daniels, *Alien Justice,* 205; Wendy Ng, *Japanese American Internment during World War II: A History and Reference Guide* (Westport, Conn.: Greenwood Press, 2002), chap. 3.

93. Jensen, *Army Surveillance,* 240–47.

94. See generally Jonathan A. Schmidt-Davis, *The Origins of the Posse Comitatus Act of 1878* (Chapel Hill, N.C.: unpublished MA thesis, University of North Carolina, 1999) (on file with the University of North Carolina at Chapel Hill Library); Dunlap, "The Thick Green Line," 34–40. For a general discussion of policy reasons not to use the military to enforce civilian laws, see Hammond, "Posse Comitatus Act," 953–84.

95. Ibid., 953.

96. Ibid., 973.

97. Timothy J. Dunn, "Waging War on Immigrants at the U.S.-Mexico Border: Human Rights Implications," in *Militarizing the American Criminal Justice System,* 65.

98. Ibid., 76–77; Elaine M. Grossman, "U.S.-Mexico Border Control a Wild Card for New Homeland Command," *Inside the Pentagon* (September 26, 2002); Tim Weiner, "U.S. and Mexico Coordinate Military Efforts for Mutual Protection against Terror," *New York Times* (March 23, 2003): B13.

99. See Carl Levin, *Opening Statement of Senator Carl Levin, Chairman, Committee on Armed Services, Hearing on The Role of the Department of Defense in Homeland Security* (October 25, 2001), available at http://levin.senate.gov/floor/102501cs1.htm; interview by Dan Sagalyn with U.S. Air Force General Ralph Eberhart, *Online NewsHour.*

100. Quoted in William Matthews, "Aldridge Calls for Study of U.S. Military's Role in Homeland Defense," *DefenseNews.com* (January 16, 2001). See also Ken Guggenheim, "Warner Wants to Bow Military Role," *AP Online* (November 13, 2002).

101. See, for example, Lawlor, "Military Support of Civil Authorities."

102. The possibilities of internal surveillance and some implications for civil liberties are depicted in Matthew Brzezinski, "Fortress America," *New York Times Magazine* 38 (February 23, 2003): 38.

103. See Jonathan Lurie, "The Role of the Federal Judiciary in the Governance of the American Military: The United States Supreme Court and 'Civil Rights and Supervision' over the Armed Forces," in Kohn, ed., *The United States Military under the Constitution,* 405; William H. Rehnquist, *All the Laws but One: Civil Liberties in Wartime* (New York: Knopf, 1998), 221–25; Diane H. Mazur, "Rehnquist's Vietnam: Constitutional Separation and the Stealth Advance of Martial Law," *Indiana Law Journal* 77 (2002): 701; Lewis, "Marbury v. Madison v. Ashcroft," A17.

104. Mazur, "Rehnquist's Vietnam," 743, quoting Rehnquist in *Parker v. Levy,* 417 US (1974), 733, 744. See also ibid., 745, 754, 759, 765, 767, 769, 773, 785 (discussing various ways in which Rehnquist places the military beyond civilian and constitutional oversight).

105. The words are James Madison's, recounting Franklin's remark. Madison's notes (September 17, 1787), reprinted in Max Farrand, ed., *The Records of the Federal Convention of 1787,* revised edition, vol. 2 (New Haven: Yale University Press, 1937), 648.

106. James McHenry's notes, "Papers of Dr. James McHenry on the Federal Convention of 1787," *American Historical Review* 11 (1900): 595, 618 (punctuation added).

ABOUT THE CONTRIBUTORS

ROBERT J. ART is the Christian A. Herter Professor of International Relations at Brandeis University. Professor Art is a former member of the Secretary of Defense's Long Range Planning Staff (1982) and a former Dean of the Graduate School of Arts and Sciences at Brandeis. His publications include *The United States and Coercive Diplomacy* (co-editor with Patrick Cronin; U.S. Institute for Peace, 2003) and *A Grand Strategy for America* (Cornell University Press, 2003). He earned his Ph.D. from Harvard University in 1967.

ROGER W. BARNETT is professor emeritus at the U.S. Naval War College. A retired U.S. Navy captain, he held a variety of operational and staff posts, including the command of a guided-missile destroyer and the head of both the Strategic Concepts and Extended Planning Branch for the Chief of Naval Operations. He has published a wide range of essays, articles, and reviews on naval affairs, national military strategy, arms control, and security policy. With Colin S. Gray he co-edited *Seapower and Strategy* (Naval Institute Press, 1989). His M.A. and Ph.D. degrees were earned at the University of Southern California.

THOMAS P. M. BARNETT is a senior strategic researcher and professor in the Warfare Analysis & Research Department, Center for Naval Warfare Studies, U.S. Naval War College. From November 2001 to June of 2003, Dr. Barnett was on temporary assignment as the Assistant for Strategic Futures, Office of Force Transformation (OFT), Office of the Secretary of Defense. He is the author of *The Pentagon's New Map: War and Peace in the Twenty-First Century* (G. P. Putnam's Sons, 2004). Dr. Barnett received his Ph.D. in political science from Harvard University.

STEPHEN BIDDLE is research professor of national security studies at the Strategic Studies Institute of the U.S. Army War College. He is on leave from the University of North Carolina and has held research positions at the Institute for Defense Analyses, the Harvard University Center for Science and International Affairs, and the Kennedy School of Government's Office of National Security Programs. Dr. Biddle's articles have appeared in such journals as *Foreign Affairs, International Security,* and *Survival.* He is the author of *Military Power: Explaining Victory and Defeat in Modern Battle* (Princeton University Press, 2004). Dr. Biddle received his Ph.D. in Public Policy from Harvard University.

HANS BINNENDIJK holds the Roosevelt Chair of National Security Policy at the National Defense University (NDU). He has served on the National Security Council as special assistant to the president and senior director for Defense Policy and Arms Control and as the director of NDU's Institute for National Strategic Studies. With over ninety publications as author or co-author, Dr. Binnendijk's most recent product is an edited volume with Stuart E. Johnson on *Transforming for Stabilization and Reconstruction Operations* (NDU Press, 2004). He received his Ph.D. in international relations from the Fletcher School of Law and Diplomacy, Tufts University.

KURT M. CAMPBELL is a senior vice president at the Center for Strategic and International Studies (CSIS) and director of the Aspen Strategy Group. He formerly served as deputy assistant secretary of defense for Asia and Pacific Affairs, was a director on the National Security Staff, and served as a faculty member at the John F. Kennedy School of Government. He is the author or editor of several books, including *To Prevail: An American Strategy for the Campaign against Terrorism* (CSIS, 2001). Dr. Campbell received his Ph.D. in international relations from Oxford University.

PAUL O. CARRESE is professor of political science at the U.S. Air Force Academy. He is co-editor of John Marshall's one-volume *The Life of George Washington: Special Edition for Schools* (Liberty Fund, 2000) and author of *The Cloaking of Power: Montesquieu, Blackstone, and the Rise of Judicial Activism* (University of Chicago Press, 2003). A Rhodes Scholar, he holds degrees in politics and philosophy and in theology from Oxford University and a Ph.D. in political science from Boston College.

STEPHEN J. CIMBALA is a distinguished professor of political science at Penn State University (Delaware County). He has been a robust contributor to the literature of national security, defense policy, peace operations, arms control, and international affairs. His books include *Clausewitz and Chaos* (Greenwood, 2000) and *Russia's Military Way into the Twenty-First Century* (Taylor and Francis, 2001), in which he was a contributing editor. Beyond his academic contributions, he has served as a consultant to U.S. government agencies and private defense contractors. He earned his Ph.D. from the University of Wisconsin–Madison.

ELIOT A. COHEN is director of the Center for Strategic Studies at the Paul H. Nitze School of Advanced International Studies at the Johns Hopkins University, as well as a member of the editorial board of *Joint Force Quarterly* and the Defense Policy Board. He was director and editor of the *Gulf War Air Power Survey* (1991–93), and he authored *Supreme Command: Soldiers, Statesmen and Leadership in Wartime* (The Free Press, 2002). Dr. Cohen received his Ph.D. in political science from Harvard University.

JOSEPH J. COLLINS is currently the deputy assistant secretary of defense for Stability Operations. He retired in 1998 as a colonel in the U.S. Army after 28 years of service. Following his military service, Dr. Collins was a senior fellow at the Center for Strategic and International Studies. His works include *The Soviet Invasion of Afghanistan* (Simon and Schuster, 1986) and *American Military Culture in the Twenty-First Century* (Center for Strategic and International Studies, 2000), co-authored with Owen Jackson and retired Lieutenant General Walter F. Ulmer. He earned his Ph.D. in political science from Columbia University.

ANTHONY H. CORDESMAN is the Arleigh A. Burke Chair in Strategy at the Center for Strategic and International Studies (CSIS), Washington, D.C. He has served in several government positions, including director of intelligence assessment for the Office of the Secretary of Defense. He is also a national security analyst appearing on ABC News. He has authored more than twenty books, including a four-volume series on the lessons of modern war. Several of his studies on U.S. security policy, energy policy, and Middle East policy may be downloaded from the CSIS website (www.csis.org). Dr. Cordesman is a former adjunct professor of national security studies at Georgetown University and has twice been selected as a fellow at the Woodrow Wilson Center for Scholars, the Smithsonian Institution, Washington, D.C.

PHILIP E. COYLE is senior advisor to the president of the Center for Defense Information, Washington, D.C. Previously, Mr. Coyle served as associate director of the Lawrence Livermore National Laboratory in Livermore, California (1959–79, 1981–93) and as assistant secretary of defense and director of Operational Test and Evaluation (1994-2001). In 2000, *Aviation Week* magazine selected Mr. Coyle as one of its "Laurels" honorees for outstanding contributions in the aerospace field.

PETER D. FEAVER is the Alexander F. Heymeyer Professor of Political Science and Public Policy at Duke University and director of the Triangle Institute for Security Studies. His works include *Soldiers and Civilians: The Civil Military Gap and American National Security* (co-edited with Richard H. Kohn; MIT Press, 2001) and *Armed Servants: Agency, Oversight, and Civil Military Relations* (Harvard University Press, 2003). Dr. Feaver received his Ph.D. in political science from Harvard University.

LOUIS FISHER is the senior specialist in separation of powers for the Congressional Research Service of the Library of Congress. His books include *American Constitutional Law* (5th edition, Carolina Academic Press, 2003) and *Presidential War Powers* (University of Kansas Press, 2004). As co-editor with Leonard Levy, Dr. Fisher received the 1995 Dartmouth Medal, awarded by the American Library Association, for their four-volume set, *Encyclopedia of the American Presidency* (Prentice Hall, 1994). He earned his Ph.D. from the New School University.

JOHN LEWIS GADDIS is the Robert A. Lovett Professor of Military and Naval History at Yale University. A renowned Cold War historian, Dr. Gaddis has also taught at Ohio University, the U.S. Naval War College, the University of Helsinki, Princeton University, and Oxford University, and served as a senior fellow of the Hoover Institution. His most recent book is *Surprise, Security, and the American Experience* (Harvard University Press, 2004). Dr. Gaddis received his Ph.D. in history at the University of Texas at Austin.

DAVID C. HENDRICKSON is a professor of political science at Colorado College. His books include *Peace Pact: The Lost World of the American Founding* (University Press of Kansas, 2003) and *The Imperial Temptation: The New World Order and America's Purpose* (with Robert W. Tucker; Council on Foreign Relations, 1992). Dr. Hendrickson received his Ph.D. from the Johns Hopkins University.

BRUCE HOFFMAN is acting director of the RAND Center for Middle East Public Policy and editor-in-chief for the journal *Studies in Conflict and Terrorism*. Among other organizations, Dr. Hoffman has served as a consultant for the Argentina National Congress, the U.S. National Academy of Sciences, the U.S. Department of Energy, and the U.K. Ministry of Defence. He also served as a member of the U.S. Department of Defense Counter-Terrorism Advisory Board. In addition to RAND reports and articles in publications such as the *Atlantic Monthly* and *Foreign Policy*, he is the author of *Inside Terrorism* (Columbia University Press, 1998). Dr. Hoffman received his Ph.D. in international relations from the University of Oxford, England.

TOM HONE serves as the assistant director for the U.S. Department of Defense, Office of Force Transformation. Previously he has served as the principal deputy director, Program Analysis and Evaluation, of the Office of the Secretary of Defense, and he is a former professor of defense acquisition at the Industrial College of the Armed Forces, Fort McNair, Washington, D.C. He received his Ph.D. in political science from the University of Wisconsin–Madison.

STUART E. JOHNSON is a distinguished research professor at the National Defense University Center for Technology and National Security Policy. Previously he was director of International Security and Defense Policy programs at the RAND Corporation, where he supervised a program of policy and strategy research for the Office of the Secretary of Defense, the Joint Staff, and the regional commanders. His most recent book, *New Challenges, New Tools for Defense Decisionmaking* was published by the RAND Press in April 2003. He received his Ph.D. from the Massachusetts Institute of Technology.

FREDERICK W. KAGAN is an associate professor of history at the U.S. Military Academy at West Point and has published articles on issues of national security in the *Wall Street Journal,* the *National Interest,* the *Weekly Standard,* and *Commentary.* His most recent book is *While America Sleeps: Self-Delusion, Military Weakness, and the Threat to Peace Today* (St. Martin's Press, 2000). He earned a Ph.D. in Russian and Soviet military history from Yale.

DANIEL J. KAUFMAN is a brigadier general in the U.S. Army and serves as dean of the U.S. Military Academy's Academic Board. In addition to being a tenured professor of political science at the U.S. Military Academy, his other military service includes tours with cavalry and armor units in the United States and Vietnam. He also served as a member of the National Security Council staff and in the Office of the Secretary of Defense. Earning a Ph.D. in political science from the Massachusetts Institute of Technology, his publications include *U.S. National Security Strategy for the 1990s* (The Johns Hopkins University Press, 1991) and *Understanding International Relations* (McGraw-Hill, 1999).

JAMES KITFIELD won the 1990 Gerald R. Ford Award for distinguished reporting on national defense. He previously covered the Pentagon for *Military Forum.* His work has also appeared in *Omni, New York Newsday,* the *Los Angeles Times,* and the *National Journal.* He is the author of *Prodigal Soldiers: How the Generation of Officers Born of Vietnam Revolutionized the American Style of War* (Simon & Schuster, 1995).

RICHARD H. KOHN is professor of history and chair of the Curriculum in Peace, War, and Defense at the University of North Carolina at Chapel Hill. He has taught at City College (City University of New York) and Rutgers University, as well as the National and Army War Colleges. From 1981 to 1991, he was chief of Air Force History and chief historian of the U.S. Air Force. His works include *The United States Military under the Constitution of the United States, 1789–1989* (NYU Press, 1991), and *The Exclusion of Black Soldiers from the Medal of Honor in World War II* (government report, 1997). With Peter D. Feaver, he co-edited *Soldiers and Civilians: The Civil-Military Gap and American National Security* (MIT Press, 2001). Dr. Kohn received his Ph.D. from the University of Wisconsin–Madison.

ANDREW F. KREPINEVICH serves as executive director of the Center for Strategic and Budgetary Assessments (CSBA). He writes on a wide range of defense and security issues. He is published in such periodicals as: the *National Interest,* the *Wall Street Journal, Armed Forces Journal, Joint Force Quarterly,* and *Strategic Review.* In 1987 he received the Furniss Award for his book *The Army and Vietnam* (The Johns Hopkins University Press, 1986), a critical assessment of the service's performance during the war. He has served in the Department of Defense's Office of Net Assessment and has taught national security and defense policymaking courses at West Point, George Mason University, and The Johns Hopkins University School of Advanced International Studies. A graduate of West Point, Dr. Krepinevich earned M.P.A. and Ph.D. degrees from Harvard University.

RICHARD L. KUGLER is a distinguished research professor at the Center for Technology and National Security Policy, National Defense University. His specializes in U.S. defense strategy, global security affairs, the NATO alliance, regional security priorities, force transformation and strategy issues. He is author or editor of fourteen books on U.S. national security strategy and defense planning. Additionally his articles have appeared in *Foreign Affairs, Survival,* and other professional journals. With a background in operations research and political science, he has worked for RAND and various offices on the Joint Staff and in the Office of the Secretary of Defense. He earned his Ph.D. from the Massachusetts Institute of Technology in 1975.

RICHARD A. LACQUEMENT, JR., is a lieutenant colonel in the U.S. Army. He is a professor on the faculty of the Department of Strategy and Policy, U.S. Naval War College. Previous assignments include teaching at the U.S. Military Academy's Department of Social Sciences, service as a field artillery officer and as a strategic plans and policy specialist. He has published in U.S. Naval Institute *Proceedings, Military Review,* and *Field Artillery.* Lt. Col. Lacquement is the author of *Shaping American Military Capabilities after the Cold War* (Praeger, 2003). He received his Ph.D. in international relations from the Woodrow Wilson School of Public and International Affairs, Princeton University.

ERIC V. LARSON is a senior policy analyst at RAND. His research centers on foreign affairs and national security policy. His most recent publications include: *Ambivalent Allies? A Study of South Korean*

Attitudes toward the U.S.; Primary Care: The Next Renaissance; Metrics for the Quadrennial Defense Review's Operational Goals; and *Interoperability of U.S. and NATO Allied Air Forces: Supporting Data and Case Studies.* He received his doctorate from the RAND Graduate School.

KRISTIN LEUSCHNER is a communications analyst for RAND. She has contributed to a wide range of RAND publications and is a co-author of *The Strategic Distribution in Support of Operation Enduring Freedom* (RAND, 2004).

MICHAEL A. LEVI is a science and technology fellow in Foreign Policy Studies at the Brookings Institution, Washington, D.C. He formerly served as director of the Strategic Security Project at the Federation of American Scientists, Washington, D.C. His articles on strategic matters and nuclear weapons have appeared in *Scientific American, Issues in Science & Technology,* and the *New Republic.* Mr. Levi holds an M.A. degree from Princeton University.

JAMES R. LOCHER III has served as assistant secretary of defense for Special Operations and Low Intensity Conflict and as a professional staff member on the Senate Committee on Armed Services. A graduate of the U.S. Military Academy and Harvard Business School, he is the author of *Victory on the Potomac* (Texas A&M University Press, 2002).

KARL P. MUELLER is associate political scientist at RAND, Washington, D.C., and adjunct associate professor at Georgetown University's Security Studies Program. He previously taught international relations at the University of Michigan, Kalamazoo College, and the U.S. Air Force School of Advanced Airpower Studies. His works on U.S. defense policy include *Conventional Coercion across the Spectrum of Operations: The Utility of Military Force in the Emerging Security Environment,* with David E. Johnson and William H. Taft V (RAND Report MR-1494-A). Dr. Mueller received his Ph.D. in politics from Princeton University.

CLARK A. MURDOCK is president of Murdock Associates and a senior fellow at the Center for Strategic and International Studies (CSIS), Washington, D.C. Among other planning positions, he served as counselor to U.S. Representative and later Secretary of Defense Les Aspin, deputy director of Strategic Planning for the U.S. Air Force, and Distinguished Professor at the National War College. Dr. Murdock previously taught at the State University of New York. In addition to articles and a range of public products, he is the author of *Defense Policy Formation: A Comparative Analysis of the McNamara Era* (State University of New York Press, 1974). Dr. Murdock received his Ph.D. in political science (with a minor in economics) from the University of Wisconsin–Madison.

RICHARD B. MYERS, general, U.S. Air Force, is chairman of the Joint Chiefs of Staff. His nearly 40-year career spans operational command and leadership positions in a variety of Air Force and Joint assignments, including 4100 flying hours as a command pilot and 600 combat hours in the F-4. Prior to becoming chairman, General Myers served as vice chairman of the Joint Chiefs of Staff and commander-in-chief, North American Aerospace Defense Command and U.S. Space Command. General Myers holds a master's degree in business administration from Auburn University. He has also attended the Air Command and Staff College, the U.S. Army War College, and the Program for Senior Executives in National and International Security at the John F. Kennedy School of Government, Harvard University.

REINHOLD NIEBUHR, 1892–1971, was a pastor in the Middle West before he became a professor of applied Christianity at Union Theological Seminary in New York in 1928. A prolific writer and editor, he was active for decades as a preacher and lecturer throughout the United States. His many books include *Moral Man and Immoral Society* (Charles Scribner's Sons, 1932), *The Irony of American History* (Charles Scribner's Sons, 1952), and *Christian Realism and Political Problems* (Charles Scribner's Sons, 1953).

DAVID L. NORQUIST serves as the deputy under secretary of defense (Financial Management) within the Office of the Secretary of Defense. Previously he served as a budget analyst for the Department of the Army and on the professional staff for the Subcommittee on Defense, House Appropriations Committee. Mr. Norquist holds a master's degree in public policy from the University of Michigan (1989), and a master of arts degree in national security studies from Georgetown University (1995).

JEFFREY H. NORWITZ is a civilian special agent with the Naval Criminal Investigative Service. He formerly served as an Army captain in Military Police and a deputy sheriff in El Paso County, Colorado. His work has appeared in the *Journal of Homeland Security* and *Terrorism and Counterterrorism: Understanding the New Security Environment* (McGraw-Hill, 2004). Mr. Norwitz holds a master's degree in strategic studies from the Naval War College.

DAVID T. ORLETSKY is an engineer at RAND. His research interests include a range of aerial operations, e.g., air refueling, air defense of the homeland, and air mobility. He has also examined the impact of Chinese military modernization on U.S. force structure and strategy. Mr. Orletsky has contributed to an array of RAND research reports, including *The U.S. Army and the New National Security Strategy* (RAND, 2003), *The Stryker Brigade Combat Team: Rethinking Strategic Responsiveness and Assessing Deployment Options* (RAND, 2002), and *The United*

States and Asia: Toward a New U.S. Strategy and Force Structure (RAND, 2001). He earned his master of science degree from the Massachusetts Institute of Technology in aeronautics and astronautics in 1987.

CHANTAL DE JONGE OUDRAAT is senior fellow and research program coordinator at the Center for Transatlantic Relations, Paul H. Nitze School of International Studies, Johns Hopkins University. She also serves as an adjunct professor at Georgetown University. Her research centers on the changing roles of international organizations, the United Nations, peace operations, military interventions, internal conflicts, the use of force, and economic sanctions. Her publications include *Managing Global Issues* (with P. J. Simmons; Carnegie Endowment for International Peace, 2001) and "UNSCOM: Between Iraq and a Hard Place" (*European Journal of International Law*, 2002). Dr. de Jonge Oudraat received her Ph.D. in political science from the University of Paris II (Panthéon).

MINXIN PEI is a senior associate and co-director of the China Program at the Carnegie Endowment for International Peace. He received his Ph.D. in political science from Harvard University in 1991 and was an assistant professor of politics at Princeton University from 1992 to 1998. He has written extensively on U.S.-China relations, the development of democratic political systems, the politics of economic reform, the growth of civil society, and legal institutions. He is the author of *From Reform to Revolution: The Demise of Communism in China and the Soviet Union* (Harvard University Press, 1994).

DOUGLAS PORCH earned his Ph.D. from Corpus Christi College, Cambridge University. A specialist in military history, he serves as professor of strategy at the U.S. Naval War College and lectures at the U.S. Marine Corps University at Quantico, Virginia. His publications include *French Secret Services: From the Dreyfus Affair to Desert Storm* (Farrar, Straus, & Giroux, 1995) and *The French Foreign Legion: A Complete History of the Legendary Fighting Force* (Perennial, 1991).

BARRY R. POSEN is professor of political science at the Massachusetts Institute of Technology, where he is affiliated with the Security Studies Program. He is also on the executive committee of Seminar XXI, an educational program for senior military officers, government officials, and business executives in the national security policy community. He has written two books, *Inadvertent Escalation: Conventional War and Nuclear Risks* (Cornell University Press, 1992) and *The Sources of Military Doctrine* (Cornell University Press, 1984). He received his Ph.D. in political science from the University of California–Berkeley in 1981.

ERVIN J. ROKKE is president of Moravian College, Pennsylvania. Dr. Rokke's career includes leadership positions within education, the military, and foreign affairs. He served as president of National Defense University, assistant chief of staff for intelligence at Headquarters, U.S. Air Force, staff plans officer at NATO headquarters in Brussels, associate director for support to military operations at the National Security Agency, and as dean of faculty at the U.S. Air Force Academy. He was also assigned as air attaché to the U.S. embassy in London and later served as defense attaché in the former Soviet Union. A 1962 graduate of the Air Force Academy, he later earned his M.A. and Ph.D. from Harvard University.

DENNY ROY is a senior research fellow at the Asia-Pacific Center for Security Studies. He has previously served as a faculty member or research fellow at the Naval Postgraduate School, the Australian National University, the National University of Singapore, and Brigham Young University. Dr. Roy is the author of *China's Foreign Relations* (Macmillan and Rowman & Littlefield, 1998) and *Taiwan: A Political History* (Cornell University Press, 2003). He received his Ph.D. in political science from the University of Chicago.

SAM C. SARKESIAN is emeritus professor of political science, Loyola University, Chicago. He is the author of numerous books and articles on national security, unconventional warfare/conflicts, and the profession of arms. His books include *The U.S. Military Profession into the Twenty-First Century* (with Robert E. Connor, Jr.; Frank Cass, 1999) and *Unconventional Conflicts in a New Security Era* (Greenwood Press, 1993). Professor Sarkesian received his Ph.D. from Columbia University.

MARK SAWYER is a senior analyst for ANSER, a not-for-profit research center based in Arlington, Virginia. He has over fourteen years experience in defense policy issues with the last two years emphasizing analysis of evolving homeland security policy. Mr. Sawyer holds a master's degree from the Patterson School of Diplomacy and International Commerce at the University of Kentucky.

BOB SCHAFFER is president, Colorado Alliance for Reform in Education and former U.S. House representative for Colorado's Fourth District. After graduating with a bachelor of arts degree from the University of Dayton, Mr. Schaffer, at the age of 25, became the youngest to serve in the Colorado State Senate (1986–96). During three terms in the U.S. Congress, he served actively on the Republican Study Committee, a group of sixty Representatives organized for the purpose of advancing a conservative social and economic agenda in the House of Representatives. In 2004, Mr. Schaffer ran in the Republican Party primary to represent Colorado in the U.S. Senate.

JAMES M. SMITH serves as director of the U.S. Air Force Institute for National Security Studies located at the U.S. Air Force Academy, where he is also a professor of military strategic studies. His military career included flying and operations plans assignments in Southeast Asia, Europe, and the United States. He has taught a wide rage of national security related courses at the Air Command and Staff College, the U.S. Military Academy, and the Air Force Academy. A 1970 graduate of the U.S. Air Force Academy, he earned an M.S. from the University of Southern California and a Ph.D. in public administration (public policy) from the University of Alabama.

SAM J. TANGREDI is a captain in the U.S. Navy who has served as commanding officer of the USS *Harper's Ferry* and head of the Strategy and Concepts Branch of the Office of the Chief of Naval Operations, and is now a senior military fellow in the Institute for National Strategic Studies at the National Defense University. He is the author of *All Wars Possible* (NDU Press, 2000). Captain Tangredi is a graduate of the U.S. Naval Academy and Naval Postgraduate School, and received his Ph.D. in international relations from the University of Southern California.

MARYBETH PETERSON ULRICH is associate professor of government, Department of National Security and Strategy, at the Army War College. She has written extensively in the field of strategic studies with an emphasis on national security and democratization in post-communist Europe. She is the author of numerous articles and book chapters, as well as *Democratizing Communist Militaries: The Case of Czech and Russian Armed Forces* (University of Michigan Press, 2000). Dr. Ulrich received her Ph.D. in political science from the University of Illinois, Urbana-Champaign.

MICHAEL WALZER is a professor in the School of Social Science, Institute for Advanced Study, in Princeton, New Jersey. He has also taught at Princeton University and Harvard University. Dr. Walzer is the author of numerous works, including *Just and Unjust Wars* (Basic Books, 1977) and *Arguing about War* (Yale University Press, 2004), and is the editor of *Dissent*. He received his Ph.D. from Harvard University.

CELESTE JOHNSON WARD is a fellow in the International Security Program at the Center for Strategic and International Studies, where she is an analyst and project leader on defense policy and national security issues. Ms. Ward has also served at the Congressional Budget Office and worked at DFI International. She has a master's degree from the Kennedy School of Government at Harvard University.

JOHN ALLEN WILLIAMS is professor of political science at Loyola University, Chicago, and is chair and president of the Inter-University Seminar on Armed Forces and Society. His research and publications center on civil-military relations, military culture, military professionalism, leadership, professional military education, personnel issues, military strategy, military forces and missions, catastrophic terrorism, defense organization, and strategic policy. His published works include *The Postmodern Military: Armed Forces after the Cold War* (co-editor and contributor, with Charles C. Moskos and David R. Segal; Oxford University Press, 2000) and *U.S. National Security Policy and Strategy: Documents and Policy Proposals 1987–1994* (co-editor and contributor, with Robert A. Vitas; Greenwood Press, 1996). He earned both an M.A. and a Ph.D. from the University of Pennsylvania.

ABOUT THE EDITORS

PAUL J. BOLT received his B.A. from Hope College and his M.A. and Ph.D. in political science from the University of Illinois at Urbana-Champaign. He has taught at Zhejiang University and Baicheng Normal College in the People's Republic of China, as well as the University of Illinois. He is currently a professor of political science at the U.S. Air Force Academy, where he has taught since 1997. In 2000, Dr. Bolt published *China and Southeast Asia's Ethnic Chinese: State and Diaspora in Contemporary Asia* (Praeger). He has also published in the *Journal of Contemporary China, Issues and Studies, Asian Affairs, Diaspora,* and *Airman Scholar.*

DAMON V. COLETTA is associate professor of political science at the U.S. Air Force Academy. He was first trained as an electrical engineer, working on electromagnetic compatibility issues for avionics on the C-17 aircraft in the early 1990s. Dr. Coletta went on to earn a master's degree in public policy from the Kennedy School of Government (1993), specializing in science and technology policy. He has performed

research for the American Association for the Advancement of Science, the American Enterprise Institute, the National Aeronautics and Space Administration, the Institute for Defense Analyses, and RAND Corporation. His work has appeared in *International Organization* and *Contemporary Security Policy.* Dr. Coletta received his Ph.D. in political science from Duke University.

COLLINS G. SHACKELFORD, JR., received his B.A. from the University of Mississippi, an M.A. from the University of South Dakota, and his Ph.D. in political science from the University of Illinois at Urbana-Champaign. His military service includes assignments in the space/missile career fields, nuclear command and control, and headquarters Air Force plans and programs. Currently serving as an assistant professor at the U.S. Air Force Academy, he is a coach for the women's rugby team and teaches courses in comparative politics, American government, international relations, space policy and law, and American defense policy.

INDEX